Windows Server 2016

Complete Study Guide

MCSA

Windows Server® 2016

Complete Study Guide
Exam 70-740, 70-741, 70-742

Will Panek

SYBEX®
A Wiley Brand

Senior Acquisitions Editor: Kenyon Brown
Development Editor: Kim Wimpsett
Technical Editors: Rodney R. Fournier and Chris Crayton
Senior Production Editor: Rebecca Anderson and Christine O'Connor
Copy Editor: Judy Flynn
Editorial Manager: Mary Beth Wakefield
Production Manager: Kathleen Wisor
Executive Editor: Jim Minatel
Book Designers: Bill Gibson and Judy Fung
Proofreader: Nancy Carrasco
Indexer: Jack Lewis
Project Coordinator, Cover: Brent Savage
Cover Designer: Wiley
Cover Image: Getty Images Inc./Jeremy Woodhouse

This book is dedicated to the three ladies of my life, Crystal, Alexandria, and Paige.

Acknowledgments

I would like to thank my wife and best friend, Crystal. She is always the light at the end of my tunnel. I want to thank my two daughters, Alexandria and Paige, for all of their love and support during the writing of all my books. The three of them are my support system, and I couldn't do any of this without them.

I want to thank all of my family and friends who always help me when I'm writing my books. I want to thank my brothers Rick, Gary, and Rob. I want to thank my great friends Shaun, Jeremy, and Gene.

I would like to thank all of my friends and co-workers at StormWind Studios. I want to especially thank the team who I work with on a daily basis and that includes Tom W, Dan Y, Corey F, Ronda, Dan J, Jessica, Dave, Tiffany, Tara, Ashley, Brittany, Doug, Mike, Vince, Desiree, Ryan, Ralph, Dan G, Tyler, Jeff B, Shayne, Patrick, Noemi, Michelle, Zachary, Colin, and the man who makes it all possible, Tom Graunke. Thanks to all of you for everything that you do. I would not have been able to complete this book without all of your help and support.

I want to thank everyone on my Sybex team, especially my development editor, Kim Wimpsett, who helped me make this the best book possible, and Rodney R. Fournier, who is the technical editor of many of my books. It's always good to have the very best technical guy backing you up. I want to thank Rebecca Anderson and Christine O'Connor, who were my production editors, and Judy Flynn for being the Copy Editor.

I want to also thank Chris Crayton who is my Technical Proofreader. Special thanks to my acquisitions editor, Kenyon Brown, who was the lead for the entire book. Finally, I want to thank everyone else behind the scenes that helped make this book possible. It's truly an amazing thing to have so many people work on my books to help make them the very best. I can't thank you all enough for your hard work.

About the Author

 **William Panek** holds the following certifications: MCP, MCP+I, MCSA, MCSA+ Security and Messaging, MCSE-NT (3.51 & 4.0), MCSE 2000, 2003, 2012/2012 R2, MCSE+Security and Messaging, MCDBA, MCT, MCTS, MCITP, CCNA, CCDA, and CHFI. Will is also a four-time and current Microsoft MVP winner.

After many successful years in the computer industry, Will decided that he could better use his talents and his personality as an instructor. He began teaching for schools such as Boston University and the University of Maryland, just to name a few. He has done consulting and training for some of the biggest government and corporate companies in the world, including the United States Secret Service, Cisco, United States Air Force, and US Army.

In 2015, Will became a Sr. Microsoft Instructor for StormWind Studios (www.stormwindstudios.com). He currently lives in New Hampshire with his wife and two daughters. Will was also a Representative in the New Hampshire House of Representatives from 2010 to 2012. In his spare time, he likes to do blacksmithing, shooting (trap and skeet), snowmobiling, playing racquetball, and riding his Harley. Will is also a commercially rated helicopter pilot.

Contents at a Glance

Contents

Table of Exercises

Introduction

This book is drawn from more than 20 years of IT experience. I have taken that experience and translated it into a Windows Server 2016 book that will help you not only prepare for the MCSA: Windows Server 2016 exams but also develop a clear understanding of how to install and configure Windows Server 2016 while avoiding all of the possible configuration pitfalls.

Many Microsoft books just explain the Windows operating system, but with *MCSA: Windows Server 2016 Complete Study Guide*, I go a step further by providing many in-depth, step-by-step procedures to support my explanations of how the operating system performs at its best.

Microsoft Windows Server 2016 is the newest version of Microsoft's server operating system software. Microsoft has taken the best of Windows Server 2003, Windows Server 2008, and Windows Server 2012 and combined them into the latest creation, Windows Server 2016.

Windows Server 2016 eliminates many of the problems that plagued the previous versions of Windows Server, and it includes a much faster boot time and shutdown. It is also easier to install and configure, and it barely stops to ask the user any questions during installation. In this book, I will show you what features are installed during the automated installation and where you can make changes if you need to be more in charge of your operating system and its features.

This book takes you through all the ins and outs of Windows Server 2016, including installation, configuration, Group Policy Objects, auditing, backups, and so much more.

Windows Server 2016 has improved on Microsoft's desktop environment, made networking easier, enhanced searching capability, and improved performance—and that's only scratching the surface.

When all is said and done, this is a technical book for IT professionals who want to take Windows Server 2016 to the next step and get certified. With this book, you will not only learn Windows Server 2016 and ideally pass the exams, but you will also become a Windows Server 2016 expert.

The Microsoft Certification Program

Since the inception of its certification program, Microsoft has certified more than 2 million people. As the computer network industry continues to increase in both size and complexity, this number is sure to grow—and the need for proven ability will also increase. Certifications can help companies verify the skills of prospective employees and contractors.

The Microsoft certification tracks for Windows Server 2016 include the following:

MCSA: Windows Server 2016 The MCSA is now the lowest-level certification you can achieve with Microsoft in relation to Windows Server 2016. It requires passing three exams: 70-740, 70-741, and 70-742.

MCSE: Cloud Platform and Infrastructure   The MCSE certifications, in relation to Windows Server 2016, require that you become an MCSA first and then pass two additional exams. The additional exams will vary depending on which of the two MCSE tracks you choose. For more information, visit Microsoft's website at www.microsoft.com/learning.

How Do You Become Certified on Windows Server 2016?

Attaining Microsoft certification has always been a challenge. In the past, students have been able to acquire detailed exam information—even most of the exam questions—from online "brain dumps" and third-party "cram" books or software products. For the new generation of exams, this is simply not the case.

Microsoft has taken strong steps to protect the security and integrity of its new certification tracks. Now prospective candidates must complete a course of study that develops detailed knowledge about a wide range of topics. It supplies them with the true skills needed, derived from working with the technology being tested.

The new generations of Microsoft certification programs are heavily weighted toward hands-on skills and experience. It is recommended that candidates have troubleshooting skills acquired through hands-on experience and working knowledge.

Fortunately, if you are willing to dedicate the time and effort to learn Windows Server 2016, you can prepare yourself well for the exam by using the proper tools. By working through this book, you can successfully meet the requirements to pass the Windows Server 2016 exams.

MCSA Exam Requirements

Candidates for MCSA certification on Windows Server 2016 must pass at least the following three Windows Server 2016 exams:

- **70-740:** Installation, Storage, and Compute with Windows Server 2016
- **70-741:** Networking with Windows Server 2016
- **70-742:** Identity with Windows Server 2016

For those who have a qualifying certification, they can take the Upgrading exam "Upgrading Your Skills to MCSA: Windows Server 2016" (Exam 70-743). The objectives for this exam span the three individual exams. This book covers all of the objectives for the Upgrading exam. For details about the exam, visit Microsoft's website at www.microsoft.com/learning.

Microsoft provides exam objectives to give you a general overview of possible areas of coverage on the Microsoft exams. Keep in mind, however, that exam objectives are subject to change at any time without prior notice and at Microsoft's sole discretion. Visit the Microsoft Learning website (www.microsoft.com/learning) for the most current listing of exam objectives. The published objectives and how they map to this book are listed later in this Introduction.

> For a more detailed description of the Microsoft certification programs, including a list of all the exams, visit the Microsoft Learning website at www.microsoft.com/learning.

Tips for Taking the Windows Server 2016 Exams

Here are some general tips for achieving success on your certification exam:

- Arrive early at the exam center so that you can relax and review your study materials. During this final review, you can look over tables and lists of exam-related information.

- Read the questions carefully. Do not be tempted to jump to an early conclusion. Make sure you know *exactly* what the question is asking.

- Answer all questions. If you are unsure about a question, mark it for review and come back to it at a later time.

- On simulations, do not change settings that are not directly related to the question. Also, assume the default settings if the question does not specify or imply which settings are used.

- For questions about which you're unsure, use a process of elimination to get rid of the obviously incorrect answers first. This improves your odds of selecting the correct answer when you need to make an educated guess.

Exam Registration

At the time this book was released, Microsoft exams are given two ways. You can take the exam live online or through the more than 1,000 Authorized VUE Testing Centers around the world. For the location of a testing center near you, go to VUE's website at www.vue.com. If you are outside of the United States and Canada, contact your local VUE registration center.

Find out the number of the exam that you want to take and then register with the VUE registration center nearest to you. At this point, you will be asked for advance payment for the exam. The exams are $165 each, and you must take them within one year of payment. You can schedule exams up to six weeks in advance or as late as one working day prior to the date of the exam. You can cancel or reschedule your exam if you contact the center at least two working days prior to the exam. Same-day registration is available in some locations, subject to space availability. Where same-day registration is available, you must register a minimum of two hours before test time.

When you schedule the exam, you will be provided with instructions regarding appointment and cancellation procedures, ID requirements, and information about the testing center location. In addition, you will receive a registration and payment confirmation letter from VUE.

Who Should Read This Book?

This book is intended for individuals who want to earn their MCSA: Windows Server 2016 certification.

This book will not only help anyone who is looking to pass the Microsoft exams, it will also help anyone who wants to learn the real ins and outs of the Windows Server 2016 operating system.

What's Inside?

Here is a glance at what's in each chapter:

Chapter 1: Installing Windows Server 2016   In the first chapter, I explain the requirements and steps required to install and configure Windows Server 2016.

Chapter 2: Installing in the Enterprise   This chapter shows you how to install Windows Server 2016 in an enterprise environment.

Chapter 3: Configuring Storage and Replication   I take you through the advantages and benefits of Windows Server 2016 storage and replication configurations.

Chapter 4: Understanding Hyper-V   This chapter will show you how to implement and configure Windows Server Hyper-V and virtual machines. You will learn about virtual networking, virtual hard disks, migration types, and Integration Services.

Chapter 5: Configuring High Availability   This chapter takes you through the different ways to create and manage Network Load Balancing (NLB) and high availability.

Chapter 6: Understanding Clustering   You will see the different ways that you can set up and configure clustering. I will explain how to set up clustering for applications or Hyper-V servers.

Chapter 7: Configuring Windows Containers   In this chapter I will explain the advantages of using Microsoft Containers. I will also explain how containers and images are created and managed using Docker.

Chapter 8: Maintaining Windows Server   This chapter shows you how to maintain your Windows Server 2016 system.

Chapter 9: Understanding Monitoring   This chapter will show you how to implement and configure monitoring. Monitoring allows you to look at the different resources on a system and fine-tune those resources for best performance.

Chapter 10: Configuring TCP/IP   In the first chapter, I show you how TCP/IP gets configured on a server and within a network. I also show you how to subnet an IPv4 network. I also show you how to work with IPv6.

Chapter 11: Configuring DNS   This chapter shows you how to install Windows Server 2016 DNS in an enterprise environment.

Chapter 12: Configuring DHCP   I take you through the advantages and benefits of using Windows Server 2016 DHCP.

Chapter 13: Implement IP Address Management   This chapter will show you how to implement and configure Windows Server 2016 IPAM.

Chapter 14: Configuring Network Access   This chapter takes you through the different ways to create and manage configure network access and VPN access.

Chapter 15: Understanding File Services   You will see the different ways that you can set up and configure Windows Server 2016 file servers and tools that work with file servers.

Chapter 16: Configuring High Availability   In this chapter I will explain the advantages of using Windows Server 2016 high availability. I show you how to configure NLB and high availability.

Chapter 17: Implementing Software Defined Networking   This chapter shows you how to create and maintain a Windows Server 2016 Software Defined Network.

Chapter 18: Installing Active Directory   In the first chapter, I will explain the benefits of using Active Directory. I will explain how Forests, Trees, and Domains work and I will also show you how to install Active Directory.

Chapter 19: Administer Active Directory   This chapter shows you how to create accounts in Active Directory. I will show you how to do bulk imports into Active Directory and also how to create and manage groups. I will also show you how to create and manage service accounts.

Chapter 20: Maintaining Active Directory   In this chapter I explain how to configure Active Directory components like an RODC, DFSR, and trusts. I will also show you how to configure and use Active Directory snapshots.

Chapter 21: Implementing GPOs   This chapter will show you how to implement and configure Group Policy Objects (GPOs).

Chapter 22: Understanding Certificates   This chapter takes you through the different ways to create and manage and configure certificates. I will show you how to install and configure a Certificate Server.

Chapter 23: Configure Access and Information Protection Solutions   You will see the different ways that you can set up and configure Active Directory Federation Services. I will also show you how to configure a Web Application Proxy.

What's Included with the Book

This book includes many helpful items intended to prepare you for the MCSA: Windows Server 2016 certification.

Assessment Test   There is an assessment test at the conclusion of the Introduction that can be used to evaluate quickly where you are with Windows Server 2016. This test should be taken prior to beginning your work in this book, and it should help you identify areas in which you are either strong or weak. Note that these questions are purposely more simple than the types of questions you may see on the exams.

Objective Map and Opening List of Objectives   Later in this Introduction, I include a detailed exam objective map showing you where each of the exam objectives are covered. Each chapter also includes a list of the exam objectives that are covered.

Helpful Exercises   Throughout the book, I have included step-by-step exercises of some of the more important tasks that you should be able to perform. Some of these exercises have corresponding videos that can be downloaded from the book's website. Also, in the following section I have a recommended home lab setup that will be helpful in completing these tasks.

Exam Essentials   The end of each chapter also includes a listing of exam essentials. These are essentially repeats of the objectives, but remember that any objective on the exam blueprint could show up on the exam.

Chapter Review Questions   Each chapter includes review questions. These are used to assess your understanding of the chapter and are taken directly from the chapter. These questions are based on the exam objectives, and they are similar in difficulty to items you might actually receive on the MCSA: Windows Server 2016 exams.

    The Sybex Interactive Online Test Bank, flashcards, videos, and Glossary can be accessed at http://www.wiley.com/go/sybextestprep.

Interactive Online Learning Environment and Test Bank

The interactive online learning environment that accompanies this study guide provides a test bank with study tools to help you prepare for the certification exams and increase your chances of passing them the first time! The test bank includes the following elements:

Sample Tests   All of the questions in this book are provided, including the assessment test, which you'll find at the end of this Introduction, and the chapter tests that include the review questions at the end of each chapter. In addition, there are three practice exams. Use these questions to test your knowledge of the study guide material. The online test bank runs on multiple devices.

Electronic Flashcards   One set of questions is provided in digital flashcard format (a question followed by a single correct answer). You can use the flashcards to reinforce your learning and provide last-minute test prep before the exam.

Glossary   The key terms from this book and their definitions are available as a fully searchable PDF.

Videos   Some of the exercises include corresponding videos. These videos show you how the author does the exercises. There is also a video that shows you how to set up virtualization so that you can complete the exercises within a virtualized environment. The author also has videos to help you on the Microsoft exams at www.youtube.com/c/williampanek.

Recommended Home Lab Setup

To get the most out of this book, you will want to make sure you complete the exercises throughout the chapters. To complete the exercises, you will need one of two setups. First, you can set up a machine with Windows Server 2016 and complete the labs using a regular Windows Server 2016 machine.

The second way to set up Windows Server 2016 (the way I set up Server 2016) is by using virtualization. I set up Windows Server 2016 as a virtual hard disk (VHD), and I did all the labs this way. The advantages of using virtualization are that you can always just wipe out the system and start over without losing a real server. Plus, you can set up multiple virtual servers and create a full lab environment on one machine.

I created a video for this book showing you how to set up a virtual machine and how to install Windows Server 2016 onto that virtual machine.

How to Contact Sybex/Author

Sybex strives to keep you supplied with the latest tools and information you need for your work. Please check the website at www.wiley.com/go/sybextestprep, where I'll post additional content and updates that supplement this book should the need arise.

You can contact me by going to my website at www.willpanek.com. You can also watch free videos on Microsoft networking at www.youtube.com/c/williampanek. If you would like to follow information about Windows Server 2016 from Will Panek, please visit Twitter @AuthorWillPanek.

Certification Objectives Maps

Tables I.1, I.2, and I.3 provide the objective mappings for the 70-740, 70-741, and 70-742 exams. In addition to the book chapters, you will find coverage of exam objectives in the flashcards, practice exams, and videos on the book's companion website: www.wiley.com/go/sybextestprep.

TABLE I.1   70-740 exam objectives

Objective	Chapter
Install Windows Servers in host and compute environments (10–15%)	
Install, upgrade, and migrate servers and workloads	Chapter 1
Determine Windows Server 2016 installation requirements; determine appropriate Windows Server 2016 editions per workloads; install Windows Server 2016; install Windows Server 2016 features and roles; install and configure Windows Server Core; manage Windows Server Core installations using Windows PowerShell, command line, and remote management capabilities; implement Windows PowerShell Desired State Configuration (DSC) to install and maintain integrity of installed environments; perform upgrades and migrations of servers and core workloads from Windows Server 2008 and Windows Server 2012 to Windows Server 2016; determine the appropriate activation model for server installation, such as Automatic Virtual Machine Activation (AVMA), Key Management Service (KMS), and Active Directory-based Activation	Chapter 1
Install and configure Nano Server	Chapter 1
Determine appropriate usage scenarios and requirements for Nano Server, install Nano Server, implement Roles and Features on Nano Server, manage and configure Nano Server, manage Nano Server remotely using Windows PowerShell	Chapter 1
Create, manage, and maintain images for deployment	Chapter 2
Plan for Windows Server virtualization; plan for Linux and FreeBSD deployments; assess virtualization workloads using the Microsoft Assessment and Planning (MAP) Toolkit; determine considerations for deploying workloads into virtualized environments; update images with patches, hotfixes, and drivers; install roles and features in offline images; manage and maintain Windows Server Core, Nano Server images, and VHDs using Windows PowerShell	Chapter 2
Implement storage solutions (10–15%)	
Configure disks and volumes	Chapter 3
Configure sector sizes appropriate for various workloads, configure GUID partition table (GPT) disks, create VHD and VHDX files using Server Manager or Windows PowerShell, mount virtual hard disks, determine when to use NTFS and ReFS file systems, configure NFS and SMB shares using Server Manager, configure SMB share and session settings using Windows PowerShell, configure SMB server and SMB client configuration settings using Windows PowerShell, configure file and folder permissions	Chapter 3

Objective	Chapter
Implement server storage	Chapter 3
Configure storage pools; implement simple, mirror, and parity storage layout options for disks or enclosures; expand storage pools; configure Tiered Storage; configure iSCSI target and initiator; configure iSNS; configure Datacenter Bridging (DCB); configure Multi-Path IO (MPIO); determine usage scenarios for Storage Replica; implement Storage Replica for server-to-server, cluster-to-cluster, and stretch cluster scenarios	Chapter 3
Implement data deduplication	Chapter 3
Implement and configure deduplication, determine appropriate usage scenarios for deduplication, monitor deduplication, implement a backup and restore solution with deduplication	Chapter 3
Implement Hyper-V (20–25%)	
Install and configure Hyper-V	Chapter 4
Determine hardware and compatibility requirements for installing Hyper-V, install Hyper-V, install management tools, upgrade from existing versions of Hyper-V, delegate virtual machine management, perform remote management of Hyper-V hosts, configure virtual machines using Windows PowerShell Direct, implement nested virtualization	Chapter 4
Configure virtual machine (VM) settings	Chapter 4
Add or remove memory in running a VM, configure dynamic memory, configure Non-Uniform Memory Access (NUMA) support, configure smart paging, configure Resource Metering, manage Integration Services, create and configure Generation 1 and 2 VMs and determine appropriate usage scenarios, implement Enhanced Session Mode, create Linux and FreeBSD VMs, install and configure Linux Integration Services (LIS), install and configure FreeBSD Integration Services (BIS), implement Secure Boot for Windows and Linux environments, move and convert VMs from previous versions of Hyper-V to Windows Server 2016 Hyper-V, export and import VMs, implement Discrete Device Assignment (DDA)	Chapter 4
Configure Hyper-V storage	Chapter 4
Create VHDs and VHDX files using Hyper-V Manager, create shared VHDX files, configure differencing disks, modify virtual hard disks, configure pass-through disks, resize a virtual hard disk, manage checkpoints, implement production checkpoints, implement a virtual Fibre Channel adapter, configure Storage Quality of Service (QoS)	Chapter 4

TABLE I.1 70-740 exam objectives *(continued)*

Objective	Chapter
Configure Hyper-V networking	Chapter 4
Add and remove virtual network interface cards (vNICs), configure Hyper-V virtual switches, optimize network performance, configure MAC addresses, configure network isolation, configure synthetic and legacy virtual network adapters, configure NIC Teaming in VMs, configure virtual machine queue (VMQ), enable Remote Direct Memory Access (RDMA) on network adapters bound to a Hyper-V virtual switch using Switch Embedded Teaming (SET), configure Bandwidth Management	Chapter 4
Implement Windows Containers (5–10%)	
Deploy Windows Containers	Chapter 7
Determine installation requirements and appropriate sScenarios for Windows Containers, install and configure Windows Server Container host in physical or virtualized environments, install and configure Windows Server container host to Windows Server Core or Nano Server in a physical or virtualized environment, install Docker on Windows Server and Nano Server, configure Docker daemon startup options, configure Windows PowerShell for use with Containers, install a base operating system, tag an image, uninstall an operating system image, create Windows Server Containers, create Hyper-V Containers	Chapter 7
Manage Windows Containers	Chapter 7
Containers using Windows PowerShell, manage container networking, manage container data volumes, manage Resource Control, create new Container images using Dockerfile, manage Container images using DockerHub repository for public and private scenarios, manage container images using Microsoft Azure	Chapter 7
Implement high availability (30–35%)	
Implement high availability and disaster recovery options in Hyper-V	Chapter 5
Implement Hyper-V Replica, implement Live Migration, implement Shared Nothing Live Migration, configure CredSSP or Kerberos authentication protocol for Live Migration, implement storage migration	Chapter 5
Implement Failover Clustering	Chapter 6

Objective	Chapter
Implement Workgroup, Single, and Multi-domain clusters; configure quorum; configure cluster networking; restore single node or cluster configuration; configure cluster storage; implement Cluster-Aware Updating; implement Cluster Operating System Rolling Upgrade; configure and optimize clustered shared volumes (CSVs); configure clusters without network names; implement Scale-Out File Server (SoFS); determine different scenarios for the use of SoFS vs. clustered File Server; determine usage scenarios for implementing guest clustering; implement a Clustered Storage Spaces solution using Shared SAS storage enclosures; implement Storage Replica; implement Cloud Witness; implement VM resiliency; implement shared VHDX as a storage solution for guest clusters	Chapter 6
Implement Storage Spaces Direct	Chapter 6
Determine scenario requirements for implementing Storage Spaces Direct, enable Storage Spaces direct using Windows PowerShell, implement a disaggregated Storage Spaces Direct scenario in a cluster, implement a hyper-converged Storage Spaces Direct scenario in a cluster	Chapter 6
Manage Failover Clustering	Chapter 6
Configure role-specific settings, including continuously available shares; configure VM monitoring; configure failover and preference settings; implement stretch and site-aware failover clusters; enable and configure node fairness	Chapter 6
Manage VM movement in clustered nodes	Chapter 5
Perform a live migration; perform a quick migration; perform a storage migration; import, export, and copy VMs; configure VM network health protection; configure drain on shutdown	Chapter 5
Implement Network Load Balancing (NLB)	Chapter 5
Install NLB nodes, configure NLB prerequisites, configure affinity, configure port rules, configure cluster operation mode, upgrade an NLB cluster	Chapter 5
Maintain and monitor server environments (10–15%)	
Maintain server installations	8

TABLE I.1 70-740 exam objectives *(continued)*

Objective	Chapter
Implement Windows Server Update Services (WSUS) solutions; configure WSUS groups; manage patch management in mixed environments; implement an antimalware solution with Windows Defender; integrate Windows Defender with WSUS and Windows Update; perform back up and restore operations using Windows Server Backup; determine backup strategies for different Windows Server roles and workloads, including Hyper-V Host, Hyper-V Guests, Active Directory, File Servers, and Web Servers using Windows Server 2016 native tools and solutions	8
Monitor server installations	Chapter 9
Monitor workloads using Performance Monitor; configure Data Collector Sets; determine appropriate CPU, memory, disk, and networking counters for storage and compute workloads; configure alerts; monitor workloads using Resource Monitor	Chapter 9

TABLE I.2 70-741 exam objectives

Implement Domain Name System (DNS) (15–20%)	Chapter
1.1. Install and configure DNS servers	Chapter 11
This objective may include but is not limited to: Determine DNS installation requirements; determine supported DNS deployment scenarios on Nano Server; install DNS; configure forwarders; configure Root Hints; configure delegation; implement DNS policies; implement DNS global settings using Windows PowerShell; configure Domain Name System Security Extensions (DNSSEC); configure DNS Socket Pool; configure cache locking; enable Response Rate Limiting; configure DNS-based Authentication of Named Entities (DANE); configure DNS logging; configure delegated administration; configure recursion settings; implement DNS performance tuning; configure global settings using Windows PowerShell	Chapter 11
1.2. Create and configure DNS zones and records	Chapter 11
This objective may include but is not limited to: Create primary zones; configure Active Directory integration of primary zones; create and configure secondary zones; create and configure stub zones; configure a GlobalNames zone; analyze zone-level statistics; create and configure DNS Resource Records (RR), including A, AAAA, PTR, SOA, NS, SRV, CNAME, and MX records; configure zone scavenging; configure record options, including Time To Live (TTL) and weight; configure round robin; configure secure dynamic updates; configure unknown record support; use DNS audit events and analytical (query) events for auditing and troubleshooting; configure Zone Scopes; configure records in Zone Scopes; configure policies for zones	Chapter 11

Implement Domain Name System (DNS) (15–20%)	**Chapter**

Implement DHCP (15–20%)

2.1. Install and configure DHCP	Chapter 12

This objective may include but is not limited to: Install and configure DHCP   Chapter 12
servers; authorize a DHCP server; create and configure scopes; create and
configure superscopes and multicast scopes; configure a DHCP reservation;
configure DHCP options; configure DNS options from within DHCP; configure
policies; configure client and server for PXE boot; configure DHCP Relay
Agent; implement IPv6 addressing using DHCPv6; perform export and import
of a DHCP server; perform DHCP server migration

2.2. Manage and maintain DHCP	Chapter 12

This objective may include but is not limited to: Configure a lease period;   Chapter 12
back up and restore the DHCP database; configure high availability using
DHCP failover; configure DHCP name protection; troubleshoot DHCP

Implement IP Address Management (IPAM) (15–20%)

3.1. Install and configure IP Address Management (IPAM)	Chapter 13

This objective may include but is not limited to: Provision IPAM manually   Chapter 13
or by using Group Policy; configure server discovery; create and manage IP
blocks and ranges; monitor utilization of IP address space; migrate existing
workloads to IPAM; configure IPAM database storage using SQL Server;
determine scenarios for using IPAM with System Center Virtual Machine
Manager for physical and virtual IP address space management

3.2. Manage DNS and DHCP using IPAM	Chapter 13

This objective may include but is not limited to: Manage DHCP server   Chapter 13
properties using IPAM; configure DHCP scopes and options; configure DHCP
policies and failover; manage DNS server properties using IPAM; manage
DNS zones and records; manage DNS and DHCP servers in multiple Active
Directory forests; delegate administration for DNS and DHCP using role-
based access control (RBAC)

3.3. Audit IPAM	Chapter 13

This objective may include but is not limited to: Audit the changes performed   Chapter 13
on the DNS and DHCP servers; audit the IPAM address usage trail; audit
DHCP lease events and user logon events

TABLE I.2   70-741 exam objectives *(continued)*

Implement Domain Name System (DNS) (15–20%)	Chapter
Implement Network Connectivity and Remote Access Solutions (25–30%)	
Implement network connectivity solutions	Chapter 14
This objective may include but is not limited to: Implement Network Address Translation (NAT); configure routing	Chapter 14
Implement virtual private network (VPN) and DirectAccess solutions	Chapter 14
This objective may include but is not limited to: Implement remote access and site-to-site (S2S) VPN solutions using remote access gateway; configure different VPN protocol options; configure authentication options; configure VPN reconnect; create and configure connection profiles; determine when to use remote access VPN and site-to-site VPN and configure appropriate protocols; install and configure DirectAccess; implement server requirements; implement client configuration; troubleshoot DirectAccess	Chapter 14
Implement Network Policy Server (NPS)	Chapter 14
This objective may include but is not limited to: Configure a RADIUS server including RADIUS proxy; configure RADIUS clients; configure NPS templates; configure RADIUS accounting; configure certificates; configure Connection Request Policies; configure network policies for VPN and wireless and wired clients; import and export NPS policies	Chapter 14
Implement Core and Distributed Network Solutions (10–15%)	
Implement IPv4 and IPv6 addressing	Chapter 10
This objective may include but is not limited to: Configure IPv4 addresses and options; determine and configure appropriate IPv6 addresses; configure IPv4 or IPv6 subnetting; implement IPv6 stateless addressing; configure interoperability between IPv4 and IPv6 by using ISATAP, 6to4, and Teredo scenarios; configure Border Gateway Protocol (BGP); configure IPv4 and IPv6 routing	Chapter 10
Implement Distributed File System (DFS) and Branch Office solutions	Chapter 15
This objective may include but is not limited to: Install and configure DFS namespaces; configure DFS replication targets; configure replication scheduling; configure Remote Differential Compression (RDC) settings; configure staging; configure fault tolerance; clone a Distributed File System Replication (DFSR) database; recover DFSR databases; optimize DFS Replication; install and configure BranchCache; implement distributed and hosted cache modes; implement BranchCache for web, file, and application servers; troubleshoot BranchCache	Chapter 15

Implement Domain Name System (DNS) (15–20%)	Chapter

Implement an Advanced Network Infrastructure (10–15%)

6.1 Implement high performance network solutions	Chapter 16
This objective may include but is not limited to: Implement NIC Teaming or the Switch Embedded Teaming (SET) solution and identify when to use each; enable and configure Receive Side Scaling (RSS); enable and configure network Quality of Service (QoS) with Data Center Bridging (DCB); enable and configure SMB Direct on Remote Direct Memory Access (RDMA) enabled network adapters; enable and configure SMB Multichannel; enable and configure virtual Receive Side Scaling (vRSS) on a Virtual Machine Queue (VMQ) capable network adapter; enable and configure Virtual Machine Multi-Queue (VMMQ); enable and configure Single-Root I/O Virtualization (SR-IOV) on a supported network adapter	Chapter 16
6.2. Determine scenarios and requirements for implementing Software Defined Networking (SDN)	Chapter 17
This objective may include but is not limited to: Determine deployment scenarios and network requirements for deploying SDN; determine requirements and scenarios for implementing Hyper-V Network Virtualization (HNV) using Network Virtualization Generic Route Encapsulation (NVGRE) encapsulation or Virtual Extensible LAN (VXLAN) encapsulation; determine scenarios for implementation of Software Load Balancer (SLB) for North-South and East-West load balancing; determine implementation scenarios for various types of Windows Server Gateways, including L3, GRE, and S2S, and their use; determine requirements and scenarios for distributed firewall policies and network security groups	Chapter 17

TABLE I.3   70-742 exam objectives

Objective	Chapter

Install and configure Active Directory Domain Services (AD DS) (20–25%)

Install and configure domain controllers	Chapter 18
Install a new forest, add or remove a domain controller from a domain, upgrade a domain controller, install AD DS on a Server Core installation, install a domain controller from Install from Media (IFM), resolve DNS SRV record registration issues, configure a global catalog server, transfer and seize operations master roles, install and configure a read-only domain controller (RODC), configure domain controller cloning	Chapter 18

TABLE I.3   70-742 exam objectives *(continued)*

Objective	Chapter
Create and manage Active Directory users and computers	Chapter 19
Automate the creation of Active Directory accounts; create, copy, configure, and delete users and computers; configure templates; perform bulk Active Directory operations; configure user rights; implement offline domain join; manage inactive and disabled accounts; automate unlocking of disabled accounts using Windows PowerShell; automate password resets using Windows PowerShell	Chapter 19
Create and manage Active Directory groups and organizational units (OUs)	Chapter 19
Configure group nesting; convert groups, including security, distribution, universal, domain local, and domain global; manage group membership using Group Policy; enumerate group membership; automate group membership management using Windows PowerShell; delegate the creation and management of Active Directory groups and OUs; manage default Active Directory containers; create, copy, configure, and delete groups and OUs	Chapter 19
Manage and maintain AD DS (15–20%)	
Configure service authentication and account policies	Chapter 19
Create and configure Service Accounts, create and configure Group Managed Service Accounts (gMSAs), configure Kerberos Constrained Delegation (KCD), manage Service Principal Names (SPNs), configure virtual accounts, configure domain and local user password policy settings, configure and apply Password Settings objects (PSOs), delegate password settings management, configure account lockout policy settings, configure Kerberos policy settings within Group Policy	Chapter 19
Maintain Active Directory	Chapter 20
Back up Active Directory and SYSVOL, manage Active Directory offline, perform offline defragmentation of an Active Directory database, clean up metadata, configure Active Directory snapshots, perform object- and container-level recovery, perform Active Directory restore, configure and restore objects by using the Active Directory Recycle Bin, configure replication to read-only domain controllers (RODCs), configure Password Replication Policy (PRP) for RODC, monitor and manage replication, upgrade SYSVOL replication to Distributed File System Replication (DFSR)	Chapter 20
Configure Active Directory in a complex enterprise environment	Chapter 20

TABLE I.3   70-742 exam objectives *(continued)*

Objective	Chapter
Implement Active Directory Certificate Services (AD CS) (10–15%)	
Install and configure AD CS	Chapter 22
Install Active Directory Integrated Enterprise Certificate Authority (CA), install offline root and subordinate CAs, install standalone CAs, configure Certificate Revocation List (CRL) distribution points, install and configure Online Responder, implement administrative role separation, configure CA backup and recovery	Chapter 22
Manage certificates	Chapter 22
Manage certificate templates; implement and manage certificate deployment, validation, and revocation; manage certificate renewal; manage certificate enrollment and renewal for computers and users using Group Policies; configure and manage key archival recovery	Chapter 22
Implement identity federation and access solutions (15–20%)	
Install and configure Active Directory Federation Services (AD FS)	Chapter 23
Upgrade and migrate previous AD FS workloads to Windows Server 2016; implement claims-based authentication, including Relying-Party Trusts; configure authentication policies; configure multifactor authentication; implement and configure device registration; integrate AD FS with Microsoft Passport; configure for use with Microsoft Azure and Office 365; configure AD FS to enable authentication of users stored in LDAP directories	Chapter 23
Implement Web Application Proxy (WAP)	Chapter 23
Install and configure WAP, implement WAP in pass-through mode, implement WAP as AD FS proxy, integrate WAP with AD FS, configure AD FS requirements, publish web apps via WAP, publish Remote Desktop Gateway applications, configure HTTP to HTTPS redirects, configure internal and external Fully Qualified Domain Names (FQDNs)	Chapter 23
Install and configure Active Directory Rights Management Services (AD RMS)	Chapter 23
Install a licensor certificate AD RMS server, manage AD RMS Service Connection Point (SCP), manage AD RMS templates, configure Exclusion Policies, back up and restore AD RMS	Chapter 23

Exam objectives are subject to change at any time without prior notice and at Microsoft's sole discretion. Please visit Microsoft's website (www.microsoft .com/learning) for the most current listing of exam objectives.

Assessment Test

1. Which of the following is a valid role for a Windows Server 2016 computer?
   A. Standalone server
   B. Member server
   C. Domain controller
   D. All of the above

2. You need to add a new Windows Server 2016 image to your WDS server. You want to use a command-line command to complete this task. What command would you use?
   A. WDSUTIL /Add
   B. WDSUTIL /image
   C. WDSUTIL /prepareimage
   D. WDSUTIL /addimage

3. You have been hired to help a small company set up its first Windows network. It has had the same 13 users for the entire two years it has been open, and the company has no plans to expand. What version of Windows Server 2016 would you recommend?
   A. Windows Server 2016 Datacenter (Desktop Experience)
   B. Windows Server 2016 Standard (Desktop Experience)
   C. Windows Server 2016 Datacenter
   D. Windows Server 2016 Essentials

4. You are using WDS to deploy Windows Server 2016 images across your organization, and you are using the WDSUTIL command-line utility to perform this task. You want to copy a previously created image from the image store using this utility. Which option of WDSUTIL should you use?
   A. /move
   B. /copy-image
   C. /get
   D. /enable

5. You want to install a group of 25 computers using disk images created in conjunction with the System Preparation Tool. Your plan is to create an image from a reference computer and then copy the image to all the machines. You do not want to create an SID on the destination computer when you use the image. Which Sysprep.exe command-line option should you use to set this up?
   A. /specialize
   B. /generalize
   C. /oobe
   D. /quiet

6. You have a Hyper-V host that runs Windows Server 2016. The host contains a virtual machine named Virtual1. Virtual1 has resource metering enabled. You need to use resource metering to track the amount of network traffic that Virtual1 sends to the 10.10.16.0/20 network. Which command would you run?

    A. Add-VMNetworkAdapteiAd

    B. Set-VMNetworkAdapter

    C. New-VMResourcePool

    D. Set-VMNetworkAdapterRoutingDomamMapping

7. You need to ensure that the company's two Virtual Machines, VM1 and VM2, can communicate with each other only. The solution must prevent VM1 and VM2 from communicating with Server1. Which cmdlet should you use?

    A. Set-NetNeighbor

    B. Remove-VMSwitchTeamMember

    C. Set-VMSwitch

    D. Enable-VMSwitchExtension

8. You want to make sure the hard disk space for your virtual machines is occupied only when needed. What type of virtual hard disk would you recommend?

    A. Dynamically expanding disk

    B. Fixed-size disk

    C. Differencing disk

    D. Physical or pass-through disk

9. What is the command to install Hyper-V on a Windows Server 2016 machine that was installed in Server Core?

    A. start /w ocsetup Hyper-V

    B. start /w ocsetup microsoft-hyper-v

    C. start /w ocsetup Microsoft-Hyper-V

    D. start /w ocsetup hyper-v

10. You are a network administrator for a small company that uses Hyper-V. You need to reboot your virtual machine. What PowerShell command can you use?

    A. Restart-VM

    B. Reboot-VM

    C. Shutdown-VM

    D. ShutStateOff

11. You are the administrator for a mid-size organization. You have been asked by the owner to set up an NLB cluster. You want to use PowerShell to set up the cluster. What command would you use?

    A. New-NlbCluster

    B. Create-NlbCluster

C. Setup-NlbCluster

D. Set-NlbCluster

12. Which of the following actions should be performed against an NLB cluster node if maintenance needs to be performed while not terminating current connections?

A. Evict

B. Drainstop

C. Pause

D. Stop

13. If you have a running cluster and need to run the Validate a Configuration Wizard again, which of the following tests may require cluster resources to be taken offline?

A. Network tests

B. Storage tests

C. System configuration tests

D. Inventory tests

14. What PowerShell command would you use to run a validation test on a cluster?

A. Test-Cluster

B. Validate-Cluster

C. Set-Cluster

D. Add-Cluster

15. You download the wrong image from Docker. What command allows you to delete an image?

A. docker del

B. docker rm

C. docker kill

D. docker dl

16. You have built a bunch of Containers. What PowerShell command allows you to view the Containers?

A. docker view

B. docker see

C. View-Container

D. Get-Container

17. What command allows you to see your container images?

A. docker images

B. docker info

C. docker view

D. docker see

18. You need to use an Active Directory application data partition. Which command can you use to create and manage application data partitions?

   A. DCPromo.exe

   B. NTDSUtil.exe

   C. ADUtil.exe

   D. ADSI.exe

19. What command-line command would you type to start Performance Monitor?

   A. Netmon.exe

   B. Perfmon.exe

   C. Performon.exe

   D. Resmon.exe

20. What command-line command would you type to start Resource Monitor?

   A. Netmon.exe

   B. Perfmon.exe

   C. Performon.exe

   D. Resmon.exe

21. Which of the following subnet masks is represented with the CIDR of /27?

   A. 255.255.255.254

   B. 255.255.255.248

   C. 255.255.255.224

   D. 255.255.255.240

22. You are the network administrator for a midsize organization that has installed Windows Server 2016 onto the network. You are thinking of moving all machines to Windows 10 and IPv6. You decide to set up a test environment with four subnets. What type of IPv6 addresses do you need set up?

   A. Global addresses

   B. Link-local addresses

   C. Unique local addresses

   D. Site-local addresses

23. You are the network administrator for ABC Company. You have an IPv6 prefix of 2001:DB8:BBCC:0000::/53, and you need to set up your network so that your IPv6 addressing scheme can handle 1,000 more subnets. Which network mask would you use?

   A. /60

   B. /61

   C. /62

   D. /63

24. You assign two DNS server addresses as part of the options for a scope. Later you find a client workstation that isn't using those addresses. What's the most likely cause?

   A. The client didn't get the option information as part of its lease.

   B. The client has been manually configured with a different set of DNS servers.

   C. The client has a reserved IP address in the address pool.

   D. There's a bug in the DHCP server service.

25. Your DHCP server crashed in the middle of the day. You rebooted the server, got it running within 5 minutes, and nobody but you seemed to notice that it had gone down at all. What additional steps must you take?

   A. None. If there were no lease-renewal requests during the 5-minute period in which the DHCP server was down, none of the clients will ever know that it went down.

   B. You need to renew all the leases manually.

   C. None. The DHCP server automatically assigned new addresses to all the clients on the network transparently.

   D. You must reboot all the client machines.

26. You are the administrator for a Windows Server 2016 network that uses DHCP. You notice that your DHCP database is getting too large and you want to reduce the size of the database. What should you do?

   A. From the folder containing the DHCP database, run `jetpack.exe dhcp.mdb temp.mdb`.

   B. From the folder containing the DHCP database, run `shrinkpack.exe dhcp.mdb temp.mdb`.

   C. From the folder containing the DHCP database, run `jetshrink.exe dhcp.mdb temp.mdb`.

   D. From the folder containing the DHCP database, run `shrinkjet.exe dhcp.mdb temp.mdb`.

27. You are the network admin for an Active Directory domain named Stormwind.com. You have a new security policy that states that whenever possible, you should install new Nano Servers. Which server role can be deployed on a Nano Server?

   A. Active Directory Domain Services

   B. DHCP Server

   C. Network Policy and Access Services

   D. Web Server (IIS)

28. You have been asked to explain how DHCP works. What abbreviation can you explain to show how DHCP operates?

   A. DORA

   B. RODA

   C. DHRA

   D. AORD

29. You are the network administrator for a large training company. You have been asked to set up the default gateway setting using DHCP. Which option would you configure?

    A. 003 Router

    B. 006 DNS

    C. 015 DNS Domain Name

    D. 028 Broadcast Address

30. You are the network administrator for your organization. You need to view the DNS server information from the IPAM database. What PowerShell command would you use?

    A. View-IpamDnsServer

    B. Get-IpamDnsServer

    C. View-DnsServer

    D. Get-DnsServer

31. You are the administrator for StormWind Studios online training company. You need to change the IPAM discovery configuration. What PowerShell command do you use?

    A. Get-IpamDiscovery

    B. Get-IpamDiscoveryDomain

    C. Set-IpamDiscovery

    D. Set-IpamDiscoveryDomain

32. You are the network administrator for your company. You need to use a PowerShell command to configure an IP address block in IPAM. What command do you use?

    A. Set-IpamIP

    B. Set-IpamBlock

    C. Set-IPBlock

    D. Set-IPAddressBlock

33. Your network contains an Active Directory domain named contoso.com. Network Access Protection (NAP) is deployed to the domain. You need to create NAP event trace log files on a client computer. What should you run?

    A. Register-ObjectEvent

    B. Register-EngineEvent

    C. tracert

    D. logman

34. Your network contains an Active Directory domain named Stormwind.com. The domain contains a RADIUS server named Server1 that runs Windows Server 2016. You add a VPN server named Server2 to the network. On Server1, you create several network policies. You need to configure Server1 to accept authentication requests from Server2. Which tool should you use on Server1?

    A. Set-RemoteAccessRadius

    B. CMAK

    C. NPS

    D. Routing and Remote Access

35. You are the administrator for a large communications company. Your company uses Windows Server 2016, and your user's files are encrypted using EFS. What command-line command would you use to change or modify the EFS files?

    A. Convert

    B. Cipher

    C. Gopher

    D. Encrypt

36. You want to publish a printer to Active Directory. Where would you click in order to accomplish this task?

    A. The Sharing tab

    B. The Advanced tab

    C. The Device Settings tab

    D. The Printing Preferences button

37. You have been hired by a small company to implement new Windows Server 2016 systems. The company wants you to set up a server for users' home folder locations. What type of server would you be setting up?

    A. PDC server

    B. Web server

    C. Exchange server

    D. File server

38. In a three-node cluster set to a node majority quorum model, how many cluster nodes can be offline before the quorum is lost?

    A. Zero

    B. One

    C. Two

    D. Three

39. You are the administrator for a mid-size company who wants to set up and test a cluster. What PowerShell command would you use to run a validation test on a cluster?

    A. Test-Cluster

    B. Validate-Cluster

    C. Set-Cluster

    D. Add-Cluster

40. You are a network administrator for a small company that uses Hyper-V. You need to reboot your virtual machine. What PowerShell command can you use?

A. Restart-VM

B. Reboot-VM

C. Shutdown-VM

D. ShutStateOff

41. What is the maximum number of domains that a Windows Server 2016 computer configured as a domain controller may participate in at one time?

A. Zero

B. One

C. Two

D. Any number of domains

42. Which of the following file systems are required for Active Directory?

A. FAT

B. FAT32

C. HPFS

D. NTFS

43. Which of the following services and protocols are required for Active Directory? (Choose all that apply.)

A. NetBEUI

B. TCP/IP

C. DNS

D. DHCP

44. Which of the following PowerShell commands allows you to view Active Directory users?

A. Get-ADUser

B. Get-User

C. View-User

D. See-ADUser

45. Which of the following PowerShell commands allows you to enable an Active Directory account after it's been locked out?

A. release-ADAccount

B. enable-ADAccount

C. Unlock-ADAccount

D. enable-Account

46. You need to create a new user account using the command prompt. Which command would you use?

   A. dsmodify

   B. dscreate

   C. dsnew

   D. dsadd

47. What kind of trust is set up between one domain and another domain in the same forest?

   A. External trust

   B. Forest trust

   C. Shortcut trust

   D. Domain trust

48. You need to deactivate the Global Catalog option on some of your domain controllers. At which level in Active Directory would you deactivate Global Catalogs?

   A. Server

   B. Site

   C. Domain

   D. Forest

49. You want to allow the new Sales Director to have permissions to reset passwords for all users within the sales OU. Which of the following is the best way to do this?

   A. Create a special administration account within the OU and grant it full permissions for all objects within Active Directory.

   B. Move the user's login account into the OU that he or she is to administer.

   C. Move the user's login account to an OU that contains the OU (that is, the parent OU of the one that he or she is to administer).

   D. Use the Delegation of Control Wizard to assign the necessary permissions on the OU that he or she is to administer.

50. You need to create OUs in Active Directory. In which MMCs can you accomplish this task? (Choose all that apply.)

   A. Active Directory Administrative Center

   B. Active Directory Sites and Services

   C. Active Directory Users and Computers

   D. Active Directory Domains and Trusts

51. You want a GPO to take effect immediately, and you need to use Windows PowerShell. Which PowerShell cmdlet command would you use?

   A. Invoke-GPUpdate

   B. Invoke-GPForce

   C. Invoke-GPResult

   D. Invoke-GPExecute

52. GPOs assigned at which of the following level(s) will override GPO settings at the domain level?

A. OU

B. Site

C. Domain

D. Both OU and site

53. A system administrator wants to ensure that only the GPOs set at the OU level affect the Group Policy settings for objects within the OU. Which option can they use to do this (assuming that all other GPO settings are the defaults)?

A. The Enforced option

B. The Block Policy Inheritance option

C. The Disable option

D. The Deny permission

54. To disable GPO settings for a specific security group, which of the following permissions should you apply?

A. Deny Write

B. Allow Write

C. Enable Apply Group Policy

D. Deny Apply Group Policy

55. You want to configure modifications of the Certification Authority role service to be logged. What should you enable? (Choose all that apply.)

A. Enable auditing of system events.

B. Enable logging.

C. Enable auditing of privilege use.

D. Enable auditing of object access.

E. You should consider enabling auditing of process tracking.

56. You need to add a certificate template to the Certificate Authority. What PowerShell command would you use?

A. Get-CSTemplate

B. Add-CSTemplate

C. Add-CATemplate

D. New-Template

57. You need to see all of the location sets for the CRL distribution point (CDP). What PowerShell command would you use?

A. View-CACrlDistributionPoint

B. See-CACrlDistributionPoint

C. Add-CACrlDistributionPoint

D. Get-CACrlDistributionPoint

58. You have a server named Server1 that runs Windows Server 2016. You need to configure Server1 as a Web Application Proxy. Which server role or role service should you install on Server1?

   A. Remote Access

   B. Active Directory Federation Services

   C. Web Server (IIS)

   D. DirectAccess and VPN (RAS)

59. You have installed Active Directory Federation Services server and the Web Application Proxy. Which two inbound TCP ports should you open on the firewall? Each correct answer presents part of the solution. (Choose two.)

   A. 443

   B. 390

   C. 8443

   D. 49443

60. You need to modify configuration settings for a server application role of an application in AD FS. What PowerShell command do you use?

   A. Add-AdfsServerApplication

   B. Set-AdfsServerApplication

   C. Get-AdfsServerApplication

   D. Install-AdfsServerApplication

Answers to Assessment Test

1. D. Based on the business needs of an organization, a Windows 2016 Server computer can be configured in any of the roles listed. See Chapter 1 for more information.

2. A. The WDSUTIL/Add command allows an administrator to add an image to a WDS server. See Chapter 1 for more information.

3. D. Windows Server 2016 Essentials is ideal for small businesses that have as many as 25 users and 50 devices. Windows Server 2016 Essentials has a simpler interface and preconfigured connectivity to cloud-based services but no virtualization rights. See Chapter 1 for more information.

4. B. You should use the /copy-image option of the WDSUTIL utility to copy an image from the image store. See Chapter 2 for more information.

5. B. The /generalize option prevents system-specific information from being included in the image. The Sysprep.exe command can be used with a variety of options. You can see a complete list by typing **sysprep/?** at a command-line prompt. See Chapter 2 for more information.

6. B. The Set-VMNetworkAdapter command allows an administrator to configure features of the virtual network adapter in a virtual machine or the management operating system. See Chapter 3 for more information.

7. C. The Set-VMSwitch cmdlet allows an administrator to configure a virtual switch. See Chapter 3 for more information.

8. A. The only virtual hard disk that increases in size is the dynamically expanding disk. See Chapter 4 for more information.

9. C. This question relates to the setup command used to install the Hyper-V server role on a Windows Server 2016 Server Core machine. It's important to remember that these commands are case sensitive, and that the correct command is start /wocsetup Microsoft-Hyper-V. See Chapter 4 for more information.

10. A. The PowerShell command Restart-VM restarts a virtual machine. See Chapter 4 for more information.

11. A. To create a new NLB cluster, you would use the PowerShell command New-NlbCluster. See Chapter 5 for more information.

12. B. If an administrator decides to use the drainstop command, the cluster stops after answering all of the current NLB connections. So the current NLB connections are finished but no new connections to that node are accepted. See Chapter 5 for more information.

13. B. The storage tests require the clustered disk resource to be offline. If you need to run the storage tests, the Validate a Configuration Wizard will prompt you to make sure you want to take the resources offline. See Chapter 6 for more information.

14. A. Administrators would use the `Test-Cluster` to complete validation tests for a cluster. See Chapter 6 for more information.

15. B. The `docker rm` command is the command that is used to delete an image. You should run `docker images` first and get the ID number or name of the image that you want to delete. See Chapter 7 for more information.

16. D. The `Get-Container` PowerShell command allows an administrator to view information about Containers. See Chapter 7 for more information.

17. A. The `docker images` command gives you the ability to see your images. The `docker info` command allows you to see how many images you have on a host but it does not give you details about the images. See Chapter 7 for more information.

18. B. The primary method by which system administrators create and manage application data partitions is through the `ntdsutil` tool. See Chapter 8 for more information.

19. B. `Perfmon.exe` is the command-line command to start Performance Monitor. See Chapter 9 for more information.

20. D. `Resmon.exe` is the command-line command to start Resource Monitor. See Chapter 9 for more information.

21. C. The CIDR /27 tells you that 27 1s are turned on in the subnet mask. Twenty-seven 1s equals 11111111.11111111.11111111.11100000. This would then equal 255.255.255.224. See Chapter 10 for more information.

22. C. The unique local address can be FC00 or FD00, and it is used like the private address space of IPv4. Unique local addresses are not expected to be routable on the global Internet, but they are used for private routing within an organization. See Chapter 10 for more information.

23. D. To calculate the network mask, you need to figure out which power number (2^x) is greater than or equal to the number you need. Since we are looking for 1000, $2^{10} = 1024$. You then add the power (10) to the current network mask (53 + 10 = 63). See Chapter 10 for more information.

24. B. Manual settings override DHCP options. See Chapter 11 for more information.

25. A. When the DHCP server crashed, the scope was effectively deactivated. Deactivating a scope has no effect on the client until it needs to renew the lease. See Chapter 11 for more information.

26. A. Microsoft's `jetpack.exe` utility allows you to compact a JET database. Microsoft JET databases are used for WINS and DHCP databases. See Chapter 12 for more information.

27. B. One of the nice advantages of DHCP is that it is one of the only Roles that can be installed onto a Nano Server. See Chapter 12 for more information.

28. A. The abbreviation that helps you remember how DHCP works is DORA: Discover, Offer, Request, and Acknowledge. See Chapter 12 for more information.

29. A. 003 Router is used to provide a list of available routers or default gateways on the same subnet. See Chapter 12 for more information.

30. B. The `Get-IpamDnsServer` command allows an administrator to view DNS server information from the IPAM database. See Chapter 13 for more information.

31. D. Administrators can use the `Set-IpamDiscoveryDomain` PowerShell command to change the IPAM discovery configuration. See Chapter 13 for more information.

32. B. Administrators can use the `Set-IpamBlock` PowerShell command to configure an IP address block in IPAM. See Chapter 13 for more information.

33. D. Logman creates and manages Event Trace Session and Performance logs and allows an administrator to monitor many different applications through the use of the command line. See Chapter 14 for more information.

34. C. The NPS snap-in allows you to set up RADIUS servers and which RADIUS server would accept authentication from other RADIUS servers. You can do your entire RADIUS configuration through the NPS snap-in. See Chapter 14 for more information.

35. B. Cipher is a command-line utility that allows you to configure or change EFS files and folders. See Chapter 15 for more information.

36. A. The Sharing tab contains a check box that you can use to list the printer in Active Directory. See Chapter 15 for more information.

37. D. File servers are used for storage of data, especially for users' home folders. Home folders are folder locations for your users to store data that is important and that needs to be backed up. See Chapter 15 for more information.

38. B. In a three-node cluster, only one node can be offline before the quorum is lost; a majority of the votes must be available to achieve the quorum. See Chapter 16 for more information.

39. A. Administrators would use the `Test-Cluster` to complete validation tests for a cluster. See Chapter 16 for more information.

40. A. The PowerShell command `Restart-VM` restarts a virtual machine. See Chapter 17 for more information.

41. B. A domain controller can contain Active Directory information for only one domain. If you want to use a multi-domain environment, you must use multiple domain controllers configured in either a tree or a forest setting. See Chapter 18 for more information.

42. D. NTFS has file-level security, and it makes efficient usage of disk space. Since this machine is to be configured as a domain controller, the configuration requires at least one NTFS partition to store the Sysvol information. See Chapter 18 for more information.

43. B, C. TCP/IP and DNS are both required when installing Active Directory. See Chapter 18 for more information.

44. A. The Get-ADUser command allows you to view Active Directory user accounts using PowerShell. See Chapter 19 for more information.

45. C. Administrators can use the Unlock-ADAccount command to unlock an Active Directory account. See Chapter 19 for more information.

46. D. The dsadd command allows you to add an object (user's account) to the Active Directory database. See Chapter 19 for more information.

47. C. Shortcut trusts are trusts set up between two domains in the same forest. See Chapter 20 for more information.

48. B. The NTDS settings for the site level are where you would activate and deactivate Global Catalogs. See Chapter 20 for more information.

49. D. The Delegation of Control Wizard is designed to allow administrators to set up permissions on specific Active Directory objects. See Chapter 20 for more information.

50. A, C. Administrators can create new Organizational Units (OUs) by using either the Active Directory Administrative Center or Active Directory Users and Computers. See Chapter 20 for more information.

51. A. You would use the Windows PowerShell Invoke-GPUpdate cmdlet. This PowerShell cmdlet allows you to force the GPO to reapply the policies immediately. See Chapter 21 for more information.

52. A. GPOs at the OU level take precedence over GPOs at the domain level. GPOs at the domain level, in turn, take precedence over GPOs at the site level. See Chapter 21 for more information.

53. B. The Block Policy Inheritance option prevents group policies of higher-level Active Directory objects from applying to lower-level objects as long as the Enforced option is not set. See Chapter 21 for more information.

54. D. To disable the application of Group Policy on a security group, you should deny the Apply Group Policy option. This is particularly useful when you don't want GPO settings to apply to a specific group, even though that group may be in an OU that includes the GPO settings. See Chapter 21 for more information.

55. B, D. To enable AD FS auditing, you must check the boxes for Success Audits and Failure Audits on the Events tab of the Federation Service Properties dialog box. You must also enable Object Access Auditing in Local Policy or Group Policy. See Chapter 22 for more information.

56. C. The Add-CATemplate command allows an administrator to add a certificate template to the CA. See Chapter 22 for more information.

57. D. Administrators can use the Get-CACrlDistributionPoint command to view all the locations set for the CRL distribution point (CDP). See Chapter 22 for more information.

58. A. To use the Web Application Proxy, you must install the Remote Access role. See Chapter 23 for more information.

59. A, D. To use a Web Application Proxy and AD FS, you should set your firewall to allow for ports 443 and 49443. See Chapter 23 for more information.

60. B. The `Set-AdfsServerApplication` command allows an administrator to modify configuration settings for a server application role of an application in AD FS See Chapter 23 for more information.

Chapter

1

Installing Windows Server 2016

THE FOLLOWING 70-740 EXAM OBJECTIVES ARE COVERED IN THIS CHAPTER:

✓ **Install, upgrade, and migrate servers and workloads**

- This objective may include but is not limited to: Determine Windows Server 2016 installation requirements; determine appropriate Windows Server 2016 editions per workloads; install Windows Server 2016; install Windows Server 2016 features and roles; install and configure Windows Server Core; manage Windows Server Core installations using Windows PowerShell, command line, and remote management capabilities; implement Windows PowerShell Desired State Configuration (DSC) to install and maintain integrity of installed environments; perform upgrades and migrations of servers and core workloads from Windows Server 2008 and Windows Server 2012 to Windows Server 2016; determine the appropriate activation model for server installation, such as Automatic Virtual Machine Activation (AVMA), Key Management Service (KMS), and Active Directory-based Activation.

✓ **Install and configure Nano Server**

- This objective may include but is not limited to: Determine appropriate usage scenarios and requirements for Nano Server; install Nano Server; implement Roles and Features on Nano Server.

So, you have decided to start down the track of Windows Server 2016. The first question you must ask yourself is what's the first step? Well, the first step is to learn about what Windows Server 2016 features and benefits are available and how these features can help improve your organization's network.

So that's where I am going to start. I will talk about the different Windows Server 2016 versions and what version may be best for you. After I show you some of the new and improved Windows Server 2016 features, I will then show you how to install these different versions onto your network.

I will also show you how to use some PowerShell commands in the Windows Server 2016 installation. Let's dive right into the server by talking about some of the new features and advantages of Windows Server 2016.

 The Windows Server 2016 installations will all be done on a virtual server. You can use any virtual software as long as its supports Windows Server 2016 and 64-bit processors.

Features and Advantages of Windows Server 2016

Before I show how to install and configure Windows Server 2016, let's take a look at some of the new features and the advantages it offers. Microsoft has stated that Windows Server 2016 is "the cloud-ready operating system." This means that many of the features of Windows Server 2016 are built and evolve around cloud based software and networking.

 Since many of you will be upgrading from previous versions of Windows Server, these are the new and/or improved features introduced by Microsoft since then. I will specifically identify any new features or advantages that are new to Windows Server 2016 only.

I will talk about all of these features in greater detail throughout this book. What follows are merely brief descriptions.

Built-in Security   Microsoft has always tried to make sure that their operating systems are as secure as possible, but with Windows Server 2016, Microsoft has included built-in breach resistance. This feature helps stop attackers on your system and allows a company to meet any compliance requirements.

Active Directory Certificate Services   *Active Directory Certificate Services (AD CS)* provides a customizable set of services that allow you to issue and manage *public key infrastructure (PKI) certificates*. These certificates can be used in software security systems that employ public key technologies.

Active Directory Domain Services   *Active Directory Domain Services (AD DS)* includes new features that make deploying domain controllers simpler and that let you implement them faster. AD DS also makes the domain controllers more flexible, both to audit and to authorize for access to files. Moreover, AD DS has been designed to make performing administrative tasks easier through consistent graphical and scripted management experiences.

Active Directory Rights Management Services   *Active Directory Rights Management Services (AD RMS)* provides management and development tools that let you work with industry security technologies, including encryption, certificates, and authentication. Using these technologies allows organizations to create reliable information protection solutions.

BitLocker   *BitLocker* is a tool that allows you to encrypt the hard drives of your computer. By encrypting the hard drives, you can provide enhanced protection against data theft or unauthorized exposure of your computers or removable drives that are lost or stolen.

BranchCache   *BranchCache* allows data from files and web servers on a wide area network (WAN) to be cached on computers at a local branch office. By using BranchCache, you can improve application response times while also reducing WAN traffic. Cached data can be either distributed across peer client computers (distributed cache mode) or centrally hosted on a server (hosted cache mode). BranchCache is included with Windows Server 2016 and Windows 10.

Containers   Windows Server 2016 has started focusing on an isolated operating system environment called Dockers. Dockers allow applications to run in isolated environments called Containers. Containers are a separate location where applications can operate without affecting other applications or other operating system resources. To understand Dockers and Containers, think of virtualization.

Virtual machines are operating systems that run in their own space on top of another operating system. Well Dockers and Containers allow an application to run in its own space and because of this, it doesn't affect other applications. There are two different types of containers to focus on.

Windows Server Containers   Windows Server 2016 allows for an isolated application to run by using a technology called process and namespace isolation. Windows Server 2016 containers allow applications to share the system's kernel with their container and all other containers running on the same host.

Hyper-V Containers   Windows Server 2016 Hyper-V Containers add another virtual layer by isolating applications in their own optimized virtual machine. Hyper-V Containers work differently than Windows Server Containers in the fact that the Hyper-V Containers do not share the system's kernel with other Hyper-V Containers.

Credential Guard   Credential Guard helps protect a system's credentials and this helps avoid pass the hash attacks. Credential Guard offers better protection against advanced persistent threats by protecting credentials on the system from being stolen by a compromised administrator or malware.

Credential Guard can also be enabled on Remote Desktop Services servers and Virtual Desktop Infrastructure so that the credentials for users connecting to their sessions are protected.

DHCP   *Dynamic Host Configuration Protocol (DHCP)* is an Internet standard that allows organizations to reduce the administrative overhead of configuring hosts on a TCP/IP-based network. Some of the features are DHCP failover, policy-based assignment, and the ability to use Windows PowerShell for DHCP Server.

DNS   *Domain Name System (DNS)* services are used in TCP/IP networks. DNS will convert a computer name or fully qualified domain name (FQDN) to an IP address. DNS also has the ability to do a reverse lookup and convert an IP address to a computer name. DNS allows you to locate computers and services through user-friendly names.

Failover Clustering   *Failover Clustering* gives an organization the ability to provide high availability and scalability to networked servers. Failover clusters can include file share storage for server applications, such as Hyper-V and Microsoft SQL Server, and those that run on physical servers or virtual machines.

File Server Resource Manager   *File Server Resource Manager* is a set of tools that allows administrators to manage and control the amount and type of data stored on the organization's servers. By using File Server Resource Manager, administrators have the ability to set up file management tasks, use quota management, get detailed reports, set up a file classification infrastructure, and configure file-screening management.

Group Policy Objects   *Group Policy Objects* are a set of rules and management configuration options that you can control through the Group Policy settings. These policy settings can be placed on users' computers throughout the organization.

Hyper-V   *Hyper-V* is one of the most changed features in Windows Server 2016. Hyper-V allows an organization to consolidate servers by creating and managing a virtualized computing environment. It does this by using virtualization technology that is built into Windows Server 2016.

Hyper-V allows you to run multiple operating systems simultaneously on one physical computer. Each virtual operating system runs in its own virtual machine environment.

Windows Server 2016 Hyper-V now allows an administrator to protect their corporate virtual machines using the new feature called Shielded Virtual Machine. Shielded Virtual Machines are encrypted using BitLocker and the VMs can only run on approved Hyper-V host systems.

Hyper-V also now includes a new feature called containers. Containers add a new unique additional layer of isolation for a containerized applications.

IPAM   *IP Address Management (IPAM)* is one of the features introduced with Windows Server 2012. IPAM allows an administrator to customize and monitor the IP address infrastructure on a corporate network.

Kerberos Authentication Windows Server 2016 uses the *Kerberos authentication* (version 5) protocol and extensions for password-based and public key authentication. The Kerberos client is installed as a *security support provider (SSP)*, and it can be accessed through the *Security Support Provider Interface (SSPI)*.

Managed Service Accounts (gMSAs) Stand-alone *group managed service accounts*, originally created for Windows Server 2008 R2 and Windows 7, are configured domain accounts that allow automatic password management and *service principal names (SPNs)* management, including the ability to delegate management to other administrators. Service accounts are accounts that an administrator creates so that the account can be used to start a service. Managed service accounts are accounts that are created using PowerShell, and then Active Directory manages the account. This includes changing the password on a regular frequency.

Nano Server Windows Server 2016 has introduced a brand-new type of server installation called Nano Server. Nano Server allows an administrator to remotely administer the server operating system. It was primarily designed and optimized for private clouds and datacenters. Nano Server is very similar to Server Core, but the Nano Server operating system uses significantly less hard drive space, has no local logon capability, and only supports 64-bit applications and tools.

Nested Virtualization Windows Server 2016 introduces a new Hyper-V feature called Nested Virtualization. Nested Virtualization allows administrators to create virtual machines within virtual machines. As an instructor, I think this is an awesome new feature. Now I can build a Windows Server 2016 Hyper-V server with a training virtual machine. Then when I get to the part when I need to teach Hyper-V, I can just do that right in the classroom virtual machine. There are numerous possibilities and we will talk more about them throughout this book.

Networking There are many networking technologies and features in Windows Server 2016, including BranchCache, Data Center Bridging (DCB), NIC Teaming, and many more.

PowerShell Direct Windows Server 2016 includes a new simple way to manage Hyper-V virtual machines called PowerShell Direct. PowerShell Direct is a new powerful set of parameters for the PSSession cmdlet called VMName. This will be discussed in greater detail in the Hyper-V chapters.

Remote Desktop Services Before Windows Server 2008, we used to refer to this as Terminal Services. *Remote Desktop Services* allows users to connect to virtual desktops, RemoteApp programs, and session-based desktops. Using Remote Desktop Services allows users to access remote connections from within a corporate network or from the Internet.

Security Auditing *Security auditing* gives an organization the ability to help maintain the security of an enterprise. By using security audits, you can verify authorized or unauthorized access to machines, resources, applications, and services. One of the best advantages of security audits is to verify regulatory compliance.

Smart Cards Using *smart cards* (referred to as *two-factor authentication*) and their associated *personal identification numbers (PINs)* is a popular, reliable, and cost-effective way to provide authentication. When using smart cards, the user not only must have the physical card but also must know the PIN to be able to gain access to network resources. This is effective because even if the smart card is stolen, thieves can't access the network unless they know the PIN.

TLS/SSL (Schannel SSP)   *Schannel* is a security support provider (SSP) that uses the *Secure Sockets Layer (SSL)* and *Transport Layer Security (TLS)* Internet standard authentication protocols together. The Security Support Provider Interface is an API used by Windows systems to allow security-related functionality, including authentication.

Windows Deployment Services   *Windows Deployment Services* allows an administrator to install Windows operating systems remotely. Administrators can use Windows Deployment Services to set up new computers by using a network-based installation.

Windows PowerShell Desired State Configuration   Windows Server 2016 created a new PowerShell management platform called Windows PowerShell Desired State Configuration (DSC). DSC enables the deploying and managing of configuration data for software services and it also helps manage the environment in which these services run.

DSC allows administrators to use Windows PowerShell language extensions along with new Windows PowerShell cmdlets, and resources. DSC allows you to declaratively specify how a corporation wants their software environment to be configured and maintained.

DSC allows you to automate tasks like enabling or disabling server roles and features, manage Registry settings, manage files and directories, manage groups and users, deploy software, and run PowerShell scripts to just name a few.

Windows Server Backup Feature   The *Windows Server Backup* feature gives an organization a way to back up and restore Windows servers. You can use Windows Server Backup to back up the entire server (all volumes), selected volumes, the system state, or specific files or folders.

Planning the Windows Server 2016 Installation

Before you install Windows Server 2016, you must first ask yourself these important questions: What type of server do I need? Will the server be a domain controller? What roles do I need to install on this server?

Once you have figured out what you need the server to do, you can make a game plan for the installation. So, let's start by looking at some of the server roles and technologies that can be installed on a Windows Server 2016 computer.

Server Roles in Windows Server 2016

When you install Windows Server 2016, you have to decide which roles and features are going to be installed onto that server. This is an important decision in the computer world. Many administrators not only overuse a server but also underutilize servers in their organization.

For example, many administrators refuse to put any other roles or features on a domain controller. This may not be a good use of a server. Domain controllers help authenticate users onto the network, but after that the domain controllers are really not very busy all day long. Domain controllers have tasks that they must perform all day, but the server on which they reside is not heavily used when compared to a SQL Server machine or an Exchange mail server. This is where monitoring your server can be useful.

If your domain controller is a virtual machine or if you have more than enough servers, then having a domain controller with no other applications on it (except DNS) may be fine. But if servers are limited, then think about putting other services or applications on your server if the server can handle them. Just remember, some applications work better on member servers than on domain controllers. So before just adding any application to a domain controller, make sure you research the application and find out best practices.

Now let's take a look at some of the roles and features you can install onto a Windows Server 2016 machine. Knowing the different roles and features you can install will help you to design, deploy, manage, and troubleshoot technologies in Windows Server 2016. Figure 1.1 shows the Add Roles and Features Wizard in Server Manager. It shows you just some of the roles that can be installed on a Windows Server 2016 machine.

FIGURE 1.1   Available roles in Windows Server 2016

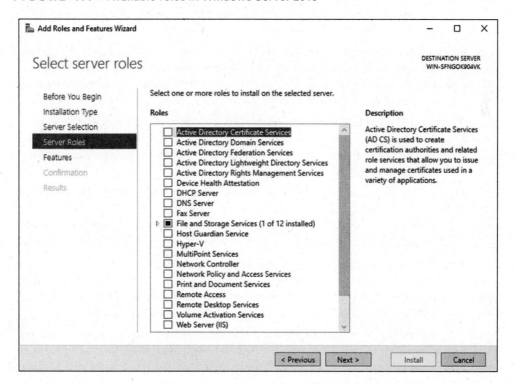

Roles and Features

Many of these roles were discussed in the section "Features and Advantages of Windows Server 2016." I include them here again because they are also *roles* that can also be installed on Windows Server 2016.

The following roles are available in Windows Server 2016:

Active Directory Certificate Services   The AD CS server role in Windows Server 2016 allows you to build a PKI and provide public key cryptography, digital certificates, and digital signature capabilities for your organization.

> **Feature**   AD CS provides a customizable set of services that allows you to issue and manage PKI certificates. These certificates can be used in software security systems that employ public key technologies.

> **Role**   AD CS in Windows Server 2016 is the server role that allows you to build a PKI and provide public key cryptography, digital certificates, and digital signature capabilities for your organization.

Active Directory Domain Services   The AD DS server role allows you to create a scalable, secure, and manageable infrastructure for user and resource management and to provide support for directory-enabled applications, such as Microsoft Exchange Server.

Active Directory Federation Services   *Active Directory Federation Services (AD FS)* provides Internet-based clients with a secure identity access solution that works on both Windows and non-Windows operating systems. AD FS gives users the ability to do a *single sign-on (SSO)* and access applications on other networks without needing a secondary password.

Active Directory Lightweight Directory Services   *Active Directory Lightweight Directory Services (AD LDS)* is a *Lightweight Directory Access Protocol (LDAP)* directory service that provides flexible support for directory-enabled applications, without the dependencies and domain-related restrictions of AD DS.

Active Directory Rights Management Services   Active Directory Rights Management Services (AD RMS) in Windows Server 2016 is the server role that provides you with management and development tools that work with industry security technologies including encryption, certificates, and authentication to help organizations create reliable information protection solutions.

Device Health Attestation   The Device Health Attestation helps protect your corporate network by verifying that client systems meet corporate policy. For example, you can make sure that all computers that connect to your network have their proper updates, antivirus, and proper configuration policies before connecting to the network.

DHCP   *Dynamic Host Configuration Protocol (DHCP)* is an Internet standard that allows organizations to reduce the administrative overhead of configuring hosts on a TCP/IP-based network. Some of the features are DHCP failover, policy-based assignment, and the ability to use Windows PowerShell for DHCP Server.

DNS   *Domain Name System (DNS)* services are used in TCP/IP networks. DNS will convert a computer name or fully qualified domain name (FQDN) to an IP address. DNS also has the ability to do a reverse lookup and convert an IP address to a computer name. DNS allows you to locate computers and services through user-friendly names.

Fax Server   The fax server allows you to send and receive faxes, and it also allows you to manage fax resources such as jobs, settings, reports, and fax devices on a specific computer or on the network.

File and Storage Services   *File and Storage Services* allows an administrator to set up and manage one or more file servers. These servers can provide a central location on your network where you can store files and then share those files with network users. If users require access to the same files and applications or if centralized backup and file management are important issues for your organization, administrators should set up network servers as a file server.

Host Guardian Service   The Host Guardian Service (HGS) allows you to have a more secure environment for your network's virtual machines. The HGS role provides the Attestation & Key Protection services that enable Guarded Hosts to run Shielded virtual machines.

Hyper-V   The Hyper-V role allows administrators to create and manage a virtualized environment by taking advantage of the technology built into the Windows Server 2016 operating system. When an administrator installs the Hyper-V role, all required virtualization components are installed.

Some of the required components include the Windows hypervisor, Virtual Machine Management Service, the virtualization WMI provider, the virtual machine bus (VMbus), the virtualization service provider (VSP), and the virtual infrastructure driver (VID).

MultiPoint Services   MultiPoint Services allows multiple users, each with their own independent and familiar Windows experience, to simultaneously share one computer.

Network Controller   The Network Controller provides the point of automation needed for continual configuration, monitoring, and diagnostics of virtual networks, physical networks, network services, network topology, address management, and so on within a datacenter.

Network Policy and Access Services   Use the *Network Policy and Access Services* server role to install and configure *Network Policy Server (NPS)*, which helps safeguard the security of your network.

Print and Document Services   *Print and Document Services* allows an administrator to centralize print server and network printer tasks. This role also allows you to receive scanned documents from network scanners and route the documents to a shared network resource, Windows SharePoint Services site, or email addresses. Print and Document Services also provides fax servers with the ability to send and receive faxes while also giving the administrator the ability to manage fax resources such as jobs, settings, reports, and fax devices on the fax server.

Remote Access   Remote Access provides connectivity through DirectAccess, VPN, and Web Application Proxies. DirectAccess provides an Always On and Always Managed experience. Remote Access provides VPN access including site-to-site connectivity. Web Application

Proxies enable web-based applications from your corporate network to client devices outside of the corporate network. Remote Access also includes routing capabilities, including Network Address Translation (NAT).

Remote Desktop Services   Remote Desktop Services allows for faster desktop and application deployments to any device, improving remote user effectiveness while helping to keep critical data secure. Remote Desktop Services allows for both a *virtual desktop infrastructure (VDI)* and session-based desktops, allowing users to connect from anywhere.

Volume Activation Services   Windows Server 2016 *Volume Activation Services* will help your organization benefit from using this service to deploy and manage volume licenses for a medium to large number of computers.

Web Server (IIS)   The *Web Server (IIS)* role in Windows Server 2016 allows an administrator to set up a secure, easy-to-manage, modular, and extensible platform for reliably hosting websites, services, and applications.

Windows Deployment Services   Windows Deployment Services allows an administrator to install a Windows operating system over the network. Administrators do not have to install each operating system directly from a CD or DVD.

Windows Server Essentials Experience   Windows Server Essentials Experience allows an administrator to set up the IT infrastructure, and it also provides powerful functions such as PC backups to help protect your corporate data and Remote Web Access that allows access to business information from anywhere in the world. Windows Server Essentials Experience also allows you to easily connect to cloud-based applications and services.

Windows Server Update Services   *Windows Server Update Services (WSUS)* allows administrators to deploy application and operating system updates. By deploying WSUS, administrators have the ability to manage updates that are released through Microsoft Update to computers in their network. This feature is integrated with the operating system as a server role on a Windows Server 2016 system.

Migrating Roles and Features to Windows Server 2016

Once you decide on which roles and features you are going to install onto your Windows Server 2016 system, then you either have to install those roles and features from scratch or migrate them from a previous version of Windows server.

Windows Server 2016 includes a set of migration tools that administrators can use to help ease the process of migrating server roles, features, operating system settings, and data. Administrators can migrate this data from an existing server that are running Windows Server 2008 R2, Windows Server 2012, Windows Server 2012 R2, or Windows Server 2016 to a computer that is running Windows Server 2016.

Using Windows Server Migration Tools to migrate roles, role services, and features can simplify the deployment of new servers. You can migrate roles and features on any server, including Server Core, installation option of Windows Server 2016, and virtual servers. By using Windows Server Migration Tools, an administrator can reduce migration downtime, increase the accuracy of the migration process, and help eliminate conflicts that could otherwise occur during the migration process.

One advantage of using the migration tools is that most of them support cross-architecture migrations (x86-based to x64-based computing platforms), migrations between physical and virtual environments, and migrations between both the full and Server Core installation options of the Windows Server operating system. In Windows Server 2016, Windows Server Migration Tools also supports cross-subnet migrations.

To use Windows Server Migration Tools, the feature must be installed on both the source and destination computers. Windows Server Migration Tools installation and preparation can be divided into the following stages:

1. Installing Windows Server Migration Tools on destination servers that run Windows Server 2016

2. Creating deployment folders on destination servers that run Windows Server 2016 for copying to source servers

3. Copying deployment folders from destination servers to source servers

4. Registering Windows Server Migration Tools on source servers

If you plan to use Windows Server Migration Tools, you must be a member of the Administrators group on both the source and destination servers to install, remove, or set up the tools.

Administrators can install Windows Server Migration Tools 2016 by using either the Add Roles Or Features Wizard in Server Manager or Windows PowerShell deployment cmdlets for Server Manager.

To install Windows Server Migration Tools on a Server Core installation of Windows Server 2016, you would complete the following steps:

1. Open a Windows PowerShell session by typing **powershell.exe** in the current command prompt session and then pressing Enter.

2. In the Windows PowerShell session, install Windows Server Migration Tools by using the Windows PowerShell `Install-WindowsFeature` cmdlet for Server Manager. In the Windows PowerShell session, type the following, and then press Enter. (Omit the `ComputerName` parameter if you are installing the Windows Server Migration Tools on the local server.)

```
Install-WindowsFeature Migration –ComputerName computer_name
```

Deciding Which Windows Server 2016 Versions to Use

You may be wondering which version of Windows Server 2016 is best for your organization. After all, Microsoft offers the following six versions of Windows Server 2016.

At the time this book was written, there were six versions of Windows Server 2016. But Microsoft is always improving and creating new versions of their products. Be sure to check out Microsoft's website for any other versions or changes.

Windows Server 2016 Datacenter This version is designed for organizations that are looking to migrate to a highly virtualized, private cloud environment. Windows Server 2016 Datacenter has full Windows Server functionality with unlimited virtual instances.

Windows Server 2016 Standard This version is designed for organizations with physical or minimally virtualized environments. Windows Server 2016 Standard has full Windows Server functionality with two virtual instances.

Windows Server 2016 Essentials This version is ideal for small businesses that have as many as 25 users and 50 devices. Windows Server 2016 Essentials has a simpler interface and preconfigured connectivity to cloud-based services but no virtualization rights.

Windows Hyper-V Server 2016 Microsoft Hyper-V Server 2016 has the exact same Hyper-V role components as Windows Server 2016. Hyper-V 2016 Server is a stand-alone version that has the Windows hypervisor, the Windows Server driver model, and the other virtualization components only. Windows Hyper-V Server 2016 allows you to have a simple virtualization solution which allows you to reduce costs.

Windows Storage Server 2016 Windows Storage Server 2016 is not openly available for sale to the general public. Windows Storage Server 2016 is only available as an integrated hardware offering or as an available field upgrade from your hardware manufacturer. Windows Storage Server 2016 fully supports upgrades from previous versions.

Windows MultiPoint Premium 2016 Server Windows MultiPoint Premium Server 2016 is a Stand-Alone Windows product designed for environments that have multiple users simultaneously sharing one computer. Windows MultiPoint Premium 2016 Server is the same as a Windows Server 2016 with Multipoint Services Installed. MultiPoint Services allows multiple users, each with their own independent and familiar Windows experience to simultaneously share one computer.

Once you choose what roles are going on your server, you must then decide how you're going to install Windows Server 2016. There are two ways to install Windows Server 2016. You can upgrade a Windows Server 2012 or Windows Server 2012 R2 machine to Windows Server 2016, or you can do a clean install of Windows Server 2016. If you decide that you are going to upgrade, there are specific upgrade paths you must follow.

Your choice of Windows Server 2016 version is dictated by how your current network is designed. If you are building a network from scratch, then it's pretty straightforward. Just choose the Windows Server 2016 version based on your server's tasks. However, if you already have a version of Windows Server 2012 installed, you should follow the recommendations in Table 1.1, which briefly summarize the supported upgrade paths to Windows Server 2016.

TABLE 1.1 Supported Windows Server 2016 upgrade path recommendations

Current System	Upgraded System
Windows Server 2012 Standard	Windows Server 2016 Standard or Datacenter
Windows Server 2012 Datacenter	Windows Server 2016 Datacenter

Current System	Upgraded System
Windows Server 2012 R2 Standard	Windows Server 2016 Standard or Datacenter
Windows Server 2012 R2 Datacenter	Windows Server 2016 Datacenter
Windows Server 2012 R2 Essentials	Windows Server 2016 Essentials
Hyper-V Server 2012 R2	Hyper-V Server 2016
Windows Storage Server 2012 Standard	Windows Storage Server 2016 Standard
Windows Storage Server 2012 Workgroup	Windows Storage Server 2016 Workgroup
Windows Storage Server 2012 R2 Workgroup	Windows Storage Server 2016 Workgroup

 If your version of Microsoft Windows Server is not 64-bit, you can't upgrade to Windows Server 2016.

Deciding on the Type of Installation

One of the final choices you must make before installing Windows Server 2016 is what type of installation you want. There are three ways to install Windows Server 2016.

Windows Server 2016 (Desktop Experience)   This is the version with which most administrators are familiar. This is the version that uses *Microsoft Management Console (MMC)* windows, and it is the version that allows the use of a mouse to navigate through the installation.

Windows Server 2016 Server Core   This is a bare-bones installation of Windows Server 2016. You can think of it this way: If Windows Server 2016 (Desktop Experience) is a top-of-the-line luxury car, then Windows Server 2016 Server Core is the stripped-down model with no air-conditioning, manual windows, and cloth seats. It might not be pretty to look at, but it gets the job done.

Windows Server 2016 Nano Server   Windows Server 2016 has introduced a brand new type of server installation called Nano Server. Nano Server allows an administrator to remotely administer the server operating system. It was primarily designed and optimized for private clouds and datacenters. Nano Server is very similar to Server Core, but the Nano Server operating system uses significantly smaller hard drive space, has no local logon capability, and only supports 64-bit applications and tools.

Real World Scenario

Server Core

Here is an explanation of Server Core that I have used ever since it was introduced in Windows Server 2008.

I am a *huge* sports fan. I love watching sports on TV, and I enjoy going to games. If you have ever been to a hockey game, you know what a hockey goal looks like. Between hockey periods, the stadium workers often bring out a huge piece of Plexiglas onto the ice. There is a tiny square cut out of the bottom of the glass. The square is just a bit bigger than a hockey puck itself.

Now they pick some lucky fan out of the stands, give them a puck at center ice, and then ask them to shoot the puck into the net with the Plexiglas in front of it. If they get it through that tiny little square at the bottom of the Plexiglas, they win a car or some such great prize.

Well, Windows Server 2016 (Desktop Experience) is like regular hockey with a net, and Windows Server 2016 Server Core is the Plexiglas version.

Server Core supports a limited number of roles:

- Active Directory Certificate Services (AD CS)
- Active Directory Domain Services (AD DS)
- Active Directory Federation Services (AD FS)
- Active Directory Lightweight Directory Services (AD LDS)
- Active Directory Rights Management Services (AD RMS)
- DHCP Server
- DNS Server
- Fax Server
- File and Storage Services
- BITS Server
- BranchCache
- Hyper-V
- Network Policy and Access Services
- Print and Document Services
- Remote Access

- Remote Desktop Services

- Volume Activation Services

- Web Server (IIS)

- Windows Deployment Services

- Windows Server Update Services

- .NET Framework 3.5 Features

- .NET Framework 4.6 Features

- Streaming Media Services

- Failover Clustering

- iSCSI

- Network Load Balancing

- MPIO

- qWave

- Telnet Server/Client

- Windows Server Migration Tools

- Windows PowerShell 4.0

Server Core does not have the normal Windows interface or GUI. Almost everything has to be configured via the command line or, in some cases, using the Remote Server Administration Tools from a full version of Windows Server 2016. While this might scare off some administrators, it has the following benefits:

Reduced Management   Because Server Core has a minimum number of applications installed, it reduces management effort.

Minimal Maintenance   Only basic systems can be installed on Server Core, so it reduces the upkeep you would need to perform in a normal server installation.

Smaller Footprint   Server Core requires only 1GB of disk space to install and 2GB of free space for operations.

Tighter Security   With only a few applications running on a server, it is less vulnerable to attacks.

The prerequisites for Server Core are basic. It requires the Windows Server 2016 installation media, a product key, and the hardware on which to install it.

After you install the base operating system, you use PowerShell or the remote administrative tools to configure the network settings, add the machine to the domain, create and format disks, and install roles and features. It takes only a few minutes to install Server Core, depending on the hardware.

Real World Scenario

Better Security

When I started in this industry more than 20 years ago, I was a programmer. I used to program computer hospital systems. When I switched to the networking world, I continued to work under contract with hospitals and with doctors' offices.

One problem I ran into is that many doctors are affiliated with hospitals, but they don't actually have offices within the hospital. Generally, they have offices either near the hospital or, in some cases, right across the street.

Here is the issue: Do we put servers in the doctors' offices, or do we make the doctor log into the hospital network through a remote connection? Doctors' offices normally don't have computer rooms, and we don't want to place a domain controller or server on someone's desk. It's just unsafe!

This is where Windows Server 2016 Server Core can come into play. Since it is a slimmed-down version of Windows and there is no GUI, it makes it harder for anyone in the office to hack into the system. Also, Microsoft has a domain controller in Windows Server 2016 called a *read-only domain controller (RODC)*. As its name suggests, it is a read-only version of a domain controller.

With Server Core and an RODC, you can feel safer placing a server on someone's desk or in any office. Server Core systems allow you to place servers in areas that you would never have placed them before. This can be a great advantage to businesses that have small, remote locations without full server rooms.

NIC Teaming

NIC Teaming, also known as *load balancing and failover (LBFO)*, gives an administrator the ability to allow multiple network adapters on a system to be placed into a team. Independent hardware vendors (IHVs) have required NIC Teaming, but until Windows Server 2012, NIC Teaming was *not* part of the Windows Server Operating System.

To be able to use NIC Teaming, the computer system must have at least one Ethernet adapter. If you want to provide fault protection, an administrator must have a minimum of two Ethernet adapters. One advantage of Windows Server 2016 is that an administrator can setup 32 network adapters in a NIC Team.

NIC Teaming is a very common practice when setting up virtualization. It is one way that you can have load balancing with Hyper-V.

NIC Teaming gives an administrator the ability to allow a virtual machine to use virtual network adapters in Hyper-V. The advantage of using NIC Teaming in Hyper-V is that the administrator can use it to connect to more than one Hyper-V switch. This allows Hyper-V to maintain connectivity even if the network adapter under the Hyper-V switch gets disconnected.

An administrator can configure NIC Teaming in either Server Manager or PowerShell.

Installing Windows Server 2016

In the following sections, I am going to walk you through two different types of installs. I will show you how to do a full install of Windows Server 2016 Datacenter (Desktop Experience), and then I will show you how to install the Server Core version of the same software and Nano Server.

 For these labs, I am using the full release of Windows Server 2016 Datacenter, but you can use Windows Server 2016 Standard.

Installing with the Desktop Experience

In Exercise 1.1, I will show you how to install Windows Server 2016 Datacenter (Desktop Experience). This installation will have a Graphical User Interface (GUI) and this means that an administrator will be able to control the applications on the Desktop and the operating system functions with a mouse.

Windows Installation

At the time of this writing, I used the first full release of Windows Server 2016 Datacenter. For this reason, there may be screens that have changed somewhat since this book was published.

EXERCISE 1.1

Installing Windows Server 2016 Datacenter (Desktop Experience)

1. Insert the Windows Server 2016 installation DVD, and restart the machine from the installation media.

2. At the first screen, Windows Server 2016 (see Figure 1.2) will ask you to configure your language, time and currency, and keyboard. Make your selections, and click Next.

3. At the next screen, click Install Now.

4. Depending on what version of Windows Server 2016 you have (MSDN, TechNet, and so on), you may be asked to enter a product key. If this screen appears, enter your product key, and click Next. If this screen does not appear, just go to step 5.

FIGURE 1.2 Windows Server 2016 Setup

5. The Select The Operating System That You Want To Install screen then appears. Choose the Windows Server 2016 Datacenter (Desktop Experience) selection (see Figure 1.3) and click Next.

FIGURE 1.3 Windows Server Edition

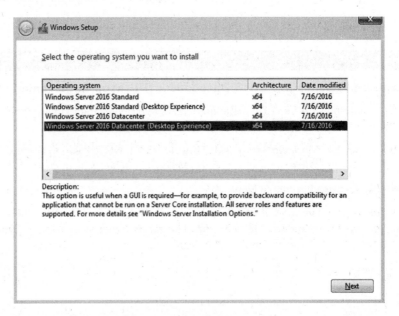

6. The license terms screen appears. After reading the Windows Server 2016 license agreement, check the I Accept The License Terms check box, and click Next.

7. On the Which type of installation do you want? Screen (see Figure 1.4), choose Custom: Install Windows Only (Advanced).

FIGURE 1.4   Windows Server Installation

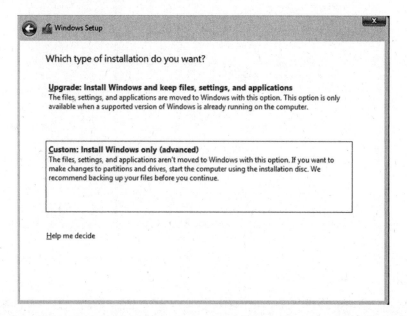

8. The next screen will ask you where you want to install Windows. If your hard disk is already formatted as NTFS, click the drive, and then click Next. If the hard disk is not yet set up or formatted, choose the New link, and create a partition. After creating the partition, click the Format link. Once the format is done, make sure you choose the new partition, and click Next.

9. The Installing Windows screen will appear next. This is where the files from your media will be installed onto the system (see Figure 1.5). The machine will reboot during this installation.

10. After the machine is finished rebooting, a screen requesting the administrator password will appear (see Figure 1.6). Type in your password. (P@ssword is used in this exercise.) Your password must meet the password complexity requirements. (Three of the following four are needed for complexity: one capitalized letter, one lowercase letter, one number, and/or one special character.) Click Finish.

FIGURE 1.5 Installing Windows screen

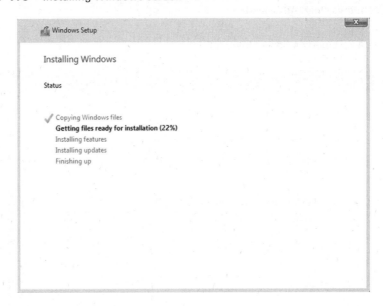

FIGURE 1.6 Customize settings

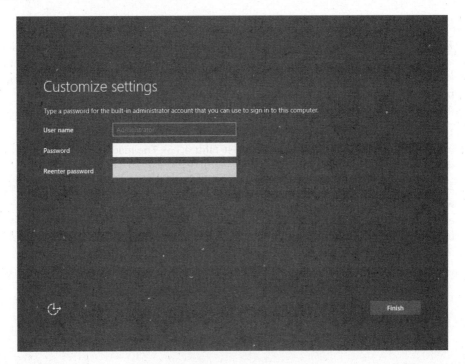

11. Next, log into the system. Press Ctrl+Alt+Del, and type in the administrator password. The machine will set up the properties of the administrator account.

12. Notice that the Server Manager dashboard automatically appears. Your Windows Server 2016 installation is now complete.

13. Close Server Manager.

After you have logged into the Windows Server 2016 Datacenter system, you will notice some features right away. The first is that there is a Start button in the lower-left corner of the screen.

Administrators can also access the Start button by pressing the Windows key on a standard keyboard.

Installing Windows Server 2016 Server Core

In Exercise 1.2, you will learn how to install Windows Server 2016 Server Core. You'll notice that the steps are similar to the ones in Exercise 1.1, with a couple of exceptions. As mentioned earlier, Server Core is a command line configuration of Windows Server 2016.

EXERCISE 1.2

Installing Windows Server 2016 Using Server Core

1. Insert the Windows Server 2016 installation DVD, and restart the machine from the installation media.

2. At the first screen, Windows Server 2016 will prompt you to configure your language, time and currency, and keyboard. Make your selections, and click Next.

3. At the next screen, click Install Now.

4. Depending on what version of Windows Server 2016 you have (MSDN, TechNet, and so on), you may be asked to enter a product key. If this screen appears, enter your product key, and click Next. If this screen does not appear, just go to step 5.

5. The Select The Operating System That You Want To Install screen then appears. Choose the Windows Server 2016 Datacenter selection (see Figure 1.7) and click Next.

6. The license terms screen appears. After reading the Windows Server 2016 license agreement, check the I Accept The License Terms check box and click Next.

7. At the Which Type Of Installation Do You Want? screen, choose Custom: Install Windows Only (Advanced).

FIGURE 1.7 Windows Server Edition

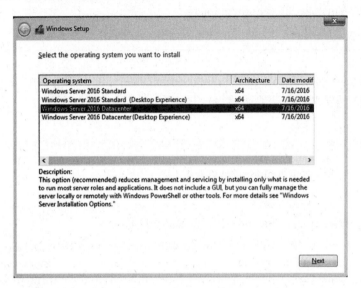

8. The next screen will ask you where you want to install Windows. If your hard disk is already formatted as NTFS, click the drive and then click Next. If the hard disk is not set up or formatted, choose the New link and create a partition. After creating the partition, click the Format link. Once the format is done, make sure you choose the new partition and click Next.

9. The Installing Windows screen will appear next. This is where the files from your media will be installed onto the system. The machine will reboot during this installation.

10. After the machine is finished rebooting, a screen requesting the administrator password will appear. Click OK (see Figure 1.8) and then type in your password. (P@ssword is used in this exercise.) Your password must meet the password complexity requirements (one capitalized letter, one number, and/or one special character).

FIGURE 1.8 Change Password Screen

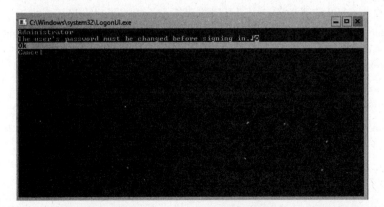

11. After the password is changed, a screen will appear telling you that the password has changed (see Figure 1.9). Hit the Enter key.

FIGURE 1.9   Password Changed Screen

12. You will automatically get logged in. You will notice that the command prompt will automatically appear (see Figure 1.10). Your Windows Server 2016 Server Core installation is now complete. To turn off the machine, type **Shutdown /s /t 0**.

FIGURE 1.10   Server Core Command Prompt

We will be showing many PowerShell commands throughout this book. The new Windows Server 2016 exams will be PowerShell intensive. I will show you the PowerShell commands needed to configure and maintain Windows Server 2016 Server Core throughout this entire book.

Installing Windows Server 2016 Nano Server

With the release of Windows Server 2016, Microsoft has released a brand new installation option called Nano Server. Nano Server is a version of Windows Server 2016 that is controlled remotely and it was specifically designed to optimize the Windows Server for private cloud and Datacenter installations.

Windows Server 2016 Nano Server is a lot like Server Core but the advantage is that it is even a smaller installation of the operating system. Nano Server has *NO* local logon or GUI capabilities and it will allow only 64-bit applications and utilities.

Since Nano Server takes much less hard drive space and does not have many of the normal server components, its allows Nano Server to be much faster when it comes to setups, reboots, and even updates. Nano Server is available for both Standard and Datacenter editions of Windows Server 2016.

When Microsoft created Nano Server, they had some very specific ideas of how companies would use this version. For example, Nano Server is a good option for a DNS server, an IIS server, an application server for cloud based applications, or even a storage machine for file servers.

Now that you have seen some of the options on how to use Nano Server, let take a look at some of the disadvantages of Nano Servers. The first downside to using a Nano Server is that it cannot act as Domain Controller (this is a server with a copy of Active Directory installed onto the system). Also, Group Policy Objects (rules that you can put on machines or users) are also not supported on Nano Servers. Finally, Nano Servers can't be configured to use System Center Configuration Manager, System Center Data Protection Manager, NIC Teaming, or as proxy servers. Nano Servers also use a version of Windows PowerShell which has many differences as a server with regular PowerShell.

At the time this book was written, Nano Server only supports the Current Branch for Business (CBB) licensing model. But be sure to check the Microsoft website before taking any of the Microsoft Windows Server 2016 exams to make sure that this has not changed.

When it comes to installing Nano Servers, there are a few different options. There is no downloadable version of just Windows Server 2016 Nano Server. Nano Server is included on the Windows Server 2016 Standard or Datacenter physical media. Both server versions have a folder called NanoServer. The NanoServer folders contain a .wim image and a subfolder called Packages. The Packages subfolder is needed when you want to add server roles and features to the image.

But if you want a real easy way to create a Nano Server virtual hard drive (VHD), you can just download the Nano Server Image Builder. This software will help you easily create a Nano Server VHD that you can then use to boot up a server with or use in Microsoft's Hyper-V server.

In Exercise 1.3, you will learn how to install the Nano Server Image Builder and build a Nano Server VHD. For this exercise, you must have a copy of Windows Server 2016 downloaded.

EXERCISE 1.3

Creating a Nano Server VHD

1. Download the Nano Server Image Builder (see Figure 1.11) at Microsoft's website (https://www.microsoft.com/en-us/download/details.aspx?id=54065) by clicking the Download button. I saved the downloaded file under my Windows Server 2016 Downloads folder.

FIGURE 1.11   Nano Server Image Builder

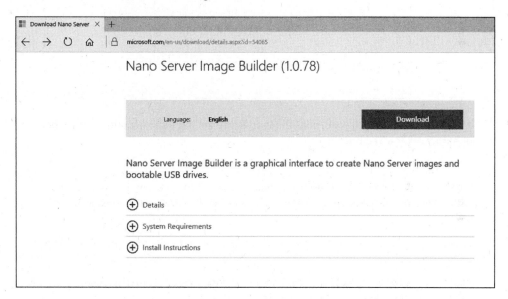

2. A file named NanoServerImageBuilder.msi will be created. Double-click on the file. If an Open File Security Warning Dialog box appears, click the Run button.

3. The Nano Server Image Builder Setup wizard will begin. Click Next at the intro screen.

4. At the Licensing screen, click the I accept the terms checkbox and click Next.

5. At the Destination Folder screen, choose the directory where you want to install the Nano Server Image Builder files (see Figure 1.12). Click Next.

FIGURE 1.12 Nano Server Image Builder Destination

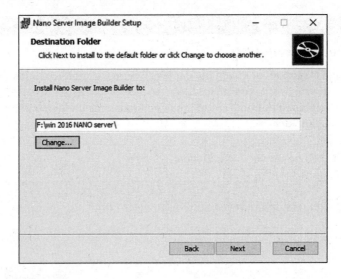

6. At the Ready to Install screen, click the Install Button. If a User Account Control box appears, click the Yes button.

7. Once the Installation is complete, click the Finish Button.

8. Open Windows Explorer and go to the destination folder that you chose in step 5. Double-click the NanoServerImageBuilder.exe file. If a UAC dialog box appears, click Yes.

9. For the Image Builder to work, you must also download the Windows ADK kit. This can be done at

   https://developer.microsoft.com/en-us/windows/hardware/windows-assessment-deployment-kit

   Click the get Windows ADK Download button.

10. It will ask you if you want to run or save the file. I saved the file to the same destination folder as the Nano Server Image Builder. Once it's downloaded, double-click the adksetup.exe file. If a dialog box appears, click Run.

11. Specify the destination of where you want the Windows ADK files to install and click Next.

12. At the Windows Kit Privacy screen, you can choose either option. By choosing Yes, you will participate in Microsoft's feedback program. For this exercise, I chose No. Click Next.

13. At the License Agreement screen, click Accept.

14. At the Features screen, accept the defaults and click Install. If a UAC screen appears, click Yes.

15. After the installation is complete, click the Close button.

16. Double-click on the `NanoServerImageBuilder.exe` file. When the UAC screen appears, click Yes.

17. So we now have the ability to create a Nano Server image or a bootable USB. We are going to create an Image. So click on the top choice "Create a new Nano Server image" (see Figure 1.13).

FIGURE 1.13   Nano Server Image Choice

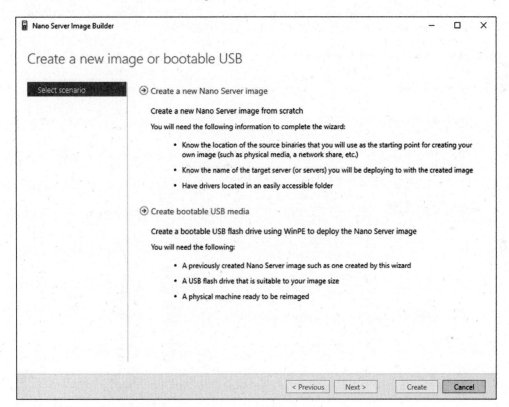

18. At the Before you begin screen, click Next.

19. At the Select Installation Media screen, point the folder to your Windows Server 2016 installation files where the NanoServer Folder resides. Click Next.

If you only have a Windows Server 2016 .ISO image, right click on the ISO image and choose Open With ➤ Windows Explorer. Then copy the NanoServer folder to another location. Then in step 20, just point to the location of the NanoServer folder.

20. At the License agreement screen, click the box that states I have read and agree to the terms. Then click Next.

21. At the Deployment type screen. I am going to choose to create a Virtual machine image named Pluto.vhd. I am keeping the default of 8 GB and I am placing the VHD in my Win 2016 Nano Server folder (see Figure 1.14). Click Next.

FIGURE 1.14   Deployment Type

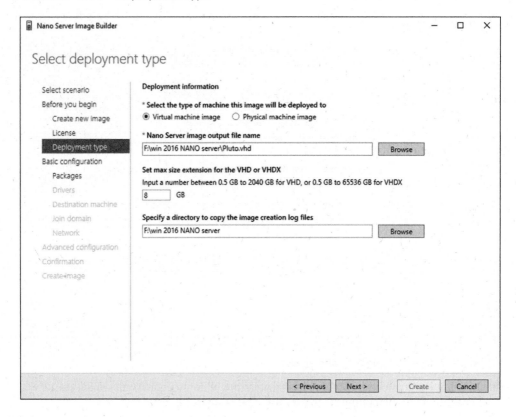

22. At the Basic Installation screen, click Next.

23. At the Select Optional Packages screen, you can choose any other options you want to install like DNS, IIS, etc. I am just going to click Next.

24. At the Drivers screen, add any drivers that may be needed for your installation and click Next.

25. Next the Destination screen will appear. Here is where you will enter the name of the computer and the Administrator's password. I am using Pluto as the computer name and P@ssw0rd as the password. Make sure your Time Zone is correct and click Next.

26. At this time, I am not going to join a domain. So I am just going to click Next.

27. I will leave the default network settings and click Next.

28. At the Advanced Configuration Screen, I am going to choose the top option "Create a Basic Nano Server Image" (see Figure 1.15).

FIGURE 1.15   Advanced Configuration Screen

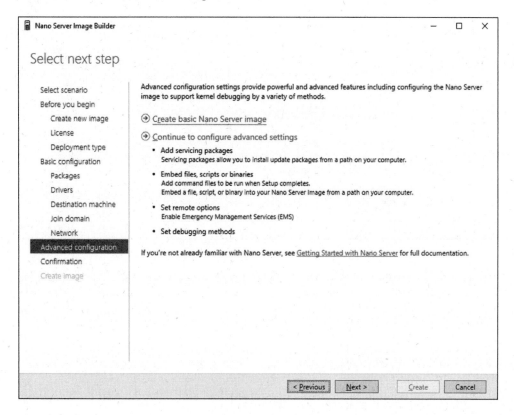

29. After you click the link, it will automatically take you to a Confirmation screen. Just click the Create button.

30. Once the image is complete, click the Close button.

31. Open Windows Explorer and go to the folder where you created the VHD (see Figure 1.16). Make sure the VHD (My VHD is named Pluto.vhd) has been created. You can now run this VHD in Microsoft Hyper-V.

FIGURE 1.16 Verifying the Created VHD

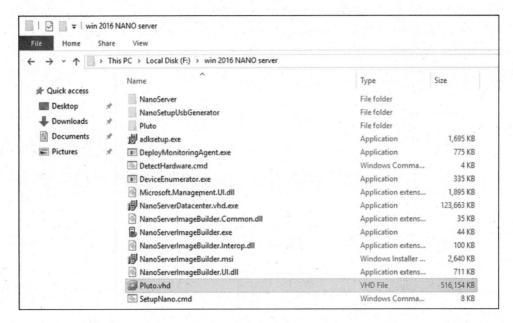

During the installation of the VHD image in Exercise 1.3, at the end of the exercise, the Nano Server Image Builder automatically created a PowerShell command to do the same installation that we just did during the exercise. The following is the PowerShell output that the Nano Server Image Builder automatically created:

```
New-NanoServerImage -MediaPath 'F:\win 2016 NANO server' -Edition 'Datacenter'
-DeploymentType Guest -TargetPath 'F:\win 2016 NANO server\Pluto.vhd' -MaxSize
8589934592 -ComputerName 'Pluto' -SetupCompleteCommand ('tzutil.exe /s
"Eastern Standard Time"') -LogPath 'C:\Users\StormWind\AppData\Local\Temp\
NanoServerImageBuilder\Logs\2016-11-13 17-48'
```

At the time this book was written, Nano Server PowerShell did not allow the following features (this list was taken directly from Microsoft's website);

- ADSI, ADO, and WMI type adapters
- Enable-PSRemoting, Disable-PSRemoting (PowerShell remoting is enabled by default.)
- Scheduled jobs and PSScheduledJob module

- Computer cmdlets for joining a domain { Add | Remove }
- Reset-ComputerMachinePassword, Test-ComputerSecureChannel
- Profiles (You can add a startup script for incoming remote connections with Set-PSSessionConfiguration.)
- Clipboard cmdlets
- EventLog cmdlets { Clear | Get | Limit | New | Remove | Show | Write } (Use the New-WinEvent and Get-WinEvent cmdlets instead.)
- Get-PfxCertificate cmdlet
- TraceSource cmdlets { Get | Set }
- Counter cmdlets { Get | Export | Import }
- Some web-related cmdlets { New-WebServiceProxy, Send-MailMessage, ConvertTo-Html }
- Logging and tracing using PSDiagnostics module
- Get-HotFix
- Implicit remoting cmdlets { Export-PSSession | Import-PSSession }
- New-PSTransportOption
- PowerShell transactions and Transaction cmdlets { Complete | Get | Start | Undo | Use }
- PowerShell Workflow infrastructure, modules, and cmdlets
- Out-Printer
- Update-List
- WMI v1 cmdlets: Get-WmiObject, Invoke-WmiMethod, Register-WmiEvent, Remove-WmiObject, Set-WmiInstance (Use CimCmdlets module instead.)

After Windows Server 2016 server is installed, you need to look at how to activate the server. In the next section, you will learn about the different ways you can activate a Windows Server 2016 system.

Activating and Servicing Windows

After you complete the installation of Windows Server 2016, the next step is activating the operating system. Windows Server 2016 gives you a few different options when it comes to activation.

In the past, many administrators would use the Volume Activation Management Tool (VMAT) to activate both Microsoft operating systems and Microsoft products like Office. Administrators can still use VMAT to activate Microsoft products like Office but with the release of Windows Server 2016, there are some new ways to help administrators activate the operating systems.

So let's take a look at some of the different activation options that you have with the Windows Server 2016 operating system.

Key Management Service

Windows Server 2016 Key Management Service (KMS) gives your Windows computers an easy and automated way to get activated. KMS allows your computers to get activated right on your local network without the need of contacting Microsoft. For this to happen, you must setup a KMS client-server network. KMS clients are able to contact KMS servers as long as your network uses either a static TCP/IP configuration or you have a Domain Name System (DNS) server setup.

To configure KMS hosts systems, you must configure and retrieve Volume Activation information. This is done by using a Software License Manager (referred to as SL Manager) script (Slmgr.vbs). This script can be run on a local system or a remote system but it needs to be run from a user's account that uses an elevated command prompt. KMS host systems can be any Windows client operating system running Windows Vista or higher and any Server above Windows Server 2003.

To create or modify the slmgr.vbs script, an administrator can use either the Wscript.exe or Cscript.exe application. Slmgr.vbs uses the Wscript.exe scripting engine by default. After an administrator makes any changes to the Slmgr.vbs script, the Software Licensing Service must be restarted. This can be done by using the Services Microsoft Management Console (MMC) or by running the net stop and net start commands at an elevated command prompt (net stop sppsvc and net start sppsvc).

The Slmgr.vbs script has different command line switches that you can use. Table 1.2 shows you some of the different switches that you can use with the Slmgr.vbs script.

TABLE 1.2   Slmgr.vbs switches

Parameter	Description
/ato	This switch is used for retail and volume systems editions with a KMS host key or a Multiple Activation Key (MAK) installed. The /ato command prompts Windows to try to do an online activation. For any systems that are using a Generic Volume License Key (GVLK), this will make the system attempt to do a KMS activation.
/cdns	This switch allows an administrator to disable KMS host automatic DNS publishing.
/cpri	Administrators can use this switch to lower the priority of KMS host processes.
/dli	Administrators can use this switch on the KMS host to view the current KMS activation count.
/dlv	When an administrator uses this switch, the license information for the installed operating system is displayed.

Parameter	Description
/ipk	This command will try to install a 5x5 product key.
/sai activationInterval	This switch allows an administrator to change how often a KMS client attempts to activate itself when it cannot find a KMS host. The default setting is 120 minutes, but you can change the interval by replacing ActivationInterval with the number of minutes you want to set.
/sdns	This switch allows an administrator to enable KMS host automatic DNS publishing.
/spri	This allows an administrator to set the CPU priority of the KMS host processes to Normal.
/sprt PortNumber	Using this switch allows an administrator to change the default TCP communications port on a KMS host from 1688 to whichever port the admin wants to use. To change the default port number, replace the PortNumber switch with the TCP port number to use.
/sri RenewalInterval	This switch allows an administrator to change how often a KMS client attempts to renew its activation by contacting a KMS host. If you need to change the default of 10080 (7 days), just replace RenewalInterval with a number of minutes you want to use.

To run Slmgr.vbs remotely, administrators must supply additional parameters. They must include the computer name of the target computer as well as a username and password of a user account that has local administrator rights on the target computer. If run remotely without a specified username and password, the script uses the credentials of the user running the script.

```
slmgr.vbs TargetComputerName [username] [password] /parameter [options]
```

Automatic Virtual Machine Activation

Another Windows Server 2016 activation method is called Automatic Virtual Machine Activation (AVMA). The main advantage of AVMA is that is works the same way a proof-of-purchase works. Once that there is proof that the Windows Server 2016 operating system is used in accordance with Microsoft Software License terms, AVMA allows you to install virtual machines on that Windows Server operating system without the need of using or managing product keys for each virtual machine.

AVMA attaches the virtual machine activation to the properly activated Hyper-V machine during the startup process. One of the nice advantages to using AVMA is that AVMA will provide administrators with real time reporting data. When your virtual servers are properly activated using volume or OEM licensing, AVMA gives an organization many benefits, like activating virtual machines in remote areas and also activating virtual machines even if no Internet connection is present.

One advantage to AVMA activations is that virtual machines are activated as long as the Hyper-V server is legally licensed. This helps consulting companies in the fact that they do not need to access client virtual machines to activate the machines as long as the Hyper-V server is properly licensed. Also, hosting companies can use the server logs to help keep the virtual machines running properly.

AVMA requires Windows Server 2016 with the Hyper-V role installed. AVMA can also run on Windows Server 2012 and Windows Server 2012 R2 if needed. Table 1.3 shows the Windows Server 2016 AVMA (5x5) Keys that are available from Microsoft's website.

TABLE 1.3 Windows Server 2016 AVMA Keys

Edition	AVMA Key
Datacenter	TMJ3Y-NTRTM-FJYXT-T22BY-CWG3J
Standard	C3RCX-M6NRP-6CXC9-TW2F2-4RHYD
Essentials	B4YNW-62DX9-W8V6M-82649-MHBKQ

Active Directory–Based Activation

One of the best advantages of using Windows Servers is the ability to install Active Directory onto your corporate network. Active Directory is just a centralized database of objects for a corporation called a domain.

For companies running Active Directory, administrators can use this towards their advantage when it comes to activation. Active Directory-Based Activation (ADBA) allows administrators to activate computers right through the domain connection.

Many organizations have remote locations and at these locations there is company owned software that needs to be registered. Normally administrators would use a retail key or a Multiple Activation Key (MAK) to get these products activated. The nice thing about ADBA is that as long as the computers are connected to the domain, the software and products can be activated through the domain.

When an Administrator joins a Windows computer to the domain, the ADBA will automatically activate the computers version of Windows either online with Microsoft or through the use of an activation proxy.

Servicing Windows Server 2016

Now that we looked at some of the ways to activate your Windows Server 2016 systems, let's take a look at how you can service your Windows Server systems. Table 1.4 will show the different versions for Windows Server 2016 and which servicing model each version uses.

TABLE 1.4 Servicing Models for Windows Server 2016

Installation Option	LTSB Servicing	CBB Servicing
Desktop Experience	Yes	No
Server Core	Yes	No
Nano Server	No	Yes

Long Term Servicing Branch

Before the release of Windows Server 2016, Windows operating systems used the "5+5" servicing models. What this meant was there were 5 years of mainstream support and 5 years of extended support for the different versions of the Windows operating systems. This model will continue to be used in Windows Server 2016 (Desktop Support and Server Core) but it will be known as Long Term Servicing Branch (LTSB).

Current Branch for Business

Administrators who decide to install Windows sever 2016 Nano Server will be choosing to use the Current Branch for Business (CBB) servicing model. This version of servicing is a more aggressive version and it was specifically designed with the cloud in mind. As the cloud continues to quickly evolve, the CBB servicing model is meant for that lifecycle. The CBB servicing model will continue to provide new features and functions to Windows Server allowing the server to evolve and grow with the rapidly changing industry. Microsoft's goal is to release updates multiple times per year for Nano Server thus keeping it changing with the industry.

Using Windows Deployment Services

Another way that many IT departments deploy operating systems has been through the use of Windows Deployment Services (WDS). WDS allows an IT administrator to install a Windows operating system without using an installation disc. Using WDS allows you to deploy the operating system through a network installation. WDS can deploy Windows XP, Windows Server 2003, Windows Vista, Windows 7, Windows 8, Windows 10, Windows Server 2008/2008 R2, Windows Server 2012, Windows Server 2012 R2, and Microsoft Windows Server 2016.

The following are some of the advantages of using WDS for automated installation:

- You can remotely install Windows 7/8/10.

- The procedure simplifies management of the server image by allowing you to access Windows 7/8/10 distribution files from a distribution server.

- You can quickly recover the operating system in the event of a computer failure.

Here are the basic steps of the WDS process from a PXE-enabled WDS client:

1. The WDS client initiates a special boot process through the PXE network adapter (and the computer's BIOS configured for a network boot). On a PXE client, the user presses F12 to start the PXE boot process and to indicate that they want to perform a WDS installation.

2. A list of available Windows PE boot images is displayed. The user should select the appropriate Windows PE boot image from the boot menu.

3. The Windows Welcome screen is displayed. The user should click the Next button.

4. The WDS user is prompted to enter credentials for accessing and installing images from the WDS server.

5. A list of available operating system images is displayed. The user should select the appropriate image file to install.

6. The WDS user is prompted to enter the product key for the selected image.

7. The Partition And Configure The Disk screen is displayed. This screen provides the ability to install a mass storage device driver, if needed, by pressing F6.

8. The image copy process is initiated, and the selected image is copied to the WDS client computer.

The following sections describe how to set up the WDS server and the WDS clients and how to install Windows 7/8/10 through WDS.

Preparing the WDS Server

With the WDS server, you can manage and distribute Windows 7/8/10 operating system images to WDS client computers. The WDS server contains any files necessary for PXE booting, Windows PE boot images, and the Windows 7/8/10 images to be deployed.

The following steps for preparing the WDS server are discussed in the upcoming sections:

1. Make sure that the server meets the requirements for running WDS.

2. Install WDS.

3. Configure and start WDS.

4. Configure the WDS server to respond to client computers (if this was not configured when WDS was installed).

For WDS to work, the server on which you will install WDS must meet the requirements for WDS and be able to access the required network services.

WDS Server Requirements

The WDS server must meet these requirements:

- The computer must be a domain controller or a member of an Active Directory domain.
- At least one partition on the server must be formatted as NTFS.

- WDS must be installed on the server.
- The operating system must be Windows Server 2003, Windows Server 2008/2008 R2, Windows Server 2012 / 2012 R2, or Windows Server 2016.
- A network adapter must be installed.

Network Services

The following network services must be running on the WDS server or be accessible to the WDS server from another network server:

- TCP/IP installed and configured
- A DHCP server, which is used to assign DHCP addresses to WDS clients (Ensure that your DHCP scope has enough addresses to accommodate all of the WDS clients that will need IP addresses.)
- A DNS server, which is used to locate the Active Directory controller
- Active Directory, which is used to locate WDS servers and WDS clients as well as authorize WDS clients and manage WDS configuration settings and client installation options

Installing the WDS Server Components

You can configure WDS on a Windows Server 2003/2008/2008 R2, Windows Server 2012 / 2012 R2, or Windows Server 2016 computer by using the Windows Deployment Services Configuration Wizard or by using the WDSUTIL command line utility. Table 1.5 describes the WDSUTIL command line options.

TABLE 1.5 WDSUTIL command line options

WDSUTIL Option	Description
/initialize-server	Initializes the configuration of the WDS server
/uninitialized-server	Undoes any changes made during the initialization of the WDS server
/add	Adds images and devices to the WDS server
/convert-ripimage	Converts Remote Installation Preparation (RIPrep) images to WIM images
/remove	Removes images from the server
/set	Sets information in images, image groups, WDS servers, and WDS devices

TABLE 1.5 WDSUTIL command line options *(continued)*

WDSUTIL Option	Description
/get	Gets information from images, image groups, WDS servers, and WDS devices
/new	Creates new capture images or discover images
/copy-image	Copies images from the image store
/export-image	Exports to WIM files images contained within the image store
/start	Starts WDS services
/stop	Stops WDS services
/disable	Disables WDS services
/enable	Enables WDS services
/approve-autoadddevices	Approves Auto-Add devices
/reject-autoadddevices	Rejects Auto-Add devices
/delete-autoadddevices	Deletes records from the Auto-Add database
/update	Uses a known good resource to update a server resource

The first step in setting up WDS to deploy operating systems to the clients is to install the WDS role. You do this by using Server Manager.

One of the advantages of using the Windows deployment server is that WDS can work with Windows image (.wim) files. Windows image files can be created through the use of the Windows Sysprep utility.

One component to which you need to pay attention when using the Windows deployment server is *Preboot Execution Environment (PXE)* network devices. PXE boot devices are network interface cards (NICs) that can talk to a network without the need for an operating system. PXE boot NIC adapters are network adapters that have a set of preboot commands within the boot firmware.

This is important when using WDS because PXE boot adapters connect to a WDS server and request the data needed to load the operating system remotely. Remember, most of the machines for which you are using WDS do not have an operating system on the computer. You need NIC adapters that can connect to a network without the need for an operating system for WDS to work properly.

For the same reason, you must set up DHCP to accept PXE machines. Those machines need a valid TCP/IP address so that they can connect to the WDS server.

Preparing the WDS Client

The WDS client is the computer on which Windows 7/8/10 will be installed. WDS clients rely on a technology called PXE, which allows the client computer to boot remotely and connect to a WDS server.

To act as a WDS client, the computer must meet all of the hardware requirements for Windows 7/8/10 and have a PXE-capable network adapter installed, and a WDS server must be present on the network. Additionally, the user account used to install the image must be a member of the Domain Users group in Active Directory.

After the WDS server has been installed and configured, you can install Windows 7/8/10 on a WDS client that uses a PXE-compliant network card.

To install Windows 7/8/10 on the WDS client, follow these steps:

1. Start the computer. When prompted, press F12 for a network service boot. The Windows PE appears.

2. The Windows Welcome screen appears. Click the Next button to start the installation process.

3. Enter the username and password of an account that has permission to access and install images from the WDS server.

4. A list of available operating system images stored on the WDS server appears. Select the image to install and click Next.

5. Enter the product key for the selected Windows 7/8/10 image and click Next.

6. The Partition And Configure The Disk screen appears. Select the desired disk-partitioning options, or click OK to use the default options.

7. Click Next to initiate the image-copying process. The Windows Setup process will begin after the image is copied to the WDS client computer.

Understanding Features On Demand

One of the problems in previous versions of Windows Server was how roles and features were stored on the hard disk. Before the introduction of Windows Server 2012, even if a server role or feature was disabled on a server, the binary files for that role or feature were still present on the disk. The problem with this approach is that, even if you disable the role, it still consumes space on your hard drive.

Features On Demand in Windows Server 2012 solves this issue because not only can administrators disable a role or feature, they can also completely remove the role or feature's files. Windows Server 2016 has continued with Features on Demand and administrators can choose what Roles and Features they want to use, when they want to use them.

Once this is done, a state of Removed is shown in Server Manager, or the state of Disabled With Payload Removed is shown in the Deployment Image Servicing and Management (Dism.exe) utility. To reinstall a role or feature that has been completely removed, you must have access to the installation files.

NOTE   The Deployment Image Servicing and Management (Dism.exe) utility is talked about throughout this entire book. DISM will be discussed in great detail when we discuss Windows imaging.

If you want to remove a role or feature completely from the system, use -Remove with the Uninstall-WindowsFeature cmdlet of Windows PowerShell.

If you want to reinstall a role or feature that has been removed completely, use the Windows PowerShell -Source option of the Install-WindowsFeature Server Manager cmdlet. Using the -Source option states the path where the WIM image files and the index number of the image will be located. If an administrator decides not to use the -Source option, Windows will use Windows Update by default.

When you're using the Features On Demand configuration, if feature files are not available on the server computer and the installation requires those feature files, Windows Server 2016 can be directed to get those files from a side-by-side feature store, which is a shared folder that contains feature files. It is available to the server on the network, from Windows Update, or from installation media. This can be overwritten using the -Source option in the Windows PowerShell utility.

Source Files for Roles or Features

Offline virtual hard disks (VHDs) cannot be used as a source for installing roles or features that have been completely removed. Only sources for the same version of Windows Server 2016 are supported.

To install a removed role or feature using a WIM image, follow these steps:

1. Run the following command:

   Get-windowsimage -*imagepath* \install.wim

   In step 1, *imagepath* is the path where the WIM files are located.

2. Run the following command:

   Install-WindowsFeature *featurename* -Source wim: *path*:*index*

   In step 2, *featurename* is the name of the role or feature from Get-WindowsFeature. *path* is the path to the WIM mount point, and *index* is the index of the server image from step 1.

To add or remove a role or feature, you must have administrative rights to the Windows Server 2016 machine.

Summary

In this chapter, you studied the latest advantages of using Windows Server 2016. You also learned about the different roles and features you can install on a Windows Server 2016 machine. You also explored how to migrate those roles and features from a Windows Server 2008, 2008 R2, and Windows Server 2012 machine to a Windows Server 2016 machine.

I discussed the different upgrade paths that are available and which upgrades are best for your current network setup. You learned that another important issue to decide when installing Windows Server 2016 is whether to use Server Core or the GUI installation.

You learned how to install Windows Server 2016 Datacenter (Desktop Experience), and you installed the Windows Server 2016 Server Core. Remember, Server Core is a slimmed-down version of Windows Server. With no GUI desktop available, it's a safer alternative to a normal Windows install.

I discussed a feature called Features On Demand. This feature allows you to remove roles and features from the operating system and remove the associated files completely from the hard drive, thus saving disk space.

Video Resources

There are videos available for the following exercises:

    1.1

    1.2

You can access the videos at `http://sybextestbanks.wiley.com` on the Other Study Tools tab.

Exam Essentials

Understand the upgrade paths.   It's important to make sure you understand the different upgrade paths from Windows Server 2012 and Windows Server 2012 R2 to Windows Server 2016.

Understand Windows Server 2016 server roles.   Understand what the Windows Server 2016 server roles do for an organization and its users.

Understand Features On Demand.   Understand the feature called Features On Demand. Microsoft loves to ask exam questions about its new features, and this will be no exception. Understand how features and roles stay on the system until you physically remove them from the hard drive.

Understand Windows Deployment Services.   Know how to install and configure a Windows Deployment Services (WDS) server. Know the WDS network requirements and components.

Review Questions

1. You are the administrator for the ABC Company. You are looking to install Windows Server 2016, and you need to decide which version to install. You need to install a version of Windows that is just for logon authentication and nothing else. You want the most secure option and cost is not an issue. What should you install?

   A. Windows Server 2016 Datacenter (Desktop Experience)

   B. Windows Server 2016 Datacenter Server Core

   C. Windows Server 2016 Standard (Desktop Experience)

   D. Windows Server 2016 Web Server Core

2. You are the IT manager for a large organization. One of your co-workers installed a new Windows Server 2016 Datacenter Server Core machine, but now the IT team has decided that it should be a Windows Server 2016 Datacenter (Desktop Experience). What should you do?

   A. Reinstall Windows Server 2016 Datacenter Server Core on the same machine.

   B. Install a new machine with Windows Server 2016 Datacenter Server Core.

   C. Convert the current Windows Server 2016 Datacenter Server Core to the Windows Server 2016 Datacenter (Desktop Experience) version.

   D. Dual-boot the machine with both Windows Server 2016 Datacenter Server Core and Windows Server 2016 Datacenter (Desktop Experience).

3. You are the administrator for your company, and you are looking at upgrading your Windows Server 2012 Standard with GUI to Windows Server 2016. Which version of Windows Server 2016 does Microsoft recommend you use to keep the GUI interface?

   A. Windows Server 2016 Datacenter (Desktop Experience)

   B. Windows Server 2016 Standard (Desktop Experience)

   C. Windows Server 2016 Datacenter

   D. Windows Server 2016 Standard

4. You are looking at upgrading your Windows Server 2012 R2 Datacenter with GUI machine to Windows Server 2016. Your organization is considering virtualizing its entire server room, which has 25 servers. To which version of Windows Server 2016 would you upgrade while keeping the GUI interface?

   A. Windows Server 2016 Datacenter (Desktop Experience)

   B. Windows Server 2016 Standard (Desktop Experience)

   C. Windows Server 2016 Datacenter

   D. Windows Server 2016 Standard

5. You have been hired to help a small company set up its first Windows network. It has had the same 13 users for the entire two years it has been open, and the company has no plans to expand. What version of Windows Server 2016 would you recommend?

   A. Windows Server 2016 Datacenter (Desktop Experience)

   B. Windows Server 2016 Standard (Desktop Experience)

   C. Windows Server 2016 Datacenter

   D. Windows Server 2016 Essentials

6. You have been hired to help a small company set up its Windows network. It has 20 users, and it has no plans to expand. What version of Windows Server 2016 would you recommend?

   A. Windows Server 2016 Datacenter

   B. Windows Server 2016 Standard

   C. Windows Server 2016 Essentials

   D. Windows Server 2016 Datacenter (Desktop Experience)

7. Which of the following are benefits of using Windows Server 2016 Server Core? (Choose all that apply.)

   A. Reduced management

   B. Minimal maintenance

   C. Smaller footprint

   D. Tighter security

8. You are a server administrator, and you are trying to save hard drive space on your Windows Server 2016 Datacenter machine. Which feature can help you save hard disk space?

   A. HDSaver.exe

   B. Features On Demand

   C. ADDS

   D. WinRM

9. You are the IT Director for your company. Your company needs to install a version of Windows Server 2016 that uses the Current Branch for Business servicing model. What version would you install?

   A. Windows Server 2016 Datacenter

   B. Windows Server 2016 Standard

   C. Windows Server 2016 Essentials

   D. Windows Server 2016 Nano Server

10. What type of domain controller would you install into an area where physical security is a concern?

   A. Primary domain controller

   B. Backup domain controller

   C. Read-only domain controller

   D. Locked-down domain controller

Chapter

2

Installing in the Enterprise

THE FOLLOWING 70-740 EXAM OBJECTIVES ARE COVERED IN THIS CHAPTER:

✓ **Create, manage, and maintain images for deployment.**

- This objective may include but is not limited to the following subobjectives: Plan for Windows Server virtualization; plan for Linux and FreeBSD deployments; assess virtualization workloads using the Microsoft Assessment and Planning (MAP) Toolkit; determine considerations for deploying workloads into virtualized environments; update images with patches, hotfixes, and drivers; install roles and features in offline images; manage and maintain Windows Server Core, Nano Server images, and VHDs using Windows PowerShell

Installing Windows Server 2016 is quick and easy, but as an IT manager or IT professional, you may have to install dozens of copies of Windows Server 2016. It is not a good practice to install them one at a time. It's important to understand how to automate a Windows Server 2016 deployment for the Windows Server 2016 (70-740) exam, but you'll also use automated deployments in a corporate environment. Many companies use third-party tools to create and deploy Windows Server 2016 machines, but there are other ways.

You can automate the installation of Windows Server 2016 in several ways. You can install Windows Server 2016 by using an unattended installation, by using Windows Deployment Services (WDS) to remotely deploy unattended installations, by using Hyper-V, or by using the System Preparation Tool for disk imaging. To help customize these options for automating remote installations, you can also use answer files to provide answers to the questions that are normally asked during the installation process. After you've installed Windows Server 2016, you can also automate the installation of applications by using Windows Installer packages.

This chapter includes an overview of the automated deployment options available with Windows Server 2016. Also included in this chapter is information on how to access the deployment tools available for Windows Server 2016 and the use of unattended installation, how the System Preparation Tool (along with Deployment Image Servicing and Management DISM utility) is used to create disk images for automated installation, and how to use Windows System Image Manager (SIM) to create unattended answer files.

Understanding Automated Deployment Options

If you need to install Windows Server 2016 on multiple computers, you could manually install the operating system on each computer, as described in Chapter 1, "Installing Windows Server 2016." However, automating the deployment process will make your job easier, more efficient, and more cost effective if you have a large number of client computers on which to install Windows Server 2016.

Windows Server 2016 comes with several utilities that can be used for deploying and automating the Windows Server 2016 installation. With access to multiple utilities with different functionality, administrators have increased flexibility in determining how to best deploy Windows Server 2016 within a large corporate environment.

The following sections contain overviews of the automated deployment options, which will help you choose which solution is best for your requirements and environment. The options for automated deployment of Windows Server 2016 are as follows:

- Microsoft Deployment Toolkit (MDT) 2013 Update 2
- Unattended installation, or unattended setup, which uses Setup.exe
- Microsoft Assessment and Planning (MAP) Toolkit
- Windows Automated Installation Kit (Windows AIK)
- Windows Assessment and Deployment Kit for Windows Server 2016
- WDS (covered in Chapter 1 "Installing Windows Server 2016")
- System Preparation Tool (Sysprep.exe), which is used to set up a machine to be imaged or cloned
- Deployment Image Servicing and Management (DISM)

> Another option that you have to deploy Windows Server 2016 is through System Center Configuration Manager (SCCM). Since SCCM is its own application with an additional cost, it is beyond the scope of this book. You can learn more about SCCM on the Microsoft website at https://technet .microsoft.com/en-us/system-center-docs/system-center.

An Overview of the Microsoft Deployment Toolkit 2013 Update 2

Microsoft released a deployment assistance toolset called the *Microsoft Deployment Toolkit (MDT) 2013 Update 2*. It is used to automate desktop and server deployment. The MDT provides an administrator with the following benefits:

- Administrative tools that allow for the deployment of desktops and servers through the use of a common console (see Figure 2.1)
- Quicker deployments and the capabilities of having standardized desktop and server images and security
- Zero-touch deployments of Windows Server 2016, Windows Server 2012/2012 R2, Windows Server 2008/2008 R2, Windows 10/8/7

To install the MDT 2013 package onto your computer (regardless of the operating system being deployed), you must first meet the minimum requirements of MDT. These components need to be installed only on the computer where MDT 2013 is being installed:

- Windows Server 2016, Windows Server 2012/2012 R2, Windows Server 2008/2008 R2, Windows 10, Windows 8.1, Windows 8, or Windows 7.
- The Windows Assessment and Deployment Kit (ADK) for Windows Server 2016 is required for all deployment scenarios.

- System Center 2016 Configuration Manager Service Pack 1 with the Windows ADK for Windows Server 2016 is required for zero-touch installation (ZTI) and user-driven installation (UDI) scenarios.

- If you are using ZTI and/or UDI, you are allowed to add the MDT SQL database to any version of System Center Configuration Manager with SQL Technology; if you are using LTI, you must use a separately licensed SQL Server product to host your MDT SQL database.

FIGURE 2.1   Microsoft Deployment Toolkit console

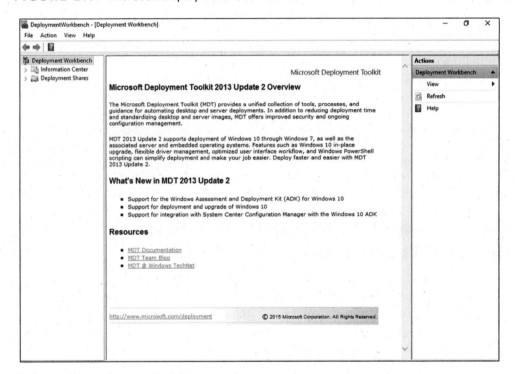

You can install MDT 2013 without installing Windows (ADK) first, but you will not be able to use the package fully until Windows (ADK) is installed. I will explain all of the benefits of Windows (ADK) in the section called "Overview of the Windows Assessment and Deployment Kit" later in this chapter. I recommend you install Windows ADK first at `https://developer.microsoft` `.com/en-us/windows/hardware/windows-assessment-deployment-kit`.

In Exercise 2.1, you will download and install MDT 2013. You can install MDT 2013 on the Windows Server 2016 operating system machine that you installed in Chapter 1. If you decide to install the MDT 2013 onto a server or production machine, I recommend that you perform a full backup before completing Exercise 2.1. Installing MDT 2013 will replace any previous version of MDT that the machine may currently be using.

EXERCISE 2.1

Downloading and Installing MDT 2013

To download and install MDT 2013, follow these steps:

1. Download the MDT 2013 Update 1 utility from Microsoft's website (https://www.microsoft.com/en-us/download/details.aspx?id=48595).

2. Click the Download button (see Figure 2.2).

FIGURE 2.2   Microsoft Deployment Toolkit Download

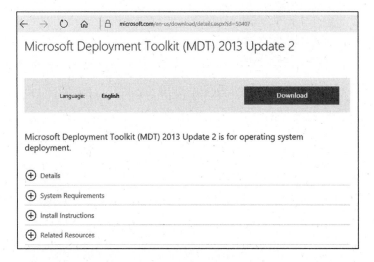

3. You get a screen asking "Choose the download you want". Choose the x64 or x86 version (I chose the x64 version). Click Next.

4. A message box may appear asking if you want to run or save the MDT. I clicked the down arrow next to Save As and saved the files into the downloads directory.

5. Double-click MicrosoftDeploymentToolkit_xxx.exe you choose to start the installation.

6. At the Welcome screen, click Next as shown in Figure 2.3.

7. At the License screen, click the I Accept The Terms In The License Agreement radio button and click Next.

8. At the Custom Setup screen, click the down arrow next to Microsoft Deployment Toolkit and choose Entire Feature Will Be Installed On Local Hard Drive. Click Next as shown on Figure 2.4.

EXERCISE 2.1 *(continued)*

FIGURE 2.3   Microsoft Deployment Toolkit Setup Screen

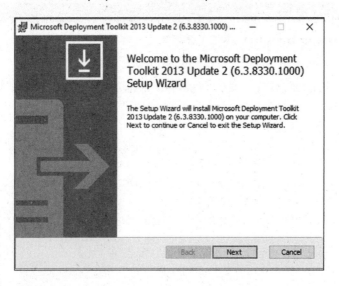

FIGURE 2.4   Microsoft Deployment Toolkit Setup Screen

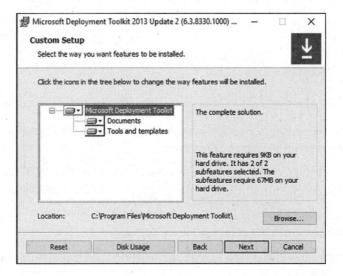

9. At the Customer Experience Improvement Program screen, choose if you want to participate or not and choose Next.

10. At the Ready To Install screen, click the Install button (shown in Figure 2.5).

FIGURE 2.5 Ready to Install Screen

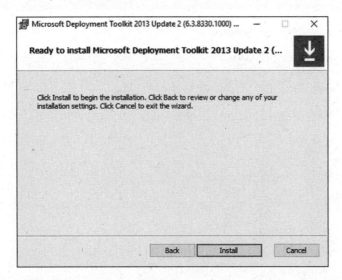

11. If a User Account Control dialog box appears, click the Yes button.

12. When the installation completes, click the Finish button.

Now that you have installed MDT 2013, you are going to configure the package. In Exercise 2.2, you will configure MDT 2013 and set up a distribution share and database. I am creating the MDT 2013 on a Windows Server 2016 so that we can distribute Windows Server 2016. Make sure the Windows Assessment and Deployment Kit (ADK) for Windows Server 2016 is installed because it is required for all deployment scenarios.

EXERCISE 2.2

Configuring MDT 2013

To configure MDT 2013, follow these steps:

1. Create a shared folder on your network called Distribution, and give the Everyone group full control to the folder for this exercise.

2. Open the MDT workbench by choosing Start ➢ Microsoft Development Toolkit ➢ Deployment Workbench (see Figure 2.6).

3. In the left-hand pane, click Deployment Shares, and then right-click the deployment shares and choose New Deployment Share.

4. The New Deployment Share Wizard begins (As shown in Figure 2.7). At the first screen, you will choose the directory where the deployments will be stored. Click the Browse button and choose the Distribution share that you created in step 1. Then click Next.

FIGURE 2.6   Deployment Workbench

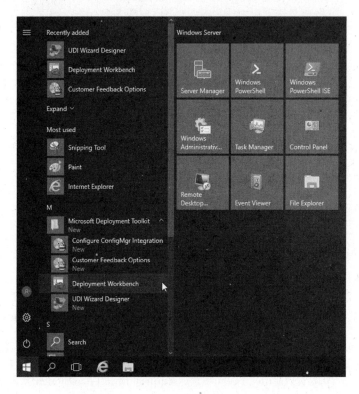

FIGURE 2.7   Microsoft Deployment Toolkit Setup Screen

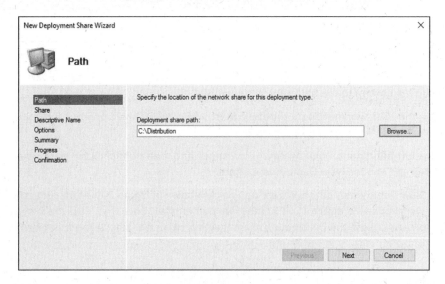

5. At the Share Name screen, accept the default, Distribution. Click Next.

6. At the Descriptive Name screen, accept the default description name (as shown in Figure 2.8) and click Next.

FIGURE 2.8   Descriptive Name Screen

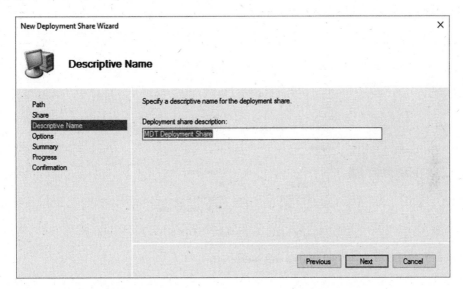

7. At the Options Screen, Make sure all check boxes are checked as shown in Figure 2.9.

FIGURE 2.9   Options Screen

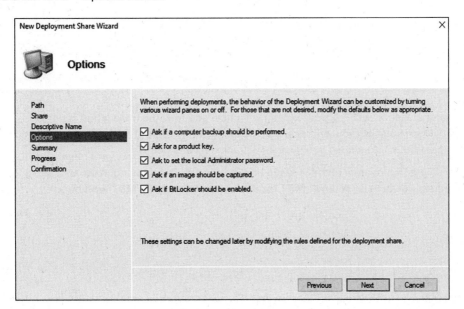

8. At the Summary screen, look over the options and choose the Next button (shown in Figure 2.10).

FIGURE 2.10   Summary Screen

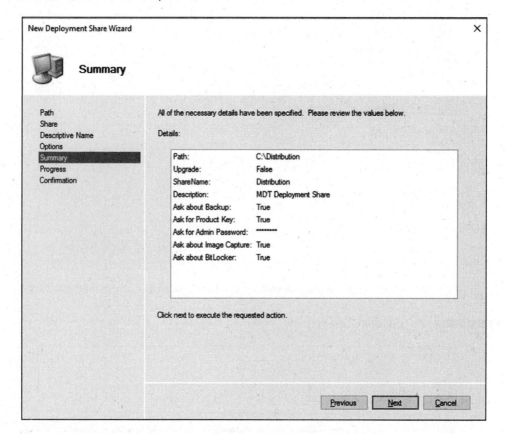

9. The installation will Progress screen will show you how the installation is performing. Once finished, you will receive a message stating that "The process completed successfully" (as shown in Figure 2.11). Click the Finish button.

10. The new Deployment share is setup and ready to start deploying. Now an operating system needs to be setup in MDT for deployment. Close the MDT workbench.

FIGURE 2.11   Confirmation Screen

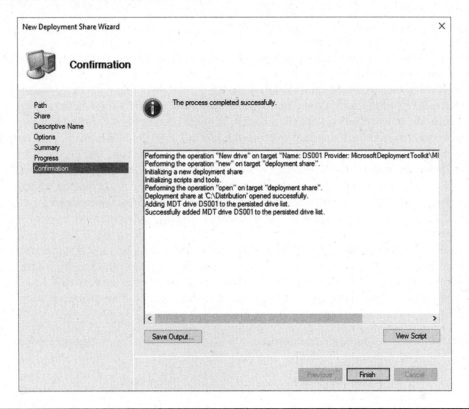

Now that you have seen how to install the MDT 2013 utility, let's take a look at some other ways to automatically install Windows Server 2016.

An Overview of Unattended Installation

Unattended installation is a practical method of automating deployments when you have a large number of clients to install and the computers require different hardware and software configurations. Unattended installations allow you to create customized installations that are specific to your environment. Custom installations can support custom hardware and software installations.

Unattended installations utilize an answer file called Autounattend.xml to provide configuration information during the installation process. Think about the Windows Server 2016 installation from the previous chapter. You are asked for your locale, type of installation, and so on. The answer file allows these questions to be answered without user interaction. In addition to providing standard Windows Server 2016 configuration information, the answer file can provide installation instructions for applications, additional language support, service packs, and device drivers.

With an unattended installation, you can use a distribution share to install Windows Server 2016 on the target computers. You can also use a Windows Server 2016 DVD with an answer file located on the root of the DVD, on a floppy disk, or on a universal flash device (UFD), such as an external USB flash drive.

Unattended installations allow you to create customized installations that are specific to your environment. Custom installations can support custom hardware and software installations. Since the answer file for Windows Server 2016 is in XML format, all custom configuration information can be contained within the `Autounattend.xml` file. This is different from past versions of Windows, where creating automated installation routines for custom installations required multiple files to be used. In addition to providing standard Windows Server 2016 configuration information, you can use the answer file to provide installation instructions for applications, additional language support, service packs, and device drivers.

If you use a distribution share, it should contain the Windows Server 2016 operating system image and the answer file to respond to installation configuration queries. The target computer must be able to connect to the distribution share over the network. After the distribution share and target computers are connected, you can initiate the installation process. Figure 2.12 illustrates the unattended installation process.

FIGURE 2.12   Unattended installation with distribution share and a target computer

Distribution Share
Windows Server 2016

Target Machine

Images Stored:
Windows 10
Windows Server 2016
Answer File (Unattend.xml)

Requires:
Network Connection

Advantages of Unattended Installation

In a midsize or large organization, it just makes sense to use automated setups. As stated earlier, it is nearly impossible to install Windows Server 2016 one at a time on hundreds of machines. But there are many advantages to using unattended installations as a method for automating Windows Server 2016:

- Unattended installation saves time and money because users do not have to interactively respond to each installation query.

- It can be configured to provide an automated query response while still selectively allowing users to provide specified input during installations.

- It can be used to install clean copies of Windows Server 2016 or upgrade an existing operating system (providing it is on the list of permitted operating systems) to Windows Server 2016.

- It can be expanded to include installation instructions for applications, additional language support, service packs, and device drivers.

- The physical media for Windows Server 2016 does not need to be distributed to all computers on which it will be installed.

Disadvantages of Unattended Installation

As stated earlier, a manual installation is not practical for mass installations. But one of the biggest disadvantages to performing an unattended installation is that an administrator does not physically walk through the installation of Windows Server 2016. A client operating system is one of the most important items that you will install onto a machine. As an IT manager and consultant, I have always felt better physically installing a client operating system. This way, if there are any glitches, I can see and deal with them immediately. If something happens during an unattended install, you may never know it, but the end user may experience small issues throughout the lifetime of the machine.

Two other disadvantages of using unattended installations as a method for automating Windows Server 2016 installations are listed here:

- They require more initial setup than a standard installation of Windows Server 2016.

- Someone must have access to each client computer and must initiate the unattended installation process on the client side.

An Overview of the System Preparation Tool and Disk Imaging

The *System Preparation Tool,* or *Sysprep* (Sysprep.exe), is used to prepare a computer for disk imaging, and the disk image can then be captured using any image capturing software including DISM or third-party imaging software.

Sysprep is a free utility that comes on all Windows operating systems. By default, the Sysprep utility can be found on Windows Server 2016 and Windows Server 2016 operating systems in the \Windows\system32\sysprep directory.

Disk imaging is the process of taking a checkpoint of a computer and then using those checkpoints to create new computers, thus allowing for automated deployments. The reference, or source, computer has Windows Server 2016 installed and is configured with the settings and applications that should be installed on the target computers. The image (checkpoints) is then created and can be transferred to other computers, thus installing the operating system, settings, and applications that were defined on the reference computer.

Using Imaging Software

Using the System Preparation Tool and disk imaging is a good choice (and the one most commonly used in the real world) for automatic deployment when you have a large number of computers with similar configuration requirements or machines that need to be rebuilt frequently.

For example, StormWind Studios, an online computer education company, reinstalls the same software every few week for new classes. Imaging is a fast and easy way to simplify the deployment process.

Most organizations use images to create new machines quickly and easily, but they also use them to reimage end users' machines that crash.

In most companies, end users will have space on a server (home folders) to allow them to store data. We give our end users space on the server because this way we need to back up only the servers at night and not the end users' machines. If your end users place all of their important documents on the server, that information gets backed up.

Now, if we are also using images in our company and an end user's machine crashes, we just reload the image and they are back up and running in minutes. Since their documents are being saved on the server, they do not lose any of their information.

Many organizations use third-party imaging software (such as Ghost) instead of using Sysprep.exe and Image Capture Wizard. This is another good way of imaging your Windows Server 2016 machines. Just make sure your third-party software supports the Windows Server 2016 operating system.

To perform an unattended installation, the System Preparation Tool prepares the reference computer by stripping away any computer-specific data, such as the security identifier (SID), which is used to uniquely identify each computer on the network; any event logs; and any other unique system information. The System Preparation Tool also detects any Plug and Play devices that are installed can adjust dynamically for any computers that have different hardware installed.

When the client computer starts an installation using a disk image, you can customize what is displayed on the Windows Welcome screen and the options that are displayed through the setup process. You can also fully automate when and how the Windows Welcome screen is displayed during the installation process by using the /oobe option with the System Preparation Tool and an answer file named Oobe.xml.

Sysprep is a utility that is good only for setting up a new machine. You do not use Sysprep to image a computer for upgrading a current machine. There are a few switches that you can use in conjunction with Sysprep to configure the Sysprep utility for your specific needs. Table 2.1 shows you the important Sysprep switches and what they will do for you when used.

TABLE 2.1   Sysprep switches

Switch	Explanation
/pnp	Forces a mini-setup wizard to start at reboot so that all Plug and Play devices can be recognized.
/generalize	This allows Sysprep to remove all system-specific data from the Sysprep image. If you're running the GUI version of Sysprep, this is a checkbox option.
/oobe	Initiates the Windows Welcome screen at the next reboot.
/audit	Initiates Sysprep in audit mode.
/nosidgen	Sysprep does not generate a new SID on the computer restart. Forces a mini-setup on restart.
/reboot	Stops and restarts the computer system.
/quiet	Runs without any confirmation dialog messages being displayed.
/mini	Tells Sysprep to run the mini-setup on the next reboot.

 **Real World Scenario**

The SID Problem with Deployment Software

For many years, when you had to create many machines that each had a Microsoft operating system on it, you would have to use files to help deploy the multiple systems.

Then, multiple third-party companies came out with software that allowed you to take a picture of the Microsoft operating system, and you could deploy that picture to other machines. One advantage of this is that all the software that is installed on the system could also be part of that picture. This was a great way to copy all the software on a machine over to another machine.

There was one major problem for years—*security identifier (SID)* numbers. All computers get assigned a unique SID that represents them on a domain network. The problem for a long time was that when you copied a machine to another machine, the SID number was also copied.

Microsoft released Sysprep many years ago, and that helped solve this problem. Sysprep would allow you to remove the SID number so that a third-party software package could image it to another machine. Many third-party image software products now also remove the SID numbers, but Sysprep was one of the first utilities to help solve this problem.

When you decide to use Sysprep to set up your images, there are a few rules that you must follow for Sysprep to work properly:

▪ You can use images to restart the Windows activation clock. The Windows activation clock starts to decrease as soon as Windows starts for the first time. You can restart the Windows activation clock only three times using Sysprep.

▪ The computer on which you're running Sysprep has to be a member of a workgroup. The machine can't be part of a domain. If the computer is a member of the domain, when you run Sysprep, the computer will automatically be removed from the domain.

▪ It simplifies the addition of user-specific or computer-specific configuration information.

▪ When installing the image, the system will prompt you for a product key. During the install you can use an answer file, which in turn will have all the information needed for the install, and you will not be prompted for any information.

▪ A third-party utility or Image Capture Wizard is required to deploy the image that is created from Sysprep.

▪ If you are using Sysprep to capture an NTFS partition, any files or folders that are encrypted will become corrupt and unreadable.

One advantage to Sysprep and Windows Server 2016 is that you can use Sysprep to prepare a new machine for duplication. You can use Sysprep to image a Windows Server 2016 machine. The following steps are necessary to image a new machine:

1. Install the Windows Server 2016 operating system.

2. Install all components on the OS.

3. Run Sysprep /generalize to create the image.

When you image a computer using the Windows Sysprep utility, a Windows image (.wim) file is created. Most third-party imaging software products can work with the Windows image file.

Advantages of the System Preparation Tool

The following are advantages of using the System Preparation Tool as a method for automating Windows Server 2016 installations:

▪ For large numbers of computers with similar hardware, it greatly reduces deployment time by copying the operating system, applications, and Desktop settings from a reference computer to an image, which can then be deployed to multiple computers.

▪ Using disk imaging facilitates the standardization of Desktops, administrative policies, and restrictions throughout an organization.

▪ Reference images can be copied across a network connection or through DVDs that are physically distributed to client computers.

Disadvantages of the System Preparation Tool

There are some disadvantages of using the System Preparation Tool as a method for automating Windows Server 2016 installations:

- Image Capture Wizard, third-party imaging software, or hardware disk-duplication devices must be used for an image-based setup.

- The version of the System Preparation Tool that shipped with Windows Server 2016 must be used. An older version of Sysprep cannot be used on a Windows Server 2016 image.

- The System Preparation Tool will not detect any hardware that is not Plug and Play compliant.

Overview of the Windows Assessment and Deployment Kit

Another way to install Windows Server 2016 is to use the *Windows Assessment and Deployment Kit (ADK)*. The Windows (ADK) is a set of utilities and documentation that allows an administrator to configure and deploy Windows operating systems. An administrator can use the Windows (ADK) to do the following:

- Windows Imaging and Configuration Designer (ICD)
- Windows Assessment Toolkit
- Windows Performance Toolkit

The Windows (ADK) can be installed and configured on the following operating systems:

- Windows Server 2016
- Windows 7 / 8 / 8.1 / 10
- Windows Server 2012 R2
- Windows Server 2012

The Windows (ADK) is a good solution for organizations that need to customize the Windows deployment environments. The Windows (ADK) allows an administrator to have the flexibility needed for mass deployments of Windows operating systems. Since every organization's needs are different, the Windows (ADK) allows you to use all or just some of the deployment tools available. It allows you to manage deployments by using some additional tools.

Windows Imaging and Configuration Designer (ICD)   The tools included with this part of the Windows (ADK) will allow an administrator to easily deploy and configure Windows operating systems and images.

Windows Assessment Toolkit   When new Windows operating systems are installed, applications that ran on the previous version of Windows may not work properly. The Application Compatibility Toolkit allows an administrator to help solve these issues before they occur.

Windows Performance Toolkit   The Windows Performance Toolkit is a utility that will locate computers on a network and then perform a thorough inventory of them. This inventory can then be used to determine which machines can have Windows Server 2016 installed.

Windows Imaging and Configuration Designer

The Windows Imaging and Configuration Designer (ICD) allows an administrator to work with images. The ICD allows an IT Department to do the following;

- View and configure all of the settings and policies for a Windows Server 2016 image or provisioning package.
- Create Windows provisioning answer files.
- Allow an answer file to add third-party drivers, apps, or other assets.
- Create variants and specify the settings that apply to each variant.
- Build and flash a Windows image.
- Build a provisioning package.

The Windows (ICD) gives an IT department many options on how to deploy and setup Windows Server 2016 clients. Here are some of the following tools included with the Windows (ICD).

- Configure and edit images by using the Deployment Image Servicing and Management (DISM) utility
- Create Windows Preinstallation Environment (Windows PE) images
- Migrate user data and profiles using the User State Migration Tool (USMT)
- Windows Imaging and Configuration Designer (Windows ICD)

Summary of Windows Server 2016 Deployment Options

Table 2.2 summarizes the installation tools and files that are used with unattended, automated installations of Windows Server 2016, the associated installation method, and a description of each tool.

TABLE 2.2   Summary of Windows Server 2016 unattended deployment utilities

Tool or File	Automated Installation Option	Description
WDS	Unattended or attended installations	Program installed onto a Windows Server 2016 server (discussed in Chapter 1 "Installing Windows Server 2016").

Tool or File	Automated Installation Option	Description
Setup.exe	Unattended installation	Program used to initiate the installation process.
Autounattend.xml	Unattended installation	Answer file used to customize installation queries.
Windows System Image Manager	Unattended installation	Program used to create answer files to be used for unattended installations.
Windows Deployment Services Image Capture Wizard	Sysprep	Utility that is initiated by using the F8 button at startup. This utility can work in conjunction with Sysprep to create and manage Windows Server 2016 image files for deployment.
Sysprep.exe	Sysprep	System Preparation Tool, which prepares a source reference computer that will be used in conjunction with a distribution share or with disk duplication through Image Capture Wizard, third-party software, or hardware disk-duplication devices.

The Windows Server 2016 installation utilities and resources relating to automated deployment are found in a variety of locations. Table 2.3 provides a quick reference for each utility or resource and its location.

TABLE 2.3   Location of Windows Server 2016 deployment utilities and resources

Utility	Location
Sysprep.exe	Included with Windows Server 2016; installed to %WINDIR% \system32\sysprep.
Image Configuration Designer	Installed with the WAIK; installed to C:\ProgramFiles(x86) \Windows Kits\10\Assessment and Deployment Kits \ Imaging and Configuration Designer\x86\ICD.exe.
Windows System Image Manager	Installed with WAIK; installed to C:\ProgramFiles(x86) \Windows Kits\10\Assessment and Deployment Kits \Imaging and Configuration Designer\x86\ICD.exe.

Deploying Unattended Installations

You can deploy Windows Server 2016 installations or upgrades through a Windows Server 2016 distribution DVD or through a distribution server that contains Windows Server 2016 images and associated files, such as Autounattend.xml for unattended installations. Using a DVD can be advantageous if the computer on which you want to install Windows Server 2016 is not connected to the network or is connected via a low-bandwidth network. It is also typically faster to install a Windows Server 2016 image from DVD than to use a network connection.

Unattended installations rely on options configured in an answer file that is deployed with the Windows Server 2016 image. Answer files are XML files that contain the settings that are typically supplied by the installer during attended installations of Windows Server 2016. Answer files can also contain instructions for how programs and applications should be run.

The Windows Setup program is run to install or upgrade to Windows Server 2016 from computers that are running compatible versions of Windows, as discussed in Chapter 1. In fact, Windows Setup is the basis for the other types of installation procedures I'll be discussing in this chapter, including unattended installations, WDS, and image-based installations.

The Windows Setup program (Setup.exe) replaces Winnt32.exe and Winnt.exe, which are the setup programs used in versions of Windows prior to Windows 7 / 8. Although it's a graphical tool, Windows Setup can be run from the command line. For example, you can use the following command to initiate an unattended installation of Windows Server 2016:

```
setup.exe /unattend:answerfile
```

The Windows Setup program has several command-line options that can be applied. Table 2.4 describes the Setup.exe command-line options.

TABLE 2.4 Setup.exe command-line options and descriptions

Setup.exe Option	Description
/1394debug: *channel* [baudrate:*baudrate*]	Enables kernel debugging over a FireWire (IEEE 1394) port for troubleshooting purposes. The [baudrate] optional parameter specifies the baud rate for data transfer during the debugging process.
/debug:*port* [*baudrate:baudrate*]	Enables kernel debugging over the specified port for troubleshooting purposes. The [baudrate] optional parameter specifies the baud rate for data transfer during the debugging process.

Setup.exe Option	Description
/emsport:{com1|com 2|usebiossettings|off} [/emsbaudrate:*baudrate*]	Configures EMS to be enabled or disabled. The [baudrate] optional parameter specifies the baud rate for data transfer during the debugging process.
/m:*folder_name*	Used with Setup to specify that replacement files should be copied from the specified location. If the files are not present, Setup will use the default location.
/noreboot	Normally, when the down-level phase of Setup.exe is complete, the computer restarts. This option specifies that the computer should not restart so that you can execute another command prior to the restart.
/tempdrive:*drive letter*	Specifies the location that will be used to store the temporary files for Windows Server 2016 and the installation partition for Windows Server 2016.
/unattend:[*answerfile*]	Specifies that you will be using an unattended installation for Windows Server 2016. The answerfile variable points to the custom answer file you will use for installation.

Next we'll look at the System Preparation Tool (Sysprep); using it is one of many ways to install Windows Server 2016 automatically.

Using the System Preparation Tool to Prepare an Installation for Imaging

You can use disk images to install Windows Server 2016 on computers that have similar hardware configurations. Also, if a computer is having technical difficulties, you can use a disk image to quickly restore it to a baseline configuration.

To create a disk image, you install Windows Server 2016 on the source computer with the configuration that you want to copy and use the System Preparation Tool to prepare the installation for imaging. The source computer's configuration should also include any applications that should be installed on target computers.

Once you have prepared the installation for imaging, you can use imaging software such as Image Capture Wizard to create an image of the installation.

The System Preparation Tool (Sysprep.exe) is included with Windows Server 2016, in the %WINDIR%\system32\sysprep directory. When you run this utility on the source computer, it strips out information that is unique for each computer, such as the SID. Table 2.5 defines the command options that you can use to customize the Sysprep.exe operation.

TABLE 2.5   System Preparation Tool command-line options

Switch	Description
/audit	Configures the computer to restart into audit mode, which allows you to add drivers and applications to Windows or test the installation prior to deployment.
/generalize	Removes any unique system information from the image, including the SID and log information.
/oobe	Specifies that the Windows Welcome screen should be displayed when the computer reboots.
/quiet	Runs the installation with no user interaction.
/quit	Specifies that the System Preparation Tool should quit after the specified operations have been completed.
/reboot	Restarts the target computer after the System Preparation Tool completes.
/shutdown	Specifies that the computer should shut down after the specified operations have been completed.
/unattend	Indicates the name and location of the answer file to use.

In the following sections, you will learn how to create a disk image and how to copy and install from it.

Preparing a Windows Server 2016 Installation

To run the System Preparation Tool and prepare an installation for imaging, take the following steps:

1. Install Windows Server 2016 on a source computer. The computer should have a similar hardware configuration to that of the destination computer(s). The source computer should not be a member of a domain. (See Chapter 1 for instructions on installing Windows Server 2016.)

2. Log on to the source computer as Administrator and, if desired, install and configure any applications, files (such as newer versions of Plug and Play drivers), or custom settings (for example, a custom Desktop) that will be applied to the target computer(s).

3. Verify that your image meets the specified configuration criteria and that all applications are properly installed and working.

4. Select Start ➤ Computer, and navigate to C:\%WINDIR%\System32\sysprep. Double-click the Sysprep application icon.

5. The Windows System Preparation Tool dialog box appears. Select the appropriate options for your configuration.

6. If configured to do so, Windows Server 2016 will be rebooted into setup mode, and you will be prompted to enter the appropriate setup information.

7. You will now be able to use imaging software to create an image of the computer to deploy to other computers.

In Exercise 2.3, you will use the System Preparation Tool to prepare the computer for disk imaging. The Sysprep utility must be run on a machine with a clean version of Windows Server 2016. If you upgraded a Windows Server 2012 R2 machine to Windows Server 2016, you will not be able to run the Sysprep utility.

EXERCISE 2.3

Prepare a System for Imaging by Using the System Preparation Tool

1. Log on to the source computer as Administrator and, if desired, install and configure any applications that should also be installed on the target computer.

2. Select Start ➢ Computer, and navigate to C:\%WINDIR%\System32\sysprep. Double-click the Sysprep application icon.

3. In the System Preparation Tool dialog box, select Enter System Out-Of-Box Experience (OOBE) in the system cleanup action.

4. Under the shutdown options, depending on the options selected, the System Preparation Tool will quit, the computer will shut down, or the computer will be rebooted into setup mode, where you will need to configure the setup options. Choose the Reboot option. Click OK.

5. After you configure the Sysprep utility, you can use an imaging tool like DISM to capture the image.

After creating the Sysprep image, you need to use some type of third-party software to capture it. Windows includes a utility called Image Capture Wizard for just that purpose.

Using Windows Imaging and Configuration Designer (Windows ICD) to Create a Disk Image

After you've run the System Preparation Tool on the source computer, you can create an image from the installation, and you can then install the image on target computers. To create an image, you can use Image Capture Wizard, which is a utility that can be used to create and manage Windows image (.wim) files.

At the time this book was written, The Windows ICD supports disk images for Windows 10 Desktop editions, Windows 10, Mobile editions, and Windows 10 IoT Core images. Windows ICD Does not support the configuration of Windows Server 2016 editions.

To run the Image Capture Wizard utility to create a disk image of a Windows Server 2016 installation, follow these steps:

 To install Windows ICD and configure images for Windows 10, you must install the Windows Assessment and Deployment Kit (ADK) for Windows 10.

1. From the Windows ICD Start page, select Simple Provisioning.

2. In the Enter Project Details window, specify a Name and Location for your project. Optionally, you can also enter a brief Description to describe your project.

3. Click Next.

4. In the Enter Project Details window, you need to enter the Name of your project and the location of the project. You can also enter a description. Click Next.

5. In the Choose which settings to view and configure window, select the Windows edition that you want to do a provision package. Then click Next.

6. Optional. If you have a provisioning package that contains customizations already configured in a different project and you want to reuse the customizations from this package, click Browse in the Import a provisioning package screen to locate the provisioning package that was exported from another project.

7. Click Finish.

There is also a Command Line version of the Windows (ICD) tool (C:\Program Files(x86)\Windows Kits\10\Assessment and Deployment Kit\Imaging and Configuration Designer\x86) that you can use. The Microsoft exams have started using a lot of command line utilities on their tests. So let us take a look at the Windows (ICD) command line utility. The command that we use for this is icd.exe:

```
icd.exe <command> <parameters>
```

Table 2.6 shows you the icd.exe command and some of the switches that you can use to configure the images.

 To see a list of all ICD switches and commands, please visit Microsoft's website at:

https://msdn.microsoft.com/en-us/library/windows/hardware
/dn916115(v=vs.85).aspx

TABLE 2.6   ICD.exe Switches

Switch	Description
/CustomizationXML	This command identifies the location of the Windows provisioning XML file. This file holds the information for customization assets and settings.
/PackagePath	Identifies the location and the built provisioning package name where the package will be saved.
/StoreFile	This command allows IT administrators to use their own settings store instead of the default store used by Windows ICD. If an IT administrator does not determine their own store, a default store that's common to all Windows editions will be loaded by Windows ICD.
/MSPackageRoot	Identifies the location of the root directory that holds the Microsoft packages that you downloaded from the Windows Portal.
/OEMInputXML	Identifies the location to the OEMInput.xml file. This file defines a subset of settings that can be designed based on the image type.
/Variables	Identifies a macro pair that is separated by semicolon <name> and <value>.
Encrypted	Indicates if the provisioning package should be created with encryption or not. Windows ICD will then automatically generate a decryption password that is included with the output.
Overwrite	Indicates whether or not to overwrite the existing provisioning package.
/?	This command is used to access the ICD help. The help lists the switches and their descriptions for the ICD command-line tool.

After you create the disk image, the next step is to install it. In the next section, you'll learn how to install the disk image on a new machine.

Installing from a Disk Image

After you've run the System Preparation Tool and Image Capture Wizard on the source computer, you can copy the image and then install it on the target computer.

Once the image is copied, you should boot the destination computer into the Windows PE. If the computer has been used previously, it may be necessary to reformat the hard drive, which you can do using the diskpart command in Windows PE. If the image is stored over the network, you should then copy the image to the destination computer by using the net use [*dir*] [*network share*] and copy [*file*] [*dir*] commands. Then, you should use the /apply option of the Image Capture Wizard utility to apply the image to the local computer. If an answer file has not been deployed along with the image, you may have to apply such information as regional settings, the product key, the computer name, and the password to the new computer after the destination computer is rebooted.

In Exercise 2.4, you will use the stripped image that was created in Exercise 2.3 to simulate the process of continuing an installation from a disk image.

EXERCISE 2.4

Installing Windows Server 2016 from a Disk Image

1. Boot the target computer into Windows PE.

2. Copy the image created in Exercise 2.3 to the local computer by using the following commands:

```
net use z: \\Server\Images
copy  Z:\Images\image.wim C:
```

3. Apply the image to the target computer using the following Image Capture Wizard command:

```
D:\ICD.exe /apply C:\Images\image.wim C:
```

When you install Windows Server 2016, the installation wizard asks you questions such as your username and computer name. There is a way to answer these questions without actually being in front of the computer. As you'll see in the next section, you can do this by using an answer file.

Using the Deployment Image Servicing and Management Tool

Deployment Image Servicing and Management (DISM.exe) is a PowerShell and command-line utility that allows you to manipulate a Windows image. DISM also allows you to prepare a Windows PE image. DISM replaces multiple programs that were included with Windows 7/8. These programs include Package Manager (Pkgmgr.exe), PEimg, and Intlcfg. These tools have been consolidated into one tool (DISM.exe), and new functionality has been added to improve the experience for offline servicing.

DISM provides additional functionality when used with Windows Server 2016 and Windows Server 2012/2012 R2. You can use DISM to do the following:

- Add, remove, and enumerate packages
- Add, remove, and enumerate drivers

- Enable or disable Windows features
- Apply changes to an Unattend.xml answer file
- Configure international settings
- Upgrade a Windows image to a different edition
- Prepare a Windows PE 3.0 image
- Works with all platforms (32-bit, 64-bit, and Itanium)
- Allows for the use of Package Manager scripts

DISM and Command-Line Commands

As stated above, DISM can work as a command line utility or a PowerShell utility. In this first section, I will show you how to use DISM with command line switches. Table 2.7 shows the different commands that can be used with DISM.exe. To see all DISM commands, type DISM in a command prompt.

TABLE 2.7   DISM.exe command-line commands

Command	Description
/Split-Image	Splits an existing .wim or .ffu file into multiple files.
/Apply-Image	Applies an image.
/Get-MountedImageInfo	Displays basic information about mounted WIM and VHD images.
/Get-ImageInfo	Displays information about images in a WIM or VHD file.
/commit-Image	Saves changes to a mounted WIM or VHD image.
/Unmount-Image	Unmounts a mounted WIM or VHD image.
/mount-image	Mounts an image from a WIM or VHD file.
/Remount-Image	Recovers an orphaned image mount directory.
/List-Image	Displays a list of files and folders in a specific image.
/Delete-Image	Deletes the specified image.
/Append-Image	Adds another image to a WIM file.
/Capture-Image	Captures an image of a drive into a new WIM file. Captures all directories, including folders and subfolders.

DISM and PowerShell

Now that we had a chance to see how DISM works in the command-line application, we need to now examine how DISM works with PowerShell. DISM has evolved over the last few years and it has become a much more powerful tool than when it was first released. To show this, Table 2.8 will show just some of the PowerShell commands that can be used to configure and manipulate images.

The table I used for this section was from Microsoft's website. To see the complete list of DISM PowerShell cmdlets, please visit `https://technet.microsoft.com/en-us/library/dn376474.aspx`.

TABLE 2.8   DISM and PowerShell

PowerShell cmdlet	Description
Add-AppxProvisionedPackage	This cmdlet allows an administrator to add an app package (.appx) that will install for each new user to a Windows image.
Add-WindowsDriver	Administrators can use this cmdlet to add a driver to an offline Windows image.
Add-WindowsImage	This allows an administrator to add an additional image to an existing image (.wim) file.
Add-WindowsPackage	Allows an administrator to add a single .cab or .msu file to an existing Windows image.
Disable-WindowsOptionalFeature	Administrators can use this cmdlet to disable a feature in a Windows image.
Enable-WindowsOptionalFeature	Administrators can use this cmdlet to enable a feature in a Windows image.
Expand-WindowsImage	This cmdlet allows an admin to expand an image to a specified location.
Export-WindowsImage	Allows an administrator to export a copy of the specified image to another file.
Get-WindowsCapability	Shows the Windows capabilities for an image or a running operating system.
Get-WindowsDriver	Allows you to see information about drivers in a Windows image.

PowerShell cmdlet	Description
Get-WindowsEdition	Administrators can view edition information about a Windows image.
Get-WindowsImage	Allows an admin to see information about a Windows image in a WIM or VHD file.
Get-WindowsImageContent	Used to display a list of the files and folders in a specified image.
Get-WindowsOptionalFeature	This shows you information about optional features in a Windows image.
New-WindowsImage	Allows an administrator to capture an image of a drive to a new WIM file.
Remove-WindowsDriver	Allows you to remove a driver from an offline Windows image.
Remove-WindowsImage	Administrators can remove a specified volume image from a WIM file that has multiple volume images.
Remove-WindowsPackage	Allows you to remove a package from a Windows image.
Repair-WindowsImage	Allows an administrator to repair a Windows image in a WIM or VHD file.
Save-WindowsImage	Allows you to apply changes made to a mounted image to its WIM or VHD file.
Set-WindowsEdition	Allows an administrator to change a Windows image to a higher Windows edition.
Set-WindowsProductKey	An administrator can set the product key for the Windows image.
Split-WindowsImage	Allows an administrator to split an existing .wim file into multiple read-only split .wim files.

Using Windows System Image Manager to Create Answer Files

Answer files are automated installation scripts used to answer the questions that appear during a normal Windows Server 2016 installation. You can use answer files with Windows Server 2016 unattended installations, disk image installations, or WDS installations. Setting up answer files allows you to easily deploy Windows Server 2016 to computers that may not be configured in the same manner, with little or no user intervention. Because answer files are associated with image files, you can validate the settings within an answer file against the image file.

You can create answer files by using the Windows System Image Manager (Windows SIM) utility. There are several advantages to using Windows SIM to create answer files:

- You can easily create and edit answer files through a graphical interface, which reduces syntax errors.

- You can validate existing answer files against newly created images.

- You can include additional application and device drivers in the answer file.

In the following sections, you will learn about options that can be configured through Windows SIM, how to create answer files with Windows SIM, how to format an answer file, and how to manually edit answer files.

Configuring Components through Windows System Image Manager

You can use Windows SIM to configure a wide variety of installation options. The following list defines which components can be configured through Windows SIM and gives a short description of each component:

auditSystem   Adds additional device drivers, specifies firewall settings, and applies a name to the system when the image is booted into audit mode. Audit mode is initiated by using the sysprep/audit command.

auditUser   Executes RunSynchronous or RunAsynchronous commands when the image is booted into audit mode. Audit mode is initiated by using the sysprep/audit command.

generalize   Removes system-specific information from an image so that the image can be used as a reference image. The settings specified in the generalize component will be applied only if the sysprep/generalize command is used.

offlineServicing   Specifies the language packs and packages to apply to an image prior to the image being extracted to the hard disk.

oobeSystem   Specifies the settings to apply to the computer the first time the computer is booted into the Windows Welcome screen, which is also known as the Out-Of-Box Experience (OOBE). To boot to the Welcome screen, the sysprep/oobe command should be used.

specialize   Configures the specific settings for the target computer, such as network settings and domain information. This configuration pass is used in conjunction with the generalize configuration pass.

Windows PE   Sets the Windows PE–specific configuration settings, as well as several Windows Setup settings, such as partitioning and formatting the hard disk, selecting an image, and applying a product key.

Microsoft Assessment and Planning (MAP) Toolkit

This chapter is all about installing Windows Server 2016 the easiest way possible. One utility that you can use to help design your network is the *Microsoft Assessment and Planning (MAP) Toolkit*. MAP is a utility that will locate computers on a network and then perform a thorough inventory of these computers. To obtain this inventory, MAP uses multiple utilities like the Windows Management Instrumentation (WMI), the Remote Registry Service, or the Simple Network Management Protocol (SNMP).

Having this information will allow an administrator to determine if the machines on their network will be able to load Microsoft Windows clients (including Vista, Windows 7/8/10, or Windows Server 2008/2008 R2/2012/2012 R2/2016, Microsoft Office, and Microsoft Application Virtualization. One advantage of using MAP when determining the needs for Windows is that MAP will also advise you of any hardware upgrades needed for a machine or device driver availability.

Anyone who has been in the industry for a while can see the potential of using MAP. Having a utility go out and discover your network hardware and then advise you of needed resources to allow the operating system to operate properly is a tool that should be in every administrator's arsenal.

When deciding to locate the computers on your network, you have multiple ways to do this. The following are your discovery options and how they try to discover the computers:

- Use Active Directory Domain Services

  - Select this check box to find computer objects in Active Directory.

- Use The Windows Networking Protocols.

  - Select this check box to find computers in workgroups and Windows NT 4.0 domains.

- Import Computer Names From A File

  - Select this check box to import computer names from a file.

- Scan An IP Address Range

  - Select this check box to find computers within a specified IP address range.

- Manually Enter Computer Names And Credentials

  - Select this check box to enter computer names individually.

As a network administrator, one thing that is always difficult to determine is how many servers are needed for your Windows end users and where to place them on your network. An included feature with MAP is the ability to obtain performance metric data from the computers. MAP will also generate a report that recommends which machines can be used for Windows clients.

MAP generates your report in both Microsoft Excel and Microsoft Word. These reports can provide information to you in both summary and full detail modes. MAP can generate reports for you for some of the following scenarios:

- Identify currently installed client operating systems and their requirements for migrating to Windows 10.

- Identify currently installed Windows Server systems and their requirements for migrating to Windows Server 2016.

- Identify currently installed Microsoft Office software and their requirements for migrating to Microsoft Office 2016.

- Server performance by using the Performance Metrics Wizard.

- Hyper-V server consolidation and placement.

- Assessment of machines (Clients, Servers) for installation of Microsoft Application Virtualization (formally known as SoftGrid).

To install MAP, we must first take a look at the system requirements.

MAP System Requirements

- **Supported Operating Systems:** Windows Server 2012 or above and/or Windows 7 and above.

- **CPU Architecture:** One advantage to the Microsoft Assessment and Planning Solution Accelerator is that it can be installed on both the 32-Bit and 64-bit versions of any of the operating systems listed above.

- **Hardware Requirements:**

  - 1.6 GHz or faster processor minimum or dual-core for Windows 7

  - 2.0GB for Windows 7

  - Minimum 1 GB of available hard-disk space

  - Network card that supports 10/100 Mbps

Microsoft Assessment and Planning Toolkit is free to use but it must be downloaded from Microsoft's website or installed from the Windows AIK installation disk. In Exercise 2.5 will walk you through the steps to install the Microsoft Assessment and Planning Toolkit from the Windows AIK installation utility. You can download the newest MAP toolkit at https://www.microsoft.com/en-in/download/details.aspx?id=7826.

EXERCISE 2.5

Installing the Microsoft Assessment and Planning Toolkit

1. Download the MAP Toolkit (MapSetup.exe).

2. When you get the message "Do you want to run MapSetup.exe," click the Run button.

3. The Welcome to the Setup Wizard for Microsoft Assessment and Planning Toolkit. Click Next.

4. Accept the License Agreement and click Next.

5. At the Installation Folder screen, just accept the default location by clicking Next.

6. You will be asked to Join the Customer Experience. Click the Do not Join the program at this time radio button and click Next.

7. At the Begin to Install screen, click the Install button.

8. After the installation is complete, the Installation Successful screen will appear. Click the Finish button.

Now that we have installed the Microsoft Assessment and Planning toolkit, it's now time to configure and test our server. In Exercise 2.6, we will create our database for testing.

Configuring MAP

1. Start the Microsoft Assessment and Planning toolkit by clicking Start, Recently added and then Microsoft Planning and Assessment Toolkit.

2. The first thing we need to do is select our database. We are going to create our database at this time. To accomplish this, click on select a database in either the center or right window panes.

3. The Create or select a database screen will appear. Make sure that the Create an inventory database radio button is clicked. In the Name Field, type in **Windows 10** and click the OK button.

After your database is created, you now have the ability to run the different options to test the machines and servers. This is where you decide which scenarios you would like to test for your network.

As a consultant and system administrator for many years, it is very useful to have a utility like MAP to help you not only detect your network and its operating systems, but also recommend enhancements.

Understanding Hyper-V

In the following sections, I'll introduce you to Hyper-V. In Chapter 4 "Understanding Hyper-V" I will show you how to completely install and configure Hyper-V. But to understand Hyper-V images and deploying servers using these images, I need to give you a brief understanding of how Hyper-V works.

Hyper-V is very easy to understand. Hyper-V allows you to run multiple operating systems on the same hardware. The Windows Server 2016 machine with the Hyper-V role installed is called the Hyper-V Host. The Windows operating systems that run within Hyper-V are referred to as Hyper-V guests (also called Virtual Machines).

What Is Virtualization?

Virtualization is a method for abstracting physical resources from the way they interact with other resources. For example, if you abstract the physical hardware from the operating system, you get the benefit of being able to move the operating system between different physical systems.

This is called *server virtualization*. But there are also other forms of virtualization available, such as presentation virtualization, desktop virtualization, and application virtualization. I will now briefly explain the differences between these forms of virtualization:

Server Virtualization   This basically enables multiple operating systems to run on the same physical server. Hyper-V is a server virtualization tool that allows you to move physical machines to virtual machines and manage them on a few physical servers. Thus, you will be able to consolidate physical servers.

Presentation Virtualization   When you use *presentation virtualization*, your applications run on a different computer and only the screen information is transferred to your computer. An example of presentation virtualization is Microsoft Remote Desktop Services in Windows Server 2016.

Desktop Virtualization   *Desktop virtualization* provides you with a virtual machine on your desktop, comparable to server virtualization. You run your complete operating system and applications in a virtual machine so that your local physical machine just needs to run a very basic operating system. An example of this form of virtualization is Microsoft Windows 10 Hyper-V.

Application Virtualization   *Application virtualization* helps prevent conflicts between applications on the same PC. Thus it helps you to isolate the application running environment from the operating system installation requirements by creating application-specific copies of all shared resources, and it helps reduce application-to-application incompatibility and testing needs. An example of an application virtualization tool is Microsoft Application Virtualization (App-V).

Now that I have given you a brief understanding of virtualization, let's look at how we can install Hyper-V. In Chapter 4, "Understanding Hyper-V," I will have exercises showing you how to do full installations of Hyper-V on a Windows Server 2016.

There are multiple ways that you can install Hyper-V onto a Windows Server 2016 system. The first and easiest way to install Hyper-V is to use Server Manager and choose the Hyper-V role. Another way is to install Hyper-V role is by using PowerShell. The following is the command that is run while in Windows PowerShell to install Hyper-V:

```
Enable-WindowsOptionalFeature -Online -FeatureName Microsoft-Hyper-V –All
```

Linux and FreeBSD Image Deployments

One of the new features of Windows 2016 is the ability for Hyper-V to support Linux and FreeBSD virtual machines. Hyper-V now can support these new virtual machines because Hyper-V has the ability to emulate Linux and FreeBSD devices. Because Hyper-V now has the ability to emulate these two devices, no additional software needs to be installed on Hyper-V.

Unfortunately, because Hyper-V has to emulate these devices, you lose some of the Hyper-V functionality like high performance and full management of the virtual machines. So it's a trade-off. You get to run Linux and FreeBSD type Hyper-V virtual machines but you lose some of the benefits of Hyper-V.

But wait. There is a way to get your Hyper-V functionality back. This issue can be resolved as long as you install Hyper-V on machines that can support Linux and FreeBSD operating systems. The drivers that are needed on Hyper-V are called Linux Integration Services (LIS) and FreeBSD Integrated Services (FIS). By putting these drivers on a device that can handle Linux and FreeBSD, you can then have Hyper-V with all of the features Microsoft offers.

To get these drivers and make Hyper-V work will all of its functionality, you must make sure that you install a newer release of Linux that includes LIS. To get the most out of FreeBSD, you must get a version after 10.0. For FreeBSD versions that are older than 10.0, Microsoft offers ports that work with BIS drivers that need to be installed. Hyper-V will work with Linux and FreeBSD without the need of any additional drivers or equipment. By having drivers and equipment that supports Linux and FreeBSD, you just get all of the Hyper-V features that your origination may need.

Summary

In this chapter, we discussed automated installation of Windows Server 2016. Installing Windows Server 2016 through an automated process is an effective way to install the Windows Server 2016 operating system on multiple computers.

There are several methods for automated installation: unattended installations, Windows Assessment and Deployment Kit (ADK), third-party applications, unattended installations, and using the System Preparation Tool along with DISM.

The Windows (ADK) is a set of utilities and documentation that allows an administrator to configure and deploy Windows operating systems.

You can use unattended answer files to automatically respond to the queries that are generated during the normal installation process.

You can also prepare an installation for imaging by using the System Preparation Tool (Sysprep.exe) and creating a disk image by using the Image Capture Wizard utility or a third-party utility.

Microsoft Deployment Toolkit (MDT) 2013 Update 2 is a way of automating desktop and server deployment. With the MDT, an administrator can deploy desktops and servers through the use of a common console, which allows for quicker deployments, having standardized desktop and server images and security and zero-touch deployments of Windows Server 2016, Windows 8, Windows 7, Windows Server 2008, Windows Server 2008 R2, Windows Server 2012, Windows Server 2012 R2, and Windows Server 2016.

Video Resources

There are no videos available for this chapter.

Exam Essentials

Know the difference between the various unattended installation methods.   Understand the various options available for unattended installations of Windows Server 2016 and when it is appropriate to use each installation method.

Be able to use disk images for unattended installations.   Know how to perform unattended installations of Windows Server 2016 using the System Preparation Tool and disk images.

Know how to use Windows System Image Manager to create and edit answer files.   Understand how to access and use Windows System Image Manager to create answer files. Be able to edit the answer files and know the basic options that can be configured for them.

Understand the Microsoft Deployment Toolkit (MDT) 2013 Update 2.   Know that the MDT is a way of automating desktop and server deployment. Understand that the MDT allows an administrator to deploy desktops and servers through the use of a common console.

Review Questions

1. You are the network administrator for your organization. You have a reference computer that runs Windows Server 2016. You need to create and deploy an image of the Windows Server 2016 computer. You create an answer file named answer.xml. You have to make sure that the installation applies the answer file after you deploy the image. Which command should you run before you capture the image?

   A. ICD.exe /append answer.xml/check

   B. ICD.exe /mount answer.xml/verify

   C. Sysprep.exe/reboot/audit/unattend:answer.xml

   D. Sysprep.exe/generalize/oobe/unattend:answer.xml

2. You have a Windows Server 2016 Windows Image (WIM) that is mounted. You need to display information about the image. What should you do?

   A. Run DISM and specify the /get-ImageInfo parameter.

   B. Run Driverquery.exe and use the /si parameter.

   C. From Device Manager, view all hidden drivers.

   D. From Windows Explorer, open the mount folder.

3. You are a network technician for your company, and you need to deploy Windows Server 2016 to multiple computers. You want to automate the installation of Windows Server 2016 so that no user interaction is required during the installation process. Which of the following utilities could you use?

   A. Windows SIM

   B. Image Capture Wizard

   C. System Preparation Tool

   D. WDSUTIL

4. Will is the network manager for a large company. He has been tasked with creating a deployment plan to automate installations for 100 computers that need to have Windows Server 2016 installed. Will wants to use WDS for the installations. To fully automate the installations, he needs to create an answer file. Will does not want to create the answer files with a text editor. What other program can he use to create unattended answer files via a GUI interface?

   A. Image Capture Wizard

   B. Answer Manager

   C. Windows System Image Manager

   D. System Preparation Tool

5. You want to initiate a new installation of Windows Server 2016 from the command line. You plan to accomplish this by using the Setup.exe command-line setup utility. You want to use an answer file with this command. Which command-line option should you use?

   A. /unattend

   B. /apply

   C. /noreboot

   D. /generalize

6. You run a training department that needs the same software installed from scratch on the training computers each week. You decide to use Image Capture Wizard to deploy disk images. Which Windows Server 2016 utility can you use in conjunction with Image Capture Wizard to create these disk images?

   A. UAF

   B. Answer Manager

   C. Setup Manager

   D. System Preparation Tool

7. You are trying to decide whether you want to use WDS as a method of installing Windows Server 2016 within your company. Which of the following options is *not* an advantage to using a WDS automated installation?

   A. The Windows Server 2016 security is retained when you restart the computer.

   B. Windows Server 2016 installation media does not need to be deployed to each computer.

   C. Unique information is stripped out of the installation image so that it can be copied to other computers.

   D. You can quickly recover the operating system in the event of a system failure.

8. You are the network manager of XYZ Corporation. You are in charge of developing an automated deployment strategy for rolling out new Windows Server 2016 computers. You want to install a WDS server and are evaluating whether an existing server can be used as a WDS server for Windows Server 2016 deployment. Which of the following is *not* a requirement for configuring the WDS server?

   A. The remote installation folder must be NTFS version 3.0 or later.

   B. The remote installation folder must reside on the system partition.

   C. RIS must be installed on the server.

   D. The existing server must run Windows Server 2003 with Service Pack 1 installed.

9. You are planning on deploying a new Windows Server 2016 image to 100 client computers that are similarly configured. You are using the Windows SIM tool to create an answer file that will be used to automate the installation process. You want each computer to contain two partitions, one for the system partition and one that will function as a data partition. You need to modify the answer file to support this configuration. Which component of the answer file will you need to modify?

A. oobeSystem

B. auditSystem

C. Windows PE

D. specialize

10. You want to install a group of 25 computers using disk images created in conjunction with the System Preparation Tool. Your plan is to create an image from a reference computer and then copy the image to all the machines. You do not want to create an SID on the destination computer when you use the image. Which Sysprep.exe command-line option should you use to set this up?

A. /specialize

B. /generalize

C. /oobe

D. /quiet

Chapter

3

Configuring Storage and Replication

THE FOLLOWING 70-740 EXAM OBJECTIVES ARE COVERED IN THIS CHAPTER:

✓ **Configure disks and volumes**

- This objective may include but is not limited to: Configure sector sizes appropriate for various workloads; configure GUID partition table (GPT) disks; create VHD and VHDX files using Server Manager or Windows PowerShell Storage module cmdlets; mount virtual hard disks; determine when to use NTFS and ReFS file systems; configure NFS and SMB shares using Server Manager; configure SMB share and session settings using Windows PowerShell; configure SMB server and SMB client configuration settings using Windows PowerShell; configure file and folder permissions.

✓ **Implement server storage**

- This objective may include but is not limited to: Configure storage pools; implement simple, mirror, and parity storage layout options for disks or enclosures; expand storage pools; configure Tiered Storage; configure iSCSI target and initiator; configure iSNS; configure Datacenter Bridging (DCB); configure Multi-Path IO (MPIO).

✓ **Implement data deduplication**

- This objective may include but is not limited to: Implement and configure deduplication; determine appropriate usage scenarios for deduplication; monitor deduplication; implement a backup and restore solution with deduplication.

This chapter explains how to set up your servers so that your network users have something to access. Before you can set up a server, you have to determine the purpose of it. Is it going to be a print server, a file storage server, a remote access server, or a domain controller?

After you have decided how the machine is going to help your network, you must implement your decision. In this chapter, I'll show you how to set up a print server and a file server. In addition, I will discuss how to set up permissions and security for these servers and how you can limit the amount of space your users can have on a server.

Finally in the chapter, I will show you how to setup and use data duplication. I will explain the benefits of duplication and how to use data duplication for backups. I will also show you how to monitor the data that is being duplicated.

But I am going to start the chapter by introducing you to the different Windows File Systems. So let's begin.

Understanding File Systems

When we start the discussion about understanding Windows files systems, we have to first think about how the Windows Server 2016 machine will be used. There are four (4) supported file systems: FAT, FAT32, NTFS, and ReFS. FAT and FAT32 partitions may not always be an available option. As you can see in Figure 3.1, all 4 file systems are available because the partition is under 4 GB.

FIGURE 3.1 Format options on Windows Server 2016

New Simple Volume Wizard	✕

Format Partition
To store data on this partition, you must format it first.

Choose whether you want to format this volume, and if so, what settings you want to use.

○ Do not format this volume

◉ Format this volume with the following settings:

File system:	NTFS ∨
	FAT
Allocation unit size:	FAT32
	NTFS
Volume label:	ReFS

☑ Perform a quick format

☐ Enable file and folder compression

< Back   Next >   Cancel

FAT has a max partition size of 4GB and FAT32 has a max partition size of 32 GB. In Figure 3.1, since it's a 3 GB partition, all four options are available. But since most drives today are much larger than 32 GB, we will continue our focus on just NTFS and ReFS.

When you're planning your Active Directory deployment, the file system that the operating system uses is an important concern for two reasons. First, the file system can provide the ultimate level of security for all the information stored on the server itself. Second, it is responsible for managing and tracking all of this data. The Windows Server 2016 platform supports two main file systems:

- Windows NT File System (NTFS)
- Resilient File System (ReFS)

Although ReFS was new to Windows Server 2012, NTFS has been around for many years, and NTFS in Windows Server 2016 has been improved for better performance.

Resilient File System (ReFS)

Windows Server 2016 includes a file system called *Resilient File System (ReFS)*. ReFS was created to help Windows Server 2016 maximize the availability of data and online operation. ReFS allows the Windows Server 2016 system to continue to function despite some errors that would normally cause data to be lost or the system to go down. ReFS uses data integrity to protect your data from errors and also to make sure that all of your important data is online when that data is needed.

One of the issues that IT members have had to face over the years is the problem of rapidly growing data sizes. As we continue to rely more and more on computers, our data continues to get larger and larger. This is where ReFS can help an IT department. ReFS was designed specifically with the issues of scalability and performance in mind, which resulted in some of the following ReFS features:

Availability   If your hard disk becomes corrupt, ReFS has the ability to implement a salvage strategy that removes the data that has been corrupted. This feature allows the healthy data to continue to be available while the unhealthy data is removed. All of this can be done without taking the hard disk offline.

Scalability   One of the main advantages of ReFS is the ability to support volume sizes up to 2^{78} bytes using 16 KB cluster sizes, while Windows stack addressing allows 2^{64} bytes. ReFS also supports file sizes of $2^{64}-1$ bytes, 2^{64} files in a directory, and the same number of directories in a volume.

Robust Disk Updating   ReFS uses a disk updating system referred to as an *allocate-on-write transactional model* (also known as *copy on write*). This model helps to avoid many hard disk issues while data is written to the disk because ReFS updates data using disk writes to multiple locations in an atomic manner instead of updating data in place.

Data Integrity   ReFS uses a check-summed system to verify that all data that is being written and stored is accurate and reliable. ReFS always uses allocate-on-write for updates to the data, and it uses checksums to detect disk corruption.

Application Compatibility   ReFS allows for most NTFS features and also supports the Win32 API. Because of this, ReFS is compatible with most Windows applications.

NTFS

Let's start with some of the features of NTFS. There are many benefits to using NTFS, including support for the following:

Disk Quotas   To restrict the amount of disk space used by users on the network, system administrators can establish *disk quotas*. By default, Windows Server 2016 supports disk quota restrictions at the volume level. That is, you can restrict the amount of storage space that a specific user uses on a single disk volume. Third-party solutions that allow more granular quota settings are also available.

File System Encryption   One of the fundamental problems with network operating systems (NOSs) is that system administrators are often given full permission to view all files and data stored on hard disks, which can be a security and privacy concern. In some cases, this is necessary. For example, to perform backup, recovery, and disk management functions, at least one user must have all permissions. Windows Server 2016 and NTFS address these issues by allowing for *file system encryption*. Encryption essentially scrambles all of the data stored within files before they are written to the disk. When an authorized user requests the files, they are transparently decrypted and provided. By using encryption, you can prevent the data from being used in case it is stolen or intercepted by an unauthorized user—even a system administrator.

Dynamic Volumes   Protecting against disk failures is an important concern for production servers. Although earlier versions of Windows NT supported various levels of Redundant Array of Independent Disks (RAID) technology, software-based solutions had some shortcomings. Perhaps the most significant was that administrators needed to perform server reboots to change RAID configurations. Also, you could not make some configuration changes without completely reinstalling the operating system. With Windows Server 2016 support for *dynamic volumes*, system administrators can change RAID and other disk configuration settings without needing to reboot or reinstall the server. The result is greater data protection, increased scalability, and increased uptime. Dynamic volumes are also included with ReFS.

Mounted Drives   By using *mounted drives*, system administrators can map a local disk drive to an NTFS directory name. This helps them organize disk space on servers and increase manageability. By using mounted drives, you can mount the C:\Users directory to an actual physical disk. If that disk becomes full, you can copy all of the files to another, larger drive without changing the directory path name or reconfiguring applications.

Remote Storage   System administrators often notice that as soon as they add more space, they must plan the next upgrade. One way to recover disk space is to move infrequently used files to external hard drives. However, backing up and restoring these files can be quite difficult and time-consuming. System administrators can use the *remote storage* features supported by NTFS to off-load seldom-used data automatically to a backup system or other devices. The files, however, remain available to users. If a user requests an archived file,

Windows Server 2016 can automatically restore the file from a remote storage device and make it available. Using remote storage like this frees up system administrators' time and allows them to focus on tasks other than micromanaging disk space.

Self-healing NTFS   In previous versions of the Windows Server operating system, if you had to fix a corrupted NTFS volume, you used a tool called Chkdsk.exe. The disadvantage of this tool is that the Windows Server's availability was disrupted. If this server was your domain controller, that could stop domain logon authentication.

To help protect the Windows Server 2016 NTFS file system, Microsoft now uses a feature called self-healing NTFS. *Self-healing NTFS* attempts to fix corrupted NTFS file systems without taking them offline. Self-healing NTFS allows an NTFS file system to be corrected without running the Chkdsk.exe utility. New features added to the NTFS kernel code allow disk inconsistencies to be corrected without system downtime.

Security   NTFS allows you to configure not only folder-level security but also file-level security. NTFS security is one of the biggest reasons most companies use NTFS. ReFS also allows folder- and file-level security.

Setting Up the NTFS Partition

Although the features mentioned in the previous section likely compel most system administrators to use NTFS, additional reasons make using it mandatory. The most important reason is that the Active Directory data store must reside on an NTFS partition. Therefore, before you begin installing Active Directory, make sure you have at least one NTFS partition available. Also, be sure you have a reasonable amount of disk space available (at least 4 GB). Because the size of the Active Directory data store will grow as you add objects to it, also be sure that you have adequate space for the future.

Exercise 3.1 shows you how to use the administrative tools to view and modify disk configuration.

WARNING   Before you make any disk configuration changes, be sure you completely understand their potential effects; then perform the test in a lab environment and make sure you have good, verifiable backups handy. Changing partition sizes and adding and removing partitions can result in a total loss of all information on one or more partitions.

If you want to convert an existing partition from FAT or FAT32 to NTFS, you need to use the CONVERT command-line utility. For example, the following command converts the C: partition from FAT to NTFS:

```
CONVERT c: /fs:ntfs
```

EXERCISE 3.1

Viewing Disk Configurations

1. Right-click the Start button and then choose Disk Management (shown in Figure 3.2).

FIGURE 3.2   Disk Management

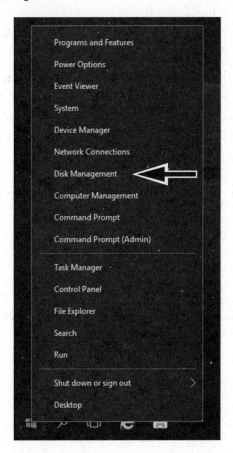

The Disk Management program shows you the logical and physical disks that are currently configured on your system. Note that information about the size of each partition
is also displayed (in the Capacity column).

2. To see the available options for modifying partition settings, right-click any of the
    disks or partitions and choose Properties. This step is optional.

3. Close Disk Management.

Storage in Windows Server 2016

As an IT administrator, you'll need to ask many questions before you start setting up a server. What type of disks should be used? What type of RAID sets should be made? What type of hardware platform should be purchased? These are all questions you must ask when planning for storage in a Windows Server 2016 server. In the following sections, I will answer these questions so that you can make the best decisions for storage in your network's environment.

Initializing Disks

To begin, I must first discuss how to add disk drives to a server. Once a disk drive has been physically installed, it must be initialized by selecting the type of partition. Different types of partition styles are used to initialize disks: *Master Boot Record (MBR)* and *GUID Partition Table (GPT)*.

MBR has a partition table that indicates where the partitions are located on the disk drive, and with this particular partition style, only volumes up to 2 TB (2,048 GB) are supported. An MBR drive can have up to four primary partitions or can have three primary partitions and one extended partition that can be divided into unlimited logical drives.

Windows Server 2016 can only boot off an MBR disk unless it is based on the Extensible Firmware Interface (EFI); then it can boot from GPT. An Itanium server is an example of an EFI-based system. GPT is not constrained by the same limitations as MBR. In fact, a GPT disk drive can support volumes of up to 18EB (18,874,368 million terabytes) and 128 partitions. As a result, GPT is recommended for disks larger than 2TB or disks used on Itanium-based computers. Exercise 3.2 demonstrates the process of initializing additional disk drives to an active computer running Windows Server 2016. If you're not adding a new drive, then stop after step 4. I am completing this exercise using Computer Management, but you also can do this exercise using Server Manager.

EXERCISE 3.2

Initializing Disk Drives

1. Open Computer Management under Administrative Tools.

2. Select Disk Management.

3. After disk drives have been installed, right-click Disk Management and select Rescan Disks.

4. A pop-up box appears indicating that the server is scanning for new disks. If you did not add a new disk, go to step 9.

5. After the server has completed the scan, the new disk appears as Unknown.

6. Right-click the Unknown disk, and select Initialize Disk.

7. A pop-up box appears asking for the partition style. For this exercise, choose MBR.

8. Click OK.

9. Close Computer Management.

The disk will now appear online as a basic disk with unallocated space.

Configuring Basic and Dynamic Disks

Windows Server 2016 supports two types of disk configurations: basic and dynamic. Basic disks are divided into partitions and can be used with previous versions of Windows. Dynamic disks are divided into volumes and can be used with Windows 2000 Server and newer releases.

When a disk is initialized, it is automatically created as a basic disk, but when a new fault-tolerant (RAID) volume set is created, the disks in the set are converted to dynamic disks. Fault-tolerance features and the ability to modify disks without having to reboot the server are what distinguish dynamic disks from basic disks.

> Fault tolerance (RAID) is discussed in detail later in this chapter in the "Redundant Array of Independent Disks" section.

A basic disk can simply be converted to a dynamic disk without loss of data. When a basic disk is converted, the partitions are automatically changed to the appropriate volumes. However, converting a dynamic disk back to a basic disk is not as simple. First, all the data on the dynamic disk must be backed up or moved. Then, all the volumes on the dynamic disk have to be deleted. The dynamic disk can then be converted to a basic disk. Partitions and logical drives can be created, and the data can be restored.

The following are actions that can be performed on basic disks:

- Formatting partitions
- Marking partitions as active
- Creating and deleting primary and extended partitions
- Creating and deleting logical drives
- Converting from a basic disk to a dynamic disk

The following are actions that can be performed on dynamic disks:

- Creating and deleting simple, striped, spanned, mirrored, or RAID-5 volumes
- Removing or breaking a mirrored volume
- Extending simple or spanned volumes
- Repairing mirrored or RAID-5 volumes
- Converting from a dynamic disk to a basic disk after deleting all volumes

In Exercise 3.3, you'll convert a basic disk to a dynamic disk.

EXERCISE 3.3

Converting a Basic Disk to a Dynamic Disk

1. Open Computer Management under Administrative Tools.

2. Select Disk Management.

3. Right-click a basic disk that you want to convert and select Convert To Dynamic Disk, as shown in Figure 3.3.

FIGURE 3.3 Converting a disk

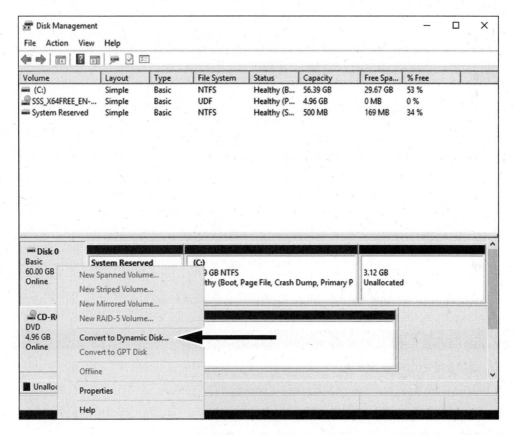

4. The Convert To Dynamic Disk dialog box appears. From here, select all of the disks that you want to convert to dynamic disks. In this exercise, only one disk will be converted.

5. Click OK.

6. The Convert To Dynamic Disk dialog box changes to the Disks To Convert dialog box and shows the disk/disks that will be converted to dynamic disks.

7. Click Convert.

8. Disk Management will warn that if you convert the disk to dynamic, you will not be able to start the installed operating system from any volume on the disk (except the current boot volume). Click Yes.

9. Close Computer Management.

The converted disk will now show as Dynamic in Disk Management.

Managing Volumes

A *volume set* is created from volumes that span multiple drives by using the free space from those drives to construct what will appear to be a single drive. The following list includes the various types of volume sets and their definitions:

- *Simple volume* uses only one disk or a portion of a disk.

- *Spanned volume* is a simple volume that spans multiple disks, with a maximum of 32. Use a spanned volume if the volume needs are too great for a single disk.

- *Striped volume* stores data in stripes across two or more disks. A striped volume gives you fast access to data but is not fault tolerant, nor can it be extended or mirrored. If one disk in the striped set fails, the entire volume fails.

- *Mirrored volume* duplicates data across two disks. This type of volume is fault tolerant because if one drive fails, the data on the other disk is unaffected.

- *RAID-5 volume* stores data in stripes across three or more disks. This type of volume is fault tolerant because if a drive fails, the data can be re-created from the parity off of the remaining disk drives. Operating system files and boot files cannot reside on the RAID-5 disks.

Exercise 3.4 illustrates the procedure for creating a volume set.

Creating a Volume Set

1. Open Computer Management under Administrative Tools.

2. Select Disk Management.

3. Select and right-click a disk that has unallocated space. If there are no disk drives available for a particular volume set, that volume set will be grayed out as a selectable option. In this exercise, you'll choose a spanned volume set, but the process after the volume set selection is the same regardless of which kind you choose. The only thing that differs is the number of disk drives chosen.

4. The Welcome page of the New Spanned Volume Wizard appears and explains the type of volume set chosen. Click Next.

5. The Select Disks page appears. Select the disk that will be included with the volume set and click Add. Repeat this process until all of the desired disks have been added. Click Next.

6. The Assign Drive Letter Or Path page appears. From here you can select the desired drive letter for the volume, mount the volume in an empty NTFS folder, or choose not to assign a drive letter. The new volume is labeled as E. Click Next.

7. The Format Volume page appears. Choose to format the new volume. Click Next.

8. Click Finish.

9. If the disks have not been converted to dynamic, you will be asked to convert the disks. Click Yes.

The new volume will appear as a healthy spanned dynamic volume with the new available disk space of the new volume set.

Storage Spaces in Windows Server 2016

Windows Server 2016 includes a technology called *Storage Spaces*. Windows Server 2016 allows an administrator to virtualize storage by grouping disks into storage pools. These storage pools can then be turned into virtual disks called *storage spaces*.

The Storage Spaces technology allows an administrator to have a highly available, scalable, low-cost, and flexible solution for both physical and virtual installations. Storage Spaces allows you to set up this advantage on either a single server or in scalable multinode mode. So, before going any further, let's look at these two terms that you must understand.

Storage Pools   *Storage pools* are a group of physical disks that allows an administrator to delegate administration, expand disk sizes, and group disks together.

Storage Spaces   *Storage spaces* allow an administrator to take free space from storage pools and create virtual disks called storage spaces. Storage spaces give administrators the ability to have precise control, resiliency, and storage tiers.

Storage spaces and storage pools can be managed by an administrator through the use of the Windows Storage Management API, Server Manager, or Windows PowerShell.

One of the advantages of using the Storage Spaces technology is the ability to set up resiliency. There are three types of Storage Space resiliency: mirror, parity, and simple (no resiliency).

 Fault tolerance (RAID) is discussed in detail in the "Redundant Array of Independent Disks" section.

Now that you understand what storage spaces and storage pools do, let's take a look at some of the other advantages of using these features in Windows Server 2016.

Availability   One advantage to the Storage Spaces technology is the ability to fully integrate the storage space with failover clustering. This advantage allows administrators to achieve service deployments that are continuously available. Administrators have the ability to set up storage pools to be clustered across multiple nodes within a single cluster.

Tiered Storage   The Storage Spaces technology allows virtual disks to be created with a two-tier storage setup. For data that is used often, you have an SSD tier; for data that is not used often, you use an HDD tier. The Storage Spaces technology will automatically transfer data at a subfile level between the two different tiers based on how often the data is used. Because of tiered storage, performance is greatly increased for data that is used most often, and data that is not used often still gets the advantage of being stored on a low-cost storage option.

Delegation   One advantage of using storage pools is that administrators have the ability to control access by using access control lists (ACLs). What is nice about this advantage is that each storage pool can have its own unique access control lists. Storage pools are fully integrated with Active Directory Domain Services.

Redundant Array of Independent Disks

The ability to support drive sets and arrays using *Redundant Array of Independent Disks (RAID)* technology is built into Windows Server 2016. RAID can be used to enhance data performance, or it can be used to provide fault tolerance to maintain data integrity in case of a hard disk failure. Windows Server 2016 supports three types of RAID technologies: RAID-0, RAID-1, and RAID-5.

RAID-0 (Disk Striping)   *Disk striping* is using two or more volumes on independent disks created as a single striped set. There can be a maximum of 32 disks. In a striped set, data is divided into blocks that are distributed sequentially across all of the drives in the set. With RAID-0 disk striping, you get very fast read and write performance because multiple blocks of data can be accessed from multiple drives simultaneously. However, RAID-0 does not offer the ability to maintain data integrity during a single disk failure. In other words, RAID-0 is not fault tolerant; a single disk event will cause the entire striped set to be lost, and it will have to be re-created through some type of recovery process, such as a tape backup.

RAID-1 (Disk Mirroring)   *Disk mirroring* is two logical volumes on two separate identical disks created as a duplicate disk set. Data is written on two disks at the same time; that way, in the event of a disk failure, data integrity is maintained and available. Although this fault tolerance gives administrators data redundancy, it comes with a price because it diminishes the amount of available storage space by half. For example, if an administrator wants to create a 300GB mirrored set, they would have to install two 300GB hard drives into the server, thus doubling the cost for the same available space.

RAID-5 Volume (Disk Striping with Parity)   With a RAID-5 volume, you have the ability to use a minimum of three disks and a maximum of 32 disks. RAID-5 volumes allow data to be striped across all of the disks with an additional block of error-correction called parity. *Parity* is used to reconstruct the data in the event of a disk failure. RAID-5 has slower write performance than the other RAID types because the OS must calculate the parity information for each stripe that is written, but the read performance is equivalent to a stripe set, RAID-0, because the parity information is not read. Like RAID-1, RAID-5 comes with additional cost considerations. For every RAID-5 set, roughly an entire hard disk is consumed for storing the parity information. For example, a minimum RAID-5 set requires three hard disks, and if those disks are 300GB each, approximately 600GB of disk space is available to the OS and 300GB is consumed by parity information, which equates to 33.3 percent of the available space. Similarly, in a five-disk RAID-5 set of 300GB disks, approximately 1,200GB of disk space is available to the OS, which means that 20 percent of the total available space is consumed by the parity information. The words *roughly* and *approximately* are used when calculating disk space because a 300GB disk will really be only about 279GB of space. This is because vendors define a gigabyte as 1 billion bytes, but the OS defines it as 2^{30} (1,073,741,824) bytes. Also, remember that file systems and volume managers have overhead as well.

Software RAID is a nice option for a small company, but hardware RAID is definitely a better option if the money is available.

Table 3.1 breaks down the various aspects of the supported RAID types in Windows Server 2016.

TABLE 3.1   Supported RAID-level properties in Windows Server 2016

RAID Level	RAID Type	Fault Tolerant	Advantages	Minimum Number of Disks	Maximum Number of Disks
0	Disk striping	No	Fast reads and writes	2	32
1	Disk mirroring	Yes	Data redundancy and faster writes than RAID-5	2	2
5	Disk striping with parity	Yes	Data redundancy with less overhead and faster reads than RAID-1	3	32

Creating RAID Sets

Now that you understand the concepts of RAID and how to use it, you can look at the creation of RAID sets in Windows Server 2016. The process of creating a RAID set is the same as the process for creating a simple or spanned volume set, except for the minimum disk requirements associated with each RAID type.

Creating a mirrored volume set is basically the same as creating a volume set except that you will select New Mirrored Volume. It is after the disk select wizard appears that you'll begin to see the difference. Since a new mirrored volume is being created, the volume requires two disks.

During the disk select process, if only one disk is selected, the Next button will be unavailable because the disk minimum has not been met. Refer to Figure 3.4 to view the Select Disks page of the New Mirrored Volume Wizard during the creation of a new mirrored volume, and notice that the Next button is not available.

FIGURE 3.4   Select Disks page of the New Mirrored Volume Wizard

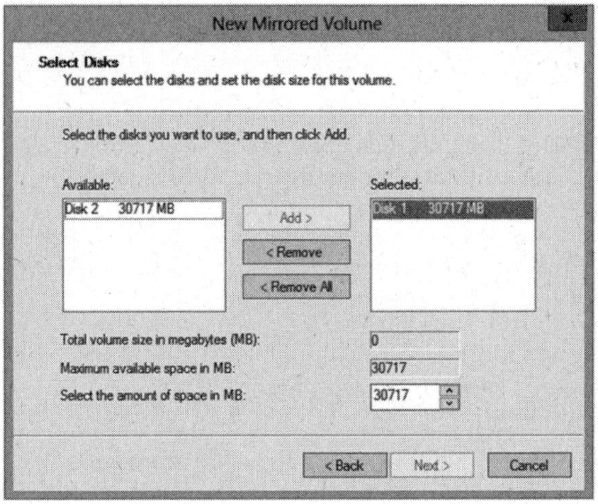

To complete the process, you must select a second disk by highlighting the appropriate disk and adding it to the volume set. Once the second disk has been added, the Next button is available to complete the mirrored volume set creation.

A drive letter will have to be assigned, and the volume will need to be formatted. The new mirrored volume set will appear in Disk Management. In Figure 3.5, notice that the capacity of the volume equals one disk even though two disks have been selected.

To create a RAID-5 volume set, you use the same process that you use to create a mirrored volume set. The only difference is that a RAID-5 volume set requires that a minimum of three disks be selected to complete the volume creation. The process is simple: Select New RAID-5 Volume, select the three disks that will be used in the volume set, assign a drive letter, and format the volume.

FIGURE 3.5   Newly created mirrored volume set

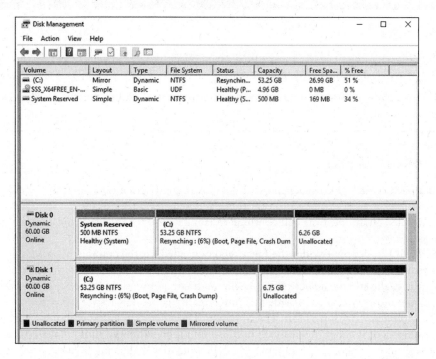

Mount Points

With the ever-increasing demands of storage, mount points are used to surpass the limitation of 26 drive letters and to join two volumes into a folder on a separate physical disk drive. A *mount point* allows you to configure a volume to be accessed from a folder on another existing disk.

Through Disk Management, a mount point folder can be assigned to a drive instead of using a drive letter, and it can be used on basic or dynamic volumes that are formatted with NTFS. However, mount point folders can be created only on empty folders within a volume. Additionally, mount point folder paths cannot be modified; they can be removed only once they have been created. Exercise 3.5 shows the steps to create a mount point.

EXERCISE 3.5

Creating Mount Points

1. Right click the Start button and select Disk Management.

2. Right-click the volume where the mount point folder will be assigned, and select Change Drive Letter And Paths.

3. Click Add.

4. Either type the path to an empty folder on an NTFS volume or click Browse to select or make a new folder for the mount point.

When you explore the drive, you'll see the new folder created. Notice that the icon indicates that it is a mount point.

Microsoft MPIO

Multipath I/O (MPIO) is associated with high availability because a computer will be able to use a solution with redundant physical paths connected to a storage device. Thus, if one path fails, an application will continue to run because it can access the data across the other path.

The MPIO software provides the functionality needed for the computer to take advantage of the redundant storage paths. MPIO solutions can also load-balance data traffic across both paths to the storage device, virtually eliminating bandwidth bottlenecks to the computer. What allows MPIO to provide this functionality is the new native *Microsoft Device Specific Module (Microsoft DSM)*. The Microsoft DSM is a driver that communicates with storage devices—iSCSI, Fibre Channel, or SAS—and it provides the chosen load-balancing policies. Windows Server 2016 supports the following load-balancing policies:

Failover   In a failover configuration, there is no load balancing. There is a primary path that is established for all requests and subsequent standby paths. If the primary path fails, one of the standby paths will be used.

Failback   This is similar to failover in that it has primary and standby paths. However, with failback you designate a preferred path that will handle all process requests until it fails, after which the standby path will become active until the primary reestablishes a connection and automatically regains control.

Round Robin   In a round-robin configuration, all available paths will be active and will be used to distribute I/O in a balanced round-robin fashion.

Round Robin with a Subset of Paths   In this configuration, a specific set of paths will be designated as a primary set and another as standby paths. All I/O will use the primary set of paths in a round-robin fashion until all of the sets fail. Only at this time will the standby paths become active.

Dynamic Least Queue Depth   In a dynamic least queue depth configuration, I/O will route to the path with the least number of outstanding requests.

Weighted Path   In a weighted path configuration, paths are assigned a numbered weight. I/O requests will use the path with the least weight—the higher the number, the lower the priority.

Exercise 3.6 demonstrates the process of installing the Microsoft MPIO feature for Windows Server 2016.

EXERCISE 3.6

Installing Microsoft MPIO

1. Choose Server Manager by clicking the Server Manager icon on the Taskbar.

2. Click number 2, Add Roles And Features.

3. Choose role-based or feature-based installation and click Next.

4. Choose your server and click Next.

5. Click Next on the Roles screen.

6. On the Select Features screen, choose the Multipath I/O check box (see Figure 3.6). Click Next.

FIGURE 3.6   Multipath I/O

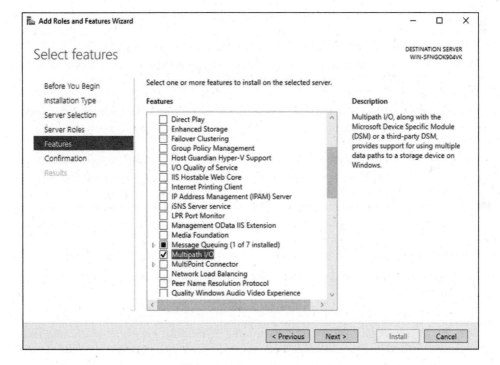

7. On the Confirm Installation Selections page, verify that Multipath I/O is the feature that will be installed. Click Install.

8. After the installation completes, the Installation Results page appears stating that the server must be rebooted to finish the installation process.

9. Click Close.

10. Restart the system.

Typically, most storage arrays work with the Microsoft DSM. However, some hardware vendors require DSM software that is specific to their products. Third-party DSM software is installed through the MPIO utility as follows:

1. Open Administrative Tools ➢ MPIO.

2. Select the DSM Install tab.

3. Add the path of the INF file and click Install.

Configuring iSCSI Target

Internet Small Computer System Interface (iSCSI) is an interconnect protocol used to establish and manage a connection between a computer (initiator) and a storage device (target). It does this by using a connection through TCP port 3260, which allows it to be used over a LAN, a WAN, or the Internet. Each initiator is identified by its iSCSI Qualified Name (iqn), and it is used to establish its connection to an iSCSI target.

iSCSI was developed to allow block-level access to a storage device over a network. This is different from using a network attached storage (NAS) device that connects through the use of Common Internet File System (CIFS) or Network File System (NFS).

Block-level access is important to many applications that require direct access to storage. Microsoft Exchange and Microsoft SQL are examples of applications that require direct access to storage.

By being able to leverage the existing network infrastructure, iSCSI was also developed as an alternative to Fibre Channel storage by alleviating the additional hardware costs associated with a Fibre Channel storage solution.

iSCSI also has another advantage over Fibre Channel in that it can provide security for the storage devices. iSCSI can use Challenge Handshake Authentication Protocol (CHAP or MS-CHAP) for authentication and Internet Protocol Security (IPsec) for encryption. Windows Server 2016 is able to connect an iSCSI storage device out of the box with no additional software needing to be installed. This is because the Microsoft iSCSI initiator is built into the operating system.

Windows Server 2016 supports two different ways to initiate an iSCSI session.

- Through the native Microsoft iSCSI software initiator that resides on Windows Server 2016

- Using a hardware iSCSI host bus adapter (HBA) that is installed in the computer

Both the Microsoft iSCSI software initiator and iSCSI HBA present an iSCSI qualified name that identifies the host initiator. When the Microsoft iSCSI software initiator is used, the CPU utilization may be as much as 30 percent higher than on a computer with a hardware iSCSI HBA. This is because all of the iSCSI process requests are handled within the operating system. Using a hardware iSCSI HBA, process requests can be offloaded to the adapter, thus freeing the CPU overhead associated with the Microsoft iSCSI software initiator. However, iSCSI HBAs can be expensive, whereas the Microsoft iSCSI software initiator is free.

It is worthwhile to install the Microsoft iSCSI software initiator and perform load testing to see how much overhead the computer will have prior to purchasing an iSCSI HBA or HBAs, depending on the redundancy level. Exercise 3.7 explains how to install and configure an iSCSI connection.

EXERCISE 3.7

Configuring iSCSI Storage Connection

1. Right-click the Start button ➢ Control Panel ➢ Administrative Tools ➢ iSCSI Initiator.

2. If a dialog box appears, click Yes to start the service.

3. Click the Discovery tab.

4. In the Target Portals portion of the page, click Discover Portal.

5. Enter the IP address of the target portal and click OK.

6. The IP address of the target portal appears in the Target Portals box.

7. Click OK.

Internet Storage Name Service

Internet Storage Name Service (iSNS) allows for central registration of an iSCSI environment because it automatically discovers available targets on the network. The purpose of iSNS is to help find available targets on a large iSCSI network.

The Microsoft iSCSI initiator includes an iSNS client that is used to register with the iSNS. The iSNS feature maintains a database of clients that it has registered either through DCHP discovery or through manual registration. iSNS DHCP is available after the installation of the service, and it is used to allow iSNS clients to discover the location of the iSNS. However, if iSNS DHCP is not configured, iSNS clients must be registered manually with the iscsicli command.

To execute the command, launch a command prompt on a computer hosting the Microsoft iSCSI and type **iscsicli addisnsserver server_name**, where **server_name** is the name of the computer hosting iSNS. Exercise 3.8 walks you through the steps required to install the iSNS feature on Windows Server 2016, and then it explains the different tabs in iSNS.

EXERCISE 3.8

Installing the iSNS Feature

1. Choose Server Manager by clicking the Server Manager icon on the Taskbar.

2. Click number 2 ➢ Add Roles And Features.

3. Choose role-based or featured-based installation and click Next.

4. Choose your server and click Next.

5. Click Next on the Roles screen.

6. On the Select Features screen, choose the iSNS Server Service check box. Click Next.

7. On the Confirmation screen, click the Install button.

8. Click the Close button. Close Server Manager and reboot.

9. Log in and open the iSNS server under Administrative Tools.

10. Click the General tab. This tab displays the list of registered initiators and targets. In addition to their iSCSI qualified name, it lists storage node type (Target or Initiator), alias string, and entity identifier (the Fully Qualified Domain Name [FQDN] of the machine hosting the iSNS client).

11. Click the Discovery Domains tab (see Figure 3.7). The purpose of Discovery Domains is to provide a way to separate and group nodes. This is similar to zoning in Fibre Channel. The following options are available on the Discovery Domains tab:

    ▪ *Create* is used to create a new discovery domain.

    ▪ *Refresh* is used to repopulate the Discovery Domain drop-down list.

    ▪ *Delete* is used to delete the currently selected discovery domain.

    ▪ *Add* is used to add nodes that are already registered in iSNS to the currently selected discovery domain.

    ▪ *Add New* is used to add nodes by entering the iSCSI Qualified Name (iQN) of the node. These nodes do not have to be currently registered.

    ▪ *Remove Used* is used to remove selected nodes from the discovery domain.

12. Click the Discovery Domain Sets tab. The purpose of discovery domain sets is to separate further discovery domains. Discovery domains can be enabled or disabled, giving administrators the ability to restrict further the visibility of all initiators and targets. The options on the Discovery Domain Sets tab are as follows:

    ▪ The *Enable* check box is used to indicate the status of the discovery domain sets and to turn them off and on.

    ▪ *Create* is used to create new discovery domain sets.

    ▪ *Refresh* is used to repopulate the Discovery Domain Sets drop-down list.

    ▪ *Delete* is used to delete the currently selected discovery domain set.

    ▪ *Add* is used to add discovery domains to the currently selected discovery domain set.

    ▪ *Remove* is used to remove selected nodes from the discovery domain sets.

FIGURE 3.7   Discovery Domain Tab

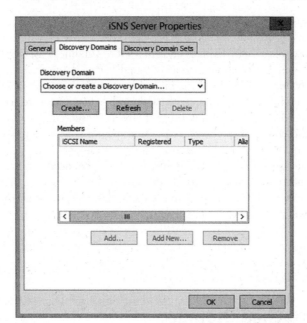

13. Close the iSNS server.

Implement Thin Provisioning and Trim

Thin provisioning and trim can be useful features that allow organizations to get the most out of their storage arrays. These solutions apply directly to a virtualized environment using virtual disks that are thin provisioned.

Thin provisioning is a way of providing what is known as just-in-time allocations. Blocks of data are written to disk only as they are used instead of zeroing out all of the blocks of data that have been allocated to the virtual disk configuration. Thin provisioning is tricky to manage properly because you could easily find yourself in a position where you have an over-provisioned environment because of over-allocation.

For example, you have 100 VMs that are all provisioned with 40GB thin-provisioned virtual disks. Each VM is currently utilizing only 20GB of the total 40GB that has been allocated. The problem is that you have only 2TB worth of storage. Without realizing it, you've over-provisioned your environment by 200 percent because of thin provisioning.

This is where trim comes in to help us manage thin provisioning. *Trim* automatically reclaims free space that is not being used. In addition to trim, Windows Server 2016 provides standardized notifications that will alert administrators when certain storage thresholds are crossed.

Fibre Channel

Fibre Channel storage devices are similar to iSCSI storage devices in that they both allow block-level access to their data sets and can provide MPIO policies with the proper hardware configurations. However, Fibre Channel requires a Fibre Channel HBA, fiber-optic cables, and Fibre Channel switches to connect to a storage device.

A *World Wide Name (WWN)* from the Fibre Channel HBA is used from the host and device so that they can communicate directly with each other, similar to using a NIC's MAC address. In other words, a logical unit number (LUN) is presented from a Fibre Channel storage device to the WWN of the host's HBA. Fibre Channel has been the preferred method of storage because of the available connection bandwidth between the storage and the host.

Fibre Channel devices support 1Gb/s, 2Gb/s, and 4Gb/s connections, and they soon will support 8Gb/s connections, but now that 10Gb/s Ethernet networks are becoming more prevalent in many datacenters, iSCSI can be a suitable alternative. It is important to consider that 10Gb/s network switches can be more expensive than comparable Fibre Channel switches.

N-Port Identification Virtualization (NPIV) is a Fibre Channel facility allowing multiple N-port IDs to share a single physical N-Port. This allows multiple Fibre Channel initiators to occupy a single physical port. By using a single port, this eases hardware requirements in storage area network (SAN) design.

Network Attached Storage

The concept of a *network attached storage (NAS)* solution is that it is a low-cost device for storing data and serving files through the use of an Ethernet LAN connection. A NAS device accesses data at the file level via a communication protocol such as NFS, CIFS, or even HTTP, which is different from iSCSI or FC Fibre Channel storage devices that access the data at the block level. NAS devices are best used in file-storing applications, and they do not require a storage expert to install and maintain the device. In most cases, the only setup that is required is an IP address and an Ethernet connection.

Virtual Disk Service

Virtual Disk Service (VDS) was created to ease the administrative efforts involved in managing all of the various types of storage devices. Many storage hardware providers used their own applications for installation and management, and this made administering all of these various devices very cumbersome.

VDS is a set of application programming interfaces (APIs) that provides a centralized interface for managing all of the various storage devices. The native VDS API enables the management of disks and volumes at an OS level, and hardware-vendor-supplied APIs manage the storage devices at a RAID level. These are known as software and hardware providers.

A *software provider* is host based, and it interacts with Plug and Play Manager because each disk is discovered and operates on volumes, disks, and disk partitions. VDS includes two software providers: basic and dynamic. The basic software provider manages basic disks with no fault tolerance, whereas the dynamic software providers manage dynamic disks with fault management. A hardware provider translates the VDS APIs into instructions specific to the storage hardware. This is how storage management applications are able to communicate with the storage hardware to create LUNs or Fibre Channel HBAs to view the WWN. The following are Windows Server 2016 storage management applications that use VDS:

- The *Disk Management snap-in* is an application that allows you to configure and manage the disk drives on the host computer. You have already seen this application in use when you initialized disks and created volume sets.

- DiskPart is a command-line utility that configures and manages disks, volumes, and partitions on the host computer. It can also be used to script many of the storage management commands. DiskPart is a robust tool that you should study on your own because it is beyond the scope of this book. Figure 3.8 shows the various commands and their function in the DiskPart utility.

FIGURE 3.8   DiskPart commands

- DiskRAID is also a scriptable command-line utility that configures and manages hardware RAID storage systems. However, at least one VDS hardware provider must be installed for DiskRAID to be functional. DiskRAID is another useful utility that you should study on your own because it's beyond the scope of this book.

Understanding Data Center Bridging

I think the easiest way to understanding Data Center Bridging (DCB) is to understand NIC bridging. Many of us who have used laptops have used both the Wireless and Wired networks at the same time. This is bridging network adapter cards to work as one. Well, Data Center Bridging is the same thing but just done on a larger scale.

The Institute of Electrical and Electronic Engineers (IEEE) created a suite of standards called Data Center Bridging. DCB allows the same ethernet infrastructure to work throughout the datacenter. This means that all of the network servers, clusters, and datacenter will share the same ethernet infrastructure. DCB works through the use of hardware based bandwidth allocation. This means that the hardware controls the flow of data through DCB.

DCB is nice because when you setup the hardware based flow control, you can determine which type of traffic gets a higher priority to the allocated bandwidth. This can be very useful for data that bypasses the operating system and accesses the network adapters directly (like virtualization can). DCB can work with different types of network adapters including Remote Direct Memory Access (RDMA) over Converged Ethernet, Internet Small Computer System Interface (iSCSI), or Fiber Channel over Ethernet (FCoE).

The reason that the IEEE has developed the DCB standard is because many third party and hardware manufacturers do not work together well. By having an industry standard of hardware based flow control protocol, many IT datacenters can use DCB to make different vendors work together. Also, Windows Server 2016 makes it very easy to deploy and manage DCB. There are a couple of requirements that are needed when deploying DCB through Windows Server 2016:

- The Ethernet adapters installed into the Windows Server 2016 systems must be DCB compatible.
- The Hardware switches that are deployed to your infrastructure must also be DCB compatible.

DCB can be installed onto a Windows Server two ways: through Server Manager or through PowerShell. Here are the steps for both ways.

Installing DCB Using PowerShell

If you would like to install and use DCB through PowerShell, you need to complete the following steps:

1. Click the Start button, then right-click Windows PowerShell ➤ More ➤ Run As Administrator.

2. In the Windows PowerShell console, enter the following command followed by the Enter key:

   ```
   Install-WindowsFeature "data-center-bridging"
   ```

Installing DCB Using Server Manager

If you would like to install and use DCB through Server Manager, you need to complete the following steps:

1. On the Windows Server 2016 system, open Server Manager.

2. Click the Add Roles And Features link.

3. At the Before You Begin screen, click Next.

4. At the Select Installation Type screen, choose Role-based or feature-based installation and then click Next.

5. The Select Destination Server screen will be next. Make sure the server that you want to install DCB on is selected and then click Next.

6. On the Select Server Roles screen, just click Next.

7. On the Select Features screen, check the box for Data Center Bridging. If a dialog box appears asking to install additional features, click the Add Feature button. Then click Next.

8. At the Confirmation screen, verify that everything is OK and then click the Install button.

Configuring Permissions

Before I can dive into how permissions work, let's first talk about how clients and servers talk to each other. In the Microsoft Windows world, clients and servers talk to each other using the Server Message Block (SMB) protocol. So let's start our discussion there.

Understanding SMB

Server Message Block (SMB) is a network-sharing protocol that allows Windows machines (either client- or server-based operating systems) that are running applications to read and write data to files. SMB also allows systems to request services or resources that are running on remote servers. The one advantage to SMB is that it doesn't matter what network protocol you are using (TCP/IP, etc.), SMB runs on top of the network protocol that is being used on your corporate infrastructure.

It's important to understand what protocols work with client- and server-based systems because it can affect your network's performance. For example, when Microsoft released Windows Server 2012, it released SMB 3.0. The issue that many users had was that SMB 3.0 was not compatible with Macintosh-based systems. So if you were running Apple Macintosh on your network and upgraded to Windows Server 2012, your Apple-based systems would not communicate properly. This issue was eventually resolved, but this is why it's important to understand that SMB file sharing is used between Windows client and server systems.

I will show you how to use Windows PowerShell for configuring SMB shares in the section called "Windows PowerShell" later in this chapter. For a complete list of SMB PowerShell commands, visit Microsoft's website at `https://technet.microsoft.com/en-us/library/jj635726(v=wps.630).aspx`.

Now that you understand how Windows clients and servers communicate with each other, let's look at how we can protect the files and folders that clients access. You can add security to a folder in two ways: NTFS security or shared permissions. But when it comes to securing files, you can secure files in only one way: NTFS Security. So let's take a look at these methods and how they work independently and then together.

Understanding NTFS

NTFS is an option that you have when you are formatting a hard drive. You can format a hard drive for a Microsoft operating system in three ways:

- File Allocation Table (FAT) is supported on older operating systems only (Server 2003, Server 2000, XP, and so on).
- FAT32 is supported in Windows Server 2016.
- NTFS is supported in Windows Server 2016.

NTFS has many advantages over FAT and FAT32. They include the following:

Compression   Compression helps compact files or folders to allow for more efficient use of hard drive space. For example, a file that usually takes up 20 MB of space might use only 13 MB after compression. To enable compression, just open the Advanced Attributes dialog box for a folder and check the Compress Contents To Save Disk Space box (see Figure 3.9).

FIGURE 3.9   Setting up compression on a folder

Quotas   *Quotas* allow you to limit how much hard drive space users can have on a server. Quotas are discussed in greater detail in the section "Configuring Disk Quotas."

Encryption   *Encrypting File System (EFS)* allows a user or administrator to secure files or folders by using encryption. Encryption employs the user's security identification (SID) number to secure the file or folder. To implement encryption, open the Advanced Attributes dialog box for a folder and check the Encrypt Contents To Secure Data box (see Figure 3.10).

FIGURE 3.10   Setting up encryption on a folder

If files are encrypted using EFS and an administrator has to unencrypt the files, there are two ways to do this. First, you can log in using the user's account (the account that encrypted the files) and unencrypt the files. Second, you can become a recovery agent and manually unencrypt the files.

If you use EFS, it's best not to delete users immediately when they leave a company. Administrators have the ability to recover encrypted files, but it is much easier to gain access to the user's encrypted files by logging in as the user who left the company and unchecking the encryption box.

Security   One of the biggest advantages of NTFS is security. Security is one of the most important aspects of an IT administrator's job. An advantage of NTFS security is that the security can be placed on individual files and folders. It does not matter whether you are local to the share (in front of the machine where the data is stored) or remote to the share (coming across the network to access the data); the security is always in place with NTFS.

The default security permission is Users = Read on new folders or shares.

NTFS security is *additive*. In other words, if you are a member of three groups (Marketing, Sales, and R&D) and these three groups have different security settings, you get the highest level of permissions. For example, let's say you have a user by the name of wpanek who belongs to all three groups (Marketing, Sales, and R&D). Figure 3.11 shows this user's permissions. The Marketing group has Read and Execute permissions to the StormWind Documents folder. The Sales group has Read and Write, and the R&D group has Full Control. Since wpanek is a member of all three groups, wpanek would get Full Control (the highest level).

FIGURE 3.11   Security settings on the StormWind Documents folder

Marketing	**Sales**	**R&D**
RX	RW	FC

The only time this does not apply is with the Deny permission. Deny overrides any other group setting. Taking the same example, if Sales has Deny permission for the StormWind Documents folder, the user wpanek would be denied access to that folder. The only way around this Deny is if you added wpanek directly to the folder and gave him individual permissions (see Figure 3.12). Individual permissions override a group Deny. In this example, the individual right of wpanek would override the Sales group's Deny. The user's security permission for the StormWind Documents folder would be Full Control.

FIGURE 3.12   Individual permissions

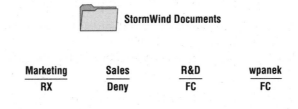

Marketing	**Sales**	**R&D**	**wpanek**
RX	Deny	FC	FC

Give users only the permissions necessary to do their jobs. Do not give them higher levels than they need.

Understanding Shared Permissions

When you set up a folder to be shared, you have the ability to assign that folder's permissions. *Shared permissions* can be placed only on the folder and not on individual files. Files have the ability to inherit their permissions from the parent folder.

Shared folder permissions are in effect only when users are remote to the shared data. In other words, if computer A shares a folder called Test Share and assigns that folder shared permissions, those permissions would apply only if you connected to that share from a machine other than computer A. If you were sitting in front of computer A, the shared permissions would not apply.

Like NTFS permissions (discussed in the previous section), shared permissions are additive, so users receive the highest level of permissions granted by the groups of which they are members.

Also, as with NTFS permissions, the Deny permission (see Figure 3.13) overrides any group permission, and an individual permission overrides a group Deny.

FIGURE 3.13   Setting up permissions on a shared folder

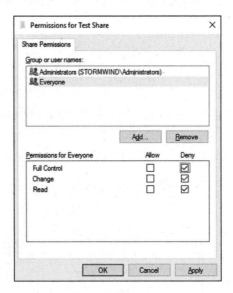

The default shared permission is Administrators = Full Control. The shared permissions going from lowest to highest are Read, Change, Full Control, and Deny. Table 3.2 compares the two different types of permissions and security.

TABLE 3.2   NTFS security vs. shared permissions

Description	NTFS	Shared
Folder-level security.	Yes	Yes
File-level security.	Yes	No
In effect when local to the data.	Yes	No
In effect when remote to the data.	Yes	Yes
Permissions are additive.	Yes	Yes
Group Deny overrides all other group settings.	Yes	Yes
Individual settings override group settings.	Yes	Yes

How NTFS Security and Shared Permissions Work Together

When you set up a shared folder, you need to set up shared permissions on that folder. If you're using NTFS, you will also need to set up NTFS security on the folder. Since both shared permissions and NTFS security are in effect when the user is remote, what happens when the two conflict?

These are the two basic rules of thumb:

- The local permission is the NTFS permission.

- The remote permission is the more restrictive set of permissions between NTFS and shared.

This is easy to do as long as you do it in steps. Let's look at Figure 3.14 and walk through the process of figuring out what wpanek has for rights.

FIGURE 3.14   NTFS security and shared permissions example

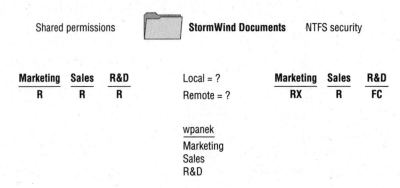

As you can see, wpanek belongs to three groups (Marketing, Sales, and R&D), and all three groups have settings for the StormWind Documents folder. In the figure, you will notice that there are two questions: Remote = ? and Local = ? That's what you need to figure out—what are wpanek's effective permissions when he is sitting at the computer that shares the folder, and what are his effective permissions when he connects to the folder from another computer (remotely)? To figure this out, follow these steps:

1. Add up the permissions on each side separately.

    Remember, permissions and security are *additive*. You get the highest permission. So, if you look at each side, the highest shared permission is the Read permission. The NTFS security side should add up to equal Full Control. Thus, now you have Read permission on shared and Full Control on NTFS.

2. Determine the local permissions.

    Shared permissions do not apply when you are local to the data. Only NTFS would apply. Thus, the local permission would be Full Control.

3. Determine the remote permissions.

Remember, the remote permission is the most restrictive set of permissions between NTFS and shared. Since Read is more restrictive than Full Control, the remote permission would be Read.

Let's try another. Look at Figure 3.15, and see whether you can come up with wpanek's local and remote permissions.

FIGURE 3.15   NTFS security and shared permissions

Shared permissions			StormWind Documents		NTFS security		
Marketing	**Sales**	**R&D**			**Marketing**	**Sales**	**R&D**
R	R	R	Local = ?		R	R	R
			Remote = ?				

wpanek
Marketing
Sales
R&D

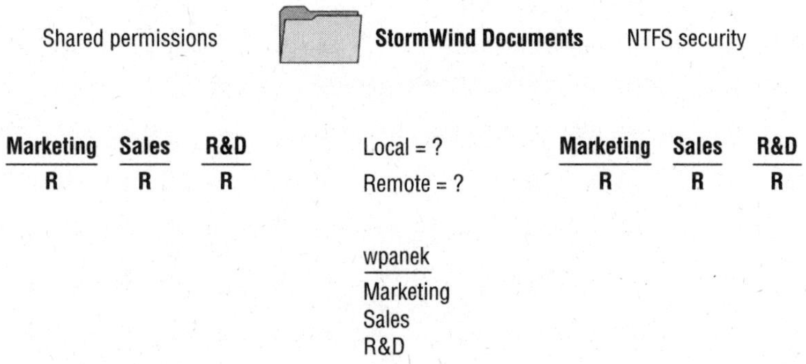

Your answer should match the following:

Local = Read

Remote = Read

Remember, first you add up each side to get the highest level of rights. NTFS would be Read, and shared would be Full Control. The local permission is always just NTFS (shared does not apply to local permissions), and remote permission is whichever permission (NTFS or shared) is the most restrictive (which would be Read on the NTFS side).

Exercise 3.9 walks you through the process of setting both NTFS and shared permissions. This exercise assumes that you have Active Directory installed on the server and you have some groups created. If you do not, go to Computer Management (right-click Start ➢ Computer Management) and under Local Users and Groups, create a new group that can be used in this exercise.

EXERCISE 3.9

Configuring Shared and NTFS Settings

1. Create a new folder in the root directory of your C: partition and name it Test Share.

2. Right-click the Test Share folder you created and choose Properties.

3. Click the Sharing tab and then click the Advanced Sharing button. Click the box Share This Folder. Make sure the share name is Test Share (see Figure 3.16).

FIGURE 3.16 Advanced Sharing

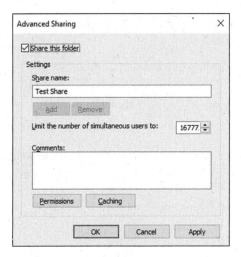

4. Click the Permissions button. Click the Add button. When the Select User page appears, choose a group from Active Directory or from the local group you created. (I used the Sales group.) Once you find your group, click OK.

5. The Permissions dialog box appears. With your group highlighted, click the Allow check box next to Full Control and click OK. (All of the other Allow check boxes will automatically become checked.)

6. On the Advanced Sharing page, click OK. Now click the Security tab. (This allows you to set the NTFS security settings.)

7. Click the Edit button. That takes you to the Permissions page. Now click the Add button. When the Select User page appears, choose a group from Active Directory. (I used the Everyone group.) Once you find your group, choose OK.

8. The Permissions dialog box appears. With your group highlighted, click the Allow check box next to Modify, and click OK. (All of the check boxes below Modify will automatically become checked.)

9. Click Close.

Understanding NFS Shares

The NFS role service and feature set gives IT administrators the ability to integrate a Windows Server–based environment with Unix-based operating systems. Most corporate environments today consist of a mixed operating system infrastructure to some extent. Using a

Windows NFS file server, you can configure file shares for use by multiple operating systems throughout the environment.

Windows Server 2016 takes those capabilities even further by enabling you to integrate with platforms such as ESXi. ESXi is VMware's exclusive operating system–independent hypervisor. ESXi is referred to as a *bare-metal* operating system because once it is installed on server virtualization hardware, guest virtual machines can be installed without requiring the use of any other underlying operating system. With Windows Server 2016, you can use an NFS share efficiently as an ESXi data store to house all of your guest virtual machines. Let's take a look at configuring an NFS data store in Exercise 3.10.

For this exercise, you will need the following:

- A Windows Server 2016 server

- A VMware ESXi 5 server

EXERCISE 3.10

Configure the NFS Data Store

1. Open Server Manager on your Windows Server 2016 machine.

2. Launch the Add Roles And Features Wizard from the dashboard.

3. Install the Server for NFS role on the server. A reboot is not required.

4. Create a new folder on your server named NFS_Datastore, right-click and select Properties, and then navigate to the NFS Sharing tab.

5. Click the Manage NFS Sharing button to open the NFS Advanced Sharing page and then check the Share This Folder box. Notice how enabling the share also enables the share's default settings. The share settings let you configure share authentication and user access further if the need arises. The default settings will work just fine for this exercise.

6. Click the Permissions tab to open the NFS Share Permissions page. This is where you will configure the type of access that will be allowed by machines accessing this NFS data store. By default, the NFS share permissions are set to Read-Only and do not include root access. For this exercise, you will need to change the type of access to Read-Write and check the box to allow root access.

7. Click OK to close the NFS Share Permissions page and then click Apply and OK on the NFS Advanced Sharing page. Your new NFS share is now built, ready to be presented as an NFS data store to a VMware ESXi host. Be sure to record the network path displayed on the NFS Sharing tab of the share's Properties page. You will need that information to perform a proper mount on the ESXi host.

8. Switch to your ESXi host and launch the Add Storage Wizard from the Configuration tab.

9. On the Select Storage Type page of the wizard, select the Network File System storage type; click Next to continue to the Locate Network File System page.

EXERCISE 3.10 *(continued)*

10. On this page of the wizard, you will fill in the server and folder information for the NFS share that you will be using as a vSphere data store. Using the information recorded from step 7, properly fill out the server and folder fields and then name your new data store.

11. Click Next to continue to the Ready To Complete page of the wizard. Review the information and click Finish. Once the Create NAS data store task completes on the ESXi host, you are ready to use your Windows Server 2016 shared folder as a vSphere ESXi data store.

The previous exercise shows how versatile Windows Server 2016 shares can be. The same principles can be applied to making Windows Server shares available to other Unix-based operating systems such as ESXi.

I will show you how to use Windows PowerShell for configuring NFS shares in the section below called "Windows PowerShell." If you would like to see a more complete list of NFS PowerShell commands, please visit Microsoft's website at https://technet.microsoft.com/en-us/library/jj603081(v=wps.630).aspx.

Configuring Disk Quotas

In this chapter so far, you have learned how to set up permissions and security and how NTFS and shared permissions work with each other. It's time to learn how to limit users' hard drive space on the servers.

Disk quotas give administrators the ability to limit how much storage space a user can have on a hard drive. As mentioned earlier in this chapter, disk quotas are an advantage of using NTFS over FAT32. If you decide to use FAT32 on a volume or partition, quotas will not be available.

You have a few options available to you when you set up disk quotas. You can set up disk quotas based on volume or on users.

A good rule of thumb is to set up an umbrella quota policy that covers the entire volume and then let individual users exceed the umbrella as needed.

Setting Quotas by Volume One way to set up disk quotas is by setting the quota by volume, on a per-volume basis. This means that if you have a hard drive with C:, D:, and E: volumes, you would have to set up three individual quotas—one for each volume. This is your umbrella. This is where you set up an entire disk quota based on the volume for all users.

Setting Quotas by User   You have the ability to set up quotas on volumes by user. Here is where you would individually let users have independent quotas that exceed your umbrella quota.

Specifying Quota Entries   You use quota entries to configure the volume and user quotas. You do this on the Quotas tab of the volume's Properties dialog box. (See Exercise 3.11.)

Creating Quota Templates   Quota templates are predefined ways to set up quotas. Templates allow you to set up disk quotas without needing to create a disk quota from scratch. One advantage of using a template is that when you want to set up disk quotas on multiple volumes (C:, D:, and E:) on the same hard drive, you do not need to re-create the quota on each volume.

Exercise 3.11 will show you how to set up an umbrella quota for all users and then have an individual account in your Active Directory exceed this quota.

EXERCISE 3.11

Configuring Disk Quotas

1. Open Windows Explorer.

2. Right-click the local disk (C:) and choose Properties.

3. Click the Quotas tab.

4. Check the Enable Quota Management check box. Also check the Deny Disk Space To Users Exceeding Quota Limit box.

5. Click the Limit Disk Space To option and enter **1000MB** in the box.

6. Enter **750MB** in the Set Warning Level To boxes.

7. Click the Apply button. If a warning box appears, click OK. This warning is just informing you that the disk may need to be rescanned for the quota.

8. Now that you have set up an umbrella quota to cover everyone, you'll set up a quota that exceeds the umbrella. Click the Quota Entries button.

9. The Quotas Entries for (C:) window appears. You will see some users already listed. These are users who are already using space on the volume. Click the Quota menu at the top and choose New Quota Entry.

10. Notice the N/A entry in the Percent Used column. This belongs to the administrator account, which by default has no limit.

11. On the Select User page, choose a user that you want to allow to exceed the quota (for this example, I used the wpanek account). Click OK.

12. This opens the Add New Quota Entry dialog box. Click the Do Not Limit Disk Usage option and click OK.

13. You will notice that the new user has no limit. Close the disk quota tool.

Windows PowerShell

Windows PowerShell is a task-based, command-line scripting utility that allows you to execute commands locally or remotely on a Windows Server 2016 machine. It was specifically designed for system administrators to allow for local or remote administration.

> Microsoft asks a lot of questions on the exam about Windows PowerShell. Therefore, I will be discussing PowerShell throughout this book because of its importance on all of the Windows Server 2016 exams.

Most operating system shells, including Cmd.exe and the SH, KSH, CSH, and BASH Unix shells, work by running a command or utility in a new process and then presenting the results to the user as text. These system shells also have commands that are built into the shell and execute in the shell process. In most system shells, because there are only a few built-in commands, many utilities have been created over the years to complete tasks.

Windows PowerShell contains an interactive prompt and a scripting environment that can be used independently or in combination. Unlike the previously mentioned system shells, which accept and return text, Windows PowerShell is built using the *.NET Framework common language runtime (CLR)* and the .NET Framework. Because of this, Windows PowerShell accepts and returns .NET Framework objects. This important change in the shell allows you to use entirely new tools and methods to manage and configure Windows.

Windows PowerShell introduced the concept of using cmdlets (pronounced "command-lets"). Cmdlets are simple, single-function command-line tools built into the shell. Administrators can use the cmdlets independently, or they can combine these tools to execute complex tasks and harness the true power of PowerShell. Windows PowerShell includes more than a hundred core cmdlets, but the true advantage of PowerShell is that anyone can write their own cmdlets and share them with other users.

Administrators often automate the management of their multicomputer environments by running sequences of long-running tasks, or *workflows*, which can affect multiple managed computers or devices at the same time. Windows PowerShell can help administrators accomplish workflows in a more effective way. Windows PowerShell includes some of the following advantages:

Windows PowerShell Scripting Syntax   Administrators can use Windows PowerShell scripting expertise to create script-based tasks by using the extensible Windows PowerShell language. Windows PowerShell script-based tasks are easy to create, and IT members can share them easily by entering them into an email or publishing them on a web page.

Day-to-Day Management Tasks   Windows PowerShell allows administrators to configure and maintain servers. PowerShell allows you to pre-create scripts or use ready-to-use scripts to handle day-to-day tasks. This way, an administrator can just run a script to complete server configurations or management.

Multiserver Management   Administrators can concurrently apply workflow tasks to hundreds of managed servers and computers. Windows PowerShell includes common parameters to set workflows automatically, such as `PSComputerName`, to enable multicomputer administrative scenarios. You can also use PowerShell to help you create new servers by creating new virtual hard drive (`.vhd`) files.

Single Task to Manage Complex, End-to-End Processes   Administrators can combine related scripts or commands that act upon an entire scenario into a single workflow. The status of activities within the workflow can be viewed at any time.

Automated Failure Recovery   Using Windows PowerShell allows workflows to survive both planned and unplanned interruptions, such as computer restarts. Administrators have the ability to suspend workflow operations and then restart or resume the workflow from the exact point at which it was suspended. Administrators can then create checkpoints as part of their workflow process so that they can resume the workflow from the last persisted task (or checkpoint) instead of restarting the workflow from the beginning.

Activity Retries   Administrators can create workflows that also specify activities that must rerun if the activity does not get completed on one or more managed computers (for example, if a target node was not online at the time the activity was running).

Connect and Disconnect   Administrators can connect and disconnect from the node that is executing the workflow, but the workflow will continue to run.

Configuring Non-Domain Servers   Another advantage of PowerShell is the ability to configure non-domain servers from a Windows Server 2016 server (domain member). When you are running commands on the non-domain machine, you must have access to the non-domain machine's system administrator account. Another way to configure a non-domain server is to connect through remote desktop into the non-domain server and then configure the machine or run PowerShell commands while connected through remote desktop.

Task Scheduling   Workflow tasks have the ability to be scheduled and started when specific conditions are met. This is also true for any other Windows PowerShell cmdlet or script.

Table 3.3 defines a few of the cmdlets available in Windows PowerShell. Again, there are hundreds of cmdlets, and the ones listed in the table are just some of the more common ones. You can retrieve a list of all the cmdlets starting here:

```
http://technet.microsoft.com/en-us/scriptcenter/dd772285.aspx
```

TABLE 3.3   Windows PowerShell cmdlets

Cmdlet	Definition
Add-VMHardDiskDrive	Allows you to add a .vhd file to a virtual machine.
Block-SmbShareAccess	This cmdlet allows an administrator to add a deny access control entry (ACE) to the security descriptor for the Server Message Block (SMB) share.

TABLE 3.3 Windows PowerShell cmdlets *(continued)*

Cmdlet	Definition
Clear-History	Deletes entries from the command history.
Close-SmbOpenFile	This allows an administrator to forcibly close an open file by one of the clients of the Server Message Block (SMB) server.
Close-SmbSession	This allows an administrator to forcibly kill a Server Message Block (SMB) session.
Format-table	Shows the results in a table format.
Get-Date	Shows the date and time.
Get-event	Shows an event in the event queue.
Get-Help Install-WindowsFeature	Shows the syntax and accepted parameters for the Install-WindowsFeature cmdlet.
Get-NetIPAddress	Shows information about IP address configuration.
Get-NfsClientConfiguration	Shows configuration settings for an NFS client.
Get-NfsMappedIdentity	Shows an NFS mapped identity.
Get-NfsMappingStore	Shows the configuration settings for the identity mapping store.
Get-NfsNetgroup	Shows the netgroup.
Get-NfsSession	Shows the information about client systems that are currently connected to a shares on an NFS server.
Get-NfsShare	Shows an NFS share on the NFS server.
Get-NfsSharePermission	Shows you the NFS shares permissions that are on a NFS server.
Get-Package	This command allows an administrator to view a list of all software packages that have been installed by using Package Management.
Get-ShieldedVMProvisioningStatus	This command allows you to view the provisioning status of a shielded virtual machine.

Cmdlet	Definition
Get-SmbOpenFile	Allows an admin to see basic information about the files that are open on the Server Message Block (SMB) server.
Get-SmbShare	Allows an administrator to see the Server Message Block (SMB) shares on the computer.
Get-WindowsFeature	Shows a list of available and installed roles and features on the local server.
Get-WindowsFeature -ServerName	Shows a list of available and installed roles and features on a remote server.
Import-Module	Adds modules to the current session.
Install-Windowsfeature	This command allows you to installs a role, role service, or feature on the local or a specified remote server that is running Windows Server 2016.
Invoke-command	Runs commands on local or remote computers.
New-NfsShare	Allows you to create an NFS file share.
New-event	Creates a new event.
New-SmbShare	Allows an admin to create a new SMB share.
New-VHD	Allows you to create a new .vhd file.
Optimize-VHD	This command allows an administrator to optimize the allocation of space in virtual hard disk files, except for fixed virtual hard disks.
Out-file	Sends the job results to a file.
Receive-job	Gets the results of a Windows PowerShell background job.
Remove-job	Deletes a Windows PowerShell background job.
Remove-NfsShare	Allows you to delete an NFS file share.
Remove-SmbShare	Allows an admin to delete an SMB share.
Set-Date	Sets the system time and date on a computer.

TABLE 3.3 Windows PowerShell cmdlets *(continued)*

Cmdlet	Definition
Set-NetIPAddress	Modifies IP address configuration properties of an existing IP address.
Set-NetIPv4Protocol	Modifies information about the IPv4 protocol configuration.
Set-SmbShare	Allows an administrator to modify the properties of the Server Message Block (SMB) share.
Set-VM	This command allows you to configure some virtual machine settings, like configuring the locations for snap shot storage and smart paging.
Set-VMDvdDrive	Allows you to set a virtual machine to use a DVD or .ISO file.
Set-VMHost	This command allows an administrator to configure a Hyper-V host.
Set-VMMemory	This command allows you to set the RAM for a virtual machine.
Set-VMNetworkAdapter	This command allows an administrator to configure features of the virtual network adapter in a virtual machine or the management operating system.
Set-VMProcessor	This command allows an admin to configure the processors of a virtual machine. This command is also used for nested virtualization. While the virtual machine is OFF, run the Set-VMProcessor command on the physical Hyper-V host to enable nested virtualization for the virtual machine.
Set-VMSwitch	This command allows an administrator to configure a virtual switch.
Start-job	Starts a Windows PowerShell background job.
Stop-job	Stops a Windows PowerShell background job.
Trace-command	Configures and starts a trace of a command on a machine.
Uninstall-WindowsFeature	Removes a role or feature.

Windows PowerShell Commands

I will show you Windows PowerShell commands throughout this book. If I show you how to install a role or feature in Server Manager, I will also try to include the Windows PowerShell equivalent.

Another advantage of Windows PowerShell is that it allows you to gain access to a file system on a computer and to access the Registry, digital certificate stores, and other data stores.

Complete Exercise 3.12 to start the Windows PowerShell utility in the Windows Server 2016 Server Core machine.

EXERCISE 3.12

Starting the Windows PowerShell Utility

1. Type **Start PowerShell** at the Windows Server 2016 Server Core command prompt.

2. When the Windows PowerShell utility starts, type **Help** and press Enter. This will show you the Windows PowerShell syntax and some of the commands included in Windows PowerShell.

3. At the Windows PowerShell command prompt, type **Get-Date**. This will show you the system's date and time.

4. At the Windows command prompt, type **Help ***. This will show you all of the cmdlets you can use.

5. Close the Windows PowerShell utility by typing **Exit**.

Using Server Manager

Server Manager is a very powerful MMC snap-in. If you want to install any features using a GUI interface, you will be using Server Manager. But what a lot of users don't know is that you can use Server Manager to configure and manage the features that are installed on a server.

This also includes configuring disks. The one advantage of using Server Manager is that it is included with every GUI version of Windows Server 2016. When it comes to hard disks, Server Manager allows you to manage and create disks from within the Server Manager program (see Figure 3.17).

FIGURE 3.17   Using Server Manager

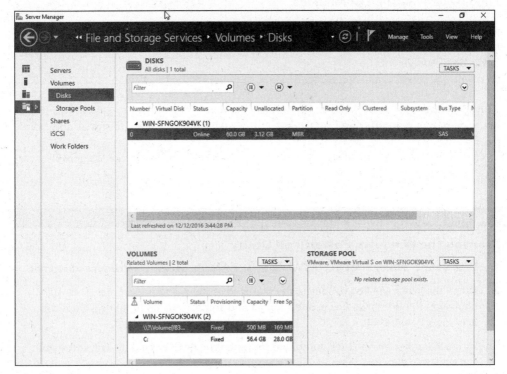

Once you are in the Server Manager application, click the File and Storage Services link on the left side. Once you are in the File and Storage Services section, you can create volumes, .vhd files, storage pools, shares, iSCSI targets, and work folders. You can also manage disk quotas from Server Manager.

One of the nice advantages of Server Manager is that you can configure and manage other Windows Servers from Server Manager. You need to add the server to Server Manager but once this is done, you can configure those servers. This is very helpful for machines that are running Server Core. If you need to install a Windows Serve without the GUI installed, you can still configure that server by using Server Manager.

Booting from a VHD

Now that I have shown you how to create a .VHD file by using PowerShell or by using Server Manager (Disk Administrator), I need to show you how to boot a machine up using that .VHD. To do this, we will work with the Boot Configuration Data store.

The Boot Configuration Data (BCD) store contains boot information parameters that were previously found in `boot.ini` in older versions of Windows (Windows Server 2003 and previous). To edit the boot options in the BCD store, use the `bcdedit` utility, which can be launched only from a command prompt. To open a command prompt window, do the following:

1. Launch `\Windows\system32\cmd.exe`.
2. Open the Run command by pressing the Windows key plus the R key and then entering **cmd**.
3. Type **cmd.exe** in the Search Programs And Files box and press Enter.

After the command prompt window is open, type **bcdedit** to launch the bcdedit utility. You can also type **bcdedit /?** to see all of the different bcdedit commands. To boot from a VHD file, you can use the following command:

```
bcdedit /set {GUID} description="Windows 2016 VHD"
```

You can also use the `bcdboot` command to change how the Boot Configuration Data store boots from another Windows directory or VHD. So, for example, let's say that you copied the bootable VHD drive to the V: drive. You would then use the following command to boot from the VHD file:

```
bcdboot V:\Windows.vhd
```

Understanding Data Deduplication

Data deduplication involves finding and removing duplicate data within the company network without compromising its integrity. The object is to store more data in less space by segmenting files into small chunks, identifying duplicate chunks, and maintaining a single copy of each chunk.

Data deduplication allows redundant copies of data chunks and then it references those multiple copies into a single copy. The data is first compressed and then the data is configured into a file system container in the System Volume Information folder.

After the data deduplication is completed, the data files will no longer be stored as independent files. The data files are replaced with markers that direct the computer system to the data blocks within the data store. Because the duplicate files are now migrated into a single data point, the data is only stored once and thus saves space on the servers.

When the files are then accessed, the data blocks are transparently re-assembled to fulfill the data request. This is all done without the users or applications having any knowledge that the data has been transformed into a single spot. This is a nice advantage to administrators because they do not have to worry that the data will be impacted in any negative way by using data deduplication.

To enable data deduplication, you enable a volume for duplication and then the data is automatically optimized. After this happens, the volume will contain the following:

Optimized Files   The volume will contain files that are optimized, and that means that these files will have pointers to map the data to its respective areas of the chunk store.

Unoptimized files   Some files will not meet the standards for data deduplication. These files will remain as Unoptimized files. For example, encrypted files are not eligible to be optimized. So these encrypted files will remain Unoptimized on the volume.

Chunk Store   This is the location that the data duplicated files will be stored and optimized.

Free Space   Because data files are optimized and require less space, your volumes will have additional free space that the administrator can use for users or applications.

Backup and Restoring Deduplicated Volumes

One issue that every administrator has faced in their career has to do with how we are going to protect our data by using backups. Backups are a million dollar industry because every backup company knows the importance of protecting your data. Well the issue that we, as IT administrators, deal with is backup space.

This is where data deduplication can help us out. Because the files are optimized, the files will require less space used on backups. This doesn't matter if its cloud-based or tape-based backups. The backups will use less space and this in turn will allow us to retain the data longer without requiring more space. Also, because the data is optimized (thus being smaller), the backups will be quicker, and if any restores are needed, they will also be faster.

Any backup system that uses block-based backup applications should work without any modifications to the backup systems. File-based backups may be an issue because file-based backups normally copy the files in their original data form. If you are using file-based backups, you must have enough backup space available to handle the files in their original form.

If your organization is using the Windows Server 2016 backup software, your backups will have the ability to back up the files as optimized files and no other changes will be needed. Since most of us don't use Windows backup, make sure your backup can handle data deduplication if you are planning on using it.

If you decide to use Windows backup, the following steps will help you backup and restore data duplicated files.

1. You will need to install Windows Server Backup on the machines running data deduplication. This can be done through Server Manager or by running the following PowerShell command:

    ```
    Add-WindowsFeature -name Windows-Server-Backup
    ```

2. Administrators can then run a backup by using the following PowerShell command (this command is backing up the E: volume to the F: drive):

```
wbadmin start backup -include:E: -backuptarget:F:
```

3. You will then want to get the version ID of the backup you just created. You can do this by running the following command:

```
wbadmin get versions
```

4. After you run the wbadmin get version command, you will be given the date and time of the backup. This will be needed if you are going to do a restore. The following is an example of the output: 04/24/2017-14:30. To restore the volume you would run the following command:

```
Wbadmin start recovery -version:04/24/2017-14:30 -itemtype:
Volume  -items:E: -recoveryTarget:E:
```

To restore just a part of a volume or folder, you would run the following command (for example, the E:\WPanek folder):

```
Wbadmin start recovery -version:04/24/2017-14:30 -itemtype:
File  -items:E:\WPanek  -recursive
```

Installing and Enabling Data Deduplication

To install data deduplication, there are two ways to do the install. You can install data deduplication through Server Manager or through PowerShell. Let's take a look at each way.

To install data deduplication by using Server Manager:

1. On the Windows Server 2016 system, open Server Manager.

2. Click the Add Roles and Features link.

3. At the Before You Begin screen, click Next.

4. At the Select Installation Type screen, choose Role-based or feature-based installation and then click Next.

5. Choose the server where you want to install Data Deduplication and click Next.

6. On the Select Server Roles screen, select File And Storage Services ➢ File And iSCSI Services and then select the Data Deduplication check box (shown in Figure 3.18). Click Next.

7. Click Next on the Selected Features screen.

8. Then click the Install button once you confirmed that all options are correct.

9. Once completed, close Server Manager.

To install data deduplication by using PowerShell:

1. Click the Start button, then right-click Windows PowerShell ➤ More ➤ Run As Administrator.

2. In the Windows PowerShell console, enter the following commands (one at a time) followed by the Enter key:

    1. `Import-Module ServerManager`

    2. `Add-WindowsFeature -name FS-Data-Deduplication`

    3. `Import-Module Deduplication`

FIGURE 3.18 Selecting Data Deduplication

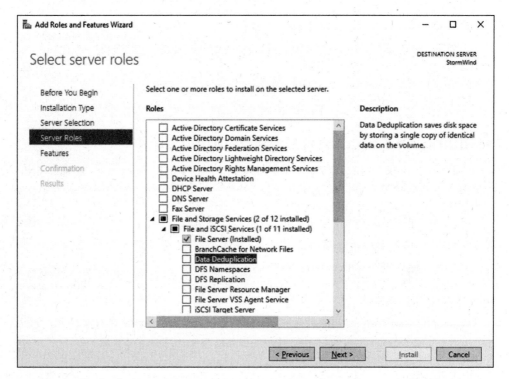

After you have installed data deduplication, you must then enable it on the servers. To enable data deduplication in Server Manager, you would need to complete the following steps:

1. In Server Manager, click File And Storage Services.

2. Click Volumes. On the right side, click the volume on which you want to set up Data Deduplication. Right-click the volume and choose Configure Data Deduplication (see Figure 3.19).

FIGURE 3.19   Enabling Data Deduplication

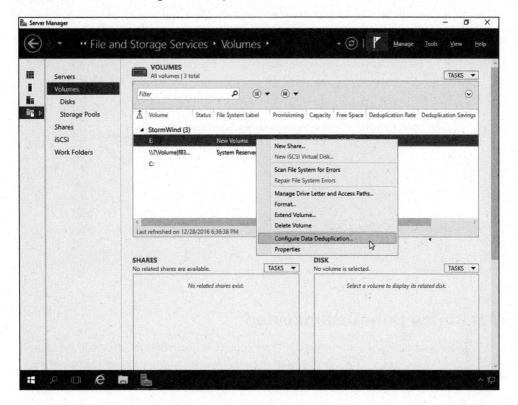

3. The New Volume Deduplication Settings Wizard will start. Under the Data Deduplication pulldown, choose General Purpose File Server (shown in Figure 3.20). Enter the number of days that should elapse from the date of file creation until files are duplicated (I used 3 days), enter the extensions of any file types that should not be duplicated (I used .exe), and then click Add to browse to any folders with files that should not be duplicated (I included \test share). Click OK once completed. You can also set a Deduplication Schedule by clicking the Set Deduplication Schedule button.

FIGURE 3.20   Data Deduplication setup

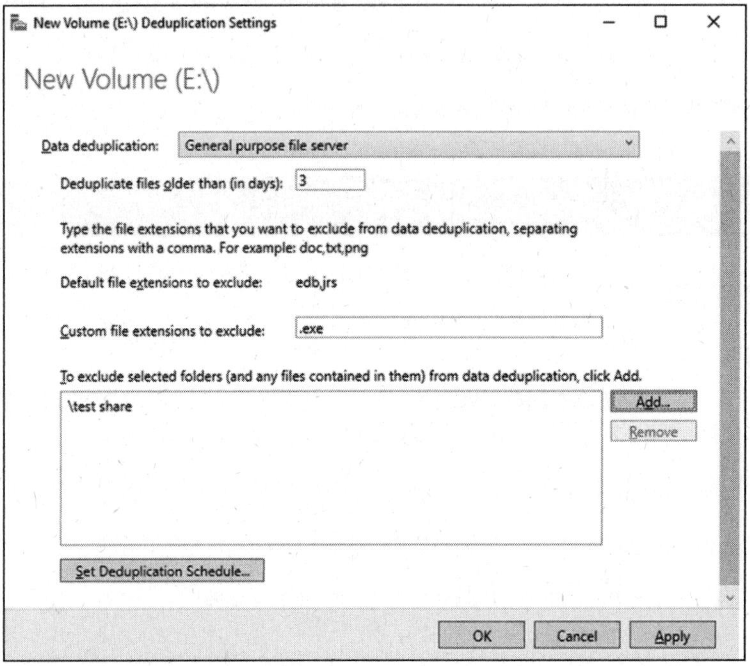

Monitoring Data Deduplicated

Finally, after data deduplication is installed and configured, an administrator will want to monitor the progress of the data deduplication jobs. To do this, you can run the following PowerShell commands (this command will show you the status of the deduplication process):

```
Get-DedupStatus
Get-DedupVolume
```

Summary

In this chapter, I discussed file servers and how they can be effective on your network. I also discussed sharing folders for users to access, and then I discussed how to publish those shared folders to Active Directory.

You learned about NTFS security versus shared folder permissions and how to limit users' hard drive space by setting up disk quotas. The chapter also covered the Encrypting File System (EFS) and how users can encrypt and compress files.

I also discussed how configuring file and storage solutions can be highly effective within your organization. You now have a better understanding of how Windows Server 2016 can provide you with extended functionality for effectively controlling corporate data.

Finally, I finished the chapter by talking about data deduplication and how data deduplication can help protect your corporate data and also provide a company with a backup solution.

Video Resources

There are videos available for the following exercises:

    3.3

    3.6

    3.12

You can access the videos at http://sybextestbanks.wiley.com on the Other Study Tools tab.

Exam Essentials

Know storage technologies.   Understand how to use the Fibre Channel, iSCSI, and NAS storage technologies. Know how to configure an iSCSI initiator and how to establish a connection to a target. Practice configuring tiered storage and using thin provisioning and trim.

Know how to configure NTFS security.   One of the major advantages of using NTFS over FAT32 is access to additional security features. NTFS allows you to put security at the file and folder layers. NTFS security is in effect whether the user is remote or local to the computer with the data.

Know how to configure shared permissions.   Shared permissions allow you to determine the access a user will receive when connecting to a shared folder. Shared permissions are allowed only at the folder layer and are in effect only when the user is remote to the computer with the shared data.

Understand how NTFS and shared permissions work together.   NTFS and shared permissions are individually additive—you get the highest level of security and permissions within each type. NTFS is always in effect, and it is the only security available locally. Shared permissions are in effect only when connecting remotely to access the shared data. When the two types of permissions meet, the most restrictive set of permissions applies.

Know how to configure disk quotas.   Disk quotas allow an organization to determine the amount of disk space that users can have on a volume of a server. An administrator can set up disk quotas based on volumes or by users. Each volume must have its own separate set of disk quotas.

Understand Windows PowerShell.   Understanding Windows PowerShell is not only important for the exam, it will also allow you to configure Server Core more efficiently. Windows PowerShell is a command-line utility that allows you run single cmdlets as well as run complex tasks to exploit the full power from PowerShell.

Understand data deduplication.   Understand that data deduplication involves finding and removing duplicate data within the company network without compromising its integrity. Understand that the goal is to store more data in less space by segmenting files into small chunks, identifying duplicate chunks, and maintaining a single copy of each chunk.

Review Questions

1. What is the default TCP port for iSCSI?

   A. 3260

   B. 1433

   C. 21

   D. 3389

2. You have a Windows Server 2016 Hyper-V host named Jupiter. You want to deploy several shielded virtual machines on Jupiter. You deploy a Host Guardian on a new server. You need to view the process of the shielded virtual machines installation. What should you run to see the progress of the shielded VM?

   A. `Get-ShieldedVMProvisioningStatus` cmdlet

   B. the `Diskpart` command

   C. the `Set-VHD` cmdlet

   D. the `Set-VM` cmdlet

3. You are the administrator of a mid-size network. You have a Hyper-V host that runs Windows Server 2016. The host contains a virtual machine named Virtual1. Virtual1 has resource metering enabled. You need to use resource metering to track the amount of network traffic that Virtual1 sends to the 10.10.16.0/20 network. Which command would you run?

   A. `Add-VMNetworkAdapteiAd`

   B. `Set-VMNetworkAdapter`

   C. `New-VMResourcePool`

   D. `Set-VMNetworkAdapterRoutingDomamMapping`

4. You are the administrator for an organization that has started using Hyper-V. You have a Hyper-V host named Server1 that runs Windows Server 2016. Server1 contains a virtual machine named Earth. You need to make sure that you can use nested virtualization on Earth. What should you run on Server1?

   A. The `Mount-VHD` cmdlet

   B. The `DiskPart` command

   C. The `Set-VMProcessor` cmdlet

   D. The `Set-VM` cmdlet

5. You need to ensure that VM1 and VM2 can communicate with each other only. The solution must prevent VM1 and VM2 from communicating with Server1. Which cmdlet should you use?

   A. `Set-NetNeighbor`

   B. `Remove-VMSwitchTeamMember`

   C. `Set-VMSwitch`

   D. `Enable-VMSwitchExtension`

6. You are the admin for a mid-size company. You have a Hyper-V host named Server1 that runs Windows Server 2016. Server1 has a dynamically expanding virtual hard disk (VHD) file that is 950 GB. The VHD currently contains around 450 GB of free space. You want to reduce the amount of disk space used by the VHD. What command should you run?

    A. The Mount-VHD cmdlet

    B. The DiskPart command

    C. The Set-VHD cmdlet

    D. The Optimize-VHD cmdlet

7. You have a Nano Server named Nano1. Which cmdlet should you use to identify whether the DNS Server role is installed on Nano1?

    A. Find-ServerPackage

    B. Get-Package

    C. Find-Package

    D. Get-WindowsOptionalFeature

8. You are working on a Windows Server 2016 Datacenter Server system. You need to view which roles and services are installed on the machine. Which PowerShell cmdlet can you use to see this?

    A. Get-event

    B. New-event

    C. Trace-command

    D. Get-WindowsFeature

9. What command would be used to register an iSCSI initiator manually to an iSNS server?

    A. iscsicli refreshisnsserver server_name

    B. iscsicli listisnsservers server_name

    C. iscsicli removeisnsserver server_name

    D. iscsicli addisnsserver server_name

10. You are an administrator who has set up two Hyper-V servers named Server1 (Windows Server 2016) and Server2 (Windows Server 2012 R2). Each Hyper-V server has multiple network cards. Each network card is connected to a different TCP/IP subnet. Server1 contains a dedicated migration network. Server2 contains a virtual machine named VM1. You plan to perform a live migration of VM1 to Server1. You need to ensure that Server1 uses all of the available networks to perform the live migration of VM1. What should you run to complete this task?

    A. The Mount-VHD cmdlet

    B. The DiskPart command

    C. The Set-VHD cmdlet

    D. The Set-VMHost cmdlet

Chapter 4

Understanding Hyper-V

THE FOLLOWING 70-740 EXAM OBJECTIVES ARE COVERED IN THIS CHAPTER:

✓ **Install and configure Hyper-V**

- This objective may include but is not limited to: Determine hardware and compatibility requirements for installing Hyper-V; install Hyper-V; install management tools; upgrade from existing versions of Hyper-V; delegate virtual machine management; perform remote management of Hyper-V hosts; configure virtual machines using Windows Power-Shell Direct; implement nested virtualization.

✓ **Configure virtual machine (VM) settings**

- This objective may include but is not limited to: Add or remove memory in running a VM; configure dynamic memory; configure Non-Uniform Memory Access (NUMA) support; configure smart paging; configure Resource Metering; manage Integration Services; create and configure Generation 1 and 2 VMs and determine appropriate usage scenarios; implement enhanced session mode; create Linux and FreeBSD VMs; install and configure Linux Integration Services (LIS); install and configure FreeBSD Integration Services (BIS); implement Secure Boot for Windows and Linux environments; move and convert VMs from previous versions of Hyper-V to Windows Server 2016 Hyper-V; export and import VMs; implement Discrete Device Assignment (DDA).

✓ **Configure Hyper-V storage**

- This objective may include but is not limited to: Create VHDs and VHDX files using Hyper-V Manager; create shared VHDX files; configure differencing disks; modify virtual hard disks; configure pass-through disks; resize a virtual hard disk; manage checkpoints; implement production checkpoints; implement a virtual Fibre Channel adapter; configure storage Quality of Service (QoS).

✓ Configure Hyper-V networking

- This objective may include but is not limited to: Add and remove virtual network interface cards (vNICs); configure Hyper-V virtual switches; optimize network performance; configure MAC addresses; configure network isolation; configure synthetic and legacy virtual network adapters; configure NIC teaming in VMs; configure virtual machine queue (VMQ); enable Remote Direct Memory Access (RDMA) on network adapters bound to a Hyper-V virtual switch using Switch Embedded Teaming (SET); configure Bandwidth Management.

One of the greatest improvements to Microsoft's servers over the past few versions is its implementation of their Virtual Server called Hyper-V.

Hyper-V is a server role in Windows Server 2016 that allows you to virtualize your environment and therefore run multiple virtual operating system instances simultaneously on a physical server. This not only helps you to improve server utilization but also helps you to create a more cost-effective and dynamic system.

Hyper-V allows an organization of any size to act and compete with other organizations of any size. A small company can buy a single server and then virtualize that server into multiple servers. Hyper-V gives a small company the ability to run multiple servers on a single box and compete with a company of any size.

For the large organizations, an administrator can consolidate multiple servers onto Hyper-V servers thus saving an organization time and money by using less physical boxes but still having all the servers needed to run the business.

In this chapter, you will learn the basic concepts and features of Hyper-V that a Windows Server 2016 technical specialist must know. You will also get a solid understanding of what is important in virtualization and in what areas of your work life you can use it.

Hyper-V Overview

In the following sections, I'll introduce you to Hyper-V. To begin, you'll take a look at virtualization and what types of virtualization exist. I will then discuss Hyper-V features and the Hyper-V architecture before finishing up with the Hyper-V requirements for software and hardware.

What Is Virtualization?

Virtualization is a method for abstracting physical resources from the way that they interact with other resources. For example, if you abstract the physical hardware from the operating system, you get the benefit of being able to move the operating system between different physical systems.

This is called *server virtualization*. But there are also other forms of virtualization available, such as presentation virtualization, desktop virtualization, and application virtualization. I will now briefly explain the differences between these forms of virtualization:

Server Virtualization This basically enables multiple servers to run on the same physical server. Hyper-V is a server virtualization tool that allows you to move physical machines to virtual machines and manage them on a few physical servers. Thus, you will be able to consolidate physical servers.

Presentation Virtualization   When you use *presentation virtualization*, your applications run on a different computer, and only the screen information is transferred to your computer. An example of presentation virtualization is Microsoft Remote Desktop Services in Windows Server 2016.

Desktop Virtualization   *Desktop virtualization* provides you with a virtual machine on your desktop, comparable to server virtualization. You run your complete operating system and applications in a virtual machine so that your local physical machine just needs to run a very basic operating system. An example of this form of virtualization is Microsoft Virtual PC.

Application Virtualization   *Application virtualization* helps prevent conflicts between applications on the same PC. Thus, it helps you to isolate the application running environment from the operating system installation requirements by creating application-specific copies of all shared resources. It also helps reduce application-to-application incompatibility and testing needs. An example of an application virtualization tool is Microsoft Application Virtualization (App-V).

Hyper-V Features

As a lead-in to the virtualization topic and Hyper-V, I will start with a list of key features, followed by a list of supported guest operating systems. This should provide you with a quick, high-level view of this feature before you dig deeper into the technology.

Key Features of Hyper-V

The following are just some of the key features of Hyper-V:

> The following features are just some of the new and improved features for Windows Server 2016 Hyper-V. To see a complete list of features, please visit Microsoft's website at:
>
> https://technet.microsoft.com/en-us/windows-server-docs/compute/ hyper-v/what-s-new-in-hyper-v-on-windows?f=255&MSPPError=-2147217396

Architecture   The hypervisor-based architecture, which has a 64-bit micro-kernel, provides a new array of device support as well as performance and security improvements.

Operating System Support   Both 32-bit and 64-bit operating systems can run simultaneously in Hyper-V. Also, different platforms like Windows, Linux, and others are supported.

Support for Symmetric Multiprocessors   Support for up to 64 processors in a virtual machine environment provides you with the ability to run applications as well as multiple virtual machines faster.

Compatible with Connected Standby   If an administrator installs the Hyper-V role on a computer that has the Always On/Always Connected (AOAC) power model configured, the

Connected Standby power state is now available. The Connected Standby power state is a low-power state that allows Windows to function more like a tablet than a PC.

Encryption Support for Generation 1 VMs   Administrators now have the ability to encrypt the operating system disk in generation 1 virtual machines by using BitLocker drive encryption. This is possible because of a new Hyper-V feature called key storage. Key storage creates a small, dedicated drive to store the system drive's BitLocker key. When you want to decrypt the disk and start the virtual machine, the Hyper-V host will need to be either a part of an authorized guarded fabric or use a private key from one of the virtual machine's guardians. Version 8 virtual machines must be used for key storage to function properly.

Host Resource Protection   Administrators can enable this feature to ensure that a virtual machine does not use more than its share of the host machine's system resources. Enabling this feature ensures that no one virtual machine can cause a performance issue on the host or on any other virtual machines. This feature is off by default. To enable this feature, an administrator will need to run the following Windows PowerShell command:

```
Set-VMProcessor -EnableHostResourceProtection $true
```

Network Load Balancing   Hyper-V provides support for *Windows Network Load Balancing (NLB)* to balance the network load across virtual machines on different servers.

Hardware Architecture   Hyper-V's architecture provides improved utilization of resources such as networking, memory, and disks.

Quick Migration   Hyper-V's *quick migration* feature provides you with the functionality to run virtual machines in a clustered environment with switchover capabilities when there is a failure. Thus, you can reduce downtime and achieve higher availability of your virtual machines.

Virtual Machine Checkpoint   You can take checkpoints of running virtual machines, which provides you with the capability to recover to any previous virtual machine checkpoint state quickly and easily.

Resource Metering   Hyper-V *resource metering* allows an organization to track usage within the businesses departments. It allows an organization to create a usage-based billing solution that adjusts to the provider's business model and strategy.

Scripting   Using the Windows Management Instrumentation (WMI) interfaces and APIs, you can easily build custom scripts to automate processes in your virtual machines.

RemoteFX   Windows Server 2016 Hyper-V RemoteFX allows for an enhanced user experience for RemoteFX desktops by providing a 3D virtual adapter, intelligent codecs, and the ability to redirect USB devices in virtual machines.

Fibre Channel   The virtual Fibre Channel feature allows you to connect to the Fibre Channel storage unit from within the virtual machine. *Virtual Fibre Channel* allows an administrator to use their existing Fibre Channel to support virtualized workloads. Hyper-V users have the ability to use Fibre Channel storage area networks (SANs) to virtualize the workloads that require direct access to SAN logical unit numbers (LUNs).

Enhanced Session Mode   *Enhanced Session Mode* enhances the interactive session of the Virtual Machine Connection for Hyper-V administrators who want to connect to their virtual machines. It gives administrators the same functionality as a remote desktop connection when the administrator is interacting with a virtual machine.

In previous versions of Hyper-V, the virtual machine connection gave you limited functionality while you connected to the virtual machine screen, keyboard, and mouse. An administrator could use an RDP connection to get full redirection abilities, but that would require a network connection to the virtual machine host.

Enhanced Session Mode gives administrators the following benefits for local resource redirection:

- Display configuration
- Audio
- Printers
- Clipboard
- Smart cards
- Drives
- USB devices
- Supported Plug and Play devices

Shared Virtual Hard Disk   Windows Server 2016 Hyper-V has a feature called Shared Virtual Hard Disk. *Shared Virtual Hard Disk* allows an administrator to cluster virtual machines by using Shared Virtual Hard Disk (VHDX) files.

Shared virtual hard disks allow an administrator to build a high availability infrastructure, which is important if you are setting up either a private cloud deployment or a cloud-hosted environment for managing large workloads. Shared virtual hard disks allow two or more virtual machines to access the same virtual hard disk (VHDX) file.

Automatic Virtual Machine Activation (AVMA)   *Automatic Virtual Machine Activation (AVMA)* is a feature that allows administrators to install virtual machines on a properly activated Windows Server 2016 system without the need to manage individual product keys for each virtual machine. When using AVMA, virtual machines get bound to the licensed Hyper-V server as soon as the virtual machine starts.

Network Isolation   One nice feature of using Microsoft Hyper-V network virtualization is the ability of Hyper-V to keep virtual networks isolated from the physical network infrastructure of the hosted system. Because administrators can set up Hyper-V software–defined virtualization policies, you are no longer limited by the IP address assignment or VLAN isolation requirements of the physical network. Hyper-V allows for built-in network isolation to keep the virtual network separated from the virtual network.

Discrete Device Assignment   One feature of Windows Server 2016 is the ability to use Discrete Device Assignment (DDA). DDA allows an administrator to take full advantage of performance and application compatibility improvements in the user experience by allowing the system's graphic cards to be directly assigned to a virtual machine. This allows the graphic card processor to be fully available to the virtual desktops that are utilizing the native driver of the graphics card processor.

Non-Uniform Memory Access   Non-Uniform Memory Access (NUMA) is a multiprocessor memory architecture that allows a processor to access its local memory quicker than memory located on another processor. NUMA allows a system to access memory quickly by providing separate memory on each processor. Processor can access their local assigned memory thus speeding the system performance. Normally a multi-processor system runs into performance issues when multiple processors access the same memory at the same time. NUMA helps prevent this by allowing processors to access their own memory. Memory that is dedicated to a processor is referred to as a NUMA node.

Dynamic Memory   *Dynamic Memory* is a feature of Hyper-V that allows it to balance memory automatically among running virtual machines. Dynamic Memory allows Hyper-V to adjust the amount of memory available to the virtual machines in response to the needs of the virtual machines. It is currently available for Hyper-V in Windows Server 2016.

Virtual Machine Queue   Windows Server 2016 Hyper-V includes a feature called Virtual machine queue (VMQ) as long as the hardware is VMQ compatible network hardware. VMQ uses packet filtering to provide data from an external virtual machine network directly to virtual machines. This helps reduce the overhead of routing packets from the management operating system to the virtual machine.

Once VMQ is enabled on Hyper-V, a dedicated queue is created on the physical network adapter for each virtual network adapter to use. When data arrives for the virtual network adapter, the physical network adapter places that data in a queue and once the system is available, all of the data in the queue is delivered to the virtual network adapter.

To enable the virtual machine queue on a specific virtual machine, enter the settings for the virtual machine and expand Network Adapter. Click Hardware Acceleration and on the right hand window, check the box for Enable virtual machine queue.

Hyper-V Nesting   Windows Server 2016 has introduced a new feature of Hyper-V called Hyper-V nesting. Hyper-V nesting allows you to run a virtual machine in a virtual machine. So let's say that you build a new 2016 Hyper-V server. You install Windows Server 2016 into a virtual machine. Then in that virtual machine, you can install Hyper-V and build other virtual machines within the first virtual machine. This is new to Windows Server 2016 and can be very useful in training situations. You can install a Windows Server 2016 virtual machine and still show others how to install and create virtual machines in the original virtual machine. To enable Hyper-V nesting, you would run the following PowerShell command on the Hyper-V Host. The virtual machines must be in the OFF State when this command is run (this means the virtual machines must be turned off):

```
Set-VMProcessor -VMName <VMName> -ExposeVirtualizationExtensions $true
```

Supported Guest Operating Systems

The following guest operating systems have been successfully tested on Hyper-V and are hypervisor-aware. Table 4.1 shows all of the guest server operating systems and the maximum number of virtual processors. Table 4.2 shows all of the guest client operating systems and the maximum number of virtual processors.

TABLE 4.1   Hyper-V guest server operating systems

Guest Operating System (Server)	Maximum Number of Virtual Processors
Windows Server 2016	64
Windows Server 2012 and Server 2012 R2	64
Windows Server 2008 R2 with Service Pack 1 (SP1)	64
Windows Server 2008 R2	64
Windows Server 2008 with Service Pack 2 (SP2)	8
Windows Home Server 2011	4
Windows Small Business Server 2011	Essentials edition: 2 Standard edition: 4
Windows Server 2003 R2 with Service Pack 2 (SP2)	2
Windows Server 2003 with Service Pack 2 (SP2)	2
Red Hat Enterprise Linux 5.7 and 5.8	64
Red Hat Enterprise Linux 6.0–6.3	64
SUSE Linux Enterprise Server 11 SP2	64
Open SUSE 12.1	64
Ubuntu 12.04	64

TABLE 4.2   Hyper-V guest client operating systems

Guest Operating System (Client)	Maximum Number of Virtual Processors
Windows 10	32
Windows 8 / 8.1	32
Windows 7 with Service Pack 1 (SP1)	4
Windows 7	4
Windows Vista with Service Pack 2 (SP2)	2
Windows XP with Service Pack 3 (SP3)	2
Windows XP x64 Edition with Service Pack 2 (SP2)	2
CentOS 5.7 and 5.8	64
CentOS 6.0–6.3	64
Red Hat Enterprise Linux 5.7 and 5.8	64
Red Hat Enterprise Linux 6.0–6.3	64
SUSE Linux Enterprise Server 11 SP2	64
Open SUSE 12.1	64
Ubuntu 12.04	64

The list of supported guest operating systems may always be extended. Please check the official Microsoft Hyper-V site to obtain a current list of supported operating systems: www.microsoft.com/virtualization.

Hyper-V Architecture

This section will provide you with an overview of the Hyper-V architecture (see Figure 4.1). I'll explain the differences between a hypervisor-aware and a non-hypervisor-aware child partition.

FIGURE 4.1   Hyper-V architecture

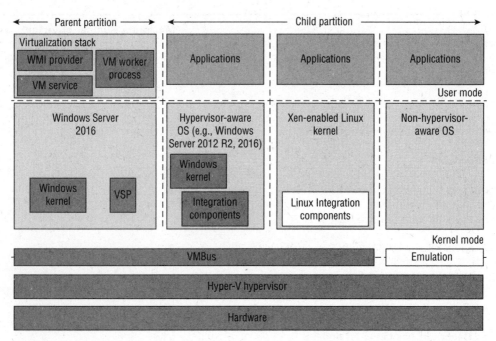

As you can see, Hyper-V is based on the microkernel architecture. Hyper-V provides a virtualization layer called a *hypervisor* that runs directly on the system hardware. You can see that the hypervisor is similar to what the kernel is to Windows. It is a software layer responsible for the interaction with the core hardware and works in conjunction with an optimized instance of Windows Server 2016 that allows running multiple operating systems on a physical server simultaneously. The Hyper-V architecture consists of the hypervisor and parent and child partitions.

The Windows Server 2016 operating system runs in the parent partition, and it delivers the WMI provider for scripting as well as the VM service.

Virtual machines each run in their own child partitions. Child partitions do not have direct access to hardware resources; instead, they have a virtual view of the resources, which are called *virtual devices*.

If you're running a hypervisor-aware operating system like Windows Server 2003, Windows Server 2008, Windows Server 2008 R2, Windows Server 2012, or Windows Server 2016 in your virtual machine, any request to the virtual devices is redirected via the high-speed bus to the devices in the parent partition, which will manage the requests.

By default, only Windows Server 2008 R2, Server 2012, and Server 2012 R2 are hypervisor-aware operating systems. Once you install Hyper-V Integration Components on an operating system other than Windows Server 2008 R2 and newer, it will be hypervisor-aware. Microsoft provides a hypervisor adapter to make Linux hypervisor aware.

Non-hypervisor-aware operating systems (for example, Windows NT 4.0) use an emulator to communicate with the Windows hypervisor, which is slower than molasses in the winter.

Hyper-V Requirements

The following sections will describe the hardware and software requirements for installing the Hyper-V server role. It is important to understand these requirements for obtaining your software license as well as for planning for server hardware. When you understand the requirements, you can design and configure a Hyper-V solution that will meet the needs of your applications.

Hardware Requirements

In addition to the basic hardware requirements for Windows Server 2016, there are requirements for running the Hyper-V server role on your Windows server. They are listed in Table 4.3.

TABLE 4.3   Hardware requirements for Hyper-V

Requirement Area	Definition
CPU	x64-compatible processor with Intel VT or AMD-V technology enabled. Hardware Data Execution Prevention (DEP), specifically Intel XD bit (execute disable bit) or AMD NX bit (no execute bit), must be available and enabled. Minimum: 1.4 GHz. Recommended: 2 GHz or faster.
Memory	Minimum: 1 GB RAM. Recommended: 2 GB RAM or greater. (Additional RAM is required for each running guest operating system.) Maximum: 1 TB.
Hard disk	Minimum: 8 GB. Recommended: 20 GB or greater. (Additional disk space needed for each guest operating system.)

The Add Roles Wizard in Server Manager additionally verifies the hardware requirements. A good starting point is to check your hardware against the Microsoft hardware list to make sure that Windows Server 2016 supports your hardware. If you try to install the Hyper-V server role on a computer that does not meet the CPU requirements, you'll get a warning window that looks like Figure 4.2.

FIGURE 4.2 Warning window that Hyper-V cannot be installed

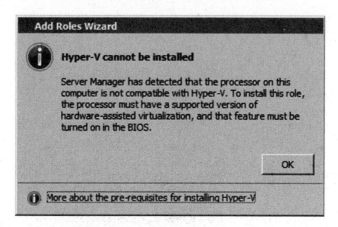

Software Requirements

To use virtualization in Windows Server 2016, you need to consider the basic software requirements for Hyper-V. Hyper-V runs only on the following editions of the Windows Server 2016 operating system:

- Windows Server 2016 Standard edition
- Windows Server 2016 Datacenter edition
- Microsoft Hyper-V Server 2012 R2 edition
- Windows Server 2016 Hyper-V edition

Hyper-V Installation and Configuration

The following sections explain how to install the Hyper-V role using Server Manager in Windows Server 2016 Full installation mode or the command-line mode in Windows Server 2016 Server Core. We will then take a look at Hyper-V as part of Server Manager before discussing how to use the Hyper-V Manager. Finally, we will look at the Hyper-V server settings and then cover two important areas for Hyper-V: virtual networks and virtual hard disks.

Install the Hyper-V Role

Now it's time to see how to install the Hyper-V server role on the two installation options of Windows Server 2016, namely, a Full installation and a Server Core installation.

Installing Hyper-V in Full Installation Mode

You can install the Hyper-V server role on any Windows Server 2016 installation for which the Full option was chosen. In addition, the server must meet both the hardware and software requirements. The installation process is simple, as Exercise 4.1 demonstrates.

Installing Hyper-V in Full Installation Mode

1. Open Server Manager.

2. In Server Manager, choose option 2, Add Roles And Features.

3. At the Select Installation Type page, choose the role-based or feature-based installation. Click Next.

4. On the Select Destination Server screen, choose Select A Server From The Server Pool and choose the server to which you want to add this role. Click Next.

5. On the Select Server Roles screen, click the check box next to Hyper-V (see Figure 4.3). When the Add Features dialog box appears, click the Add Features button. Then click Next.

FIGURE 4.3   Server Manager Add Features

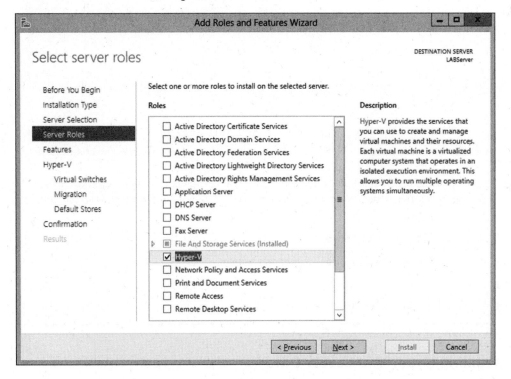

6. At the Select Features screen, click Next.

7. At the Hyper-V introduction screen, click Next.

8. At the Create Virtual Switches screen, choose your adapter and click Next (see Figure 4.4).

FIGURE 4.4   Virtual switch screen

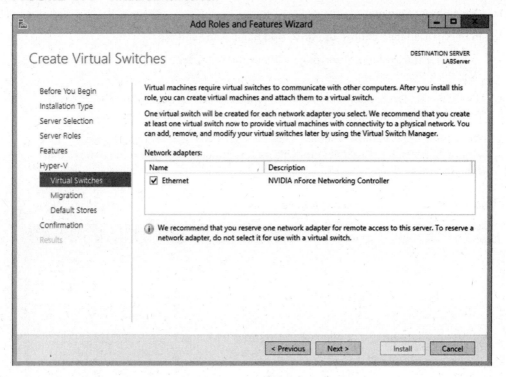

9. At the Virtual Machine Migration screen, click Next. You want to use migration only if you have multiple Hyper-V servers. Since we will have only one for this exercise, just skip this screen.

10. At the Default Stores screen, accept the defaults and click Next.

11. At the Confirmation screen, click the Install button.

12. After the installation is complete, click the Close button.

13. Restart your server.

Installing Hyper-V in Server Core

The Server Core installation option is introduced in Windows Server 2008. It creates an operating system installation without a GUI shell. You can either manage the server remotely from another system or use the Server Core's command-line interface.

This installation option provides the following benefits:

- Reduces attack surface (because fewer applications are running on the server)

- Reduces maintenance and management (because only the required options are installed)

- Requires less disk space and produces less processor utilization
- Provides a minimal parent partition
- Reduces system resources required by the operating system as well as the attack surface

By using Hyper-V on a Server Core installation, you can fundamentally improve availability because the attack surface is reduced and the downtime required for installing patches is optimized. It will thus be more secure and reliable with less management.

To install Hyper-V for a Windows Server 2016 installation, you must execute the following command in the command-line interface:

```
Dism /online /enable-feature /featurename:Microsoft-Hyper-V
```

Hyper-V in Server Manager

As with all of the other Windows Server 2016 roles, the Hyper-V role neatly integrates into Server Manager. Server Manager filters the information just for the specific role and thus displays only the required information. As you can see in Figure 4.5, the Hyper-V Summary page shows related event log entries, the state of the system services for Hyper-V, and useful resources and support.

FIGURE 4.5   Hyper-V in Server Manager

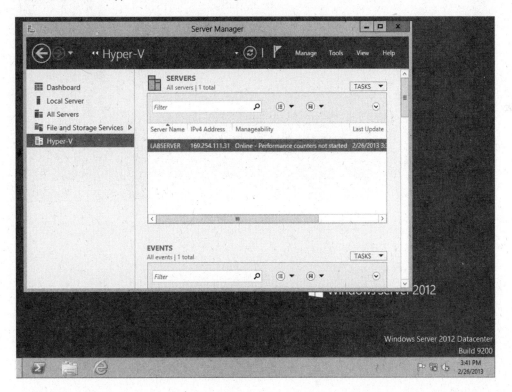

Using Hyper-V Manager

Hyper-V Manager is the central management console to configure your server and create and manage your virtual machines, virtual networks, and virtual hard disks. Hyper-V Manager is managed through a Microsoft Management Console (MMC) snap-in. You can access it either in Server Manager or by using Administrative Tools ➤ Hyper-V Manager. Figure 4.6 shows how Hyper-V Manager looks once you start it.

FIGURE 4.6   Hyper-V Manager

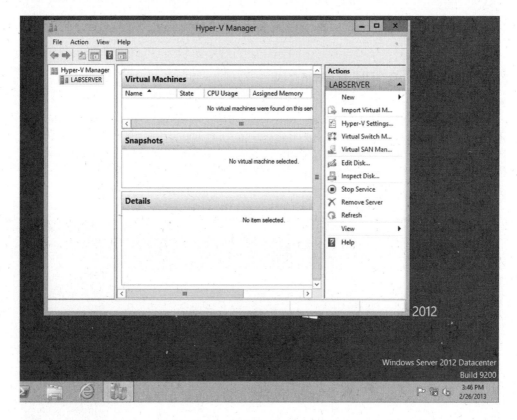

Hyper-V Manager is available for the following operating systems:

- Windows Server 2016

- Windows Server 2012 R2

- Windows Server 2012

- Windows Server 2008 R2

- Windows Server 2008

- Windows 8

- Windows 10

- Windows 8.1

- Windows 7
- Windows Vista with Service Pack 1 (SP1)

Hyper-V Manager is installed on a Windows Server 2016 machine only when you install Hyper-V on it. On Windows Server 2012 R2/2012/2008/2008 R2/ 2003, Windows 10/8/7, or Windows Vista, you will need to install the Hyper-V Manager MMC using the Remote Server Administration Tools (RSAT).

You can use Hyper-V Manager to connect to any Full or Server Core installation remotely. Besides Hyper-V Manager, you can use the WMI interface for scripting Hyper-V.

Configure Hyper-V Settings

In this section, you will get an overview of the available Hyper-V settings for the server. You configure all server-side default configuration settings like default locations of your configuration files or the release key. You can open the Hyper-V Settings page (see Figure 4.7) in Hyper-V Manager by clicking Hyper-V Settings in the Actions pane.

FIGURE 4.7   Hyper-V Settings

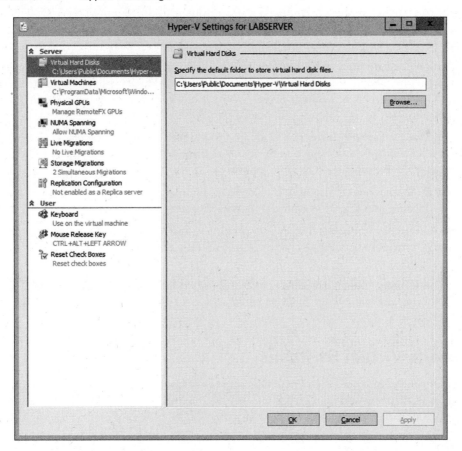

The Hyper-V Settings page includes the following settings:

Virtual Hard Disks   Specifies the default location of your virtual hard disk files (`.vhd` and `.vhdx`).

Virtual Machines   Specifies the default location of your virtual machine configuration files. It includes the Virtual Machine XML configuration files (part of the `Virtual Machines` folder) as well as related checkpoints (part of the `Checkpoints` folder).

Physical GPUs   This feature allows for graphical processing unit (GPU) accelerated video within a virtual machine. The GPU will allow you to support 3D GPU accelerated graphics.

NUMA Spanning   An administrator can configure Hyper-V to allow virtual machines to span nonuniform memory architecture (NUMA) nodes. When the physical computer has NUMA nodes, this setting provides virtual machines with additional computing resources. Spanning NUMA nodes can help you run more virtual machines at the same time. However, using NUMA can decrease overall performance.

Live Migrations   *Live migration* allows a Hyper-V administrator to relocate running virtual machines easily from one node of the failover cluster to another node in the same cluster.

Storage Migrations   *Storage Migration* allows an administrator to move their virtual machine storage from one location to another. This setting allows you to specify how many storage migrations can be performed at the same time on this system.

Replication Configuration   This setting allows you to configure this computer as a Replica Server to another Hyper-V server. Hyper-V Replica allows administrators to replicate their Hyper-V virtual machines from one Hyper-V host at a primary site to another Hyper-V host at the Replica site.

Each node of the failover cluster that is involved in Replica must have the Hyper-V server role installed. One of the servers in the Hyper-V replication needs to be set up as a Replica Broker to allow the replication to work properly.

Keyboard   Defines how to use Windows key combinations. Options are Physical Computer, Virtual Machine, and Virtual Machine Only When Running Full Screen.

Mouse Release Key   Specifies the key combination to release the mouse in your virtual machine. Options are Ctrl+Alt+left arrow, Ctrl+Alt+right arrow, Ctrl+Alt+space, and Ctrl+Alt+Shift.

Reset Check Boxes   Resets any check boxes that hide pages and messages when checked. This will bring any window up again on which you checked the Do Not Show This Window Again check box.

Manage Virtual Switches

A *virtual network* provides the virtual links between nodes in either a virtual or physical network. Virtual networking in Hyper-V is provided in a secure and dynamic way because you can granularly define virtual network switches for their required usage. For example, you can define a private or internal virtual network if you don't want to allow your virtual machines to send packages to the physical network.

To allow your virtual machines to communicate with each other, you need virtual networks. Just like normal networks, virtual networks exist only on the host computer and allow you to configure how virtual machines communicate with each other, with the host, and with the network or the Internet. You manage virtual networks in Hyper-V using Virtual Switch Manager, as shown in Figure 4.8.

FIGURE 4.8   Virtual Network Manager

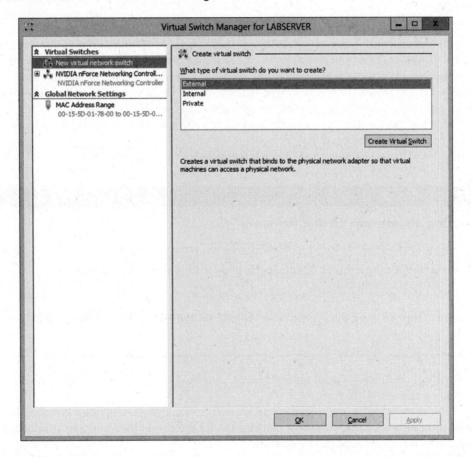

Using *Virtual Switch Manager*, you can create, manage, and delete virtual switches. You can define the network type as external, internal only, or private.

External   Any virtual machine connected to this virtual switch can access the physical network. You would use this option if you want to allow your virtual machines to access, for example, other servers on the network or the Internet. This option is used in production environments where your clients connect directly to the virtual machines.

Internal   This option allows virtual machines to communicate with each other as well as the host system but not with the physical network. When you create an internal network, it also creates a local area connection in Network Connections that allows the host machine to communicate with the virtual machines. You can use this if you want to separate your host's network from your virtual networks.

Private   When you use this option, virtual machines can communicate with each other but not with the host system or the physical network; thus, no network packets are hitting the wire. You can use this to define internal virtual networks for test environments or labs, for example.

On the external and internal-only virtual networks, you also can enable virtual LAN (VLAN) identification. You can use VLANs to partition your network into multiple subnets using a VLAN ID. When you enable virtual LAN identification, the NIC that is connected to the switch will never see packets tagged with VLAN IDs. Instead, all packets traveling from the NIC to the switch will be tagged with the access mode VLAN ID as they leave the switch port. All packets traveling from the switch port to the NIC will have their VLAN tags removed. You can use this if you are already logically segmenting your physical machines and also use it for your virtual ones.

Exercise 4.2 explains how to create an internal-only virtual switch.

EXERCISE 4.2

Creating an Internal Virtual Network

1. Click the Windows Key ➢ Administrative Tools ➢ Hyper-V Manager.

2. In Hyper-V Manager, in the Actions pane, choose Virtual Switch Manager.

3. On the Virtual Switch page, select Private and click the Create Virtual Switch button.

4. On the New Virtual Switch page, enter **Private Virtual Network** in the Name field.

5. Click OK.

When you create the internal virtual switch, a network device is created in Network Connections, as shown in Figure 4.9.

This is also the case when you create an external virtual network because it will replace the physical network card of the host machine to give the parent partition a virtual network card that is also used in the child partitions.

Hyper-V binds the virtual network service to a physical network adapter only when an external virtual network is created. The benefit of this is that the performance is better if you do not use the external virtual network option. The downside, however, is that there will be a network disruption when you create or delete an external virtual network.

FIGURE 4.9   Virtual network card

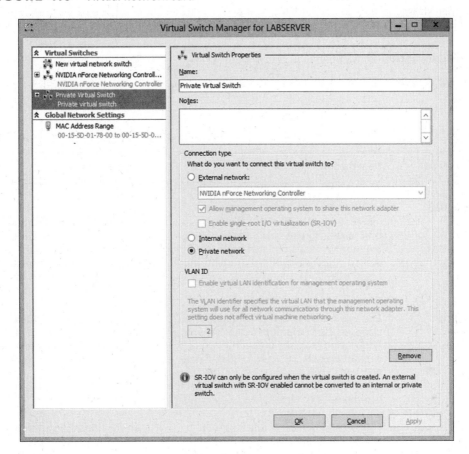

Communication between the virtual machine and the local host computer is not configured automatically. Once you install a virtual machine, you need to make sure that the TCP/IP settings are in agreement with the settings you define in the virtual network card. Start with a successful ping from your host machine to the virtual machines to verify that communication is working.

Managing Virtual Hard Disks

In addition to virtual networks, you need to manage virtual hard disks that you attach to your virtual machines. A virtual hard disk in Hyper-V, apart from a pass-through disk, is a VHD or VHDX file that basically simulates a hard drive on your virtual machine.

The following sections will first show you what types of virtual hard disks are available and then show you how to create them. You will also learn about what options are available to manage virtual hard disks.

Types of Hard Disks

Depending on how you want to use the disk, Hyper-V offers various types, as described in Table 4.4.

TABLE 4.4 Virtual hard disks in Hyper-V

Type of Disk	Description	When to Use It
Dynamically expanding	This disk starts with a small VHD file and expands it on demand once an installation takes place. It can grow to the maximum size you defined during creation. You can use this type of disk to clone a local hard drive during creation.	This option is effective when you don't know the exact space needed on the disk and when you want to preserve hard disk space on the host machine. Unfortunately, it is the slowest disk type.
Fixed size	The size of the VHD file is fixed to the size specified when the disk is created. This option is faster than a dynamically expanding disk. However, a fixed-size disk uses up the maximum defined space immediately. This type is ideal for cloning a local hard drive.	A fixed-size disk provides faster access than dynamically expanding or differencing disks, but it is slower than a physical disk.
Differencing	This type of disk is associated in a parent-child relationship with another disk. The differencing disk is the child, and the associated virtual disk is the parent. Differencing disks include only the differences to the parent disk. By using this type, you can save a lot of disk space in similar virtual machines. This option is suitable if you have multiple virtual machines with similar operating systems.	Differencing disks are most commonly found in test environments and should not be used in production environments.
Physical (or pass-through disk)	The virtual machine receives direct pass-through access to the physical disk for exclusive use. This type provides the highest performance of all disk types and thus should be used for production servers where performance is the top priority. The drive is not available for other guest systems.	This type is used in high-end datacenters to provide optimum performance for VMs. It's also used in failover cluster environments.

Creating Virtual Hard Disks

To help you gain practice in creating virtual hard disks, the following three exercises will teach you how to create a differencing hard disk, how to clone an existing disk by creating a new disk, and how to configure a physical or pass-through disk to your virtual machine. First, in Exercise 4.3, you will learn how to create a differencing virtual hard disk.

EXERCISE 4.3

Creating a Differencing Hard Disk

1. Open Hyper-V Manager.

2. In Hyper-V Manager, on the Actions pane, choose New ➢ Hard Disk.

3. In the New Virtual Hard Disk Wizard, click Next on the Before You Begin page.

4. At the Choose Disk Format screen, choose VHDX and click Next. The size of your VHDs depends on which format you choose. If you're going to have a VHD larger than 2,040 GB, use VHDX. If your VHD is less than 2,040 GB, then you should use VHD.

5. On the Choose Disk Type page, select Fixed Size and click Next.

6. On the Specify Name And Location page, enter the new name of the child disk (for example, **newvirtualharddisk.vhdx**). You can also modify the default location of the new VHDX file if you want. Click Next to continue.

7. Next, on the Configure Disk page, you need to specify the size of the VHDX file. Choose a size based on your hard disk and then click Next to continue. I used 60 GB as our test size.

8. On the Completing The New Virtual Hard Disk Wizard page, verify that all settings are correct and click Finish to create the hard disk.

The process to add a physical or pass-through disk to a virtual machine is quite different. For this, first you need to create the virtual machine, and then you open the virtual machine settings to configure the physical disk. If you want to add a physical disk to a virtual machine, the physical disk must be set as Offline in Disk Management, as shown in Figure 4.10.

To access Disk Management, click the Windows key, choose Administrative Tools ➢ Computer Management, expand Storage in the left pane, and click Disk Management.

You cannot share a physical disk among multiple virtual machines or with the host system.

FIGURE 4.10   In Disk Management, you can set disks as Offline.

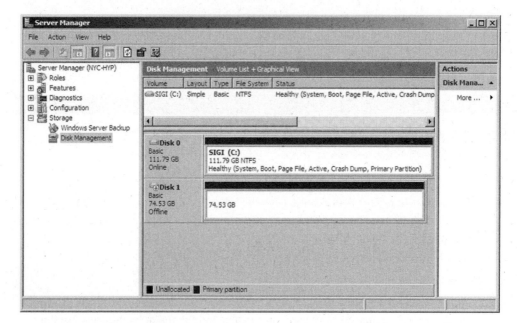

Physical or pass-through disks might not be that important if your use of virtualization is based on test environments, but they become crucial when you need to plan for highly available virtual datacenters. This is especially true if you consider using failover clusters to provide the Quick Migration feature, which is when you should consider matching one logical unit number (LUN) from your enterprise storage system or storage area network (SAN) as one physical disk. This provides you with the optimum performance you need in such an environment.

Managing Virtual Hard Disks

Hyper-V also provides two tools to manage virtual hard disks: Inspect Disk and Edit Disk. These tools are available on the Actions pane in Hyper-V Manager.

Inspect Disk   This provides you with information about the virtual hard disk. It shows you not only the type of the disk but also information such as the maximum size for dynamically expanding disks and the parent VHD for differencing disks.

Edit Disk   This provides you with the Edit Virtual Hard Disk Wizard, which you can use to compact, convert, expand, merge, or reconnect hard disks. Figure 4.11 shows you the wizard's options when you select a dynamically expanding disk.

FIGURE 4.11 The Edit Virtual Hard Disk Wizard

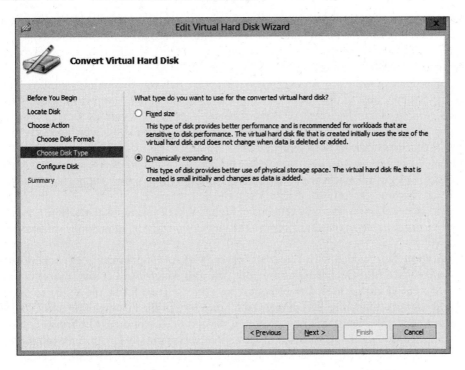

Table 4.5 provides you with an overview of what you can do with the wizard.

TABLE 4.5 Edit Disk overview

Action	Description
Compact	Reduces the size of a dynamically expanding or differencing disk by removing blank space from deleted files.
Convert	Converts a dynamically expanding disk to a fixed disk or vice versa.
Expand	Increases the storage capacity of a dynamically expanding disk or a fixed virtual hard disk.
Merge	Merges the changes from a differencing disk into either the parent disk or another disk (applies to differencing disks only!).
Reconnect	If a differencing disk no longer finds its referring parent disk, this option can reconnect the parent to the disk.

Generation 1 vs. Generation 2 VHDs

Previous versions of Hyper-V had some pretty major drawbacks. One big drawback was that Hyper-V could not boot a virtual machine from a virtual hard drive that was SCSI. Believe it or not, SCSI controllers were not even recognized by Hyper-V unless you installed the Integration Services component.

Another issue that the previous versions of Hyper-V had was the inability to copy files from the Hyper-V host to the virtual machines without the use of a network connection in the virtual machine. The older versions of Hyper-V, prior to Windows Server 2016, are now considered generation 1 versions. Why is it so important to know which generations of Hyper-V you should use or need to use?

Hyper-V generations help determine what functionality and what virtual hardware you can use in your virtual machine. Windows Server 2016 Hyper-V now supports two different virtual machine generations: generation 1 and generation 2.

As already explained, previous versions of Hyper-V are considered generation 1, and this provides the same virtual hardware to the virtual machine as in previous versions of Hyper-V.

Generation 2 is included with Windows Server 2016, and it provides better functionality on the virtual machines including secure boot (which is enabled by default), the ability to boot from a SCSI virtual hard disk or boot from a SCSI virtual DVD, the ability to use a standard network adapter to PXE boot, and Unified Extensible Firmware Interface (UEFI) firmware support. Generation 2 now gives you the ability to support UEFI firmware instead of BIOS-based firmware. On a virtual machine that is Generation 2, you can configure Secure Boot, Enable TPM, and set security policies by clicking on the Security section of the virtual machines properties.

So when you create VHDs in Windows Server 2016, one of your choices will be the ability to create the VHDs as a generation 1 or generation 2 VHD. If you need the ability to have your VHDs run on older versions of Hyper-V, make them a generation 1 VHD. If they are going to run only on Windows Server 2016, make your VHDs generation 2 and take advantage of all the new features and functionality.

Configuring Virtual Machines

The following sections cover the topics of creating and managing virtual machines as well as how to back up and restore virtual machines using features such as Import and Export and Checkpoint. You'll also briefly look at Hyper-V's Live Migration feature.

Creating and Managing Virtual Machines

It is important to learn how to create a virtual machine, how to change its configuration, and how to delete it. You will take a look at the Virtual Machine Connection tool and install the Hyper-V Integration Components onto a virtual machine.

Virtual Machines

Virtual machines define the child partitions in which you run operating system instances. Each virtual machine is separate and can communicate with the others only by using a virtual network. You can assign hard drives, virtual networks, DVD drives, and other system components to it. A virtual machine is similar to an existing physical server, but it no longer runs on dedicated hardware—it shares the hardware of the host system with the other virtual machines that run on the host.

Exercise 4.4 shows you how to create a new virtual machine. Before completing this exercise, download an eval copy of Windows Server from Microsoft's website (www.microsoft.com/downloads). Make sure the file downloaded is an image file (.iso). You will use this image to install the operating system into the virtual machine.

EXERCISE 4.4

Creating a New Virtual Machine

1.   Open Hyper-V Manager (see Figure 4.12).

FIGURE 4.12   Hyper-V Manager

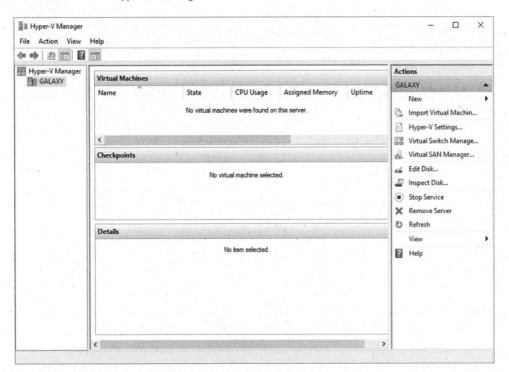

2. In Hyper-V Manager, on the Actions pane, choose New ➢ Virtual Machine.

3. In the New Virtual Machine Wizard, click Next on the Before You Begin page.

4. On the Specify Name And Location page, give your virtual machine a name and change the default location of the virtual machine configuration files. Click Next to continue.

5. The Specify Generation screen is next. Choose Generation 2 (see Figure 4.13) and click Next.

FIGURE 4.13 Specify Generation screen

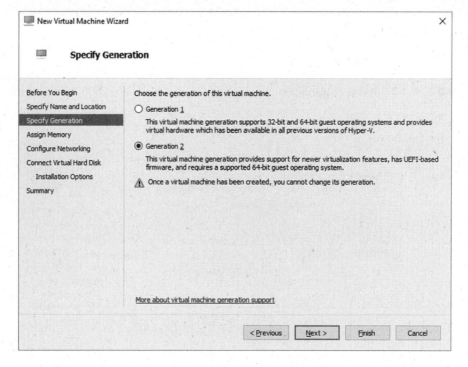

6. On the Assign Memory page (see Figure 4.14), define how much of your host computer's memory you want to assign to this virtual machine. Remember that once your virtual machine uses up all of your physical memory, it will start swapping to disk, thus reducing the performance of all virtual machines. Click Next to continue.

7. On the Configure Networking page, select the virtual network that you previously configured using Virtual Network Manager (see Figure 4.15). Click Next to continue.

FIGURE 4.14   VM RAM

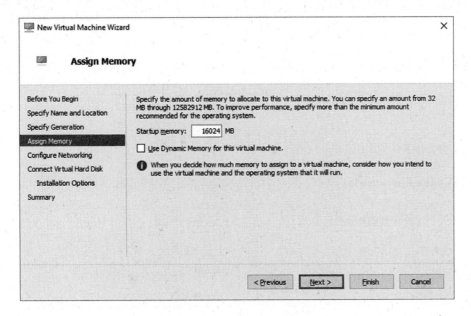

FIGURE 4.15   Networking page

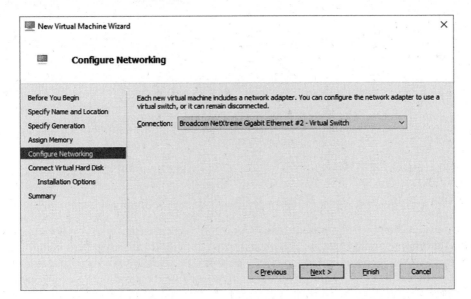

8.   On the next page, you configure your virtual hard disk (see Figure 4.16). You can create a new virtual hard disk, select an existing disk, or choose to attach the hard disk later. Be aware that you can create only a dynamically expanding virtual disk on this page; you cannot create a differencing, physical, or fixed virtual hard disk there. However, if you created the virtual hard disk already, you can, of course, select it. Click Next to continue.

FIGURE 4.16   Virtual Hard Disk page

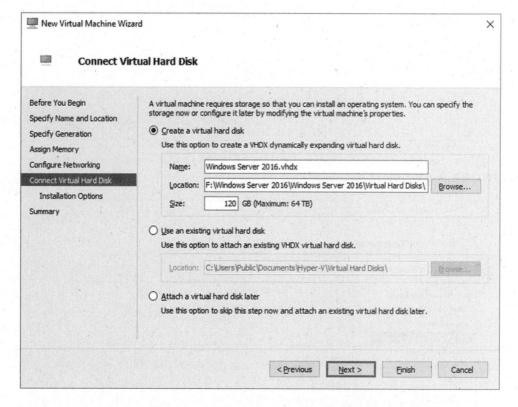

9.   On the Installation Options page (see Figure 4.17), you can select how you want to install your operating system. You have the option to install an operating system later, install the operating system from a boot CD/DVD-ROM where you can select a physical device or an image file (ISO file), install an operating system from a floppy disk image (VFD file, or a virtual boot floppy disk), or install an operating system from a network-based installation server. The last option will install a legacy network adapter to your virtual machine so that you can boot from the network adapter. Select Install An Operating System from a bootable CD/DVD-ROM and choose Image File (.iso). Then click Next.

FIGURE 4.17 Installing OS screen

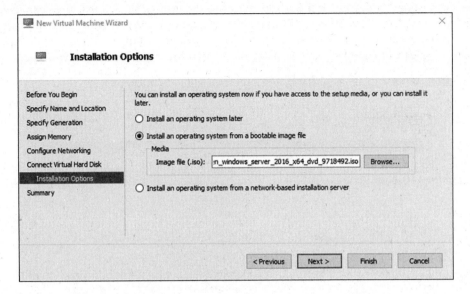

10. On the Completing The New Virtual Machine Wizard summary page, verify that all settings are correct (see Figure 4.18). You also have the option to start the virtual machine immediately after creation. Click Next to create the virtual machine.

FIGURE 4.18 Completing the New Virtual Machine Wizard screen

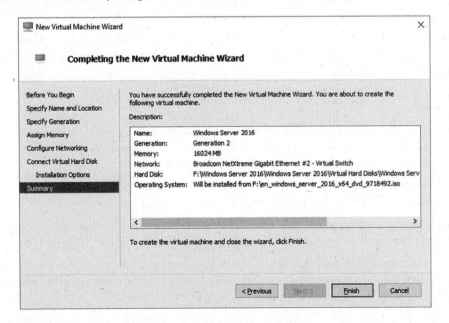

11. Repeat this process and create a few more virtual machines.

After completing Exercise 4.4, you will have a virtual machine available in Hyper-V Manager. Initially, the state of the virtual machine will be Off. Virtual machines can have the following states: Off, Starting, Running, Paused, and Saved. You can change the state of a virtual machine in the Virtual Machines pane by right-clicking the virtual machine's name, as shown in Figure 4.19, or by using the Virtual Machine Connection window.

FIGURE 4.19   Options available when right-clicking a virtual machine

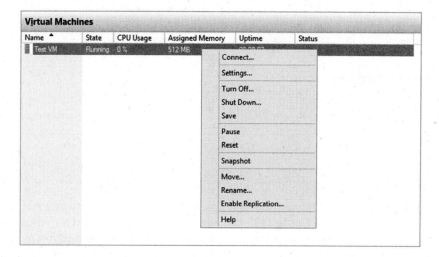

Here is a list of some of the state options (when the VM is running) available for a virtual machine:

Start   Turn on the virtual machine. This is similar to pressing the power button when the machine is turned off. This option is available when your virtual machine is Off or in Saved state.

Turn Off   Turn off the virtual machine. This is similar to pressing the power-off button on the computer. This option is available when your virtual machine is in Running, Saved, or Paused state.

Shut Down   This option shuts down your operating system. You need to have the Hyper-V Integration Components installed on the operating system; otherwise, Hyper-V will not be able to shut down the system.

Save   The virtual machine is saved to disk in its current state. This option is available when your virtual machine is in Running or Paused state.

Pause   Pause the current virtual machine, but do not save the state to disk. You can use this option to release processor utilization quickly from this virtual machine to the host system.

Reset   Reset the virtual machine. This is like pressing the reset button on your computer. You will lose the current state and any unsaved data in the virtual machine. This option is available when your virtual machine is in Running or Paused state.

Resume   When your virtual machine is paused, you can resume it and bring it online again.

Changing Configuration on an Existing Virtual Machine

To change the configuration settings on an existing virtual machine, you right-click your virtual machine's name in the Virtual Machines pane in Hyper-V Manager and choose Settings. You can change settings such as memory allocation and hard drive configuration. All items that you can configure are described in the following list:

Add Hardware Add devices to your virtual machine, namely, a SCSI controller, a network adapter, or a legacy network adapter. A legacy network adapter is required if you want to perform a network-based installation of an operating system.

Firmware This is the replacement of the virtual machine's BIOS. Because you can no longer enter the BIOS during startup, you need to configure it with this setting. You can turn Num Lock on or off and change the basic startup order of the devices.

Security This setting allows an administrator to set up the Secure Boot option along with enabling the Trusted Platform Module (TPM). TPM is a special-purpose microprocessor which provides cryptographic services. You can also set virtual machine shielding in the security section.

Memory Change the amount of random access memory (RAM) allocated to the virtual machine.

Processor Change the number of logical processors this virtual machine can use and define resource control to balance resources among virtual machines by using a relative weight.

SCSI Controller Configure all hard drives that are connected to the SCSI controller. You can add up to 63 hard drives to each SCSI controller, and you can have multiple SCSI controllers available.

Hard Drive Select a controller to attach to this device as well as to specify the media to use with your virtual hard disk. The available options are Virtual Hard Disk File (with additional buttons labeled New, Edit, Inspect, and Browse that are explained in the virtual hard disk section) and Physical Hard Disk. You can also remove the device here.

DVD Drive Select a controller to attach to this device and specify the media to use with your virtual CD/DVD drive. The available options are None, Image File (ISO Image), and Physical CD/DVD Drive Connected To The Host Computer. You also can remove the device here.

Network Adapter Specify the configuration of the network adapter or remove it. You can also configure the virtual network and MAC address for each adapter and enable virtual LAN identification. The network adapter section also allows you to control Bandwidth Management.

Bandwidth Management allows an administrator to specify how the network adapter will utilize network bandwidth. Administrators have the ability to set a minimum network bandwidth that a network adapter can use and a maximum bandwidth. This gives administrators greater control over how much bandwidth a virtual network adapter can use.

Name Edit the name of the virtual machine and provide some notes about it.

Integration Services   Define what integration services are available to your virtual machine. Options are Operating System Shutdown, Time Synchronization, Data Exchange, Heartbeat, and Backup (Volume Checkpoint).

Checkpoints   Define the default file location of your checkpoint files. Virtual machine checkpoints allow an administrator to restore a virtual machine to a previous state. After checkpoints are created, an administrator would use the "Recover action" to restore a virtual machine back to the time the checkpoint was created.

Smart Paging File Location   This area allows you to set up a paging file for your virtual machine. Windows Server 2016 has a Hyper-V feature called *Smart Paging*. If you have a virtual machine that has a smaller amount of memory than what it needs for startup memory, when the virtual machine gets restarted, Hyper-V then needs additional memory to restart the virtual machine. Smart Paging is used to bridge the memory gap between minimum memory and startup memory. This allows your virtual machines to restart properly.

Automatic Start   Define what this virtual machine will do when the physical computer starts. Options are Nothing, Automatically Start If The Service Was Running, and Always Start This Virtual Machine. You also can define a start delay here.

Automatic Stop   Define what this virtual machine will do when the physical computer shuts down. Options are Save State, Turn Off, and Shut Down.

Please be aware that only some settings can be changed when the virtual machine's state is Running. It is best practice to shut down the virtual machine before you modify any setting.

Deleting Virtual Machines

You can also delete virtual machines using Hyper-V Manager. This deletes all of the configuration files, as shown in Figure 4.20.

FIGURE 4.20   Delete Virtual Machine warning window

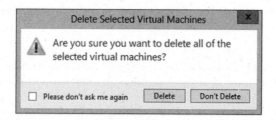

Make sure you manually delete any virtual disks that were part of the virtual machines to free up disk space. Virtual disks are *not* deleted when you delete a virtual machine.

Virtual Machine Connection

Hyper-V comes with Virtual Machine Connection to connect to virtual machines that run on a local or remote server. You can use it to log onto the virtual machine and use your computer's mouse and keyboard to interact with the virtual machine. You can open Virtual Machine Connection in Hyper-V Manager by double-clicking a virtual machine or by right-clicking a virtual machine and selecting Connect. If your virtual machine is turned off, you might see a window similar to the one in Figure 4.21.

FIGURE 4.21　Virtual Machine Connection window when the machine is turned off

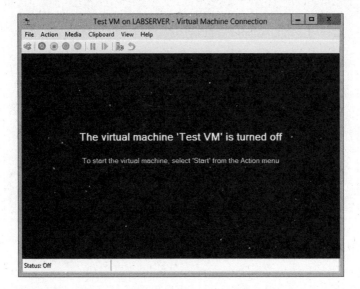

Virtual Machine Connection not only provides you with functionality similar to that of Hyper-V Manager, such as being able to change the state of a virtual machine, but it also provides you with additional features that are especially useful when you want to work with a virtual machine.

File Access Settings or Exit Virtual Machine Connection　Change the state of a virtual machine and create or revert a checkpoint. Additionally, you have the options to send Ctrl+Alt+Delete to your virtual machine and Insert Integration Services Setup Disk.

Context-Sensitive Buttons Provide Quick Access to Key Features　These buttons are available under the menu bar to provide you with fast access to the most important features, as you can see in Figure 4.22. It shows the connection of a running VM, but the VM has not had an operating system installed yet, so the figure shows the Windows Server 2016 Setup screen.

FIGURE 4.22   Virtual Machine Connection window showing a running Windows Server 2016 virtual machine

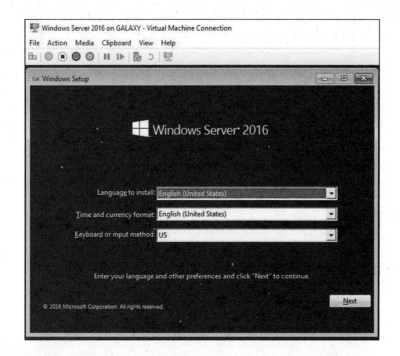

NIC Teaming

NIC Teaming, also known as load balancing and failover (LBFO), gives an administrator the ability to allow multiple network adapters on a system to be placed into a team. Independent hardware vendors (IHVs) have required NIC Teaming, but until Windows Server 2012, NIC Teaming was *not* part of the Windows Server operating system.

To be able to use NIC Teaming, the computer system must have at least one Ethernet adapter. If you want to provide fault protection, an administrator must have a minimum of two Ethernet adapters. One advantage of Windows Server 2016 is that an administrator can set up 32 network adapters in a NIC team.

NIC Teaming is a common practice when setting up virtualization. This is one way that you can have load balancing with Hyper-V.

NIC Teaming gives an administrator the ability to allow a virtual machine to use virtual network adapters in Hyper-V. The advantage of using NIC Teaming in Hyper-V is that the administrator can use NIC Teaming to connect to more than one Hyper-V switch. This allows Hyper-V still to have connectivity even if the network adapter under the Hyper-V switch gets disconnected.

An administrator can configure NIC Teaming in either Server Manager or PowerShell. NIC Teaming can be configured in different configuration models including Switch Independent or Switch Dependent. Switch Independent means that each NIC adapter is connected into a different switch. Switch Dependent means that all NIC adapters are connected into the same switch. If you use Switch Independent NIC Teaming then you must connect your NICs to different switches but both switches must be on the same subnet.

Remote Direct Memory Access

When most of us think of Hyper-V, we think of a group of virtual machines sharing access to a systems resource. With Windows Server 2016, Hyper-V includes Remote Direct Memory Access (RDMA).

RDMA allows one computer to directly access memory from the memory of another computer without the need of interfacing with either one's operating system. This gives systems the ability to have high throughput and low-latency networking. This is very useful when it comes to clustering systems (including Hyper-V).

Windows Server 2012 R2 RDMA services couldn't be bound to a Hyper-V Virtual Switch and because of this, Remote Direct Memory Access and Hyper-V had to be on the same computer as the network adapters. Because of this, there was a need for a higher number of physical network adapters that were required to be installed on the Hyper-V host.

Because of the improvements of RDMA on Windows Server 2016, administrators can use less network adapters while using RDMA.

Switch Embedded Teaming

Earlier we discussed NIC Teaming but we also have the ability to do Switch Embedded Teaming (SET). SET can be an alternative to using NIC Teaming in environments that include Hyper-V and the Software Defined Networking (SDN) stack in Windows Server 2016. SET is available in all versions of Windows Server 2016 that include Hyper-V and SDN stack.

SET does use some of the functionality of NIC Teaming into the Hyper-V Virtual Switch but SET allows an administrator to combine a group of physical adapters (minimum of 1 adapter and a maximum of 8 adapters) into software based virtual adapters.

By using virtual adapters, you get better performance and greater fault tolerance in the event of a network adapter going bad. For SET to be enabled, all of the physical network adapters must be installed on the same physical Hyper-V host.

One of the requirements of SET is that all network adapters that are members of the SET group be identical adapters. This means that they need to be the same adapter types from the same manufacturers.

One main difference between NIC Teaming and Set is that SET only supports Switch Independent mode setups. Again this means that the NIC adapters are connected to different switches.

Administrators need to create a SET team at the same time that they create the Hyper-V Virtual Switch. Administrators can do this by using the Windows PowerShell command New-VMSwitch.

At the time an administrator creates a Hyper-V Virtual Switch, the administrator needs to include the EnableEmbeddedTeaming parameter in their command syntax. The following example shows a Hyper-V switch named StormSwitch.

```
New-VMSwitch -Name StormSwitch -NetAdapterName "NIC 1","NIC 2"
-EnableEmbeddedTeaming $true
```

Administrators also have the ability to remove a SET team by using the following PowerShell command. This example removes a Virtual Switch named StormSwitch.

```
Remove-VMSwitch [StormSwitch]
```

Storage Quality of Service

Windows Server 2016 Hyper-V includes a feature called *Storage Quality of Service (QoS)*. Storage QoS allows a Hyper-V administrator to manage how virtual machines access storage throughput for virtual hard disks.

Storage QoS gives an administrator the ability to guarantee that the storage throughput of a single VHD cannot adversely affect the performance of another VHD on the same host. It does this by giving administrators the ability to specify the maximum and minimum I/O loads based on I/O operations per second (IOPS) for each virtual disk in your virtual machines.

To configure Storage QoS, you would set the maximum IOPS values (or limits) and set the minimum values (or reserves) on virtual hard disks for virtual machines.

 If you are using shared virtual hard disks, Storage QoS will not be available.

Installing Hyper-V Integration Components

Hyper-V *Integration Components*, also called *Integration Services*, are required to make your guest operating system hypervisor-aware. These components improve the performance of the guest operating system once they are installed. From an architectural perspective, virtual devices are redirected directly via the VMBus; thus, quicker access to resources and devices is provided.

If you do not install the Hyper-V Integration Components, the guest operating system uses emulation to communicate with the host's devices, which of course makes the guest operating system slower.

Exercise 4.5 shows you how to install Hyper-V Integration Components on one of your virtual machines running Windows Server 2016.

EXERCISE 4.5

Installing Hyper-V Integration Components

1. Open Hyper-V Manager.

2. In Hyper-V Manager, in the Virtual Machines pane, right-click the virtual machine on which you want to install Hyper-V Integration Components and click Start.

3. Right-click the virtual machine again and click Connect. Meanwhile, your virtual machine should already be booting.

4. If you need to log into the operating system of your virtual machine, you should do so.

5. Once the Windows Desktop appears, you need to select Insert Integration Services Setup Disk from the Actions menu of your Virtual Machine Connection window.

6. Once the Hyper-V Integration Components are installed, you are asked to perform a reboot.

After the reboot, Hyper-V Integration Components are installed on your operating system, and you will be able to use them.

Linux and FreeBSD Image Deployments

One of the features of Windows 2016 is the ability for Hyper-V to support Linux and FreeBSD virtual machines. Hyper-V now can support these new virtual machines because Hyper-V has the ability to emulate Linux and FreeBSD devices. Because Hyper-V now has the ability to emulate these two devices, no additional software needs to be installed on Hyper-V.

Unfortunately, because Hyper-V has to emulate these devices, you lose some of the Hyper-V functionality like high performance and full management of the virtual machines. So it's a tradeoff. You get to run Linux and FreeBSD type Hyper-V virtual machines but you lose some of the benefits of Hyper-V.

But wait; there is a way to get your Hyper-V functionality back. This issue can be resolved as long as you install Hyper-V on machines that can support Linux and FreeBSD operating systems. The drivers that are needed on Hyper-V are called Linux Integration Services (LIS) and FreeBSD Integrated Services (FIS). By putting these drivers on a device that can handle Linux and FreeBSD, you can then have Hyper-V with all of the features Microsoft offers.

To get these drivers and make Hyper-V work will all of its functionality, you must make sure that you install a newer release of Linux that includes LIS. To get the most out of FreeBSD you must get a version after 10.0. For FreeBSD versions that are older than 10.0, Microsoft offers ports that work with BIS drivers that need to be installed. Hyper-V will work with Linux and FreeBSD without the need of any additional drivers or equipment. By having drivers and equipment that supports Linux and FreeBSD, you just get all of the Hyper-V features that your organization may need.

In Exercise 4.6, I will show you how to install Linux into a virtual machine. I will then walk you through a full installation of a Linux Server. Before you complete this lab, you must download a copy of Linux. For this exercise, I downloaded a free copy of Linux Ubuntu Server as an image file (.iso). If you choose a different version of Linux, the installation screens during the exercise may be different.

EXERCISE 4.6

Creating a Linux Virtual Machine

1. Open Hyper-V Manager.

2. In the right hand window under Actions, click New ➢ Virtual Machine (see Figure 4.23).

FIGURE 4.23 New Virtual Machine

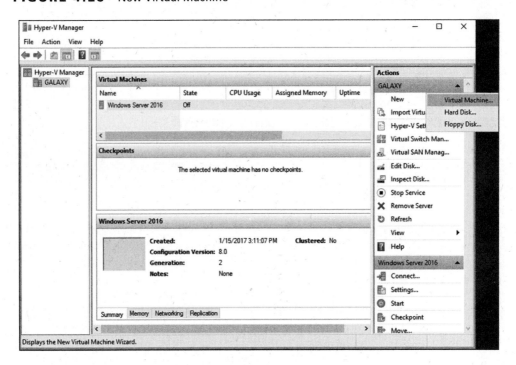

3. At the Before you Begin screen, just choose Next.

4. At the Specify Name and Location screen, enter in the name of the Linux virtual machine and the location you would like to store the virtual machine files. Then click Next.

5. At the Generation screen, choose Generation 2 and click Next.

6. At the Assign Memory screen, enter in the amount of memory you want to allocate to this virtual machine. I am using 12GB (12000MB). Click Next.

7. Choose which network connection you want to use and click Next.

8. At the Connect Virtual Hard Disk screen, choose Create a virtual hard disk. Set the location of where you want the files to reside and also how much space you want to use (I chose 127GB). Click Next.

9. At the Installation Options screen, choose Install an Operating system from a bootable image file and point to your Linux .iso download. Click Next.

10. At the Completing the New Virtual Machine Wizard screen, make sure all of the settings are correct and choose Finish.

11. After the virtual machine was created, click the virtual machine and on the right side under Linux, click Start.

12. When the Linux install starts, click your Language.

13. At the Ubuntu menu, choose Install Ubuntu Server.

14. Again, you will need to choose your language for the install.

15. Choose your country.

16. On the detect keyboard layout, choose No. Choose your keyboard (ours is US Normal). The installation will Continue.

17. Next you will choose a hostname. I am keeping the default of Ubuntu. Click Continue.

18. Enter your user account (full name) and click Continue.

19. Enter your username. First name is fine and click Continue.

20. Type in your password and click Continue. Do not choose to show your password in clear. You will then be asked to re-enter your password and click Continue.

21. When it asks you to encrypt your home directory, choose No.

22. The install will try to figure out your time zone. If it picks correctly, chose Yes. If it doesn't, choose No and enter your time zone.

23. The next screen will ask you about setting up a Partition disk. I am going to allow Linux to configure the disk (Guided) and I will allow it to use the entire drive with a Logical Volume Manager (LVM). So I am choosing Guided—use entire disk and set up LVM.

24. It will then ask about partition type. I am choosing SCSI3.

25. The next screen will verify your choices for partitioning. Choose Yes.

26. It will then verify your disk size and then if you want to continue. Choose the disk size and then choose Yes to continue.

27. The next screen will ask you if you use a Proxy server for Internet access. If you use a Proxy, put it in and if you don't, just click Continue.

28. You will be asked about updates for Linux. Choose how you want to do your updates. Since this is a test virtual machine, I am choosing No automatic updates.

29. At the Software selection screen, choose what software you want installed during this process. I chose DNS, Samba File Server, and standard system utilities. Click Continue.

30. At the GRUB boot screen, click Yes to install the GRUB boot loader. This is OK since we have no other operating system on this virtual machine.

31. Once the installation is complete, choose Continue. At this point, Linux will restart and ask you for your login and password. After you enter them, you will be at a Linux prompt.

32. Type shutdown at the prompt to shut down the virtual machine.

Now that we have installed Linux (or FreeBSD), the next step is to help improve the Hyper-V performance. As I stated earlier, this issue will be resolved as long as we install the drivers that are needed on Hyper-V called Linux Integration Services (LIS) and FreeBSD Integrated Services (FIS). By putting these drivers on a device that can handle Linux and FreeBSD, you can then have Hyper-V with all of the features Microsoft offers.

Depending on what version of Linux or FreeBSD that you installed, you will need to download some additional updates to get the best performance out of Hyper-V. The following Microsoft website has a list of links for the different versions of Linux and FreeBSD updates: https://technet.microsoft.com/windows-server-docs/compute/ hyper-v/supported-linux-and-freebsd-virtual-machines-for -hyper-v-on-windows?f=255&MSPPError=-2147217396.

In Exercise 4.7, I will show you how to install the additional updates needed for the Linux Ubuntu version (16.10) that I installed in Exercise 4.6.

EXERCISE 4.7

Updating Linux Ubuntu 16.10

1. Open Hyper-V Manager.

2. Start the Linux virtual machine by clicking on the Linux virtual machine and clicking Start on the right hand menu.

3. At the Ubuntu login, enter the login and password that you created in Exercise 4.6.

4. Since we are using Ubuntu 16.10, we need to install the latest virtual kernel to have up-to-date Hyper-V capabilities. To install the virtual HWE kernel, run the following command as root (or sudo):

    `sudo apt-get update`

5. You will be asked for your password. Enter your password.

6. Next type in the following command:

    `sudo apt-get install linux-image-virtual`

7. You will be asked to confirm your choice by typing Y and hit enter.

8. Type in the following command:

    `sudo apt-get install linux-tools-virtual linux-cloud-tools-virtual`

9. You will be asked to confirm your choice by typing Y and hit enter.

10. After everything is installed, you are ready to go. You can clear the screen by typing `Clear` and hit enter. To shut down the system, type `shutdown`.

Finally, if you want to setup the Linux or FreeBSD virtual machines to use the advantages of secure boot, you would need to run the following PowerShell command on the Hyper-V server:

```
Set-VMFirmware -VMName "VMname" -EnableSecureBoot Off
```

PowerShell Commands

One of the things that Microsoft has stated is that the exams are going to be more PowerShell intensive. So, I wanted to add a PowerShell section showing the different PowerShell commands that you can use for Hyper-V. This table has been taken directly from Microsoft's websites. Table 4.6 explains just some of the PowerShell commands that you can use with Hyper-V.

 Table 4.6 shows you just some of the PowerShell commands for Hyper-V. To see a more comprehensive list, please visit Microsoft's website at https://technet.microsoft.com/en-us/library/hh848559.aspx.

TABLE 4.6 Hyper-V PowerShell commands

Command	Explanation
Add-VMDvdDrive	Adds a DVD drive to a virtual machine.
Add-VMHardDiskDrive	Adds a hard disk drive to a virtual machine.
Add-VMMigrationNetwork	Adds a network for virtual machine migration on one or more virtual machine hosts.
Add-VMNetworkAdapter	Adds a virtual network adapter to a virtual machine.
Add-VMSwitch	Adds a virtual switch to an Ethernet resource pool.
Checkpoint-VM	Creates a checkpoint of a virtual machine.
Convert-VHD	Converts the format, version type, and block size of a virtual hard disk file.
Copy-VMFile	Copies a file to a virtual machine.
Debug-VM	Debugs a virtual machine.

TABLE 4.6 Hyper-V PowerShell commands *(continued)*

Command	Explanation
Disable-VMConsoleSupport	Disables keyboard, video, and mouse for virtual machines.
Disable-VMMigration	Disables migration on one or more virtual machine hosts.
Dismount-VHD	Dismounts a virtual hard disk.
Enable-VMConsoleSupport	Enables keyboard, video, and mouse for virtual machines.
Enable-VMMigration	Enables migration on one or more virtual machine hosts.
Enable-VMReplication	Enables replication of a virtual machine.
Enable-VMResourceMetering	Collects resource utilization data for a virtual machine or resource pool.
Export-VM	Exports a virtual machine to disk.
Export-VMSnapshot	Exports a virtual machine checkpoint to disk.
Get-VHD	Gets the virtual hard disk object associated with a virtual hard disk.
Get-VHDSet	Gets information about a VHD set.
Get-VHDSnapshot	Gets information about a checkpoint in a VHD set.
Get-VM	Gets the virtual machines from one or more Hyper-V hosts.
Get-VMDvdDrive	Gets the DVD drives attached to a virtual machine or checkpoint.
Get-VMHardDiskDrive	Gets the virtual hard disk drives attached to one or more virtual machines.
Get-VMMemory	Gets the memory of a virtual machine or checkpoint.
Get-VMNetworkAdapter	Gets the virtual network adapters of a virtual machine, checkpoint, or management operating system or of a virtual machine and management operating system.
Get-VMProcessor	Gets the processor of a virtual machine or checkpoint.

Command	Explanation
Get-VMReplication	Gets the replication settings for a virtual machine.
Get-VMSwitch	Gets virtual switches from one or more virtual Hyper-V hosts.
Merge-VHD	Merges virtual hard disks.
Mount-VHD	Mounts one or more virtual hard disks.
Move-VM	Moves a virtual machine to a new Hyper-V host.
New-VHD	Creates one or more new virtual hard disks.
New-VM	Creates a new virtual machine.
New-VMGroup	Creates a virtual machine group.
New-VMSwitch	Creates a new virtual switch on one or more virtual machine hosts.
Remove-VHDSnapshot	Removes a checkpoint from a VHD set file.
Remove-VM	Deletes a virtual machine.
Remove-VMHardDiskDrive	Deletes one or more virtual hard disks (VHDs) from a virtual machine (VM).
Remove-VMNetworkAdapter	Removes one or more virtual network adapters from a virtual machine.
Remove-VMReplication	Removes the replication relationship of a virtual machine.
Remove-VMSan	Removes a virtual storage area network (SAN) from a Hyper-V host.
Remove-VMSwitch	Deletes a virtual switch.
Rename-VM	Renames a virtual machine.
Rename-VMGroup	Renames virtual machine groups.
Resize-VHD	Resizes a virtual hard disk.
Restart-VM	Restarts a virtual machine.

TABLE 4.6 Hyper-V PowerShell commands *(continued)*

Command	Explanation
Save-VM	Saves a virtual machine.
Set-VHD	Sets properties associated with a virtual hard disk.
Set-VM	Configures a virtual machine.
Set-VMBios	Configures the BIOS of a Generation 1 virtual machine.
Set-VMMemory	Configures the memory of a virtual machine.
Set-VMNetworkAdapter	Configures features of the virtual network adapter in a virtual machine or the management operating system.
Set-VMProcessor	Configures one or more processors of a virtual machine. The Set-VMProcessor command also allows an administrator to configure nested virtualization. While the virtual machine is in the OFF state, run the Set-VMProcessor command on the physical Hyper-V host. This will enable nested virtualization for the virtual machine.
Set-VMReplicationServer	Configures a host as a Replica server.
Set-VMSan	Configures a virtual storage area network (SAN) on one or more Hyper-V hosts.
Set-VMSwitch	Configures a virtual switch.
Stop-VM	Shuts down, turns off, or saves a virtual machine.
Suspend-VM	Suspends, or pauses, a virtual machine.

Summary

Virtualization is quickly becoming a hot topic in information technology. The potential for consolidation is tremendous, and thus it will become more and more important.

After reading this chapter, you should have a good understanding of the Hyper-V architecture and what is required to install Hyper-V.

The section about installation and configuration covered various basic aspects of configuring the virtualization environment. You learned about the different types of virtual networks that are available, the options for installing the Hyper-V role, and the various types of virtual hard disks that you can use to optimize virtualization for your specific scenario.

You also learned how to configure virtual machines using the Hyper-V environment and how to create your own virtual datacenter on top of your Hyper-V machines. I showed you how to create and manage virtual machines, how to use Virtual Machine Connection to control a virtual machine remotely, and how to install Hyper-V Integration Components. You also learned how to export and import virtual machines as well as how to do checkpoints of your virtual machine.

If you have never worked with virtualization software before, the information in this chapter may have been completely new to you. You should now be well prepared to try Hyper-V in your own environment.

Video Resources

There are videos available for the following exercises:

> 4.1
>
> 4.4

You can access the videos at http://sybextestbanks.wiley.com on the Other Study Tools tab.

Exam Essentials

Understand Hyper-V's architecture.   When you have a good understanding of Hyper-V's architecture, especially when an operating system in a virtual machine is hypervisor-aware versus non-hypervisor-aware, you have a solid understanding of what is important from an architectural perspective.

You should know about the Hyper-V Integration Components and how they change the behavior of a virtual machine. Also know for which operating systems the integration components are available.

Know Hyper-V's requirements and how to install it.   Know the hardware and software requirements as well as how to install Hyper-V. Hyper-V requires an x64-based processor and Data Execution Protection (DEP). Hardware-assisted virtualization must be enabled—don't forget this! Also remember that you can install Hyper-V two ways: using Server Manager or using the command line in Server Core.

Understand virtual networks and virtual hard disks.   Virtual networks and hard disks are the two most tested topics. You definitely should know the types of virtual networks available (that is, external, internal only, and private virtual network) as well as all types of virtual hard disks (namely, dynamically expanding, fixed size, differential, and physical or pass-through). You should be able to apply the correct one when needed. Don't forget the Edit Virtual Hard Disk Wizard, which is also a good source for questions in the exam.

Know how to create and manage virtual machines.   You should be able to explain how to create a virtual machine, what options are available to install an operating system in a virtual machine, and how to install the Hyper-V Integration Components on a virtual machine. Don't forget about the virtual machine states and the virtual machine settings!

Understand how to back up and restore virtual machines.   Have a good understanding of the concept of exporting and importing virtual machines, how checkpoints work, and what lies behind a quick migration. Understand how you can export a virtual machine, what you should consider when moving it to a new host machine, and what happens after importing it to the import folder. The same applies to checkpoints: You need to know what options you have available and what each option will do. Especially recognize the difference between applying and reverting a checkpoint.

Review Questions

1. On which of the following x64 editions of Windows Server 2016 does Hyper-V run? (Choose all that apply.)

    A. Windows Server 2016 Web Edition

    B. Windows Server 2016 Standard Edition

    C. Windows Server 2016 Itanium Edition

    D. Windows Server 2016 Datacenter Edition

2. You want to build a test environment based on virtual machines on a single Windows Server 2016 machine, but you also want to make sure the virtual machines communicate with only each other. What type of virtual network do you need to configure?

    A. External

    B. Internal only

    C. Private virtual machine network

    D. Public virtual machine network

3. Andy wants to change the memory of a virtual machine that is currently powered up. What does he need to do?

    A. Shut down the virtual machine, use the virtual machine's settings to change the memory, and start it again.

    B. Use the virtual machine's settings to change the memory.

    C. Pause the virtual machine, use the virtual machine's settings to change the memory, and resume it.

    D. Save the virtual machine, use the virtual machine's settings to change the memory, and resume it.

4. You want to make sure the hard disk space for your virtual machines is occupied only when needed. What type of virtual hard disk would you recommend?

    A. Dynamically expanding disk

    B. Fixed-size disk

    C. Differencing disk

    D. Physical or pass-through disk

5. How do you add a physical disk to a virtual machine?

    A. Use the Virtual Hard Disk Wizard.

    B. Use the Edit Virtual Hard Disk Wizard.

    C. Use the virtual machine's settings.

    D. Use the New Virtual Machine Wizard.

6. Rich bought a new server with an Itanium IA-64 processor, 4 GB RAM, and a SAN that provides 1 TB hard disk space. After installing Windows Server 2016 for Itanium-based systems, he wants to install Hyper-V on this server. Can Hyper-V be installed on this system?

    A. Yes

    B. No

7. What are the minimum CPU requirements for running Hyper-V on a machine? (Choose all that apply.)

    A. An x64-based processor (Intel or AMD).

    B. Hardware Data Execution Protection (DEP) must be enabled.

    C. Hardware-assisted virtualization must be enabled.

    D. The processor must at least have a dual core.

8. What is the command to install Hyper-V on a Windows Server 2016 machine that was installed in Server Core?

    A. `start /w ocsetup Hyper-V`

    B. `start /w ocsetup microsoft-hyper-v`

    C. `start /w ocsetup Microsoft-Hyper-V`

    D. `start /w ocsetup hyper-v`

9. On what operating systems can you install the Hyper-V Manager MMC? (Choose all that apply.)

    A. Windows Server 2012 R2

    B. Windows Server 2003

    C. Windows 10

    D. Windows 7, Windows 8

10. What statement is correct for an external virtual network?

    A. The virtual machines can communicate with each other and with the host machine.

    B. The virtual machines can communicate with each other only.

    C. The virtual machines can communicate with each other, with the host machine, and with an external network.

    D. The virtual machines cannot communicate with each other.

Chapter

5

Configuring High Availability

THE FOLLOWING 70-740 EXAM OBJECTIVES ARE COVERED IN THIS CHAPTER:

✓ **Implement high availability and disaster recovery options in Hyper-V**

- This objective may include, but is not limited to: Implement Hyper-V Replica; implement Live Migration; implement Shared Nothing Live Migration; configure CredSSP or Kerberos authentication protocol for Live Migration; implement storage migration.

✓ **Implement Network Load Balancing (NLB)**

- This objective may include, but is not limited to: Install NLB nodes; configure NLB prerequisites; configure affinity; configure port rules; configure cluster operation mode; upgrade an NLB cluster.

✓ **Manage VM movement in clustered nodes**

- This objective may include but is not limited to: Perform a live migration; perform a quick migration; perform a storage migration; import, export, and copy VMs; configure VM network health protection; configure drain on shutdown.

It is now time to start talking about keeping our servers up and running as much as possible. So with this in mind, this chapter and Chapter 6, "Understanding Clustering," work hand in hand together.

In this chapter, I will start introducing you to some of the techniques and components of high availability. I will explain how to set up high availability using Network Load Balancing. I will talk about some of the reasons why you would choose to use Network Load Balancing over using a failover cluster and which applications or servers work better with Network Load Balancing. I will also show you how to use PowerShell for NLB.

I will continue the chapter by explaining how to keep your Hyper-V servers up and running by implementing high availability and disaster recovery options in Hyper-V. Finally, I will show you the PowerShell commands for Hyper-V high availability.

Components of High Availability

High availability is a buzzword that many application and hardware vendors like to throw around to get you to purchase their products. Many different options are available to achieve high availability, and there also seem to be a number of definitions and variations that help vendors sell their products as high-availability solutions.

When it comes right down to it, however, high availability simply means providing services with maximum uptime by avoiding unplanned downtime. Often, *disaster recovery (DR)* is also closely lumped into discussions of high availability, but DR encompasses the business and technical processes that are used to recover once a disaster has happened.

Defining a high availability plan usually starts with a *service level agreement (SLA)*. At its most basic, an SLA defines the services and metrics that must be met for the availability and performance of an application or service. Often, an SLA is created for an IT department or service provider to deliver a specific level of service. An example of this might be an SLA for a Microsoft Exchange server. The SLA for an Exchange server might have uptime metrics on how much time during the month the mailboxes need to be available to end users, or it might define performance metrics for the amount of time it takes for email messages to be delivered.

When determining what goes into an SLA, two other factors need to be considered. However, you will often see them discussed only in the context of disaster recovery, even though they are important for designing a highly available solution. These factors are the *recovery point objective (RPO)* and the *recovery time objective (RTO)*.

An RTO is the length of time an application can be unavailable before service must be restored to meet the SLA. For example, a single component failure would have an RTO of less than five minutes, and a full-site failure might have an RTO of three hours. An RPO is essentially the amount of data that must be restored in the event of a failure. For example, in a single server or component failure, the RPO would be 0, but in a site failure, the RPO might allow for up to 20 minutes of lost data.

SLAs, on the other hand, are usually expressed in percentages of the time the application is available. These percentages are also often referred to by the number of nines the percentage includes. So if someone told you that you need to make sure that the router has a rating of Five 9s, that would mean that the router could only be down for 5.26 minutes a year. Table 5.1 shows you some of the different nines rating and what each rating allows for downtime.

TABLE 5.1   Availability percentages

Availability Rating	Allowed Unplanned Downtime/Year
99 (two nines) percent	3.65 days
99.9 (three nines) percent	8.76 hours
99.99 (four nines) percent	52.56 minutes
99.999 (five nines) percent	5.26 minutes
99.9999 (six nines) percent	31.5 seconds
99.99999 (seven nines) percent	3.15 seconds

Two important factors that affect an SLA are the *mean time between failure (MTBF)* and the *mean time to recovery (MTTR)*. To be able to reduce the amount of unplanned downtime, the time between failures must be increased, and the time it takes to recover must be reduced. Modifying these two factors will be addressed in the next several sections of this chapter.

Achieving High Availability

Windows Server 2016 is the most secure and reliable Windows version to date. It also is the most stable, mature, and capable of any version of Windows. Although similar claims have been made for previous versions of Windows Server, you can rest assured that Windows Server 2016 is much better than previous versions for a variety of reasons.

An honest look at the feature set and real-world use should prove that this latest version of Windows provides the most suitable foundation for creating a highly available solution. However, more than just good software is needed to be able to offer high availability for applications.

High Availability Foundation

Just as a house needs a good foundation, a highly available Windows server needs a stable and reliable hardware platform on which to run. Although Windows Server 2016 will technically run on desktop-class hardware, high availability is more easily achieved with server-class hardware. What differentiates desktop-class from server-class hardware? *Server-class hardware* has more management and monitoring features built into it so that the health of the hardware is capable of being monitored and maintained.

Another large difference is that server-class hardware has redundancy options. Server-class hardware often has options to protect from drive failures, such as RAID controllers, and to protect against power supply failures, such as multiple power supplies. Enterprise-class servers have even more protection.

More needs to be done than just installing Windows Server 2016 to ensure that the applications remain running with the best availability possible. Just as a house needs maintenance and upkeep to keep the structure in proper repair, so too does a server. In the case of a highly available server, this means *patch management*.

Installing Patches

Microsoft releases monthly updates to fix security problems with its software, both for operating system fixes and for applications. To ensure that your highly available applications are immune to known vulnerabilities, these patches need to be applied in a timely manner during a scheduled maintenance window. Also, to address stability and performance issues, updates and service packs are released regularly for many applications, such as Microsoft SQL Server, Exchange Server, and SharePoint Portal Server. Many companies have a set schedule—daily, weekly, or monthly—to apply these patches and updates after they are tested and approved.

Desired Configuration Manager (DCM), an option in Microsoft System Center Configuration Manager, is a great tool for helping to validate that your cluster nodes are patched. It can leverage the SCCM client to collect installed patches and help reporting within the enterprise on compliancy with desired system states based on the software installed.

To continue with the house analogy, if you were planning to have the master bath remodeled, would you rather hire a college student on spring break looking to make some extra money to do the job or a seasoned artisan? Of course, you would want someone with experience and a proven record of accomplishment to remodel your master bath.

Likewise, with any work that needs to be done on your highly available applications, it's best to hire only decidedly qualified individuals. This is why obtaining a Microsoft certification is definitely an excellent start to becoming qualified to configure a highly available server properly. There is no substitute for real-life and hands-on experience. Working with highly available configurations in a lab and in production will help you know not only what configurations are available but also how the changes should be made.

For example, it may be possible to use Failover Clustering for a DNS server, but in practice DNS replication may be easier to support and require less expensive hardware in order to provide high availability. This is something you would know only if you had enough experience to make this decision.

As with your house, once you have a firm and stable foundation built by skilled artisans and a maintenance plan has been put into place, you need to ascertain what more is needed. If you can't achieve enough uptime with proper server configuration and mature operational processes, a cluster may be needed.

Windows Server 2016 provides two types of high availability: *Failover Clustering* and *Network Load Balancing (NLB)*. Failover clustering is used for applications and services such as SQL Server and Exchange Server. Network Load Balancing is used for network-based services such as web and FTP servers. The remaining sections of this chapter will cover NLB and Hyper-V high availability in depth. Chapter 6 "Understanding Clustering" will cover all of the clustering aspects.

Understanding Network Load Balancing

So the first thing we have to discuss is why an administrator would choose to use NLB. NLB allows an administrator to configure two or more servers as a single virtual cluster. NLB is designed for high availability and scalability of Internet server applications. So this means that Windows Server 2016 NLB is designed to work with web servers, FTP servers, firewalls, proxy servers, and virtual private networks (VPNs).

Administrators can use NLB for other mission-critical servers, but you can also use failover clusters on many of these servers. So after these two chapters are done, hopefully you will be able to choose the appropriate high availability server setup for your network and applications.

Network Load Balancing is a form of clustering where the nodes are highly available for a network-based service. This is typically a port listener configuration where a farm of, say, Microsoft Internet Information Services servers all listen on ports 80 and 443 for incoming web traffic from client endpoints. These nodes, while not fully clustered in a technical sense, are load balanced, where each node handles some of the distributed network traffic.

The NLB feature uses the TCP/IP networking protocol to distribute traffic. For web servers and other necessary servers, NLB can provide performance and consistency when two or more computers are combined into a single virtual cluster.

Hosts are servers that make up an NLB cluster. Each host runs their own individual copy of the server applications. The incoming client requests are distributed by NLB to each of the hosts in the cluster. The administrator can configure the load so that it is handled by each host. Hosts can be added to the cluster to increase the load. If NLB has all traffic directed to a specific single host, then it is called a default host.

With the use of NLB, all the computers in a cluster can use the same set of IP addresses while each host maintains its own exclusive IP address. When a host fails for load-balanced applications, the computers still in operation will receive the workload automatically. When the down computer is ready to rejoin the cluster, it comes back online and will regain its share of the workload. This allows the rest of the computers in the cluster to handle less traffic.

NLB is beneficial in that stateless applications (for example, web servers) are available with little downtime and it allows for scalability.

Scalability is the capability of a system, network, or process to handle a growing amount of work, or its potential to be enlarged in order to accommodate growth. Scalability, when used for NLB clusters, is the ability to add one or more systems to an existing cluster when the need arises. An administrator can do the following with NLB to support scalability:

- A single cluster can support up to 32 computers.
- Handle multiple server load requests from across multiple hosts in a cluster.
- For single TCP/IP services, balance load requests across the NLB cluster.
- As the workload grows, be able to add hosts to the NLB cluster without failure.
- When the workload declines, be able to remove hosts from the cluster.
- Allow higher performance and lower overhead by utilizing a pipelined implementation. Pipelining allows requests to be sent to the NLB cluster without waiting for a response.
- Use NLB Manager or Windows PowerShell cmdlets to manage and configure NLB clusters and hosts from a single computer.
- Determine port rules for each website. Port rules allow you to configure which ports are going to be enabled or disabled. Ports are doorways that applications can use to access resources. For example, DNS traffic uses port 53 for all DNS traffic. Here are some of the more common port numbers:
  - FTP uses ports 20/21.
  - Secure Shell uses port 22.
  - SMTP (mail) uses port 25.
  - DNS uses port 53.
  - HTTP uses port 80.
  - POPv3 uses port 110.
  - HTTPS uses port 443.

- Determine load-balancing behavior using port management rules for an IP port or group of ports.

- Use an optional, single-host rule that will direct all client requests to a single host. NLB will route client requests to a specific host that is running particular applications.

- Allow certain IP ports to block unwanted network access.

- When operating in multicast mode, enable Internet Group Management Protocol (IGMP) support on the cluster host. This will control switch port flooding (when all incoming network packets are sent to all ports on the switch).

- Use Windows PowerShell to start, stop, and control NLB actions remotely.

- Check NLB events using Windows Event Log. All NLB actions and cluster changes are logged in the Event Log.

NLB Requirements

The NLB cluster hardware requirements are as follows:

- All hosts must be on the same subnet.

- For each host, there is no limitation to the number of network adapters.

- All network adapters must be multicast or unicast within the cluster. Mixed environments, within a single cluster, are NOT supported.

- If using unicast mode, the network adapter used to handle client-to-cluster traffic must support media access control (MAC) address changing.

NLB cluster software requirements:

- The adapter on which NLB is enabled can only support TCP/IP.

- Must have a static IP address on the servers in the cluster.

Installing NLB Nodes

You can install NLB nodes like any other server build. Administrators can install NLB by using either Server Manager or the Windows PowerShell commands for NLB.

Administrators should first make sure that all NLB servers have the most current updates, provisioned with appropriate resources (typically with multiple network interface cards for capacity and responsiveness), and monitored for health and reliability. In Exercise 5.1, I will walk you through the installation of your NLB nodes.

EXERCISE 5.1

Installing NLB Nodes

1. Once you have multiple hosts ready for the installation of NLB, simply run the Add roles and features Wizard and select Network Load Balancing in the Features area of the wizard. If the Add Features dialog box appears, click the Add Features button.

2. Click the Next button. At the Confirmation screen, click the Install button. After the installation is finished, click the Close button and then close Server Manager.

3. This wizard places a new application in your Start menu under Windows Administrative Tools, the Network Load Balancing Manager (see Figure 5.1).

FIGURE 5.1   Network Load Balancing

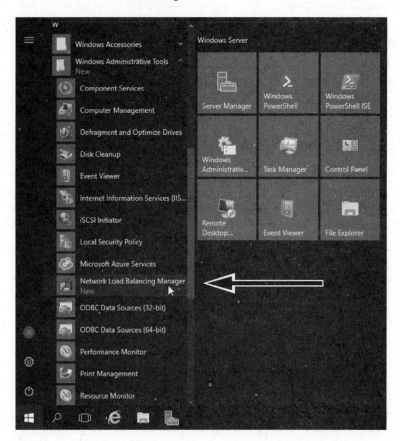

4. Right-click Network Load Balancing Clusters and select New Cluster (see Figure 5.2).

5. You are then presented with the New Cluster: Connect wizard where you can specify the name of one of your hosts. Type in the name of one of your cluster nodes and hit connect (see Figure 5.3). After the connection is made the TCP/IP address will be shown. Click Next.

FIGURE 5.2   New Cluster

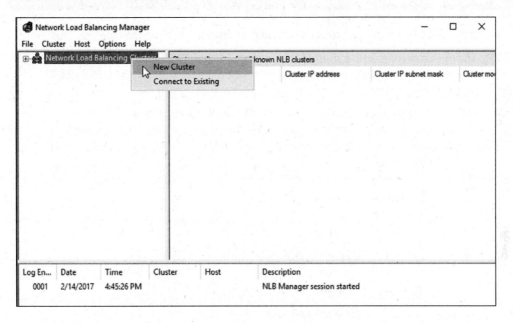

FIGURE 5.3   Host Name setup

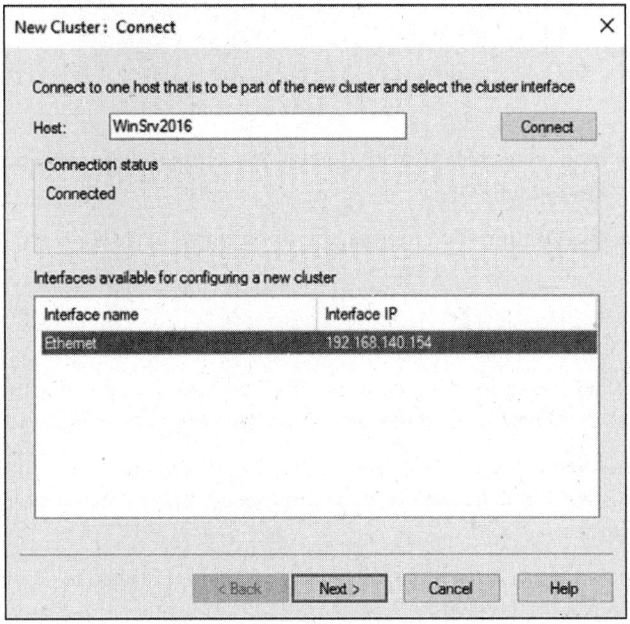

6. If you get a DHCP dialog box, you will want to disable DHCP on this adapter. Click OK.

7. The next screen reveals a prompt to add any additional IPs and assign a priority level. You can do all this later, so hit Next. If you get a dialog box about No Dedicated IP Addresses, click Yes.

8. The next wizard screen is where you specify the cluster IP address. This is the address that the endpoints or clients or users of the NLB cluster will contact. Typically the network team will assign a cluster IP address for this use (see Figure 5.4). Click OK. Then Click Next.

FIGURE 5.4   Add IP address

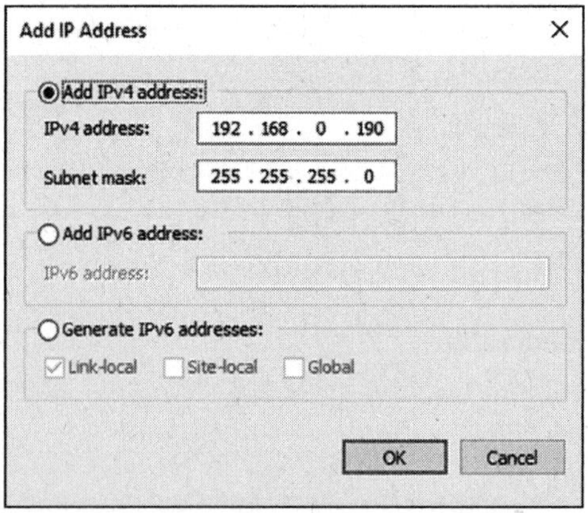

Add IP Address	×
⊙ Add IPv4 address:	
IPv4 address:	192 . 168 . 0 . 190
Subnet mask:	255 . 255 . 255 . 0
○ Add IPv6 address:	
IPv6 address:	
○ Generate IPv6 addresses:	
☑ Link-local ☐ Site-local ☐ Global	
	OK Cancel

9. On the next screen, you configure the Cluster operation mode (see Figure 5.5) and specify a Full internet name.

With regard to the cluster operation modes, the differences between them are as follows:

Unicast

The cluster adapters for all nodes are assigned the same MAC address.

The outgoing MAC address for each packet is modified based on priority to prevent upstream switches from discovering that all nodes have the same MAC address.

Communication between cluster nodes (other than heartbeat and other administrative NLB traffic) is not possible unless there are additional adapters (because all nodes have the same MAC address).

Depending on load, this configuration can cause switch flooding since all inbound packets are sent to all ports on the switch.

FIGURE 5.5   Cluster Parameters

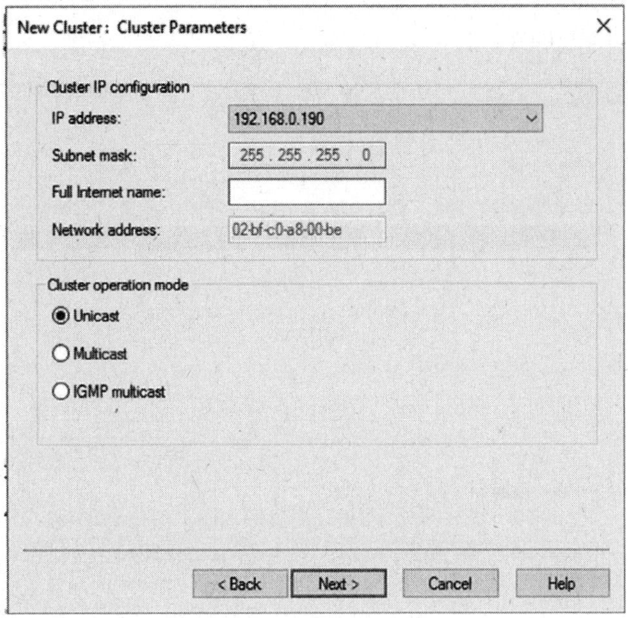

Multicast

The cluster adapters for all nodes are assigned their own MAC unicast address.

The cluster adapters for all nodes are assigned a multicast MAC address (derived from the IP of the cluster).

Non-NLB network traffic between cluster nodes works fine since they all have their own MAC address.

IGMP Multicast

This is much like multicast, but the MAC traffic goes only to the switch ports of the NLB cluster, preventing switch flooding.

10. After selecting the appropriate settings, the next page is where port rules (see Figure 5.6) are configured. By default, it is set up to be wide open. Most implementations will limit NLB ports to just the ports needed for the application. For example, a web server would need port 80 enabled. It is also in this area where you can configure filtering mode.

    The affinity sets a client's preference to a particular NLB host. It is not recommended to set affinity to None when UDP is an expected traffic type.

FIGURE 5.6   Port Rules

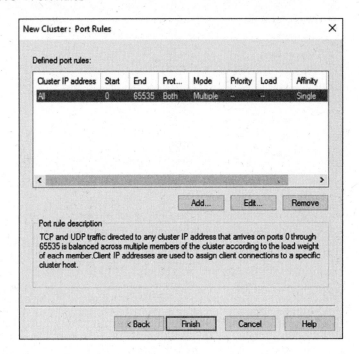

11. Click the Finish button. Close the NLB Manager.

If you decide that you want to install NLB using Windows PowerShell commands, you would open an elevated Windows PowerShell prompt and type in the following command:

```
Install-WindowsFeature NLB -IncludeManagementTools
```

Upgrading an NLB Cluster

Upgrading an NLB cluster is a fairly straightforward process. The first thing that you have to do is stop the NLB cluster. There are two ways to stop a NLB cluster: stop or drainstop.

If an administrator decides to use the stop command, the cluster stops immediately. This also means that any current connections to the NLB cluster are killed.

If an administrator decides to use the drainstop command, the cluster stops after answering all of the current NLB connections. So the current NLB connections are finished but no new connections to that node are accepted.

So to do your upgrade, you should execute a stop or drainstop on the NLB cluster node that you want to upgrade or remove existing connections to the application on the local host. After the NLB cluster is stopped you then perform an in-place upgrade in a rolling manner.

If you want to stop the entire cluster from running, while in the NLB manager (type NLBmgr in Run command), you would right click on the cluster, point to Control Hosts, and then choose Stop.

If you want to stop a single node in the cluster from running, while in the NLB manager (type NLBmgr in Run command), you would right click on the node, point to Control Hosts, and then choose Stop.

PowerShell Commands for an NLB Cluster

In Table 5.2, I will show you some of the different PowerShell commands that you can use to manage the NLB cluster.

TABLE 5.2   PowerShell Commands for NLB

PowerShell Command	Description
Add-NlbClusterNode	This command adds a new node to the NLB cluster.
Add-NlbClusterNodeDip	This command will add a dedicated IP address to a cluster.
Add-NlbClusterPortRule	This command adds a new port rule to a cluster.
Add-NlbClusterVip	This command adds a virtual IP address to a cluster.
Disable-NlbClusterPortRule	This command disables a port rule on a Network Load Balancing (NLB) cluster.
Enable-NlbClusterPortRule	This command enables a port rule on a cluster.
Get-NlbCluster	This command allows you to view information about the Network Load Balancing (NLB) cluster.
Get-NlbClusterDriverInfo	This command allows you to see information about the NLB drivers on a machine.
Get-NlbClusterNode	This command gets the information about the cluster object.
Get-NlbClusterPortRule	This command gets the port rule objects.
New-NlbCluster	This command creates a cluster on the specified interface.
New-NlbClusterIpv6Address	This command generates IPv6 addresses to create cluster virtual IP addresses.

TABLE 5.2   PowerShell Commands for NLB *(continued)*

PowerShell Command	Description
Remove-NlbCluster	This command deletes a cluster.
Remove-NlbClusterNode	This command removes a node from a cluster.
Remove-NlbClusterPortRule	This command deletes a port rule from a cluster.
Resume-NlbCluster	This command resumes all nodes in the cluster.
Set-NlbCluster	This command allows you to edit the configuration of an NLB cluster.
Set-NlbClusterNode	This command allows an administrator to edit the NLB cluster node settings.
Set-NlbClusterPortRule	This command allows you to edit the NLB port rules.
Start-NlbCluster	This command will start all of the nodes in a cluster.
Start-NlbClusterNode	This command will start one of the nodes in a cluster.
Stop-NlbCluster	This command stops all nodes in the cluster.
Stop-NlbClusterNode	This command will stop one of the nodes in a cluster.

Achieving High Availability with Hyper-V

One of the nice advantages of using Hyper-V is the ability to run an operating server within another server. Virtualization allows you to run multiple servers on top of a single Hyper-V server. But we need to make sure that these servers stay up and running.

That is where Hyper-V high availability comes into play. Having the ability to ensure that your Hyper-V servers are going to continue to run even if there is a hardware issue is an important step in guaranteeing the success of your network.

There are many ways that you can ensure that your virtual machines will continue to operate. One is to set up clustering (discussed in Chapter 6) and another is to set up Hyper-V high availability without clustering.

To set up reliability without clustering requires that your Hyper-V servers have replica copies that can automatically start up if the virtual machine errors out. This is referred to as Live Migration and replica servers.

Implementing a Hyper-V Replica

Hyper-V Replica is an important part of the Hyper-V role. It replicates the Hyper-V virtual machines from the primary site to the replica secondary sites simultaneously.

Once an administrator enables Hyper-V Replica for a particular virtual machine on the primary Hyper-V host server, the Hyper-V Replica will begin to create an exact copy of the virtual machine for the secondary site. After this replication, Hyper-V Replica creates a log file for the virtual machine VHDs. This log file is rerun in reverse order to the replica VHD. This is done using replication frequency. The log files and reverse order helps ensure that the latest changes are stored and copied asynchronously. If there is an issue with the replication frequency then the administrator will receive an alert.

On the virtual machine, an administrator can establish resynchronization settings. This can be setup to be done manually, automatically or automatically on an explicit schedule. To fix constant synchronization issues an administrator may choose to set up automatic resynchronization.

Hyper-V Replica will aid in a disaster recovery strategy by replicating virtual machines from one host to other while keeping workloads accessible. Hyper-V Replica can create a copy of a running virtual machine to a replica offline virtual machine.

Hyper-V Hosts

With replication over a WAN link the primary and secondary host servers can be located in the same physical location or at different geographical locations. Hyper-V hosts can be standalone, clustered or a combination of both. Hyper-V hosts are not dependent upon Active Directory and there is no need to be domain members.

Replication and Change Tracking

When an administrator enables Hyper-V Replica on a particular virtual machine an identical copy of the virtual machine is created on a secondary host server. Once this happens, the Hyper-V Replica will create a log file that will track changes made on a virtual machine VHD. The log file is rerun in reverse order to the replica VHD. This is based on the replication frequency settings. This ensures that the latest changes are created and replicated asynchronously. This can be done over HTTP or HTTPS.

Extended (Chained) Replication

Extended (chained) Replication allows an administrator to replicate a virtual machine from a primary host to a secondary host and then replicate the secondary host to a third host. It is not possible to replicate from the primary host directly to the second and third hosts.

Extended (Chained) Replication aids in disaster recovery in that an administrator can recover from both the primary and extended replica. Extended Replication will also aid if the primary and secondary locations go offline. It must be noted that the extended replica does not support application-consistent replication and it must use the same VHD that the secondary replica uses.

Setting the Affinity

NLB allows an administrator to configure three types of affinity settings to help response times between NLB clients. Each affinity setting determines a method of distributing NLB client requests. There are three different affinity settings: None, Single, and Class C. The New Cluster Wizard sets the default affinity to Single.

No Affinity (None)   When setting the affinity to No Affinity (None), NLB will not assign a NLB client with any specific member. When a request is sent to the NLB, the requests are balanced among all of the nodes. The No Affinity provides greater performance but there may be issues with clients establishing sessions. This happens because the request may be load balanced between NLB nodes and session information may not be present.

Single Affinity   Setting the cluster affinity to Single will send all traffic from a specific IP address to a single cluster node. This will keep a client on a specific node where the client should not have to authenticate again. Setting the affinity mode to Single would remove the authentication problem but would not distribute the load to other servers unless the initial server was down. Setting the affinity to Single allows a client's IP address to always connect to the same NLB node. This setting allows clients using an intranet to get the best performance.

Class C Affinity   When setting the affinity to Class C, NLB links clients with a specific member based on the Class C part of the client's IP address. This allows an administrator to setup NLB so that clients from the same Class C address range can access the same NLB member. This affinity is best for NLB clusters using the internet.

Failover

If the primary or the secondary (extended) host server locations goes offline an administrator can manually initiate failover. Failover is not automatic. There are several different types of manually initiating failover:

Test Failover   Use Test Failover to verify that the replica virtual machine can successfully start in the secondary site. It will create a copy test virtual machine during failover and does not affect standard replication. After the test failover, if the administrator selects Failover on the replica test virtual machine the test failover will be deleted.

Planned Failover   Use Planned Failover during scheduled downtime. The administrator will have to turn off the primary machine before performing a planned failover. Once the machine fails over the Hyper-V Replica will start replicating changes back to the primary server. The changes are tracked and sent to ensure that there is no data lost. Once the planned failover is complete, the reverse replication begins so that the primary virtual machine become the secondary and vice versa. This ensures that the hosts are synchronized.

Unplanned Failover   Use Unplanned Failover during unforeseen outages. Unplanned failover is started on the replica virtual machine. This should only be used if the primary machine goes offline. A check will confirm whether the primary machine is running. If the administrator has recovery history enabled then it is possible to recover to an earlier point in time. During failover an administrator should ensure that the recovery point is acceptable and then finish the failover to ensure that recovery points are combined.

Virtual Machine Advanced Features

One nice feature of virtual machines is the ability to setup advanced features. In the Advanced Features section (see Figure 5.7), there are multiple settings that you can configure.

FIGURE 5.7   VM Advanced Features

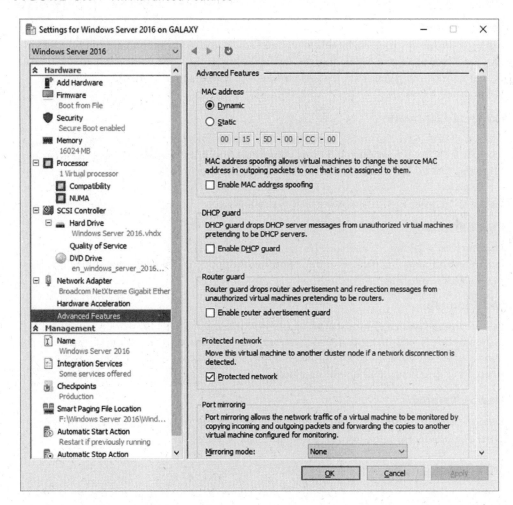

MAC Addressing

The first thing that you can configure in the Advanced Features section is setting a MAC address. The MAC address is a physical address that is associated to the NIC adapter. Administrators have the ability to set the MAC address to Dynamic (creates its own MAC addresses) or Static (this is where you can set a MAC address).

You also have the ability to do MAC spoofing. This is where a VM can change the source MAC address in outgoing packets to one that is not assigned to the NIC adapters.

DHCP Guard

DHCP guard drops DHCP server messages from unauthorized virtual machines pretending to be a DHCP server. So what does this mean to you? If a server tries to pretend to be a DHCP server, your virtual machine will drop any messages that are sent by that DHCP server.

Router Guard

Router guard drops router advertisement and redirection messages from unauthorized virtual machines pretending to be routers. It almost works the same way DHCP guard works. If an unauthorized router tries to send messages to a virtual machine, that VM will not accept those messages.

Protected Network

Administrators have the ability to set Network Health Detection at the virtual machine level for a Hyper-V host cluster. This is configured as a Protected Network. By setting the Protected Network check box, the virtual machine will be moved to another cluster node if a network disconnection is detected. If the health of a network connection is showing as disconnected, the VM will be automatically moved.

Port Mirroring

Port mirroring allows the network traffic of a virtual machine to be monitored by copying incoming and outgoing packets and forwarding the copies to another virtual machine configured for monitoring.

NIC Teaming

NIC Teaming gives an administrator the ability to allow multiple network adapters on a system to be placed into a team. You can establish NIC Teaming in the guest operating system to aggregate bandwidth and provide redundancy. This is useful if teaming is not configured in the management operating system.

Device Naming

Device naming causes the name of the network adapter to be propagated into supported guest operating systems.

VM Checkpoints

One thing that you may want to setup on your Hyper-V server is recovery points or checkpoints. A checkpoint is a snapshot in time from when an administrator can recover a virtual machine. It's like taking a picture of the virtual machine and using that picture to recover the VM. Administrators can create multiple checkpoints of a VM and then recover back to any of those checkpoints if there is an issue. Using a more recent recovery point will result in less data lost. Checkpoints can be accessed from up to 24 hours ago.

If you want to enable these checkpoints in time for Hyper-V, you just need to follow the steps below:

1. In Hyper-V Manager, right-click on the virtual machine and then click Settings.

2. Under the Management section, choose Checkpoints.

3. To enable checkpoints for a VM, check the box Enable checkpoints. If you want to disable checkpoints, just clear box.

4. Once finished, Click Apply. Once you are finished, click OK and close the Hyper-V Manager.

Software Load Balancing

Windows Server 2016 Hyper-V also allows an administrator to distribute virtual network traffic using Software Load Balancing (SLB). Software Load Balancing allows administrators to have multiple servers hosting the same virtual networking workload in a multitenant environment. This allows an administrator to setup high availability.

Using SLB allows an organization to load balance virtual machines on the same Hyper-V server. So let's take a look at how SLB works. SLB is possible because it sets up a virtual IP address (VIP) that is automatically mapped to the dynamic IP addresses (DIP) of the virtual machines. The DIP addresses are the IP addresses of the virtual machines that are part of the load balancing setup.

So when someone tries to access the resources in the load balancing setup, they access it by using the VIP address. The VIP request then gets sent to the DIP address of the virtual machines. So users use the single VIP address and that address gets sent to the load balancing virtual machines.

Understanding Live Migration

Before we can implement Live Migration, first you need to understand what Live Migration does for Hyper-V. Hyper-V live migration transfers a running virtual machine from one physical server to another. The real nice advantage of Live Migration is that during the move of the virtual machine, there is no impact on the network's users. The virtual machine will continue to operate even during the move. This is different from using Quick Migrations. Quick Migrations require a pause in the Hyper-V VM while it's being moved.

Live Migrations allow administrators to move virtual machines between servers. This is very useful when a Hyper-V server starts having issues. For example, if a Hyper-V machine is starting to have hardware issues, you can move the virtual machines from that Hyper-V server to another server that is running properly.

When setting up VM migrations, you have a few options. You can Live Migrate a VM, Quick Migrate a VM, or just move a VM. As stated before, Live Migration requires no interruption of the VM. Quick Migration requires that you first pause the VM, then save the VM, then move the VM and finally re-start the VM. Moving a virtual machine means that you are going to copy a VM from one Hyper-V server to another while the virtual machine is turned off.

So if you decide to setup and use Live Migrations, there are a few things that you should understand before setting it up. So let's take a look at some of the configuration settings that you can configure.

Configure CredSSP or Kerberos authentication

When choosing to setup Live Migrations, one of the settings that you get to manipulate is the type of authentication you can use. Choosing the authentication type is a feature listed under the Advanced Features of Live Migration. Administrators can choose two types of authentication (as shown in Figure 5.8): Kerberos or Credential Security Support Provider (CredSSP).

FIGURE 5.8 Live Migration Advanced Features

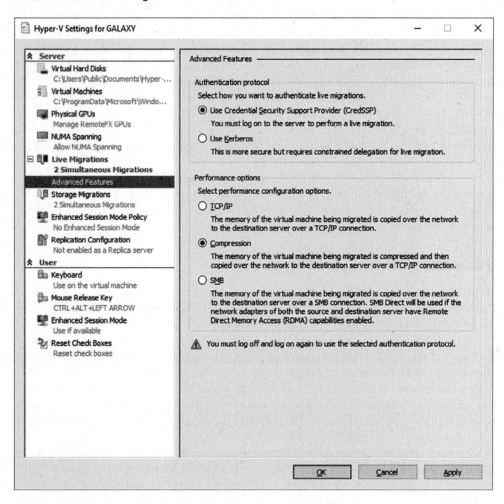

Authentication is choosing which protocol you will use to guarantee that live migration traffic between the source and destination servers are verified. Let's take a look at both options.

- Use Credential Security Support Provider (CredSSP)

  - This option allows an administrator to setup better security but requires constrained delegation for Live Migration. Administrators have the ability to sign in to the source server. Administrators can sign in to the source server by using a local console session, a Remote Desktop session, or a remote Windows PowerShell session.

- Use Kerberos

  - This option allows an administrator to avoid having to sign in to the server, but requires constrained delegation to be set up.

Another section that you setup in the Advanced Features of Live Migrations is the Performance options. This section allows you to choose how the network traffic for Live Migrations will be configured. There are three options that you can choose from:

TCP/IP   The memory of the virtual machine being migrated is copied over the network to the destination server over a TCP/IP connection.

Compression   The memory of the virtual machine being migrated is compressed and then copied over the network to the destination server over a TCP/IP connection.

SMB   The memory of the virtual machine is copied over the network to the destination server over a SMB (Server Message Block) connection. SMB Direct will be used if the network adapters of both the source and destination server have Remote Direct Memory Access (RDMA) capabilities enabled.

Implementing Live Migration

You will need the following to set up non-clustered hosts for live migration:

- A user account in the local Hyper-V Administrators group or the Administrators group on both the source and destination computers. Membership in the Domain Administrators group.

- The Hyper-V role in Windows Server 2016 or Windows Server 2012 R2 installed on both the source and destination servers. Live migration can be done if the virtual machine is at least version 5.

- The source and destination computers must belong to the same Active Directory domain or belong to trusted domains.

- The Hyper-V management tools installed on the server. Computer must be running Windows Server 2016 or Windows 10.

If an administrator wants to setup the source and destination of the live migration, they would need to use the following steps in Hyper-V Manager:

1. Open Hyper-V Manager. (click Start ➤ Administrative Tools ➤ Hyper-V Manager.)

2. In the navigation pane, click on one of the servers. Right click on the server ➤ Hyper-V Settings ➤ Live Migrations.

3. Click on the Live Migrations pane. Check the box Enable incoming and outgoing live migrations.

4. Under the section Simultaneous live migrations, specify the number of Simultaneous live migrations (the default is 2).

5. Under Incoming live migrations, administrators can choose to accept any network for live migrations or specify the IP address you want to use for live migration. If you want to use an IP address, click the Add button and type in the IP address information. Click OK once you're finished.

6. For Kerberos and performance options, expand Live Migrations (click the plus sign next to Live Migrations) and then select Advanced Features.

    ▪ Under Authentication protocol, select either Use CredSSP or Use Kerberos.

    ▪ Under Performance options, Select performance configuration options (either TCP/IP, Compression, or SMB).

7. Click OK.

8. If you have any other servers that you want to setup for Live Migrations, select the server and repeat the steps.

Implement Shared Nothing Live Migration

Administrators can now Live Migrate virtual machines even if the Hyper-V host is not part of a cluster. Before using Live Migrate without a Windows Cluster an administrator will need to configure the servers. Either choose Kerberos or Credential Security Support Provider (CredSSP) to authenticate the Live Migration.

To trigger a Shared Nothing Live Migration remotely, the administrator will need to enable Kerberos constrained delegation.

Constrained delegation is configured through Active Directory Users and Computers in the Delegation tab for each computer taking part in the Shared Nothing Live Migration.

Implementing Storage Migration

Hyper-V supports moving virtual machine storage without downtime by allowing the administrator to move storage while the virtual machine is running. This can be performed by using Hyper-V Manager or Windows PowerShell.

An administrator can add storage to a Hyper-V cluster or a stand-alone computer, and then move virtual machines to the new storage while the virtual machines continue to run.

An administrator can move virtual machine storage between physical storage devices to respond to a decrease in performance that results from bottlenecks.

Storage Migration Requirements

The following will be needed to utilize Hyper-V functionality of moving virtual machine storage:

▪ One or more installations of Windows Server 2016 with the Hyper-V role installed.

- A server that is capable of running Hyper-V.
- Virtual machines that are configured to use only virtual hard disks for storage.

Storage Migration allows administrators to move the virtual hard disks of a virtual machine while the virtual hard disks are still able to be used by the running virtual machine (see Figure 5.9). When an administrator moves a running virtual machine's virtual hard disks, Hyper-V performs the following steps:

1. Disk reads and writes utilize the source virtual hard disk.

2. When reads and writes occur on the source virtual hard disk, the disk data is copied to the new destination virtual hard disk.

3. Once the initial disk copy is complete, the disk writes are mirrored to both the source and destination virtual hard disks while outstanding disk changes are replicated.

4. After the source and destination virtual hard disks are entirely synchronized, the virtual machine changes over to using the destination virtual hard disk.

5. The source virtual hard disk is deleted.

FIGURE 5.9   Storage Migration Settings

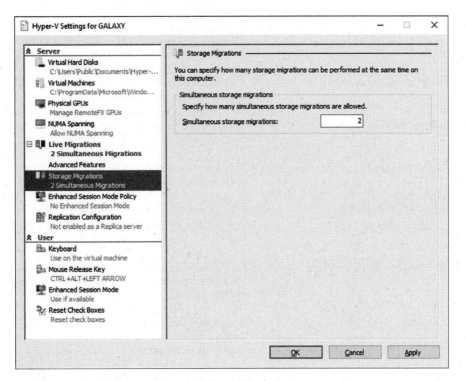

PowerShell Commands for Hyper-V High Availability

When configuring Hyper-V high availability, you may want to setup some of the components using PowerShell. Table 5.3 shows you some of the available PowerShell commands available for setting up Hyper-V high availability.

TABLE 5.3 PowerShell Commands for High Availability

PowerShell Command	Description
Complete-VMFailover	This command helps finish a virtual machine's failover process on the Replica server.
Disable-VMMigration	This command allows an administrator to disable virtual machine migration on a virtual machine host.
Enable-VMMigration	This command allows an administrator to enable virtual machine migration on a virtual machine host.
Enable-VMReplication	This command allows an administrator to enable replication of a virtual machine.
Get-VMMigrationNetwork	This command shows you the virtual machine networks used for migration.
Get-VMReplication	This command shows an administrator the replication settings for a virtual machine.
Get-VMReplicationAuthorizationEntry	This command shows an administrator the authorization entries of a Replica server.
Get-VMReplicationServer	This command shows an administrator the replication and authentication settings of a Replica server.
Import-VMInitialReplication	This command imports initial replication files for a Replica virtual machine when using external media.
Measure-VMReplication	This command shows an administrator the replication statistics and information associated with a virtual machine.
New-VMReplicationAuthorizationEntry	This command allows you to create an authorization entry to replicate data to a specified Replica server.

PowerShell Command	Description
Remove-VMMigrationNetwork	This command allows an administrator to remove a network from use in migration.
Remove-VMReplication	This command removes the replication from a specific virtual machine.
Reset-VMReplicationStatistics	This command allows an administrator to reset the replication statistics of a virtual machine.
Resume-VMReplication	This command allows an administrator to resume virtual machine replication after an error, a pause, a suspension, or a resynchronization is required.
Set-VMProcessor	This command allows an administrator to configure which processors are used for a virtual machine.
Set-VMReplication	This command allows an administrator to modify the replication settings of a virtual machine.
Set-VMReplicationServer	This command allows an admin to configure a host as a Replica server.
Start-VMInitialReplication	This command starts replication of a virtual machine.
Stop-VMReplication	This command stops replication of a virtual machine.
Suspend-VMReplication	This command suspends replication of a virtual machine.
Test-VMReplicationConnection	This command allows an administrator to test the connection of a primary server and a Replica server.

Summary

High availability is more than just clustering. It is achieved through improved hardware, software, and processes. This chapter focused on how to configure Failover Clustering and Network Load Balancing in order to achieve high availability and scalability.

High availability should be approached through proper hardware configuration, training, and operational discipline. Failover Clustering provides a highly available base for many applications, such as databases and mail servers.

Network load-balanced clusters are used to provide high availability and scalability for network-based applications, such as VPNs and web servers. Network load-balanced clusters can be configured with any edition of Windows Server 2016 except for the Windows Server 2016 Hyper-V Edition.

Windows Server 2016 Hyper-V can also have high availability set up on it without using clustering. Administrators have the ability to set up Live Migrations on Hyper-V virtual machines.

Live Migration allows you to move a virtual machine from one server to another without any impact on the users. This can be very useful if you have a Hyper-V server that is starting to show hardware issues. Administrators can move the virtual machine from the server with issues to a server without any issues.

Video Resources

There are no videos available for this chapter.

Exam Essentials

Know the hardware requirements for Network Load Balancing.   Network Load Balancing has distinct hardware requirements. Know the requirements for NLB.

Know the PowerShell commands for NLB.   Make sure you know the different PowerShell commands for Network Load Balancing. Understand which command is used to create, manage, and stop NLB clusters.

Understanding Live Migration.   Understand how Live Migrations work and why we use them. Understand that Live Migrations allow an administrator to move a virtual machine from one server to another without any impact on the users.

Know PowerShell for VM Replication   Make sure you know the different PowerShell commands for Virtual Machine Replication. Understand which commands are used to create, manage, and stop VM Replication.

Review Questions

1. You are the administrator for a mid-size organization. You have been asked by the owner to set up a NLB cluster. You want to use PowerShell to set up the cluster. What command would you use?

   A. `New-NlbCluster`

   B. `Create-NlbCluster`

   C. `Setup-NlbCluster`

   D. `Set-NlbCluster`

2. You are the administrator for your company. You have an application named AppA. AppA is distributed in a multitenant setup across multiple Hyper-V virtual machines. You need to ensure that the traffic is distributed evenly among the virtual machines that host AppA. What should you include in the environment?

   A. Router and Windows Server Network Load Balancing (NLB) nodes

   B. Router and Windows Server Software Load Balancing (SLB) nodes

   C. RAS Gateway and Windows Server Network Load Balancing (NLB) nodes

   D. RAS Gateway and Windows Server Software Load Balancing (SLB) nodes

3. What is the maximum number of nodes that can participate in a Windows Server 2016 NLB single cluster?

   A. 32

   B. 4

   C. 16

   D. 64

4. Which of the following actions should be performed against an NLB cluster node if maintenance needs to be performed while not terminating current connections?

   A. Evict

   B. Drainstop

   C. Pause

   D. Stop

5. Which of the following actions should be performed against an NLB cluster node if maintenance needs to be performed and all connections must be terminated immediately?

   A. Evict

   B. Drainstop

   C. Pause

   D. Stop

6. You are the network administrator for your organization and you want to stop virtual machine replication. What PowerShell command would you use?

   A. `Stop-VMReplication`

   B. `Terminate-VMReplication`

   C. `Kill-VMReplication`

   D. `Drainstop-VMReplication`

7. You are the network administrator for a company that has a Windows Server 2016 Hyper-V failover cluster. This cluster contains two nodes named ServerA and ServerB. On ServerA, you create a virtual machine named VirtualMachineA by using Hyper-V Manager. You need to configure VirtualMachineA to move to ServerB automatically if ServerA becomes unavailable. What should you do?

   A. In the Failover Cluster manager, run the configure Role actions.

   B. In the Hyper-V Manager, click VirtualMachineA and click Enable Replication.

   C. In the Hyper-V Manager, click ServerA and modify the hyper-V settings.

   D. Using Windows PowerShell, run the `Enable-VMReplication` cmdlet.

8. To configure an NLB cluster with unicast, what is the minimum number of network adapters required in each node?

   A. One

   B. Two

   C. Three

   D. Six

9. Users who are connecting to an NLB cluster have been complaining that after using the site for a few minutes they are prompted to log in using their username. What should you do to fix the problem and retain scalability?

   A. Create a port rule to allow only ports 80 and 443.

   B. Set the cluster affinity to None.

   C. Set the filtering mode to Single Host.

   D. Set the cluster affinity to Single.

10. Users who are connecting to an NLB cluster through the Internet are complaining that they keep connecting to different NLB nodes in different locations. You want to keep Internet users connecting to the same NLB members each time they connect. What should you do to fix the problem?

    A. Create a port rule to allow only ports 80 and 443.

    B. Set the cluster affinity to None.

    C. Set the cluster affinity to Class C.

    D. Set the cluster affinity to Single.

Chapter

6

Understanding Clustering

THE FOLLOWING 70-740 EXAM OBJECTIVES ARE COVERED IN THIS CHAPTER:

✓ **Implement failover clustering**

- This objective may include but is not limited to: Implement Workgroup, Single, and Multi-Domain clusters; configure quorum; configure cluster networking; restore single node or cluster configuration; configure cluster storage; implement Cluster-Aware Updating; implement Cluster Operating System Rolling Upgrade; configure and optimize clustered shared volumes (CSVs); configure clusters without network names; implement Scale-Out File Server (SoFS); determine different scenarios for the use of SoFS vs. clustered File Server; determine usage scenarios for implementing guest clustering; implement a Clustered Storage Spaces solution using Shared SAS storage enclosures; implement Storage Replica; implement Cloud Witness; implement VM resiliency; implement shared VHDX as a storage solution for guest clusters.

✓ **Implement Storage Spaces Direct**

- This objective may include but is not limited to: Determine scenario requirements for implementing Storage Spaces Direct; enable Storage Spaces direct using Windows PowerShell; implement a disaggregated Storage Spaces Direct scenario in a cluster; implement a hyper-converged Storage Spaces Direct scenario in a cluster.

✓ **Manage failover clustering**

- This objective may include but is not limited to: Configure role-specific settings, including continuously available shares; configure VM monitoring; configure failover and preference settings; implement stretch and site-aware failover clusters; enable and configure node fairness.

As I started to explain in the last chapter, keeping servers up and running 24/7 is one of the most important jobs that we have in IT. There are many ways that we can be sure that our servers are always going to be available. I started explaining one way in the last chapter with NLB and keeping servers highly available.

Well now I am going to keep that discussion going with clustering. There are different ways that you can set up clustering. You can set up high availability clusters and you can also set up failover clusters.

In this chapter, I will show you the different types of clusters that you can set up and configure. I will also explain some of the different situations in which each cluster would be best used. So let's continue our discussion on keeping our servers up and running 24/7 with clustering.

Achieving High Availability with Failover Clustering

Taking high availability to the next level for enterprise services often means creating a failover cluster. In a failover cluster, all of the clustered application or service resources are assigned to one node or server in the cluster. Commonly clustered applications are SQL Server and Exchange Server; commonly clustered services are File and Print. Since the differences between a clustered application and a clustered service are primarily related to the number of functions or features, for simplicity's sake I will refer to both as *clustered applications*. Another, more frequently, clustered resource is a Hyper-V virtual machine.

If there is a failure of the primary node or if the primary node is taken offline for maintenance, the clustered application is started on another cluster node. The client requests are then automatically redirected to the new cluster node to minimize the impact of the failure.

How does Failover Clustering improve availability? By increasing the number of server nodes available on which the application or virtual machine can run, you can move the application or virtual machine to a healthy server if there is a problem, if maintenance needs to be completed on the hardware or the operating system, or if patches need to be applied. The clustered application being moved will have to restart on the new server regardless of whether the move was intentional. This is why the term *highly available* is used instead of *fault tolerant*. Virtual machines, however, can be moved from one node to another node using a process known as *live migration*. Live migration is where one or more virtual machines are intentionally moved from one node to another with their current memory state intact through the cluster network with no indicators to the virtual machine consumer that the virtual machine has moved from one server to another. However, in the event of a cluster node or virtual machine failure, the virtual machine will still fail and will then be brought online again on another healthy cluster node.

Figure 6.1 shows an example of SQL Server running on the first node of a Windows Server 2016 failover cluster.

FIGURE 6.1 Using Failover Clustering to cluster SQL Server

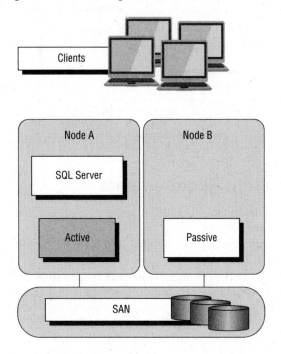

The clustered SQL Server in Figure 6.2 can be failed over to another node in the cluster and still service database requests. However, the database will be restarted.

Failover clustering is notorious for being complicated and expensive. Windows Server 2016 makes strides in removing both of these concerns. Troubleshooting and other advanced concepts are outside of the scope of the Microsoft MCSA exams and thus this book, so I will cover only the basic requirements and concepts needed to configure a failover cluster.

FIGURE 6.2 Failing the SQL Server service to another node

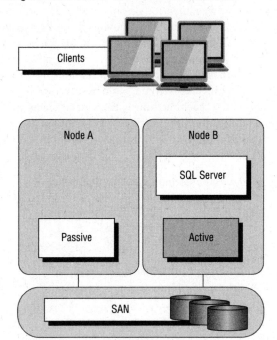

Failover Clustering Requirements

The Failover Clustering feature is available in the Datacenter, Standard, and Hyper-V editions of Windows Server 2016.

To be able to configure a failover cluster, you must have the required components. A single failover cluster can have up to 64 nodes when using Windows Server 2016, however, and the clustered service or application must support that number of nodes.

To create a failover cluster, an administrator must make sure that all the hardware involved meets the cluster requirements. To be supported by Microsoft, all hardware must be certified for Windows Server 2016, and the complete failover cluster solution must pass all tests in the Validate a Configuration Wizard. Although the exact hardware will depend on the clustered application, a few requirements are standard:

- Server components must be marked with the "Certified for Windows Server 2016" logo.

- Although not explicitly required, server hardware should match and contain the same or similar components.

- All of the Validate a Configuration Wizard tests must pass.

The requirements for Failover Clustering storage have changed from previous versions of Windows. For example, Parallel SCSI is no longer a supported storage technology for any of the clustered disks. There are, however, additional requirements that need to be met for the storage components:

- Disks available for the cluster must be Fibre Channel, iSCSI, or Serial Attached SCSI.
- Each cluster node must have a dedicated network interface card for iSCSI connectivity. The network interface card you use for iSCSI should not be used for network communication.
- Multipath software must be based on Microsoft's Multipath I/O (MPIO).
- Storage drivers must be based on `storport.sys`.
- Drivers and firmware for the storage controllers on each server node in the cluster should be identical.
- Storage components must be marked with the "Certified for Windows Server 2016" logo.

In addition, there are network requirements that must be met for Failover Clustering:

- Cluster nodes should be connected to multiple networks for communication redundancy.
- Network adapters should be the same make, use the same driver, and have the firmware version in each cluster node.
- Network components must be marked with the "Certified for Windows Server 2016" logo.

There are two types of network connections in a failover cluster. These should have adequate redundancy because total failure of either could cause loss of functionality of the cluster. The two types are as follows:

Public Network   This is the network through which clients are able to connect to the clustered service application.

Private Network   This is the network used by the nodes to communicate with each other.

To provide redundancy for these two network types, additional network adapters would need to be added to the node and configured to connect to the networks.

In previous versions of Windows Server, support was given only when the entire cluster configuration was tested and listed on the Hardware Compatibility List. The tested configuration listed the server and storage configuration down to the firmware and driver versions. This proved to be difficult and expensive from both a vendor and a consumer perspective to deploy supported Windows clusters.

When problems did arise and Microsoft support was needed, it caused undue troubleshooting complexity as well. With Windows Server 2016 Failover Clustering and simplified requirements, including the "Certified for Windows Server 2016" logo program and the Validate a Configuration Wizard, it all but eliminates the guesswork of getting the cluster components configured in a way that follows best practices and allows Microsoft support to assist you easily when needed.

Workgroup and Multi-Domain Clusters

One nice new advantage of using Windows Server 2016 is the ability to set up a cluster on systems not part of the same domain. In Window Server 2012 R2 and previous versions, clusters could only be created on machines that were part of the same domain. Windows

Server 2016 allows you to set up a cluster without using Active Directory dependencies. Administrators can create clusters in the following situations:

Single-Domain Cluster   All nodes in cluster are part of the same domain.

Multi-Domain Cluster   Nodes in cluster are part of a different domain.

Workgroup Cluster   Nodes are member servers and part of a workgroup.

Site-Aware, Stretched, or Geographically Dispersed Clusters (Geoclustering)

One nice advantage of Windows Server 2016 clustering is that you can set up site-aware failover clusters. Site-Aware clustering allows an administrator to expand clustered nodes to different geographic locations (sites). Site-aware failover clusters allow you to setup clusters in remote locations for failover, placement policies, Cross-Site Heartbeating, and for quorum placement.

One of the issues with previous clusters was the heartbeat. The cluster heartbeat is a signal sent between servers so that they know that the machines are up and running. Servers send heartbeats and if after 5 non-responsive heartbeats, the cluster would assume that the node was offline. So if you had nodes in remote locations, the heartbeats would not get the response they needed.

But now Windows Server 2016 includes Cross-Site Heartbeating and it allows you to setup delays so that remote nodes can answer the heartbeat within time. The following two PowerShell commands allow you to setup the delay necessary for Cross-Site Heartbeating.

```
(Get-Cluster).CrossSiteDelay = <value>
(Get-Cluster).CrossSiteThreshold = <value>
```

The first PowerShell command (CrossSiteDelay) is what is used to set the amount of time between each heartbeat sent to nodes. This value is done in milliseconds (default is 1000).

The second PowerShell command (CrossSiteThreshold) is the value that you set for the number of missed heartbeats (default is 20) before the node is considered offline.

One issue you may face is if you have multiple sites or if the cluster is geographically dispersed. If the failover cluster does not have a shared common disk, data replication between nodes might not pass the cluster validation "storage" tests.

Setting up a cluster in a site-aware, stretched, or geocluster (these terms can be used interchangeably) configuration is a common practice. As long as the cluster solution does not require external storage to fail over, it will not need to pass the storage test to function properly.

Cluster Quorum

When a group of people set out to accomplish a single task or goal, a method for settling disagreements and for making decisions is required. In the case of a cluster, the goal is to provide a highly available service in spite of failures. When a problem occurs and a cluster node loses communication with the other nodes because of a network error, the functioning nodes are supposed to try to bring the redundant service back online.

How, though, is it determined which node should bring the clustered service back online? If all the nodes are functional despite the network communications issue, each one might try. Just like a group of people with their own ideas, a method must be put in place to determine which idea, or node, to grant control of the cluster. Windows Server 2016 Failover Clustering, like other clustering technologies, requires that a quorum exist between the cluster nodes before a cluster becomes available.

A *quorum* is a consensus of the status of each of the nodes in the cluster. Quorum must be achieved in order for a clustered application to come online by obtaining a majority of the votes available (see Figure 6.3). Windows Server 2016 has four models, or methods, for determining the quorum and for adjusting the number and types of votes available:

- Node majority (no witness)
- Node majority with witness (disk or file share)
- Node and file share majority
- No majority (disk witness only)

FIGURE 6.3 Majority needed

When a majority of the nodes are communicating, the cluster is functional.

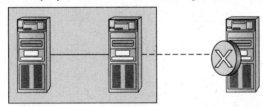

When a majority of the nodes are not communicating, the cluster stops.

Witness Configuration

Most administrators follow some basic rules. For example, when you configure a quorum, the voting components in the cluster should be an odd number. For example, if I set up a quorum for five elements and I lose one element, I continue to work. If I lose two elements, I continue to work. If I lose three elements, the cluster stops—as soon as it hits half plus 1, the cluster stops. This works well with an odd number.

If the cluster contains an even number of voting elements, an administrator should then configure a disk witness or a file share witness. The advantage of using a witness (disk or file share) is that the cluster will continue to run even if half of the cluster nodes simultaneously go down or are disconnected. The ability to configure a disk witness is possible only if the storage vendor supports read-write access from all sites to the replicated storage.

One of the advantages of Windows Server 2016 is the advanced quorum configuration option. This option allows you to assign or remove quorum votes on a per-node basis. Administrators now have the ability to remove votes from nodes in certain configurations. For example, if your organization uses a site-aware cluster, you may choose to remove votes from the nodes in the backup site. This way, those backup nodes would not affect your quorum calculations.

There are different ways that you can setup quorum witnesses. Here are some of the options that you can choose from:

Configure a Disk Witness   Choosing the quorum disk witness is normally setup if all nodes can see the disks. To set this disk witness up, the cluster must be able to see the Dedicated LUN. The LUN needs to store a copy of the cluster database and it's most useful for clusters that are using shared storage. The following list is just some of the requirements when setting up a Disk Witness:

- LUN needs to be at least 512 MB minimum.
- The disk must be dedicated to cluster use only.
- Must pass disk storage validation tests.
- The disk can't be used is a Cluster Shared Volume (CSV).
- You must use a single volume for Basic disks.
- No drive letter needed.
- Drive must be formatted using NTFS or ReFS.
- Can be used with hardware RAID.
- Should not be used with Antivirus or backup software

Configure a File Share Witness   Administrators should choose to use the File Share Witness when you need to think about multi-site disaster recovery and the file server must be using the SMB file share.

The following list is just some of the requirements when setting up a File Share Witness:

- Minimum of 5 MB of free space required.
- File share must be dedicated to the cluster and not used to store user data or application data.

Configure a Cloud Witness   Windows Server 2016 Cloud Witness is a new type of Failover Cluster quorum witness that leverages Microsoft Azure as the intercession point. The Cloud Witness gets a vote just like any other quorum witness. Administrators can setup the cloud witness as a quorum witness using the Configure a Cluster Quorum Wizard.

Dynamic Quorum Management

Another advantage in Windows Server 2016 is dynamic quorum management. *Dynamic quorum management* automatically manages the vote assignment to nodes. With this feature enabled, votes are automatically added or removed from nodes when that node either joins or leaves a cluster. In Windows Server 2016, dynamic quorum management is enabled by default.

Validating a Cluster Configuration

Configuring a failover cluster in Windows Server 2016 is much simpler than in previous versions of Windows Server. Before a cluster can be configured, the Validate A Configuration Wizard should be run to verify that the hardware is configured in a fashion that is supportable. Before you can run the Validate A Configuration Wizard, however, the Failover Clustering feature needs to be installed using Server Manager. The account that is used to create a cluster must have administrative rights on each of the cluster nodes and have permissions to create a cluster name object in Active Directory. Follow these steps:

1. Prepare the hardware and software perquisites.

2. Install the Failover Clustering feature on each server.

3. Log in with the appropriate user ID and run the Validate A Configuration Wizard.

4. Create a cluster.

5. Install and cluster applications and services.

To install the Failover Clustering feature on a cluster node, follow the steps outlined in Exercise 6.1.

EXERCISE 6.1

Installing the Failover Cluster Feature

1. Press the Windows key and select Administrative Tools ➢ Server Manager.

2. Select number 2, Add Roles And Features.

3. At the Select Installation Type screen, choose a role-based or feature-based installation.

4. At the Select Destination Server screen, choose Select A Server From The Server Pool and click Next.

5. At the Select Server Roles screen, click Next.

6. At the Select Features screen, click the Failover Clustering (see Figure 6.4) check box. If the Add Features dialog box appears, click the Add Features button. Click Next.

7. At the confirmation screen (see Figure 6.5), click the Install button.

FIGURE 6.4 Failover Cluster feature

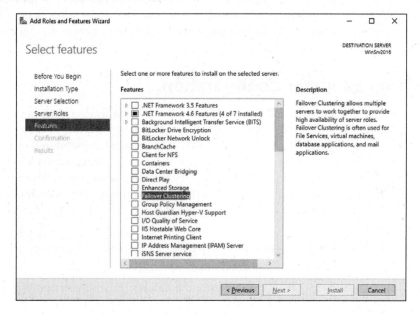

FIGURE 6.5 Confirmation screen

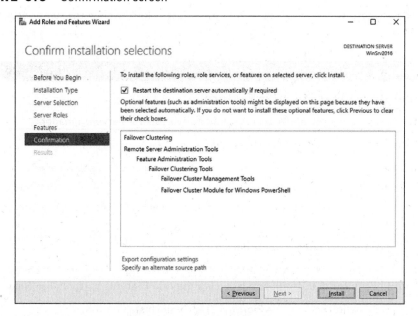

8. Once the installation is complete, click the Close button.

9. Close Server Manager.

Using the Validate A Configuration Wizard before creating a cluster is highly recommended. This wizard validates that the hardware configuration and the software configuration for the potential cluster nodes are in a supported configuration. Even if the configuration passes the tests, take care to review all warnings and informational messages so that they can be addressed or documented before the cluster is created.

Running the Validate A Configuration Wizard does the following:

- Conducts four types of tests (software and hardware inventory, network, storage, and system configuration)

- Confirms that the hardware and software settings are supportable by Microsoft support staff

You should run the Validate A Configuration Wizard before creating a cluster or after making any major hardware or software changes to the cluster. Doing this will help you identify any misconfigurations that could cause problems with the failover cluster.

Running the Validate a Configuration Wizard

The Validate A Configuration Wizard, shown in Figure 6.6, is simple and straightforward to use, as its "wizard" name would suggest. It should be run after the Failover Clustering feature has been installed on each of the cluster nodes, and it can be run as many times as required.

FIGURE 6.6   The Validate A Configuration Wizard

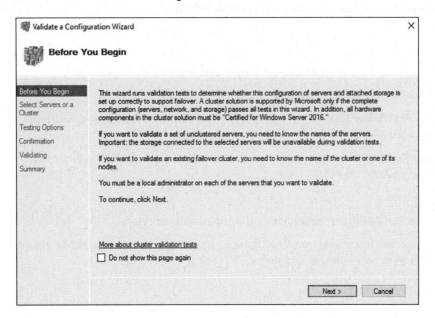

When you are troubleshooting cluster problems or have changed the configuration of the cluster hardware, it is a good idea to run the Validate A Configuration Wizard again to help pinpoint potential cluster configuration problems.

If you already have a cluster configured and want to run the Validate A Configuration Wizard, you can do so; however, you will not be able to run all of the storage tests without taking the clustered resources offline. You will be prompted either to skip the disruptive tests or to take the clustered resources offline so that the tests can complete.

Exercise 6.2 shows the exact steps to follow to run the Validate A Configuration Wizard successfully on clusters named NODEA and NODEB, which are not yet clustered.

I am using servers called NODEA and NODEB in the exercises. You need to replace these two nodes with your own two servers to complete these exercises.

EXERCISE 6.2

Running the Validate A Configuration Wizard

1. Press the Windows key and select Administrative Tools ➢ Failover Cluster Management.

2. In the Actions pane (right side of screen), click Validate Configuration.

3. At the Before You Begin screen, click Next.

4. Type **First Server Name** (this is your server's name) in the Enter Name field and click Add.

5. Type **Second Server Name** (this is the second server's name) in the Enter Name field and click Add.

6. Click Next.

7. Leave Run All Tests (Recommended) selected and click Next.

8. You will see tests being run (see Figure 6.7). Let the test complete, review the report in the Summary window, and then click Finish.

FIGURE 6.7   Cluster Tests

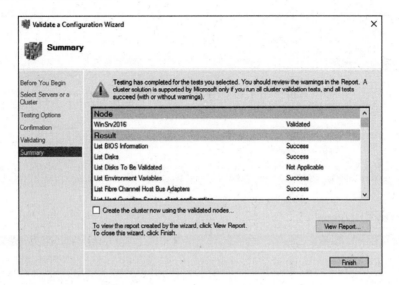

9.   Close the Failover Cluster Wizard.

Addressing Problems Reported by the Validate A Configuration Wizard

After the Validate A Configuration Wizard has been run, it will show the results, as shown in Figure 6.8. This report can also be viewed in detail later using a web browser. The report is named with the date and time the wizard was run, and it is stored in %windir%\cluster\ Reports.

How should errors listed in the report be addressed? Often, the errors reported by the Validate A Configuration Wizard are self-explanatory; however, sometimes additional help is required. The following three guidelines should help troubleshoot the errors:

- Read all of the errors because multiple errors may be related.

- Use the checklists available in the Windows Server help files to ensure that all the steps have been completed.

- Contact the hardware vendor for updated drivers, firmware, and guidance for using the hardware in a cluster.

FIGURE 6.8 Validate A Configuration Wizard results

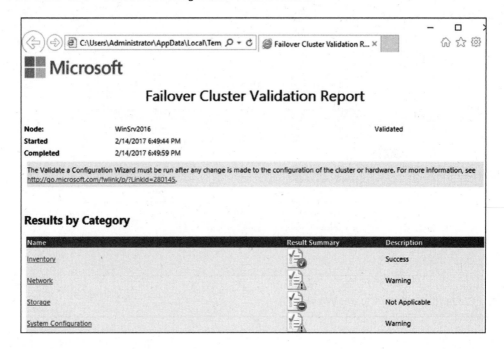

Creating a Cluster

After you have successfully validated a configuration and the cluster hardware is in a supportable state, you can create a cluster. The process for creating a cluster is straightforward and similar to the process of running the Validate A Configuration Wizard. To create a cluster with two servers, follow the instructions in Exercise 6.3.

EXERCISE 6.3

Creating a Cluster

1. Open the Failover Cluster Management MMC.

2. In the Management section of the center pane, select Create A Cluster.

3. Read the Before You Begin information and click Next.

4. In the Enter Server Name box, type **Your Server** and then click Add.

5. Again, in the Enter Server Name box, type **Your Second Server** and then click Add. Click Next.

6. At the Validation screen, choose No for this exercise and then click Next.

7. In the Access Point For Administering The Cluster section, enter **Cluster1** for the cluster name.

8. Type an IP address and then click Next. This IP address will be the IP address of the cluster.

9. In the Confirmation dialog box, verify the information and then click Next.

10. On the Summary page, click Finish.

Working with Cluster Nodes

Once a cluster is created, a couple of actions are available. First, you can add another node to the cluster by using the Add Node Wizard from the Failover Cluster Management Actions pane.

At this point, you also have the option to pause a node, which prevents resources from being failed over or moved to the node. You typically would pause a node when the node is involved in maintenance or troubleshooting. After a node is paused, it must be resumed to allow resources to be run on it again.

Another action available to perform on a node at this time is *evict*. Eviction is an irreversible process. Once you evict the node, it must be re-added to the cluster. You would evict a node when it is damaged beyond repair or is no longer needed in the cluster. If you evict a damaged node, you can repair or rebuild it and then add it back to the cluster using the Add Node Wizard.

Clustering Roles, Services, and Applications

Once the cluster is created, applications, services, and roles can be clustered. Windows Server 2016 includes a number of built-in roles and features that can be clustered (see Figure 6.9).

- DFS Namespace Server
- DHCP Server
- Distributed Transaction Coordinator (DTC)
- File Server
- Generic Application
- Generic Script
- Generic Service
- Hyper-V Replica Broker
- iSCSI Target Server
- iSNS Server
- Message Queuing
- Other Server
- Virtual Machine

FIGURE 6.9 High availability roles

In addition, other common services and applications can be clustered on Windows Server 2016 clusters:

- Enterprise database services, such as Microsoft SQL Server
- Enterprise messaging services, such as Microsoft Exchange Server

To cluster a role or feature such as Print Services, the first step is to install the role or feature on each node of the cluster. The next step is to use the Configure A Service Or Application Wizard in the Failover Cluster Management tool. Exercise 6.4 shows you how to cluster the Print Services role once an appropriate disk has been presented to the cluster. To complete this exercise, you must have a cluster created.

EXERCISE 6.4

Clustering the Print Services Role

1. Open the Failover Cluster Management MMC.

2. In the console tree, click the arrow next to the cluster name to expand the items underneath it.

3. Right-click Roles and choose Configure Role.

4. Click Next on the Before You Begin page.

5. Click Other Server on the Select Role screen and then click Next.

6. Type the name of the print server, such as **Print1**, and type in the IP address that will be used to access the print service, such as **80.0.0.34**. Then click Next.

7. At the Select Storage page, just click Next.

8. Click Next at the Confirmation page.

9. After the wizard runs and the Summary page appears, you can view a report of the tasks the wizard performed by clicking View Report.

10. Close the report and click Finish.

The built-in roles and features all are configured in a similar fashion. Other applications, such as Microsoft Exchange Server 2016, have specialized cluster configuration routines that are outside the scope of this exam. Applications that are not developed to be clustered can also be clustered using the Generic Application, Generic Script, or Generic Service option in the Configure A Service Or Application Wizard, as shown in Figure 6.10.

FIGURE 6.10   Configuring a generic application

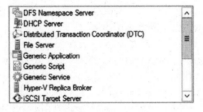

Clustered Application Settings

Windows Server 2016 has options that allow an administrator to fine-tune the failover process to meet the needs of their business. These options will be covered in the next few sections.

Failover occurs when a clustered application or service moves from one node to another. The process can be triggered automatically because of a failure or server maintenance or can be done manually by an administrator. The failover process works as follows:

1. The cluster service takes all of the resources in the role offline in the order set in the dependency hierarchy.

2. The cluster service transfers the role to the node that is listed next on the application's list of preferred host nodes.

3. The cluster service attempts to bring all of the role's resources online, starting at the bottom of the dependency hierarchy.

These steps can change depending on the use of Live Migration.

In a cluster that is hosting multiple applications, it may be important to set specific nodes to be primarily responsible for each clustered application. This can be helpful from a troubleshooting perspective since a specific node is targeted for the hosting service. To set a preferred node and an order of preference for failover, use the General tab in the Properties dialog box of the clustered application.

Also, the order of failover is set in this same dialog box by moving the order in which the nodes are listed. If NODEA should be the primary node and NODEC should be the server that the application fails to first, NODEA should be listed first and selected as the preferred owner. NODEC should be listed second, and the remaining cluster nodes should be listed after NODEC.

A number of failover settings can be configured for the clustered service. The failover settings control the number of times a clustered application can fail in a period of time before the cluster stops trying to restart it. Typically, if a clustered application fails a number of times, some sort of manual intervention will be required to return the application to a stable state.

Specifying the maximum number of failures will keep the application from trying to restart until it is manually brought back online after the problem has been resolved. This is beneficial because if the application continues to be brought online and then fails, it may show as being functional to the monitoring system, even though it continues to fail. After the application is put in a failed state, the monitoring system will not be able to contact the application and should report it as being offline.

Failback settings control whether and when a clustered application would fail back to the preferred cluster node once it becomes available. The default setting is Prevent Failback. If failback is allowed, two additional options are available, either to fail back immediately after the preferred node is available or to fail back within a specified time.

The time is specified in the 24-hour format. If you want to allow failback between 10 p.m. and 11 p.m., you would set the failback time to be between 22 and 23. Setting a failback time to off-hours is an excellent way to ensure that your clustered applications are running on the designated nodes and automatically scheduling the failover process for a time when it will impact the fewest users.

One tool that is valuable in determining how resources affect other resources is the dependency viewer. The *dependency viewer* visualizes the dependency hierarchy created for an application or service. Using this tool can help when troubleshooting why specific resources are causing failures and allow an administrator to visualize the current configuration better and adjust it to meet business needs. Exercise 6.5 will show you how to run the dependency viewer.

EXERCISE 6.5

Using the Dependency Viewer

1. Open the Failover Cluster Management MMC.

2. In the console tree, click the arrow to expand the cluster.

3. Click Roles.

4. Under the Roles section in the center of the screen, click one of the roles (such as Print1).

5. Right-click the role and under More Actions click Show Dependency Report.

6. Review the dependency report.

7. Close the Dependency Report and close the Failover Cluster Manager.

Exercise 6.5 generated a dependency report that shows how the print service is dependent on a network name and a clustered disk resource. The network name is then dependent on an IP address.

Resource Properties

Resources are physical or logical objects, such as a file share or IP address, which the failover cluster manages. They may be a service or application available to clients, or they may be part of the cluster. Resources include physical hardware devices such as disks and logical items such as network names. They are the smallest configurable unit in a cluster and can run on only a single node in a cluster at a time.

Like clustered applications, resources have a number of properties available for meeting business requirements for high availability. This section covers resource dependencies and policies.

Dependencies can be set on individual resources and control how resources are brought online and offline. Simply put, a dependent resource is brought online after the resources that it depends on, and it is taken offline before those resources. As shown in Figure 6.11, dependencies can be set on a specific resource, such as the Generic Application.

FIGURE 6.11 Resource dependencies

Resource policies are settings that control how resources respond when a failure occurs and how resources are monitored for failures. Figure 6.12 shows the Policies tab of a resource's Properties dialog box.

FIGURE 6.12 Resource policies

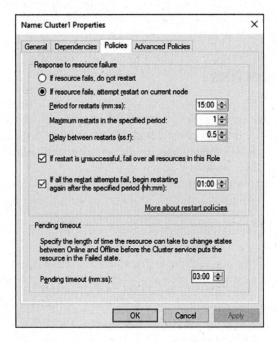

The Policies tab sets configuration options for how a resource should respond in the event of a failure. The options available are as follows:

If Resource Fails, Do Not Restart This option, as it would lead you to believe, leaves the failed resource offline.

If Resource Fails, Attempt Restart On Current Node With this option set, the resource tries to restart if it fails on the node on which it is currently running. There are two additional options if this is selected so that the number of restarts can be limited. They set the number of times the resource should restart on the current node in a specified length of time. For example, if you specify 5 for Maximum Restarts In The Specified Period and 10:00 (mm:ss) for Period For Restarts, the cluster service will try to restart the resource five times during that 10-minute period. After the fifth restart, the cluster service will no longer attempt to restart the service on the active node.

If Restart Is Unsuccessful, Fail Over All Resources In This Service Or Application If this option is selected, when the cluster service is no longer trying to restart the resource on the active node, it will fail the entire service or application to another cluster node. If you wanted to leave the application or service with a failed resource on the current node, you would clear this check box.

If All The Restart Attempts Fail, Begin Restarting Again After The Specified Period (hh:mm) If this option is selected, the cluster service will restart the resource at a specified interval if all previous attempts have failed.

Pending Timeout This option is used to set the amount of time in minutes and seconds that the cluster service should wait for this resource to respond to a change in states. If a resource takes longer than the cluster expects to change states, the cluster will mark it as having failed. If a resource consistently takes longer than this and the problem cannot be resolved, you may need to increase this value. Figure 6.13 shows the Advanced Policies tab.

FIGURE 6.13 Resource Advanced Policies

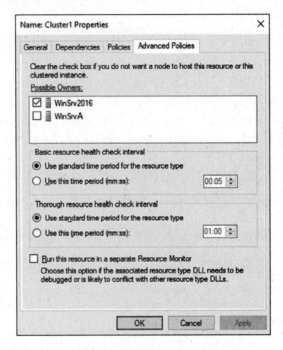

The options available on the Advanced Policies tab are as follows:

Possible Owners This option allows an administrator to remove specific cluster nodes from running this resource. Using this option is valuable when there are issues with a resource on a particular node and the administrator wants to keep the applications from failing over to that node until the problem can be repaired.

Basic Resource Health Check Interval This option allows an administrator to customize the health check interval for this resource.

Thorough Resource Health Check Interval This option allows an administrator to customize the thorough health check interval for this resource.

Run This Resource In A Separate Resource Monitor If the resource needs to be debugged by a support engineer or if the resource conflicts with other resources, this option may need to be used.

Windows Server 2016 Clustering Features

Many new features are included in the Windows Server 2016 release for clustering. It is a rich feature set of high availability with greatly improved flexibility based on the needs of IT organizations. The new features relate to quorum behavior, virtual machine hosting, Active Directory–detached clusters, and a new dashboard.

Windows PowerShell Cmdlets for Failover Clusters   As I have explained throughout this book, Windows PowerShell is a command-line shell and scripting tool. Windows Server 2016 clustering has new cmdlets that provide powerful ways to script cluster configuration and management tasks. Windows PowerShell cmdlets have now replaced the Cluster.exe command-line interface.

Cluster Shared Volumes   *Cluster Shared Volumes (CSV)* allows for the configuration of clustered virtual machines. CSV allows you to do the following:

- Reduce the number of LUNs (disks) required for your virtual machines.

- Make better use of disk space. Any VHD file on that LUN can use the free space on a CSV volume.

- More easily track the paths to VHD files and other files used by virtual machines.

- Use a few CSV volumes to create a configuration that supports many clustered virtual machines.

CSV volumes also are utilized for the Scale-Out File Server cluster role.

Management of Large-Scale Clusters   One advantage of Windows Server 2016 clusters is the ability for Server Manager to discover and manage the nodes in a cluster. By starting the Failover Cluster Manager from Server Manager, you can do remote multiserver management and role and feature installation. Administrators now have the ability to manage a cluster from one convenient location.

Management and Mobility of Clustered Virtual Machines   Microsoft, as well as the industry as a whole, is moving toward the cloud and virtualization. With that in mind, administrators can now configure settings such as prioritizing the starting or placement of virtual machines in the clustered workloads. This allows administrators to allocate resources efficiently to your cluster.

Cluster-Aware Updating   One issue that every administrator has dealt with is updating a system or application while it is running. For example, if you are running Microsoft Exchange and you want to do an Exchange update, when do you take the server offline to do the update? It always seems that someone is on the system 24 hours a day. Well, Windows Server 2016 clustering has a solution. *Cluster-Aware Updating (CAU)* is a new automated feature that allows system updates to be applied automatically while the cluster remains available during the entire update process.

Cluster Node Fairness   Virtual Machine Load Balancing feature is new to Windows Server 2016. This new load balancing feature helps optimize the nodes in a cluster. When an organization builds a virtual machine cluster, there will be times when that cluster needs to have maintenance and certain virtual machines will be taken offline. When this happens, an unbalanced cluster (this is when some nodes are hosting VMs more often than others) may occur. This is where the VM Load Balancing feature (Node Fairness) helps the cluster. The Balancer will re-distribute VMs from an over balance node to an under balanced node. To setup Node Fairness, you would use the PowerShell command `AutoBalancerLevel` (shown below). The value input is a 1, 2, or 3. 1 is equivalent to the Low setting (move the host when showing more than 80% loaded), 2 is equivalent to Medium (move the host when more than 70% loaded) and 3 is equivalent to High (average nodes and move the host when showing more than 5% above the average).

```
(Get-Cluster).AutoBalancerLevel = <value>
```

Cluster Operating System Rolling Upgrade   One of the problems that many IT people face is the issue with downtime while their servers get upgraded to a new operating system. Windows Server 2016 includes a new feature called Cluster Operating System Rolling Upgrade. This new feature allows an administrator to upgrade a Hyper-V or Scale-Out File Server cluster from Windows Server 2012 R2 to Windows Server 2016 without stopping the servers.

Scale-Out File Server for Application Data   By utilizing *Microsoft Storage Spaces*, you can create a highly available clustered file share that utilizes SMB 3.0 and CSV to provide scalable access to data.

Scale-Out File Servers are useful for storing the following application data:

- Hyper-V virtual machine storage
- SQL Server database files

Be aware that Scale-Out File Servers are not useful at all for typical file share data because they benefit only from applications that require a persistent connection to their storage.

Shared Virtual Hard Disks   In the previous versions of Windows, Failover Cluster nodes running as virtual machines had to use iSCSI or virtual HBAs to connect directly to SAN-based storage. With Windows Server 2016, you can set your Hyper-V virtualized cluster to use a shared VHDX virtual disk. Shared virtual hard disks can reside on the following:

- A Scale-Out File Server failover cluster
- Cluster CSV volumes

Shared virtual hard disks are extremely useful in providing highly available shared storage for the following virtualized workloads:

- SQL Server
- Virtual Machine Manager
- Exchange Server

Virtual Machine Drain on Shutdown   When needing to perform maintenance on a Hyper-V failover cluster, you may have a lot of virtual machines on one node of a cluster. Inevitably, you will need to restart a cluster node for updates or shut it down for maintenance.

In previous versions of Windows, virtual machines running on the cluster would save their state, and then the cluster node would shut down. Windows Server 2016 helps alleviate this issue by automatically draining the virtual machines running on a node before it shuts down or restarts. Windows does this by attempting to live migrate all virtual machines on the cluster node to other nodes in the cluster when at all possible.

This feature is turned on by default, but it can be disabled through PowerShell.

Active Directory–Detached Clusters   Previous versions of Windows Failover Clustering have depended on Active Directory to provide computer objects for the cluster name object as well as virtual computer objects. With Active Directory–detached failover clusters, communication to the cluster-form clients will use NTLM authentication rather than the normal Kerberos authentication. This is useful in maintaining high availability should a person accidently delete a virtual computer object in Active Directory that a clustered resource depends on for Kerberos authentication.

Dynamic Witness   Earlier in this chapter, I mentioned the Dynamic Quorum model and how votes were dynamically adjusted based on the number of nodes in a cluster. In Windows Server 2016, there is a new feature called *dynamic witness* that is enabled by default when the cluster is configured to use a dynamic quorum. Since it is preferred to have an odd number of votes at any one time in a cluster, the dynamic witness will turn on or off the witness vote in order to ensure that there are an odd number of votes in the cluster.

Tie Breaker For 50% Node Split   Like the *dynamic witness* feature just described, the Tie Breaker For 50% Node Split option in Windows Server 2016 dynamically adjusts cluster node votes in order to maintain an odd number of votes in a cluster where no witness is being used.

This is useful for a cluster in a site-aware, stretched, or geocluster configuration.

Global Update Manager Mode   Since the first release of Microsoft Cluster Services appearing in Windows NT 4.0 Enterprise, all nodes in a cluster maintain a local database that keeps a copy of the cluster configuration. The *Global Update Manager (GUM)* is a component of the cluster that ensures that before a change is marked as being committed for the entire cluster, all nodes have received and committed that change to their local cluster database. If one or more nodes do not report back or commit a change, the cluster node is kicked out of being a member of the cluster. Another issue that can occur is that for various clustered applications, such as SQL and Exchange, their performance can be negatively impacted by the time it takes the GUM to coordinate with all the nodes of a cluster for any changes. The GUM is only as fast as the slowest node in the cluster.

With Windows Server 2016, a new feature was added to Failover Clustering called *Global Update Manager mode*. This feature allows you to configure the GUM read-write modes manually in order to greatly speed up the processing of changes by the GUM and to improve the performance of certain clustered resources.

Turn Off IPsec Encryption For Inter-Node Cluster Communications   In network environments where IPsec is used, slow Group Policy updates and other issues can cause Active Directory Domain Services to be temporarily unavailable to cluster nodes. If the cluster intracluster communications protocol uses IPsec encryption, then these delays could cause cluster nodes to drop out of the cluster for failure to communicate in a timely manner with the rest of the nodes in the cluster. Windows Server 2016 now provides a way to turn off IPsec encryption on the cluster communication network.

Cluster Dashboard   Starting with Windows Server 2012, Failover Clustering supports up to 64 nodes in a cluster. Keeping track of the status and resources on all of these nodes can be an administrative headache! Managing more than one failover cluster and determining what a certain cluster hosts can be painful as well. Fortunately, in Windows Server 2016, the *Failover Cluster Manager*'s main dashboard has been updated to make it easier to see the status and health of multiple clusters.

Hyper-V Replica Broker   Starting with Windows Server 2012, Hyper-V supported continuous replication of virtual machines to another server or cluster for disaster recovery purposes. The Hyper-V Recovery Broker allows for virtual machines in a cluster to be replicated. The Hyper-V Recovery Broker keeps track of which cluster nodes virtual machines are residing on and ensures that replication is maintained.

Hyper-V Manager Integration into Failover Cluster Manager   In Windows Server 2016, the Hyper-V Management Console is integrated with Failover Cluster Manager for managing virtual machines that are clustered. Normal Hyper-V operations such as configuring, exporting, importing, configuring replication, stopping, starting, and live migrating virtual machines are supported directly through Failover Cluster Manager.

Virtual Machine Monitoring   Starting with Windows Server 2012, Failover Clustering supports Virtual Machine Monitoring for Windows Server virtual machines. Virtual Machine Monitoring monitors administrator-selected Windows services running within a virtual machine and will automatically restart a service if it should fail. If the service does not start for the configured number of restart attempts, the virtual machine will fail over to another node and then restart. For example, you can configure Failover Clustering to monitor the Print Spooler service on a Windows Server 2016 virtual machine. If the Print Spooler service goes offline, then the cluster will attempt to restart the Print Spooler service within the virtual machine. If the service still fails, Failover Clustering will move the virtual machine to another node.

PowerShell Commands for Clustering

Table 6.1 is just some of the PowerShell commands that you can use to configure and manage Windows Server 2016 clustering.

TABLE 6.1 Storage Spaces Direct PowerShell commands

PowerShell Command	Description
Add-ClusterDisk	This command allows an admin to add a new disk to a failover cluster. The disk's logical unit number (LUN) must be visible to all cluster nodes.
Add-ClusterFileServerRole	This command allows an admin to create a clustered file server.
Add-ClusterGenericApplicationRole	This command allows you to configure high availability for an application that is normally not designed for clustering.
Add-ClusterGroup	This command allows an admin to add a resource group to the failover cluster.
Add-ClusterNode	This command allows an admin to add a node to a failover cluster.
Add-ClusterResource	This command allows an admin to add a resource to a failover cluster.
Add-ClusterResourceDependency	This command allows an admin to add a resource dependency to a failover cluster.
Add-ClusterServerRole	This command allows you to add the cluster server role to a server.
Block-ClusterAccess	This command allows an admin to block the specified users from accessing a cluster.
Get-Cluster	This command shows you the information about a failover clusters.
Get-ClusterAccess	This command shows you the permissions for a failover clusters.
Get-ClusterNode	This command shows you the information about the servers in a failover clusters.
Get-ClusterQuorum	This command shows you the information about the cluster quorum in a clusters.
New-Cluster	This command allows you to create a new failover cluster.
Remove-Cluster	This command allows you to remove a failover cluster.

PowerShell Command	Description
Remove-ClusterAccess	This command allows an admin to remove a user's access from the cluster.
Remove-ClusterNode	This command allows you to remove a node from a failover cluster.
Start-Cluster	This command allows an admin to start the Cluster service on all nodes.
Stop-Cluster	This command allows an admin to stop the Cluster service on all nodes.
Stop-ClusterNode	This command stops the Cluster service on a node.
Test-Cluster	This command allows an admin to complete validation tests for a cluster.

Implementing Storage Spaces Direct

Storage Spaces Direct use local-attached drives on servers to create highly available storage at a minimal cost of traditional storage devices (SAN or NAS). Storage Spaces Direct use regular hard drives that are connected to a single node of the failover cluster and these disks can be used as storage for the cluster.

To understand how Storage Spaces Direct truly works, I think it is better to first understand some other technology terms for Windows Server 2016. When an IT administrator takes a bunch of physical disks and puts them together it is called a storage pool. Storage spaces are virtual disks that are created from storage pools. Storage Spaces Direct is the evolution of Storage Spaces.

Many of the same features are used in Windows Server 2016 like Failover Clustering, Cluster Shared Volumes, and SMB.

Storage Spaces Direct utilizes disks that are connected to one node of a failover cluster and allows for the creation of pools using those disks by Storage Spaces. Storage Spaces Direct streamlines deployment by using converged or hyper-converged architecture.

Virtual Disks (Spaces) that are constructed on a pool will have their mirrors or parity (redundant data) span across the disks using different nodes of the cluster. Since replicas of the data are spread across the disks this allows for access to data in the event a node fails or is going down for maintenance.

You can implement Storage Spaces Direct in virtual machines with each VM configured with two or more virtual disks connected to the VM's SCSI Controller. Each node of the cluster running inside the virtual machine can connect to its own disks but utilizing Storage Spaces Direct allows all the disks to be part of the Storage Pool that spans the entire cluster node.

For the redundant data (mirror or parity spaces) to be spread across the nodes, Storage Spaces Direct uses SMB3 as the protocol transport.

Networking Hardware   To communicate between servers, Storage Spaces Direct uses SMB3, including SMB Direct and SMB Multichannel over Ethernet. It is recommended to use 10+Gbe with Remote-Direct Memory Access (RDMA), or either internet Wide Area RDMA Protocol (iWARP) or RDMA over Converged Ethernet (RoCE).

Storage Hardware   The following list shows the Storage requirements.

- 2–16 servers with locally attached SATA, SAS, or NVMe drives
- Must have at least two solid-state drives on each server and at least four additional drives.
- SATA and SAS device should be following a Host-Bus Adapter (HBA) and SAS expander.

Failover Clustering   To connect the servers, Windows Server 2016 uses the built-in clustering feature.

Software Storage Bus   Storage Spaces Direct has a new feature called Software Storage Bus. This allows all the servers to see all of each other's local drives by spanning the cluster and establishing a software-defined storage structure.

Storage Bus Layer Cache   The Software Storage Bus joins the fastest drives available to the slower drives to provide server-side read/write caching that speeds up the IO and boosts data.

Storage Pool   The storage pool is the collection of drives that form the Storage Space. It is created automatically and all qualified drives are discovered and added. It is recommended that an administrator use the default settings on one pool per cluster.

Storage Spaces   Storage Spaces offers fault tolerance to virtual disk using mirroring, erasure coding, or both. It is thought of as distributed, software-defined RAID utilizing the drives in the pool. These virtual disks normally have resiliency when two synchronized drives or servers fail.

Resilient File System (ReFS)   The Resilient File System (ReFS) is Microsoft's latest file system which was designed to maximize data availability, efficiently scale to large data sets across varied workloads, and provide data integrity. It includes hastening the .vhdx file operations such as creating, expanding, checkpoint merging, and built-in checksums to distinguish and fix bit errors. ReFS also introduced real-time tiers, based on usage, which will rotate data between "hot" and "cold" storage tiers.

Cluster Shared Volumes   The Cluster Shared Volumes (CSV) file system unites all the ReFS volumes into a single namespace available through any server. This namespace allows every server and every volume to look and act like it's mounted locally.

Scale-Out File Server   In converged deployments only is this necessary. It offers remote file access by using the SMB3 protocol to clients over the network. This essentially turns Storage Spaces Direct into network-attached storage (NAS).

> To see step-by-step instructions on configuring and deploying Storage Spaces Direct, visit Microsoft's website at https://technet.microsoft.com/en-us/windows-server-docs/ storage/storage-spaces/hyper-converged-solution-using-storage- spaces-direct.

The Benefits of Storage Spaces Direct

The following are just some of the benefits of using Storage Spaces Direct with Windows Server 2016:

Simplicity   In less than 15 minutes, an administrator can go from a standard server running Windows Server 2016 to creating a Storage Spaces Direct cluster. It's just the click of a check box if an administrator is using System Center.

Unrivaled Performance   Storage Spaces Direct exceeds 150,000 mixed 4k random IOPS per server with reliability, low latency, built-in read/write cache, and support for NVMe drives that are mounted directly on the PCIe bus.

Fault Tolerance   Constantly available built-in resiliency that will handle drives, servers, or component failures. Chassis and rack fault tolerance can also be configured for larger deployments. There are no complex management steps needed when hardware fails. Simply change it out for another one and the software will fix itself.

Resource Efficiency   Greater resource efficiency with Erasure coding delivering up to 2.4x more storage. Using Local Reconstruction Codes and ReFS, real-time tiers extend to hard disk drives and mixed hot/cold workloads, all while reducing CPU usage to give the resources back to the virtual machines where they are needed.

Manageability   Keep excessively active virtual machines in order by using Storage QoS Controls with minimum and maximum per-VM IOPS limits. Continuously monitor and alert by using the built-in Health Service. There are also new APIs that make it easier to collect cluster-wide performance statistics and capacity metrics.

Scalability   For multiple petabytes of storage per cluster, an administrator can increase up to 16 servers and add over 400 drives. To scale out, an administrator will just need to add drives or add more servers. Storage Spaces Direct will automatically add the new drives and begin to utilize them.

Deployment Options

When using Windows Server 2016 and installing Storage Spaces Direct, there are two deployment options that you can choose from:

Converged

In converged, there are separate clusters for each storage and compute. The converged deployment option, also called "disaggregated," puts a Scale-Out File Server (SoFS) on top of Storage Spaces Direct to provide Network-Attached Storage (NAS) over SMB3 file shares. This allows for scaling computer/workloads separately from the storage cluster. This is essential when working with large-scale deployments such as Hyper-V Infrastructure as a Service (IaaS).

Hyper-Converged

In hyper-converged, there is only one cluster for storage and compute. The hyper-converged deployment option runs the Hyper-V virtual machines or SQL Server databases directly on the servers delivering the storage, storing of files all on the local volumes. This removes the need to configure file server access and permissions. It also reduces the hardware costs associated for small-to-medium business or remote office/branch office deployments.

Requirements to Set Up Storage Spaces Direct

To set up Storage Spaces Direct properly, you must make sure that all of your hardware components meet the minimum requirements. Table 6.2 was taken directly from Microsoft's website for the requirements needed and also what is actually recommended by Microsoft for proper configuration of Storage Spaces Direct.

TABLE 6.2   Storage Space Direct requirements

Component	Requirements
Servers	Minimum of 2 servers, maximum of 16 servers.
	All servers should be the same make and model.
CPU	Minimum of Intel Nehalem or later compatible processor.
Memory	4 GB of RAM per terabyte (TB) of cache drive capacity on each server, to store Storage Spaces Direct metadata.
	Any memory used by Windows Server, VMs, and other apps or workloads.
Networking	Minimum of 10 Gbps network interface for intra-cluster communication.
	Recommended: Two NICs for redundancy and performance
	Recommended: NICS that are remote-direct memory access (RDMA) capable, iWARP or RoCE

Component	Requirements
Drives	Use local-attached SATA, SAS, or NVMe drives.
	Every drive must be physically connected to only one server.
	All servers must have the same drive types.
	Recommended: All servers have the same drive configuration.
	SSDs must have power-loss protection, i.e., they are "enterprise-grade."
	Recommended: SSDs used for cache have high endurance, providing minimum of 5 drive-writes-per-day (DWPD).
	Add capacity drives in multiples of the number of NVMe or SSD cache devices.
	Not supported: Multi-path IO (MPIO) or physically connecting drives via multiple paths.
Host-bus adapter (HBA)	Simple pass-through SAS HBA for both SAS and SATA drives.
	SCSI Enclosure Services (SES) for SAS and SATA drives.
	Any direct-attached storage enclosures must present Unique ID.
	Not Supported: RAID HBA controllers or SAN (Fibre Channel, iSCSI, FCoE) devices.

Storage Spaces Direct Using Windows PowerShell

Table 6.3 includes just some of the PowerShell commands that you can use to configure and manage Storage Spaces Direct.

TABLE 6.3   Storage Spaces Direct PowerShell commands

PowerShell Command	Description
`Disable-NetQosFlowControl`	This command allows an administrator to turn off flow control.
`Enable-ClusterStorageSpacesDirect`	This command enables Storage Spaces Direct.
`Enable-NetAdapterQos`	This command allows an administrator to apply network QoS policies to the target adapters.
`Enable-NetAdapterRDMA`	This command allows an administrator to enable remote direct memory access (RDMA) on a network adapter.
`Enable-NetQosFlowControl`	This command allows an administrator to turn on flow control.

TABLE 6.3   Storage Spaces Direct PowerShell commands *(continued)*

PowerShell Command	Description
Enable-ClusterStorageSpacesDirect	This command allows an administrator to enable highly available storage spaces that use directly attached storage, Storage Spaces Direct (S2D), on a cluster.
Get-ClusterAvailableDisk	This command allows an administrator to view the information about the disks that can support Failover Clustering and are visible to all nodes. But these disks are not yet part of the set of clustered disks.
Get-ClusterParameter	This command allows you to view detailed information about an object in a failover cluster. Administrators use this command to manage private properties for a cluster object.
Get-NetAdapter	This command will retrieve a list of the network adapters.
Get-StoragePool	This command allows you to see a specific storage pool, or a set of StoragePool objects.
Get-StorageTier	This command allows you to see storage tiers on Windows Storage subsystems. Use this command to see Storage Spaces Direct default tier templates called Performance and Capacity.
New-Cluster	This command creates a new cluster.
New-NetQosPolicy	This command allows an admin to create a new network QoS policy.
New-NetQosTrafficClass	This command allows you to create a traffic class (like SMB).
New-Volume	This command creates a new volume.
Set-Item	This command allows an administrator to configure the trusted hosts to all hosts.
Test-Cluster	This command allows an administrator to test a set of servers for use as a Storage Spaces Direct cluster.
Update-StorageProviderCache	This command allows you to update the cache of the service for a particular provider and associated child objects.

Summary

High availability is more than just clustering. It is achieved through improved hardware, software, and processes. This chapter focused on how to configure Failover Clustering in order to achieve high availability and scalability.

High availability should be approached through proper hardware configuration, training, and operational discipline. Failover Clustering provides a highly available base for many applications, such as databases and mail servers.

Finally, I showed you the benefits of using Storage Spaces Direct and I also explained how to implement Storage Spaces Direct using PowerShell commands for Windows Server 2016.

Video Resources

There are videos available for the following exercises:

6.1

6.4

You can access the videos at http://sybextestbanks.wiley.com on the Other Study Tools tab.

Exam Essentials

Know how to modify failover and failback settings. These settings are set on the clustered service or application, but they can be modified by settings on the resources.

Know the hardware requirements for Failover Clustering. Failover Clustering has very distinct hardware requirements. Know all of the components needed to set up and manage a cluster.

Understand Storage Spaces Direct. Storage Spaces Direct uses local-attached drives on servers to create highly available storage at a minimal cost of traditional storage devices (SAN or NAS).

Know the PowerShell commands for clustering. Make sure that you know how to install and manage clustering using Windows PowerShell.

Know Storage Spaces Direct PowerShell commands. Make sure that you know how to install and manage Storage Spaces Direct using Windows PowerShell.

Review Questions

1. You have a Windows Server 2016 Hyper-V failover cluster that contains two nodes named NodeA and NodeB. On NodeA, you create a virtual machine named VM01 by using Hyper-V Manager. You need to configure VM01 to move to NodeB automatically if NodeA becomes unavailable. What should you do?

   A. In the Failover Cluster manager, configure Role actions.

   B. In the Hyper-V Manager, click VM01 and click Enable Replication.

   C. In the Hyper-V Manager, click NodeA and modify the Hyper-V settings.

   D. Run the PowerShell command Enable-VMReplication.

2. You are the administrator for a large organization that wants to implement site-aware clustering. What two PowerShell commands would you use to help you set up site-aware clustering?

   A. (Get-Cluster).CrossSiteDelay = <value>

   B. (Get-Cluster).CrossSiteThreshold = <value>

   C. (Add-Cluster).CrossSiteDelay = <value>

   D. (Add-Cluster).CrossSiteThreshold = <value>

3. What is the maximum number of nodes that can participate in a Windows Server 2016 failover cluster?

   A. 2

   B. 4

   C. 16

   D. 64

4. As an administrator, you need to create highly available storage spaces that connect to directly attached storage on the hosts. Which PowerShell command would you use?

   A. Enable-ClusterStorageSpacesDirect

   B. Set-StoragePool

   C. Add-ClusterDisk

   D. Update-ClusterVirtualMachineConfiguration

5. If you have a running cluster and need to run the Validate a Configuration Wizard again, which of the following tests may require cluster resources to be taken offline?

   A. Network tests

   B. Storage tests

   C. System configuration tests

   D. Inventory tests

6. Which of the following applications would be better suited on a failover cluster instead of a network load-balanced cluster? (Choose all that apply.)

   A. SQL Server

   B. Website

   C. Exchange Mailbox Server

   D. VPN services

7. You are the administrator for a mid-size company who wants to set up and test a cluster. What PowerShell command would you use to run a validation test on a cluster?

   A. Test-Cluster

   B. Validate-Cluster

   C. Set-Cluster

   D. Add-Cluster

8. What is the mechanism that is used in clustering to see if a node is online or if the node is not responding?

   A. Testbeat

   B. Heartbeat

   C. Testnode

   D. Pulse

9. In a four-node cluster set to a Node And File Share Majority quorum model, how many votes can be lost before a quorum is lost?

   A. One

   B. Two

   C. Three

   D. Four

10. In a three-node cluster set to a Node Majority quorum model, how many cluster nodes can be offline before the quorum is lost?

   A. Zero

   B. One

   C. Two

   D. Three

Chapter

7

Configuring Windows Containers

THE FOLLOWING 70-740 EXAM OBJECTIVES ARE COVERED IN THIS CHAPTER:

✓ **Deploy Windows containers**

- This objective may include but is not limited to: Determine installation requirements and appropriate scenarios for Windows Containers; install and configure Windows Server container host in physical or virtualized environments; install and configure Windows Server container host to Windows Server Core or Nano Server in a physical or virtualized environment; install Docker on Windows Server and Nano Server; configure Docker daemon start-up options; configure Windows PowerShell for use with containers; install a base operating system; tag an image; uninstall an operating system image; create Windows Server containers; create Hyper-V containers.

✓ **Manage Windows containers**

- This objective may include but is not limited to: Manage Windows or Linux containers using the Docker daemon; manage Windows or Linux containers using Windows PowerShell; manage container networking; manage container data volumes; manage Resource Control; create new container images using Dockerfile; manage container images using DockerHub repository for public and private scenarios; manage container images using Microsoft Azure.

When reading a Windows Server book, there will always be things in that book that you will already know because previous versions of Windows had the same type of functionality. This chapter is not going to be like that.

In this chapter, I will introduce you to Windows Containers. Windows Containers are brand new to Windows Server 2016 or some versions of Windows 10.

I will teach you how to install, configure, and maintain your Windows Containers. I will also show you all of the components needed to work with containers. Unless you have already started to learn about containers, this entire chapter will be brand new material. So let's start learning about Windows Containers.

Understanding Windows Containers

Windows Containers are independent and isolated environments that run an operating system. These isolated environments allow an administrator to place an application into its own container thus not affecting any other applications or containers.

Think of containers as virtual environments that are used to run independent applications. They load much faster than virtual machines and you can run as many containers as needed for all of the different applications that you run.

One of the nice advantages of using Windows Containers is that the containers can be managed the same way an administrator can manage an operating system. A container works the same way as a newly installed physical or virtual machine. So once you know how to configure these containers, management is much easier than configuring a physical machine.

There are two different types of containers that the Windows Container can use.

Windows Server Containers This container allows an administrator to isolate applications so applications can run in their own space and not affect other applications. The question that you may be asking is why not use a virtual machine? Well the advantage of Windows Server Containers is that they are already pre-built and you don't need all of the other services that a virtual machine would need to run. So Windows Containers are smaller, faster, and more efficient when isolating applications. In a Windows Server Container, the kernel is shared between all of the different Windows Containers.

Hyper-V Containers Hyper-V Containers and Windows Containers work the same way. The difference between the two is that Hyper-V Containers run within a virtual machine and the Windows Containers don't need to run in a Hyper-V environment. In a Hyper-V Container the container host's kernel is not shared between the other Hyper-V Containers.

Container Terminology

As with any new technology, it is important to understand the terminology that goes along with that new technology. The first thing that you may have noticed is that a container works a lot like a virtual machine. Just like a virtual machine, the container has a running operating system within the container.

The container has a file system and the container can also be accessed through the network the same way a virtual machine does. The advantage is that a container is a more efficient operating system. But to truly understand how containers work, you need to understand all of the different components that allow containers to function properly.

Container Host   This component can be on a physical or virtual machine and it's the component that is configured with the Windows Container feature. So the Windows Container sits on top of the Container Host.

Container OS Image   This component provides the operating system to the container. Containers are made up from multiple images that are stacked on top of each other within the container.

Container Image   This is the component that contains all of the layers of the container. So the Container Image contains the operating system, the application, and all of the services required to make that application function properly.

Container Registry   This component is the heart and brain of the container. The container images are kept within the container's registry. The advantage of doing containers this way is that you can download other registries to automatically add other applications or services quickly.

Docker Daemon   This is the component that runs the docker application. The docker daemon is automatically installed after you complete the installation of the docker application. If you need to configure the docker daemon, you would use the docker daemon file. This file is in a JSON format.

Dockerfile   This component is used to create the container images. The advantage of using the Dockerfile is that you can automate how containers are created. Dockerfiles are batches of instructions (within a txt file) and commands that are called on when an image is assembled.

Docker Hub Repositories   This component is a location where all of your images are stored. By having a central location for stored images, the images can be used among coworkers, customers, or the for the entire IT community. There are docker hub repositories on the internet and these locations allow you to grab and use images for your organization.

Install and Configure Server Containers

So now that we have talked about what the different components are of a container, it's time that we look at installing containers on our Windows Server 2016 system. When it comes to Microsoft, it really doesn't matter if we are installing containers on a GUI based system or non-GUI based system. We are going to install the components needed by using Windows PowerShell.

But before we can look at installing and using containers, I need to show you what is required on the Windows Server 2016 system. So the first step in using containers is looking at what we need on our network and computers for containers to run properly.

Requirements

Now that you have decided to work with containers, you need to make sure that your network meets the minimum requirements to install and work with Windows Containers. The following are the requirements for installing and working with containers:

- Computer systems (physical or virtual machines) running Windows Server 2016 (Core and with Desktop Experience), Nano Server, or Windows 10 Professional and Enterprise (Anniversary Edition).

- The boot partition must be on the C: drive (this does not apply if only Hyper-V Containers will be deployed).

- All critical updates must be installed on the system running the Windows Container feature.

- Docker application needs to be installed.

The following are the requirements needed if you are going to be running virtualization with containers.

- For systems running the Hyper-V containers, the Hyper-V role must be installed on the system.

- If you are going to run a Windows Container host from a Hyper-V virtual machine (also you will be hosting Hyper-V Containers), you will need to enable nested virtualization. Nested virtualization also has some requirements:

  - Operating system that allows nested virtualization (Windows Server 2016).

  - Minimum of 4 GB RAM available to the virtualized Hyper-V host.

  - The processor needs to use Intel VT-x (this is only available for Intel processors).

  - 2 virtual processors for the container host VM.

Supported Images for Windows Containers

When I talk about setting up containers and you are getting ready to start using containers, there is one major requirement that we need to consider. The operating system on the host machine needs to be the same operating system that is used in the Windows Container. If you install a different operating system in the Windows Container, the container may load but you will most likely start to see errors and there is no guarantee that all of the container's functionality will work.

So it is very important to make sure that the version of Windows Server 2016 that you install onto the host system is the same version as you run in the Windows Container. One nice advantage to using Microsoft Windows is that you can check what version of Windows you are using.

To see what Windows version you have installed, enter into the system's Registry (Regedit.exe) and search the following Registry key (see Figure 7.1):

```
HKEY_LOCAL_MACHINE\Software\Microsoft\Windows NT\CurrentVersion
```

FIGURE 7.1 Regedit version

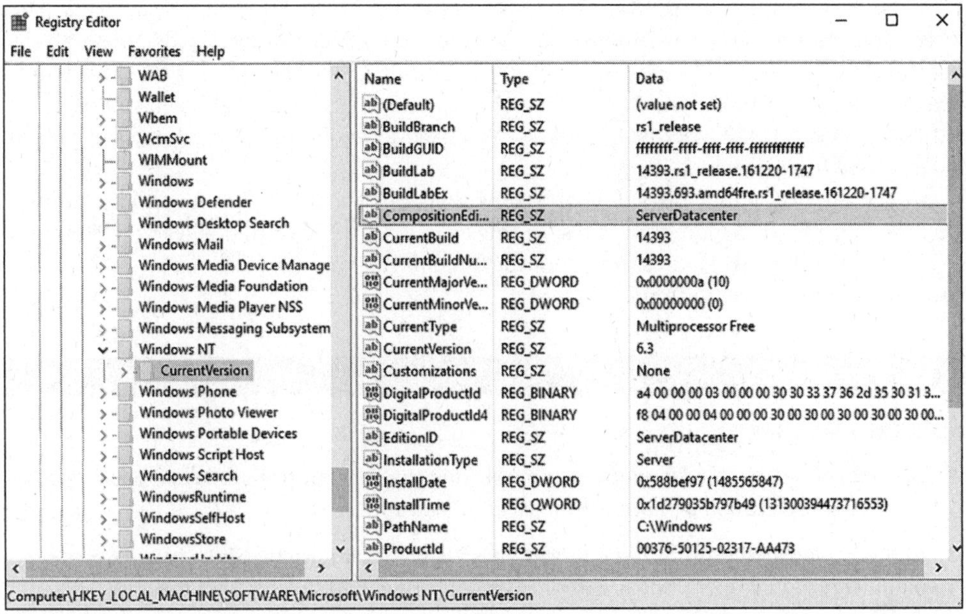

Depending on which host operating system that you are going to run will determine what operating systems you can run in the Windows Server Container or Hyper-V container. Not all operating systems are available depending on the host OS image. Table 7.1 shows you all of the supported configurations for each host operating system.

TABLE 7.1 Supported Base Images

Host Operating System	Windows Server Container	Hyper-V Container
Windows Server 2016 with Desktop	Server Core / Nano Server	Server Core / Nano Server
Windows Server 2016 Core	Server Core / Nano Server	Server Core / Nano Server
Nano Server	Nano Server	Server Core / Nano Server
Windows 10 Pro / Enterprise	Not Available	Server Core / Nano Server

Installing Docker

So the first step in setting up our Windows Containers is to install Docker. Docker is the software package that allows you to create and manipulate containers and images.

Docker is the software package that you install and the docker daemon is the application that you use to do your configuration and management. After you install docker, the docker daemon is automatically installed and configured with default settings.

Docker is a third party application that Microsoft has started using for containers. The docker application consists of a docker engine and a docker client (docker daemon). So the first thing that we need to do is install docker. To do this, you need to first download and install the docker application. Another item that needs to be completed when installing and using docker, is the Microsoft updates. You need to make sure that all of the current updates have been installed.

In Exercise 7.1, I will show you how to download and install docker. I will also show you how to get your Windows updates. In this exercise, I will install docker to a Windows Server 2016 (with GUI) Datacenter operating system. But this installation can be done on a Nano Server or a Server with no GUI.

EXERCISE 7.1

Installing Docker

1. Open an elevated command prompt by clicking the Start button and right clicking on Windows PowerShell ➤ More ➤ Run as Administrator.

2. At the PowerShell prompt, type **Sconfig**. This will bring up the Server Configuration Menu (see Figure 7.2). Choose option 6 by entering 6 and hitting the Enter key. This will do an update on Windows Server 2016.

FIGURE 7.2 Server Configuration screen

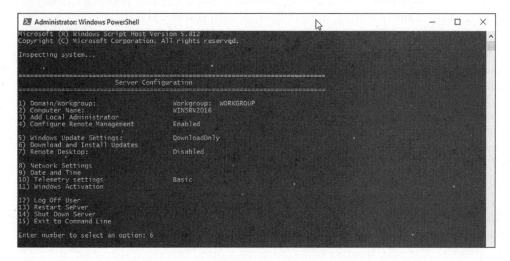

3. A screen should appear asking if you want to install (A)ll updates or (R)ecommended updates only. Choose A for All updates and hit Enter. If there are any updates available, click A for installing all updates and hit Enter. The updates will be downloaded and installed.

4. If there were no updates, go to step 6. After all updates have been installed, choose option 13 to restart the server. A box will appear asking if you are sure you want to Reboot. Click Yes.

5. Login and restart the PowerShell with administrative rights.

6. At the PowerShell prompt, type the following command and hit enter to download the docker software.

   ```
   Install-Module -Name DockerMsftProvider -Repository PSGallery -Force
   ```

7. If you get a message that NuGet provider needs to be installed (see Figure 7.3), choose Y and hit Enter. If this message doesn't appear, go to step 9.

FIGURE 7.3 Install NuGet

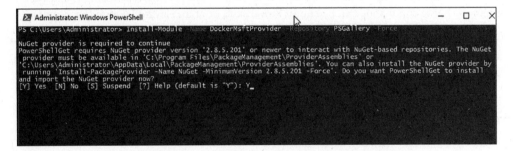

8. If you needed to install NuGet, then re-enter the following command:

   ```
   Install-Module -Name DockerMsftProvider -Repository PSGallery -Force
   ```

9. Now that you have downloaded docker, it's time to install it. At the PowerShell prompt, type the following command (see Figure 7.4) and hit Enter.

   ```
   Install-Package -Name docker -ProviderName DockerMsftProvider
   ```

FIGURE 7.4 Install Docker

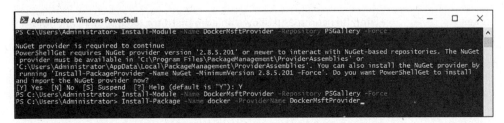

10. A message will appear that states that the package is not trusted Are you sure you want to install software from DockerDefault? Click Y and hit enter.

11. Now that docker is installed, you need to check for updates again and then reboot. So type Sconfig and choose option 6. Click A for checking for All updates. If there are any updates, click A for installing All updates.

12. After the updates complete, you will return back to the Server Configuration screen. Choose option 13. Click Yes to reboot.

13. Login to the server.

Docker is now downloaded and installed onto the Windows Server 2016 machine. The next step is to work with docker to install and configure containers.

When using Docker, there are some switches that you can use to work with Docker. Table 7.2 shows some of the Docker switches and what each switch does. These commands are what is needed if you want to manage Windows or Linux containers using the docker daemon. These commands can be run in PowerShell or at an elevated command prompt.

 Table 7.2 is just a partial list of Docker commands. To see a more complete list, go to Microsoft's website at https://docs.docker.com/engine/reference/run/. In the left-hand window, the entire list is under Engine (Docker) CLI.

TABLE 7.2   Docker PowerShell and command-line commands

Command	Description
docker attach	This command allows an administrator to attach to a running container.
docker build	Using this command allows you to build an image from a Docker file.
docker checkpoint	Administrators can use this command to manage a Docker checkpoint.
docker commit	This command allows an administrator to debug and build a new image.
docker container	This command allows you to manage containers.
docker cp	Using this command allows an administrator to copy files and folders between the container and the local computer system.
docker create	This command gives you the ability to create a new container.
docker deploy	Administrators can use this command to create and modify a stack.
docker diff	This command allows an administrator to view changes to files or directories in the container's filesystem.

Command	Description
docker events	This command allows an administrator to see a server's events in real time.
docker exec	Administrators can use this command to run a new command in an existing container.
docker image	This command (along with its options) allows you to manage your images.
docker info	Using this command allows an administrator to view system information of the Docker installation.
docker kill	This command allows you to terminate running containers.
docker login	Administrators can use this command to log in to the docker registry of a server.
docker pause	This command allows an administrator to pause all processes within a container.
docker port	Use this command to view the port mappings for a container.
docker ps	This command allows you to view all of the containers.
docker pull	Administrators can use this command to pull an image from a registry.
docker push	This command allows you to push an image to a registry.
docker rename	This command allows you to rename a container.
docker restart	Using this command allows you to restart a container.
docker rm	Administrators can use this command to remove a container.
docker run	Using this command (along with the Options), an administrator can add to or override the image settings set by a developer.
docker save	This command allows an administrator to save images to an archive.
docker search	This command allows you to search the Docker Hub for images.
docker start	This command allows an administrator to start a stopped container.
docker stop	This command allows an administrator to stop a running container.
docker update	Administrators can use this command to update the configuration of a container.
docker version	This command allows an administrator to view the Docker version information.

After docker is installed, you may want to configure the docker daemon for how docker will start and stop after a system restart or when the system needs to reboot. If you want to set a restart policy, you will want to use the -restart flag on the Docker run command.

Table 7.3 shows you all of the different startup policies that you can set on a container.

TABLE 7.3   Docker Restart Policy

Policy	Result
no	This setting will not automatically restart the container. This is the default setting for a container.
on-failure[:max-retries]	This setting will restart the container only if the container has a non-zero exit status. Also you have the ability to limit the number of restart retries that the docker daemon will attempt.
always	This setting will always restart the container. When the setting is set to always, docker will try to restart the container indefinitely. The container will also always start on daemon startup.
unless-stopped	This setting will always restart the container unless the container was stopped before the restart.

Install and Configure Windows Containers

So now that you have installed docker on your Windows Server 2016 system, let's take a look at how you install and configure containers.

In Exercise 7.2, I will show you how to make sure your Docker service is started. I will then show you how to install a base operating system image onto your host. I will also show you how to create Windows Server Containers.

 There are dozens of pre-made Docker images. You can look at all of the different docker components at the Docker Store. Go to https://store.docker.com to see all of the available docker downloads (including pre-made images).

EXERCISE 7.2

Installing a Base Operating System

1. Open the Services MMC by clicking Start ➢ Windows Administrative Tools ➢ Services.

2. Scroll down until you see Docker. Make sure that the Docker Service is started (see Figure 7.5). If it's not started, right click on Docker and choose Start.

3. Close Services.

4. Open Windows PowerShell with administrative privileges. To do this, click on Start and then right click on Windows PowerShell ➢ More ➢ Run as administrator.

FIGURE 7.5   Checking the Docker service

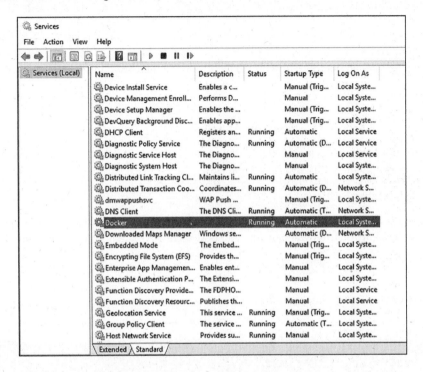

5. Now we are going to look to see if any containers are running. To do this, type Docker info in PowerShell and hit Enter. You will see a report (see Figure 7.6) that will show you if you have any containers running.

FIGURE 7.6   Docker Info

```
Administrator: Windows PowerShell                                         —   □   ×

Windows PowerShell
Copyright (C) 2016 Microsoft Corporation. All rights reserved.

PS C:\Users\Administrator> Docker info
Containers: 0
 Running: 0
 Paused: 0
 Stopped: 0
Images: 0
Server Version: 1.13.1-cs1
Storage Driver: windowsfilter
 Windows:
Logging Driver: json-file
Plugins:
 Volume: local
 Network: l2bridge l2tunnel nat null overlay transparent
Swarm: inactive
Default Isolation: process
Kernel Version: 10.0 14393 (14393.693.amd64fre.rs1_release.161220-1747)
Operating System: Windows Server 2016,Datacenter
OSType: windows
Architecture: x86_64
CPUs: 4
Total Memory: 8 GiB
Name: WinSrv2016
ID: PURT:4ZQW:TMYH:DKG4:EZBN:ALUW:CM6U:6U6V:OFEX:SRAD:IVZA:6EOI
Docker Root Dir: C:\ProgramData\docker
Debug Mode (client): false
Debug Mode (server): false
Registry: https://index.docker.io/v1/
Experimental: false
Insecure Registries:
 127.0.0.0/8
Live Restore Enabled: false
PS C:\Users\Administrator>
```

EXERCISE 7.2 *(continued)*

6. So now you are going to install a Container image for either Microsoft Nano Server or Windows Server Core from the online Package repository. To do this, type in one of the following command into PowerShell (choose the command for the operating system that you want):

```
Docker pull microsoft/nanoserver
docker pull microsoft/windowsservercore
```

7. After your container is installed, let's go ahead and restart the Docker service. Type the following command into PowerShell:

```
Restart-Service docker
```

8. Now let's take a look at your docker information again by typing **`Docker Info`** at the PowerShell prompt. As you can see, you now have an image that you didn't have before (see Figure 7.7).

FIGURE 7.7 Docker information

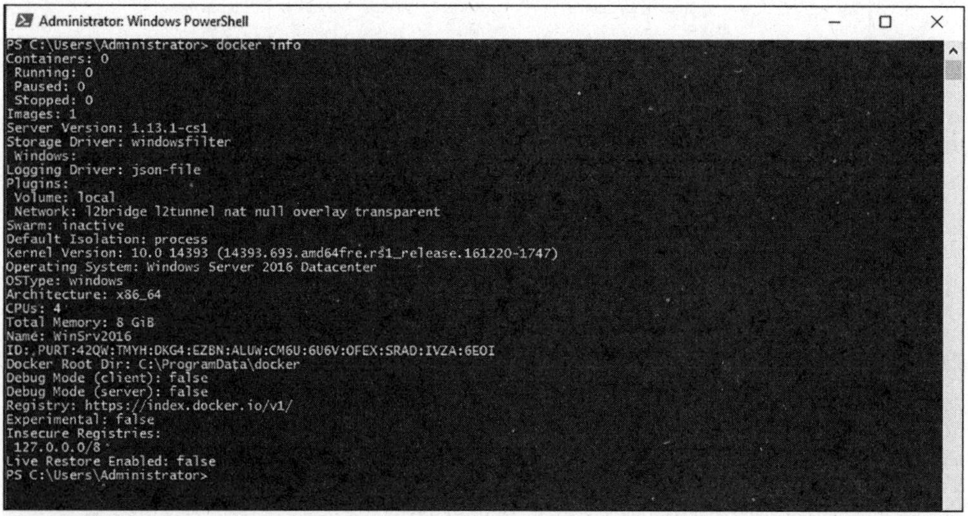

9. To see all of the images that you have on your system, at the PowerShell prompt type **docker images** (see Figure 7.8).

FIGURE 7.8   Docker images

10. So now that you have seen how to grab a base image from docker, let's create a Windows Server Container with Nano Server installed. At the PowerShell prompt, type the following command:

    docker run microsoft/dotnet-samples:dotnetapp-nanoserver

11. If the installation worked properly, you should see what looks like to be a small alien on your screen (see Figure 7.9). Type **docker info** at the PowerShell prompt and you will see that you now have a container. You will also notice that you have two images now. The one you downloaded earlier and the one you just downloaded.

FIGURE 7.9   Container created

12. Close PowerShell.

Now that you have seen how to download an image to the systems repository, you need to see how you can turn an image into a container. To do this, you need to just use the docker run command to get the image into a container. Also there may be a time when you need to remove an image from a container. This is done using the docker rm command.

But first you need to know which image that you want to put into a container. Exercise 7.3 will show you how to see your images and then how to add an image into a container. To complete Exercise 7.3, you must have completed Exercise 7.2.

EXERCISE 7.3

Adding an Image to a Container

1. Open a PowerShell window with Administrative rights.

2. Type **docker info** into the PowerShell prompt. You should only have one container at this time.

3. Next you need to do is see what images are in our Repository. To do this, type **docker images** at the PowerShell window. This will show you your docker images (see Figure 7.10).

FIGURE 7.10 Docker images

4. We need the Image ID from the Nano server or Server core that you downloaded in exercise 7.2. The Image ID for my Nano server is d9bccb9d4cac. We will use this ID to turn the image into a container. Type the following into a PowerShell prompt (your Image ID will be different) and hit enter (see Figure 7.11).

   docker run d9bccb9d4cac

FIGURE 7.11 Docker run command

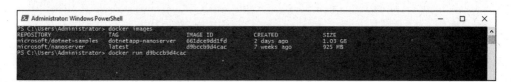

5. Type **Docker info** at the PowerShell prompt. You should now have two containers instead of just one (see Figure 7.12).

FIGURE 7.12   Docker info command

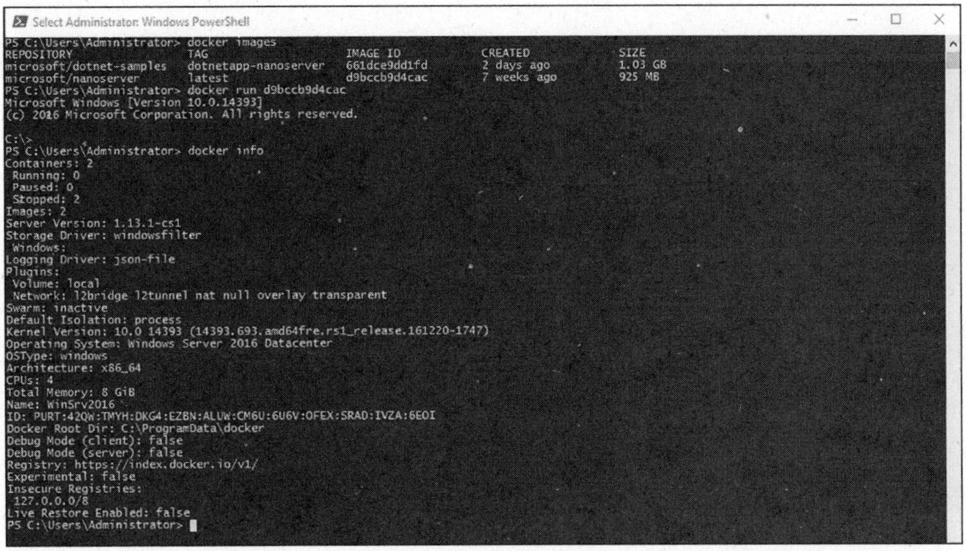

```
PS C:\Users\Administrator> docker images
REPOSITORY                 TAG                  IMAGE ID          CREATED          SIZE
microsoft/dotnet-samples   dotnetapp-nanoserver 661dce9dd1fd      2 days ago       1.03 GB
microsoft/nanoserver       latest               d9bccb9d4cac      7 weeks ago      925 MB
PS C:\Users\Administrator> docker run d9bccb9d4cac
Microsoft Windows [Version 10.0.14393]
(c) 2016 Microsoft Corporation. All rights reserved.

C:\>
PS C:\Users\Administrator> docker info
Containers: 2
 Running: 0
 Paused: 0
 Stopped: 2
Images: 2
Server Version: 1.13.1-cs1
Storage Driver: windowsfilter
 Windows:
Logging Driver: json-file
Plugins:
 Volume: local
 Network: l2bridge l2tunnel nat null overlay transparent
Swarm: inactive
Default Isolation: process
Kernel Version: 10.0 14393 (14393.693.amd64fre.rs1_release.161220-1747)
Operating System: Windows Server 2016 Datacenter
OSType: windows
Architecture: x86_64
CPUs: 4
Total Memory: 8 GiB
Name: WinSrv2016
ID: PURT:42QW:TMYH:DKG4:EZBN:ALUW:CM6U:6U6V:OFEX:SRAD:IVZA:6EOI
Docker Root Dir: C:\ProgramData\docker
Debug Mode (client): false
Debug Mode (server): false
Registry: https://index.docker.io/v1/
Experimental: false
Insecure Registries:
 127.0.0.0/8
Live Restore Enabled: false
PS C:\Users\Administrator>
```

6. Close PowerShell.

Tagging an Image

Administrators have the ability to change the tags associated with the images. Many administrators use tag names as version names so that they can keep track of the different images on their machine.

By having tags that you create, it allows you to easily access the images later by its tag name. To tag an image, you use the -t parameter. So the following is tagging an image as WillPanekImage.

```
docker build -t WillPanekImage
```

Uninstall an Operating System Image

One of the maintenance issues that many IT administrators must deal with is hard drive space. As you are downloading and using images, there may be a time when you need to remove images from our server that are no longer being used.

If you continue to download and use multiple images files, you will need to make sure that every once in a while that you look at all of your images and delete any images that are no longer valid or no longer in use.

Exercise 7.4 will show you how to remove an image file from your host system. To complete this exercise, make sure that you have completed the earlier exercises in this chapter.

EXERCISE 7.4

Uninstalling an Image

1. Open a PowerShell window with Administrative rights.

2. Type **docker images** and get the ID number of the Nano server Image.

3. Type **docker rm d9bccb9d4cac** (your ID number should go where the d9bccb9d4cac number is).

4. Type docker images. The image is now gone.

5. Close PowerShell

Creating New Images Using Dockerfile

One nice advantage of using docker is that you can go out to Docker's website and look at the different images that are available. There are images for operating systems, applications, and software.

But what if you can't find an image that you need? Well, then you can build your own images using Dockerfiles. When an administrator installs docker, the docker engine includes tools that the IT department can use to create these Dockerfiles. Dockerfiles are just text files that are manually created and they are compiled and turned into an image file.

If your organization decides that they want to build their own Dockerfiles, then they will get some benefits while doing just that. Some of the advantages of building your own Dockerfiles are as follows:

- Administrators can store images as code.

- Your organization can have rapid recreation of images. These images can then be used for maintenance and upgrade cycles.

- Customization for exactly what your organization wants.

So once you have installed docker, there will be some components that are included so that you can create your own Dockerfiles. These two docker components include the docker engine and the compiler (docker build command).

So if you have ever built .ini files or even a host file, then you understand how building a file can work. Same as many programming codes or .ini files, you can use the pound (#) to show comments in the file. This is very useful.

Many years ago, before I got into networking, I was a programmer. One thing that most programmers hate is when you look at someone else's coding and you have no idea what they were doing. When a coder takes the time to put in comments so that anyone can follow them and work on the code, it makes following that coder a thousand times easier. This is what the comments in the Dockerfile do. Using the pound (#) for making comments and stating exactly why each line is included, helps someone following you or if someone is trying to learn what you do.

So let's take a look at an example of a Dockerfile:

```
# Sample Dockerfile for WillPanek
# We will be using Windows Server Core as our base image.
FROM microsoft/windowsservercore
# Uses dism.exe to install the DNS role.
RUN dism.exe /online /enable-feature /all /featurename: : DNS-Server-Full-Role /NoRestart
# Sets a command or process that will run each time a container is run from the new image.
CMD [ "cmd" ]
```

So now that we can see a Dockerfile, lets break down some of the different sections that you can configure. Table 7.4 will show you some of the configuration settings that you can use.

TABLE 7.4 Dockerfile Commands

Command	Description
Add	This setting will copy new files, directories, or remote file URLs from a source (<src>) location to the filesystem of the image destination <dest>.
CMD	This setting sets the default commands that will be executed when deploying the container image.
Copy	This setting will copy new files or directories from a source (<src>) location to the filesystem of the image destination <dest>.
Escape	This setting is used to escape characters in a line and to escape a newline. Normally, the escape command is followed by the character that will represent a new line. For example: escape=\. This means that when a \ (backslash) is in the file, it will represent a new line.
ENV	This setting allows you to add an environmental variable.
Expose	This setting tells Docker that the container is listening on the specified network ports during runtime.

TABLE 7.4 Dockerfile Commands *(continued)*

Command	Description
From	This setting shows the location of the container image that will be used during the image creation process.
Label	This setting adds metadata to an image.
Onbuild	This setting allows you to set a trigger that gets executed when the image is used as the base for another build.
Run	This setting will specify what commands are to be run in the Dockerfile process. These commands can include software installation and file, directory, and environment creation.
User	This setting allows you to set up a user's account that will be used during the runtime.
Volume	This setting allows an administrator to create a mount point and externally mounted volumes from host systems or other containers.
Workdir	This setting allows you to set the working directory that will be used during the runtime.

Understanding Hyper-V Containers

So far in this chapter we have discussed Windows Containers, but now we are going to look at Hyper-V Containers. As I stated earlier, Windows Containers share the system's kernel between all containers and the host. Hyper-V Containers are different because each Hyper-V Containers utilizes their own instance of the Windows kernel.

Since Hyper-V containers utilizing their own instance of the Windows kernel, administrators can use different versions of Windows between the host system and the image version.

Also the Windows host system needs to have the Microsoft Hyper-V role installed onto the host system. Windows Server 2016 and Windows 10 Professional and Enterprise (Anniversary Editions) both allow you to create containers and Hyper-V.

The one nice feature is that both container types, Windows Containers and Hyper-V Containers, are created, managed, and function the exact same way. The only difference is how the Hyper-V Containers have better isolation to the kernel.

When you are working with Hyper-V containers in Docker, the settings are identical to managing Windows Server containers. The one difference that you want to include in the Hyper-V Container is using the --isolation=hyperv parameter. The following is an example of the docker command with the Hyper-V parameters:

```
docker run -it --isolation=hyperv microsoft/nanoserver cmd
```

Managing Container Networking

One of the features included with building containers is the ability to access the servers and data within the container the same way you would on a normal network server or Hyper-V server.

Once you have installed Docker, there will be three networks that are created automatically. You can see these networks by typing **docker network ls** in PowerShell (see Figure 7.13) or at an elevated command prompt.

FIGURE 7.13 Docker Network Info

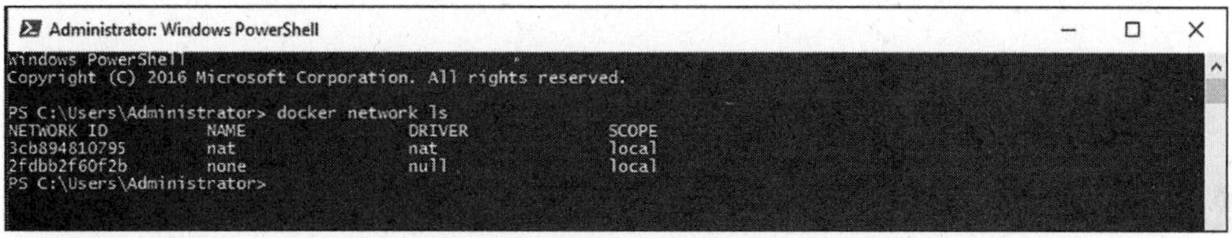

If you would like to get even more details about a specific network (see Figure 7.14), after you run the docker network ls command, you will need to grab the Network ID number. Then type the following PowerShell command followed by the Network ID number (my Network ID is 3cb894810795):

Docker network inspect 3cb894810795

FIGURE 7.14 Docker Network Info

One nice thing about working with networks within containers is that these three networks are always available to you even when you choose only one to be part of your container. You can specify which network you want your container to run on by using the --Network flag setting.

When you create a container, the host network adds the container onto the host's network stack. When you are dealing with the containers network, there are very few reasons why you would even need to manage or manipulate the container's network. The only network that you may need to work with is the bridge network. The docker default bridge is created as soon as you install the Docker Engine. It creates your bridge network and its name is bridge.

Using Docker Hub Repository

One really nice advantage of using containers is that there are hundreds of images that you can use. Docker has a public database of images that you can access.

The DockerHub repository has images for Microsoft, UNIX, Linux, and hundreds more. If you want to see what a vendor has out on the repository, just type in docker search vendorname. So let us take a look at what Microsoft has for you in the repository. Type **docker search Microsoft** (see Figure 7.15).

FIGURE 7.15   Docker Search Microsoft

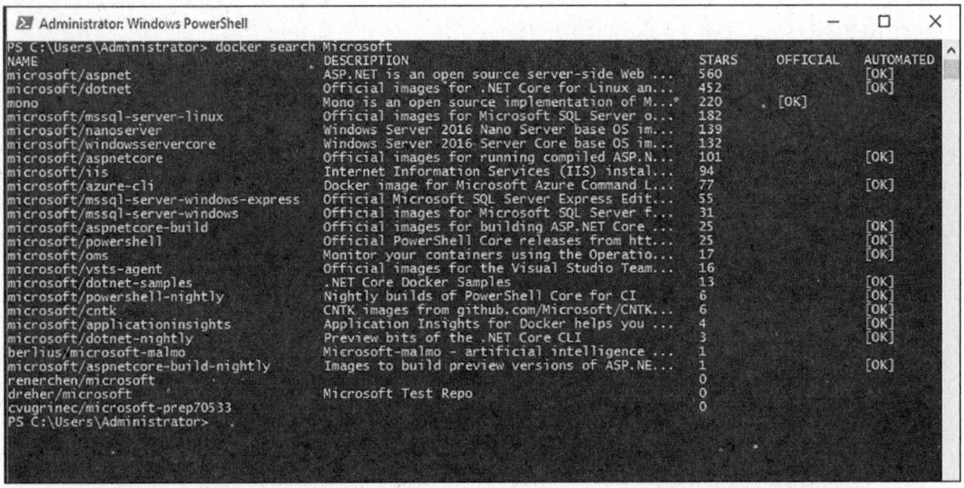

Administrators have the ability to setup a private repository so that co-workers can share and use the images that you create. After you create your images using the Docker Daemon, you can then push those images to your corporate Docker Hub repository. Administrators can add users and accounts to the Docker Hub to verify that only the organization's users are accessing the images.

If you are building images and placing those images on GitHub or Bitbucket, you can then use the Automatic build repository that is included with the Docker Hub service.

So when you are ready to start uploading corporate images to the Docker Hub, you will first need to create a Docker Hub user account (`https://cloud.docker.com/`). After you have created your account, click the Create ↓ and choose "Create Repository."

You will then be asked to put in a Docker ID namespace for your organization. The repository name needs to be unique and it can be up to 255 characters. The namespace will only allow letters, numbers, or the dash (-) and underscore (_). You are then allowed to put in a Short Description (100 characters or less) and a Full Description. Then you click the Create button and you are finished.

After your repository is created, you can push images to the repository by putting in the name of your image, your Docker Hub username, the repository name that you created earlier, and the image tag. The following is an example of the docker push command:

```
docker push <hub-user>/<repo-name>:<tag>
```

Using Microsoft Azure for Images

If you decide to run container applications within a cluster of virtual machines, you can use the Azure Container Service. The Azure Container Service allows you to easily create, configure, and manage your virtual machine cluster of containers. The Azure Container Service uses open-source scheduling and management tools.

By using open-source tools, the Azure Container Service connects you with thousands of other users who are also designing, building, and maintaining container images.

The Azure Container Service uses the Docker format but it is also compatible with Marathon, DC/OS, Kubernetes, or Docker Swarm. Because the Azure Container Service works with all of these different formats, you have the ability to work with thousands of applications and images. But since this is Microsoft's Azure platform, you get all of the security benefits and features that Azure has to offer.

To setup the Azure Container Service, you must first setup an Azure Container Service cluster through the Microsoft portal. Once you have entered the portal, you would need to use the Azure Resource Manager template for Docker Swarm, DC/OS, and Kubernetes, or you would need to use the Azure Command Line Interface.

 To setup an Azure account or to find out more information on using the Azure Container Service, visit Microsoft's website at: https://azure.microsoft.com/en-us/services/container-service/.

Using PowerShell for Containers

The following table (Table 7.5) will show you just some of the available PowerShell commands that are available for using containers and Docker.

TABLE 7.5   PowerShell Commands

PowerShell Command	Description
Add-ContainerNetworkAdapter	This command allows an administrator to add a virtual network adapter to a container.
Connect-ContainerNetworkAdapter	Administrators can use this command to connect a virtual network adapter to a virtual switch.
Disconnect-ContainerNetworkAdapter	This command allows an administrator to disconnect a virtual network adapter from a virtual switch.
Export-ContainerImage	Administrators can use this command to export a container image to a file.
Get-Container	This command allows an administrator to view information about containers.
Get-ContainerHost	This command allows an administrator to view information about the host.
Get-ContainerImage	Administrators can use this command to view local container images.
Get-ContainerNetworkAdapter	Administrators can use this command to view the virtual network adapter of a container.
Import-ContainerImage	Administrators can use this command to import a container image from a file.
Install-ContainerOSImage	This command allows an administrator to install the operating system image to a base container.
Install-Module	Administrators can use this command to download a module from an online gallery. This module can then be installed on the local computer.
Install-Package	Administrators can use this command to install a software package on a computer.
Install-PackageProvider	This command allows an administrator to install a Package Management package providers.
Move-ContainerImageRepository	Administrators can use this command to move the local container image repository.

PowerShell Command	Description
New-Container	This command allows an administrator to create a container image from an existing container.
Remove-Container	Administrators can use this command to delete a container.
Remove-ContainerImage	This command allows an administrator to remove a container image.
Remove-ContainerNetworkAdapter	This command allows an administrator to remove a virtual network adapter from a container.
Restart-Computer	Administrators can use this command to restart a local and remote computer.
Set-ContainerNetworkAdapter	Administrators can use this command to configure the features of the virtual network adapter within a container.
Start-Container	Administrators can use this command to start a container.
Stop-Container	Administrators can use this command to stop a container.
Test-ContainerImage	This command allows an administrator to test for issues with a container image.
Uninstall-ContainerOSImage	Administrators can use this command to uninstall the container operating system image.

Summary

In this chapter, I started introducing you to Windows Containers. Windows Containers are a brand-new technology to Windows Server 2016 or some versions of Windows 10.

I also showed you how to install, configure, and maintain your Windows Containers. And I talked to you about the components that are needed to work with containers.

I then showed you some exercises for configuring Windows Server 2016 containers and also how to download and work with image files. These image files can be used to create Windows and Hyper-V containers.

In addition, I showed you how to install and work with Docker. Docker is the technology used to manage and maintain Windows Containers. I showed you how to work with Docker PowerShell and command-line switches and also how to use PowerShell to work with Windows Containers.

Video Resources

There are videos available for the following exercises:

> 7.1
>
> 7.2

You can access the videos at http://sybextestbanks.wiley.com on the Other Study Tools tab.

Exam Essentials

Understand Windows Containers. Windows Containers work a lot like virtual machines except that when you build a virtual machine, you need all of the services that make that VM run properly. Windows Containers are fast operating system builds that allow you to run applications in their own environment.

Know the requirements for Windows Containers. Understand that you have to have Windows Server 2016 with Docker installed. You must also make sure that all updates are current on the system. You can install containers on Windows 10 Professional and Enterprise (Anniversary Edition).

Know the PowerShell commands used for Containers. The Microsoft exams are going to focus on PowerShell commands. Make sure you know the PowerShell commands that are used for Docker and containers.

Understand Docker technology. Understand that Docker is the technology that is used to manage and maintain Windows Containers. There are preset images on Docker that you can pull down and run. Microsoft has preset Docker images that you can use and manipulate.

Know the different Docker switches. Understand how docker switches are used and know the main docker switches. Understand that docker switches can be run in PowerShell or at an elevated command prompt.

Review Questions

1. You have a Windows Server 2016 server named Server. You install the Docker daemon on Server1. You need to configure the Docker daemon to accept connections only on TCP port 64500. What should you do?

   A. Use the `New-NetFirewallRulecmdlet`.

   B. Use the `View-ServiceWindows` PowerShell cmdlet.

   C. Edit the `daemon.json` file.

   D. Create a new configuration file.

2. You are the network administrator for a company that has decided to start using Windows Containers. You want to create a new container. What command allows you to create a container?

   A. `docker create`

   B. `docker build container`

   C. `docker new`

   D. `docker build`

3. You are the network administrator for a company that has decided to start using Windows Containers. You have built a bunch of containers. What PowerShell command allows you to view the containers?

   A. `docker view`

   B. `docker see`

   C. `View-Container`

   D. `Get-Container`

4. You have a Nano Server named Nano1. You deploy several containers to Nano1 that use an image named Image1. You need to deploy a new container to Nano1 that uses Image1. What should you run?

   A. `Install-NanoServerPackage` cmdlet

   B. `Install-WindowsFeaturecmdlet` cmdlet

   C. `docker load`

   D. `docker run`

5. You are the network administrator for a company that has decided to start using Windows Containers. You have created some images. What command allows you to see your images?

   A. `docker images`

   B. `docker info`

   C. `docker view`

   D. `docker see`

6. You are the administrator for your organization, which has started using containers. You need to build and use a Dockerfile. You need to compile and create an image using the Dockerfile. What command would you use?

   A. Docker run

   B. Docker rm

   C. Docker build

   D. Docker compile

7. You are the administrator for your organization, which has started using containers. You need to build and use a Dockerfile. You need to execute commands within the Dockerfile. What command would you use?

   A. Docker run

   B. Docker rm

   C. Docker build

   D. Docker compile

8. You are the network administrator for a company that has decided to start using Windows Containers. You want to delete a container. What PowerShell command allows you to delete a container?

   A. docker delete

   B. docker kill container

   C. Remove-Container

   D. Delete-docker-Container

9. You are the administrator for your organization, which has started using containers. You need to build a new image using Windows Server Core. What command would you use to get a Windows Server Core image?

   A. Docker run microsoft/windowsservercore

   B. docker pull microsoft/windowsservercore

   C. Docker build microsoft/windowsservercore

   D. Docker get microsoft/windowsservercore

10. You have been asked to start using Windows containers in your organization. Your manager wants to know what client operating systems can host containers. Which of the following client operating systems will allow for containers?

   A. Windows 10 Home

   B. Windows 7 Professional

   C. Windows 10 Enterprise (Anniversary Edition)

   D. Windows 8.1 Enterprise

Chapter

8

Maintaining Windows Server

THE FOLLOWING 70-740 EXAM OBJECTIVES ARE COVERED IN THIS CHAPTER:

✓ **Install, upgrade, and migrate servers and workloads**

- This objective may include but is not limited to: Implement Windows Server Update Services (WSUS) solutions; configure WSUS groups; manage patch management in mixed environments; implement an antimalware solution with Windows Defender; integrate Windows Defender with WSUS and Windows Update; perform backup and restore operations using Windows Server Backup; determine backup strategies for different Windows Server roles and workloads, including Hyper-V Host, Hyper-V Guests, Active Directory, File Servers, and Web Servers using Windows Server 2016 native tools and solutions

In this chapter, we will start with keeping your systems updated using Windows Server Update Services (WSUS). Making sure that your users have Windows operating systems with the most current updates is one of the most important things that we can do in IT.

Microsoft is continually working to make their operating systems better and more secure. IT departments need to make sure that we keep our clients up-to-date with all of these Microsoft improvements. WSUS allows us to setup a server that deploys updates to your users.

Another important task of an IT team is to keep the network up and running quickly and efficiently. Keeping your network running is one way to make sure your end users continue to use the network and its resources without problems or interruptions. Backups are one way to make sure we can recover our network quickly and efficiently.

Remember, everyone has clients—salespeople have theirs, accountants have theirs, and so do we as system administrators. Our clients are the end users, and it's our job to make sure that our clients can always do their jobs by keeping the data secure and the network running.

When you are working with servers, it is important you make sure that your system's information is safely and efficiently backed up. Backups become useful when data gets lost due to system failures, file corruptions, or accidental deletions of information. As an IT Director, I can tell you from experience that backups are among the most important tasks that an IT person performs daily.

Configuring Windows Server Updates

When Microsoft releases a new operating system, users may encounter issues and security deficiencies. Both of these can cause your network to have many problems. So to help fix these issues, Microsoft will release updates and security fixes on a weekly and/or monthly basis. It is important for an IT department to keep their network systems up-to-date with these fixes.

Well there are two main ways to do this. You can let your users all connect to Microsoft's website one at a time and grab updates or you can setup a Windows Server Update Services (WSUS) server to get these updates. Then that WSUS server can release the updates to your users. This helps a company because when all your users connect to Microsoft to get the same updates, it's a waste of bandwidth and time. Also, as an IT person, we may not want all of the Microsoft updates to be deployed to our clients without viewing and testing them first.

I can tell you from first hand experience that there has been times when I deployed an update from Microsoft and it caused more issues than it fixed. So having the ability to view and test updates on a test system ensures that the updates that we are deploying work the way that they are supposed to. So let's take a look at some of the tools that you need to understand when dealing with updates.

Windows Update   This utility attaches to the Microsoft website through a user-initiated process, and it allows Windows users to update their operating systems by downloading updated files (critical and noncritical software updates).

Windows Server Update Services (WSUS)   This utility is used to deploy a limited version of Windows Update to a corporate server, which in turn provides the Windows updates to client computers within the corporate network. This allows clients that are limited to what they can access through a firewall to be able to keep their Windows operating systems up-to-date.

Windows Update

Windows Update is available for most Windows operating systems and it allows the system to receive updates from Microsoft. Examples of updates include security fixes, critical updates, updated help files, and updated drivers.

If you want to use Windows Update, an administrator would click Start ➢ Settings ➢ Update & security. You would then see the following options:

When the Last Updates Were Done   When you enter into the Windows Update settings, the first thing you will see is when the last updates were done (if any).

Check For Updates Button   This allows you to manually check to see if any updates are available for the operating system. When an administrator clicks this button (shown in Figure 8.1), the system will check for updates. If any updates are found, they will be downloaded and installed.

FIGURE 8.1   Windows Update control panel

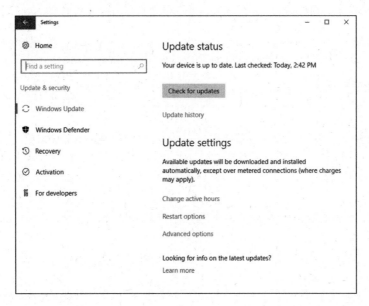

Update History   This allows you to track all of the updates that you have applied to your server.

Change Active Hours   This setting allows you to set your active hours on the system. So for example, you worked on this system or the server was most active from 8:00am to 6:00pm, you can set those hours so that the Windows Update knows when to download and install updates.

Restart Options   This setting allows you to customize when the system will restart after the machine receives its updates.

Advanced Options   This customizes what updates you receive when you use Windows Update.

> The information that is collected by Windows Update includes the operating system and version number, the Internet Explorer version, the software version information for any software that can be updated through Windows Update, the Plug and Play ID numbers for installed hardware, and the region and language settings. Windows Update will also collect the product ID and product key to confirm that you are running a licensed copy of Windows, but this information is retained only during the Windows Update session and it is not stored. No personal information that can be used to identify users of the Windows Update service is collected.

Windows Server 2016 updates will recognize when you have a network connection and will automatically search for any updates for your computer from the Windows Update website (as long as an internet connection is available) or from a WSUS server (explained below).

If any updates are identified, they will be downloaded using *Background Intelligent Transfer Services (BITS)*. BITS is a bandwidth-throttling technology that allows downloads to occur using idle bandwidth only. This means that downloading automatic updates will not interfere with any other Internet traffic.

If Updates detects any updates for your computer, you will see an update icon in the notification area of the Taskbar.

As stated before, an administrator configures Updates by selecting Start ➤ Settings ➤ Update & security. You can manually check for updates by clicking the Check For Updates button.

After you click the link to see if there are any updates available, you can then choose to install the updates. After you click to install the updates, you will see a status window showing you the update status of the updates being downloaded and installed (see Figure 8.2).

FIGURE 8.2 Seeing the Update Status

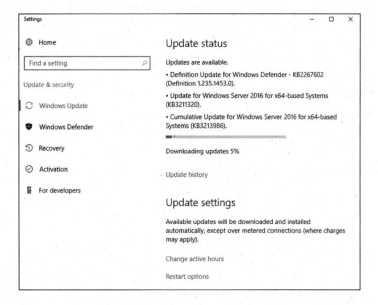

Once updates have been installed, you can click the link Update History to see all of the previous updates. When you click this link, you will be shown the updates that have been installed and also have the ability to uninstall any updates (see Figure 8.3).

FIGURE 8.3 Viewing your Update History

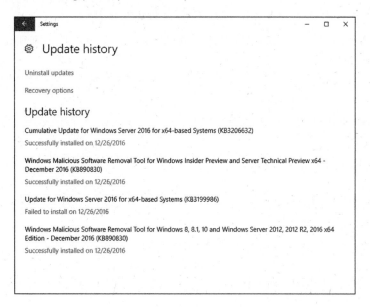

You also have the ability to set advanced options in the Updates section. One of the advanced options is to download other Microsoft updates for other Microsoft products (for example, you get Office updates at the same time you get operating system updates). Administrators also have the ability to defer updates (see Figure 8.4).

FIGURE 8.4   Viewing Advanced Options

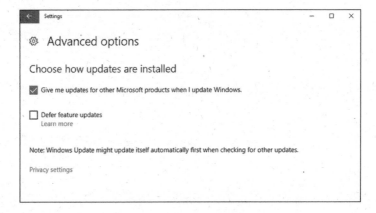

When you decide to defer updates, new Windows features will not be downloaded or installed during the upgrade process. Deferring updates will not affect the Windows Server 2016 system from getting security updates. Deferring updates will only prevent you from getting the newest Windows features as soon as they are released.

Using Windows Server Update Services

Windows Server Update Services (WSUS), formerly known as Software Update Services (SUS), is used to leverage the features of Windows Update within a corporate environment. WSUS downloads Windows updates to a corporate server, which in turn provides the updates to the internal corporate clients. This allows administrators to test and have full control over what updates are deployed within the corporate environment. WSUS is designed to work in medium-sized corporate networks that are not using System Center Essentials 2016.

Advantages of Using WSUS

Using WSUS has many advantages:

- It allows an internal server within a private intranet to act as a virtual Windows Update server.

- Administrators have selective control over what updates are posted and deployed from the public Windows Update site. No updates are deployed to client computers unless an administrator first approves them.

- Administrators can control the synchronization of updates from the public Windows Update site to the WSUS server either manually or automatically.

- Administrators can configure Automatic Updates on client computers to access the local WSUS server as opposed to the public Windows Update site.

- WSUS checks each update to verify that Microsoft has digitally signed it. Any updates that are not digitally signed are discarded.

- Administrators can selectively specify whether clients can access updated files from the intranet or from Microsoft's public Windows Update site, which is used to support remote clients.

- Administrators can deploy updates to clients in multiple languages.

- Administrators can configure client-side targeting to help client machines get updates. Client-side targeting allows your organization's computers to automatically add themselves to the computer groups that were created in the WSUS console.

- Administrators can configure a WSUS statistics server to log update access, which allows them to track which clients have installed updates. The WSUS server and the WSUS statistics server can coexist on the same computer.

- Administrators can manage WSUS servers remotely using HTTP or HTTPS if their web browser is Internet Explorer 6.0 or newer.

WSUS Server Requirements

To act as a WSUS server, the server must meet the following requirements:

- It must be running Windows 2008, Windows Server 2008 R2, Windows Server 2012, Windows Server 2012 R2, or Windows Server 2016.

- It must have all of the most current security patches applied.

- It must be running Internet Information Services (IIS).

- It must be connected to the network.

- It must have an NTFS partition with 100 MB free disk space to install the WSUS server software, and it must have 6 GB of free space to store all of the update files.

- It must use BITS version 2.0.

- It must use Microsoft Management Console 3.0.

- It must use Microsoft Report Viewer Redistributable 2008.

- Windows Defender should be enabled on the WSUS server.

Installing the WSUS Server

WSUS should run on a dedicated server, meaning that the server will not run any other applications except IIS, which is required. Microsoft recommends that you install a clean or new version of Windows Server 2008, Windows Server 2008 R2, Windows Server 2012, Windows Server 2012 R2, or Windows Server 2016 and apply any service packs or security-related patches.

Exercise 8.1 walks you through the installation process for WSUS.

EXERCISE 8.1

Installing a WSUS Server

1. Choose Server Manager by clicking the Server Manager icon on the Taskbar.

2. Click option number 2, Add Roles And Features. If a Before You Begin screen appears, just click Next.

3. Choose role-based or featured-based installation and click Next.

4. Choose your server and click Next.

5. Choose Windows Server Update Services (see Figure 8.5). Click the Add Features button when the dialog box appears. Then click Next.

FIGURE 8.5 Choosing to install WSUS

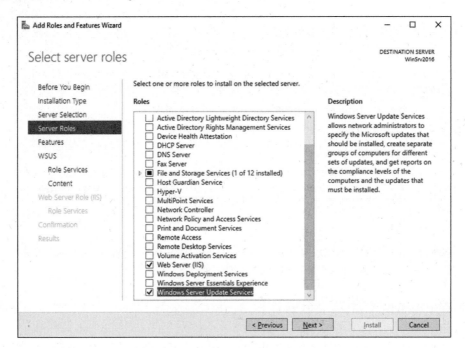

6. At the Select Features screen, just click Next.

7. At the Windows Server Update Services screen, click Next.

8. At the Select Role Services screen, make sure that WID Connectivity and WSUS Services are both checked (see Figure 8.6). Click Next.

FIGURE 8.6 Select Role screen

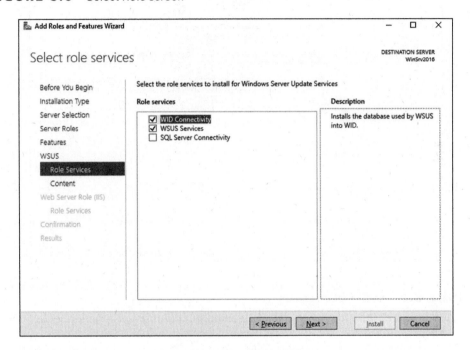

9. At the Content Location Selection screen, uncheck the box Store Updates In The Following Location and click Next (see Figure 8.7). When you uncheck this box, updates are not stored locally. They are downloaded from Microsoft only once they are approved. This will help save hard drive space.

10. At the Web Server Role screen, click Next.

11. At the Role Services screen, just accept the defaults and click Next.

12. At the confirmation screen, shown in Figure 8.8, check the box to restart the destination server automatically if required. If a dialog box appears, click Yes. Then click the Install button.

FIGURE 8.7 Content Location Selection screen

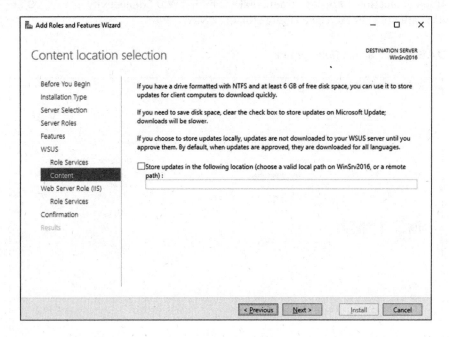

FIGURE 8.8 Confirmation screen

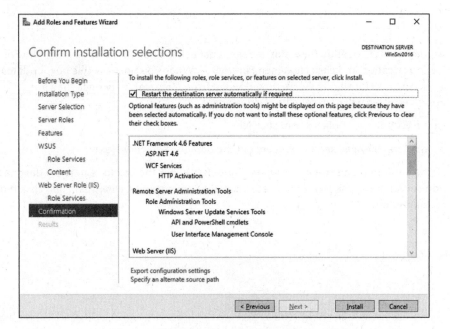

13. The installation will begin (shown in Figure 8.9), and you will see the progress. Once the installation is complete, click Close.

FIGURE 8.9   Status screen

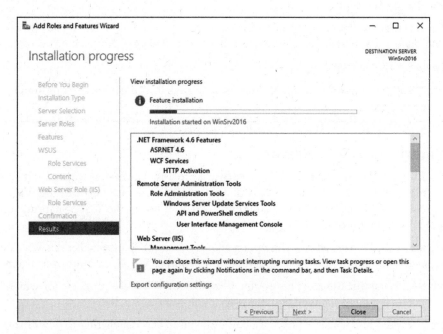

14. In Server Manager, click the WSUS link on the left side. Then click the More link (see Figure 8.10) next to Configuration Required For Windows Server Update Services.

FIGURE 8.10   Status screen

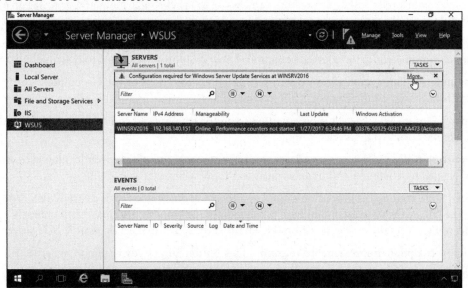

15. At the All Servers Task Details And Notifications screen, click the Launch Post-Installation Tasks link.

16. The installation process will automatically continue. Once it is finished, you will see Complete under Stage. Close the All Servers Task Details And Notifications screen.

17. Close Server Manager.

18. If a WSUS Configure Options box appears, just close it. You will set options in the next exercise.

Configuring a WSUS Server

Configuring a WSUS machine is a straightforward process. The easiest way to do it is to use the WSUS Server Configuration Wizard. This wizard walks you through the WSUS setup process, and it makes it easy to configure WSUS. When in the WSUS snap-in, you can configure different options.

Update Source And Proxy Server   This option allows you to configure whether this WSUS server synchronizes either from Microsoft Update or from another WSUS server on your network.

Products And Classifications   This option allows you to select the products for which you want to get updates and the type of updates that you want to receive.

Update Files And Languages   This option allows you to choose whether to download update files and where to store these update files. This option also allows you to choose which update languages you want downloaded.

Synchronization Schedule   This option allows you to configure how and when you synchronize your updates. Administrators can choose to synchronize manually or to set up a schedule for daily automatic synchronization.

Automatic Approvals   This option allows you to specify how to approve installation of updates automatically for selected groups and how to approve revisions to existing updates.

Computers   This option allows you to set computers to groups or use Group Policy or Registry settings on the computer to receive updates.

Server Cleanup Wizard   This option allows you to clean out old computers, updates, and update files from your server.

Reporting Rollup   This option allows you to choose whether to have replica downstream servers roll up computer and update status to this WSUS server.

Email Notifications   This option allows you to set up email notifications for WSUS. You can be notified when new updates are synchronized, or you can get email status reports. This option also allows you to set up the email server's information on your WSUS server.

Microsoft Update Improvement Program   This option allows you to choose whether you want to participate in the Microsoft Update Improvement program. When you choose to participate in this program, your WSUS server will automatically send information to Microsoft about the quality of your updates. This following information is included:

- How many computers are in the organization
- How many computers successfully installed each update
- How many computers failed to install each update

Personalization   This option allows you to personalize the way that information is displayed for this server. This option also allows you to set up a to-do list for WSUS.

WSUS Server Configuration Wizard   This option allows you to set up many of the preceding options by just using this one setup wizard.

In Exercise 8.2, you will learn how to set up some of the WSUS server options. To complete this exercise, you need to have an Internet connection that can communicate with Microsoft.

EXERCISE 8.2

Setting WSUS Server Options

1. Open the Windows Server Update Services snap-in from Administrative Tools by pressing the Start key and then choosing Administrative Tools (see Figure 8.11). The Windows Server Update Services snap-in will be at the bottom of the list alphabetically.

FIGURE 8.11   Administrative Tools

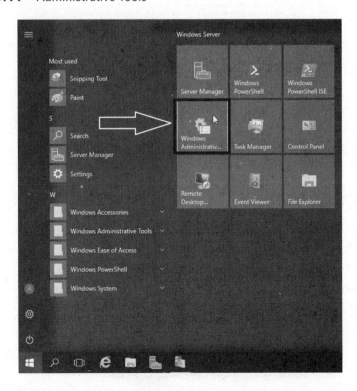

2. On the left side, click the name of your server to expand the list. Then click the Options link (shown in Figure 8.12).

FIGURE 8.12 WSUS Options

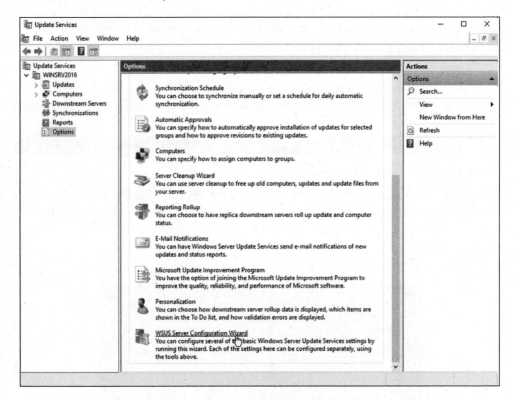

3. WSUS Server Configuration Wizard appears at the bottom of the options list. Click this link.

4. Click Next at the Before You Begin screen.

5. At the Join Microsoft Update Improvement Program screen, uncheck the Yes box and click Next.

6. At the Choose Upstream Server screen, choose Synchronize From Microsoft Update and click Next.

7. Fill in the information at the Specify Proxy Server screen if you need to use a proxy server. If you do not need a proxy server, just click Next.

8. At the Connect To Upstream Server screen, click the Start Connecting button (see Figure 8.13). This step can take a while depending on your connection speed. Once it's finished connecting, click Next.

FIGURE 8.13   Connect to Upstream Server

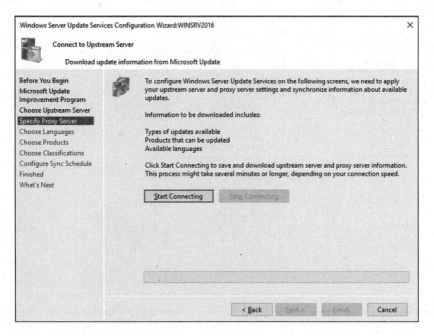

9. At the Choose Products screen (Figure 8.14), scroll down and choose the products for which you want to receive updates. Then click Next. You should only choose the products that you have in your organization. The more items you choose, the more space your network will need.

10. At the Choose Classifications screen, choose the classifications of updates you would like and click Next.

11. The Set Sync Schedule screen will appear next. At this screen, you can choose whether you want manual or automatic synchronizations. For this exercise, choose Synchronize Manually and click Next.

12. At the Finish screen, you can click Begin Initial Synchronization and click Finish. Be advised, this initial sync can take some time to finish. So if you don't have time to complete it now, you can always synchronize later.

13. Close WSUS.

FIGURE 8.14   Choose Products screen

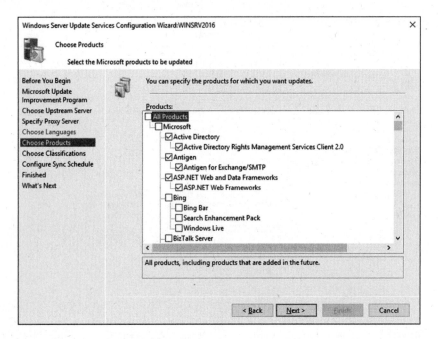

Testing and Approving Updates

The administrator should test and approve updates before they are deployed to WSUS clients. The testing should be done on a test machine that is not used for daily tasks.

You also want to make sure that the WSUS test client has Windows Defender or a third-party antivirus-type software on it. This ensures that when the updates are loaded onto this test system, the updates will be checked against possible viruses, antimalware, spyware, or any other type of malicious software.

There are many reasons why you should pre-test the updates. There have been times in the past (and it doesn't happen a lot) when Microsoft has released an update that has caused issues on a network. Microsoft does its very best job to ensure that all updates are tested before deploying them but depending on how your network is setup; the update may not perform the same way as it was intended. So by testing updates before deploying them, you ensure that the updates will not cause your network any unseen issues.

To approve updates, from the Welcome screen, click Updates on the site's toolbar. Make your settings on the Updates page that appears.

Viewing the Synchronization Log

To view the synchronization log, click the Reports button on the site's toolbar from the Welcome screen. The Reports page will appear. Click Synchronization Results to view the results.

Configuring a Disconnected Network

You have the ability to use WSUS on a disconnected network. To do so, you download the updates to the Internet-connected WSUS server. After the download is complete, you can export the updates and then import the updates to the disconnected network.

Choosing Products to Update

One of the toughest decisions that you will have to make when setting up a network and a WSUS server is which products are we (the IT department) going to allow in my network environment. The more Microsoft products that we choose, the more updates we will need.

But you have to make sure you choose the products that are needed and make sure those updates get done. Some of the products that we need to look at may not be things we think of right away. For example, we want to make sure that when we choose our products that we include Windows Defender.

As stated in the Testing and Approving Updates section, Windows Defender protects your systems against viruses, spyware, antimalware, and other malicious software. As new viruses get released, we need to make sure we protect our network systems against those viruses. By making sure we always have the up-to-date protection ensures that we can battle against these attacks.

Also, as new operating systems come out (for example, Windows Server 2016), we as IT members want to make sure that we have the latest security updates and improvements. This will not only ensure that our network runs at peak performance but it will also ensure that we fix any security loopholes that hackers may have figured out in the operating system.

WSUS Client Requirements

WSUS clients run a special version of Automatic Updates that is designed to support WSUS. The following enhancements to Automatic Updates are included:

- Clients can receive updates from a WSUS server as opposed to the public Microsoft Windows Update site.

- The administrator can schedule when the downloading of updated files will occur.

- Clients can be configured via Group Policy or through editing the Registry.

- Updates can occur when an administrative account or nonadministrative account is logged on.

  The following client platforms are the only ones that WSUS currently supports:

- Windows XP Home Edition (with Service Pack 3)

- Windows XP Professional (with Service Pack 3)

- Windows Server 2003 (SP1 or newer)

- Windows Vista

- Windows 7

- Windows 8

- Windows 8.1

- Windows 10

- Windows Server 2008 and 2008 R2
- Windows Server 2012 and 2012 R2
- Windows Server 2016

Configuring the WSUS Clients

You can configure WSUS clients in two ways. The method you use depends on whether you use Active Directory in your network.

In a nonenterprise network (not running Active Directory), you would configure Automatic Updates through the Control Panel. Each client's registry would then be edited to reflect the location of the server providing the automatic updates.

Within an enterprise network, using Active Directory, you would typically see Automatic Updates configured through Group Policy. Group Policy is used to manage configuration and security settings via Active Directory. Group Policy is also used to specify what server a client will use for Automatic Updates. If Automatic Updates is configured through Group Policy, the user will not be able to change Automatic Updates settings by choosing Control Panel ➢ Windows Update (for Windows 8, Windows 7, Windows Server 2008, Windows Server 2008 R2, Windows Server 2012, Windows Server 2012 R2, and Windows Server 2016).

Configuring a Client in a Non–Active Directory Network

The easiest way to configure the client to use Automatic Updates is through the Control Panel. However, you can also configure Automatic Updates through the Registry. The Registry is a database of all your server settings. You can access it by choosing Start ➢ Run and typing **regedit** in the Run dialog box. Automatic Updates settings are defined through HKEY_LOCAL_MACHINE\Software\Policies\Microsoft\Windows\WindowsUpdate\AU.

Table 8.1 lists some of the Registry options that you can configure for Automatic Updates.

TABLE 8.1   Selected Registry keys and values for Automatic Updates

Registry key	Options for values
NoAutoUpdate	0: Automatic Updates are enabled (default).
	1: Automatic Updates are disabled.
	2: Notify of download and installation.
	3: Autodownload and notify of installation.
	4: Autodownload and schedule installation.
	5: Automatic Updates are required, but end users can configure.

Registry key	Options for values
ScheduledInstallDay	1: Sunday
	2: Monday
	3: Tuesday
	4: Wednesday
	5: Thursday
	6: Friday
	7: Saturday
UseWUServer	0: Use public Microsoft Windows Update site.
	1: Use server specified in WUServer entry.

To specify what server will be used as the Windows Update server, you edit two Registry keys, which are found here:

HKEY_LOCAL_MACHINE\Software\Policies\Microsoft\Windows\WindowsUpdate

- The WUServer key sets the Windows Update server using the server's HTTP name—for example, http://intranetSUS.
- The WUStatusServer key sets the Windows Update intranet WSUS statistics server by using the server's HTTP name—for example, http://intranetSUS.

Configuring a Client in an Active Directory Network

If the WSUS client is part of an enterprise network using Active Directory, you would configure the client via Group Policy. In Exercise 8.3, I will walk you through the steps needed to configure the Group Policy Object (GPO) for WSUS clients. The *Group Policy Management Console (GPMC)* needs to be installed to complete this exercise. If you don't have the GPMC installed, you can install it using the Server Manager utility.

EXERCISE 8.3

Configuring a GPO for WSUS

1. Open the GPMC by pressing the Windows key and selecting Administrative Tools ➤ Group Policy Management.

2. Expand the forest, domains, and your domain name. Under your domain name, right-click and choose Create And Link GPO Here. Name the GPO **WSUS**, and hit Enter. Right-click the WSUS GPO and choose Edit.

3. Under the Computer Configuration section, expand Policies ➢ AdministrativeTemplates ➢ Windows Components ➢ Windows Update.

4. In the right pane, double-click the Configure Automatic Updates option. The Configure Automatic Updates Properties dialog box appears. Click the Enabled button. Then, in the drop-down list, choose Auto Download And Notify For Install. Click OK.

5. Double-click Specify Intranet Microsoft Update Service Location Properties. This setting allows you to specify the server from which the clients will get the updates. Click Enabled. In the two server name boxes, enter **//servername** (the name of the server on which you installed WSUS in Exercise 8.1). Click OK.

6. To configure the rescheduling of automatic updates, double-click Reschedule Automatic Updates Scheduled Installations. You can enable and schedule the amount of time that Automatic Updates waits after system startup before it attempts to proceed with a scheduled installation that was previously missed. Click Enabled. Enter **10** in the Startup (Minutes) box. Click OK.

7. To configure auto-restart for scheduled Automatic Updates installations, double-click No Auto-Restart For Scheduled Automatic Updates Installations. When you enable this option, the computer is not required to restart after an update. Enable this option and click OK.

8. Close the GPMC.

Configuring Client-Side Targeting

Administrators can use a GPO to enable client-side targeting. Client machines can be automatically added into the proper computer group once the client computer connects to the WSUS server. Client-side targeting can be a very useful tool when an administrator has multiple client computers and the administrator needs to automate the process of assigning those computers to computer groups.

Administrators can enable client-side targeting on the WSUS server by clicking the Use Group Policy Or Registry Settings On Client Computers option on the Computers Options page.

1. On the WSUS console toolbar, click Options and then click Computer Options.

2. In Computer Options, choose one of the following options:

    ▪ If an administrator wants to create groups and assign computers through the WSUS console (server-side targeting), click Use The Move Computers Task In Windows Server Update Services.

    ▪ If an administrator wants to create groups and assign computers by using Group Policy settings on the client computer (client-side targeting), click Use Group Policy Or Registry Settings On Computers.

3. Under Tasks, click the Save Settings button and then click OK.

Understanding Backups

One of the most important jobs of an IT administrator is to protect the company's data. Doesn't matter if it's setting up security and permissions or installing a new firewall, we are trying to protect our data. It truly is our number one job.

Knowing that protecting our data is our primary task means that our IT departments have to ensure that we can recover that data in the event of a major catastrophe (like a fire in the server room) or hardware failure.

If you have deployed Active Directory in your network environment, your users now depend on it to function properly in order to do their jobs. From network authentications to file access to print and web services, Active Directory has become a mission-critical component of your business. Therefore, the importance of backing up the Active Directory data store should be evident.

Backups are just good common sense, but here are several specific reasons to back up data:

Protect Against Hardware Failures   Computer hardware devices have finite lifetimes, and all hardware eventually fails. *Mean Time Between Failures (MTBF)* is the average time a device will function before it actually fails. There is also a rating derived from benchmark testing of hard disk devices that tells you when you may be at risk for an unavoidable disaster. Some types of failures, such as corrupted hard disk drives, can result in significant data loss.

Protect Against Accidental Deletion or Modification of Data   Although the threat of hardware failures is very real, in most environments, mistakes in modifying or deleting data are much more common. For example, suppose a system administrator accidentally deletes all of the objects within a specific OU. Clearly, it's very important to be able to retrieve this information from a backup.

Protect Against a Major Catastrophe   As IT administrators, it's tough to think that a major catastrophe would ever happen to our company, but we have to make sure we protect our company in the event of that very possibility. Fires, earthquakes, flooding, and tornados are just some of the events that we have to consider. Because of these types of events, we have to make sure that not only do we back up our data, we also get that data offsite. When I talk about offsite, I don't mean another building on the campus. It needs to be in another city or in a very safe location (like a safety deposit box).

Keeping Historical Information   Users and system administrators sometimes modify files and then later find out that they require access to an older version of the file. Or a file is accidentally deleted, and a user does not discover that fact until much later. By keeping multiple backups over time, you can recover information from prior backups when necessary.

Protect Against Malicious Deletion or Modification of Data   Even in the most secure environments, it is conceivable that unauthorized users (or authorized ones with malicious intent!) could delete or modify information. In such cases, the loss of data might require valid backups from which to restore critical information.

Windows Server 2016 includes a Backup utility (called wbadmin) that is designed to back up operating system files and the Active Directory data store. It allows for basic backup functionality, such as scheduling backup jobs and selecting which files to back up. Figure 8.15 shows the main screen of the Windows Server 2016 Backup utility (wbadmin).

FIGURE 8.15   The main screen of the Windows Server 2016 Backup utility

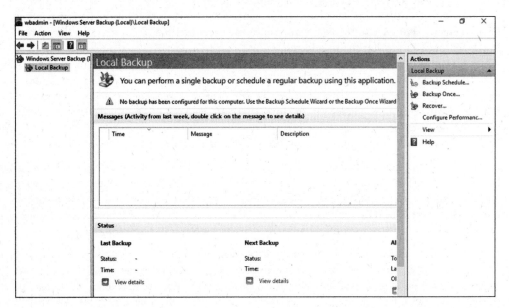

In the following sections, we'll look at the details of using the Windows Server 2016 Backup utility and how you can restore Active Directory when problems do occur.

Overview of the Windows Server 2016 Backup Utility

Although the general purpose behind performing backup operations—protecting information—is straightforward, system administrators must consider many options when determining the optimal backup-and-recovery scenario for their environment. Factors include what to back up, how often to back up, and when the backups should be performed.

In this section, you'll see how the Windows Server 2016 Backup utility makes it easy to implement a backup plan for many network environments.

Although the Windows Server 2016 Backup utility provides the basic function-ality required to back up your files, you may want to investigate third-party products that provide additional functionality. These applications can provide options for specific types of backups (such as those for Exchange Server and SQL Server) as well as disaster recovery options, networking functionality, centralized management, and support for more advanced hardware.

Backup Types

One of the most important issues you will have to deal with when you are performing backups is keeping track of which files you have backed up and which files you need to back up. Whenever a backup of a file is made, the archive bit for the file is set. You can view the attributes of system files by right-clicking them and selecting Properties. By clicking the Advanced button in the Properties dialog box, you will access the Advanced Attributes dialog box. Here you will see the option Folder Is Ready For Archiving. Figure 8.16 shows an example of the attributes for a folder.

FIGURE 8.16   Viewing the Archive attributes for a folder

Although it is possible to back up all of the files in the file system during each backup operation, it's sometimes more convenient to back up only selected files (such as those that have changed since the last backup operation). When performing backups, you can back up to removable media (DVD) or to a network location.

It is recommended by Microsoft to do a backup to a network location or removable media. The reason for this is that if your company suffers from a disaster (fire, hurricane, and so forth), your data can all still be lost—including the backup. If you back up to a removable media source, a copy of the backup can be taken offsite. This protects against a major disaster. Several types of backups can be performed:

Although Windows Server 2016 does not support all of these backup types, it's very important that you understand the most common backup types. Most administrators use third-party software for their backups. That's why it's important to know all of the different types.

Normal   Normal backups (also referred to as *system* or *full backups*) back up all of the selected files and then mark them as backed up. This option is usually used when a full system backup is made. Windows Server 2016 supports this backup.

Copy *Copy backups* back up all of the selected files but do not mark them as backed up. This is useful when you want to make additional backups of files for moving files offsite or you want to make multiple copies of the same data for archival purposes.

Incremental *Incremental backups* copy any selected files that are marked as ready for backup (typically because they have not been backed up or they have been changed since the last backup) and then mark the files as backed up. When the next incremental backup is run, only the files that are not marked as having been backed up are stored. Incremental backups are used in conjunction with normal (full) backups.

The most common backup process is to make a full backup and then make subsequent incremental backups. The benefit to this method is that only files that have changed since the last full or incremental backup will be stored. This can reduce backup times and disk or tape storage space requirements.

When recovering information from this type of backup method, a system administrator must first restore the full backup and then restore each of the incremental backups.

Differential *Differential backups* are similar in purpose to incremental backups with one important exception: Differential backups copy all of the files that are marked for backup but do not mark the files as backed up. When restoring files in a situation that uses normal and differential backups, you need only restore the normal backup and the latest differential backup.

Daily *Daily backups* back up all of the files that have changed during a single day. This operation uses the file time/date stamps to determine which files should be backed up and does not mark the files as having been backed up.

Backing Up System State Data

When you are planning to back up and restore Active Directory, be aware that the most important component is known as the *System State data*. System State data includes the components upon which the Windows Server 2016 operating system relies for normal operations. The Windows Server 2016 Backup utility offers you the ability to back up the System State data to another type of media (such as a hard disk or network share). Specifically, it will back up the following components for a Windows Server 2016 domain controller:

Active Directory The *Active Directory data store* is at the heart of Active Directory. It contains all of the information necessary to create and manage network resources, such as users and computers. In most environments that use Active Directory, users and system administrators rely on the proper functioning of these services in order to do their jobs.

Boot Files *Boot files* are the files required for booting the Windows Server 2016 operating system and can be used in the case of boot file corruption.

COM+ Class Registration Database The *COM+ Class Registration database* is a listing of all of the COM+ Class registrations stored on the computer. Applications that run on a Windows Server 2016 computer might require the registration of various share code components. As part of the System State backup process, Windows Server 2016 stores all of the information related to Component Object Model+ (COM+) components so that it can be quickly and easily restored.

Registry   The Windows Server 2016 *Registry* is a central repository of information related to the operating system configuration (such as desktop and network settings), user settings, and application settings. Therefore, the Registry is absolutely vital to the proper functioning of Windows Server 2016.

***Sysvol* Directory**   The *Sysvol directory* includes data and files that are shared between the domain controllers within an Active Directory domain. Many operating system services rely on this information in order to function properly.

Bare Metal Backups and Restores

One of the options you have in Windows Server 2016 is to do a *Bare Metal Restore (BMR)*. This is a restore of a machine after the machine has been completely wiped out and formatted. This type of restore is done usually after a catastrophic machine failure or crash.

Windows Server 2016 gives you the ability to back up all of the files needed for a Bare Metal Restore by choosing the Bare Metal Recovery check box (see Figure 8.17).

FIGURE 8.17   Bare Metal Restore option

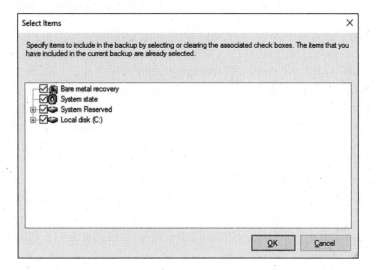

When you choose the Bare Metal Restore option in Windows Server 2016, all of the sub-options (System State, System Reserved, and Local Disk) automatically get checked.

When preparing your network for a Bare Metal Backup, you want to make sure that you have everything you need on hand to complete this type of restore. You may want to keep a copy of the server software, server drivers, and so forth on hand and ready to go, just in case you have to do a full restore.

Scheduling Backups

In addition to specifying which files to back up, you can schedule backup jobs to occur at specific times. Planning *when* to perform backups is just as important as deciding *what* to back up. Performing backup operations can reduce overall system performance; therefore, you should plan to back up information during times of minimal activity on your servers.

To add a backup operation to the schedule, you can simply click the Add button on the Specify Backup Time window.

Restoring System State Data

In some cases, the Active Directory data store or other System State data may become corrupt or unavailable. This could be due to many different reasons. A hard disk failure might, for example, result in the loss of data. Or the accidental deletion of an Organizational Unit (OU) and all of its objects might require a restore operation to be performed.

The actual steps involved in restoring System State data are based on the details of what has caused the data loss and what effect this data loss has had on the system. In the best-case scenario, the System State data is corrupt or inaccurate but the operating system can still boot. If this is the case, all you must do is boot into a special *Directory Services Restore Mode (DSRM)* and then restore the System State data from a backup. This process will replace the current System State data with that from the backup. Therefore, any changes that have been made since the last backup will be completely lost and must be redone.

In a worst-case scenario, all of the information on a server has been lost or a hardware failure is preventing the machine from properly booting. If this is the case, here are several steps that you must take in order to recover System State data:

1. Fix any hardware problem that might prevent the computer from booting (for example, replace any failed hard disks).

2. Reinstall the Windows Server 2016 operating system. This should be performed like a regular installation on a new system.

3. Reinstall any device drivers that may be required by your backup device. If you backed up information to the file system, this will not apply.

4. Restore the System State data using the Windows Server 2016 Backup utility.

I'll cover the technical details of performing restores later in this chapter. For now, however, you should understand the importance of backing up information and, whenever possible, testing the validity of backups.

Backing Up and Restoring Group Policy Objects

Group Policy Objects (GPOs) are a major part of Active Directory. When you back up Active Directory, GPOs can also get backed up. You also have the ability to back up GPOs through the Group Policy Management Console (GPMC). This gives you the ability to back up and restore individual GPOs.

To back up all GPOs, open the GPMC and right-click the Group Policy Objects container. You will see the option Back Up All. After you choose this option, a wizard will start, asking you for the backup location. Choose a location and click Backup.

To back up an individual GPO, right-click the GPO (in the Group Policy Objects container) and choose Backup. Again, after you choose this option, a wizard will start, asking you for the backup location. Choose a location and click Backup.

To restore a GPO, it's the same process as above (backing up GPOs) except, instead of choosing Backup, you will either choose Manage Backups (to restore all GPOs) or Restore (for an individual GPO).

Setting Up an Active Directory Backup

The Windows Server 2016 Backup utility makes it easy to back up the System data (including Active Directory) as part of a normal backup operation. We've already covered the ideas behind the different backup types and why and when they are used.

Exercise 8.4 walks you through the process of backing up the domain controller. In order to complete this exercise, the local machine must be a domain controller, and you must have a DVD burner or network location to back up the System State.

 The Windows Server 2016 Backup utility is not installed by default. If you have already installed the Windows Server 2016 Backup utility, skip to step 9.

EXERCISE 8.4

Backing Up Active Directory

1. To install the Windows Server 2016 Backup utility, click the Start key ➢ Server Manager.

2. In the center console, click the link for # 2, Add Roles And Features. Click Next at the Before You Begin screen (if it appears).

3. At the Select Installation Type screen, choose role-based or feature-based installation and click Next.

4. The Select Destination Server screen appears. Choose Select A Server From The Server Pool, and choose your server under Server Pool. Click Next.

5. Click Next at the Select Server Roles screen.

6. At the Select Features screen (see Figure 8.18), scroll down and check the box next to Windows Server Backup. Click Next.

FIGURE 8.18 Selecting Windows Server Backup

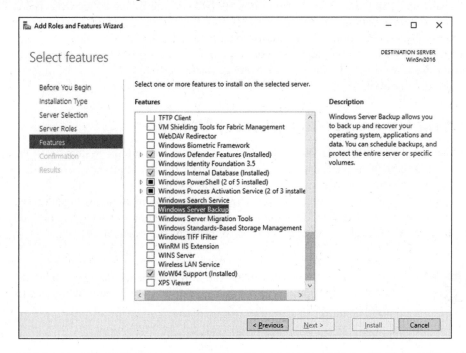

7. At the Confirmation screen, click the check box to restart the destination server automatically. This will bring up a dialog box. Click Yes, and then click the Install button.

8. Click the Close button when finished. Close Server Manager.

9. Open Windows Backup by clicking Start ➢ Administrative Tools ➢ Windows Server Backup.

10. On the left-hand side, click Local Backup. Then, under Actions, click Backup Once.

11. When the Backup Once Wizard appears, click Different Options (see Figure 8.19) and click Next.

12. At the Select Backup Configuration screen, choose Custom and click Next.

13. Click the Add Items button (see Figure 8.20). Choose System State and click OK. Click Next.

FIGURE 8.19   Backup Options screen

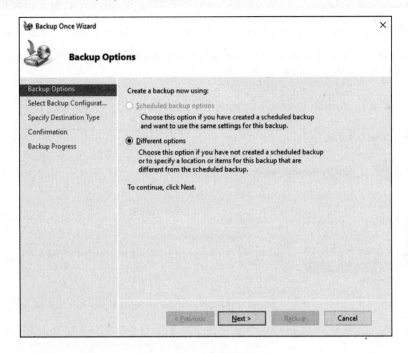

FIGURE 8.20   Select Items for Backup screen

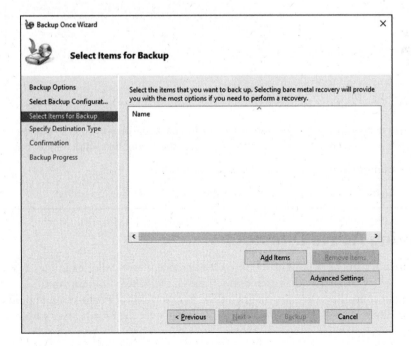

14. At the Specify Destination Type screen, choose Remote Shared Folder. Click Next.

15. Put in the shared path you want to use. Make sure the Do Not Inherit radio button is selected and click Next (see Figure 8.21).

FIGURE 8.21   Specify Destination screen

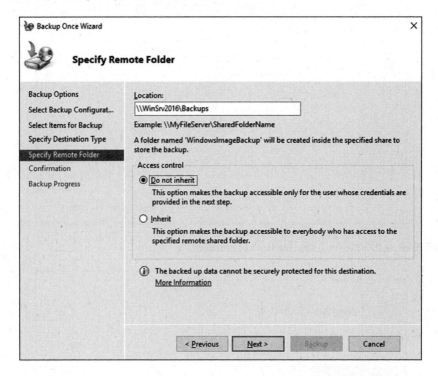

16. You will need to provide user credentials for the backup. You will need to use these credentials in the event of a restore. After you enter the credentials, click the OK button.

17. At the Confirmation screen, click the Backup button.

18. Once the backup is complete, close the Windows Server Backup utility.

Restoring Active Directory

Active Directory has been designed with fault tolerance in mind. For example, it is highly recommended by Microsoft that each domain have at least two domain controllers. Each of these domain controllers contains a copy of the Active Directory data store. Should one of the domain controllers fail, the available one can take over the failed server's functionality.

When the failed server is repaired, it can then be promoted to a domain controller in the existing environment. This process effectively restores the failed domain controller without incurring any downtime for end users because all of the Active Directory data is replicated to the repaired server in the next scheduled replication.

In some cases, you might need to restore Active Directory from a backup. For example, suppose a system administrator accidentally deletes several hundred users from the domain and does not realize it until the change has been propagated to all of the other domain controllers. Manually re-creating the accounts is not an option because the objects' security identifiers will be different (and all permissions must be reset). Clearly, a method for restoring from backup is the best solution. You can elect to make the Active Directory restore authoritative or nonauthoritative, as described in the following sections.

Overview of Authoritative Restore

Restoring Active Directory and other System State data is an important process should system files or the Active Directory data store become corrupt or otherwise unavailable. Fortunately, the Windows Server 2016 Backup utility allows you to restore data easily from a backup, should the need arise.

I mentioned earlier that in the case of the accidental deletion of information from Active Directory, you might need to restore Active Directory from a recent backup. But what happens if there is more than one domain controller in the environment? Even if you did perform a restore, the information on this domain controller would be seen as outdated and it would be overwritten by the data from another domain controller. This data from the older domain controller is exactly the information you want to replace. The domain controller that was reloaded using a backup would have an older time stamp, and the other domain controllers would re-delete the information from the backup.

Fortunately, Windows Server 2016 and Active Directory allow you to perform what is called an *authoritative restore*. The authoritative restore process specifies a domain controller as having the authoritative (or master) copy of the Active Directory data store. When other domain controllers communicate with this domain controller, their information will be overwritten with Active Directory data stored on the local machine.

Now that you have an idea of how an authoritative restore is supposed to work, let's move on to looking at the details of performing the process.

Performing an Authoritative Restore

When you are restoring Active Directory information on a Windows Server 2016 domain controller, make sure that Active Directory services are not running. This is because the restore of System State data requires full access to system files and the Active Directory data store. If you attempt to restore System State data while the domain controller is active, you will see an error message.

In general, restoring data and operating system files is a straightforward process. It is important to note that restoring a System State backup will replace the existing Registry, Sysvol, and Active Directory files, so that any changes you made since the last backup will be lost.

In addition to restoring the entire Active Directory database, you can also restore only specific subtrees within Active Directory using the restoresubtree command in the ntdsutil utility. This allows you to restore specific information, and it is useful in case of accidental deletion of isolated material.

Following the authoritative restore process, Active Directory should be updated to the time of the last backup. Furthermore, all of the other domain controllers for this domain will have their Active Directory information overwritten by the results of the restore operation. The result is an Active Directory environment that has been recovered from media.

Overview of Nonauthoritative Restore

Now that you understand why you would use an authoritative restore and how it is performed, it's an easy conceptual jump to understand a *nonauthoritative restore*. Remember that by making a restore authoritative, you are simply telling other domain controllers in the domain to recognize the restored machine as the newest copy of Active Directory for replication purposes. If you only have one domain controller, the authoritative restore process becomes moot; you can simply skip the steps required to make the restore authoritative and begin using the domain controller immediately after the normal restore is complete.

If you have more than one domain controller in the domain and you need to perform a nonauthoritative restore, simply allow the domain controller to receive Active Directory database information from other domain controllers in the domain using normal replication methods.

Active Directory Recycle Bin

The Active Directory Recycle Bin is a great feature that allows an administrator to restore an Active Directory object that has been deleted. This feature is only available on domain controllers.

Let's say that you have a junior administrator who has been making changes to Active Directory for hours. The junior admin then deletes an OU from Active Directory. You would then have to reload the OU from a tape backup, or even worse, you may have to reload the entire Active Directory (depending on your backup software), thus losing the hours of work the junior admin has completed.

The problem here is that when you delete a security object from Active Directory, the object's security ID (SID) gets removed. All users' rights and permissions are associated with the users' SID number and not their account name. This is where the AD Recycle Bin can help.

The *Active Directory Recycle Bin* allows you to preserve and restore accidentally deleted Active Directory objects without the need of using a backup.

The Active Directory Recycle Bin works for both the Active Directory Domain Services (AD DS) and the Active Directory Lightweight Directory Services (AD LDS) environments.

By enabling (disabled by default) the Active Directory Recycle Bin, any deleted Active Directory objects are preserved and Active Directory objects can be restored, in their entirety, to the same condition that they were in immediately before deletion. This means that all group memberships and access rights that an object had before deletion will remain intact.

To enable the Active Directory Recycle Bin, you must do the following (you must be a member of the Schema Admins group):

- Run the adprep /forestprep command to prepare the forest on the server that holds the schema master to update the schema.

- Run the adprep /domainprep /gpprep command to prepare the domain on the server that holds the infrastructure operations master role.

- If a read-only domain controller (RODC) is present in your environment, you must also run the adprep /rodcprep command.

- Make sure that all domain controllers in your Active Directory forest are running Windows Server 2016, Windows Server 2012 R2, Windows Server 2012, or Windows Server 2008 R2.

- Make sure that the forest functional level is set to Windows Server 2016, Windows Server 2012 R2, Windows Server 2012, or Windows Server 2008 R2.

Understanding the *ntdsutil* Utility

As you learned in the preceding section, there are times when you have to be offline to do maintenance. For example, you need to perform authoritative and nonauthoritative restores while the domain controller is offline. The main utility we use for offline maintenance is ntdsutil.

Ntdsutil.exe

The primary method by which system administrators can do offline maintenance is through the ntdsutil command-line tool. You can launch this tool by simply entering **ntdsutil** at a command prompt. For the commands to work properly, you must start the command prompt with elevated privileges. The ntdsutil command is both interactive and context sensitive. That is, once you launch the utility, you'll see an ntdsutil command prompt. At this prompt, you can enter various commands that set your context within the application. For example, if you enter **domain management**, you'll be able to enter domain-related commands. Several operations also require you to connect to a domain, a domain controller, or an Active Directory object before you perform a command.

Table 8.2 provides a list of some of the domain-management commands supported by the ntdsutil tool. You can access this functionality by typing the command at an elevated command prompt. Once you are in the ntdsutil prompt, you can use the question mark to see all of the commands available.

TABLE 8.2   Ntdsutil offline maintenance commands

Ntdsutil **Command**	**Purpose**
Help or ?	Displays information about the commands that are available within the Domain Management menu of the ntdsutil utility.
Activate instance %s	Sets NTDS or a specific AD LDS instance as the active instance.

TABLE 8.2   Ntdsutil offline maintenance commands *(continued)*

Ntdsutil **Command**	**Purpose**
Authoritative restore	Sets the domain controller for the authoritative restore of the Active Directory database.
Change service account	This allows an administrator to change the AD LDS service account to user name and password. You can use a "NULL" for a blank password, and you can use * to prompt the user to enter a password.
configurable settings	Allows an administrator to manage configurable settings.
DS behavior	Allows an administrator to view and modify AD DS or AD LDS behavior.
files	This command allows an administrator to manage the AD DS or AD LDS database files.
Group Membership Evaluation	Allows an administrator to evaluate the security IDs (SIDs) in a token for a given user or group.
LDAP policies	Administrators can manage the Lightweight Directory Access Protocol (LDAP) protocol policies.
metadata cleanup	Removes metadata from decommissioned domain controllers.
security account management	This command allows an administrator to manage SIDs.
Set DSRM Password	Resets the Directory Service Restore mode administrator account password.

Wbadmin Command-Line Utility

The wbadmin command allows you to back up and restore your operating system, volumes, files, folders, and applications from a command prompt.

You must be a member of the Administrators group to configure a backup schedule. You must be a member of the Backup Operators or the Administrators group (or you must have been delegated the appropriate permissions) to perform all other tasks using the wbadmin command.

To use the wbadmin command, you must run wbadmin from an elevated command prompt (to open an elevated command prompt, click Start, right-click Command Prompt, and then click Run As Administrator). Table 8.3 shows some of the wbadmin commands.

TABLE 8.3 Wbadmin commands

Command	Description
Wbadmin enable backup	Configures and enables a daily backup schedule.
Wbadmin disable backup	Disables your daily backups.
Wbadmin start backup	Runs a one-time backup.
Wbadmin stop job	Stops the currently running backup or recovery operation.
Wbadmin get items	Lists the items included in a specific backup.
Wbadmin start recovery	Runs a recovery of the volumes, applications, files, or folders specified.
Wbadmin get status	Shows the status of the currently running backup or recovery operation.
Wbadmin start systemstaterecovery	Runs a system state recovery.
Wbadmin start systemstatebackup	Runs a system state backup.
Wbadmin start sysrecovery	Runs a recovery of the full system state.

Backing Up Virtual Machines

One of the main questions that you have to ask yourself when it comes to backing up a Hyper-V server is, Do I back up the Hyper-V server and the virtual machines as files, or do I back up each virtual machine as its own server?

Virtual machines and the virtual hard drives that work with those virtual machines are just files that reside on a Microsoft Hyper-V server. But when they are running, they work as normal servers within the virtual environment.

Some people like to back up the Hyper-V server and its files and some like to back up the virtual machines as servers. So what is best for your company? Well, it depends on what the virtual machines do and how much storage space you have.

I have set up many companies and I have set up dozens of virtual machines and I personally like to back up the virtual machines as normal servers. I do have good reasons for this decision.

Let's say we set up a Windows Server 2016 server that works as a Hyper-V host. We then decide to load a virtual machine that will be a file server. We will do our normal daily backups once a day at night, and maybe we will even do a backup during the day at 1p.m.

At 11:30 a.m., one of your users deletes a file that was created yesterday. Before deleting the file, the user had created 25 new documents. But that one file needs to be recovered. If we back up the virtual machines as files, depending on our backup software, we will need to restore the virtual machine file from last night. Okay, problem solved, but is it? Well actually it's not. Because when we restored last night's virtual machine files, we also lost all of our changes that have happened today.

If we backed up the virtual machines as servers, we would then just need to restore the single file that was lost on that server. This would save us a lot of time and issues. But it can also cause some issues. By backing each virtual machine up as a server, your backups will require more space. So if your backup server, software, tapes, or cloud storage is large enough, then it may be best to back up each virtual machine as its own server.

PowerShell Commands

As I have stated in other chapters, Microsoft has announced that the Windows Server 2016 exams are going to be PowerShell intensive. So in this section, I will show you some of the available PowerShell commands for updates and for backups.

So Table 8.4 will show you some of the different PowerShell commands that are available for WSUS administration.

Table 8.4 is just a partial list of PowerShell commands for WSUS. To see a complete list, visit Microsoft's website at

https://technet.microsoft.com/en-us/library/hh826166.aspx

TABLE 8.4   WSUS administration commands

PowerShell Command	Description
Add-WsusComputer	This command allows an administrator to add a client computer to a WSUS target group.
Approve-WsusUpdate	This allows an administrator to approve an update that can then be applied to clients.
Deny-WsusUpdate	This allows an administrator to deny an update.
Get-WsusClassification	Administrators can use this command to get the list of all WSUS classifications available on the server.
Get-WsusProduct	Administrators can use this command to get the list of all WSUS products available on the server.

PowerShell Command	Description
Get-WsusUpdate	This command shows you the WSUS update object and the details about that update.
Invoke-WsusServerCleanup	Allows an administrator to initiate the cleanup process on the WSUS server.
Set-WsusClassification	Sets whether the classifications of updates are enabled on the WSUS server.

Now that you have viewed the PowerShell commands for WSUS administration, let's go ahead and take a look at the backups and recovery.

So Table 8.5 will show you some of the different PowerShell commands that are available for Backup administration.

Table 8.5 is just a partial list of PowerShell commands for backups and restores. To see a complete list, visit Microsoft's website at https://technet.microsoft.com/en-us/library/jj902428 (v=wps.630).aspx

TABLE 8.5   Backup and restore commands

PowerShell Command	Description
Add-WBBackupTarget	This command allows an administrator to add a backup target to a backup.
Add-WBBareMetalRecovery	Allows you to select a bare metal backup to a backup so that administrators can perform bare metal recoveries.
Add-WBSystemState	This command includes the system state components to the backup.
Add-WBVirtualMachine	This command allows you to include a virtual machine file to a backup.
Add-WBVolume	This command adds a volume to a backup.
Get-WBBackupSet	Administrators can use this command to view the backups for a server.
Get-WBDisk	This command shows the hard drives of a computer.

TABLE 8.5   Backup and restore commands *(continued)*

PowerShell Command	Description
Get-WBJob	Shows an administrator the current backup job.
Get-WBSchedule	Shows an administrator the current backup schedule.
Get-WBVolume	Shows the administrator the volumes on a system.
New-WBPolicy	This command creates a new backup policy.
Remove-WBFileSpec	Deletes a backup file specification from a backup.
Remove-WBPolicy	This allows you to delete a backup policy.
Remove-WBSystemState	Deletes the system state components from a backup.
Remove-WBVolume	Deletes a volume from a backup.
Resume-WBBackup	This command allows you to resume a backup.
Set-WBPolicy	With this command, you can set a new policy on a backup.
Set-WBSchedule	Administrators can set the backup schedule.
Start-WBBackup	This command starts a manual backup job.
Stop-WBJob	This command allows you to stop a backup job.

Summary

This chapter began with a discussion of WSUS and what Windows Update can do for your network. You learned why you would want to use a WSUS server instead of having clients manually connect to the Internet to receive their updates.

I talked about the importance of choosing which updates and which products you want to update. Also, I talked about the importance of testing updates before deploying them.

You learned about how important it is to back up and restore a Windows Server 2016 server in the event of a hardware or software failure. I also explained how some of the features, such as the Active Directory Recycle Bin and ntdsutil, are part of Windows Server 2016 domain controller and how these utilities make an administrator's life easier by restoring an Active Directory object or the entire Active Directory database.

Video Resources

There are videos available for the following exercises:

8.1

8.2

You can access the videos at http://sybextestbanks.wiley.com on the Other Study Tools tab.

Exam Essentials

Understand WSUS.   Using Windows Server Update Services is one way to have your end users receive important updates from Microsoft. WSUS gives administrators the ability to download, test, and approve updates before they get released onto the network.

Understand the various backup types available with the Windows Server 2016 Backup utility.   The Windows Server 2016 Backup utility can perform full and incremental backup operations. Some third-party backup utilities also support differential and daily backups. You can use each of these operations as part of an efficient backup strategy.

Know how to back up Active Directory.   The data within the Active Directory database on a domain controller is part of the system state data. You can back up the system state data to a file using the Windows Server 2016 Backup utility.

Know how to restore Active Directory.   Restoring the Active Directory database is considerably different from other restore operations. To restore some or the entire Active Directory database, you must first boot the machine into Directory Services Restore mode.

Understand the importance of an authoritative restore process.   You use an authoritative restore when you want to restore earlier information from an Active Directory backup and you want the older information to be propagated to other domain controllers in the environment.

Understand offline maintenance using ntdsutil.   The ntdsutil command-line tool is a primary method by which system administrators perform offline maintenance. Understand how to launch this tool by entering **ntdsutil** at a command prompt.

Review Questions

1. You are the network administrator for a Fortune 500 company. You are responsible for all client computers at the central campus. You want to make sure that all of the client computers have the most current software installed for their operating systems, including software in the categories Critical Updates and Service Packs, Windows Server 2016 Family, and Driver Updates. You want to automate the process as much as possible, and you want the client computers to download the updates from a central server that you are managing. You decide to use Windows Server Update Services. The WSUS server software has been installed on a server called WSUSServer. You want to test the WSUS server before you set up group policies within the domain. You install Windows 10. Which of the following Registry entries needs to be made for the client to specify that the client should use WSUSServer for Windows Update? (Choose all that apply.)

   A. Use HKEY_LOCAL_MACHINE\Software\Policies\Microsoft\Windows\WindowsUpdate\AU\UseWUServer, and specify 0 data.

   B. Use HKEY_LOCAL_MACHINE\Software\Policies\Microsoft\Windows\WindowsUpdate\AU\UseWUServer, and specify 1 for data.

   C. Use HKEY_LOCAL_MACHINE\Software\Policies\Microsoft\Windows\WindowsUpdate\AU\WUServer, and specify http://WSUSServer.

   D. Use HKEY_LOCAL_MACHINE\Software\Policies\Microsoft\Windows\WindowsUpdate\AU\WUServer, and specify WSUSServer.

   E. Use HKEY_LOCAL_MACHINE\Software\Policies\Microsoft\Windows\WindowsUpdate\WUServer, and specify http://WSUSServer.

   F. Use HKEY_LOCAL_MACHINE\Software\Policies\Microsoft\Windows\WindowsUpdate\WUServer, and specify WSUSServer.

2. You are the administrator of a new Windows Server 2016 machine. You need to install WSUS. From where do you install WSUS?

   A. Add/Remove Programs

   B. Programs

   C. Server Manager

   D. Administrative Tools

3. You are a network administrator for your company. The network consists of a single Active Directory domain. All servers run Windows Server 2016. Windows Server Update Services (WSUS) is installed on two servers, SERVERA and SERVERB. SERVERA receives software updates from Microsoft Windows Update servers. You manually synchronized SERVERB with the Windows Update servers, and now you need to complete the WSUS configuration on SERVERB. Which of the following is *not* a step you might take to complete the configuration of WSUS on SERVERB?

   A. Approve the current updates.

   B. Set SERVERB to receive updates from SERVERA and automatically synchronize with approved updates on SERVERA.

C. Set SERVERB to draw updates automatically from whichever sources SERVERA is set to draw from.

D. Set SERVERB to receive daily updates automatically at a given time.

4. You are the network administrator for your company. The network consists of a single Active Directory domain. All servers run Windows Server 2016. All client computers run Windows 10. The company has 16 mobile sales representatives who are all members of the Power Users local group on their computers. From 6 p.m. until 7 a.m., the sales representatives' laptops are usually turned off and disconnected from the corporate network. The mobile sales representatives' computers must receive software updates every day with minimal user interaction. While verifying the recent updates on one of the laptops, you notice that the updates from the Windows Update servers were not applied. On the Automatic Updates tab of the System Properties dialog box of the mobile computer, what should you do to make sure that software updates are applied to the computer? (Choose three.)

A. Set the scheduled time to every day at 12 a.m.

B. Select the option Automatically Download The Updates, And Install Them On The Schedule That I Specify.

C. Select the option Notify Me Before Downloading Any Updates And Notify Me Again Before Installing Them On My Computer.

D. Select the Keep My Computer Up To Date check box.

E. Select the option Download The Updates Automatically And Notify Me When They Are Ready To Be Installed.

F. Set the scheduled time to every day at 12 p.m.

5. You are responsible for managing several Windows Server 2016 domain controller computers in your environment. Recently, a single hard disk on one of these machines failed, and the Active Directory database was lost. You want to perform the following tasks:

- Determine which partitions on the server are still accessible.

- Restore as much of the system configuration (including the Active Directory database) as possible.

Which of the following could be used to help meet these requirements?

A. Event Viewer

B. Performance Monitor

C. A hard disk from another server that is not configured as a domain controller

D. A valid system state backup from the server

6. While setting up WSUS, you need to configure the server from which you will be getting your Microsoft updates. Under which option would you set this up?

A. Products And Classifications

B. Update Files And Languages

C. Update Source And Proxy Server

D. Synchronization Schedule

7. You are the administrator of a large company and you need to ensure that you can recover your Windows Server 2016 Active Directory configuration and data if the computer's hard disk fails. What should you do?

A. Create a complete PC Backup and Restore image.

B. Create a backup of all file categories.

C. Perform an Automated System Recovery (ASR) backup.

D. Create a system restore point.

8. You need to back up the existing data on a computer before you install a new application. You also need to ensure that you are able to recover individual user files that are replaced or deleted during the installation. What should you do?

A. Create a System Restore point.

B. Perform an Automated System Recovery (ASR) backup and restore.

C. In the Windows Server Backup utility, click the Backup Once link.

D. In the Backup And Restore Center window, click the Back Up Computer button.

9. You are the administrator of a large organization. While setting up your Windows Server 2016 domain controller, you are creating a data recovery strategy that must meet the following requirements:

▪ Back up all data files and folders in C:\Data.

▪ Restore individual files and folders in C:\Data.

▪ Ensure that data is backed up to and restored from external media.

What should you do?

A. Use the Previous Versions feature to restore the files and folders.

B. Use the System Restore feature to perform backup and restore operations.

C. Use the NTBackup utility to back up and restore individual files and folders.

D. Use the Windows Server Backup to back up and restore files.

10. Your manager has decided that your organization needs to use an Active Directory application data partition. Which command can you use to create and manage application data partitions?

A. DCPromo.exe

B. NTDSUtil.exe

C. ADUtil.exe

D. ADSI.exe

Chapter

9

Understanding Monitoring

THE FOLLOWING 70-740 EXAM OBJECTIVES ARE COVERED IN THIS CHAPTER:

✓ **Monitor server installations**

- This objective may include but is not limited to: Monitor workloads using Performance Monitor; configure Data Collector Sets; determine appropriate CPU, memory, disk, and networking counters for storage and compute workloads; configure alerts; monitor workloads using Resource Monitor

A very important task of an IT team is to keep the network up and running quickly and efficiently. Keeping your network running at its peak performance is one way to make sure your end users continue to use the network and its resources without problems or interruptions.

Sometimes, performance optimization can feel like a luxury, especially if you can't get your domain controllers to the point where they are actually performing the services for which you intended them, such as servicing printers or allowing users to share and work on files. The Windows Server 2016 operating system has been specifically designed to provide high-availability services solely intended to keep your mission-critical applications and data accessible, even in times of disaster.

The most common cause of such problems is a hardware configuration issue. Poorly written device drivers and unsupported hardware can cause problems with system stability. Failed hardware components (such as system memory) may do so as well. Memory chips can be faulty, electrostatic discharge can ruin them, and other hardware issues can occur. No matter what, a problem with your memory chip spells disaster for your server.

Third-party hardware vendors usually provide utility programs with their computers that can be used for performing hardware diagnostics on machines to help you find problems. These utilities are a good first step in resolving intermittent server crashes. When these utility programs are used in combination with the troubleshooting tips provided in this and other chapters of this book, you should be able to pinpoint most network-related problems that might occur.

In this chapter, I'll cover the tools and methods used for measuring performance and troubleshooting failures in Windows Server 2016. Before you dive into the technical details, however, you should thoroughly understand what you're trying to accomplish and how you'll meet this goal.

Knowing How to Locate and Isolate Problems

In a book such as this, it would be almost impossible to cover everything that could go wrong with your Windows Server 2016 system. This book covers many of the most common issues that you might come across, but almost anything is possible. Make sure you focus on the methodology used and the steps required to locate and isolate a problem—even if you are not 100 percent sure about the cause of the problem. Use online resources to help you locate and troubleshoot the problem, but don't believe everything you read (some things that are posted online can be wrong or misleading).

Test your changes in a lab environment, and try to read multiple sources. Always use Microsoft Support (http://support.microsoft.com/) as one of your sources because this site is most likely the right source for information. You won't be able to find and fix everything, but knowing where to find critical information that will help you in your efforts never hurts. One of the tools that many of us in the industry use is *Microsoft TechNet*. The full version of TechNet (a paid subscription) is a resource that will help you find and fix many real-world issues.

Overview of Windows Server 2016 Performance Monitoring

The first step in any performance optimization strategy is to measure performance accurately and consistently. The insight that you'll gain from monitoring factors such as network and system utilization will be extremely useful when you measure the effects of any changes.

The overall performance monitoring process usually involves the following steps:

1. Establish a baseline of current performance.
2. Identify the bottlenecks.
3. Plan for and implement changes.
4. Measure the effects of the changes.
5. Repeat the process based on business needs.

Note that the performance optimization process is never really finished because you can always try to gain more performance from your system by modifying settings and applying other well-known tweaks.

Before you get discouraged, realize that you'll reach some level of performance that you and your network and system users consider acceptable and that it's not worth the additional effort it will take to optimize performance any further. Also note that as your network and system load increases (more users or users doing more), so too will the need to reiterate this process. By continuing to monitor, measure, and optimize, you will keep ahead of the pack and keep your end users happy.

Now that you have an idea of the overall process, let's focus on how changes should be made. It's important to keep in mind the following ideas when monitoring performance:

Plan Changes Carefully   Here's a rule of thumb that you should always try to follow: An hour of planning can save a week of work. When you are working in an easy-to-use GUI-based operating system like Windows Server 2016, it's tempting to remove a check mark here or there and then retest the performance. You should resist the urge to do this because some changes can cause large decreases in performance or can impact functionality. Before you make haphazard changes (especially on production servers), take the time to learn about, plan for, and test your changes. Plan for outages and testing accordingly.

Utilize a Test Environment   Test in a test lab that simulates a production environment. Do not make changes on production environments without first giving warning. Ideally, change production environments in off-hours when fewer network and system users will be affected. Making haphazard changes in a production environment can cause serious problems. These problems will likely outweigh any benefits that you may receive from making performance tweaks.

Make Only One Change at a Time   The golden rule of scientific experiments is that you should always keep track of as many variables as possible. When the topic is server optimization, this roughly translates into making only one change at a time.

One of the problems with making multiple system changes is that although you may have improved overall performance, it's hard to determine exactly *which* change created the positive effects. It's also possible, for example, that changing one parameter increased performance greatly while changing another decreased it only slightly. Although the overall result was an increase in performance, you should identify the second, performance-reducing option so that the same mistake is not made again. To reduce the chance of obtaining misleading results, always try to make only one change at a time.

The main reason to make one change at a time, however, is that if you do make a mistake or create an unexpected issue, you can easily "back out" of the change. If you make two or three changes at the same time and are not sure which one created the problem, you will have to undo all of the changes and then make one alteration at a time to find the problem. If you make only one change at a time and follow that methodology every time, you won't find yourself in this situation.

It's important to remember that many changes (such as Registry changes) take place immediately; they do not need to be applied explicitly. Once the change is made, it's live. Be careful to plan your changes wisely.

Ensure Consistency in Measurements   When you are monitoring performance, consistency is extremely important. You should strive to have repeatable and accurate measurements. Controlling variables, such as system load at various times during the day, can help.

Assume, for instance, that you want to measure the number of transactions that you can simulate on the accounting database server within an hour. The results would be widely different if you ran the test during the month-end accounting close than if you ran the test on a Sunday morning. By running the same tests when the server is under a relatively static load, you will be able to get more accurate measurements.

Maintain a Performance History   In the introduction to this chapter, I mentioned that the performance optimization cycle is a continuous improvement process. Because many changes may be made over time, it is important to keep track of the changes that have been made and the results you have experienced. Documenting this knowledge will help solve similar problems if they arise. I understand that many IT professionals do not like to document, but documentation can make life much easier in the long run.

As you can see, you need to keep a lot of factors in mind when optimizing performance. Although this might seem like a lot to digest and remember, do not fear. As a system administrator, you will learn some of the rules you need to know to keep your system running optimally. Fortunately, the tools included with Windows Server 2016 can help you organize the process and take measurements. Now that you have a good overview of the process, let's move on to look at the tools that can be used to set it in motion.

Using Windows Server 2016 Performance Tools

Because performance monitoring and optimization are vital functions in network environments of any size, Windows Server 2016 includes several performance-related tools.

Introducing Performance Monitor

The first and most useful tool is the Windows Server 2016 *Performance Monitor*, which was designed to allow users and system administrators to monitor performance statistics for various operating system parameters. Specifically, you can collect, store, and analyze information about CPU, memory, disk, and network resources using this tool, and these are only a handful of the things that you can monitor. By collecting and analyzing performance values, system administrators can identify many potential problems.

You can use the Performance Monitor in the following ways:

Performance Monitor ActiveX Control   The Windows Server 2016 Performance Monitor is an ActiveX control that you can place within other applications. Examples of applications that can host the Performance Monitor control include web browsers and client programs such as Microsoft Word or Microsoft Excel. This functionality can make it easy for applications developers and system administrators to incorporate the Performance Monitor into their own tools and applications.

Performance Monitor MMC   For more common performance monitoring functions, you'll want to use the built-in Microsoft Management Console (MMC) version of the Performance Monitor.

System Stability Index   The *System Stability Index* is a numerical value from 1 (least stable) to 10 (most stable) that represents the stability of your network. Performance Monitor calculates and creates the System Stability Index. You can view a graph of this index value. The graph can help a network administrator identify when the network started encountering problems. The System Stability Index also offers side-by-side comparisons. An administrator can view when system changes occurred (installing applications, devices, or drivers) and when system problems started to occur. This way, you can determine whether any system changes caused the problems that you are encountering.

Data Collector Sets Windows Server 2016 Performance Monitor includes the Data Collector Set. This tool works with performance logs, telling Performance Monitor where the logs are stored and when the log needs to run. The Data Collector Sets also define the credentials used to run the set.

To access the Performance Monitor MMC, you open Administrative Tools and then choose Performance Monitor. This launches the Performance MMC and loads and initializes Performance Monitor with a handful of default counters.

You can choose from many different methods of monitoring performance when you are using Performance Monitor. A couple of examples are listed here:

- You can look at a snapshot of current activity for a few of the most important counters. This allows you to find areas of potential bottlenecks and monitor the load on your servers at a certain point in time.

- You can save information to a log file for historical reporting and later analysis. This type of information is useful, for example, if you want to compare the load on your servers from three months ago to the current load.

You'll get to take a closer look at this method and many others as you examine Performance Monitor in more detail.

In the following sections, you'll learn about the basics of working with the Windows Server 2016 Performance Monitor and other performance tools. Then you'll apply these tools and techniques when you monitor the performance of your network.

 Your Performance Monitor grows as your system grows, and whenever you add services to Windows Server 2016 (such as installing Exchange Server), you also add to what you can monitor. You should make sure that, as you install services, you take a look at what it is you can monitor.

Deciding What to Monitor

The first step in monitoring performance is to decide *what* you want to monitor. In Windows Server 2016, the operating system and related services include hundreds of performance statistics that you can track easily. For example, you may want to monitor IPsec by monitoring connection security rules. This is just one of many items that can be monitored. All performance statistics fall into three main categories that you can choose to measure:

Performance Objects A *performance object* within Performance Monitor is a collection of various performance statistics that you can monitor. Performance objects are based on various areas of system resources. For example, there are performance objects for the processor and memory as well as for specific services such as web services.

Counters *Counters* are the actual parameters measured by Performance Monitor. They are specific items that are grouped within performance objects. For example, within the Processor performance object, there is a counter for % Processor Time. This counter displays one type of detailed information about the Processor performance object (specifically, the amount of total CPU time all of the processes on the system are using). Another set of counters you can use will allow you to monitor print servers.

Instances Some counters will have instances. An *instance* further identifies which performance parameter the counter is measuring. A simple example is a server with two CPUs. If you decide you want to monitor processor usage (using the Processor performance object)—specifically, utilization (the % Total Utilization counter)—you must still specify *which* CPU(s) you want to measure. In this example, you would have the choice of monitoring either of the two CPUs or a total value for both (using the Total instance).

One important thing that you want to watch when monitoring objects and counters is the average number. For example, there will be times when your CPU is at 100%. This doesn't mean that you need to buy a newer CPU or add an additional CPU. The number that you want to watch is the average CPU usage. If that is over 80% on average, then your CPU can't handle the workload of the server. If the Hard Page Faults per second average more than 5 per second, you don't have enough RAM. Make sure to watch the averages and not just whats happening at this moment.

To specify which performance objects, counters, and instances you want to monitor, you add them to Performance Monitor using the Add Counters dialog box. Figure 9.1 shows the various options that are available when you add new counters to monitor using Performance Monitor.

FIGURE 9.1 Adding a new Performance Monitor counter

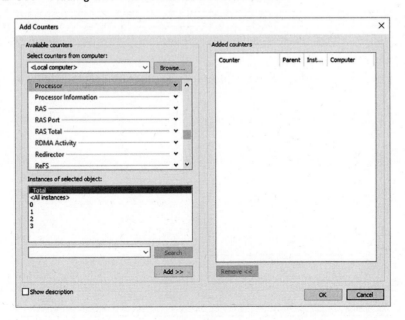

The items that you will be able to monitor will be based on your hardware and software configuration. For example, if you have not installed and configured the IIS, the options available within the Web Server performance object will not be available. Or, if you have multiple network adapters or CPUs in the server, you will have the option of viewing each instance separately or as part of the total value.

Viewing Performance Information   The Windows Server 2016 Performance Monitor was designed to show information in a clear and easy-to-understand format. Performance objects, counters, and instances may be displayed in each of three views. This flexibility allows system administrators to define quickly and easily the information they want to see once and then choose how it will be displayed based on specific needs. Most likely, you will use only one view, but it's helpful to know what other views are available depending on what it is you are trying to assess.

You can use the following main views to review statistics and information on performance:

Line View   The Line view (also referred to as the Graph view) is the default display that is presented when you first access the Windows Server 2016 Performance Monitor. The chart displays values using the vertical axis and displays time using the horizontal axis. This view is useful if you want to display values over a period of time or see the changes in these values over that time period. Each point that is plotted on the graph is based on an average value calculated during the sample interval for the measurement being made. For example, you may notice overall CPU utilization starting at a low value at the beginning of the chart and then becoming much higher during later measurements. This indicates that the server has become busier (specifically, with CPU-intensive processes). Figure 9.2 provides an example of the Graph view.

FIGURE 9.2   Viewing information in Performance Monitor Line view

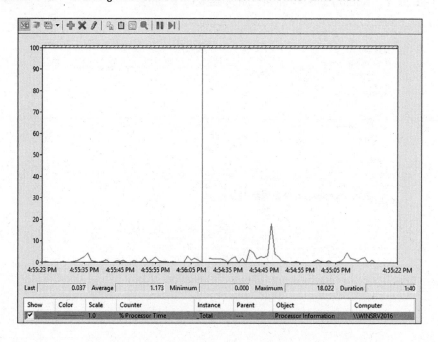

Histogram View   The *Histogram view* shows performance statistics and information using a set of relative bar charts. This view is useful if you want to see a snapshot of the latest value for a given counter. For example, if you were interested in viewing a snapshot of current system performance statistics during each refresh interval, the length of each of the bars in the display would give you a visual representation of each value. It would also allow you to compare measurements visually relative to each other. You can set the histogram to display an average measurement as well as minimum and maximum thresholds. Figure 9.3 shows a typical Histogram view.

FIGURE 9.3   Viewing information in Performance Monitor Histogram view

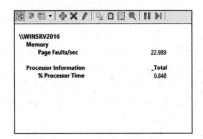

Report View   Like the Histogram view, the *Report view* shows performance statistics based on the latest measurement. You can see an average measurement as well as minimum and maximum thresholds. This view is most useful for determining exact values because it provides information in numeric terms, whereas the Chart and Histogram views provide information graphically. Figure 9.4 provides an example of the type of information you'll see in the Report view.

FIGURE 9.4   Viewing information in Performance Monitor Report view

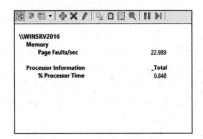

Managing Performance Monitor Properties

You can specify additional settings for viewing performance information within the properties of Performance Monitor. You can access these options by clicking the Properties button in the Taskbar or by right-clicking the Performance Monitor display and selecting Properties. You can change these additional settings by using the following tabs:

General Tab On the General tab (shown in Figure 9.5), you can specify several options that relate to Performance Monitor views:

▪ You can enable or disable legends (which display information about the various counters), the value bar, and the toolbar.

▪ For the Report and Histogram views, you can choose which type of information is displayed. The options are Default, Current, Minimum, Maximum, and Average. What you see with each of these options depends on the type of data being collected. These options are not available for the Graph view because the Graph view displays an average value over a period of time (the sample interval).

▪ You can also choose the graph elements. By default, the display will be set to update every second. If you want to update less often, you should increase the number of seconds between updates.

FIGURE 9.5 General tab of the Performance Monitor Properties dialog box

Source Tab On the Source tab (shown in Figure 9.6), you can specify the source for the performance information you want to view. Options include current activity (the default setting) or data from a log file. If you choose to analyze information from a log file, you can also specify the time range for which you want to view statistics. We'll cover these selections in the next section.

FIGURE 9.6   Source tab of the Performance Monitor Properties dialog box

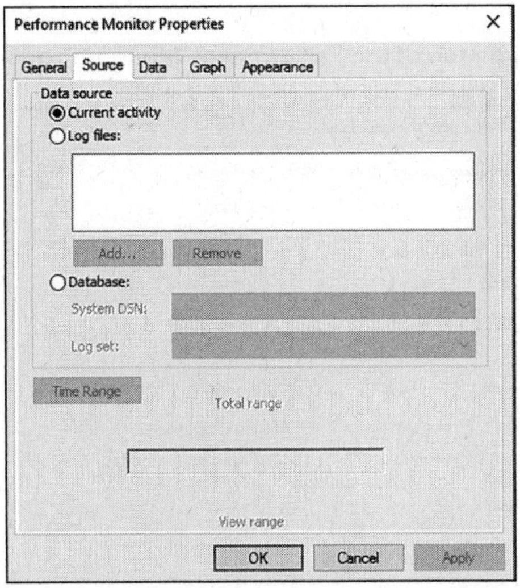

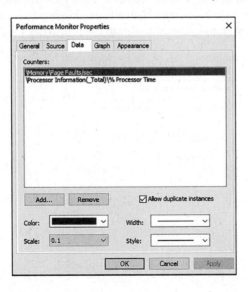

Data Tab   The Data tab (shown in Figure 9.7) lists the counters that have been added to the Performance Monitor display. These counters apply to the Chart, Histogram, and Report views. Using this interface, you can also add or remove any of the counters and change the properties, such as the width, style, and color of the line and the scale used for display.

FIGURE 9.7   The Data tab of the Performance Monitor Properties dialog box

Graph Tab   On the Graph tab (shown in Figure 9.8), you can specify certain options that will allow you to customize the display of Performance Monitor views. First you can specify what type of view you want to see (Line, Histogram, or Report). Then you can add a title for the graph, specify a label for the vertical axis, choose to display grids, and specify the vertical scale range.

FIGURE 9.8 The Graph tab of the Performance Monitor Properties dialog box

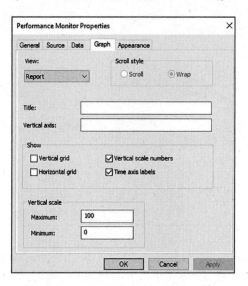

Appearance Tab Using the Appearance tab (see Figure 9.9), you can specify the colors for the areas of the display, such as the background and foreground. You can also specify the fonts that are used to display counter values in Performance Monitor views. You can change settings to find a suitable balance between readability and the amount of information shown on one screen. Finally, you can set up the properties for a border.

FIGURE 9.9 The Appearance tab of the Performance Monitor Properties dialog box

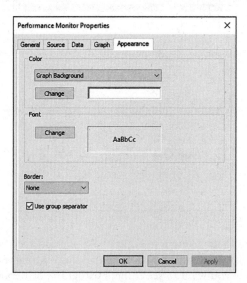

Now that you have an idea of the types of information Performance Monitor tracks and how this data is displayed, you'll take a look at another feature—saving and analyzing performance data.

Saving and Analyzing Data with Performance Logs and Alerts

One of the most important aspects of monitoring performance is that it should be done over a given period of time (referred to as a *baseline*). So far, I have shown you how you can use Performance Monitor to view statistics in real time. I have, however, also alluded to using Performance Monitor to save data for later analysis. Now let's take a look at how you can do this.

When viewing information in Performance Monitor, you have two main options with respect to the data on display:

View Current Activity When you first open the Performance icon from the Administrative Tools folder, the default option is to view data obtained from current system information. This method of viewing measures and displays various real-time statistics on the system's performance.

View Log File Data This option allows you to view information that was previously saved to a log file. Although the performance objects, counters, and instances may appear to be the same as those viewed using the View Current Activity option, the information itself was actually captured at a previous point in time and stored into a log file.

Log files for the View Log File Data option are created in the Performance Logs And Alerts section of the Windows Server 2016 Performance tool.

Three items allow you to customize how the data is collected in the log files:

Counter Logs *Counter logs* record performance statistics based on the various performance objects, counters, and instances available in Performance Monitor. The values are updated based on a time interval setting and are saved to a file for later analysis.

Circular Logging In *circular logging*, the data that is stored within a file is overwritten as new data is entered into the log. This is a useful method of logging if you want to record information only for a certain time frame (for example, the past four hours). Circular logging also conserves disk space by ensuring that the performance log file will not continue to grow over certain limits.

Linear Logging In *linear logging*, data is never deleted from the log files, and new information is added to the end of the log file. The result is a log file that continually grows. The benefit is that all historical information is retained.

Now that you have an idea of the types of functions that are supported by the Windows Server 2016 Performance tools, you can learn how you can apply this information to the task at hand—monitoring and troubleshooting your Windows network.

Real World Scenario

Real-World Performance Monitoring

In our daily jobs as system engineers and administrators, we come across systems that are in need of our help. . . and may even ask for it. You, of course, check your Event Viewer and Performance Monitor and perform other tasks that help you troubleshoot. But what is really the most common problem that occurs? From my experience, I'd say that you suffer performance problems many times if your Windows Server 2016 operating system is installed on a subpar system. Either the server hardware isn't enterprise class or the minimum hardware requirements weren't addressed. Most production servers suffer from slow response times, lagging, and so on because money wasn't spent where it should have been in the first place—on the server's hardware requirements.

In Exercise 9.1, I will show you how to use Performance Monitor. I will also show you how to add objects and counters and then view those items in the Line view.

EXERCISE 9.1

Using Performance Monitor

1. Right-click on the Start and choose Run. Type in Perfmon.exe and hit the Enter key.

2. On the left-hand side under Monitoring Tools, click Performance Monitor.

3. In the center window, click the green plus sign. This will allow you to add a counter.

4. Under Available Counters, make sure Local Computer is chosen. Then expand Processor and choose % Processor Time. Click the Add button. Click OK.

5. Choose any other counters that you want to watch. If you would like to change the view, use the pull-down arrow next to the green plus sign.

6. Once you're completed, close Performance Monitor.

Using Other Monitoring Tools

Performance Monitor allows you to monitor different parameters of the Windows Server 2016 operating system and associated services and applications. However, you can also use three other tools to monitor performance in Windows Server 2016. They are Microsoft Message Analyzer, Task Manager, and Event Viewer. All three of these tools are useful for monitoring different areas of overall system performance and for examining details related to specific system events. In the following sections, you'll take a quick look at these tools and how you can best use them.

Microsoft Message Analyzer

Although Performance Monitor is a great tool for viewing overall network performance statistics, it isn't equipped for packet-level analysis and doesn't give you much insight into what types of network traffic are traveling on the wire. That's where the Microsoft Message Analyzer (MMA) tool comes in.

The Microsoft Message Analyzer Agent is available for use with Windows 7, Windows 8, Windows 10, Windows Server 2008 R2, Windows Server 2012, Windows Server 2012 R2, and Windows Server 2016. The agent allows you to track network packets. When you install the Microsoft Message Analyzer Agent, you will also be able to access the Network Segment System Monitor counter.

On Windows Server 2016 computers, you'll see the Microsoft Message Analyzer icon appear in the Administrative Tools program group. You can use the Microsoft Message Analyzer tool to capture data as it travels on your network.

> The full version of Microsoft Message Analyzer is available at Microsoft's download server. For more information, see www.microsoft.com/downloads/.

Once you have captured the data of interest, you can save it to a capture file or further analyze it using Microsoft Message Analyzer. Experienced network and system administrators can use this information to determine how applications are communicating and the types of data that are being passed via the network.

> For the exam, you don't need to understand the detailed information that Microsoft Message Analyzer displays, but you should be aware of the types of information that you can view and when you should use Microsoft Message Analyzer.

Wireshark

Normally I would never talk about a third party product in a Microsoft certification book. Especially when the third party product will not be on the exam. But when we talk about Microsoft Message Analyzer, we need to mention Wireshark. Wireshark is a free downloadable software that allows you to view network packets (same as Microsoft Message Analyzer). But Wireshark has many advantages over Microsoft Message Analyzer including ease of use and ease of reading the details.

The down side to Microsoft Message Analyzer is that it is very difficult to read and understand the results. If this is something that you do daily, then you will easily understand the results. But if it's something that is done only once in a while, then Wireshark may be better for you. Wireshark is an easier networking monitor tool.

One thing that you need to make sure of when it comes to any Microsoft Message Analyzer tools is who is using them. If you go by someone's office and you see them using any Microsoft Message Analyzer tools, you need to put a stop to that instantly. Unless that person is part of IT or security, no one should be monitoring live network packets.

Task Manager

Performance Monitor is designed to allow you to keep track of specific aspects of system performance over time. But what do you do if you want to get a quick snapshot of what the local system is doing? Creating a System Monitor chart, adding counters, and choosing a view is overkill. Fortunately, the Windows Server 2016 Task Manager has been designed to provide a quick overview of important system performance statistics without requiring any configuration. Better yet, it's always readily available.

You can easily access Task Manager in several ways:

- Right-click the Windows Taskbar and then click Task Manager.
- Press the Windows Key + R
- Press Ctrl+Alt+Del and then select Task Manager.
- Press Ctrl+Shift+Esc.

Each of these methods allows you to access a snapshot of the current system performance quickly.

Once you access Task Manager, you will see the following five tabs:

Processes Tab   The Processes tab shows you all of the processes that are currently running on the local computer. By default, you'll be able to view how much CPU time and memory a particular process is using. By clicking any of the columns, you can quickly sort by the data values in that particular column. This is useful, for example, if you want to find out which processes are using the most memory on your server.

By accessing the performance objects in the View menu, you can add columns to the Processes tab. Figure 9.10 shows a list of the current processes running on a Windows Server 2016 computer.

FIGURE 9.10   Viewing process statistics and information using Task Manager

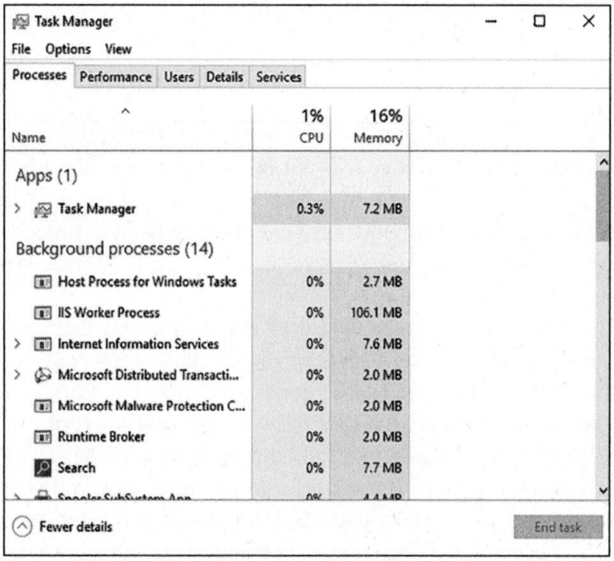

Performance Tab   One of the problems with using Performance Monitor to get a quick snapshot of system performance is that you have to add counters to a chart. Most system administrators are too busy to take the time to do this when all they need is basic CPU and memory information. That's where the Performance tab of Task Manager comes in. Using the Performance tab, you can view details about how memory is allocated on the computer and how much of the CPU is utilized (see Figure 9.11).

FIGURE 9.11   Viewing CPU and memory performance information using Task Manager

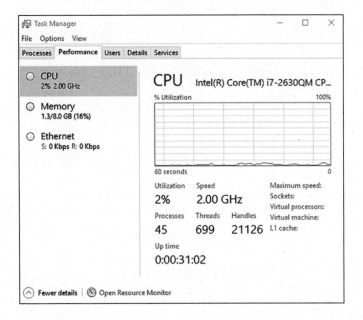

Users Tab   The Users tab (see Figure 9.12) lists the currently active user accounts. This is particularly helpful if you want to see who is online and quickly log off or disconnect users. You can also view all of the services and applications that are being used by that user. As you can see in Figure 9.12, the Administrator account has a lot of services that are running on this system.

Details Tab   The Details tab (see Figure 9.13) shows you what applications are currently running on the system. From this location, you can stop an application from running by right-clicking the application and choosing Stop. You also have the ability to set your affinity level here. By setting the affinity, you can choose which applications will use which processors on your system.

Services Tab   The Services tab (see Figure 9.14) shows you what services are currently running on the system. From this location, you can stop a service from running by right-clicking the service and choosing Stop. The Open Services link launches the Services MMC.

FIGURE 9.12 Viewing user information using Task Manager

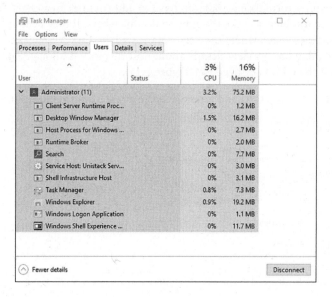

FIGURE 9.13 Viewing applications that are currently running using Task Manager

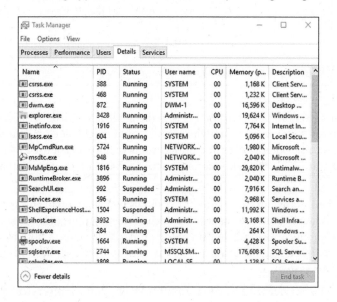

FIGURE 9.14   Viewing services information using Task Manager

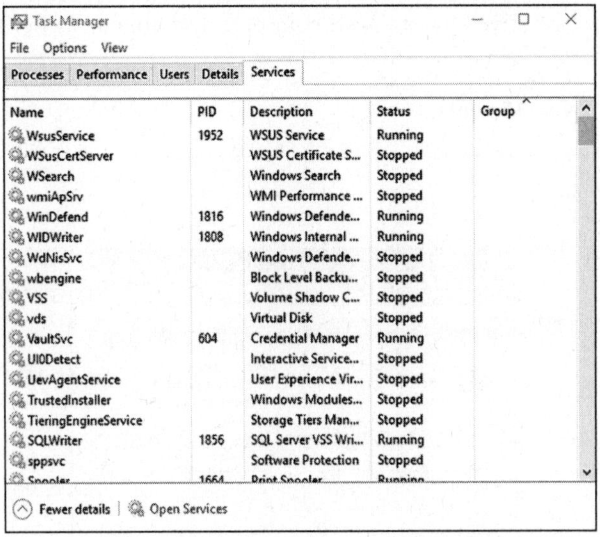

Task Manager					— □ ✕

File   Options   View

Processes	Performance	Users	Details	**Services**	

Name	PID	Description	Status	Group	
WsusService	1952	WSUS Service	Running		
WSusCertServer		WSUS Certificate S...	Stopped		
WSearch		Windows Search	Stopped		
wmiApSrv		WMI Performance ...	Stopped		
WinDefend	1816	Windows Defende...	Running		
WIDWriter	1808	Windows Internal ...	Running		
WdNisSvc		Windows Defende...	Stopped		
wbengine		Block Level Backu...	Stopped		
VSS		Volume Shadow C...	Stopped		
vds		Virtual Disk	Stopped		
VaultSvc	604	Credential Manager	Running		
UI0Detect		Interactive Service...	Stopped		
UevAgentService		User Experience Vir...	Stopped		
TrustedInstaller		Windows Modules...	Stopped		
TieringEngineService		Storage Tiers Man...	Stopped		
SQLWriter	1856	SQL Server VSS Wri...	Running		
sppsvc		Software Protection	Stopped		
Spooler	1664	Print Spooler	Running		

⌃ Fewer details | Open Services

The Task Manager tabs can be different on Windows client machines. For example, Windows 7 has six tabs and Windows 10 has seven tabs.

As you can see, Task Manager is useful for providing important information about the system quickly. Once you get used to using Task Manager, you won't be able to get by without it!

Make sure that you use Task Manager and familiarize yourself with all that it can do; you can end processes that have become intermittent, kill applications that may hang the system, view NIC performance, and so on. In addition, you can access this tool quickly to get an idea of what could be causing you problems. Event Viewer, Microsoft Message Analyzer, and Performance Monitor are all great tools for getting granular information on potential problems.

Event Viewer

Event Viewer is also useful for monitoring network information. Specifically, you can use the logs to view any information, warnings, or alerts related to the proper functioning of the network. You can access Event Viewer by selecting Administrative Tools ➤ Event Viewer. Clicking any of the items in the left pane displays the various events that have been logged for each item. Figure 9.15 shows the contents of the Directory Service log.

Each event is preceded by a blue *i* icon. That icon designates that these events are informational and do not indicate problems with the network. Rather, they record benign events such as Active Directory startup or a domain controller finding a global catalog server.

FIGURE 9.15 Event Viewer

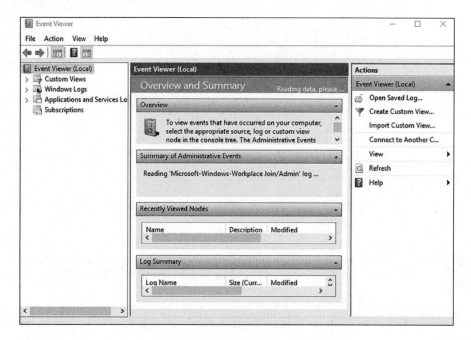

A yellow warning icon or a red error icon, both of which are shown in Figure 9.16, indicate problematic or potentially problematic events. Warnings usually indicate a problem that wouldn't prevent a service from running but might cause undesired effects with the service in question. For example, I was configuring a site with some fictional domain controllers and IP addresses. My local domain controller's IP address wasn't associated with any of the sites, and Event Viewer generated a warning. In this case, the local domain controller could still function as a domain controller, but the site configuration could produce undesirable results.

Error events almost always indicate a failed service, application, or function. For instance, if the dynamic registration of a DNS client fails, Event Viewer will generate an error. As you can see, errors are more severe than warnings because, in this case, the DNS client cannot participate in DNS at all.

Double-clicking any event opens the Event Properties dialog box, as shown in Figure 9.17, which displays a detailed description of the event.

FIGURE 9.16   Information, errors, and warnings in Event Viewer

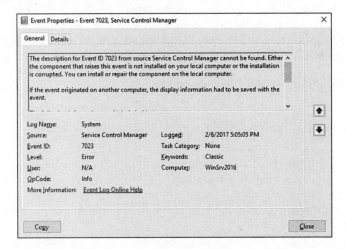

FIGURE 9.17   An Event Properties dialog box

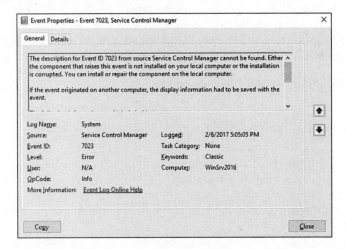

Event Viewer can display thousands of different events, so it would be impossible to list them all here. The important points of which you should be aware are the following:

- Information events are always benign.
- Warnings indicate noncritical problems.
- Errors indicate show-stopping events.

Let's discuss some of the logs and the ways you can view data:

Applications and Services The *applications and services logs* are part of Event Viewer where applications (for example, Exchange) and services (DNS) log their events. DNS events would be logged in this part of Event Viewer. An important log in this section is the DNS Server log (see Figure 9.18). This is where all of your DNS events get stored.

FIGURE 9.18   The applications and services DNS Server log

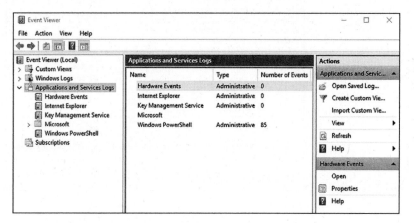

Custom Views *Custom views* allow you to filter events (see Figure 9.19) to create your own customized look. You can filter events by event level (critical, error, warning, and so on), by logs, and by source. You also have the ability to view events occurring within a specific timeframe. This allows you to look only at the events that are important to you.

FIGURE 9.19   Create Custom View dialog box

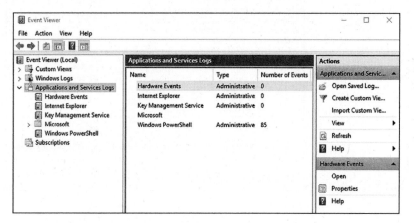

Subscriptions *Subscriptions* allow a user to receive alerts about events that you predefine. In the Subscription Properties dialog box (see Figure 9.20), you can define what type of events you want notifications about and the notification method. The Subscriptions section is an advanced alerting service to help you watch for events.

FIGURE 9.20 Subscription Properties dialog box

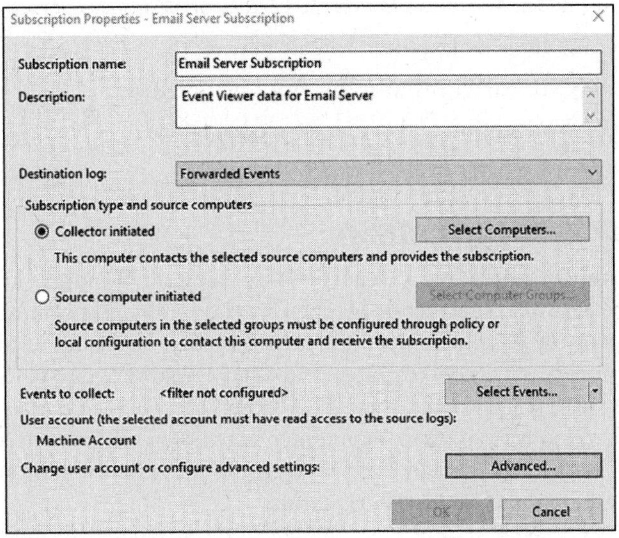

Microsoft Baseline Security Analyzer

The *Microsoft Baseline Security Analyzer (MBSA)* is a security assessment utility that you can download from the Microsoft website at the following location:

`https://www.microsoft.com/en-us/download/details.aspx?id=755`

The filename of the download is `mbsasetup.msi`. It verifies whether your computer has the latest security updates and whether any common security violation configurations have been applied to your computer. MBSA can scan the following programs and operating systems:

- Windows 7
- Windows 8
- Windows 10
- Windows Server 2008 R2
- Windows Server 2012
- Windows Server 2012 R2
- Windows Server 2016
- IIS 5 or newer
- Internet Explorer, versions 6.0 and newer

- SQL Server 7 or newer
- Microsoft Office 2007 or newer
- Windows Media Player, versions 6.4 and newer

To use MBSA, the computer must meet the following requirements:

- It must be running Windows 7, Windows 8, Windows 10, Windows Server 2008 R2, Windows Server 2012, Windows Server 2012 R2, or Windows Server 2016.
- It must be running Internet Explorer 5.01 or newer.
- It must have an XML parser installed for full functionality.
- It must have the Workstation and Server services enabled.
- It must have Client for Microsoft Networks installed.

Using the GUI Version of MBSA

Once you have installed MBSA, you can access it by using the Windows key and choosing Microsoft Baseline Security Analyzer or by opening the command prompt and executing `mbsa.exe`. This opens the Baseline Security Analyzer utility. You can select from Scan A Computer, Scan More Than One Computer, and View Existing Security Reports.

When you click Scan A Computer, the Pick A Computer To Scan dialog box appears. You can specify that you want to scan a computer based on a computer name or IP address. You can also specify the name of the security report that will be generated.

The following are options for the security scan:

- Check For Windows Vulnerabilities
- Check For Weak Passwords
- Check For IIS Vulnerabilities
- Check For SQL Vulnerabilities
- Check For Security Updates

If you use the Check For Security Updates option and are using WSUS, you can specify the name of the WSUS server that should be checked for the security updates.

Once you have made your selections, click Start Scan. When the scan is complete, the security report will be automatically displayed. If you have scanned multiple computers, you can sort the security reports based on issue name or score (worst first or best first).

Using the MBSA Command-Line Utility *mbsacli.exe*

After Microsoft Baseline Security Analyzer has been installed, you can use the command-line utility `mbsacli.exe`. Enter **mbsacli.exe/hf** and then customize the command execution with any of the options defined in Table 9.1.

TABLE 9.1 `mbsacli.exe` `/hf` command-line options

Option	Description
-h *host name[, host name, . . .]*	Scans the specified host. You can specify that you want to scan multiple host computers by separating the hostnames with commas.
-fh *filename*	Scans the NetBIOS name of each computer that is to be scanned, and it saves the information as text within a file specified by `filename`.
-i *xxxx.xxxx.xxxx.xxxx[, xxxx.xxxx.xxxx.xxxx, . . .]*	Scans a computer based on the specified IP address. You can scan multiple computers by IP address by separating the IP addresses with commas.
-fip *filename*	Looks in the text file specified by `filename` for IP addresses and scans the computers with those IP addresses. The file can have up to a maximum of 256 IP addresses.
-d *domainname*	Scans the specified domain.
-n	Scans all of the computers on the local network.

Simple Network Management Protocol

The *Simple Network Management Protocol (SNMP)* is a TCP/IP protocol monitor. The SNMP service creates trap messages that are then sent to a trap destination. One way you might use SNMP is to trap messages that don't contain an appropriate hostname for a particular service.

When you set up SNMP, you set up communities. *Communities* are groupings of computers that help monitor each other.

Windows Server 2016 includes SNMP with the operating system. To install the service, you must use Server Manager. In Exercise 9.2, you will walk through the process of installing the SNMP service.

EXERCISE 9.2

Installing SNMP

1. Open Server Manager.

2. Click option number 2, Add Roles And Features. If you see the Before You Begin screen, just click Next.

3. Choose role-based or feature-based installation and click Next.

EXERCISE 9.2 *(continued)*

4. Choose your server and click Next.

5. Click Next at the Select Server Roles screen.

6. When the Select Features window appears, click the SNMP Services check box. If an ADD Features dialog box appears, click the Add Features button. Click Next.

7. The Confirm Installation page appears. Click Install.

8. Click Close. Exit the Server Manager application.

Now that you have installed the SNMP service, you have to set up your community so that you can start trapping messages. As stated earlier, communities are a grouping of computers to help monitor each other. After you have created the initial community, you can add other computer systems to the community.

In Exercise 9.3, you will walk through the steps to set up the SNMP service and also set up your first community name. To complete this exercise, you must have completed Exercise 9.2.

EXERCISE 9.3

Configuring SNMP

1. Open Computer Management by pressing the keyboard's Windows key and selecting Administrative Tools ➢ Computer Management.

2. Expand Services And Applications. Click Services. In the right pane, double-click SNMP Service.

3. The SNMP Service Properties window will open. Click the Traps tab. In the Community Name box, enter **Community1**. Click the Add To List button.

4. Click the General tab. Click the Start button to start the service. Click OK.

5. Close Computer Management.

Using Resource Monitor

The Resource Monitor is another utility that allows you to view some of the resources on your server. You can access the Resource Monitor by going into the Administrative tools and choosing Resource Monitor or by typing **Resmon.exe** in the Run box.

Resource Monitor is a method of viewing Performance Monitoring data in a quick to view format. One advantage to using the Resource Monitor is that you can choose items that are affecting the systems performance and the view will change to show that item along with the totals.

As seen in Figure 9.21, you can use Resource Monitor to watch the system's CPU, Memory, Disk, and Network. There are 5 tabs that show you the different components. Figure 9.21 shows the Overview tab. The Overview tab allows you to watch all four hardware components in one window. Now let's take a look at each tab (which represents a component).

FIGURE 9.21   Resource Monitor

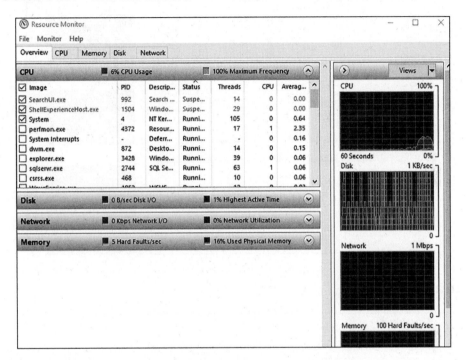

CPU   The CPU tab (shown in Figure 9.22) will show you the total percentage of the CPU being used in a green color and it will show you the Maximum Frequency of the CPU in blue.

Memory   This tab (shown in Figure 9.23) will show you how much memory is being used. When looking at the Resource Overview Memory window, there are two colors that you need to monitor. The current physical memory that is being used will be shown in the color green. The standby memory is shown in the color blue.

Disk   The Disk tab (shown in Figure 9.24) will show you the total current input/output in the color green and it will show you the highest activity time. The current disk activity will be shown in green and the highest activity is shown in blue.

FIGURE 9.22   Resource Monitor CPU tab

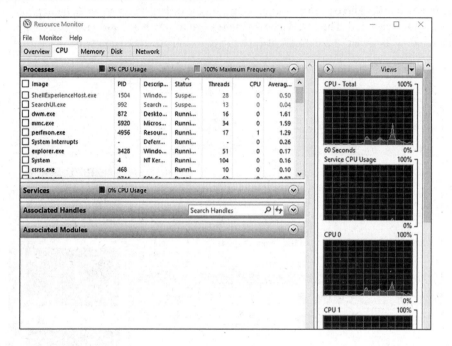

FIGURE 9.23   Resource Monitor Memory tab

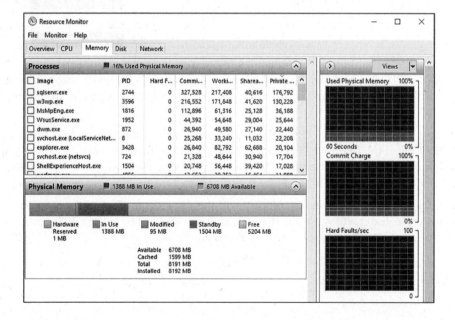

FIGURE 9.24   Resource Monitor Disk tab

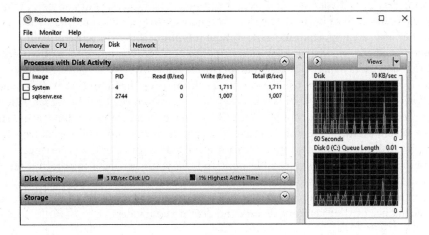

Network   The Network tab (shown in Figure 9.25) shows you how the network traffic is operating. The window will show you the percentage of network capacity and the total current network traffic.

FIGURE 9.25   Resource Monitor Network tab

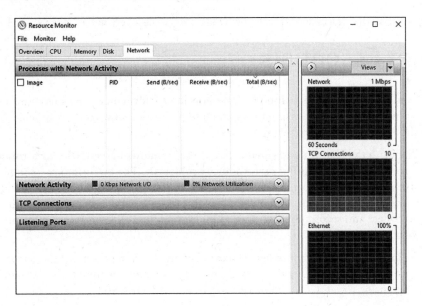

Summary

This chapter began with a discussion of server optimization and reliability, including a look at many tools that can help you monitor and manage your systems and the basics of troubleshooting the network in times of disaster.

Monitoring performance on servers is imperative to rooting out any issues that may affect your network. If your systems are not running at their best, your end users may experience issues such as latency, or worse, you may experience corruption in your network data. Either way, it's important to know how to monitor the performance of your servers. You also looked at ways system administrators can optimize the operations of servers to ensure that end users experience adequate performance.

You also examined how to use the various performance-related tools that are included with Windows Server 2016. Tools such as Performance Monitor, Task Manager, Microsoft Message Analyzer, Resource Monitor, and Event Viewer can help you diagnose and troubleshoot system performance issues. These tools will help you find typical problems related to memory, disk space, and any other hardware-related issues you may experience.

Knowing how to use tools to troubleshoot and test your systems is imperative, not only to passing the exam but also to performing your duties at work. To have a smoothly running network environment, it is vital that you understand the issues related to the reliability and performance of your network servers and domain controllers.

Video Resources

There are videos available for the following exercises:

9.1

You can access the videos at http://sybextestbanks.wiley.com on the Other Study Tools tab.

Exam Essentials

Understand the methodology behind troubleshooting performance.   By following a set of steps that involves making measurements and finding bottlenecks, you can systematically troubleshoot performance problems.

Be familiar with the features and capabilities of the Windows Server 2016 Performance Monitor tool for troubleshooting performance problems.   The Performance Monitor administrative tool is a powerful method for collecting data about all areas of system performance. Through the use of performance objects, counters, and instances, you can choose to collect and record only the data of interest and use this information for pinpointing performance problems.

Know the importance of common performance counters.   Several important performance-related counters deal with general system performance. Know the importance of monitoring memory, print server, CPU, and network usage on a busy server.

Understand the role of other troubleshooting tools.   Windows Task Manager, Microsoft Message Analyzer, SNMP, Baseline Security Analyzer, and Event Viewer can all be used to diagnose and troubleshoot configuration- and performance-related issues.

Understand how to troubleshoot common sources of server reliability problems.
Windows Server 2016 has been designed to be a stable, robust, and reliable operating system. Should you experience intermittent failures, you should know how to troubleshoot device drivers and buggy system-level software.

Review Questions

1. You need to stop an application from running in Task Manager. Which tab would you use to stop an application from running?

   A. Performance

   B. Users

   C. Options

   D. Details

2. You are the network administrator for a Fortune 500 company. You are responsible for all client computers at the central campus. You want to make sure that all of the client computers are secure. You decide to use MBSA to scan your client computers for possible security violations. You want to use the command-line version of MBSA to scan your computers based on IP address. Which of the following commands should you use?

   A. `mdsacli.exe /hf -i xxxx.xxxx.xxxx.xxxx`

   B. `mdsacli.exe /ip xxxx.xxxx.xxxx.xxxx`

   C. `mbsa.exe /hf -ip xxxx.xxxx.xxxx.xxxx`

   D. `mbsa.exe /ip xxxx.xxxx.xxxx.xxxx`

3. You are the network administrator for your company. You want to look at some of the resources on the network. Specifically, you want to watch the CPU and Memory. Which tool can you use to get the most detailed information about the resources?

   A. Performance Monitor

   B. System Hardware Monitor

   C. Event Viewer

   D. Server Manager

4. What command-line command would you type to start Performance Monitor?

   A. `Netmon.exe`

   B. `Perfmon.exe`

   C. `Performon.exe`

   D. `Resmon.exe`

5. You need to view which users are running applications on a server. Which application can you use to see what users are currently connected to the server?

   A. System Information

   B. Resource Monitor

   C. Performance Monitor

   D. Task Manager

6. You are the network administrator for a large organization. You need to watch some of the main components on a server. These include the Memory, CPU, Network, and Disk. What utility can you use to get a quick overview of these four components?

A. System Monitor

B. Resource Monitor

C. System Configuration

D. Event Viewer

7. What command-line command would you type to start Resource Monitor?

A. `Netmon.exe`

B. `Perfmon.exe`

C. `Performon.exe`

D. `Resmon.exe`

8. You have been hired as a consultant to research a network-related problem at a small organization. The environment supports many custom-developed applications that are not well documented. A manager suspects that some computers on the network are generating excessive traffic and bogging down the network. You want to do the following:

- Determine which computers are causing the problems.

- Record and examine network packets that are coming to/from specific machines.

- View data related only to specific types of network packets.

What tool should you use to accomplish all of the requirements?

A. Task Manager

B. Performance Monitor

C. Event Viewer

D. Microsoft Message Analyzer

9. You need to install Microsoft Baseline Security Analyzer. How do you need to do the install?

A. Download MBSA from Microsoft's website.

B. Install from Server Manager.

C. Use Add/Remove Programs.

D. Programs

10. You need to disconnect a user running applications on a server. Which application can you use to disconnect a user currently connected to the server?

A. System Information

B. Resource Monitor

C. Performance Monitor

D. Task Manager

Chapter

10

Configuring TCP/IP

THE FOLLOWING 70-741 EXAM OBJECTIVES ARE COVERED IN THIS CHAPTER:

✓ **Configure IPv4 and IPv6 addressing**

- Configure IP address options
- Configure IPv4 or IPv6 subnetting
- Configure supernetting
- Configure interoperability between IPv4 and IPv6
- Configure ISATAP
- Configure Teredo

In this chapter, I will discuss the most important protocol used in a Microsoft Windows Server 2016 network: *Transmission Control Protocol/Internet Protocol (TCP/IP)*.

TCP/IP is actually two protocols bundled together: the Transmission Control Protocol (TCP) and the Internet Protocol (IP). TCP/IP is a suite of protocols developed by the US Department of Defense's Advanced Research Projects Agency in 1969.

This chapter is divided into two main topics: First I'll talk about TCP/IP version 4, and then I'll discuss TCP/IP version 6. TCP/IP version 4 is still used in Windows Server 2016, and it was the primary version of TCP/IP in all previous versions of Windows. However, TCP/IP version 6 is the latest release of TCP/IP, and it has been incorporated into Windows Server 2016.

Understanding TCP/IP

I mentioned that TCP/IP is actually two protocols bundled together: TCP and IP. These protocols sit on a four-layer TCP/IP model.

Details of the TCP/IP Model

The four layers of the TCP/IP model are as follows (see Figure 10.1):

Application Layer   The *Application layer* is where the applications that use the protocol stack reside. These applications include File Transfer Protocol (FTP), Trivial File Transfer Protocol (TFTP), Simple Mail Transfer Protocol (SMTP), and Hypertext Transfer Protocol (HTTP).

Transport Layer   The *Transport layer* is where the two Transport layer protocols reside. These are TCP and the User Datagram Protocol (UDP). TCP is a connection-oriented protocol, and delivery is guaranteed. UDP is a connectionless protocol. This means that UDP does its best job to deliver the message, but there is no guarantee.

Internet Layer   The *Internet layer* is where IP resides. *IP* is a connectionless protocol that relies on the upper layer (Transport layer) for guaranteeing delivery. *Address Resolution Protocol (ARP)* also resides on this layer. ARP turns an IP address into a Media Access Control (MAC) address. All upper and lower layers travel through the IP protocol.

Link Layer   The data link protocols like Ethernet and Token Ring reside in the *Link layer*. This layer is also referred to as the *Network Access layer*.

FIGURE 10.1   TCP/IP model

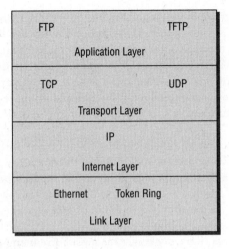

How TCP/IP Layers Communicate

When an application like FTP is called upon, the application moves down the layers and TCP is retrieved. TCP then connects itself to the IP protocol and gets released onto the network through the Link layer (see Figure 10.2). This is a connection-oriented protocol because TCP is the protocol that guarantees delivery.

FIGURE 10.2   TCP/IP process

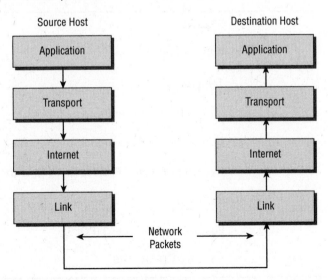

When an application like TFTP gets called, the application moves down the layers, and UDP is retrieved. UDP then connects itself to the IP protocol and gets released onto the network through the Link layer. This is a connectionless protocol because UDP does not have guaranteed delivery.

Understanding Port Numbers

TCP and UDP rely on port numbers assigned by the *Internet Assigned Numbers Authority (IANA)* to forward packets to the appropriate application process. Port numbers are 16-bit integers that are part of a message header. They identify the application software process with which the packet should be associated. For example, let's say that a client has a copy of Internet Explorer and a copy of Mail open at the same time. Both applications are sending TCP requests across the Internet to retrieve web pages and email, respectively. How does the computer know which return packets to forward to Internet Explorer and which packets to forward to Mail?

When making a connection, the client chooses a source port for the communication that is usually in the range 1024–65535 (or sometimes in the range 1–65535). This source port then communicates with a destination port of 80 or 110 on the server side. Every packet destined for Internet Explorer has a source port number of 80 in the header, and every packet destined for Mail has a source port number of 110 in the header.

Table 10.1 describes the most common port numbers (you might need to know these for the exam). You can visit www.iana.org to get the most current and complete list of port numbers. It's good to become familiar with specific port numbers because it's a benefit to be able to determine from memory the ports that, for example, allow or block specific protocols in a firewall. Allowing only port 80, for instance, does not ensure that all web traffic will be allowed. You must also allow port 443 for certain secure web traffic.

TABLE 10.1 Common port numbers

Port Number	Description
20	FTP data
21	FTP control
23	Telnet
25	Simple Mail Transfer Protocol (SMTP)
53	Domain Name System (DNS)
80	Hypertext Transfer Protocol (HTTP), Web
88	Kerberos
110	Post Office Protocol v3 (POP3)
443	Secure HTTP (HTTPS)

Simply because a port is "well known" doesn't mean that a given service must run on it. It's technically valid to run any service on any port, but doing so is usually a bad idea. For example, if you chose to run your web server on TCP port 25, clients would need to type www.example.com:25 to reach your website from most browsers.

Understanding IP Addressing

Understanding IP addressing is critical to understanding how IP works. An IP address is a numeric identifier assigned to each device on an IP network. This type of address is a logical software address that designates the device's location on the network. It isn't the physical hardware address hard-coded in the device's network interface card.

In the following sections, you will see how IP addresses are used to identify uniquely every machine on the network (MAC address).

The Hierarchical IP Addressing Scheme

An IP address consists of 32 bits of information. These bits are divided into four sections (sometimes called *octets* or *quads*) containing 1 byte (8 bits) each. There are three common methods for specifying an IP address:

- Dotted-decimal, as in 130.57.30.56

- Binary, as in 10000010.00111001.00011110.00111000

- Hexadecimal, as in 82 39 1E 38

All of these examples represent the same IP address.

The 32-bit IP address is a structured, or hierarchical, address as opposed to a flat, or nonhierarchical, address. Although IP could have used either *flat addressing* or *hierarchical addressing*, its designers elected to use the latter for a very good reason, as you will now see.

 Real World Scenario

Why Hierarchical Addressing Is Used

What's the difference between flat and hierarchical addressing? A good example of a flat addressing scheme is a US state driver's license number. There's no partitioning to it; the range of legal numbers isn't broken up in any meaningful way (say, by county of residence or date of issue). If this method had been used for IP addressing, every machine on the Internet would have needed a totally unique address, just as each driver's license number in a particular state is unique.

continued

The good news about flat addressing is that it can handle a large number of addresses in 32 bits of data, namely, 4.3 billion. A 32-bit address space with two possible values for each position—either 0 (zero) or 1 (one)—gives you 2^{32} values, which equals approximately 4.3 billion.

The bad news—and the reason flat addressing isn't used in IP—relates to routing. If every address were totally unique, every router on the Internet would need to store the address of every other machine on the Internet. It would be fair to say that this would make efficient routing impossible, even if only a fraction of the possible addresses were used.

The solution to this dilemma is to use a hierarchical addressing scheme that breaks the address space into ordered chunks. Telephone numbers are a great example of this type of addressing. The first section of a US telephone number, the area code, designates a very large area. The area code is followed by the prefix, which narrows the scope to a local calling area. The final segment, the customer number, zooms in on the specific connection. By looking at a number such as 603-766-xxxx, you can quickly determine that the number is located in the southern part of New Hampshire (area code 603) in the Portsmouth area (the 766 exchange).

IP Address Structure

IP addressing works the same way. Instead of the entire 32 bits being treated as a unique identifier, one part of the IP address is designated as the network address (or network ID) and the other part as a node address (or host ID), giving it a layered, hierarchical structure. Together, the IP address, the network address, and the node address uniquely identify a device within an IP network.

The network address—the first two sets of numbers in an IP address—uniquely identifies each network. Every machine on the same network shares that network address as part of its IP address, just as the address of every house on a street shares the same street name. In the IP address 130.57.30.56, for example, 130.57 is the network address.

The node address—the second two sets of numbers—is assigned to, and uniquely identifies, each machine in a network, just as each house on the same street has a different house number. This part of the address must be unique because it identifies a particular machine—an individual, as opposed to a network. This number can also be referred to as a *host address*. In the sample IP address 130.57.30.56, the node address is .30.56.

Understanding Network Classes

The designers of the Internet decided to create classes of networks based on network size. For the small number of networks possessing a very large number of nodes, they created the Class A network. At the other extreme is the Class C network, reserved for the numerous networks with small numbers of nodes. The class of networks in between the very large and very small ones is predictably called the Class B network.

The default subdivision of an IP address into a network and node address is determined by the class designation of your network. Table 10.2 summarizes the three classes of networks, which will be described in more detail in the following sections.

TABLE 10.2 Network address classes

Class	Mask Bits	Leading Bit Pattern	Decimal Range of First Octet of IP Address	Assignable Networks	Maximum Nodes per Network
A	8	0	1–126	126	16,777,214
B	16	10	128–191	16,384	65,534
C	24	110	192–223	2,097,152	254

Classless Inter-Domain Routing (CIDR), explained in detail later in this chapter, has effectively done away with these class designations. You will still hear and should still know the meaning behind the class designations of addresses because they are important to understanding IP addressing. However, when you're working with IP addressing in practice, CIDR is more important to know.

To ensure efficient routing, Internet designers defined a mandate for the leading bits section of the address for each different network class. For example, because a router knows that a Class A network address always starts with a 0, it can quickly apply the default mask, if necessary, after reading only the first bit of the address. Table 10.2 illustrates how the leading bits of a network address are defined. When considering the subnet masking between network and host addresses, the number of bits to mask is important. For example, in a Class A network, 8 bits are masked, making the default subnet mask 255.0.0.0; in a Class C, 24 bits are masked, making the default subnet mask 255.255.255.0.

Some IP addresses are reserved for special purposes and shouldn't be assigned to nodes. Table 10.3 describes some of the reserved IP addresses. See RFC 3330 for others.

TABLE 10.3 Special network addresses

Address	Function
Entire IP address set to all 0s	Depending on the mask, this network (that is, the network or subnet of which you are currently a part) or this host on this network.
A routing table entry of all 0s with a mask of all 0s	Used as the default gateway entry. Any destination address masked by all 0s produces a match for the all 0s reference address. Because the mask has no 1s, this is the least desirable entry, but it will be used when no other match exists.
Network address 127	Reserved for loopback tests. Designates the local node, and it allows that node to send a test packet to itself without generating network traffic.

TABLE 10.3 Special network addresses *(continued)*

Address	Function
Node address of all 0s	Used when referencing a network without referring to any specific nodes on that network. Usually used in routing tables.
Node address of all 1s	Broadcast address for all nodes on the specified network, also known as a *directed broadcast*. For example, 128.2.255.255 means all nodes on the Class B network 128.2. Routing this broadcast is configurable on certain routers.
169.254.0.0 with a mask of 255.255.0.0	The "link-local" block used for autoconfiguration and communication between devices on a single link. Communication cannot occur across routers. Microsoft uses this block for Automatic Private IP Addressing (APIPA).
Entire IP address set to all 1s (same as 255.255.255.255) 10.0.0.0/8 172.16.0.0 to 172.31.255.255	Broadcast to all nodes on the current network; sometimes called a limited broadcast or an all-1s broadcast. *This broadcast is not routable.*
192.168.0.0/16	The private-use blocks for Classes A, B, and C. As noted in RFC 1918, the addresses in these blocks must never be allowed into the Internet, making them acceptable for simultaneous use behind NAT servers and non-Internet-connected IP networks.

In the following sections, you will look at the three network types.

Class A Networks

In a Class A network, the first byte is the network address, and the three remaining bytes are used for the node addresses. The Class A format is Network.Node.Node.Node.

For example, in the IP address 49.22.102.70, 49 is the network address, and 22.102.70 is the node address. Every machine on this particular network would have the distinctive network address of 49. Within that network, however, you could have a large number of machines.

There are 126 possible Class A network addresses. Why? The length of a Class A network address is 1 byte, and the first bit of that byte is reserved, so 7 bits in the first byte remain available for manipulation. This means that the maximum number of Class A networks is 128. (Each of the 7 bit positions that can be manipulated can be either a 0 or a 1, and this gives you a total of 2^7 positions, or 128.) But to complicate things further, it was also decided that the network address of all 0s (0000 0000) would be reserved. This means that the actual number of usable Class A network addresses is 128 minus 1, or 127. Also, 127 is a reserved number (a network address of 0 followed by all 1s [0111 1111], so you actually start with 128 addresses minus the 2 reserved, and you're left with 126 possible Class A network addresses.

Each Class A network has 3 bytes (24 bit positions) for the node address of a machine, which means that there are 2^{24}, or 16,777,216, unique combinations. Because addresses with the two patterns of all 0s and all 1s in the node bits are reserved, the actual maximum usable number of nodes for a Class A network is 2^{24} minus 2, which equals 16,777,214.

Class B Networks

In a Class B network, the first 2 bytes are assigned to the network address, and the remaining 2 bytes are used for node addresses. The format is Network.Network.Node.Node.

For example, in the IP address 130.57.30.56, the network address is 130.57, and the node address is 30.56.

The network address is 2 bytes, so there would be 2^{16} unique combinations. But the Internet designers decided that all Class B networks should start with the binary digits 10. This leaves 14 bit positions to manipulate; therefore, there are 16,384 (or 2^{14}) unique Class B networks.

This gives you an easy way to recognize Class B addresses. If the first 2 bits of the first byte can be only 10, that gives you a decimal range from 128 up to 191 in the first octet of the IP address. Remember that you can always easily recognize a Class B network by looking at its first byte, even though there are 16,384 different Class B networks. If the first octet in the address falls between 128 and 191, it is a Class B network, regardless of the value of the second octet.

A Class B network has 2 bytes to use for node addresses. This is 2^{16} minus the two patterns in the reserved-exclusive club (all 0s and all 1s in the node bits) for a total of 65,534 possible node addresses for each Class B network.

Class C Networks

The first 3 bytes of a Class C network are dedicated to the network portion of the address, with only 1 byte remaining for the node address. The format is Network.Network.Network.Node.

In the example IP address 198.21.74.102, the network address is 198.21.74, and the node address is 102.

In a Class C network, the first three bit positions are always binary 110. Three bytes, or 24 bits, minus 3 reserved positions leaves 21 positions. There are therefore 2^{21} (or 2,097,152) possible Class C networks.

The lead bit pattern of 110 equates to decimal 192 and runs through 223. Remembering our handy easy-recognition method, this means you can always spot a Class C address if the first byte is in the range 192–223, regardless of the values of the second and third bytes of the IP address.

Each unique Class C network has 1 byte to use for node addresses. This leads to 2^8, or 256, minus the two special patterns of all 0s and all 1s, for a total of 254 node addresses for each Class C network.

Class D networks, used for multicasting only, use the address range 224.0.0.0 to 239.255.255.255 and are used, as in broadcasting, as destination addresses only. Class E networks (reserved for future use at this point) cover 240.0.0.0 to 255.255.255.255. Addresses in the Class E range are considered within the experimental range.

Subnetting a Network

If an organization is large and has lots of computers or if its computers are geographically dispersed, it makes good sense to divide its colossal network into smaller ones connected by routers. These smaller networks are called *subnets*. The benefits of using subnets are as follows:

Reduced Network Traffic We all appreciate less traffic of any kind, and so do networks. Without routers, packet traffic could choke the entire network. Most traffic will stay on the local network—only packets destined for other networks will pass through the router and to another subnet. This traffic reduction also improves overall performance.

Simplified Management It's easier to identify and isolate network problems in a group of smaller networks connected together than within one gigantic one.

Understanding the Benefits of Subnetting

To understand one benefit of subnetting, consider a hotel or office building. Say that a hotel has 1,000 rooms with 75 rooms to a floor. You could start at the first room on the first floor and number it 1; then when you get to the first room on the second floor, you could number it 76 and keep going until you reach room 1,000. But someone looking for room 521 would have to guess on which floor that room is located. If you were to "subnet" the hotel, you would identify the first room on the first floor with the number 101 (1 = Floor 1 and 01 = Room 1), the first room on the second floor with 201, and so on. The guest looking for room 521 would go to the fifth floor and look for room 21.

An organization with a single network address (comparable to the hotel building mentioned in the sidebar "Understanding the Benefits of Subnetting") can have a subnet address for each individual physical network (comparable to a floor in the hotel building). Each subnet is still part of the shared network address, but it also has an additional identifier denoting its individual subnetwork number. This identifier is called a *subnet address*.

Subnetting solves several addressing problems:

- If an organization has several physical networks but only one IP network address, it can handle the situation by creating subnets.

- Because subnetting allows many physical networks to be grouped together, fewer entries in a routing table are required, notably reducing network overhead.
- These things combine collectively to yield greatly enhanced network efficiency.

The original designers of the Internet Protocol envisioned a small Internet with only tens of networks and hundreds of hosts. Their addressing scheme used a network address for each physical network. As you can imagine, this scheme and the unforeseen growth of the Internet created a few problems. The following are two examples:

Not Enough Addresses   A single network address can be used to refer to multiple physical networks, but an organization can request individual network addresses for each one of its physical networks. If all of these requests were granted, there wouldn't be enough addresses to go around.

Gigantic Routing Tables   If each router on the Internet needed to know about every physical network, routing tables would be impossibly huge. There would be an overwhelming amount of administrative overhead to maintain those tables, and the resulting physical overhead on the routers would be massive (CPU cycles, memory, disk space, and so on). Because routers exchange routing information with each other, an additional, related consequence is that a terrific overabundance of network traffic would result.

Although there's more than one way to approach these problems, the principal solution is the one that I'll cover in this book—subnetting. As you might guess, *subnetting* is the process of carving a single IP network into smaller logical subnetworks. This trick is achieved by subdividing the host portion of an IP address to create a subnet address. The actual subdivision is accomplished through the use of a subnet mask (covered later in the chapter).

In the following sections, you will see exactly how to calculate and apply subnetting.

Implementing Subnetting

Before you can implement subnetting, you need to determine your current requirements and plan on how best to implement your subnet scheme.

How to Determine Your Subnetting Requirements

Follow these guidelines to calculate the requirements of your subnet:

1. Determine the number of required network IDs: one for each subnet and one for each wide area network (WAN) connection.
2. Determine the number of required host IDs per subnet: one for each TCP/IP device, including, for example, computers, network printers, and router interfaces.
3. Based on these two data points, create the following:
   - One subnet mask for your entire network
   - A unique subnet ID for each physical segment
   - A range of host IDs for each unique subnet

How to Implement Subnetting

Subnetting is implemented by assigning a subnet address to each machine on a given physical network. For example, in Figure 10.3, each machine on subnet 1 has a subnet address of 1.

FIGURE 10.3   A sample subnet

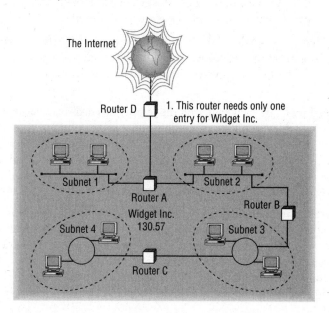

The default network portion of an IP address can't be altered without encroaching on another administrative domain's address space, unless you are assigned multiple consecutive classful addresses. To maximize the efficient use of the assigned address space, machines on a particular network share the same network address. In Figure 10.3, you can see that all of the Widget Inc. machines have a network address of 130.57. That principle is constant. In subnetting, it's the host address that's manipulated—the network address doesn't change. The subnet address scheme takes a part of the host address and recycles it as a subnet address. Bit positions are stolen from the host address to be used for the subnet identifier. Figure 10.4 shows how an IP address can be given a subnet address.

Because the Widget Inc. network is a Class B network, the first two bytes specify the network address and are shared by all machines on the network, regardless of their particular subnet. Here every machine's address on the subnet must have its third byte read 0000 0001. The fourth byte, the host address, is the unique number that identifies the actual host within that subnet. Figure 10.5 illustrates how a network address and a subnet address can be used together.

FIGURE 10.4   Network vs. host addresses

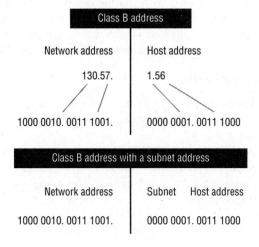

FIGURE 10.5   The network address and its subnet

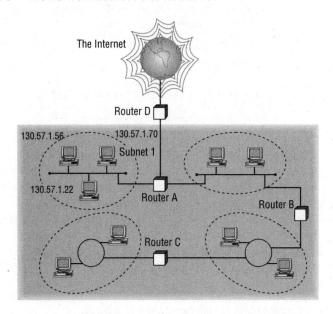

When implementing subnetting, you need some type of hardware installed onto the network. Most of us will just use a router. But if you do not want to purchase an expensive router, there is another way.

One way that you can implement subnetting is by using a Windows Server 2016 machine with multiple NIC adapters configured with routing enabled on the server. This type of router is called a *multihomed router*. This is an inexpensive way to set up a router using a Microsoft server, but it may not be the best way. Many companies specialize in routers, and these routers offer many more features and more flexibility than a multihomed router.

How to Use Subnet Masks

For the subnet address scheme to work, every machine on the network must know which part of the host address will be used as the network address. This is accomplished by assigning each machine a subnet mask.

The network administrator creates a 32-bit subnet mask comprising 1s and 0s. The 1s in the subnet mask represent the positions in the IP address that refer to the network and subnet addresses. The 0s represent the positions that refer to the host part of the address. Figure 10.6 illustrates this combination.

FIGURE 10.6   The subnet mask revealed

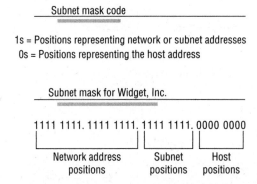

In the Widget Inc. example, the first two bytes of the subnet mask are 1s because Widget's network address is a Class B address, formatted as Network.Network.Node. Node. The third byte, normally assigned as part of the host address, is now used to represent the subnet address. Hence, those bit positions are represented with 1s in the subnet mask. The fourth byte is the only part of the example that represents the host address.

The subnet mask can also be expressed using the decimal equivalents of the binary patterns. The binary pattern of 1111 1111 is the same as decimal 255. Consequently, the subnet mask in the example can be denoted in two ways, as shown in Figure 10.7.

FIGURE 10.7   Different ways to represent the same mask

Subnet mask in binary: 1111 1111. 1111 1111. 1111 1111. 0000 0000

Subnet mask in decimal: 255   .   255   .   255   .   0

(The spaces in the above example are only for illustrative purposes.
The subnet mask in decimal would actually appear as 255.255.255.0.)

Not all networks need to have subnets, and therefore they don't need to use custom subnet masks. In this case, they are said to have a *default* subnet mask. This is basically the same as saying that they don't have any subnets except for the one main subnet on which the network is running. Table 10.4 shows the default subnet masks for the different classes of networks.

TABLE 10.4 Default subnet masks

Class	Format	Default Subnet Mask
A	Network.Node.Node.Node	255.0.0.0
B	Network.Network.Node.Node	255.255.0.0
C	Network.Network.Network.Node	255.255.255.0

Once the network administrator has created the subnet mask and has assigned it to each machine, the IP software applies the subnet mask to the IP address to determine its subnet address. The word *mask* carries the implied meaning of "lens" in this case; that is, the IP software looks at its IP address through the lens of its subnet mask to see its subnet address. Figure 10.8 illustrates an IP address being viewed through a subnet mask.

FIGURE 10.8 Applying the subnet mask

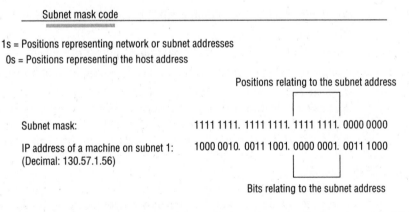

In this example, the IP software learns through the subnet mask that, instead of being part of the host address, the third byte of its IP address is now going to be used as a subnet address. The IP software then looks in its IP address at the bit positions that correspond to the mask, which are 0000 0001.

The final step is for the subnet bit values to be matched up with the binary numbering convention and converted to decimal. In the Widget Inc. example, the binary-to-decimal conversion is simple, as illustrated in Figure 10.9.

FIGURE 10.9   Converting the subnet mask to decimal

Binary numbering convention

Position/value: ◄— (continued)	128 64 32 16 8 4 2 1
Widget third byte:	0 0 0 0 0 0 0 1
Decimal equivalent:	0 + 1 = 1
Subnet address:	1

By using the entire third byte of a Class B address as the subnet address, it is easy to set and determine the subnet address. For example, if Widget Inc. wants to have a subnet 6, the third byte of all machines on that subnet will be 0000 0110 (decimal 6 in binary).

Using the entire third byte of a Class B network address for the subnet allows for a fair number of available subnet addresses. One byte dedicated to the subnet provides eight bit positions. Each position can be either a 1 or a 0, so the calculation is 2^8, or 256. Thus, Widget Inc. can have up to 256 total subnetworks, each with up to 254 hosts.

Although RFC 950 prohibits the use of binary all 0s and all 1s as subnet addresses, today almost all products actually permit this usage. Microsoft's TCP/IP stack allows it, as does the software in most routers (provided you enable this feature, which sometimes is not the case by default). This gives you two additional subnets. However, you should not use a subnet of 0 (all 0s) unless all the software on your network recognizes this convention.

How to Calculate the Number of Subnets

The formulas for calculating the maximum number of subnets and the maximum number of hosts per subnet are as follows:

2 × number of masked bits in subnet mask = maximum number of subnets

2 × number of unmasked bits in subnet mask − 2 = maximum number of hosts per subnet

In the formulas, *masked* refers to bit positions of 1, and *unmasked* refers to bit positions of 0. The downside to using an entire byte of a node address as your subnet address is that you reduce the possible number of node addresses on each subnet. As explained earlier, without a subnet, a Class B address has 65,534 unique combinations of 1s and 0s that can be used for node addresses. The question then is why would you ever want 65,534 hosts on a single physical network?

The trade-off is acceptable to most who ask themselves this question. If you use an entire byte of the node address for a subnet, you then have only 1 byte for the host addresses, leaving only 254 possible host addresses. If any of your subnets are populated with more than 254 machines, you'll have a problem. To solve it, you would then need to shorten the subnet mask, thereby lengthening the number of host bits and increasing the number of host addresses. This gives you more available host addresses on each subnet. A side effect of this solution is that it shrinks the number of possible subnets.

Figure 10.10 shows an example of using a smaller subnet address. A company called Acme Inc. expects to need a maximum of 14 subnets. In this case, Acme does not need to take an entire byte from the host address for the subnet address. To get its 14 different subnet addresses, it needs to snatch only 4 bits from the host address ($2^4 = 16$). The host portion of the address has 12 usable bits remaining ($2^{12} - 2 = 4,094$). Each of Acme's 16 subnets could then potentially have a total of 4,094 host addresses, and 4,094 machines on each subnet should be plenty.

FIGURE 10.10   An example of a smaller subnet address

Acme, Inc.

Network address:	132.8 (Class B; net.net.host.host)
Example IP address:	1000 0100. 0000 1000. 0001 0010. 0011 1100
Decimal:	132 . 8 . 18 . 60

Subnet Mask Code

1s = Positions representing network or subnet addresses
0s = Positions representing the host address

Subnet mask:
Binary: 1111 1111. 1111 1111. 1111 0000. 0000 0000
Decimal: 255 . 255 . 240 . 0
(The decimal 240 is equal to the binary 1111 0000.)

Positions relating to the subnet address

Subnet mask: 1111 1111. 1111 1111. 1111 0000. 0000 0000

IP address of an Acme machine: 1000 0100. 0000 1000. 0001 0010. 0011 1100
(Decimal: 132.8.18.60)

Bits relating to the subnet address

Binary-to-Decimal Conversions for Subnet Address

Subnet mask positions:	1	1	1	1	0	0	0	0
Position/value: ← (continue)	128	64	32	16	8	4	2	1
Third byte of IP address:	0	0	0	1	0	0	1	0
Decimal equivalent:						0 + 16 = 16		
Subnet address for this IP address:							16	

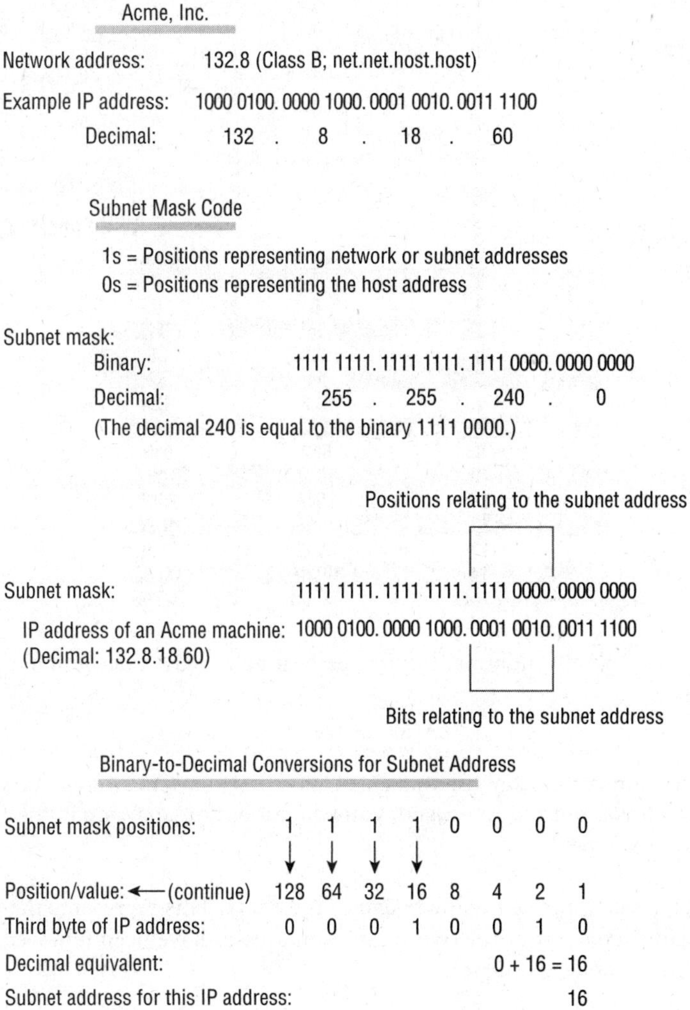

An Easier Way to Apply Subnetting

Now that you have the basics of how to subnet down, you'll learn an easier way. If you have learned a different way and it works for you, stick with it. It does not matter how you get to the finish line, just as long as you get there. But if you are new to subnetting, Figure 10.11 will make it easier for you.

FIGURE 10.11   Will's IPv4 subnetting chart

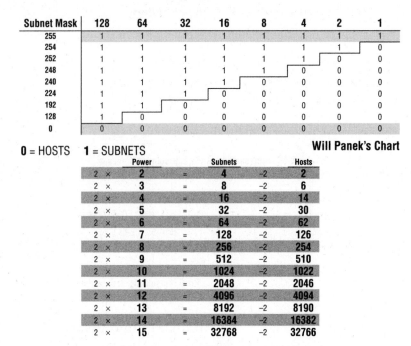

Subnet Mask	128	64	32	16	8	4	2	1
255	1	1	1	1	1	1	1	1
254	1	1	1	1	1	1	1	0
252	1	1	1	1	1	1	0	0
248	1	1	1	1	1	0	0	0
240	1	1	1	1	0	0	0	0
224	1	1	1	0	0	0	0	0
192	1	1	0	0	0	0	0	0
128	1	0	0	0	0	0	0	0
0	0	0	0	0	0	0	0	0

0 = HOSTS   **1** = SUBNETS   **Will Panek's Chart**

	Power		Subnets		Hosts
2 ×	2	=	4	−2	2
2 ×	3	=	8	−2	6
2 ×	4	=	16	−2	14
2 ×	5	=	32	−2	30
2 ×	6	=	64	−2	62
2 ×	7	=	128	−2	126
2 ×	8	=	256	−2	254
2 ×	9	=	512	−2	510
2 ×	10	=	1024	−2	1022
2 ×	11	=	2048	−2	2046
2 ×	12	=	4096	−2	4094
2 ×	13	=	8192	−2	8190
2 ×	14	=	16384	−2	16382
2 ×	15	=	32768	−2	32766

This chart may look intimidating, but it's really simple to use once you have done it a few times.

> Remember that, on this chart, 1s equal subnets and 0s equal hosts. If you get this confused, you will get wrong answers in the following exercises.

Watch the Hosts column on the lower end of the chart. This represents the number of addresses available to you after the two reserved addresses have been removed. The following exercises provide some examples.

SUBNET MASK EXERCISE 10.1

Class C, 10 Hosts per Subnet

You have a Class C address, and you require 10 hosts per subnet.

1. Write down the following:

    255.255.255.____

    The blank is the number you need to fill in.

2. Look under the Hosts column and choose the first number that is larger than 10 (the number of hosts per subnet you need). You should have come up with 14.

3. Move across the page and look at the number in the Power column. The power number is 4.

4. Go to the top of the chart and look for the row with exactly four 0s (hosts). Find the number at the beginning of the row.

The number at the beginning of the row is 240. That's your answer. The subnet mask should be 255.255.255.240.

SUBNET MASK EXERCISE 10.2

Class C, 20 Hosts per Subnet

You have a Class C address, and you need 20 hosts per subnet.

1. Write down the following:

    255.255.255.___

2. Look under the Hosts column and find the first number that covers 20. (This should be 30.)

3. Go across to the power number (5).

4. Go to the top part of the chart and find the row with exactly five 0s from right to left.

The number at the beginning of the row is 224. Your answer should be 255.255.255.224.

SUBNET MASK EXERCISE 10.3

Class C, Five Subnets

Now you have a Class C address, and you need five subnets. Remember that subnets are represented by 1s in the chart.

1. Write down the following:

   255.255.255.___

2. Look under the Subnets column and find the first number that covers 5. (This should be 8.)

3. Go across to the power number. (This should be 3.)

4. Go to the top part of the chart and find out which row has exactly three 1s (remember, 1s are for subnets) from left to right.

Your answer should be 255.255.255.224.

SUBNET MASK EXERCISE 10.4

Class B, 1,500 Hosts per Subnet

This one is a bit harder. You have a Class B address, and you need 1,500 hosts per subnet. Because you have a Class B address, you need to fill in the third octet of numbers. The fourth octet contains eight 0s.

1. Write down the following:

   255.255.___.0

2. Look at the Hosts column and find the first number that covers 1,500. (This should be 2,046.)

3. Go across and find the power number. (This should be 11.)

4. Remember, you already have eight 0s in the last octet. So, you need only three more. Find the row with three 0s.

You should come up with an answer of 255.255.248.0. This actually breaks down to 11111111.11111111.11111000.00000000, and that's how you got the 11 zeros.

SUBNET MASK EXERCISE 10.5

Class B, 3,500 Hosts per Subnet

You have a Class B address, and you need 3,500 hosts per subnet.

1. Write down the following:

   255.255.___.0

2. Look at the Hosts column and find the first number that covers 3,500. (This should be 4,094.)

3. Go across and find the power number. (This should be 12.)

4. Remember, you already have eight 0s in the last octet, so you need only four more. Count for four zeros from right to left.

You should come up with an answer of 255.255.240.0. Again, this actually breaks down to 11111111.11111111.11110000.00000000, and that's how you got the 12 zeros.

 If you get a question that gives you both the hosts and the subnets, always figure out the larger number first. Then, depending on the mask you have decided to use, make sure that the lower number is also correct with that mask.

Now try some more subnet mask exercises using the data that follows:

Class B address

1,000 hosts per subnet

Class C address

45 hosts per subnet

192.168.0.0

10 subnets

Class B address

25 subnets

Class B address

4,000 hosts per subnet

Class B address

2,000 hosts per subnet

25 subnets

Here are the answers. If any of your answers are wrong, follow the previous examples and try to work through them again.

Class B address

1,000 hosts per subnet 255.255.252.0

Class C address

45 hosts per subnet 255.255.255.192

192.168.0.0

10 subnets 255.255.255.240

Class B address

25 subnets 255.255.248.0

Class B address

4,000 hosts per subnet 255.255.240.0

Class B address

2,000 hosts per subnet

25 subnets 255.255.248.0

Applying Subnetting the Traditional Way

Sometimes subnetting can be confusing. After all, it can be quite difficult to remember all of those numbers. You can step back a minute and take a look at the primary classes of networks and how to subnet each one. Let's start with Class C because it uses only 8 bits for the node address, so it's the easiest to calculate. In the following sections, I will explain how to subnet the various types of networks.

Subnetting Class C

If you recall, a Class C network uses the first 3 bytes (24 bits) to define the network address. This leaves you 1 byte (8 bits) with which to address hosts. So if you want to create subnets, your options are limited because of the small number of bits available.

If you break down your subnets into chunks smaller than the default Class C, then figuring out the subnet mask, network number, broadcast address, and router address can be confusing. To build a sturdy base for subnetting, study the following techniques for determining these special values for each subnet, but also learn and use the more efficient technique presented in the later section "Quickly Identifying Subnet Characteristics Using CIDR" and the earlier section "An Easier Way to Apply Subnetting." Table 10.5 summarizes how you can break down a Class C network into one, two, four, or eight smaller subnets, and it gives you the subnet masks, network numbers, broadcast addresses, and router addresses. The first three bytes have simply been designated x.y.z. (Note that the table assumes you can use the all-0s and all-1s subnets too.)

TABLE 10.5   Setting up Class C subnets

Number of Desired Subnets	Subnet Mask	Network Number	Router Address	Broadcast Address	Remaining Number of IP Addresses
1	255.255.255.0	x.y.z.0	x.y.z.1	x.y.z.255	253
2	255.255.255.128	x.y.z.0	x.y.z.1	x.y.z.127	125
	255.255.255.128	x.y.z.128	x.y.z.129	x.y.z.255	125
4	255.255.255.192	x.y.z.0	x.y.z.1	x.y.z.63	61
	255.255.255.192	x.y.z.64	x.y.z.65	x.y.z.127	61
	255.255.255.192	x.y.z.128	x.y.z.129	x.y.z.191	61
	255.255.255.192	x.y.z.192	x.y.z.193	x.y.z.255	61
8	255.255.255.224	x.y.z.0	x.y.z.1	x.y.z.31	29

Number of Desired Subnets	Subnet Mask	Network Number	Router Address	Broadcast Address	Remaining Number of IP Addresses
	255.255.255.224	x.y.z.32	x.y.z.33	x.y.z.63	29
	255.255.255.224	x.y.z.64	x.y.z.65	x.y.z.95	29
	255.255.255.224	x.y.z.96	x.y.z.97	x.y.z.127	29
	255.255.255.224	x.y.z.128	x.y.z.129	x.y.z.159	29
	255.255.255.224	x.y.z.160	x.y.z.161	x.y.z.191	29
	255.255.255.224	x.y.z.192	x.y.z.193	x.y.z.223	29
	255.255.255.224	x.y.z.224	x.y.z.225	x.y.z.255	29

For example, suppose you want to chop up a Class C network, 200.211.192.*x*, into two subnets. As you can see in the table, you'd use a subnet mask of 255.255.255.128 for each subnet. The first subnet would have the network number 200.211.192.0, router address 200.211.192.1, and broadcast address 200.211.192.127. You could assign IP addresses 200.211.192.2 through 200.211.192.126—that's 125 additional different IP addresses.

Heavily subnetting a network results in the loss of a progressively greater percentage of addresses to the network number, broadcast address, and router address.

The second subnet would have the network number 200.211.192.128, router address 200.211.192.129, and broadcast address 200.211.192.255.

Why It's Best to Use Routers That Support Subnet 0

When subnetting a Class C network using the method in Table 10.5, if you use the $2^x - 2$ calculation, the subnet 128 in the table doesn't make sense. It turns out that there's a legitimate and popular reason to do it this way, however.

- Remember that using subnet 0 is not allowed according to the RFC standards, but by using it you can subnet your Class C network with a subnet mask of 128. This uses only 1 bit, and according to your calculator $2^1 - 2 = 0$, giving you zero subnets.

- By using routers that support subnet 0, you can assign 1–126 for hosts and 129–254 for hosts, as stated in the table. This saves a bunch of addresses! If you were to stick to the method defined by the RFC standards, the best you could gain is a subnet mask of 192 (2 bits), which allows you only two subnets ($2^2 - 2 = 2$).

Determining the Subnet Numbers for a Class C Subnet

The first subnet always has a 0 in the interesting octet. In the example, it would be 200.211.192.0, the same as the original nonsubnetted network address. To determine the subnet numbers for the additional subnets, first you have to determine the incremental value:

1. Begin with the octet that has an interesting value (other than 0 or 255) in the subnet mask. Then subtract the interesting value from 256. The result is the incremental value.

   If again you use the network 200.211.192.*x* and a mask of 255.255.255.192, the example yields the following equation: 256 − 192 = 64. Thus, 64 is your incremental value in the interesting octet—the fourth octet in this case. Why the fourth octet? That's the octet with the interesting value, 192, in the mask.

2. To determine the second subnet number, add the incremental value to the 0 in the fourth octet of the first subnet.

   In the example, it would be 200.211.192.64.

3. To determine the third subnet number, add the incremental value to the interesting octet of the second subnet number.

   In the example, it would be 200.211.192.128.

4. Keep adding the incremental value in this fashion until you reach the actual subnet mask number.

   For example, 0 + 64 = 64, so your second subnet is 64. And 64 + 64 is 128, so your third subnet is 128. And 128 + 64 is 192, so your fourth subnet is 192. Because 192 is the subnet mask, this is your last subnet. If you tried to add 64 again, you'd come up with 256, an unusable octet value, which is always where you end up when you've gone too far. This means your valid subnets are 0, 64, 128, and 192 (total of 4 subnets on your network).

The numbers between the subnets are your valid host and broadcast addresses. For example, the following are valid hosts for two of the subnets in a Class C network with a subnet mask of 192:

- The valid hosts for subnet 64 are in the range 65–126, which gives you 62 hosts per subnet.

  (You can't use 127 as a host because that would mean your host bits would be all 1s. The all-1s format is reserved as the broadcast address for that subnet.)

- The valid hosts for subnet 128 are in the range 129–190, with a broadcast address of 191.

As you can see, this solution wastes a few addresses—six more than not subnetting at all, to be exact. In a Class C network, this should not be hard to justify. The 255.255.255.128 subnet mask is an even better solution if you need only two subnets and expect to need close to 126 host addresses per subnet.

Calculating Values for an Eight-Subnet Class C Network

What happens if you need eight subnets in your Class C network?

By using the calculation of $2x$, where x is the number of subnet bits, you would need 3 subnet bits to get eight subnets ($2^3 = 8$). What are the valid subnets, and what are the valid hosts of each subnet? Let's figure it out.

11100000 is 224 in binary, and it would be the interesting value in the fourth octet of the subnet mask. This must be the same on all workstations.

> You're likely to see test questions that ask you to identify the problem with a given configuration. If a workstation has the wrong subnet mask, the router could "think" that the workstation is on a different subnet than it actually is. When that happens, the misguided router won't forward packets to the workstation in question. Similarly, if the mask is incorrectly specified in the workstation's configuration, that workstation will observe the mask and send packets to the default gateway when it shouldn't.

To figure out the valid subnets, subtract the interesting octet value from 256 (256 − 224 = 32), so 32 is your incremental value for the fourth octet. Of course, the 0 subnet is your first subnet, as always. The other subnets would be 32, 64, 96, 128, 160, 192, and 224. The valid hosts are the numbers between the subnet numbers, except the numbers that equal all 1s in the host bits. These numbers would be 31, 63, 95, 127, 159, 191, 223, and 255. Remember that using all 1s in the host bits is reserved for the broadcast address of each subnet.

The valid subnets, hosts, and broadcasts are as follows:

Subnet	Hosts	Broadcast
0	1–30	31
32	33–62	63
64	65–94	95
96	97–126	127
128	129–158	159
160	161–190	191
192	193–222	223
224	225–254	255

You can add one more bit to the subnet mask just for fun. You were using 3 bits, which gave you 224. By adding the next bit, the mask now becomes 240 (11110000).

By using 4 bits for the subnet mask, you get 16 subnets because $2^4 = 16$. This subnet mask also gives you only 4 bits for the host addresses, or $2^4 - 2 = 14$ hosts per subnet. As you can see, the number of hosts per subnet gets reduced rather quickly for each host bit that gets reallocated for subnet use.

The first valid subnet for subnet 240 is 0, as always. Because 256 − 240 = 16, your remaining subnets are then 16, 32, 48, 64, 80, 96, 112, 128, 144, 160, 176, 192, 208, 224, and 240. Remember that the actual interesting octet value also represents the last valid subnet, so 240 is the last valid subnet number. The valid hosts are the numbers between the subnets, except for the numbers that are all 1s—the broadcast address for the subnet.

Table 10.6 shows the numbers in the interesting (fourth) octet for a Class C network with eight subnets.

TABLE 10.6 Fourth octet addresses for a Class C network with eight subnets

Subnet	Hosts	Broadcast
0	1–14	15
16	17–30	31
32	33–46	47
48	49–62	63
64	65–78	79
80	81–94	95
96	97–110	111
112	113–126	127
128	129–142	143
144	145–158	159
160	161–174	175
176	177–190	191
192	193–206	207
208	209–222	223
224	225–238	239
240	241–254	255

Subnetting Class B

Because a Class B network has 16 bits for host addresses, you have plenty of available bits to play with when figuring out a subnet mask. Remember that you have to start with the leftmost bit and work toward the right. For example, a Class B network would look like x.y.0.0, with the default mask of 255.255.0.0. Using the default mask would give you one network with 65,534 hosts.

The default mask in binary is 11111111.11111111.00000000.00000000. The 1s represent the corresponding network bits in the IP address, and the 0s represent the host bits. When you're creating a subnet mask, the leftmost bit(s) will be borrowed from the host bits (0s will be turned into 1s) to become the subnet mask. You then use the remaining bits that are still set to 0 for host addresses.

If you use only 1 bit to create a subnet mask, you have a mask of 255.255.128.0. If you use 2 bits, you have a mask of 255.255.192.0, or 11111111.11111111.11000000.00000000.

As with subnetting a Class C address, you now have three parts of the IP address: the network address, the subnet address, and the host address. You figure out the subnet mask numbers the same way as you did with a Class C network (see the previous section, "Calculating Values for an Eight-Subnet Class C Network"), but you'll end up with a lot more hosts per subnet.

There are four subnets, because $2^2 = 4$. The valid third-octet values for the subnets are 0, 64, 128, and 192 (256 − 192 = 64, so the incremental value of the third octet is 64). However, there are 14 bits (0s) left over for host addressing. This gives you 16,382 hosts per subnet ($2^{14} − 2 = 16,382$).

The valid subnets and hosts are as follows:

Subnet	Hosts	Broadcast
x.y.0.0	x.y.0.1 through x.y. 63.254	x.y.63.255
x.y.64.0	x.y.64.1 through x.y.127.254	x.y.127.255
x.y.128.0	x.y.128.1 through x.y.191.254	x.y.191.255
x.y.192.0	x.y.192.1 through x.y.255.254	x.y.255.255

You can add another bit to the subnet mask, making it 11111111.11111111.11100000 .00000000, or 255.255.224.0. This gives you eight subnets ($2^3 = 8$) and 8,190 hosts. The valid subnets are 0, 32, 64, 96, 128, 160, 192, and 224 (256 − 224 = 32). The subnets, valid hosts, and broadcasts are listed here:

Subnet	Hosts	Broadcast
x.y.0.0	x.y.0.1 through x.y.31.254	x.y.31.255
x.y.32.0	x.y.32.1 through x.y.63.254	x.y.63.255
x.y.64.0	x.y.64.1 through x.y.95.254	x.y.95.255
x.y.96.0	x.y.96.1 through x.y.127.254	x.y.127.255
x.y.128.0	x.y.128.1 through x.y.159.254	x.y.159.255
x.y.160.0	x.y.160.1 through x.y.191.254	x.y.191.255
x.y.192.0	x.y.192.1 through x.y.223.254	x.y.223.255
x.y.224.0	x.y.224.1 through x.y.255.254	x.y.255.255

The following are the breakdowns for a 9-bit mask and a 14-bit mask:

- If you use 9 bits for the mask, it gives you 512 subnets (2^9). With only 7 bits for hosts, you still have 126 hosts per subnet ($2^7 - 2 = 126$). The mask looks like this:

  11111111.11111111.11111111.10000000, or 255.255.255.128

- If you use 14 bits for the subnet mask, you get 16,384 subnets (2^{14}) but only two hosts per subnet ($2^2 - 2 = 2$). The subnet mask would look like this:

  11111111.11111111.11111111.11111100, or 255.255.255.252

 **Real World Scenario**

Subnet Mask Use in an ISP

You may be wondering why you would use a 14-bit subnet mask with a Class B address. This approach is actually very common. Let's say you have a Class B network and use a subnet mask of 255.255.255.0. You'd have 256 subnets and 254 hosts per subnet. Imagine also that you are an Internet service provider (ISP) and have a network with many WAN links, a different one between you and each customer. Typically, you'd have a direct connection between each site. Each of these links must be on its own subnet or network. There will be two hosts on these subnets—one address for each router port. If you used the mask described earlier (255.255.255.0), you would waste 252 host addresses per subnet. But by using the 255.255.255.252 subnet mask, you have more subnets available, which means more customers—each subnet with only two hosts, which is the maximum allowed on a point-to-point circuit.

You can use the 255.255.255.252 subnet mask only if you are running a routing algorithm such as Enhanced Interior Gateway Routing Protocol (EIGRP) or Open Shortest Path First (OSPF). These routing protocols allow what is called *Variable Length Subnet Masking (VLSM)*. VLSM allows you to run the 255.255.255.252 subnet mask on your interfaces to the WANs and run 255.255.255.0 on your router interfaces in your local area network (LAN) using the same classful network address for all subnets. It works because these routing protocols transmit the subnet mask information in the update packets that they send to the other routers. Classful routing protocols, such as RIP version 1, don't transmit the subnet mask and therefore cannot employ VLSM.

Subnetting Class A

Class A networks have even more bits available than Class B and Class C networks. A default Class A network subnet mask is only 8 bits, or 255.0.0.0, giving you a whopping 24 bits for hosts to play with. Knowing which hosts and subnets are valid is a lot more complicated than it was for either Class B or Class C networks.

If you use a mask of 11111111.11111111.00000000.00000000, or 255.255.0.0, you'll have 8 bits for subnets, or 256 subnets (2^8). This leaves 16 bits for hosts, or 65,534 hosts per subnet ($2^{16} - 2 = 65534$).

If you split the 24 bits evenly between subnets and hosts, you would give each one 12 bits. The mask would look like this: 11111111.11111111.11110000.00000000, or 255.255.240.0. How many valid subnets and hosts would you have? The answer is 4,096 subnets each with 4,094 hosts ($2^{12} - 2 = 4,094$).

The second octet will be somewhere between 0 and 255. However, you will need to figure out the third octet. Because the third octet has a 240 mask, you get 16 (256 − 240 = 16) as your incremental value in the third octet. The third octet must start with 0 for the first subnet, the second subnet will have 16 in the third octet, and so on. This means that some of your valid subnets are as follows (not in order):

Subnet	Hosts	Broadcast
x.0-255.0.0	x.0-255.0.1 through x.0-255.15.254	x.0-255.15.255
x.0-255.16.0	x.0-255.16.1 through x.0-255.31.254	x.0-255.31.255
x.0-255.32.0	x.0-255.32.1 through x.0-255.47.254	x.0-255.47.255
x.0-255.48.0	x.0-255.48.1 through x.0-255.63.254	x.0-255.63.255

They go on in this way for the remaining third-octet values through 224 in the subnet column.

Working with Classless Inter-Domain Routing

Microsoft uses an alternate way to write address ranges, called *Classless Inter-Domain Routing* (*CIDR*; pronounced "cider"). CIDR is a shorthand version of the subnet mask. For example, an address of 131.107.2.0 with a subnet mask of 255.255.255.0 is listed in CIDR as 131.107.2.0/24 because the subnet mask contains 24 1s. An address listed as 141.10.32.0/19 would have a subnet mask of 255.255.224.0, or 19 1s (the default subnet mask for Class B plus 3 bits). This is the nomenclature used in all Microsoft exams (see Figure 10.12).

FIGURE 10.12   Subnet mask represented by 1s

Subnet mask in binary: 1111 1111. 1111 1111. 1111 1111. 0000 0000

Subnet mask in decimal: 255   .   255   .   255   .   0

(The spaces in the above example are only for illustrative purposes.
The subnet mask in decimal would actually appear as 255.255.255.0.)

Let's say an Internet company has assigned you the following Class C address and CIDR number: 192.168.10.0/24. This represents the Class C address of 192.168.10.0 and a subnet mask of 255.255.255.0.

Again, CIDR represents the number of 1s turned on in a subnet mask. For example, a CIDR number of /16 stands for 255.255.0.0 (11111111.11111111.00000000.00000000).

The following is a list of all of the CIDR numbers (starting with a Class A default subnet mask) and their corresponding subnet masks:

CIDR	Mask	CIDR	Mask	CIDR	Mask
/8	255.0.0.0	/17	255.255.128.0	/25	255.255.255.128
/9	255.128.0.0	/18	255.255.192.0	/26	255.255.255.192
/10	255.192.0.0	/19	255.255.224.0	/27	255.255.255.224
/11	255.224.0.0	/20	255.255.240.0	/28	255.255.255.240
/12	255.240.0.0	/21	255.255.248.0	/29	255.255.255.248
/13	255.248.0.0	/22	255.255.252.0	/30	255.255.255.252
/14	255.252.0.0	/23	255.255.254.0	/31	255.255.255.254
/15	255.254.0.0	/24	255.255.255.0	/32	255.255.255.255
/16	255.255.0.0				

Quickly Identifying Subnet Characteristics Using CIDR

Given the limited time you have to dispatch questions in the structured environment of a Microsoft certification exam, every shortcut to coming up with the correct answer is a plus. The following method, using CIDR notation, can shave minutes off the time it takes you to complete a single question. Since you already understand the underlying binary technology at the heart of subnetting, you can use the following shortcuts, one for each address class, to come up with the correct answer without working in binary.

Identifying Class C Subnet Characteristics

Consider the host address 192.168.10.50/27. The following steps flesh out the details of the subnet of which this address is a member:

1. Obtain the CIDR-notation prefix length for the address by converting the dotted-decimal mask to CIDR notation.

   In this case, /27 corresponds to a mask of 255.255.255.224. Practice converting between these notations until it becomes second nature.

2. Using the closest multiple of 8 that is greater than or equal to the prefix length, compute the interesting octet (the octet that increases from one subnet to the next in increments other than 1 or 0). Divide this multiple by 8. The result is a number corresponding to the octet that is interesting.

   In this case, the next multiple of 8 greater than 27 is 32. Dividing 32 by 8 produces the number 4, pointing to the fourth octet as the interesting one.

3. To compute the incremental value in the interesting octet, subtract the prefix length from the next higher multiple of 8, which in this case is 32. The result (32 – 27) is 5. Raise 2 to the computed value ($2^5 = 32$). The result is the incremental value of the interesting octet.

4. Recall the value of the interesting octet from the original address (50 in this case). Starting with 0, increment by the incremental value until the value is exceeded. The values then are 0, 32, 64, and so on.

5. The subnet in question extends from the increment that is immediately less than or equal to the address's interesting octet value to the address immediately before the next increment. In this example, 192.168.10.50/27 belongs to the subnet 192.168.10.32, and this subnet extends to the address immediately preceding 192.168.10.64, which is its broadcast address, 192.168.10.63.

    Note that if the interesting octet is not the fourth octet, all octets after the interesting octet must be set to 0 for the subnet address.

6. The usable range of addresses for the subnet in question extends from one higher than the subnet address to one less than the broadcast address, making the range for the subnet in question 192.168.10.33 through 192.168.10.62. As you can see, 192.168.10.50/27 definitely falls within the subnet 192.168.10.32/27.

Identifying Class B Subnet Characteristics

Using the steps in the previous section, find the subnet in which the address 172.16.76.12 with a mask of 255.255.240.0 belongs.

1. The corresponding CIDR notation prefix length is /20.

2. The next multiple of 8 that is greater than 20 is 24. 24/8 = 3. Octet 3 is interesting.

3. 24 – 20 = 4, so the incremental value is $2^4 = 16$.

4. The increments in the third octet are 0, 16, 32, 48, 64, 80, and so on.

5. The increments of 64 and 80 bracket the address's third-octet value of 76, making the subnet in question 172.16.64.0, after setting all octets after the interesting octet to 0. This subnet's broadcast address is 172.16.79.255, which comes right before the next subnet address of 172.16.80.0.

6. The usable address range then extends from 172.16.64.1 through 172.16.79.254.

Identifying Class A Subnet Characteristics

Try it one more time with 10.6.127.255/14. Combine some of the related steps if possible:

1. The prefix length is 14. The next multiple of 8 that is greater than or equal to 14 is 16. 16/8 = 2, so the second octet is interesting.

2. 16 – 14 = 2, so the incremental value in the second octet is $2^2 = 4$.

3. The corresponding second-octet value of 6 in the address falls between the 4 and 8 increments. This means that the subnet in question is 10.4.0.0 (setting octets after the second one to 0) and its broadcast address is 10.7.255.255.

4. The usable address range is from 10.4.0.1 through 10.7.255.254.

Determining Quantities of Subnets and Hosts

The general technique described in the previous sections is also useful when trying to determine the total number of subnets and hosts produced by a given mask with respect to the default mask of the class of address in question.

For example, consider the Class B address 172.16.0.0 with a subnet mask of 255.255.254.0.

This is a prefix length of 23 bits. When you subtract the default prefix length for a Class B address of 16 from 23, you get the value 7. Raising 2 to the 7th power results in the value 128, which is the number of subnets you get when you subnet a Class B address with the 255.255.254.0 mask.

Determining the number of hosts available in each of these 128 subnets is simple because you always subtract the prefix length that the subnet mask produces, 23 in this example, from the value 32, which represents the total number of bits in any IP address. The difference, 9, represents the remaining number of 0s, or host bits, in the subnet mask. Raising 2 to this value produces the total possible number of host IDs per subnet that this subnet mask allows. Remember to subtract 2 from this result to account for the subnet and broadcast addresses for each subnet. This gives you the actual number of usable host IDs per subnet. In this case, this value is $2^9 - 2 = 510$.

Repeated practice with this technique will reduce your time to obtain the desired answer to mere seconds, leaving time for the more challenging tasks in each question. You have a wealth of examples and scenarios in this chapter, as well as in the review questions, on which to try your technique and build your trust in this faster method.

Supernetting

Let's take a look at a different type of subnetting. Class B addresses give you 65,534 addresses, but let's say that you have 1,000 users. Would you really need a Class B address? Not if you use supernetting.

Supernetting allows you to have two or more blocks of contiguous subnetwork addresses. So what does that actually mean? Class C addresses give you 254 usable addresses. So if you needed 1,000 users, you could set up supernetting of 4 Class C addresses that are contiguous.

Example:
192.168.16.0
192.168.17.0
192.168.18.0
192.168.19.0

When you set up supernetting for a Class C, you would use a Class B subnet mask. When you set up supernetting for a Class B, you would use a Class A subnet mask. This allows you to use multiple classes to get a larger number of hosts without taking up an entire class.

So the subnet mask for the above example would be 255.255.252.0 or /22. The reason we used this subnet mask is because a 252 subnet mask allows for 4 subnets. Each of the above Class C numbers would equal one subnet on this network.

Understanding IPv6

Internet Protocol version 6 (IPv6) is the first major revamping of IP since RFC 791 was accepted in 1981. Yes, the operation of IP has improved, and there have been a few bells and whistles added (such as NAT, for example), but the basic structure is still being used as it was originally intended. IPv6 has actually been available to use in Microsoft operating systems since NT 4.0, but it always had to be manually enabled. Windows Vista was the first Microsoft operating system to have it enabled by default. It is also enabled by default in Windows 7, Windows 10, Windows Server 2008, Windows Server 2008 R2, and Windows Server 2016, and it probably will be in all Microsoft operating systems from this point on.

TCP and UDP—as well as the IP applications, such as HTTP, FTP, SNMP, and the rest—are still being used in IPv4. So, you might ask, why change to the new version? What does IPv6 bring to your networking infrastructure? What is the structure of an IPv6 address? How is it implemented and used within Windows Server 2016? I'll answer all of those questions and more in the following sections.

IPv6 History and Need

In the late 1970s, as the IP specifications were being put together, the vision of the interconnected devices was limited compared to what we actually have today. To get an idea of the growth of the Internet, take a look at Hobbes' Internet Timeline in RFC 2235 (www.faqs .org/rfcs/rfc2235.html). As you can see, in 1984, the number of hosts finally surpassed 1,000—two years after TCP and IP were introduced. With 32 bits of addressing available in IPv4, it handled the 1,000+ hosts just fine. And even with the number of hosts breaking the 10,000 mark in 1987 and then 100,000 in 1989, there were still plenty of IP addresses to go around. But when the number of hosts exceeded 2 million in 1992 and 3 million in 1994, concern in the industry started to build. So in 1994, a working group was formed to come up with a solution to the quickly dwindling usable address availability in the IPv4 space. Internet Protocol next generation (IPng) was started.

Have you heard of IP address depletion being a problem today? Probably not as much. When the working group realized that it could not have IPv6 standardized before the available addresses might run out, they developed and standardized *Network Address Translation (NAT)* as an interim solution. NAT, or more specifically an implementation of NAT called *Port Address Translation (PAT)*, took care of a big portion of the problem.

NAT works very well, but it does have some limitations, including issues of peer-to-peer applications with their IPv4 addresses embedded in the data, issues of end-to-end traceability, and issues of overlapping addresses when two networks merge. Because all devices in an IPv6 network will have a unique address and no network address translation will take place, the global addressing concept of IPv4 will be brought back (the address put on by the source device will stay all the way to the destination). Thus, with the new-and-improved functionality of IPv6, the drawbacks of NAT and the limitations of IPv4 will be eliminated.

New and Improved IPv6 Concepts

Several elements of the IPv4 protocol could use some enhancements. Fortunately, IPv6 incorporates those enhancements as well as new features directly into the protocol specification to provide better and additional functionality.

The following list includes new concepts and new implementations of old concepts in IPv6:

- Larger address space (128-bit vs. 32-bit).

- Autoconfiguration of Internet-accessible addresses with or without DHCP. (Without DHCP, it's called *stateless autoconfiguration*.)

- More efficient IP header (fewer fields and no checksum).

- Fixed-length IP header (the IPv4 header is variable length) with extension headers beyond the standard fixed length to provide enhancements.

- Built-in IP mobility and security. (Although available in IPv4, the IPv6 implementation is a much better implementation.)

- Built-in transition schemes to allow integration of the IPv4 and IPv6 spaces.

- ARP broadcast messages replaced with multicast request.

Here are more details about these features:

128-Bit Address Space   The new 128-bit address space will provide unique addresses for the foreseeable future. Although I would like to say that we will never use up all of the addresses, history may prove me wrong. The number of unique addresses in the IPv6 space is 2^{128}, or 3.4×10^{38}, addresses. How big is that number? It's enough for toasters and refrigerators (and maybe even cars) to all have their own addresses.

As a point of reference, the nearest black hole to Earth is 1,600 light years away. If you were to stack 4mm BB pellets from here to the nearest black hole and back, you would need 1.51×10^{22} BBs. This means you could uniquely address each BB from Earth to the black hole and back and still have quite a few addresses left over.

Another way to look at it is that the IPv6 address space is big enough to provide more than 1 million addresses per square inch of the surface area of the earth (oceans included).

Autoconfiguration and Stateless Autoconfiguration   Autoconfiguration is another added/improved feature of IPv6. We've used DHCP for a while to assign IP addresses to client machines. You should even remember that APIPA can be used to assign addresses automatically to Microsoft DHCP client machines in the absence of a DHCP server. The problem with APIPA is that it confines communication between machines to a local LAN (no default gateway). What if a client machine could ask whether there was a router on the LAN and what network it was on? If the client machine knew that, it could not only assign itself an address, it could also choose the appropriate network and default gateway. The stateless autoconfiguration functionality of IPv6 allows the clients to do this.

Improved IPv6 Header   The IPv6 header is more efficient than the IPv4 header because it is fixed length (with extensions possible) and has only a few fields. The IPv6 header consists of a total of 40 bytes:

32 bytes   Source and destination IPv6 addresses

8 bytes   Version field, traffic class field, flow label field, payload length field, next header field, and hop limit field

You don't have to waste your time with a checksum validation anymore, and you don't have to include the length of the IP header (it's fixed in IPv6; the IP header is variable length in IPv4, so the length must be included as a field).

IPv6 Mobility   IPv6 is only a replacement of the OSI layer 3 component, so you'll continue to use the TCP (and UDP) components as they currently exist. IPv6 addresses a TCP issue, though. Specifically, TCP is connection oriented, meaning that you establish an end-to-end communication path with sequencing and acknowledgments before you ever send any data, and then you have to acknowledge all of the pieces of data sent. You do this through a combination of an IP address, port number, and port type (socket).

If the source IP address changes, the TCP connection may be disrupted. But then how often does this happen? Well, it happens more and more often because more people are walking around with a wireless laptop or a wireless Voice over IP (VoIP) telephone. IPv6 mobility establishes a TCP connection with a home address and, when changing networks, it continues to communicate with the original endpoint from a care-of address as it changes LANs, which sends all traffic back through the home address. The handing off of network addresses does not disrupt the TCP connection state (the original TCP port number and address remain intact).

Improved Security   Unlike IPv4, IPv6 has security built in. *Internet Protocol Security (IPsec)* is a component used today to authenticate and encrypt secure tunnels from a source to a destination. This can be from the client to the server or between gateways. IPv4 lets you do this by enhancing IP header functionality (basically adding a second IP header while encrypting everything behind it). In IPv6, you add this as standard functionality by using extension headers. Extension headers are inserted into the packet only if they are needed. Each header has a "next header" field, which identifies the next piece of information. The extension headers currently identified for IPv6 are Hop-By-Hop Options, Routing, Fragment, Destination Options, Authentication, and Encapsulating Security Payload. The Authentication header and the Encapsulating Security Payload header are the IPsec-specific control headers.

IPv4 to IPv6 Interoperability   Several mechanisms in IPv6 make the IPv4-to-IPv6 transition easy.

- A simple dual-stack implementation where both IPv4 and IPv6 are installed and used is certainly an option. In most situations (so far), this doesn't work so well because most of us aren't connected to an IPv6 network and our Internet connection is not IPv6 even if we're using IPv6 internally. Therefore, Microsoft includes other mechanisms that can be used in several different circumstances.

- *Intra-Site Automatic Tunnel Addressing Protocol (ISATAP)* is an automatic tunneling mechanism used to connect an IPv6 network to an IPv4 address space (not using NAT). ISATAP treats the IPv4 space as one big logical link connection space.

- *6to4* is a mechanism used to transition to IPv4. This method, like ISATAP, treats the IPv4 address space as a logical link layer with each IPv6 space in transition using a 6to4 router to create endpoints using the IPv4 space as a point-to-point connection (kind of like a WAN, eh?). 6to4 implementations still do not work well through a NAT, although a 6to4 implementation using an Application layer gateway (ALG) is certainly doable.

- *Teredo* is a mechanism that allows users behind a NAT to access the IPv6 space by tunneling IPv6 packets in UDP.

Pseudo-interfaces are used in these mechanisms to create a usable interface for the operating system. Another interesting feature of IPv6 is that addresses are assigned to interfaces (or pseudo-interfaces), not simply to the end node. Your Windows Server 2016 will have several unique IPv6 addresses assigned.

New Broadcast Methods   IPv6 has moved away from using broadcasting. The three types of packets used in IPv6 are unicast, multicast, and anycast. IPv6 clients then must use one of these types to get the MAC address of the next Ethernet hop (default gateway). IPv6 makes use of multicasting for this along with the new functionality called *neighbor discovery*. Not only does ARP utilize new functionality, but ICMP (also a layer 3 protocol) has been redone and is now known as ICMP6. *ICMP6* is used for messaging (packet too large, time exceeded, and so on) as it was in IPv4, but now it's also used for the messaging of IPv6 mobility. ICMP6 echo request and ICMP6 echo reply are still used for ping.

IPv6 Addressing Concepts

You need to consider several concepts when using IPv6 addressing. For starters, the format of the address has changed. Three types of addresses are used in IPv6, with some predefined values within the address space. You need to get used to seeing these addresses and be able to identify their uses.

IPv6 Address Format

For the design of IPv4 addresses, you present addresses as octets or the decimal (base 10) representation of 8 bits. Four octets add up to the 32 bits required. IPv6 expands the address space to 128 bits, and the representation is for the most part shown in hexadecimal (a notation used to represent 8 bits using the values 0–9 and A–F). Figure 10.13 compares IPv4 to IPv6.

A full IPv6 address looks like this example:

2001:0DB8:0000:0000:1234:0000:A9FE:133E

FIGURE 10.13   IPv4/IPv6 comparison

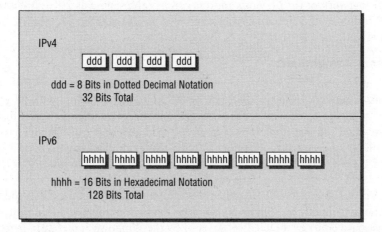

You can tell the implementation of DNS will make life a lot easier even for those who like to ping the address in lieu of the name. Fortunately, DNS already has the ability to handle IPv6 addresses with the use of an AAAA record. (*A* is short for *alias*.) An A record in IPv4's addressing space is 32 bits, so an AAAA record, or four *A*s, is 128 bits. The Windows Server 2016 DNS server handles the AAAA and the reverse pointer (PTR) records for IPv6.

IPv6 Address Shortcuts

There are several shortcuts for writing an IPv6 address. These are described in the following list:

- :0: stands for :0000:.

- You can omit preceding 0s in any 16-bit word. For example, :DB8: and :0DB8: are equivalent.

- :: is a variable standing for enough zeros to round out the address to 128 bits. :: can be used only once in an address.

You can use these shortcuts to represent the example address 2001:0DB8:0000:0000:1234:0000:A9FE:133E, as shown here:

- Compress :0000: into :0::
  2001:0DB8:0000:0000:1234:0:A9FE:133E

- Eliminate preceding zeros:
  2001:DB8:0000:0000:1234:0:A9FE:133E

- Use the special variable shortcut for multiple 0s:
  2001:DB8::1234:0:A9FE:133E

You now also use prefix notation or slash notation when discussing IPv6 networks. For example, the network of the previous address can be represented as 2001:DB8:0000:0000:0000:0000:0000:0000. This can also be expressed as 2001:DB8:: /32. The /32 indicates 32 bits of network, and 2001:DB8: is 32 bits of network.

IPv6 Address Assignment

So, do you subnet IPv6? The answer depends on your definition of subnetting. If you are given 32 bits of network from your ISP, you have 96 bits with which to work. If you use some of the 96 bits to route within your network infrastructure, then you are subnetting. In this context, you do subnet IPv6. However, given the huge number of bits you have available, you will no longer need to implement VLSM. For example, Microsoft has a network space of 2001:4898:: /32. That gives the administrators a space of 96 bits (2^{96} = 79,228,162,514,264,337,593,543,950,336 unique addresses using all 96 bits) with which to work.

You can let Windows Server 2016 dynamically/automatically assign its IPv6 address, or you can still assign it manually (see Figure 10.14). With dynamic/automatic assignment, the IPv6 address is assigned either by a DHCPv6 server or by the Windows Server 2016 machine. If no DHCPv6 server is configured, the Windows Server 2016 machine can query the local LAN segment to find a router with a configured IPv6 interface. If so, the server will assign itself an address on the same IPv6 network as the router interface and set its default gateway to the router interface's IPv6 address. Figure 10.14 shows that you have the same dynamic and manual choices as you do in IPv4; however, the input values for IPv6 must conform to the new format.

FIGURE 10.14 TCP/IPv6 Properties window

To see your configured IP addresses (IPv4 and IPv6), you can still use the ipconfig command. For example, I have configured a static IPv4 address and an IPv6 address on my server. The IPv6 address is the same as the one used in the earlier IPv6 example address. Figure 10.15 shows the result of this command on Windows Server 2016 for my server.

FIGURE 10.15   IPv6 configuration as seen from the command prompt

```
Administrator: C:\Windows\system32\cmd.exe                              _ □ ×
Ethernet adapter Local Area Connection:

    Connection-specific DNS Suffix  . :
    Description . . . . . . . . . . . : Intel 21140-Based PCI Fast Ethernet Adapt
er (Emulated)
    Physical Address. . . . . . . . . : 00-03-FF-11-02-CD
    DHCP Enabled. . . . . . . . . . . : No
    Autoconfiguration Enabled . . . . : Yes
    IPv6 Address. . . . . . . . . . . : 2001:db8::1234:0:a9fe:133e(Preferred)
    Link-local IPv6 Address . . . . . : fe80::a425:ab9d:7da4:ccba%10(Preferred)
    IPv4 Address. . . . . . . . . . . : 192.168.1.200(Preferred)
    Subnet Mask . . . . . . . . . . . : 255.255.255.0
    Default Gateway . . . . . . . . . : 2001:db8::1234:0:0:1
                                        0.0.0.0
                                        192.168.1.1
    DNS Servers . . . . . . . . . . . : ::1
                                        192.168.1.1
    NetBIOS over Tcpip. . . . . . . . : Enabled
```

IPv6 Address Types

As stated earlier, there are three types of addresses in IPv6: anycast, unicast, and multicast. A description of each of these types of IPv6 addresses follows.

> Note the absence of the broadcast type, which is included in IPv4. You can't use broadcasts in IPv6; they've been replaced with multicasts.

Anycast Addresses   Anycast addresses are not really new. The concept of anycast existed in IPv4 but was not widely used. An *anycast address* is an IPv6 address assigned to multiple devices (usually different devices). When an anycast packet is sent, it is delivered to one of the devices, usually the closest one.

Unicast Addresses   A *unicast packet* uniquely identifies an interface of an IPv6 device. The interface can be a virtual interface or pseudo-interface or a real (physical) interface.

Unicast addresses come in several types, as described in the following list:

Global Unicast Address   As of this writing, the global unicast address space is defined as 2000:: /3. The 2001::/32 networks are the IPv6 addresses currently being issued to business entities. As mentioned, Microsoft has been allocated 2001:4898:: /32. A Microsoft DHCPv6 server would be set up with scopes (ranges of addresses to be assigned) within this address space. There are some special addresses and address formats that you will see in use as well. You'll find most example addresses listed as 2001:DB8:: /32; this space has been reserved for documentation. Do you remember the loopback address in IPv4, 127.0.0.1? In IPv6 the loopback address is ::1 (or 0:0:0:0:0:0:0:0001). You may also see an address with dotted-decimal used. A dual-stack Windows Server 2016 machine may also show you FE80::5EFE:192.168.1.200. This address form is used in an integration/migration model of IPv6 (or if you just can't leave the dotted-decimal era, I suppose).

Link-Local Address   Link-local addresses are defined as FE80:: /10. If you refer to Figure 10.15 showing the ipconfig command, you will see the link-local IPv6 address as fe80::a425:ab9d:7da4:ccba. The last 8 bytes (64 bits) are random to ensure a high probability of randomness for the link-local address. The link-local address is to be used on a single link (network segment) and should never be routed.

There is another form of the local-link IPv6 address called the *Extended User Interface 64-bit (EUI-64)* format. This is derived by using the MAC address of the physical interface and inserting an FFFE between the third and fourth bytes of the MAC. The first byte is also made 02 (this sets the universal/local, or U/L, bit to 1 as defined in IEEE 802 frame specification). Again looking at Figure 10.15, the EUI-64 address would take the physical (MAC) address 00-03-FF-11-02-CD and make the link-local IPv6 address FE80::0203:FFFF:FE11:02CD. (I've left the preceding zeros in the link-local IPv6 address to make it easier for you to pick out the MAC address with the FFFE inserted.)

AnonymousAddress   Microsoft Server 2016 uses the random address by default instead of EUI-64. The random value is called the *AnonymousAddress* in Microsoft Server 2016. It can be modified to allow the use of EUI-64.

Unique Local Address   The *unique local address* can be Fc00 or FD00, and it is used like the private address space of IPv4. RFC 4193 describes unique local addresses. They are not expected to be routable on the global Internet. They are used for private routing within an organization.

Multicast Address   *Multicast addresses* are one-to-many communication packets. Multicast packets are identifiable by their first byte (most significant byte, leftmost byte, leftmost 2 nibbles, leftmost 8 bits, and so on). A multicast address is defined as FF00::/8.

In the second byte shown (the 00 of FF00), the second 0 is what's called the *scope*. Interface-local is 01, and link-local is 02. FF01:: is an interface-local multicast.

There are several well-known (already defined) multicast addresses. For example, if you want to send a packet to all nodes in the link-local scope, you send the packet to FF02::1 (also shown as FF02:0:0:0:0:0:0:1). The all-routers multicast address is FF02::2.

You can also use multicasting to get the logical link layer address (MAC address) of a device with which you are trying to communicate. Instead of using the ARP mechanism of IPv4, IPv6 uses the ICMPv6 neighbor solicitation (NS) and neighbor advertisement (NA) messages. The NS and NA ICMPv6 messages are all part of the new *Neighbor Discovery Protocol (NDP)*. This new ICMPv6 functionality also includes router solicitation and router advertisements as well as redirect messages (similar to the IPv4 redirect functionality).

Table 10.7 outlines the IPv6 address space known prefixes and some well-known addresses.

Unicast vs. Anycast

Unicast and anycast addresses look the same and may be indistinguishable from each other; it just depends on how many devices have the same address. If only one device has a globally unique IPv6 address, it's a unicast address. If more than one device has the same address, it's an anycast address. Both unicast and anycast are considered one-to-one communication, although you could say that anycast is one-to-"one of many."

TABLE 10.7   IPv6 address space known prefixes and addresses

Address Prefix	Scope of Use
2000:: /3	Global unicast space prefix
FE80:: /10	Link-local address prefix
FC00:: /7	Unique local unicast prefix
FD00:: /8	Unique local unicast prefix
FF00:: /8	Multicast prefix
2001:DB8:: /32	Global unicast prefix used for documentation
::1	Reserved local loopback address
2001:0000: /32	Teredo prefix (discussed later in this chapter)
2002:: /16	6to4 prefix

IPv6 Integration/Migration

It's time to get into the mind-set of integrating IPv6 into your existing infrastructure with the longer goal of migrating to IPv6. In other words, this is not going to be an "OK, Friday the Internet is changing over" rollout. You have to bring about the change as a controlled implementation. It could easily take three to five years before a solid migration occurs and probably longer. I think the migration will take slightly less time than getting the world to migrate to the metric system on the overall timeline. The process of integration/migration consists of several mechanisms.

Dual Stack   Simply running both IPv4 and IPv6 on the same network, utilizing the IPv4 address space for devices using only IPv4 addresses and utilizing the IPv6 address space for devices using IPv6 addresses

Tunneling   Using an encapsulation scheme for transporting one address space inside another

Address Translation   Using a higher-level application to change one address type (IPv4 or IPv6) to the other transparently so that end devices are unaware one address space is talking to another

I elaborate on these three mechanisms in the following sections.

IPv6 Dual Stack

The default implementation in Windows Server 2016 is an enabled IPv6 configuration along with IPv4; this is dual stack. The implementation can be dual IP layer or dual TCP/IP stack. Windows Server 2016 uses the dual IP layer implementation (see Figure 10.16). When an application queries a DNS server to resolve a hostname to an IP address, the DNS server may respond with an IPv4 address or an IPv6 address. If the DNS server responds with both, Windows Server 2016 will prefer the IPv6 address. Windows Server 2016 can use both IPv4 and IPv6 addresses as necessary for network communication. When looking at the output of the ipconfig command, you will see both address spaces displayed.

FIGURE 10.16   IPv6 dual IP layer diagram

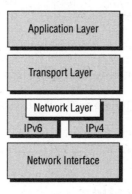

IPv6 Tunneling

Windows Server 2016 includes several tunneling mechanisms for tunneling IPv6 through the IPv4 address space. They include the following:

- Intra-Site Automatic Tunnel Addressing Protocol (ISATAP), which is used for unicast IPv6 communication across an IPv4 infrastructure. ISATAP is enabled by default in Windows Server 2016.

- 6to4, which is used for unicast IPv6 communication across an IPv4 infrastructure.

- Teredo, which is used for unicast IPv6 communication with an IPv4 NAT implementation across an IPv4 infrastructure.

With multiple tunneling protocols available and enabled by default, you might ask, what's the difference, and why is one used over the others? They all allow you to tunnel IPv6 packets through the IPv4 address space (a really cool thing if you're trying to integrate/migrate). Here are the details of these tunneling mechanisms:

ISATAP   *Intra-Site Automatic Tunnel Addressing Protocol (ISATAP)* is the automatic tunnel addressing protocol providing IPv6 addresses based on the IPv4 address of the end interface (node). The IPv6 address is automatically configured on the local device, and the dual stack machine can use either its IPv4 or IPv6 address to communicate on the local network (within the local network infrastructure). ISATAP can use the neighbor discovery mechanism to determine the router ID and network prefix where the device is located, thus making intra-site communication possible even in a routed infrastructure.

The format of an ISATAP address is as follows:

[64 bits of prefix] [32 bits indicating ISATAP] [32 bits IPv4 address]

The center 32 bits indicating ISATAP are actually 0000:5EFE (when using private IPv4 addresses). The ISATAP address of the example Windows Server 2016 machine using the link-local IPv6 address is FE80::5EFE:192.168.1.200. Each node participating in the ISATAP infrastructure must support ISATAP. If you're routing through an IPv4 cloud, a border router (a router transitioning from an IPv6 to IPv4 space) must support ISATAP. Windows Server 2016 can be configured as a border router, and it will forward ISATAP packets. ISATAP is experimental and is defined in RFC 4214.

6to4   *6to4* specifies a procedure for IPv6 networks to communicate with each other through an IPv4 space without the IPv6 nodes having to know what's happening. The IPv6 nodes do not need to be dual stacked to make this happen. The border router is the device responsible for knowing about the IPv6-to-IPv4 transition. The IPv6 packets are encapsulated at the border router (and decapsulated at the other end or on the way back). There is an assigned prefix for the 6to4 implementation: 2002:: /16. 6to4 is defined in RFC 3056.

Teredo   *Teredo* (named after a kind of shipworm that drills holes in the wood of ships) is a protocol designed to allow IPv6 addresses to be available to hosts through one or more layers of NAT. Teredo uses a process of tunneling packets through the IPv4 space using UDP. The Teredo service encapsulates the IPv6 data within a UDP segment (packet) and uses IPv4 addressing to get through the IPv4 cloud. Having layer 4 (Transport layer) available to use as translation functionality is what gives you the ability to be behind a NAT. Teredo provides host-to-host communication and dynamic addressing for IPv6 nodes (dual stack), allowing the nodes to have access to resources in an IPv6 network and the IPv6 devices to have access to the IPv6 devices that have only connectivity to the IPv4 space (like home users who have an IPv6-enabled operating system connecting to IPv6 resources while their home ISP has only IPv4 capabilities). Teredo is defined in RFC 4380.

In Windows Server 2016, an IPv4 Teredo server is identified and configured (using the `netsh` command interface). The Teredo server provides connectivity resources (address) to the Teredo client (the node that has access to the IPv4 Internet and needs access to an IPv6 network/Internet). A Teredo relay is a component used by the IPv6 router to receive traffic destined for Teredo clients and forward the traffic appropriately. The defined prefix for a Teredo address is 2001:0000:: /32. Teredo does add overhead like all the other implementations discussed. It is generally accepted that you should use the simplest model available. However, in the process of integration/migration for most of us behind a NAT, Teredo will be the process to choose.

From Windows Server 2016, use the `ipconfig /all` command to view the default configurations including IPv4 and IPv6. You may notice a notation that I didn't discuss, the percent sign at the end of the IPv6 address (see Figure 10.17). The number after the percent sign is the virtual interface identifier used by Windows Server 2016.

FIGURE 10.17   IPv6 interface identifier for ipconfig display

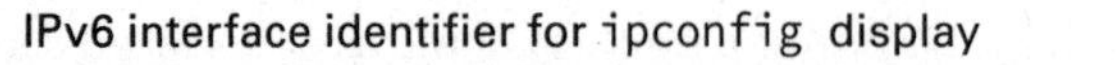

```
Link local IPv6 Address . . . . . : fe80::a425:ab9d:7da4:ccba%10
```

Useful IPv6 Information Commands

You can use numerous commands to view, verify, and configure the network parameters of Windows Server 2016. Specifically, you can use the netsh command set and the route command set as well as the standard ping and tracert functions.

Use the netsh command interface (as well as the provided dialog boxes, if you want) to examine and configure IPv6 functionality. The netsh command issued from the command interpreter changes into a network shell (netsh) where you can configure and view both IPv4 and IPv6 components.

Don't forget to use the ever-popular route print command to see the Windows Server 2016 routing tables (IPv4 and IPv6). The other diagnostic commands are still available for IPv4 as well as IPv6. In previous versions of Microsoft operating systems, ping was the IPv4 command, and ping6 was the IPv6 command. This has changed in Windows Server 2016; ping works for both IPv4 and IPv6 to test layer 3 connectivity to remote devices. The IPv4 tracert command was tracert6 for IPv6. The command is now tracert for both IPv4 and IPv6, and it will show you every layer 3 (IP) hop from source to destination. (This assumes that all of the administrators from here to there want you to see the hops and are not blocking ICMP. It also assumes that there are no IP tunnels, which your packets are traversing; you won't see the router hops in the tunnel either.)

Overall, the consortium of people developing the Internet and the Internet Protocol have tried to make all of the changes to communication infrastructures easy to implement. (This is a daunting task with the many vendors and various infrastructures currently in place.) The goal is not to daze and confuse administrators; it's designed to provide maximum flexibility with the greatest functionality. IPv6 is going to provide the needed layer 3 (Network layer, global addressing layer, logical addressing layer...call it what you like) functionality for the foreseeable future.

Subnetting with IPv6

Subnetting with IPv6 is a lot like subnetting with IPv4. You need to know how many bits you are going to use for the network mask to subnet it correctly.

For example, let's say you have an IPv6 prefix of 2001:DB8:BBCC:0000::/53 and you need to set up your network so that your IPv6 addressing scheme can handle 1,500 more subnets. How would you figure this out?

When determining any number of hosts or subnets, the calculation is 2 to the power (2^x). The first power number that is greater than or equal to the number you need is the power number that you add to the current network mask. Thus, in the previous question, to get to 1,500 subnets, you would need to determine which 2^x is the first one that is greater than or equal to 1,500. If you calculate your powers correctly, 2^{11} (2^{11} = 2,048) is the first one that is greater than or equal to 1,500. So, you would add the power of 11 to the /53 in the previous address, and you would now use /64 as your network mask. Table 10.8 shows you some of the power numbers for the power of 2.

TABLE 10.8 Powers of 2

Power	Equals
2^2	4
2^3	8
2^4	16
2^5	32
2^6	64
2^7	128
2^8	256
2^9	512
2^{10}	1,024
2^{11}	2,048
2^{12}	4,096

Summary

Why TCP/IP is the primary protocol in use today is one of the important topics covered in this chapter. You also learned that the 32-bit IPv4 address is a structured and hierarchical one that is used to identify uniquely every machine on a network. You learned how to determine available IP addresses and implement subnetting. In addition, you learned how the new layer 3 IPv6 protocol is implemented, including the structure of the IPv6 address. Finally, I discussed the new functionality included in IPv6 addressing as well as several Windows Server 2016 integration/migration implementations.

Exam Essentials

Understand what subnetting is and when to use it.   If an organization is large and has many computers or if its computers are geographically dispersed, it's sensible to divide its large network into smaller ones connected by routers. These smaller networks are called *subnets*. Subnetting is the process of carving a single IP network into smaller, logical subnetworks.

Understand subnet masks.   For the subnet address scheme to work, every machine on the network must know which part of the host address will be used as the subnet address. The network administrator creates a 32-bit subnet mask consisting of 1s and 0s. The 1s in the subnet mask represent the positions that refer to the network or subnet addresses. The 0s represent the positions that refer to the host portion of the address.

Understand IPv6.   Understand the structure of an IPv6 address and how it's displayed. Know the shortcuts and rules (such as for displaying 0s) for writing IPv6 addresses. Know the integration/migration components for IPv6 included in Windows Server 2016, including tunneling and dual stack.

Review Questions

1. You are the network administrator for ABC Company. You have an IPv6 prefix of 2001:DB8:BBCC:0000::/53, and you need to set up your network so that your IPv6 addressing scheme can handle 1,000 more subnets. Which network mask would you use?

   A. /60

   B. /61

   C. /62

   D. /63

   E. /64

2. You are the network administrator for Stellacon Corporation. Stellacon has a Windows Server 2016 machine that needs to be able to communicate with all computers on the internal network. Stellacon has decided to add 15 new segments to its IPv6 network. How would you configure the IPv6 so that the server can communicate with all the segments?

   A. Configure the IPv6 address as fd00::2b0:e0ff:dee9:4143/8.

   B. Configure the IPv6 address as fe80::2b0:e0ff:dee9:4143/32.

   C. Configure the IPv6 address as ff80::2b0:e0ff:dee9:4143/64.

   D. Configure the IPv6 address as fe80::2b0:e0ff:dee9:4143/64.

3. You are the network administrator for a mid-size organization that has installed Windows Server 2016 onto the network. You are thinking of moving all machines to Windows 10 and IPv6. You decide to set up a test environment with four subnets. What type of IPv6 addresses do you need to set up?

   A. Global addresses

   B. Link-local addresses

   C. Unique local addresses

   D. Site-local addresses

4. You have a large IP-routed network using the address 137.25.0.0; it is composed of 20 subnets, with a maximum of 300 hosts on each subnet. Your company continues on a merger-and-acquisitions spree, and your manager has told you to prepare for an increase to 50 subnets with some containing more than 600 hosts. Using the existing network address, which of the following subnet masks would work for the requirement set by your manager?

   A. 255.255.252.0

   B. 255.255.254.0

   C. 255.255.248.0

   D. 255.255.240.0

5. Your company is growing dramatically via acquisitions of other companies. As the network administrator, you need to keep up with the changes because they affect the workstations and you need to support them. When you started, there were 15 locations connected via routers, and now there are 25. As new companies are acquired, they are migrated to Windows Server 2016 and brought into the same domain as another site. Management says that they are going to acquire at least 10 more companies in the next two years. The engineers have also told you that they are redesigning the company's Class B address into an IP addressing scheme that will support these requirements and that there will never be more than 1,000 network devices on any subnet. What is the appropriate subnet mask to support this network when the changes are completed?

A. 255.255.252.0

B. 255.255.248.0

C. 255.255.255.0

D. 255.255.255.128

6. You work for a small printing company that has 75 workstations. Most of them run standard office applications such as word processing, spreadsheet, and accounting programs. Fifteen of the workstations are constantly processing huge graphics files and then sending print jobs to industrial-sized laser printers. The performance of the network has always been an issue, but you have never addressed it. You have now migrated your network to Windows 10 and Windows Server 2016 and have decided to take advantage of the routing capability built into Windows Server 2016. You choose the appropriate server and place two NICs in the machine, but you realize that you have only one network address, 201.102.34.0, which you obtained years ago. How should you subnet this address to segment the bandwidth hogs from the rest of the network while giving everyone access to the entire network?

A. 255.255.255.192

B. 255.255.255.224

C. 255.255.255.252

D. 255.255.255.240

7. You work for Carpathian Worldwide Enterprises, which has more than 50 administrative and manufacturing locations around the world. The size of these organizations varies greatly, with the number of computers per location ranging from 15 to slightly fewer than 1,000. The sales operations use more than 1,000 facilities, each of which contains 2 to 5 computers. Carpathian is also in merger talks with another large organization. If the merger materializes as planned, you will have to accommodate another 100 manufacturing and administrative locations, each with a maximum of 600 computers, as well as 2,000 additional sales facilities. You don't have any numbers for the future growth of the company, but you are told to keep growth in mind. You decide to implement a private addressing plan for the entire organization. More than half of your routers don't support Variable Length Subnet Masking. Which subnet masks would work for this situation? (Choose all that apply.)

A. 255.255.224.0

B. 255.255.240.0

C. 255.255.248.0

D. 255.255.252.0

E. 255.255.254.0

8. Which of the following subnet masks are represented with the CIDR of /27?

   A. 255.255.255.254

   B. 255.255.255.248

   C. 255.255.255.224

   D. 255.255.255.240

9. You have 3,500 client computers on a single subnet. You need to select a subnet mask that will support all the client computers. You need to minimize the number of unused addresses. Which subnet mask should you choose?

   A. 255.255.248.0

   B. 255.255.254.0

   C. 255.255.240.0

   D. 255.255.252.0

10. You ask one of your technicians to get the IPv6 address of a new Windows Server 2016 machine, and she hands you a note with FE80::0203:FFFF:FE11:2CD on it. What can you tell from this address? (Choose two.)

   A. This is a globally unique IPv6 address.

   B. This is a link-local IPv6 address.

   C. This is a multicast IPv6 address.

   D. In EUI-64 format, you can see the MAC address of the node.

   E. In EUI-64 format, you can see the IPv4 address of the node.

Chapter

11

Configuring DNS

THE FOLLOWING 70-741 EXAM OBJECTIVES ARE COVERED IN THIS CHAPTER:

✓ **Install and configure DNS servers**

■ This objective may include but is not limited to: Determine DNS installation requirements; determine supported DNS deployment scenarios on Nano Server; install DNS; configure forwarders; configure Root Hints; configure delegation; implement DNS policies; implement DNS global settings using Windows PowerShell; configure Domain Name System Security Extensions (DNSSEC); configure DNS Socket Pool; configure cache locking; enable Response Rate Limiting; configure DNS-based Authentication of Named Entities (DANE); configure DNS logging; configure delegated administration; configure recursion settings; implement DNS performance tuning; configure global settings using Windows PowerShell.

✓ **Create and configure DNS zones and records**

■ This objective may include but is not limited to: Create primary zones; configure Active Directory integration of primary zones; create and configure secondary zones; create and configure stub zones; configure a GlobalNames zone; analyze zone-level statistics; create and configure DNS Resource Records (RR), including A, AAAA, PTR, SOA, NS, SRV, CNAME, and MX records; configure zone scavenging; configure record options, including Time To Live (TTL) and weight; configure round robin; configure secure dynamic updates; configure unknown record support; use DNS audit events and analytical (query) events for auditing and troubleshooting; configure Zone Scopes; configure records in Zone Scopes; configure policies for zones.

The Domain Name System (DNS) is one of the most important networking services that you can put on your network, and it's also one of the key topics that you'll need to understand if you plan to take any of the Microsoft Windows Server 2016 exams.

By the end of this chapter, you should have a deeper understanding of how DNS works, how to set it up properly, how to configure DNS, proper management of the DNS server, and how to troubleshoot DNS issues quickly and easily in Microsoft Windows Server 2016.

Introducing DNS

The *Domain Name System (DNS)* is a service that allows you to resolve a hostname to an Internet Protocol (IP) address. One of the inherent complexities of operating in networked environments is working with multiple protocols and network addresses. Owing largely to the tremendous rise in the popularity of the Internet, however, most environments have transitioned to use *Transmission Control Protocol/Internet Protocol (TCP/IP)* as their primary networking protocol. Microsoft is no exception when it comes to supporting TCP/IP in its workstation and server products. All current versions of Microsoft's operating systems support TCP/IP, as do most other modern operating systems.

An easy way to understand DNS is to think about making a telephone call. If you wanted to call Microsoft and did not know the phone number, you could call information, tell the operator the name (Microsoft), and get the telephone number. You would then make the call. Now think about trying to connect to Server1. You don't know the TCP/IP number (the computer's telephone number), so your computer asks DNS (information) for the number of Server1. DNS returns the number, and your system makes the connection (call). DNS is your network's 411, or information, and it returns the TCP/IP data for your network.

TCP/IP is actually a collection of different technologies (protocols and services) that allow computers to function together on a single, large, and heterogeneous network. Some of the major advantages of this protocol include widespread support for hardware, software, and network devices; reliance on a system of standards; and scalability. TCP handles tasks such as sequenced acknowledgments. IP involves many jobs, such as logical subnet assignment and routing.

The Form of an IP Address

To understand DNS, you must first understand how TCP/IP addresses are formed. Because DNS is strictly on a network to support TCP/IP, understanding the basics of TCP/IP is extremely important.

An *IP address* is a logical number that uniquely identifies a computer on a TCP/IP network. TCP/IP allows a computer packet to reach the correct host. Windows Server 2016 works with two versions of TCP/IP: IPv4 and IPv6. An IPv4 address takes the form of four octets (eight binary bits), each of which is represented by a decimal number between 0 and 255. The four numbers are separated by decimal points. For example, all of the following are valid IP addresses:

- 128.45.23.17
- 230.212.43.100
- 10.1.1.1

The dotted-decimal notation was created to make it easier for users to deal with IP addresses, but this idea did not go far enough. As a result, another abstraction layer was developed, which used names to represent the dotted decimal notation—the domain name. For example, the IP address 11000000 10101000 00000001 00010101 maps to 192.168.1.21, which in turn might map to server1.company.org, which is how the computer's address is usually presented to the user or application.

As stated earlier, IPv4 addresses are made up of octets, or the decimal (base 10) representation of 8 bits. It takes four octets to add up to the 32 bits required. IPv6 expands the address space to 128 bits. The address is usually represented in hexadecimal notation as follows:

```
2001:0DB8:0000:0000:1234:0000:A9FE:133E
```

You can tell that the implementation of DNS would make life a lot easier for everyone, even those of us who like to use alphanumeric values. (For example, some of us enjoy pinging the address in lieu of the name.) Fortunately, DNS already has the ability to handle IPv6 addresses using an AAAA record. An A record in IPv4's addressing space is 32 bits, and an AAAA record (4 As) in IPv6's is 128 bits.

Nowadays, most computer users are quite familiar with navigating to DNS-based resources, such as www.microsoft.com. To resolve these "friendly" names to TCP/IP addresses that the network stack can use, you need a method for mapping them. Originally, ASCII flat files (often called *HOSTS files*, as shown in Figure 11.1) were used for this purpose. In some cases, they are still used today in small networks, and they can be useful in helping to troubleshoot name resolution problems.

As the number of machines and network devices grew, it became unwieldy for administrators to manage all of the manual updates required to enter new mappings to a master HOSTS file and distribute it. Clearly, a better system was needed.

FIGURE 11.1   HOSTS file

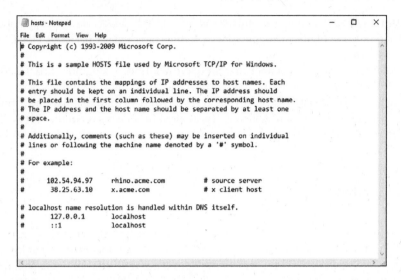

As you can see from the sample HOSTS file in Figure 11.1, you can conduct a quick test of the email server's name resolution as follows:

1. Open the HOSTS file: `C:\Windows\Systems32\drivers\etc`.

2. Add the IP-address-to-hostname mapping.

3. Try to ping the server using the hostname to verify that you can reach it using an easy-to-remember name.

Following these steps should drive home the concept of DNS for you because you can see it working to make your life easier. Now you don't have to remember 10.0.0.10; you only need to remember `exchange03`. However, you can also see how this method can become unwieldy if you have many hosts that want to use easy-to-remember names instead of IP addresses to locate resources on your network.

When dealing with large networks, users and network administrators must be able to locate the resources they require with minimal searching. Users don't care about the actual physical or logical network address of the machine; they just want to be able to connect to it using a simple name that they can remember.

From a network administrator's standpoint, however, each machine must have its own logical address that makes it part of the network on which it resides. Therefore, some scalable and easy-to-manage method for resolving a machine's logical name to an IP address and then to a domain name is required. DNS was created just for this purpose.

DNS is defined by a number of requests for comments (RFCs), though primarily by RFC 1034 and RFC 1035.

DNS is a hierarchically distributed database. In other words, its layers are arranged in a definite order, and its data is distributed across a wide range of machines, each of which can exert control over a portion of the database. DNS is a standard set of protocols that defines the following:

- A mechanism for querying and updating address information in the database
- A mechanism for replicating the information in the database among servers
- A schema of the database

DNS was originally developed in the early days of the Internet (called ARPAnet at the time) when it was a small network created by the Department of Defense for research purposes. Before DNS, computer names, or hostnames, were manually entered into a HOSTS file located on a centrally administered server. Each site that needed to resolve hostnames outside of its organization had to download this file. As the number of computers on the Internet grew, so did the size of this HOSTS file—and along with it the problems of its management. The need for a new system that would offer features such as scalability, decentralized administration, and support for various data types became more and more obvious. DNS, introduced in 1984, became this new system.

With DNS, the hostnames reside in a database that can be distributed among multiple servers, decreasing the load on any one server and providing the ability to administer this naming system on a per-partition basis. DNS supports hierarchical names and allows for the registration of various data types in addition to the hostname-to-IP-address mapping used in HOSTS files. Database performance is ensured through its distributed nature as well as through caching.

The DNS distributed database establishes an inverted logical tree structure called the *domain namespace*. Each node, or domain, in that space has a unique name. At the top of the tree is the root. This may not sound quite right, which is why the DNS hierarchical model is described as being an inverted tree, with the root at the top. The root is represented by the null set: "". When written, the root node is represented by a single dot (.).

Each node in the DNS can branch out to any number of nodes below it. For example, below the root node are a number of other nodes, commonly referred to as *top-level domains (TLDs)*. These are the familiar .com, .net, .org, .gov, .edu, and other such names. Table 11.1 lists some of these TLDs.

TABLE 11.1   Common top-level DNS domains

Domain Name	Type of Organization
com	Commercial (for example, stormwind.com for StormWind Training Corporation).
edu	Educational (for example, gatech.edu for the Georgia Institute of Technology).
gov	Government (for example, whitehouse.gov for the White House in Washington, D.C.).

TABLE 11.1   Common top-level DNS domains *(continued)*

Domain Name	Type of Organization
int	International organizations (for example, nato.int for NATO); this top-level domain is fairly rare.
mil	Military organizations (for example, usmc.mil for the Marine Corps); there is a separate set of root name servers for this domain.
net	Networking organizations and Internet providers (for example, hiWAAY.net for HiWAAY Information Systems); many commercial organizations have registered names under this domain too.
org	Noncommercial organizations (for example, fidonet.org for FidoNet).
au	Australia
uk	United Kingdom
ca	Canada
us	United States
jp	Japan

Each of these nodes then branches out into another set of domains, and they combine to form what we refer to as *domain names,* such as microsoft.com. A domain name identifies the domain's position in the logical DNS hierarchy in relation to its parent domain by separating each branch of the tree with a dot. Figure 11.2 shows a few of the top-level domains, where the Microsoft domain fits, and a host called Tigger within the microsoft.com domain. If someone wanted to contact that host, they would use the *fully qualified domain name (FQDN),* tigger.microsoft.com.

An FQDN includes the trailing dot (.) to indicate the root node, but it's commonly left off in practice.

As previously stated, one of the strengths of DNS is the ability to delegate control over portions of the DNS namespace to multiple organizations. For example, the Internet Corporation for Assigned Names and Numbers (ICANN) assigns the control over TLDs to one or more organizations. In turn, those organizations delegate portions of the DNS namespace to other organizations. For example, when you register a domain name, let's call it example.com, you control the DNS for the portion of the DNS namespace within example.com. The registrar controlling the .com TLD has delegated control over the example.com node in the DNS tree. No other node can be named example directly below the .com within the DNS database.

FIGURE 11.2   The DNS hierarchy

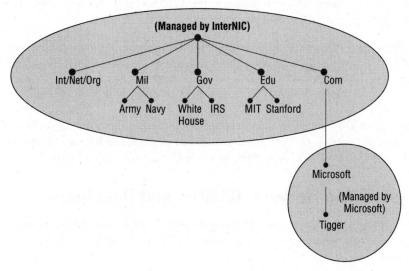

Within the portion of the domain namespace that you control (example.com), you could create host and other records (more on these later). You could also further subdivide example.com and delegate control over those divisions to other organizations or departments. These divisions are called *subdomains*. For example, you might create subdomains named for the cities in which the company has branch offices and then delegate control over those subdomains to the branch offices. The subdomains might be named losangeles.example.com, chicago.example.com, portsmouth.example.com, and so on.

Each domain (or delegated subdomain) is associated with DNS name servers. In other words, for every node in the DNS, one or more servers can give an authoritative answer to queries about that domain. At the root of the domain namespace are the root servers, which I'll cover later in the chapter.

Domain names and hostnames must contain only characters a to z, A to Z, 0 to 9, and - (hyphen). Other common and useful characters, such as the & (ampersand), / (slash), . (period), and _ (underscore) characters, are not allowed. This is in conflict with NetBIOS's naming restrictions. However, you'll find that Windows Server 2016 is smart enough to take a NetBIOS name, like Server_1, and turn it into a legal DNS name, like server1.example.com.

DNS servers work together to resolve hierarchical names. If a server already has information about a name, it simply fulfills the query for the client. Otherwise, it queries other DNS servers for the appropriate information. The system works well because it distributes the authority over separate parts of the DNS structure to specific servers. A DNS zone is a portion of the DNS namespace over which a specific DNS server has authority. (DNS zone types are discussed in detail later in this chapter.)

> There is an important distinction to make between DNS zones and Active Directory (AD) domains. Although both use hierarchical names and require name resolution, DNS zones do not map directly to AD domains.

Within a given DNS zone, resource records (RRs) contain the hosts and other database information that make up the data for the zone. For example, an RR might contain the host entry for www.example.com, pointing it to the IP address 192.168.1.10.

Understanding Servers, Clients, and Resolvers

You will need to know a few terms and concepts in order to manage a DNS server. Understanding these terms will make it easier to understand how the Windows Server 2016 DNS server works:

DNS Server   Any computer providing domain name services is a *DNS name server*. No matter where the server resides in the DNS namespace, it's still a DNS name server. For example, 13 root name servers at the top of the DNS tree are responsible for delegating the TLDs. The *root servers* provide referrals to name servers for the TLDs, which in turn provides referrals to an authoritative name server for a given domain.

> The Berkeley Internet Name Domain (BIND) was originally the only software available for running the root servers on the Internet. However, a few years ago the organizations responsible for the root servers undertook an effort to diversify the software running on these important machines. Today, root servers run multiple types of name server software. BIND is still primarily on Unix-based machines, and it is also the most popular for Internet providers. None of the root servers run Windows DNS.

Any DNS server implementation supporting Service Location Resource Records (see RFC 2782) and Dynamic Updates (RFC 2136) is sufficient to provide the name service for any operating system running Windows 2003 software and newer.

DNS Client   A *DNS client* is any machine that issues queries to a DNS server. The client hostname may or may not be registered in a DNS database. Clients issue DNS requests through processes called *resolvers*. You'll sometimes see the terms *client* and *resolver* used synonymously.

Resolver   *Resolvers* are software processes, sometimes implemented in software libraries, which handles the actual process of finding the answers to queries for DNS data. The resolver is also built into many larger pieces of software so that external libraries don't have to be called to make and process DNS queries. Resolvers can be what you'd consider client computers or other DNS servers attempting to resolve an answer on behalf of a client (for example, Internet Explorer).

Query A *query* is a request for information sent to a DNS server. Three types of queries can be made to a DNS server: recursive, inverse, and iterative. I'll discuss the differences between these query types in the section "DNS Queries" a bit later in the chapter.

Understanding the DNS Process

To help you understand the DNS process, I will start by covering the differences between Dynamic DNS and Non-Dynamic DNS. During this discussion, you will learn how Dynamic DNS populates the DNS database. You'll also see how to implement security for Dynamic DNS. I will then talk about the workings of different types of DNS queries. Finally, I will discuss caching and time to live (TTL). You'll learn how to determine the best setting for your organization.

Dynamic DNS and Non-Dynamic DNS

To understand Dynamic DNS and Non-Dynamic DNS, you must go back in time (here is where the TV screen always used to get wavy). Many years ago when we all worked on NT 3.51 and NT 4.0, most networks used Windows Internet Name Service (WINS) to do their TCP/IP name resolution. Windows versions 95/98 and NT 4.0 Professional were all built on the idea of using WINS. This worked out well for administrators because WINS was dynamic (which meant that once it was installed, it automatically built its own database). Back then, there was no such thing as Dynamic DNS; administrators had to enter DNS records into the server manually. This is important to know even today. If you have clients still running any of these older operating systems (95/98 or NT 4), these clients cannot use Dynamic DNS.

Now let's move forward in time to the release of Windows Server 2000. Microsoft announced that DNS was going to be the name resolution method of choice. Many administrators (me included) did not look forward to the switch. Because there was no such thing as Dynamic DNS, most administrators had nightmares about manually entering records. However, luckily for us, when Microsoft released Windows Server 2000, DNS had the ability to operate dynamically. Now when you're setting up Windows Server 2016 DNS, you can choose what type of dynamic update you would like to use, if any. Let's talk about why you would want to choose one over the other.

The *Dynamic DNS (DDNS) standard*, described in RFC 2136, allows DNS clients to update information in the DNS database files. For example, a Windows Server 2016 DHCP server can automatically tell a DDNS server which IP addresses it has assigned to what machines. Windows 2000 (and higher) and Windows 7 (and higher) DHCP clients can do this too. For security reasons, however, it's better to let the DHCP server do it. The result: IP addresses and DNS records stay in sync so that you can use DNS and DHCP together seamlessly. Because DDNS is a proposed Internet standard, you can even use the Windows Server 2016 DDNS-aware parts with Unix/Linux-based DNS servers.

Non-Dynamic DNS (NDDNS) does not automatically populate the DNS database. The client systems do not have the ability to update to DNS. If you decide to use Non-Dynamic DNS, an administrator will need to populate the DNS database manually. Non-Dynamic DNS is a reasonable choice if your organization is small to midsize and you do not want extra network traffic (clients updating to the DNS server) or if you need to enter the computer's TCP/IP information manually because of strict security measures.

> Dynamic DNS has the ability to be secure, and the chances are slim that a rogue system (a computer that does not belong in your DNS database) could update to a secure DNS server. Nevertheless, some organizations have to follow stricter security measures and are not allowed to have dynamic updates.

The major downside to entering records into DNS manually occurs when the organization is using the *Dynamic Host Configuration Protocol (DHCP)*. When using DHCP, it is possible for users to end up with different TCP/IP addresses every day. This means that an administrator has to update DNS manually each day to keep it accurate.

If you choose to allow Dynamic DNS, you need to decide how you want to set it up. When setting up dynamic updates on your DNS server, you have three choices (see Figure 11.3).

FIGURE 11.3 Setting the Dynamic Updates option

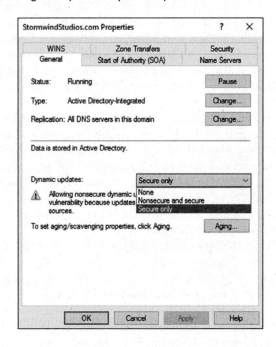

None   This means your DNS server is Non-Dynamic.

Nonsecure and Secure   This means that any machine (even if it does not have a domain account) can register with DNS. Using this setting could allow rogue systems to enter records into your DNS server.

Secure Only   This means that only machines with accounts in Active Directory can register with DNS. Before DNS registers any account in its database, it checks Active Directory to make sure that account is an authorized domain computer.

How Dynamic DNS Populates the DNS Database

TCP/IP is the protocol used for network communications on a Microsoft Windows Server 2016 network. Users have two ways to receive a TCP/IP number:

- Static (administrators manually enter the TCP/IP information)
- Dynamic (using DHCP)

When an administrator sets up TCP/IP, DNS can also be configured.

Once a client gets the address of the DNS server, if that client is allowed to update with DNS, the client sends a registration to DNS or requests DHCP to send the registration. DNS then does one of two things, depending on which Dynamic Updates option is specified:

- Check with Active Directory to see if that computer has an account (Secure Only updates) and, if it does, enter the record into the database.
- Enter the record into its database (nonsecure and secure updates).

What if you have clients that cannot update DNS? Well, there is a solution—DHCP. In the DNS tab of the IPv4 Properties window, check the option labeled "Dynamically update DNS records for DHCP clients that do not request updates (for example, clients running Windows NT 4.0)," which is shown in Figure 11.4.

FIGURE 11.4   DHCP settings for DNS

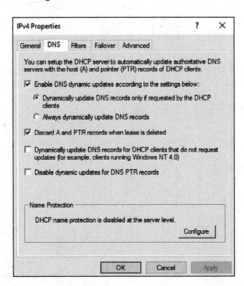

DHCP, along with Dynamic DNS clients, allows an organization to update its DNS database dynamically without the time and effort of having an administrator manually enter DNS records.

DNS Queries

As stated earlier, a client can make three types of queries to a DNS server: recursive, inverse, and iterative. Remember that the client of a DNS server can be a resolver (what you'd normally call a client) or another DNS server.

Iterative Queries

Iterative queries are the easiest to understand: A client asks the DNS server for an answer, and the server returns the best answer. This information likely comes from the server's cache. The server never sends out an additional query in response to an iterative query. If the server doesn't know the answer, it may direct the client to another server through a referral.

Recursive Queries

In a *recursive query*, the client sends a query to a name server, asking it to respond either with the requested answer or with an error message. The error states one of two things:

- The server can't come up with the right answer.

- The domain name doesn't exist.

In a recursive query, the name server isn't allowed to just refer the client to some other name server. Most resolvers use recursive queries. In addition, if your DNS server uses a forwarder, the requests sent by your server to the forwarder will be recursive queries.

Figure 11.5 shows an example of both recursive and iterative queries. In this example, a client within the Microsoft Corporation is querying its DNS server for the IP address for www.whitehouse.gov.

FIGURE 11.5   A sample DNS query

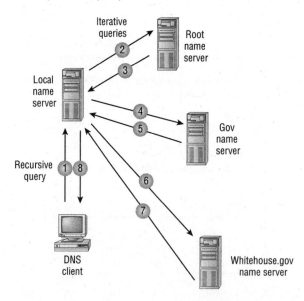

Here's what happens to resolve the request:

1. The resolver sends a recursive DNS query to its local DNS server asking for the IP address of www.whitehouse.gov. The local name server is responsible for resolving the name, and it cannot refer the resolver to another name server.

2. The local name server checks its zones, and it finds no zones corresponding to the requested domain name.

3. The root name server has authority for the root domain and will reply with the IP address of a name server for the .gov top-level domain.

4. The local name server sends an iterative query for www.whitehouse.gov to the Gov name server.

5. The Gov name server replies with the IP address of the name server servicing the whitehouse.gov domain.

6. The local name server sends an iterative query for www.whitehouse.gov to the whitehouse.gov name server.

7. The whitehouse.gov name server replies with the IP address corresponding to www.whitehouse.gov.

8. The local name server sends the IP address of www.whitehouse.gov back to the original resolver.

Inverse Queries

Inverse queries use pointer (PTR) records. Instead of supplying a name and then asking for an IP address, the client first provides the IP address and then asks for the name. Because there's no direct correlation in the DNS namespace between a domain name and its associated IP address, this search would be fruitless without the use of the in-addr.arpa domain. Nodes in the in-addr.arpa domain are named after the numbers in the dotted-octet representation of IP addresses. However, because IP addresses get more specific from left to right and domain names get less specific from left to right, the order of IP address octets must be reversed when building the in-addr.arpa tree. With this arrangement, administration of the lower limbs of the DNS in-addr.arpa tree can be given to companies as they are assigned their Class A, B, or C subnet address or delegated even further down thanks to Variable Length Subnet Masking (VLSM).

Once the domain tree is built into the DNS database, a special PTR record is added to associate the IP addresses with the corresponding hostnames. In other words, to find a hostname for the IP address 206.131.234.1, the resolver would query the DNS server for a PTR record for 1.234.131.206.in-addr.arpa. If this IP address is outside the local domain, the DNS server will start at the root and sequentially resolve the domain nodes until arriving at 234.131.206.in-addr.arpa, which would contain the PTR record for the desired host.

Caching and Time to Live

When a name server is processing a recursive query, it may be required to send out several queries to find the definitive answer. Name servers, acting as resolvers, are allowed to cache all of the received information during this process; each record contains information called *time to live (TTL)*. The TTL specifies how long the record will be held in the local cache until it must be resolved again. If a query comes in that can be satisfied by this cached data, the TTL that's returned with it equals the current amount of time left before the data is flushed.

There is also a negative cache TTL. The *negative cache TTL* is used when an authoritative server responds to a query indicating that the record queried doesn't exist, and it indicates the amount of time that this negative answer may be held. Negative caching is quite helpful in preventing repeated queries for names that don't exist.

The administrator for the DNS zone sets TTL values for the entire zone. The value can be the same across the zone, or the administrator can set a separate TTL for each RR within the zone. Client resolvers also have data caches and honor the TTL value so that they know when to flush.

Choosing Appropriate TTL Values

For zones that you administer, you can choose the TTL values for the entire zone, for negative caching, and for individual records. Choosing an appropriate TTL depends on a number of factors, including the following:

- Amount of change you anticipate for the records within the zone

- Amount of time that you can withstand an outage that might require changing an IP address

- Amount of traffic that you believe the DNS server can handle

Resolvers query the name server every time the TTL expires for a given record. A low TTL, say 60 seconds, can burden the name server, especially for popular DNS records. (DNS queries aren't particularly intensive for a server to handle, but they can add up quickly if you mistakenly use 60 seconds instead of 600 seconds for the TTL on a popular record.) Set a low TTL only when you need to respond quickly to a changing environment.

A high TTL, say 604,800 seconds (that's one week), means that if you need to make a change to the DNS record, clients might not see the change for up to a week. This consideration is especially important when making changes to the network, and it's one that's all too frequently overlooked. I can't count the number of times I've worked with clients who have recently made a DNS change to a new IP for their email or website only to ask why it's not working for some clients. The answer can be found in the TTL value. If the record is being cached, then the only thing that can solve their problem is time.

You should choose a TTL that's appropriate for your environment. Take the following factors into account:

- The amount of time that you can afford to be offline if you need to make a change to a DNS record that's being cached

- The amount of load that a low TTL will cause on the DNS server

In addition, you should plan well ahead of any major infrastructure changes and change the TTL to a lower value to lessen the effect of the downtime by reducing the amount of time that the record(s) can be cached.

Introducing DNS Database Zones

As mentioned earlier in this chapter, a DNS zone is a portion of the DNS namespace over which a specific DNS server has authority. Within a given DNS zone, there are resource records that define the hosts and other types of information that make up the database for the zone. You can choose from several different zone types. Understanding the characteristics of each will help you choose which is right for your organization.

> The DNS zones discussed in this book are all Microsoft Windows Server 2012/2016 zones. Non-Windows (for example, Unix) systems set up their DNS zones differently.

In the following sections, I will discuss the different zone types and their characteristics.

Understanding Primary Zones

When you're learning about zone types, things can get a bit confusing. But it's really not difficult to understand how they work and why you would want to choose one type of zone over another. Zones are databases that store records. By choosing one zone type over another, you are basically just choosing how the database works and how it will be stored on the server.

The primary zone is responsible for maintaining all of the records for the DNS zone. It contains the primary copy of the DNS database. All record updates occur on the primary zone. You will want to create and add primary zones whenever you create a new DNS domain.

There are two types of primary zones:

- Primary zone
- Primary zone with Active Directory Integration (Active Directory DNS)

> From this point forward, I refer to a primary zone with Active Directory Integration as an *Active Directory DNS*. When I use only the term *primary zone,* Active Directory is not included.

To install DNS as a primary zone, first you must install DNS using the Server Manager MMC. Once DNS is installed and running, you create a new zone and specify it as a primary zone.

> The process of installing DNS and its zones will be discussed later in this chapter. In addition, there will be step-by-step exercises to walk you through how to install these components.

Primary zones have advantages and disadvantages. Knowing the characteristics of a primary zone will help you decide when you need the zone and when it fits into your organization.

Local Database

Primary DNS zones get stored locally in a file (with the suffix .dns) on the server. This allows you to store a primary zone on a domain controller or a member server. In addition, by loading DNS onto a member server, you can help a small organization conserve resources. Such an organization may not have the resources to load DNS on an Active Directory domain controller.

Unfortunately, the local database has many disadvantages:

Lack of Fault Tolerance   Think of a primary zone as a contact list on your smartphone. All of the contacts in the list are the records in your database. The problem is that if you lose your phone or the phone breaks, you lose your contact list. Until your phone gets fixed or you swap out your phone card, the contacts are unavailable.

It works the same way with a primary zone. If the server goes down or you lose the hard drive, DNS records on that machine are unreachable. An administrator can install a secondary zone (explained in the next section), and that provides temporary fault tolerance. Unfortunately, if the primary zone is down for an extended period of time, the secondary server's information will no longer be valid.

Additional Network Traffic   Let's imagine that you are looking for a contact number for John Smith. John Smith is not listed in your cell phone directory, but he is listed in your partner's cell phone. You have to contact your partner to get the listing. You cannot directly access your partner's cell contacts.

When a resolver sends a request to DNS to get the TCP/IP address for Jsmith (in this case Jsmith is a computer name) and the DNS server does not have an answer, it does not have the ability to check the other server's database directly to get an answer. Thus, it forwards the request to another DNS. When DNS servers are replicating zone databases with other DNS servers, this causes additional network traffic.

No Security   Staying with the cell phone example, let's say that you call your partner looking for John Smith's phone number. When your partner gives you the phone number over your wireless phone, someone with a scanner can pick up your conversation. Unfortunately, wireless telephone calls are not very secure.

Now a resolver asks a primary zone for the Jsmith TCP/IP address. If someone on the network has a packet sniffer, they can steal the information in the DNS packets being sent over the network. The packets are not secure unless you implement some form of secondary security. Also, the DNS server has the ability to be dynamic. A primary zone accepts all updates from DNS servers. You cannot set it to accept secure updates only.

Understanding Secondary Zones

In Windows Server 2016 DNS, you have the ability to use secondary DNS zones. Secondary zones are noneditable copies of the DNS database. You use them for *load balancing* (also referred to as *load sharing*), which is a way of managing network overloads on a single server. A secondary zone gets its database from a primary zone.

A *secondary zone* contains a database with all of the same information as the primary zone, and it can be used to resolve DNS requests. Secondary zones have the following advantages:

- A secondary zone provides fault tolerance, so if the primary zone server becomes unavailable, name resolution can still occur using the secondary zone server.

- Secondary DNS servers can also increase network performance by offloading some of the traffic that would otherwise go to the primary server.

Secondary servers are often placed within the parts of an organization that have high-speed network access. This prevents DNS queries from having to run across slow wide area network (WAN) connections. For example, if there are two remote offices within the stormwind.com organization, you may want to place a secondary DNS server in each remote office. This way, when clients require name resolution, they will contact the nearest server for this IP address information, thus preventing unnecessary WAN traffic.

> Having too many secondary zone servers can actually cause an increase in network traffic because of replication (especially if DNS changes are fairly frequent). Therefore, you should always weigh the benefits and drawbacks and properly plan for secondary zone servers.

Configure Zone Delegation

One advantage of DNS is the ability of turning a namespace into one or more zones. These zones can be replicated to each other or other DNS servers. As an administrator, you must decide when you want to break your DNS into multiple zones. When considering this option, there are a few things to think about:

- You want the management of your DNS namespace to be delegated by another location or department in your organization.

- You want to load-balance your traffic among multiple servers by turning a large zone into many smaller zones. This will help improve performance and create redundancy among your DNS servers.

- You have remote offices opening up, and you want to expand your DNS namespace.

To create a new zone delegation, you would complete the following steps:

1. Open the DNS console.

2. In the console tree, right-click the applicable subdomain and then click New Delegation.

3. Follow the instructions provided in the New Delegation Wizard to finish creating the newly delegated domain.

Understanding Active Directory Integrated DNS

Windows Server 2000 introduced *Active Directory Integrated DNS* to the world. This zone type was unique, and it was a separate choice during setup. In Windows Server 2003, this zone type became an add-on to a primary zone. In Windows Server 2016, it works the same way. After choosing to set up a primary zone, you check the box Store The Zone In Active Directory (see Figure 11.6).

FIGURE 11.6   Setting up an Active Directory Integrated zone

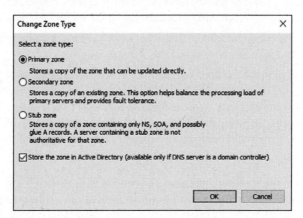

Disadvantages of Active Directory Integrated DNS

The main disadvantage of Active Directory Integrated DNS is that it has to reside on a domain controller because the DNS database is stored in Active Directory. As a result, you cannot load this zone type on a member server, and small organizations might not have the resources to set up a dedicated domain controller.

Advantages of Active Directory Integrated DNS

The advantages of using an Active Directory Integrated DNS zone well outweigh the disadvantages just discussed. The following are some of the major advantages to an Active Directory Integrated zone:

Full Fault Tolerance   Think of an Active Directory Integrated zone as a database on your server that stores contact information for all your clients. If you need to retrieve John Smith's phone number, as long as it was entered, you can look it up on the software.

If John Smith's phone number was stored only on your computer and your computer stopped working, no one could access John Smith's phone number. But since John Smith's phone number is stored in a database to which everyone has access, if your computer stops working, other users can still retrieve John Smith's phone number.

An Active Directory Integrated zone works the same way. Since the DNS database is stored in Active Directory, all Active Directory DNS servers can have access to the same data. If one server goes down or you lose a hard drive, all other Active Directory DNS servers can still retrieve DNS records.

No Additional Network Traffic   As previously discussed, an Active Directory Integrated zone is stored in Active Directory. Since all records are now stored in Active Directory, when a resolver needs a TCP/IP address for Jsmith, any Active Directory DNS server can access Jsmith's address and respond to the resolver.

When you choose an Active Directory Integrated zone, DNS zone data can be replicated automatically to other DNS servers during the normal Active Directory replication process.

DNS Security   An Active Directory Integrated zone has a few security advantages over a primary zone:

- An Active Directory Integrated zone can use secure dynamic updates.

- As explained earlier, the Dynamic DNS standard allows secure-only updates or dynamic updates, not both.

- If you choose secure updates, then only machines with accounts in Active Directory can register with DNS. Before DNS registers any account in its database, it checks Active Directory to make sure that it is an authorized domain computer.

- An Active Directory Integrated zone stores and replicates its database through Active Directory replication. Because of this, the data gets encrypted as it is sent from one DNS server to another.

Background Zone Loading   Background zone loading (discussed in more detail later in this chapter) allows an Active Directory Integrated DNS zone to load in the background. As a result, a DNS server can service client requests while the zone is still loading into memory.

Understanding Stub Zones

Stub zones work a lot like secondary zones—the database is a noneditable copy of a primary zone. The difference is that the stub zone's database contains only the information necessary (three record types) to identify the authoritative DNS servers for a zone (see Figure 11.7). You should not use stub zones to replace secondary zones, nor should you use them for redundancy and load balancing.

FIGURE 11.7   DNS stub zone type

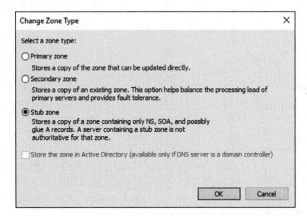

Stub zone databases contain only three record types: name server (NS), start of authority (SOA), and glue host (A) records. Understanding these records will help you on the Microsoft certification exams. Microsoft asks many questions about stub zones on all DNS-related exams.

When to Use Stub Zones

Stub zones become particularly useful in a couple of different scenarios. Consider what happens when two large companies merge: example.com and example.net. In most cases, the DNS zone information from both companies must be available to every employee. You could set up a new zone on each side that acts as a secondary for the other side's primary zone, but administrators tend to be very protective of their DNS databases and probably wouldn't agree to this plan.

A better solution is to add to each side a stub zone that points to the primary server on the other side. When a client in example.com (which you help administer) makes a request for a name in example.net, the stub zone on the example.com DNS server would send the client to the primary DNS server for example.net without actually resolving the name. At this point, it would be up to example.net's primary server to resolve the name.

An added benefit is that, even if the administrators over at example.net change their configuration, you won't have to do anything because the changes will automatically replicate to the stub zone, just as they would for a secondary server.

Stub zones can also be useful when you administer two domains across a slow connection. Let's change the previous example a bit and assume that you have full control over example.com and example.net but they connect through a 56 Kbps line. In this case, you wouldn't necessarily mind using secondary zones because you personally administer the entire network. However, it could get messy to replicate an entire zone file across that slow line. Instead, stub zones would refer clients to the appropriate primary server at the other site.

GlobalName Zones

Earlier in this chapter, I talked about organizations using WINS to resolve NetBIOS names (also referred to as *computer names*) to TCP/IP addresses. Even today, many organizations still use WINS along with DNS for name resolution. Unfortunately, WINS is slowly becoming obsolete.

To help organizations move forward with an all-DNS network, Microsoft Windows Server 2016 DNS supports *GlobalName zones*. These use single-label names (DNS names that do not contain a suffix such as .com, .net, and so on). GlobalName zones are not intended to support peer-to-peer networks and workstation name resolution, and they don't support dynamic DNS updates.

GlobalName zones are designed to be used with servers. Because GlobalName zones are not dynamic, an administrator has to enter the records into the zone database manually. In most organizations, the servers have static TCP/IP addresses, and this works well with the GlobalName zone design. GlobalName zones are usually used to map single-label CNAME (alias) resource records to an FQDN.

Zone Transfers and Replication

DNS is such an important part of the network that you should not just use a single DNS server. With a single DNS server, you also have a single point of failure, and in fact, many domain registrars encourage the use of more than two name servers for a domain. Secondary servers or multiple primary Active Directory Integrated servers play an integral role in providing DNS information for an entire domain.

As previously stated, secondary DNS servers receive their zone databases through zone transfers. When you configure a secondary server for the first time, you must specify the primary server that is authoritative for the zone and will send the zone transfer. The primary server must also permit the secondary server to request the zone transfer.

Zone transfers occur in one of two ways: *full zone transfers (AXFR)* and *incremental zone transfers (IXFR)*.

When a new secondary server is configured for the first time, it receives a full zone transfer from the primary DNS server. The full zone transfer contains all of the information in the DNS database. Some DNS implementations always receive full zone transfers.

After the secondary server receives its first full zone transfer, subsequent zone transfers are incremental. The primary name server compares its zone version number with that of the secondary server, and it sends only the changes that have been made in the interim. This significantly reduces network traffic generated by zone transfers.

The secondary server typically initiates zone transfers when the refresh interval time for the zone expires or when the secondary or stub server boots. Alternatively, you can configure notify lists on the primary server that send a message to the secondary or stub servers whenever any changes to the zone database occur.

When you consider your DNS strategy, you must carefully consider the layout of your network. If you have a single domain with offices in separate cities, you want to reduce the number of zone transfers across the potentially slow or expensive WAN links, although this is becoming less of a concern because of continuous increases in bandwidth.

Active Directory Integrated zones do away with traditional zone transfers altogether. Instead, they replicate across Active Directory with all of the other AD information. This replication is secure and encrypted because it uses the Active Directory security.

How DNS Notify Works

Windows Server 2016 supports DNS Notify. *DNS Notify* is a mechanism that allows the process of initiating notifications to secondary servers when zone changes occur (RFC 1996). DNS Notify uses a push mechanism for communicating to a select set of secondary zone servers when their zone information is updated. (DNS Notify does not allow you to configure a notify list for a stub zone.)

After being notified of the changes, secondary servers can then start a pull zone transfer and update their local copies of the database.

NOTE Many different mechanisms use the push/pull relationship. Normally, one object pushes information to another, and the second object pulls the information from the first. Most applications push replication on a change value and pull it on a time value. For example, a system can push replication after 10 updates, or it can be pulled every 30 minutes.

To configure the DNS Notify process, you create a list of secondary servers to notify. List the IP address of the server in the primary master's Notify dialog box (see Figure 11.8). The Notify dialog box is located under the Zone Transfers tab, which is located in the zone Properties dialog box (see Figure 11.9).

FIGURE 11.8   DNS Notify dialog box

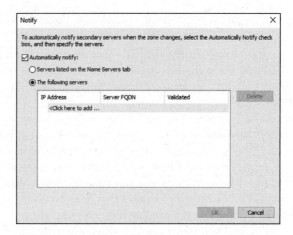

FIGURE 11.9   DNS Zone Transfers tab

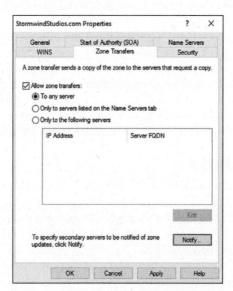

Configuring Stub Zone Transfers with Zone Replication

In the preceding section, I talked about how to configure secondary server zone transfers. What if you wanted to configure settings for stub zone transfers? This is where zone replication scope comes in.

Only Active Directory–integrated primary and stub zones can configure their replication scope. Secondary servers do not have this ability.

You can configure zone replication scope configurations in two ways. An administrator can set configuration options through the DNS snap-in or through a command-line tool called DNSCmd.

To configure zone replication scope through the DNS snap-in, follow these steps:

1. Click Start ➢ Administrative Tools ➢ DNS.

2. Right-click the zone that you want to set up.

3. Choose Properties.

4. In the Properties dialog box, click the Change button next to Replication (see Figure 11.10).

5. Choose the replication scope that fits your organization.

FIGURE 11.10 DNS zone replication scope

Advantages of DNS in Windows Server 2016

DNS in Microsoft Windows Server 2016 has some great advantages over many other versions of Microsoft DNS. Here are some of the improvements of DNS in Windows Server 2016 (some of these became available in previous versions of Windows Server):

- Background zone loading
- Support for TCP/IP version 6 (IPv6)
- Read-only domain controllers
- GlobalName zone
- DNS socket pools
- DNS cache locking
- Response Rate Limiting (RRL)
- Unknown Record Support
- IPv6 Root Hints
- DNS Security Extensions (DNSSEC)
- DNS devolution
- Record weighting
- Netmask ordering
- DnsUpdateProxy group
- DNS Policies

Background Zone Loading

If an organization had to restart a DNS server with an extremely large Active Directory Integrated DNS zones database in the past, DNS had a common problem with an Active Directory Integrated DNS zone. After the DNS restart, it could take hours for DNS data to be retrieved from Active Directory. During this time, the DNS server was unable to service any client requests.

Microsoft Windows Server 2008 DNS addressed this problem by implementing background zone loading, and Windows Server 2016 has taken it a step further. As the DNS restarts, the Active Directory zone data populates the database in the background. This allows the DNS server to service client requests for data from other zones almost immediately after a restart.

Background zone loading accomplishes this task by loading the DNS zone using separate threads. This allows a DNS server to service requests while still loading the rest of the zone. If a client sends a request to the DNS server for a computer that has not yet loaded into memory, the DNS server retrieves the data from Active Directory and updates the record.

Support for IPv6 Addresses

Over the past few years, the Internet has starting running into a problem that was not foreseen when it was first created—it started running out of TCP/IP addresses. As you probably know, when the Internet was created, it was used for government and academic purposes only. Then, seemingly overnight, it grew to be the information superhighway. Nowadays, asking someone for their email address is almost more common as asking for their phone number.

Version 4 (IPv4) was the common version of TCP/IP. The release of TCP/IP version 6 (IPv6) has solved the lack-of-IP-addresses problem. IPv4 addresses are 32 bits long, but IPv6 addresses are 128 bits in length. The longer lengths allow for a much greater number of globally unique TCP/IP addresses.

Microsoft Windows Server 2016 DNS has built-in support to accommodate both IPv4 and IPv6 address records (DNS records are explained later in this chapter). DHCP can also issue IPv6 addresses, which lets administrators allow DHCP to register the client with DNS, or the IPv6 client can register their address with the DNS server.

Support for Read-Only Domain Controllers

Windows Server 2008 introduced a new type of domain controller called the *read-only domain controller (RODC)*. This is a full copy of the Active Directory database without the ability to write to Active Directory. The RODC gives an organization the ability to install a domain controller in a location (onsite or offsite) where security is a concern.

Microsoft Windows Server 2016 DNS has implemented a type of zone to help support an RODC. A primary read-only zone allows a DNS server to receive a copy of the application partition (including ForestDNSZones and DomainDNSZones) that DNS uses. This allows DNS to support an RODC because DNS now has a full copy of all DNS zones stored in Active Directory.

A primary, read-only zone is just what it says—a read-only zone; so to make any changes to it, you have to change the primary zones located on the Active Directory Integrated DNS server.

DNS Socket Pools

If your server is running Windows Server 2016, you will be able to take advantage of DNS socket pools. *DNS socket pools* allow source port randomization to protect against DNS cache-poisoning attacks.

If you choose to use source port randomization, when the DNS service starts, the DNS server will randomly pick a source port from a pool of available sockets. This is an advantage because instead of DNS using a well-known source port when issuing queries, the DNS server uses a random port selected from the socket pool. This helps guard against attacks because a hacker must correctly access the source port of the DNS query. The socket pool is automatically enabled in DNS with the default settings.

When using the DNS socket pool, the default size of the DNS socket pool is 2,500. When configuring the socket pool, you have the ability to choose a size value from 0 to

10,000. The larger the value, the greater the protection you will have against DNS spoofing attacks. If you decide to configure your socket pool size with a zero value, only a single socket for remote DNS queries will be used.

DNS Cache Locking

Windows Server 2016 *DNS cache locking* allows cached DNS records to remain safe for the duration of the record's time to live (TTL) value. This means that the cached DNS records cannot be overwritten or changed. Because of this new DNS feature, it's tougher for hackers to perform cache-poisoning attacks against your DNS server.

DNS administrators can set how long a record will remain safe in cache. The configuration is based on a percent value. For example, if you set your cache locking value to 50 percent, then the cached records cannot be overwritten until half of the TTL has been reached. DNS cache locking is set to 100 percent by default. This means that the cached records never get overwritten.

Response Rate Limiting

Response Rate Limiting (RRL) allows an administrator to help prevent the possibility of hackers using your corporate DNS servers to initiate a denial of service attack on your corporate DNS clients.

Administrators have the ability to configure their RRL settings so that they can control how requests are responded to by DNS servers when these servers receive multiple requests by the same clients. When an administrator configures these settings, it helps prevent hackers from sending a denial of service (DoS) attack using your corporate DNS servers. When configuring RRL, an administrator can manipulate the following settings:

Responses Per Second   This setting allows administrators to set the maximum number of times the same response will be given to a client per second.

Errors Per Second   This setting allows administrators to set the maximum number of times an error response will be sent to the same client per second.

Window   This setting allows administrators to set the number of requests that are made by a client. This setting sets the number of seconds for which responses to a client will be suspended if too many requests are made.

Leak Rate   This setting allows administrators to set how often the DNS server will respond to a query during the suspended time responses. For example, if the DNS server suspends a response to a client for 20 seconds and the leak rate is 10, then the server will still respond to one query for every 10 queries sent. This will ensure that the appropriate clients get responses even when the DNS server is applying response rate limiting.

TC Rate   Administrators can set this setting to inform clients who are trying to connect using TCP when responses to the client are suspended. For example, if the TC rate is 3 and the DNS server suspends responses to a client, the server will issue a request for TCP connection for every three queries. Administrators want to set the value of the TC rate lower than the leak rate. This gives clients the option to connect using TCP before the leak rate applies.

Maximum Responses   This setting allows administrators to set the maximum number of responses a DNS server will issue to a client while responses are suspended.

White List Domains   Administrators can set the list of domains that are to be excluded from RRL settings.

White List Subnets   Administrators can set the list of subnets that are to be excluded from RRL settings.

White List Server Interfaces   Administrators can set the list of DNS server interfaces that are to be excluded from RRL settings.

Unknown Record Support

There are times when a DNS server does not recognize the RDATA format of a resource record. These resource records are known as Unknown Records.

Windows Server 2016 now supports Unknown Records (RFC 3597). This now means that administrators can add these unsupported record types into the Windows DNS server zone. Administrators can add these records using the binary on-wire supported format.

Windows caching resolvers already have the ability to support these unknown record types but DNS servers do not do any processing of these unknown records. What happens is after administrators add the unknown record types to the DNS zone, the DNS servers will respond back to the clients when queries are received.

IPv6 Root Hints

Windows Server 2016 DNS now supports root hints as published by the IANA. DNS name queries now have the ability to use IPv6 root servers for completing name resolution.

DNS Security Extensions

One major issue that you must always look at is keeping your DNS safe. Think about it: DNS is a database of computer names and IP addresses. As a hacker, if I control DNS, I can control your company. In organizations that do not support extra security like IPsec, DNS security is even more important. This is where *Domain Name System Security Extensions (DNSSEC)* can help.

Windows Server 2016 can use a suite of extensions that will help add security to DNS, and that suite is called DNSSEC, which was introduced in Windows Server 2008 R2. The DNSSEC protocol allows your DNS servers to be secure by validating DNS responses. DNSSEC secures your DNS resource records by accompanying the records with a digital signature.

To allow your DNS resource records to receive digital signatures, DNSSEC is applied to your DNS server by a procedure called *zone signing*. This process begins when a DNS resolver initiates a DNS query for a resource record in a signed DNS zone. When a response is returned, a digital signature (RRSIG) accompanies the response, and this allows the response to be verified. If the verification is successful, then the DNS resolver knows that the data has not been modified or tampered with in any way.

Once you implement a zone with DNSSEC, all of the records that are contained within that zone get individually signed. Since all of the records in the zone get individually signed, this gives administrators the ability to add, modify, or delete records without re-signing the entire zone. The only requirement is to re-sign any updated records.

DNS-based Authentication of Named Entities

Another RFC that deals with DNS security is RFC 6698. RFC 6698 explains DNS-based Authentication of Named Entities (DANE). DANE is a protocol that is based on Transport Layer Security Authentication (TLSA). The TLSA records then provide information to DNS clients telling the clients which CA server they should expect their certificate from. By knowing your CA, hackers can't corrupt your DNS cache. Man in the middle attackers can change your cache. This would then point you to their websites. DANE stops these types of attacks. DANE support is now included with Windows Server 2016.

Trust Anchors

Trust anchors are an important part of the DNSSEC process because trust anchors allow the DNS servers to validate the DNSKEY resource records. *Trust anchors* are preconfigured public keys that are linked to a DNS zone. For a DNS server to perform validation, one or more trust anchors must be configured. If you are running an Active Directory Integrated zone, trust anchors can be stored in the Active Directory Domain Services directory partition of the forest. If you decide to store the trust anchors in the directory partition, then all DNS servers that reside on a domain controller get a copy of this trust anchor. On DNS servers that reside on standalone servers, trust anchors are stored in a file called TrustAnchors.dns.

If your servers are running Windows Server 2016, then you can view trust anchors in the DNS Manager Console tree in the Trust Points container. You can also use Windows PowerShell or Dnscmd.exe to view trust anchors. Windows PowerShell is the recommended command-line method for viewing trust anchors. The following line is a PowerShell command to view the trust anchors for Contoso.com:

```
get-dnsservertrustanchor sec.contoso.com
```

DNSSEC Clients

Windows 7, Windows 8/8.1, Windows 10, Windows Server 2008/2008 R2, and Windows Server 2012/2016 are all DNS clients that receive a response to a DNS query, examine the response, and then evaluate whether the response has been validated by a DNS server. The DNS client itself is nonvalidating, and the DNS client relies on the local DNS server to indicate that validation was successful. If the server doesn't perform validation, then the DNS client service can be configured to return no results.

DNS Devolution

Using *DNS devolution*, if a client computer is a member of a child namespace, the client computer will be able to access resources in the parent namespace without the need to explicitly provide the fully qualified domain name of the resource. DNS devolution removes the leftmost label of the namespace to get to the parent suffix. DNS devolution allows the

DNS resolver to create the new FQDNs. DNS devolution works by appending the single-label, unqualified domain name with the parent suffix of the primary DNS suffix name.

Record Weighting

Weighting DNS records will allow an administrator to place a value on DNS SRV records. Clients will then randomly choose SRV records proportional to the weight value assigned.

Netmask Ordering

If round robin is enabled, when a client requests name resolution, the first address entered in the database is returned to the resolver, and it is then sent to the end of the list. The next time a client attempts to resolve the name, the DNS server returns the second name in the database (which is now the first name) and then sends it to the end of the list, and so on. Round robin is enabled by default.

Netmask ordering is a part of the round robin process. When an administrator configures netmask ordering, the DNS server will detect the subnet of the querying client. The DNS server will then return a host address available for the same subnet. Netmask ordering is enabled through the DNS Manager console on the Advanced tab of the server Properties dialog box.

DnsUpdateProxy Group

As mentioned previously, the DHCP server can be configured to register host (A) and pointer (PTR) resource records dynamically on behalf of DHCP clients. Because of this, the DNS server can end up with stale resources. To help solve this issue, an administrator can use the built-in security group called *DnsUpdateProxy*.

To use the DnsUpdateProxy group, an administrator must first create a dedicated user account and configure the DHCP servers with its credentials. This will protect against the creation of unsecured records. Also, when you create the dedicated user account, members of the DnsUpdateProxy group will be able to register records in zones that allow only secured dynamic updates. Multiple DHCP servers can use the same credentials of one dedicated user account.

DNS Policies

One of the newest advantages to Windows Server 2016 DNS is the ability to set up DNS Policies. Administrators can set up policies based on location, time of day, deployment types, queries, application load balancing, and more. The following are just some of the items that you can configure:

Application Load Balancing   There are many times in a corporate environment when you have multiple copies of the same application running in different locations. Application Load Balancing allows DNS to pass client requests for the same applications (even when they are in different locations) to multiple servers hosting that application. This allows DNS to give an application load balancing.

Location Based Traffic Management   Administrators can set DNS to work off of locations and help direct users to resources that are closer to their location. Administrators can set up DNS policies so that a DNS server will respond to a DNS client's query based on geographic location of the client and the IP address of the nearest requested resource.

Split Brain DNS   Another new DNS policy that an administrator can set up is the ability to have DNS split zones. Split zones allow a DNS server to respond to a client based on whether the clients are internal or external clients. Active Directory zones or standalone DNS servers can be configured as Split Brain DNS servers.

Filtering   Administrators now have the ability to set up policies to create query filters that are based on criteria that an administrator supplies. Query filters allow an administrator to set up the DNS server to send a custom response based on a specific type of DNS query and/ or DNS client.

Forensics   Administrators also have the ability to set up a DNS honeypot. A honeypot allows a DNS server to redirect a malicious DNS client to an IP address that does not exist.

Time of Day Based Redirection   Administrators can set up a DNS policy to distribute application traffic between different locations. DNS will be able to do this because the policy that you set for an application will be based on the time of day. So for example, when its 1:00 p.m., a server that has a copy of the application gets all client requests, and at 7:00 p.m., a different server that has a copy of the application gets all of the client requests.

Now that you have learned about some of the new features of Windows Server 2016 DNS, let's take a look at some of the DNS record types.

Introducing DNS Record Types

No matter where your zone information is stored, you can rest assured that it contains a variety of DNS information. Although the DNS snap-in makes it unlikely that you'll ever need to edit these files by hand, it's good to know exactly what data is contained there.

As stated previously, zone files consist of a number of resource records. You need to know about several types of resource records to manage your DNS servers effectively. They are discussed in the following sections.

Part of the resource record is its class. *Classes* define the type of network for the resource record. There are three classes: Internet, Chaosnet, and Hesoid. By far, the Internet class is the most popular. In fact, it's doubtful that you'll see either Chaosnet or Hesoid classes in the wild.

The following are some of the more important resource records in a DNS database. For a complete listing of records in a Microsoft DNS database, visit Microsoft's website at https://technet.microsoft.com/en-us/library/cc958958.aspx.

Start of Authority (SOA) Records

The first record in a database file is the *start of authority (SOA) record*. The SOA defines the general parameters for the DNS zone, including the identity of the authoritative server for the zone.

The SOA appears in the following format:

```
@ IN SOA primary_mastercontact_e-mailserial_number
refresh_timeretry_timeexpiration_timetime_to_live
```

Here is a sample SOA from the domain example.com:

```
@ IN SOA win2k3r2.example.com. hostmaster.example.com. (
                     5              ; serial number
                     900            ; refresh
                     600            ; retry
                     86400          ; expire
                     3600        )  ; default TTL
```

Table 11.2 lists the attributes stored in the SOA record.

TABLE 11.2 The SOA record structure

Field	Meaning
Current zone	The current zone for the SOA. This can be represented by an @ symbol to indicate the current zone or by naming the zone itself. In the example, the current zone is example.com. The trailing dot (.com.) indicates the zone's place relative to the root of the DNS.
Class	This will almost always be the letters *IN* for the Internet class.
Type of record	The type of record follows. In this case, it's SOA.
Primary master	The primary master for the zone on which this file is maintained.
Contact email	The Internet email address for the person responsible for this domain's database file. There is no @ symbol in this contact email address because @ is a special character in zone files. The contact email address is separated by a single dot (.). So, the email address of root@example.com would be represented by root.example.com in a zone file.
Serial number	This is the "version number" of this database file. It increases each time the database file is changed.
Refresh time	The amount of time (in seconds) that a secondary server will wait between checks to its master server to see whether the database file has changed and a zone transfer should be requested.

TABLE 11.3   The SOA record structure *(continued)*

Field	Meaning
Retry time	The amount of time (in seconds) that a secondary server will wait before retrying a failed zone transfer.
Expiration time	The amount of time (in seconds) that a secondary server will spend trying to download a zone. Once this time limit expires, the old zone information will be discarded.
Time to live	The amount of time (in seconds) that another DNS server is allowed to cache any resource records from this database file. This is the value that is sent out with all query responses from this zone file when the individual resource record doesn't contain an overriding value.

Name Server Records

Name server (NS) records list the name servers for a domain. This record allows other name servers to look up names in your domain. A zone file may contain more than one name server record. The format of these records is simple:

```
example.com.    IN     NS      Hostname.example.com
```

Table 11.3 explains the attributes stored in the NS record.

TABLE 11.3   The NS record structure

Field	Meaning
Name	The domain that will be serviced by this name server. In this case I used example.com.
AddressClass	Internet (IN)
RecordType	Name server (NS)
Name Server Name	The FQDN of the server responsible for the domain

Any domain name in the database file that is not terminated with a period will have the root domain appended to the end. For example, an entry that just has the name *sales* will be expanded by adding the root domain to the end, whereas the entry sales.example.com. won't be expanded.

Host Record

A *host record* (also called an *A record* for IPv4 and *AAAA record* for IPv6) is used to associate statically a host's name to its IP addresses. The format is pretty simple:

```
host_nameoptional_TTL IN  A  IP_Address
```

Here's an example from my DNS database:

```
www  IN  A  192.168.0.204
SMTP IN  A  192.168.3.144
```

The A or AAAA record ties a hostname (which is part of an FQDN) to a specific IP address. This makes these records suitable for use when you have devices with statically assigned IP addresses. In this case, you create these records manually using the DNS snap-in. As it turns out, if you enable DDNS, your DHCP server can create these for you. This automatic creation is what enables DDNS to work.

Notice that an optional TTL field is available for each resource record in the DNS. This value is used to set a TTL that is different from the default TTL for the domain. For example, if you wanted a 60-second TTL for the www A or AAAA record, it would look like this:

```
www 60 IN  A  192.168.0.204
```

Alias Record

Closely related to the host record is the *alias record*, or *canonical name (CNAME) record*. The syntax of an alias record is as follows:

```
aliasoptional_TTL  IN  CNAME  hostname
```

Aliases are used to point more than one DNS record toward a host for which an A record already exists. For example, if the hostname of your web server was actually chaos, you would likely have an A record such as this:

```
chaos IN A 192.168.1.10
```

Then you could make an alias or CNAME for the record so that www.example.com would point to chaos:

```
www IN CNAME chaos.example.com.
```

Note the trailing dot (.) on the end of the CNAME record. This means the root domain is not appended to the entry.

Pointer Record

A or AAAA records are probably the most visible component of the DNS database because Internet users depend on them to turn FQDNs like www.microsoft.com into the IP addresses that browsers and other components require to find Internet resources. However, the host record has a lesser-known but still important twin: the *pointer (PTR) record*. The format of a PTR record appears as follows:

```
reversed_address.in-addr.arpa. optional_TTL IN PTR targeted_domain_name
```

The A or AAAA record maps a hostname to an IP address, and the PTR record does just the opposite—mapping an IP address to a hostname through the use of the `in-addr.arpa` zone.

The PTR record is necessary because IP addresses begin with the least-specific portion first (the network) and end with the most-specific portion (the host), whereas hostnames begin with the most-specific portion at the beginning and the least-specific portion at the end.

Consider the example 192.168.1.10 with a subnet mask 255.255.255.0. The portion 192.168.1 defines the network and the final .10 defines the host, or the most-specific portion of the address. DNS is just the opposite: The hostname `www.example.com.` defines the most-specific portion, `www`, at the beginning and then traverses the DNS tree to the least-specific part, the dot (.), at the root of the tree.

Reverse DNS records, therefore, need to be represented in this most-specific-to-least-specific manner. The PTR record for mapping 192.168.1.10 to `www.example.com` would look like this:

```
10.1.168.192.in-addr.arpa. IN PTR www.example.com.
```

Now a DNS query for that record can follow the logical DNS hierarchy from the root of the DNS tree all the way to the most-specific portion.

Mail Exchanger Record

The *mail exchanger (MX) record* is used to specify which servers accept mail for this domain. Each MX record contains two parameters—a preference and a mail server, as shown in the following example:

```
domain IN MX preference mailserver_host
```

The MX record uses the preference value to specify which server should be used if more than one MX record is present. The preference value is a number. The lower the number, the more preferred the server. Here's an example:

```
example.com.    IN  MX  0  mail.example.com.
example.com.    IN  MX  10 backupmail.example.com.
```

In the example, `mail.example.com` is the default mail server for the domain. If that server goes down for any reason, the `backupmail.example.com` mail server is used by emailers.

Service Record

Windows Server 2016 depends on some other services, like the Lightweight Directory Access Protocol (LDAP) and Kerberos. Using a service record, which is another type of DNS record, a Windows 2000, XP, Vista, Windows 7, Windows 8 / 8.1, or Windows 10 client can query

DNS servers for the location of a domain controller. This makes it much easier (for both the client and the administrator) to manage and distribute logon traffic in large-scale networks. For this approach to work, Microsoft has to have some way to register the presence of a service in DNS. Enter the service (SRV) record.

Service (SRV) records tie together the location of a service (like a domain controller) with information about how to contact the service. SRV records provide seven items of information. Let's review an example to help clarify this powerful concept. (Table 11.4 explains the fields in the following example.)

```
ldap.tcp.example.com.   86400 IN SRV   10   100   389   hsv.example.com
ldap.tcp.example.com.   86400 IN SRV   20   100   389   msy.example.com
```

TABLE 11.4 The SRV record structure

Field	Meaning
Domain name	Domain for which this record is valid (`ldap.tcp.example.com.`).
TTL	Time to live (86,400 seconds).
Class	This field is always IN, which stands for Internet.
Record type	Type of record (SRV).
Priority	Specifies a preference, similar to the Preference field in an MX record. The SRV record with the lowest priority is used first (10).
Weight	Service records with equal priority are chosen according to their weight (100).
Port number	The port where the server is listening for this service (389).
Target	The FQDN of the host computer (`hsv.example.com` and `msy.example.com`).

You can define other types of service records. If your applications support them, they can query DNS to find the services they need.

Configuring DNS

In the following sections, you'll begin to learn about the actual DNS server. You will start by installing DNS. Then I will talk about different zone configuration options and what they mean. Finally, you'll complete an exercise that covers configuring Dynamic DNS, delegating zones, and manually entering records.

Installing DNS

If DNS is already installed onto your server, you can skip this exercise. But if you have not installed DNS, let's start by installing DNS. Installing DNS is an important part of running a network. Exercise 11.1 walks you through the installation of a DNS server.

 If you are using a Dynamic TCP/IP address, please change your TCP/IP number to static.

EXERCISE 11.1

Installing and Configuring the DNS Service

1. Open Server Manager.

2. On the Server Manager dashboard, click the Add Roles And Features link.

3. If a Before You Begin screen appears, click Next.

4. On the Selection type page, choose Role-Based Or Feature-Based Installation and click Next.

5. Click the Select A Server From The Server Pool radio button and choose the server under the Server Pool section. Click Next.

6. Click the DNS Server Item in the Server Role list. If a pop-up window appears telling you that you need to add additional features, click the Add Features button. Click Next to continue.

7. On the Add Features page, just click Next.

8. Click Next on the DNS Server information screen.

9. On the Confirm Installation screen, choose the Restart The Destination Server Automatically If Required check box and then click the Install button.

10. At the Installation progress screen, click Close after the DNS server is installed.

11. Close Server Manager.

Load Balancing with Round Robin

Like other DNS implementations, the Windows Server 2016 implementation of DNS supports load balancing through the use of round robin. Load balancing distributes the network load among multiple network hosts if they are available. You set up round-robin load balancing by creating multiple resource records with the same hostname but different IP addresses for multiple computers. Depending on the options that you select, the DNS server responds with the addresses of one of the host computers.

If round robin is enabled, when a client requests name resolution, the first address entered in the database is returned to the resolver and is then sent to the end of the list. The next time a client attempts to resolve the name, the DNS server returns the second name in the database (which is now the first name) and then sends it to the end of the list, and so on. Round robin is enabled by default.

Configuring a Caching-Only Server

Although all DNS name servers cache queries that they have resolved, caching-only servers are DNS name servers that only perform queries, cache the answers, and return the results. They are not authoritative for any domains, and the information that they contain is limited to what has been cached while resolving queries. Accordingly, they don't have any zone files, and they don't participate in zone transfers. When a caching-only server is first started, it has no information in its cache; the cache is gradually built over time.

Caching-only servers are easy to configure. After installing the DNS service, simply make sure the root hints are configured properly. One new advantage to Windows Server 2016 is the ability to also support IPv6 root hints.

1. Right-click your DNS server and choose the Properties command.

2. When the Properties dialog box appears, switch to the Root Hints tab (see Figure 11.11).

3. If your server is connected to the Internet, you should see a list of root hints for the root servers maintained by ICANN and the Internet Assigned Numbers Authority (IANA). If not, click the Add button to add root hints as defined in the cache.dns file.

FIGURE 11.11   The Root Hints tab of the DNS server's Properties dialog box

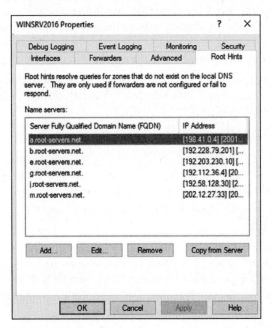

You can obtain current cache.dns files on the Internet by using a search engine. Just search for *cache.dns* and download one. (I always try to get cache·dns files from a university or a company that manages domain names.)

Setting Zone Properties

There are six tabs on the Properties dialog box for a forward or reverse lookup zone. You only use the Security tab to control who can change properties and to make dynamic updates to records on that zone. The other tabs are discussed in the following sections.

 Secondary zones don't have a Security tab, and their SOA tab shows you the contents of the master SOA record, which you can't change.

General Tab

The General tab includes the following:

- The Status indicator and the associated Pause button let you see and control whether this zone can be used to answer queries. When the zone is running, the server can use it to answer client queries; when it's paused, the server won't answer any queries it gets for that particular zone.

- The Type indicator and its Change button allow you to select the zone type. The options are Standard Primary, Standard Secondary, and AD-Integrated. (See "Introducing DNS Database Zones" earlier in this chapter.) As you change the type, the controls you see below the horizontal dividing line change too. For primary zones, you'll see a field that lets you select the zone filename; for secondary zones, you'll get controls that allow you to specify the IP addresses of the primary servers. But the most interesting controls are the ones you see for AD Integrated zones. When you change to the AD Integrated zones, you have the ability to make the dynamic zones Secure Only.

- The Replication indicator and its Change button allow you to change the replication scope if the zone is stored in Active Directory. You can choose to replicate the zone data to any of the following:

  - All DNS servers in the Active Directory forest

  - All DNS servers in a specified domain

  - All domain controllers in the Active Directory domain (required if you use Windows 2000 domain controllers in your domain)

  - All domain controllers specified in the replication scope of the application directory partition

- The Dynamic Updates field gives you a way to specify whether you want to support Dynamic DNS updates from compatible DHCP servers. As you learned earlier in the section "Dynamic DNS and Non-Dynamic DNS," the DHCP server or DHCP client must know about and support Dynamic DNS in order to use it, but the DNS server has to participate too. You can turn dynamic updates on or off, or you can require that updates be secured.

Start Of Authority (SOA) Tab

The following options in the Start Of Authority (SOA) tab, shown in Figure 11.12, control the contents of the SOA record for this zone.

- The Serial Number field indicates which version of the SOA record the server currently holds. Every time you change another field, you should increment the serial number so that other servers will notice the change and get a copy of the updated record.

- The Primary Server and Responsible Person fields indicate the location of the primary name server for this zone and the email address of the administrator responsible for the maintenance of this zone, respectively. The standard username for this is hostmaster.

- The Refresh Interval field controls how often any secondary zones of this zone must contact the primary zone server and get any changes that have been posted since the last update.

- The Retry Interval field controls how long secondary servers will wait after a zone transfer fails before they try again. They'll keep trying at the interval you specify (which should be shorter than the refresh interval) until they eventually succeed in transferring zone data.

- The Expires After field tells the secondary servers when to throw away zone data. The default of 1 day (24 hours) means that a secondary server that hasn't gotten an update in 24 hours will delete its local copy of the zone data.

- The Minimum (Default) TTL field sets the default TTL for all RRs created in the zone. You can assign specific TTLs to individual records if you want.

- The TTL For This Record field controls the TTL for the SOA record itself.

FIGURE 11.12   The Start Of Authority (SOA) tab of the zone Properties dialog box

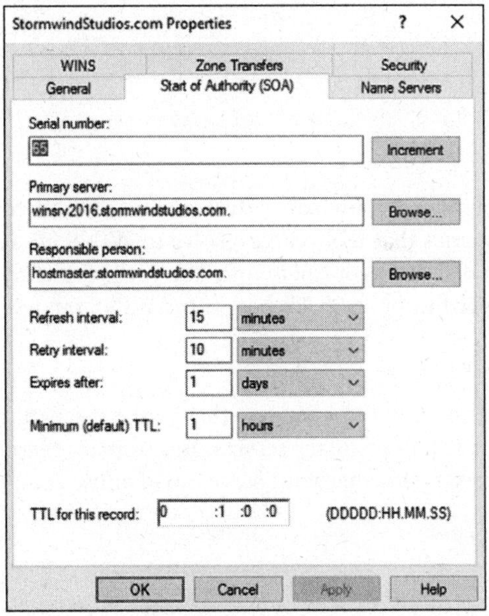

Name Servers Tab

The *name server (NS) record* for a zone indicates which name servers are authoritative for the zone. That normally means the zone primary server and any secondary servers you've configured for the zone. (Remember, secondary servers are authoritative read-only copies of the zone.) You edit the NS record for a zone using the Name Servers tab (see Figure 11.13). The tab shows you which servers are currently listed, and you use the Add, Edit, and Remove buttons to specify which name servers you want included in the zone's NS record.

FIGURE 11.13   The Name Servers tab of the zone Properties dialog box

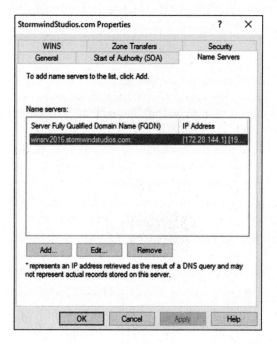

WINS Tab

The WINS tab allows you to control whether this zone uses WINS forward lookups or not. These lookups pass on queries that DNS can't resolve to WINS for action. This is a useful setup if you're still using WINS on your network. You must explicitly turn this option on with the Use WINS Forward Lookup check box in the WINS tab for a particular zone.

Zone Transfers Tab

Zone transfers are necessary and useful because they're the mechanism used to propagate zone data between primary and secondary servers. For primary servers (whether AD Integrated or not), you can specify whether your servers will allow zone transfers and, if so, to whom.

You can use the following controls on the Zone Transfers tab to configure these settings per zone:

- The Allow Zone Transfers check box controls whether the server answers zone transfer requests for this zone at all—when it's not checked, no zone data is transferred. The Allow Zone Transfers selections are as follows:

  - To Any Server allows any server anywhere on the Internet to request a copy of your zone data.

  - Only To Servers Listed On The Name Servers Tab (the default) limits transfers to servers you specify. This is a more secure setting than To Any Server because it limits transfers to other servers for the same zone.

  - Only To The Following Servers allows you to specify exactly which servers are allowed to request zone transfers. This list can be larger or smaller than the list specified on the Name Servers tab.

- The Notify button is for setting up automatic notification triggers that are sent to secondary servers for this zone. Those triggers signal the secondary servers that changes have occurred on the primary server so that the secondary servers can request updates sooner than their normally scheduled interval. The options in the Notify dialog box are similar to those in the Zone Transfers tab. You can enable automatic notification and then choose either Servers Listed On The Name Servers Tab or The Following Servers.

Configuring Zones for Dynamic Updates

In Exercise 11.2, you will create and then modify the properties of a forward lookup zone. In addition, you'll configure the zone to allow dynamic updates.

EXERCISE 11.2

Configuring a Zone for Dynamic Updates

1. Open the DNS management snap-in by selecting Server Manager. Once in Server Manager, click DNS on the left side. In the Servers window (center screen), right-click your server name and choose DNS Manager.

2. Click the DNS server to expand it and then click the Forward Lookup Zones folder. Right-click the Forward Lookup Zones folder and choose New Zone.

3. At the New Zone Welcome screen, click Next.

4. At the Zone Type screen, choose the Primary Zone option. If your DNS server is also a domain controller, do not check the box to store the zone in Active Directory. Click Next when you are ready.

5. Enter a new zone name in the Zone Name field and click Next. (I used my last name— Panek.com.)

EXERCISE 11.2 *(continued)*

6. Leave the default zone filename and click Next.

7. Select the Do Not Allow Dynamic Updates radio button and click Next.

8. Click Finish to end the wizard.

9. Right-click the zone you just created and choose the Properties command.

10. Click the down arrow next to Dynamic Updates. Notice that there are only two options (None and Nonsecure And Secure). The Secure Only option is not available because you are not using Active Directory Integrated. Make sure Nonsecure And Secure is chosen.

11. Click OK to close the Properties box.

12. Close the DNS management snap-in.

13. Close the Server Manager snap-in.

Delegating Zones for DNS

DNS provides the ability to divide the namespace into one or more zones, which can then be stored, distributed, and replicated to other DNS servers. When deciding whether to divide your DNS namespace to make additional zones, consider the following reasons to use additional zones:

- A need to delegate management of part of your DNS namespace to another location or department within your organization

- A need to divide one large zone into smaller zones for distributing traffic loads among multiple servers, for improving DNS name-resolution performance, or for creating a more fault-tolerant DNS environment

- A need to extend the namespace by adding numerous subdomains at once, such as to accommodate the opening of a new branch or site

Each newly delegated zone requires a primary DNS server just as a regular DNS zone does. When delegating zones within your namespace, be aware that for each new zone you create, you need to place delegation records in other zones that point to the authoritative DNS servers for the new zone. This is necessary both to transfer authority and to provide correct referral to other DNS servers and clients of the new servers being made authoritative for the new zone.

In Exercise 11.3, you'll create a delegated subdomain of the domain you created in Exercise 11.2. Note that the name of the server to which you want to delegate the subdomain must be stored in an A or CNAME record in the parent domain.

EXERCISE 11.3

Creating a Delegated DNS Zone

1. Open the DNS management snap-in by selecting Server Manager. Once in Server Manager, click DNS on the left side. In the Servers window (center screen), right-click your server name and choose DNS Manager.

2. Expand the DNS server and locate the zone you created in Exercise 11.2.

3. Right-click the zone and choose the New Delegation command.

4. The New Delegation Wizard appears. Click Next to dismiss the initial wizard page.

5. Enter **ns1** (or whatever other name you like) in the Delegated Domain field of the Delegated Domain Name page. This is the name of the domain for which you want to delegate authority to another DNS server. It should be a subdomain of the primary domain (for example, to delegate authority for farmington.example.net, you'd enter **farmington** in the Delegated Domain field). Click Next to complete this step.

6. When the Name Servers page appears, click the Add button to add the names and IP addresses of the servers that will be hosting the newly delegated zone. For the purpose of this exercise, enter the server name you used in Exercise 11.2. Click the Resolve button to resolve this domain name's IP address automatically into the IP address field. Click OK when you are finished. Click Next to continue with the wizard.

7. Click the Finish button. The New Delegation Wizard disappears, and you'll see the new zone you just created appear beneath the zone you selected in step 3. The newly delegated zone's folder icon is drawn in gray to indicate that control of the zone is delegated.

DNS Forwarding

If a DNS server does not have an answer to a DNS request, it may be necessary to send that request to another DNS server. This is called *DNS forwarding*. You need to understand the two main types of forwarding:

External Forwarding   When a DNS server forwards an external DNS request to a DNS server outside of your organization, this is considered *external forwarding*. For example, a resolver requests the host www.microsoft.com. Most likely, your internal DNS server is not going to have Microsoft's web address in its DNS database. So, your DNS server is going to send the request to an external DNS (most likely your ISP).

Conditional Forwarding   *Conditional forwarding* is a lot like external forwarding except that you are going to forward requests to specific DNS servers based on a condition. Usually this is an excellent setup for internal DNS resolution. For example, let's say that you have two companies, Stormwind.com and Stormtest.com. If a request comes in for Stormwind.com, it gets forwarded to the Stormwind DNS server, and any requests for Stormtest.com will get forwarded to the Stormtest DNS server. Requests are forwarded to a specific DNS server depending on the condition that an administrator sets up.

Manually Creating DNS Records

From time to time you may find it necessary to add resource records manually to your Windows Server 2016 DNS servers. Although Dynamic DNS frees you from the need to fiddle with A and PTR records for clients and other such entries, you still have to create other resource types (including MX records, required for the proper flow of SMTP email) manually. You can manually create A, PTR, MX, SRV, and many other record types.

There are only two important things to remember for manually creating DNS records:

- You must right-click the zone and choose either the New Record command or the Other New Records command.

- You must know how to fill in the fields of whatever record type you're using.

  For example, to create an MX record, you need three pieces of information (the domain, the mail server, and the priority). To create an SRV record, however, you need several more pieces of information.

In Exercise 11.4, you will manually create an MX record for a mailtest server in the zone you created in Exercise 11.2.

EXERCISE 11.4

Manually Creating DNS RRs

1. Open the DNS management snap-in by selecting Server Manager. Once in Server Manager, click DNS on the left side. In the Servers window (center screen), right-click your server name and choose DNS Manager.

2. Expand your DNS server, right-click its zone, and choose New Host (A record).

3. Enter **mailtest** in the Name field. Enter a TCP/IP number in the IP Address field. (You can use any number for this exercise, such as, for example, 192.168.1.254.) Click the Add Host button.

4. A dialog box appears stating that the host record was created successfully. Click OK. Click Done.

5. Right-click your zone name and choose New Mail Exchanger (MX).

6. Enter **mailtest** in the Host Or Child Domain field and enter **mailtest.yourDomain.com** (or whatever domain name you used in Exercise 11.2) in the Fully-Qualified Domain Name (FQDN) Of Mail Server field and then click OK. Notice that the new record is already visible.

7. Next create an alias (or CNAME) record to point to the mail server. (It is assumed that you already have an A record for mailtest in your zone.) Right-click your zone and choose New Alias (CNAME).

8. Type **mail** into the Alias Name field.

9. Type **mailtest.yourDomain.com** into the Fully-Qualified Domain Name (FQDN) For Target Host field.

10. Click the OK button.

11. Close the DNS management snap-in.

DNS Aging and Scavenging

When using dynamic updates, computers (or DHCP) will register a resource record with DNS. These records get removed when a computer is shut down properly. A major problem in the industry is that laptops are frequently removed from the network without a proper shutdown. Therefore, their resource records continue to live in the DNS database.

Windows Server 2016 DNS supports two features called *DNS aging* and *DNS scavenging*. These features are used to clean up and remove stale resource records. DNS zone or DNS server aging and scavenging flag old resource records that have not been updated in a certain amount of time (determined by the scavenging interval). These stale records will be scavenged at the next cleanup interval. DNS uses time stamps on the resource records to determine how long they have been listed in the DNS database.

By default, DNS aging and scavenging are disabled by default. Microsoft states that these features should only be enabled if you have users that are not logging off the network properly. If your users are all using desktops or if your users log off the network properly every day, you should keep these features disabled.

The issue that you can run into if this feature is enabled and DNS deletes records that should not be deleted, is that this can stop users from access resources on the network because their DNS records have been deleted improperly.

If you decide that you want to enable DNS aging and scavenging, you must enable these features on both at the DNS server and on the zone.

DNS aging and scavenging is done by using time stamps. Time stamps are a date and time value that is used by the DNS server. The date and time is used to determine removal of the resource record when it performs the aging and scavenging operations.

Monitoring and Troubleshooting DNS

Now that you have set up and configured your DNS name server and created some resource records, you will want to confirm that it is resolving and replying to client DNS requests. A couple of tools allow you to do some basic monitoring and managing. Once you are able to monitor DNS, you'll want to start troubleshooting.

The simplest test is to use the ping command to make sure that the server is alive. A more thorough test would be to use nslookup to verify that you can actually resolve addresses for items on your DNS server.

In the following sections, you'll look at some of these monitoring and management tools and how to troubleshoot DNS.

Monitoring DNS with the DNS Snap-In

You can use the DNS snap-in to do some basic server testing and monitoring. More important, you use the snap-in to monitor and set logging options. On the Event Logging tab of the server's Properties dialog box (see Figure 11.14), you can pick which events you want logged. The more events you select, the more logging information you'll get. This is useful when you're trying to track what's happening with your servers, but it can result in a very large log file if you're not careful.

FIGURE 11.14   The Event Logging tab of the server's Properties dialog box

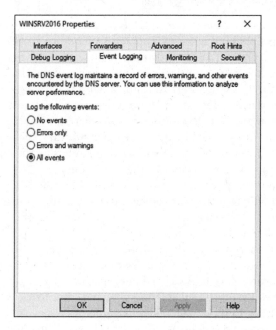

The Monitoring tab (see Figure 11.15) gives you some testing tools. When the check box labeled A Simple Query Against This DNS Server is checked, a test is performed that asks for a single record from the local DNS server. It's useful for verifying that the service is running and listening to queries, but not much else. When the check box labeled A Recursive Query To Other DNS Servers is checked, the test is more sophisticated—a recursive query checks whether forwarding is working okay. The Test Now button and the Perform Automatic Testing At The Following Interval check box allow you to run these tests now or later as you require.

Another tab in the server's properties that allows you to monitor the activity of the DNS server is the Debug Logging tab. The Debug Logging tab allows you to monitor all outbound and inbound DNS traffic, packet content, packet type, and which transport protocol (TCP or UDP) you want to monitor on the DNS server.

FIGURE 11.15   The Monitoring tab of the server's Properties dialog box

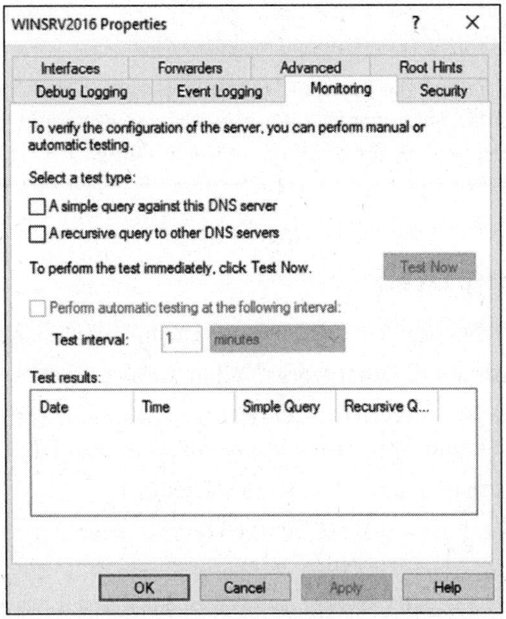

WINSRV2016 Properties   ?   ×

| Interfaces | Forwarders | Advanced | Root Hints |
| Debug Logging | Event Logging | Monitoring | Security |

To verify the configuration of the server, you can perform manual or
automatic testing.

Select a test type:

☐ A simple query against this DNS server

☐ A recursive query to other DNS servers

To perform the test immediately, click Test Now.   [Test Now]

☐ Perform automatic testing at the following interval:

Test interval: 1   minutes

Test results:

Date	Time	Simple Query	Recursive Q...

[OK]   [Cancel]   [Apply]   [Help]

If the simple query fails, check that the local server contains the zone
1.0.0.127.in-addr.arpa. If the recursive query fails, check that your root
hints are correct and that your root servers are running.

In Exercise 11.5, you will enable logging, use the DNS MMC to test the DNS server, and view the contents of the DNS log.

EXERCISE 11.5

Simple DNS Testing

1. Open the DNS management snap-in by selecting Server Manager. Once in Server Manager, click DNS on the left side. In the Servers window (center screen), right-click your server name and choose DNS Manager.

2. Right-click the DNS server name on the top left and select Properties.

3. Switch to the Debug Logging tab, check all the debug logging options except Filter Packets By IP Address and enter a full path and filename in the File Path And Name field. Click the Apply button.

4. Switch to the Monitoring tab and check both A Simple Query Against This DNS Server and A Recursive Query To Other DNS Servers.

EXERCISE 11.5 *(continued)*

5.   Click the Test Now button several times and then click OK.

6.   Press the Windows key on the keyboard (left side between the Ctrl and Alt keys) and then choose Computer. Navigate to the folder that you specified in step 3 and use WordPad or Notepad to view the contents of the log file.

Troubleshooting DNS

When troubleshooting DNS problems, ask yourself the following basic questions:

- What application is failing? What works? What doesn't work?

- Is the problem basic IP connectivity, or is it name resolution? If the problem is name resolution, does the failing application use NetBIOS names, DNS names, or hostnames?

- How are the things that do and don't work related?

- Have the things that don't work ever worked on this computer or network? If so, what has changed since they last worked?

Windows Server 2016 provides several useful tools, discussed in the following sections, which can help you answer these questions:

- Nslookup is used to perform DNS queries and to examine the contents of zone files on local and remote servers.

- DNSLint is a command-line utility used for troubleshooting many common DNS issues.

- Ipconfig allows you to perform the following tasks:

    - View DNS client settings

    - Display and flush the resolver cache

    - Force a dynamic update client to register its DNS records

- The DNS log file monitors certain DNS server events and logs them for your edification.

Using *Nslookup*

Nslookup is a standard command-line tool provided in most DNS server implementations, including Windows Server 2016. Windows Server 2016 gives you the ability to launch nslookup from the DNS snap-in.

When nslookup is launched from the DNS snap-in, a command prompt window opens automatically. You enter nslookup commands in this window.

Nslookup offers you the ability to perform query testing of DNS servers and to obtain detailed responses at the command prompt. This information can be useful for diagnosing and solving name resolution problems, for verifying that resource records are added or updated correctly in a zone, and for debugging other server-related problems. You can do a number of useful things with nslookup:

- Use it in noninteractive mode to look up a single piece of data
- Enter interactive mode and use the debug feature
- Perform the following from within interactive mode:
  - Set options for your query
  - Look up a name
  - Look up records in a zone
  - Perform zone transfers
  - Exit nslookup

 When you are entering queries, it is generally a good idea to enter FQDNs so that you can control what name is submitted to the server. However, if you want to know which suffixes are added to unqualified names before they are submitted to the server, you can enter **nslookup** in debug mode and then enter an unqualified name.

Using *Nslookup* on the Command Line

To use nslookup in plain-old command-line mode, enter the following in the command prompt window:

```
nslookup DNS_name_or_IP_address server_IP_address
```

This command will look up a DNS name or address using a server at the IP address you specify.

Using *Nslookup* in Interactive Mode

Nslookup is a lot more useful in interactive mode because you can enter several commands in sequence. Entering **nslookup** by itself (without specifying a query or server) puts it in interactive mode, where it will stay until you type **exit** and press Enter. Before that point, you can look up lots of useful stuff. The following are some of the tasks that you can perform with nslookup in interactive mode:

Setting Options with the set Command   While in interactive mode, you can use the set command to configure how the resolver will carry out queries. Table 11.5 shows a few of the options available with set.

TABLE 11.5 Command-line options available with the `set` command

Option	Purpose
`set all`	Shows all the options available.
`set d2`	Puts `nslookup` in debug mode so that you can examine the query and response packets between the resolver and the server.
`set domain=`*domain name*	Tells the resolver what domain name to append for unqualified queries.
`set timeout=`*timeout*	Tells the resolver how long to keep trying to contact the server. This option is useful for slow links where queries frequently time out and the wait time must be lengthened.
`set type=`*record type*	Tells the resolver which type of resource records to search for (for example, A, PTR, or SRV). If you want the resolver to query for all types of resource records, type **settype=all**.

Looking Up a Name   While in interactive mode, you can look up a name just by typing it: **stormwind.com**. In this example, `stormwind` is the owner name for the record for which you are searching, and `.com` is the server that you want to query.

You can use the wildcard character (*) in your query. For example, if you want to look for all resource records that have *k* as the first letter, just type **k****** as your query.

Looking Up a Record Type   If you want to query a particular type of record (for instance, an MX record), use the `set type` command. The command `set type=mx` tells `nslookup` that you're interested only in seeing MX records that meet your search criteria.

Listing the Contents of a Domain   To get a list of the contents of an entire domain, use the `ls` command. To find all the hosts in your domain, you'd type **set type=a** and then type **ls -t yourdomain.com**.

Troubleshooting Zone Transfers   You can simulate zone transfers by using the `ls` command with the `-d` switch. This can help you determine whether the server you are querying allows zone transfers to your computer. To do this, type the following: **ls -d domain__name**.

Nslookup Responses and Error Messages

A successful `nslookup` response looks like this:

```
Server: Name_of_DNS_server
Address: IP_address_of_DNS_server
Response_data
```

Nslookup might also return an error message. Some common messages are listed in Table 11.6.

TABLE 11.6   Common nslookup error messages

Error message	Meaning
DNS request timed out. Timeout was *x* seconds. *** Can't find server name for address *IP_Address*: Timed out *** Default servers are not available Default Server: Unknown Address: *IP_address_of_DNS_server*	The resolver did not locate a PTR resource record (containing the hostname) for the server IP address you specified. Nslookup can still query the DNS server, and the DNS server can still answer queries.
*** Request to Server timed-out	A request was not fulfilled in the allotted time. This might happen, for example, if the DNS service was not running on the DNS server that is authoritative for the name.
*** Server can't find *Name_or_IP_address_queried_for*: No response from server	The server is not receiving requests on User Datagram Protocol (UDP) port 53.
*** Server can't find *Name_or_IP_address_queried_for:* Non-existent domain	The DNS server was unable to find the name or IP address in the authoritative domain. The authoritative domain might be on the remote DNS server or on another DNS server that this DNS server is unable to reach.
*** Server can't find *Name_or_IP_address_queried_for*: Server failed	The DNS server is running, but it is not working properly. For example, it might include a corrupted packet, or the zone in which you are querying for a record might be paused. However, this message can also be returned if the client queries for a host in a domain for which the DNS server is not authoritative. You will also receive the error if the DNS server cannot contact its root servers, it is not connected to the Internet, or it has no root hints.

In Exercise 11.6, you'll get some hands-on practice with the nslookup tool.

EXERCISE 11.6

Using the nslookup Command

1. Press the Windows key on the keyboard and then choose Computer. Navigate to the C:\Windows\System32 folder and double-click CMD.exe. (When you get to this file, you can right-click the file and choose Send To Desktop. The shortcut will then always be available on the desktop.)

2. Type **nslookup** and press the Enter key. (For the rest of the exercise, use the Enter key to terminate each command.)

3. Try looking up a well-known address: Type www.microsoft.com.

4. Try looking up a nonexistent host: Type **www.example.ccccc**. Notice that your server indicates that it can't find the address and times out. This is normal behavior.

5. Type **Exit** at the prompt. Type **Exit** again to leave the command prompt.

Using *DNSLint*

Microsoft Windows Server 2016 DNS can use the DNSLint command-line utility to help diagnose some common DNS name-resolution issues and to help diagnose potential problems of incorrect delegation. You need to download DNSLint from the Microsoft Download Center.

DNSLint uses three main functions to verify DNS records and to generate a report in HTML:

dnslint /d This function helps diagnose the reasons for "lame delegation" and other related DNS problems.

dnslint /ql This function helps verify a user-defined set of DNS records on multiple DNS servers.

dnslint /ad This function helps verify DNS records pertaining to Active Directory replication.

Here is the syntax for DNSLint:

```
dnslint /d domain_name | /ad [LDAP_IP_address] | /ql input_file
[/c [smtp,pop,imap]] [/no_open] [/r report_name]
[/t] [/test_tcp] [/s DNS_IP_address] [/v] [/y]
```

The following are some sample queries:

```
dnslint /d stormwind.com
dnslint /ad /s 192.168.36.201
dnslint /ql dns_server.txt
dnslint /ql autocreate
dnslint /v /d stormwind.com
dnslint /r newfile /d stormwind.com
dnslint /y /d stormwind.com
dnslint /no_open /d stormwind.com
```

Table 11.7 explains the command options.

TABLE 11.7   DNSLint command options

Command option	Meaning
/d	Domain name that is being tested.
/ad	Resolves DNS records that are used for Active Directory forest replication.
/s	TCP/IP address of host.
/ql	Requests DNS query tests from a list. This switch sends DNS queries specified in an input file.
/v	Turns on verbose mode.
/r filename	Allows you to create a report file.
/y	Overwrites an existing report file without being prompted.
/no_open	Prevents a report from opening automatically.

Using *Ipconfig*

You can use the command-line tool ipconfig to view your DNS client settings, to view and reset cached information used locally for resolving DNS name queries, and to register the resource records for a dynamic update client. If you use the ipconfig command with no parameters, it displays DNS information for each adapter, including the domain name and DNS servers used for that adapter. Table 11.8 shows some command-line options available with ipconfig.

TABLE 11.8   Command-line options available for the `ipconfig` command

Command	What It Does
ipconfig /all	Displays additional information about DNS, including the FQDN and the DNS suffix search list.
ipconfig /flushdns	Flushes and resets the DNS resolver cache. For more information about this option, see the section "Configuring DNS" earlier in this chapter.
ipconfig /displaydns	Displays the contents of the DNS resolver cache. For more information about this option, see "Configuring DNS" earlier in this chapter.
ipconfig /registerdns	Refreshes all DHCP leases and registers any related DNS names. This option is available only on Windows 2000 and newer computers that run the DHCP client service.

 You should know and be comfortable with the `ipconfig` commands related to DNS for the exam.

Using *DNSCmd*

DNSCmd allows you to display and change the properties of DNS servers, zones, and resource records through the use of command-line commands. The DNSCmd utility allows you to modify, create, and delete resource records and/or zones manually, and it allows you to force replication between two DNS servers.

Table 11.9 lists some of the DNSCmd commands and their explanations.

TABLE 11.9   DNSCmd command-line options

Command	Explanation
dnscmd /clearcache	Clears the DNS server cache
dnscmd /config	Resets DNS server or zone configuration
dnscmd /createdirectorypartition	Creates a DNS application directory partition
dnscmd /deletedirectorypartition	Deletes a DNS application directory partition
dnscmd /enumrecords	Shows the resource records in a zone

Command	Explanation
dnscmd /exportsettings	Creates a text file of all server configuration information
dnscmd /info	Displays server information
dnscmd /recordadd	Adds a resource record to a zone
dnscmd /recorddelete	Deletes a resource record from a zone
dnscmd /zoneadd	Creates a new DNS zone
dnscmd /zonedelete	Deletes a DNS zone
dnscmd /zoneexport	Creates a text file of all resource records in the zone
dnscmd /zoneinfo	Displays zone information
dnscmd /zonerefresh	Forces replication of the master zone to the secondary zone

Using the DNS Log File

You can configure the DNS server to create a log file that records the following information:

- Queries
- Notification messages from other servers
- Dynamic updates
- Content of the question section for DNS query messages
- Content of the answer section for DNS query messages
- Number of queries this server sends
- Number of queries this server has received
- Number of DNS requests received over a UDP port
- Number of DNS requests received over a TCP port
- Number of full packets sent by the server
- Number of packets written through by the server and back to the zone

The DNS log appears in systemroot\System32\dns\Dns.log. Because the log is in RTF format, you must use WordPad or Word to view it.

Once the log file reaches the maximum size, Windows Server 2016 writes over the beginning of the file. You can change the maximum size of the log. If you increase the size value, data persists for a longer time period, but the log file consumes more disk space. If you decrease the value, the log file uses less disk space, but the data persists for a shorter time period.

WARNING Do not leave DNS logging turned on during normal operation because it sucks up both processing and hard disk resources. Enable it only when diagnosing and solving DNS problems.

Troubleshooting the .(*root*) Zone

The *DNS root zone* is the top-level DNS zone in the DNS hierarchy. Windows Server 2016–based DNS servers will build a .(root) zone when a connection to the Internet can't be found.

Because of this, the .(root) zone may prevent access to the Internet. The DNS forwarding option and DNS root hints will not be configurable. If you want your DNS to work as a DNS forwarder or you want to use root hints, you must remove the .(root) zone.

Issues with Non-Microsoft DNS Servers

Another troubleshooting problem that you may run into is working with both Microsoft DNS servers and non-Microsoft DNS servers. One of the most common non-Microsoft DNS servers is the Unix-based BIND DNS server.

If you need to complete a zone transfer from Microsoft DNS to a BIND DNS server, you need to enable BIND Secondaries on the Microsoft DNS server (see Figure 11.16).

FIGURE 11.16 Enabling BIND Secondaries

If you need to enable Bind Secondaries, complete the following steps:

1. Open DNS management.
2. Right-click the server name and choose Properties.
3. Click the Advanced tab.
4. Check the Enable BIND Secondaries box.
5. Click OK.

Integrating Dynamic DNS and IPv4 DHCP

DHCP integration with Dynamic DNS is a simple concept but powerful in action. By setting up this integration, you can pass addresses to DHCP clients while still maintaining the integrity of your DNS services.

The DNS server can be updated in two ways. One way is for the DHCP client to tell the DNS server its address. Another way is for the DHCP server to tell the DNS server when it registers a new client.

Neither of these updates will take place, however, unless you configure the DNS server to use Dynamic DNS. You can make this change in two ways:

- If you change it at the scope level, it will apply only to the scope.
- If you change it at the server level, it will apply to all scopes and superscopes served by the server.

Which of these options you choose depends on how widely you want to support Dynamic DNS; most of the sites I visit have enabled DNS updates at the server level.

To update the settings at either the server or scope level, you need to open the scope or server properties by right-clicking the appropriate object and choosing Properties. The DNS tab of the Properties dialog box includes the following options:

Enable DNS Dynamic Updates According To The Settings Below   This check box controls whether this DHCP server will attempt to register lease information with a DNS server. It must be checked to enable Dynamic DNS.

Dynamically Update DNS A And PTR Records Only If Requested By The DHCP Clients This radio button (which is on by default) tells the DHCP server to register the update only if the DHCP client asks for DNS registration. When this button is active, DHCP clients that aren't hip to DDNS won't have their DNS records updated. However, Windows 2000, XP, Vista, Windows 7, Windows 8 / 8.1, Windows 10, Server 2003, Server 2008/2008 R2, and Server 2012/2016 DHCP clients are smart enough to ask for the updates.

Always Dynamically Update DNS A And PTR Records   This radio button forces the DHCP server to register any client to which it issues a lease. This setting may add DNS registrations for DHCP-enabled devices that don't really need them, such as print servers. However, it allows other clients (such as Mac OS, Windows NT, and Linux machines) to have their DNS information automatically updated.

Discard A And PTR Records When Lease Is Deleted This check box has a long name but a simple function. When a DHCP lease expires, what should happen to the DNS registration? Obviously, it would be nice if the DNS record associated with a lease vanished when the lease expired. When this check box is checked (as it is by default), that's exactly what happens. If you uncheck this box, your DNS will contain entries for expired leases that are no longer valid. When a particular IP address is reissued on a new lease, the DNS will be updated, but in between leases you'll have incorrect data in your DNS—something that's always best to avoid.

Dynamically Update DNS A And PTR Records For DHCP Clients That Do Not Request Updates This check box lets you handle these older clients graciously by making the updates using a separate mechanism.

In Exercise 11.7, you will enable a scope to participate in Dynamic DNS updates.

EXERCISE 11.7

Enabling DHCP-DNS Integration

1. Open the DHCP snap-in by selecting Administrative Tools ➤ DHCP.

2. Right-click the IPv4 item, and select Properties.

3. The Server Properties dialog box appears. Click the DNS tab.

4. Verify that the check box labeled Enable DNS Dynamic Updates According To The Settings Below is checked, and verify that the radio button labeled Dynamically Update DNS A And PTR Records Only If Requested By The DHCP Clients is selected.

5. Verify that the check box labeled Discard A And PTR Records When Lease Is Deleted is checked. If not, then check it.

6. Click the OK button to apply your changes and close the Server Properties dialog box.

DNS PowerShell Commands

When talking about PowerShell commands for DNS, I must let you know that there are dozens of commands that you can use to configure and maintain a DNS server. Before I show you the table of DNS PowerShell commands, let's look at two commands first.

When we install DNS onto a server, we can use PowerShell to do the install. But when we are talking about Nano server, the PowerShell commands are a bit different.

Let's first look at how you install DNS on a regular Windows server using PowerShell. The following command is the command used to install DNS on a Windows Server.

```
Install-WindowsFeature DNS -IncludeManagementTools
```

Now let's take a look at the PowerShell command for installing DNS on a Nano server. The following commands are used to install DNS on a Nano server. The first command downloads DNS to the Nano server and the second command installs it on the server.

```
Install-NanoServerPackage Microsoft-NanoServer-DNS-Package -Culture en-us
Enable-WindowsOptionalFeature -Online -FeatureName DNS-Server-Full-Role
```

Nano servers have no GUI interface and all installations have to be done using remote tools or PowerShell commands. There are dozens of possible PowerShell commands. Nano servers are excellent servers to use as DNS servers. Just be sure that you know what Roles can be installed onto a Nano server and which Roles can't be installed on a Nano server (like DHCP).

In Table 11.10, I will show you just some of the possible PowerShell commands that are available for DNS.

For a complete list of DNS PowerShell commands, please visit Microsoft's website at https://technet.microsoft.com/itpro/powershell/windows/dnsserver/dnsserver.

TABLE 11.10 PowerShell Commands for DNS

PowerShell Command	Description
Add-DnsServerClientSubnet	This command allows an administrator to add a client subnet to a DNS server.
Add-DnsServerConditionalForwarderZone	Administrators can use this command to add a conditional forwarder to a DNS server.
Add-DnsServerForwarder	This command allows an administrator to add forwarders to a DNS server.
Add-DnsServerPrimaryZone	Administrators can use this command to add a primary zone to a DNS server.
Add-DnsServerQueryResolutionPolicy	This command allows an administrator to add a query resolution policy to DNS.
Add-DnsServerResourceRecord	Administrators can use this command to add a resource record to a DNS zone.
Add-DnsServerResourceRecordA	This command allows an administrator to add an A record to a DNS zone.
Add-DnsServerResourceRecordAAAA	This command allows an administrator to add an AAAA record to a DNS zone.

TABLE 11.10   PowerShell Commands for DNS *(continued)*

PowerShell Command	Description
Add-DnsServerResourceRecordCName	This command allows an administrator to add a CNAME record to a DNS zone.
Add-DnsServerResourceRecordDnsKey	Administrators can use this command to add a DNSKEY record to a DNS zone.
Add-DnsServerResourceRecordDS	This command allows an administrator to add a DS record to a DNS zone.
Add-DnsServerResourceRecordMX	This command allows an administrator to add a MX record to a DNS zone.
Add-DnsServerResourceRecordPtr	This command allows an administrator to add a PTR record to a DNS zone.
Add-DnsServerSecondaryZone	Administrators can use this command to add a secondary zone.
Add-DnsServerSigningKey	This command adds a KSK or ZSK to a signed zone.
Add-DnsServerStubZone	This command adds a stub zone to a DNS server.
Add-DnsServerTrustAnchor	Admins can use this command to add a trust anchor to a DNS server.
Add-DnsServerZoneDelegation	This command allows an administrator to add a new delegated DNS zone to an existing zone.
Clear-DnsServerCache	Administrators use this command to clear resource records from a DNS cache.
ConvertTo-DnsServerPrimaryZone	This command converts a zone to a primary zone.
Get-DnsServer	This command retrieves configuration information for a DNS server.
Get-DnsServerDsSetting	This command allows you to gather information about DNS Active Directory settings.
Get-DnsServerRootHint	Administrators use this command to view root hints on a DNS server.

PowerShell Command	Description
`Get-DnsServerScavenging`	Administrators use this command to view DNS aging and scavenging settings.
`Get-DnsServerSetting`	This command allows you to view DNS server settings.
`Get-DnsServerSigningKey`	This command allows you to view zone signing keys.
`Import-DnsServerResourceRecordDS`	This command allows an administrator to import DNS resource records from a file.
`Import-DnsServerRootHint`	This command imports root hints from a DNS server.
`Remove-DnsServerZone`	Administrators use this command to remove a DNS zone from a server.
`Resume-DnsServerZone`	This command allows you to resume resolution on a suspended zone.
`Set-DnsServer`	Administrators can use this command to set the DNS server configuration.
`Set-DnsServerRootHint`	This command allows an administrator to replace a server's root hints.
`Set-DnsServerSetting`	Administrators can use this command to change DNS server settings.
`Test-DnsServer`	This command allows an administrator to test a functioning DNS server.

Summary

DNS was designed to be a robust, scalable, and high-performance system for resolving friendly names to TCP/IP host addresses. This chapter presented an overview of the basics of DNS and how DNS names are generated. You then looked at the many new features available in the Microsoft Windows Server 2016 version of DNS, and you learned how to install, configure, and manage the necessary services. Microsoft's DNS is based on a widely accepted set of industry standards. Because of this, Microsoft's DNS can work with both Windows- and non-Windows-based networks.

Exam Essentials

Understand the purpose of DNS.   DNS is a standard set of protocols that defines a mechanism for querying and updating address information in the database, a mechanism for replicating the information in the database among servers, and a schema of the database.

Understand the different parts of the DNS database.   The SOA record defines the general parameters for the DNS zone, including who is the authoritative server. NS records list the name servers for a domain; they allow other name servers to look up names in your domain. A host record (also called an address record or an A record) statically associates a host's name with its IP addresses. Pointer records (PTRs) map an IP address to a hostname, making it possible to do reverse lookups. Alias records allow you to use more than one name to point to a single host. The MX record tells you which servers can accept mail bound for a domain. SRV records tie together the location of a service (like a domain controller) with information about how to contact the service.

Know how DNS resolves names.   With iterative queries, a client asks the DNS server for an answer, and the client, or resolver, returns the best kind of answer it has. In a recursive query, the client sends a query to one name server, asking it to respond either with the requested answer or with an error. The error states either that the server can't come up with the right answer or that the domain name doesn't exist. With inverse queries, instead of supplying a name and then asking for an IP address, the client first provides the IP address and then asks for the name.

Understand the differences among DNS servers, clients, and resolvers.   Any computer providing domain name services is a DNS server. A DNS client is any machine issuing queries to a DNS server. A resolver handles the process of mapping a symbolic name to an actual network address.

Know how to install and configure DNS.   DNS can be installed before, during, or after installing the Active Directory service. When you install the DNS server, the DNS snap-in is installed too. Configuring a DNS server ranges from easy to difficult, depending on what you're trying to make it do. In the simplest configuration, for a caching-only server, you don't have to do anything except to make sure that the server's root hints are set correctly. You can also configure a root server, a normal forward lookup server, and a reverse lookup server.

Know how to create new forward and reverse lookup zones.   You can use the New Zone Wizard to create a new forward or reverse lookup zone. The process is basically the same for both types, but the specific steps and wizard pages differ somewhat. The wizard walks you through the steps, such as specifying a name for the zone (in the case of forward lookup zones) or the network ID portion of the network that the zone covers (in the case of reverse lookup zones).

Know how to configure zones for dynamic updates.   The DNS service allows dynamic updates to be enabled or disabled on a per-zone basis at each server. This is easily done in the DNS snap-in.

Know how to delegate zones for DNS.   DNS provides the ability to divide the namespace into one or more zones; these can then be stored, distributed, and replicated to other DNS servers. When delegating zones within your namespace, be aware that for each new zone you create, you need delegation records in other zones that point to the authoritative DNS servers for the new zone.

Understand the tools that are available for monitoring and troubleshooting DNS.   You can use the DNS snap-in to do some basic server testing and monitoring. More important, you use the snap-in to monitor and set logging options. Windows Server 2016 automatically logs DNS events in the event log under a distinct DNS server heading. Nslookup offers the ability to perform query testing of DNS servers and to obtain detailed responses at the command prompt. You can use the command-line tool ipconfig to view your DNS client settings, to view and reset cached information used locally for resolving DNS name queries, and to register the resource records for a dynamic update client. Finally, you can configure the DNS server to create a log file that records queries, notification messages, dynamic updates, and various other DNS information.

Review Questions

1. You are the network administrator for the ABC Company. Your network consists of two DNS servers named *DNS1* and *DNS2*. The users who are configured to use DNS2 complain because they are unable to connect to Internet websites. The following table shows the configuration of both servers.

   DNS1   DNS2

   _msdcs.abc.comabc.com   .(root)_msdcs.abc.comabc.com

   The users connected to DNS2 need to be able to access the Internet. What needs to be done?

   A. Build a new Active Directory Integrated zone on DNS2.

   B. Delete the .(root) zone from DNS2, and configure conditional forwarding on DNS2.

   C. Delete the current cache.dns file.

   D. Update your cache.dns file and root hints.

2. You are the network administrator for a large company that has one main site and one branch office. Your company has a single Active Directory forest, ABC.com. You have a single domain controller (ServerA) in the main site that has the DNS role installed. ServerA is configured as a primary DNS zone. You have decided to place a domain controller (ServerB) in the remote site and implement the DNS role on that server. You want to configure DNS so that, if the WAN link fails, users in both sites can still update records and resolve any DNS queries. How should you configure the DNS servers?

   A. Configure ServerB as a secondary DNS server. Set replication to occur every 5 minutes.

   B. Configure ServerB as a stub zone.

   C. Configure ServerB as an Active Directory Integrated zone, and convert ServerA to an Active Directory Integrated zone.

   D. Convert ServerA to an Active Directory Integrated zone, and configure ServerB as a secondary zone.

3. You are the network administrator for a mid-size computer company. You have a single Active Directory forest, and your DNS servers are configured as Active Directory Integrated zones. When you look at the DNS records in Active Directory, you notice that there are many records for computers that do not exist on your domain. You want to make sure only domain computers register with your DNS servers. What should you do to resolve this issue?

   A. Set dynamic updates to None.

   B. Set dynamic updates to Nonsecure And Secure.

   C. Set dynamic updates to Domain Users Only.

   D. Set dynamic updates to Secure Only.

4. Your company consists of a single Active Directory forest. You have a Windows Server 2016 domain controller that also has the DNS role installed. You also have a Unix-based DNS server at the same location. You need to configure your Windows DNS server to allow zone transfers to the Unix-based DNS server. What should you do?

    A. Enable BIND secondaries.

    B. Configure the Unix machine as a stub zone.

    C. Convert the DNS server to Active Directory Integrated.

    D. Configure the Microsoft DNS server to forward all requests to the Unix DNS server.

5. You are the network administrator for Stormwind Corporation. Stormwind has two trees in its Active Directory forest, Stormwind.com and abc.com. Company policy does not allow DNS zone transfers between the two trees. You need to make sure that when anyone in abc.com tries to access the Stormwind.com domain, all names are resolved from the Stormwind.com DNS server. What should you do?

    A. Create a new secondary zone in abc.com for Stormwind.com.

    B. Configure conditional forwarding on the abc.com DNS server for Stormwind.com.

    C. Create a new secondary zone in Stormwind.com for abc.com.

    D. Configure conditional forwarding on the Stormwind.com DNS server for abc.com.

6. You are the network administrator for your organization. A new company policy states that all inbound DNS queries need to be recorded. What can you do to verify that the IT department is compliant with this new policy?

    A. Enable Server Auditing - Object Access.

    B. Enable DNS debug logging.

    C. Enable server database query logging.

    D. Enable DNS Auditing - Object Access.

7. You are the network administrator for a small company with two DNS servers: DNS1 and DNS2. Both DNS servers reside on domain controllers. DNS1 is set up as a standard primary zone, and DNS2 is set up as a secondary zone. A new security policy was written stating that all DNS zone transfers must be encrypted. How can you implement the new security policy?

    A. Enable the Secure Only setting on DNS1.

    B. Enable the Secure Only setting on DNS2.

    C. Configure Secure Only on the Zone Transfers tab for both servers.

    D. Delete the secondary zone on DNS2. Convert both DNS servers to use Active Directory Integrated zones.

8. You are responsible for DNS in your organization. You look at the DNS database and see a large number of older records on the server. These records are no longer valid. What should you do?

   A. In the zone properties, enable Zone Aging and Scavenging.

   B. In the server properties, enable Zone Aging and Scavenging.

   C. Manually delete all the old records.

   D. Set Dynamic Updates to None.

9. Your IT team has been informed by the compliance team that they need copies of the DNS Active Directory Integrated zones for security reasons. You need to give the Compliance department a copy of the DNS zone. How should you accomplish this goal?

   A. Run dnscmd /zonecopy.

   B. Run dnscmd /zoneinfo.

   C. Run dnscmd /zoneexport.

   D. Run dnscmd /zonefile.

10. You are the network administrator for a Windows Server 2016 network. You have multiple remote locations connected to your main office by slow satellite links. You want to install DNS into these offices so that clients can locate authoritative DNS servers in the main location. What type of DNS servers should be installed in the remote locations?

   A. Primary DNS zones

   B. Secondary DNS zones

   C. Active Directory Integrated zones

   D. Stub zones

Chapter

12

Configuring DHCP

THE FOLLOWING 70-741 EXAM OBJECTIVES ARE COVERED IN THIS CHAPTER:

✓ **Install and configure DHCP**

- This objective may include but is not limited to: Install and configure DHCP servers; authorize a DHCP server; create and configure scopes; create and configure superscopes and multicast scopes; configure a DHCP reservation; configure DHCP options; configure DNS options from within DHCP; configure policies; configure client and server for PXE boot; configure DHCP Relay Agent; implement IPv6 addressing using DHCPv6; perform export and import of a DHCP server; perform DHCP server migration.

✓ **Manage and maintain DHCP**

- This objective may include but is not limited to: Configure a lease period; back up and restore the DHCP database; configure high availability using DHCP failover; configure DHCP name protection; troubleshoot DHCP.

In this chapter, I will show you the different methods of setting up an IP address network. If you want systems to be able to share network resources, the computers must all talk the same type of language. This is where DHCP comes into play.

DHCP allows your users to get the required information so that they can properly communicate on the network. I will show you how to install and configure DHCP. I will also show you the advantages of using DHCP and how DHCP can save you hours of configuration time.

Understanding DHCP

When you're setting up a network, the computers need to communicate with each other using the same type of computer language. This is referred to as a protocol. TCP/IP is the priority protocol for Windows Server 2016. For all of your machines to work using TCP/IP, each system must have its own unique IP address. There are two ways to have clients and servers get TCP/IP addresses:

- You can manually assign the addresses.
- The addresses can be assigned automatically.

Manually assigning addresses is a fairly simple process. An administrator goes to each of the machines on the network and assigns TCP/IP addresses. The problem with this method arises when the network becomes midsized or larger. Think of an administrator trying to individually assign 4,000 TCP/IP addresses, subnet masks, default gateways, and all other configuration options needed to run the network.

DHCP's job is to centralize the process of IP address and option assignment. You can configure a DHCP server with a range of addresses (called a *pool*) and other configuration information and let it assign all of the IP parameters—addresses, default gateways, DNS server addresses, and so on.

One of the nice advantages of DHCP is that you can install DHCP onto a Server Core server. DHCP is one of the roles that can be deployed onto a Server Core server. At the time this book was written, DHCP was not supported on a Nano Server. So you can NOT load DHCP on a Windows Server 2016 Nano Server.

DHCP is defined by a series of Request for Comments documents, notably 2131 and 2132.

Introducing the DORA Process

An easy way to remember how DHCP works is to learn the acronym DORA. *DORA* stands for Discover, Offer, Request, and Acknowledge. In brief, here is DHCP's DORA process:

1. **Discover:** When IP networking starts up on a DHCP-enabled client, a special message called a DHCPDISCOVER is broadcast within the local physical subnet.

2. **Offer:** Any DHCP server that hears the request checks its internal database and replies with a message called a DHCPOFFER, which contains an available IP address.

    The contents of this message depend on how the DHCP server is configured—there are numerous options aside from an IP address that you can specify to pass to the client on a Windows Server DHCP server.

3. **Request:** The client receives one or more DHCPOFFERs (depending on how many DHCP servers exist on the local subnet), chooses an address from one of the offers, and sends a DHCPREQUEST message to the server to signal acceptance of the DHCPOFFER.

    This message might also request additional configuration parameters.

    Other DHCP servers that sent offers take the request message as an acknowledgment that the client didn't accept their offer.

4. **Acknowledge:** When the DHCP server receives the DHCPREQUEST, it marks the IP address as being in use (that is, usually, though it's not required). Then it sends a DHCPACK to the client.

    The acknowledgment message might contain requested configuration parameters.

    If the server is unable to accept the DHCPREQUEST for any reason, it sends a DHCPNAK message. If a client receives a DHCPNAK, it begins the configuration process over again.

5. When the client accepts the IP offer, the address is assigned to the client for a specified period of time, called a *lease*. After receiving the DHCPACK message, the client performs a final check on the parameters (sometimes it sends an ARP request for the offered IP address) and makes note of the duration of the lease. The client is now configured. If the client detects that the address is already in use, it sends a DHCPDECLINE.

    If the DHCP server has given out all of the IP addresses in its pool, it won't make an offer. If no other servers make an offer, the client's IP network initialization will fail, and the client will use Automatic Private IP Addressing (APIPA).

DHCP Lease Renewal

No matter how long the lease period, the client sends a new lease request message directly to the DHCP server when the lease period is half over (give or take some randomness required by RFC 2131). This period goes by the name *T1* (not to be confused with the T1 type of network connection). If the server hears the request message and there's no reason to reject it, it sends a DHCPACK to the client. This resets the lease period.

If the DHCP server isn't available, the client realizes that the lease can't be renewed. The client continues to use the address, and once 87.5 percent of the lease period has elapsed (again, give or take some randomness), the client sends out another renewal request. This interval is known as *T2*. At that point, any DHCP server that hears the renewal can respond to this *DHCP request message* (which is a request for a lease renewal) with a DHCPACK and renew the lease. If at any time during this process the client gets a negative DHCPNACK message, it must stop using its IP address immediately and start the leasing process over from the beginning by requesting a new lease.

When a client initializes its IP networking, it always attempts to renew its old address. If the client has time left on the lease, it continues to use the lease until its end. If the client is unable to get a new lease by that time, all IP communications with the network will stop until a new, valid address can be obtained.

DHCP Lease Release

Although leases can be renewed repeatedly, at some point they might run out. Furthermore, the lease process is "at will." That is, the client or server can cancel the lease before it ends. In addition, if the client doesn't succeed in renewing the lease before it expires, the client loses its lease and reverts to APIPA. This release process is important for reclaiming extinct IP addresses used by systems that have moved or switched to a non-DHCP address.

Advantages and Disadvantages of DHCP

DHCP was designed from the start to simplify network management. It has some significant advantages, but it also has some drawbacks.

Advantages of DHCP

The following are advantages of DHCP:

- Configuration of large and even midsized networks is much simpler. If a DNS server address or some other change is necessary to the client, the administrator doesn't have to touch each device in the network physically to reconfigure it with the new settings.

- Once you enter the IP configuration information in one place—the server—it's automatically propagated to clients, eliminating the risk that a user will misconfigure some parameters and require you to fix them.

- IP addresses are conserved because DHCP assigns them only when requested.

- IP configuration becomes almost completely automatic. In most cases, you can plug in a new system (or move one) and then watch as it receives a configuration from the server. For example, when you install new network changes, such as a gateway or DNS server, the client configuration is done at only one location—the DHCP server.

- It allows a preboot execution environment (PXE) client to get a TCP/IP address from DHCP. PXE clients (also called Microsoft Windows Deployment Services [WDS] clients) can get an IP address without needing to have an operating system installed. This allows WDS clients to connect to a WDS server through the TCP/IP protocol and download an operating system remotely.

Disadvantages of DHCP

Unfortunately, there are a few drawbacks with DHCP:

- DHCP can become a single point of failure for your network. If you have only one DHCP server and it's not available, clients can't request or renew leases.

- If the DHCP server contains incorrect information, the misinformation will automatically be delivered to all of your DHCP clients.

- If you want to use DHCP on a multisegment network, you must put either a DHCP server or a relay agent on each segment, or you must ensure that your router can forward Bootstrap Protocol (BOOTP) broadcasts.

Ipconfig Lease Options

The ipconfig command-line tool is useful for working with network settings. Its /renew and /release switches make it particularly handy for DHCP clients. These switches allow you to request renewal of, or give up, your machine's existing address lease. You can do the same thing by toggling the Obtain An IP Address Automatically button in the Internet Protocol (TCP/IP) Properties dialog box, but the command-line option is useful especially when you're setting up a new network.

For example, I spend about a third of my time teaching MCSA or MCSE classes, usually in temporary classrooms set up at conferences, hotels, and so on. Laptops are used in these classes, with one brawny one set up as a DNS/DHCP/DC server. Occasionally, a client will lose its DHCP lease (or not get one, perhaps because a cable has come loose). The quickest way to fix it is to pop open a command-line window and type **ipconfig /renew**.

You can configure DHCP to assign options only to certain classes. *Classes*, defined by an administrator, are groups of computers that require identical DHCP options. The /setclassid*classID* switch of ipconfig is the only way to assign a machine to a class.

More specifically, the switches do the following:

ipconfig /renew   Instructs the DHCP client to request a lease renewal. If the client already has a lease, it requests a renewal from the server that issued the current lease. This is equivalent to what happens when the client reaches the half-life of its lease. Alternatively, if the client doesn't currently have a lease, it is equivalent to what happens when you boot a DHCP client for the first time. It initiates the DHCP mating dance, listens for lease offers, and chooses one it likes.

ipconfig /release   Forces the client to give up its lease immediately by sending the server a DHCP release notification. The server updates its status information and marks the client's old IP address as "available," leaving the client with no address bound to its network interface. When you use this command, most of the time it will be immediately followed by ipconfig/renew. The combination releases the existing lease and gets a new one, probably with a different address. (It's also a handy way to force your client to get a new set of settings from the server before the lease expiration time.)

ipconfig /setclassid*classID* Sets a new class ID for the client. You will see how to configure class options later in the section "Setting Scope Options for IPv4." For now, you should know that the only way to add a client machine to a class is to use this command. Note that you need to renew the client lease for the class assignment to take effect.

If you have multiple network adapters in a single machine, you can provide the name of the adapter (or adapters) upon which you want the command to work, including an asterisk (*) as a wildcard. For example, one of my servers has two network cards: an Intel EtherExpress (ELNK1) and a generic 100 Mbps card. If you want to renew DHCP settings for both adapters, you can type **ipconfig/renew *.** If you just want to renew the Intel EtherExpress card, you can type **ipconfig/renew ELNK1.**

Understanding Scope Details

By now you should have a good grasp of what a lease is and how it works. To learn how to configure your servers to hand out those leases, however, you need to have a complete understanding of some additional topics: scopes, superscopes, exclusions, reservations, address pool, and relay agents.

Scope

Let's start with the concept of a *scope*, which is a contiguous range of addresses. There's usually one scope per physical subnet, and a scope can cover a Class A, Class B, or Class C network address or a TCP/IP v6 address. DHCP uses scopes as the basis for managing and assigning IP addressing information.

Each scope has a set of parameters, or scope options, that you can configure. *Scope options* control what data is delivered to DHCP clients when they're completing the DHCP negotiation process with a particular server. For example, the DNS server name, default gateway, and default network time server are all separate options that can be assigned. These settings are called *option types*. You can use any of the types provided with Windows Server 2016, or you can specify your own.

Superscope

A *superscope* enables the DHCP server to provide addresses from more than one scope to clients on the same physical subnet. This is helpful when clients within the same subnet have more than one IP network and thus need IPs from more than one address pool. Microsoft's DHCP snap-in allows you to manage IP address assignment in the superscope, though you must still configure other scope options individually for each child scope.

Exclusions and Reservations

The scope defines what IP addresses could potentially be assigned, but you can influence the assignment process in two additional ways by specifying exclusions and reservations:

Exclusions   These are IP addresses within the range that you never want automatically assigned. These excluded addresses are off-limits to DHCP. You'll typically use exclusions to tag any addresses that you never want the DHCP server to assign at all. You might use exclusions to set aside addresses that you want to assign permanently to servers that play a vital role in your organization.

Reservations   These are IP addresses within the range for which you want a permanent DHCP lease. They essentially reserve a particular IP address for a particular device. The device still goes through the DHCP process (that is, its lease expires and it asks for a new one), but it always obtains the same addressing information from the DHCP server.

Exclusions are useful for addresses that you don't want to participate in DHCP at all. *Reservations* are helpful for situations in which you want a client to get the same settings each time they obtain an address.

An address cannot be simultaneously reserved and excluded. Be aware of this fact for the exam, possibly relating to a troubleshooting question.

 Real World Scenario

Using Reservations and Exclusions

Deciding when to assign a reservation or exclusion can sometimes be confusing. In practice, you'll find that certain computers in the network greatly benefit by having static IP network information. Servers such as DNS servers, the DHCP server itself, SMTP servers, and other low-level infrastructure servers are good candidates for static assignment. There are usually so few of these servers that the administrator is not overburdened if a change in network settings requires going out to reconfigure each individually. Chances are that the administrator would still need to reconfigure these servers manually (by using ipconfig /release and then ipconfig /renew), even if they did not have IP addresses reserved. Even in large installations, I find it preferable to manage these vital servers by hand rather than to rely on DHCP.

Reservations are also appropriate for application servers and other special but nonvital infrastructure servers. With a reservation in DHCP, the client device will still go through the DHCP process but will always obtain the same addressing information from the DHCP server. The premise behind this strategy is that these nonvital servers can withstand a short outage if DHCP settings change or if the DHCP server fails.

Address Pool

The range of IP addresses that the DHCP server can assign is called its *address pool*. For example, let's say you set up a new DHCP scope covering the 192.168.1 subnet. That gives you 255 IP addresses in the pool. After adding an exclusion from 192.168.1.240 to 192.168.1.254, you're left with 241 (255 – 14) IP addresses in the pool. That means (in theory, at least) that you can service 241 unique clients at a time before you run out of IP addresses.

DHCP Relay Agent

By design, DHCP is intended to work with clients and servers on a single IP network. But RFC 1542 sets out how BOOTP (on which DHCP is based) should work in circumstances in which the client and server are on different IP networks. If no DHCP server is available on the client's network, you can use a DHCP relay agent to forward DHCP broadcasts from the client's network to the DHCP server. The relay agent acts like a radio repeater, listening for DHCP client requests and retransmitting them through the router to the server.

Installing and Authorizing DHCP

Installing DHCP is easy using the Windows Server 2016/2012 R2 installation mechanism. Unlike some other services discussed in this book, the installation process installs just the service and its associated snap-in, starting it when the installation is complete. At that point, it's not delivering any DHCP service, but you don't have to reboot.

Installing DHCP

Exercise 12.1 shows you how to install a DHCP Server using Server Manager. This exercise was completed on a Windows Server 2016 Member Server since Active Directory is not installed yet.

EXERCISE 12.1

Installing the DHCP Service

1. Choose Server Manager by clicking the Server Manager icon on the Taskbar.

2. Click Add Roles And Features.

3. Choose role-based or feature-based installation and click Next.

4. Choose your server and click Next.

5. Choose DHCP (as shown in Figure 12.1) and click Next.

FIGURE 12.1   Choosing DHCP

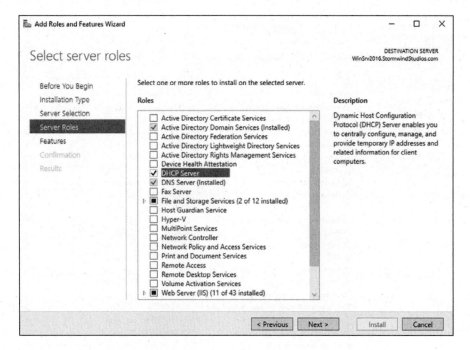

6.   At the Features screen, click Next.

7.   Click Next at the DHCP screen.

8.   At the DHCP confirmation screen, click the Install button.

9.   When the installation is complete, click the Close button.

10. On the left side, click the DHCP link.

11. Click the More link next to Configuration Required For DHCP Server.

12. Under Action, click Complete DHCP Configuration.

13. At the DHCP Description page, click Commit.

14. Click Close at the Summary screen.

15. Close Server Manager.

Introducing the DHCP Snap-In

When you install the DHCP server, the DHCP snap-in is also installed. You can open it by selecting Administrative Tools ➤ DHCP. Figure 12.2 shows the snap-in.

FIGURE 12.2 DHCP snap-in

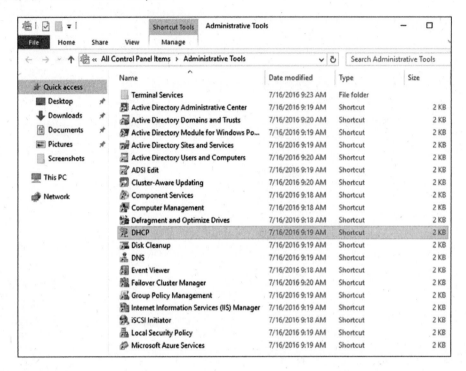

As you can see, the snap-in follows the standard MMC model. The left pane displays IPv4 and IPv6 sections and which servers are available; you can connect to servers other than the one to which you're already connected. A Server Options folder contains options that are specific to a particular DHCP server. Each server contains subordinate items grouped into folders. Each scope has a folder named after the scope's IP address range. Within each scope, four subordinate views show you interesting things about the scope, such as the following:

- The Address Pool view shows what the address pool looks like.

- The Address Leases view shows one entry for each current lease. Each lease shows the computer name to which the lease was issued, the corresponding IP address, and the current lease expiration time.

- The Reservations view shows the IP addresses that are reserved and which devices hold them.

- The Scope Options view lists the set of options you've defined for this scope.

Authorizing DHCP for Active Directory

Authorization creates an Active Directory object representing the new server. It helps keep unauthorized servers off your network. Unauthorized servers can cause two kinds of problems. They may hand out bogus leases, or they may fraudulently deny renewal requests from legitimate clients.

When you install a DHCP server using Windows Server 2016 and Active Directory is present on your network, the server won't be allowed to provide DHCP services to clients until it has been authorized. If you install DHCP on a member server in an Active Directory domain or on a stand-alone server, you'll have to authorize the server manually. When you authorize a server, you're adding its IP address to the Active Directory object that contains the IP addresses of all authorized DHCP servers.

> You also have the ability to authorize a DHCP server during the installation of DHCP if you are installing DHCP onto an Active Directory machine.

At start time, each DHCP server queries the directory, looking for its IP address on the "authorized" list. If it can't find the list or if it can't find its IP address on the list, the DHCP service fails to start. Instead, it adds a message to the event log, indicating that it couldn't service client requests because the server wasn't authorized.

Exercise 12.2 and Exercise 12.3 show you how to authorize and unauthorize a DHCP server onto a network with Active Directory. If you installed DHCP onto a network with a domain, you can complete the following two exercises, but if you are still on a member server, you *cannot* do these exercises. These are here to show you how to do it after you have Active Directory on your network.

EXERCISE 12.2

Authorizing a DHCP Server

1. From Administrative Tools, choose DHCP to open the DHCP snap-in.

2. Right-click the server you want to authorize and choose the Authorize command (see Figure 12.3).

FIGURE 12.3   Choosing Authorize

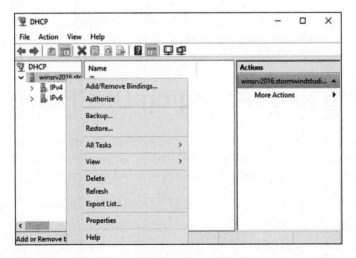

3. Wait a few seconds and then hit F5. This will refresh the server. You should now see that the red down arrows are now green.

Unauthorizing a DHCP Server

1. From Administrative Tools, choose DHCP to open the DHCP snap-in.

2. Right-click the server you want to authorize and choose the Unauthorize command (as shown in Figure 12.4).

FIGURE 12.4   Choosing Unauthorize

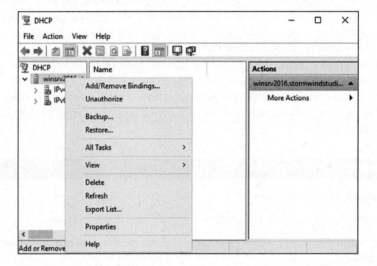

3. Wait a few seconds and then hit F5. This will refresh the server. You should now see that the green arrows are now red.

4. Now let's reauthorize the server. Right-click the server and choose the Authorize command. Wait a few seconds and hit F5.

Creating and Managing DHCP Scopes

You can use any number of DHCP servers on a single physical network if you divide the range of addresses that you want assigned into multiple scopes. Each scope contains a number of useful pieces of data, but before you can understand them, you need to know some additional terminology.

You can perform the following management tasks on DHCP scopes:

- Create a scope
- Configure scope properties
- Configure reservations and exclusions

- Set scope options
- Activate and deactivate scopes
- Create a superscope
- Create a multicast scope
- Integrate Dynamic DNS and DHCP

I will cover each task in the following sections.

Creating a New Scope in IPv4

Like many other things in Windows Server 2016, a wizard drives the process of creating a new scope. You will most likely create a scope while installing DHCP, but you may need to create more than one. The overall process is simple, as long as you know beforehand what the wizard is going to ask. If you think about what defines a scope, you'll be well prepared. You need to know the following:

- The IP address range for the scope you want to create.
- Which IP addresses, if any, you want to exclude from the address pool.
- Which IP addresses, if any, you want to reserve.
- Values for the DHCP options you want to set, if any. This item isn't strictly necessary for creating a scope. However, to create a useful scope, you'll need to have some options to specify for the clients.

To create a scope, under the server name, right-click the IPv4 option in the DHCP snap-in, and use the Action ➤ New Scope command. This starts the New Scope Wizard (see Figure 12.5). You will look at each page of the wizard in the following sections.

FIGURE 12.5   Welcome page of the New Scope Wizard

Setting the Screen Name

The Scope Name page allows you to enter a name and description for your scope. These will be displayed by the DHCP snap-in.

> It's a good idea to pick sensible names for your scopes so that other administrators will be able to figure out the purpose of the scope. For example, the name DHCP is likely not very helpful, whereas a name like 1st Floor Subnet is more descriptive and can help in troubleshooting.

Defining the IP Address Range

The IP Address Range page (see Figure 12.6) is where you enter the start and end IP addresses for your range. The wizard does minimal checking on the addresses you enter, and it automatically calculates the appropriate subnet mask for the range. You can modify the subnet mask if you know what you're doing.

FIGURE 12.6   IP Address Range page of the New Scope Wizard

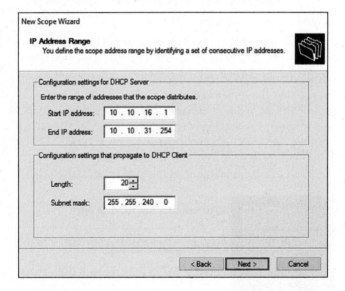

Adding Exclusions and Delay

The Add Exclusions And Delay page (see Figure 12.7) allows you to create exclusion ranges. Exclusions are TCP/IP numbers that are in the pool, but they do not get issued to clients. To exclude one address, put it in the Start IP Address field. To exclude a range, also fill in the

End IP Address field. The delay setting is a time duration by which the server will delay the transmission of a DHCPOFFER message.

FIGURE 12.7   Add Exclusions And Delay page of the New Scope Wizard

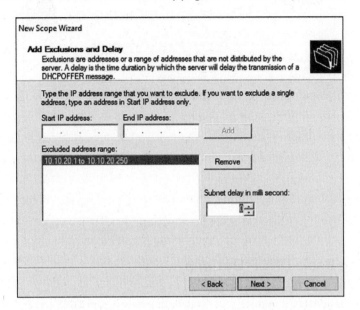

 Although you can always add exclusions later, it's best to include them when you create the scope so that no excluded addresses are ever passed out to clients.

Setting a Lease Duration

The Lease Duration page (see Figure 12.8) allows you to set how long a device gets to use an assigned IP address before it has to renew its lease. The default lease duration is eight days. You may find that a shorter or longer duration makes sense for your network. If your network is highly dynamic, with lots of arrivals, departures, and moving computers, set a shorter lease duration; if it's less active, make it longer.

 Remember that renewal attempts begin when approximately half of the lease period is over (give or take a random interval), so don't set them too short.

FIGURE 12.8   Lease Duration page of the New Scope Wizard

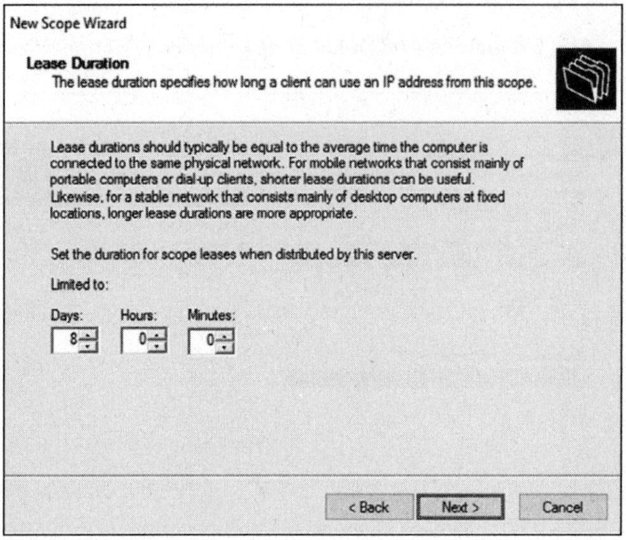

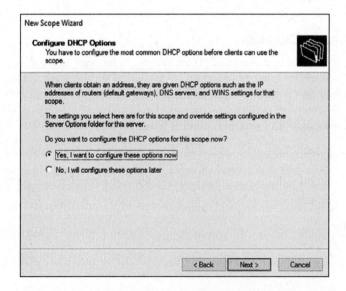

Configuring Basic DHCP Options

The Configure DHCP Options page (see Figure 12.9) allows you to choose whether you want to set up basic DHCP options such as default gateway and DNS settings. The options are described in the following sections. If you choose not to configure options, you can always do so later. However, you should not activate the scope until you've configured the options you want assigned.

FIGURE 12.9   Configure DHCP Options page of the New Scope Wizard

Configuring a Router

The first option configuration page is the Router (Default Gateway) page (see Figure 12.10), in which you enter the IP addresses of one or more routers (more commonly referred to as *default gateways*) that you want to use for outbound traffic. After entering the IP addresses of the routers, use the Up and Down buttons to order the addresses. Clients will use the routers in the order specified when attempting to send outgoing packets.

FIGURE 12.10 Router (Default Gateway) page of the New Scope Wizard

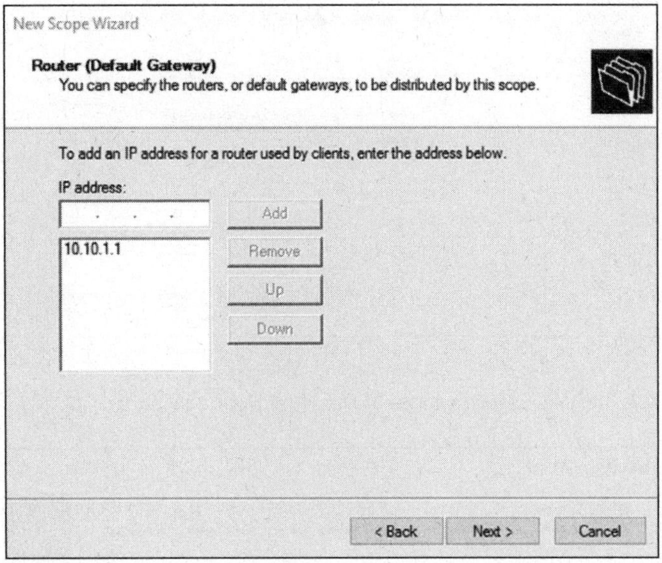

Providing DNS Settings

On the Domain Name And DNS Servers page (see Figure 12.11), you specify the set of DNS servers and the parent domain you want passed down to DHCP clients. Normally, you'll want to specify at least one DNS server by filling in its DNS name or IP address. You can also specify the domain suffix that you want clients to use as the base domain for all connections that aren't fully qualified. For example, if your clients are used to navigating based on server name alone rather than the fully qualified domain name (FQDN) of server.willpanek.com, then you'll want to place your domain here.

Providing WINS Settings

If you're still using Windows Internet Name Service (WINS) on your network, you can configure DHCP so that it passes WINS server addresses to your Windows clients. (If you want the Windows clients to honor it, you'll also need to define the WINS/NBT Node Type option for the scope.) As on the DNS server page, on the WINS Servers page (see Figure 12.12) you can enter the addresses of several servers and move them into the order in which you want clients to try them. You can enter the DNS or NetBIOS name of each server, or you can enter an IP address.

FIGURE 12.11   Domain Name And DNS Servers page of the New Scope Wizard

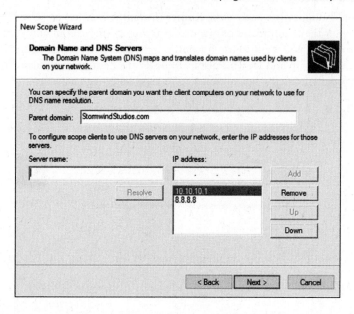

FIGURE 12.12   WINS Servers page of the New Scope Wizard

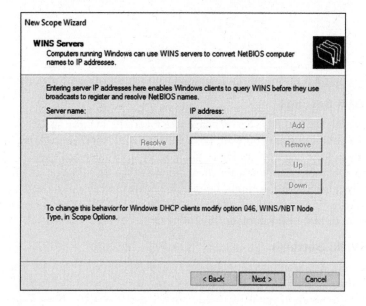

Here are some of the more common options you can set on a DHCP server:

003 Router   Used to provide a list of available routers or default gateways on the same subnet.

006 DNS Servers   Used to provide a list of DNS servers.

015 DNS Domain Name   Used to provide the DNS suffix.

028 Broadcast Address   Used to configure the broadcast address, if different than the default, based on the subnet mask.

44 WINS/NBNS Servers   Used to configure the IP addresses of WINS servers.

46 WINS/NBT Node Type   Used to configure the preferred NetBIOS name resolution method. There are four settings for node type:

B node (0x1)   Broadcast for NetBIOS resolution

P node (0x2)   Peer-to-peer (WINS) server for NetBIOS resolution

M node (0x4)   Mixed node (does a B node and then a P node)

H node (0x8)   Hybrid node (does a P node and then a B node)

051 Lease   Used to configure a special lease duration.

Activating the Scope

The Activate Scope page (see Figure 12.13) gives you the option to activate the scope immediately after creating it. By default, the wizard assumes that you want the scope activated unless you select the No, I Will Activate This Scope Later radio button, in which case the scope will remain dormant until you activate it manually.

FIGURE 12.13   Activate Scope page of the New Scope Wizard

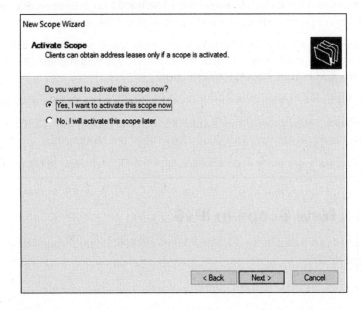

WARNING   Be sure to verify that there are no other DHCP servers assigned to the address range you choose!

In Exercise 12.4, you will create a new scope for the 192.168.0.xprivate Class C network. First you need to complete Exercise 12.1 before beginning this exercise.

EXERCISE 12.4

Creating a New Scope

1. Open the DHCP snap-in by selecting Administrative Tools ≻ DHCP.

2. Right-click the IPv4 folder and choose New Scope. The New Scope Wizard appears.

3. Click the Next button on the welcome page.

4. Enter a name and a description for your new scope and click the Next button.

5. On the IP Address Range page, enter **192.168.0.2** as the start IP address for the scope and **192.168.0.250** as the end IP address. Leave the subnet mask controls alone (though when creating a scope on a production network, you might need to change them). Click the Next button.

6. On the Add Exclusions And Delay page, click Next without adding any excluded addresses or delays.

7. On the Lease Duration page, set the lease duration to 3 days and click the Next button.

8. On the Configure DHCP Options page, click the Next button to indicate you want to configure default options for this scope.

9. On the Router (Default Gateway) page, enter **192.168.0.1** for the router IP address and then click the Add button. Once the address is added, click the Next button.

10. On the Domain Name And DNS Servers page, enter the IP address of a DNS server on your network in the IP Address field (for example, you might enter **192.168.0.251**) and click the Add button. Click the Next button.

11. On the WINS Servers page, click the Next button to leave the WINS options unset.

12. On the Activate Scope page, if your network is currently using the 192.168.0.x range, select Yes, I Want To Activate This Scope Now. Click the Next button.

13. When the wizard's summary page appears, click the Finish button to create the scope.

Creating a New Scope in IPv6

Now that you have seen how to create a new scope in IPv4, I'll go through the steps to create a new scope in IPv6.

To create a scope, right-click the IPv6 option in the DHCP snap-in under the server name and select the Action ➤ New Scope command. This starts the New Scope Wizard. Just as with creating a scope in IPv4, the welcome page of the wizard tells you that you've launched the New Scope Wizard. You will look at each page of the wizard in the following sections.

Setting the Screen Name

The Scope Name page (see Figure 12.14) allows you to enter a name and description for your scope. These will be displayed by the DHCP snap-in.

FIGURE 12.14   IPv6 Scope Name page of the New Scope Wizard

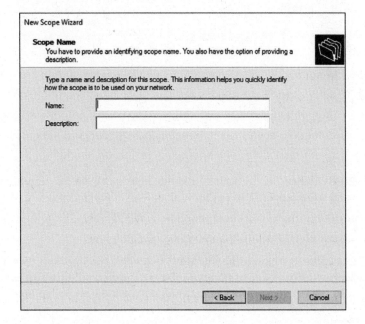

It's a good idea to pick a sensible name for your scopes so that other administrators will be able to figure out what the scope is used for.

Scope Prefix

The Scope Prefix page (see Figure 12.15) gets you started creating the IPv6 scope. IPv6 has three types of addresses, which can be categorized by type and scope.

FIGURE 12.15 Scope Prefix page of the New Scope Wizard

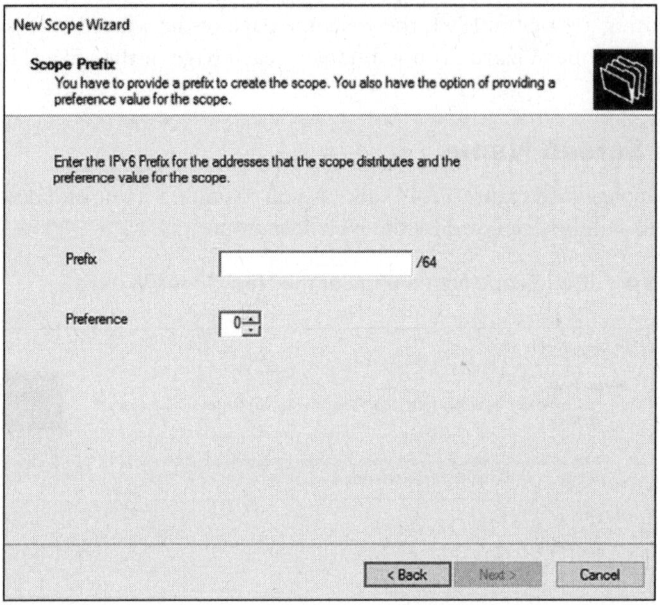

Unicast Addresses *One-to-one*: A packet from one host is delivered to another host. The following are some examples of IPv6 unicast:

- The unicast prefix for site-local addresses is FEC0::/48.
- The unicast prefix for link-local addresses is FE80::/64.

The 6to4 address allows communication between two hosts running both IPv4 and IPv6. The way to calculate the 6to4 address is by combining the global prefix 2002::/16 with the 32 bits of a public IPv4 address of the host. This gives you a 48-bit prefix. 6to4 is described in RFC 3056.

Multicast addresses *One-to-many*: A packet from one host is delivered to multiple hosts (but not everyone). The prefix for multicast addresses is FF00::/8.

Anycast addresses A packet from one host is delivered to the nearest of multiple hosts (in terms of routing distance).

Adding Exclusions

As with the IPv4 New Scope Wizard, the Add Exclusions page allows you to create exclusion ranges. *Exclusions* are TCP/IP numbers that are in the pool but do not get issued to clients. To exclude one address, put it in the Start IPv6 Address field. To exclude a range, also fill in the End IPv6 Address field.

Setting a Lease Duration

The Scope Lease page allows you to set how long a device gets to use an assigned IP address before it has to renew its lease. You can set two different lease durations. The section labeled Non Temporary Address (IANA) is the lease time for your more permanent hosts (such as printers and server towers). The one labeled Temporary Address (IATA) is for hosts that might disconnect at any time, such as laptops.

Activating the Scope

The Completing The New Scope Wizard page gives you the option to activate the scope immediately after creating it. By default, the wizard will assume you want the scope activated. If you want to wait to activate the scope, choose No in the Activate Scope Now box.

Changing Scope Properties (IPv4 and IPv6)

Each scope has a set of properties associated with it. Except for the set of options assigned by the scope, you can find these properties on the General tab of the scope's Properties dialog box (see Figure 12.16). Some of these properties, such as the scope name and description, are self-explanatory. Others require a little more explanation.

- The Start IP Address and End IP Address fields allow you to set the range of the scope.
- For IPv4 scopes, the settings in the section Lease Duration For DHCP Clients control how long leases in this scope are valid.

    The IPv6 scope dialog box includes a Lease tab where you set the lease properties.

FIGURE 12.16   General tab of the scope's Properties dialog box for an IPv4 scope

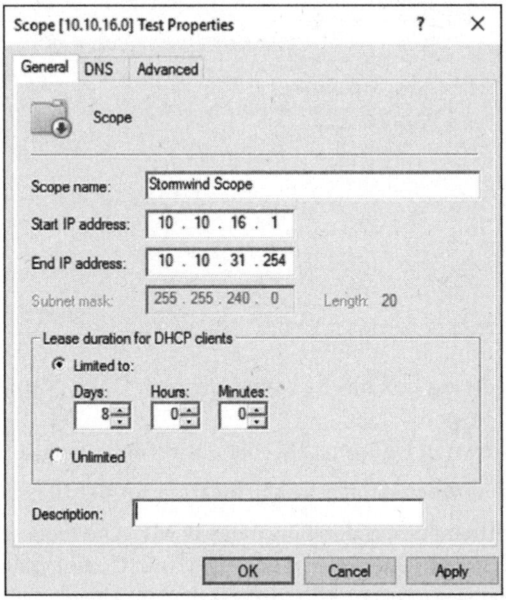

When you make changes to these properties, they have no effect on existing leases. For example, say you create a scope from 172.30.1.1 to 172.30.1.199. You use that scope for a while and then edit its properties to reduce the range from 172.30.1.1 to 172.30.1.150. If a client has been assigned the address 172.30.1.180, which was part of the scope before you changed it, the client will retain that address until the lease expires but will not be able to renew it.

Changing Server Properties

Just as each scope has its own set of properties, so too does the server itself. You access the server properties by right-clicking the IPv4 or IPv6 object within the DHCP management console and selecting Properties.

IPv4 Server Properties

Figure 12.17 shows the IPv4 Properties dialog box.

FIGURE 12.17   General tab of the IPv4 Properties dialog box for the server

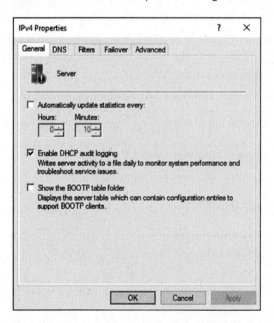

The IPv4 Properties dialog box has five tabs: General, DNS, Network Access Protection, and Advanced.

The Advanced tab, shown in Figure 12.18, contains the following configuration parameters:

- Audit Log File Path is where you enter the location for log files.

- Conflict Detection Attempts specifies how many ICMP echo requests (pings) the server sends for an address it is about to offer. The default is 0. Conflict detection is a way to verify that the DHCP server is not issuing IP addresses that are already being used on the network.

FIGURE 12.18   Advanced tab of the IPv4 Properties dialog box for the server

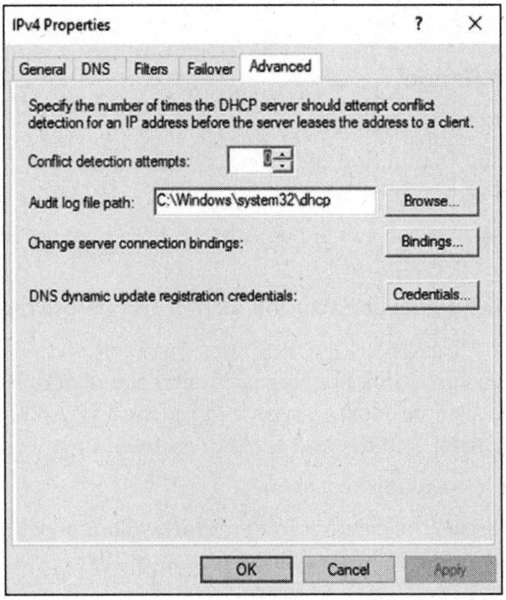

IPv6 Server Properties

The IPv6 Properties dialog box for the server has two tabs: General and Advanced. On the General tab, you can configure the following settings:

- Frequency with which statistics are updated
- DHCP auditing

The Advanced tab allows you to configure the following settings:

- Database path for the audit log file path.
- Connection bindings.
- Registration credentials for dynamic DNS. The registration credential is the user account that DHCP will use to register clients with Active Directory.

Managing Reservations and Exclusions

After defining the address pool for your scope, the next step is to create reservations and exclusions, which reduce the size of the pool. In the following sections, you will learn how to add and remove exclusions and reservations.

Adding and Removing Exclusions

When you want to exclude an entire range of IP addresses, you need to add that range as an exclusion. Ordinarily, you'll want to do this before you enable a scope because that prevents any of the IP addresses you want excluded from being leased before you have a chance to exclude them. In fact, you can't create an exclusion that includes a leased address—you have to get rid of the lease first.

Adding an Exclusion Range

Here's how to add an exclusion range:

1. Open the DHCP snap-in and find the scope to which you want to add an exclusion (either IPv4 or IPv6).

2. Expand the scope so that you can see its Address Pool item for IPv4 or the Exclusion section for IPv6.

3. Right-click the Address Pool or Exclusion section and choose the New Exclusion Range command.

4. When the Add Exclusion dialog box appears, enter the IP addresses you want to exclude. To exclude a single address, type it in the Start IP Address field. To exclude a range of addresses, also fill in the End IP Address field.

5. Click the Add button to add the exclusion.

When you add exclusions, they appear in the Address Pool node, which is under the Scope section for IPv4 and under the Exclusion section of IPv6.

Removing an Exclusion Range

To remove an exclusion, just right-click it and choose the Delete command. After confirming your command, the snap-in removes the excluded range and the addresses become immediately available for issuance.

Adding and Removing Reservations

Adding a reservation is simple as long as you have the MAC address of the device for which you want to create a reservation. Because reservations belong to a single scope, you create and remove them within the Reservations node beneath each scope.

Adding a Reservation

To add a reservation, perform the following tasks:

1. Right-click the scope and select New Reservation.

   This displays the New Reservation dialog box, shown in Figure 12.19.

2. Enter the IP address and MAC address or ID for the reservation.

To find the MAC address of the local computer, use the `ipconfig` command. To find the MAC address of a remote machine, use the `nbtstat-acomputername` command.

3. If you want, you can also enter a name and description.

4. For IPv4, in the Supported Types section, choose whether the reservation will be made by DHCP only, BOOTP only (useful for remote-access devices), or both.

FIGURE 12.19   New Reservation dialog box for IPv4 and IPv6

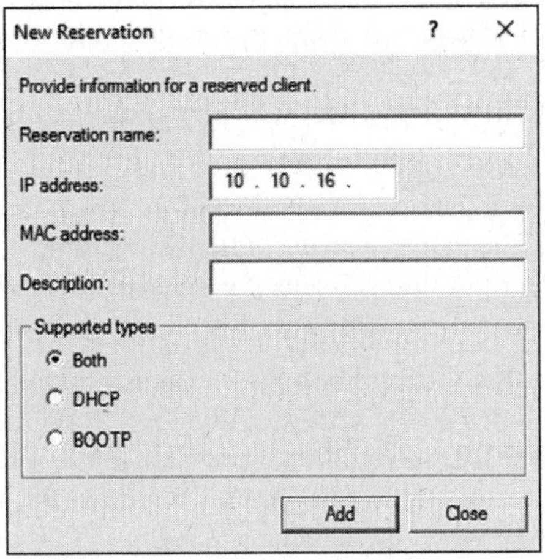

New Reservation	? ✕

Provide information for a reserved client.

Reservation name:	
IP address:	10 . 10 . 16 .
MAC address:	
Description:	

Supported types
- ⦿ Both
- ◯ DHCP
- ◯ BOOTP

[Add]   [Close]

Removing a Reservation

To remove a reservation, right-click it and select Delete. This removes the reservation but does nothing to the client device.

 There's no way to change a reservation once it has been created. If you want to change any of the associated settings, you'll have to delete and re-create the reservation.

Setting Scope Options for IPv4

Once you've installed a server, authorized it in Active Directory, and fixed up the address pool, the next step is to set scope options that you want sent out to clients, such as router (that is, default gateway) and DNS server addresses. You must configure the options you want sent out before you activate a scope. If you don't, clients may register in the scope without getting any options, rendering them virtually useless. Thus, configure the scope options, along with the IP address and subnet mask that you configured earlier in this chapter.

In the following sections, you will learn how to configure and assign scope options on the DHCP server.

Understanding Option Assignment

You can control which DHCP options are doled out to clients in five (slightly overlapping) ways:

Predefined Options   *Predefined options* are templates that are available in the Server, Scope, or Client Options dialog box.

Server Options   *Server options* are assigned to all scopes and clients of a particular server. That means if there's some setting you want all clients of a DHCP server to have, no matter what scope they're in, this is where you assign it. Specific options (those that are set at the class, scope, or client level) will override server-level options. That gives you an escape valve; it's a better idea, though, to be careful about which options you assign if your server manages multiple scopes.

Scope Options   If you want a particular option value assigned only to those clients in a certain subnet, you should assign it as a *scope option*. For example, it's common to specify different routers for different physical subnets; if you have two scopes corresponding to different subnets, each scope would probably have a separate value for the router option.

Class Options   You can assign different options to clients of different types, that is, *class options*. For example, Windows 2000, XP, Vista, Windows 7, Windows 8/8.1, Windows 10, Server 2003, Server 2003 R2, Server 2008, Server 2008 R2, and Server 2016/2012 R2 machines recognize a number of DHCP options that Windows 98, Windows NT, and Mac OS machines ignore, and vice versa. By defining a Windows 2000 or newer class (using the `ipconfig /setclassid` command you saw earlier), you could assign those options only to machines that report themselves as being in that class.

Client Options   If a client is using DHCP reservations, you can assign certain options to that specific client. You attach *client options* to a particular reservation. Client options override scope, server, and class options. The only way to override a client option is to configure the client manually. The DHCP server manages client options.

Client options override class options, class options override scope options, and scope options override server options.

Assigning Options

You can use the DHCP snap-in to assign options at the scope, server, reserved address, or class level. The mechanism you use to assign these options is the same for each; the only difference is where you set the options.

When you create an option assignment, remember that it applies to all of the clients in the server or the scope from that point forward. Option assignments aren't retroactive, and they don't migrate from one scope to another.

Creating and Assigning a New Option

To create a new option and have it assigned, follow these steps:

1.   Select the scope or server where you want the option assigned.

2.   Select the corresponding Options node and choose Action ➢ Configure Options.

   To set options for a reserved client, right-click its entry in the Reservations node and select Configure Options.

   Then you'll see the Scope Options dialog box, which lists all of the options that you might want to configure.

3. To select an individual option, check the box next to it and then use the controls in the Data Entry control group to enter the value you want associated with the option.

4. Continue to add options until you've specified all of the ones you want attached to the server or scope. Then click OK.

Configuring the DHCP Server for Classes

Now it is time for you to learn how to configure the DHCP server to recognize your customized classes and configure options for them. In Exercise 12.5, you will create a new user class and configure options for the new class. Before you begin, make sure that the computers you want to use in the class have been configured with the ipconfig /setclassid command.

EXERCISE 12.5

Configuring User Class Options

1. Open the DHCP snap-in by selecting Administrative Tools ➤ DHCP.

2. Right-click the IPv4 item and select Define User Classes.

3. Click the Add button in the DHCP User Classes dialog box.

4. In the New Class dialog box, enter a descriptive name for the class in the Display Name field. Enter a class ID in the ID field. (Typically, you will enter the class ID in the ASCII portion of the ID field.) When you have finished, click OK.

5. The new class appears in the DHCP User Classes dialog box. Click the Close button to return to the DHCP snap-in.

6. Right-click the Scope Options node and select Configure Options.

7. Click the Advanced tab. Select the class you defined in step 4 from the User Class pop-up menu.

8. Configure the options you want to set for the class. Click OK when you have finished. Notice that the options you configured (and the class with which they are associated) appear in the right pane of the DHCP window.

About the Default Routing and Remote Access Predefined User Class

Windows Server 2016 includes a predefined user class called the *Default Routing and Remote Access class*. This class includes options important to clients connecting to Routing and Remote Access, notably the 051 Lease option.

 Be sure to know that the 051 Lease option is included within this class and that it can be used to assign a shorter lease duration for clients connecting to Routing and Remote Access.

Activating and Deactivating Scopes

When you've completed the steps in Exercise 12.4 and you're ready to unleash your new scope so that it can be used to make client assignments, the final required step is activating the scope. When you activate a scope, you're just telling the server that it's OK to start handing out addresses from that scope's address pool. As soon as you activate a scope, addresses from its pool may be assigned to clients. Of course, this is a necessary precondition to getting any use out of your scope.

If you later want to stop using a scope, you can, but be aware that it's a permanent change. When you deactivate a scope, DHCP tells all clients registered with the scope that they need to release their leases immediately and renew them someplace else—the equivalent of a landlord who evicts tenants when the building is condemned!

 WARNING Don't deactivate a scope unless you want clients to stop using it immediately.

Creating a Superscope for IPv4

A *superscope* allows the DHCP server to provide multiple logical subnet addresses to DHCP clients on a single physical network. You create superscopes with the New Superscope command, which triggers the New Superscope Wizard.

 NOTE You can have only one superscope per server.

The steps in Exercise 12.6 take you through the process of creating a superscope.

EXERCISE 12.6

Creating a Superscope

1. Open the DHCP snap-in by selecting Administrative Tools ➢ DHCP.

2. Follow the instructions in Exercise 12.4 to create two scopes: one for 192.168.0.2 through 192.168.0.127 and one for 192.168.1.12 through 192.168.1.127.

3. Right-click IPv4 and choose the New Superscope command. The New Superscope Wizard appears. Click the Next button.

4. On the Superscope Name page, name your superscope and click the Next button.

5. The Select Scopes page appears, listing all scopes on the current server. Select the two scopes you created in step 2 and then click the Next button.

6. The wizard's summary page appears. Click the Finish button to create your scope.

7. Verify that your new superscope appears in the DHCP snap-in.

Deleting a Superscope

You can delete a superscope by right-clicking it and choosing the Delete command. A superscope is just an administrative convenience, so you can safely delete one at any time—it doesn't affect the "real" scopes that make up the superscope.

Adding a Scope to a Superscope

To add a scope to an existing superscope, find the scope you want to add, right-click it, and choose Action ➤ Add To Superscope. A dialog box appears, listing all of the superscopes known to this server. Pick the one to which you want the current scope appended and click the OK button.

Removing a Scope from a Superscope

To remove a scope from a superscope, open the superscope and right-click the target scope. The pop-up menu provides a Remove From Superscope command that will do the deed.

Activating and Deactivating Superscopes

Just as with regular scopes, you can activate and deactivate superscopes. The same restrictions and guidelines apply. You must activate a superscope before it can be used, and you must not deactivate it until you want all of your clients to lose their existing leases and be forced to request new ones.

To activate or deactivate a superscope, right-click the superscope name and select Activate or Deactivate, respectively, from the pop-up menu.

Creating IPv4 Multicast Scopes

Multicasting occurs when one machine communicates to a network of subscribed computers rather than specifically addressing each computer on the destination network. It's much more efficient to multicast a video or audio stream to multiple destinations than it is to unicast it to the same number of clients, and the increased demand for multicast-friendly network hardware has resulted in some head scratching about how to automate the multicast configuration.

In the following sections, you will learn about MADCAP, the protocol that controls multicasting, and about how to build and configure a multicast scope.

Understanding the Multicast Address Dynamic Client Allocation Protocol

DHCP is usually used to assign IP configuration information for *unicast* (or one-to-one) network communications. With multicast, there's a separate type of address space assigned from 224.0.0.0 through 239.255.255.255. Addresses in this space are known as *Class D addresses*, or simply *multicast addresses*. Clients can participate in a multicast just by knowing (and using) the multicast address for the content they want to receive. However, multicast clients also need to have an ordinary IP address.

How do clients know what address to use? Ordinary DHCP won't help because it's designed to assign IP addresses and option information to one client at a time. Realizing this, the Internet Engineering Task Force (IETF) defined a new protocol: *Multicast Address Dynamic Client Allocation Protocol (MADCAP)*. MADCAP provides an analog to DHCP but for multicast use. A MADCAP server issues leases for multicast addresses only. MADCAP clients can request a multicast lease when they want to participate in a multicast.

DHCP and MADCAP have some important differences. First you have to realize that the two are totally separate. A single server can be a DHCP server, a MADCAP server, or both; no implied or actual relation exists between the two. Likewise, clients can use DHCP and/or MADCAP at the same time—the only requirement is that every MADCAP client has to get a unicast IP address from somewhere.

> Remember that DHCP can assign options as part of the lease process but MADCAP cannot. The only thing MADCAP does is dynamically assign multicast addresses.

Building Multicast Scopes

Most of the steps you go through when creating a multicast scope are identical to those required for an ordinary unicast scope. Exercise 12.7 highlights the differences.

EXERCISE 12.7

Creating a New Multicast Scope

1. Open the DHCP snap-in by selecting Administrative Tools ➢ DHCP.

2. Right-click IPv4 and choose New Multicast Scope. The New Multicast Scope Wizard appears. Click the Next button on the welcome page.

3. In the Multicast Scope Name page, name your multicast scope (and add a description if you'd like). Click the Next button.

4. The IP Address Range page appears. Enter a start IP address of **224.0.0.0** and an end IP address of **224.255.0.0**. Adjust the TTL to 1 to make sure that no multicast packets escape your local network segment. Click the Next button when you're finished.

5. The Add Exclusions page appears; click its Next button.

6. The Lease Duration page appears. Since multicast addresses are used for video and audio, you'd ordinarily leave multicast scope assignments in place somewhat longer than you would with a regular unicast scope, so the default lease length is 30 days (instead of 8 days for a unicast scope). Click the Next button.

7. The wizard asks you if you want to activate the scope now. Click the No radio button and then the Next button.

8. The wizard's summary page appears; click the Finish button to create your scope.

9. Verify that your new multicast scope appears in the DHCP snap-in.

Setting Multicast Scope Properties

Once you create a multicast scope, you can adjust its properties by right-clicking the scope name and selecting Properties.

The Multicast Scope Properties dialog box has two tabs. The General tab allows you to change the scope's name, its start and end addresses, its Time To Live (TTL) value, its lease duration, and its description—in essence, all of the settings you provided when you created it in the first place.

The Lifetime tab allows you to limit how long your multicast scope will be active. By default, a newly created multicast scope will live forever, but if you're creating a scope to provide MADCAP assignments for a single event (or a set of events of limited duration), you can specify an expiration time for the scope. When that time is reached, the scope disappears from the server but not before making all of its clients give up their multicast address leases. This is a nice way to make sure that the lease cleans up after itself when you're finished with it.

Integrating Dynamic DNS and IPv4 DHCP

DHCP integration with Dynamic DNS is a simple concept but powerful in action. By setting up this integration, you can pass addresses to DHCP clients while still maintaining the integrity of your DNS services.

The DNS server can be updated in two ways. One way is for the DHCP client to tell the DNS server its address. Another way is for the DHCP server to tell the DNS server when it registers a new client.

Neither of these updates will take place, however, unless you configure the DNS server to use Dynamic DNS. You can make this change in two ways:

- If you change it at the scope level, it will apply only to the scope.

- If you change it at the server level, it will apply to all scopes and superscopes served by the server.

Which of these options you choose depends on how widely you want to support Dynamic DNS; most of the sites I visit have enabled DNS updates at the server level.

To update the settings at either the server or scope level, you need to open the scope or server properties by right-clicking the appropriate object and choosing Properties. The DNS tab of the Properties dialog box (see Figure 12.20) includes the following options:

Enable DNS Dynamic Updates According To The Settings Below   This check box controls whether this DHCP server will attempt to register lease information with a DNS server. It must be checked to enable Dynamic DNS.

Dynamically Update DNS A And PTR Records Only If Requested By The DHCP Clients
This radio button (which is on by default) tells the DHCP server to register the update only if the DHCP client asks for DNS registration. When this button is active, DHCP clients that aren't hip to DDNS won't have their DNS records updated. However, Windows 2000, XP, Vista, Windows 7, Windows 8/8.1, Windows 10, Server 2003/2003 R2, Server 2008/2008 R2, and Server 2016/2012 R2 DHCP clients are smart enough to ask for the updates.

FIGURE 12.20   DNS tab of the scope's IPv4 Properties dialog box

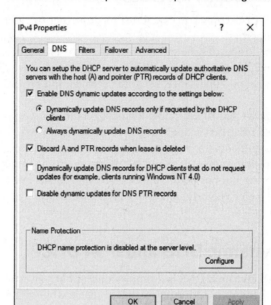

Always Dynamically Update DNS A And PTR Records   This radio button forces the DHCP server to register any client to which it issues a lease. This setting may add DNS registrations for DHCP-enabled devices that don't really need them, such as print servers. However, it allows other clients (such as Mac OS, Windows NT, and Linux machines) to have their DNS information automatically updated.

Discard A And PTR Records When Lease Is Deleted   This check box has a long name but a simple function. When a DHCP lease expires, what should happen to the DNS registration? Obviously, it would be nice if the DNS record associated with a lease vanished when the lease expired. When this check box is checked (as it is by default), that's exactly what happens. If you uncheck this box, your DNS will contain entries for expired leases that are no longer valid. When a particular IP address is reissued on a new lease, the DNS will be updated, but in between leases you'll have incorrect data in your DNS—something that's always best to avoid.

Dynamically Update DNS A And PTR Records For DHCP Clients That Do Not Request Updates   This check box lets you handle these older clients graciously by making the updates using a separate mechanism.

In Exercise 12.8, you will enable a scope to participate in Dynamic DNS updates.

EXERCISE 12.8

Enabling DHCP-DNS Integration

1.   Open the DHCP snap-in by selecting Administrative Tools ➢ DHCP.

2.   Right-click the IPv4 item and select Properties.

3. The Server Properties dialog box appears. Click the DNS tab.

4. Verify that the check box labeled Enable DNS Dynamic Updates According To The
    Settings Below is checked and verify that the radio button labeled Dynamically
    Update DNS A And PTR Records Only If Requested By The DHCP Clients is selected.

5. Verify that the check box labeled Discard A And PTR Records When Lease Is Deleted
    is checked. If not, then check it.

6. Click the OK button to apply your changes and close the Server Properties dialog box.

Using DHCP Failover Architecture

DHCP can become a single point of failure within a network if there is only one DHCP
server. If that server becomes unavailable, clients will not be able to obtain new leases or renew existing leases. For this reason, it is recommended that you have more than one DHCP
server in the network. However, more than one DHCP server can create problems if they
both are configured to use the same scope or set of addresses. Microsoft recommends the
80/20 rule for redundancy of DHCP services in a network.

Implementing the 80/20 rule calls for one DHCP server to make approximately 80
percent of the addresses for a given subnet available through DHCP while another server
makes the remaining 20 percent of the addresses available. For example, with a /24 network of 254 addresses, say 192.168.1.1 to 192.168.1.254, you might have Server 1 offer
192.168.1.10 to 192.168.1.210 while Server 2 offers 192.168.1.211 to 192.168.254.

DHCP Load Sharing

Load sharing is the normal default way that you use multiple DHCP servers (as explained
earlier). Both servers cover the same subnets (remember that a DHCP server can handle
multiple subnets at the same time) simultaneously, and both servers assign IP addresses and
options to clients on the assigned subnets. The client requests are load balanced and shared
between the two servers.

This is a good option for a company that has multiple DHCP servers in the same physical location. The DHCP servers are set up in a failover relationship at the same site, and
both servers respond to all DHCP client requests from the subnets to which they are associated. The DHCP server administrator can set the load distribution ratio between the multiple DHCP servers.

DHCP Hot Standby

When thinking of a DHCP hot standby setup, think of the old server failover cluster. You
have two servers where one server does all of the work and the other server is a standby
server in the event that the first server crashes or goes down.

In a DHCP hot standby situation, the two DHCP servers operate in a failover relationship where one server acts as an active server and is responsible for leasing IP addresses to
all clients in a scope or subnet. The secondary DHCP server assumes the standby role, and
it is ready to go in the event that the primary DHCP server becomes unavailable. If the primary
server becomes unavailable, the secondary DHCP server is given the role of the primary
DHCP server and takes over all the responsibilities of the primary DHCP server.

This failover situation is best suited to DHCP deployments where a company has DHCP servers in multiple locations.

To learn more about DHCP failover situations, please visit Microsoft at http://technet.microsoft.com/en-us/library/hh831385.aspx. Microsoft has been known for taking questions right off its websites, and this website is the perfect solution for doing this.

Working with the DHCP Database Files

DHCP uses a set of database files to maintain its knowledge of scopes, superscopes, and client leases. These files, which live in the *systemroot*\System32\DHCP folder, are always open when the DHCP service is running. DHCP servers use Joint Engine Technology (JET) databases to maintain their records.

You shouldn't modify or alter the DHCP database files when the service is running.

The primary database file is dhcp.mdb—it has all of the scope data in it.

The following files are also part of the DHCP database:

Dhcp.tmp This is a backup copy of the database file created during reindexing of the database. You normally won't see this file, but if the service fails during reindexing, it may not remove the file when it should.

J50.log This file (plus a number of files named J50*xxxxx*.log, where *xxxxx* stands for 00001, 00002, 00003, and so on) is a log file that stores changes before they're written to the database. The DHCP database engine can recover some changes from these files when it restarts.

J50.chk This is a checkpoint file that tells the DHCP engine which log files it still needs to recover.

In the following sections, you will see how to manipulate the DHCP database files.

Removing the Database Files

If you're convinced that your database is corrupt because the lease information that you see doesn't match what's on the network, the easiest repair mechanism is to remove the database files and start over with an empty database.

If you think the database is corrupt because the DHCP service fails at startup, you should check the event log.

To start over, follow these steps:

1. Stop the DHCP service by typing **net stop dhcpserver** at the command prompt.

2. Remove all of the files from the *systemroot*\system32\DHCP folder.

3. Restart the service (at command prompt, type **net start dhcpserver**).

4. Reconcile the scope.

Changing the Database Backup Interval

By default, the DHCP service backs up its databases every 60 minutes. You can adjust this setting by editing the Backup Interval value under HKEY_LOCAL_MACHINE\SYSTEM\ CurrentControlSet\Services\DHCPServer\Parameters. This allows you to make backups either more frequently (if your database changes a lot or if you seem to have ongoing corruption problems) or less often (if everything seems to be on an even keel).

Moving the DHCP Database Files

You may find that you need to dismantle or change the role of your DHCP server and offload the DHCP functions to another computer. Rather than spend the time re-creating the DHCP database on the new machine by hand, you can copy the database files and use them directly. This is especially helpful if you have a complicated DHCP database with lots of reservations and option assignments.

By copying the files, you also minimize the amount of human error that could be introduced by reentering the information by hand.

Compacting the DHCP Database Files

There may be a time when you need to compact the DHCP database. Microsoft has a utility called jetpack.exe that allows you to compact the JET database. Microsoft JET databases are used for WINS and DHCP databases. If you wanted to use the jetpack command, the proper syntax is:

```
JETPACK.EXE <database name><temp database name>
```

After you compact the database, you rename the temp database to dhcp.mdb.

Working with Advanced DHCP Configuration Options

DHCP makes the life of an administrator easy when it comes to managing the IP addresses of devices within an organization. Could you imagine having to keep track of each device and that device's IP manually? With Windows Server 2016's DHCP high availability and load balancing options available, life gets even easier. The next few sections will cover how to implement advanced DHCP solutions in detail.

Implement DHCPv6

In Windows Server 2016, administrators can create and manage both IPv4 and IPv6 DHCP scopes for their organization. Even though they are managed separately, they have the same capabilities of being able to configure reservations, exclusions, and other DHCP options. Unlike an IPv4 client, a DHCPv6 client uses a device unique identifier (DUID) instead of a MAC address to get an IP address from the DHCP server.

DHCPv6 supports both stateful address configuration and stateless address configuration. An easy way to think of the difference between a stateful configuration and a stateless configuration is that, with a stateful configuration, the DHCPv6 client receives its IPv6 address and its additional DHCP options from the DHCPv6 server. With a stateless configuration, the IPv6 client can automatically assign itself an IPv6 address without ever having to communicate with the DHCPv6 server. The stateless configuration process is also known as *DHCPv6 autoconfiguration*. Exercise 12.9 will walk you through the process of creating and activating a new DHCPv6 scope.

EXERCISE 12.9

Creating and Activating a New DHCPv6 Scope

1. Open the DHCP Management Console.

2. Right-click IPv6 and choose the New Scope command. The New Scope Wizard appears. Click the Next button.

3. On the Welcome To The New Scope Wizard page, click the Next button.

4. On the Scope Name page, provide a name and description for your new DHCPv6 scope. Click the Next button.

5. On the Scope Prefix page, input the corresponding prefix for your organization's IPv6 network settings. In the event that you have more than one DHCPv6 server, you can set a preference value that will indicate your server priority. The lower the preference value, the higher the server priority. Click Next.

6. On the Add Exclusions page of the wizard, you can configure either a single IP exclusion or a range of IPs to exclude from obtaining an address automatically. Exclusions should include any device or range of devices that have been manually set with a static IP on that particular scope. Click Next.

7. Keep the default selections on the Scope Lease page. Click Next.

8. Make sure the Activate Scope Now radio button is toggled to Yes. Click Finish to complete the creation and activation of your new DHCPv6 scope.

9. Verify that your new scope appears in the DHCP Management Console to complete this exercise.

Configure High Availability for DHCP, Including DHCP Failover and Split Scopes

DHCP failover provides load balancing and redundancy for DHCP services, enabling administrators to deploy a highly resilient DHCP service for their organization. The idea is to share your DHCP IPV4 scopes between two Windows Server 2016 servers so that if one of the failover partners goes down, then the other failover partner will continue providing DHCP services throughout the environment. DHCP failover supports large-scale DHCP deployments without the challenges of a split-scope DHCP environment.

Here are a few of the benefits that DHCP failover provides:

Multisite DHCP failover supports a deployment architecture that includes multiple sites. DHCP failover partner servers do not need to be located at the same physical site.

Flexibility DHCP failover can be configured to provide redundancy in hot standby mode; or, with load balancing mode, client requests can be distributed between two DHCP servers.

Seamless DHCP servers share lease information, allowing one server to assume the responsibility for servicing clients if the other server is unavailable. DHCP clients can keep the same IP address when a lease is renewed, even if a different DHCP server issues the lease.

Simplicity A wizard is provided to create DHCP failover relationships between DHCP servers. The wizard automatically replicates scopes and settings from the primary server to the failover partner.

Configuring DHCP Failover

One of the nice things about DHCP failover is that the configured scope is replicated between both clustered DHCP nodes whether or not you are running the cluster in hot standby or load balancing mode. If one server fails, the other can manage the entire pool of IP addresses on behalf of the environment. Exercise 12.10 provides step-by-step DHCP failover configuration in Windows Server 2016.

EXERCISE 12.10

Configuring DHCP Failover

1. Open the DHCP Management Console.

2. Right-click IPv4 and choose the Configure Failover command to launch the Configure Failover Wizard. Click Next on the Introduction page.

3. On the Specify The Partner Server To Use For Failover page, select your partner DHCP server from the drop-down menu or by browsing the Add Server directory. Click Next.

4. On the Create A New Failover Relationship page, provide a relationship name, select the Load Balance mode from the drop-down, and provide a shared secret password that will be used to authenticate the DHCP failover relationship between the two servers in the failover cluster. Click Next.

5. Review your configuration settings and click the Finish button to configure your new DHCP failover configuration. Click Close upon successful completion.

6. After the wizard successfully completes on the primary DHCP server, verify that the new failover scope has been created and activated on the secondary DHCP server in the DHCP Management Console to complete this exercise.

You can always go back in and change the properties of the failover scope if you want. Test both hot standby and load balancing modes to decide which deployment configuration option best suits your organization's needs. Expect to see exam scenarios discussing both DHCP failover configuration modes and the differences between them.

DHCP Split Scopes

Even though you have the capabilities of DHCP failover in Windows Server 2016, for exam purposes you will need to understand how DHCP split scopes work. Split scopes are configurable only on IPv4 IP addresses and cannot be configured on IPv6 scopes. The idea of DHCP split scopes is to have two stand-alone DHCP servers that are individually responsible for only a percentage of the IP addresses on a particular subnet.

For example, DHCP Server 1 would be responsible for 70 percent of the IP addresses, and DHCP Server 2 would be responsible for the other 30 percent of IP addresses. The two DHCP servers in a split-scope configuration do not share any lease information between one another, and they do not take over for one another in the event that one of the two DHCP servers fails. As you can see, a split-scope configuration is less fault tolerant than a full DHCP failover configuration. However, a split-scope configuration does split the load of DHCP leases and renewals between two servers, providing a basic level of native load balancing in a Windows Server 2016 environment.

DHCP Allow and Deny Filtering

One of the nice things about DHCP is that administrators can use allow or deny filtering to control which devices get an IP address and which devices do not on your network. DHCP filtering is controlled by recording a client's MAC address in a list and then enabling either the Allow or Deny filter. One thing to keep in mind about DHCP filtering is that by enabling the allow list, you automatically deny DHCP addresses to any client computer not on the list. In Exercise 12.11, you will configure DHCP filtering by adding a client machine to the Deny filter by MAC address.

Configuring DHCP Filtering

1. Open the DHCP Management Console.

2. Expand IPv4 until you reach the Deny filter object in your DHCP hierarchy.

3. Right-click the Deny filter object and select New Filter.

4. Enter the MAC address of the device you want to exclude from your network, provide a description such as Unwanted Device, click Add, and then click Close.

5. Right-click the Deny filter and select Enable to complete this exercise.

One of the good things about these filters is that you can move devices from one filter to the other quite easily at any time by right-clicking the device in the list and selecting either Move To Allow or Move To Deny. Test both Allow and Deny filters thoroughly while preparing for the exam. You will most likely see multiple scenarios surrounding DHCP filtering.

Configure DHCP Name Protection

DHCP name protection is an additional configuration option that administrators should consider when working DHCP within their environment. Name protection protects a DHCP leased machine's name from being overwritten by another machine with the same name during DNS dynamic updates so that you can configure a Windows 2016 DHCP server to verify and update the DNS records of a client machine during the lease renewal process. If the DHCP server detects that a machine's DNS A and PTR records already exist in the environment when a DHCP update occurs, then that DHCP update will fail on that client machine, making sure not to overwrite the existing server name. There are just a few simple steps needed in order to configure DHCP name protection. Exercise 12.12 will walk you through these steps.

EXERCISE 12.12

Enabling DHCP Name Protection

1. Open the DHCP Management Console.

2. Right-click IPv4 and select Properties.

3. The Server Properties dialog box appears. Click the DNS tab.

4. Verify that Enable DNS Dynamic Updates According To The Settings Below is checked, and verify that the radio button labeled Dynamically Update DNS A And PTR Records Only If Requested By The DHCP Clients is selected.

5. Verify that Discard A And PTR Records When Lease Is Deleted is checked. If not, then check it.

6. Click Configure under Name Protection, and select Enable Name Protection.

7. Click OK twice to complete this exercise.

PowerShell Commands

When talking about PowerShell commands for DHCP, I must let you know that there are dozens of commands that you can use to configure and maintain a DHCP server.

In Table 12.1, I will show you just some of the possible PowerShell commands that are available for DHCP.

> The following list are just some of the PowerShell commands available for DHCP. To see the complete list, visit Microsoft's website at https://technet.microsoft.com/en-us/itpro/powershell/windows/dhcpserver/dhcpserver.

TABLE 12.1   DHCP PowerShell commands

Command	Description
Add-DhcpServerInDC	This command allows an administrator to authorize the DHCP server services in Active Directory.
Add-DhcpServerv4Class	This command allows an administrator to add an IPv4 vendor or user class.
Add-DhcpServerv4ExclusionRange	Administrators can use this command to add an exclusion range to an IPv4 scope.
Add-DhcpServerv4Failover	Administrators can use this command to add an IPv4 failover.
Add-DhcpServerv4Lease	This command allows an administrator to add a new IPv4 address lease.
Add-DhcpServerv4MulticastScope	Administrators use this command to add a multicast scope server.
Add-DhcpServerv4OptionDefinition	This command allows an administrator to add a DHCPv4 option definition.
Add-DhcpServerv4Policy	Admins can use this command to add a new policy to either the server or scope level.
Add-DhcpServerv4Reservation	This command allows an admin to reserve a client IPv4 address in the scope.
Add-DhcpServerv4Scope	This command adds an IPv4 scope.

Command	Description
Add-DhcpServerv6Class	This command allows an administrator to add an IPv6 vendor or user class.
Add-DhcpServerv6ExclusionRange	Administrators can use this command to add an exclusion range to an IPv6 scope.
Add-DhcpServerv6Lease	This command allows an administrator to add a new IPv6 address lease.
Add-DhcpServerv6OptionDefinition	This command allows an administrator to add a DHCPv6 option definition.
Add-DhcpServerv6Reservation	This command allows an admin to reserve a client IPv6 address in the scope.
Add-DhcpServerv6Scope	This command adds an IPv6 scope.
Backup-DhcpServer	Administrators can use this command to back up the DHCP database.
Export-DhcpServer	This command allows an administrator to export the DHCP server configuration and lease data.
Get-DhcpServerAuditLog	This command shows you the audit log for the DHCP configuration.
Get-DhcpServerDatabase	Administrators can use this command to view the configuration parameters of the DHCP database.
Get-DhcpServerSetting	This command allows an admin to view the configuration parameters of the DHCP database.
Get-DhcpServerv4Class	Administrators use this command to view the IPv4 vendor or user class settings.
Set-DhcpServerDatabase	This command allows an administrator to modify configuration settings of the DHCP database.
Set-DhcpServerDnsCredential	Administrators can set the credentials of the DHCP Server service, which help register or deregister client records.
Set-DhcpServerSetting	This command allows an administrator to configure the server-level settings.

TABLE 12.1 DHCP PowerShell commands *(continued)*

Command	Description
Set-DhcpServerv4Class	This command allows an administrator to configure the IPv4 vendor class or user class settings.
Set-DhcpServerv4Failover	This command allows an admin to configure the settings for an existing failover relationship.
Set-DhcpServerv4Policy	Administrators can use this command to configure the settings of a DHCP policy.
Set-DhcpServerv4Reservation	This command allows an administrator to configure an IPv4 reservation.
Set-DhcpServerv4Scope	Admins can use this command to configure the settings of an existing IPv4 scope.
Set-DhcpServerv6Reservation	This command allows an administrator to configure an IPv4 reservation.
Set-DhcpServerv6Scope	Admins can use this command to configure the settings of an existing IPv6 scope.

Summary

In this chapter, I explained how DHCP can help your company by issuing all of the TCP/IP settings to your corporate clients. There are two ways to set up a TCP/IP network: manually or automatic. Manually means that an administrator needs to set up the TCP/IP for each client. Automatic means that your corporate clients get their TCP/IP settings from DHCP.

This chapter covered the DHCP lease process as it relates to TCP/IP configuration information for clients. The following stages were covered: IP discovery, IP lease offer, IP lease selection, and IP lease acknowledgment. I showed you how to install and configure the DHCP server on Windows Server 2016 and how to create and manage DHCP scopes and scope options.

I also discussed the authorization of DHCP servers within Active Directory and scopes for IPv4 and IPv6, and then I showed you how to create them. I also covered superscopes as well as managing client leases with their options.

Exam Essentials

Know how to install and authorize a DHCP server.   You install the DHCP Server service using the Add/Remove Windows Components Wizard. You authorize the DHCP server using the DHCP snap-in. When you authorize a server, you're actually adding its IP address to the Active Directory object that contains a list of the IP addresses of all authorized DHCP servers.

Know how to create a DHCP scope.   You use the New Scope Wizard to create a new scope for both IPv4 and IPv6. Before you start, you'll need to know the IP address range for the scope you want to create; which IP addresses, if any, you want to exclude from the address pool; which IP addresses, if any, you want to reserve; and the values for the DHCP options you want to set, if any.

Understand how relay agents help with multiple physical network segments.   A question about relay agents on the exam may appear to be a DHCP-related question. Relay agents assist DHCP message propagation across network or router boundaries where such messages ordinarily wouldn't pass.

Understand the difference between exclusions and reservations.   When you want to exclude an entire range of IP addresses, you need to add that range as an exclusion. Any IP addresses within the range for which you want a permanent DHCP lease are known as reservations. Remember that exclusions are TCP/IP numbers in a pool that do not get issued and reservations are numbers in a TCP/IP pool that get issued only to the same client each time.

Understand DHCP Failover.   DHCP failover (and load sharing) is one of the hottest new features in Windows Server 2016. It is easy to deploy, and it provides an added level of redundancy when compared to using a DHCP split-scope configuration.

Know How to Configure DHCP Name Protection.   DHCP name protection protects DNS Host A records from being overwritten by other clients' Host A records during DNS dynamic updates. DHCP name protection is configured using the DHCP Management Console.

Review Questions

1. You are the network administrator for a midsize computer company. You have a single Active Directory forest, and you have a requirement to implement DHCP for the organization. You need to ensure that your DHCP deployment configuration is both fault tolerant and redundant. Out of the options provided, which is the most reliable DHCP configuration that you could implement?

    A. DHCP split scope

    B. DHCP multicast scope

    C. DHCP failover

    D. DHCP super scope

2. You are the network administrator for your organization. You need to configure the settings of an existing IPv4 scope. What PowerShell cmdlet would you use?

    A. Set-DhcpServerScope

    B. Set-Serverv4Scope

    C. Set-DhcpServerv4Scope

    D. Set-DhcpScope

3. You have decided to split the DHCP scope between two DHCP servers. What is the recommended split that Microsoft states that you should use?

    A. 50/50

    B. 60/40

    C. 70/30

    D. 80/20

4. You are the network administrator for an organization with two servers. The servers are named Server1 and Server2. Server2 is a DHCP server. You want Server1 to help lease addresses for Server2. You add the DHCP role to Server1. What should you do next?

    A. In the DHCP console, run the Configure Failover Wizard.

    B. In the DHCP console, run the Configure Zone Wizard.

    C. On Server2, set the DHCP role to Enabled.

    D. On Server1, start the Share Zone Information Wizard.

5. True or False? You can load DHCP on a Nano Server.

    A. True

    B. False

6. You are the network administrator for a large training company. You have been asked to set up the default gateway setting using DHCP. Which option would you configure?

    A. 003 Router

    B. 006 DNS

      C. 015 DNS Domain Name

      D. 028 Broadcast Address

7. You are the network administrator for your organization. Your DHCP server (Server1) has a scope of 10.10.16.0 to 10.10.16.254 with a subnet mask of /20. You need to ensure that all of the client computers obtain an IP address from Server1. What PowerShell cmdlet would you use?

      A. `Reconcile-DHCPServerv4IPRecord`

      B. `Get-Serverv4Scope`

      C. `Get- DHCPServerv4IPRecord`

      D. `Set-DhcpServerv4Scope`

8. You are the network administrator for a large training company. You have been asked to set up the DNS setting of all your clients using DHCP. Which option would you configure?

      A. 003 Router

      B. 006 DNS

      C. 015 DNS Domain Name

      D. 028 Broadcast Address

9. Your network contains two servers named ServerA and ServerB that run Windows Server 2016. ServerA is a DHCP server that is configured to have a scope named Scope1. ServerB is configured to obtain an IP address automatically. In the scope on ServerA, you create a reservation named ServerB_Reservation for ServerB. A technician replaces the network adapter on ServerB. You need to make sure that ServerB can obtain the same IP address as it did before the network card got replaced. What should you modify on Server1?

      A. The Advanced settings of ServerB_Reservation

      B. The MAC address of ServerB_Reservation

      C. The Network Access Protection settings of Scope1

      D. The Name Protection settings of Scope1

10. You are the network administrator for a large training company. You have one DHCP server called DHCP1. DHCP1 has an IPv4 scope named Scope1. Users report that when they boot up their systems, it takes a long time to access the network. After auditing your network, you notice that it takes a long time for computers to receive their IP addresses from DHCP because the DHCP server sends out five (5) pings before issuing the IP address to the client machine. How do you reduce the amount of time it takes for computers to receive their IP addresses?

      A. Run the DHCP Configuration Wizard.

      B. Create a new IPv4 filter.

      C. Modify the Conflict Detection Attempts setting.

      D. Modify the Ethernet properties of DHCP1.

Chapter

13

Implement IP Address Management

THE FOLLOWING 70-741 EXAM OBJECTIVES ARE COVERED IN THIS CHAPTER:

✓ **Install and configure IP Address Management (IPAM)**

 ▪ This objective may include but is not limited to: Provision IPAM manually or by using Group Policy; configure server discovery; create and manage IP blocks and ranges; monitor utilization of IP address space; migrate existing workloads to IPAM; configure IPAM database storage using SQL Server; determine scenarios for using IPAM with System Center Virtual Machine Manager for physical and virtual IP address space managementDeploy and manage IPAM.

✓ **Manage DNS and DHCP using IPAM**

 ▪ This objective may include but is not limited to: Manage DHCP server properties using IPAM; configure DHCP scopes and options; configure DHCP policies and failover; manage DNS server properties using IPAM; manage DNS zones and records; manage DNS and DHCP servers in multiple Active Directory forests; delegate administration for DNS and DHCP using role-based access control (RBAC); Create and manage IP blocks and ranges.

✓ **Audit IPAM Migrate to IPAM**

 ▪ This objective may include but is not limited to: Audit the changes performed on the DNS and DHCP servers; audit the IPAM address usage trail; audit DHCP lease events and user logon events.

In this book, I have shown you how to work with and configure protocols and services like TCP/IP, DNS, and DHCP. In this chapter, I will show you a tool that allows you to manage and manipulate these services and protocols from one application.

I will show you how you can use the IP Address Management application to manage and configure all of your TCP/IP services. I will show you how you can use this application to do your entire TCP/IP configuration from one location.

Understanding IPAM

One of the great features of Windows Server 2016 is the *IP Address Management (IPAM)* utility. IPAM is a built-in utility that allows an administrator to discover, monitor, audit, and manage the TCP/IP schema used on your network. IPAM provides an administrator with the ability to observe and administer the servers that are running the Dynamic Host Configuration Protocol (DHCP) and the Domain Name System (DNS). IPAM includes some of the following advantages:

Automatic IP Address Infrastructure Discovery IPAM has the ability to discover automatically the domain's DHCP servers, DNS servers, and domain controllers. IPAM can do the discovery for any of the domains you specify. Administrators also have the ability to enable or disable management of these servers using the IPAM utility.

Management of DHCP and DNS Services IPAM gives administrators the capability to monitor and manage Microsoft DHCP and DNS servers across an entire network using the IPAM console. IPAM allows you to configure things as easy as adding a resource record to DNS or as complex as configuring DHCP policies and failover servers.

Custom IP Address Management Administrators now have the ability to customize the display of IP addresses and tracking and utilization data. IPAM allows the IP address space to be organized into IP address blocks, IP address ranges, and individual IP addresses. To help you organize the IP address space further, built-in or user-defined fields are also assigned to the IP addresses.

Multiple Active Directory Forest Support Administrators can manage multiple Active Directory forests using IPAM as long as there is a two-way trust between the two forests.

There may be times when an organization needs to have multiple forests in their structure or when a company purchases another company. Once both forests are connected by a trust, administrators can manage both companies IP services through one application.

Purge Utilization Data   Administrators now have the ability to reduce the size of the IPAM database. This is done by purging the IP address utilization data older than the date that the administrator specifies.

Auditing and Tracking of IP Address   IPAM allows administrators to track and audit IP addresses through the use of the IPAM console. IPAM allows IP addresses to be tracked using DHCP lease events and user logon events. These events are collected from the Network Policy Server (NPS) servers, domain controllers, and DHCP servers. Administrators can track IP data by following the IP address, client ID, hostname, or username.

PowerShell Support   Windows Server 2016 now allows an administrator to manage access scopes on IPAM objects using PowerShell commands.

As an administrator, you should understand a few things before installing the IPAM feature. There are three main methods to deploy an IPAM server:

Distributed   This method allows an IPAM server deployment at every site in an enterprise network.

Centralized   This method allows only one IPAM server in an enterprise network.

Hybrid   This method uses a central IPAM server deployment along with dedicated IPAM servers at each site in the enterprise network.

Installing IPAM

Now that I have started explaining what IPAM can do for your organization, the next step is to install IPAM. When you are thinking of installing IPAM, there are a few considerations that you must think about. So let's start with looking at the hardware and software requirements needed for IPAM.

IPAM Hardware and Software Requirements

So let's start with the main requirement. IPAM must be loaded onto a Windows Server. Since this is a Windows Server 2016 book, I would recommend that you use Windows Server 2016. However, you can load IPAM onto a Windows Server 2008, 2008 R2, 2012, or 2012 R2 system.

You can also load an IPAM client (this allows you to remotely operate IPAM) onto any Windows 7 or higher system. Before the IPAM client can be used, you must first install the Remote Server Administration Tools (RSAT). You need to make sure that you install the proper version of RSAT based on the version of Windows you have installed.

Your network needs to be a domain. Workgroup networks are not supported by IPAM. So the server on which you decide to install IPAM needs to be part of a domain but it can't be a domain controller. Domain controllers are servers that are part of a domain and have a copy of the Active Directory database. When you install IPAM, you HAVE to load it on a Member Server.

IPAM will work on both an IPv4 and IPv6 network. The member server that you install IPAM onto must be able to see and connect to the other servers on your network. If the IPAM server is not able to access the other servers (like DNS and DHCP), the IPAM server will not be able to help monitor and maintain these servers.

One of the advantages of IPAM is that the IPAM server will automatically discover other servers on your network. Server discovery requires the IPAM server to be able to access at least one domain controller and an authoritative DNS server.

Microsoft's best practices are to place the IPAM server onto its own server. You should *NOT* put the IPAM server on a server with other network services like DNS or DHCP. For example, DHCP server discovery will be automatically disabled if you install IPAM and DHCP onto the same server.

This makes IPAM a good candidate for virtual machines or containers. By using a virtual machine or container for the IPAM installation, you don't give up all of the hardware resources of a powerful server for just one feature. Some other IPAM specifications and features are as follows:

- Server discovery for IPAM is limited to a single Active Directory forest.

- IPAM can manage DNS and DHCP servers belonging to a different AD forest as long as a two-way trust relationship is set up between your forest and the other forest. The servers in the other forest will need to be manually entered into IPAM.

- IPAM only works with Microsoft servers (domain controllers, DHCP, DNS, and NPS) using Windows Server 2008 and above.

- IPAM only supports Microsoft-based systems. IPAM does not support non-Microsoft network devices.

- IPAM only supports Windows Internal Database (WID) or SQL Server. Other database engines are not supported.

- Windows Server 2016 IPAM now supports /31, /32, and /128 subnets.

- Windows Server 2016 IPAM now supports DNS resource records, conditional forwarders, and DNS zone management for both primary zones and primary zones with Active Directory integration.

- You can now purge IP address utilization data, thus reducing the size of the IPAM database.

So let's go ahead and install the IPAM feature. Exercise 13.1 will show you how to install the IPAM feature. You will install and configure the IPAM feature using Server Manager. Remember, this exercise has to be done on a member server.

EXERCISE 13.1

Installing the IPAM Feature

1. Open Server Manager.

2. Click the number 2 link, Add Roles And Features. If the Before You Begin screen appears, just click Next.

3. Choose a role-based or feature-based installation and click Next.

4. Choose your server and click Next.

5. On the Roles screen, just click Next.

6. On the Features screen, click the box for the IP Address Management (IPAM) server (see Figure 13.1). Click the Add Features button when the box appears. Click Next.

FIGURE 13.1   Choosing the IPAM feature

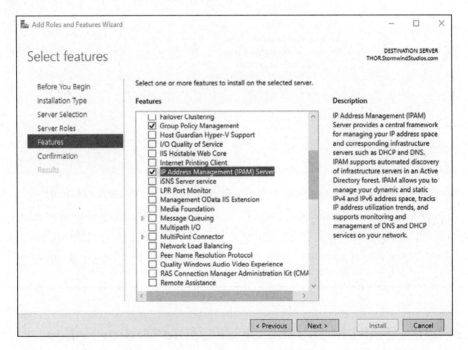

7. At the Confirmation screen, make sure the check box Restart The Destination Server Automatically If Required is selected (see Figure 13.2) and then click the Install button.

FIGURE 13.2   Confirmation Screen

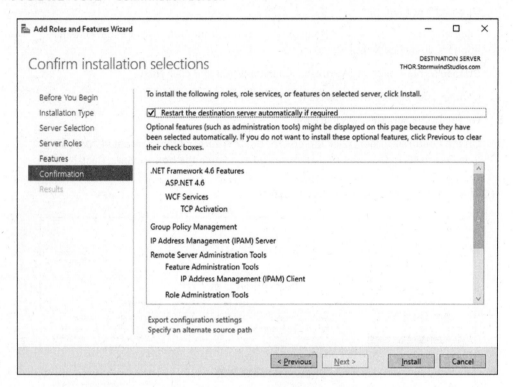

8. Once the installation is complete, click the Close button. Close Server Manager.

9. In the Add Servers box, click the DNS tab. In the search box, type the name of your DNS server and click the magnifying glass.

10. Under Name, double-click the server name. The server will be added to the right-side box. Click OK. Close Server Manager.

Provision IPAM Manually or by Using Group Policy

When setting up an IPAM server, you must determine how the IPAM server will communicate with your other servers. This is called IPAM provisioning. IPAM provisioning can be set up two ways, manually or by using GPOs.

IPAM will try to locate your DNS servers, DHCP servers, and domain controllers as long as those servers are within the searching scope that you have configured. An administrator can configure whether the servers (DNS, DHCP, and domain controllers) are managed by IPAM or unmanaged. Please note that this will work only with Microsoft products; it won't find Infoblox or Unix-based DNS/DHCP.

If you want your servers to be managed by IPAM, you must make sure you set up the network and the servers properly. For example, you will need to configure the security settings and firewall ports properly on the servers (DNS, DHCP, and domain controllers) in order to allow IPAM to access these servers and perform its configuration and monitoring.

Once you have decided to use the Group Policy provisioning method, you will be required to create a GPO name prefix in the provisioning wizard (I use IPAM1 in Exercise 13.2). Once you have set up the GPO name prefix, the provisioning wizard will show you the names of the GPOs that you will need to create. You will be required to either manually create or automatically create (using PowerShell) the GPOs for the different servers.

If you decide to manually create the GPOs, then you will need to open the Group Policy Management Console and then create a GPO for each of the different server types that IPAM will manage. This is a more difficult way to create the GPOs. It is easier to create the provisioned GPOs automatically.

To create these provisioned GPOs automatically, you will need to use the `Invoke-IpamGpoProvisioning` cmdlet at an elevated Windows PowerShell prompt.

The following is an example of the `Invoke-IpamGpoProvisioning` command. In this example, the IPAM server is named IPAMServer. The name of our domain is StormWindStudios.com and the GPO Prefix name will be IPAM1. As you will see in the command, I added a `-Force` switch to the end of the command. This switch forces the PowerShell command to run without asking the user for confirmation.

```
Invoke-IpamGPOProvioning -Domain StormWindStudios.com -GpoPrefixName IPAM1
-IpamServerFqdn IPAMServer.StormWindStudios.com -Force
```

After you run the `Invoke-IpamGpoProvisioning` command, new GPOs will be created based on your network setup. For example, I am running a domain controller and NPS together. So the GPOs may look like the following:

- <GPO-prefix>_DHCP
- <GPO-prefix>_DNS
- <GPO-prefix>_DC_NPS

The created GPOs will all have the GPO prefix name that you used in the `Invoke-IpamGpoProvisioning` command. For example, I used IPAM1 in the above `Invoke-IpamGPOProvisioning` command. So my actual GPOs look like the following:

- IPAM1_DHCP
- IPAM1_DNS
- IPAM1_DC_NPS

In order for IPAM to automatically manage these servers, you must create these GPOs. After the GPOs are created, IPAM will be able to manage these servers through the IPAM console. When an IPAM server no longer manages these servers (servers will be shown as unmanaged), the GPOs can be removed.

The IPAM server needs to be able to manipulate the GPOs directly. To ensure that IPAM can manage the GPOs directly, you must make sure that the GPO security filtering includes the IPAM servers. If the IPAM servers are not added to the security filtering for the GPOs, the IPAM server will not be able to manage these other servers (DNS, DHCP, and NPS).

In Exercise 13.2, I will walk you through the process of provisioning your IPAM server. I will also show you how to create the GPOs needed for the IPAM provisioning and then I will show you how to add the IPAM servers to the GPOs security filter. To complete this exercise properly, you will need to log into the IPAM server with a domain admin account or higher.

EXERCISE 13.2

Provisioning an IPAM Server

1. Open Server Manager.

2. Click the IPAM link on the left side. This opens the IPAM Overview page.

3. Click number 2, Provision the IPAM Server (see Figure 13.3).

FIGURE 13.3 IPAM Overview screen

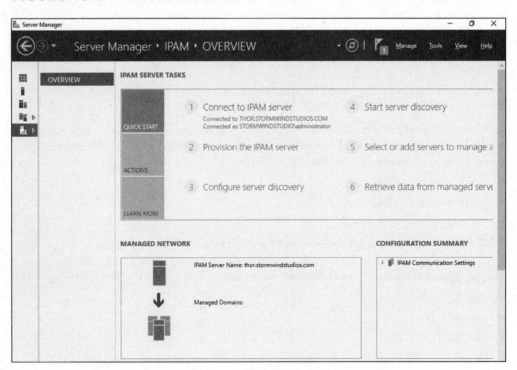

4.   Click Next at the Before You Begin screen.

5.   At this screen, you will need to setup a database for IPAM. You can either use the Windows Internal Database (WID) or a Microsoft SQL Server. If you choose to use a WID (I am using a WID in this exercise), you will need to put in a location for the database storage. Make your database selection on the Configure Database screen and click Next.

6.   At the Select Provisioning Method screen, choose GPO and put in a GPO suffix name. I used IPAM1 for the GPO suffix name (see Figure 13.4).

FIGURE 13.4   Select Provisioning

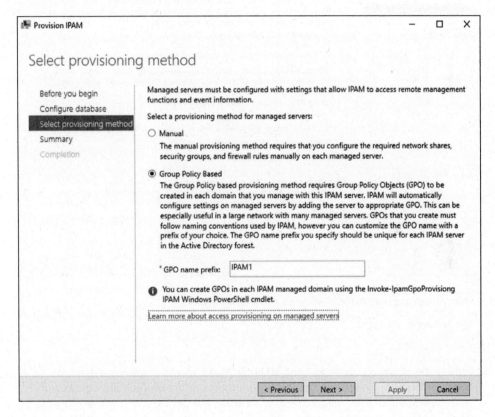

7.   At the Summary screen, write down the names of the GPOs that you need to create (see Figure 13.5). Click the Apply button.

FIGURE 13.5   GPOs Needed

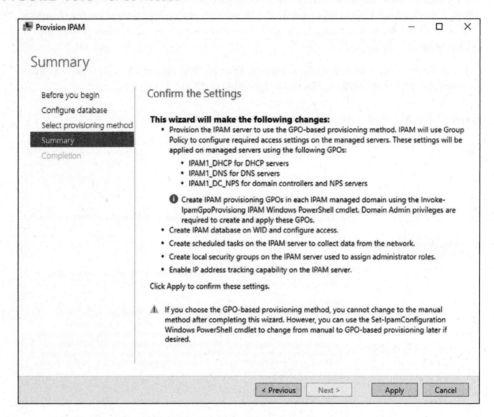

8. Once the process is completed, click the Close button.

9. Close Server Manager.

10. Open PowerShell

11. Type in the following command and hit Enter. Make sure to change the domain name, GPO suffix name, and the IPAM server name to match your settings. I used StormWindStudios.com as my domain, IPAM1 as my GPO Prefix name, and Mercury as my IPAM server name.

    ```
    Invoke-IpamGPOProvisioning -Domain StormwindStudios.com
    -GPOPrefixName IPAM1 -IpamServerFqdn Mercury.StormwindStudios.com -Force
    ```

12. You will be asked to confirm the installation of the GPOs. This is normally asked three times. When asked to confirm, click Y and hit Enter for all three.

13. After the command has finished, close PowerShell.

14. On your domain controller, open the Group Policy Management Console.

15. Under the Forest, expand Domains and then expand the name of your domain. You should now see the three new GPOs (see Figure 13.6).

FIGURE 13.6   New GPOs

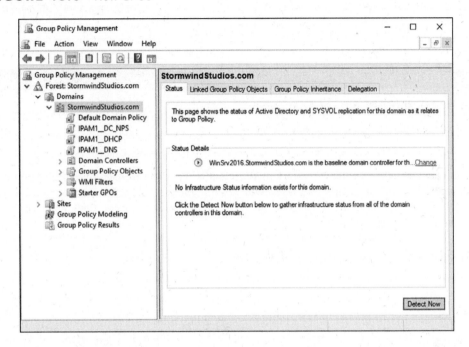

16. Click on the GPO that you want to configure. For example, if you are adding a managed DHCP server, click the GPO name ending in _DHCP.

17. On the Scope tab, under the Security Filtering section, click the Add button.

18. In the Select User, Computer, or Group window, click the Object Types button.

19. Select the Computers check box, and then click OK.

20. Under the section called Enter The Object Name To Select, type the name of the IPAM server and click the Check Names button. If the name is proper, the server name will become underlined. Click OK.

21. Repeat steps 16 through 20 for the other IPAM GPOs. Only do these steps for every server that you currently have. For example, if you only have a DHCP and DNS server, do these steps for just these two servers.

22. When you've completed the GPOs, close the Group Policy Management Console.

Configure Server Discovery

Once you have successfully installed and provisioned the IPAM feature on your Windows Server 2016 machine, you can begin server discovery. One of the great things about IPAM is that you can define multiple domains within the same forest to be managed by a single IPAM server.

Once initiated, server discovery will automatically search for all of the machines running on the specified domain. Administrator privileges are required for the domain against which you are running server discovery. Exercise 13.3 will walk you through the server discovery process.

EXERCISE 13.3

Configuring IPAM Server Discovery

1. Open Server Manager and select IPAM.

2. On the IPAM Overview page, select option 3, Configure Server Discovery.

3. On the Configure Server Discovery page, select and add the forest and domains you want to discover and click OK. When you add the domain, it should appear under the Select The Server Roles To Discover section and Domain Controller, DNS, and DHCP should be checked (see Figure 13.7).

FIGURE 13.7   Configuring server discovery

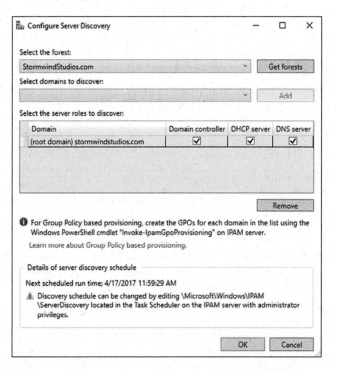

4. On the IPAM Overview page, select option 4, Start Server Discovery. The task will run in the background. You will receive notification once server discovery has completed.

5. On the IPAM home page, select Server Inventory to review the now-completed server discovery of the requested domain (see Figure 13.8). This may take a few minutes and you may need to refresh Server Manager.

FIGURE 13.8 Server Inventory screen

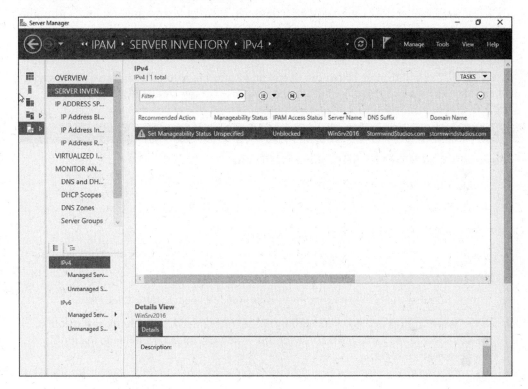

6. Close Server Manager.

Create and Manage IP Blocks and Ranges

In IPAM, IP address space is divided into addresses, ranges, and blocks. Blocks are groups of ranges, and ranges are groups of IP Addresses. Here you will find a breakdown of each IP Management space found within IPAM:

IP Addresses   Individual IP addresses map to a single IP address range. When you map an IP address to a range, it enables actions to be taken on a range that affect all IP addresses in the range, such as adding, updating, or deleting IP address fields.

IP Address Ranges   IP address ranges are smaller chunks of IP addresses that typically correspond to a DHCP scope. IP address ranges are contained within, or "mapped to," IP address blocks. IP address ranges cannot map to multiple IP address blocks, and ranges that map to the same block cannot overlap.

IP Address Blocks   IP address blocks are large chunks of IP addresses that are used to organize address space at a high level. For example, you might use one IP address block for all private IP addresses in your organization and another block for public IP addresses. You can think of IP address blocks as containers that hold IP address ranges. IP address blocks are not deployed and managed on the network like IP address ranges or individual IP addresses.

When you have an IPAM-managed DHCP server, the IP address ranges found within the scopes of that DHCP server are automatically entered into the IPAM database during the discovery process. Individual IP addresses and IP blocks are not automatically added to the IPAM database.

Exercise 13.4 will demonstrate how to add an IP address manually and also on how to add an IP address block. I will be adding the IP address of my DNS/DHCP server.

EXERCISE 13.4

Manually Add IPAM IP Address and Blocks

1. Open Server Manager and select IPAM.

2. Select IP Address Blocks.

3. Right-click IPv4 and select Add IP Address.

4. Enter the IP address of the device that is to be managed by IPAM. Keep all other defaults.

5. Click Apply.

6. On the Summary page, verify that the task completed successfully. Click OK.

7. Your new IP address is now managed by IPAM. You can now both create and delete DHCP reservations and DNS records for this IP address space from inside the IPAM management console.

8. Right-click IPv4 and select Add IP Address Block.

9. Fill in the following fields and click OK:

   Network ID: 10.10.16.0

   Leave all other fields as defaults.

10. Close Server Manager.

Managing Services

One of the nicest advantages of using IPAM is the ability to manage and maintain your DNS and DHCP servers from one location. Normally in a corporate environment, the IT department will use the DNS console and the DHCP console to configure these services. With IPAM, you can open one application and configure many of the IP services from one location.

So let's start by learning how to configure and manage your DNS servers from IPAM.

Managing DNS

Domain Name System (DNS) is the default name resolution service used by Windows Server 2016. Let's talk about TCP/IP for a moment. TCP/IP is just like a telephone number. Every computer gets its own telephone number (TCP/IP address). Now just like the telephone system, when you don't know a number, you call information and ask for the number. This is exactly what DNS does. DNS turns a host name into a TCP/IP number.

There are many different ways to configure and manage a DNS server. IPAM is just another tool for doing DNS management but the nice advantage of using IPAM is the ability to also manage other IP services.

In Windows Server 2016, IPAM allows an administrator to configure DNS resource record, conditional forwarder, server properties, and DNS zone management. IPAM allows an administrator to manage DNS for both Active Directory integration and file based DNS servers (see Figure 13.9). Finally, IPAM can manage and maintain DNS servers in multiple Active Directory forests.

FIGURE 13.9 IPAM DNS Management

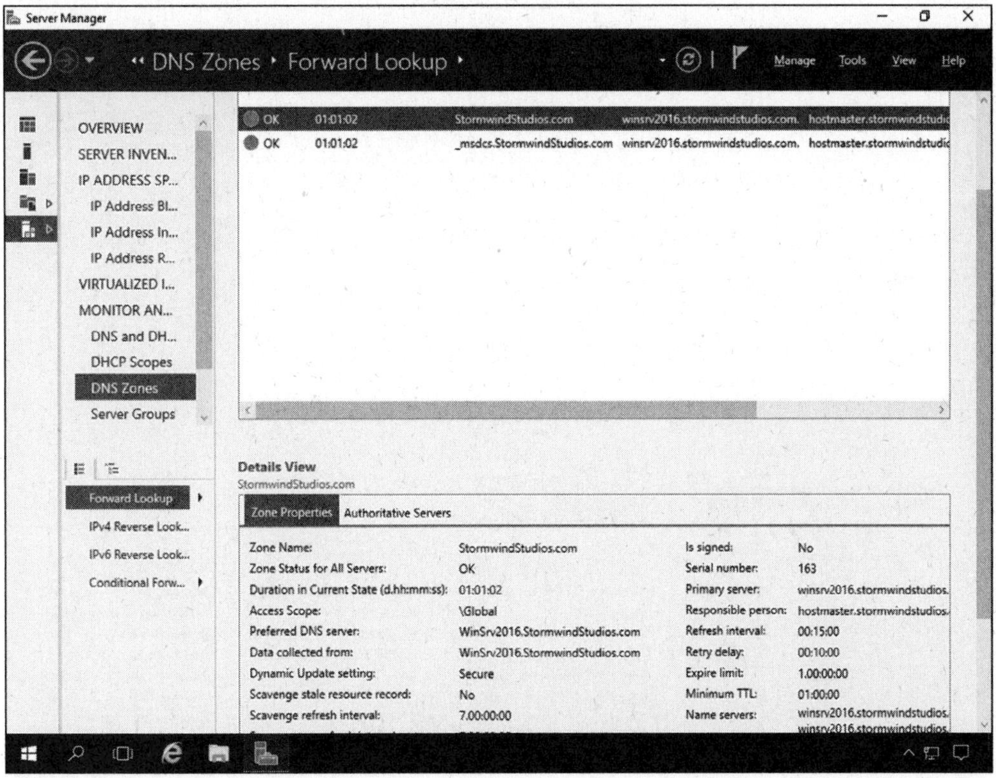

When using the IPAM console to configure DNS, it's easy to manage and maintain the DNS settings. Let's start with some of the basics like adding DNS resource records.

Resource records are the database records used by DNS. There are many types of records including Host records (A or AAAA), Reverse Lookup records (PTR), Mail Exchange records (MX), and Name Server records (NS) to just name a few.

In Exercise 13.5, I will show you how to add a few resource records to the DNS zone using IPAM.

EXERCISE 13.5

Adding Resource Records

1. Open Server Manager.

2. Click on the IPAM section and choose DNS Zones (under Monitor and Manage).

3. Right click the name of your zone and choose Add DNS Resource record (see Figure 13.10).

FIGURE 13.10   Adding DNS records

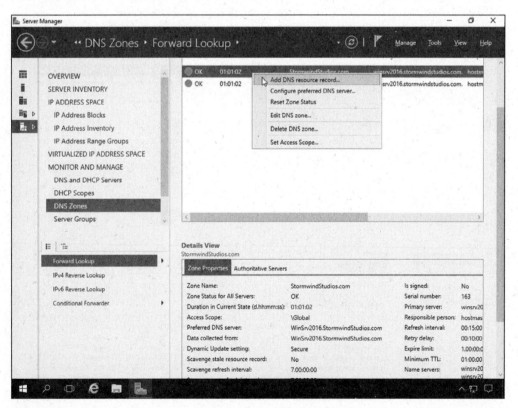

4. When the Add Resource Record wizard starts, make sure the DNS zone is chosen along with the DNS server. Click the New button.

5. Fill in the following properties and click Create Resource record (see Figure 13.11);

   Resource record type: A

   Name: TestBox

   FQDN: Testbox.YourDNSDomain.xxx

   IP Address: Enter an IP address of an Unused IP.

   Make sure the Checkbox is checked for Create assoiciated pointer (PTR) record.

FIGURE 13.11   Adding A Record

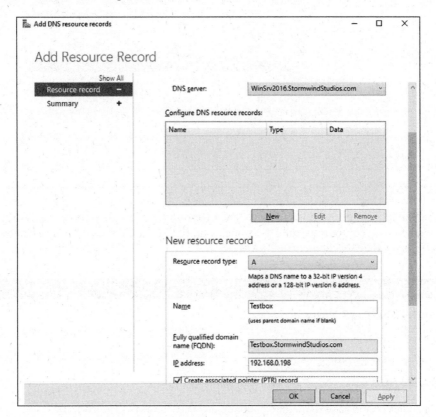

6. Once the record is added to the list, click the OK button for the wizard.

7. Open your DNS server and verify that the record is created as shown in Figure 13.12.

EXERCISE 13.5 *(continued)*

FIGURE 13.12 Verifying the DNS record

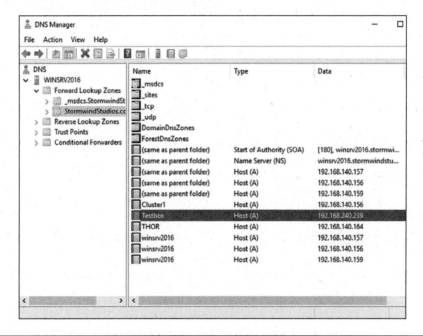

In Exercise 13.5, I showed you how to add a Resource Record to DNS using IPAM. Now let's take a look at configuring the DNS zone using IPAM. In Exercise 13.6, I will show you how to manage the DNS zone using IPAM.

EXERCISE 13.6

Managing the DNS Zone

1. Open Server Manager.

2. Click on IPAM on left side.

3. Click on DNS Zones under Monitor and Manage.

4. Right click on the zone name and choose Edit DNS Zone (see Figure 13.13).

5. The Edit DNS Zone wizard appears. Make sure all zone information is correct. Click on Advanced.

6. In the Advanced settings, set the No-refresh interval and Refresh interval for 5 days (see Figure 13.14). Make sure all the other settings are correct. Once everything is verified, click on the SOA link.

FIGURE 13.13   Managing the DNS Zone

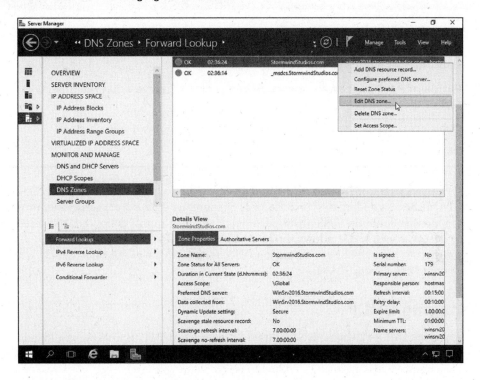

FIGURE 13.14   DNS Zone Advanced Properties

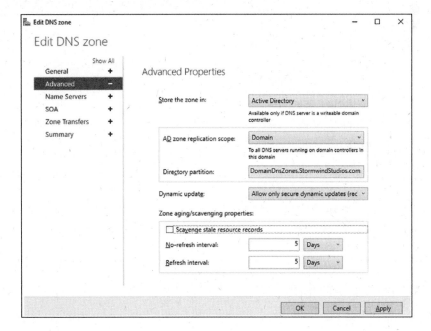

7. Check all of the values under the SOA page and make sure that everything is setup correctly. If you would like to force replication between DNS servers, increase the Serial Number by 1. Then click on Zone Transfers.

8. Make sure that the zone transfers are setup to only DNS servers that you trust. Click on the Summary link.

9. At this point, you will need to click on the Apply button to save your changes.

10. Close Server Manager.

As you have seen from exercises 13.5 and 13.6, you can manage and manipulate DNS from IPAM. Besides adding Resource Records or changing the zone properties, administrators can also configure the DNS preferred server, reset zone status, delete the DNS zone, and set access scopes. IPAM allows you to configure both IPv4 and IPv6 networks.

Now that we have looked at configuring DNS using IPAM, now it's time to look at how to configure DHCP using IPAM.

Managing DHCP

In the section called "Managing DNS," I used an example of TCP/IP working just like the telephone system. DHCP in this example would be the telephone company that issues you a telephone number. DHCP issues TCP/IP addresses to all of your users.

Administrators can use IPAM to configure many of the DHCP options. For example, you can use IPAM to configure the following DHCP options (as seen in Figure 13.15):

- DHCP Server Properties
- DHCP Server Options
- Create DHCP Scope
- Configure Predefined DHCP Options
- Configure DHCP User Classes
- Configure DHCP Vendor Classes
- Configure DHCP Policy
- Import DHCP Policy
- Add DHCP MAC Address Filtering
- Launch the DHCP Console
- Activate or Deactivate Policies

- Setup DHCP Failover Servers
- Replicate DHCP Servers
- Set Access Scope
- Retrieve Server Data

FIGURE 13.15   Configuring DHCP using IPAM

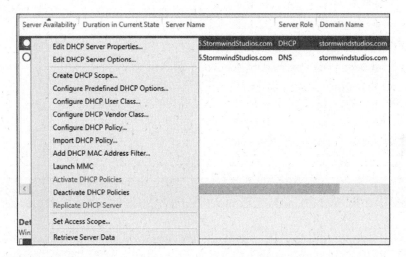

In Exercise 13.7, I will show you how to start configuring DHCP using IPAM. I will start by showing you how to use IPAM to create a new DHCP Scope.

EXERCISE 13.7

Creating a DHCP Scope

1. Open Server Manager.
2. Click on IPAM.
3. Click on DNS and DHCP Servers link under Monitor and Manage.
4. Right click on the DHCP server in the right hand window. Choose Create DHCP Scope (see Figure 13.16).
5. When the Create Scope wizard appears, fill in the following information (as seen in Figure 13.17).

   Scope Name: Scope1

   Description: Scope for Sybex Book

EXERCISE 13.7 *(continued)*

Start IP: 10.10.16.1

Ending IP: 10.10.31.254

Subnet Mask: 255.255.240.0

DHCP Lease: 8 Days

Activate Scope on Creation: NO

All DNS Settings leave blank.

> Under Scope Options, add the following information:
>
>> 003 Router: 10.10.10.1
>>
>> 006 DNS: 10.10.10.2

FIGURE 13.16   Create DHCP Scope

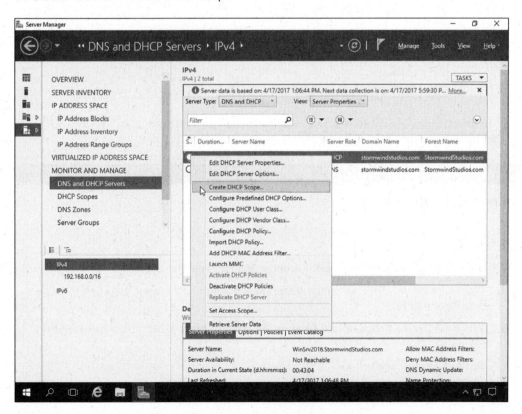

FIGURE 13.17   DHCP Scope settings

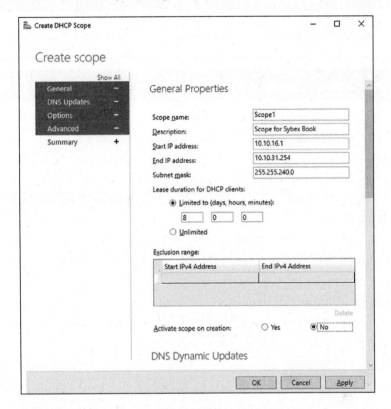

6. Once all the settings are completed, click OK.

7. Once the wizard completes, close Server Manager.

Now that you have setup your DHCP Scope using IPAM, now I will show you how to setup DHCP Policies. In Exercise 13.8, I will show you how to setup DHCP Policies for MAC addresses and lease times. What this will do for us is give us a shorter lease for any system with the same beginning MAC address.

EXERCISE 13.8

Setting Up DHCP Policies

1. Open Server Manager.

2. Click on IPAM.

3. Click on DNS and DHCP Servers link under Monitor and Manage.

4. Right click on the DHCP server in the right hand window. Choose Configure DHCP Policy (see Figure 13.18).

FIGURE 13.18   Configuring DHCP Policy

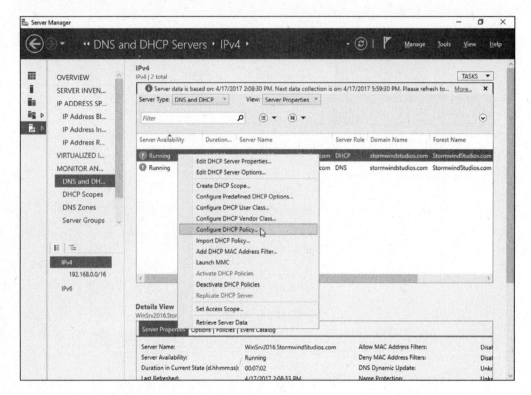

5. Fill in the following properties (see Figure 13.19):

    Name: Test Policy

    Description: DHCP Policy for Sybex Book

    Set lease duration for Policy Checked and set for 1 day

    Under Policy Conditions - Click the New button

    Criteria: MAC Address

    Operation: Equals

    Value: 462F68

    Use Wildcard (*): Checked

    Click the Add button next to Value. Then click the Add Condition button. Then hit the OK button.

FIGURE 13.19   DHCP Policy settings

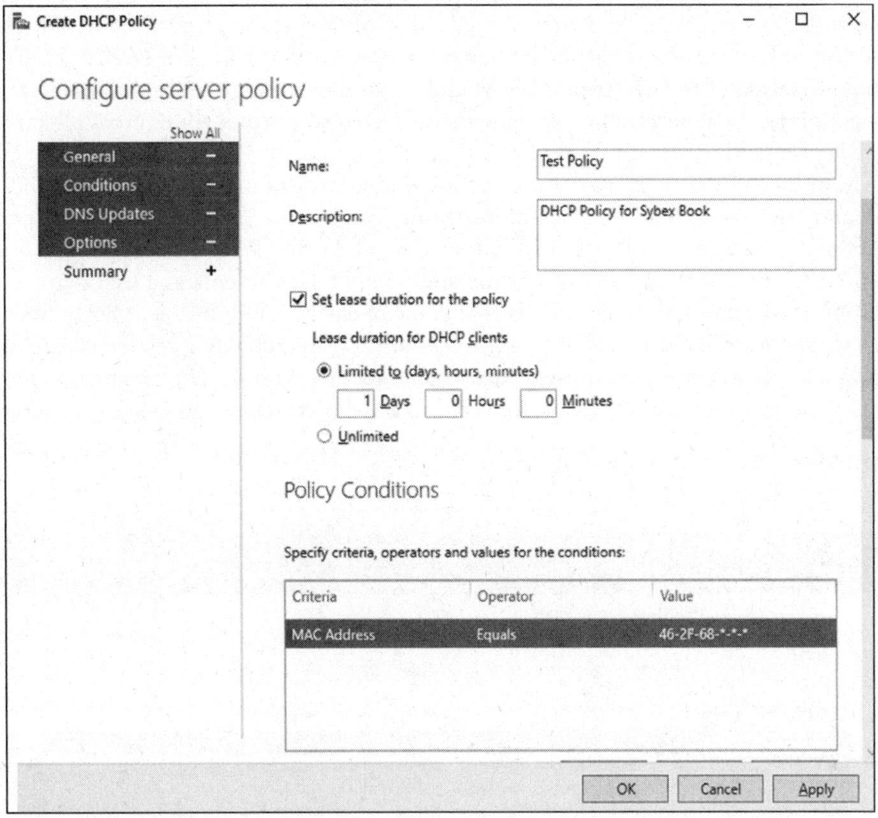

6.   Close Server Manager.

Now that I have shown you how to use IPAM to configure DNS and DHCP, I will now show you how to setup IPAM auditing.

IPAM Access and Auditing

It is essential for network administrators to be able to monitor and manage their IP address infrastructure well. This grows increasingly difficult as your network gets bigger and becomes more complex. Unfortunately, quite a few administrators still rely on spreadsheets and basic database applications for IP tracking and usage. The problem is that manual tracking is time-consuming and prone to error.

IPAM tracks the service status of the DNS and DHCP servers on the network. By aggregating multiple DHCP servers, the Multiserver Management (MSM) module enables an administrator to perform editing and configuration of important properties on multiple DHCP servers and scopes. It also facilitates surveillance and tracking of DHCP service status and utilization of DHCP scopes. IPAM allows for monitoring the condition of a DNS zone on multiple DNS servers by exposing the collected status of a zone across all authoritative DNS servers.

IPAM also comes with its own event catalog that allows administrators to track both DHCP and DNS correlated events. Administrators can use the event catalog to audit the changes performed on the DNS and DHCP servers, audit the IPAM address usage trail, monitor utilization of IP address space, and audit DHCP lease events and user logon events.

The nice thing about this event log is that you can easily search by client hostname, client ID, username, or IP address for a full list of both DNS and DHCP related events on that client. You can also export these event logs to an Excel workbook. The event catalog (see Figure 13.20) is found toward the bottom of the IPAM hierarchical navigation window.

FIGURE 13.20 IPAM event catalog

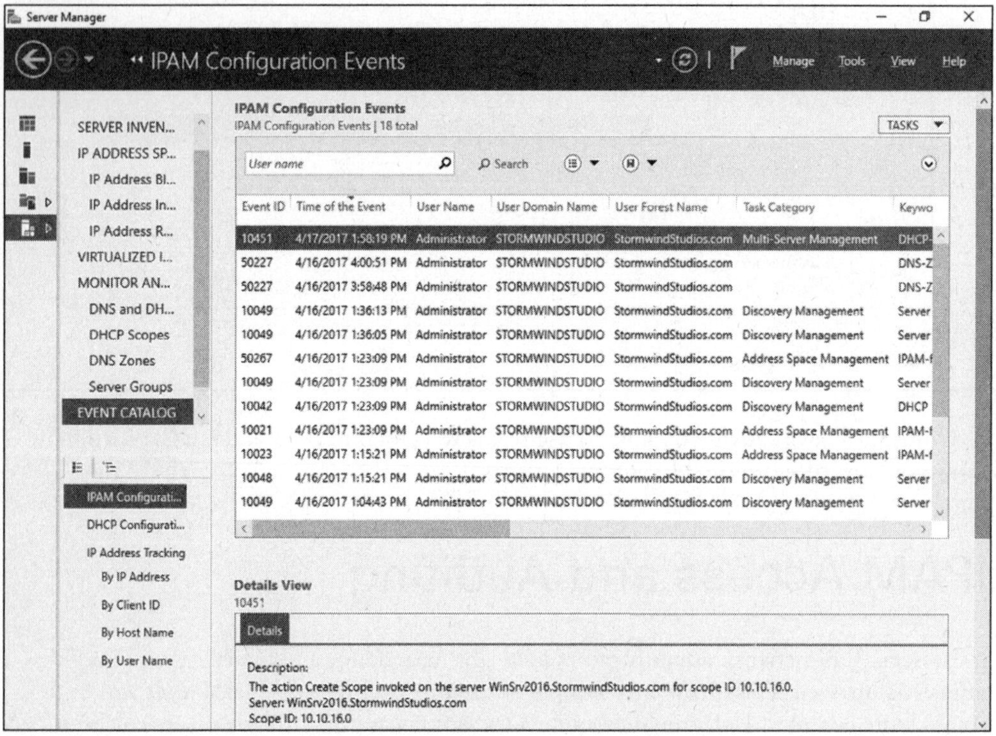

If you want to use the event catalog to check errors or issues with DNS and DHCP, click on the event message. You want to look at the event ID and the task category. You can enter these into TechNet or your favorite search engine and see what the event issue is and how to fix it.

When I first starting using TechNet in Windows NT 4.0, I learned how valuable it could be to help me locate and fix issues with my server. Microsoft still uses TechNet on the Internet, and you can search the event IDs and find out how to solve many of your issues.

 If you would like to use Microsoft TechNet, go to the following Microsoft website and enter your search in the search bar: `https://technet` `.microsoft.com/en-us/`.

Migrate to IPAM

There are two possible IPAM database storage solutions. An administrator can use either a Windows Internal Database (WID) or a dedicated Microsoft SQL Server instance for their IPAM configuration. For smaller networks, a WID backend will work just fine for the initial IPAM deployment. If in the future the need arises to expand past a WID to a SQL database, then you already know that IPAM comes with migration functionality just for that situation. The database configuration options are chosen during the provisioning steps of an IPAM deployment.

Fully deploy and test the capabilities of the IPAM feature set to help track and forecast IP address utilization within your organization. IPAM is a great way to discover, monitor, and manage all of the TCP/IP devices on your network.

The situation may arise in which you must migrate your IPAM database infrastructure either from a Windows Internal Database (WID) to a Microsoft SQL database or from one SQL server to another. Windows Server 2016 IPAM comes with the functionality to migrate an IPAM database via PowerShell. The Move-IpamDatabase cmdlet is used to complete this operation. When this cmdlet is run, a new IPAM schema is created, and then all of the IP address information is copied over. You can also use the Get-IpamDatabase cmdlet to review and compare pre- and post-database configuration settings during an IPAM database migration.

Delegate IPAM Administration

The delegation of IPAM administration is similar to the delegation of DNS. When IPAM is installed and provisioned, new security groups become available to administrators to configure role-based access control (RBAC) within your IPAM infrastructure. The five security groups for IPAM administration are as follows:

IPAM Administrators   Members of this group have full permissions to manage and administer an IPAM infrastructure.

IPAM IP Audit Administrators   Members of this group can perform common IPAM management tasks and can carry out IPAM audits.

IPAM ASM Administrators Members of this group can perform tasks related to IP address space management (ASM) functionality.

IPAM MSM Administrator Members of this group can perform tasks across multiple IPAM servers through the IPAM multiserver management (MSM) functionality.

IPAM Users Members of this group can only view information about server discovery, ASM, and MSM in IPAM. They can also view operational events, but they have no access to tracking or auditing information.

One new feature to Windows Server 2016 IPAM is the ability to configure Role Based Access Control using Windows PowerShell. IPAM also comes with an Access Control feature, which allows administrators to get even more granular with IPAM permissions by using up to eight different preconfigured roles.

You can also create your own custom IPAM administration roles for full IPAM permissions flexibility within your environment. Figure 13.21 illustrates the new Access Control panel for IPAM delegation of administration. Take the time to add and remove users from each of these groups and roles to get used to IPAM permission sets.

FIGURE 13.21 IPAM Access Control

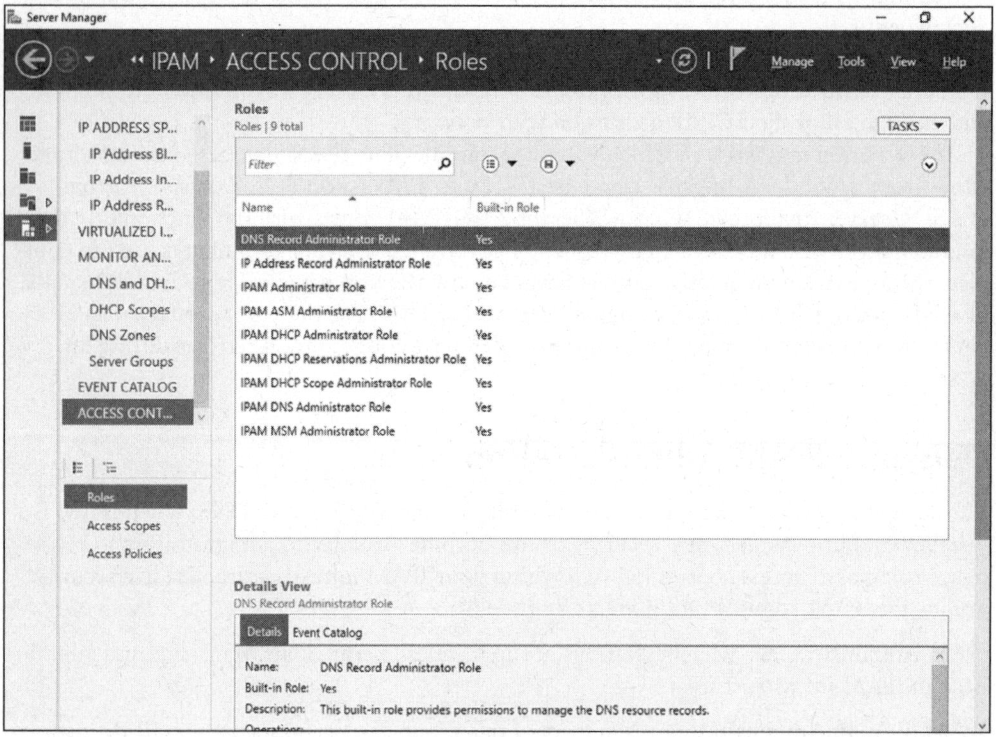

In Exercise 13.9, I will show you how to configure RBAC for IPAM using Server Manager.

EXERCISE 13.9

Configuring Role-Based Access Control

1. Open Server Manager.

2. Click on IPAM.

3. Click Access Control in the navigation window. Click Roles in the lower navigation window.

4. Right-click Roles and choose Add User Role (see Figure 13.22).

FIGURE 13.22   Add User Role

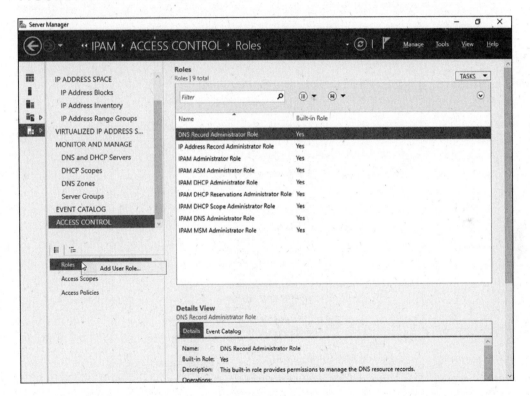

5. Fill in the following fields and check boxes (see Figure 13.23). Then click OK. In the Operations section, you can expand any of the operations and choose more fine-grained options. I am choosing a few random operations. You can choose whichever operations you want this account to have access to.

Name: IPAM_TeamMember

Description: IPAM Role for IT Team

EXERCISE 13.9 *(continued)*

Operations:

DHCP Server Operations

DHCP Scope Operations

DHCP Reservation Operations

DNS Zone Operations

IP Address Subnet Operations

IP Address Operations

DNS Server Operations

FIGURE 13.23 User Operations

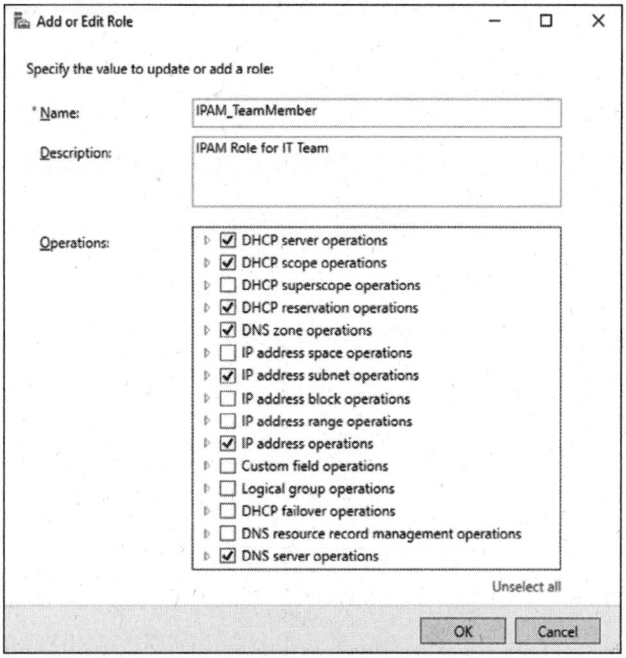

6. You should be able to see your new role under the Roles section. Close Server Manager.

Manage IPAM Collections

In IPAM, server groups are logical groups used to organize managed DHCP and DNS servers. Servers are members of a server group based on values of custom fields that are assigned to the server. Having servers of the same type sorted into their own IPAM collections makes it easier to manage your server lists within the IPAM Management Console. Drop-down menus will allow you to filter server and task lists by IPAM service categories such as DNS or DHCP servers.

Virtual Machine Manager and IPAM

IPAM gives you the ability to work with virtual machines and set up and monitor both physical and virtual IP address spaces. Inside the IPAM console, there is a link called Virtualized IP Address Space. Once you have clicked on this link, you can then add or view both customer and provider IP address spaces. For example, administrators have the ability to view logical networks under the Provider IP Address Space.

Administrators can also create a logical network within IPAM. To do this, an administrator would click Virtualized IP Address Space in the IPAM console and then right-click Provider IP Address Space in the lower navigation window. They would then choose Add IP Address Space and then need to fill in all of the fields.

 If you would like to see all the steps needed for creating a virtual and logical network, visit Microsoft's website at

`https://technet.microsoft.com/en-us/library/`
`dn783485(v=ws.11).aspx`

There may be times when you want to have your virtual machines and your IPAM server to work even more closely together. You can do this by integrating System Center Virtual Machine Manager (SCVMM) and IPAM. To do this, you need to first configure a user account (you must be part of the Administrators group or higher) that can be used on both the IPAM server and the System Center Virtual Machine Manager server. Then you need to configure the IPAM network service plug-in in VMM.

You must then give permission for the VMM server to be able to view and configure the IP address space in the IPAM server. The VMM server must also be able to perform management of the IPAM server remotely. To set this up, the VMM server uses the "Run As" account to achieve the permissions needed to configure the IPAM network service plug-in.

The following are the steps needed to create the VMM user account.

1. Open an elevated command prompt on the IPAM server. At the command prompt, type **lusrmgr.msc** and press Enter. This will open the Local Users and Groups MMC.

2. You need to create a new group. To do this, right-click Groups and choose New Group.

3. When the New Group dialog box appears, type **VMM Users** in the Group Name spot.

4. In the Enter The Object Names To Select section, click Add. Then type in the username of the user account that you will use for the VMM server and click OK.

5. Click Create to create the group and then click Close.

6. Close the Local Users and Groups MMC.

After the group is created, you need to next assign the necessary permissions to the VMM user account that you chose in the previous steps:

1. On the IPAM server, open Server Manager and choose the IPAM server console.

2. Choose Access Control in the upper navigation pane.

3. In the lower navigation windows, Right-click on Access Policies and then click Add Access Policy.

4. Click the Add button and then add the name of the VMM Users group that you created previously. Then click the OK button.

5. Next you need to click on Access Settings. Then click New and then from the drop-down list under Select Role, choose the IPAM ASM Administrator Role. Make sure the Global Access Scope is selected and then click the OK button.

6. Right-click Remote Management Users in the Local Users and Groups console, and then click Add to Group.

7. Next you will need to click the Add button and then type in the VMM user account under Enter the object names to select. Click the OK button.

8. Close the Remote Management Users Properties by clicking the OK button.

Finally, you need to configure the VMM server. To configure the server, you would need to complete the following steps:

1. Expand the Networking node in the Fabric workspace and then click Network Service.

2. Right-click Network Service and then click Add Network Service. This will start the Add Network Service Wizard.

3. On the Name page, type **IPAM** next to Name. You can add something to the Description field or leave it blank. Click Next.

4. The Manufacturer And Model screen is next. Choose Microsoft next to Manufacturer and choose Microsoft Windows Server IP Address Management next to the Model field. Click Next.

5. When the Credentials page appears, click the Browse button next to Run As Account. Click the Create Run As Account button.

6. When the Create Run As Account page appears, type a name for the account. I used VMM User1. Enter the username and password created earlier on the IPAM server. Click OK once you're finished.

7. At the Select A Run As Account dialog box, click the OK button to close. Click Next.

8. At the Connection String screen, enter the fully qualified domain name (FQDN) of the IPAM server. Then click Next.

9. The Provider screen will be next. Make sure the Microsoft IPAM Provider is chosen (at the Configuration provider field) and then click Test.

10. Make sure that there is a Passed message next to the Test open connection, Test capability discovery, and Test system info sections. Click Next.

11. On the Host Group screen, select the check box All Hosts. This enables IPAM integration with SCVMM. Click Next.

12. Click the Finish button at the Summary screen.

13. Make sure that the Completed status is next to the Add network service device and Create new RunAs Account fields. Close all applications.

Auditing IPAM

One of the nicest advantages to IPAM is the ability to audit the different services that you are monitoring. In today's complex IT world, we all have many different servers and applications that we are running to get our job done. We use Microsoft products and non-Microsoft products to accomplish the tasks that help our end users do their jobs more efficiently.

One of the issues that we have because of using all of these different servers and applications is knowing how they all operate and making sure we are keeping these products operating at max performance.

As an IT member today, you have to be a jack-of-all-trades when it comes to networking technologies. This is where auditing really comes into play. Being able to audit a server, services, or applications allows us to make sure that we are running these products the way they should be run.

Once you decide that you are going to be using IPAM for all of your IP based services, you now also get a single application to monitor all of these services.

IPAM allows you to audit the changes performed on the DNS and DHCP servers, audit the IPAM address usage trail, audit DHCP lease events, and audit user logon events (to just name a few).

This is very easy to do since we are using the same IPAM console that we have used for everything else IPAM related. That's the nice advantage. Normally if you want to audit these services, you have to open a different application. With IPAM, the auditing is located in the same console as the rest of the IPAM services.

IPAM allows you to audit all of the IPAM events using the Event Catalog (see Figure 13.24) or you can audit events just for the individual services like DHCP (see Figure 13.25).

In Exercise 13.10 I will show you how to configure auditing for IPAM using Server Manager. I will show you how to audit the changes performed on the DNS and DHCP servers, audit the IPAM address usage trail, audit DHCP lease events, and audit user logon events.

FIGURE 13.24 Event Catalog

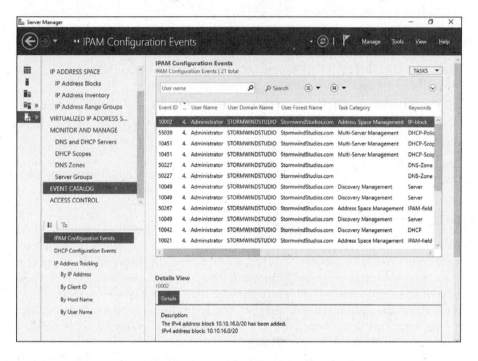

FIGURE 13.25 DHCP Event Catalog

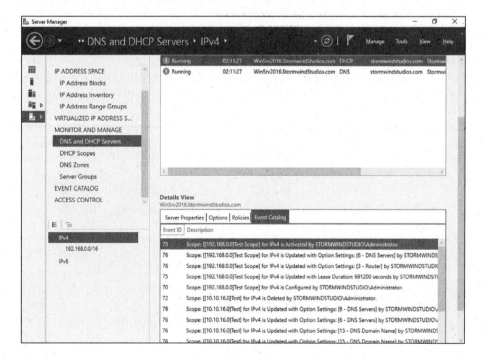

EXERCISE 13.10

Configuring Auditing

1. Open Server Manager.

2. Click on IPAM.

3. Click Event Catalog in the navigation window. In the right hand side under IPAM Configuration Event, you will see all of the IPAM configuration events that have been logged.

4. In the lower window, click on DHCP configuration events. This will show you any configuration changes made to the DHCP servers.

5. Now click on IP address tracking. This allows you to audit the IP address usage. You can search this By IP Address, By Client ID, By Host Name or By User Name. Click on any of the categories to view the DHCP events.

6. Under the Monitor and Manage section, click on DNS and DHCP servers. In the right hand windows, click either of the two servers and then choose Event Catalog under the Details View (see Figure 13.26). This allows you to monitor DNS and DHCP events independently. You can look at DHCP lease events or look at DNS zone events. It just depends on which server you are monitoring.

FIGURE 13.26 DNS Event Catalog

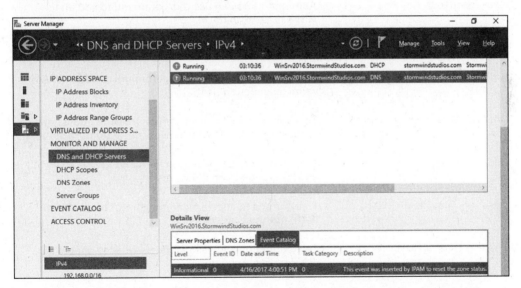

7. Under the Monitor and Manage section, you can choose any server that you want to monitor, including your domain controllers. Just click on the server and then choose Event Catalog under the Details View. You can search DCs for user logon information or you can choose NPS and see policy changes that were performed.

8. Once you are finished looking at all of the different servers you have in IPAM, close Server Manager.

PowerShell Commands for IPAM

As I have shown you in most chapters, PowerShell is a big part of the Microsoft management process. In Table 13.1, I will show you some of the possible PowerShell commands for IPAM.

For a complete list of IPAM PowerShell commands, please visit Microsoft's website at https://technet.microsoft.com/en-us/itpro/powershell/windows/ipamserver/ipamserver.

TABLE 13.1   PowerShell commands for IPAM

Command	Description
Add-IpamAddress	This command allows an administrator to add an IP address to IPAM.
Add-IpamAddressSpace	This command allows an administrator to add an address space to IPAM.
Add-IpamBlock	Administrators can use this command to add an IP address block to IPAM.
Add-IpamCustomField	This command is used to add a custom field to IPAM.
Add-IpamCustomValue	Administrators can use this command to add an IPAM value to a custom field.
Add-IpamDiscoveryDomain	This command allows an administrator to add a new domain in which IPAM discovers infrastructure servers.
Add-IpamRange	Administrators can use this command to add an IP address range to an IPAM server.
Disable-IpamCapability	This command allows an administrator to disable an IPAM optional capability.
Enable-IpamCapability	This command allows an administrator to enable an IPAM optional capability.
Export-IpamAddress	Administrators can use this command to export IP addresses from an IPAM server.

Command	Description
Export-IpamRange	Administrators can use this command to export all of the IP address ranges.
Export-IpamSubnet	This command allows an administrator to export the subnets of an IP address.
Find-IpamFreeAddress	This command will show you the available subnets for allocation, given an IP block, prefix length, and number of requested subnets.
Get-IpamAddress	This command shows an administrator a requested IP addresses from IPAM.
Get-IpamAddressSpace	This command shows an administrator an address spaces in IPAM.
Get-IpamBlock	This command shows an administrator a set of address blocks from IPAM.
Get-IpamDatabase	Administrators can use this command to view the IPAM database configuration settings.
Get-IpamDhcpScope	Administrators can use this command to view DHCP scopes on an IPAM server.
Get-IpamDhcpServer	This command allows an administrator to view DHCP server information from an IPAM database.
Get-IpamDnsResourceRecord	Administrators can use this command to view DNS resource records in an IPAM database.
Get-IpamDnsServer	This command allows an administrator to view DNS server information from an IPAM database.
Get-IpamDnsZone	This command allows an administrator to view DNS zone information from an IPAM database.
Get-IpamIpAddressAuditEvent	Administrators can use this command to view IP address audit events in IPAM.
Import-IpamAddress	This command allows an admin to import an IP address into the IPAM server.
Import-IpamRange	This command allows an admin to import an IP address range into the IPAM server.

TABLE 13.1 PowerShell commands for IPAM *(continued)*

Command	Description
Import-IpamSubnet	This command allows an admin to import an IP address subnet into the IPAM server.
Invoke-IpamGpoProvisioning	Administrators can create and link IPAM group policies (GPOs) for provisioning.
Move-IpamDatabase	This command allows an admin to move an IPAM database to a SQL Server database.
Remove-IpamAddress	Administrators use this command on an IPAM server to remove a set of IP addresses.
Remove-IpamAddressSpace	Administrators use this command on an IPAM server to remove a set of IP address spaces.
Set-IpamAccessScope	This command allows an administrator to set up an IPAM access scope.
Set-IpamAddress	Administrators can use this command to configure an IP address in IPAM.
Set-IpamAddressSpace	Administrators can use this command to configure an IP address space in IPAM.
Set-IpamBlock	Administrators can use this command to configure an IP address block in IPAM.
Set-IpamConfiguration	Administrators can adjust the configuration of a computer that hosts the IPAM server.
Set-IpamDatabase	This command allows an administrator to change the settings on how IPAM connects to the IPAM database.
Set-IpamDiscoveryDomain	Administrators use this command to change the IPAM discovery configuration.
Set-IpamRange	This command is used to modify an existing IP address range.
Set-IpamSubnet	This command is used to modify an existing IP subnet.
Update-IpamServer	Administrators can use this command to update the IPAM server after an operating system upgrade.

Summary

This chapter talked about the advanced configuration options of IPAM. You learned step-by-step how to configure core network services and features using the IPAM console. IPAM allows an administrator to manage TCP/IP network services easily in a large or complex environment.

I showed you how to install and configure IPAM. I explained how you need to setup the required GPOs using PowerShell and the different types of role-based administration IPAM allows.

Understanding how DHCP, DNS, and IPAM all work together is essential for ensuring success when taking the exam. Focus your attention on completing the labs found within the chapter and learning the ins and outs of managing TCP/IP services using IPAM administration.

Exam Essentials

Understand IP Address Management.   IPAM allows administrators to track and audit IP addresses through the use of the IPAM console. IPAM allows IP addresses to be tracked using DHCP lease events and user logon events.

Know how to provision IPAM and configure server discovery.   IPAM is managed and monitored in Server Manager. Know that there are two separate provisioning models—manual and GPO—and know how to configure each. Know how to configure IPAM server discovery.

Know how to delegate IPAM administration.   Active Directory has specific security groups for IPAM. IPAM has its own internal delegation of administration. A user does not need to be a member of the Domain Admins group in order to manage IPAM.

Video Resources

There are videos available for the following exercises:

    Exercise 13.1

    Exercise 13.2

    Exercise 13.3

You can access the videos at http://sybextestbanks.wiley.com on the Other Study Tools tab.

Review Questions

1. You are the network administrator for your company. You need to use a PowerShell command to configure an IP address block in IPAM. What command do you use?

   A. `Set-IpamIP`

   B. `Set-IpamBlock`

   C. `Set-IPBlock`

   D. `Set-IPAddressBlock`

2. You are the network administrator for your company. You need to use a PowerShell command to add an IP address range to an IPAM server. What command do you use?

   A. `Get-IpRange`

   B. `Set-IpRange`

   C. `Add-IpamRange`

   D. `Set-IPBlock`

3. You are the administrator for StormWind Studios online training company. You need to change the IPAM discovery configuration. What PowerShell command do you use?

   A. `Get-IpamDiscovery`

   B. `Get-IpamDiscoveryDomain`

   C. `Set-IpamDiscovery`

   D. `Set-IpamDiscoveryDomain`

4. You are the network administrator for a large training company. You need to view the DNS zone information from the IPAM database. What PowerShell command do you use?

   A. `Get-IpamDnsZone`

   B. `Add-IpamDnsZone`

   C. `Set-IpamDnsZone`

   D. `View-IpamDnsZone`

5. You are the administrator for StormWind Studios. You are installing and configuring IPAM. You have already installed IPAM and now you need to set up the GPOs for IPAM Provisioning. What PowerShell command creates the Provisioned GPOs needed for IPAM to function properly?

   A. `Get-IpamGpoProvisioning`

   B. `Add-IpamGpoProvisioning`

   C. `Invoke-IpamGpoProvisioning`

   D. `Set-IpamGpoProvisioning`

6. You are the infrastructure team lead for a high-tech hardware development company. You need to delegate some of the team's IPAM administration responsibilities between team members. You decide that Noelle will be managing IPAM address spaces, but she will not

be managing IP address tracking and auditing. Which IPAM security group would best fit Noelle's new responsibilities?

A. IPAM Administrators

B. IPAM Users

C. IPAM ASM Administrators

D. IPAM MSM Administrators

7. You are the network administrator for a large communications company. You have recently decided to implement IPAM within your organization with the release of Windows Server 2016. You want to set up your IPAM infrastructure so that one primary server can manage your entire enterprise. Which IPAM deployment method would fulfill this requirement?

A. Isolated

B. Centralized

C. Hybrid

D. Distributed

8. You are the administrator of a company who is using IPAM. You need to change the IPAM GPO prefix. What command would you use?

A. `Set-IPAMConfiguration`

B. `Set-IPAM`

C. `Get-IPAMConfiguration`

D. `Get-IPAM`

9. You are the lead network administrator for a web hosting company. You have recently made the decision to implement IPAM within your organization. You have already installed and provisioned the IPAM feature on your dedicated Windows Server 2016 server. What is the next logical step in your IPAM deployment?

A. Create a new IP block.

B. Delegate IPAM administration.

C. Configure server discovery.

D. Create a new IP range.

10. You are a system administrator for the Stellacon Corporation. Because of the unusual growth of TCP/IP devices on your corporate network over the last year, you need to scale out your IPAM database capabilities. You are currently using a Windows Internal Database (WID) for your IPAM infrastructure, and you want to migrate your IPAM database to a Microsoft SQL Server. Which PowerShell cmdlet would you use to verify current IPAM database configuration settings?

A. `Move-IpamDatabase`

B. `Show-IpamDatabaseConfig`

C. `Show-IpamStatistics`

D. `Get-IpamMigrationSettings`

Chapter

14

Configuring Network Access

THE FOLLOWING 70-741 EXAM OBJECTIVES ARE COVERED IN THIS CHAPTER:

✓ **Implement network connectivity solutions**

- This objective may include but is not limited to: Implement Network Address Translation (NAT); configure routing.

✓ **Implement virtual private network (VPN) and DirectAccess solutions**

- This objective may include but is not limited to: Implement remote access and site-to-site (S2S) VPN solutions using remote access gateway; configure different VPN protocol options; configure authentication options; configure VPN reconnect; create and configure connection profiles; determine when to use remote access VPN and site-to-site VPN and configure appropriate protocols; install and configure DirectAccess; implement server requirements; implement client configuration; troubleshoot DirectAccess; Configure Network Access Protection (NAP).

✓ **Implement Network Policy Server (NPS)**

- This objective may include but is not limited to: Configure a RADIUS server including RADIUS proxy; configure RADIUS clients; configure NPS templates; configure RADIUS accounting; configure certificates; configure Connection Request Policies; configure network policies for VPN and wireless and wired clients; import and export NPS policies.

So in the first few chapters, I talked about using TCP/IP and the services that help support TCP/IP. Now I will show you how to access your network both locally and remotely.

Routing and Remote Access Services (RRAS) includes some security features necessary to provide remote access effectively. For example, you'll probably want the ability to restrict user dial-up access by group membership, time of day, or other factors. You'll also need a way to specify the various callback, authentication, and encryption options that the protocols support.

In this chapter, you'll learn about *virtual private networks (VPNs)*, which provide remote access to private networks across public connections. That is, using the Internet, clients can dial in to an Internet service provider (ISP) and connect to your private network.

The main benefit of VPNs is reduced cost because it means that long-distance calls are unnecessary. VPNs are becoming more popular because of the increased popularity of high-speed Internet connections, such as cable and digital subscriber line (DSL) connections.

I will also talk to you about a VPN replacement called DirectAccess. DirectAccess allows a user to remotely access your network without the need for the user to initiate the remote connection.

I will also talk about how to protect your network by using the Network Policy Server. Network Policy Server allows you to put rules on the way your users access your network.

Before I can get into the details of what these features do and how to configure them to provide remote access for your network, you need to understand some of the basic terms and concepts specific to RRAS. That's where you'll begin in this chapter, and then you'll move on to learning about the features and configuration settings that you need to understand to meet the exam objectives.

Overview of Dial-Up Networking

LANs provide relatively high-speed connectivity to attached machines, but where does that leave those of us who work from home, who travel, or who need to access data on a remote computer? Until wireless access is available worldwide, we have the option of using dial-up networking in which the client computer uses a modem to dial in and connect to a remote server. Once the connection is established, a variety of protocols and services make it possible for us to view web pages, transfer files and email, and do pretty much anything we could do with a hardwired LAN connection, albeit at a reduced speed.

In the following sections, you will learn more about what dial-up networking does and how it works by examining the specific technologies and protocols associated with remote access.

What DUN Does

At this point in the book, you should understand that Windows Server 2016 network protocols are actually implemented as drivers. These drivers normally work with hardware network interfaces to get data from point A to point B. How do dial-up connections fit in? Many people may read this and say, "Who still uses dial-up?" Well, as a person who lives in New Hampshire, I can tell you that we still have many areas that can't get broadband or even satellite access.

Think back to the OSI model. Each layer has a function, and each layer serves as an intermediary between the layer above it and the one below it. By substituting one driver for another at some level in the stack, you can dramatically change how things work. That's exactly what the Windows Server 2016's *Dial-Up Networking (DUN)* subsystem does. It makes the dial-up connection appear to be just another network adapter.

The DUN driver takes care of the task of making a slow asynchronous modem appear to work just like a fast LAN interface. Applications and services that use TCP/IP on your DUN connection never know the difference. In fact, you can configure Windows Server 2016 to use your primary connection first and then to pass traffic over a secondary connection (such as a dial-up link) if the primary connection is down. This does not affect the applications with which you're working (except that they might run more slowly).

Depending on how you configure the DUN server, users who dial in can see the whole network or only specific resources on the server. You also get to control who can log on, when they can log on, and what they can do once they've logged on. As far as Windows Server 2016 is concerned, a user connected via DUN is no different from one using resources over your LAN, so all the access controls and permissions you apply remain in force for DUN users.

How DUN Works

A lot of pieces are required to complete a dial-up call successfully from your computer to a server at another physical location. Understanding what these pieces are, how they work, and what they do for you is important. The following sections will cover the DUN infrastructure, how the *Point-to-Point Protocol (PPP)* helps with this connection, the relationship between PPP and the network protocols, and how multilink can be used to increase the speed and efficiency of your remote connections.

The DUN Infrastructure

This section covers the physical layer that underlies voice and data calls. Most of the following material will be familiar to anyone who has ever used a modem, but you should still understand the details you may not have considered before.

Plain Old Telephone Service

Plain Old Telephone Service (POTS) connections offer a theoretical maximum speed of 56 Kbps; in practice, many users routinely get connections at 51 Kbps or 52 Kbps.

The word *modem* is actually short for *modulator-demodulator*. The original Bell System modems took digital data and modulated it into screechy analog audio tones suitable for use on regular phone lines. Because phone lines are purposely designed to pass only the low end of the audible frequency range that most can hear, the amount of data was limited. However, in the early 1990s, an engineer discovered that you could communicate much faster when the path between the sender and receiver was all digital.

An all-digital path doesn't have any analog components that induce signal loss, so it preserves the original signal quality faithfully. This in turn makes it possible to put more information into the original signal. As it happens, phone companies nationwide were in the process of making major upgrades to replace their analog equipment with newer and better digital equivalents. These upgrades made it possible for people in most areas to get almost 56 Kbps speeds without changing any of the wiring in their homes or offices. The connection between the house and the phone office was still analog, but the connections between phone offices were digital, ensuring high-quality connections.

Integrated Services Digital Network

In the mid-1970s, *Integrated Services Digital Network (ISDN)* was designed. At the time, no one had any idea that you'd be able to get 56 Kbps speeds out of an ordinary phone line. ISDN speeds of up to 128 Kbps over a single pair of copper wires seemed pretty revolutionary. In addition, ISDN had features such as call forwarding, caller ID, and multiple directory numbers (so you could have more than one number, perhaps with different ringing patterns, associated with a single line).

Unfortunately, ISDN requires an all-digital signal path. It also requires special equipment on both ends of the connection. The phone companies were slow to promote ISDN as a faster alternative to regular dial-up service, so customers avoided it.

ISDN still has some advantages, though. Because it's all digital, call setup times are much shorter than they are for analog modems—it takes only about half a second to establish a new ISDN call. Modern ISDN adapters and ISDN-capable routers can seamlessly stitch together multiple ISDN channels to deliver bandwidth in 64 Kbps increments. Because you can use ISDN lines for regular analog voice, data, and fax traffic, you can make a single ISDN act like two voice lines, a single 128 Kbps data line, or a 64 Kbps data line plus a voice line.

   ISDN is quickly being replaced by faster broadband services such as DSL and cable modems. In fact, you should resort to ISDN only if these other solutions are not available in your area. Note that DSL (a misnomer because they are all digital) and cable modems do not use PPP (discussed later), so they are technically not considered dial-up connections.

Other Connection Methods

Any other on-demand connection that's established using the Point-to-Point Protocol can be thought of as a dial-up connection, and Windows Server 2016 doesn't make any distinction between POTS, ISDN, and other dial-ups—they're all treated identically.

Connecting with PPP

The Point-to-Point Protocol enables any two devices to establish a TCP/IP connection over a serial link. That usually means a dial-up modem connection, but it could just as easily be a direct serial cable connection, an infrared connection, or any other type of serial connection. When one machine dials another, the machine that initiates the connection is referred to as a *client*, and the machine that receives the call is referred to as a *server*—even though PPP itself makes no such distinction.

PPP negotiation involves three phases that are required to establish a remote access connection. Actually, at least six distinct protocols run on top of PPP. Understanding what they do helps to make the actual PPP negotiation process clearer. These protocols are as follows:

The Link Control Protocol   The *Link Control Protocol (LCP)* handles the details of establishing and configuring the lowest-level PPP link. In that regard, you can think of LCP as if it were almost part of the Physical layer. When one PPP device calls another, the devices use LCP to agree that they want to establish a PPP connection.

The Challenge Handshake Authentication Protocol   *The Challenge Handshake Authentication Protocol (CHAP)*—as well as MS-CHAPv2 and PAP—allow the client to authenticate itself to the server. This authentication functions much like a regular network logon; once the client presents its logon credentials, the server can figure out what access to grant.

The Callback Control Protocol   The *Callback Control Protocol (CBCP)* is used to negotiate whether a callback is required, whether it's permitted, and when it happens. Once the client has authenticated itself, the server can decide whether it should hang up and call the client back. The client can also request a callback at a number it provides. Although this isn't as secure as having the server place a call to a predetermined number, it provides some additional flexibility. If a callback occurs, the connection is reestablished and reauthenticated, but the CBCP stage is skipped.

The Compression Control Protocol   The *Compression Control Protocol (CCP)* allows the two sides of the connection to determine what kind of compression, if any, they want to use on the network data. Because PPP traffic actually consists of wrapped-up IP datagrams and because IP datagram headers tend to be fairly compressible, negotiating effective compression can significantly improve overall PPP throughput.

The IP Control Protocol   At this point in the call, the two sides have agreed to authentication, compression, and a callback. They haven't yet agreed on what IP parameters to use for the connection. These parameters, which include the maximum packet size to be sent over the link (the *maximum transmission unit*, or *MTU*), have a great impact on the overall link performance, so the client and server use the *IP Control Protocol (IPCP)* to negotiate them based on the traffic they expect to be passed.

The Internet Protocol   Once the IPCP negotiation has been completed, each end has complete knowledge of how to communicate with its peer. That knowledge allows the two sides to begin exchanging Internet Protocol (IP) datagrams over the link, just as they would over a standard LAN connection.

The Relationship Between PPP and Network Protocols

Usually, when you hear about network communication, you hear about using TCP/IP on a hardwired LAN. How does this protocol fit in with PPP? In the case of TCP/IP, that's an easy question to answer: The client routes all (or some) of its outgoing TCP/IP traffic to its PPP peer, which can then inspect the IP datagrams it gets back from the PPP stack to analyze and route them properly.

Windows Server 2016 supports only TCP/IP, so consider what has to happen when a client using AppleTalk needs to connect via dial-up. Because the server will not use those other protocols, it will drop the call or cause the client to warn its user (that's what Windows Server 2016 does). After the other PPP setup steps are finished, the client and server can wrap other types of network traffic inside an IP datagram. This process, called *encapsulation*, allows the client to take a packet with some kind of private content, wrap it inside an IP datagram, and send it to the server. The server, in turn, processes the IP datagram, routing real datagrams normally and handling any encapsulated packets with the appropriate protocol. At that point, the client can communicate with the server without knowing that its non-TCP/IP packets are being encapsulated in any way—that detail is hidden deep in the layers of the OSI model.

Understanding the Benefits of Multilink

Many parts of the world don't have high-speed broadband access yet. In fact, many places don't have ISDN or even phone lines that support 56 Kbps modems. The *multilink extensions* to the Point-to-Point Protocol provide a way to take several independent PPP connections and make them look like one line so that they act as a single connection.

For example, if you use two phone lines and modems to place a two-line multilink call to your ISP, instead of getting the usual 48 Kbps connection, you would end up with an apparent bandwidth of 96 Kbps. The multilink PPP software on your Windows Server 2016 machine and on the ISP's router takes care of stringing all of the packets together to make this process seamless. Windows Server 2012's RRAS supports multilink PPP for inbound and outbound calls.

 The primary drawback to multilink calls is that they take up more than one phone line apiece.

Overview of Virtual Private Networks

Private networks offer superior security. You own the wires, so you have control over what they're used for, who can use them, and what kind of data passes over them. However, they're not very flexible because they require you to configure and manage costly leased lines between remote locations. To make things worse, most private networks face a dilemma: Implementing enough capacity to handle peak loads almost guarantees that much of that capacity will remain idle much of the time, even though it still has to be paid for.

One way to work around this problem is to maintain private dial-up services. Such services allow, for example, a field rep in Chicago to dial into the home office in Boston. But dial-ups are expensive, and they have the same excess capacity problem as truly private networks. As an added detriment, someone has to pay long-distance or toll-free number charges.

Virtual private networks (VPNs) offer a solution. You get the security of a true private network with the flexibility, ubiquity, and low cost of the Internet. In the following sections, I will cover VPNs, including what they are used for and how they work (in general and with Windows Server 2016).

What VPNs Do

At any time, two parties can create a connection over the Internet. The idea behind a VPN is that you can use these connections to let two parties establish an *encrypted tunnel* between them using the Internet as a transportation medium. The VPN software on each end takes care of encrypting the VPN packets as they go; when the packets leave one end of the tunnel, their payloads are encrypted and encapsulated inside regular IP packets that cause them to be delivered to the remote machine. Figure 14.1 shows one way to conceptualize this process.

FIGURE 14.1   Drilling a tunnel through the Internet

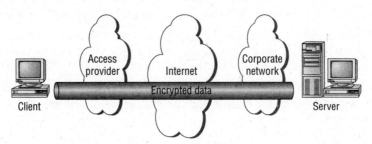

As an example, let's say you're in the field at a client site. As long as you're somewhere that your ISP serves, you can dial into the client's local point of presence and get connected to the Internet. At that point, you can open a VPN connection back to the servers at your office and do whatever you could do when sitting in front of a regular desktop machine.

VPNs and Windows Server 2016

Windows Server 2016 includes support for Microsoft's proprietary *Point-to-Point Tunneling Protocol* and Layer 2 Tunneling Protocol. *Layer 2 Tunneling Protocol (L2TP)* provides a more generic tunneling mechanism than PPTP, and when combined with IPsec, L2TP also allows you to establish VPNs using a wide range of Microsoft or non-Microsoft hardware and software products, including routers and access devices from companies such as Cisco, Red Creek, and Nortel.

Windows Server 2016's VPN support includes the following worthwhile features:

- You can set up account lockout policies for dial-up and VPN users. This capacity has existed for network and console users for some time.

- The *Extensible Authentication Protocol (EAP)* allows Microsoft or third parties to write modules that implement new authentication methods and retrofit them to servers. One example is the EAP-TLS module, which implements access control based on smart cards and certificates for VPN and dial-up users.

How you enable VPN support on your Windows Server 2016 machine depends on whether you're using a server or a client (Windows XP, Windows Vista, Windows 7, Windows 8, and so on).

Client configuration is easy. Just install the Dial-Up Networking service and then use the Make New Connection Wizard to create a new VPN connection. On the server side, you'll need to install and configure RRAS and then enable it to accept incoming VPN connections.

How VPNs Work

The VPN client assumes that the VPN server is already connected to the Internet in some way. Here's how the VPN connection process works:

1. The client establishes a connection to the Internet. Dial-up networking or any other connection method can be used for this connection. The client must be able to send packets to the Internet.

2. The client sends a VPN connection request to the server. The exact format of the request varies, depending on whether the VPN is using PPTP, L2TP, or SSTP.

3. The client authenticates itself to the server. Again, the exact process varies according to the VPN protocol in use. If the client can't provide valid credentials, the connection is terminated.

4. The client and server negotiate parameters for the VPN session. This negotiation allows the two ends to agree on an encryption algorithm and strength.

5. The client and server go through the PPP negotiation process because both L2TP and PPTP depend on the lower-level PPP.

Because the contents of data passed around in step 2 and step 3 vary according to the tunneling protocol in use, I'll explain the differences. First, though, you should understand encapsulation and how VPNs use it to wrap one kind of data inside another.

An Encapsulation Primer

Most of yesterday's networks could carry only one kind of data. Each network vendor had its own protocol, and most of the time there was no way to intermingle data using different protocols on the same line. Over time, vendors began to find ways to allow a single network to carry many different types of traffic, resulting in the current assortment of traffic types found on most large networks. However, the Internet works only with IP, which is why it's called *Internet Protocol*. If you need to send other types of traffic, such as AppleTalk, across the Internet, you can encapsulate it within IP.

How does encapsulation work? Software at each level of the OSI model has to see header information to figure out where a packet is coming from and where it's going. However, the payload contents aren't important to most of those components, and the payload is what's encapsulated. By fabricating the right kind of header and prepending it for whatever you want in the payload, you can route foreign traffic types through IP networks with no trouble.

VPNs depend on encapsulation because their security method depends on being able to keep the payload information encrypted. The following steps demonstrate what happens to a typical packet as it goes from being a regular IP datagram to a PPTP packet (see Figure 14.2).

FIGURE 14.2   The encapsulation process

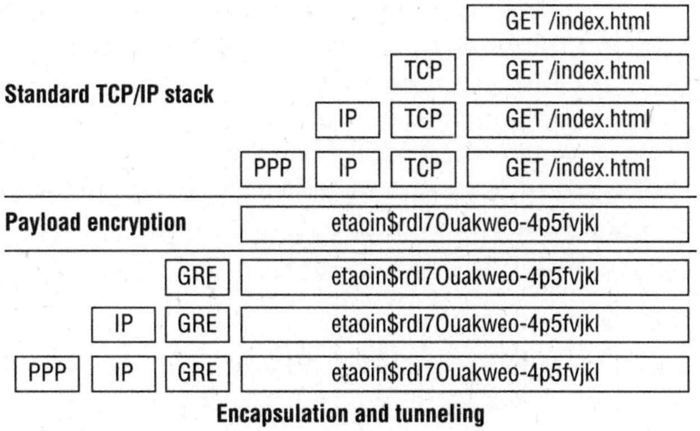

1. An application creates a block of data bound for a remote host. In this case, it's a web browser.

2. The client-side IP stack takes the application's data and turns it into an IP packet, first by adding a TCP header and then by adding an IP header. This is called the *IP datagram* because it contains all of the necessary addressing information to be delivered by IP.

3. The client is connected via PPP, so it adds a PPP header to the IP datagram. This PPP+IP combination is called a *PPP frame.*

4. If you are using PPP instead of a VPN protocol, the packet goes across the PPP link without further modification. When you are using a VPN (as in this example), the next step is for the VPN to encrypt the PPP frame, turning it into unreadable information to be transported over the Internet.

5. A *Generic Routing Encapsulation (GRE) header* is combined with the encrypted payload. GRE really is generic; in this case, the protocol ID field in the GRE header says that this is an encapsulated PPTP packet.

6. Now that there is a tag to tell you what's in the payload, the PPTP stack can add an IP header (specifying the destination address of the VPN server) and a PPP header.

7. Now the packet can be sent out over your PPP connection. The IP header specifies that it should be routed to the VPN server.

8. When the packet arrives at the VPN server, the server reverses steps 1 through 6 to extract the payload.

Encapsulation allows the use of VPN data inside ordinary-looking IP datagrams, which is part of what makes VPNs so powerful—you don't have to change any of your applications, routers, or network components (unless they have to be configured to recognize and pass GRE packets).

PPTP Tunneling

PPTP is a pretty straightforward protocol. It works by encapsulating packets using the mechanism described in the previous section, "An Encapsulation Primer," and performs encryption (step 4) using the *Microsoft Point-to-Point Encryption (MPPE) algorithm.* The encryption keys used to encrypt the packets are generated dynamically for each connection; in fact, the keys can be changed periodically during the connection.

When the client and server have successfully established a PPTP tunnel, the authorization process begins. This process is an exchange of credentials that allows the server to decide whether the client is permitted to connect:

1. The server sends a challenge message to the client.

2. The client answers with an encrypted response.

3. The server checks the response to see whether the answer is right. The challenge-response process allows the server to determine which account is trying to make a connection.

4. The server determines whether the user account is authorized to make a connection.

5. If the account is authorized, the server accepts the inbound connection; any access controls or remote access restrictions still apply.

L2TP/IPsec Tunneling

L2TP is much more flexible than PPTP, but it's also more complicated. It was designed to be a general-purpose tunneling protocol not limited to VPN use.

L2TP itself doesn't offer any kind of security. When you use L2TP, you're setting up an unencrypted, unauthenticated tunnel. Using L2TP by itself over the Internet, therefore, would be dangerous because anyone who wanted to could read your traffic.

The overall flow of an L2TP/IPsec tunnel session looks a little different from that of a PPTP session because IPsec security is different. Here's how the L2TP/IPsec combination works:

1. The client and server establish an IPsec security association using the ISAKMP and Oakley protocols. At this point, the two machines have an encrypted channel between them.

2. The client builds a new L2TP tunnel to the server. Because this happens after the channel has been encrypted, there's no security risk.

3. The server sends an authentication challenge to the client.

4. The client encrypts its answer to the challenge and returns it to the server.

5. The server checks the challenge response to see whether it's valid; if so, the server can determine which account is connecting. At this point, the server can accept the inbound connection, subject to whatever access policies you've put in place.

Note that steps 3 through 5 mirror the steps described for PPTP tunneling. This is because the authorization process is a function of the remote access server, not the VPN stack. All the VPN does is to provide a secure communications channel, and something else has to decide who gets to use it.

SSTP Tunneling

The *Secure Sockets Tunneling Protocol (SSTP)* is a secure way to make a VPN connection using the Secure Sockets Layer v.3 (SSL) port 443. The following steps show how SSTP operates and functions:

1. The client connects to the server through the Internet using port 443.

2. During the TCP session, SSL negotiation takes place.

3. During the SSL authentication phase, the client machine receives the server certificate.

4. The client machine will send HTTPS requests on top of the encrypted SSL session.

5. The client machine will then also send SSTP control packets on top of the HTTPS session.

6. PPP negotiation now takes place on both ends of the connection.

7. After PPP is finished, both ends are ready to send IP packets to each other.

Configuring Your Remote Access Server

Most of the configuration necessary for a remote access server happens at the server level. You use the server's Properties dialog box to control whether the server allows remote connections, what protocols and options it supports, and so forth. Because all of the protocols are carried via PPP, you can set some generic PPP options as well. I will cover these options in the following sections. You also have to configure settings for your users, which you'll read about in the next section, and you will install and configure the Remote Access role for the server in the first exercise.

Configuring PPP Options

You can use the PPP tab of the RRAS server's Properties dialog box (see Figure 14.3) to control the PPP layer options available to clients that call in. The settings you specify here control whether the related PPP options are available to clients; you can use remote access policies to control whether individual connections can use them.

FIGURE 14.3   The PPP tab of the RRAS server's Properties dialog box

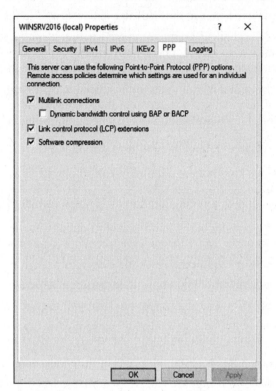

This tab has four check boxes:

- The Multilink Connections check box, which is selected by default, controls whether the server will allow clients to establish multilink connections when they call in.

- The Dynamic Bandwidth Control Using BAP Or BACP check box determines whether clients and servers are allowed to add or remove links dynamically during a multilink session. If you enable this feature, you can throttle the amount of available bandwidth up or down on demand. It's available only when the Multilink Connections check box is selected. (BAP stands for Bandwidth Allocation Protocol, and BACP stands for Bandwidth Allocation Control Protocol.)

- The Link Control Protocol (LCP) is used to establish a PPP link and negotiate its settings. A variety of LCP extensions are defined in various RFCs; these extensions allow a client and server to agree dynamically about which protocols are being passed back and forth, among other things. The Link Control Protocol (LCP) Extensions check box controls whether these extensions are available. Windows 9x, NT, 2000, Vista, XP, Windows 7, Windows 8/8.1, and Windows 10 clients depend on the LCP extensions, so you should leave this check box selected.

- The Software Compression check box controls whether RRAS will allow a remote client to use the Compression Control Protocol (CCP) to compress PPP traffic. In some cases, hardware compression at the modem level is more efficient, but not everyone has a compression-capable modem. You should leave this check box selected as well.

Configuring IP-Based Connections

TCP/IP is far and away the most commonly used remote access protocol; coincidentally, it's also the most configurable of the protocols that Windows Server 2016 supports. Both of these facts are reflected in the IPv4 and IPv6 tabs of the server's Properties dialog box. Figure 14.4 shows the IPv4 tab.

FIGURE 14.4   The IPv4 tab of the RRAS server's Properties dialog box

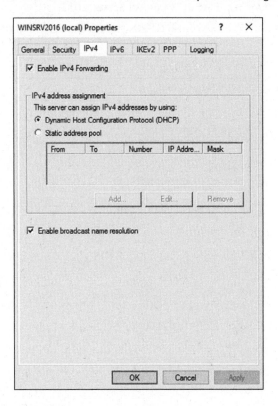

The controls on the IPv4 tab do the following:

- The Enable IPv4 Forwarding check box controls whether RRAS will route IPv4 packets between the remote client and other interfaces on your RRAS server. When this box is checked, as it is by default, remote clients' packets can go to the RRAS server or to any other host to which the RRAS server has a route. To allow clients to access resources on the RRAS server only, uncheck this box.

- The IP Address Assignment control group lets you specify how you want remote clients to get their IP addresses. The default settings here depend on what you told the RRAS Setup Wizard during setup:

  - If you want to use a DHCP server on your network as the source of IP addresses for remote clients, select the Dynamic Host Configuration Protocol (DHCP) radio button and make sure that you have the DHCP relay agent installed and running.

  - If you'd rather use static address allocation, select the Static Address Pool radio button. Then, in the list below, specify which IP address ranges you want issued to clients.

  - The Enable Broadcast Name Resolution option allows remote clients to resolve TCP/IP names without the use of a WINS or DNS server. This feature is enabled by default, and it was new in Windows Server 2012.

Figure 14.5 shows the IPv6 tab of the RRAS server's Properties dialog box.

FIGURE 14.5 The IPv6 tab of the RRAS Server's Properties dialog box

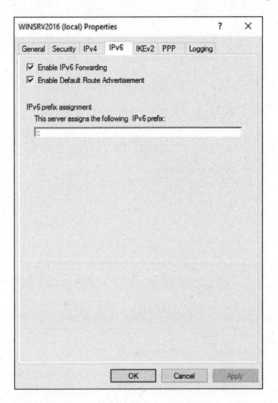

The controls on the IPv6 tab do the following:

- The Enable IPv6 Forwarding check box controls whether RRAS will route IPv6 packets between the remote client and other interfaces on your RRAS server. When this box is checked, as it is by default, remote clients' packets can go to the RRAS server or to any other host to which the RRAS server has a route. To allow clients to access resources on the RRAS server only, uncheck this box.

- The Enable Default Route Advertisement check box (enabled by default) makes the *Border Gateway Protocol (BGP)* routing protocol available. BGP can exchange routing information between Windows Server 2016 routers. When this box is checked, your Windows Server 2016 router can announce its route to other routers.

- On the IPv6 tab, you can also set up your IPv6 prefix assignment.

In Exercise 14.1, I will show you how to install and configure the Remote Access role onto your server. Just as with many of our installations, you will use Server Manager to install the Remote Access role. This role also installs the DirectAccess role onto your server.

EXERCISE 14.1

Installing the Remote Access Role

1. Open Server Manager.

2. On the Server Manager dashboard, click the Add Roles And Features link (number 2).

3. If a Before You Begin screen appears, click Next.

4. On the Selection type page, choose a role-based or feature-based installation and click Next.

5. Click the top radio button, Select A Server From The Server Pool, and choose the server in the Server Pool section. Click Next.

6. On the Select Server Roles screen, click the Remote Access check box (see Figure 14.6). If a pop-up window appears telling you that you need to add features, click the Add Features button. Click Next.

7. On the Add Features page, click Next.

8. On the Remote Access page, click Next.

9. On the Select Role Services page, choose the first two check boxes: DirectAccess And VPN (RAS) and Routing (see Figure 14.7). If a pop-up window appears telling you that you need to add additional features, click the Add Features button. Click Next.

10. At the Confirmation screen, click the Install button.

11. After the Installation screen finishes, click the Close button.

12. In Server Manager, click the Remote Access link on the left window pane.

FIGURE 14.6 Remote Access check box

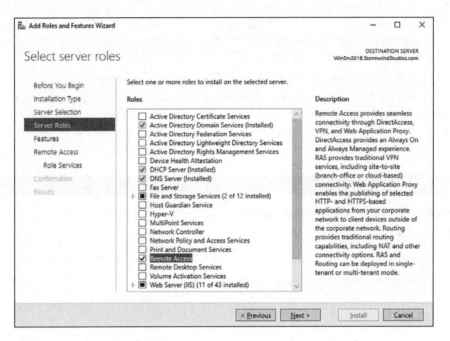

FIGURE 14.7 Remote Access

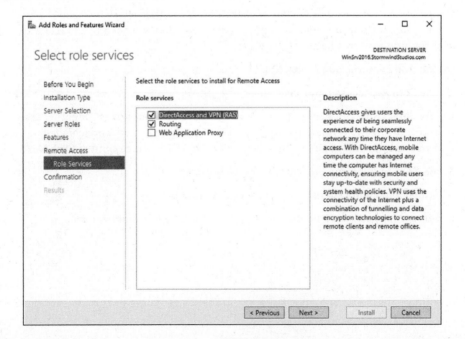

13. Click the more link (see Figure 14.8).

FIGURE 14.8   Remote Access configuration needed

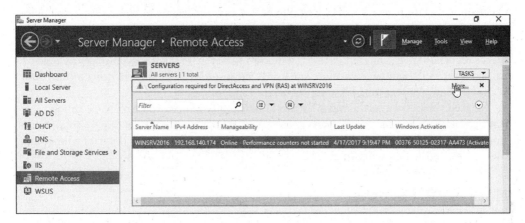

14. At the Post-deployment Configuration task, click the link for Open The Getting Started Wizard (see Figure 14.9).

FIGURE 14.9   Opening the Getting Started Wizard

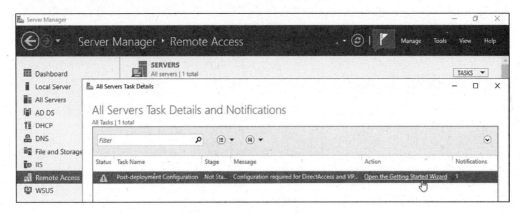

15. At the Configure Remote Access screen, choose the Deploy VPN Only link.

16. At this point we can configure the Remote Access VPN role. We will configure this role in a later exercise. Close Server Manager.

Understanding a VPN

Conventional dial-up access works well, but as you saw earlier, it can be expensive to implement, painful to manage, and extremely slow by today's standards. VPNs offer a way around these problems by providing low initial and ongoing costs, easy management, and excellent speeds (depending on your connection). Windows Server 2012's RRAS component includes two complete VPN implementations: one using Microsoft's PPTP and one using a combination of the Internet-standard IPsec protocol and L2TP or SSTP.

The basic process of setting up a VPN is simple, but you need to think some things through before plunging ahead. Getting the VPN installation right may require small hardware or networking changes plus proper configuration of the VPN service. You will look at this process in the following sections.

How a VPN Works

A VPN sits between your internal network and the Internet, accepting connections from clients in the outside world. In Figure 14.10, clients 1 and 2 are using different ISPs (probably because they're at different physical locations). For example, a packet from client 1 goes from its computer to its ISP and then through some route, unknown to you, that eventually delivers it to the VPN server, which transforms it into a packet suitable for use on the internal network.

FIGURE 14.10   VPNs provide private connections between clients and servers across the Internet.

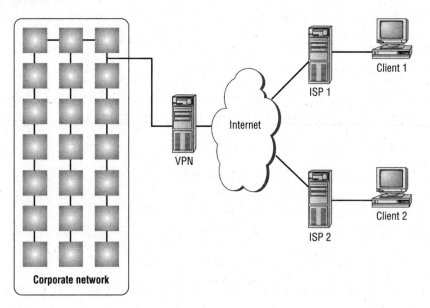

Imagine a line around the internal network, and think of it as a security boundary. In general, you'll want your VPN server to be outside any firewalls or network security measures that you have in place. The most common configuration is to use two NICs: One connects to the Internet, and the other connects either to the private network or to an intermediate network that itself connects to the private network. Of course, you can use any type of Internet connection you want for the VPN server, such as cable modem, DSL, T1, satellite, or whatever.

The point behind giving the VPN its own network adapter is that your VPN clients need a public IP address to which they can connect, and you probably don't want them calling directly into your internal network. That also means that things will be easiest for your VPN users if the IP address for your VPN server's external interface is statically assigned so that it won't be changing on them when they least expect it.

Enabling RRAS as a VPN

If you're already using RRAS for IP routing or remote access, you can enable it as a VPN server without reinstalling.

The General tab of the server's Properties dialog box allows you to specify whether your RRAS server is a router, a remote access server, or both. The first step in converting your existing RRAS server to handle VPN traffic is to make sure that the IPv4 Remote Access Server or IPv6 Remote Access Server check box is selected on this tab.

Making this change requires you to stop and restart the RRAS service, but that's OK because the snap-in will do it for you. Then you must configure VPN ports, as shown in the following sections.

Configuring a VPN

VPN configuration is extremely simple, at least for PPTP. Either a server can accept VPN calls or it can't. If it can, it will have a certain number of VPN ports, all of which are configured identically. You don't have to change or tweak much to get a VPN server set up, but you can adjust a few things as you like.

Configuring VPN Ports

The biggest opportunity to configure your VPN server is to adjust the number and kind of VPN ports available for clients to use. You can enable or disable either PPTP or L2TP, depending on what you want your remote users to be able to access. You accomplish this through the Ports Properties dialog box.

For conventional remote access servers, this dialog box shows you a list of hardware ports, but for servers that support VPN connections, there are two WAN Miniport device selections: one for PPTP and one for L2TP. (These aren't really devices; they're actually virtual ports maintained by RRAS for accepting VPN connections.) You configure these ports by selecting one and clicking the Configure button, which displays the Configure Device – WAN Miniport (PPTP) dialog box.

Three controls are pertinent to a VPN configuration:

- The Remote Access Connections (Inbound Only) check box must be activated in order to accept VPN connections with this port type. To disable a VPN type (for instance, if you want to turn off L2TP), uncheck this box.

- The Demand-Dial Routing Connections (Inbound And Outbound) check box controls whether this VPN type can be used for demand-dial connections. By default, this box is checked; you'll need to uncheck it if you don't want to use VPN connections to link your network with other networks.

- The Maximum Ports control lets you set the number of inbound connections that this port type will support. By default, you get 5 PPTP and 5 L2TP ports when you install RRAS; you can use from 0 to 250 ports of each type by adjusting the number here.

You can also use the Phone Number For This Device field to enter the IP address of the public interface to which VPN clients connect. You might want to do this if your remote access policies accept or reject connections based on the number called by the client. Because you can assign multiple IP addresses to a single adapter, you can control VPN traffic by throttling which clients can connect to which addresses through a policy.

Troubleshooting VPNs

The two primary problems you might encounter with VPN are as follows:

- Inability to establish a connection at all
- Inability to reach some needed resource once connected

There's a lot of common ground between the process of troubleshooting a VPN connection and the process of troubleshooting an ordinary remote access connection.

The following are some extremely simple—but sometimes overlooked—things to check when your VPN clients can't connect. First, make sure your clients can make the underlying connection to their ISP; then, check the following:

- Is RRAS installed and configured on the server?

    - Is the server configured to allow remote access? Check the General tab of the server's Properties dialog box.

    - Is the server configured to allow VPN traffic? Check the Ports Properties dialog box to make sure that the appropriate VPN protocol is enabled and that the number of ports for that protocol is greater than 0.

    - Are there any available VPN ports? If you have 10 L2TP ports allocated, the 11th caller will not be able to connect.

- Do the client and server match?
  - Is the VPN protocol used by the client enabled on the server? Windows 2000 and newer clients will try L2TP first and switch to PPTP as a second choice. However, clients on other OSs (including Windows NT) can normally expect L2TP, PPTP, or SSTP (2008 or higher).
- Are the client and server authenticated correctly?
  - Are the username and password correct?
  - Does the user account in question have remote access permissions, either directly on the account or through a policy?
  - Do the authentication settings in the server's policies (if any) match the supported set of authentication protocols?

If you check all of the simple stuff and find nothing wrong, it's time to move on to checking more complex issues. These tend to affect more than one user, as opposed to the simple (and generally user-specific) issues just outlined. The problems include the following:

Policy Problems   If you're using a native-mode Windows Server 2016 domain and you're using policies, those policies may cause some subtle problems that show up under some circumstances:

- Are there any policies whose Allow or Deny settings conflict with each other? Remember that all conditions of all policies must match to gain user access; if any condition of any policy fails or if there are any policies that deny access, the connection will be denied.
- Does the user match all of the necessary conditions that are in place, such as time and date?

Network Problems   If you're using dynamic IP addressing, are there any addresses left in the pool? If the VPN server can't assign an address, it won't accept the connection.

Domain Problems   Windows Server 2016 RRAS servers can coexist with Windows NT RRAS servers, and both of them can interoperate with RADIUS servers from Microsoft and other vendors. Sometimes, though, this interoperation doesn't work exactly as you'd expect. Here are some questions to ask:

- Is the RRAS server's domain membership correct? Your RRAS servers don't have to be domain members unless you want to use native-mode features such as remote access policies.
- If you're in a domain, are the server's group memberships correct? The server account must be a member of the RAS group and Internet Authentication Servers security group.

So now that you understand what a VPN does, let's go ahead and configure your VPN server. In Exercise 14.2, I will show you how to configure your VPN server.

EXERCISE 14.2

Setting Up a VPN Server

1. Open Routing and Remote Access by clicking the Start button and choosing Administrative tools and then choose Routing and Remote Access.

2. Right-click on the server name and choose Configure and Enable Routing and Remote Access.

3. The Routing and Remote Access wizard starts. Click Next at the Welcome screen.

4. At the Configuration screen, choose the first option Remote access (dial-up or VPN) as shown in Figure 14.11.

FIGURE 14.11   Remote access choice

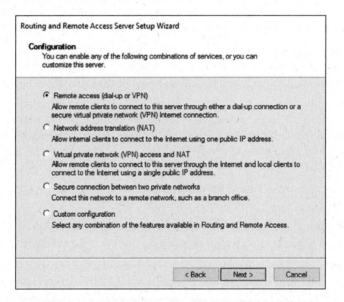

5. At the Remote Access screen, choose the VPN check box. Click Next.

6. Click the Ethernet adapter that will be connected to the internet. Make sure the check box for Enable security on the selected interface is selected. Click Next.

7. At the IP Address Assignment screen, choose Automatically and choose Next.

8. At the Managing Multiple Remote Access Servers screen, click the No button and click Next.

9. At the Summary screen, click the Finish button.

10. If you get a message about setting up a DHCP Relay Agent, click OK.

Managing Your Remote Access Server

RRAS server management is generally pretty easy because, in most cases, there's not much to manage. You set up the server, and it answers calls. You'll probably find it necessary to monitor the server's ongoing activity, however, and you may find it necessary to log activity for accounting or security purposes.

You can monitor your server's activity in a number of ways, including having the server keep local copies of its logs or having it send logging data to a remote RADIUS server. In addition, you can monitor the current status of any of the ports on your system.

Microsoft's documentation distinguishes between event logging, which records significant things that happen such as the RRAS service starting up and shutting down, and authentication and accounting logging, which tracks things like when a user logged on and logged off. The settings for both types of logging are intermingled in the RRAS snap-in.

Managing Remote Users with a RADIUS Server

Remote Authentication Dial-In User Service (RADIUS) allows for maintaining and managing your remote users. A RADIUS server allows Remote Access Service (RAS) clients and dial-up routers to be authenticated.

Network Policy Server (NPS) is Microsoft's implementation of a RADIUS server in Windows Server 2016. NPS replaced Windows Server 2003 Internet Authentication Service (IAS) in Windows Server 2008. NPS, working as a RADIUS server, allows for authentication, authorization, and accounting for wireless and VPN networks.

NPS allows a server to perform the duties of a RADIUS proxy. A RADIUS proxy allows the routing of RADIUS messages between RADIUS clients (RAS) and RADIUS servers. NPS also gives you the ability to record information about forwarded messages in an accounting log.

Monitoring Overall Activity

The Server Status node in the RRAS snap-in shows you a summary of all the RRAS servers known to the system. When you select the Server Status item, the right pane of the MMC will list each known RRAS server. Each entry in the list tells you whether the server is up, what kind of server it is, how many ports it has, how many ports are currently in use, and how long the server has been up. You can right-click any Windows Server 2016 RRAS server in this view to start, stop, restart, pause, or resume its RRAS service; disable RRAS on the server; or remove the server's advertisement from Active Directory (provided, of course, that you're using Active Directory).

Controlling Remote Access Logging

A standard RRAS installation will always log some data locally, but that's pretty useless unless you know what gets logged and where it goes. Each RRAS server on your network has its own set of logs, which you manage through the Remote Access Logging folder. Within that folder, you'll usually see a single item labeled *Local File*, which is the log file stored on that particular server.

If you don't have Windows accounting or Windows authentication turned on, you won't have a local log file. Depending on whether you're using RADIUS accounting and logging, you may see additional entries.

Setting Server Logging Properties

You can control server logging at the server level. You use the Logging tab to control what level of detail you want in the server's event log.

These controls regulate all logging by RRAS, not just remote access log entries.

You have four choices for the level of logged detail:

- The Log Errors Only radio button instructs the server to log errors and nothing else. This gives you an adequate indication of problems after they happen, but it doesn't point out potential problems noted by warning messages.

- The Log Errors And Warnings radio button is the default choice. This forces the server to log error and warning messages to the event log, giving you a nice balance between information content and log volume.

- The Log All Events radio button causes the RRAS service to log mass quantities of messages, literally covering everything the server does. Although this voluminous output is useful for troubleshooting (or even for getting a better understanding of how remote access works), it's overkill for everyday use.

- The Do Not Log Any Events radio button turns off all event logging for RRAS.

Don't use the Do Not Log Any Events option. The service's logs are important in case of a problem.

The Log Additional Routing And Remote Access Information check box allows you to turn on the logging of all PPP negotiations and connections. This can provide valuable information when you're trying to figure out what's wrong, but it adds a lot of unnecessary bulk to your log files. Don't turn it on unless you're trying to pin down a problem.

Setting Log File Properties

By selecting an individual log file in the snap-in, you can change what events will be logged in that file. The Local Log File Properties dialog box has two tabs:

- The Settings tab controls what gets logged in the file:
    - Accounting Requests governs whether events related to the service will be logged (as well as accounting data). You should always leave this checked.

- Authentication Requests adjusts whether successful and failed logon requests are logged. You should always leave this checked.

- Periodic Status controls whether interim accounting packets are permanently stored on disk. You should usually leave this checked.

- Periodic Authentication Requests adjusts whether successful and failed logon requests are periodically logged. You should always leave this checked.

- The Log File tab (see Figure 14.12) controls the format of the file, specifically, how the log file is written to disk. You use this tab to designate three things:

  - The Directory field shows where the log file is stored. By default, each server logs its data in *systemroot*\system32\LogFiles. You can change this location to wherever you want.

  - The Format controls determine the format of the log file. By default, Windows Server 2016 uses the database-compatible file format ODBC (legacy) as shown in Figure 14.12. This format makes it easy for you to take log data and store it in a database, enabling more sophisticated post-processing for things such as billing and chargebacks.

  - The Create A New Log File section determines how often new log files are created. For example, some administrators prefer to start a new log file each week or each month, whereas others are content to let the log file grow without end. You can choose to have RRAS start new log files every day, week, month, never, or when the log file reaches a certain size.

FIGURE 14.12   The Log File tab

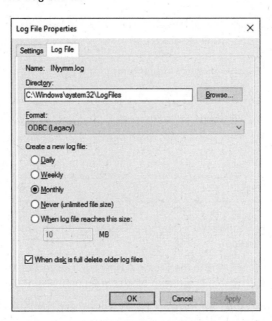

Having correct accounting and authorization data is critical to maintaining a good level of security. Exercise 14.3 walks you through configuring remote access logging.

EXERCISE 14.3

Changing Remote Access Logging Settings

1. Open the RRAS MMC snap-in by pressing the Windows key and selecting Administrative Tools ➢ Routing And Remote Access.

2. Navigate to the `Remote Access Logging and Policies` folder. Right-click the folder and select Launch NPS.

3. On the left pane, click Accounting. On the right side, click Change Log File Properties (see Figure 14.13).

FIGURE 14.13   Change Log File Properties

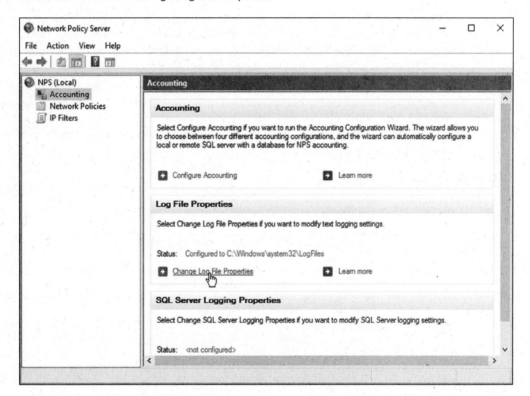

4. The Local File Logging dialog box appears. On the Settings tab, make sure that all check boxes are marked.

5. Switch to the Log File tab, and in the Create A New Log File section, select the When Log File Reaches This Size option. Enter **50** to set the maximum size of the log file to 50 MB.

6. Click the OK button. Close the Network Policy Server window.

Reviewing the Remote Access Event Log

You use the Log File tab to specify the format, size, and location of the log file. Once you have a log file, however, what do you do with the log information? Windows Server 2016 online help has an exhaustive list of all of the fields logged for each connection attempt and accounting record. Because of the availability of online help, you don't need to have all of those fields memorized, and you don't have to remember exactly how to make sense of the log entries.

Why bother reviewing the logs? One nice feature is that each entry in the authentication log indicates which remote access policy was applied (either to accept or to reject the connection). This is a good way to identify problems with policies because sometimes multiple policies can combine to have an effect that you didn't expect.

Furthermore, if it's desirable in your environment, you can use the logged data to generate accounting reports to tell you things such as the average utilization of your dial-in ports, the top 10 users of dial-in connect time, or how much online time accounts or certain Windows groups use.

Monitoring Ports and Port Activity

You can monitor port status and activity from the RRAS snap-in. The Ports folder under the server contains one entry for each defined port. When you select the Ports folder, you'll see a list of the ports and their current status. The list indicates whether each port is a dial-in or VPN port and whether it's active, so you can get a quick summary of your server's workload at any time.

Double-clicking an individual port displays the Port Status dialog box (see Figure 14.14). This dialog box shows information such as a port's line speed (Line BPS), the amount of transmitted and received data (Bytes In and Bytes Out), and the network address for each protocol being carried on the port. This is a useful tool for verifying whether a port is in active use, and it gives you a count of the number of transmission and reception errors on the port.

FIGURE 14.14   The Port Status dialog box

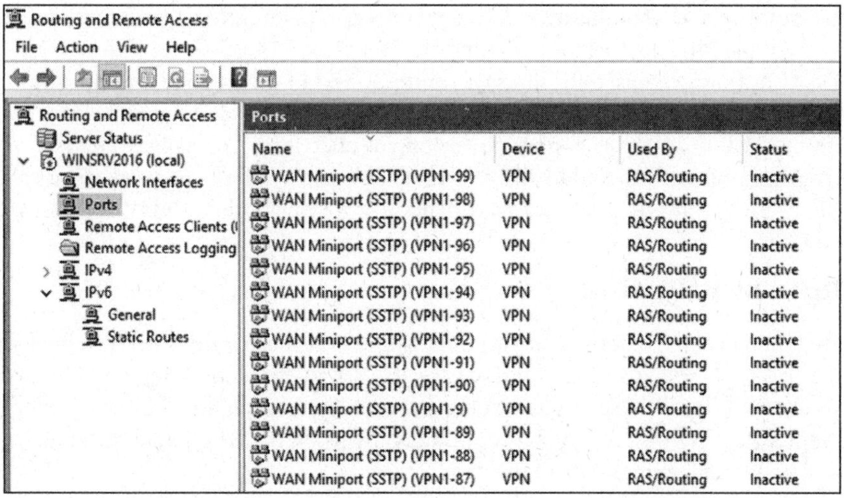

Network Address Translation

Network Address Translation (NAT) provides an advantage with routing and tunneling. NAT (also referred to as network masquerading) allows a router to translate one IP address to another across the tunnel. This allows you to use private IP addressing internally but use pubic addresses between the tunnels.

The huge advantage of NAT is the ability for you to share a single public IP address and single Internet connection between multiple locations using private IP addressing schemes. The nodes on the private network use nonroutable private addresses. NAT maps the private addresses to the public address.

Implementing NAT

Implementing NAT is an easy process. I am going to show you the steps needed to implement NAT, but I am not going to do it as an exercise. To set up NAT in an exercise without a tunnel or without multiple networks is not always an easy thing to do. So, I will just show you how to implement NAT in case you need to do it at work. To run these steps, you must be a member of at least the local Administrators group or higher. The following steps show you how to implement NAT:

1. Start the Routing and Remote Access MMC snap-in (under Administrative Tools). Right-click your server name and choose Configure And Enable Routing And Remote Access.

2. At the Welcome Screen, click Next.

3. Choose the Custom Configuration radio button. Click Next.

4. Click NAT and click Next.

5. Start Service.

6. Expand your server name.

7. Expand IPv4.

At this point, you can configure NAT. If you need to install NAT, you must have a system with multiple NIC devices or a demand-dial setup.

NAT is also commonly used for Internet connections, but this is done through your firewall or router. For example, let's say you have an Internet service provider that issues you only four valid Internet TCP/IP addresses for you to use on your network. You can set up NAT and program it to use those four valid addresses. Then, when a user from the network wants to access the Internet, NAT swaps the user's internal IP address for one of the valid IP addresses.

Configuring Routes

If you are familiar with routers, then you understand that most routers need to have their routing tables built. Well, using a Microsoft Server as a router is no different. When you decide to use a multihomed server as a router, you have to decide how you want to set up the routing table. The routers can be programmed by using the Routing and Remote Access MMC or by using a command prompt.

Any subnet that is connected directly to the router does not need programming. Since the router can see the subnet, it knows what computers can be on that subnet. But you need to program any subnets that are not directly connected to the router.

If I have three subnets, subnet A, subnet B, and subnet C and router1 is connected to subnet A and subnet B, then I have to program router1 to know how to get to subnet C. I don't need to program router1 for subnets A or B. If I have a router (router2) connected to subnet B and subnet C, then router2 needs a route for subnet A.

To program the route in the Microsoft router, you would need to use the Route command. To add a route, you would type in **Route add** and the parameters of the route path. Let's take a look at Figure 14.15.

FIGURE 14.15 Network Layout

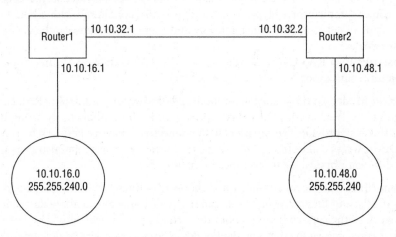

Router1 can NOT see the 10.10.48.0 subnet and Router2 can NOT see 10.10.16.0. So you would need to use the Route command to set these routes up. To use the Route command, you state what you are doing (Route add, Route delete, etc.). Then you put in the subnet you are trying to get to, the mask, and the gateway that you use to get to that subnet. So for Router1 you would use the following command:

Route add 10.10.48.0 mask 255.255.240.0 10.10.32.2 -p

As you can see in this command, you are trying to program for the 10.10.48.0 subnet. The mask is 255.255.240.0 and the gateway you would use from Router1 is the next router (10.10.32.2). The -p stands for persistent and it puts the route into the registry. This is important because when you type Route commands, they are put into Cache. So if the machine reboots, you lose your routes. By using the -p, these routes are entered into the registry and the routes will be reloaded if the server reboots. If you were on Router2, the command would be as follows:

Route add 10.10.16.0 mask 255.255.240.0 10.10.32.1 -p

Now you do have a second option to programming the router. Not do it. You can add a router protocol that will automatically build the routing tables. Microsoft uses the Routing Information Protocol (RIP) to automatically program routes. RIP is a broadcast-based protocol and it can be added to any Microsoft router. The downside to using RIP is the extra broadcast traffic. So if you only have a few routers, it's best to just configure the routes manually. On a large network with many subnets, you may want to consider using RIP.

RAS Gateway

In Windows Server 2016, RAS Gateways are a software router and gateway that routes network traffic between your physical and virtual networks. No matter where the resources are located. So let's say you have a physical and virtual network located at the same physical location. You can implement a Hyper-V server that is also configured with a RAS Gateway virtual machine to act as a forwarding gateway and route traffic between the virtual and physical networks.

When setting up a RAS Gateway, you can use the RAS Gateway in either single tenant mode or multitenant mode.

Single Tenant Mode   In the single tenant mode, administrators can deploy RAS Gateways as an edge VPN server, an edge DirectAccess server, or both simultaneously. Using RAS Gateways this way provides remote users with connectivity to your network by using either VPN or DirectAccess connections. Also, single tenant mode allows administrators to connect offices at different physical locations through the Internet.

Multitenant Mode   When an administrator chooses Multitenant mode, Cloud Service Providers (CSPs) and Enterprise networks can use RAS Gateways to allow datacenter and cloud network traffic routing between both the virtual and physical networks. For multitenant mode, it is recommended that you deploy RAS Gateways on virtual machines that are running Windows Server 2016.

Configuring a VPN Client

Dial-up RAS clients and VPN clients are similar. Almost all of the options that are available when you set up a RAS client are also available when you set up a VPN client. The main differences are as follows:

- VPN clients specify the server's IP address, whereas RAS clients specify the server's phone number.
- VPN clients require an underlying connection to the Internet.

Client configuration is not a focus of the exam, so in this chapter you will learn how to configure a VPN client but not a RAS client. Just remember that the RAS client configuration is extremely similar and that RAS clients are slowly fading away. Thus, here I will focus on VPN settings only.

VPN connections are almost always created on client workstations, so this section describes the settings in Windows 7 / 8 / 8.1 / 10.

When you establish a virtual private network connection, you're actually building an encrypted tunnel between you and some other machine. The tunneled data is carried over an insecure network, such as the Internet.

Once you've created a connection, you can change its properties at any time by opening its Properties dialog box. The Dial-Up Connection Properties dialog box has a total of five tabs that you can use to adjust all of the pertinent settings for each connection.

Don't confuse these settings with the ones in the Local Area Connection Properties dialog box; they serve entirely different purposes.

The General Tab

The General tab of the Connection Properties dialog box (the box is called Dial-Up Connections or VPN Connections, depending on whether you're configuring dial-up RAS or VPN) is where you specify either the IP address of the VPN server or the modem and phone number to use with this particular connection. Some fields have been filled in already from when you used the Network Connection Wizard. Figure 14.16 shows the VPN settings.

FIGURE 14.16   General tab of the VPN Connection Properties dialog box

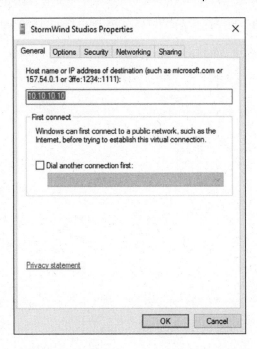

The General tab has a field where you enter the VPN server address or hostname. The First Connect group lets you specify which dial-up connection, if any, you want brought up before the VPN connection is established.

With the General tab, you can also do the following:

- Set VPN options:

  - Enter the VPN server address or hostname.

  - Specify whether to dial another connection automatically first and then specify the connection to dial.

- Set RAS options:

  - Change the modem this connection uses, or the settings for the modem you already have, with the Configure button.

When configuring dial-up, you can also use the Phone And Modem Options control panel to adjust a broader range of modem settings.

The Options Tab

The Options tab holds settings that control how DUN dials and redials the connection. The controls in this dialog box are segregated into two groups. The Dialing Options group holds controls that govern DUN's interface behavior while dialing, and the Redialing Options group controls whether and how DUN will redial if it doesn't immediately connect (see Figure 14.17).

FIGURE 14.17   Options tab of the VPN Connection Properties dialog box

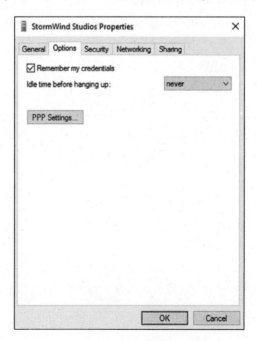

Dialing Options

Four dialing options are available in the Dialing Options group:

- The Display Progress While Connecting check box (selected by default) instructs DUN to keep you updated on its progress as it attempts to raise the connection.

- The Prompt For Name And Password, Certificate, Etc. check box is also selected by default. When it's on, Windows will prompt you for any credentials it needs to authenticate your connection to the remote server. This may be a username, a password, a public key certificate, or some combination of the three, depending on what the remote end requires.

- The Include Windows Logon Domain check box is unchecked by default. It forces DUN to include the domain name of the domain to which you're logged on as part of the authentication credential. Leave this unchecked unless you're dialing into a Windows NT/2000 network that has a trust relationship with your logon domain.

- For RAS connections, a Prompt For Phone Number check box tells DUN to display the phone number in the connection dialog box. This box is checked by default. This gives you a chance to edit the phone number before dialing; you may want to uncheck it if you (or your users) are prone to making accidental changes.

Redialing Options

The settings in the Redialing Options group control how DUN will attempt to redial the specified number if the remote end is busy or doesn't answer with a recognizable carrier tone. These settings are as follows:

- The Redial Attempts field controls how many attempts DUN will make to raise the other end before giving up. The default value is 3, but you can set any value from 0 (meaning that DUN won't attempt to redial) to 999,999,999.

- The Time Between Redial Attempts drop-down menu controls how long DUN will wait after each failed call before it tries again. Values in the drop-down menu range from 1 second all the way up to 10 minutes, with various increments in between.

- The Idle Time Before Hanging Up drop-down menu lets you specify an inactivity timer. If your connection is idle for longer than the specified period, your client will terminate the call. Note that the remote end may drop the call sooner than your client, depending on how it's configured. By default, this drop-down menu is set to Never, meaning that your client will never drop a call. If you want an inactivity timer, you can pick values ranging from 1 minute to 24 hours.

- The Redial If Line Is Dropped check box automatically redials the number if you are disconnected.

The Security Tab

How useful you find the Security tab will depend on whom you're calling. The default settings it provides will work fine with most Internet service providers and corporate dial-up facilities, but Windows 7 / 8 / 8.1 / 10 have a broad range of security settings that you can change if you require. The Security Options group contains controls that directly affect the security of your connection. The Advanced (Custom Settings) radio button controls settings such as encryption and authentication protocols.

Security Options

The controls in the Security Options group are pretty straightforward. The security settings in effect for this connection are governed by your choice between the Typical (Recommended Settings) and Advanced (Custom Settings) radio buttons (see Figure 14.18).

FIGURE 14.18   Security tab of the VPN Connection Properties dialog box

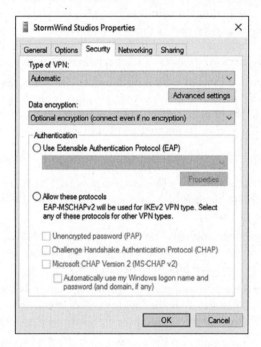

Typical (Recommended Settings)

Usually, it's best to stick with the Typical (Recommended Settings) option and use its subordinate controls to pick a canned setting that matches your needs. These subordinate controls are as follows:

- The Validate My Identity As Follows drop-down menu lets you choose among the following authentication methods:
  - Unsecured passwords (the default, and the only type of authentication that most networks support)
  - Secured passwords
  - Smart card authentication (useful only when calling another Windows network)

- If you choose to require a secured password, the Automatically Use My Windows Logon Name And Password (And Domain If Any) check box instructs DUN to offer to the remote end the logon credentials you used to log on to the computer or domain. This is useful only if you're dialing into a network that has access to your domain authentication information.

- If you require a secured password or smart card authentication, the Require Encryption (Disconnect If None) check box allows you to have either an encrypted connection or none at all. If you check this box, your client and the remote server will attempt to negotiate a common encryption method. If they can't (perhaps because the remote end doesn't offer encryption), your client will hang up.

Advanced (Custom Settings)

If you select the Advanced (Custom Settings) radio button and then click the Settings button, you'll see the Advanced Security Settings dialog box. Its controls are more complex than the ones on the Security tab.

The first field is the Data Encryption drop-down menu. Windows 10 offers you the opportunity to encrypt both sides of network connections using IPsec. This capability extends to dial-up connections too. The drop-down menu gives you the following four choices:

- No Encryption Allowed means that the server will drop your call if it requires encryption because you can't provide it.

- Optional Encryption tells the client to request encryption but to continue the call if it's not available.

- Require Encryption tells the client to request encryption and to refuse to communicate with servers that don't support it.

- Maximum Strength Encryption tells the client to communicate only with servers that offer the same strength encryption it does. For example, with this setting in force, a North American Windows Server 2016 machine running 3DES won't communicate with a French Windows XP machine because the French machine uses the weaker exportable encryption routines.

The Authentication section controls which authentication protocols this client can use. The default setting, Use Extensible Authentication Protocol (EAP), is for standard Windows authentication (using the MD5-Challenge method) or certificate-based authentication (using the Smart Card Or Other Certificate choice in the drop-down menu).

The Allow These Protocols radio button is followed by a long list of authentication protocols. Although the specifics of how they work are different, the basic idea behind all of these protocols is the same. Each provides a secure way for a client to prove its identity to a server. By selecting the appropriate check boxes, you can make your client use the same protocols as the remote end.

The Networking Tab

You use the Networking tab (see Figure 14.19) to control which protocols your client will attempt to use when communicating with other servers.

FIGURE 14.19   Networking tab of the VPN Connection Properties dialog box

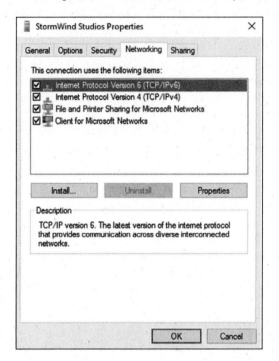

The list box in the middle of the tab shows the network protocols installed on the client. Protocols marked with a check are available for use with this connection. Usually, when configuring RAS, you'll see TCP/IP and Client For Microsoft Networks marked, which indicates that those two protocols can be used over the connection.

The Install, Uninstall, and Properties buttons work just as they do in the Local Area Connection Properties dialog box. By using them, you can control which protocols are on your machine and their settings.

It's worth mentioning that selecting Internet Protocol (TCP/IP) in the protocols list and opening its Properties dialog box gives you access to a set of properties that are completely distinct from any TCP/IP settings that may apply to your LAN interfaces. Usually, the dial-up TCP/IP settings are configured to obtain an IP address and DNS information from the remote server, although if you need to, you can override these settings.

The Sharing Tab

Internet Connection Sharing allows other users to connect to the Internet through this machine. The machine on which you enable this feature works like a gateway to the Internet (see Figure 14.20).

FIGURE 14.20   Sharing tab of the VPN Connection Properties dialog box

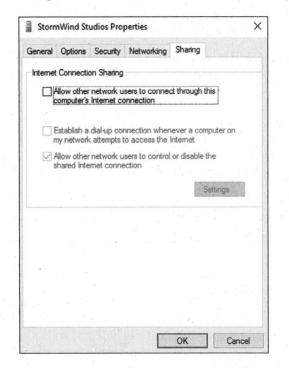

Configuring a Web Application Proxy

One of the new advantages of using the Remote Access role service in Windows Server 2016 is the Web Application Proxy. Normally, your users access applications on the Internet from your corporate network. The *Web Application Proxy* reverses this feature, and it allows your corporate users to access applications from any device outside the network.

Administrators can choose which applications to provide reverse proxy features, and this allows administrators the ability to give access selectively to corporate users for the desired application that you want to set up for the Web Application Proxy service.

The Web Application Proxy feature allows applications running on servers inside the corporate network to be accessed by any device outside the corporate network. The process of allowing an application to be available to users outside of the corporate network is known as *publishing*.

Publishing Applications

One disadvantage to corporate networks are that the machines that access the network are normally devices issued by the organization. That's where Web Application Proxy publishing can help.

Web Application Proxy allows an administrator to publish an organization's applications, thus allowing corporate end users the ability to access the applications from their own devices. This is becoming a big trend in the computer industry, called *bring your own device (BYOD)*.

In today's technology world, users are buying and using many of their own devices, even for business work. Because of this, the users are comfortable with their own devices. Web Application Proxy allows an organization to set up applications and enable their corporate users to use these applications with the devices the users already own, including computers, tablets, and smartphones.

The client side is easy to use as long as the end user has a standard browser or Office client. End users can also use apps from the Microsoft Windows Store that allow the client system to connect to the Web Application Proxy.

Configuring Pass-Through Authentication

Now when setting up the Web Application Proxy so that your users can access applications, you must have some kind of security or everyone with a device would be able to access and use your applications.

Because of this, Active Directory Federation Services (AD FS) must always be deployed with Web Application Proxy. AD FS gives you features such as single sign-on (SSO). *Single sign-on* allows you to log in one time with a set of credentials and use that set of credentials to access the applications over and over.

Pass-through authentication is truly a great benefit for your end users. Think of having a network where a user has to log in every time that user wants to access an application. The more times you make your end users log into an application, the more chances there are that the end user will encounter possible issues. Pass-through authentication works in the following way:

1. The client enters a URL address on their device, and the client system attempts to access the published web application.

2. The Web Application Proxy sends the request to the proxy server.

3. If the backend server needs the user to authenticate, the end user needs to enter their credentials only once.

4. After the server authenticates the credentials, the client has access to the published web application.

 When an administrator sets up applications to use pass-through preauthentication, additional features of AD FS will not function. For example, you will not be able to use AD FS Workplace Join, multifactor authentication (MFA), and multifactor access control.

Understanding DirectAccess

DirectAccess was a new technology that was introduced in the Windows Server 2008 R2 and Windows 7 operating systems. DirectAccess has been improved upon, and it is also available for Windows 10 and Windows Server 2016.

DirectAccess allows a remote user to work on their corporate network when they are away from the office without the need for a VPN. As long as the remote user is connected to the Internet, DirectAccess will automatically connect the remote user to the corporate network without the need for any user intervention.

When a user's DirectAccess-enabled laptop is connected to the Internet, a bidirectional connection is automatically established with the user's corporate network. Because the connection is bidirectional, the IT administrator can also remotely manage the Windows 10 machine while the machine is away from the network.

DirectAccess vs. VPNs

There really is no debate between VPN or DirectAccess—DirectAccess is the better way to go. The downside to DirectAccess is that it requires a great deal of time, resources, and knowledge to set it up properly.

There are a few problems with using VPNs to connect to a network. One issue is that when a user gets disconnected from their VPN connection, they must reestablish the VPN connection.

Another issue with VPNs is that many organizations filter VPN connection traffic. It may not be possible for an organization to open a firewall to allow VPN traffic. Also, if your intranet and your Internet connections are the same as your VPN connections, this can cause your Internet to be slower.

DirectAccess does not face the same limitations of a VPN. DirectAccess allows a laptop or desktop that is configured properly to connect automatically using a bidirectional connection between the client and the server.

To establish this connection, DirectAccess uses Internet Protocol Security (IPsec) and IPv6. IPsec provides a high level of security between the client and the server, and IPv6 is the protocol that the machines use.

Understanding the DirectAccess Process

Before you can set up the features and benefits of DirectAccess, there are some prerequisites that I must first go over. DirectAccess is a great way to get your users to access the network from the road, but it is not the easiest thing to set up, and it must be done correctly.

DirectAccess Prerequisites

As with any software package, role, or feature, when you install any one of these, there are always prerequisites that you must deal with. DirectAccess is no different. The following is a list of DirectAccess Server with Advanced Settings prerequisites:

- A public key infrastructure must be deployed.

- ISATAP in the corporate network is not supported. If you are using ISATAP, you should remove it and use native IPv6.

- Computers that are running the following operating systems are supported as DirectAccess clients:

  - Windows Server 2016

  - Windows Server 2012 R2

  - Windows Server 2012

  - Windows Server 2008 R2

  - Windows 10 Enterprise

  - Windows 8.1 Enterprise

  - Windows 8 Enterprise

  - Windows 7 Ultimate

  - Windows 7 Enterprise

- Force tunnel configuration is not supported with KerbProxy authentication.

- Changing policies by using a feature other than the DirectAccess management console or Windows PowerShell cmdlets is not supported.

- Separating NAT64/DNS64 and IPHTTPS server roles on another server is not supported.

The following is the list of prerequisites if you want to manage DirectAccess clients remotely:

- Windows Firewall must be enabled on all profiles.

- ISATAP in the corporate network is not supported. If you are using ISATAP, you should remove it and use native IPv6.

- Computers that are running the following operating systems are supported as DirectAccess clients:

  - Windows Server 2016

  - Windows Server 2012 R2

  - Windows Server 2012

  - Windows Server 2008 R2

  - Windows 10 Enterprise

  - Windows 8.1 Enterprise

- Windows 8 Enterprise
- Windows 7 Ultimate
- Windows 7 Enterprise
- Changing policies by using a feature other than the DirectAccess management console or Windows PowerShell cmdlets is not supported.

Understanding DirectAccess

To understand DirectAccess better, it helps to understand the process involved with how DirectAccess operates. The following steps, taken from the Microsoft white papers, show how DirectAccess operates.

1. The Windows 8 DirectAccess client determines whether the machine is connected to a network or the Internet.
2. The Windows 8 DirectAccess computer tries to connect to the web server specified during the DirectAccess setup configuration.
3. The Windows 8 DirectAccess client computer connects to the Windows Server 2016 DirectAccess server using IPv6 and IPsec. Because most users connect to the Internet using IPv4, the client establishes an IPv6-over-IPv4 tunnel using 6to4 or Teredo.
4. If an organization has a firewall that prevents the DirectAccess client computer using 6to4 or Teredo from connecting to the DirectAccess server, the Windows 8 client automatically attempts to connect using the IP-HTTPS protocol.
5. As part of establishing the IPsec session, the Windows 8 DirectAccess client and server authenticate each other using computer certificates for authentication.
6. The DirectAccess server uses Active Directory membership, and the DirectAccess server verifies that the computer and user are authorized to connect using DirectAccess.
7. The DirectAccess server begins forwarding traffic from the DirectAccess client to the intranet resources to which the user has been granted access.

Now that you understand how DirectAccess works, let's look at the requirements for setting up DirectAccess on your network.

Knowing the DirectAccess Infrastructure Requirements

To set up DirectAccess, you must make sure that your network infrastructure meets some minimum requirements. The following are the requirements for setting up DirectAccess:

- Windows Server 2016 configured to use DirectAccess. The Windows Server 2016 machine will be set up as a multihomed system. This means your server will need two network adapters so that one adapter is connected directly to the Internet and a second adapter is connected to the intranet. Each network adapter will be configured with its own TCP/IP address.
- Windows 7 / 8 / 8.1 / 10 client machines configured to use DirectAccess.

- Minimum of one domain controller and one Domain Name System (DNS) server running Windows Server 2008 SP2, Windows Server 2008 R2, Windows Server 2012, Windows Server 2012 R2, or Windows Server 2016.

- Certificate authority (CA) server that will issue computer certificates, smart card certificates, or health certificates.

- IPsec policies to specify protection for traffic.

- IPv6 on the DirectAccess server that uses ISATAP, Teredo, or 6to4.

Overview of Wireless Access

In today's computer world, it seems like everyone has a laptop. We all do a lot of traveling, and at any airport it seems like everyone is working on a laptop while waiting for a plane.

Because laptops have grown in popularity, IT professionals must account for them on their networks. Laptops offer IT administrators a unique set of challenges that must be dealt with on a day-to-day basis.

One major concern for IT administrators is security. Years ago, we never had to worry about users copying documents to a desktop computer and then walking out with the computer. However, today users can copy company documents to laptop computers and then walk out the door with the computer and the documents. So, I will discuss wireless networks, protocols, and security.

Windows 7 / 8 / 8.1 / 10, Windows 2008 / 2008 R2, Windows Server 2012 / 2012 R2, and Windows Server 2016 have enhanced the IEEE 802.11 wireless support to include some of the following changes:

- Single sign-on

- 802.11 wireless diagnostics

- WPA2 support

- Native Wi-Fi architecture

- User interface improvements for wireless connections

- Wireless Group Policy enhancements

- Changes in wireless auto-configuration

- Integration with Network Access Protection when using 802.1X authentication

- EAP host infrastructure

- Command-line support for configuring wireless settings

- Network location awareness and network profiles

- Next-generation TCP/IP stack enhancements for wireless environments

Configuring Wireless Access

Windows 7 / 8 / 8.1 / 10, Windows 2008 / 2008 R2, Windows Server 2012 / 2012 R2, and Windows Server 2016 provide built-in support for 802.11 wireless LAN networking. Inside the Network Connections folder, an installed 802.11 wireless LAN network adapter appears as a wireless network connection. The following are some of the items you can configure:

Operating Modes   There are two types of operating modes:

Infrastructure Mode   This mode uses at least one wireless access point (WAP) and/or a device that bridges the wireless computers to each other.

Ad Hoc Mode   Using this mode, wireless network computers connect directly to each other without the use of an access point (AP) or bridge.

Wired Equivalent Privacy   All of us (on a laptop) have tried to find a wireless network at one time or another. *Wired Equivalent Privacy (WEP)* is a wireless encryption that was originally defined in 802.11. WEP helps to prevent unauthorized wireless users from accessing your wireless network by the use of a shared secret key:

- If your wireless network is using the infrastructure mode, the WEP key must be configured on the wireless AP and all of the wireless clients.

- If your wireless network is using the ad hoc mode, the WEP key must be configured on all of the wireless clients.

The WEP key can be either 40-bit or 104-bit, depending on what your hardware can accommodate.

Wi-Fi Protected Access   An organization of wireless equipment vendors called the Wi-Fi Alliance created an interim standard called *Wi-Fi Protected Access (WPA)* while the IEEE 802.11i wireless LAN security standard was still being completed. WPA uses a strong encryption method called the *Temporal Key Integrity Protocol (TKIP)* to replace the weaker WEP standard. You have the ability to use the *Advanced Encryption Standard (AES)* for encryption that is provided by WPA.

WPA can be used in two different mode types:

WPA-Personal   This is used for a home office or small company. In the WPA-Personal model, you would use a preshared or passphrase code to gain authorization onto the network.

WPA-Enterprise   This was designed for a midsize to large organization. WPA-Enterprise has all of the same features as WPA-Personal, but it also includes the ability to use a 802.1X RADIUS server.

Wi-Fi Protected Access 2   Wi-Fi Protected Access 2 (WPA2) was officially designed to replace the WEP standard. WPA2 certifies that equipment used in a wireless network is compatible with the IEEE 802.11i standard. This certification is used to help standardize the use of the additional security features of the IEEE 802.11i standard that are not already included in WPA.

WPA2 can be used in two different mode types:

WPA2-Personal This is used for a home office or small company. In the WPA-Personal model, you would use a preshared or passphrase code to gain authorization onto the network.

WPA2-Enterprise This was designed for a midsize to large organization. WPA-Enterprise has all of the same features as WPA-Personal, but it also includes the ability to use a 802.1X RADIUS server.

Service Set Identifier To specify a wireless network by name, you specify the *service set identifier (SSID)*, also known as the *wireless network name*:

Infrastructure Mode The SSID is configured on the wireless access point.

Ad Hoc Mode The SSID is configured on the initial wireless client.

To help wireless clients discover and join the wireless network, the wireless AP or the initial wireless client periodically advertises the SSID. (This can be disabled for security.)

Group Policies for Wireless You have the ability to use Group Policy settings for Vista, Windows 7, Windows 8, Windows 10, Windows 2008/2008 R2, Windows Server 2012/2012 R2, and Windows Server 2016 for WPA2. Group Policy settings allow you to configure WPA2 options at the server for all wireless clients.

Remote Access Security

In the past, remote access was seldom part of most companies' networks. It was too hard to implement, too hard to manage, and too hard to secure. It's reasonably easy to secure your networks from unauthorized physical access, but it was perceived to be much harder to do so for remote access. Recently, a number of security policies, protocols, and technologies have been developed to ease this problem. First I'll discuss the user authentication protocols.

User Authentication

One of the first steps in establishing a secure remote access connection involves allowing the user to present some credentials to the server. You can use any or all of the following authentication protocols that Windows Server 2016 supports:

Password Authentication Protocol The *Password Authentication Protocol (PAP)* is the simplest authentication protocol. It transmits all authentication information in cleartext with no encryption, which makes it vulnerable to snooping if attackers can put themselves between the modem bank and the remote access server. However, this type of attack is unlikely in most networks. The security risk with PAP is largely overemphasized considering the difficulty of setting up a sniffer in between the modems and the remote access server. If an attacker has the ability to install a sniffer this deep in the network, you have larger problems to address. PAP is the most widely supported authentication protocol, and therefore you may find that you need to leave it enabled.

Microsoft CHAPv2   Microsoft created *Microsoft CHAPv2 (MS-CHAPv2)* as an extension of the CHAP protocol to allow the use of Windows authentication information. Version 2 is more secure than version 1, and version 1 is not supported by Windows Server 2008 and newer. Some other operating systems (besides Microsoft) support MS-CHAP version 1.

Extensible Authentication Protocol   The *Extensible Authentication Protocol (EAP)* doesn't provide any authentication itself. Instead, it relies on external third-party authentication methods that you can retrofit to your existing servers. Instead of hardwiring any one authentication protocol, a client-server pair that understands EAP can negotiate an authentication method. The computer that asks for authentication (the *authenticator*) is free to ask for several pieces of information, making a separate query for each one. This allows the use of almost any authentication method, including smart cards, secure access tokens such as SecurID, one-time password systems such as S/Key, or ordinary username/password systems.

Each authentication scheme supported in EAP is called an *EAP type*. Each EAP type is implemented as a plug-in module. Windows Server 2016 can support any number of EAP types at once; the Routing and Remote Access Services (RRAS) server can use any EAP type to authenticate if you've allowed that module to be used and the client has the module in question.

Windows Server 2016 comes with *EAP-Transport Level Security (EAP-TLS)*. This EAP type allows you to use public key certificates as an authenticator. TLS is similar to the familiar Secure Sockets Layer (SSL) protocol used for web browsers. When EAP-TLS is turned on, the client and server send TLS-encrypted messages back and forth. EAP-TLS is the strongest authentication method you can use; as a bonus, it supports smart cards. However, EAP-TLS requires your RRAS server to be part of a Windows 2000, Windows Server 2003, Windows Server 2008/2008 R2, Windows Server 2012/2012 R2, or Windows Server 2016 domain.

EAP-RADIUS is another authentication method included with Windows Server 2016. EAP-RADIUS is a fake EAP type that passes any incoming message to a Remote Authentication Dial-In User Service (RADIUS) server for authentication.

PEAP-MS-CHAP v2   This protocol is founded on the authenticated wireless access design, and it's based on Protected Extensible Authentication Protocol Microsoft Challenge Handshake Authentication Protocol version 2 (PEAP-MS-CHAP v2). This authentication protocol utilizes the user account credentials (username and password) stored in Active Directory Domain Services to authenticate wireless access clients instead of using smart cards or user and computer certificates for client authentication.

PEAP-MS-CHAP v2 is an EAP-type protocol that is easier to deploy than Extensible Authentication Protocol with Transport Level Security (EAP-TLS). It is easier because user authentication is accomplished by using password-based credentials (username and password) instead of digital certificates or smart cards. Only servers running Network Policy Server or PEAP-MS-CHAP v2 are required to have a certificate. The server certificate used by NPS can be issued by your organization's private trusted root CA deployed on your network or by a public CA that is already trusted by the client computer.

Just in case you missed the very important line above, I will say it again: Servers that are running Network Policy Server or PEAP-MS-CHAP v2 are *required* to have a certificate.

TLS/SSL (Schannel) *TLS/SSL (Schannel)* implements both the Secure Sockets Layer and Transport Layer Security Internet standard authentication protocols. Administrators can use TLS/SSL to authenticate servers and client computers. Administrators also have the ability to use the protocol to encrypt messages between the authenticated parties (client and server).

The Transport Layer Security protocol, Secure Sockets Layer protocol, Datagram Transport Layer Security (DTLS), and Private Communications Transport (PCT) protocol are all based on the public key cryptography. The Security Channel authentication protocol suite provides these protocols, and this protocol is based on the client-server model.

NTLMv2 *NTLMv2* (Windows NT LAN Manager) helps the authentication process for Windows NT 4 systems or earlier, and it allows for transactions between any two computers running these older systems. Networks that use NTLMv2 are referred to as *mixed mode*.

Kerberos The *Kerberos authentication protocol* is used to perform Active Directory domain authentication. By default, all computers joined to a Windows Server 2016 domain use the Kerberos authentication protocol. Kerberos allows for a single sign-on to network resources on a domain or on a trusted domain. Administrators have the ability to control certain parameters through the Kerberos security settings of the account policies.

802.1X The IEEE has a standard for wireless authentication called 802.1X. 802.1X allows wireless networks to authenticate onto wired Ethernet networks or wireless 802.11 networks. The IEEE 802.1X standard uses EAP for exchanging messages during the authentication process.

Connection Security

You can use some additional features to provide connection-level security for your remote access clients:

- The *Callback Control Protocol (CBCP)* allows your RRAS servers or clients to negotiate a callback with the other end. When CBCP is enabled, either the client or the server can ask the server at the other end to call the client back at a number supplied by the client or a prearranged number stored on the server.

- You can program the RRAS server to accept or reject calls based on the caller ID or automatic number identification (ANI) information transmitted by the phone company. For example, you can instruct your primary RRAS server to accept calls from only your home analog line. This means you can't call the server when you're on the road, and it also keeps the server from talking to strangers.

- You can specify various types and levels of encryption to protect your connection from interception or tampering.

🌐 Real World Scenario

The Limits of Caller ID

It's risky to rely on ANI information for any type of authentication or caller verification. First, caller ID information can be forged. Therefore, if an attacker knows the telephone numbers from which your network accepted calls, they could make their ANI report as one of those numbers and be authenticated onto the network.

Another problem with relying on ANI for authentication is that not all telephone companies pass ANI information with the call. Therefore, if your users are in remote locations (which is why they'd be dialing in anyway), they might not be able to authenticate. Even when ANI information is sent, some telephone companies pass different pieces of the information, which can also result in authentication failures.

Finally, not all incoming line types support ANI. If your site uses a network access server or modem bank that doesn't receive this information based on the type of T1 connection used for incoming calls, the ANI information might not be there at all.

Access Control

Apart from the connection-level measures that you can use to prohibit outside callers from talking to your servers, you can restrict which users can make remote connections in a number of ways:

- You can allow or disallow remote access from individual user accounts. This is the same limited control you have in Windows NT, but it's just the start for Windows Server 2016.

- You can use network access policies to control whether users can get access.

  Like group policies, network access policies give you an easy way to apply a consistent set of policies to groups of users. However, the policy mechanism is a little different: You create rules that include or exclude the users whom you want in the policy.

  Unlike group policies, network access policies are available only in Windows 2003 or higher domain functional level.

  In the next sections, you will learn how to configure user access control.

Configuring User Access

Now it's time to determine who can actually use the remote access services. You do this in two ways:

- By setting up remote access profiles on individual accounts
- By creating and managing network access policies that apply to groups of users

This distinction is subtle but important because you manage and apply profiles and policies in different places.

Setting Up User Profiles

Windows Server 2016 stores a lot of information for each user account. Collectively, this information is known as the account's *profile*, and it's normally stored in Active Directory. Some settings in the user's profile are available through one of the two user-management snap-ins:

▪ If your RRAS server is part of an Active Directory domain, the user profile settings are in the Active Directory Users and Computers snap-in.

▪ If your RRAS server is *not* part of an Active Directory domain, the user profile settings are in the Local Users and Groups snap-in.

In either case, the interesting part of the profile is the Dial-In tab of the user's Properties dialog box (see Figure 14.21). This tab has a number of controls that regulate how the user account can be used for dial-in access.

FIGURE 14.21 The Dial-In tab of the user's Properties dialog box

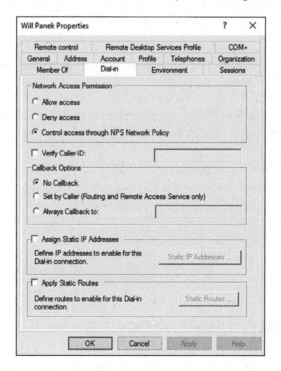

These controls include the following:

Network Access Permission Control Group   The first, and probably most familiar, controls on this tab are in the Network Access Permission control group. These options control whether the user has dial-in permission. Windows Server 2016 has a feature that, in addition to explicitly allowing or denying access, lets you control access through Network Access Protection.

Verify Caller-ID Check Box   RRAS can verify a user's caller ID information and use the results to allow or deny access. When you check the Verify Caller-ID check box and enter a phone number in the field, you're telling RRAS to reject a call from anyone who provides that username and password but whose caller ID information doesn't match what you enter. This means the user can call in only from a single phone number.

Callback Options Control Group   The Callback Options control group gives you three choices for regulating callback:

No Callback   This is the default setting. It means that the server will never honor callback requests from this account.

Set By Caller   This setting allows the calling system to specify a number at which it wants to be called back. The RRAS server will call the client back at that number.

Always Callback To   This setting allows you to enter a number that the server will call back no matter from where the client is actually calling. This option is less flexible but more secure than the Set By Caller option.

Assign Static IP Addresses Check Box   If you want this user always to get the same static IP address, you can arrange to do so by selecting the Assign Static IP Addresses check box and then entering the desired IP address. This allows you to set up nondynamic DNS records for individual users, guaranteeing that their machines will always have a valid DNS entry. On the other hand, this can be more prone to typographical errors on setup than the dynamic DNS-DHCP combination you could use instead.

Apply Static Routes Check Box   In an ordinary LAN, you don't have to do anything special to clients to enable them to route packets—just configure them with a default gateway, and the gateway handles the rest. For dial-up connections, though, you may want to define a list of static routes that will enable the remote client to reach hosts on your network, or elsewhere, without requiring that packets be sent to a gateway in between. Depending on the remote access server, though, the client may be able to use Address Resolution Protocol (ARP) for local devices too. If you want to define a set of static routes on the client, you'll have to do it manually. If you want to assign static routes on the server, select the Apply Static Routes check box and then use the Static Routes button to add and remove routes as necessary.

Remember that these settings apply to individual users, so you can assign different routes, caller ID, or callback settings to each user.

Using Network Access Policies

Windows Server 2016 includes support for additional configuration systems:

- Network access policies (which used to be called *remote access policy*).

- Remote access profiles.

- Network Policy Server (NPS) is the Microsoft implementation of a Remote Authentication Dial-in User Service (RADIUS) server and proxy in Windows Server 2012. NPS is the replacement for Internet Authentication Service (IAS) in Windows Server 2003.

Policies determine who can and cannot connect; you define rules with conditions that the system evaluates to see whether a particular user can connect.

You can have any number of policies in a native Windows Server 2016 domain; each policy must have exactly one profile associated with it.

Settings in an individual user's profile override settings in a network access policy.

You manage network access policies through the Remote Access Logging & Policies folder in the RRAS snap-in. Policies contain conditions that you pick from a list. When a caller connects, the policy's conditions are evaluated, one by one, to see whether the caller gets in. All of the conditions in the policy must match for the user to gain access. If there are multiple policies, they're evaluated according to an order you specify.

In the following sections, you will see how to create and configure network access policies.

Network Policy Attributes

To create a policy, right-click the Remote Access Logging & Policies folder and select Launch NPS. Then right-click Network Policies and choose New. This command starts the New Network Policy Wizard, which uses a series of steps to help you define the policy.

The Select Condition dialog box is part of the New Network Policy Wizard. It lists the attributes you can evaluate in a policy. Table 14.1 describes the attributes that you can set. These attributes are drawn from the RADIUS standards, so you can (and in some cases, should) intermix your Windows Server 2016 RRAS servers with RADIUS servers.

When setting up any policies, you must base your policy on company rules and standards. Remember, policies can allow or restrict users from remotely accessing your network. The needs of the organization determine the policy and when to use it.

Once you choose an attribute and click the Add button, its corresponding editor appears. You use the editor to set the value of the attribute. For example, if you select the Day And Time Restrictions attribute, you'll see the Time Of Day Constraints dialog box, which offers a calendar grid that lets you select which days and times are available for logging on.

TABLE 14.1   Network access policy attributes

Attribute Name	What It Specifies
Authentication Type	Specifies the authentication methods required to match this policy.
Allowed EAP Types	Specifies the EAP types required for the client computer authentication method configuration to match this policy.
Called Station ID	Specifies the phone number of the remote access port called by the caller.
Calling Station ID	Specifies the caller's phone number.
Client Friendly Name	Specifies the name of the RADIUS server that's attempting to validate the connection.
Client IP Address (IPv4 and IPv6)	Specifies the IP address of the RADIUS server that's attempting to validate the connection.
Client Vendor	Specifies the vendor of the remote access server that originally accepted the connection. This is used to set different policies for different hardware.
Day And Time Restrictions	Specifies the weekdays and times when connection attempts are accepted or rejected.
Framed Protocol	Specifies the protocol to be used for framing incoming packets (for example, PPP, SLIP, and so on).
HCAP (Host Credential Authorization Protocol) User Groups	Used for communications between NPS and some third-party network access servers (NASs).
Location Groups	Specifies the HCAP location groups required to match this policy. This is used for communications between HCAP and some third-party network access servers (NASs).
MS RAS Vendor	Specifies the vendor identification number of the network access server (NAS) that is requesting authentication.
NAS Identifier	Specifies the friendly name of the remote access server that originally accepted the connection.
NAS IP Address (IPv4 and IPv6)	Specifies the IP address of the remote access server that originally accepted the connection.

TABLE 14.1   Network access policy attributes *(continued)*

Attribute Name	What It Specifies
NAS Port Type	Specifies the physical connection (for example, ISDN, POTS) used by the caller.
Service Type	Specifies Framed or Async (for PPP) or login (Telnet).
Tunnel Type	Specifies which tunneling protocol should be used (L2TP or PPTP).
Windows Groups	Specifies which Windows groups are allowed access.

After you select an attribute and give it a value, you can add more attributes or move to the next page by clicking the Next button on the Select Condition page.

Once you're finished setting attributes, you arrive at the Specify Access Permission page of the wizard. This page has only two radio buttons: Grant Remote Access Permissions and Deny Remote Access Permissions. These buttons specify whether the policy you create *allows* users to connect or *prevents* users from connecting. The page also includes an Access Is Determined By User Dial-In Properties check box. If this box is checked and there is a conflict between the network policy and user dial-in properties, the user dial-in properties take precedence.

Creating a Network Access Policy

In Exercise 14.4, you'll create an adjunct policy that adds time and day restrictions to the default policy. (An *adjunct policy* is one used in conjunction with another policy.) This exercise requires that you have completed the previous exercises in this chapter.

EXERCISE 14.4

Creating a Network Access Policy

1. Open the RRAS MMC snap-in by pressing the Windows key and selecting Administrative Tools ➢ Routing And Remote Access.

2. Expand the server you want to configure in the left pane of the MMC.

3. Right-click the Remote Access Logging And Policies folder.

4. Right-click and then select Launch NPS.

5. Once the Network Policy Server page appears, right-click Network Policies and then choose New.

6. The New Network Policy Wizard starts. In the Policy Name box, enter **Test Policy** and then click Next (leave the other settings as they are).

7. On the Specify Conditions page, click the Add button.

8. In the Select Condition dialog box, scroll down and click Day And Time Restrictions. Click Add.

9. The Time Of Day Constraints dialog box appears. Use the calendar controls to allow remote access Monday through Saturday from 7 a.m. to 7 p.m. and then click the OK button.

10. The Select Conditions dialog box reappears, this time with the new condition listed. Click the Next button.

11. The Specify Access Permission page appears. Select the Access Granted radio button and click Next to continue.

12. The Configure Authentication Methods page appears next. This page is where you choose which authentication methods will be used for this connection. Make sure that MS-CHAP and MS-CHAPv2 are both checked, along with the check boxes associated with them. Click Next.

13. The Configure Constraints page appears. Under Constraints, click Session Timeout. On the right side, click the Disconnect After The Following Maximum Session Time box, and type **60** in the field (the value represents minutes). Click Next.

14. The Configure Settings page appears. This page allows you to configure any additional settings for this network policy. Click Next.

15. On the Completing New Network Policy page, click Finish.

NPS as a RADIUS Proxy Server

When a user tries to log into a domain through the use of a RADIUS server, the RADIUS server processes the connection request and helps the user log into the network.

RADIUS proxy servers work in a different way. When a connection request comes into a RADIUS proxy server, the RADIUS proxy server forwards the request to another RADIUS server for authentication onto the network. Servers that are running Network Policy Server can act both as a RADIUS server and as a RADIUS proxy.

When an administrator sets up NPS as a RADIUS server, NPS provides some of the following actions to help the RADIUS server work properly:

- RADIUS clients send an access request to the central authentication and authorization service. NPS uses Active Directory to authenticate the user's credentials. NPS accesses the Active Directory user's dial-in properties and policies to authorize the connection.

- When using NPS, the RADIUS server also records all accounting information on how much the RADIUS server is used. This is helpful when you have to bill other departments for the RADIUS use. Many organizations require that each department pay for its RADIUS use for its users, and using NPS allows an administrator to do this.

When you set up NPS as a RADIUS proxy, NPS provides all of the routing between all of the RADIUS servers and RADIUS clients. NPS is the main switching and routing service when you use RADIUS as a proxy server.

NPS Configuration

Now that you know that NPS can be set up as a RADIUS server, let's take a look at some of those details of how to do it. When an administrator sets up NPS as a RADIUS proxy, network access servers are then configured as the RADIUS clients. The RADIUS proxy server receives requests from the RADIUS clients, and then the RADIUS server forwards those requests to the appropriate servers. Using NPS to set up a RADIUS proxy should be done when the following conditions are needed:

- If you are the administrator of an organization that offers VPN or wireless network access to multiple clients, the RADIUS server can authenticate and authorize the user through their authentication server.

- If you are an administrator of a domain and you want users who are not members of your domain to authenticate into your domain, you can use an NPS server with a RADIUS proxy. To make this situation work, you must set up a two-way trust (two one-way trusts in opposite directions).

- Another great example of when to set up a RADIUS proxy server is when you are using a non-Microsoft-based database. RADIUS servers have the ability to communicate with different types of databases, allowing users still to be authenticated even when it's not a Microsoft authentication database; an example is a Novell Directory Services (NDS) database.

Another configuration that you may need to set when configuring NPS and RADIUS is the priority. The higher the RADIUS priority number, the less that the RADIUS server gets used. For example, if I have two RADIUS servers named Server1 and Server2 and I want Server2 used only when Server1 is unavailable, I would set the RADIUS priority from 1 to 10. This way it will get used only when Server1 is having issues or is unresponsive.

RADIUS Clients

Network access servers that are RADIUS RFC compliant (2865 and 2866) are considered RADIUS clients when used with NPS and a RADIUS server or proxy.

NPS allows an administrator to enable the use of wireless, switches, remote access, or VPN equipment as long as they are heterogeneous or homogenous sets. Network administrators can allow authentication and authorization through the use of NPS network connection requests as long as administrators deploy the following types of network access servers and technologies:

- Wired access with 802.1X-secured and RADIUS-compliant authenticating switches
- Wireless access with 802.1X-secured and RADIUS-compliant wireless access points

NPS Templates

Templates can be a valuable tool when used properly. Templates allow you to create something once and then use that template to create the same thing over and over again.

You can use templates when creating Active Directory users, when setting up GPOs, and now even when setting up NPS. NPS templates allow an administrator to save time and thus also save the cost required to manage and configure NPS on multiple servers. Multiple NPS templates are available in the Templates Management MMC for an administrator to configure:

- Shared Secrets
- RADIUS Clients
- Remote RADIUS Servers
- IP Filters
- Health Policies
- Remediation Server Groups

One advantage of creating a template is that once the template is created, there is no interference with the actual NPS server's performance. Creating templates does not affect an operational NPS server in any way. Once you load the template to the appropriate location, the template becomes active.

Creating Templates

To create a template in the Template Management MMC, right-click the template type you want to create (such as Health Policies) and click New. The New Template dialog box appears, and you just fill in all of your configuration information.

Importing and Exporting NPS Policies

Importing/exporting NPS is a pretty easy thing. It just happens to depend on which version of Windows you are exporting from. In the following examples, I will explain how to export from Windows Server 2012 R2 using the Windows MMC and how to import into Windows Server 2016.

Exporting from Windows Server 2012 R2

To export NPS from Windows Server 2012 R2, follow these steps:

1. On the source server, open Server Manager.
2. In the Server Manager console tree, open Roles\Network Policy and Access Services\NPS.
3. Right-click NPS and then click Export Configuration.
4. In the dialog box that appears, select the check box I Am Aware That I Am Exporting All Shared Secrets and then click OK.

5. For File Name, type **file.xml**, navigate to the migration store file location, and then click Save.

6. In the console tree, right-click Templates Management and then click Export Templates To A File.

7. For File Name, type **iastemplates.xml**, navigate to the migration store file location, and then click Save.

8. If you have configured SQL logging, you must manually record detailed SQL configuration settings.

    To record these settings, follow these steps:

    a. In the NPS console tree, click Accounting and then click Change SQL Server Logging Properties.

    b. Record the configuration settings on the Settings tab and then click Configure.

    c. Manually record all configuration settings from the Connection and Advanced tabs by copying them into the sql.txt file. Alternatively, you can click the All tab and enter Name and Value settings displayed on each line into the sql.txt file.

9. Copy the file.xml, iastemplates.xml, and sql.txt files to the migration store file location. This information will be required to configure the destination server.

Importing to Windows Server 2016

To import NPS from Windows Server 2016, follow these steps:

1. Copy the configuration files file.xml, iastemplates.xml, and sql.txt that were exported to the migration store file location to the destination NPS server. Alternatively, you can import configuration settings directly from the migration store file location by supplying the appropriate path to the file in the import command. If you have custom settings that were recorded using the NPS Server Migration: Appendix A—Data Collection Worksheet, they must be configured manually on the destination server.

2. On the destination server, open Server Manager.

3. In the Server Manager console tree, click All Servers; then, from the list of servers in the right pane, right-click the relevant server and select Network Policy Server.

4. To import template configuration settings, complete the remaining steps in this list. If you do not have template settings, skip to step 7.

5. In the console tree, right-click Templates Management and then click Import Templates from a file.

6. Select the template configuration file iastemplates.xml that you copied from the source server and then click Open.

7. In the console tree, right-click NPS and then click Import Configuration.

8. Select the configuration file file.xml or ias.txt that you copied from the source server and then click Open.

9. Verify that a message appears indicating the import was successful.

10. Configure SQL accounting if required using the `sql.txt` file and the data collection worksheet. To configure SQL accounting, complete the remaining steps in this list.

11. In the NPS console tree, click Accounting and then click Change SQL Server Logging Properties in the details pane.

12. Modify the properties on the Settings tab if required and then click Configure to enter detailed settings.

13. Using information recorded in the `sql.txt` file, enter the required settings on the Connection and Advanced tabs and then click OK.

Using Remote Access Profiles

Remote access profiles are an integral part of network access policies. Profiles determine what happens during call setup and completion. Each policy has a profile associated with it; the profile determines what settings will be applied to connections that meet the conditions stated in the policy.

For security reasons, it's usually a good idea to limit access to the administrative accounts on your network. In particular, as a consultant, I usually tell clients to restrict remote access for the administrator account; that way, the potential exposure from a dial-up compromise is reduced. In Exercise 14.5, you will learn how to configure the administrator account's user profile to restrict dial-up access.

EXERCISE 14.5

Restricting a User Profile for Dial-In Access

1. Log on to your computer using an account that has administrative privileges.

2. If you're using an RRAS server that's part of an Active Directory domain, open the Active Directory Users and Computers snap-in by pressing the Windows key and selecting Administrative Tools ➤ Active Directory Users And Computers. If not, open the Local Users and Groups snap-in by pressing the Windows key and selecting Administrative Tools ➤ Computer Management ➤ Local Users And Groups.

3. Expand the tree to the Users folder. Right-click the Administrator account in the right pane and choose Properties. The Administrator Properties dialog box appears.

4. Switch to the Dial-In tab. On machines that participate in Active Directory, make sure the Control Access Through NPS Network Policy option (in the Permissions group) is selected.

5. Click the Deny Access radio button to prevent the use of this account over a dial-in connection.

6. Click the OK button.

You can create one profile for each policy. The profile contains settings that fit into specific areas. Each area has its own link in the profile's Properties dialog box.

The Constraints Tab

The Constraints tab has most of the settings that you think of when you consider dial-in access controls. The controls here allow you to adjust how long the connection can be idle before it gets dropped, how long it can be up, the dates and times for establishing the connection, and what dial-in port and medium can be used to connect.

Authentication Link

In the Authentication Methods pane, you can specify which authentication methods are allowed on this specific policy. Note that these settings, like the other policy settings, will be useful only if the server's settings match. For example, if you turn EAP authentication off in the server's Properties dialog box, turning it on in the Authentication Methods pane of the profile's Properties dialog box will have no effect.

You'll notice that each authentication method has a check box. Check the appropriate boxes to control the protocols that you want this profile to use. If you enable EAP, you can also choose which specific EAP type you want the profile to support. You can also choose to allow totally unauthenticated access (which is unchecked by default).

Settings Tab

The Settings tab of the policy's Properties dialog box has several useful sections, which are described in the following list:

IP Settings Pane   The IP Settings pane gives you control over the IP-related settings associated with an incoming call. If you think back to the server-specific settings covered earlier, you'll remember that the server preferences include settings for protocols other than IP; this is not so in the network access profile. In this pane, you can specify where the client gets its IP address.

Multilink And Bandwidth Allocation Protocol (BAP) Pane   The profile mechanism gives you a degree of control over how the server handles multilink calls. You exert this control through the Multilink And Bandwidth Allocation Protocol (BAP) pane of the profile Properties dialog box. Your first choice is to decide whether to allow multilink calls at all and, if so, how many ports you want to let a single client use at once. Normally, this setting is configured so that the server-specific settings take precedence, but you can override them.

Bandwidth Allocation Protocol Group   The Bandwidth Allocation Protocol control group gives you a way to control what happens during a multilink call when the bandwidth usage drops below a certain threshold. For example, why tie up three analog lines to provide 168 Kbps of bandwidth when the connection is using only 56 Kbps? You can tweak the capacity and time thresholds. By default, a multilink call will drop one line every time the bandwidth usage falls to less than 50 percent of the available bandwidth and stays there for two minutes. The Require BAP For Dynamic Multilink Requests check box allows you to refuse calls from clients that don't support BAP. This is an easy way to make sure that no client can hog your multilink bandwidth.

Encryption Pane   The Encryption pane of the Settings tab controls which type of encryption you want your remote users to be able to access.

The following radio buttons are on the Encryption pane:

- Basic Encryption (MPPE 40-Bit) means single Data Encryption Standard (DES) for IPsec or 40-bit Microsoft Point-to-Point Encryption (MPPE) for Point-to-Point Tunneling Protocol (PPTP).

- Strong Encryption (MPPE 56-Bit) means 56-bit encryption (single DES for IPsec; 56-bit MPPE for PPTP).

- Strongest Encryption (MPPE 128-Bit) means triple DES for IPsec or 128-bit MPPE for PPTP connections.

- No Encryption allows users to connect using no encryption at all. Unless this button is selected, a remote connection must be encrypted or it'll be rejected.

In Exercise 14.6, you'll force all connections to your server to use encryption. Any client that can't use encryption will be dropped. You must complete Exercise 14.4 before you do this exercise.

WARNING   Don't do this exercise on your production RRAS server unless you're sure that all of your clients are encryption-capable.

EXERCISE 14.6

Configuring Encryption

1. Open the RRAS MMC snap-in by pressing the Windows key and selecting Administrative Tools ➢ Routing And Remote Access.

2. Expand the server you want to configure in the left pane of the MMC.

3. Right-click the `Remote Access Logging & Policies` folder.

4. Select Launch NPS.

5. Once the Network Policy Server page appears, click the hours policy you created in Exercise 14.4. (I named mine Test Policy.)

6. Select Action ➢ Properties. The policy's Properties dialog box appears.

7. Click the Settings tab. Select Encryption in the left pane.

8. In the right pane, uncheck the No Encryption check box. Make sure that the Basic, Strong, and Strongest check boxes are all selected.

9. Click the OK button. When the policy Properties dialog box reappears, click the OK button.

Setting Up a VPN Network Access Policy

Earlier in this chapter, you learned how to use the Network Access Policy mechanism on a Windows Server 2016 domain. Now it's time to apply what you've learned to a virtual private network (VPN). Recall that you have two ways to control which specific users can access a remote access server:

- You can grant and deny dial-up permission to individual users in each user's Properties dialog box.

- You can create a network access policy that embodies whatever restrictions you want to impose.

It turns out that you can do the same thing for VPN connections, but there are a few additional things to consider.

Granting and Denying Per-User Access

To grant or deny VPN access to individual users, all you have to do is make the appropriate change on the Dial-In tab of each user's Properties dialog box. Although this is the easiest method to understand, it gets tedious quickly if you need to change VPN permissions for more than a few users. Furthermore, this method offers you no way to distinguish between dial-in and VPN permissions.

Creating a Network Access Policy for VPNs

You may find it helpful to create network access policies that enforce the permissions that you want end users to have. You can accomplish this result in a number of ways; which one you use will depend on your overall use of network access policies.

The simplest way is to create a policy that allows all of your users to use a VPN. Earlier in this chapter, you learned how to create network access policies and specify settings for them; one thing you may have noticed was that there's a NAS-Port-Type attribute that you can use in the policy's conditions. That attribute is the cornerstone of building a policy that allows or denies remote access via VPN because you use it to accept or reject connections arriving over a particular type of VPN connection. For best results, you'll use the Tunnel-Type attribute in conjunction with the NAS-Port-Type attribute, as described in Exercise 14.7.

EXERCISE 14.7

Creating a VPN Network Access Policy

1. Open the RRAS MMC snap-in by pressing the Windows key and selecting Administrative Tools ➢ Routing And Remote Access.

2. Expand the server you want to configure in the left pane of the MMC.

3. Right-click the Remote Access Logging & Policies folder.

4. Select Launch NPS.

5. Once the Network Policy Server page appears, right-click Network Policies and choose New.

6. The New Network Policy Wizard starts. In the Policy Name box, enter VPN Network Policy and click Next (leave the other settings as they are).

7. On the Specify Conditions page, click the Add button.

8. On the Select Condition page, scroll down, click NAS-Port-Type Attribute, and click Add. When the NAS Port Type page appears, click Virtual VPN in the Common Dial-Up And VPN Tunnel Types box. Click OK and then click the Next button.

9. The Specify Conditions page reappears, this time with the new condition listed. Click the Next button.

10. The Specify Access Permission page appears. Select the Access Granted radio button and click Next to continue.

11. Next the Configure Authentication Methods page will appear. This page is where you choose which authentication methods will be used for this connection. Make sure that MS-CHAP and MS-CHAPv2 are both checked along with their associated check boxes. Click Next.

12. The Configure Constraints page appears. Under Constraints, click Session Timeout. On the right side, click the Disconnect After The Following Maximum Session Time box and type 60 in the box (the value specifies minutes). Click Next.

13. The Configure Settings page appears. This page allows you to configure any additional settings for this network policy. Click Next.

14. At the Completing New Network Policy page, click Finish.

If you don't want to grant VPN access to everyone, you can make some changes to the process in Exercise 14.7 to fine-tune it. First you'll probably want to move the VPN policy to the top of the list. (When you first add the policy described in the exercise, it is placed at the end of the policy list. Unless you move it, the default policies will take effect before the VPN-specific policy does.)

Next you can create an Active Directory group and put your VPN users in it. You can then create a policy using the two conditions outlined in Exercise 14.7 plus a condition that uses the Windows-Groups attribute to specify the new group. You can also use this process to allow everyone dial-up access and reserve VPN capability for a smaller group.

Connection Manager

To help administrators create and manage remote access connections, Microsoft includes a suite of components called Connection Manager within Windows Server 2016. Connection Manager is not installed by default. You can install the Connection Manager using Server Manager ➤ Add Roles ➤ Network Access Services.

Connection Manager allows an administrator to create remote access connections called *service profiles*. These profiles then appear on client machines as network connections. You can use these network connections to connect client machines to VPNs or remote networks.

Configuring Security

When configuring remote access security, you must consider several aspects, the most fundamental of which involves configuring the types of authentication and encryption that the server will use when accepting client requests. You will look at each of these in the following sections.

Controlling Server Security

The Security tab of the server's Properties dialog box (see Figure 14.22) allows you to specify which authentication and accounting methods RRAS uses. You can choose one of two authentication providers by using the Authentication Provider drop-down list.

FIGURE 14.22   The Security tab of the RRAS server's Properties dialog box

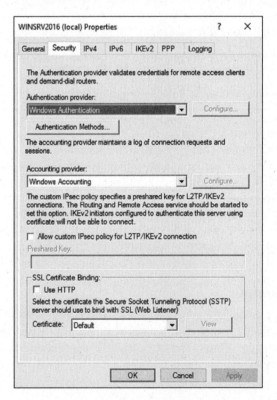

Your choices include the following:

Windows Authentication   This is a built-in authentication suite included with Windows Server 2016.

RADIUS Authentication   This authentication allows you to send all authentication requests heard by your server to a RADIUS server for approval or denial.

You can also use the Accounting Provider drop-down list on the Security tab to choose between the following:

Windows Accounting   With this type of accounting, connection requests are maintained in the event log.

RADIUS Accounting   In this type of accounting, all accounting events, such as call start and call stop, are sent to a RADIUS server for action.

RADIUS Authentication Settings

When you select the RADIUS Authentication option from the Authentication Provider drop-down menu, you are enabling a RADIUS client that passes authentication duties to a RADIUS server. This communication is sent via UDP on port 1645 or 1812, depending on the version of RADIUS being used.

Click the Configure button to open the RADIUS Authentication dialog box. From here, you can set the following options:

- Click the Add button to add the name or address of a RADIUS server to which the RAS server will pass authentication duties.

- You must also enter the correct secret, which is initially set by the RADIUS server.

- The Time-Out option determines how long the RRAS server will attempt to authenticate the remote user before giving up.

- The Initial Score option is similar to the cost value used by routers. The RAS server will attempt to authenticate users on the RADIUS server with the highest score first. If that attempt fails, the RAS server will use the RADIUS server with the next highest score, and so on.

- Although the Port option can be changed, the default setting is part of RFC 2866, "RADIUS Accounting," and it should not be altered unless extraordinary circumstances call for it.

   The Internet Assigned Numbers Authority (IANA) is the official source for port number assignment. You can view current port number assignments and other valuable information at www.iana.org/assignments/port-numbers.

Windows Authentication Settings

Select the Windows Authentication option from the Authentication Provider drop-down menu if you want the local machine to authenticate your remote access users. To configure the server by telling it which authentication methods you want it to use, click the Authentication Methods button, which displays the Authentication Methods dialog box. If you look at the list of authentication protocols earlier in the chapter, you'll find that each one has a corresponding check box here: EAP, MS-CHAPv2, CHAP, and PAP. You can also turn on unauthenticated access by checking the Allow Remote Systems To Connect Without Authentication box, but that is not recommended because it allows anyone to connect to, and use, your server (and thus by extension your network).

There's actually a special set of requirements for using CHAP because it requires access to each user's encrypted password. Windows Server 2016 normally doesn't store user passwords in a format that CHAP can use, so you have to take some additional steps if you want to use CHAP:

1. Enable CHAP at the server and policy levels.

2. Edit the default domain GPO's Password Policy object to turn on the Store Password Using Reversible Encryption policy setting.

3. Change or reset each user's password, which forces Windows Server 2016 to store the password using reversible encryption.

After these steps are completed for an account, that account can be used with CHAP.

 These steps aren't required for MS-CHAPv2; for that protocol, you just enable MS-CHAPv2 at the server and policy levels.

Configuring Network Access Protection

Another way that you can have security is to allow users to access resources based on the identity of the client computer. This security solution is called *Network Access Protection (NAP)*. Determined by the client needs, network administrators now have the ability to define granular levels of network access using NAP. NAP also allows administrators to determine client access based on compliancy with corporate governance policies. The following are some of the NAP features:

Network Layer Protection   *Network layer protection* is the ability to secure communications at the Network layer of the OSI model.

All communications travel through the seven layers of the OSI model. Starting at the top (layer 7), the seven layers are the Application, Presentation, Session, Transport, Network, Data-Link, and Physical layers.

VPN Enforcement   VPN enforcement verifies the compliancy of the system before the VPN connection is given full access to the network.

IPsec Enforcement   *IPsec enforcement* will allow a computer to communicate with other computers as long as the computers are IPsec compliant. You have the ability to configure the requirements for secure communications between the two compliant computer systems. You can configure the IPsec communications based on IP address or TCP/UDP port numbers.

802.1X Enforcement   For a computer system to have 802.1X unlimited access to network connections (Ethernet 802.11 or wireless access point), the computer system must be 802.1X compliant. *802.1X enforcement* verifies that the connecting system is 802.1X connection compliant. Noncompliant computers will obtain only limited access to network connections.

Flexible Host Isolation   *Flexible host isolation* allows a server and domain to isolate computers to help make it possible to design a layer of security between computers or networks. Even if a hacker gains access to your network using an authorized username and password, the server and domain isolation can stop the attack because the computer is not an authorized domain computer.

Multiconfiguration System Health Validator   This feature allows you to specify multiple configurations of a *system health validator (SHV)*. When an administrator configures a network policy for health evaluation, the administrator will select a specific health policy. Using this feature allows you to specify different network policies for different sets of health requirements based on a specific configuration of the SHV. For example, an administrator can create a network policy that specifies that all internal computers must have antivirus software enabled and a different network policy that specifies that VPN-connected computers must have their antivirus software enabled and signature files up-to-date.

NAP Monitoring

There may be many times when you will need to monitor how NAP is running and what NAP policies are being enforced. There are multiple ways that you can monitor NAP. You can use the Network Access Protection MMC snap-in to look at how things are running.

But there is another tool that you can use called Logman. Logman creates and manages Event Trace Session and Performance logs and allows an administrator to monitor many different applications through the use of the command line. Table 14.2 shows some of the different Logman switches you can use.

TABLE 14.2   Logman switches

Switch	Description
Logman create	Creates a counter, trace, configuration data collector, or API
Logman query	Queries data collector properties
Logman start | stop	Starts or stops data collection
Logman delete	Deletes an existing data collector
Logman update	Updates the properties of an existing data collector
Logman import | export	Imports a data collector set from an XML file or exports a data collector set to an XML file

PowerShell for Remote Access

There may be times when you need to use PowerShell to configure Remote Access. Table 14.3 is just some of the PowerShell commands that you can use to configure and manage remote access.

 To see the entire list of Remote Access PowerShell commands, visit Microsoft's website at https://technet.microsoft.com/en-us/itpro/powershell/windows/remoteaccess/remoteaccess.

TABLE 14.3 PowerShell commands for RAS

Command	Description
Add-DAAppServer	This command allows an administrator to add a new application server security group to the DirectAccess.
Add-DAClient	Administrators use this command to add client computer security groups (SGs) to the DirectAccess (DA).
Add-DAEntryPoint	This command allows you to add an entry point to a multisite deployment.
Add-RemoteAccessIpFilter	Administrators use this command to add filters for network traffic that passes through a particular interface.
Add-RemoteAccessRadius	This command allows an administrator to add a new external RADIUS server for VPN or DirectAccess connectivity.
Disconnect-VpnUser	Administrators can use this command to disconnect a VPN user.
Enable-DAMultiSite	This command allows an admin to enable and configure a multisite deployment while also adding the first entry point.
Get-BgpPeer	Administrators can use this command to show the configuration information for BGP peers.
Get-BgpRouter	This command allows you to see the configuration information for BGP routers.
Get-DAClient	Administrators use this command to see the list of client security groups that are part of the DirectAccess deployment and the client properties.

Command	Description
Get-DAEntryPoint	This command shows the settings for an entry point.
Get-DAServer	Admins can use this command to see the properties of the DirectAccess server.
Get-RemoteAccess	This command shows the configuration of a DirectAccess and VPN server.
Remove-BgpPeer	Administrators can use this command to remove a BGP peer from a router.
Set-DAServer	This command allows an administrator to set the properties specific to the DirectAccess server.
Set-VpnAuthType	Administrators use this command to set the authentication type to be used for a VPN connection.
Set-VpnServerConfiguration	This command allows you to update the S2S server parameters.
Set-VpnSstpProxyRule	Administrators use this command for updating the tenant ID to gateway mapping for SSTP Proxy.
Update-DAMgmtServer	This command is used to update the list of management servers of the DirectAccess deployment.

Summary

In this chapter, you learned how to install and configure Routing and Remote Access Services to handle dial-in connections, how to configure appropriate encryption and security settings so that communication between the client and server is encrypted and authenticated, how to install RRAS to provide VPN service using the PPTP and L2TP protocols, how to configure VPN services on the server and client, and, finally, how to troubleshoot common problems with VPNs. I explained the benefits of DirectAccess and how DirectAccess works.

I talked about the different ways that you can secure your remote access connections. You learned how to configure appropriate security settings so that communication between the client and server is secure because of NAP and NPS settings.

I talked about how to verify that client machines meet the minimum requirements in order to gain either full or limited access to your network.

I also discussed wireless networking and what types of security encryption you can use to help support your wireless network. You learned about the different components of wireless access and using group policies to configure wireless clients.

Exam Essentials

Know how to install and configure RAS at the server level.   The RAS installation process is driven by the Routing and Remote Access Server Setup Wizard, which you use to set up a dial-up server. You can specify whether the server acts as a remote access server, specify what authentication providers and settings you want the server to use, control the settings applied to each protocol you have installed, specify which PPP protocols (including multilink) the clients on this server are allowed to use, and control what level of log detail is kept for incoming connections.

Know how to install and configure a VPN server.   If you don't have RRAS installed, you'll need to install it, activate it, and configure it as a VPN server. If you're already using RRAS for IP routing or remote access, you can enable it as a VPN server without reinstalling. VPN configuration is extremely simple, at least for PPTP. Either a server can accept VPN calls or it can't. If it can, it will have a certain number of VPN ports, all of which are configured identically.

Know how to configure an RRAS client.   Most client connections are made on Windows 8, Windows 7, Windows Vista, or Windows XP Professional workstations. Dial-in and VPN connections are configured similarly, but when creating a VPN connection, you must substitute an IP address for a phone number.

Understand what NAP can do for your network.   Understand that NAP allows administrators to determine client access based on compliancy with corporate governance policies. Some of the settings are Network Layer Protection, VPN Enforcement, IPsec Enforcement, 802.1X Enforcement, Flexible Host Isolation, and Multi-configuration System Health Validator.

Understand what NPS can do for your network.   Understand how to use NPS to manage network access centrally through a variety of network access servers, including RADIUS-compliant 802.1X-capable wireless access points, VPN servers, dial-up servers, and 802.1X-capable Ethernet switches.

Video Resources

There are videos available for the following exercises:

> Exercise 14.1
>
> Exercise 14.2

You can access the videos at http://sybextestbanks.wiley.com on the Other Study Tools tab.

Review Questions

1. You are the network administrator for StormWind Studios. You deploy a RAS Gateway server as an edge VPN server and as an edge DirectAccess server. Your users can now access the corporate network by using either VPN or DirectAccess connections. Which RAS Gateway mode is being described?

   A. Multitenant mode

   B. Single tenant mode

2. What PowerShell command would you use to see the configuration information for your BGP routers?

   A. `Get-BgpRouter`

   B. `Get-Router`

   C. `Set-RouterClient`

   D. `Add-BgpClient`

3. You are the administrator of StormWind. You need to see a list of client security groups that are a part of the DirectAccess deployment. What PowerShell command would you use?

   A. `Get-Client`

   B. `Get-DAClient`

   C. `Get-VPNClient`

   D. `Get-RASClient`

4. Your network contains an Active Directory domain named StormWind.com. Network Access Protection (NAP) is deployed to the domain. You need to create NAP event trace log files on a client computer. What should you run?

   A. Register-ObjectEvent

   B. Register-EngineEvent

   C. tracert

   D. logman

5. Your network contains four Network Policy Server (NPS) servers named ServerA, ServerB, ServerC, and ServerD. Server1 is configured as a RADIUS proxy that forwards connection requests to a remote RADIUS server group named Group1. You need to ensure that ServerB and ServerC receive connection requests. ServerD should receive connection requests only if both ServerB and ServerC are unavailable. How should you configure Group1?

   A. Change the weight of ServerB and ServerC to 10.

   B. Change the weight of ServerD to 10.

   C. Change the priority of ServerB and ServerC to 10.

   D. Change the priority of ServerD to 10.

6. You have a Windows Server 2016 server named ServerA. ServerA is located on the perimeter network and only uses inbound TCP port 443 is allowed to connect ServerA from the Internet. You install the Remote Access server role on ServerA. You need to configure ServerA to accept VPN connections over port 443. Which VPN protocol should you use?

    A. PPTP

    B. SSTP

    C. L2TP

    D. IKEv2

7. What PowerShell command would you use to view the configuration of a DirectAccess or VPN server?

    A. Get-Server

    B. View-Server

    C. Get-RemoteAccess

    D. Get-RASAccess

8. You are the administrator of a large company. You need to set the setting of your DirectAccess server. What PowerShell command would you use?

    A. Set-DirectAccessServer

    B. Set-DAServer

    C. Set-DirectServer

    D. Set-RASServer

9. You have decided to implement a VPN server. You want to set the authentication type for the VPN connect. What PowerShell command would you use?

    A. Set-VPNType

    B. Set-AuthType

    C. Set-VPNAuthType

    D. Set-VPNAuth

10. You are the network administrator for a mid-size company. You need to add a new external RADIUS server for VPN connectivity. What PowerShell command would you use?

    A. Add-RemoteAccessServer

    B. Add-RemoteAccess

    C. Add-RASServer

    D. Add-RemoteAccessRadius

Chapter

15

Understanding File Services

THE FOLLOWING 70-741 EXAM OBJECTIVES ARE COVERED IN THIS CHAPTER:

✓ **Implement Distributed File System (DFS) and Branch Office solutions**

 ▪ This objective may include but is not limited to: Install and configure DFS namespaces; configure DFS replication targets; configure replication scheduling; configure Remote Differential Compression (RDC) settings; configure staging; configure fault tolerance; clone a Distributed File System Replication (DFSR) database; recover DFSR databases; optimize DFS Replication; install and configure BranchCache; implement distributed and hosted cache modes; implement BranchCache for web, file, and application servers; troubleshoot BranchCache.

In this chapter, I will talk about the services that we can use with file servers. File servers are servers that are set up to host files for your organization. Once you have set up a basic server and decided that the server will host files, it's now time to add some other features to that server.

I will start the chapter talking about using the File Server Resource Manager. This is a utility that allows an administrator to manage and configure file servers. This includes setting up how much space your users will get on the file servers. I will also show you how to set up and manage encrypted files using the Encrypting File System (EFS).

I will then introduce you to the Distributed File System (DFS) setup. I will show you how to install and set up a DFS namespace. I will then show you how to add shared folders to the DFS structure.

Configuring File Server Resource Manager

As an administrator, when you need to control and manage the amount and type of data stored on your servers, Microsoft delivers the tools to help you do just that. The *File Server Resource Manager (FSRM)* is a suite of tools that allows an administrator to place quotas on folders or volumes, filter file types, and create detailed storage reports. These tools allow an administrator to properly plan and implement policies on data as needed.

FSRM Features

Many of the advantages of using FSRM come from all of the included features, which allow administrators to manage the data that is stored on their file servers. Some of the advantages included with FSRM are as follows:

Configure File Management Tasks   FSRM allows an administrator to apply a policy or action to data files. Some of the actions that can be performed include the ability to encrypt files or run a custom command.

Configure Quotas   Quotas give an administrator the ability to limit how much disk space a user can use on a file server. Administrators have the ability to limit space to an entire volume or to specific folders.

File Classification Infrastructure   Administrators can set file classifications and then manage the data more effectively by using these classifications. Classifying files, and then setting policies to those classifications, allows an administrator to set policies on those classifications. These policies include restricting file access, file encryption, and file expirations.

Configure File Screens   Administrators can set file screening on a server and limit the types of files that are being stored on that server. For example, an administrator can set a file screen on a server so that any file ending in .bmp gets rejected.

Configure Reports   Administrators can create reports that show them how data is classified and accessed. They also have the ability to see which users are trying to save unauthorized file extensions.

Installing the FSRM Role Service

Installing FSRM is easy when using either Server Manager or PowerShell. To install using Server Manager, you go into Add Roles And Features and choose File And Storage Services ➢ File Services ➢ File Server Resource Manager. To install FSRM using PowerShell, you use the following command:

```
Install-WindowsFeature -Name FS-Resource-Manager -IncludeManagementTools
```

Configuring FSRM using the Windows GUI version is straightforward, but setting up FSRM using PowerShell is a bit more challenging. Table 15.1 describes some of the PowerShell commands for FSRM.

TABLE 15.1   PowerShell commands for FSRM

PowerShell Cmdlet	Description
Get-FsrmAutoQuota	Gets auto-apply quotas on a server
Get-FsrmClassification	Gets the status of the running file classification
Get-FsrmClassificationRule	Gets classification rules
Get-FsrmFileGroup	Gets file groups
Get-FsrmFileScreen	Gets file screens
Get-FsrmFileScreenException	Gets file screen exceptions
Get-FsrmQuota	Gets quotas on the server
Get-FsrmSetting	Gets the current FSRM settings

TABLE 15.1 PowerShell commands for FSRM *(continued)*

PowerShell Cmdlet	Description
Get-FsrmStorageReport	Gets storage reports
New-FsrmAutoQuota	Creates an auto-apply quota
New-FsrmFileGroup	Creates a file group
New-FsrmFileScreen	Creates a file screen
New-FsrmQuota	Creates an FSRM quota
New-FsrmQuotaTemplate	Creates a quota template
Remove-FsrmClassificationRule	Removes classification rules
Remove-FsrmFileScreen	Removes a file screen
Remove-FsrmQuota	Removes an FSRM quota from the server
Set-FsrmFileScreen	Changes the configuration settings of a file screen
Set-FsrmQuota	Changes the configuration settings for an FSRM quota

Configure File and Disk Encryption

Hardware and software encryption are some of the most important actions you can take as an administrator. You must make sure that if anyone steals hardware from your company or from your server rooms that the data they are stealing is secured and cannot be used. This is where BitLocker can help.

Using BitLocker Drive Encryption

To prevent individuals from stealing your computer and viewing personal and sensitive data found on your hard disk, some editions of Windows come with a new feature called *BitLocker Drive Encryption*. BitLocker encrypts the entire system drive. New files added to this drive are encrypted automatically, and files moved from this drive to another drive or computers are decrypted automatically.

Only Windows 7 Enterprise, Windows 7 Ultimate, Windows 8 Pro, Windows 8 Enterprise, Windows 10 Enterprise, Windows 10 Pro, Windows Server 2008, Windows Server 2008 R2,

Windows Server 2012, Windows Server 2012 R2, and Windows Server 2016 include BitLocker Drive Encryption, and only the operating system drive (usually C:) or internal hard drives can be encrypted with BitLocker. Files on other types of drives must be encrypted using BitLocker To Go. BitLocker To Go allows you to put BitLocker on removable media such as external hard disks or USB drives.

BitLocker Recovery Password

The BitLocker recovery password is important. Do not lose it, or you may not be able to unlock the drive. Even if you do not have a TPM, be sure to keep your recovery password in case your USB drive becomes lost or corrupted.

BitLocker uses a *Trusted Platform Module (TPM)* version 1.2 or newer to store the security key. A TPM is a chip that is found in newer computers. If you do not have a computer with a TPM, you can store the key on a removable USB drive. The USB drive will be required each time you start the computer so that the system drive can be decrypted.

If the TPM discovers a potential security risk, such as a disk error or changes made to the BIOS, hardware, system files, or startup components, the system drive will not be unlocked until you enter the 48-digit BitLocker recovery password or use a USB drive with a recovery key as a recovery agent.

BitLocker must be set up either within the Local Group Policy editor or through the BitLocker icon in the Control Panel. One advantage of using BitLocker is that you can prevent any unencrypted data from being copied onto a removable disk, thus protecting the computer.

BitLocker requires that you have a hard disk with at least two partitions, both formatted with NTFS. One partition will be the system partition that will be encrypted. The other partition will be the active partition that is used to start the computer. This partition will remain unencrypted.

Features of BitLocker

As with any version of Windows, Microsoft continues to improve on the technologies used in Windows Server 2016 and Windows 10. The following sections cover some of the features of BitLocker.

BitLocker Provisioning

In previous versions of BitLocker (Windows Vista and Windows 7), BitLocker provisioning (system and data volumes) was completed during the post installation of the BitLocker utility. BitLocker provisioning was done through either the command-line interface (CLI) or the Control Panel. In the Windows 8/Windows Server 2016 version of BitLocker, an administrator can choose to provision BitLocker before the operating system is even installed.

Administrators have the ability to enable BitLocker prior to the operating system deployment from the Windows Preinstallation Environment (WinPE). BitLocker is applied to the formatted volume, and BitLocker encrypts the volume prior to running the Windows setup process.

If an administrator wants to check the status of BitLocker on a particular volume, the administrator can view the status of the drive either in the BitLocker Control Panel applet or in File Explorer.

Used Disk Space–Only Encryption

Windows 7 BitLocker requires that all data and free space on the drive must be encrypted. Because of this requirement, the encryption process can take a long time on larger volumes. In Windows 10 BitLocker, administrators have the ability to encrypt either the entire volume or just the space being used. When you choose the Used Disk Space Only option, only the section of the drive that contains data will be encrypted. Because of this, encryption is completed much faster.

Standard User PIN and Password Change

One issue that BitLocker has had in the past is that you need to be an administrator to configure BitLocker on operating system drives. This could become an issue in a large organization because deploying TPM + PIN to a large number of computers can be challenging.

Even with the new operating system changes, administrative privileges are still needed to configure BitLocker, but now your users have the ability to change the BitLocker PIN for the operating system or change the password on the data volumes.

When a user gets to choose their own PIN and password, they normally choose something that has meaning to them and something that is easy to remember. That is a good and bad thing at the same time. It's a good thing because when your users choose their own PIN and password, they normally don't need to write it down—they just know it. It's a bad thing because if anyone knows the user well, they can have an easier time figuring out the person's PIN and password. Even when you allow your users to choose their own PIN and password, make sure you set a GPO to require password complexity.

Network Unlock

One of the features of BitLocker is called Network Unlock. *Network Unlock* allows administrators to easily manage desktop and servers that are configured to use BitLocker. Network Unlock allows an administrator to configure BitLocker to automatically unlock an encrypted hard drive during a system reboot when that hard drive is connected to their trusted corporate environment. For this to function properly on a machine, there has to be a DHCP driver implementation in the system's firmware.

If your operating system volume is also protected by the TPM + PIN protection, the administrator has to be sure to enter the PIN at the time of the reboot. This protection can actually make using Network Unlock more difficult to use, but they can be used in combination.

Support for Encrypted Hard Drives for Windows

One of the new advantages of using BitLocker is *Full Volume Encryption (FVE)*. BitLocker provides built-in encryption for Windows data files and Windows operating system files. The advantage of this type of encryption is that encrypted hard drives that use *Full Disk Encryption (FDE)* get each block of the physical disk space encrypted. Because each physical block gets encrypted, it offers much better encryption. The only downside to this is that because each physical block is encrypted, it degrades the hard drive speed somewhat. So, as an administrator, you have to decide whether you want better speed or better security on your hard disk.

Windows 7 and 2008 R2 vs. Windows 10 and 2016

The real question is what's the difference between Windows 7/Windows 2008 R2 and Windows 10/Windows Server 2016? Table 15.2 shows you many of the common features and how they work then and now.

TABLE 15.2   BitLocker then and now

Feature	Windows 7/Server 2008 R2	Windows 10/Server 2016
Resetting the BitLocker PIN or password	The user's privileges must be set to an administrator if you want to reset the BitLocker PIN on an operating system drive and the password on a fixed or removable data drive.	Standard users now have the ability to reset the BitLocker PIN and password on operating system drives, fixed data drives, and removable data drives.
Disk encryption	When BitLocker is enabled, the entire disk is encrypted.	When BitLocker is enabled, users have the ability to choose whether to encrypt the entire disk or only the used space on the disk.
Hardware-encrypted drive support	Not supported.	If the Windows logo hard drive comes preencrypted from the manufacturer, BitLocker is supported.
Unlocking using a network-based key to provide dual-factor authentication	Not available.	If a computer is rebooted on a trusted corporate wired-network key protector, then this feature allows a key to unlock and skip the PIN entry.

TABLE 15.2 BitLocker then and now *(continued)*

Feature	Windows 7/Server 2008 R2	Windows 10/Server 2016
Protection for clusters	Not available.	Windows Server 2016 BitLocker includes the ability to support cluster-shared volumes and failover clusters as long as they are running in a domain that was established by a Windows Server 2016 domain controller with the Kerberos Key Distribution Center Service enabled.
Linking a BitLocker key protector to an Active Directory account	Not available.	BitLocker allows a user, group, or computer account in Active Directory to be tied to a key protector. This key protector allows protected data volumes to be unlocked.

In Exercise 15.1, you will enable BitLocker on the Windows Server 2016 system.

EXERCISE 15.1

Enabling BitLocker in Windows Server 2016

1. Open Server Manager by selecting the Server Manager icon or running servermanager.exe.

2. Select Add Roles And Features from the dashboard.

3. Select Next at the Before You Begin pane (if shown).

4. Select role-based or feature-based installation and select Next to continue.

5. Select the Select A Server From The Server Pool option and click Next.

6. At the Select Server Roles screen, click Next.

7. At the Select Features screen, click the BitLocker Drive Encryption check box. When the Add Roles and Features dialog box appears, click the Add Features button. Then click Next.

8. Select the Install button on the Confirmation pane of the Add Roles and Features Wizard to begin BitLocker feature installation. The BitLocker feature requires a restart

to complete. Selecting the Restart The Destination Server Automatically If Required option in the Confirmation pane will force a restart of the computer after installation is complete.

9. If the Restart The Destination Server Automatically If Required check box is not selected, the Results pane of the Add Roles And Features Wizard will display the success or failure of the BitLocker feature installation. If required, a notification of additional action necessary to complete the feature installation, such as the restart of the computer, will be displayed in the results text.

You also can install BitLocker by using the Windows PowerShell utility. To install BitLocker, use the following PowerShell commands:

```
Install-WindowsFeature BitLocker -IncludeAllSubFeature -IncludeManagementTools
-Restart
```

Using EFS Drive Encryption

If you have been in the computer industry long enough, you may remember the days when only servers used NTFS. Years ago, most client systems used FAT or FAT32, but NTFS had some key benefits over FAT/FAT32. The main advantages were NTFS security, quotas, compression, and encryption. Encryption is available on a system because you are using a file structure (for example, NTFS) that allows encryption. Windows Server 2016 NTFS allows administrators to use these four advantages including encryption.

Encrypting File System (EFS) allows a user or administrator to secure files or folders by using encryption. Encryption employs the user's security identification (SID) number to secure the file or folder. Encryption is the strongest protection that Windows provides to help you keep your information secure. Some key features of EFS are as follows:

- Encrypting is simple; just select a check box in the file or folder's properties to turn it on.

- You have control over who can read the files.

- Files are encrypted when you close them but are automatically ready to use when you open them.

- If you change your mind about encrypting a file, clear the check box in the file's properties.

To implement encryption, open the Advanced Attributes dialog box for a folder and check the Encrypt Contents To Secure Data box.

If files are encrypted using EFS and an administrator has to unencrypt the files, there are two ways to do this. You can log in using the user's account (the account that encrypted the files) and unencrypt the files using the Cipher command. Alternatively, you can become a recovery agent and manually unencrypt the files.

If you use EFS, it's best not to delete users immediately when they leave a company. Administrators have the ability to recover encrypted files, but it is much easier to gain access to the user's encrypted files by logging in as the user who left the company and unchecking the encryption box.

Using the Cipher Command

The Cipher command is useful when it comes to EFS. Cipher is a command-line utility that allows you to change and/or configure EFS. When it comes to using the Cipher command, you should be aware of a few things:

- Administrators can decrypt files by running Cipher.exe in the Command Prompt window (advanced users).

- Administrators can use Cipher to modify an EFS-encrypted file.

- Administrators can use Cipher to import EFS certificates and keys.

- Administrators can also use Cipher to back up EFS certificates and keys.

Let's take a look at some of the different switches that you can use with Cipher. Table 15.3 describes many of the different Cipher switches you can use. This table comes from Microsoft's TechNet site. Microsoft continues to add and improve switches, so make sure you check Microsoft's website to see whether there are any changes.

TABLE 15.3 Using the cipher switches

Cipher switch	Description
/e	This switch allows an administrator to encrypt specified folders. With this folder encrypted, any files added to this folder will automatically be encrypted.
/d	This switch allows an administrator to decrypt specified folders.
/s: dir	By using this switch, the operation you are running will be performed in the specified folder and all subfolders.
/i	By default, when an error occurs, Cipher automatically halts. By using this switch, Cipher will continue to operate even after errors occur.
/f	The force switch (/f) will encrypt or decrypt all of the specified objects, even if the files have been modified by using encryption previously. Cipher, by default, does not touch files that have been encrypted or decrypted previously.

Cipher switch	Description
/q	This switch shows you a report about the most critical information of the EFS object.
/h	Normally, system or hidden files are not touched by encryption. By using this switch, you can display files with hidden or system attributes.
/k	This switch will create a new file encryption key based on the user currently running the Cipher command.
/?	This shows the Cipher help command.

Configuring Distributed File System

One problem that network administrators have is deciding how to share folders and communicating to end users how to find the shares. For example, if you share a folder called StormWind Documents on server A, how do you make sure your users will find the folder and the files within it? The users have to know the server name and the share name. This can be a huge problem if you have hundreds of shares on multiple servers. If you want to have multiple copies of the folder called StormWind Documents for fault tolerance and load balancing, the problem becomes even more complicated.

Distributed File System (DFS) in Windows Server 2016 offers a simplified way for users to access geographically dispersed files. DFS allows you to set up a tree structure of virtual directories that allows users to connect to shared folders throughout the entire network.

Administrators have the ability to take shared folders that are located on different servers and transparently connect them to one or more DFS namespaces—virtual trees of shared folders throughout an organization. The advantage of using DFS is that if one of the folders becomes unavailable, DFS has failover capability that will allow your users to connect to the data on a different server.

Administrators can use the DFS tools to choose which shared folders will appear in the namespace and also to decide how the names of these shared folders will show up in the virtual tree listing.

Advantages of DFS

One of the advantages of DFS is that when a user views this virtual tree, the shared folders appear to be located on a single machine. These are some of the other advantages of DFS:

Simplified Data Migration   DFS gives you the ability to move data from one location to another without the user needing to know the physical location of the data. Because the users do not need to know the physical location of the shared data, administrators can simply move data from one location to another.

Security Integration   Administrators do not need to configure additional security for the DFS shared folders. The shared folders use the NTFS and shared folder permissions that an administrator has already assigned when the share was set up.

Access-Based Enumeration (ABE)   This DFS feature (disabled by default) displays only the files and folders that a user has permissions to access. If a user does not have access to a folder, Windows hides the folder from the user's DFS view. This feature is not active if the user is viewing the files and folders locally.

Types of DFS

The following are types of DFS:

DFS Replication (DFSR)   Administrators have the ability to manage replication scheduling and bandwidth throttling using the DFS management console. Replication is the process of sharing data between multiple machines. As explained earlier in the section, replicated shared folders allow you to balance the load and have fault tolerance. DFS also has read-only replication folders.

DFS Namespace   The DFS Namespace service is the virtual tree listing in the DFS server. An administrator can set up multiple namespaces on the DFS, allowing for multiple virtual trees within DFS. The DFS Namespace service was once known as *Distributed File System* in Windows 2000 Server and Windows Server 2003 (in case you still use Server 2003).

In Exercise 15.2, you will install the DFS Namespace service on the file server. You need to start the installation using the Server Manager MMC.

EXERCISE 15.2

Installing the DFS Namespace Service

1.   Open Server Manager by selecting the Server Manager icon or running `servermanager.exe`.

2.   Select Add Roles And Features from the dashboard.

3.   Select Next at the Before You Begin pane (if shown).

4.   Select Role-Based or Feature-Based installation and select Next to continue.

5.   Select the Select A Server From The Server Pool option and click Next.

6. At the Select Server Roles screen, expand File And Storage Services and check the DFS Namespace and DFS Replication check boxes (See Figure 15.1). Then click Next. If a dialog box appears, click the Add Features button.

FIGURE 15.1   Select Server Roles

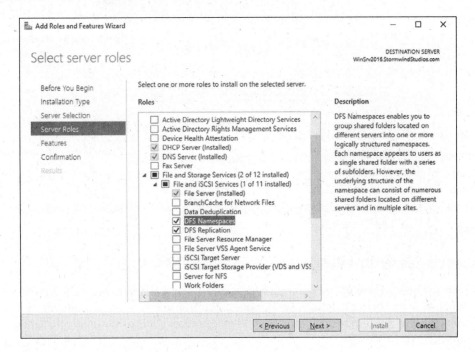

7. At the Select Features screen, click Next.

8. At the Confirmation screen, click the Install button.

9. After the installation is complete, click the Close button.

10. Close Server Manager.

Once you have installed DFS, it's time to learn how to manage DFS with the DFS Management MMC. The DFS Management console (see Figure 15.2) gives you one place to do all of your DFS configurations. The DFS Management console allows you to set up DFS Replication and DFS Namespace. Another task you can do in the DFS Management console is to add a folder target—a folder that you add to the DFS namespace (the virtual tree) for all your users to share.

FIGURE 15.2 DFS Management console

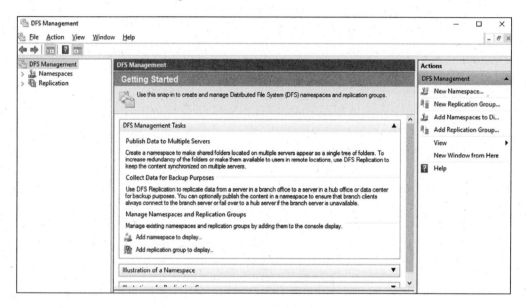

What's New in Windows Server 2016

As with any new version of an operating system, Microsoft is trying to make each version of Windows Server better than the previous ones. This is also true with DFS. Microsoft has added many new features to DFS, and the following are just some of the major changes of Windows Server 2016 DFS.

Windows PowerShell Module for DFS Replication

Windows PowerShell cmdlets for DFS replication modules can help administrators perform the majority of their DFS replication tasks. Administrators can use Windows PowerShell cmdlets to perform common administrative tasks such as creating, modifying, and removing DFS replication settings by using Window PowerShell scripts.

One of the nice new advantages of using Windows PowerShell for DFS is the ability to clone DFS replication databases and also to have the ability to restore those DFS databases in the event of an issue or crash.

Administrators have the ability to manage DFS management and replication through the use of the DNS Management and DFS Replication command-line utilities. Administrators who use the command-line tools are not doing anything incorrectly, but it is an inefficient way to do these tasks as well as being extremely time-consuming.

Administrators can use Windows PowerShell instead of command-line utilities and run hundreds of scripted commands, thus making their jobs easier and more efficient.

For an administrator who wants to use the Windows PowerShell cmdlets, the computer system installed with the DFS Management tools must be running Windows Server 2012

R2 or Windows 8.1 or newer. The DFS Management tools are part of the Remote Server Administration tools.

DFS Replication Windows Management Infrastructure Provider

In this book, I have spoken many times about using Windows Remote Management (WinRM) and how WinRM can help you administer a server remotely.

Windows Management Infrastructure (referred to as WMI v2) allows an administrator, using a properly configured firewall, to provide functionality and which provides programmatic access to manage DFS Replication (DFSR).

Database Cloning

For the first time ever in DFS, Windows Server 2016 includes a new DFS database cloning function. This new feature allows administrators to accelerate replication when creating folders, servers, or recovery systems.

Administrators will now have the ability to extract the DFS database from a single DFS server and then clone that database to multiple DFS servers.

Administrators can use PowerShell and the `Export-DfsrClone` cmdlet to export the volume that contains the DFS database and configuration `.xml` file settings. When executing this PowerShell cmdlet, a trigger is engaged that exports the DFS service, and the system will not proceed until the service is completed. Administrators would then use the PowerShell cmdlet `Import-DfsrClone` to import the data to a specific volume. The service will then validate that the replication was transferred completely.

Recovering a DFS Database

Windows Server 2016 DFS database recovery is a feature that allows DFS to detect a corrupted database, thus allowing DFS to rebuild the database automatically and continue with normal operations of DFS replication. One advantage to this is that when DFS detects and fixes a corrupt database, it does so with no file conflicts.

Prior to this new feature, if a DFS database were determined to be corrupt, DFS Replication would delete the database and start again with an initial nonauthoritative sync process. This would cause newer file versions to be overwritten by older data causing real data loss.

DFS in Windows Server 2016 uses local files and an update sequence number (USN) to fix a corrupt database, allowing for no loss of data.

Optimizing DFS

Windows Server 2016 DFS allows an administrator to configure variable file staging sizes on individual DFS servers. This allows an administrator to set a minimum file size for a file to stage. This increases the staging size of files, and that in turn increases the performance of the replication.

Prior to Windows Server 2016, DFS Replication used a hard-coded 256KB file size to determine staging requirements. If a file size were larger than 256KB, that file would be staged before it replicated. The more file staging that you have, the longer replication takes on a DFS system.

Remote Differential Compression

One issue that can arise occurs when files are changed. There has to be some mechanism that helps files stay accurate. That's where the *Remote Differential Compression (RDC)* feature comes into play. RDC is a group of application programming interfaces (APIs) that programs can use to determine whether files have changed. Once RDC determines that there has been a change, RDC then helps to detect which portions of the files contain the changes. RDC has the ability to detect insertions, removals, and rearrangements of data in files. This feature becomes helpful with limited-bandwidth networks when they replicate changes.

To install the RDC feature, use Server Manager and then run the Add Features Wizard, or type the following command at an elevated command prompt:

```
Servermanagercmd -Install Rdc
```

Now that I have shown you how to install DFS and how DFS works, let's go ahead and setup DFS. In exercise 15.3, I will show you how to configure a DFS Namespace and how to add a shared folder to DFS.

EXERCISE 15.3

Setting Up a DFS Namespace

1. Open DFS Management (Start ➤ Administrative Tools ➤ DFS Management).

2. Right-click Namespaces (see Figure 15.3) and choose New Namespace.

FIGURE 15.3   Adding a Namespace

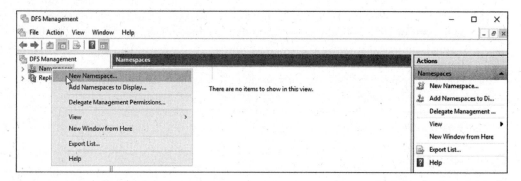

3. In the Server box, enter the name of the server that will host this namespace (I am using the DFS server). Click Next.

4. At the Namespace screen, enter the namespace you want (see Figure 15.4) to use and hit the Next button.

FIGURE 15.4   Adding a Namespace

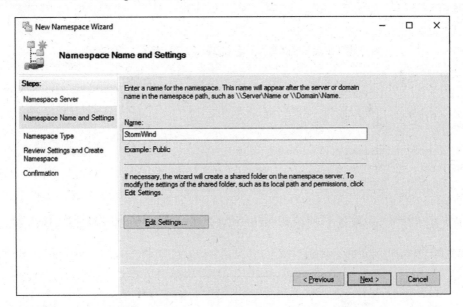

5. Under Namespace Type screen, choose Stand-Alone or Domain Based and click Next. In my lab, I am using a Stand-Alone DFS.

6. At the Review Screen, click Create.

7. Click the Close button. Leave DFS open.

8. Go to Windows Explorer by hitting the Windows Key + E.

9. Create a new folder called Home and share the folder.

10. In DFS under the Actions section (right hand side), choose New Folder (see Figure 15.5).

11. When the New Folder screen appears, Type in the Name for this folder and then hit Add.

12. Add the shared Home Folder and hit OK.

FIGURE 15.5   New Folder

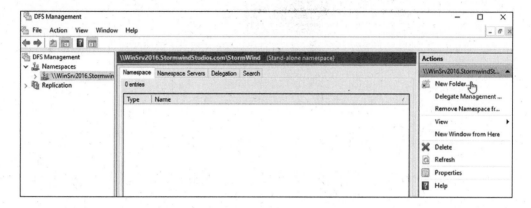

13. After you have entered a name and put in the Home folder (see Figure 15.6), click OK.

FIGURE 15.6   Home Folder

14. The namespace has been created and you have added a shared folder to the namespace. Add any of your other shared folders and then close DFS.

Configure Advanced File Services

Windows Server has come a long way in terms of its file and storage capabilities. I have talked quite a bit about the new features and functionality provided in Windows Server 2016. In this section, you will take a closer look at some of the advanced configuration options available in the Network File System (NFS), BranchCache, and the File Server Resource Manager (FSRM).

Configure the NFS Data Store

The NFS role service and feature set gives IT administrators the ability to integrate a Windows Server–based environment with Unix-based operating systems. Most corporate environments today consist of a mixed operating system infrastructure to some extent. Using a Windows NFS file server, you can configure file shares for use by multiple operating systems throughout the environment.

Windows Server 2016 takes those capabilities even further by enabling you to integrate with platforms such as ESXi. ESXi is VMware's exclusive operating system–independent hypervisor. ESXi is referred to as a *bare-metal* operating system because once it is installed on server virtualization hardware, guest virtual machines can be installed without requiring the use of any other underlying operating system. With Windows Server 2016, you can use an NFS share efficiently as an ESXi data store to house all of your guest virtual machines. Let's take a look at configuring an NFS data store in Exercise 15.4.

For this exercise, you will need the following:

- A Windows Server 2016 server
- A VMware ESXi 5 server

EXERCISE 15.4

Configure the NFS Data Store

1. Open Server Manager on your Windows Server 2016 machine.

2. Launch the Add Roles And Features Wizard from the dashboard.

3. Install the Server for NFS role on the server. A reboot is not required.

4. Create a new folder on your server named NFS_Datastore, right-click and select Properties, and then navigate to the NFS Sharing tab.

5. Click the Manage NFS Sharing button to open the NFS Advanced Sharing page and then check the Share This Folder box. Notice how enabling the share also enables the share's default settings. The share settings let you configure share authentication and user access further if the need arises. The default settings will work just fine for this exercise.

6. Click the Permissions tab to open the NFS Share Permissions page. This is where you will configure the type of access that will be allowed by machines accessing this NFS data store. By default, the NFS share permissions are set to Read-Only and do not include root access. For this exercise, you will need to change the type of access to Read-Write and check the box to allow root access.

7. Click OK to close the NFS Share Permissions page and then click Apply and OK on the NFS Advanced Sharing page. Your new NFS share is now built, ready to be presented as an NFS data store to a VMware ESXi host. Be sure to record the network path displayed on the NFS Sharing tab of the share's Properties page. You will need that information to perform a proper mount on the ESXi host.

8. Switch to your ESXi host and launch the Add Storage Wizard from the Configuration tab.

9. On the Select Storage Type page of the wizard, select the Network File System storage type; click Next to continue to the Locate Network File System page.

10. On this page of the wizard, you will fill in the server and folder information for the NFS share that you will be using as a vSphere data store. Using the information recorded from step 7, properly fill out the server and folder fields and then name your new data store.

11. Click Next to continue to the Ready To Complete page of the wizard. Review the information and click Finish. Once the Create NAS data store task completes on the ESXi host, you are ready to use your Windows Server 2016 shared folder as a vSphere ESXi data store.

The previous exercise shows how versatile Windows Server 2016 shares can be. The same principals can be applied to making Windows Server shares available to other Unix-based operating systems such as ESXi. Now that you have configured a NFS data store, let's take a look at what BranchCache has to offer.

Configure BranchCache

BranchCache is a technology that was introduced with Windows Server 2008 R2 and Windows 7. BranchCache allows an organization with slower links between offices to cache data so that downloads between offices do not have to occur each time a file is accessed.

For example, John comes into work and logs into the network. John accesses the corporate website and downloads a media file that takes four minutes to download. With BranchCache enabled, when Judy comes into work, connects to the corporate website, and tries to download the same media file, the file will be cached from the previous download and Judy will have immediate access to the file.

You can set up two types of BranchCache configurations:

Distributed Cache Mode   In the distributed cache mode configuration, all Windows 7, Windows 8/8.1, and Windows 10 client machines cache the files locally on the client machines. Thus, in the previous example, after John downloaded the media file, Judy would receive the cached media file from John's Windows 7, Windows 8/8.1, or Windows 10 machine.

Hosted Mode   In the hosted mode configuration, the cache files are cached on a local (within the site) Windows Server 2016 machine. So, in the previous example, after John downloads the media file, the cached file would be placed on a Windows Server 2016 machine by default, and all other users (Judy) would download the media file from the Windows Server 2016 machine.

Distributed Cache Mode Requirements

If you decide to install BranchCache in the distributed cache mode configuration, a hosted cache server running Windows Server 2016 is not required at the branch office. To set up distributed cache mode, the client machines must be running Windows 7 Enterprise, Windows 7 Ultimate, Windows 8/8.1 Pro, Windows 8/8.1 Enterprise, Windows 10 Pro or Windows 10 Enterprise.

The Windows client machines would download the data files from the content computer at the main branch office, and then these machines become the local cache servers. To set up distributed cache mode, you must install a content computer (the computer that will hold the original content) at the main office first. After the content server is installed, physical connections (WAN or VPN connections) between the sites and branch offices must be established.

Client computers running Windows 7 Enterprise or higher (from versions listed above) have BranchCache installed by default. However, you must enable and configure BranchCache and configure firewall exceptions. Complete Exercise 15.5 to configure BranchCache firewall rule exceptions.

EXERCISE 15.5

Configuring BranchCache Firewall Exceptions

1. On a domain controller, open the Group Policy Management Console.

2. In the Group Policy Management Console, expand the following path: Forest ➤ Domains ➤ Group Policy Objects. Make sure the domain you choose contains the BranchCache Windows 7/Windows 8/Windows 10 client computer accounts that you want to configure.

EXERCISE 15.5 *(continued)*

3. In the Group Policy Management Console, right-click Group Policy Objects and select New. Name the policy **BranchCache Client** and click OK. Right-click BranchCache Client and click Edit. The Group Policy Management Editor console opens.

4. In the Group Policy Management Editor console, expand the following path: Computer Configuration ➢ Policies ➢ Windows Settings ➢ Security Settings ➢ Windows Firewall With Advanced Security ➢ Windows Firewall With Advanced Security – LDAP ➢ Inbound Rules.

5. Right-click Inbound Rules and then click New Rule. The New Inbound Rule Wizard opens.

6. On the Rule Type screen, click Predefined, expand the list of choices, and then click BranchCache – Content Retrieval (Uses HTTP). Click Next.

7. On the Predefined Rules screen, click Next.

8. On the Action screen, ensure that Allow The Connection is selected and then click Finish. You must select Allow The Connection for the BranchCache client to be able to receive traffic on this port.

9. To create the WS-Discovery firewall exception, right-click Inbound Rules and click New Rule. The New Inbound Rule Wizard opens.

10. On the Rule Type screen, click Predefined, expand the list of choices, and then click BranchCache – Peer Discovery (Uses WSD). Click Next.

11. On the Predefined Rules screen, click Next.

12. On the Action screen, ensure that Allow The Connection is selected and then click Finish.

13. In the Group Policy Management Editor console, right-click Outbound Rules and then click New Rule. The New Outbound Rule Wizard opens.

14. On the Rule Type screen, click Predefined, expand the list of choices, and then click BranchCache – Content Retrieval (Uses HTTP). Click Next.

15. On the Predefined Rules screen, click Next.

16. On the Action screen, make sure that Allow The Connection is selected and then click Finish.

17. Create the WS-Discovery firewall exception by right-clicking Outbound Rules and then clicking New Rule. The New Outbound Rule Wizard opens.

18. On the Rule Type screen, click Predefined, expand the list of choices, and then click BranchCache – Peer Discovery (Uses WSD). Click Next.

19. On the Predefined Rules screen, click Next.

20. On the Action screen, make sure that Allow The Connection is selected and then click Finish. Close the Group Policy Management console.

Now that you have looked at the distributed cache mode configuration, let's take a look at the hosted mode configuration.

Hosted Mode Requirements

To set up a hosted mode BranchCache configuration, you must first set up a Windows Server 2016 hosted cache server at the main and branch offices. You also need to be running Windows 7 Enterprise, Windows 7 Ultimate, Windows 8/8.1 Pro, Windows 8/8.1 Enterprise, Windows 10 Pro, or Windows 10 Enterprise computers at the branch offices.

The Windows client machines download the data from the main cache server, and then the hosted cache servers at the branch offices obtain a copy of the downloaded data for other users to access.

Your network infrastructure must also allow for physical connections between the main office and the branch offices. These connections can be VPNs or some type of WAN links. After these requirements are met, your cache server must obtain a server certificate so that the client computers in the branch offices can positively identify the cache servers.

Exercise 15.6 walks you through the process of installing the BranchCache feature on a Windows Server 2016 machine. To begin this exercise, you must be logged into the Windows Server 2016 machine as an administrator.

EXERCISE 15.6

Installing BranchCache on Windows Server 2016

1. Open Server Manager by selecting the Server Manager icon or by running servermanager.exe.

2. Select Add Roles And Features.

3. Select Next at the Before You Begin pane (if shown).

4. Select Role-Based Or Feature-Based Installation and select Next to continue.

5. Select the Select A Server From The Server Pool option and click Next.

6. At the Select Server Roles screen, click Next.

7. At the Select Features screen, click the check box for BranchCache (see Figure 15.7). Then click Next.

FIGURE 15.7   BranchCache Option

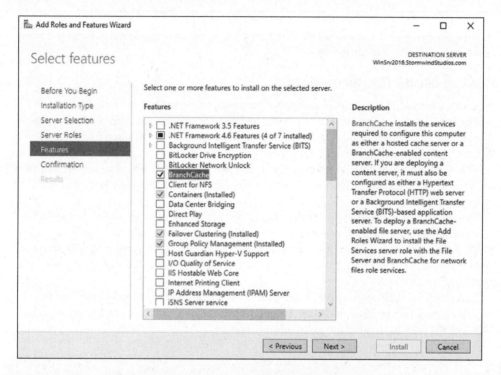

8. Check the Restart The Destination Server If Required box and then click the Install button. If a dialog box appears about restarting, click the Yes button. The system should restart.

9. After the system restarts, log in as the administrator.

Make sure to repeat this exercise on all branch office cache servers. One of the requirements for BranchCache is a physical connection between the main office and the branch offices.

BranchCache and PowerShell

As stated throughout this book, PowerShell is a command-line shell and scripting tool. BranchCache has many different PowerShell cmdlets that allow you to configure and maintain the BranchCache feature. Table 15.4 shows just some of the different PowerShell cmdlets for BranchCache.

TABLE 15.4   PowerShell cmdlets for BranchCache

Cmdlet	Description
Add-BCDataCacheExtension	Increases the amount of cache storage space that is available on a hosted cache server by adding a new cache file
Clear-BCCache	Deletes all data in all data and hash files
Disable-BC	Disables the BranchCache service
Disable-BCDowngrading	Disables downgrading so that client computers that are running Windows 10 do not request Windows 7/8 specific versions of content information from content servers
Enable-BCDistributed	Enables BranchCache and configures a computer to operate in distributed cache mode
Enable-BCHostedClient	Configures BranchCache to operate in hosted cache client mode
Enable-BCHostedServer	Configures BranchCache to operate in hosted cache server mode
Enable-BCLocal	Enables the BranchCache service in local caching mode
Export-BCCachePackage	Exports a cache package
Export-BCSecretKey	Exports a secret key to a file
Get-BCClientConfiguration	Gets the current BranchCache client computer settings
Get-BCContentServerConfiguration	Gets the current BranchCache content server settings
Get-BCDataCache	Gets the BranchCache data cache
Get-BCStatus	Gets a set of objects that provide BranchCache status and configuration information
Import-BCCachePackage	Imports a cache package into BranchCache
Import-BCSecretKey	Imports the cryptographic key that BranchCache uses for generating segment secrets

TABLE 15.4 PowerShell cmdlets for BranchCache *(continued)*

Cmdlet	Description
Set-BCAuthentication	Specifies the BranchCache computer authentication mode
Set-BCCache	Modifies the cache file configuration
Set-BCSecretKey	Sets the cryptographic key used in the generation of segment secrets

Enhanced Features in Windows Server 2016 BranchCache

Microsoft continues to improve on many of the features of Windows Server, and BranchCache is no different. Microsoft has improved BranchCache in Windows Server 2016 and Windows 8/10. The following list includes some of the enhanced features:

Office sizes and the number of branch offices are not limited. Windows Server 2016 BranchCache allows any number of offices along with any number of users once an administrator deploys hosted cache mode with multiple hosted cache servers.

There are no requirements for a Group Policy object (GPO) for each office location, streamlining deployment. All that is required to deploy BranchCache is a single GPO that contains a small number of settings.

Client computer configuration is easy. Administrators have the ability to configure their clients through the use of a Group Policy object. If this is done, client configuration will automatically be configured through the GPO, and if a client can't find a hosted cache server, the client will automatically self-configure as a hosted cache mode client.

BranchCache is deeply integrated with the Windows file server. BranchCache is automatically integrated with Windows file server technology. Because of this, the process of finding duplicate pieces in independent files is greatly improved.

Duplicate content is stored and downloaded only once. BranchCache stores only one instance of the content on a hosted cache server or content server, and because of this, you get greater disk storage savings. Since client computers at the remote offices download only one instance of any content, your network saves on additional WAN bandwidth.

Small changes to large files produce bandwidth savings. One advantage of BranchCache is the file server chunking system that helps divide files and web pages into smaller parts. Now when a file is changed, only the part of that file that has been changed gets replicated. This allows BranchCache to use lower bandwidth requirements.

Offline content creation improves performance. When BranchCache is deployed as content or file servers, the data is calculated offline before a client even has the chance to request it. Because of this, the systems get faster performance and bandwidth.

Cache encryption is enabled automatically. BranchCache stores its cached data as encrypted data. This guarantees data security without the need to encrypt the entire drive.

You can deploy multiple hosted cache servers. In Windows 7 and Windows Server 2008 R2, BranchCache was able to deploy only one hosted cache server per office location. Windows Server 2016 allows you to deploy as many hosted cache servers as are needed at a location.

Implementing an Audit Policy

One of the most important aspects of controlling security in networked environments is ensuring that only authorized users are able to access specific resources. Although system administrators often spend much time managing security permissions, it is almost always possible for a security problem to occur.

Sometimes the best way to find possible security breaches is actually to record the actions that specific users take. Then, in the case of a security breach (the unauthorized shutdown of a server, for example), system administrators can examine the log to find the cause of the problem.

The Windows Server 2016 operating system and Active Directory offer you the ability to audit a wide range of actions. In the following sections, you'll see how to implement auditing for Active Directory.

Overview of Auditing

The act of *auditing* relates to recording specific actions. From a security standpoint, auditing is used to detect any possible misuse of network resources. Although auditing does not necessarily prevent resources from being misused, it does help determine when security violations have occurred (or were attempted). Furthermore, just the fact that others know that you have implemented auditing may prevent them from attempting to circumvent security.

You need to complete several steps in order to implement auditing using Windows Server 2016:

1. Configure the size and storage settings for the audit logs.

2. Enable categories of events to audit.

3. Specify which objects and actions should be recorded in the audit log.

Note that there are trade-offs to implementing auditing. First, recording auditing information can consume system resources. This can decrease overall system performance and use up valuable disk space. Second, auditing many events can make the audit log impractical to view. If too much detail is provided, system administrators are unlikely to scrutinize all of the recorded events. For these reasons, you should always be sure to find a balance between the level of auditing detail provided and the performance-management implications of these settings.

Implementing Auditing

Auditing is not an all-or-none type of process. As is the case with security in general, system administrators must choose specifically which objects and actions they want to audit.

The main categories for auditing include the following:

- Audit account logon events
- Audit account management
- Audit directory service access
- Audit logon events
- Audit object access
- Audit policy change
- Audit privilege use
- Audit process tracking
- Audit system events

In this list of categories, many of the categories are related to Active Directory. Let's discuss these auditing categories in more detail.

Audit Account Logon Events   You enable this auditing event if you want to audit when a user authenticates with a domain controller and logs onto the domain. This event is logged in the security log on the domain controller.

Audit Account Management   This auditing event is used when you want to watch what changes are being made to Active Directory accounts. For example, when another administrator creates or deletes a user account, it would be an audited event.

Audit Directory Service Access   This auditing event occurs whenever a user or administrator accesses Active Directory objects. Let's say an administrator opens Active Directory and clicks a user account; even if nothing is changed on that account, an event is logged.

Audit Logon Events   Account logon events are created for domain account activity. For example, you have a user who logs on to a server so that they can access files; the act of logging onto the server creates this audit event.

Audit Object Access   Audit object access allows you to audit objects within your network such as folders, files, and printers. If you suspect someone is trying to hack into an object (for example, the finance folder), this is the type of auditing that you would use. You still would need to enable auditing on the actual object (for example, the finance folder).

Audit Policy Change   Audit policy change allows you to audit changes to user rights' assignment policies, audit policies, or trust policies. This auditing allows you to see whether anyone changes any of the other audit policies.

Audit Privilege Use   Setting the audit privilege use allows an administrator to audit each instance of a user exercising a user right. For example, if a user changes the system time on a machine, this is a user right. Log on locally is another common user right.

To audit access to objects stored within Active Directory, you must enable the Audit Directory Service Access option. Then you must specify which objects and actions should be tracked.

Exercise 15.7 walks through the steps you must take to implement auditing of Active Directory objects on domain controllers.

EXERCISE 15.7

Enabling Auditing of Active Directory Objects

1. Open the Local Security Policy tool (located in the Administrative Tools program group).

2. Expand Local Policies ➤ Audit Policy.

3. Double-click the setting for Audit Directory Service Access.

4. In the Audit Directory Service Access Properties dialog box, place check marks next to Success and Failure. Click OK to save the settings.

5. Close the Local Security Policy tool.

Viewing Auditing Information

One of the most important aspects of auditing is regularly monitoring the audit logs. If this step is ignored, as it often is in poorly managed environments, the act of auditing is useless. Fortunately, Windows Server 2016 includes the *Event Viewer* tool, which allows system administrators to view audited events quickly and easily. Using the filtering capabilities of Event Viewer, they can find specific events of interest.

Exercise 15.8 walks you through the steps that you must take to generate some auditing events and to examine the data collected for these actions. In this exercise, you will perform some actions that will be audited, and then you will view the information recorded within the audit logs.

EXERCISE 15.8

Generating and Viewing Audit Logs

1. Open the Active Directory Users and Computers tool.

2. Within the Engineering OU, right-click any user account and select Properties.

3. On the user's Properties dialog box, add the middle initial *A* for this user account and specify **Software Developer** in the Description box. Click OK to save the changes.

4. Within the Engineering OU, right-click the Robert Admin user account and select Properties.

5. In the Robert Properties dialog box, add the description **Engineering IT Admin** and click OK.

6. Close the Active Directory Users and Computers tool.

7. Open the Event Viewer tool from the Administrative Tools program group. Select the Security item under Windows Logs. You will see a list of audited events categorized under Directory Service Access. Note that you can obtain more details about a specific item by double-clicking it.

8. When you have finished viewing the security log, close the Event Viewer tool.

Using the *Auditpol.exe* Command

There may be a time when you need to look at your actual auditing policies set on a user or a system. This is where an administrator can use the Auditpol.exe command. *Auditpol* gives administrators the ability not only to view an audit policy but also allows an administrator to set, configure, modify, restore, and even remove an audit policy. Auditpol is a command-line utility, and there are multiple switches that can be used with Auditpol. The following is the syntax used with Auditpol.

```
Auditpol command [<sub-command><options>]
```

Here's an example of using the command:

```
Auditpol /get /user:wpanek /category:"Detailed Tracking" /r
```

Table 15.5 describes some of the switches.

TABLE 15.5 Auditpol commands

Command	Description
/backup	Allows an administrator to save the audit policy to a file
/clear	Allows an administrator to clear an audit policy
/get	Gives administrators the ability to view the current audit policy
/list	Allows you to view selectable policy elements
/remove	Removes all per-user audit policy settings and disables all system audit policy settings

Command	Description
/restore	Allows an administrator to restore an audit policy from a file that was previously created using `auditpol /backup`
/set	Gives an administrator the ability to set an audit policy
/?	Displays help

Windows Server 2016 Auditing Features

Auditing in Windows Server 2016 and Windows 10 has been enhanced in many ways. Microsoft has increased the level of detail in the security auditing logs. Microsoft has also simplified the deployment and management of auditing policies. The following list includes some of the major enhancements:

Global Object Access Auditing   Administrators using Windows Server 2016 and Windows 10 have the ability to define computer-wide system access control lists (SACLs). Administrators can define SACLs for either the file system or the registry. After the specified SACL is defined, the SACL is then applied automatically to every single object of that type. This can be helpful to administrators in verifying that all critical files, folders, and registry settings on a computer are protected. This is also helpful for identifying when an issue occurs with a system resource.

"Reason for Access" Reporting   When an administrator is performing auditing in Windows Server 2016 and Windows 10, they can see the reason why an operation was successful or unsuccessful. Previously, they lacked the ability to see the reason why an operation succeeded or failed.

Advanced Audit Policy Settings   In Windows Server 2016, there are hundreds of Advanced Audit Policy settings that can be used in place of the nine basic auditing settings. These advanced audit settings also help eliminate the unnecessary auditing activities that can make audit logs difficult to manage and decipher.

Expression-Based Audit Policies   Administrators have the ability, because of Dynamic Access Control, to create targeted audit policies by using expressions based on user, computer, and resource claims. For example, an administrator has the ability to create an audit policy that tracks all Read and Write operations for files that are considered high-business impact. Expression-based audit policies can be directly created on a file or folder or created through the use of a Group Policy.

Removable Storage Device Auditing   Administrators have the ability to monitor attempts to use a removable storage device on your network. If an administrator decides to implement this policy, an audit event is created every time one of your users attempts to copy, move, or save a network resource onto a removable storage device.

Configure and Optimize Storage

Disk storage is a requirement for just about every computer and application used in any corporate environment. Administrators have some familiarity with storage, whether it is internal storage, a locally attached set of disks, or network attached storage (NAS). In this section, you will examine the various aspects of Windows Server 2016 file and storage solutions. Though I'll discuss the various types of file and storage technologies, this section will primarily focus on iSCSI because of the native features in Windows Server 2016. You will also look at some of the advanced configuration options of implementing thin provisioning and trim, managing server free space, and configuring tiered storage.

Configure iSCSI Target and Initiator

Internet Small Computer System Interface (iSCSI) is an Internet protocol used to establish and manage a connection between a computer (initiator) and a storage device (target). It does this by using a connection through TCP port 3260, which allows it to be used over a LAN, a WAN, or the Internet. Each initiator is identified by its iSCSI Qualified Name (iqn), and it is used to establish its connection to an iSCSI target.

iSCSI was developed to allow block-level access to a storage device over a network. This is different from using a NAS device that connects through the use of Common Internet File System (CIFS) or NFS.

Block-level access is important to many applications that require direct access to storage. Microsoft Exchange and Microsoft SQL are examples of applications that require direct access to storage.

By being able to leverage the existing network infrastructure, iSCSI was also developed as an alternative to Fibre Channel storage by alleviating the additional hardware costs associated with a Fibre Channel storage solution.

iSCSI also has another advantage over Fibre Channel in that it can provide security for the storage devices. iSCSI can use Microsoft Challenge Handshake Authentication Protocol (CHAP or MS-CHAP) for authentication and Internet Protocol Security (IPsec) for encryption. Windows Server 2016 is able to connect an iSCSI storage device out of the box with no additional software needing to be installed. This is because the Microsoft iSCSI initiator is built into the operating system.

Windows Server 2016 supports two different ways to initiate an iSCSI session:

- Through the native Microsoft iSCSI software initiator that resides on Windows Server 2016

- Using a hardware iSCSI host bus adapter (HBA) that is installed in the computer

Both the Microsoft iSCSI software initiator and iSCSI HBA present an iSCSI qualified name that identifies the host initiator. When the Microsoft iSCSI software initiator is used, the CPU utilization may be as much as 30 percent higher than on a computer with a hardware iSCSI HBA. This is because all of the iSCSI process requests are handled within the operating system. Using a hardware iSCSI HBA, process requests can be offloaded to the adapter, thus freeing the CPU overhead associated with the Microsoft iSCSI software initiator. However, iSCSI HBAs can be expensive, whereas the Microsoft iSCSI software initiator is free.

It is worthwhile installing the Microsoft iSCSI software initiator and performing load testing to see how much overhead the computer will have prior to purchasing an iSCSI HBA or HBAs, depending on the redundancy level. Exercise 15.9 explains how to install and configure an iSCSI connection.

EXERCISE 15.9

Configuring iSCSI Storage Connection

1. Press the Windows key or the Start button in the lower-left corner and select Administrative Tools ➢ iSCSI Initiator.

2. If a dialog box appears, click Yes to start the service.

3. Click the Discovery tab.

4. In the Target Portals portion of the page, click Discover Portal.

5. Enter the IP address of the target portal and click OK.

6. The IP address of the target portal appears in the Target Portals box.

7. Click OK.

    To use the storage that has now been presented to the server, you must create a volume on it and format the space.

Configure Internet Storage Name Server

Internet Storage Name Service (iSNS) allows for the central registration of an iSCSI environment because it automatically discovers available targets on the network. The purpose of iSNS is to help find available targets on a large iSCSI network.

The Microsoft iSCSI initiator includes an iSNS client that is used to register with the iSNS. The iSNS feature maintains a database of clients that it has registered either through DCHP discovery or through manual registration. iSNS DHCP is available after the installation of the service, and it is used to allow iSNS clients to discover the location of the iSNS. However, if iSNS DHCP is not configured, iSNS clients must be registered manually with the `iscsicli` command.

To execute the command, launch a command prompt on a computer hosting the Microsoft iSCSI and type **`iscsicli addisnsserver server_name`**, where server_name is the name of the computer hosting iSNS. Exercise 15.10 walks you through the steps required to install the iSNS feature on Windows Server 2016, and then it explains the different tabs in iSNS.

EXERCISE 15.10

Installing the iSNS Feature on Windows Server 2016

1. Open Server Manager.

2. Launch the Add Roles And Features Wizard.

3. Choose role-based or featured-based installation and click Next.

4. Choose your server and click Next.

5. Click Next at the Roles screen.

6. At the Select Features screen, choose the iSNS Server Service check box. Click Next.

7. At the Confirmation screen, click the Install button.

8. Click the Close button. Close Server Manager and reboot.

9. Log in and open the iSNS server under Administrative Tools.

10. Click the General tab. This tab displays the list of registered initiators and targets. In addition to their iSCSI qualified names, it lists storage node type (Target or Initiator), alias string, and entity identifier (the fully qualified domain name [FQDN] of the machine hosting the iSNS client).

11. Click the Discovery Domains tab. The purpose of discovery domains is to provide a way to separate and group nodes. This is similar to zoning in Fibre Channel.

    The following options are available on the Discovery Domains tab:

    Create creates a new discovery domain.

    Refresh repopulates the Discovery Domain drop-down list.

    Delete deletes the currently selected discovery domain.

    Add adds nodes that are already registered in iSNS to the currently selected discovery domain.

    Add New adds nodes by entering the iSCSI qualified name of the node. These nodes do not have to be currently registered.

    Remove Used removes selected nodes from the discovery domain.

12. Click the Discovery Domain Sets tab. The purpose of discovery domain sets is to separate further discovery domains. Discovery domains can be enabled or disabled, giving administrators the ability to restrict further the visibility of all initiators and targets.

    The options on the Discovery Domain Sets tab are as follows:

    The *Enable* check box indicates the status of the discovery domain sets and turns them off and on.

      Create creates new discovery domain sets.

      Refresh repopulates the Discovery Domain Sets drop-down list.

      Delete deletes the currently selected discovery domain set.

      Add adds discovery domains to the currently selected discovery domain set.

      Remove removes selected nodes from the discovery domain sets.

13. Close the iSNS server.

Implement Thin Provisioning and Trim

Thin provisioning and trim can be useful features that allow organizations to get the most out of their storage arrays. These solutions apply directly to a virtualized environment using virtual disks that are thin provisioned.

Thin provisioning is a way of providing what is known as just-in-time allocations. Blocks of data are written to disk only as they are used instead of zeroing out all of the blocks of data that have been allocated to the virtual disk configuration. Thin provisioning is tricky to manage properly because you could easily find yourself in a position where you have an over-provisioned environment because of over-allocation.

For example, you have 100 VMs that are all provisioned with 40 GB thin-provisioned virtual disks. Each VM is currently utilizing only 20 GB of the total 40 GB that has been allocated. The problem is that you have only 2 TB worth of storage. Without realizing it, you've over-provisioned your environment by 200 percent because of thin provisioning.

This is where trim comes in to help us manage thin provisioning. *Trim* automatically reclaims free space that is not being used. In addition to trim, Windows Server 2016 provides standardized notifications that will alert administrators when certain storage thresholds are crossed.

Manage Server Free Space Using Features on Demand

Features on Demand was first introduced in Windows Server 2012. This feature lets you conserve disk space within the environment by installing only basic operating system components with every new installation of a Windows Server 2016 or Windows 10 machine. Instead of loading unnecessary payload files, those files are stored in a central repository and used as needed to install roles and features. When I talk about *payload files*, I am talking about the binaries for all permissions, settings, and components of a feature. Features on Demand gives you the ability not only to disable Windows Server features but also to remove all of the payloads. This lets administrators keep a tighter security footprint at the operating system level, which is similar to a Server Core installation but without the limitation of not being able to control which source files are loaded during operating system installation.

Configure Tiered Storage

Tiered storage is an excellent new feature in Windows Server 2016 that gives administrators the ability to use solid-state drives (SSDs) and conventional hard-disk drives (HDDs) within the same storage pool. You can configure virtual disks that span SSD and HDD tiers, which are presented as a single LUN. One of the really nice things about this feature is that with Windows Server 2016, data is automatically saved to either an SSD or an HDD based on actual usage within the environment. Most frequently accessed data is stored on an SSD, and the less frequently accessed data is stored on an HDD.

Quite a few organizations these days use some sort of charge-back or show-back application to track and even charge for hosted solutions and services. Having the capability to tier storage gives users more options in selecting a plan that works for them. It also makes it possible for administrators to keep high I/O servers and applications on faster and better-performing drives without having to move data manually across multiple tiers of storage.

Summary

This chapter took you through the use of many server tools and utilities such as DFS, Encryption, and auditing. Distributed File System allows an administrator to set up a tree structure of virtual directories that allow users to connect to a shared folder anywhere throughout the entire network.

You also learned about EFS and how to use Cipher to modify or configure EFS in a command window. Cipher is the best way to change encrypted directories and files.

This chapter also covered auditing. You looked at what needs to be audited if you are watching Active Directory and its objects. You looked at Auditpol and many of the switches that you would use when configuring Auditpol.

I discussed how configuring file and storage solutions can be highly effective within your organization. You now have a better understanding of how Windows Server 2016 can provide you with extended functionality for effectively controlling corporate data. Quite a few of these solutions are essential to managing a Windows Server environment to the best of your ability. Take the time to complete each exercise thoroughly until you are comfortable with performing the majority of these tasks without documentation.

Exam Essentials

Know how to configure DFS.   Distributed File System in Windows Server 2016 offers a simplified way for users to access geographically dispersed files. The DFS Namespace service allows you to set up a tree structure of virtual directories that lets users connect to shared folders throughout the entire network.

Understand EFS and Cipher.   Users can encrypt their directories and files by using EFS. Understand how Cipher can help an administrator configure or modify an EFS object while in the command prompt.

Understand the purpose and function of auditing.   Auditing helps determine the cause of security violations and helps troubleshoot permissions-related problems. Configure and test the effects of auditing within a file share hierarchy in a lab environment.

Know storage technologies.   Understand how to use the Fibre Channel, iSCSI, and NAS storage technologies. Know how to configure an iSCSI initiator and how to establish a connection to a target. Practice configuring tiered storage and using thin provisioning and trim.

Understand the features and functionality of BranchCache.   BranchCache helps eliminate the problems of slow access and bandwidth issues when sharing data across multiple, geographically disparate locations. By syncing and caching data between sites, users can use company-wide shared resources more efficiently when slower site links exist between site locations.

Review Questions

1. The company for which you work has a multilevel administrative team that is segmented by departments and locations. There are four major locations, and you are in the Northeast group. You have been assigned to the administrative group that is responsible for creating and maintaining network shares for files and printers in your region. The last place you worked was a large Windows Server 2012 network, where you had a much wider range of responsibilities. You are excited about the chance to learn more about Windows Server 2016.

   For your first task, you have been given a list of file and printer shares that need to be created for the users in your region. You ask how to create them in Windows Server 2016, and you are told that the process of creating a share is the same as with Windows Server 2012. You create the shares and use NETUSE to test them. Everything appears to work fine, so you send a message that the shares are available. The next day, you start receiving calls from users who say they cannot see any of resources you created. What is the most likely reason for the calls from the users?

   A. You forgot to enable NetBIOS for the shares.

   B. You need to force replication for the shares to appear in the directory.

   C. You need to publish the shares in the directory.

   D. The shares will appear within the normal replication period.

2. You want to publish a printer to Active Directory. Where would you click in order to accomplish this task?

   A. The Sharing tab

   B. The Advanced tab

   C. The Device Settings tab

   D. The Printing Preferences button

3. You are the network administrator for a large organization. You have implemented FSRM on your network. You need to view the quotas on FSRM. Which PowerShell command would you use?

   A. `Get-Quota`

   B. `Get-FsrmQuota`

   C. `View-Quota`

   D. `View-FsrmQuota`

4. You are the administrator for a company that uses FSRM. You need to create a file group. What PowerShell command would you use?

   A. `New-FsrmGroup`

   B. `New-FsrmFile`

   C. `New-FsrmFileGroup`

   D. `New-FileGroup`

5. You are the administrator for a company who is using FSRM. You want to create a quota template to use in the future. What PowerShell command would you use to create a FSRM quota template?

    A. `New-FsrmQuotaTemplate`

    B. `New-FsrmTemplate`

    C. `New-QuotaTemplate`

    D. `New-FsrmQuota`

6. You are an administrator for an organization that uses FSRM. Your boss has asked you to remove a FSRM classification rule. Which PowerShell command allows you to do this?

    A. `Delete-FsrmClassificationRule`

    B. `Delete-FsrmClassRule`

    C. `Remove-FsrmClassificationRule`

    D. `Kill-FsrmClassRule`

7. You are the administrator of a company with four Windows 2016 servers, and all of the clients are running Windows 10. All of your sales people use laptops to do their work away from the office. What should you configure to help them work when away from the office?

    A. Online file access

    B. Offline file access

    C. Share permissions

    D. NTFS permissions

8. Your company has decided to implement an external hard drive. The company IT manager before you always used FAT32 as the system partition. Your company wants to know whether it should move to NTFS. Which of the following are some advantages of NTFS? (Choose all that apply.)

    A. Security

    B. Quotas

    C. Compression

    D. Encryption

9. You are the administrator of your network, which consists of two Windows Server 2016 systems. One of the servers is a domain controller, and the other server is a file server for data storage. The hard drive of the file server is starting to fill up. You do not have the ability to install another hard drive, so you decide to limit the amount of space everyone gets on the hard drive. What do you need to implement to solve your problem?

    A. Disk spacing

    B. Disk quotas

    C. Disk hardening

    D. Disk limitations

10. You are the administrator for a large communications company. Your company uses Windows Server 2016, and your users' files are encrypted using EFS. What command-line command would you use to change or modify the EFS files?

   A. Convert

   B. Cipher

   C. Gopher

   D. Encrypt

Chapter

16

Configuring High Availability

THE FOLLOWING 70-741 EXAM OBJECTIVES ARE COVERED IN THIS CHAPTER:

✓ **Implement high performance network solutions**

- This objective may include but is not limited to: Implement NIC Teaming or the Switch Embedded Teaming (SET) solution and identify when to use each; enable and configure Receive Side Scaling (RSS); enable and configure network Quality of Service (QoS) with Data Center Bridging (DCB); enable and configure SMB Direct on Remote Direct Memory Access (RDMA) enabled network adapters; enable and configure SMB Multichannel; enable and configure virtual Receive Side Scaling (vRSS) on a Virtual Machine Queue (VMQ) capable network adapter; enable and configure Virtual Machine Multi-Queue (VMMQ); enable and configure Single Root I/O Virtualization (SR-IOV) on a supported network adapter.

In this chapter, I will show you some of the techniques and components of high availability. I will explain how to set up high availability and I will talk about some of the reasons why you would choose to use high availability. I will also show you how to use PowerShell for high availability.

I will continue the chapter by explaining how to keep your Hyper-V servers up and running by implementing high availability and disaster recovery options in Hyper-V. Finally I will show you the PowerShell commands for Hyper-V high availability.

Components of High Availability

High availability is a buzzword that many application and hardware vendors like to throw around to get you to purchase their products. Many different options are available to achieve high availability, and there also seems to be a number of definitions and variations that help vendors sell their products as high-availability solutions.

When it comes right down to it, however, high availability simply means providing services with maximum uptime by avoiding unplanned downtime. Often, *disaster recovery (DR)* is also closely lumped into discussions of high availability, but DR encompasses the business and technical processes that are used to recover once a disaster has happened.

Defining a high availability plan usually starts with a *service level agreement (SLA)*. At its most basic, an SLA defines the services and metrics that must be met for the availability and performance of an application or service. Often, an SLA is created for an IT department or service provider to deliver a specific level of service. An example of this might be an SLA for a Microsoft Exchange Server. The SLA for an Exchange Server might have uptime metrics on how much time during the month the mailboxes need to be available to end users, or it might define performance metrics for the amount of time it takes for email messages to be delivered.

When determining what goes into an SLA, two other factors need to be considered. However, you will often see them discussed only in the context of disaster recovery, even though they are important for designing a highly available solution. These factors are the *recovery point objective (RPO)* and the *recovery time objective (RTO)*.

An RTO is the length of time an application can be unavailable before service must be restored to meet the SLA. For example, a single component failure would have an RTO of less than five minutes, and a full-site failure might have an RTO of three hours. An RPO is essentially the amount of data that must be restored in the event of a failure. For example, in a single server or component failure, the RPO would be 0, but in a site failure, the RPO might allow for up to 20 minutes of lost data.

SLAs, on the other hand, are usually expressed in percentages of the time the application is available. These percentages are also often referred to by the number of nines the percentage includes. So if someone told you that you need to make sure that the router has a rating of Five 9s, that would mean that the router could only be down for 5.26 minutes a year. Table 16.1 shows you some of the different nines ratings and what each rating allows for downtime.

TABLE 16.1   Availability percentages

Availability Rating	Allowed Unplanned Downtime/Year
99 (two nines) percent	3.65 days
99.9 (three nines) percent	8.76 hours
99.99 (four nines) percent	52.56 minutes
99.999 (five nines) percent	5.26 minutes
99.9999 (six nines) percent	31.5 seconds
99.99999 (seven nines) percent	3.15 seconds

Two important factors that affect an SLA are the *mean time between failure (MTBF)* and the *mean time to recovery (MTTR)*. To be able to reduce the amount of unplanned downtime, the time between failures must be increased, and the time it takes to recover must be reduced. Modifying these two factors will be addressed in the next several sections of this chapter.

Achieving High Availability

Windows Server 2016 is the most secure and reliable Windows version to date. It also is the most stable, mature, and capable of any version of Windows. Although similar claims have been made for previous versions of Windows Server, you can rest assured that Windows Server 2016 is much better than previous versions for a variety of reasons.

An honest look at the feature set and real-world use should prove that this latest version of Windows provides the most suitable foundation for creating a highly available solution. However, more than just good software is needed to be able to offer high availability for applications.

High Availability Foundation

Just as a house needs a good foundation, a highly available Windows server needs a stable and reliable hardware platform on which to run. Although Windows Server 2016 will technically run on desktop-class hardware, high availability is more easily achieved with server-class hardware. What differentiates desktop-class from server-class hardware? *Server-class hardware* has more management and monitoring features built into it so that the health of the hardware is capable of being monitored and maintained.

Another large difference is that server-class hardware has redundancy options. Server-class hardware often has options to protect from drive failures, such as RAID controllers, and to protect against power supply failures, such as multiple power supplies. Enterprise-class servers have even more protection.

More needs to be done than just installing Windows Server 2016 to ensure that the applications remain running with the best availability possible. Just as a house needs maintenance and upkeep to keep the structure in proper repair, so too does a server. In the case of a highly available server, this means *patch management*.

Installing Patches

Microsoft releases monthly updates to fix security problems with its software, both for operating system fixes and for applications. To ensure that your highly available applications are immune to known vulnerabilities, these patches need to be applied in a timely manner during a scheduled maintenance window. Also, to address stability and performance issues, updates and service packs are released regularly for many applications, such as Microsoft SQL Server, Exchange Server, and SharePoint Portal Server. Many companies have a set schedule—daily, weekly, or monthly—to apply these patches and updates after they are tested and approved.

Desired Configuration Manager (DCM), an option in Microsoft System Center Configuration Manager, is a great tool for helping to validate that your cluster nodes are patched. It can leverage the SCCM client to collect installed patches and help reporting within the enterprise on compliancy with desired system states based on the software installed.

To continue with the house analogy, if you were planning to have the master bath remodeled, would you rather hire a college student on spring break looking to make some extra money to do the job or a seasoned artisan? Of course, you would want someone with experience and a proven record of accomplishment to remodel your master bath.

Likewise, with any work that needs to be done on your highly available applications, it's best to hire only decidedly qualified individuals. This is why obtaining a Microsoft certification is definitely an excellent start to becoming qualified to configure a highly available server properly. There is no substitute for real-life and hands-on experience. Working with highly available configurations in a lab and in production will help you know not only what configurations are available but also how the changes should be made.

For example, it may be possible to use Failover Clustering for a DNS server, but in practice DNS replication may be easier to support and require less expensive hardware in order to provide high availability. This is something you would know only if you had enough experience to make this decision.

As with your house, once you have a firm and stable foundation built by skilled artisans and a maintenance plan has been put into place, you need to ascertain what more is needed. If you can't achieve enough uptime with proper server configuration and mature operational processes, a cluster may be needed.

Windows Server 2016 provides two types of high availability: *Failover Clustering* and *Network Load Balancing (NLB)*. Failover clustering is used for applications and services such as SQL Server and Exchange Server. Network Load Balancing is used for network-based services such as web and FTP servers. The remaining sections of this chapter will cover NLB and Hyper-V high availability in depth.

Understanding Network Load Balancing

So the first thing we have to discuss is why an administrator would choose to use NLB. NLB allows an administrator to configure two or more servers as a single virtual cluster. NLB is designed for high availability and scalability of Internet server applications. So this means that Windows Server 2016 NLB is designed to work with web servers, FTP servers, firewalls, proxy servers, and virtual private networks (VPNs).

Network Load Balancing is a form of clustering where the nodes are highly available for a network-based service. This is typically a port listener configuration where a farm of, say, Microsoft Internet Information Services servers all listen on ports 80 and 443 for incoming web traffic from client endpoints. These nodes, while not fully clustered in a technical sense, are load balanced, where each node handles some of the distributed network traffic.

The NLB feature uses the TCP/IP networking protocol to distribute traffic. For web servers and other necessary servers, NLB can provide performance and consistency when two or more computers are combined into a single virtual cluster.

Hosts are servers that make up an NLB cluster. Each host runs their own individual copy of the server applications. The incoming client requests are distributed by NLB to each of the hosts in the cluster. The administrator can configure the load so that it is handled by each host. Hosts can be added to the cluster to increase the load. If NLB has all traffic directed to a specific single host, then it is called a default host.

With the use of NLB, all the computers in a cluster can use the same set of IP addresses while each host maintains its own exclusive IP address. When a host fails for load-balanced applications, the computers still in operation will receive the workload automatically. When the down computer is ready to rejoin the cluster it comes back online and will regain its share of the workload. This allows the rest of the computers in the cluster to handle less traffic.

NLB is beneficial in that stateless applications (for example, web servers) are available with little downtime and it allows for scalability.

Scalability is the capability of a system, network, or process to handle a growing amount of work, or its potential to be enlarged in order to accommodate growth. Scalability, when used for NLB clusters, is the ability to add one or more systems to an existing cluster when the need arises. An administrator can do the following with NLB to support scalability:

- A single cluster can support up to 32 computers.

- Handle multiple server load requests from across multiple hosts in a cluster.

- For single TCP/IP services, balance load requests across the NLB cluster.

- As the workload grows, be able to add hosts to the NLB cluster without failure.

- When the workload declines, be able to remove hosts from the cluster.

- Allow higher performance and lower overhead by utilizing a pipelined implementation. Pipelining allows requests to be sent to the NLB cluster without waiting for a response.

- Use NLB Manager or Windows PowerShell cmdlets to manage and configure NLB clusters and hosts from a single computer.

- Determine port rules for each website. Port rules allow you to configure which ports are going to be enabled or disabled. Ports are doorways that applications can use to access resources. For example, DNS traffic uses port 53 for all DNS traffic. Here are some of the more common port numbers:

  - FTP uses ports 20/21

  - Secure Shell uses port 22

  - SMTP (mail) uses port 25

  - DNS uses port 53

  - HTTP uses port 80

  - POPv3 uses port 110

  - HTTPS uses port 443

- Determine load balancing behavior using port management rules for an IP port or group of ports.

- Use an optional, single-host rule that will direct all client requests to a single host. NLB will route client requests to a specific host that is running particular applications.

- Allow certain IP ports to block unwanted network access.

- When operating in multicast mode, enable Internet Group Management Protocol (IGMP) support on the cluster host. This will control switch port flooding (when all incoming network packets are sent to all ports on the switch).

- Use Windows PowerShell to start, stop and control NLB actions remotely.

- Check NLB events using Windows Event Log. All NLB actions and cluster changes are logged in the Event Log.

NLB Requirements

NLB cluster hardware requirements:

- All hosts must be on the same subnet.

- For each host, there is no limitation to the number of network adapters.

- All network adapters must be multicast or unicast within the cluster. Mixed environments, within a single cluster, are NOT supported.

- If using unicast mode, the network adapter used to handle client-to-cluster traffic must support media access control (MAC) address changing.

   NLB cluster software requirements:

- The adapter on which NLB is enabled can only support TCP/IP.

- Must have a static IP address on the servers in the cluster.

Installing NLB Nodes

You can install NLB nodes like any other server build. Administrators can install NLB by using either Server Manager or the Windows PowerShell commands for NLB.

   Administrators should first make sure that all NLB servers have the most current updates, provisioned with appropriate resources (typically with multiple network interface cards for capacity and responsiveness), and monitored for health and reliability. In Exercise 16.1, I will walk you through the installation of your NLB nodes.

EXERCISE 16.1

Installing NLB Nodes

1. Once you have multiple hosts ready for the installation of NLB, simply run the Add Roles and Features Wizard and select Network Load Balancing in the Features area of the wizard. If the Add Features dialog box appears, click the Add Features button.

2. Click the Next button. At the Confirmation screen, click the Install button. After the installation is finished, click the Close button and then close Server Manager.

3. This wizard places a new application in your Start menu under Windows Administrative Tools, the Network Load Balancing Manager (see Figure 16.1).

EXERCISE 16.1 *(continued)*

FIGURE 16.1   Network Load Balancing

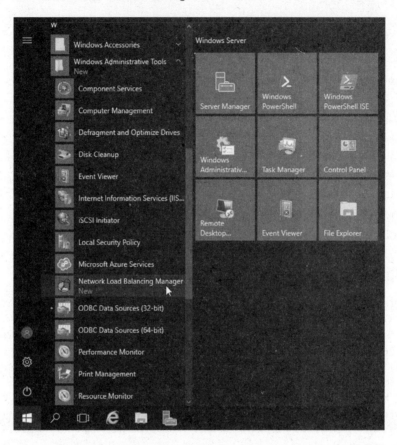

4. Right-click Network Load Balancing Clusters and select New Cluster (see Figure 16.2).

5. You are then presented with the New Cluster: Connect wizard where you can specify the name of one of your hosts. Type in the name of one of your cluster nodes and hit connect (see Figure 16.3). After the connection is made the TCP/IP address will be shown. Click Next.

6. If you get a DHCP dialog box, you will want to disable DHCP on this adapter. Click OK.

FIGURE 16.2 New Cluster

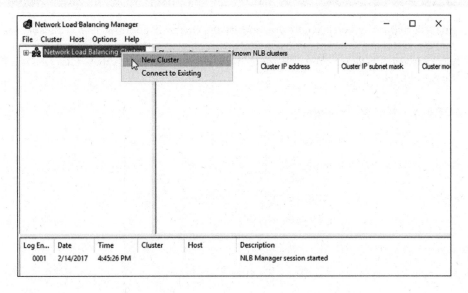

FIGURE 16.3 Host Name setup

7. The next screen reveals a prompt to add any additional IPs and assign a priority level. You can do all this later, so hit Next. If you get a dialog box about No Dedicated IP Addresses, click Yes.

EXERCISE 16.1 *(continued)*

8. The next wizard screen is where you specify the cluster IP address. This is the address that the endpoints or clients or users of the NLB cluster will contact. Typically the network team will assign a cluster IP address for this use (see Figure 16.4). Click OK. Then Click Next.

FIGURE 16.4   Add IP address

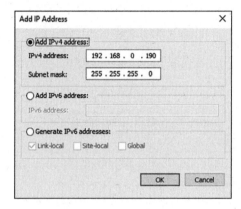

9. On the next screen, you configure the Cluster operation mode (see Figure 16.5) and specify a Full Internet name.

FIGURE 16.5   Cluster Parameters

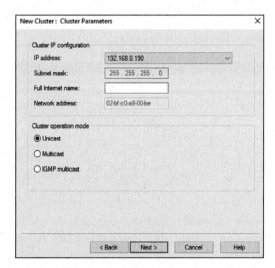

With regard to the cluster operation modes, the differences between them are as follows:

Unicast

The cluster adapters for all nodes are assigned the same MAC address.

The outgoing MAC address for each packet is modified based on priority to prevent upstream switches from discovering that all nodes have the same MAC address.

Communication between cluster nodes (other than heartbeat and other administrative NLB traffic) is not possible unless there are additional adapters (because all nodes have the same MAC address).

Depending on load, this configuration can cause switch flooding since all inbound packets are sent to all ports on the switch.

Multicast

The cluster adapters for all nodes are assigned their own MAC unicast address.

The cluster adapters for all nodes are assigned a multicast MAC address (derived from the IP of the cluster).

Non-NLB network traffic between cluster nodes works fine since they all have their own MAC address.

IGMP Multicast

This is much like multicast, but the MAC traffic goes only to the switch ports of the NLB cluster, preventing switch flooding.

10. After selecting the appropriate settings, the next page is where port rules (see Figure 16.6) are configured. By default, it is set up to be wide open. Most implementations will limit NLB ports to just the ports needed for the application. For example, a web server would need port 80 enabled. It is also in this area where you can configure filtering mode.

FIGURE 16.6   Port Rules

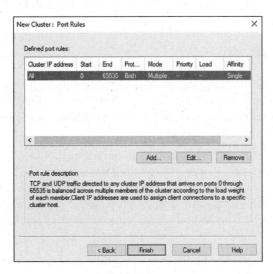

The affinity sets a client's preference to a particular NLB host. It is not recommended to set affinity to None when UDP is an expected traffic type.

11. Click the Finish button. Close the NLB Manager.

If you decide that you want to install NLB using Windows PowerShell commands, you would open an elevated Windows PowerShell prompt and type in the following command:

```
Install-WindowsFeature NLB -IncludeManagementTools
```

Upgrading an NLB Cluster

Upgrading an NLB cluster is a fairly straightforward process. The first thing that you have to do is stop the NLB cluster. There are two ways to stop a NLB cluster: stop or drainstop.

If an administrator decides to use the stop command, the cluster stops immediately. This also means that any current connections to the NLB cluster are killed.

If an administrator decides to use the drainstop command, the cluster stops after answering all of the current NLB connections. So the current NLB connections are finished but no new connections to that node are accepted.

So to do your upgrade, you should execute a stop or drainstop on the NLB cluster node that you want to upgrade or remove existing connections to the application on the local host. After the NLB cluster is stopped you then perform an in-place upgrade in a rolling manner.

If you want to stop the entire cluster from running, while in the NLB manager (type **NLBmgr** in Run command), you would right-click on the cluster, point to Control Hosts, and then choose Stop.

If you want to stop a single node in the cluster from running, while in the NLB manager (type **NLBmgr** in Run command), you would right-click on the node, point to Control Hoss, and then choose Stop.

Setting the Affinity

NLB allows an administrator to configure three types of affinity settings to help response times between NLB clients. Each affinity setting determines a method of distributing NLB client requests. There are three different affinity settings: None, Single, and Class C. The New Cluster Wizard sets the default affinity to Single.

No Affinity (None)   When setting the affinity to No Affinity (None), NLB will not assign a NLB client with any specific member. When a request is sent to the NLB, the requests are balanced among all of the nodes. The No Affinity provides greater performance but there may be issues with clients establishing sessions. This happens because the request may be load balanced between NLB nodes and session information may not be present.

Single Affinity   Setting the cluster affinity to Single will send all traffic from a specific IP address to a single cluster node. This will keep a client on a specific node where the client should not have to authenticate again. Setting the affinity mode to Single would remove the authentication problem but would not distribute the load to other servers unless the initial server was down. Setting the affinity to Single allows a client's IP address to always connect to the same NLB node. This setting allows clients using an intranet to get the best performance.

Class C Affinity   When setting the affinity to Class C, NLB links clients with a specific member based on the Class C part of the client's IP address. This allows an administrator to setup NLB so that clients from the same Class C address range can access the same NLB member. This affinity is best for NLB clusters using the Internet.

PowerShell Commands for an NLB Cluster

In Table 16.2, I will show you some of the different PowerShell commands that you can use to manage the NLB cluster.

TABLE 16.2   PowerShell Commands for NLB

PowerShell Command	Description
Add-NlbClusterNode	This command adds a new node to the NLB cluster.
Add-NlbClusterNodeDip	This command will add a dedicated IP address to a cluster.
Add-NlbClusterPortRule	This command adds a new port rule to a cluster.
Add-NlbClusterVip	This command adds a virtual IP address to a cluster.
Disable-NlbClusterPortRule	This command disables a port rule on a Network Load Balancing (NLB) cluster.
Enable-NlbClusterPortRule	This command enables a port rule on a cluster.
Get-NlbCluster	This command allows you to view information about the Network Load Balancing (NLB) cluster.
Get-NlbClusterDriverInfo	This command allows you to see information about the NLB drivers on a machine.
Get-NlbClusterNode	This command gets the information about the cluster object.
Get-NlbClusterPortRule	This command gets the port rule objects.

TABLE 16.2 PowerShell Commands for NLB *(continued)*

PowerShell Command	Description
New-NlbCluster	This command creates a cluster on the specified interface.
New-NlbClusterIpv6Address	This command generates IPv6 addresses to create cluster virtual IP addresses.
Remove-NlbCluster	This command deletes a cluster.
Remove-NlbClusterNode	This command removes a node from a cluster.
Remove-NlbClusterPortRule	This command deletes a port rule from a cluster.
Resume-NlbCluster	This command resumes all nodes in the cluster.
Set-NlbCluster	This command allows you to edit the configuration of a NLB cluster.
Set-NlbClusterNode	This command allows an administrator to edit the NLB cluster node settings.
Set-NlbClusterPortRule	This command allows you to edit the NLB port rules.
Start-NlbCluster	This command will start all of the nodes in a cluster.
Start-NlbClusterNode	This command will start one of the nodes in a cluster.
Stop-NlbCluster	This command stops all nodes in the cluster.
Stop-NlbClusterNode	This command will stop one of the nodes in a cluster.

Achieving High Availability with Failover Clustering

Taking high availability to the next level for enterprise services often means creating a failover cluster. In a failover cluster, all of the clustered application or service resources are assigned to one node or server in the cluster. Commonly clustered applications are SQL Server and Exchange Server; commonly clustered services are File and Print. Since the differences between a clustered application and a clustered service are primarily related to the number of functions or features, for simplicity's sake I will refer to both as *clustered applications*. Another, more frequently, clustered resource is a Hyper-V virtual machine.

If there is a failure of the primary node or if the primary node is taken offline for maintenance, the clustered application is started on another cluster node. The client requests are then automatically redirected to the new cluster node to minimize the impact of the failure.

How does Failover Clustering improve availability? By increasing the number of server nodes available on which the application or virtual machine can run, you can move the application or virtual machine to a healthy server if there is a problem, if maintenance needs to be completed on the hardware or the operating system, or if patches need to be applied. The clustered application being moved will have to restart on the new server regardless of whether the move was intentional. This is why the term *highly available* is used instead of *fault tolerant*. Virtual machines, however, can be moved from one node to another node using a process known as *live migration*. Live migration is where one or more virtual machines are intentionally moved from one node to another with their current memory state intact through the cluster network with no indicators to the virtual machine consumer that the virtual machine has moved from one server to another. However, in the event of a cluster node or virtual machine failure, the virtual machine will still fail and will then be brought online again on another healthy cluster node.

Figure 16.7 shows an example of SQL Server running on the first node of a Windows Server 2016 failover cluster.

FIGURE 16.7 Using Failover Clustering to cluster SQL Server

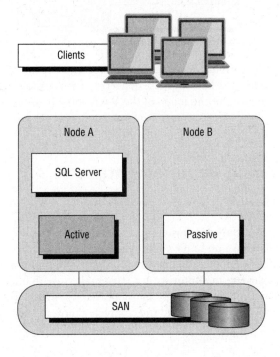

The clustered SQL Server in Figure 16.8 can be failed over to another node in the cluster and still service database requests. However, the database will be restarted.

FIGURE 16.8 Failing the SQL Server service to another node

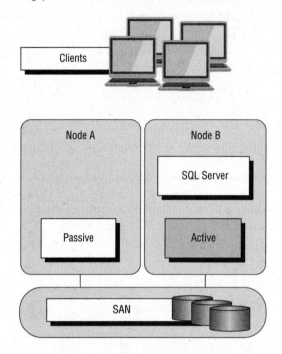

Failover clustering is notorious for being complicated and expensive. Windows Server 2016 makes strides in removing both of these concerns. Troubleshooting and other advanced concepts are outside of the scope of the Microsoft MCSA exams and thus this book, so I will cover only the basic requirements and concepts needed to configure a failover cluster.

Failover Clustering Requirements

The Failover Clustering feature is available in the Datacenter, Standard, and Hyper-V editions of Windows Server 2016.

To be able to configure a failover cluster, you must have the required components. A single failover cluster can have up to 64 nodes when using Windows Server 2016, however, and the clustered service or application must support that number of nodes.

To create a failover cluster, an administrator must make sure that all the hardware involved meets the cluster requirements. To be supported by Microsoft, all hardware must be certified for Windows Server 2016, and the complete failover cluster solution must pass all tests in the Validate a Configuration Wizard. Although the exact hardware will depend on the clustered application, a few requirements are standard:

- Server components must be marked with the "Certified for Windows Server 2016" logo.

- Although not explicitly required, server hardware should match and contain the same or similar components.

- All of the Validate a Configuration Wizard tests must pass.

The requirements for Failover Clustering storage have changed from previous versions of Windows. For example, Parallel SCSI is no longer a supported storage technology for any of the clustered disks. There are, however, additional requirements that need to be met for the storage components:

- Disks available for the cluster must be Fibre Channel, iSCSI, or Serial Attached SCSI.

- Each cluster node must have a dedicated network interface card for iSCSI connectivity. The network interface card you use for iSCSI should not be used for network communication.

- Multipath software must be based on Microsoft's Multipath I/O (MPIO).

- Storage drivers must be based on `storport.sys`.

- Drivers and firmware for the storage controllers on each server node in the cluster should be identical.

- Storage components must be marked with the "Certified for Windows Server 2016" logo.

In addition, there are network requirements that must be met for Failover Clustering:

- Cluster nodes should be connected to multiple networks for communication redundancy.

- Network adapters should be the same make, use the same driver, and have the firmware version in each cluster node.

- Network components must be marked with the "Certified for Windows Server 2016" logo.

There are two types of network connections in a failover cluster. These should have adequate redundancy because total failure of either could cause loss of functionality of the cluster. The two types are as follows:

Public Network This is the network through which clients are able to connect to the clustered service application.

Private Network This is the network used by the nodes to communicate with each other.

To provide redundancy for these two network types, additional network adapters would need to be added to the node and configured to connect to the networks.

In previous versions of Windows Server, support was given only when the entire cluster configuration was tested and listed on the Hardware Compatibility List. The tested configuration listed the server and storage configuration down to the firmware and driver versions. This proved to be difficult and expensive from both a vendor and a consumer perspective to deploy supported Windows clusters.

When problems did arise and Microsoft support was needed, it caused undue troubleshooting complexity as well. With Windows Server 2016 Failover Clustering and simplified requirements, including the "Certified for Windows Server 2016" logo program and the Validate a Configuration Wizard, it all but eliminates the guesswork of getting the cluster components configured in a way that follows best practices and allows Microsoft support to assist you easily when needed.

Workgroup and Multi-Domain Clusters

One nice new advantage of using Windows Server 2016 is the ability to set up a cluster on systems not part of the same domain. In Window Server 2012 R2 and previous versions, clusters could only be created on machines that were part of the same domain. Windows Server 2016 allows you to set up a cluster without using Active Directory dependencies. Administrators can create clusters in the following situations:

Single-Domain Cluster   All nodes in a cluster are part of the same domain.

Multi-Domain Cluster   Nodes in a cluster are part of a different domain.

Workgroup Cluster   Nodes are member servers and part of a workgroup.

Site-Aware, Stretched, or Geographically Dispersed Clusters (Geoclustering)

One nice advantage of Windows Server 2016 clustering is that you can set up site-aware failover clusters. Site-aware clustering allows an administrator to expand clustered nodes to different geographic locations (sites). Site-aware failover clusters allow you to set up clusters in remote locations for failover, placement policies, Cross-Site Heartbeating, and for quorum placement.

One of the issues with previous clusters was the heartbeat. The cluster heartbeat is a signal sent between servers so that they know that the machines are up and running. Servers send heartbeats and if after 5 non-responsive heartbeats, the cluster would assume that the node was offline. So if you had nodes in remote locations, the heartbeats would not get the response they needed.

But now Windows Server 2016 includes Cross-Site Heartbeating and it allows you to setup delays so that remote nodes can answer the heartbeat within time. The following two PowerShell commands allow you to setup the delay necessary for Cross-Site Heartbeating.

```
(Get-Cluster).CrossSiteDelay = <value>
(Get-Cluster).CrossSiteThreshold = <value>
```

The first PowerShell command (`CrossSiteDelay`) is what is used to set the amount of time between each heartbeat sent to nodes. This value is done in milliseconds (default is 1000).

The second PowerShell command (`CrossSiteThreshold`) is the value that you set for the number of missed heartbeats (default is 20) before the node is considered offline.

One issue you may face is if you have multiple sites or if the cluster is geographically dispersed. If the failover cluster does not have a shared common disk, data replication between nodes might not pass the cluster validation "storage" tests.

Setting up a cluster in a site-aware, stretched, or geocluster (these terms can be used interchangeably) configuration is a common practice. As long as the cluster solution does not require external storage to fail over, it will not need to pass the storage test to function properly.

Cluster Quorum

When a group of people sets out to accomplish a single task or goal, a method for settling disagreements and for making decisions is required. In the case of a cluster, the goal is to provide a highly available service in spite of failures. When a problem occurs and a cluster node loses communication with the other nodes because of a network error, the functioning nodes are supposed to try to bring the redundant service back online.

How, though, is it determined which node should bring the clustered service back online? If all the nodes are functional despite the network communications issue, each one might try. Just like a group of people with their own ideas, a method must be put in place to determine which idea, or node, to grant control of the cluster. Windows Server 2016 Failover Clustering, like other clustering technologies, requires that a quorum exist between the cluster nodes before a cluster becomes available.

A *quorum* is a consensus of the status of each of the nodes in the cluster. Quorum must be achieved in order for a clustered application to come online by obtaining a majority of the votes available (see Figure 16.9). Windows Server 2016 has four quorum models, or methods, for determining a quorum and for adjusting the number and types of votes available:

- Node majority (no witness)
- Node majority with witness (disk or file share)
- Node and file share majority
- No majority (disk witness only)

Witness Configuration

Most administrators follow some basic rules. For example, when you configure a quorum, the voting components in the cluster should be an odd number. For example, if I set up a quorum for five elements and I lose one element, I continue to work. If I lose two elements, I continue to work. If I lose three elements, the cluster stops—as soon as it hits half plus 1, the cluster stops. This works well with an odd number.

FIGURE 16.9   Majority needed

When a majority of the nodes are communicating, the cluster is functional.

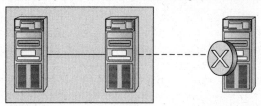

When a majority of the nodes are not communicating, the cluster stops.

If the cluster contains an even number of voting elements, an administrator should then configure a disk witness or a file share witness. The advantage of using a witness (disk or file share) is that the cluster will continue to run even if half of the cluster nodes simultaneously go down or are disconnected. The ability to configure a disk witness is possible only if the storage vendor supports read-write access from all sites to the replicated storage.

One of the advantages of Windows Server 2016 is the advanced quorum configuration option. This option allows you to assign or remove quorum votes on a per-node basis. Administrators now have the ability to remove votes from nodes in certain configurations. For example, if your organization uses a site-aware cluster, you may choose to remove votes from the nodes in the backup site. This way, those backup nodes would not affect your quorum calculations.

There are different ways that you can setup quorum witnesses. Here are some of the options that you can choose from:

Configure a Disk Witness   Choosing the quorum disk witness is normally setup if all nodes can see the disks. To set this disk witness up, the cluster must be able to see the Dedicated LUN. The LUN needs to store a copy of the cluster database and it's most useful for clusters that are using shared storage. The following list is just some of the requirements when setting up a Disk Witness:

- LUN needs to be at least 512 MB minimum.
- The disk must be dedicated to cluster use only.
- Must pass disk storage validation tests.
- The disk can't be used in a Cluster Shared Volume (CSV).
- You must use a single volume for Basic disks.

- No drive letter needed.
- Drive must be formatted using NTFS or ReFS.
- Can be used with hardware RAID.
- Should not be used with Antivirus or backup software

Configure a File Share Witness   Administrators should choose to use the File Share Witness when you need to think about multi-site disaster recovery and the file server must be using the SMB file share.

The following list is just some of the requirements when setting up a File Share Witness:

- Minimum of 5 MB of free space required.
- File share must be dedicated to the cluster and not used to store user data or application data.

Configure a Cloud Witness   Windows Server 2016 Cloud Witness is a new type of Failover Cluster quorum witness that leverages Microsoft Azure as the intercession point. The Cloud Witness gets a vote just like any other quorum witness. Administrators can setup the cloud witness as a quorum witness using the Configure a Cluster Quorum Wizard.

Dynamic Quorum Management

Another advantage in Windows Server 2016 is dynamic quorum management. *Dynamic quorum management* automatically manages the vote assignment to nodes. With this feature enabled, votes are automatically added or removed from nodes when that node either joins or leaves a cluster. In Windows Server 2016, dynamic quorum management is enabled by default.

Validating a Cluster Configuration

Configuring a failover cluster in Windows Server 2016 is much simpler than in previous versions of Windows Server. Before a cluster can be configured, the Validate a Configuration Wizard should be run to verify that the hardware is configured in a fashion that is supportable. Before you can run the Validate a Configuration Wizard, however, the Failover Clustering feature needs to be installed using Server Manager. The account that is used to create a cluster must have administrative rights on each of the cluster nodes and have permissions to create a cluster name object in Active Directory (if using Active Directory). Follow these steps:

1. Prepare the hardware and software perquisites.
2. Install the Failover Clustering feature on each server.
3. Log in with the appropriate user ID and run the Validate a Configuration Wizard.
4. Create a cluster.
5. Install and cluster applications and services.

To install the Failover Clustering feature on a cluster node, follow the steps outlined in Exercise 16.2.

EXERCISE 16.2

Installing the Failover Cluster Feature

1. Press the Windows key and select Administrative Tools ➢ Server Manager.

2. Select number 2, Add Roles And Features.

3. At the Select Installation Type screen, choose a role-based or feature-based installation.

4. At the Select Destination Server screen, choose Select A Server From The Server Pool and click Next.

5. At the Select Server Roles screen, click Next.

6. At the Select Features screen, click the Failover Clustering (see Figure 16.10) check box. If the Add Features dialog box appears, click the Add Features button. Click Next.

FIGURE 16.10 Failover Cluster Feature

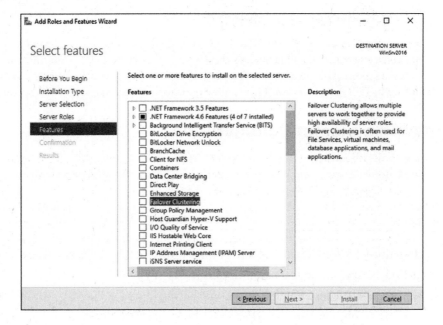

7. At the Confirmation screen (see Figure 16.11), click the Install button.

FIGURE 16.11   Confirmation Screen

8. Once the installation is complete, click the Close button.

9. Close Server Manager.

Using the Validate a Configuration Wizard before creating a cluster is highly recommended. This wizard validates that the hardware configuration and the software configuration for the potential cluster nodes are in a supported configuration. Even if the configuration passes the tests, take care to review all warnings and informational messages so that they can be addressed or documented before the cluster is created.

Running the Validate a Configuration Wizard does the following:

- Conducts four types of tests (software and hardware inventory, network, storage, and system configuration)
- Confirms that the hardware and software settings are supportable by Microsoft support staff

You should run the Validate a Configuration Wizard before creating a cluster or after making any major hardware or software changes to the cluster. Doing this will help you identify any misconfigurations that could cause problems with the failover cluster.

Running the Validate a Configuration Wizard

The Validate a Configuration Wizard, shown in Figure 16.12, is simple and straightforward to use, as its "wizard" name would suggest. It should be run after the Failover Clustering feature has been installed on each of the cluster nodes, and it can be run as many times as required.

FIGURE 16.12 The Validate a Configuration Wizard

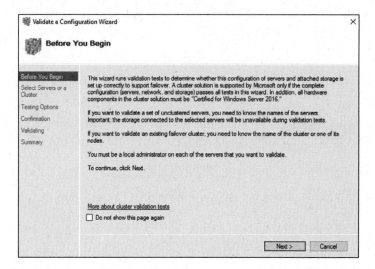

 When you are troubleshooting cluster problems or have changed the configuration of the cluster hardware, it is a good idea to run the Validate a Configuration Wizard again to help pinpoint potential cluster configuration problems.

If you already have a cluster configured and want to run the Validate a Configuration Wizard, you can do so; however, you will not be able to run all of the storage tests without taking the clustered resources offline. You will be prompted either to skip the disruptive tests or to take the clustered resources offline so that the tests can complete.

Exercise 16.3 shows the exact steps to follow to run the Validate a Configuration Wizard successfully on clusters named NODEA and NODEB, which are not yet clustered.

 I am using NODEA and NODEB in the exercises. You need to replace these two nodes with your own two servers to complete these exercises.

EXERCISE 16.3

Running the Validate a Configuration Wizard

1. Press the Windows key and select Administrative Tools ➢ Failover Cluster Management.

2. In the Actions pane (right side of screen), click Validate Configuration.

3. At the Before You Begin screen, click Next.

4. Type **First Server Name** (this is your server's name) in the Enter Name field and click Add.

5. Type **Second Server Name** (this is the second server's name) in the Enter Name field and click Add.

6. Click Next.

7. Leave Run All Tests (Recommended) selected and click Next.

8. You will see tests being run (see Figure 16.13). Let the test complete, review the report in the Summary window, and then click Finish.

FIGURE 16.13   Cluster Tests

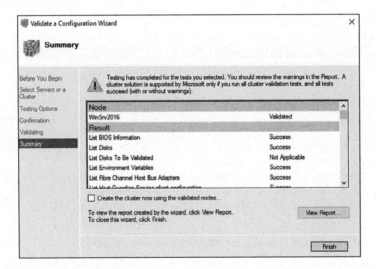

9. Close the Failover Cluster Wizard.

Addressing Problems Reported by the Validate a Configuration Wizard

After the Validate a Configuration Wizard has been run, it will show the results, as shown in Figure 16.14. This report can also be viewed in detail later using a web browser. The report is named with the date and time the wizard was run, and it is stored in %windir%\cluster\Reports.

FIGURE 16.14   Validate a Configuration Wizard results

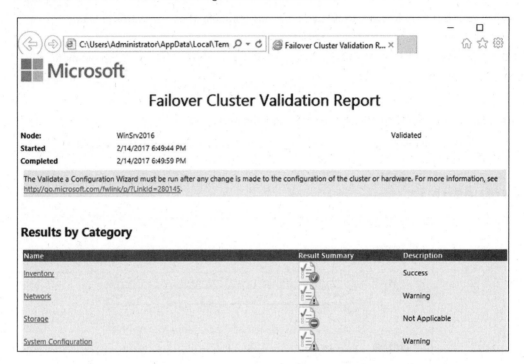

How should errors listed in the report be addressed? Often, the errors reported by the Validate a Configuration Wizard are self-explanatory; however, sometimes additional help is required. The following three guidelines should help troubleshoot the errors:

- Read all of the errors because multiple errors may be related.

- Use the checklists available in the Windows Server help files to ensure that all the steps have been completed.

- Contact the hardware vendor for updated drivers, firmware, and guidance for using the hardware in a cluster.

Creating a Cluster

After you have successfully validated a configuration and the cluster hardware is in a supportable state, you can create a cluster. The process for creating a cluster is straightforward and similar to the process of running the Validate a Configuration Wizard. To create a cluster with two servers, follow the instructions in Exercise 16.4.

EXERCISE 16.4

Creating a Cluster

1. Open the Failover Cluster Management MMC.

2. In the Management section of the center pane, select Create A Cluster.

3. Read the Before You Begin information and click Next.

4. In the Enter Server Name box, type **Your Server** and then click Add.

5. Again, in the Enter Server Name box, type **Your Second Server** and then click Add. Click Next.

6. At the Validation screen, choose No for this exercise and then click Next.

7. In the Access Point For Administering The Cluster section, enter **Cluster1** for the cluster name.

8. Type an IP address and then click Next. This IP address will be the IP address of the cluster.

9. In the Confirmation dialog box, verify the information and then click Next.

10. On the Summary page, click Finish.

Working with Cluster Nodes

Once a cluster is created, a couple of actions are available. First you can add another node to the cluster by using the Add Node Wizard from the Failover Cluster Management Actions pane.

At this point, you also have the option to pause a node, which prevents resources from being failed over or moved to the node. You typically would pause a node when the node is involved in maintenance or troubleshooting. After a node is paused, it must be resumed to allow resources to be run on it again.

Another action available to perform on a node at this time is *evict*. Eviction is an irreversible process. Once you evict the node, it must be re-added to the cluster. You would evict a node when it is damaged beyond repair or is no longer needed in the cluster. If you evict a damaged node, you can repair or rebuild it and then add it back to the cluster using the Add Node Wizard.

Clustering Roles, Services, and Applications

Once the cluster is created, applications, services, and roles can be clustered. Windows Server 2016 includes a number of built-in roles and features that can be clustered.

The following roles and features can be clustered in Windows Server 2016 (see Figure 16.15):

- DFS Namespace Server
- DHCP Server
- Distributed Transaction Coordinator (DTC)

- File Server
- Generic Application
- Generic Script
- Generic Service
- Hyper-V Replica Broker
- iSCSI Target Server
- iSNS Server
- Message Queuing
- Other Server
- Virtual Machine

FIGURE 16.15   High availability roles

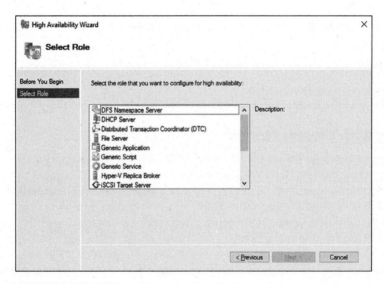

In addition, other common services and applications can be clustered on Windows Server 2016 clusters:

- Enterprise database services, such as Microsoft SQL Server
- Enterprise messaging services, such as Microsoft Exchange Server

To cluster a role or feature such as Print Services, the first step is to install the role or feature on each node of the cluster. The next step is to use the Configure a Service or Application Wizard in the Failover Cluster Management tool. Exercise 16.5 shows you how to cluster the Print Services role once an appropriate disk has been presented to the cluster. To complete this exercise, you must have a cluster created.

EXERCISE 16.5

Clustering the Print Services Role

1. Open the Failover Cluster Management MMC.

2. In the console tree, click the arrow next to the cluster name to expand the items underneath it.

3. Right-click Roles and choose Configure Role.

4. Click Next on the Before You Begin page.

5. Click Other Server on the Select Role screen and then click Next.

6. Type the name of the print server, such as **Print1**, and type in the IP address that will be used to access the print service, such as **80.0.0.34**. Then click Next.

7. At the Select Storage page, just click Next.

8. Click Next at the Confirmation page.

9. After the wizard runs and the Summary page appears, you can view a report of the tasks the wizard performed by clicking View Report.

10. Close the report and click Finish.

The built-in roles and features all are configured in a similar fashion. Other applications, such as Microsoft Exchange Server 2016, have specialized cluster configuration routines that are outside the scope of this exam. Applications that are not developed to be clustered can also be clustered using the Generic Application, Generic Script, or Generic Service option in the Configure a Service or Application Wizard, as shown in Figure 16.16.

FIGURE 16.16   Configuring a generic application

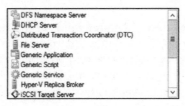

Clustered Application Settings

Windows Server 2016 has options that allow an administrator to fine-tune the failover process to meet the needs of their business. These options will be covered in the next few sections.

Failover occurs when a clustered application or service moves from one node to another. The process can be triggered automatically because of a failure or server maintenance or can be done manually by an administrator. The failover process works as follows:

1. The cluster service takes all of the resources in the application offline in the order set in the dependency hierarchy.

2. The cluster service transfers the application to the node that is listed next on the application's list of preferred host nodes.

3. The cluster service attempts to bring all of the application's resources online, starting at the bottom of the dependency hierarchy.

   These steps can change depending on the use of Live Migration.

In a cluster that is hosting multiple applications, it may be important to set specific nodes to be primarily responsible for each clustered application. This can be helpful from a troubleshooting perspective since a specific node is targeted for a hosting service. To set a preferred node and an order of preference for failover, use the General tab in the Properties dialog box of the clustered application.

Also, the order of failover is set in this same dialog box by moving the order in which the nodes are listed. If NODEA should be the primary node and NODEB should be the server that the application fails to first, NODEA should be listed first and selected as the preferred owner. NODEB should be listed second, and the remaining cluster nodes should be listed after NODEB.

A number of failover settings can be configured for the clustered service. The failover settings control the number of times a clustered application can fail in a period of time before the cluster stops trying to restart it. Typically, if a clustered application fails a number of times, some sort of manual intervention will be required to return the application to a stable state.

Specifying the maximum number of failures will keep the application from trying to restart until it is manually brought back online after the problem has been resolved. This is beneficial because if the application continues to be brought online and then fails, it may show as being functional to the monitoring system, even though it continues to fail. After the application is put in a failed state, the monitoring system will not be able to contact the application and should report it as being offline.

Failback settings control whether and when a clustered application would fail back to the preferred cluster node once it becomes available. The default setting is Prevent Failback. If failback is allowed, two additional options are available, either to fail back immediately after the preferred node is available or to fail back within a specified time.

The time is specified in the 24-hour format. If you want to allow failback between 10 p.m. and 11 p.m., you would set the failback time to be between 22 and 23. Setting a failback time to off-hours is an excellent way to ensure that your clustered applications are running on the designated nodes and automatically scheduling the failover process for a time when it will impact the fewest users.

One tool that is valuable in determining how resources affect other resources is the dependency viewer. The *dependency viewer* visualizes the dependency hierarchy created for an application or service. Using this tool can help when troubleshooting why specific resources are causing failures and allow an administrator to visualize the current configuration better and adjust it to meet business needs. Exercise 16.6 will show you how to run the dependency viewer.

EXERCISE 16.6

Using the Dependency Viewer

1. Open the Failover Cluster Management MMC.

2. In the console tree, click the arrow to expand the cluster.

3. Click Roles.

4. Under the Roles section in the center of the screen, click one of the roles (such as Print1).

5. Right-click the role and under More Actions click Show Dependency Report.

6. Review the dependency report.

7. Close the Dependency Report and close the Failover Cluster Manager.

Exercise 16.6 generated a dependency report that shows how the print service is dependent on a network name and a clustered disk resource. The network name is then dependent on an IP address.

Resource Properties

Resources are physical or logical objects, such as a file share or IP address, which the failover cluster manages. They may be services or applications available to clients, or they may be part of the cluster. Resources include physical hardware devices such as disks and logical items such as network names. They are the smallest configurable unit in a cluster and can run on only a single node in a cluster at a time.

Like clustered applications, resources have a number of properties available for meeting business requirements for high availability. This section covers resource dependencies and policies.

Dependencies can be set on individual resources and control how resources are brought online and offline. Simply put, a dependent resource is brought online after the resources that it depends on, and it is taken offline before those resources. As shown in Figure 16.17, dependencies can be set on a specific resource, such as the Generic Application.

FIGURE 16.17 Resource dependencies

Resource policies are settings that control how resources respond when a failure occurs and how resources are monitored for failures. Figure 16.18 shows the Policies tab of a resource's Properties dialog box.

FIGURE 16.18 Resource policies

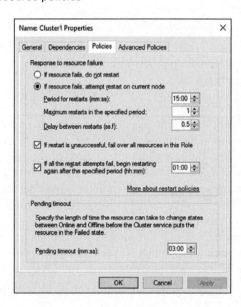

The Policies tab sets configuration options for how a resource should respond in the event of a failure. The options available are as follows:

If Resource Fails, Do Not Restart   This option, as it would lead you to believe, leaves the failed resource offline.

If Resource Fails, Attempt Restart On Current Node   With this option set, the resource tries to restart if it fails on the node on which it is currently running. There are two additional options if this is selected so that the number of restarts can be limited. They set the number of times the resource should restart on the current node in a specified length of time. For example, if you specify 5 for Maximum Restarts In The Specified Period and 10:00 (mm:ss) for Period For Restarts, the cluster service will try to restart the resource five times during that 10-minute period. After the fifth restart, the cluster service will no longer attempt to restart the service on the active node.

If Restart Is Unsuccessful, Fail Over All Resources In This Service Or Application   If this option is selected, when the cluster service is no longer trying to restart the resource on the active node, it will fail the entire service or application to another cluster node. If you wanted to leave the application or service with a failed resource on the current node, you would clear this check box.

If All The Restart Attempts Fail, Begin Restarting Again After The Specified Period (hh:mm)   If this option is selected, the cluster service will restart the resource at a specified interval if all previous attempts have failed.

Pending Timeout   This option is used to set the amount of time in minutes and seconds that the cluster service should wait for this resource to respond to a change in states. If a resource takes longer than the cluster expects to change states, the cluster will mark it as having failed. If a resource consistently takes longer than this and the problem cannot be resolved, you may need to increase this value. Figure 16.19 shows the Advanced Policies tab.

FIGURE 16.19   Resource Advanced Policies

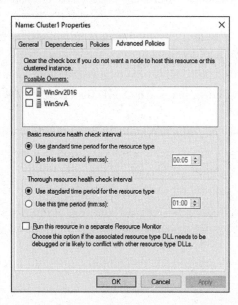

The options available on the Advanced Policies tab are as follows:

Possible Owners   This option allows an administrator to remove specific cluster nodes from running this resource. Using this option is valuable when there are issues with a resource on a particular node and the administrator wants to keep the applications from failing over to that node until the problem can be repaired.

Basic Resource Health Check Interval   This option allows an administrator to customize the health check interval for this resource.

Thorough Resource Health Check Interval   This option allows an administrator to customize the thorough health check interval for this resource.

Run This Resource In A Separate Resource Monitor   If the resource needs to be debugged by a support engineer or if the resource conflicts with other resources, this option may need to be used.

Windows Server 2016 Clustering Features

Many new features are included in the Windows Server 2016 release for clustering. It is a rich feature set of high availability with greatly improved flexibility based on the needs of IT organizations. The new features relate to quorum behavior, virtual machine hosting, Active Directory–detached clusters, and a new dashboard.

Windows PowerShell Cmdlets for Failover Clusters   As I have explained throughout this book, Windows PowerShell is a command-line shell and scripting tool. Windows Server 2016 clustering has new cmdlets that provide powerful ways to script cluster configuration and management tasks. Windows PowerShell cmdlets have now replaced the Cluster.exe command-line interface.

Cluster Shared Volumes   *Cluster Shared Volumes (CSV)* allows for the configuration of clustered virtual machines. CSV allows you to do the following:

- Reduce the number of LUNs (disks) required for your virtual machines.
- Make better use of disk space. Any VHD file on that LUN can use the free space on a CSV volume.
- More easily track the paths to VHD files and other files used by virtual machines.
- Use a few CSV volumes to create a configuration that supports many clustered virtual machines.

CSV volumes also are utilized for the Scale-Out-File-Server cluster role.

Management of Large-Scale Clusters   One advantage of Windows Server 2016 clusters is the ability for Server Manager to discover and manage the nodes in a cluster. By starting the

Failover Cluster Manager from Server Manager, you can do remote multiserver management and role and feature installation. Administrators now have the ability to manage a cluster from one convenient location.

Management and Mobility of Clustered Virtual Machines   Microsoft, as well as the industry as a whole, is moving toward the cloud and virtualization. With that in mind, administrators can now configure settings such as prioritizing the starting or placement of virtual machines in the clustered workloads. This allows administrators to allocate resources efficiently to your cluster.

Cluster-Aware Updating   One issue that every administrator has dealt with is updating a system or application while it is running. For example, if you are running Microsoft Exchange and you want to do an Exchange update, when do you take the server offline to do the update? It always seems that someone is on the system 24 hours a day. Well, Windows Server 2016 clustering has a solution. *Cluster-Aware Updating (CAU)* is a new automated feature that allows system updates to be applied automatically while the cluster remains available during the entire update process.

Cluster Node Fairness   Virtual Machine Load Balancing feature is new to Windows Server 2016. This new load balancing feature helps optimize the nodes in a cluster. When an organization builds a virtual machine cluster, there will be times when that cluster needs to have maintenance and certain virtual machines will be taken offline. When this happens, an unbalanced cluster (this is when some nodes are hosting VMs more often than others) may occur. This is where the VM Load Balancing feature (Node Fairness) helps the cluster. The Balancer will re-distribute VMs from an over balance node to an under balanced node. To setup Node Fairness, you would use the PowerShell command AutoBalancerLevel (shown below). The value input is a 1, 2, or 3. 1 is equivalent to the Low setting (move the host when showing more than 80% loaded), 2 is equivalent to Medium (move the host when more than 70% loaded) and 3 is equivalent to High (average nodes and move the host when showing more than 5% above the average).

```
(Get-Cluster).AutoBalancerLevel = <value>
```

Cluster Operating System Rolling Upgrade   One of the problems that many IT people face is the issue with downtime while their servers get upgraded to a new operating system. Windows Server 2016 includes a new feature called Cluster Operating System Rolling Upgrade. This new feature allows an administrator to upgrade a Hyper-V or Scale-Out File Server cluster from Windows Server 2012 R2 to Windows Server 2016 without stopping the servers.

Scale-Out File Server for Application Data   By utilizing *Microsoft Storage Spaces*, you can create a highly available clustered file share that utilizes SMB 3.0 and CSV to provide scalable access to data.

Scale-out file servers are useful for storing the following application data:

- Hyper-V virtual machine storage
- SQL Server database files

Be aware that scale-out file servers are not useful at all for typical file share data because they benefit only from applications that require a persistent connection to their storage.

Shared Virtual Hard Disks   In the previous versions of Windows, Failover Cluster nodes running as virtual machines had to use iSCSI or virtual HBAs to connect directly to SAN-based storage. With Windows Server 2016, you can set your Hyper-V virtualized cluster to use a shared VHDX virtual disk. Shared virtual hard disks can reside on the following:

- A scale-out file server failover cluster
- Cluster CSV volumes

Shared virtual hard disks are extremely useful in providing highly available shared storage for the following virtualized workloads:

- SQL Server
- Virtual Machine Manager
- Exchange Server

Virtual Machine Drain on Shutdown   When needing to perform maintenance on a Hyper-V failover cluster, you may have a lot of virtual machines on one node of a cluster. Inevitably, you will need to restart a cluster node for updates or shut it down for maintenance.

In previous versions of Windows, virtual machines running on the cluster would save their state, and then the cluster node would shut down. Windows Server 2016 helps alleviate this issue by automatically draining the virtual machines running on a node before it shuts down or restarts. Windows does this by attempting to live migrate all virtual machines on the cluster node to other nodes in the cluster when at all possible.

This feature is turned on by default, but it can be disabled through PowerShell.

Active Directory–Detached Clusters   Previous versions of Windows Failover Clustering have depended on Active Directory to provide computer objects for the cluster name object as well as virtual computer objects. With Active Directory–detached failover clusters, communication to the cluster-form clients will use NTLM authentication rather than the normal Kerberos authentication. This is useful in maintaining high availability should a person accidently delete a virtual computer object in Active Directory that a clustered resource depends on for Kerberos authentication.

Dynamic Witness   Earlier in this chapter, I mentioned the Dynamic Quorum model and how votes were dynamically adjusted based on the number of nodes in a cluster. In Windows Server 2016, there is a new feature called *dynamic witness* that is enabled by default when the cluster is configured to use a dynamic quorum. Since it is preferred to have an odd number of votes at any one time in a cluster, the dynamic witness will turn on or off the witness vote in order to ensure that there are an odd number of votes in the cluster.

Tie Breaker For 50% Node Split   Like the *dynamic witness* feature just described, the Tie Breaker For 50% Node Split option in Windows Server 2016 dynamically adjusts cluster node votes in order to maintain an odd number of votes in a cluster where no witness is being used.

This is useful for a cluster in a site-aware, stretched, or geocluster configuration.

Global Update Manager Mode   Since the first release of Microsoft Cluster Services appearing in Windows NT 4.0 Enterprise, all nodes in a cluster maintain a local database that keeps a copy of the cluster configuration. The *Global Update Manager (GUM)* is a component of the cluster that ensures that before a change is marked as being committed for the entire cluster, all nodes have received and committed that change to their local cluster database. If one or more nodes do not report back or commit a change, the cluster node is kicked out of being a member of the cluster. Another issue that can occur is that for various clustered applications, such as SQL and Exchange, their performance can be negatively impacted by the time it takes the GUM to coordinate with all the nodes of a cluster for any changes. The GUM is only as fast as the slowest node in the cluster.

With Windows Server 2016, a new feature was added to Failover Clustering called *Global Update Manager mode*. This feature allows you to configure the GUM read-write modes manually in order to greatly speed up the processing of changes by the GUM and to improve the performance of certain clustered resources.

Turn Off IPsec Encryption for Inter-Node Cluster Communications   In network environments where IPsec is used, slow Group Policy updates and other issues can cause Active Directory Domain Services to be temporarily unavailable to cluster nodes. If the cluster intracluster communications protocol uses IPsec encryption, then these delays could cause cluster nodes to drop out of the cluster for failure to communicate in a timely manner with the rest of the nodes in the cluster. Windows Server 2016 now provides a way to turn off IPsec encryption on the cluster communication network.

Cluster Dashboard   Starting with Windows Server 2012, Failover Clustering supports up to 64 nodes in a cluster. Keeping track of the status and resources on all of these nodes can be an administrative headache! Managing more than one failover cluster and determining what a certain cluster hosts can be painful as well. Fortunately, in Windows Server 2016, the *Failover Cluster Manager*'s main dashboard has been updated to make it easier to see the status and health of multiple clusters.

Hyper-V Replica Broker   Starting with Windows Server 2012, Hyper-V supported continuous replication of virtual machines to another server or cluster for disaster recovery purposes. The Hyper-V Recovery Broker allows for virtual machines in a cluster to be replicated. The Hyper-V Recovery Broker keeps track of which cluster nodes virtual machines are residing on and ensures that replication is maintained.

Hyper-V Manager Integration into Failover Cluster Manager   In Windows Server 2016, the Hyper-V Management Console is integrated with Failover Cluster Manager for managing virtual machines that are clustered. Normal Hyper-V operations such as configuring, exporting, importing, configuring replication, stopping, starting, and live migrating virtual machines are supported directly through Failover Cluster Manager.

Virtual Machine Monitoring   Starting with Windows Server 2012, Failover Clustering supports Virtual Machine Monitoring for Windows Server virtual machines. Virtual Machine Monitoring monitors administrator-selected Windows services running within a virtual machine and will automatically restart a service if it should fail. If the service does not start for the configured number of restart attempts, the virtual machine will fail over to another node and then restart. For example, you can configure Failover Clustering to monitor the Print Spooler service on a Windows Server 2016 virtual machine. If the Print Spooler service goes offline, then the cluster will attempt to restart the Print Spooler service within the virtual machine. If the service still fails, Failover Clustering will move the virtual machine to another node.

PowerShell Commands for Clustering

The following table (Table 16.3) is just some of the PowerShell commands that you can use to configure and manage Windows Server 2016 clustering.

TABLE 16.3   Clustering PowerShell Commands

PowerShell Command	Description
Add-ClusterDisk	This command allows an admin to add a new disk to a failover cluster. The disk's logical unit number (LUN) must be visible to all cluster nodes.
Add-ClusterFileServerRole	This command allows an admin to create a clustered file server.
Add-ClusterGenericApplicationRole	This command allows you to configure high availability for an application that is normally not designed for clustering.
Add-ClusterGroup	This command allows an admin to add a resource group to the failover cluster.
Add-ClusterNode	This command allows an admin to add a node to a failover cluster.
Add-ClusterResource	This command allows an admin to add a resource to a failover cluster.
Add-ClusterResourceDependency	This command allows an admin to add a resource dependency to a failover cluster.
Add-ClusterServerRole	This command allows you to add the cluster server role to a server.
Block-ClusterAccess	This command allows an admin to block the specified users from accessing a cluster.

PowerShell Command	Description
Get-Cluster	This command shows you the information about a failover clusters.
Get-ClusterAccess	This command shows you the permissions for a failover clusters.
Get-ClusterNode	This command shows you the information about the servers in a failover clusters.
Get-ClusterQuorum	This command shows you the information about the cluster quorum in a clusters.
New-Cluster	This command allows you to create a new failover cluster.
Remove-Cluster	This command allows you to remove a failover cluster.
Remove-ClusterAccess	This command allows an admin to remove a user's access from the cluster.
Remove-ClusterNode	This command allows you to remove a node from a failover cluster.
Start-Cluster	This command allows an admin to start the Cluster service on all nodes.
Stop-Cluster	This command allows an admin to stop the Cluster service on all nodes.
Stop-ClusterNode	This command stops the Cluster service on a node.
Test-Cluster	This command allows an admin to complete validation tests for a cluster.

Implementing Storage Spaces Direct

Storage Spaces Direct uses local-attached drives on servers to create highly available storage at a minimal cost of traditional storage devices (SAN or NAS). Storage Spaces Direct uses regular hard drives that are connected to a single node of the failover cluster and these disks can be used as storage for the cluster.

To understand how Storage Spaces Direct truly works, I think it is better to first under-stand some other technology terms for Windows Server 2016. When an IT administrator takes a bunch of physical disks and puts them together it is called a storage pool. Storage spaces are virtual disks that are created from storage pools. Storage Spaces Direct is the evolution of Storage Spaces.

Many of the same features are used in Windows Server 2016 like Failover Clustering, Cluster Shared Volumes, and SMB.

Storage Spaces Direct utilizes disks that are connected to one node of a failover cluster and allows for the creation of pools using those disks by Storage Spaces. Storage Spaces Direct streamlines deployment by using converged or hyper-converged architecture.

Virtual Disks (Spaces) that are constructed on a pool will have their mirrors or parity (redundant data) span across the disks using different nodes of the cluster. Since replicas of the data are spread across the disks, this allows for access to data in the event a node fails or is going down for maintenance.

You can implement Storage Spaces Direct in virtual machines with each VM configured with two or more virtual disks connected to the VM's SCSI Controller. Each node of the cluster running inside the virtual machine can connect to its own disks, but utilizing Storage Spaces Direct allows all the disks to be part of the Storage Pool that spans the entire cluster node.

For the redundant data (mirror or parity spaces) to be spread across the nodes, Storage Spaces Direct uses SMB3 as the protocol transport.

Networking Hardware   To communicate between servers Storage Spaces Direct uses SMB3, including SMB Direct and SMB Multichannel over Ethernet. It is recommended to use 10+Gbe with Remote-Direct Memory Access (RDMA), or either Internet Wide Area RDMA Protocol (iWARP) or RDMA over Converged Ethernet (RoCE).

Storage Hardware

- 2 – 16 servers with locally-attached SATA, SAS, or NVMe (non-volatile memory express) drives
- Must have at least 2 solid-state drives on each server and at least 4 additional drives.
- SATA and SAS device should be following a Host-Bus Adapter (HBA) and SAS expander.

Failover Clustering   To connect the servers, Windows Server 2016 uses the built-in cluster-ing feature.

Software Storage Bus   Storage Spaces Direct has a new feature called Software Storage Bus. This allows all the servers to see all of each other's local drives by spanning the cluster and establishing a software-defined storage structure.

Storage Bus Layer Cache   The Software Storage Bus joins the fastest drives available to the slower drives to provide server-side read/write caching that speeds up the IO and boosts data.

Storage Pool   The storage pool is the collection of drives that form the Storage Space. It is created automatically and all qualified drives are discovered and added. It is recommended that an administrator use the default settings on one pool per cluster.

Storage Spaces   Storage Spaces offers fault tolerance to a virtual disk using mirroring, erasure coding, or both. It is thought of as distributed, software-defined RAID utilizing the drives in the pool. These virtual disks normally have resiliency when two synchronized drives or servers fail.

Resilient File System (ReFS)   The Resilient File System (ReFS) is Microsoft's latest file system which was designed to maximize data availability, efficiently scale to large data sets across varied workloads, and provide data integrity. It includes hastening the .vhdx file operations such as creating, expanding, checkpoint merging, and built-in checksums to distinguish and fix bit errors. ReFS also introduced real-time tiers, based on usage, which will rotate data between "hot" and "cold" storage-tiers.

Cluster Shared Volumes   The Cluster Shared Volumes (CSV) file system unites all the ReFS volumes into a single namespace available through any server. This namespace allows every server and every volume to look and act like it's mounted locally.

Scale-Out File Server   In converged deployments only is this necessary. It offers remote file access by using the SMB3 protocol to clients over the network. This essentially turns Storage Spaces Direct into Network-Attached Storage (NAS).

To see step-by-step instructions on configuring and deploying Storage Spaces Direct, visit Microsoft's website at:

```
https://technet.microsoft.com/en-us/windows-server-docs/
storage/storage-spaces/
hyper-converged-solution-using-storage-spaces-direct
```

The Benefits of Storage Spaces Direct

The following are just some of the benefits of using Storage Spaces Direct with Windows Server 2016:

Simplicity   In less than 15 minutes, an administrator can go from a standard server running Windows Server 2016 to creating a Storage Spaces Direct cluster. It's just the click of a check box if an administrator is using System Center.

Unrivaled Performance   Storage Spaces Direct exceeds 150,000 mixed 4k random IOPS per server with reliability, low latency, built-in read/write cache, and support for NVMe drives that are mounted directly on the PCIe bus.

Fault Tolerance   Constantly available built-in resiliency that will handle drives, servers, or component failures. Chassis and rack fault tolerance can also be configured for larger deployments. There are no complex management steps needed when hardware fails. Simply change it out for another one and the software will fix itself.

Resource Efficiency   Greater resource efficiency with Erasure coding delivering up to 2.4x more storage. Using Local Reconstruction Codes and ReFS, real-time tiers extend to hard disk drives and mixed hot/cold workloads, all while reducing CPU usage to give the resources back to the virtual machines where they are needed.

Manageability   Keep excessively active virtual machines in order by using Storage QoS Controls with minimum and maximum per-VM IOPS limits. Continuously monitor and alert by using the built-in Health Service. There are also new APIs that make it easier to collect cluster-wide performance statistics and capacity metrics.

Scalability   For multiple petabytes of storage per cluster, an administrator can increase up to 16 servers and add over 400 drives. To scale out, an administrator will just need to add drives or add more servers. Storage Spaces Direct will automatically add the new drives and begin to utilize them.

Deployment Options

When using Windows Server 2016 and installing Storage Spaces Direct, there are two deployment options that you can choose from:

Converged

In converged, there are separate clusters for each storage and compute. The converged deployment option, also called "disaggregated," puts a Scale-Out File Server (SoFS) on top of Storage Spaces Direct to provide Network-Attached Storage (NAS) over SMB3 file shares. This allows for scaling computer/workloads separately from the storage cluster. This is essential when working with large-scale deployments such as Hyper-V Infrastructure as a Service (IaaS).

Hyper-Converged

In hyper-converged, there is only one cluster for storage and compute. The hyper-converged deployment option runs the Hyper-V virtual machines or SQL Server databases directly on the servers delivering the storage, storing files all on the local volumes. This removes the need to configure file server access and permissions. It also reduces the hardware costs associated for small-to-medium business or remote office/branch office deployments.

Requirements to Set up Storage Spaces Direct

To setup Storage Spaces Direct properly, you must make sure that all of your hardware components meet the minimum requirements. Table 16.4 was taken directly from Microsoft's website for the requirements needed and also what is actually recommended by Microsoft for proper configuration of Storage Spaces Direct.

TABLE 16.4   Storage Space Direct Requirements

Component	Requirements
Servers	Minimum of 2 servers, maximum of 16 servers
	All servers should be the same make and model.
CPU	Minimum of Intel Nehalem or later compatible processor
Memory	4 GB of RAM per terabyte (TB) of cache drive capacity on each server, to store Storage Spaces Direct metadata.
	Any memory used by Windows Server, VMs, and other apps or workloads.
Networking	Minimum of 10 Gbps network interface for intra-cluster communication.
	Recommended: Two NICs for redundancy and performance
	Recommended: NICS that are remote-direct memory access (RDMA) capable, iWARP or RoCE
Drives	Use local-attached SATA, SAS, or NVMe drives.
	Every drive must be physically connected to only one server.
	All servers must have the same drive types.
	Recommended: All servers have the same drive configuration.
	SSDs must have power-loss protection, i.e. they are "enterprise-grade."
	Recommended: SSDs used for cache have high endurance, providing a minimum of 5 drive-writes-per-day (DWPD).
	Add capacity drives in multiples of the number of NVMe or SSD cache devices.
	Not supported: Multi-path IO (MPIO) or physically connecting drives via multiple paths.
Host-bus adapter (HBA)	Simple pass-through SAS HBA for both SAS and SATA drives.
	SCSI Enclosure Services (SES) for SAS and SATA drives.
	Any direct-attached storage enclosures must present Unique ID.
	Not Supported: RAID HBA controllers or SAN (Fibre Channel, iSCSI, FCoE) devices.

Storage Spaces Direct Using Windows PowerShell

The following table (Table 16.5) is just some of the PowerShell commands that you can use to configure and manage Storage Spaces Direct.

TABLE 16.5 Storage Spaces Direct PowerShell commands

PowerShell Command	Description
Disable-NetQosFlowControl	This command allows an administrator to turn off flow control.
Enable-ClusterStorageSpacesDirect	This command enables Storage Spaces Direct.
Enable-NetAdapterQos	This command allows an administrator to apply network QoS policies to the target adapters.
Enable-NetAdapterRDMA	This command allows an administrator to enable remote direct memory access (RDMA) on a network adapter.
Enable-NetQosFlowControl	This command allows an administrator to turn on flow control.
Get-NetAdapter	This command will retrieve a list of the network adapters.
Get-StoragePool	This command allows you to see a specific storage pool, or a set of StoragePool objects.
Get-StorageTier	This command allows you to see storage tiers on Windows Storage subsystems. Use this command to see Storage Spaces Direct default tier templates called Performance and Capacity.
New-Cluster	This command creates a new cluster.
New-NetQosPolicy	This command allows an admin to create a new network QoS policy.
New-NetQosTrafficClass	This command allows you to create a traffic class (like SMB).
New-Volume	This command creates a new volume.
Set-Item	This command allows an administrator to configure the trusted hosts to all hosts.
Test-Cluster	This command allows an administrator to test a set of servers for use as a Storage Spaces Direct cluster.
Update-StorageProviderCache	This command allows you to update the cache of the service for a particular provider and associated child objects.

Achieving High Availability with Hyper-V

One of the nice advantages of using Hyper-V is the ability to run an operating server within another server. Virtualization allows you to run multiple servers on top of a single Hyper-V server. But we need to make sure that these servers stay up and running.

That is where Hyper-V high availability comes into play. Having the ability to ensure that your Hyper-V servers are going to continue to run even if there is a hardware issue is an important step in guaranteeing the success of your network.

There are many ways that you can ensure that your virtual machines will continue to operate. One is to set up clustering and another is to set up Hyper-V high availability without clustering.

To set up reliability without clustering requires that your Hyper-V servers have replica copies that can automatically start up if the virtual machine errors out. This is referred to as Live Migration and replica servers.

Implementing a Hyper-V Replica

Hyper-V Replica is an important part of the Hyper-V role. It replicates the Hyper-V virtual machines from the primary site to the replica secondary sites simultaneously.

Once an administrator enables Hyper-V Replica for a particular virtual machine on the primary Hyper-V host server, the Hyper-V replica will begin to create an exact copy of the virtual machine for the secondary site. After this replication, Hyper-V Replica creates a log file for the virtual machine VHDs. This log file is rerun in reverse order to the replica VHD. This is done using replication frequency. The log files and reverse order helps ensure that the latest changes are stored and copied asynchronously. If there is an issue with the replication frequency, then the administrator will receive an alert.

On the virtual machine, an administrator can establish resynchronization settings. This can be setup to be done manually, automatically, or automatically on an explicit schedule. To fix constant synchronization issues an administrator may choose to set up automatic resynchronization.

Hyper-V Replica will aid in a disaster recovery strategy by replicating virtual machines from one host to another while keeping workloads accessible. Hyper-V Replica can create a copy of a running virtual machine to a replica offline virtual machine.

Hyper-V Hosts

With replication over a WAN link the primary and secondary host servers can be located in the same physical location or at different geographical locations. Hyper-V hosts can be standalone, clustered, or a combination of both. Hyper-V Hosts are not dependent upon Active Directory and there is no need to be domain members.

Replication and Change Tracking

When an administrator enables Hyper-V Replica on a particular virtual machine an identical copy of the virtual machine is created on a secondary host server. Once this happens, the Hyper-V Replica will create a log file that will track changes made on a virtual machine VHD. The log file is rerun in reverse order to the replica VHD. This is based on the replication frequency settings. This ensures that the latest changes are created and replicated asynchronously. This can be done over HTTP or HTTPS.

Extended (Chained) Replication

Extended (chained) Replication allows an administrator to replicate a virtual machine from a primary host to a secondary host and then replicate the secondary host to a third host. It is not possible to replicate from the primary host directly to the second and third hosts.

Extended (Chained) Replication aids in disaster recovery in that an administrator can recover from both the primary and extended replica. Extended Replication will also aid if the primary and secondary locations go offline. It must be noted that the extended replica does not support application-consistent replication and it must use the same VHD that the secondary replica uses.

Failover

If the primary or the secondary (extended) host server locations go offline, an administrator can manually initiate failover. Failover is not automatic. There are several different types of manually initiating failover:

Test Failover   Use Test Failover to verify that the replica virtual machine can successfully start in the secondary site. It will create a copy test virtual machine during failover and does not affect standard replication. After the test failover, if the administrator selects Failover on the replica test virtual machine the test failover will be deleted.

Planned Failover   Use Planned Failover during scheduled downtime. The administrator will have to turn off the primary machine before performing a planned failover. Once the machine fails over, the Hyper-V Replica will start replicating changes back to the primary server. The changes are tracked and sent to ensure that there is no data lost. Once the planned failover is complete, the reverse replication begins so that the primary virtual machine becomes the secondary and vice versa. This ensures that the hosts are synchronized.

Unplanned Failover   Use Unplanned Failover during unforeseen outages. Unplanned failover is started on the replica virtual machine. This should only be used if the primary machine goes offline. A check will confirm whether the primary machine is running. If the administrator has recovery history enabled, then it is possible to recover to an earlier point in time. During failover an administrator should ensure that the recovery point is acceptable and then finish the failover to ensure that recovery points are combined.

Virtual Machine Advanced Features

One nice feature of virtual machines is the ability to setup advanced features. In the Advanced Features section (see Figure 16.20), there are multiple settings that you can configure.

FIGURE 16.20   VM Advanced Features

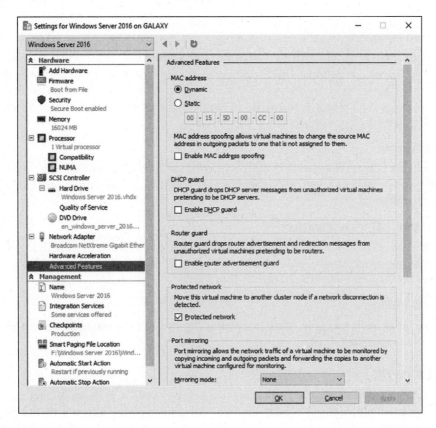

MAC Addressing

The first thing that you can configure in the Advanced Features section is setting a MAC address. The MAC address is a physical address that is associated to the NIC adapter. Administrators have the ability to set the MAC address to Dynamic (creates its own MAC addresses) or Static (this is where you can set a MAC address).

You also have the ability to do MAC spoofing. This is where a VM can change the source MAC address in outgoing packets to one that is not assigned to the NIC adapters.

DHCP Guard

DHCP guard drops DHCP server messages from unauthorized virtual machines pretending to be a DHCP server. So what does this mean to you? If a server tries to pretend to be a DHCP server, your virtual machine will drop any messages that are sent by that DHCP server.

Router Guard

Router guard drops router advertisement and redirection messages from unauthorized virtual machines pretending to be routers. It almost works the same way DHCP guard works. If an unauthorized router tries to send messages to a virtual machine, that VM will not accept those messages.

Protected Network

Administrators have the ability to set Network Health Detection at the virtual machine level for a Hyper-V host cluster. This is configured as a Protected Network. By setting the Protected Network checkbox, the virtual machine will be moved to another cluster node if a network disconnection is detected. If the health of a network connection is showing as disconnected, the VM will be automatically moved.

Port Mirroring

Port mirroring allows the network traffic of a virtual machine to be monitored by copying incoming and outgoing packets and forwarding the copies to another virtual machine configured for monitoring.

Single Root I/O Virtualization

The single root I/O virtualization (SR-IOV) interface is a continuation of the PCI Express (PCIe) interface specification. SR-IOV allows a device (like a network adapter) to separate its resources between multiple PCIe hardware functions.

Device Naming

Device naming causes the name of the network adapter to be propagated into supported guest operating systems.

NIC Teaming

NIC Teaming, also known as load balancing and failover (LBFO), gives an administrator the ability to allow multiple network adapters on a system to be placed into a team. Independent hardware vendors (IHVs) have required NIC Teaming, but until Windows Server 2012, NIC Teaming was *not* part of the Windows Server operating system.

To be able to use NIC Teaming, the computer system must have at least one Ethernet adapter. If you want to provide fault protection, an administrator must have a minimum of two Ethernet adapters. One advantage of Windows Server 2016 is that an administrator can set up 32 network adapters in a NIC team.

NIC Teaming is a common practice when setting up virtualization. This is one way that you can have load balancing with Hyper-V.

NIC Teaming gives an administrator the ability to allow a virtual machine to use virtual network adapters in Hyper-V. The advantage of using NIC Teaming in Hyper-V is that the administrator can use NIC Teaming to connect to more than one Hyper-V switch. This allows Hyper-V still to have connectivity even if the network adapter under the Hyper-V switch gets disconnected.

An administrator can configure NIC Teaming in either Server Manager or PowerShell. NIC teaming can be configured in different configuration models including Switch Independent or Switch Dependent. Switch Independent means that each NIC adapter is connected into a different switch. Switch Dependent means that all NIC adapters are connected into the same switch. If you use Switch Independent NIC Teaming, then you must connect your NICs to different switches, but both switches must be on the same subnet.

Remote Direct Memory Access

When most of us think of Hyper-V, we think of a group of virtual machines sharing access to a systems resource. With Windows Server 2016, Hyper-V includes Remote Direct Memory Access (RDMA).

RDMA allows one computer to directly access memory from the memory of another computer without the need of interfacing with either one's operating system. This gives systems the ability to have high throughput and low-latency networking. This is very useful when it comes to clustering systems (including Hyper-V).

Windows Server 2012 R2 RDMA services couldn't be bound to a Hyper-V Virtual Switch and because of this, Remote Direct Memory Access and Hyper-V had to be on the same computer as the network adapters. Because of this, there was a need for a higher number of physical network adapters that were required to be installed on the Hyper-V host.

Because of the improvements of RDMA on Windows Server 2016, administrators can use less network adapters while using RDMA.

Switch Embedded Teaming

Earlier we discussed NIC Teaming but we also have the ability to do Switch Embedded Teaming (SET). SET can be an alternative to using NIC Teaming in environments that include Hyper-V and the Software Defined Networking (SDN) stack in Windows Server 2016.

SET does use some of the functionality of NIC Teaming in the Hyper-V Virtual Switch, but SET allows an administrator to combine a group of physical adapters (minimum of 1 adapter and a maximum of 8 adapters) into software based virtual adapters.

By using virtual adapters, you get better performance and greater fault tolerance in the event of a network adapter going bad. For SET to be enabled, all of the physical network adapters must be installed on the same physical Hyper-V host.

One of the requirements of SET is that all network adapters that are members of the SET group be identical adapters. This means that they need to be the same adapter types from the same manufacturer.

One main difference between NIC Teaming and Set is that SET only supports Switch Independent mode setups. Again this means that the NIC adapters are connected to different switches.

Administrators need to create a SET team at the same time that they create the Hyper-V Virtual Switch. Administrators can do this by using the Windows PowerShell command New-VMSwitch.

At the time an administrator creates a Hyper-V Virtual Switch, the administrator needs to include the EnableEmbeddedTeaming parameter in their command syntax. The following example shows a Hyper-V switch named StormSwitch:

```
New-VMSwitch -Name StormSwitch -NetAdapterName "NIC 1","NIC 2"
-EnableEmbeddedTeaming $true
```

Administrators also have the ability to remove a SET team by using the following PowerShell command. This example removes a Virtual Switch named StormSwitch.

```
Remove-VMSwitch "StormSwitch
```

Virtual Machine Queue

Windows Server 2016 Hyper-V includes a feature called Virtual machine queue (VMQ) as long as the hardware is VMQ compatible network hardware. VMQ uses packet filtering to provide data from an external virtual machine network directly to virtual machines. This helps reduce the overhead of routing packets from the management operating system to the virtual machine.

Once VMQ is enabled on Hyper-V, a dedicated queue is created on the physical network adapter for each virtual network adapter to use. When data arrives for the virtual network adapter, the physical network adapter places that data in a queue and once the system is available, all of the data in the queue is delivered to the virtual network adapter.

To enable the virtual machine queue on a specific virtual machine, enter the settings for the virtual machine and expand Network Adapter. Click on Hardware Acceleration and on the right hand window; check the box for Enable virtual machine queue.

To enable VMQ on a physical network adapter:

1. Open Device Manager.

2. Expand the Network adapters section and right-click the name of the network adapter. Choose Properties.

3. On the Advanced tab in the properties, locate the setting for virtual machine queues and make sure it is enabled. If the setting is not available, the adapter does not support VMQ.

Receive Side Scaling

Receive Side Scaling (RSS) allows a system's network adapter to spread the network processing between multiple processor cores in systems that have a multi-core processor. Due to the fact that RSS can distribute the networking load across multiple processors, the system can handle more network traffic.

RSS has the ability to work with systems that have more than sixty four (64) processors. RSS can do this because it spreads the load across all of the processors. Because RSS can spread the network load, you end up with TCP load balancing. RSS also has the ability to load balance non-TCP traffic like UDP and multicast messages. RSS also allows an administrator to have better auditing and management capabilities.

With the release of Windows Server 2012, RSS started working with load balancing across Non-Uniform Memory Access (NUMA) systems. RSS also includes some of the following capabilities:

▪ Event tracing for RSS logs

▪ RSS configuration information

▪ Windows Management Instrumentation (WMI) for RSS

- PowerShell for RSS
- Dynamic load balancing
- RSS profiles
- Benefits for working with low latency

If you want to enable or disable RSS, you would complete the following steps.

1. Open an elevated Command prompt by right clicking Command Prompt, and then choosing Run as administrator.

2. At the Command Prompt, type the following command and hit Enter.

   netsh interface tcp set global rss=enabled

3. Close the Command Prompt window.

4. Open Device Manager (right click Start and then click Device Manager).

5. Expand Network adapters, right-click the network adapter you want to work with, and then click Properties.

6. In the network adapter properties, click on the Advanced tab. On the Receive-side scaling setting, make sure it is enabled or disabled (depending on what you need to do).

Virtual Receive-Side Scaling

Virtual Receive-side scaling (VRSS) is the virtual equivalent of RSS. VRSS is a Windows Server 2016 feature that allows a virtual network adapter to distribute the load across multiple virtual processors in a virtual machine.

VRSS works with many different types of technologies including:

- IPv4 and IPv6
- TCP and UDP
- LBFO (NIC Teaming)
- Live Migration
- Network Virtualization using Generic Routing Encapsulation (NVGRE)

VRSS is not enabled by default. VRSS is easily enabled or disabled inside of the virtual machine or on a physical host by using PowerShell cmdlets. If you are going to enable VRSS in a virtual machine, the Windows operating system of the virtual machine must be one of the following:

- Windows 8.1
- Windows 8.1 with integration components installed.
- Windows 10
- Windows Server 2012 R2
- Windows Server 2012 R2 with integration components installed.
- Windows Server 2016.

To enable VRSS using PowerShell, you would need to run one of the following commands from PowerShell. Either PowerShell command will enable VRSS.

```
Enable-NetAdapterRSS -Name "AdapterName"
Set-NetAdapterRSS -Name "AdapterName" -Enabled $True
```

To disable VRSS using PowerShell, you would need to run one of the following commands from PowerShell. Either PowerShell command will disable VRSS.

```
Disable-NetAdapterRSS -Name "AdapterName"
Set-NetAdapterRSS -Name "AdapterName" -Enabled $False
```

Virtual Machine Multi-Queue

Windows Server 2016 Hyper-V includes a new feature called Virtual Machine Multi-Queue (VMMQ). VMMQ was created using previous versions of RSS and VMQ.

Today's network adapters have more queues than the virtual machines they work with. In previous versions of virtualization (before Windows Server 2012 R2) a single virtual machine could be assigned to a single virtual machine queue. This single queue would have a set affinity to a single processor. So what this means is that even though network adapters can handle multiple queues, the virtual machines could only send traffic using a single queue.

VMMQ helps resolve this issue. VMMQ allocates multiple queues to a single virtual machine and each queue will have its own affinity settings to a core. For this to operate properly, the virtual machine must have the ability to work with multiple virtual CPUs (vCPUs).

Virtual Machine Quality of Service

There may be times when you want to control the traffic that is generated by a virtual machine. Virtual Machine Quality of Service (vmQoS) is a Hyper-V features that does just that.

Virtual Machine Quality of Service allows an administrator to set the bandwidth limits generated by a virtual machine. Administrators can also use vmQoS to set a bandwidth reserve on an external network connection. This helps stop a single virtual machine from chocking the bandwidth of another virtual machine. Administrators have the ability to set minimum and maximum bandwidth limits.

Administrators that have the ability to set performance levels can use these features when service level agreements (SLAs) need to be enforced between your organization and your clients. This allows you to guarantee certain bandwidth levels for your customers and it makes sure that no other customer's bandwidth is compromised. Hyper-V QoS gives an administrator the ability to:

- Enforce minimum and maximum bandwidth limits for traffic flow. This is identified with a port number in the Hyper-V Virtual Switch.

- Configure Hyper-V virtual switch port minimum and maximum bandwidth by using either PowerShell cmdlets or Windows Management Instrumentation (WMI).

- Configure multiple Hyper-V virtual network adapters and specify the QoS on each virtual network adapter independently.

Windows Server 2016 Hyper-V QoS also allows an administrator to use compatible hardware for Data Center Bridging (DCB).

DCB is a suite of Institute of Electrical and Electronics Engineers (IEEE) standards that allow multiple infrastructure technologies (i.e. storage, data networking, Inter-Process Communication (IPC), and management traffic) to all share the same Ethernet network infrastructure. To enable DCB, you would use the following PowerShell cmdlet:

```
Install-WindowsFeature -Name Data-Center-Bridging -IncludeManagementTools
```

By using DCB, administrators can unite multiple types of network traffic onto a single network adapter. This allows administrators to have a guaranteed level of service for every type of network traffic.

To enable the vmQoS features, an administrator can use Windows PowerShell. Administrators can configure these features manually or by writing a script to automate the installation.

VM Checkpoints

One thing that you may want to setup on your Hyper-V server is recovery points or checkpoints. A checkpoint is a snap shot in time from when an administrator can recover a virtual machine. It's like taking a picture of the virtual machine and using that picture to recover the VM. Administrators can create multiple checkpoints of a VM and then recover back to any of those checkpoints if there is an issue. Using a more recent recovery point will result in less data lost. Checkpoints can be accessed from up to 24 hours ago.

If you want to enable these checkpoints in time for Hyper-V, you just need to follow the steps below:

1. In Hyper-V Manager, right-click on the virtual machine and then click Settings.

2. Under the Management section, choose Checkpoints.

3. To enable checkpoints for a VM, check the box Enable checkpoints. If you want to disable checkpoints, just clear the box.

4. Once finished, Click Apply. Once you are finished, click OK and close the Hyper-V Manager.

Understanding Live Migration

Before we can implement Live Migration, first you need to understand what Live Migration does for Hyper-V. Hyper-V live migration transfers a running virtual machine from one physical server to another. The real nice advantage of Live Migration is that during the move of the virtual machine, there is no impact on the network's users. The virtual machine will continue to operate even during the move. This is different from using Quick Migrations. Quick Migrations require a pause in the Hyper-V VM while it's being moved.

Live Migrations allow administrators to move virtual machines between servers. This is very useful when a Hyper-V server starts having issues. For example, if a Hyper-V machine is starting to have hardware issues, you can move the virtual machines from that Hyper-V server to another server that is running properly.

When setting up VM migrations, you have a few options. You can Live Migrate a VM, Quick Migrate a VM, or just move a VM. As stated before, Live Migration requires no interruption of the VM. Quick Migration requires that you first pause the VM, then save the VM, then move the VM and finally re-start the VM. Moving a virtual machine means that you are going to copy a VM from one Hyper-V server to another while the virtual machine is turned off.

So if you decide to setup and use Live Migrations, there are a few things that you should understand before setting it up. So let's take a look at some of the configuration settings that you can configure.

Configure CredSSP or Kerberos authentication

When choosing to setup Live Migrations, one of the settings that you get to manipulate is the type of authentication you can use. Choosing the authentication type is a feature listed under the Advanced Features of Live Migration. Administrators can choose two types of authentication (as shown in Figure 16.21): Kerberos or Credential Security Support Provider (CredSSP).

FIGURE 16.21 Live Migration Advanced Features

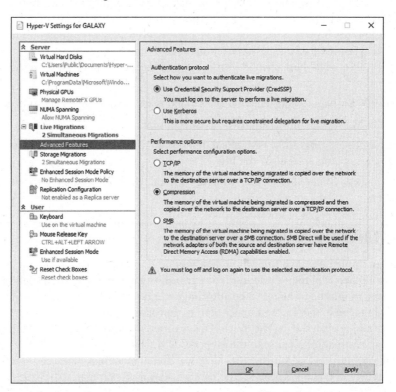

Authentication is choosing which protocol you will use to guarantee that live migration traffic between the source and destination servers are verified. Let's take a look at both options.

- Use Credential Security Support Provider (CredSSP):

  - This option allows an administrator to setup better security but requires constrained delegation for Live Migration. Administrators have the ability to sign in to the source server. Administrators can sign in to the source server by using a local console session, a Remote Desktop session, or a remote Windows PowerShell session.

- Use Kerberos:

  - This option allows an administrator to avoid having to sign in to the server, but requires constrained delegation to be set up.

Another section that you setup in the Advanced Features of Live Migrations is the Performance options. This section allows you to choose how the network traffic for Live Migrations will be configured. There are three options that you can choose from:

TCP/IP   The memory of the virtual machine being migrated is copied over the network to the destination server over a TCP/IP connection.

Compression   The memory of the virtual machine being migrated is compressed and then copied over the network to the destination server over a TCP/IP connection.

SMB   The memory of the virtual machine is copied over the network to the destination server over a SMB (Server Message Block) connection. SMB Direct will be used if the network adapters of both the source and destination server have Remote Direct Memory Access (RDMA) capabilities enabled.

Implementing Live Migration

You will need the following to set up non-clustered hosts for live migration:

- A user account in the local Hyper-V Administrators group or the Administrators group on both the source and destination computers. Membership in the Domain Administrators group (if using a domain).

- The Hyper-V role in Windows Server 2016 or Windows Server 2012 R2 installed on both the source and destination servers. Live migration can be done if the virtual machine is at least version 5.

- The source and destination computers must belong to the same Workgroup or Active Directory domain or belong to trusted domains.

- The Hyper-V management tools installed on the server. Computer must be running Windows Server 2016 or Windows 10.

If an administrator wants to setup the source and destination of the live migration, they would need to use the following steps in Hyper-V Manager:

1. Open Hyper-V Manager. (Click Start ➢ Administrative Tools ➢ Hyper-V Manager.)

2. In the navigation pane, click on one of the servers. Right click on the server ➢ Hyper-V Settings ➢ Live Migrations.

3. Click on the Live Migrations pane. Check the box Enable incoming and outgoing live migrations.

4. Under the section Simultaneous live migrations, specify the number of Simultaneous live migrations (the default is 2).

5. Under Incoming live migrations, administrators can choose to accept any network for live migrations or specifically the IP address you want to use for live migration. If you want to use an IP address, click the Add button and type in the IP address information. Click OK once you're finished.

6. For Kerberos and performance options, expand Live Migrations (click the plus sign next to Live Migrations) and then select Advanced Features.

    ▪ Under Authentication protocol, select either Use CredSSP or Use Kerberos.

    ▪ Under Performance options, Select performance configuration options (either TCP/IP, Compression, or SMB).

7. Click OK.

8. If you have any other servers that you want to setup for Live Migrations, select the server and repeat the steps.

Implement Shared Nothing Live Migration

Administrators can now Live Migrate virtual machines even if the Hyper-V host is not part of a cluster. Before using Live Migrate without a Windows Cluster an administrator will need to configure the servers. Either choose Kerberos or Credential Security Support Provider (CredSSP) to authenticate the Live Migration.

To trigger a Shared Nothing Live Migration remotely, the administrator will need to enable Kerberos constrained delegation.

Constrained delegation is configured through Active Directory Users and Computers in the Delegation tab for each computer taking part in the Shared Nothing Live Migration.

Implementing Storage Migration

Hyper-V supports moving virtual machine storage without downtime by allowing the administrator to move storage while the virtual machine is running. This can be performed by using Hyper-V Manager or Windows PowerShell.

An administrator can add storage to a Hyper-V cluster or a standalone computer, and then move virtual machines to the new storage while the virtual machines continue to run.

An administrator can move virtual machine storage between physical storage devices to respond to a decrease in performance that results from bottlenecks.

Storage Migration Requirements

The following will be needed to utilize Hyper-V functionality of moving virtual machine storage:

- One or more installations of Windows Server 2016 with the Hyper-V role installed.
- A server that is capable of running Hyper-V.
- Virtual machines that are configured to use only virtual hard disks for storage.

Storage Migration allows administrators to move the virtual hard disks of a virtual machine while the virtual hard disks are still able to be used by the running virtual machine (see Figure 16.22). When an administrator moves a running virtual machine's virtual hard disks, Hyper-V performs the following steps:

1. Disk reads and writes utilize the source virtual hard disk.

2. When reads and writes occur on the source virtual hard disk, the disk data is copied to the new destination virtual hard disk.

3. Once the initial disk copy is complete, the disk writes are mirrored to both the source and destination virtual hard disks, while outstanding disk changes are replicated.

4. After the source and destination virtual hard disks are entirely synchronized, the virtual machine changes over to using the destination virtual hard disk.

5. The source virtual hard disk is deleted.

FIGURE 16.22   Storage Migration Settings

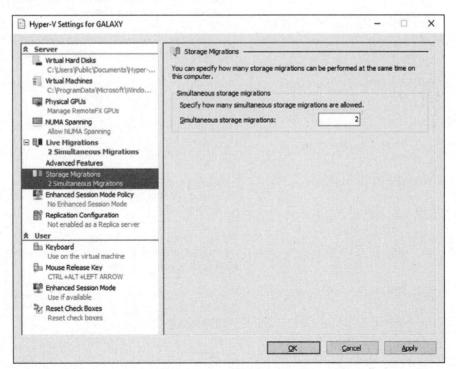

PowerShell Commands for Hyper-V High Availability

When configuring Hyper-V high availability, you may want to setup some of the components using PowerShell. Table 16.6 shows you some of the available PowerShell commands available for setting up Hyper-V high availability.

TABLE 16.6 PowerShell Commands for High Availability

PowerShell Command	Description
Complete-VMFailover	This command helps finish a virtual machine's failover process on the replica server.
Disable-VMMigration	This command allows an administrator to disable virtual machine migration on a virtual machine host.
Enable-VMMigration	This command allows an administrator to enable virtual machine migration on a virtual machine host.
Enable-VMReplication	This command allows an administrator to enable replication of a virtual machine.
Get-VMMigrationNetwork	This command shows you the virtual machine networks used for migration.
Get-VMReplication	This command shows an administrator the replication settings for a virtual machine.
Get-VMReplicationAuthorizationEntry	This command shows an administrator the authorization entries of a replica server.
Get-VMReplicationServer	This command shows an administrator the replication and authentication settings of a replica server.
Import-VMInitialReplication	This command imports initial replication files for a replica virtual machine when using external media.
Measure-VMReplication	This command shows an administrator the replication statistics and information associated with a virtual machine.
New-VMReplicationAuthorizationEntry	This command allows you to create an authorization entry to replicate data to a specified replica server.

PowerShell Command	Description
Remove-VMMigrationNetwork	This command allows an administrator to remove a network from use in migration.
Remove-VMReplication	This command removes the replication from a specific virtual machine.
Reset-VMReplicationStatistics	This command allows an administrator to reset the replication statistics of a virtual machine.
Resume-VMReplication	This command allows an administrator to resume virtual machine replication after an error, a pause, a suspension, or a resynchronization is required.
Set-VMProcessor	This command allows an administrator to configure which processors are used for a virtual machine.
Set-VMReplication	This command allows an administrator to modify the replication settings of a virtual machine.
Set-VMReplicationServer	This command allows an admin to configure a host as a replica server.
Start-VMInitialReplication	This command starts replication of a virtual machine.
Stop-VMReplication	This command stops replication of a virtual machine.
Suspend-VMReplication	This command suspends replication of a virtual machine.
Test-VMReplicationConnection	This command allows an administrator to test the connection of a primary server and a replica server.

Summary

High availability is more than just clustering. It is achieved through improved hardware, software, and processes. This chapter focused on how to configure Failover Clustering and Network Load Balancing in order to achieve high availability and scalability.

High availability should be approached through proper hardware configuration, training, and operational discipline. Failover clustering provides a highly available base for many applications, such as databases and mail servers.

Network load-balanced clusters are used to provide high availability and scalability for network-based applications, such as VPNs and web servers. Network load-balanced clusters can be configured with any edition of Windows Server 2016 except for the Windows Server 2016 Hyper-V Edition.

Windows Server 2016 Hyper-V can also have high availability set up on it without using clustering. Administrators have the ability to setup Live Migrations on Hyper-V virtual machines.

Live Migration allows you to move a virtual machine from one server to another without any impact on the users. This can be very useful if you have a Hyper-V server that is starting to show hardware issues. Administrators can move the virtual machine from the server with issues to a server without any issues.

Exam Essentials

Know how to modify failover and failback settings.   These settings are set on the clustered service or application, but they can be modified by settings on the resources.

Know the hardware requirements for Network Load Balancing.   Network Load Balancing has distinct hardware requirements. Know the requirements for NLB.

Know the PowerShell commands for NLB.   Make sure you know the different PowerShell commands for Network Load Balancing. Understand which command is used to create, manage, and stop NLB clusters.

Understand Live Migration.   Understand how Live Migrations work and why we use them. Understand that Live Migrations allow an administrator to move a virtual machine from one server to another without any impact on the users.

Know PowerShell for VM Replication.   Make sure you know the different PowerShell commands for Virtual Machine Replication. Understand which commands are used to create, manage, and stop VM Replication.

Video Resources

There are videos available for the following exercises:

Exercise 16.2

Exercise 16.5

You can access the videos at http://sybextestbanks.wiley.com on the Other Study Tools tab.

Review Questions

1. You are the administrator for a mid-size organization. You have been asked by the owner to set up a NLB cluster. You want to use PowerShell to set up the cluster. What command would you use?

   A. `New-NlbCluster`

   B. `Create-NlbCluster`

   C. `Setup-NlbCluster`

   D. `Set-NlbCluster`

2. Which of the following editions of Windows Server 2016 can be configured in a Network Load Balancing cluster? (Choose all that apply.)

   A. Windows Server 2016 Virtual Edition

   B. Windows Server 2016 Standard Edition

   C. Windows Server 2016 Small Business Server

   D. Windows Server 2016 Datacenter Edition

3. What is the maximum number of nodes that can participate in a Windows Server 2016 NLB single cluster?

   A. 32

   B. 4

   C. 16

   D. 64

4. Which of the following actions should be performed against an NLB cluster node if maintenance needs to be performed while not terminating current connections?

   A. Evict

   B. Drainstop

   C. Pause

   D. Stop

5. Which of the following actions should be performed against an NLB cluster node if maintenance needs to be performed and all connections must be terminated immediately?

   A. Evict

   B. Drainstop

   C. Pause

   D. Stop

6. You are the network administrator for your organization and you want to stop virtual machine replication. What PowerShell command would you use?

   A. Stop-VMReplication

   B. Terminate-VMReplication

   C. Kill-VMReplication

   D. Drainstop-VMReplication

7. Which of the following applications would be better suited on a Network Load Balancing cluster instead of a failover cluster? (Choose all that apply.)

   A. SQL Server

   B. Website

   C. Database servers

   D. Terminal Services

8. To configure an NLB cluster with unicast, what is the minimum number of network adapters required in each node?

   A. One

   B. Two

   C. Three

   D. Six

9. Users who are connecting to an NLB cluster have been complaining that after using the site for a few minutes they are prompted to log in using their username. What should you do to fix the problem and retain scalability?

   A. Create a port rule to allow only ports 80 and 443.

   B. Set the cluster affinity to None.

   C. Set the filtering mode to Single Host.

   D. Set the cluster affinity to Single.

10. Users who are connecting to an NLB cluster through the Internet are complaining that they keep connecting to different NLB nodes in different locations. You want to keep Internet users connecting to the same NLB members each time they connect. What should you do to fix the problem?

    A. Create a port rule to allow only ports 80 and 443.

    B. Set the cluster affinity to None.

    C. Set the cluster affinity to Class C.

    D. Set the cluster affinity to Single.

Chapter 17

Implementing Software Defined Networking

THE FOLLOWING 70-741 EXAM OBJECTIVES ARE COVERED IN THIS CHAPTER:

✓ **Determine scenarios and requirements for implementing Software Defined Networking (SDN)**

- This objective may include but is not limited to: Determine deployment scenarios and network requirements for deploying SDN; determine requirements and scenarios for implementing Hyper-V Network Virtualization (HNV) using Network Virtualization Generic Route Encapsulation (NVGRE) encapsulation or Virtual Extensible LAN (VXLAN) encapsulation; determine scenarios for implementation of Software Load Balancer (SLB) for North-South and East-West load balancing; determine implementation scenarios for various types of Windows Server Gateways, including L3, GRE, and S2S, and their use; determine requirements and scenarios for distributed firewall policies and network security groups.

One of the greatest improvements to Microsoft's servers over the past few versions is its implementation of their Virtual Server called Hyper-V.

Hyper-V is a server role in Windows Server 2016 that allows you to virtualize your environment and therefore run multiple virtual operating system instances simultaneously on a physical server. This not only helps you to improve server utilization but also helps you to create a more cost-effective and dynamic system.

Hyper-V allows an organization of any size to act and compete with other organizations of any size. A small company can buy a single server and then virtualize that server into multiple servers. Hyper-V gives a small company the ability to run multiple servers on a single box and compete with a company of any size.

For the large organizations, an administrator can consolidate multiple servers onto Hyper-V servers thus saving an organization time and money by using less physical boxes but still having all the servers needed to run the business.

In Windows Server 2016, Microsoft has taken virtualization to the next level with Software Defined Networking. This allows you to use virtualization and also create a virtual network (including virtual routers, switches, etc.).

In this chapter, you will learn the basic concepts and features of Software Defined Networking and Hyper-V. You will also get a solid understanding of what is important in virtualization and in what areas of your work life you can use it.

Understanding Software Defined Networking

Software Defined Networking (SDN) allows an administrator to centrally manage and control all of your virtual and physical network devices. These devices include things like datacenter switches, routers, and gateways. SDN also allows administrators to manage virtual elements like Hyper-V virtual switches and gateways. Administrators can easily manage their entire networks centrally.

Administrators that want to run Hyper-V and virtual machines using SDN servers, like Network Controllers and Software Load Balancing systems, need to use Windows Server 2016 Datacenter. Administrators can use Windows Server 2016 Standard edition if they want to run SDN controlled networks components like tenant VMs.

One of the nice advantages of using SDN is the ability to still use your current network hardware components like switches, routers, and other types of network hardware devices. SDN gives an administrator the ability to merge both virtual and physical networks together.

To understand SDN, you must first understand some of the components that SDN uses. So let's take a look at some of the available SDN components.

Network Controllers

Network Controllers are new to Windows Server 2016. Network Controllers allow an administrator to have a centralized virtual and physical datacenter infrastructure. This allows administrators to manage, configure, and troubleshoot all of their infrastructure components from one location. Administrators no longer need to manually configure each network component separately.

Network Controllers use three different application programming interface (API) languages to control all of the different hardware on your network. The Southbound API allows Network Controllers to communicate with the network and the Northbound API allows you to communicate with the Network Controller.

Administrators can use Windows PowerShell to communicate with the Representational State Transfer (REST) API (this is the management application) to manage their network infrastructure components. These components include the:

- Physical switches

- Physical routers

- Hyper-V switches and Virtual Machines (VMs)

- Datacenter Firewalls

- VPN Gateways

- Load Balancing components

If you would like to setup a Network Controller using Windows PowerShell, you would use the New-NetworkControllerNodeObject command as shown:

```
New-NetworkControllerNodeObject -Name <String> -Server <String> -FaultDomain
<String> -RestInterface <String>  [-NodeCertificate <X509Certificate2>]
[-WhatIf] [-Confirm] [<CommonParameters>]
```

The following is an example of the New-NetworkControllerNodeObject command. The name of the Network Controller Node Object is Node1. The server name is NCServer1. StormWind.com and the ethernet adapter is being used.

```
New-NetworkControllerNodeObject -Name "Node1" -Server "NCNode1.StormWind.com"
-FaultDomain "fd:/rack1/host1" -RestInterface "Ethernet"
```

Internal DNS Service (iDNS)

The Domain Name System (DNS) is a service that allows you to resolve a hostname to an Internet Protocol (IP) address. As stated in Chapter 2 "Configuring DNS", an easy way to understand DNS is to think about making a telephone call. If you wanted to call Microsoft and did not know the phone number, you could call information, tell the operator the name (Microsoft), and get the telephone number. You would then make the call.

Now think about trying to connect to Server1. You don't know the TCP/IP number (the computer's telephone number), so your computer asks DNS (information) for the number of Server1. DNS returns the number, and your system makes the connection (call). DNS is your network's 411, or information, and it returns the TCP/IP data for your network.

Organizations that work with Cloud Service Providers (CSP) or enterprise networks that use Windows Server 2016 SDNs, administrators can use DNS for their hosted virtual machines by using Internal DNS (iDNS). Windows Server 2016 SDN automatically integrates iDNS. This can provide virtual machines with DNS name resolution services for their isolated local name space and for their Internet resources.

Since the iDNS service is not available from the tenant's Virtual Network, unless it goes through the iDNS proxy, this stops the server from being vulnerable from malicious activities on tenant networks. The iDNS service includes both the iDNS server and the iDNS proxy.

iDNS Servers   The iDNS service contains DNS servers that host tenant specific data (i.e., virtual machine Resource Records). iDNS servers are the authoritative zone for the hosted virtual machines and also the resolver for external resources.

iDNS Proxy   The iDNS proxy is a Windows Server 2016 service that runs on your host server. The iDNS proxy forwards virtual network DNS traffic to the iDNS Server.

Software Load Balancer (SLB) and Network Address Translation (NAT)

Organizations that work with Cloud Service Providers (CSP) or enterprise networks that use Windows Server 2016 SDNs can use Software Load Balancing (SLB) to evenly distribute network traffic for tenants and/or tenant customers between the virtual network resources.

SLB allows an administrator to setup multiple servers that can host the same workload. This gives an organization the ability to have high availability and scalability between the server's workload.

When it comes to SLB and NAT, you may hear the terms north-south or east-west. These terms just refer to the way that your application traffic patterns go in context of your datacenter. Now it's not as simple as direction. North-south and east-west layer 4 (L4) load balancing and NAT improves your company's data by using Direct Server Return. Direct Server Return allows the return network traffic to be bypassed by the Load Balancing multiplexer.

Applications can be designed using many tiers when residing in your datacenter. Most developers use Three-tier application architecture. Three-tier architecture is the most common architecture used by developers today and it is just the way that applications talk to other applications and servers.

For example: Applications that send data to other applications within the same data center or between datacenters has an east-west traffic pattern. If your organization has an older data center where clients simply requested data from a single server, it is more likely to have a north-south data pattern.

Windows Server 2016 SLB includes some of the following capabilities.

- Layer 4 load balancing services for north-south and east-west traffic patterns.

- Load balancing for internal and public network traffic.

- Supports dynamic IP addresses (DIPs) on virtual networks.

- Support for health probes.

- Scalability for multiplexers and Host Agents.

Windows Server 2016 SLB is scalable and it supports tens of gigabytes of data per cluster along with easy provisioning models. SLB is possible because it maps virtual IP addresses (VIPs) to dynamic IP addresses (DIPs). When an administrator sets up load balancing of virtual machines, users can gain access to these VMs by using a single IP address setup by the VIPs. VIPs are IP addresses on the Internet that allows users to connect to the cloud resources. DIPs are the IP addresses that sit behind the VIPs. The DIPs are the actual IP addresses of the load balancing servers.

The easiest way to configure your SLB and NAT setup is by using System Center 2016 Virtual Machine Manager or by using Windows PowerShell commands.

To see all of the steps needed to configure SLB, please visit Microsoft's website at:

https://docs.microsoft.com/en-us/windows-server/networking/ sdn/manage/configure-slb-and-nat

Datacenter Firewall

Firewalls allow an administrator to set up policies on who or what can be allowed past the firewall. For example, if you want to allow DNS traffic to pass through the firewall, you would enable port 53. If you want the traffic to leave the firewall, you would config- ure port 53 outbound. If you want to have the traffic enter into the company, you would configure inbound.

Datacenter Firewalls are new Windows Server 2016 network layer, Stateful, multitenant firewalls. Network administrators that work with virtual network tenants can install and then configure firewall policies. These firewall policies can help protect their virtual net- works from unwanted traffic from Internet and intranet networks.

The Datacenter Firewall allows you to setup granular access control lists (ACLs) and this allows you to apply firewall policies at the VM interface level or at the subnet level. To create ACLs on the Datacenter Firewall, an administrator can use Windows PowerShell.

The following is an example of the PowerShell command that is used to assign the ACL to the AccessControlList property of the network interface.

```
$nic.properties.ipconfigurations[0].properties.AccessControlList = $acl
```

Windows Server 2016 Datacenter Firewalls give you the following tenant benefits:

- Administrators have the ability to define firewall rules that help protect Internet facing workloads on virtual networks.

- Administrators have the ability to define firewall rules to protect data between virtual machines on the same layer 2 or different layer 2 virtual subnets.

- Administrators have the ability to define firewall rules to protect and isolate network traffic between tenants on a virtual network from a service provider.

RAS Gateway

Administrators can setup Remote Access Server (RAS) gateways that you can use for bridging traffic between virtual and non-virtual networks. Gateways are used so traffic can be transferred from one type of system to another. This is very useful when you are setting up site-to-site (S2S) VPNs, forwarding gateways, and Generic Routing Encapsulation (GRE) gateways.

RAS Gateways are software-based, multitenant, and Border Gateway Protocol (BGP) capable routers available in Windows Server 2016.

One nice advantage to using Windows Server 2016 gateways is that N+M redundancy of gateways is supported. N+M is an industry standard for setting up clusters. There may be times when a single cluster is managing many services and having only one dedicated failover server may not be enough. In these situations more than one (M) standby server is needed. This is the N+M redundancy standard and Windows Server 2016 supports this type of setup.

RAS Gateways for routing traffic between virtual networks and physical networks can be deployed using Internet Key Exchange version 2 (IKEv2) site-to-site VPNs, Layer 3 (L3) VPNs, or Generic Routing Encapsulation (GRE) gateways.

RAS Gateways can be setup one of two ways: single tenant mode or multitenant mode.

Single Tenant Mode   Single tenant mode is used for organizations of any size that want to deploy RAS Gateways. In single tenant mode, the RAS Gateway is used as the exterior or Internet facing VPN or DirectAccess edge server. In single tenant mode, administrators will deploy the RAS Gateway on a Windows Server 2016 physical server or virtual machine.

Multitenant Mode   Multitenant mode is used for Cloud Service Providers (CSPs) or enterprise networks to allow datacenter or cloud network traffic routing between virtual and physical networks. This includes traffic that goes over the Internet. In multitenant mode, administrators will deploy the RAS Gateway on a Windows Server 2016 virtual machine.

Remote Direct Memory Access and Switch Embedded Teaming

If you are using any Windows version prior to Windows Server 2016, configuring RDMA on network adapters, bound to NIC teaming or Hyper-V switches, was not available. Windows Server 2016 has changed that.

Windows Server 2016 allows an administrator to enable Remote Direct Memory Access (RDMA) on the bound Hyper-V network adapters. Administrators have the ability to enable RDMA with or without using Switch Embedded Teaming (SET). Administrators can now use less network adapters when RDMA and SET are used at the same time.

Remote Direct Memory Access (RDMA) allows nodes in your network to interchange data in RAM without involving the processor, cache, or operating system. RDMA allows a system to run better because it doesn't use any of the other resources.

Before an administrator can enable RDMA it is recommended that they first enable Data Center Bridging (DCB). DCB is not required for Internet Wide Area RDMA Protocol (iWARP) networks but ethernet based RDMA networks have shown better performance when working with DCB. To enable DCB and RDMS, you would run the following PowerShell commands:

```
Install-WindowsFeature Data-Center-Bridging
Add-VMNetworkAdapter -SwitchName RDMAswitch -Name SMB_1
Enable-NetAdapterRDMA "vEthernet (SMB_1)"
```

Switch Embedded Teaming is another option to NIC teaming. SET has the ability to be used in multiple environments including Hyper-V and SDN networks in Windows Server 2016. Administrators have the ability to group physical network adapters together when using SET. SET also integrates many of the NIC Teaming functionality into the Hyper-V Virtual Switch. SET gives you the ability to group between one and eight network adapters into software based virtual adapters.

Virtual adapters allow you to have faster performance while also providing fault tolerance in the event of any of your network adapters failing. One requirement to setting up SET is that all SET group adapters need to be installed on the same physical Hyper-V host server.

Administrators have the ability to connect their teamed NICs to either the same physical switch or to different physical switches. If you decide to connect your NICs to different switches, both switches must be part of the same subnet. To setup SET using PowerShell, you would run the following command:

```
New-VMSwitch -Name SETswitch -NetAdapterName "SLOT 2","SLOT 3"
-EnableEmbeddedTeaming $true
```

To learn more about Remote Direct Memory Access and Switch Embedded Teaming, visit Microsoft's website at https://technet.microsoft.com/en-us/library/mt403349.aspx.

Windows Server Containers

Windows Containers are independent and isolated environments that run an operating system. These isolated environments allow an administrator to place an application into its own container thus not affecting any other applications or containers.

Think of containers as virtual environments that are used to run independent applications. They load much faster than virtual machines and you can run as many containers as needed for all of the different applications that you run.

Administrators can use containers to separate applications or services from other services that are running on the same host. This is possible because each container has its own operating system, processes, file system, registry, and IP address. With Windows Server 2016, you can now connect Windows Server containers to virtual networks.

One of the nice advantages of using Windows Containers is that the containers can be managed the same way an administrator can manage an operating system. A container works the same way as a newly installed physical or virtual machine. So once you know how to configure these containers, management is much easier than configuring a physical machine.

There are two different types of containers that the Windows Container can use:

Windows Server Containers   This container allows an administrator to isolate applications so applications can run in their own space and not affect other applications. The question that you may be asking is why not use a virtual machine? Well the advantage of Windows Server Containers is that they are already pre-built and you don't need all of the other services that a virtual machine would need to run. So Windows Containers are smaller, faster, and more efficient when isolating applications. In a Windows Server Container, the kernel is shared between all of the different Windows Containers.

Hyper-V Containers   Hyper-V Containers and Windows Containers work the same way. The difference between the two is that Hyper-V Containers run within a virtual machine and the Windows Containers don't need to run in a Hyper-V environment. In a Hyper-V Container the container host's kernel is not shared between the other Hyper-V Containers.

As with any new technology, it is important to understand the terminology that goes along with that new technology. The first thing that you may have noticed is that a container works a lot like a virtual machine. Just like a virtual machine, the container has a running operating system within the container.

The container has a file system and the container can also be accessed through the network the same way a virtual machine does. The advantage is that a container is a more efficient operating system. But to truly understand how containers work, you need to understand all of the different components that allow containers to function properly.

Container Host   This component can be on a physical or virtual machine and it's the component that is configured with the Windows Container feature. So the Windows Container sits on top of the Container Host.

Container OS Image   This component provides the operating system to the container. Containers are made up from multiple images that are stacked on top of each other within the container.

Container Image   This is the component that contains all of the layers of the container. So the Container Image contains the operating system, the application, and all of the services required to make that application function properly.

Container Registry   This component is the heart and brain of the container. The container images are kept within the container's registry. The advantage of doing containers this way is that you can download other registries to automatically add other applications or services quickly.

Docker Daemon   This is the component that runs the docker application. The docker daemon is automatically installed after you complete the installation of the docker application.

Dockerfile   This component is used to create the container images. The advantage of using the Dockerfile is that you can automate how containers are created. Dockerfiles are batches of instructions (within a txt file) and commands that are called on when an image is assembled.

Docker Hub Repositories   This component is a location where all of your images are stored. By having a central location for stored images, the images can be used among co-workers, customers, or for the entire IT community. There are docker hub repositories on the internet and these locations allow you to grab and use images for your organization.

To learn more about Windows Containers, Please read William Panek's Windows Server 2016 book "MCSA Windows Server 2016 Study Guide: Exam 70-740" published by Sybex, 2017.

Hyper-V Components

One of the nice advantages of SDN is the ability to work with Hyper-V components. Administrators setup a virtual network and then you configure SDN services. So to truly understand how this works, you must understand Hyper-V. So let's take a look at Windows Server 2016 Hyper-V.

Hyper-V Overview

In the following sections, I'll introduce you to Hyper-V. To begin, you'll take a look at virtualization and what types of virtualization exist. I will then discuss Hyper-V features and the Hyper-V architecture before finishing up with the Hyper-V requirements for software and hardware.

What Is Virtualization?

Virtualization is a method for abstracting physical resources from the way that they interact with other resources. For example, if you abstract the physical hardware from the operating system, you get the benefit of being able to move the operating system between different physical systems.

This is called *server virtualization*. But there are also other forms of virtualization available, such as presentation virtualization, desktop virtualization, and application virtualization. I will now briefly explain the differences between these forms of virtualization:

Server Virtualization   This basically enables multiple servers to run on the same physical server. Hyper-V is a server virtualization tool that allows you to move physical machines to virtual machines and manage them on a few physical servers. Thus, you will be able to consolidate physical servers.

Presentation Virtualization   When you use *presentation virtualization*, your applications run on a different computer, and only the screen information is transferred to your computer. An example of presentation virtualization is Microsoft Remote Desktop Services in Windows Server 2016.

Desktop Virtualization   *Desktop virtualization* provides you with a virtual machine on your desktop, comparable to server virtualization. You run your complete operating system and applications in a virtual machine so that your local physical machine just needs to run a very basic operating system. An example of this form of virtualization is Microsoft Virtual PC or Windows 10 with Hyper-V.

Application Virtualization   *Application virtualization* helps prevent conflicts between applications on the same PC. Thus, it helps you to isolate the application running environment from the operating system installation requirements by creating application-specific copies of all shared resources. It also helps reduce application-to-application incompatibility and testing needs. An example of an application virtualization tool is Microsoft Application Virtualization (App-V).

Hyper-V Features

As a lead-in to the virtualization topic and Hyper-V, I will start with a list of key features, followed by a list of supported guest operating systems. This should provide you with a quick, high-level view of this feature before you dig deeper into the technology.

Key Features of Hyper-V

The following are the key features of Hyper-V:

Architecture   The hypervisor-based architecture, which has a 64-bit micro-kernel, provides a new array of device support as well as performance and security improvements.

Operating System Support   Both 32-bit and 64-bit operating systems can run simultaneously in Hyper-V. Also, different platforms like Windows, Linux, and others are supported.

Support for Symmetric Multiprocessors   Support for up to 64 processors in a virtual machine environment provides you with the ability to run applications as well as multiple virtual machines faster.

Network Load Balancing   Hyper-V provides support for *Windows Network Load Balancing (NLB)* to balance the network load across virtual machines on different servers.

Hardware Architecture   Hyper-V's architecture provides improved utilization of resources such as networking, memory, and disks.

Quick Migration   Hyper-V's *quick migration* feature provides you with the functionality to run virtual machines in a clustered environment with switchover capabilities when there is a failure. Thus, you can reduce downtime and achieve higher availability of your virtual machines.

Virtual Machine Checkpoints   You can take checkpoints of running virtual machines, which provides you with the capability to recover to any previous virtual machine checkpoints state quickly and easily.

Resource Metering   Hyper-V *resource metering* allows an organization to track usage within the businesses departments. It allows an organization to create a usage-based billing solution that adjusts to the provider's business model and strategy.

Scripting   Using the Windows Management Instrumentation (WMI) interfaces and APIs, you can easily build custom scripts to automate processes in your virtual machines.

RemoteFX   Windows Server 2016 Hyper-V RemoteFX allows for an enhanced user experience for RemoteFX desktops by providing a 3D virtual adapter, intelligent codecs, and the ability to redirect USB devices in virtual machines.

Fibre Channel   The virtual Fibre Channel feature allows you to connect to the Fibre Channel storage unit from within the virtual machine. *Virtual Fibre Channel* allows an administrator to use their existing Fibre Channel to support virtualized workloads. Hyper-V users have the ability to use Fibre Channel storage area networks (SANs) to virtualize the workloads that require direct access to SAN logical unit numbers (LUNs).

Enhanced Session Mode   *Enhanced Session Mode* enhances the interactive session of the Virtual Machine Connection for Hyper-V administrators who want to connect to their virtual machines. It gives administrators the same functionality as a remote desktop connection when the administrator is interacting with a virtual machine.

In previous versions of Hyper-V, the virtual machine connection gave you limited functionality while you connected to the virtual machine screen, keyboard, and mouse. An administrator could use an RDP connection to get full redirection abilities, but that would require a network connection to the virtual machine host.

Enhanced Session Mode gives administrators the following benefits for local resource redirection:

- Display configuration
- Audio
- Printers
- Clipboard
- Smart cards

- Drives
- USB devices
- Supported Plug and Play devices

Shared Virtual Hard Disk   Windows Server 2016 Hyper-V has a feature called Shared Virtual Hard Disk. Shared Virtual Hard Disk allows an administrator to cluster virtual machines by using shared virtual hard disk (VHDX) files.

Shared virtual hard disks allow an administrator to build a high availability infrastructure, which is important if you are setting up either a private cloud deployment or a cloud-hosted environment for managing large workloads. Shared virtual hard disks allow two or more virtual machines to access the same virtual hard disk (VHDX) file.

Automatic Virtual Machine Activation (AVMA)   *Automatic Virtual Machine Activation (AVMA)* is a feature that allows administrators to install virtual machines on a properly activated Windows Server 2016 system without the need to manage individual product keys for each virtual machine. When using AVMA, virtual machines get bound to the licensed Hyper-V server as soon as the virtual machine starts.

Network Isolation   One nice feature of using Microsoft Hyper-V network virtualization is the ability of Hyper-V to keep virtual networks isolated from the physical network infrastructure of the hosted system. Because administrators can set up Hyper-V software–defined virtualization policies, you are no longer limited by the IP address assignment or VLAN isolation requirements of the physical network. Hyper-V allows for built-in network isolation to keep the virtual network separated from the virtual network.

Discrete Device Assignment   One feature of Windows Server 2016 is the ability to use Discrete Device Assignment (DDA). DDA allows an administrator to take full advantage of performance and application compatibility improvements in the user experience by allowing the system's graphic cards to be directly assigned to a virtual machine. This allows the graphic card processor to be fully available to the virtual desktops that are utilizing the native driver of the graphics card processor.

Non-Uniform Memory Access   Non-Uniform Memory Access (NUMA) is a multiprocessor memory architecture that allows a processor to access its local memory quicker than memory located on another processor. NUMA allows a system to access memory quickly by providing separate memory on each processor. Processors can access their local assigned memory thus speeding the system performance. Normally a multi-processor system runs into performance issues when multiple processors access the same memory at the same time. NUMA helps prevent this by allowing processors to access their own memory. Memory that is dedicated to a processor is referred to as a NUMA node.

Dynamic Memory   *Dynamic Memory* is a feature of Hyper-V that allows it to balance memory automatically among running virtual machines. Dynamic Memory allows Hyper-V to adjust the amount of memory available to the virtual machines in response to the needs of the virtual machines. It is currently available for Hyper-V in Windows Server 2016.

Virtual Machine Queue   Windows Server 2016 Hyper-V includes a feature called Virtual machine queue (VMQ) as long as the hardware is VMQ compatible network hardware. VMQ uses packet filtering to provide data from an external virtual machine network directly to virtual machines. This helps reduce the overhead of routing packets from the management operating system to the virtual machine.

Once VMQ is enabled on Hyper-V, a dedicated queue is created on the physical network adapter for each virtual network adapter to use. When data arrives for the virtual network adapter, the physical network adapter places that data in a queue and once the system is available, all of the data in the queue is delivered to the virtual network adapter.

To enable the virtual machine queue on a specific virtual machine, enter the settings for the virtual machine and expand Network Adapter. Click on Hardware Acceleration and on the right hand window; check the box for Enable virtual machine queue.

Network Virtualization using Generic Routing Encapsulation   Windows Server 2016 now supports Hyper-V Network Virtualization using Generic Routing Encapsulation (NVGRE). NVGRE is a tool that allows you to virtualize IP addresses and the virtual machine's packets are then encapsulated inside of other packets. The NVGRE header packet will then have the correct source and destination provider area (PA) IP addresses along with a 24-bit Virtual Subnet ID (VSID).

Virtual Extensible LAN   Virtual Extensible LAN (VXLAN) is an industry technology for network virtualization. VXLAN uses a VLAN compatible encapsulation method to help encapsulate MAC-based OSI layer 2 Ethernet frames within layer 4 UDP packets. The UDP packets use the default IANA-assigned destination UDP port number 4789.

Hyper-V Nesting   Windows Server 2016 has introduced a new feature of Hyper-V called Hyper-V nesting. Hyper-V nesting allows you to run a virtual machine in a virtual machine. So let's say that you build a new 2016 Hyper-V server. You install Windows Server 2016 into a virtual machine. Then in that virtual machine, you can install Hyper-V and build other virtual machines within the first virtual machine. This is new to Windows Server 2016 and can be very useful in training situations. You can install a Windows Server 2016 virtual machine and still show others how to install and create virtual machines in the original virtual machine. To enable Hyper-V nesting, you would run the following PowerShell command on the Hyper-V Host. The virtual machines must be in the OFF State when this command is run (this means the virtual machines must be turned off):

```
Set-VMProcessor -VMName <VMName> -ExposeVirtualizationExtensions $true
```

Supported Guest Operating Systems

The following guest operating systems have been successfully tested on Hyper-V and are hypervisor-aware. Table 17.1 shows all of the guest server operating systems and the maximum number of virtual processors. Table 17.2 shows all of the guest client operating systems and the maximum number of virtual processors.

TABLE 17.1   Hyper-V guest server operating systems

Guest Operating System (Server)	Maximum Number of Virtual Processors
Windows Server 2016	64
Windows Server 2012 and Server 2012 R2	64
Windows Server 2008 R2 with Service Pack 1 (SP1)	64
Windows Server 2008 R2	64
Windows Server 2008 with Service Pack 2 (SP2)	8
Windows Home Server 2011	4
Windows Small Business Server 2011	Essentials edition: 2 Standard edition: 4
Windows Server 2003 R2 with Service Pack 2 (SP2)	2
Windows Server 2003 with Service Pack 2 (SP2)	2
Red Hat Enterprise Linux 5.7 and 5.8	64
Red Hat Enterprise Linux 6.0–6.3	64
SUSE Linux Enterprise Server 11 SP2	64
Open SUSE 12.1	64
Ubuntu 12.04	64

TABLE 17.2   Hyper-V guest client operating systems

Guest Operating System (Client)	Maximum Number of Virtual Processors
Windows 10	32
Windows 8	32
Windows 7 with Service Pack 1 (SP1)	4

Guest Operating System (Client)	Maximum Number of Virtual Processors
Windows 7	4
Windows Vista with Service Pack 2 (SP2)	2
Windows XP with Service Pack 3 (SP3)	2
Windows XP x64 Edition with Service Pack 2 (SP2)	2
CentOS 5.7 and 5.8	64
CentOS 6.0–6.3	64
Red Hat Enterprise Linux 5.7 and 5.8	64
Red Hat Enterprise Linux 6.0–6.3	64
SUSE Linux Enterprise Server 11 SP2	64
Open SUSE 12.1	64
Ubuntu 12.04	64

The list of supported guest operating systems may always be extended. Please check the official Microsoft Hyper-V site to obtain a current list of supported operating systems: www.microsoft.com/virtualization.

Hyper-V Architecture

This section will provide you with an overview of the Hyper-V architecture (see Figure 17.1). I'll explain the differences between a hypervisor-aware and a non-hypervisor-aware child partition.

As you can see, Hyper-V is based on the microkernel architecture. Hyper-V provides a virtualization layer called a *hypervisor* that runs directly on the system hardware. You can see that the hypervisor is similar to what the kernel is to Windows. It is a software layer responsible for the interaction with the core hardware and works in conjunction with an optimized instance of Windows Server 2016 that allows running multiple operating systems on a physical server simultaneously. The Hyper-V architecture consists of the hypervisor and parent and child partitions.

FIGURE 17.1 Hyper-V architecture

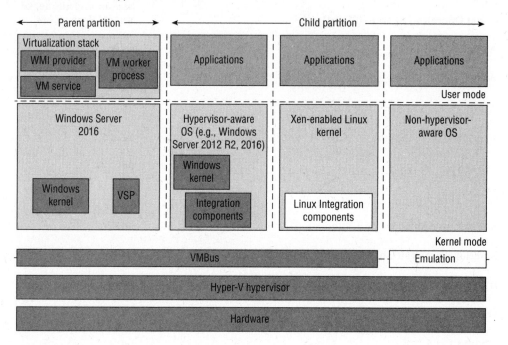

The Windows Server 2016 operating system runs in the parent partition, and it delivers the WMI provider for scripting as well as the VM service.

Virtual machines each run in their own child partitions. Child partitions do not have direct access to hardware resources; instead, they have a virtual view of the resources, which are called *virtual devices*.

If you're running a hypervisor-aware operating system like Windows Server 2003, Windows Server 2008, Windows Server 2008 R2, Windows Server 2012, or Windows Server 2016 in your virtual machine, any request to the virtual devices is redirected via the high-speed bus to the devices in the parent partition, which will manage the requests.

By default, only Windows Server 2008 R2, Server 2012, and Server 2012 R2 are hypervisor-aware operating systems. Once you install Hyper-V Integration Components on an operating system other than Windows Server 2008 R2 and newer, it will be hypervisor-aware. Microsoft provides a hypervisor adapter to make Linux hypervisor aware.

Non-hypervisor-aware operating systems (for example, Windows NT 4.0) use an emulator to communicate with the Windows hypervisor, which is slower than molasses in the winter.

Hyper-V Requirements

The following sections will describe the hardware and software requirements for installing the Hyper-V server role. It is important to understand these requirements for obtaining your software license as well as for planning for server hardware. When you understand the requirements, you can design and configure a Hyper-V solution that will meet the needs of your applications.

Hardware Requirements

In addition to the basic hardware requirements for Windows Server 2016, there are requirements for running the Hyper-V server role on your Windows server. They are listed in Table 17.3.

TABLE 17.3   Hardware requirements for Hyper-V

Requirement Area	Definition
CPU	x64-compatible processor with Intel VT or AMD-V technology enabled. Hardware Data Execution Prevention (DEP), specifically Intel XD bit (execute disable bit) or AMD NX bit (no execute bit), must be available and enabled. Minimum: 1.4 GHz. Recommended: 2 GHz or faster.
Memory	Minimum: 1 GB RAM. Recommended: 2 GB RAM or greater. (Additional RAM is required for each running guest operating system.) Maximum: 1 TB.
Hard disk	Minimum: 8 GB. Recommended: 20 GB or greater. (Additional disk space needed for each guest operating system.)

The Add Roles Wizard in Server Manager additionally verifies the hardware requirements. A good starting point is to check your hardware against the Microsoft hardware list to make sure that Windows Server 2016 supports your hardware. If you try to install the Hyper-V server role on a computer that does not meet the CPU requirements, you'll get a warning window that looks like Figure 17.2.

FIGURE 17.2   Warning window that Hyper-V cannot be installed

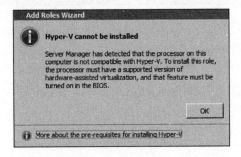

Software Requirements

To use virtualization in Windows Server 2016, you need to consider the basic software requirements for Hyper-V. Hyper-V runs only on the following editions of the Windows Server 2016 operating system:

- Windows Server 2016 Standard edition

- Windows Server 2016 Datacenter edition

- Microsoft Hyper-V Server 2016 edition

Hyper-V Installation and Configuration

The following sections explain how to install the Hyper-V role using Server Manager in Windows Server 2016 Full installation mode or the command-line mode in Windows Server 2016 Server Core. We will then take a look at Hyper-V as part of Server Manager before discussing how to use the Hyper-V Manager. Finally, we will look at the Hyper-V server settings and then cover two important areas for Hyper-V: virtual networks and virtual hard disks.

Install the Hyper-V Role

Now it's time to see how to install the Hyper-V server role on the two installation options of Windows Server 2016, namely, a Full installation and a Server Core installation.

Installing Hyper-V in Full Installation Mode

You can install the Hyper-V server role on any Windows Server 2016 installation for which the Full option was chosen. In addition, the server must meet both the hardware and software requirements. The installation process is simple, as Exercise 17.1 demonstrates.

EXERCISE 17.1

Installing Hyper-V in Full Installation Mode

1. Open Server Manager.

2. In Server Manager, choose option 2, Add Roles And Features.

3. At the Select Installation Type page, choose the role-based or feature-based installation. Click Next.

4. On the Select Destination Server screen, choose Select A Server From The Server Pool and choose the server to which you want to add this role. Click Next.

5. On the Select Server Roles screen, click the check box next to Hyper-V (see Figure 17.3). When the Add Features dialog box appears, click the Add Features button. Then click Next.

FIGURE 17.3   Server Manager Add Features

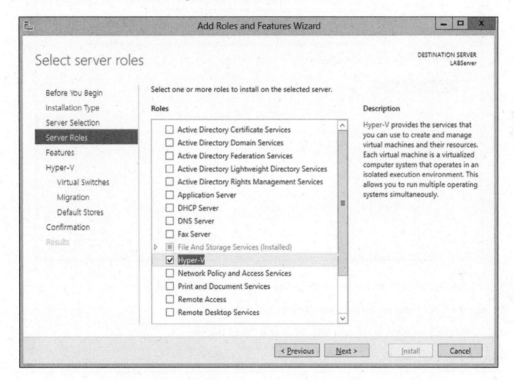

6. At the Select Features screen, click Next.

7. At the Hyper-V introduction screen, click Next.

8. At the Create Virtual Switches screen, choose your adapter (see Figure 17.4) and click Next.

9. At the Virtual Machine Migration screen, click Next. You want to use migration only if you have multiple Hyper-V servers. Since we will have only one for this exercise, just skip this screen.

EXERCISE 17.1 *(continued)*

FIGURE 17.4 Virtual Switch Screen

10. At the Default Stores screen, accept the defaults and click Next.

11. At the Confirmation screen, click the Install button.

12. After the installation is complete, click the Close button.

13. Restart your server.

Installing Hyper-V in Server Core

The Server Core installation option is introduced in Windows Server 2016. It creates an operating system installation without a GUI shell. You can either manage the server remotely from another system or use the Server Core's command-line interface.

This installation option provides the following benefits:

▪ Reduces attack surface (because fewer applications are running on the server)

▪ Reduces maintenance and management (because only the required options are installed)

- Requires less disk space and produces less processor utilization
- Provides a minimal parent partition
- Reduces system resources required by the operating system as well as the attack surface

By using Hyper-V on a Server Core installation, you can fundamentally improve availability because the attack surface is reduced and the downtime required for installing patches is optimized. It will thus be more secure and reliable with less management.

To install Hyper-V for a Windows Server 2016 installation, you must execute the following command in the command-line interface:

```
Dism /online /enable-feature /featurename:Microsoft-Hyper-V
```

Hyper-V in Server Manager

As with all of the other Windows Server 2016 roles, the Hyper-V role neatly integrates into Server Manager. Server Manager filters the information just for the specific role and thus displays only the required information. As you can see in Figure 17.5, the Hyper-V Summary page shows related event log entries, the state of the system services for Hyper-V, and useful resources and support.

FIGURE 17.5 Hyper-V in Server Manager

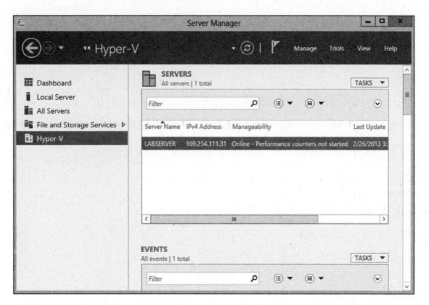

Using Hyper-V Manager

Hyper-V Manager is the central management console to configure your server and create and manage your virtual machines, virtual networks, and virtual hard disks. Unlike some other virtual servers where you managed all virtual machines through a web interface, Hyper-V Manager is managed through a Microsoft Management Console (MMC) snap-in. You can access it either in Server Manager or by using Administrative Tools ➢ Hyper-V Manager. Figure 17.6 shows how Hyper-V Manager looks once you start it.

FIGURE 17.6   Hyper-V Manager

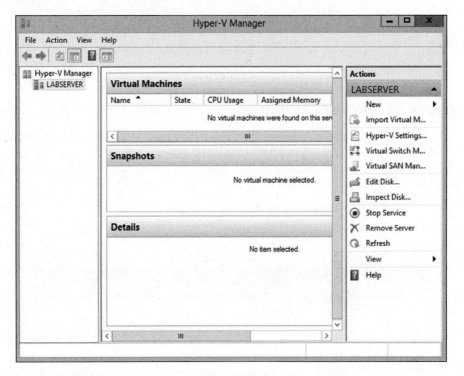

Hyper-V Manager is available for the following operating systems:

- Windows Server 2016
- Windows Server 2012 R2
- Windows Server 2012
- Windows Server 2008 R2
- Windows Server 2008
- Windows 10
- Windows 8
- Windows 7
- Windows Vista with Service Pack 1 (SP1)

Hyper-V Manager is installed on a Windows Server 2016 machine only when you install Hyper-V on it. On Windows Server 2012 R2/2012/2008/2008 R2/ 2003, Windows 10/8/7, or Windows Vista, you will need to install the Hyper-V Manager MMC.

You can use Hyper-V Manager to connect to any Full or Server Core installation remotely. Besides Hyper-V Manager, you can use the WMI interface for scripting Hyper-V.

Configure Hyper-V Settings

In this section, you will get an overview of the available Hyper-V settings for the server. You configure all server-side default configuration settings like default locations of your configuration files or the release key. You can open the Hyper-V Settings page (see Figure 17.7) in Hyper-V Manager by clicking Hyper-V Settings in the Action pane.

FIGURE 17.7   Hyper-V Settings

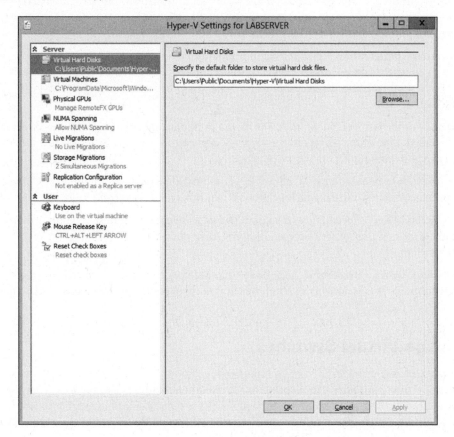

The Hyper-V Settings page includes the following settings:

Virtual Hard Disks   Specifies the default location of your virtual hard disk files (.vhd and .vdhx).

Virtual Machines   Specifies the default location of your virtual machine configuration files. It includes the Virtual Machine XML configuration files (part of the Virtual Machines folder) as well as related snapshots (part of the Snapshot folder).

Physical GPUs   This feature allows for graphical processing unit (GPU) accelerated video within a virtual machine. The GPU will allow you to support 3D GPU accelerated graphics.

NUMA Spanning   An administrator can configure Hyper-V to allow virtual machines to span nonuniform memory architecture (NUMA) nodes. When the physical computer has NUMA nodes, this setting provides virtual machines with additional computing resources. Spanning NUMA nodes can help you run more virtual machines at the same time. However, using NUMA can decrease overall performance.

Live Migrations   *Live Migration* allows a Hyper-V administrator to relocate running virtual machines easily from one node of the failover cluster to another node in the same cluster.

Storage Migrations   *Storage Migration* allows an administrator to move their virtual machine storage from one location to another. This setting allows you to specify how many storage migrations can be performed at the same time on this system.

Replication Configuration   This setting allows you to configure this computer as a Replica Server to another Hyper-V server. Hyper-V Replica allows administrators to replicate their Hyper-V virtual machines from one Hyper-V host at a primary site to another Hyper-V host at the Replica site.

Each node of the failover cluster that is involved in Replica must have the Hyper-V server role installed. One of the servers in the Hyper-V replication needs to be set up as a Replica Broker to allow the replication to work properly.

Keyboard   Defines how to use Windows key combinations. Options are Physical Computer, Virtual Machine, and Virtual Machine Only When Running Full Screen.

Mouse Release Key   Specifies the key combination to release the mouse in your virtual machine. Options are Ctrl+Alt+left arrow, Ctrl+Alt+right arrow, Ctrl+Alt+space, and Ctrl+Alt+Shift.

Reset Check Boxes   Resets any check boxes that hide pages and messages when checked. This will bring any window up again on which you checked the Do Not Show This Window Again check box.

Manage Virtual Switches

A *virtual network* provides the virtual links between nodes in either a virtual or physical network. Virtual networking in Hyper-V is provided in a secure and dynamic way because you can granularly define virtual network switches for their required usage. For example, you can define a private or internal virtual network if you don't want to allow your virtual machines to send packages to the physical network.

To allow your virtual machines to communicate with each other, you need virtual networks. Just like normal networks, virtual networks exist only on the host computer and allow you to configure how virtual machines communicate with each other, with the host, and with the network or the Internet. You manage virtual networks in Hyper-V using Virtual Switch Manager, as shown in Figure 17.8.

FIGURE 17.8   Virtual Network Manager

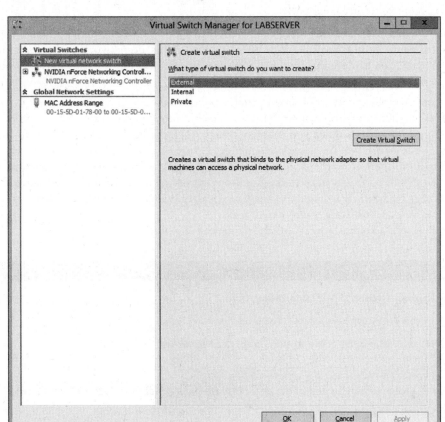

Hyper-V virtual switches are layer-2 software-based ethernet switches available in Hyper-V Manager. These switches are available as soon as you have installed the Hyper-V server role. Windows Server 2016 Hyper-V virtual switches allow you to deploy Switch Embedded Teaming (SET) and Remote Direct Memory Access (RDMA).

Using *Virtual Switch Manager*, you can create, manage, and delete virtual switches. You can define the network type as external, internal only, or private.

External   Any virtual machine connected to this virtual switch can access the physical network. You would use this option if you want to allow your virtual machines to access, for example, other servers on the network or the Internet. This option is used in production environments where your clients connect directly to the virtual machines.

Internal   This option allows virtual machines to communicate with each other as well as the host system but not with the physical network. When you create an internal network, it also creates a local area connection in Network Connections that allows the host machine to communicate with the virtual machines. You can use this if you want to separate your host's network from your virtual networks.

Private When you use this option, virtual machines can communicate with each other but not with the host system or the physical network; thus, no network packets are hitting the wire. You can use this to define internal virtual networks for test environments or labs, for example.

On the external and internal-only virtual networks, you also can enable virtual LAN (VLAN) identification. You can use VLANs to partition your network into multiple subnets using a VLAN ID. When you enable virtual LAN identification, the NIC that is connected to the switch will never see packets tagged with VLAN IDs. Instead, all packets traveling from the NIC to the switch will be tagged with the access mode VLAN ID as they leave the switch port. All packets traveling from the switch port to the NIC will have their VLAN tags removed. You can use this if you are already logically segmenting your physical machines and also use it for your virtual ones.

Exercise 17.2 explains how to create an internal-only virtual switch.

EXERCISE 17.2

Creating an Internal Virtual Network

1. Click the Windows Key ➤ Administrative Tools ➤ Hyper-V Manager.

2. In Hyper-V Manager, in the Action pane, choose Virtual Switch Manager.

3. On the Virtual Switch page, select Private and click the Create Virtual Switch button.

4. On the New Virtual Switch page, enter Private Virtual Network in the Name field.

5. Click OK.

When you create the internal virtual switch, a network device is created in Network Connections, as shown in Figure 17.9.

This is also the case when you create an external virtual network because it will replace the physical network card of the host machine to give the parent partition a virtual network card that is also used in the child partitions.

Hyper-V binds the virtual network service to a physical network adapter only when an external virtual network is created. The benefit of this is that the performance is better if you do not use the external virtual network option. The downside, however, is that there will be a network disruption when you create or delete an external virtual network.

Communication between the virtual machine and the local host computer is not configured automatically. Once you install a virtual machine, you need to make sure that the TCP/IP settings are in agreement with the settings you define in the virtual network card. Start with a ping from your host machine to the virtual machines to verify that communication is working.

FIGURE 17.9   Virtual Switch Manager

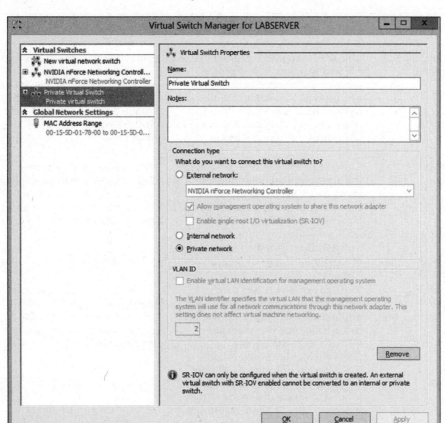

Managing Virtual Hard Disks

In addition to virtual networks, you need to manage virtual hard disks that you attach to your virtual machines. A virtual hard disk in Hyper-V, apart from a pass-through disk, is a VHD or VHDX file that basically simulates a hard drive on your virtual machine.

The following sections will first show you what types of virtual hard disks are available and then show you how to create them. You will also learn about what options are available to manage virtual hard disks.

Types of Hard Disks

Depending on how you want to use the disk, Hyper-V offers various types, as described in Table 17.4.

TABLE 17.4   Virtual hard disks in Hyper-V

Type of Disk	Description	When to Use It
Dynamically expanding	This disk starts with a small VHD file and expands it on demand once an installation takes place. It can grow to the maximum size you defined during creation. You can use this type of disk to clone a local hard drive during creation.	This option is effective when you don't know the exact space needed on the disk and when you want to preserve hard disk space on the host machine. Unfortunately, it is the slowest disk type.
Fixed size	The size of the VHD file is fixed to the size specified when the disk is created. This option is faster than a dynamically expanding disk. However, a fixed-size disk uses up the maximum defined space immediately. This type is ideal for cloning a local hard drive.	A fixed-size disk provides faster access than dynamically expanding or differencing disks, but it is slower than a physical disk.
Differencing	This type of disk is associated in a parent-child relationship with another disk. The differencing disk is the child, and the associated virtual disk is the parent. Differencing disks include only the differences to the parent disk. By using this type, you can save a lot of disk space in similar virtual machines. This option is suitable if you have multiple virtual machines with similar operating systems.	Differencing disks are most commonly found in test environments and should not be used in production environments.
Physical (or pass-through disk)	The virtual machine receives direct pass-through access to the physical disk for exclusive use. This type provides the highest performance of all disk types and thus should be used for production servers where performance is the top priority. The drive is not available for other guest systems.	This type is used in high-end datacenters to provide optimum performance for VMs. It's also used in failover cluster environments.

Creating Virtual Hard Disks

To help you gain practice in creating virtual hard disks, the following three exercises will teach you how to create a differencing hard disk, how to clone an existing disk by creating a new disk, and how to configure a physical or pass-through disk to your virtual machine. First, in Exercise 17.3, you will learn how to create a differencing virtual hard disk.

EXERCISE 17.3

Creating a Differencing Hard Disk

1. Open Hyper-V Manager.

2. In Hyper-V Manager, on the Action pane, choose New ➤ Hard Disk.

3. In the New Virtual Hard Disk Wizard, click Next on the Before You Begin page.

4. At the Choose Disk Format screen, choose VHDX and click Next. The size of your VHDs depends on which format you choose. If you're going to have a VHD larger than 2,040 GB, use VHDX. If your VHD is less than 2,040 GB, then you should use VHD.

5. On the Choose Disk Type page, select Fixed Size and click Next.

6. On the Specify Name And Location page, enter the new name of the child disk (for example, **newvirtualharddisk.vhd**). You can also modify the default location of the new VHD file if you want. Click Next to continue.

7. Next, on the Configure Disk page, you need to specify the size of the VHD file. Choose a size based on your hard disk and then click Next to continue. I used 60 GB as our test size.

8. On the Completing The New Virtual Hard Disk Wizard page, verify that all settings are correct and click Finish to create the hard disk.

The process to add a physical or pass-through disk to a virtual machine is quite different. For this, first you need to create the virtual machine, and then you open the virtual machine settings to configure the physical disk. If you want to add a physical disk to a virtual machine, the physical disk must be set as Offline in Disk Management, as shown in Figure 17.10.

To access Disk Management, click the Windows key, choose Administrative Tools ➤ Computer Management, expand Storage in the left pane, and click Disk Management.

You cannot share a physical disk among multiple virtual machines or with the host system.

Physical or pass-through disks might not be that important if your use of virtualization is based on test environments, but they become crucial when you need to plan for highly available virtual datacenters. This is especially true if you consider using failover clusters to provide the Quick Migration feature, which is when you should consider matching one logical unit number (LUN) from your enterprise storage system or storage area network (SAN) as one physical disk. This provides you with the optimum performance you need in such an environment.

FIGURE 17.10 In Disk Management, you can set disks as Offline.

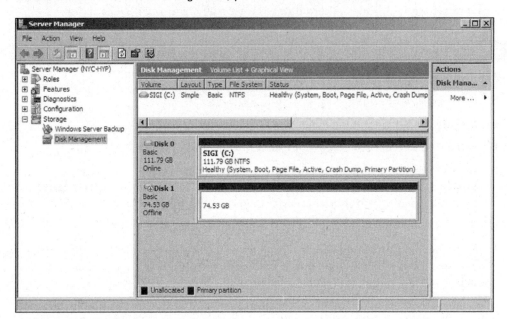

Managing Virtual Hard Disks

Hyper-V also provides two tools to manage virtual hard disks: Inspect Disk and Edit Disk. These tools are available on the Action pane in Hyper-V Manager.

Inspect Disk This provides you with information about the virtual hard disk. It shows you not only the type of the disk but also information such as the maximum size for dynamically expanding disks and the parent VHD for differencing disks.

Edit Disk This provides you with the Edit Virtual Hard Disk Wizard, which you can use to compact, convert, expand, merge, or reconnect hard disks. Figure 17.11 shows you the wizard's options when you select a dynamically expanding disk.

Table 17.5 provides you with an overview of what you can do with the wizard.

Generation 1 vs. Generation 2 VHDs

Previous versions of Hyper-V had some pretty major drawbacks. One big drawback was that Hyper-V could not boot a virtual machine from a virtual hard drive that was SCSI. Believe it or not, SCSI controllers were not even recognized by Hyper-V unless you installed the Integration Services component.

Another issue that the previous versions of Hyper-V had was the inability to copy files from the Hyper-V host to the virtual machines without the use of a network connection in the virtual machine. The older versions of Hyper-V, prior to Windows Server 2012, are now considered generation 1 versions. Why is it so important to know which generations of Hyper-V you should use or need to use?

FIGURE 17.11 The Edit Virtual Hard Disk Wizard

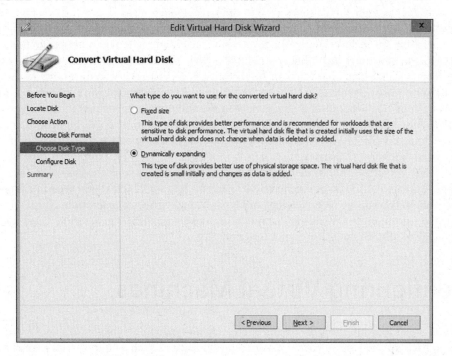

TABLE 17.5 Edit Disk overview

Action	Description
Compact	Reduces the size of a dynamically expanding or differencing disk by removing blank space from deleted files.
Convert	Converts a dynamically expanding disk to a fixed disk or vice versa.
Expand	Increases the storage capacity of a dynamically expanding disk or a fixed virtual hard disk.
Merge	Merges the changes from a differencing disk into either the parent disk or another disk (applies to differencing disks only!).
Reconnect	If a differencing disk no longer finds its referring parent disk, this option can reconnect the parent to the disk.

Hyper-V generations help determine what functionality and what virtual hardware you can use in your virtual machine. Windows Server 2016 Hyper-V now supports two different virtual machine generations: generation 1 and generation 2.

As already explained, previous versions of Hyper-V are considered generation 1, and this provides the same virtual hardware to the virtual machine as in previous versions of Hyper-V.

Generation 2 is included with Windows Server 2016, and it provides better functionality on the virtual machines including secure boot (which is enabled by default), the ability to boot from a SCSI virtual hard disk or boot from a SCSI virtual DVD, the ability to use a standard network adapter to PXE boot, and Unified Extensible Firmware Interface (UEFI) firmware support. Generation 2 now gives you the ability to support UEFI firmware instead of BIOS-based firmware. On a virtual machine that is Generation 2, you can configure Secure Boot, Enable TPM, and set security policies by clicking on the Security section of the virtual machines properties.

So when you create VHDs in Windows Server 2016, one of your choices will be the ability to create the VHDs as a generation 1 or generation 2 VHD. If you need the ability to have your VHDs run on older versions of Hyper-V, make them a generation 1 VHD. If they are going to run only on Windows Server 2016, make your VHDs generation 2 and take advantage of all the new features and functionality.

Configuring Virtual Machines

The following sections cover the topics of creating and managing virtual machines as well as how to back up and restore virtual machines using features such as Import and Export and Checkpoints. You'll also briefly look at Hyper-V's Live Migration feature.

Creating and Managing Virtual Machines

It is important to learn how to create a virtual machine, how to change its configuration, and how to delete it. You will take a look at the Virtual Machine Connection tool and install the Hyper-V Integration Components onto a virtual machine.

Virtual Machines

Virtual machines define the child partitions in which you run operating system instances. Each virtual machine is separate and can communicate with the others only by using a virtual network. You can assign hard drives, virtual networks, DVD drives, and other system components to it. A virtual machine is similar to an existing physical server, but it no longer runs on dedicated hardware—it shares the hardware of the host system with the other virtual machines that run on the host.

Exercise 17.4 shows you how to create a new virtual machine. Before completing this exercise, download an eval copy of Windows Server from Microsoft's website (www.microsoft.com/downloads). Make sure the file downloaded is an image file (.iso). You will use this image to install the operating system into the virtual machine.

EXERCISE 17.4

Creating a New Virtual Machine

1. Open Hyper-V Manager (see Figure 17.12).

FIGURE 17.12   Hyper-V Manager

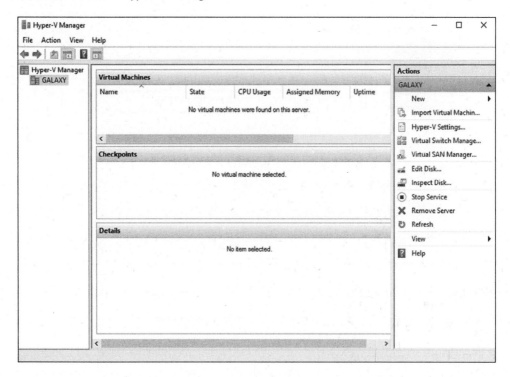

2. In Hyper-V Manager, on the Action pane, choose New ➢ Virtual Machine.

3. In the New Virtual Machine Wizard, click Next on the Before You Begin page.

4. On the Specify Name And Location page, give your virtual machine a name and change the default location of the virtual machine configuration files. Click Next to continue.

5. The Specify Generation screen is next. Choose Generation 2 (see Figure 17.13) and click Next.

6. On the Assign Memory page (see Figure 17.14), define how much of your host computer's memory you want to assign to this virtual machine. Remember that once your virtual machine uses up all of your physical memory, it will start swapping to disk, thus reducing the performance of all virtual machines. Click Next to continue.

FIGURE 17.13 Specify Generation Screen

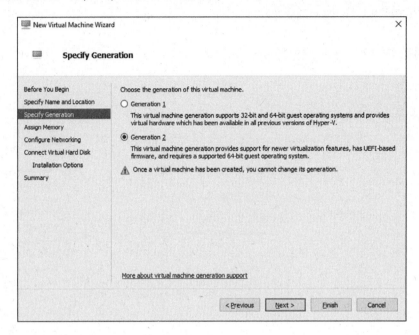

FIGURE 17.14 VM RAM

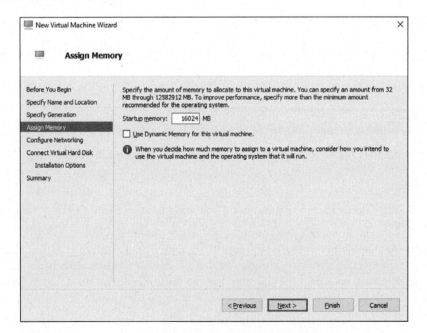

7. On the Configure Networking page, select the virtual network that you previously configured using Virtual Network Manager (see Figure 17.15). Click Next to continue.

FIGURE 17.15   Networking Page

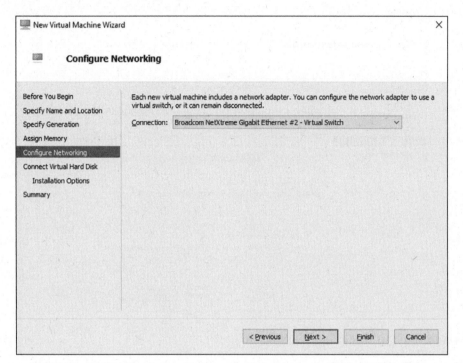

8. On the next page, you configure your virtual hard disk (see Figure 17.16). You can create a new virtual hard disk, select an existing disk, or choose to attach the hard disk later. Be aware that you can create only a dynamically expanding virtual disk on this page; you cannot create a differencing, physical, or fixed virtual hard disk there. However, if you created the virtual hard disk already, you can, of course, select it. Click Next to continue.

9. On the Installation Options page (see Figure 17.17), you can select how you want to install your operating system. You have the option to install an operating system later, install the operating system from a boot CD/DVD-ROM where you can select a physical device or an image file (.iso file), install an operating system from a floppy disk image (VFD file, or a virtual boot floppy disk), or install an operating system from a network-based installation server. The last option will install a legacy network adapter to your virtual machine so that you can boot from the network adapter. Select Install An Operating System from a bootable CD/DVD-ROM and choose Image File (.iso). Then click Next.

FIGURE 17.16   Virtual Hard Disk Page

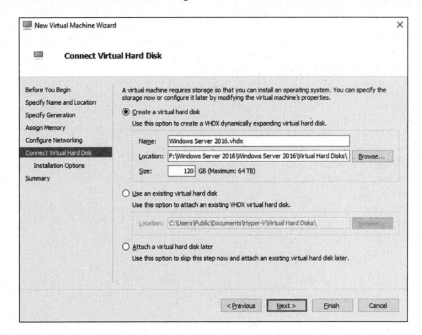

FIGURE 17.17   Installing OS screen

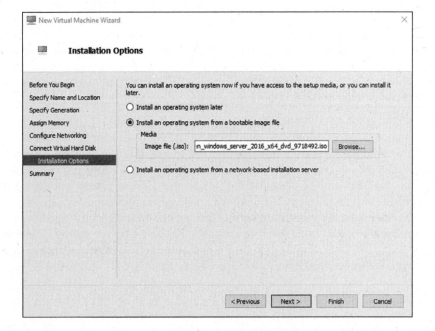

10. On the Completing The New Virtual Machine Wizard summary page, verify that all settings are correct. You also have the option to start the virtual machine immediately after creation (see Figure 17.18). Click Next to create the virtual machine.

FIGURE 17.18   Completing the New Virtual Machine Wizard screen

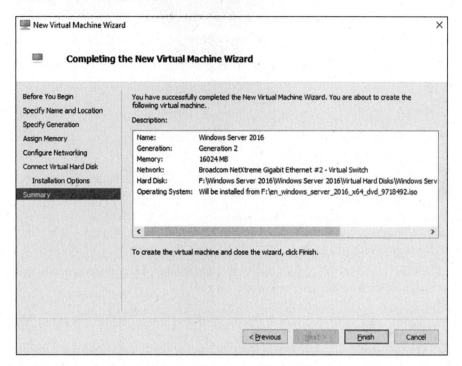

11. Repeat this process and create a few more virtual machines.

After completing Exercise 17.4, you will have a virtual machine available in Hyper-V Manager. Initially, the state of the virtual machine will be Off. Virtual machines can have the following states: Off, Starting, Running, Paused, and Saved. You can change the state of a virtual machine in the Virtual Machines pane by right-clicking the virtual machine's name, as shown in Figure 17.19, or by using the Virtual Machine Connection window.

Here is a list of some of the state options (when the VM is running) available for a virtual machine:

Start   Turn on the virtual machine. This is similar to pressing the power button when the machine is turned off. This option is available when your virtual machine is Off or in Saved state.

Turn Off   Turn off the virtual machine. This is similar to pressing the power-off button on the computer. This option is available when your virtual machine is in Running, Saved, or Paused state.

FIGURE 17.19   Options available when right-clicking a virtual machine

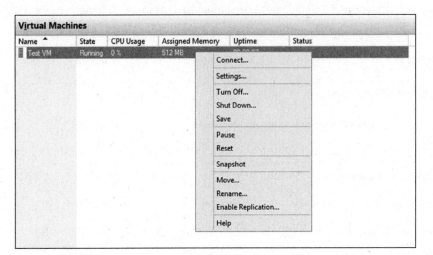

Shut Down   This option shuts down your operating system. You need to have the Hyper-V Integration Components installed on the operating system; otherwise, Hyper-V will not be able to shut down the system.

Save   The virtual machine is saved to disk in its current state. This option is available when your virtual machine is in Running or Paused state.

Pause   Pause the current virtual machine, but do not save the state to disk. You can use this option to release processor utilization quickly from this virtual machine to the host system.

Reset   Reset the virtual machine. This is like pressing the reset button on your computer. You will lose the current state and any unsaved data in the virtual machine. This option is available when your virtual machine is in Running or Paused state.

Resume   When your virtual machine is paused, you can resume it and bring it online again.

Changing Configuration on an Existing Virtual Machine

To change the configuration settings on an existing virtual machine, you right-click your virtual machine's name in the Virtual Machines pane in Hyper-V Manager and choose Settings. You can change settings such as memory allocation and hard drive configuration. All items that you can configure are described in the following list:

Add Hardware   Add devices to your virtual machine, namely, a SCSI controller, a network adapter, or a legacy network adapter. A legacy network adapter is required if you want to perform a network-based installation of an operating system.

BIOS   This is the replacement of the virtual machine's BIOS. Because you can no longer enter the BIOS during startup, you need to configure it with this setting. You can turn Num Lock on or off and change the basic startup order of the devices.

Memory Change the amount of random access memory (RAM) allocated to the virtual machine.

Processor Change the number of logical processors this virtual machine can use and define resource control to balance resources among virtual machines by using a relative weight.

IDE Controller Add/change and remove devices from the IDE controller. You can have hard drives or DVD drives as devices. Every IDE controller can have up to two devices attached, and by default, you have two IDE controllers available.

Hard Drive Select a controller to attach to this device as well as to specify the media to use with your virtual hard disk. The available options are Virtual Hard Disk File (with additional buttons labeled New, Edit, Inspect, and Browse) and Physical Hard Disk. You can also remove the device here.

DVD Drive Select a controller to attach to this device and specify the media to use with your virtual CD/DVD drive. The available options are None, Image File (ISO Image), and Physical CD/DVD Drive Connected To The Host Computer. You also can remove the device here.

SCSI Controller Configure all hard drives that are connected to the SCSI controller. You can add up to 63 hard drives to each SCSI controller, and you can have multiple SCSI controllers available.

Network Adapter Specify the configuration of the network adapter or remove it. You can also configure the virtual network and MAC address for each adapter and enable virtual LAN identification. The network adapter section also allows you to control Bandwidth Management.

Bandwidth Management allows an administrator to specify how the network adapter will utilize network bandwidth. Administrators have the ability to set a minimum network bandwidth that a network adapter can use and a maximum bandwidth. This gives administrators greater control over how much bandwidth a virtual network adapter can use.

COM1 and COM2 Configure the virtual COM port to communicate with the physical computer through a named pipe. You have COM1 and COM2 available.

Diskette Specify a virtual floppy disk file to use.

Name Edit the name of the virtual machine and provide some notes about it.

Integration Services Define what integration services are available to your virtual machine. Options are Operating System Shutdown, Time Synchronization, Data Exchange, Heartbeat, and Backup (Volume Snapshot).

Snapshot File Location Define the default file location of your snapshot files.

Smart Paging File Location This area allows you to set up a paging file for your virtual machine. Windows Server 2016 has a Hyper-V feature called Smart Paging. If you have a virtual machine that has a smaller amount of memory than what it needs for startup memory, when the virtual machine gets restarted, Hyper-V then needs additional memory to restart the virtual machine. Smart Paging is used to bridge the memory gap between minimum memory and startup memory. This allows your virtual machines to restart properly.

Automatic Start Define what this virtual machine will do when the physical computer starts. Options are Nothing, Automatically Start If The Service Was Running, and Always Start This Virtual Machine. You also can define a start delay here.

Automatic Stop Define what this virtual machine will do when the physical computer shuts down. Options are Save State, Turn Off, and Shut Down.

> Please be aware that only some settings can be changed when the virtual machine's state is Running. It is best practice to shut down the virtual machine before you modify any setting.

Deleting Virtual Machines

You can also delete virtual machines using Hyper-V Manager. This deletes all of the configuration files, as shown in Figure 17.20.

FIGURE 17.20 Delete Virtual Machine warning window

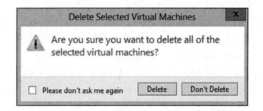

Make sure you manually delete any virtual disks that were part of the virtual machines to free up disk space. Virtual disks are *not* deleted when you delete a virtual machine.

Virtual Machine Connection

Hyper-V comes with Virtual Machine Connection to connect to virtual machines that run on a local or remote server.

You can use it to log into the virtual machine and use your computer's mouse and keyboard to interact with the virtual machine. You can open Virtual Machine Connection in Hyper-V Manager by double-clicking a virtual machine or by right-clicking a virtual machine and selecting Connect. If your virtual machine is turned off, you might see a window similar to the one in Figure 17.21.

Virtual Machine Connection not only provides you with functionality similar to that of Hyper-V Manager, such as being able to change the state of a virtual machine, but it also provides you with additional features that are especially useful when you want to work with a virtual machine.

File Access Settings or Exit Virtual Machine Connection Change the state of a virtual machine and create or revert a snapshot. Additionally, you have the options to send Ctrl+Alt+Delete to your virtual machine and Insert Integration Services Setup Disk.

FIGURE 17.21   Virtual Machine Connection window when the machine is turned off

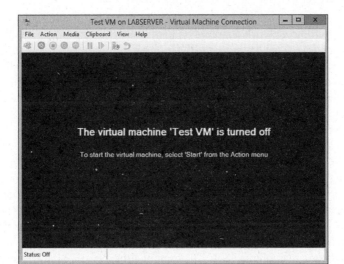

Context-Sensitive Buttons Provide Quick Access to Key Features   These buttons are available under the menu bar to provide you with fast access to the most important features, as you can see in Figure 17.22. It shows the connection of a running VM, but the VM has not had an operating system installed yet, so the figure shows the Windows Server 2016 Setup screen.

FIGURE 17.22   Virtual Machine Connection window showing a running Windows Server 2016 virtual machine

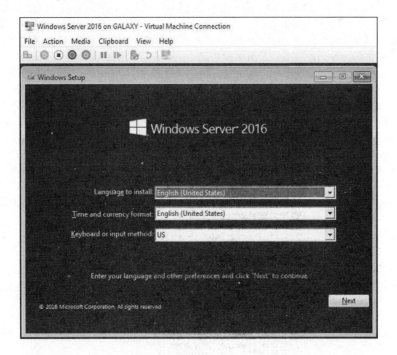

NIC Teaming

NIC Teaming, also known as load balancing and failover (LBFO), gives an administrator the ability to allow multiple network adapters on a system to be placed into a team. Independent hardware vendors (IHVs) have required NIC Teaming, but until Windows Server 2012, NIC Teaming was *not* part of the Windows Server operating system.

To be able to use NIC Teaming, the computer system must have at least one Ethernet adapter. If you want to provide fault protection, an administrator must have a minimum of two Ethernet adapters. One advantage of Windows Server 2016 is that an administrator can set up 32 network adapters in a NIC team.

NIC Teaming is a common practice when setting up virtualization. This is one way that you can have load balancing with Hyper-V.

NIC Teaming gives an administrator the ability to allow a virtual machine to use virtual network adapters in Hyper-V. The advantage of using NIC Teaming in Hyper-V is that the administrator can use NIC Teaming to connect to more than one Hyper-V switch. This allows Hyper-V still to have connectivity even if the network adapter under the Hyper-V switch gets disconnected.

An administrator can configure NIC Teaming in either Server Manager or PowerShell. NIC teaming can be configured in different configuration models including Switch Independent or Switch Dependent. Switch Independent means that each NIC adapter is connected into a different switch. Switch Dependent means that all NIC adapters are connected into the same switch. If you use Switch Independent NIC Teaming, then you must connect your NICs to different switches, but both switches must be on the same subnet.

Remote Direct Memory Access

When most of us think of Hyper-V, we think of a group of virtual machines sharing access to a systems resource. With Windows Server 2016, Hyper-V includes Remote Direct Memory Access (RDMA).

RDMA allows one computer to directly access memory from the memory of another computer without the need of interfacing with either one's operating system. This gives systems the ability to have high throughput and low-latency networking. This is very useful when it comes to clustering systems (including Hyper-V).

Windows Server 2012 R2 RDMA services couldn't be bound to a Hyper-V Virtual Switch and because of this, Remote Direct Memory Access and Hyper-V had to be on the same computer as the network adapters. Because of this, there was a need for a higher number of physical network adapters that were required to be installed on the Hyper-V host.

Because of the improvements of RDMA on Windows Server 2016, administrators can use less network adapters while using RDMA.

Switch Embedded Teaming

Earlier we discussed NIC Teaming but we also have the ability to do Switch Embedded Teaming (SET). SET can be an alternative to using NIC Teaming in environments that include Hyper-V and the Software Defined Networking (SDN) stack in Windows Server 2016. SET is available in all versions of Windows Server 2016 that include Hyper-V and SDN stack.

SET does use some of the functionality of NIC Teaming into the Hyper-V Virtual Switch but SET allows an administrator to combine a group of physical adapters (minimum of 1 adapter and a maximum of 8 adapters) into software based virtual adapters.

By using virtual adapters, you get better performance and greater fault tolerance in the event of a network adapter going bad. For SET to be enabled, all of the physical network adapters must be installed on the same physical Hyper-V host.

One of the requirements of SET is that all network adapters that are members of the SET group be identical adapters. This means that they need to be the same adapter types from the same manufacturers.

One main difference between NIC Teaming and Set is that SET only supports Switch Independent mode setups. Again this means that the NIC adapters are connected to different switches.

Administrators need to create a SET team at the same time that they create the Hyper-V Virtual Switch. Administrators can do this by using the Windows PowerShell command `New-VMSwitch`.

At the time an administrator creates a Hyper-V Virtual Switch, the administrator needs to include the EnableEmbeddedTeaming parameter in their command syntax. The following example shows a Hyper-V switch named StormSwitch.

```
New-VMSwitch -Name StormSwitch -NetAdapterName "NIC 1","NIC 2"
-EnableEmbeddedTeaming $true
```

Administrators also have the ability to remove a SET team by using the following PowerShell command. This example removes a Virtual Switch named StormSwitch.

```
Remove-VMSwitch "StormSwitch
```

Storage Quality of Service

Windows Server 2016 Hyper-V includes a feature called *Storage Quality of Service (QoS)*. Storage QoS allows a Hyper-V administrator to manage how virtual machines access storage throughput for virtual hard disks.

Storage QoS gives an administrator the ability to guarantee that the storage throughput of a single VHD cannot adversely affect the performance of another VHD on the same host. It does this by giving administrators the ability to specify the maximum and minimum I/O loads based on I/O operations per second (IOPS) for each virtual disk in your virtual machines.

To configure Storage QoS, you would set the maximum IOPS values (or limits) and set the minimum values (or reserves) on virtual hard disks for virtual machines.

 If you are using shared virtual hard disks, Storage QoS will not be available.

Installing Hyper-V Integration Components

Hyper-V *Integration Components*, also called *Integration Services*, are required to make your guest operating system hypervisor-aware. Similar to the VM Additions that were part of Microsoft Virtual Server 2005, these components improve the performance of the guest operating system once they are installed. From an architectural perspective, virtual devices are redirected directly via the VMBus; thus, quicker access to resources and devices is provided.

If you do not install the Hyper-V Integration Components, the guest operating system uses emulation to communicate with the host's devices, which of course makes the guest operating system slower.

Exercise 17.5 shows you how to install Hyper-V Integration Components on one of your virtual machines running Windows Server 2016.

EXERCISE 17.5

Installing Hyper-V Integration Components

1.   Open Hyper-V Manager.

2.   In Hyper-V Manager, in the Virtual Machines pane, right-click the virtual machine on which you want to install Hyper-V Integration Components and click Start.

3.   Right-click the virtual machine again and click Connect. Meanwhile, your virtual machine should already be booting.

4.   If you need to log into the operating system of your virtual machine, you should do so.

5.   Once the Windows Desktop appears, you need to select Insert Integration Services Setup Disk from the Actions menu of your Virtual Machine Connection window.

6.   Once the Hyper-V Integration Components are installed, you are asked to perform a reboot.

After the reboot, Hyper-V Integration Components are installed on your operating system, and you will be able to use them.

Linux and FreeBSD Image Deployments

One of the features of Windows 2016 is the ability for Hyper-V to support Linux and FreeBSD virtual machines. Hyper-V now can support these new virtual machines because Hyper-V has the ability to emulate Linux and FreeBSD devices. Because Hyper-V now has the ability to emulate these two devices, no additional software needs to be installed on Hyper-V.

Unfortunately, because Hyper-V has to emulate these devices, you lose some of the Hyper-V functionality like high performance and full management of the virtual machines. So it's a tradeoff. You get to run Linux and FreeBSD type Hyper-V virtual machines but you lose some of the benefits of Hyper-V.

But wait; there is a way to get your Hyper-V functionality back. This issue can be resolved as long as you install Hyper-V on machines that can support Linux and FreeBSD operating systems. The drivers that are needed on Hyper-V are called Linux Integration Services (LIS) and FreeBSD Integrated Services (FIS). By putting these drivers on a device that can handle Linux and FreeBSD, you can then have Hyper-V with all of the features Microsoft offers.

To get these drivers and make Hyper-V work will all of its functionality, you must make sure that you install a newer release of Linux that includes LIS. To get the most out of FreeBSD you must get a version after 10.0. For FreeBSD versions that are older than 10.0, Microsoft offers ports that work with BIS drivers that need to be installed. Hyper-V will work with Linux and FreeBSD without the need of any additional drivers or equipment. By having drivers and equipment that supports Linux and FreeBSD, you just get all of the Hyper-V features that your organization may need.

In Exercise 17.6, I will show you how to install Linux into a virtual machine. I will then walk you through a full installation of a Linux Server. Before you complete this lab, you must download a copy of Linux. For this exercise, I downloaded a free copy of Linux Ubuntu as an image file (.iso). If you choose a different version of Linux, the installation screens during the exercise may be different.

EXERCISE 17.6

Creating a Linux Virtual Machine

1. Open Hyper-V Manager.

2. In the right hand window under Actions, click New ➤ Virtual Machine (see Figure 17.23).

3. At the Before you Begin screen, just choose Next.

4. At the Specify Name and Location screen, Enter in the name of the Linux virtual machine and the location you would like to store the virtual machine files. Then click Next.

5. At the Generation screen, choose Generation 2 and click Next.

6. At the Assign Memory screen, enter in the amount of memory you want to allocate to this virtual machine. I am using 12 GB (12000 MB). Click Next.

7. Choose which network connection you want to use and click Next.

8. At the Connect Virtual Hard Disk screen, choose Create a virtual hard disk. Set the location of where you want the files to reside and also how much space you want to use (I chose 127 GB). Click Next.

9. At the Installation Options screen, choose Install an Operating system from a bootable image file and point to your Linux .iso download. Click Next.

10. At the Completing the New Virtual Machine Wizard screen, make sure all of the settings are correct and choose Finish.

FIGURE 17.23   New Virtual Machine

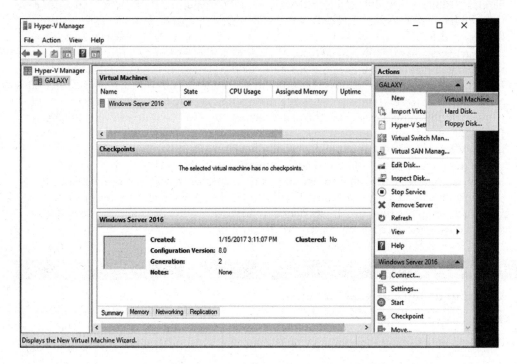

11. After the virtual machine was created, click on the virtual machine and on the right side under Linux, click Start.

12. When the Linux install starts, click your Language.

13. At the Ubuntu menu, choose Install Ubuntu Server.

14. Again, you will need to choose your language for the install.

15. Choose your country.

16. On the detect keyboard layout, choose No. Choose your keyboard (ours is US Normal). The installation will Continue.

17. Next you will choose a hostname. I am keeping the default of Ubuntu. Click Continue.

18. Enter your user account (full name) and click Continue.

19. Enter your username. First name is fine and click Continue.

20. Type in your password and click Continue. Do not choose to show your password in clear text. You will then be asked to re-enter your password and click Continue.

21. When it asks you to encrypt your home directory, choose No.

22. The install will try to figure out your time zone. If it picks correctly, chose Yes. If it doesn't, choose No and enter your time zone.

23. The next screen will ask you about setting up a Partition disk. I am going to allow Linux to configure the disk (Guided) and I will allow it to use the entire drive with a Logical Volume Manager (LVM). So I am choosing Guided - use entire disk and set up LVM.

24. It will then ask about partition type. I am choosing SCSI3.

25. The next screen will verify your choices for partitioning. Choose Yes.

26. It will then verify your disk size and then if you want to continue. Choose the disk size and then choose Yes to continue.

27. The next screen will ask you if you use a Proxy server for Internet access. If you use a Proxy, put it in and if you don't, just click Continue.

28. You will be asked about updates for Linux. Choose how you want to do your updates. Since this is a test virtual machine, I am choosing No automatic updates.

29. At the Software selection screen, choose what software you want installed during this process. I chose DNS, Samba File Server, and standard system utilities. Click Continue.

30. At the GRUB boot screen, click Yes to install the GRUB boot loader. This is OK since we have no other operating system on this virtual machine.

31. Once the installation is complete, choose Continue. At this point, Linux will restart and ask you for your login and password. After you enter them, you will be at a Linux prompt.

32. Type shutdown at the prompt to shut down the virtual machine.

Now that we have installed Linux (or FreeBSD), the next step is to help improve the Hyper-V performance. As I stated earlier, this issue will be resolved as long as we install the drivers that are needed on Hyper-V called Linux Integration Services (LIS) and FreeBSD Integrated Services (FIS). By putting these drivers on a device that can handle Linux and FreeBSD, you can then have Hyper-V with all of the features Microsoft offers.

 Depending on what version of Linux or FreeBSD that you installed, you will need to download some additional updates to get the best performance out of Hyper-V. The following Microsoft website has a list of links for the different versions of Linux and FreeBSD updates. https://technet.microsoft.com/windows-server-docs/compute/hyper-v/ supported-linux-and-freebsd-virtual-machines-for-hyper-v-on-windows ?f=255&MSPPError=-2147217396.

In Exercise 17.7, I will show you how to install the additional updates needed for the Linux Ubuntu version (16.10) that I installed in Exercise 17.6.

EXERCISE 17.7

Updating Linux Ubuntu 16.10

1. Open Hyper-V Manager.

2. Start the Linux virtual machine by clicking on the Linux virtual machine and clicking Start on the right hand menu.

3. At the Ubuntu login, enter the login and password that you created in Exercise 17.6.

4. Since we are using Ubuntu 16.10, we need to install the latest virtual kernel to have up-to-date Hyper-V capabilities. To install the virtual HWE kernel, run the following commands as root (or sudo):

   `sudo apt-get update`

5. You will be asked for your password. Enter your password.

6. Next type in the following command;

   `sudo apt-get install linux-image-virtual`

7. You will be asked to confirm your choice by typing Y and hit enter.

8. Type in the following command;

   `sudo apt-get install linux-tools-virtual linux-cloud-tools-virtual`

9. You will be asked to confirm your choice by typing Y and hit enter.

10. After everything is installed, you are ready to go. You can clear the screen by typing `Clear` and hit enter. To shut down the system, type `shutdown`.

Finally, if you want to setup the Linux or FreeBSD virtual machines to use the advantages of secure boot, you would need to run the following PowerShell command on the Hyper-V server;

`Set-VMFirmware -VMName "VMname" -EnableSecureBoot Off`

PowerShell Commands

One of the things that Microsoft has stated is that the exams are going to be more PowerShell intensive. So, I wanted to add a PowerShell section showing the different PowerShell commands that you can use for Hyper-V. This table has been taken directly from Microsoft's websites. Table 17.6 explains just some of the PowerShell commands that you can use with Hyper-V.

This table shows you just some of the PowerShell commands for Hyper-V. To see a more comprehensive list, please visit Microsoft's website at https://technet.microsoft.com/en-us/library/hh848559.aspx.

TABLE 17.6   Hyper-V PowerShell commands

Command	Explanation
Add-VMDvdDrive	Adds a DVD drive to a virtual machine
Add-VMHardDiskDrive	Adds a hard disk drive to a virtual machine
Add-VMMigrationNetwork	Adds a network for virtual machine migration on one or more virtual machine hosts
Add-VMNetworkAdapter	Adds a virtual network adapter to a virtual machine
Add-VMSwitch	Adds a virtual switch to an Ethernet resource pool
Checkpoint-VM	Creates a checkpoint of a virtual machine
Convert-VHD	Converts the format, version type, and block size of a virtual hard disk file
Copy-VMFile	Copies a file to a virtual machine
Debug-VM	Debugs a virtual machine
Disable-VMConsoleSupport	Disables keyboard, video, and mouse for virtual machines
Disable-VMMigration	Disables migration on one or more virtual machine hosts
Dismount-VHD	Dismounts a virtual hard disk
Enable-VMConsoleSupport	Enables keyboard, video, and mouse for virtual machines
Enable-VMMigration	Enables migration on one or more virtual machine hosts
Enable-VMReplication	Enables replication of a virtual machine
Enable-VMResourceMetering	Collects resource utilization data for a virtual machine or resource pool
Export-VM	Exports a virtual machine to disk
Export-VMSnapshot	Exports a virtual machine checkpoint to disk

TABLE 17.6 Hyper-V PowerShell commands *(continued)*

Command	Explanation
Get-VHD	Gets the virtual hard disk object associated with a virtual hard disk
Get-VHDSet	Gets information about a VHD set
Get-VHDSnapshot	Gets information about a checkpoint in a VHD set
Get-VM	Gets the virtual machines from one or more Hyper-V hosts
Get-VMDvdDrive	Gets the DVD drives attached to a virtual machine or snapshot
Get-VMHardDiskDrive	Gets the virtual hard disk drives attached to one or more virtual machines
Get-VMMemory	Gets the memory of a virtual machine or snapshot
Get-VMNetworkAdapter	Gets the virtual network adapters of a virtual machine, snapshot, management operating system or of a virtual machine and management operating system
Get-VMProcessor	Gets the processor of a virtual machine or snapshot
Get-VMReplication	Gets the replication settings for a virtual machine
Get-VMSwitch	Gets virtual switches from one or more virtual Hyper-V hosts
Merge-VHD	Merges virtual hard disks
Mount-VHD	Mounts one or more virtual hard disks
Move-VM	Moves a virtual machine to a new Hyper-V host
New-VHD	Creates one or more new virtual hard disks
New-VM	Creates a new virtual machine
New-VMGroup	Creates a virtual machine group
New-VMSwitch	Creates a new virtual switch on one or more virtual machine hosts
Remove-VHDSnapshot	Removes a snapshot from a VHD set file
Remove-VM	Deletes a virtual machine

Command	Explanation
Remove-VMHardDiskDrive	Deletes one or more virtual hard disks (VHDs) from a virtual machine (VM)
Remove-VMNetworkAdapter	Removes one or more virtual network adapters from a virtual machine
Remove-VMReplication	Removes the replication relationship of a virtual machine
Remove-VMSan	Removes a virtual storage area network (SAN) from a Hyper-V host
Remove-VMSwitch	Deletes a virtual switch
Rename-VM	Renames a virtual machine
Rename-VMGroup	Renames virtual machine groups
Resize-VHD	Resizes a virtual hard disk
Restart-VM	Restarts a virtual machine
Save-VM	Saves a virtual machine
Set-VHD	Sets properties associated with a virtual hard disk
Set-VM	Configures a virtual machine
Set-VMBios	Configures the BIOS of a Generation 1 virtual machine
Set-VMMemory	Configures the memory of a virtual machine
Set-VMNetworkAdapter	Configures features of the virtual network adapter in a virtual machine or the management operating system
Set-VMProcessor	Configures one or more processors of a virtual machine
Set-VMReplicationServer	Configures a host as a Replica server
Set-VMSan	Configures a virtual storage area network (SAN) on one or more Hyper-V hosts
Set-VMSwitch	Configures a virtual switch
Stop-VM	Shuts down, turns off, or saves a virtual machine
Suspend-VM	Suspends, or pauses, a virtual machine

Summary

In this chapter, I started the discussion with Software Defined Networking (SDN). I talked about Software Load Balancing (SLB), Network Controllers, NAT, and RAS Gateways. I explained how SDNs use virtualization to design and create the network.

I then showed you how to configure virtual machines using the Hyper-V environment and how to create your own virtual datacenter on top of your Hyper-V machines. I showed you how to create and manage virtual machines, how to use Virtual Machine Connection to control a virtual machine remotely, and how to install Hyper-V Integration Components. You also learned how to export and import virtual machines as well as how to do snapshots of your virtual machine.

If you have never worked with virtualization software before, the information in this chapter may have been completely new to you. You should now be well prepared to try Hyper-V in your own environment.

Exam Essentials

Understand Software Defined Networking.   Know what Software Defined Networking (SDN) is and the different components needed to setup SDN. Some of these components include Software Load Balancing, Network Controllers, NAT, and RAS Gateways.

Know Hyper-V's requirements and how to install it.   Know the hardware and software requirements as well as how to install Hyper-V. Hyper-V requires an x64-based processor and Data Execution Protection (DEP). Hardware-assisted virtualization must be enabled—don't forget this! Also remember that you can install Hyper-V two ways: using Server Manager or using the command line in Server Core.

Understand virtual networks and virtual hard disks.   Virtual networks and hard disks are the two most tested topics. You definitely should know the types of virtual networks available (that is, external, internal only, and private virtual network) as well as all types of virtual hard disks (namely, dynamically expanding, fixed size, differential, and physical or pass-through). You should be able to apply the correct one when needed. Don't forget the Edit Virtual Hard Disk Wizard, which is also a good source for questions in the exam.

Know how to create and manage virtual machines.   You should be able to explain how to create a virtual machine, what options are available to install an operating system in a virtual machine, and how to install the Hyper-V Integration Components on a virtual machine. Don't forget about the virtual machine states and the virtual machine settings!

Review Questions

1. You are the network administrator for a large organization that has decided to start using Network Controllers. What PowerShell command allows you to create a new Network Controller?

   A. `New-NetworkController`

   B. `New-NetworkControllerServerObject`

   C. `New-NetworkControllerObject`

   D. `New-NetworkControllerNodeObject`

2. You are an application developer and network admin. You create an application named App1. App1 is going to be distributed to multiple Hyper-V virtual machines in a multitenant environment for both virtual and non-virtual networks. What should you include in the environment if you need to ensure that the traffic is distributed evenly among the virtual machines that host App1?

   A. Network Controller and Windows Server Network Load Balancing (NLB) nodes.

   B. A RAS Gateway and Windows Server Software Load Balancing (SLB) nodes.

   C. A RAS Gateway and Windows Server Network Load Balancing (NLB) nodes.

   D. Network Controller and Windows Server Software Load Balancing (SLB) nodes.

3. You are the Network Administrator for your company. You have an Active Directory domain that contains multiple Hyper-V hosts that run Windows Server 2016. You plan to deploy network virtualization and to centrally manage Datacenter Firewall policies. What component must be installed for the planned deployment?

   A. Data Center Bridging feature.

   B. Network Controller server role.

   C. Routing role service.

   D. Canary Network Diagnostics feature.

4. You want to make sure the hard disk space for your virtual machines is occupied only when needed. What type of virtual hard disk would you recommend?

   A. Dynamically expanding disk

   B. Fixed-size disk

   C. Differencing disk

   D. Physical or pass-through disk

5. How do you add a physical disk to a virtual machine?

   A. Use the Virtual Hard Disk Wizard.

   B. Use the Edit Virtual Hard Disk Wizard.

   C. Use the virtual machine's settings.

   D. Use the New Virtual Machine Wizard.

6. Rich bought a new server with an Itanium IA-64 processor, 4 GB RAM, and a SAN that provides 1 TB hard disk space. After installing Windows Server 2016 for Itanium-based systems, he wants to install Hyper-V on this server. Can Hyper-V be installed on this system?

   A. Yes

   B. No

7. What are the minimum CPU requirements for running Hyper-V on a machine? (Choose all that apply.)

   A. An x64-based processor (Intel or AMD).

   B. Hardware Data Execution Protection (DEP) must be enabled.

   C. Hardware-assisted virtualization must be enabled.

   D. The processor must at least have a dual core.

8. What is the command to install Hyper-V on a Windows Server 2016 machine that was installed in Server Core?

   A. `start /w ocsetup Hyper-V`

   B. `start /w ocsetup microsoft-hyper-v`

   C. `start /w ocsetup Microsoft-Hyper-V`

   D. `start /w ocsetup hyper-v`

9. You are the network administrator for your company. You want to deploy the RAS Gateway as an edge VPN server, an edge DirectAccess server, or both simultaneously. The RAS Gateway will provide remote employees with connectivity to your network by using either VPN or DirectAccess connections. What RAS Gateway Mode type will you be setting up?

   A. Multitenant mode

   B. Single tenant mode

   C. Dual tenant mode

   D. Lone tenant mode

10. What statement is correct for an external virtual network?

   A. The virtual machines can communicate with each other and with the host machine.

   B. The virtual machines can communicate with each other only.

   C. The virtual machines can communicate with each other, with the host machine, and with an external network.

   D. The virtual machines cannot communicate with each other.

Chapter

18

Installing Active Directory

THE FOLLOWING 70-742 EXAM OBJECTIVES ARE COVERED IN THIS CHAPTER:

✓ **Install and configure domain controllers**

- This objective may include but is not limited to: Install a new forest; add or remove a domain controller from a domain; upgrade a domain controller; install AD DS on a Server Core installation; install a domain controller from Install from Media (IFM); resolve DNS SRV record registration issues; install and configure a read-only domain controller (RODC); configure domain controller cloning

One of the most important tasks that you will complete on a network is setting up your domain. To set up your domain properly, you must know how to install and configure your domain controllers.

After I show you how to install and configure your domain controller, you'll explore the concept of *domain functional levels*, which essentially determine what sorts of domain controllers you can use in your environment. For instance, in the Windows Server 2008 domain functional level, you can have Windows Server 2008/2008 R2, Windows Server 2012/2012 R2, and Windows Server 2016 domain controllers, but the functionality of the domain is severely limited. Also, you CAN NOT have any domain controllers below the domain function level (no domain controllers below 2008 in this example).

Once you understand how to plan properly for your domain environment, you will learn how to install Active Directory, which you will accomplish by promoting a Windows Server 2016 computer to a domain controller. I will also discuss a feature in Windows Server 2016 called a *read-only domain controller (RODC)*, and I will show you how to install Active Directory using Windows PowerShell.

For these exercises, I assume you are creating a Windows Server 2016 machine in a test environment and not on a live network.

Verifying the File System

When you're planning your Active Directory deployment, the file system that the operating system uses is an important concern for two reasons. First, the file system can provide the ultimate level of security for all the information stored on the server itself. Second, it is responsible for managing and tracking all of this data. The Windows Server 2016 platform supports three file systems:

- File Allocation Table 32 (FAT32)
- Windows NT File System (NTFS)
- Resilient File System (ReFS)

Although ReFS was new to Windows Server 2012, NTFS has been around for many years, and NTFS in Windows Server 2016 has been improved for better performance.

If you have been working with servers for many years, you may have noticed a few changes to the server file system choices. For example, in Windows Server 2003, you could choose between FAT, FAT32, and NTFS. In Windows Server 2016, you could choose between FAT32, NTFS, and ReFS (see Figure 18.1).

FIGURE 18.1   Format options on Windows Server 2016

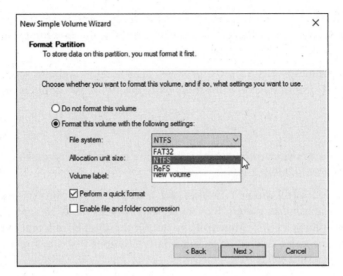

Resilient File System (ReFS)

Windows Server 2016 includes a file system called *Resilient File System (ReFS)*. ReFS was created to help Windows Server maximize the availability of data and online operation. ReFS allows the Windows Server 2016 system to continue to function despite some errors that would normally cause data to be lost or the system to go down. ReFS uses data integrity to protect your data from errors and also to make sure that all of your important data is online when that data is needed.

One of the issues that IT members have had to face over the years is the problem of rapidly growing data sizes. As we continue to rely more and more on computers, our data continues to get larger and larger. This is where ReFS can help an IT department. ReFS was designed specifically with the issues of scalability and performance in mind, which resulted in some of the following ReFS features:

Availability   If your hard disk becomes corrupt, ReFS has the ability to implement a salvage strategy that removes the data that has been corrupted. This feature allows the healthy data to continue to be available while the unhealthy data is removed. All of this can be done without taking the hard disk offline.

Scalability   One of the main advantages of ReFS is the ability to support volume sizes up to 2^{78} bytes using 16 KB cluster sizes, while Windows stack addressing allows 2^{64} bytes. ReFS also supports file sizes of $2^{64}-1$ bytes, 2^{64} files in a directory, and the same number of directories in a volume.

Robust Disk Updating   ReFS uses a disk updating system referred to as an *allocate-on-write transactional model* (also known as *copy on write*). This model helps to avoid many hard disk issues while data is written to the disk because ReFS updates data using disk writes to multiple locations in an atomic manner instead of updating data in place.

Data Integrity   ReFS uses a check-summed system to verify that all data that is being written and stored is accurate and reliable. ReFS always uses allocate-on-write for updates to the data, and it uses checksums to detect disk corruption.

Application Compatibility   ReFS allows for most NTFS features and also supports the Win32 API. Because of this, ReFS is compatible with most Windows applications.

NTFS

Let's start with some of the features of NTFS. There are many benefits to using NTFS, including support for the following:

Disk Quotas   To restrict the amount of disk space used by users on the network, system administrators can establish *disk quotas*. By default, Windows Server 2016 supports disk quota restrictions at the volume level. That is, you can restrict the amount of storage space that a specific user uses on a single disk volume. Third-party solutions that allow more granular quota settings are also available.

File System Encryption   One of the fundamental problems with network operating systems (NOSs) is that system administrators are often given full permission to view all files and data stored on hard disks, which can be a security and privacy concern. In some cases, this is necessary. For example, to perform backup, recovery, and disk management functions, at least one user must have all permissions. Windows Server 2016 and NTFS address these issues by allowing for *file system encryption*. Encryption essentially scrambles all of the data stored within files before they are written to the disk. When an authorized user requests the files, they are transparently decrypted and provided. By using encryption, you can prevent the data from being used in case it is stolen or intercepted by an unauthorized user—even a system administrator.

Dynamic Volumes   Protecting against disk failures is an important concern for production servers. Although earlier versions of Windows NT supported various levels of Redundant Array of Independent Disks (RAID) technology, software-based solutions had some shortcomings. Perhaps the most significant was that administrators needed to perform server reboots to change RAID configurations. Also, you could not make some configuration changes without completely reinstalling the operating system. With Windows Server 2016 support for *dynamic volumes*, system administrators can change RAID and other disk configuration settings without needing to reboot or reinstall the server. The result is greater data protection, increased scalability, and increased uptime. Dynamic volumes are also included with ReFS.

Mounted Drives   By using *mounted drives*, system administrators can map a local disk drive to an NTFS directory name. This helps them organize disk space on servers and increase manageability. By using mounted drives, you can mount the C:\Users directory to an actual physical disk. If that disk becomes full, you can copy all of the files to another, larger drive without changing the directory path name or reconfiguring applications.

Remote Storage   System administrators often notice that as soon as they add more space, they must plan the next upgrade. One way to recover disk space is to move infrequently used files to external hard drives. However, backing up and restoring these files can be quite difficult and time-consuming. System administrators can use the *remote storage* features supported by NTFS to off-load seldom-used data automatically to a backup system or other devices. The files, however, remain available to users. If a user requests an archived file, Windows Server 2016 can automatically restore the file from a remote storage device and make it available. Using remote storage like this frees up system administrators' time and allows them to focus on tasks other than micromanaging disk space.

Self-Healing NTFS   In previous versions of the Windows Server operating system, if you had to fix a corrupted NTFS volume, you used a tool called Chkdsk.exe. The disadvantage of this tool is that the Windows Server's availability was disrupted. If this server was your domain controller, that could stop domain logon authentication.

To help protect the Windows Server 2016 NTFS file system, Microsoft now uses a feature called self-healing NTFS. *Self-healing NTFS* attempts to fix corrupted NTFS file systems without taking them offline. Self-healing NTFS allows an NTFS file system to be corrected without running the Chkdsk.exe utility. New features added to the NTFS kernel code allow disk inconsistencies to be corrected without system downtime.

Security   NTFS allows you to configure not only folder-level security but also file-level security. NTFS security is one of the biggest reasons most companies use NTFS. ReFS also allows folder- and file-level security.

Setting Up the NTFS Partition

Although the features mentioned in the previous section likely compel most system administrators to use NTFS, additional reasons make using it mandatory. The most important reason is that the Active Directory data store must reside on an NTFS partition. Therefore, before you begin installing Active Directory, make sure you have at least one NTFS partition available. Also, be sure you have a reasonable amount of disk space available (at least 4 GB). Because the size of the Active Directory data store will grow as you add objects to it, also be sure that you have adequate space for the future.

Exercise 18.1 shows you how to use the administrative tools to view and modify disk configuration.

Before you make any disk configuration changes, be sure you completely understand their potential effects; then perform the test in a lab environment and make sure you have good, verifiable backups handy. Changing partition sizes and adding and removing partitions can result in a total loss of all information on one or more partitions.

If you want to convert an existing partition from FAT or FAT32 to NTFS, you need to use the CONVERT command-line utility. For example, the following command converts the C: partition from FAT to NTFS:

```
CONVERT c: /fs:ntfs
```

EXERCISE 18.1

Viewing the Disk Configurations

1. Right-click on the Start button and then choose Computer Management.

2. Under Storage, click Disk Management (see Figure 18.2).

FIGURE 18.2 Disk Management

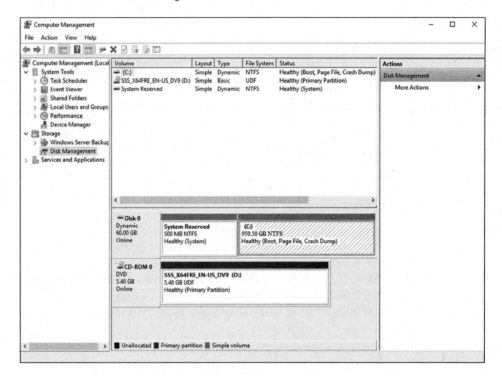

The Disk Management program shows you the logical and physical disks that are currently configured on your system.

3. Use the View menu to choose various depictions of the physical and logical drives in your system.

4. To see the available options for modifying partition settings, right-click any of the disks or partitions. This step is optional.

5. Close Computer Management.

Verifying Network Connectivity

Although a Windows Server 2016 computer can be used by itself without connecting to a network, you will not harness much of the potential of the operating system without network connectivity. Because the fundamental purpose of a network operating system is to provide resources to users, you must verify network connectivity.

Basic Connectivity Tests

Before you begin to install Active Directory, you should perform several checks of your current configuration to ensure that the server is configured properly on the network. You should test the following:

Network Adapter   At least one network adapter should be installed and properly configured on your server. A quick way to verify that a network adapter is properly installed is to use the Computer Management administrative tool. Under Device Manager, Network Adapters branch, you should have at least one network adapter listed. If you do not, use the Add Hardware icon in Control Panel to configure hardware.

TCP/IP   Make sure that TCP/IP is installed, configured, and enabled on any necessary network adapters. The server should also be given a valid IP address and subnet mask. Optionally, you may need to configure a default gateway, DNS servers, WINS servers, and other network settings. If you are using DHCP, be sure that the assigned information is correct. It is always a good idea to use a static IP address for servers because IP address changes can cause network connectivity problems if they are not handled properly.

Internet Access   If the server should have access to the Internet, verify that it is able to connect to external web servers and other machines outside of the local area network (LAN). If the server is unable to connect, you might have a problem with the TCP/IP configuration.

LAN Access   The server should be able to view other servers and workstations on the network. If other machines are not visible, make sure that the network and TCP/IP configurations are correct for your environment.

Client Access   Network client computers should be able to connect to your server and view any shared resources. A simple way to test connectivity is to create a share and test whether other machines are able to see files and folders within it. If clients cannot access the machine, make sure that both the client and the server are configured properly.

Wide Area Network Access   If you're working in a distributed environment, you should ensure that you have access to any remote sites or users who will need to connect to this machine. Usually, this is a simple test that can be performed by a network administrator.

Tools and Techniques for Testing Network Configuration

In some cases, verifying network access can be quite simple. You might have some internal and external network resources with which to test. In other cases, it might be more complicated. You can use several tools and techniques to verify that your network configuration is correct.

The Windows Server 2016 exams will include a lot of PowerShell commands. One easy way to start getting familiar with PowerShell is to use it whenever you need to run a network configuration command. All of the following commands work in PowerShell.

Using the Ipconfig **Utility**   By typing **ipconfig/all** at the command prompt, you can view information about the TCP/IP settings of a computer. Figure 18.3 shows the types of information you'll receive.

FIGURE 18.3   Viewing TCP/IP information with the ipconfig utility

```
Administrator: Windows PowerShell                                    —  □  X
Windows PowerShell
Copyright (C) 2016 Microsoft Corporation. All rights reserved.

PS C:\Users\Administrator> Ipconfig

Windows IP Configuration

Tunnel adapter Local Area Connection* 12:

   Media State . . . . . . . . . . . : Media disconnected
   Connection-specific DNS Suffix  . :

Ethernet adapter Ethernet:

   Connection-specific DNS Suffix  . : localdomain
   Link-local IPv6 Address . . . . . : fe80::4d43:2490:cc9e:83e%3
   IPv4 Address. . . . . . . . . . . : 192.168.140.180
   Subnet Mask . . . . . . . . . . . : 255.255.255.0
   Default Gateway . . . . . . . . . : 192.168.140.2

Tunnel adapter isatap.localdomain:

   Media State . . . . . . . . . . . : Media disconnected
   Connection-specific DNS Suffix  . : localdomain

Tunnel adapter Teredo Tunneling Pseudo-Interface:

   Connection-specific DNS Suffix  . :
   IPv6 Address. . . . . . . . . . . : 2001:0:9d38:953c:c23:180a:3f57:734b
   Link-local IPv6 Address . . . . . : fe80::c23:180a:3f57:734b%9
   Default Gateway . . . . . . . . . : ::
PS C:\Users\Administrator> _
```

Using the Ping **Command**   The ping command was designed to test connectivity to other computers. You can use the command simply by typing **ping** and then an IP address or hostname at the command line. The following are some steps for testing connectivity using the ping command.

Ping Other Computers on the Same Subnet   You should start by pinging a known active IP address on the network to check for a response. If you receive one, then you have connectivity to the network.

Next check to see whether you can ping another machine using its hostname. If this works, then local name resolution works properly.

Ping Computers on Different Subnets   To ensure that routing is set up properly, you should attempt to ping computers that are on other subnets (if any exist) on your network. If this test fails, try pinging the default gateway. Any errors may indicate a problem in the network configuration or a problem with a router.

When You Don't Receive a Response

Some firewalls, routers, or servers on your network or on the Internet might prevent you from receiving a successful response from a ping command. This is usually for security reasons (malicious users might attempt to disrupt network traffic using excessive pings as well as redirects and smurf attacks). If you do not receive a response, do not assume that the service is not available. Instead, try to verify connectivity in other ways. For example, you can use the TRACERT command to demonstrate connectivity beyond your subnet, even if other routers ignore Internet Control Message Protocol (ICMP) responses. Because the display of a second router implies connectivity, the path to an ultimate destination shows success even if it does not display the actual names and addresses.

Using the TraceRT **Command**   The TraceRT command works just like the ping command except that the TraceRT command shows you every hop along the way. So if one router or switch is down, the TraceRT command will show you where the trace stops.

Browsing the Network   To ensure that you have access to other computers on the network, be sure that they can be viewed by clicking Network. This verifies that your name resolution parameters are set up correctly and that other computers are accessible. Also, try connecting to resources (such as file shares or printers) on other machines.

   By default, Network Discovery is turned off. To browse the network, you must first enable Network Discovery from the Control Panel in the Network and Sharing Center ➤ Advanced Sharing settings.

Browsing the Internet You can quickly verify whether your server has access to the Internet by visiting a known website, such as www.microsoft.com. Success ensures that you have access outside of your network. If you do not have access to the web, you might need to verify your proxy server settings (if applicable) and your DNS server settings.

By performing these simple tests, you can ensure that you have a properly configured network connection and that other network resources are available.

Understanding Domain and Forest Functionality

Windows Server 2016 Active Directory uses a concept called *domain and forest functionality*. The functional level that you choose during the Active Directory installation determines which features your domain can use.

About the Domain Functional Level

Windows Server 2016 will support the following domain functional levels:

- Windows Server 2008
- Windows Server 2008 R2
- Windows Server 2012
- Windows Server 2012 R2
- Windows Server 2016

Which function level you use depends on the domain controllers you have installed on your network. This is an important fact to remember. You can use any version of Windows Server as long as those servers are member servers only. You can only use Domain Controllers as low as your function level.

For example, if the Domain Function Level is Windows Server 2012 R2, then all domain controllers must be running Windows Server 2012 R2 or higher. You can have Windows Server 2008 R2 member servers but all of your domain controllers need to be at least 2012 R2.

Windows Server 2016 no longer supports the Windows Server 2003 function levels. With Windows Server 2003 being no longer supported, the Windows Server 2003 function levels have been removed.

Table 18.1 shows the features available in Windows Server 2008, Windows Server 2008 R2, Windows Server 2012, Windows Server 2012 R2, and Windows Server 2016 domain function levels.

TABLE 18.1   Comparing domain functional levels

Domain Functional Feature	Windows Server 2008	Windows Server 2008 R2	Windows Server 2012	Windows Server 2012 R2	Windows Server 2016
Privileged access management	Disabled	Disabled	Disabled	Enabled	Enabled
Authentication assurance	Disabled	Enabled	Enabled	Enabled	Enabled
Fine-grained password policies	Enabled	Enabled	Enabled	Enabled	Enabled
Last interactive logon information	Enabled	Enabled	Enabled	Enabled	Enabled
Advanced Encryption Services (AES 128 and 256) support for the Kerberos protocol	Enabled	Enabled	Enabled	Enabled	Enabled
Distributed File System replication support for Sysvol	Enabled	Enabled	Enabled	Enabled	Enabled
Read-only domain controller (RODC)	Enabled	Enabled	Enabled	Enabled	Enabled
Ability to redirect the Users and Computers containers	Enabled	Enabled	Enabled	Enabled	Enabled
Ability to rename domain controllers	Enabled	Enabled	Enabled	Enabled	Enabled
Logon time stamp updates	Enabled	Enabled	Enabled	Enabled	Enabled
Kerberos KDC key version numbers	Enabled	Enabled	Enabled	Enabled	Enabled
Passwords for InetOrgPerson objects	Enabled	Enabled	Enabled	Enabled	Enabled
Converts NT groups to domain local and global groups	Enabled	Enabled	Enabled	Enabled	Enabled
SID history	Enabled	Enabled	Enabled	Enabled	Enabled
Group nesting	Enabled	Enabled	Enabled	Enabled	Enabled
Universal groups	Enabled	Enabled	Enabled	Enabled	Enabled

About Forest Functionality

Windows Server 2016 forest functionality applies to all of the domains in a forest. All domains have to be upgraded to Windows Server 2016 before the forest can be upgraded to Windows Server 2016.

There are five levels of forest functionality:

- Windows Server 2008
- Windows Server 2008 R2
- Windows Server 2012
- Windows Server 2012 R2
- Windows Server 2016

Windows Server 2008, Windows Server 2008 R2, Windows Server 2012, Windows Server 2012 R2, and Windows Server 2016 have many of the same forest features. Some of these features are described in the following list:

Global Catalog Replication Enhancements   When an administrator adds a new attribute to the global catalog, only those changes are replicated to other global catalogs in the forest. This can significantly reduce the amount of network traffic generated by replication.

Defunct Schema Classes and Attributes   You can never permanently remove classes and attributes from the Active Directory schema. However, you can mark them as defunct so that they cannot be used. With Windows Server 2003, Windows Server 2008/2008 R2, Windows Server 2012/2012 R2, and Windows Server 2016 forest functionality, you can redefine the defunct schema attribute so that it occupies a new role in the schema.

Forest Trusts   Previously, system administrators had no easy way of granting permission on resources in different forests. Windows Server 2003, Windows Server 2008/2008 R2, Windows Server 2012/2012 R2, and Windows Server 2016 resolve some of these difficulties by allowing trust relationships between separate Active Directory forests. Forest trusts act much like domain trusts, except that they extend to every domain in two forests. Note that all forest trusts are intransitive.

Linked Value Replication   Windows Server 2003, Windows Server 2008/2008 R2, Windows Server 2012/2012 R2, and Windows Server 2016 use a concept called *linked value replication*. With linked value replication, only the user record that has been changed is replicated (not the entire group). This can significantly reduce network traffic associated with replication.

Renaming Domains   Although the Active Directory domain structure was originally designed to be flexible, there were several limitations. Because of mergers, acquisitions, corporate reorganizations, and other business changes, you may need to rename domains. In Windows Server 2003, Windows Server 2008/2008 R2, Windows Server 2012/2012 R2, and Windows Server 2016 you can change the DNS and NetBIOS names for any domain. Note that this operation is not as simple as just issuing a rename command. Instead, there's a specific process that you must follow to make sure the operation is successful. Fortunately, when you properly follow the procedure, Microsoft supports domain renaming even though not all applications support it.

Other Features   Windows Server 2008/2008 R2, Windows Server 2012/2012 R2, and Windows Server 2016 also support the following features:

- Improved replication algorithms and dynamic auxiliary classes are designed to increase performance, scalability, and reliability.

- *Active Directory Federation Services (AD FS)*, also known as *Trustbridge*, handles federated identity management. *Federated identity management* is a standards-based information technology process that enables distributed identification, authentication, and authorization across organizational and platform boundaries. The ADFS solution in Windows Server 2008, Windows Server 2008 R2, Windows Server 2012, Windows Server 2012 R2, and Windows Server 2016 helps administrators address these challenges by enabling organizations to share a user's identity information securely.

- *Active Directory Lightweight Directory Services (AD LDS)* was developed for organizations that require flexible support for directory-enabled applications. AD LDS, which uses the Lightweight Directory Access Protocol (LDAP), is a directory service that adds flexibility and helps organizations avoid increased infrastructure costs.

- Active Directory Recycle Bin (Windows Server 2008 R2 Forest level or higher) provides administrators with the ability to restore deleted objects in their entirety while AD DS is running. Before this, if you deleted an Active Directory object, you needed to recover it from a backup. Now you can recover the object from the AD recycle bin.

 Many of the concepts related to domain and forest functional features are covered in greater detail later in this book.

Planning the Domain Structure

Once you have verified the technical configuration of your server for Active Directory, it's time to verify the Active Directory configuration for your organization. Since the content of this chapter focuses on installing the first domain in your environment, you really need to know only the following information prior to beginning setup:

- The DNS name of the domain

- The computer name or the NetBIOS name of the server (which will be used by previous versions of Windows to access server resources)

- In which domain function level the domain will operate

- Whether other DNS servers are available on the network
- What type of and how many DNS servers are available on the network

 DNS is a requirement of Active Directory. You can install DNS during the Active Directory installation. For more information about DNS, please read *MCSA Windows Server 2016 Study Guide: Exam 70-742, 2nd Edition* (Sybex, 2017), or Chapter 11 in the *MCSA Windows Server 2016 Complete Study Guide: Exam 70-740, Exam 70-741, Exam 70-742, and Exam 70-743, 2nd Edition,* by William Panek (Sybex, 2017).

However, if you will be installing additional domain controllers in your environment or will be attaching to an existing Active Directory structure, you should also have the following information:

- If this domain controller will join an existing domain, you should know the name of that domain. You will also either require a password for a member of the Enterprise Administrators group for that domain or have someone with those permissions create a domain account before promotion.

- You should know whether the new domain will join an existing tree and, if so, the name of the tree it will join.

- You should know the name of a forest to which this domain will connect (if applicable).

Installing Active Directory

Installing Active Directory is an easy and straightforward process as long as you plan adequately and make the necessary decisions beforehand. There are many ways that you can install Active Directory. You can install Active Directory by using the Windows Server 2016 installation disk (Install from Media (IFM)), using Server Manager, or using Windows PowerShell. But before you can do the actual installation, you must first make sure that your network is ready for the install.

In the following sections, you'll look at the benefits and required steps to install the first domain controller in a given environment.

New to Active Directory

As with any new version of Windows Server, Microsoft has made some improvements to Active Directory. The following changes have been made to Windows Server 2016 Active Directory:

Privileged Access Management   Privileged access management (PAM) allows you to alleviate security concerns about the Active Directory environment. Some of these security issues include credential theft techniques (pass-the-hash & spear phishing) along with other types of similar attacks. PAM allows an administrator to create new access solutions that can be configured by using Microsoft Identity Manager (MIM).

Azure AD Join   Azure Active Directory Join allows you to setup an Office 365 based Azure network and then easily join your end-users systems to that domain.

Microsoft Passport   Microsoft Passport allows your users to setup a key-based authentication that allows your users to authenticate by using more than just their password (biometrics or PIN numbers). Your users would then log on to their systems using a biometric or PIN number that is linked to a certificate or an asymmetrical key pair.

Read-Only Domain Controllers

Windows Server 2016 supports another type of domain controller called the *read-only domain controller (RODC)*. This is a full copy of the Active Directory database without the ability to write to Active Directory. The RODC gives an organization the ability to install a domain controller in a location (onsite or offsite) where security is a concern.

RODCs need to get their Active Directory database from another domain controller. If there are no domain controllers setup yet for a domain, RODCs will not be available (the option will be greyed out). Implementing an RODC is the same as adding another domain controller to a domain. The installation is exactly the same except that when you get to the screen to choose Domain Controller options, you check the box for RODC. Again, this is ONLY available if there are other domain controllers already in the domain.

Adprep

When you are adding a new user to Active Directory, you fill in fields such as First Name, Last Name, and so on. These fields are called *attributes*. The problem is that when you go to install Windows Server 2016, its version of Active Directory has newer attributes than the previous versions of Active Directory. Thus, you need to set up your current version of Active Directory so that it can accept the installation of Windows Server 2016 Active Directory. This is why you use Adprep. Adprep is required to run in order to add the first Windows Server 2016 domain controller to an existing domain or forest.

You would need to run Adprep /forestprep to add the first Windows Server 2016 domain controller to an existing forest. Adprep /forestprep must be run by an administrator who is a member of the Enterprise Admins group, the Schema Admins group, and the Domain Admins group of the domain that hosts the schema master.

You would need to run Adprep /domainprep to add the first Windows Server 2016 domain controller to an existing domain. Again, to achieve this command, you must be a member of the Domain Admins group of the domain where you are installing the Windows Server 2016 domain controller.

Adprep /rodcprep must be run to add the first Windows Server 2016 RODC to an existing forest. The administrator who runs this command must be a member of the Enterprise Admins group.

One feature that is new to the Windows Server 2016 Active Directory installation process is that, if needed, Adprep will automatically be executed during the normal Active Directory Domain Services installation.

Active Directory Prerequisites

Before you install Active Directory into your network, you must first make sure that your network and the server meet some minimum requirements. Table 18.2 will show you the requirements needed for Active Directory.

TABLE 18.2   Active Directory requirements

Requirement	Description
Adprep	When adding the first Windows Server 2016 domain controller to an existing Active Directory domain, Adprep commands run automatically as needed.
Credentials	When installing a new AD DS forest, the administrator must be set to local Administrator on the first server. To install an additional domain controller in an existing domain, you need to be a member of the Domain Admins group.
DNS	Domain Name System needs to be installed for Active Directory to function properly. You can install DNS during the Active Directory installation.
NTFS	The Windows Server 2016 drives that store the database, log files, and SYSVOL folder must be placed on a volume that is formatted with the NTFS file system.
RODCs	Read Only Domain Controllers can be installed as long as another domain controller (Windows Server 2008 or newer) already exists on the domain. Also the Forest functional level must be at least Windows Server 2003.
TCP/IP	You must configure the appropriate TCP/IP settings on your domain, and you must configure the DNS server addresses.

The Installation Process

Windows Server 2016 computers are configured as either member servers (if they are joined to a domain) or standalone servers (if they are part of a workgroup). The process of converting a server to a domain controller is known as *promotion*. Through the use of a simple and intuitive wizard in Server Manager, system administrators can quickly configure servers to be domain controllers after installation. Administrators also have the ability to promote domain controllers using Windows PowerShell.

The first step in installing Active Directory is promoting a Windows Server 2016 computer to a domain controller. The first domain controller in an environment serves as the starting point for the forest, trees, domains, and the operations master roles.

Exercise 18.2 shows the steps you need to follow to promote an existing Windows Server 2016 computer to a domain controller. To complete the steps in this exercise, you must have already installed and configured a Windows Server 2016 computer. You also need a DNS server that supports SRV records. If you do not have a DNS server available, the Active Directory Installation Wizard automatically configures one for you.

EXERCISE 18.2

Promoting a Domain Controller

1. Install the Active Directory Domain Services by clicking the Add Roles And Features link in Server Manager's Dashboard view.

2. At the Before You Begin screen, click Next.

3. The Select Installation Type screen will be next. Make sure that the Role-Based radio button is selected and click Next.

4. At the Select Destination Server screen, choose the local machine. Click Next.

5. At the Select Server Roles screen, click the check box for Active Directory Domain Services.

6. After you check the Active Directory Domain Services box, a pop-up menu will appear asking you to install additional features. Click the Add Features button.

7. Click Next.

8. At the Select Features screen, accept the defaults and click Next.

9. Click Next at the information screen.

10. Click the Install button at the Confirmation Installation screen.

11. The Installation Progress screen will show you how the installation is progressing.

12. After the installation is complete, click the Close button.

13. On the left side window, click the AD DS link.

14. Click the More link next to Configuration Required for Active Directory Domain Services.

15. Under the Post-Deployment Configuration section, click the Promote This Server To A Domain Controller link.

16. At this point, you will configure this domain controller. You are going to install a new domain controller in a new domain in a new forest. At the Deployment Configuration screen, choose the Add A New Forest radio button. You then need to add a root domain name. In this exercise, I will use StormWindAD.com (see Figure 18.4). Click Next.

FIGURE 18.4 New Forest screen

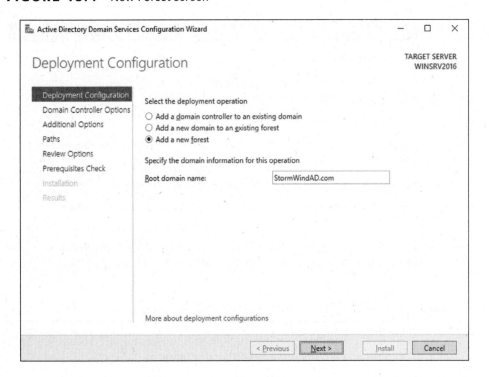

17. At the Domain Controller Options screen, set the following options (see Figure 18.5):

- Function levels: Windows Server 2012 R2 (for both)

- Verify that the DNS and Global Catalog check boxes are checked. Notice that the RODC check box is greyed out. This is because RODCs need to get their Active Directory database from another domain controller. Since this is the first domain controller in the forest, RODCs are not possible. If you need an RODC, complete the previous steps on a member server in a domain where domain controllers already exist.

- Password: **P@ssw0rd**

Then click Next.

FIGURE 18.5   Domain Controller Options

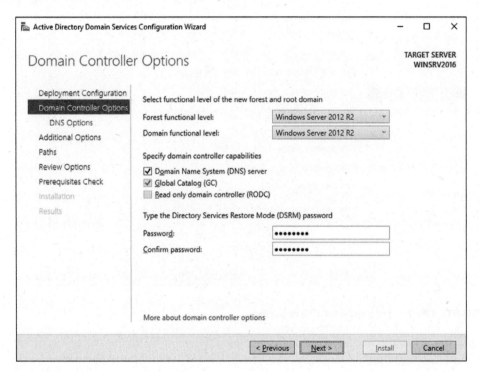

18. At the DNS screen, click Next.

19. At the additional options screen, accept the default NetBIOS domain name and click Next.

20. At the Paths screen, accept the default file locations and click Next.

21. At the Review Options screen (see Figure 18.6), verify your settings and click Next. At this screen, there is a View Script button. This button allows you to grab a PowerShell script based on the features you have just set up.

22. At the Prerequisites Check screen, click the Install button (as long as there are no errors). Warnings are OK just as long as there are no errors (see Figure 18.7).

FIGURE 18.6 Review Options screen

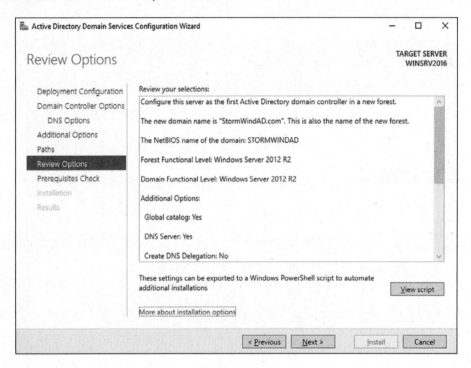

FIGURE 18.7 Prerequisites Check screen

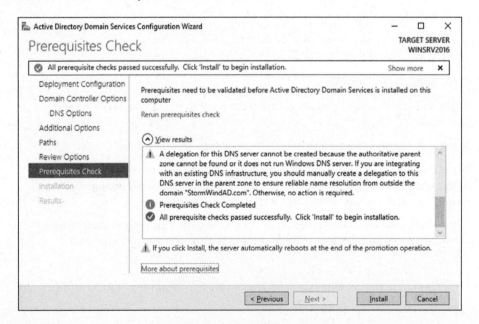

23. After the installation completes, the machine will automatically reboot. Log in as the administrator.

24. Close Server Manager.

25. Click the Start button on the keyboard and choose Administrative Tools.

26. You should see new MMC snap-ins for Active Directory.

27. Close the Administrative Tools window.

In Exercise 18.3, you will learn how to install Active Directory on a Server Core installation. You will use Windows Server 2016 Datacenter Server Core. Before actually installing AD DS, you will learn how to configure the computer name, the time, the administrator password, and a static TCP/IP address, and then you will install DNS.

Exercise 18.3 will have you install Active Directory onto a Datacenter Server Core server using Microsoft PowerShell. If you need to install Active Directory onto any Windows Server 2016 server using PowerShell, it's the same steps in this exercise.

EXERCISE 18.3

Installing AD DS on Server Core Using PowerShell

1. At the Server Core command prompt, type **cd\windows\system32** and press Enter.

2. Type **timedate.cpl** and set your date, local time zone, and time. Click OK.

3. Type **Netsh** and press Enter.

4. Type **Interface**, and press Enter.

5. Type **IPv4,** and press Enter.

6. Type **Show IP** and press Enter. This will show you the current TCP/IP address and the interface with which the TCP/IP address is associated.

7. As you can see, interface 12 is my Ethernet interface. To change this interface, type the following command and press Enter:

   ```
   Set address name="12" source=static address=192.168.0.165
   mask=255.255.255.0 gateway=192.168.0.1
   ```

   I used 192.168.0.x for my address. You can replace the address, mask, and gateway based on your local settings.

8. Type **Show IP** and press Enter. You should see that the new address is now manual and set to the IP address you set.

9. Type **Exit** and press Enter.

10. Type **Net User Administrator** * and press Enter.

EXERCISE 18.3 *(continued)*

11. Type in your password and then confirm the password. I used P@ssw0rd for my password.

12. Type the following command and press Enter:

    ```
    Netdom renamecomputer %computername% /newname:ServerA
    ```

13. Type **Y** and press Enter.

14. Type **Shutdown /R /T 0** and press Enter. This will reboot the machine. After the reboot, log back into the system.

15. Type **PowerShell** and press Enter.

16. At the PowerShell prompt, type **Add-WindowsFeature DNS** and press Enter. This will add DNS to the server.

17. At the PowerShell prompt, type **Add-WindowsFeature AD-Domain-Services** and press Enter.

18. At the PowerShell prompt, type **Import-Module ADDSDeployment**.

19. At the PowerShell prompt, type **Install-ADDSForest**.

20. Type in your domain name and press Enter. I used Sybex.com.

21. Next you will be asked for your Safe mode administrator password. Type in **P@ssw0rd** and then confirm it.

22. Type **Y** and press Enter.

Active Directory will install, and the machine will automatically reboot.

Now that we have installed Active Directory onto two different types of systems, let's take a look at how to install an RODC. In Exercise 18.4 I will show you how to add a RODC to a domain. To do this exercise, you need another domain controller in the domain.

EXERCISE 18.4

Creating an RODC Server

1. Install the Active Directory Domain Services by clicking the Add Roles And Features link in Server Manager's Dashboard view.

2. At the Before You Begin screen, click Next.

3. The Select Installation Type screen will be next. Make sure that the Role-Based radio button is selected and click Next.

4. At the Select Destination Server screen, choose the local machine. Click Next.

5. At the Select Server Roles screen, click the check box for Active Directory Domain Services.

6. After you check the Active Directory Domain Services box, a pop-up menu will appear asking you to install additional features. Click the Add Features button.

7. Click Next.

8. At the Select Features screen, accept the defaults and click Next.

9. Click Next at the information screen.

10. Click the Install button at the Confirmation Installation screen.

11. The Installation Progress screen will show you how the installation is progressing.

12. After the installation is complete, click the Close button.

13. On the left side window, click the AD DS link.

14. Click the More link next to Configuration Required for Active Directory Domain Services.

15. Under the Post-Deployment Configuration section, click the Promote This Server To A Domain Controller link.

16. At this point, you will configure this domain controller. You are going to install a new domain controller in an existing domain. At the Deployment Configuration screen, choose the Add A Domain Controller to an existing Domain. You then need to add the name of another domain controller in that domain.

17. At the Domain Controller Options screen, set the following options:

- Verify that the RODC check box is checked.

- Password: **P@ssw0rd**

    Then click Next.

18. At the Paths screen, accept the default file locations and click Next.

19. At the Review Options screen, verify your settings and click Next. At this screen, there is a View Script button. This button allows you to grab a PowerShell script based on the features you have just set up.

20. At the Prerequisites Check screen, click the Install button (as long as there are no errors). Warnings are OK just as long as there are no errors.

21. After the installation completes, the machine will automatically reboot. Log in as the administrator.

22. Close Server Manager.

Deploying Active Directory in Windows Azure

Well, before I jump into this topic, I must first explain what I am talking about. Windows Azure is a Microsoft cloud platform that allows you to put your server data into the cloud. Deploying Active Directory with Infrastructure as a Service (IaaS) means you are using virtualization for the deployment.

So, to put this in a nutshell, this type of install is actually not too far off from the install you already did. You create a virtual server and then install Active Directory. Then you upload that virtual server to the cloud.

Now that you understand what this section is about, let's talk about some of the tasks that are different from the normal way you install Active Directory virtually. There are three main differences when installing Active Directory IaaS on Windows Azure.

Windows Azure virtual machines may need to have connectivity to the corporate network. Microsoft states that you don't have to have connectivity to your onsite corporate network, but you will lose functionality. Thus, Microsoft recommends that you set up connectivity, and to do that, you must use Windows Azure Virtual Network. Windows Azure Virtual Network includes a site-to-site or site-to-point virtual private network (VPN) component capable of seamlessly connecting Windows Azure virtual machines and onsite machines.

Static IP addresses are *not* supported on Windows Azure virtual machines.   Normally, when setting up a server, we all use static IP addresses. This is actually required on a DHCP server, DNS server, and so on. But when you deploy Active Directory IaaS in Windows Azure, you must use Dynamic TCP/IP addressing, and this requires that you set up Windows Azure Virtual Network.

IP addresses for Windows Azure virtual machines are attached to Windows Azure Virtual Network, and that TCP/IP address persists for the lifetime of the virtual machine. Because of this, the Windows Server Active Directory requirements for IP addressing are met, and the requirements for DNS are also met if you want the server to have both roles.

Windows Azure allows for two distinct disk types for virtual machines.   The selection of the virtual machine disk type is important when deploying domain controllers. Windows Azure allows both "operating system disks" and "data disks." Most of the time you will use data disks when installing Active Directory on the virtual machine. Data disks use write-through caching, guaranteeing durability of writes, and this is important to the integrity of any Windows Server active machine. There are some other factors of which you should be aware when choosing your disk type. Please check Microsoft's website for more details when choosing a disk type.

Installing Additional Domain Controllers by Using Install from Media

There may be times when you need to install additional domain controllers without having a lot of additional replication traffic. When you can install a domain controller without the need of additional replication traffic, the installation is much quicker. This is the perfect time to install an additional domain controller by using the Install from Media (IFM) method.

Windows Server 2016 allows you to install a domain controller using the IFM method by using the `Ntdsutil` utility. The `Ntdsutil` utility allows you to create installation media for an additional domain controller in a domain. One issue that you must remember is that any objects that were created, modified, or deleted since the IFM was created must be replicated. By creating the IFM as close (time wise) as the installation of the domain controller guarantees that all objects will be created at the time the domain controller is installed.

One other way that you can also create the IFM is by restoring a backup of a similar domain controller in the same domain to another location.

Verifying Active Directory Installation

Once you have installed and configured Active Directory, you'll want to verify that you have done so properly. In the following sections, you'll look at methods for doing this.

Using Event Viewer

The first (and perhaps most informative) way to verify the operations of Active Directory is to query information stored in the Windows Server 2016 event log. You can do this using the Windows Server 2016 Event Viewer. Exercise 18.5 walks you through this procedure. Entries seen with the Event Viewer include errors, warnings, and informational messages.

> To complete the steps in Exercise 18.5, you must have configured the local machine as a domain controller.

EXERCISE 18.5

Viewing the Active Directory Event Log

1. Open Administrative tools by pressing the Windows key and choosing Administrative Tools.

2. Open the Event Viewer snap-in from the Administrative Tools program group.

3. In the left pane, under Applications And Services Logs, select Directory Service.

4. In the right pane, you can sort information by clicking column headings. For example, you can click the Source column to sort by the service or process that reported the event.

5. Double-click an event in the list to see the details for that item. Note that you can click the Copy button to copy the event information to the Clipboard. You can then paste the data into a document for later reference. Also, you can move between items using the up and down arrows. Click OK when you have finished viewing an event.

EXERCISE 18.5 *(continued)*

6. Filter an event list by right-clicking the Directory Service item in the left pane and selecting Filter Current Log. Note that filtering does not remove entries from the event logs—it only restricts their display.

7. To verify Active Directory installation, look for events related to the proper startup of Active Directory, such as Event ID 1000 (Active Directory Startup Complete) and 1394 (Attempts To Update The Active Directory Database Are Succeeding). Also, be sure to examine any error or warning messages because they could indicate problems with DNS or other necessary services.

8. When you've finished viewing information in the Event Viewer, close the application.

Gaining Insight Through Event Viewer

Despite its simple user interface and somewhat limited GUI functionality, the Event Viewer tool can be your best ally in isolating and troubleshooting problems with Windows Server 2016. The Event Viewer allows you to view information that is stored in various log files that are maintained by the operating system. This includes information from the following logs:

Application Stores messages generated by programs running on your system. For example, SQL Server 2012 might report the completion of a database backup job within the Application log.

Security Contains security-related information as defined by your auditing settings. For example, you could see when users have logged onto the system or when particularly sensitive files have been accessed.

System Contains operating system-related information and messages. Common messages might include a service startup failure or information about when the operating system was last rebooted.

Directory Service Stores messages and events related to how Active Directory functions. For example, you might find details related to replication here.

DNS Server Contains details about the operations of the DNS service. This log is useful for troubleshooting replication or name-resolution problems.

Other Log Files Contain various features of Windows Server 2016 and the applications that may run on this operating system, which can create additional types of logs. These files allow you to view more information about other applications or services through the familiar Event Viewer tool.

Additionally, developers can easily send custom information from their programs to the Application log. Having all of this information in one place really makes it easy to analyze operating system and application messages. Also, many third-party tools and utilities are available for analyzing log files.

Although the Event Viewer GUI does a reasonably good job of letting you find the information you need, you might want to extract information to analyze other systems or applications. One especially useful feature of the Event Viewer is its ability to save a log file in various formats. You can access this feature by clicking Action ➤ Save As. You'll be given the option of saving in various formats, including tab- and comma-delimited text files. You can then open these files in other applications (such as Microsoft Excel) for additional data analysis.

Overall, in the real world, the Event Viewer can be an excellent resource for monitoring and troubleshooting your important servers and workstations.

In addition to providing information about the status of events related to Active Directory, the Event Viewer shows you useful information about other system services and applications. You should routinely use this tool.

Using Active Directory Administrative Tools

After a server has been promoted to a domain controller, you will see that various tools are added to the Administrative Tools program group, including the following:

Active Directory Administrative Center   This is a *Microsoft Management Console (MMC)* snap-in that allows you to accomplish many Active Directory tasks from one central location. This MMC snap-in allows you to manage your directory services objects, including doing the following tasks:

- Reset user passwords
- Create or manage user accounts
- Create or manage groups
- Create or manage computer accounts
- Create or manage organizational units (OUs) and containers
- Connect to one or several domains or domain controllers in the same instance of Active Directory Administrative Center
- Filter Active Directory data

Active Directory Domains and Trusts   Use this tool to view and change information related to the various domains in an Active Directory environment. This MMC snap-in also allows you to set up shortcut trusts.

Active Directory Sites and Services   Use this tool to create and manage Active Directory sites and services to map to an organization's physical network infrastructure.

Active Directory Users and Computers   User and computer management is fundamental for an Active Directory environment. The Active Directory Users and Computers tool allows you to set machine- and user-specific settings across the domain. This tool is discussed throughout this book.

Active Directory Module for Windows PowerShell   *Windows PowerShell* is a command-line shell and scripting language. The Active Directory Module for Windows PowerShell is a group of cmdlets used to manage your Active Directory domains, Active Directory Lightweight Directory Services (AD LDS) configuration sets, and Active Directory Database Mounting Tool instances in a single, self-contained package. The Active Directory Module for Windows PowerShell is a normal PowerShell window. The only difference is that the Active Directory PowerShell module is pre-loaded when you choose the Active Directory Module for Windows PowerShell.

A good way to make sure that Active Directory is accessible and functioning properly is to run the Active Directory Users and Computers tool. When you open the tool, you should see a configuration similar to that shown in Figure 18.8. Specifically, you should make sure the name of the domain you created appears in the list. You should also click the Domain Controllers folder and make sure that the name of your local server appears in the right pane. If your configuration passes these two checks, Active Directory is present and configured.

FIGURE 18.8   Viewing Active Directory information using the Active Directory Users and Computers tool

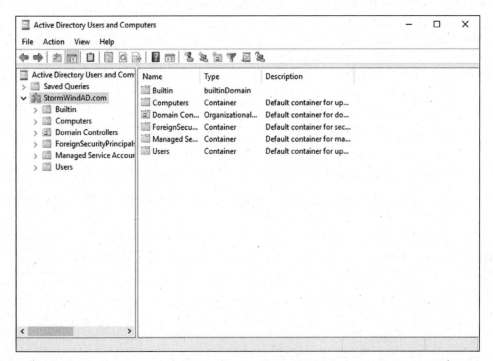

Testing from Clients

The best test of any solution is simply to verify that it works the way you had intended in your environment. When it comes to using Active Directory, a good test is to ensure that clients can view and access the various resources presented by Windows Server 2016 domain controllers. In the following sections, you'll look at several ways to verify that Active Directory is functioning properly.

Verifying Client Connectivity

If you are unable to see the recently promoted server on the network, there is likely a network configuration error. If only one or a few clients are unable to see the machine, the problem is probably related to client-side configuration. To fix this, make sure that the client computers have the appropriate TCP/IP configuration (including DNS server settings) and that they can see other computers on the network.

If the new domain controller is unavailable from any of the other client computers, you should verify the proper startup of Active Directory using the methods mentioned earlier in this chapter. If Active Directory has been started, ensure that the DNS settings are correct. Finally, test network connectivity between the server and the clients by accessing the network or by using the ping command.

Joining a Domain

If Active Directory has been properly configured, clients and other servers should be able to join the domain. Exercise 18.6 outlines the steps you need to take to join a Windows 7, Windows 8/8.1, or Windows 10 computer to the domain.

To complete this exercise, you must have already installed and properly configured at least one Active Directory domain controller and a DNS server that supports SRV records in your environment. In addition to the domain controller, you need at least one other computer, not configured as a domain controller, running one of the following operating systems: Windows 7, Windows 8, Windows 8.1, Windows 10, Windows Server 2008, Windows Server 2008 R2, Windows Server 2012, Windows Server 2012 R2, or Windows Server 2016.

Once clients are able to join the domain successfully, they should be able to view Active Directory resources using the Network icon. This test validates the proper functioning of Active Directory and ensures that you have connectivity with client computers.

 Exercise 18.6 is being done from a Windows 10 Enterprise computer.

EXERCISE 18.6

Joining a Computer to an Active Directory Domain

1. Right-click on the Start menu and choose System.

2. Go to the section called Computer Name. On the right side, click the Change Settings link.

3. Next to the section To Rename This Computer Or Change Its Domain Or Workgroup, click the Change button.

4. In the Member Of section, choose the Domain option. Type the name of the Active Directory domain that this computer should join. Click OK.

5. When prompted for the username and password of an account that has permission to join computers to the domain, enter the information for an administrator of the domain. Click OK to commit the changes. If you successfully joined the domain, you will see a dialog box welcoming you to the new domain.

6. You will be notified that you must reboot the computer before the changes take place. Select Yes when prompted to reboot.

Creating and Configuring Application Data Partitions

Organizations store many different kinds of information in various places. For the IT departments that support this information, it can be difficult to ensure that the right information is available when and where it is needed. Windows Server 2016 uses a feature called *application data partitions*, which allows system administrators and application developers to store custom information within Active Directory. The idea behind application data partitions is that since you already have a directory service that can replicate all kinds of information, you might as well use it to keep track of your own information.

Developing distributed applications that can, for example, synchronize information across an enterprise is not a trivial task. You have to come up with a way to transfer data between remote sites (some of which are located across the world), and you have to ensure that the data is properly replicated. By storing application information in Active Directory, you can take advantage of its storage mechanism and replication topology. Application-related information stored on domain controllers benefits from having fault-tolerance features and availability.

Consider the following simple example to understand how this can work. Suppose your organization has developed a customer Sales Tracking and Inventory application. The company needs to make the information that is stored by this application available to all of its branch offices and users located throughout the world. However, the goal is to do this with the least amount of IT administrative effort. Assuming that Active Directory has already been deployed throughout the organization, developers can build support into the application for storing data within Active Directory. They can then rely on Active Directory to store and synchronize the information among various sites. When users request updated data from the application, the application can obtain this information from the nearest domain controller that hosts a replica of the Sales Tracking and Inventory data.

Other types of applications can also benefit greatly from the use of application data partitions. Now that you have a good understanding of the nature of application data partitions, let's take a look at how you can create and manage them using Windows Server 2016 and Active Directory.

Creating Application Data Partitions

By default, after you create an Active Directory environment, you will not have any customer application data partitions. Therefore, the first step in making this functionality available is to create a new application data partition. You can use several tools to do this:

Third-Party Applications or Application-Specific Tools   Generally, if you are planning to install an application that can store information in the Active Directory database, you'll receive some method of administering and configuring that data along with the application. For example, the setup process for the application might assist you in the steps you need to take to set up a new application data partition and to create the necessary structures for storing data.

 Creating and managing application data partitions are advanced Active Directory–related functions. Be sure that you have a solid understanding of the Active Directory schema, Active Directory replication, LDAP, and your applications' needs before you attempt to create new application data partitions in a live environment.

Active Directory Service Interfaces   ADSI is a set of programmable objects that can be accessed through languages such as Visual Basic Scripting Edition (VBScript), Visual C#, Visual Basic .NET, and many other language technologies that support the Component Object Model (COM) standard. Through the use of ADSI, developers can create, access, and update data stored in Active Directory and in any application data partitions.

The LDP Tool   You can view and modify the contents of the Active Directory schema using LDAP-based queries. The LDP tool allows you to view information about application data partitions.

Ldp.exe is a graphical user interface (GUI) tool that allows an administrator to configure Lightweight Directory Access Protocol (LDAP) directory service. Administrators have the ability to use the LDP tool to administer an Active Directory Lightweight Directory Services (AD LDS) instance. To use the LDP tool, you must be an administrator or equivalent.

Ntdsutil   The ntdsutil utility is the main method by which system administrators create and manage application data partitions on their Windows Server 2016 domain controllers. This utility's specific commands are covered later in this chapter.

Creating and managing application data partitions can be fairly complex. Such a project's success depends on the quality of the architecture design. This is a good example of where IT staff and application developers must cooperate to ensure that data is stored effectively and that it is replicated efficiently.

You can create an application data partition in one of three different locations within an Active Directory forest:

- As a new tree in an Active Directory forest

- As a child of an Active Directory domain partition

  For example, you can create an Accounting application data partition within the Finance.MyCompany.com domain.

- As a child of another application data partition

  This method allows you to create a hierarchy of application data partitions.

As you might expect, you must be a member of the Enterprise Admins or Domain Admins group to be able to create application data partitions. Alternatively, you can be delegated the appropriate permissions to create new partitions.

Now that you have a good idea of the basic ways in which you can create application data partitions, let's look at how replicas (copies of application data partition information) are handled.

Managing Replicas

A *replica* is a copy of any data stored within Active Directory. Unlike the basic information that is stored in Active Directory, application partitions cannot contain security principals. Also, not all domain controllers automatically contain copies of the data stored in an application data partition. System administrators can define which domain controllers host copies of the application data. This is an important feature because, if replicas are used effectively, administrators can find a good balance between replication traffic and data consistency. For example, suppose that three of your organization's 30 locations require up-to-date accounting-related information. You might choose to replicate the data only to domain controllers located in the places that require the data. Limiting replication of this data reduces network traffic.

Replication is the process by which replicas are kept up-to-date. Application data can be stored and updated on designated servers in the same way basic Active Directory information (such as users and groups) is synchronized between domain controllers. Application data partition replicas are managed using the *Knowledge Consistency Checker (KCC)*, which ensures that the designated domain controllers receive updated replica information. Additionally, the KCC uses all Active Directory sites and connection objects that you create to determine the best method to handle replication.

Removing Replicas

When you perform a *demotion* on a domain controller, that server can no longer host an application data partition. If a domain controller contains a replica of application data partition information, you must remove the replica from the domain controller before you demote it. If a domain controller is the machine that hosts a replica of the application data partition, then the entire application data partition is removed and will be permanently lost. Generally, you want to do this only after you're absolutely sure that your organization no longer needs access to the data stored in the application data partition.

Using *ntdsutil* to Manage Application Data Partitions

The primary method by which system administrators create and manage application data partitions is through the ntdsutil command-line tool. You can launch this tool simply by entering **ntdsutil** at a command prompt. The ntdsutil command is both interactive and context sensitive. That is, once you launch the utility, you'll see an ntdsutil command prompt. At this prompt, you can enter various commands that set your context within the application. For example, if you enter the domain management command, you'll be able to use domain-related commands. Several operations also require you to connect to a domain, a domain controller, or an Active Directory object before you perform a command.

> For complete details on using ntdsutil, see the Windows Server 2016 Help and Support Center.

Table 18.3 describes the domain management commands supported by the ntdsutil tool. You can access this information by typing in the following sequence of commands at a command prompt:

```
ntdsutil
domain management
Help
```

TABLE 18.3   ntdsutil domain management commands

ntdsutil Domain Management Command	Purpose
Help or ?	Displays information about the commands that are available within the Domain Management menu of the ntdsutil command.
Connection or Connections	Allows you to connect to a specific domain controller. This will set the context for further operations that are performed on specific domain controllers.

TABLE 18.3 ntdsutil domain management commands *(continued)*

ntdsutil Domain Management Command	Purpose
Create NC *PartitionDistinguishedNameDNSName*	Creates a new application directory partition.
Delete NC *PartitionDistinguishedName*	Removes an application data partition.
List NC Information *PartitionDistinguishedName*	Shows information about the specified application data partition.
List NC Replicas *PartitionDistinguishedName*	Returns information about all replicas for the specific application data partition.
Precreate *PartitionDistinguishedNameServerDNSName*	Pre-creates cross-reference application data partition objects. This allows the specified DNS server to host a copy of the application data partition.
Remove NC Replica *PartitionDistinguishedNameDCDNSName*	Removes a replica from the specified domain controller.
Select Operation Target	Selects the naming context that will be used for other operations.
Set NC Reference Domain *PartitionDistinguishedName* *DomainDistinguishedName*	Specifies the reference domain for an application data partition.
Set NC Replicate NotificationDelay *PartitionDistinguishedName* *FirstDCNotificationDelay* *OtherDCNotificationDelay*	Defines settings for how often replication will occur for the specified application data partition.

The ntdsutil commands are all case insensitive. Mixed case was used in the table to make them easier to read. NC in commands stands for "naming context," referring to the fact that this is a partition of the Active Directory schema.

Figure 18.9 provides an example of working with ntdsutil. The following commands were entered to set the context for further operations:

```
ntdsutil
domain management
connections
connect to server localhost
```

```
connect to domain ADTest
quit
list
```

FIGURE 18.9   Viewing `ntdsutil` commands on the local domain controller

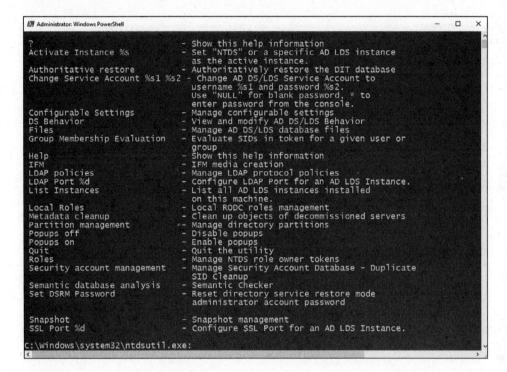

Configuring DNS Integration with Active Directory

There are many benefits to integrating Active Directory and DNS services:

- You can configure and manage replication along with other Active Directory components.

- You can automate much of the maintenance of DNS resource records through the use of dynamic updates.

- You will be able to set specific security options on the various properties of the DNS service.

Exercise 18.7 shows the steps that you must take to ensure that these integration features are enabled. You'll look at the various DNS functions that are specific to interoperability with Active Directory.

Before you begin this exercise, make sure that the local machine is configured as an Active Directory domain controller and that DNS services have been properly configured. If you instructed the Active Directory Installation Wizard to configure DNS automatically, many of the settings mentioned in this section may already be enabled. However, you should verify the configuration and be familiar with how the options can be set manually.

Configuring DNS Integration with Active Directory

1. Open Administrative Tools by pressing the Windows key and choosing Administrative Tools.

2. Open the DNS snap-in from the Administrative Tools program group.

3. Right-click the icon for the local DNS server and select Properties. Click the Security tab. Notice that you can now specify which users and groups have access to modify the configuration of the DNS server. Make any necessary changes and click OK.

4. Expand the local server branch and the Forward Lookup Zones folder.

5. Right-click the name of the Active Directory domain you created and select Properties.

6. On the General tab (see Figure 18.10), verify that the type is Active Directory–Integrated and that the Data Is Stored In Active Directory message is displayed. If this option is not currently selected, you can change it by clicking the Change button next to Type and choosing the Store The Zone In Active Directory check box on the bottom.

FIGURE 18.10 General Tab of DNS zone properties

7. Verify that the Dynamic Updates option is set to Secure Only. This ensures that all updates to the DNS resource records database are made through authenticated Active Directory accounts and processes.

   The other options are Nonsecure And Secure (accepts all updates) and None (to disallow dynamic updates).

8. Finally, notice that you can define the security permissions at the zone level by clicking the Security tab. Make any necessary changes and click OK.

Summary

This chapter covered the basics of implementing an Active Directory forest and domain structure, creating and configuring application data partitions, and setting the functional level of your domain and forest.

You are now familiar with how you can implement Active Directory. We carefully examined all of the necessary steps and conditions that you need to follow to install Active Directory on your network. First you need to prepare for the Domain Name System because Active Directory cannot be installed without the support of a DNS server.

You also need to verify that the computer you upgrade to a domain controller meets some basic file system and network connectivity requirements so that Active Directory can run smoothly and efficiently in your organization. These are some of the most common things you will have to do when you deploy Active Directory.

The chapter also covered the concept of domain functional levels, which essentially determine the kinds of domain controllers you can use in your environment.

You also learned how to install Active Directory, which you accomplish by promoting a Windows Server 2016 computer to a domain controller using Server Manager. You also learned how to verify the installation by testing Active Directory from a client computer.

This chapter was limited in scope to examining the issues related to installing and configuring the first domain in an Active Directory environment.

Exam Essentials

Know the prerequisites for promoting a server to a domain controller. You should understand the tasks that you must complete before you attempt to upgrade a server to a domain controller. Also, you should have a good idea of the information you need in order to complete the domain controller promotion process.

Understand the steps of the Active Directory Installation Wizard. When you run the Active Directory Installation Wizard, you'll be presented with many different choices. You should understand the effects of the various options provided in each step of the wizard.

Be familiar with the tools that you will use to administer Active Directory. Three main administrative tools are installed when you promote a Windows Server 2016 to a domain controller. Be sure that you know which tools to use for which types of tasks.

Understand the purpose of application data partitions. The idea behind application data partitions is that since you already have a directory service that can replicate all kinds of security information, you can also use it to keep track of application data. The main benefit of storing application information in Active Directory is that you can take advantage of its storage mechanism and replication topology. Application-related information stored on domain controllers benefits from having fault-tolerance features and availability.

Review Questions

You can find the answers in the Appendix.

1. You are the system administrator of a large organization that has recently implemented Windows Server 2016. You have a few remote sites that do not have very tight security. You have decided to implement read-only domain controllers (RODCs). What forest and function levels does the network need for you to do the install? (Choose all that apply.)

   A. Windows Server 2016

   B. Windows Server 2008 R2

   C. Windows Server 2012 R2

   D. Windows Server 2008

2. What is the maximum number of domains that a Windows Server 2016 computer configured as a domain controller may participate in at one time?

   A. Zero

   B. One

   C. Two

   D. Any number of domains

3. A system administrator is trying to determine which file system to use for a server that will become a Windows Server 2016 file server and domain controller. The company has the following requirements:

   - The file system must allow for file-level security from within Windows 2016 Server.

   - The file system must make efficient use of space on large partitions.

   - The domain controller Sysvol must be stored on the partition.

   Which of the following file systems meets these requirements?

   A. FAT

   B. FAT32

   C. HPFS

   D. NTFS

4. For security reasons, you have decided that you must convert the system partition on your removable drive from the FAT32 file system to NTFS. Which of the following steps must you take in order to convert the file system? (Choose two.)

   A. Run the command CONVERT /FS:NTFS from the command prompt.

   B. Rerun Windows Server 2016 Setup and choose to convert the partition to NTFS during the reinstallation.

   C. Boot Windows Server 2016 Setup from the installation CD-ROM and choose Rebuild File System.

   D. Reboot the computer.

5. Windows Server 2016 requires the use of which of the following protocols or services in order to support Active Directory? (Choose two.)

   A. DHCP

   B. TCP/IP

   C. NetBEUI

   D. IPX/SPX

   E. DNS

6. You are promoting a Windows Server 2016 computer to an Active Directory domain controller for test purposes. The new domain controller will be added to an existing domain. While you are using the Active Directory Installation Wizard, you receive an error message that prevents the server from being promoted. Which of the following might be the cause of the problem? (Choose all that apply.)

   A. The system does not contain an NTFS partition on which the Sysvol directory can be created.

   B. You do not have a Windows Server 2016 DNS server on the network.

   C. The TCP/IP configuration on the new server is incorrect.

   D. The domain has reached its maximum number of domain controllers.

7. Your network contains a single Active Directory domain. The domain contains five Windows Server 2008 R2 domain controllers. You plan to install a new Windows Server 2016 domain controller. Which two actions would you need to perform? (Each correct answer presents part of the solution. Choose two.)

   A. Run adprep.exe /rodcprep at the command line.

   B. Run adprep.exe /forestprep at the command line.

   C. Run adprep.exe /domainprep at the command line.

   D. From Active Directory Domains and Trusts, raise the functional level of the domain.

   E. From Active Directory Users and Computers, prestage the RODC computer account.

8. You are the network administrator for a large company that creates widgets. Management asks you to implement a new Windows Server 2016 system. You need to implement federated identity management. Which of the following will help you do this?

   A. Active Directory Federation Services

   B. Active Directory DNS Services

   C. Active Directory IIS Services

   D. Active Directory IAS Services

9. You are the system administrator responsible for your company's infrastructure. You think you have an issue with name resolution, and you need to verify that you are using the correct hostname. You want to test DNS on the local system and need to see whether the hostname server-1 resolves to the IP address 10.1.1.1. Which of the following actions provides a solution to the problem?

   A. Add a DNS server to your local subnet.

   B. Add the mapping for the hostname server-1 to the IP address 10.1.1.1 in the local system's HOSTS file.

   C. Add an A record to your local WINS server.

   D. Add an MX record to your local DNS server.

10. You have one Active Directory forest in your organization that contains one domain named WillPanek.com. You have two domain controllers configured with the DNS role installed. There are two Active Directory Integrated zones named WillPanek.com and WillPanekAD.com. One of your IT members (who is not an administrator) needs to be able to modify the WillPanek.com DNS server, but you need to prevent this user from modifying the WillPanekAD.com SOA record. How do you accomplish this?

    A. Modify the permissions of the WillPanek.com zone from the DNS Manager snap-in.

    B. Modify the permissions of the WillPanekAd.com zone from the DNS Manager snap-in.

    C. Run the Delegation Of Control Wizard in Active Directory.

    D. Run the Delegation Of Control Wizard in the DNS snap-in.

Chapter

19

Administer Active Directory

THE FOLLOWING 70-742 EXAM OBJECTIVES ARE COVERED IN THIS CHAPTER:

✓ **Create and manage Active Directory users and computers**

- This objective may include but is not limited to: Automate the creation of Active Directory accounts; create, copy, configure, and delete users and computers; configure templates; perform bulk Active Directory operations; configure user rights; implement offline domain join; manage inactive and disabled accounts; automate unlocking of disabled accounts using Windows PowerShell; automate password resets using Windows PowerShell.

✓ **Create and manage Active Directory groups and organizational units (OUs)**

- This objective may include but is not limited to: Configure group nesting; convert groups, including security, distribution, universal, domain local, and domain global; manage group membership using Group Policy; enumerate group membership; automate group membership management using Windows PowerShell; delegate the creation and management of Active Directory groups and OUs; manage default Active Directory containers; create, copy, configure, and delete groups and OUs.

✓ **Configure service authentication and account policies**

- This objective may include but is not limited to: Create and configure Service Accounts; create and configure Group Managed Service Accounts (gMSAs); configure Kerberos Constrained Delegation (KCD); manage Service Principal Names (SPNs); configure virtual accounts; configure domain and local user password policy settings; configure and apply Password Settings Objects (PSOs); delegate password settings management; configure account lockout policy settings; configure Kerberos policy settings within Group Policy.

In previous chapters, you learned how to install Active Directory, but you still haven't been introduced to the lower-level objects that exist in Active Directory.

In this chapter, you will look at the structure of the various components within a domain. You'll see how an organization's business structure can be mirrored within Active Directory through the use of organizational units for ease of use and to create a seamless look and feel. Because the concepts related to organizational units are quite simple, some system administrators may underestimate their importance and not plan to use them accordingly. Make no mistake: One of the fundamental components of a successful Active Directory installation is the proper design and deployment of organizational units.

You'll also see in this chapter the actual steps you need to take to create common Active Directory objects and then learn how to configure and manage them. Finally, you'll look at ways to publish resources and methods for creating user accounts automatically.

Active Directory Overview

One of the fundamental design goals for Active Directory is to define a single, centralized repository of users and information resources. Active Directory records information about all of the users, computers, and resources on your network. Each domain acts as a logical boundary, and members of the domain (including workstations, servers, and domain controllers) share information about the objects within them.

The information stored within Active Directory determines which resources are accessible to which users. Through the use of permissions that are assigned to Active Directory objects, you can control all aspects of network security.

Throughout this chapter, you'll learn the details of security as it pertains to Active Directory. Note, however, that Active Directory security is only one aspect of overall network security. You should also be sure that you have implemented appropriate access control settings for the file system, network devices, and other resources. Let's start by looking at the various components of network security, which include working with security principals and managing security and permissions, access control lists (ACLs), and access control entries (ACEs).

When you are setting up a network, you should always keep in mind that 90 percent of all hacks on a network are internal. This means internal permissions and security (as well as external security) need to be as strong as possible while still allowing users to do their jobs.

Understanding Active Directory Features

Active Directory is the heart and soul of a Microsoft domain, and I can never talk enough about the roles and features included with Active Directory. Let's take a look at some of the advantages of Windows Server 2016 and Active Directory.

Active Directory Certificate Services   Active Directory Certificate Services (AD CS) provides a customizable set of services that allows you to issue and manage public key infrastructure (PKI) certificates. These certificates can be used in software security systems that employ public key technologies.

Active Directory Domain Services   Active Directory Domain Services (AD DS) includes new features that make deploying domain controllers simpler and lets you implement them faster. AD DS also makes the domain controllers more flexible, both to audit and to authorize access to files. Moreover, AD DS has been designed to make performing administrative tasks easier through consistent graphical and scripted management experiences.

Active Directory Rights Management Services   Active Directory Rights Management Services (AD RMS) provides management and development tools that let you work with industry security technologies, including encryption, certificates, and authentication. Using these technologies allows organizations to create reliable information protection solutions.

Kerberos Authentication   Windows Server 2016 uses the Kerberos authentication protocol and extensions for password-based and public-key authentication. The Kerberos client is installed as a security support provider (SSP), and it can be accessed through the Security Support Provider Interface (SSPI).

Kerberos Constrained Delegation   Kerberos constrained delegation (KCD) is an authentication protocol that administrators can set up for delegating client credentials for specific service accounts. For example, KCD may be a requirement for services in SharePoint 2016. If you are planning on using SharePoint 2016 Analysis Services and Power Pivot data, you will need to configure KCD. KCD allows a service account to impersonate another service account and this allows access to specific resources.

Managed Service Accounts   The *Managed Service Accounts* is a Windows Server 2016 account that is managed by Active Directory. Regular service accounts are accounts that are created to run specific services such as Exchange and SQL Server. Normally when an administrator creates a service account, it's up to that administrator to maintain the account (including changing the password). Managed Service Accounts are accounts that administrators create, but the accounts are managed by Active Directory (including password changes). To create Managed Service Accounts, you must use the `New-ADServiceAccount` PowerShell command. You must use PowerShell in order to create a Managed Service Account.

Group Managed Service Accounts   The group Managed Service Account (gMSA) provides the same functionality within the domain as Managed Service Accounts, but gMSAs extend their functionality over multiple servers. These accounts are very useful when a service account needs to work with multiple servers, as with a server farm (for Network Load Balancing).

There are times when the authentication process requires that all instances of a service use the same service account. This is where gMSAs are used. Once group Managed Service Account are used, Windows Server 2016 will automatically manage the password for the service account. The network administrator will no longer be responsible to manage the service account password.

Security Auditing   Security auditing gives an organization the ability to help maintain the security of an enterprise. By using security audits, you can verify authorized or unauthorized access to machines, resources, applications, and services. One of the best advantages of security audits is to verify regulatory compliance.

TLS/SSL (Schannel SSP)   Schannel is a security support provider (SSP) that uses the Secure Sockets Layer (SSL) and Transport Layer Security (TLS) Internet standard authentication protocols together. The Security Support Provider Interface (SSPI) is an API used by Windows systems to allow security-related functionality, including authentication.

Windows Deployment Services   Windows Deployment Services allows an administrator to install Windows operating systems remotely. Administrators can use Windows Deployment Services to set up new computers by using a network-based installation.

Understanding Security Principals

Security principals are Active Directory objects that are assigned *security identifiers (SIDs)*. An SID is a unique identifier that is used to manage any object to which permissions can be assigned. Security principals are assigned permissions to perform certain actions and access certain network resources.

The following basic types of Active Directory objects serve as security principals:

User Accounts   User accounts identify individual users on your network by including information such as the user's name and their password. User accounts are the fundamental unit of security administration.

Groups   There are two main types of groups: security groups and distribution groups. Both types can contain user accounts. System administrators use security groups to ease the management of security permissions. They use distribution groups, on the other hand, solely to send email. Distribution groups are not security principals.

Computer Accounts   Computer accounts identify which client computers are members of particular domains. Because these computers participate in the Active Directory database, system administrators can manage security settings that affect the computer. They use computer accounts to determine whether a computer can join a domain and for authentication purposes. As you'll see later in this chapter, system administrators can also place restrictions on certain computer settings to increase security. These settings apply to the computer and, therefore, also apply to any user who is using it (regardless of the permissions granted to the user account).

Note that other objects—such as OUs—do not function as security principals. What this means is that you can apply certain settings (such as Group Policy) on all of the objects within an OU; however, you cannot specifically set permissions with respect to the OU itself. The purpose of OUs is to organize other Active Directory objects logically based on business needs, add a needed level of control for security, and create an easier way to delegate.

You can manage security by performing the following actions with security principals:

- You can assign them permissions to access various network resources.

- You can give them user rights.

- You can track their actions through auditing (covered later in this chapter).

The major types of security principals—user accounts, groups, and computer accounts— form the basis of the Active Directory security architecture. As a system administrator, you will likely spend a portion of your time managing permissions for these objects.

It is important to understand that, since a unique SID defines each security principal, deleting a security principal is an irreversible process. For example, if you delete a user account and then later re-create one with the same name, you'll need to reassign permissions and group membership settings for the new account. Once a user account is deleted, its SID is deleted. This is why you should always consider disabling accounts instead of deleting them.

An Overview of OUs

An *organizational unit (OU)* is a logical group of Active Directory objects, just as the name implies. OUs serve as containers (see Figure 19.1) within which Active Directory objects can be created, but they do not form part of the DNS namespace. They are used solely to create organization within a domain.

FIGURE 19.1   Active Directory OUs

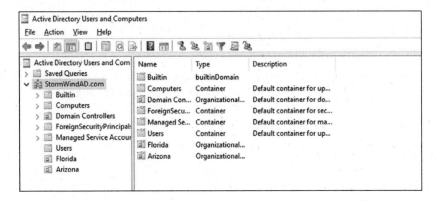

OUs can contain the following types of Active Directory objects:

- Users
- Groups
- Computers
- Shared Folder objects
- Contacts
- Printers
- InetOrgPerson objects
- Microsoft Message Queuing (MSMQ) Queue aliases
- Other OUs

Perhaps the most useful feature of OUs is that they can contain other OU objects. As a result, system administrators can hierarchically group resources and objects according to business practices. The OU structure is extremely flexible and, as you will see later in this chapter, can easily be rearranged to reflect business reorganizations.

Another advantage of OUs is that each can have its own set of policies. Administrators can create individual and unique Group Policy objects (GPOs) for each OU. GPOs are rules or policies that can apply to all of the objects within the OU.

Each type of object has its own purpose within the organization of Active Directory domains. Later in this chapter, you'll look at the specifics of User, Computer, Group, and Shared Folder objects. For now, let's focus on the purpose and benefits of using OUs.

The Purpose of OUs

OUs are mainly used to organize the objects within Active Directory. Before you dive into the details of OUs, however, you must understand how OUs, users, and groups interact. Most important, you should understand that OUs are simply containers that you can use to group various objects logically. They are not, however, groups in the classical sense. That is, they are not used for assigning security permissions. Another way of stating this is that the user accounts, computer accounts, and group accounts that are contained in OUs are considered security principals while the OUs themselves are not.

OUs do not take the place of standard user and group permissions. A good general practice is to assign users to groups and then place the groups within OUs. This enhances the benefits of setting security permissions and of using the OU hierarchy for making settings.

An OU contains objects only from within the domain in which it resides. As you'll see in the section "Delegating Administrative Control" later in this chapter, the OU is the finest level of granularity used for group policies and other administrative settings.

Benefits of OUs

There are many benefits to using OUs throughout your network environment:

- OUs are the smallest unit to which you can assign directory permissions.
- You can easily change the OU structure, and it is more flexible than the domain structure.

- The OU structure can support many different levels of hierarchy.

- Child objects can inherit OU settings.

- You can set Group Policy settings on OUs.

- You can easily delegate the administration of OUs and the objects within them to the appropriate users and groups.

   Now that you have a good idea of why you should use OUs, take a look at some general practices you can use to plan the OU structure.

Planning the OU Structure

One of the key benefits of Active Directory is the way in which it can bring organization to complex network environments. Before you can begin to implement OUs in various configurations, you must plan a structure that is compatible with business and technical needs. In the following sections, you'll learn about several factors that you should consider when planning for the structure of OUs.

Logical Grouping of Resources

The fundamental purpose of using OUs is to group resources (which exist within Active Directory) hierarchically. Fortunately, hierarchical groups are quite intuitive and widely used in most businesses. For example, a typical manufacturing business might divide its various operations into different departments as follows:

- Sales
- Marketing
- Engineering
- Research and Development
- Support
- Information Technology (IT)

   Each of these departments usually has its own goals and mission. To make the business competitive, individuals within each of the departments are assigned to various roles. The following role types might be used:

- Managers
- Clerical staff
- Technical staff
- Planners

   Each of these roles usually entails specific job responsibilities. For example, managers should provide direction to general staff members. Note that the very nature of these roles suggests that employees may fill many different positions. That is, one employee might be a manager in one department and a member of the technical staff in another. In the modern workplace, such situations are quite common.

All of this information helps you plan how to use OUs. First the structure of OUs within a given network environment should map well to the business's needs, including the political and logical structure of the organization as well as its technical needs. Figure 19.2 shows how a business organization might be mapped to the OU structure within an Active Directory domain.

FIGURE 19.2 Mapping a business organization to an OU structure

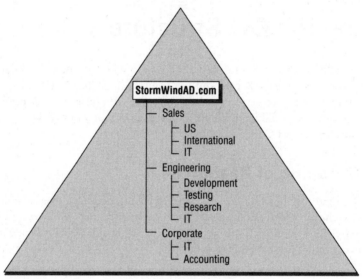

StormWindAD.com Domain

When naming OUs for your organization, you should keep several considerations and limitations in mind:

Keep the Names and Descriptions Simple The purpose of OUs is to make administering and using resources simple. Therefore, it's always a good idea to keep the names of your objects simple and descriptive. Sometimes, finding a balance between these two goals can be a challenge. For example, although a printer name like "The LaserJet located near Bob's cube" might seem descriptive, it is certainly difficult to type. Also, imagine the naming changes that you might have to make if Bob moves (or leaves the company)!

Pay Attention to Limitations The maximum length for the name of an OU is 64 characters. In most cases, this should adequately describe the OU. Remember, the name of an OU does not have to describe the object uniquely because the OU is generally referenced only as part of the overall hierarchy. For example, you can choose to create an OU named "IT" within two different parent OUs. Even though the OUs have the same name, users and administrators are able to distinguish between them based on their complete pathname.

Pay Attention to the Hierarchical Consistency   The fundamental basis of an OU structure is its position in a hierarchy. From a design standpoint, this means you cannot have two OUs with the same name at the same level. However, you can have OUs with the same name at different levels. For example, you could create an OU named "Corporate" within the North America OU and another one within the South America OU. This is because the fully qualified domain name includes information about the hierarchy. When an administrator tries to access resources in a Corporate OU, they must specify which Corporate OU they mean.

For example, if you create a North America OU, the Canada OU should logically fit under it. If you decide that you want to separate the North America and Canada OUs into completely different containers, then you might want to use other, more appropriate names. For example, you could change North America to "U.S." Users and administrators depend on the hierarchy of OUs within the domain, so make sure that it remains logically consistent.

Based on these considerations, you should have a good idea of how best to organize the OU structure for your domain.

Understanding OU Inheritance

When you rearrange OUs within the structure of Active Directory, you can change several settings. When they are moving and reorganizing OUs, system administrators must pay careful attention to automatic and unforeseen changes in security permissions and other configuration options. By default, OUs inherit the permissions of their new parent container when they are moved.

By using the built-in tools provided with Windows Server 2016 and Active Directory, you can move or copy OUs only within the same domain. You cannot use the Active Directory Users and Computers tool to move OUs between domains. To do this, use the *Active Directory Migration Tool (ADMT)*. This is one of the many Active Directory support tools.

Delegating Administrative Control

I already mentioned that OUs are the smallest component within a domain to which administrative permissions and group policies can be assigned by administrators. Now you'll take a look specifically at how administrative control is set on OUs.

Delegation occurs when a higher security authority assigns permissions to a lesser security authority. As a real-world example, assume that you are the director of IT for a large organization. Instead of doing all of the work yourself, you would probably assign roles and responsibilities to other individuals. For example, if you worked within a multidomain environment, you might make one system administrator responsible for all operations within the Sales domain and another responsible for the Engineering domain. Similarly, you could assign the permissions for managing all printers and print queue objects within your organization to one individual user while allowing another individual user to manage all security permissions for users and groups. In this way, you can distribute the various roles and responsibilities of the IT staff throughout the organization.

Businesses generally have a division of labor that handles all of the tasks involved in keeping the company's networks humming. Network operating systems (NOSs), however, often make it difficult to assign just the right permissions; in other words, they do not support very granular permission assignments. Sometimes, fine granularity is necessary to ensure that only the right permissions are assigned. A good general rule of thumb is to provide users and administrators with the minimum permissions they require to do their jobs. This way, you can ensure that accidental, malicious, and otherwise unwanted changes do not occur.

You can use auditing to log events to the Security log in the Event Viewer. This is a way to ensure that if accidental, malicious, and otherwise unwanted changes do occur, they are logged and traceable.

In the world of Active Directory, you delegate to define responsibilities for OU administrators. As a system administrator, you will occasionally be tasked with having to delegate responsibility to others—you can't do it all, although sometimes administrators believe that they can. You understand the old IT logic of doing all of the tasks yourself for job security, but this can actually make you look worse.

You can delegate control only at the OU level and not at the object level within the OU.

If you do find yourself in a role where you need to delegate, remember that Windows Server 2016 was designed to offer you the ability to do so. In its simplest definition, *delegation* allows a higher administrative authority to grant specific administrative rights for containers and subtrees to individuals and groups. What this essentially does is eliminate the need for domain administrators with sweeping authority over large segments of the user population. You can break up this control over branches within your tree, within each OU you create.

To understand delegation and rights, you should first understand the concept of *access control entries (ACEs)*. ACEs grant specific administrative rights on objects in a container to a user or group. A container's access control list (ACL) is used to store ACEs.

When you are considering implementing delegation, keep these two concerns in mind:

Parent-Child Relationships   The OU hierarchy you create will be important when you consider the maintainability of security permissions. OUs can exist in a parent-child relationship, which means that permissions and group policies set on OUs higher up in the hierarchy (parents) can interact with objects in lower-level OUs (children). When it comes to delegating permissions, this is extremely important. You can allow child containers to inherit the permissions set on parent containers automatically. For example, if the North America division of your organization contains 12 other OUs, you could delegate permissions to all of them at once (saving time and reducing the likelihood of human error) by placing security permissions on the North America division. This feature can greatly ease administration, especially in larger organizations, but it is also a reminder of the importance of properly planning the OU structure within a domain.

Inheritance Settings   Now that you've seen how you can use parent-child relationships for administration, you should consider *inheritance*, the process in which child objects take on the permissions of a parent container. When you set permissions on a parent container, all of the child objects are configured to inherit the same permissions. You can override this behavior, however, if business rules do not lend themselves well to inheritance.

Applying Group Policies

One of the strengths of the Windows operating system is that it offers users a great deal of power and flexibility. From installing new software to adding device drivers, users can make many changes to their workstation configurations. However, this level of flexibility is also a potential problem. For instance, inexperienced users might inadvertently change settings, causing problems that can require many hours to fix.

In many cases (and especially in business environments), users require only a subset of the complete functionality the operating system provides. In the past, however, the difficulty associated with implementing and managing security and policy settings has led to lax security policies. Some of the reasons for this are technical—it can be tedious and difficult to implement and manage security restrictions. Other problems have been political—users and management might feel that they should have full permissions on their local machines, despite the potential problems this might cause.

That's where the idea of group policies comes in. Simply defined, *group policies* are collections of rules that you can apply to objects within Active Directory. Specifically, Group Policy settings are assigned at the site, domain, and OU levels, and they can apply to user accounts and computer accounts. For example, a system administrator can use group policies to configure the following settings:

- Restricting users from installing new programs
- Disallowing the use of the Control Panel
- Limiting choices for display and Desktop settings

Creating OUs

Now that you have looked at several different ways in which OUs can be used to bring organization to the objects within Active Directory, it's time to look at how you can create and manage them.

Through the use of the *Active Directory Users and Computers administrative tool*, also called the *MMC (Microsoft Management Console)*, you can quickly and easily add, move, and change OUs. This graphical tool makes it easy to visualize and create the various levels of hierarchy an organization requires.

Figure 19.3 shows a geographically based OU structure that a multinational company might use. Note that the organization is based in North America and that it has a corporate office located there. In general, the other offices are much smaller than the corporate office located in North America.

FIGURE 19.3 A geographically based OU structure

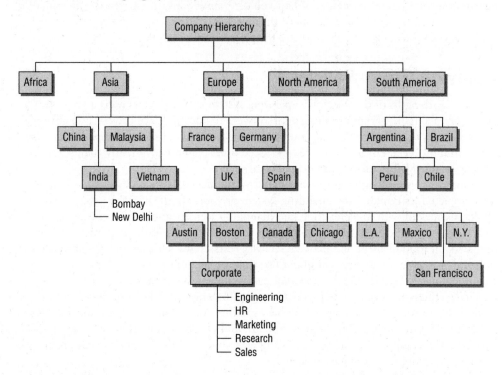

It's important to note that this OU structure could have been designed in several different ways. For example, I could have chosen to group all of the offices located in the United States within an OU named "U.S." However, because of the large size of these offices, I chose to place these objects at the same level as the Canada and Mexico OUs. This prevents an unnecessarily deep OU hierarchy while still logically grouping the offices.

One nice feature when creating an OU is the ability to protect the OU from being accidentally deleted. When you create an OU, you can check the Protect Container From Accidental Deletion check box. This check box protects against an administrator deleting the OU. To delete the OU, you must go into the advanced view of the OU and uncheck the box.

Exercise 19.1 walks you through the process of creating several OUs for a multinational business. You'll be using this OU structure in later exercises within this chapter.

To perform the exercises included in this chapter, you must have administrative access to a Windows Server 2016 domain controller.

EXERCISE 19.1

Creating an OU Structure

1. Open Active Directory Users and Computers by clicking Start ➢ Administrative Tools
   ➢ Active Directory Users And Computers.

2. Right-click the name of the local domain and choose New ➢ Organizational Unit.

3. Type **North America** for the name of the first OU (see Figure 19.4). Uncheck the box
   Protect Container From Accidental Deletion and click OK to create this object.

FIGURE 19.4   New OU dialog box

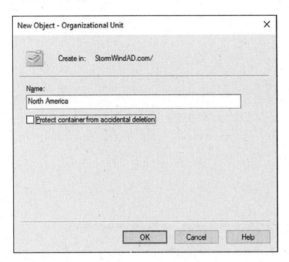

4. Create the following top-level OUs by right-clicking the name of the domain and
   choosing New ➢ Organizational Unit. Also make sure to uncheck Protect Container
   From Accidental Deletion for all OUs in these exercises because you'll be deleting
   some of these OUs in later ones.

   Africa

   Asia

   Europe

   South America

   Note that the order in which you create the OUs is not important. In this exercise, you
   are simply using a method that emphasizes the hierarchical relationship.

5. Create the following second-level OUs within the North America OU by right-clicking the North America OU and selecting New ➤ Organizational Unit:

Austin

Boston

Canada

Chicago

Corporate

Los Angeles

Mexico

New York

San Francisco

6. Create the following OUs under the Asia OU:

China

India

Malaysia

Vietnam

7. Create the following OUs under the Europe OU:

France

Germany

Spain

UK

8. Create the following OUs under the South America OU:

Argentina

Brazil

Chile

Peru

9. Create the following third-level OUs under the India OU by right-clicking India within the Asia OU and selecting New ➤ Organizational Unit:

Bombay

New Delhi

10. Within the North America Corporate OU, create the following OUs:

Engineering

HR

Marketing

Research

Sales

11. When you have completed creating the OUs, close Active Directory.

Managing OUs

Managing network environments would still be challenging, even if things rarely changed. However, in the real world, business units, departments, and employee roles change frequently. As business and technical needs change, so should the structure of Active Directory.

Fortunately, changing the structure of OUs within a domain is a relatively simple process. In the following sections, you'll look at ways to delegate control of OUs and make other changes.

Moving, Deleting, and Renaming OUs

The process of moving, deleting, and renaming OUs is a simple one. Exercise 19.2 shows how you can easily modify and reorganize OUs to reflect changes in the business organization. The specific scenario covered in this exercise includes the following changes:

- The Research and Engineering departments have been combined to form a department known as Research and Development (RD).

- The Sales department has been moved from the Corporate headquarters office to the New York office.

- The Marketing department has been moved from the Corporate headquarters office to the Chicago office.

This exercise assumes you have already completed the steps in Exercise 19.1.

EXERCISE 19.2

Modifying OU Structure

1. Open Active Directory Users and Computers by clicking Start ➢ Administrative Tools ➢ Active Directory Users And Computers.

2. Right-click the Engineering OU (located within North America ➢ Corporate) and click Delete. When you are prompted for confirmation, click Yes. Note that if this OU contained objects, they would have all been automatically deleted as well.

3. Right-click the Research OU and select Rename. Type **RD** to change the name of the OU and press Enter.

4. Right-click the Sales OU and select Move. In the Move dialog box, expand the North America branch and click the New York OU. Click OK to move the OU.

5. You will use an alternate method to move the Marketing OU. Drag the Marketing OU and drop it onto the Chicago OU.

6. When you have finished, close the Active Directory Users and Computers administrative tool.

Administering Properties of OUs

Although OUs are primarily created for organizational purposes within the Active Directory environment, they have several settings that you can modify. To modify the properties of an OU using the Active Directory Users and Computers administrative tool, right-click the name of any OU and select Properties. When you do, the OU Properties dialog box appears. In the example shown in Figure 19.5, you'll see the options on the General tab.

FIGURE 19.5   The General tab of the OUs Properties dialog box

In any organization, it helps to know who is responsible for managing an OU. You can set this information on the Managed By tab (see Figure 19.6). The information specified on this tab is convenient because it is automatically pulled from the contact information on a user record. You should consider always having a contact for each OU within your organization so that other system administrators know whom to contact if they need to make any changes.

FIGURE 19.6   The Managed By tab of the OUs Properties dialog box

Delegating Control of OUs

In simple environments, one or a few system administrators may be responsible for managing all of the settings within Active Directory. For example, a single system administrator could manage all users within all OUs in the environment. In larger organizations, however, roles and responsibilities may be divided among many different individuals. A typical situation is one in which a system administrator is responsible for objects within only a few OUs in an Active Directory domain. Alternatively, one system administrator might manage User and Group objects while another is responsible for managing file and print services.

Fortunately, using the Active Directory Users and Computers tool, you can quickly and easily ensure that specific users receive only the permissions they need. In Exercise 19.3, you will use the Delegation of Control Wizard to assign permissions to individuals. To complete these steps successfully, first you must have created the objects in the previous exercises of this chapter.

EXERCISE 19.3

Using the Delegation of Control Wizard

1. Open Active Directory Users and Computers by clicking Start ➤ Administrative Tools ➤ Active Directory Users And Computers.

2. Right-click the Corporate OU within the North America OU and select Delegate Control. This starts the Delegation of Control Wizard. Click Next to begin configuring security settings.

3. In the Users Or Groups page, click the Add button. In the Enter The Object Names To Select field, enter **Account Operators** and click the Check Names button. Click OK. Click Next to continue.

4. In the Tasks To Delegate page, select Delegate The Following Common Tasks and place a check mark next to the following items:

   Create, Delete, And Manage User Accounts

   Reset User Passwords And Force Password Change At Next Logon

   Read All User Information

   Create, Delete, And Manage Groups

   Modify The Membership Of A Group

5. Click Next to continue.

6. The Completing The Delegation Of Control Wizard page then provides a summary of the operations you have selected. To implement the changes, click Finish.

Although the common tasks available through the wizard are sufficient for many delegation operations, you may have cases in which you want more control. For example, you might want to give a particular system administrator permissions to modify only Computer objects. Exercise 19.4 uses the Delegation of Control Wizard to assign more granular permissions. To complete these steps successfully, you must have completed the previous exercises in this chapter.

EXERCISE 19.4

Delegating Custom Tasks

1. Open Active Directory Users and Computers by clicking Start ➤ Administrative Tools ➤ Active Directory Users And Computers.

2. Right-click the Corporate OU within the North America OU and select Delegate Control. This starts the Delegation of Control Wizard. Click Next to begin making security settings.

3. In the Users Or Groups page, click the Add button. In the Enter The Object Names To Select field, enter **Server Operators** and click the Check Names button. Click OK and then click Next to continue.

4. In the Tasks To Delegate page, select the Create A Custom Task To Delegate radio button and click Next to continue.

5. In the Active Directory Object Type page, choose Only The Following Objects In The Folder and place a check mark next to the following items. (You will have to scroll down to see them all.)

   User Objects

   Computer Objects

   Contact Objects

   Group Objects

   Organizational Unit Objects

   Printer Objects

6. Click Next to continue.

7. In the Permissions page, place a check mark next to the General option and make sure the other options are not checked. Note that if the various objects within your Active Directory schema had property-specific settings, you would see those options here. Place a check mark next to the following items:

   Create All Child Objects

   Read All Properties

   Write All Properties

   This gives the members of the Server Operators group the ability to create new objects within the Corporate OU and the permissions to read and write all properties for these objects.

8. Click Next to continue.

9. The Completing The Delegation Of Control Wizard page provides a summary of the operations you have selected. To implement the changes, click Finish.

🌐 **Real World Scenario**

Delegation: Who's Responsible for What?

You're the IT director for a large, multinational organization. You've been with the company for quite a while, that is, since the environment had only a handful of offices and a few network and system administrators. Times have changed, however. Now system administrators must coordinate the efforts of hundreds of IT staffers in 14 countries.

For years now, a debate has been raging among IT administrators on the question of when to create a new child domain and when to make it just an OU. For example, let's say you have a remote office in Concord, New Hampshire. Do you give the remote office its own domain (as a child domain), or do you just make the Concord office an OU? Well, it really depends on who you want to manage the resources in Concord. Do you want to create domains or OUs based on location?

Fortunately, through the proper use of OUs and delegation, you are given a lot of flexibility in determining how to handle the administration. You can structure the administration in several ways. First, if you choose to create OUs based on a geographic business structure, you could delegate control of these OUs based on the job functions of various system administrators. For example, you could use one user account to administer the Concord OU. Within the Concord OU, this system administrator could delegate control of resources represented by the Printers and Scanners OUs.

Alternatively, the OU structure may create a functional representation of the business. For example, the Engineering OU might contain other OUs that are based on office locations such as New York and Paris. A system administrator of the Engineering domain could delegate permissions based on geography or job functions to the lower OUs. Regardless of whether you build a departmental, functional, or geographical OU model, keep in mind that each model excludes other models. This is one of the most important decisions you need to make. When you are making this decision or modifying previous decisions, your overriding concern is how it will affect the management and administration of the network. The good news is that, because Active Directory has so many features, the model you choose can be based on specific business requirements rather than imposed by architectural constraints.

Troubleshooting OUs

In general, you will find using OUs to be a relatively straightforward and painless process. With adequate planning, you'll be able to implement an intuitive and useful structure for OU objects.

The most common problems with OU configuration are related to the OU structure. When troubleshooting OUs, pay careful attention to the following factors:

Inheritance   By default, Group Policy and other settings are transferred automatically from parent OUs to child OUs and objects. Even if a specific OU is not given a set of permissions, objects within that OU might still get them from parent objects.

Delegation of Administration   If you allow the wrong user accounts or groups to perform specific tasks on OUs, you might be violating your company's security policy. Be sure to verify the delegations you have made at each OU level.

Organizational Issues   Sometimes, business practices do not easily map to the structure of Active Directory. A few misplaced OUs, user accounts, computer accounts, or groups can make administration difficult or inaccurate. In many cases, it might be beneficial to rearrange the OU structure to accommodate any changes in the business organization. In others, it might make more sense to change business processes.

If you regularly consider each of these issues when troubleshooting problems with OUs, you will be much less likely to make errors in the Active Directory configuration.

Creating and Managing Active Directory Objects

Now that you are familiar with the task of creating OUs, you should find creating and managing other Active Directory objects quite simple. The following sections will examine the details.

Overview of Active Directory Objects

When you install and configure a domain controller, Active Directory sets up an organizational structure for you, and you can create and manage several types of objects.

Active Directory Organization

When you are looking at your Active Directory structure, you will see objects that look like folders in File Explorer. These objects are containers, or *organizational units (OUs)*. The difference is that an OU is a container to which you can link a GPO. Normal containers cannot have a GPO linked to them. That's what makes an OU a special container.

By default, after you install and configure a domain controller, you will see the following organizational sections within the Active Directory Users and Computers tool (they look like folders):

Built-In   The *Built-In container* includes all of the standard groups that are installed by default when you promote a domain controller. You can use these groups to administer the servers in your environment. Examples include the Administrators group, Backup Operators group, and Print Operators group.

Computers   By default, the *Computers container* contains a list of the workstations in your domain. From here, you can manage all of the computers in your domain.

Domain Controllers   The *Domain Controllers OU* includes a list of all the domain controllers for the domain.

Foreign Security Principals   In environments that have more than one domain, you may need to grant permissions to users who reside in multiple domains. Generally, you manage this using Active Directory trees and forests. However, in some cases, you may want to provide resources to users who belong to domains that are not part of the forest.

Active Directory uses the concept of foreign security principals to allow permissions to be assigned to users who are not part of an Active Directory forest. This process is automatic and does not require the intervention of system administrators. You can then add the foreign security principals to domain local groups for which, in turn, you can grant permissions for resources within the domain. You can view a list of foreign security principals by using the Active Directory Users and Computers tool.

Foreign security principals containers are any objects to which security can be assigned and that are not part of the current domain. Security principals are Active Directory objects to which permissions can be applied, and they can be used to manage permissions in Active Directory.

Managed Service Accounts   The Managed Service Accounts container is a Windows Server 2016 container. Service accounts are accounts created to run specific services such as Exchange and SQL Server. Having a Managed Service Accounts container allows you to control the service accounts better and thus allows for better service account security. To create Managed Service Accounts, you must use the New-ADServiceAccount PowerShell command.

Users   The *Users container* includes all the security accounts that are part of the domain. When you first install the domain controller, there will be several groups in this container. For example, the Domain Admins group and the administrator account are created in this container.

You want to be sure to protect the administrator account. You should rename the admin account and make sure the password is complex. Protected admin accounts can make your network safer. Every hacker knows that there is an administrator account on the server by default. Be sure to make your network safer by protecting the admin account.

Active Directory Objects

You can create and manage several different types of Active Directory objects. The following are specific object types:

Computer   *Computer objects* represent workstations that are part of the Active Directory domain. All computers within a domain share the same security database, including user and group information. Computer objects are useful for managing security permissions and enforcing Group Policy restrictions.

Contact   *Contact objects* are usually used in OUs to specify the main administrative contact. Contacts are not security principals like users. They are used to specify information about individuals outside the organization.

Group   *Group objects* are logical collections of users primarily for assigning security permissions to resources. When managing users, you should place them into groups and then assign permissions to the group. This allows for flexible management without the need to set permissions for individual users.

InetOrgPerson   The *InetOrgPerson object* is an Active Directory object that defines attributes of users in Lightweight Directory Access Protocol (LDAP) and X.500 directories.

MSIMaging-PSPs   *MSIMaging-PSPs* is a container for all Enterprise Scan Post Scan Process objects.

MSMQ Queue Alias   An *MSMQ Queue Alias object* is an Active Directory object for the MSMQ-Custom-Recipient class type. The Microsoft Message Queuing (MSMQ) Queue Alias object associates an Active Directory path and a user-defined alias with a public, private, or direct single-element format name. This allows a queue alias to be used to reference a queue that might not be listed in Active Directory Domain Services (AD DS).

Organizational Unit   An *OU object* is created to build a hierarchy within the Active Directory domain. It is the smallest unit that can be used to create administrative groupings, and it can be used to assign group policies. Generally, the OU structure within a domain reflects a company's business organization.

Printer   *Printer objects* map to printers.

Shared Folder   *Shared Folder objects* map to server shares. They are used to organize the various file resources that may be available on file/print servers. Often, Shared Folder objects are used to give logical names to specific file collections. For example, system administrators might create separate shared folders for common applications, user data, and shared public files.

User   A *User object* is the fundamental security principal on which Active Directory is based. User accounts contain information about individuals as well as password and other permission information.

Creating Objects Using the Active Directory Users and Computers Tool

Exercise 19.5 walks you through the steps necessary to create various objects within an Active Directory domain. In this exercise, you create some basic Active Directory objects. To complete this exercise, you must have access to at least one Active Directory domain controller, and you should have also completed the previous exercises in this chapter.

EXERCISE 19.5

Creating Active Directory Objects

1. Open Active Directory Users and Computers by clicking Start ➤ Administrative Tools ➤ Active Directory Users And Computers.

2. Expand the current domain to list the objects currently contained within it. For this exercise, you will use the second- and third-level OUs contained within the North America top-level OU.

3. Right-click the Corporate OU and select New ➤ User. Fill in the following information:

   First Name: **Maria**

   Initial: **D**

   Last Name: **President**

   Full Name: (leave as default)

   User Logon Name: **mdpresident** (leave default domain)

   Click Next to continue.

4. Enter **P@ssw0rd** for the password for this user and then confirm it. Note that you can also make changes to password settings here. Click Next.

5. You will see a summary of the user information. Click Finish to create the new user.

6. Click the RD container and create another user in that container with the following information:

   First Name: **John**

   Initial: **Q**

   Last Name: **Adams**

   Full Name: (leave as default)

   User Logon Name: **jqadams** (leave default domain)

   Click Next to continue.

7. Assign the password **P@ssw0rd**. Click Next and then click Finish to create the user.

8. Right-click the RD OU and select New ➤ Contact. Use the following information to fill in the properties of the Contact object:

   First Name: **Jane**

   Initials: **R**

   Last Name: **Admin**

   Display Name: **jradmin**

   Click OK to create the new Contact object.

9. Right-click the RD OU and select New ➤ Shared Folder. Enter **Software** for the name and **\\server1\applications** for the network path (also known as the Universal Naming Convention [UNC] path). Note that you can create the object even though this resource (the physical server) does not exist. Click OK to create the Shared Folder object.

10. Right-click the HR OU and select New ➤ Group. Type **All Users** for the group name. Do not change the value in the Group Name (Pre–Windows 2000) field. For Group Scope, select Global, and for Group Type, select Security. To create the group, click OK.

11. Right-click the Sales OU and select New ➤ Computer. Type **Workstation1** for the name of the computer. Notice that the pre–Windows 2000 name is automatically populated and that, by default, the members of the Domain Admins group are the only ones who can add this computer to the domain. Place a check mark in the Assign This Computer Account As A Pre-Windows 2000 Computer box and then click OK to create the Computer object.

12. Close the Active Directory Users and Computers tool.

Configuring the User Principal Name

When you log into a domain, your logon name looks like an email address (for example, wpanek@willpanek.com). This is called your *user principal name (UPN)*. A UPN is the username followed by the @ sign and the domain name. At the time the user account is created, the UPN suffix is generated by default. The UPN is created as *userName@DomainName*, but an administrator can alter or change the default UPN. If your forest has multiple domains and you need to change the UPN to a different domain, you have that ability. To change the UPN suffix, in Active Directory Users and Computers, choose a user and go into their properties. Choose the Attribute Editor tab. Scroll down to the userPrincipalName attribute and make your changes. These changes then get replicated to the global catalog.

 If your organization has multiple forests set up by a trust, you can't change the UPN to a domain in the other forest. Global catalogs are used to log on users. Because UPNs get replicated to the local forest global catalog servers, you cannot log on to other forests using the UPN.

Using Templates

Now you are going to dive into user templates. *User templates* allow an Active Directory administrator to create a default account (for example, template_sales) and use that account to create all of the other users who match it (all the salespeople).

If you are creating multiple accounts, this can save you a lot of time and resources. For example, if you need to add 35 new salespeople to your company, you'll create one template for sales and use a copy of that template for all of the other new accounts. This saves you the trouble of filling out many of the same fields over and over again. When you copy a template, some of the information does *not* get copied over. This is because it is user-specific information. Here are some of the fields that do not get copied over from a template:

- Name
- Logon Name
- Password
- Email
- Phone Numbers
- Description
- Office
- Web Page

Many of the important fields such as Member Of (groups to which the user belongs), Profile Path, Department, and Company all get copied over. There is one important item that needs to be done when creating a template: the template account needs to be disabled after creation. You do not want anyone using this account to access your network. In Exercise 19.6, you will create a Sales template to use for your Sales department.

EXERCISE 19.6

Creating a User Template

1. Open Active Directory Users and Computers by clicking Start ➤ Administrative Tools ➤ Active Directory Users And Computers.

2. Expand the current domain to list the objects contained within it. For this exercise, you will use the Sales OU. Right-click the Sales OU and choose New ➤ User.

3. Use the following properties:

   First Name: **Sales**

   Last Name: **Template**

   Username: **sales_template**

   Password: **P@ssw0rd**

4. Click Next and then click Finish.

5. In the right window, double-click the Sales Template user to open the properties.

6. On the General tab, complete the following items:

   Description: **Template Account**

   Office: **Corporate**

Telephone: **999-999-9999**

Email: **Salet@abc.com**

Web: **www.abc.com**

7.   Click the Profile tab. In the Profile Path field, type **\\ServerA\%username%**.

8.   On the Members Of tab, click the Add button. At the Enter The Object Name To Select box, type **Administrator** and click the Check Names button. (Normally you would not add salespeople to the Administrators group, but you are doing so just for this exercise.) Click OK.

9.   Click the Account tab. Scroll down in the Account Options box and check the Account Is Disabled check box.

10. Click OK in the user's Properties window to go back to the Sales OU.

11. Right-click the Sales Template account and choose Copy.

12. Enter the following information:

First Name: **Jenny**

Last Name: **Sales**

Username: **jsales**

Password: **P@ssw0rd**

Uncheck the Account Is Disabled check box.

13. In the right window, double-click the Jenny Sales user to open the properties.

14. Take a look at the Members Of tab, the General tab, and the Profile tab, and you will see that some of the fields are prefilled (including the Administrators group).

15. Close Jenny Sales Properties and exit Active Directory Users and Computers.

Importing Objects from a File

In Exercise 19.5, you created an account using the Active Directory Users and Computers tool. But what if you need to bulk import accounts? There are two main applications for doing bulk imports of accounts: the ldifde.exe utility and the csvde.exe utility. Both utilities import accounts from files.

The ldifde utility imports from line-delimited files. This utility allows an administrator to export and import data, thus allowing batch operations such as Add, Modify, and Delete to be performed in Active Directory. Windows Server 2016 includes ldifde.exe to help support batch operations.

The csvde.exe utility performs the same export functions as ldifde.exe, but csvde.exe uses a comma-separated value file format. The csvde.exe utility does not allow administrators to modify or delete objects. It only supports adding objects to Active Directory.

Active Directory Migration Tool

Another tool that administrators have used in the past is the *Active Directory Migration Tool (ADMT)*. ADMT allows an administrator to migrate users, groups, and computers from a previous version of the server to a current version of the server.

Administrators also used ADMT to migrate users, groups, and computers between Active Directory domains in different forests (interforest migration) and between Active Directory domains in the same forest (intraforest migration).

At the time this book was written, Microsoft had not yet released a new version of ADMT that is supported by Windows Server 2016. The reason I even mention it in this book is because Microsoft may be releasing a version of it soon and I wanted you to understand what it can do. Continue to check the Microsoft website to see whether a new version has been released.

Offline Domain Join of a Computer

Offline domain join gives administrators the ability to preprovision computer accounts in the domain to prepare operating systems for deployments. At startup, computers can then join the domain without the need to contact a domain controller. This helps reduce the time it takes to deploy computers in a datacenter.

Let's say your datacenter needs to have multiple virtual machines deployed. This is where offline domain join can be useful. Upon initial startup after the operating system is installed, offline domain join allows the virtual machines to join the domain automatically. No additional steps or restarts are needed.

The following are some of the benefits of using offline domain join:

- There is no additional network traffic for Active Directory state changes.

- There is no additional network traffic for computer state changes to the domain controller.

- Changes for both the Active Directory state and the computer state can be completed at a different times.

Managing Object Properties

Once you've created the necessary Active Directory objects, you'll probably need to make changes to their default properties. In addition to the settings you made when you were creating Active Directory objects, you can configure several more properties. You can also access object properties by right-clicking any object and selecting Properties from the pop-up menu.

Each object type contains a unique set of properties.

User Object Properties

The following list describes some of the properties of a User object (see Figure 19.7):

FIGURE 19.7   User Properties

General   General account information about this user

Address   Physical location information about this user

Account   User logon name and other account restrictions, such as workstation restrictions and logon hours

Profile   Information about the user's roaming profile settings

Telephones   Telephone contact information for the user

Organization   The user's title, department, and company information

Member Of   Group membership information for the user

Dial-In   Remote Access Service (RAS) permissions for the user

Environment   Logon and other network settings for the user

Sessions   Session limits, including maximum session time and idle session settings

Remote Control   Remote control options for this user's session

Remote Desktop Services Profile   Information about the user's profile for use with Remote Desktop Services

Personal Virtual Desktop   Allows you to assign a user a specific virtual machine to use as a personal virtual desktop

COM+   Specifies a COM+ partition set for the user

Computer Object Properties

Computer objects have different properties than User objects. Computer objects refer to the systems that clients are operating to be part of a domain. The following list describes some Computer object properties:

General   Information about the name of the computer, the role of the computer, and its description

(You can enable an option to allow the Local System account of this machine to request services from other servers. This is useful if the machine is a trusted and secure computer.)

Operating System   The name, version, and service pack information for the operating system running on the computer

Member Of   Active Directory groups of which this Computer object is a member

Delegation   Allows you to set services that work on behalf of another user

Location   A description of the computer's physical location

Managed By   Information about the User or Contact object that is responsible for managing this computer

Dial-In   Sets dial-in options for the computer

Setting Properties for Active Directory Objects

Now that you have seen the various properties that can be set for the Active Directory objects, let's complete an exercise on how to configure some of these properties. Exercise 19.7 walks you through how to set various properties for Active Directory objects. To complete the steps in this exercise, first you must have completed Exercise 19.5.

Although it may seem a bit tedious, it's always a good idea to enter as much information as you know about Active Directory objects when you create them. Although the name Printer1 may be meaningful to you, users will appreciate the additional information, such as location, when they are searching for objects.

EXERCISE 19.7

Managing Object Properties

1. Open Active Directory Users and Computers by clicking Start ➤ Administrative Tools ➤ Active Directory Users And Computers.

2. Expand the name of the domain and select the RD container. Right-click the John Q. Adams user account and select Properties.

3. Here you will see the various Properties tabs for the User account. Make some configuration changes based on your personal preferences. Click OK to continue.

4. Select the HR OU. Right-click the All Users group and click Properties. In the All Users Properties dialog box, you will be able to modify the membership of the group.

    Click the Members tab and then click Add. Add the Maria D. President and John Q. Admin user accounts to the group. Click OK to save the settings and then OK to accept the group modifications.

5. Select the Sales OU. Right-click the Workstation1 Computer object. Notice that you can choose to disable the account or reset it (to allow another computer to join the domain under that same name). From the context menu, choose Properties. You'll see the properties for the Computer object.

    Examine the various options and make changes based on your personal preference. After you have examined the available options, click OK to continue.

6. Select the Corporate OU. Right-click the Maria D. President user account and choose Reset Password. You will be prompted to enter a new password, and then you'll be asked to confirm it. Note that you can also force the user to change this password upon the next logon, and you can also unlock the user's account from here. For this exercise, do not enter a new password; just click Cancel.

7. Close the Active Directory Users and Computers tool.

By now, you have probably noticed that Active Directory objects have a lot of common options. For example, Group and Computer objects both have a Managed By tab.

Windows Server 2016 allows you to manage many User objects at once. For instance, you can select several User objects by holding down the Shift or Ctrl key while selecting. You can then right-click any one of the selected objects and select Properties to display the properties that are available for multiple users. Notice that not every user property is available because some properties are unique to each user. You can configure the Description field for multiple object selections that include both users and nonusers, such as computers and groups.

An important thing to think about when it comes to accounts is the difference between disabling an account and deleting an account. When you delete an account, the security ID (SID) gets deleted. Even if you later create an account with the same username, it will have a different SID number, and therefore it will be a different account. It is sometimes better to disable an account and place it into a nonactive OU called *Disabled*. This way, if you ever need to reaccess the account, you can do so.

Another object management task is the process of deprovisioning. *Deprovisioning* is the management of Active Directory objects in the container. When you remove an object from an Active Directory container, the deprovisioning process removes the object and synchronizes the container to stay current.

Understanding Groups

Now that you know how to create user accounts, it's time to learn how to create group accounts. As an instructor, I am always amazed when students (who work in the IT field) have no idea why they should use groups. This is something every organization should be using.

To illustrate their usefulness, let's say you have a Sales department user by the name of wpanek. Your organization has 100 resources shared on the network for users to access. Because wpanek is part of the Sales department, he has access to 50 of the resources. The Marketing department uses the other 50. If the organization is not using groups and wpanek moves from Sales to Marketing, how many changes do you have to make? The answer is 100. You have to move him out of the 50 resources he currently can use and place his account into the 50 new resources that he now needs.

Now let's say that you use groups. The Sales group has access to 50 resources, and the Marketing group has access to the other 50. If wpanek moves from Sales to Marketing, you need to make only two changes. You just have to take wpanek out of the Sales group and place him in the Marketing group. Once this is done, wpanek can access everything he needs to do his job.

Group Properties

Now that you understand why you should use groups, let's go over setting up groups and their properties (see Figure 19.8). When you are creating groups, it helps to understand some of the options that you need to use.

FIGURE 19.8   New Group dialog box

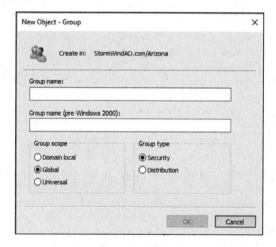

Group Type   You can choose from two group types: security groups and distribution groups.

Security Groups   These groups can have rights and permissions placed on them. For example, if you want to give a certain group of users access to a particular printer, but you want to control what they are allowed to do with this printer, you'd create a security group and then apply certain rights and permissions to this group.

Security groups can also receive emails. If someone sent an email to the group, all users within that group would receive it (as long as they have a mail system that allows for mail-enabled groups, like Exchange).

Distribution Groups   These groups are used for email *only* (as long as they have a mail system that allows for mail-enabled groups, like Exchange). You cannot place permissions and rights for objects on this group type.

Group Scope   When it comes to group scopes, you have three choices.

Domain Local Groups   Domain local groups are groups that remain in the domain in which they were created. You use these groups to grant permissions within a single domain. For example, if you create a domain local group named HPLaser, you cannot use that group in any other domain, and it has to reside in the domain in which you created it.

Global Groups   Global groups can contain other groups and accounts from the domain in which the group is created. In addition, you can give them permissions in any domain in the forest.

Universal Groups   Universal groups can include other groups and accounts from any domain in the domain tree or forest. You can give universal groups permissions in any domain in the domain tree or forest.

Creating Group Strategies

When you are creating a group strategy, think of this acronym that Microsoft likes to use in the exam: AGDLP (or AGLP). This acronym stands for a series of actions you should perform. Here is how it expands:

A   Accounts (Create your user accounts.)

G   Global groups (Put user accounts into global groups.)

DL   Domain local groups (Put global groups into domain local groups.)

P   Permissions (Assign permissions such as Deny or Apply on the domain local group.)

Another acronym that stands for a strategy you can use is AGUDLP (or AULP). Here is how it expands:

A   Accounts (Create your user accounts.)

G   Global groups (Put user accounts into global groups.)

U   Universal groups (Put the global groups into universal groups.)

DL   Domain local groups (Put universal groups into domain local groups.)

P   Permissions (Place permissions on the local group.)

Creating a Group

To create a new group, open the Active Directory Users and Computers snap-in. Click the OU where the group is going to reside. Right-click and choose New and then Group. After you create the group, just click the Members tab and choose Add. Add the users you want to reside in that group, and that's all there is to it.

Filtering and Advanced Active Directory Features

The Active Directory Users and Computers tool has a couple of other features that come in quite handy when you are managing many objects. You can access the Filter Options dialog box by clicking the View menu in the MMC and choosing Filter Options. You'll see a dialog box similar to the one shown in Figure 19.9. Here you can choose to filter objects by their specific types within the display. For example, if you are an administrator who works primarily with user accounts and groups, you can select those specific items by placing check marks in the list. In addition, you can create more complex filters by choosing Create Custom. Doing so provides you with an interface that looks similar to that of the Find command.

FIGURE 19.9   The Filter Options dialog box

Another option in the Active Directory Users and Computers tool is to view advanced options. You can enable the advanced options by choosing Advanced Features in the View menu. This adds some top-level folders to the list under the name of the domain. Let's take a look at a couple of the new top-level folders.

The System folder (shown in Figure 19.10) provides additional features that you can configure to work with Active Directory. You can configure settings for the Distributed File

System (DFS), IP Security (IPSec) policies, the File Replication Service (FRS), and more. In addition to the System folder, you'll see the LostAndFound folder. This folder contains any files that may not have been replicated properly between domain controllers. You should check this folder periodically for any files so that you can decide whether you need to move them or copy them to other locations.

FIGURE 19.10   Advanced Features in the System folder of the Active Directory Users and Computers tool

As you can see, managing Active Directory objects is generally a simple task. The Active Directory Users and Computers tool allows you to configure several objects. Let's move on to look at one more common administration function: moving objects.

Moving, Renaming, and Deleting Active Directory Objects

One of the extremely useful features of the Active Directory Users and Computers tool is its ability to move users and resources easily.

Exercise 19.8 walks you through the process of moving Active Directory objects. In this exercise, you will make several changes to the organization of Active Directory objects. To complete this exercise, first you must have completed Exercise 19.5.

EXERCISE 19.8

Moving Active Directory Objects

1. Open Active Directory Users and Computers by clicking Start ➢ Administrative Tools ➢ Active Directory Users And Computers.

2. Expand the name of the domain.

3. Select the Sales OU (under the New York OU), right-click Workstation1, and select Move. A dialog box appears. Select the RD OU and click OK to move the Computer object to that container.

4. Click the RD OU and verify that Workstation1 was moved.

5. Close the Active Directory Users and Computers tool.

In addition to moving objects within Active Directory, you can easily rename them by right-clicking an object and selecting Rename. Note that this option does not apply to all objects. You can remove objects from Active Directory by right-clicking them and choosing Delete.

Deleting an Active Directory object is an irreversible action. When an object is destroyed, any security permissions or other settings made for that object are removed as well. Because each object within Active Directory contains its own security identifier (SID), simply re-creating an object with the same name does not place any permissions on it. Before you delete an Active Directory object, be sure that you will never need it again. Windows Server 2016 has an Active Directory Recycle Bin to allow an administrator to retrieve a deleted object, but in case the Recycle Bin gets cleared, it's better to be safe than sorry. Also, the AD Recycle Bin is disabled by default, so it will be unavailable unless you turn that feature on. So, what is the moral of this story? Don't delete AD objects unless you are absolutely sure you want them gone.

Windows Server 2016 has a check box called Protect Container From Accidental Deletion for all OUs. If this check box is checked, to delete or move an OU, you must go into the Active Directory Users and Computers advanced options. Once you are in the advanced options, you can uncheck the box to move or delete the OU .

Resetting an Existing Computer Account

Every computer on the domain establishes a discrete channel of communication with the domain controller at logon time. The domain controller stores a randomly selected password (different from the user password) for authentication across the channel. The password is updated every 30 days.

Sometimes the computer's password and the domain controller's password don't match, and communication between the two machines fails. Without the ability to reset the computer account, you wouldn't be able to connect the machine to the domain. Fortunately, you can use the Active Directory Users and Computers tool to reestablish the connection.

Exercise 19.9 shows you how to reset an existing computer account. You should have completed the previous exercises in this chapter before you begin this exercise.

EXERCISE 19.9

Resetting an Existing Computer Account

1. Open Active Directory Users and Computers by clicking Start ➢ Administrative Tools ➢ Active Directory Users And Computers.

2. Expand the name of the domain.

3. Click the RD OU and then right-click the Workstation1 computer account.

4. Select Reset Account from the context menu. Click Yes to confirm your selection. Click OK at the success prompt.

5. When you reset the account, you break the connection between the computer and the domain. So, after performing this exercise, reconnect the computer to the domain if you want it to continue working on the network.

Throughout this book, I have tried to show you the PowerShell way of doing a task shown previously using an MMC snap-in. Well, this is going to be no different.

This example shows you how to reset the secure connection between the local computer and the domain to which it is joined using a PowerShell command. In this example, the domain controller that performs the operation is specified as `StormDC1.StormWindAD.com`. To execute this PowerShell command, you must run this command on the local computer:

```
Test-ComputerSecureChannel -Repair -Server StormDC1.StormWindAD.com
```

Understanding Dynamic Access Control

One of the advantages of Windows Server 2016 is the ability to apply data governance to your file server. This will help control who has access to information and auditing. You get these advantages through the use of *Dynamic Access Control (DAC)*. Dynamic Access Control allows you to identify data by using data classifications (both automatic and manual) and then control access to these files based on these classifications.

DAC also gives administrators the ability to control file access by using a central access policy. This central access policy will also allow an administrator to set up audit access to files for reporting and forensic investigation.

DAC allows an administrator to set up Active Directory Rights Management Service encryption for Microsoft Office documents. For example, you can set up encryption for any documents that contain financial information.

Dynamic Access Control gives an administrator the flexibility to configure file access and auditing to domain-based file servers. To do this, DAC controls claims in the authentication token, resource properties, and conditional expressions within permission and auditing entries.

Administrators have the ability to give users access to files and folders based on Active Directory attributes. For example, a user named Dana is given access to the file server share because in the user's Active Directory (department attribute) properties, the value contains the value Sales.

 For DAC to function properly, an administrator must enable Windows 7/8/10 computers and Windows Server 2012/2012 R2/2016 file servers to support claims and compound authentication.

Managing Security and Permissions

Now that you understand the basic issues, terms, and Active Directory objects that pertain to security, it's time to look at how you can apply this information to secure your network resources. The general practice for managing security is to assign users to groups and then grant permissions and logon parameters to the groups so that they can access certain resources.

For management ease and to implement a hierarchical structure, you can place groups within OUs. You can also assign Group Policy settings to all of the objects contained within an OU. By using this method, you can combine the benefits of a hierarchical structure (through OUs) with the use of security principals.

The primary tool you use to manage security permissions for users, groups, and computers is the Active Directory Users and Computers tool. Using this tool, you can create and manage Active Directory objects and organize them based on your business needs. Common tasks for many system administrators might include the following:

- Resetting a user's password (for example, in cases where they forget their password)

- Creating new user accounts (when, for instance, a new employee joins the company)

- Modifying group memberships based on changes in job requirements and functions

- Disabling user accounts (when, for example, users will be out of the office for long periods of time and will not require network resource access)

Once you've properly grouped your users, you need to set the actual permissions that affect the objects within Active Directory. The actual permissions that are available vary based on the type of object. Table 19.1 provides an example of some of the permissions that you can apply to various Active Directory objects and an explanation of what each permission does.

TABLE 19.1　Permissions of Active Directory objects

Permission	Explanation
Control Access	Changes security permissions on the object
Create Child	Creates objects within an OU (such as other OUs)
Delete Child	Deletes child objects within an OU
Delete Tree	Deletes an OU and the objects within it
List Contents	Views objects within an OU
List Object	Views a list of the objects within an OU
Read	Views properties of an object (such as a username)
Write	Modifies properties of an object

Using ACLs and ACEs

Each object in Active Directory has an *access control list*. The ACL is a list of user accounts and groups that are allowed to access the resource. For each ACL, there is an access control entry that defines what a user or a group can actually do with the resource. Deny permissions are always listed first. This means that if users have Deny permissions through user or group membership, they will not be allowed to access the object, even if they have explicit Allow permissions through other user or group permissions.

 Real World Scenario

Using Groups Effectively

You are a new system administrator for a medium-sized organization, and your network spans a single campus environment. The previous administrator had migrated the network from Windows Server 2008 to Windows Server 2016 and everyone seems fine with the network and new workstations. As you familiarize yourself with the network, you realize that the previous administrator applied a very ad hoc approach. Many of the permissions to resources had been given to individual accounts on request. It seems that there was no particular strategy with regard to administration.

Management tells you that the company has acquired another company, ideally the first of several acquisitions. They tell you about these plans because they do not want any hiccups in the information system as necessary changes ensue.

You immediately realize that management practices of the past must be replaced with the best practices that have been developed for networks over the years. One of the fundamental practices that you need to establish for this environment is the use of groups to apply permissions and give privileges to users throughout the network.

It is quite simple to give permissions individually, and in some cases, it seems like overkill to create a group, give permissions to the group, and then add a user to the group. Using group-based permissions really pays off in the long run, however, regardless of how small your network is today.

One constant in the networking world is that networks grow. When they grow, it is much easier to add users to a well-thought-out system of groups and consistently applied policies and permissions than it is to patch these elements together for each individual user.

Don't get caught up in the "easy" way of dealing with each request as it comes down the pike. Take the time to figure out how the system will benefit from a more structured approach. Visualize your network as already large with numerous accounts, even if it is still small; this way, when it grows, you will be well positioned to manage the network as smoothly as possible.

Using Group Policy for Security

A very useful and powerful feature of Active Directory is a technology known as a *Group Policy*. Through the use of Group Policy settings, system administrators can assign thousands of different settings and options for users, groups, and OUs. Specifically, in relation to security, you can use many different options to control how important features such as password policies, user rights, and account lockout settings can be configured.

The general process for making these settings is to create a *Group Policy object (GPO)* with the settings you want and then link it to an OU or other Active Directory object.

Table 19.2 lists many Group Policy settings that are relevant to creating a secure Active Directory environment. Note that this list is not comprehensive—many other options are available through Windows Server 2016's administrative tools.

TABLE 19.2 Group Policy settings used for security purposes

Setting section	Setting name	Purpose
Account Policies ➤ Password Policy	Enforce Password History	Specifies how many passwords will be remembered. This option prevents users from reusing the same passwords whenever they're changed.
Account Policies ➤ Password Policy	Minimum Password Length	Prevents users from using short, weak passwords by specifying the minimum number of characters that the password must include.
Account Policies ➤ Account Lockout Policy	Account Lockout Threshold	Specifies how many bad password attempts can be entered before the account gets locked out.
Account Policies ➤ Account Lockout Policy	Account Lockout Duration	Specifies how long an account will remain locked out after too many bad password attempts have been entered. By setting this option to a reasonable value (such as 30 minutes), you can reduce administrative overhead while still maintaining fairly strong security.
Account Policies ➤ Account Lockout Policy	Reset Account Lockout Counter After	Specifies how long the Account Lockout Threshold counter will hold failed logon attempts before resetting to 0.
Local Policies ➤ Security Options	Accounts: Rename Administrator Account	Often, when trying to gain unauthorized access to a computer, individuals attempt to guess the administrator password. One method for increasing security is to rename this account so that no password allows entry using this logon.
Local Policies ➤ Security Options	Domain Controller: Allow Server Operators To Schedule Tasks	This option specifies whether members of the built-in Server Operators group are allowed to schedule tasks on the server.
Local Policies ➤ Security Options	Interactive Logon: Do Not Display Last User Name	Increases security by not displaying the name of the last user who logged on to the system.
Local Policies ➤ Security Options	Shutdown: Allow System To Be Shut Down Without Having To Log On	Allows system administrators to perform remote shutdown operations without logging on to the server.

You can use several different methods to configure Group Policy settings using the tools included with Windows Server 2016. Exercise 19.10 walks through the steps required to create a basic group policy for the purpose of enforcing security settings. To complete the steps of this exercise, you must have completed Exercise 19.1.

EXERCISE 19.10

Applying Security Policies by Using Group Policy

1. Open the Group Policy Management Console tool.

2. Expand Domains and then click the domain name.

3. In the right pane, right-click the Default Domain Policy and choose Edit.

4. In the Group Policy Management Editor window, expand Computer Configuration ➤ Policies ➤ Windows Settings ➤ Security Settings ➤ Account Policies ➤ Password Policy.

5. In the right pane, double-click the Minimum Password Length setting.

6. In the Security Policy Setting dialog box, make sure the box labeled Define This Policy Setting Option is checked. Increase the Password Must Be At Least value to eight characters.

7. Click OK to return to the Group Policy Management Editor window.

8. Expand User Configuration ➤ Policies ➤ Administrative Templates ➤ Control Panel. Double-click Prohibit Access To The Control Panel And PC settings, select Enabled, and then click OK.

9. Close the Group Policy window.

Fine-Grained Password Policies

The Windows 2016 operating systems allow an organization to have different password and account lockout policies for different sets of users in a domain. In versions of Active Directory before 2008, an administrator could set up only one password policy and account lockout policy per domain.

The Default Domain policy for the domain is where these policy settings were configured. Because domains could have only one password and account lockout policy, organizations that wanted multiple password and account lockout settings had to either create a password filter or deploy multiple domains.

Fine-grained password policies allow you to specify multiple password policies within a single domain. Let's say you want administrators not to have to change their password as frequently as salespeople. Fine-grained password policies allow you to do just that.

Password Settings objects (PSOs) are created so that you can create fine-grained password policies. You create PSOs using the ADSI editor and then you can use those PSOs to create your fine-grained password policies.

Exercise 19.11 walks through the creation of a custom password policy using the ADSI Edit tool, and then you will link that policy to a group using Active Directory Users and Computers. Before completing this exercise, create a new global group named Passgroup in Active Directory Users and Computers.

 Administrators also have the ability to create fine-grained password policies using the Active Directory Administrative Center. I will show you how to create a new password policy in the section "Using the Active Directory Administrative Center" later in this chapter.

EXERCISE 19.11

Fine-Grained Password Policy

1. Open ADSI Edit by pressing the Windows key and choosing ADSI Edit.

2. Right-click ADSI Edit and then choose Connect To.

3. When the Connection Settings dialog box appears, click OK.

4. In the window on the left, expand Default Naming Context ≻ DC=yourdomainname,DC=com ≻ CN=System ≻ CN=Password Settings Container.

5. Right-click CN=Password Settings Container and choose New ≻ Object.

6. In the Select A Class box, choose msDS-PasswordSettings and click Next.

7. At the Common Name screen, type **CustomPolicy** and click Next.

8. At the Password Settings Precedence screen, enter **10** as the value. This works as a cost value. The lowest priority takes precedence.

9. At the Password Reversible Encryption Status For Users Accounts screen, set the value to False (recommended by Microsoft).

10. The Password History Length screen shows how many passwords are remembered before a password can be used again. You can set this for up to 1,024 remembered passwords. Set the value to **12**. Click Next.

11. At the Password Complexity screen, set the value to True.

12. The next screen will be the Minimum Password Length screen. Set the value to **8** and click Next.

13. At the Minimum Password Age screen, you must enter a value for the amount of time you want the password to be used at a minimum. Time is done in the I8 format, like so:

    −600000000 = 1 minute

    −36000000000 = 1 hour

    −864000000000 = 1 day

Enter **–8640000000000** (10 zeros) as your value for 10 days and click Next. You must put the – (minus) sign in the front of the value.

14. At the Maximum Password Age screen, set the value as **–51840000000000** (10 zeros). This value equals 60 days. Click Next.

15. At the Lockout Threshold screen, enter **3** and click Next.

16. At the Observation Window screen, enter **–3000000000** (5 minutes) and click Next.

17. At the Lockout Duration screen, enter **–18000000000** (30 minutes) and click Next.

18. Click Finished. If you received any errors, check all of your times to be sure the – (minus) sign appears in front of the number.

19. Close ADSI Edit.

20. Open the Active Directory Users and Computers snap-in.

21. On the View menu along the top, make sure Advanced Features is checked.

22. In the window on the left, expand Active Directory Users And Computers ➢ *yourdomain* ➢ System ➢ Password Settings Container.

23. In the details pane on the right side, right-click CustomPolicy and choose Properties.

24. Click the Attribute Editor tab.

25. Scroll down and select the msDS-PsoAppliesTo attribute. Click Edit.

26. In the Multi-valued Distinguished Name dialog box, click Add Windows Account.

27. Type in **Passgroup** (this is the group you created before the exercise) and click the Check Name button. Click OK.

28. Click OK twice more, and then you are finished. Close the Active Directory Users and Computers snap-in.

Publishing Active Directory Objects

One of the main goals of Active Directory is to make resources easy to find. Two of the most commonly used resources in a networked environment are server file shares and printers. These are so common, in fact, that most organizations have dedicated file and print servers. When it comes to managing these types of resources, Active Directory makes it easy to determine which files and printers are available to users.

With that being said, take a look at how Active Directory manages to publish shared folders and printers.

Making Active Directory Objects Available to Users

An important aspect of managing Active Directory objects is that a system administrator can control which objects users can see. The act of making an Active Directory object available is known as *publishing*. The two main types of publishable objects are Printer objects and Shared Folder objects.

The general process for creating server shares and shared printers has remained unchanged from previous versions of Windows: you create the various objects (a printer or a file system folder) and then enable them for sharing. To make these resources available via Active Directory, however, there's an additional step: you must publish the resources. Once an object has been published in Active Directory, clients will be able to use it.

When you publish objects in Active Directory, you should know the server name and share name of the resource. When system administrators use Active Directory objects, they can change the resource to which the object points, without having to reconfigure or even notify clients. For example, if you move a share from one server to another, all you need to do is to update the Shared Folder object's properties to point to the new location. Active Directory clients still refer to the resource with the same path and name that they used before.

Publishing Printers

Printers can be published easily within Active Directory. This makes them available to users in your domain.

Exercise 19.12 walks you through the steps you need to take to share and publish a Printer object by having you create and share a printer. To complete the printer installation, you need access to the Windows Server 2016 installation media (via the hard disk, a network share, or the DVD drive).

EXERCISE 19.12

Creating and Publishing a Printer

1. Click the Windows key on the keyboard and choose Control Panel.

2. Click Devices And Printers ➢ Add A Printer. This starts the Add Printer Wizard. Then click the Next button.

3. In the Choose A Local Or Network Printer page, select Add A Local Printer. This should automatically take you to the next page. If it does not, click Next.

4. On the Choose A Printer Port page, select Use An Existing Port. From the drop-down list beside that option, make sure LPT1: (Printer Port) is selected. Click Next.

5. On the Install The Printer Driver page, select Generic for the manufacturer. For the printer, highlight Generic/Text Only. Click Next.

6. On the Type A Printer Name page, type **Text Printer**. Uncheck the Set As The Default Printer box and then click Next.

7.   The Installing Printer screen appears. After the system is finished, the Printer Sharing page appears. Make sure the box labeled "Share this printer so that others on your network can find and use it" is selected, and accept the default share name of Text Printer.

8.   In the Location section, type **Building 203**, and in the Comment section, add the following comment: **This is a text-only Printer**. Click Next.

9.   On the You've Successfully Added Text Printer page, click Finish.

10. Next you need to verify that the printer will be listed in Active Directory. Right-click the Text Printer icon and select Printer Properties.

11. Select the Sharing tab and make sure that the List In The Directory box is checked. Note that you can also add additional printer drivers for other operating systems using this tab. Click OK to accept the settings.

Note that when you create and share a printer this way, an Active Directory Printer object is not displayed within the Active Directory Users and Computers tool. The printer is actually associated with the Computer object to which it is connected.

Publishing Shared Folders

Now that you've created and published a printer, you'll see how the same thing can be done to shared folders.

Exercise 19.13 walks through the steps required to create a folder, share it, and then publish it in Active Directory. This exercise assumes you are using the C: partition; however, you may want to change this based on your server configuration. This exercise assumes you have completed Exercise 19.5.

Creating and Publishing a Shared Folder

1.   Create a new folder in the root directory of your C: partition and name it **Test Share**. To do this, click the File Explorer link on the toolbar.

2.   Right-click the Test Share folder. Choose Share With ➢ Specific People.

3.   In the File Sharing dialog box, enter the names of users with whom you want to share this folder. In the upper box, enter **Everyone** and then click Add. Note that Everyone appears in the lower box. Click in the Permission Level column next to Everyone and choose Read/Write from the pop-up menu. Then click Share.

4.   You'll see a message that your folder has been shared. Click Done.

5.   Click the Windows key on the keyboard and choose Administrative Tools.

6. Open the Active Directory Users and Computers tool. Expand the current domain and right-click the RD OU. Select New ≻ Shared Folder.

7. In the New Object - Shared Folder dialog box, type **Shared Folder Test** for the name of the folder. Then type the UNC path to the share (for example, **\\server1\Test Share**). Click OK to create the share.

Once you have created and published the Shared Folder object, clients can use the My Network Places icon to find it. The Shared Folder object will be organized based on the OU in which you created it. When you use publication, you can see how this makes it easy to manage shared folders.

Querying Active Directory

So far you've created several Active Directory resources. One of the main benefits of having all of your resource information in Active Directory is that you can easily find what you're looking for using the Find dialog box. Recall that I recommended that you always enter as much information as possible when creating Active Directory objects. This is where that extra effort begins to pay off.

Exercise 19.14 walks you through the steps to find specific objects in Active Directory. To complete this exercise, you must have completed Exercise 19.5.

EXERCISE 19.14

Finding Objects in Active Directory

1. Open Active Directory Users and Computers by clicking Start ≻ Administrative Tools ≻ Active Directory Users And Computers.

2. Right-click the name of the domain and select Find.

3. In the Find Users, Contacts, And Groups dialog box, select Users, Contacts, And Groups from the Find drop-down list. For the In setting, choose Entire Directory. This searches the entire Active Directory environment for the criteria you enter.

   Note that if this is a production domain and there are many objects, searching the whole directory may be a time-consuming and network-intensive operation.

4. In the Name field, type **admin** and then click Find Now to obtain the results of the search.

5. Now that you have found several results, you can narrow down the list. Click the Advanced tab of the Find Users, Contacts, And Groups dialog box.

   In the Field drop-down list, select User ≻ Last Name. For Condition, select Starts With, and for Value, type **admin**. Click Add to add this condition to the search criteria. Click Find Now. Now only the users that have the last name Admin are shown.

6. When you have finished searching, close the Find Users, Contacts, And Groups dialog box and exit the Active Directory Users and Computers tool.

Using the many options available in the Find dialog box, you can usually narrow down the objects for which you are searching quickly and efficiently. Users and system administrators alike find this tool useful in environments of any size. Now that you have seen how to create objects in Active Directory, let's take a look at a new Windows Server 2016 feature called Active Directory Administrative Center.

Using the Active Directory Administrative Center

Windows Server 2016 has a feature called the *Active Directory Administrative Center*. This feature allows you to manage many Active Directory tasks from one central location (see Figure 19.11).

FIGURE 19.11 Administrative Center Overview screen

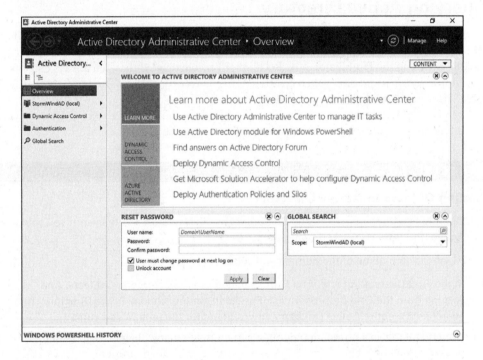

Using the Active Directory Administrative Center, here are some of the tasks that an administrator can perform:

- Reset passwords
- Create new objects
- Delete objects
- Move objects
- Perform global searches
- Configure properties for Active Directory objects

In Windows Server 2016, the Active Directory Administrative Center is just another tool in your Active Directory tool belt. It does not matter which way you create your Active Directory objects as long as you have a good understanding of how to create them.

One of the easy tasks that you can complete with the Active Directory Administrative center is the ability to create a Fine-Grained Password Policy.

Exercise 19.15 walks you through the steps to create a password policy for the IT Department. To complete this exercise, you must have a Global Security group called IT. If you do not have a group called IT, please create the IT group using Active Directory Users and Computers.

EXERCISE 19.15

Creating a PSO Using the Active Directory Administrative Center

1. Open the Active Directory Administrative Center by clicking Start ➢ Administrative Tools ➢ Active Directory Administrative Center.

2. Expand the domain, expand System, and then click Password Settings Container (see Figure 19.12).

FIGURE 19.12   Password Settings Container

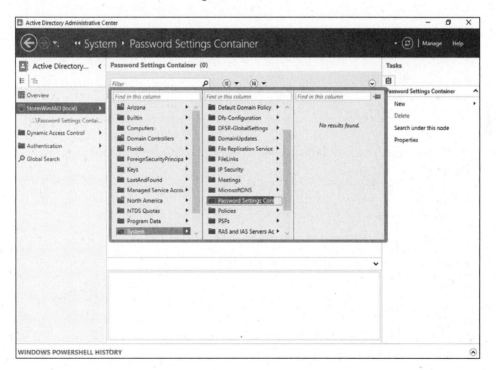

EXERCISE 19.15 *(continued)*

3. In the right-hand side under Tasks, choose New ➤ Password Settings (see Figure 19.13).

FIGURE 19.13 New Password Settings

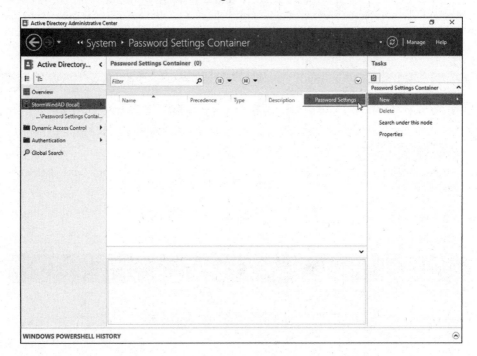

4. When the Password Settings dialog box appears, fill in the following settings (see Figure 19.14):

- Name: **ITpso**
- Precedence: **10**
- Enforce Minimum Password Length: checked
- Minimum Password Length (characters): **8**
- Enforce Password History: checked
- Number Of Passwords Remembered: **24**
- Password Must Meet Complexity Requirements: checked
- Protect From Accidental Deletion: checked

- Enforce Minimum Password Age: checked

- User Cannot Change The Password Within: **1** (for 1 day)

- Enforce Maximum Password Age: checked

- User Must Change The Password After: **60** (for 60 days)

- Enforce Account Lockout Policy: checked

- Number Of Failed Logon Attempts Allowed: **5**

- Reset Failed Logon Attempts Count After (min): **30**

- Account Will Be Locked Out : Until An Administrator Manually Unlocks The Account

- Protect From Accidental Deletion: checked

- Description: **IT Department Password Policy**

FIGURE 19.14   PSO settings

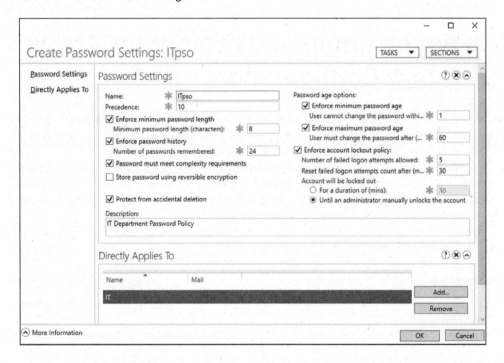

5.   Click the Add button.

6.   Type in **IT** and click the Check Names button (see Figure 19.15). Then click OK.

FIGURE 19.15   Select Users or Groups

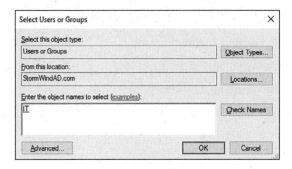

7.   Click OK to complete the PSO. Close the Active Directory Administrative Center.

Using the Command Prompt for Active Directory Configuration

Many IT administrators like to use command-line commands to configure and maintain their Active Directory environment. One advantage of using command-line commands is the ability to do multiple changes at once using batch files.

Another advantage of knowing how to manipulate Active Directory using the command prompt is working with Windows Server 2016 Server Core. Server Core is an installation of Windows Server 2016 that has no GUI windows. One of the ways to configure Server Core is to use commands in the command prompt window.

Table 19.3 shows you many of the command prompt commands and explains how each command affects Active Directory.

TABLE 19.3   Command prompt commands

Command	Explanation
Csvde	This command allows you to import and export data from Active Directory. The data gets stored in a comma-separated value (CSV) format.
Dcdiag	This troubleshooting command checks the state of your domain controllers in your forest and sends back a report of any problems.

Command	Explanation
Djoin	This command allows a computer account to join a domain, and it runs an offline domain join when a computer restarts.
Dsacls	This command allows you to see and change permissions in the access control list for objects in Active Directory Domain Services (AD DS).
Dsadd	This command allows you to add an object to the AD DS directory.
Dsamain	This command shows the Active Directory data stored in either a snapshot or a backup as if it were in a Lightweight Directory Access Protocol (LDAP) server.
Dsdbutil	This command provides database utilities for Active Directory Lightweight Directory Services (AD LDS).
Dsget	This command shows the properties of an object in the AD DS directory.
Dsmgmt	This command gives an administrator management utilities for AD LDS.
Dsmod	This command allows you to modify an AD DS object.
Dsmove	This command allows you to move an object in an Active Directory domain from its current OU to a new OU within the same forest.
Dsquery	This command allows you to query AD DS.
Dsrm	This command removes an object from the AD DS directory.
Ldifde	This command allows you to import and export data from Active Directory. The data is stored as LDAP Data Interchange Format (LDIF).
Ntdsutil	This is one of the most important commands for Active Directory. It allows you to do maintenance on the Active Directory database.
Repadmin	This command allows administrators to diagnose Active Directory replication problems between domain controllers.

PowerShell for Active Directory

Table 19.4 will show you just some of the available PowerShell commands for maintaining Active Directory. These PowerShell commands can help you do everything from unlocking disabled accounts to doing password resets.

To see a complete list of PowerShell commands for Active Directory, please visit Microsoft's website at:

https://technet.microsoft.com/en-us/library/ee617195.aspx

TABLE 19.4   PowerShell commands for Active Directory

Command	Explanation
Add-ADComputerServiceAccount	This command allows an administrator to add service accounts to Active Directory.
Add-ADGroupMember	This command allows you to add users to an Active Directory group.
Disable-ADAccount	Administrators can use this command to disable an Active Directory account.
Enable-ADAccount	Administrators can use this command to enable an Active Directory account.
Get-ADComputer	This command allows you to view one or more Active Directory computers.
Get-ADDomain	Administrators can use this command to view an Active Directory domain.
Get-ADFineGrainedPasswordPolicy	This command allows you to view the Active Directory fine-grained password policies.
Get-ADGroup	Administrators can use this command to view Active Directory groups.
Get-ADGroupMember	This command allows you to view the users in an Active Directory group.
Get-ADServiceAccount	Administrators can use this command to view the Active Directory service accounts.
Get-ADUser	This command allows you to view one or more Active Directory users.
New-ADComputer	Administrators can use this command to create a new Active Directory computer.
New-ADGroup	Administrators can use this command to create a new Active Directory group.

Command	Explanation
New-ADServiceAccount	This command is the *only* way that you can create a new Managed Service Account.
New-ADUser	Administrators can use this command to create a new Active Directory user.
Set-ADAccountPassword	This command allows you to modify the password of an Active Directory account.
Unlock-ADAccount	Administrators can use this command to unlock an Active Directory account.

Summary

This chapter covered the fundamentals of administering Active Directory. The most important part of administering Active Directory is learning about how to work with OUs. Therefore, you should be aware of the purpose of OUs; that is, they help you to organize and manage the directory. For instance, think of administrative control. If you wanted to delegate rights to another administrator (such as a sales manager), you could delegate that authority to that user within the Sales OU. As the system administrator, you would retain the rights to the castle.

You also looked at how to design an OU structure from an example. The example showed you how to design a proper OU layout. You can also create, organize, and reorganize OUs if need be.

In addition, you took a look at groups and group strategies. There are different types of groups (domain local, global, and universal groups), and you should know when each group is available and when to use each group.

Finally, this chapter covered how to use the Active Directory Users and Computers tool to manage Active Directory objects. If you're responsible for day-to-day system administration, there's a good chance that you are already familiar with this tool; if not, you should be after reading this chapter. Using this tool, you learned how to work with Active Directory objects such as User, Computer, and Group objects.

Exam Essentials

Understand the purpose of OUs.   OUs are used to create a hierarchical, logical organization for objects within an Active Directory domain.

Know the types of objects that can reside within OUs.   OUs can contain Active Directory User, Computer, Shared Folder, and other objects.

Understand how to use the Delegation of Control Wizard. The Delegation of Control Wizard is used to assign specific permissions at the level of OUs.

Understand the concept of inheritance. By default, child OUs inherit permissions and Group Policy assignments set for parent OUs. However, these settings can be overridden for more granular control of security.

Know groups and group strategies. You can use three groups: domain local, global, and universal. Understand the group strategies and when they apply.

Understand how Active Directory objects work. Active Directory objects represent some piece of information about components within a domain. The objects themselves have attributes that describe details about them.

Understand how Active Directory objects can be organized. By using the Active Directory Users and Computers tool, you can create, move, rename, and delete various objects.

Understand how to import bulk users. You can import multiple accounts by doing a bulk import. Bulk imports use files to import the data into Active Directory. Know the two utilities (ldifde.exe and csvde.exe) you need to perform the bulk imports and how to use them.

Learn how resources can be published. A design goal for Active Directory was to make network resources easier for users to find. With that in mind, you should understand how using published printers and shared folders can simplify network resource management.

Review Questions

You can find the answers in the Appendix.

1. You are the administrator of an organization with a single Active Directory domain. A user who left the company returns after 16 weeks. The user tries to log on to their old computer and receives an error stating that authentication has failed. The user's account has been enabled. You need to ensure that the user is able to log on to the domain using that computer. What do you do?

    A. Reset the computer account in Active Directory. Disjoin the computer from the domain, and then rejoin the computer to the domain.

    B. Run the ADadd command to rejoin the computer account.

    C. Run the MMC utility on the user's computer, and add the Domain Computers snap-in.

    D. Re-create the user account and reconnect the user account to the computer account.

2. You are the administrator of an organization with a single Active Directory domain. One of your senior executives tries to log on to a machine and receives the error "This user account has expired. Ask your administrator to reactivate your account." You need to make sure that this doesn't happen again to this user. What do you do?

    A. Configure the domain policy to disable account lockouts.

    B. Configure the password policy to extend the maximum password age to 0.

    C. Modify the user's properties to set the Account Never Expires setting.

    D. Modify the user's properties to extend the maximum password age to 0.

3. You need to create a new user account using the command prompt. Which command would you use?

    A. dsmodify

    B. dscreate

    C. dsnew

    D. dsadd

4. Maria is a user who belongs to the Sales distribution global group. She is not able to access the laser printer that is shared on the network. The Sales global group has full access to the laser printer. How do you fix the problem?

    A. Change the group type to a security group.

    B. Add the Sales global group to the Administrators group.

    C. Add the Sales global group to the Printer Operators group.

    D. Change the Sales group to a local group.

5. You are a domain administrator for a large domain. Recently, you have been asked to make changes to some of the permissions related to OUs within the domain. To restrict security for the Texas OU further, you remove some permissions at that level. Later, a junior system administrator mentions that she is no longer able to make changes to objects within the

Austin OU (which is located within the Texas OU). Assuming that no other changes have been made to Active Directory permissions, which of the following characteristics of OUs might have caused the change in permissions?

A. Inheritance

B. Group Policy

C. Delegation

D. Object properties

6. Isabel, a system administrator, created a new Active Directory domain in an environment that already contains two trees. During the promotion of the domain controller, she chose to create a new Active Directory forest. Isabel is a member of the Enterprise Administrators group and has full permissions over all domains. During the organization's migration to Active Directory, many updates were made to the information stored within the domains. Recently, users and other system administrators have complained about not being able to find specific Active Directory objects in one or more domains (although the objects exist in others). To investigate the problem, Isabel wants to check for any objects that have not been properly replicated among domain controllers. If possible, she would like to restore these objects to their proper place within the relevant Active Directory domains.

Which two of the following actions should she perform to be able to view the relevant information? (Choose two.)

A. Change Active Directory permissions to allow object information to be viewed in all domains.

B. Select the Advanced Features item in the View menu.

C. Promote a member server in each domain to a domain controller.

D. Rebuild all domain controllers from the latest backups.

E. Examine the contents of the LostAndFound folder using the Active Directory Users and Computers tool.

7. You are a consultant hired to evaluate an organization's Active Directory domain. The domain contains more than 200,000 objects and hundreds of OUs. You begin examining the objects within the domain, but you find that the loading of the contents of specific OUs takes a long time. Furthermore, the list of objects can be large. You want to do the following:

- Use the built-in Active Directory administrative tools and avoid the use of third-party tools or utilities.

- Limit the list of objects within an OU to only the type of objects that you're examining (for example, only Computer objects).

- Prevent any changes to the Active Directory domain or any of the objects within it.

Which one of the following actions meets these requirements?

A. Use the Filter option in the Active Directory Users and Computers tool to restrict the display of objects.

B. Use the Delegation of Control Wizard to give yourself permissions over only a certain type of object.

   C. Implement a new naming convention for objects within an OU and then sort the results using this new naming convention.

   D. Use the Active Directory Domains and Trusts tool to view information from only selected domain controllers.

   E. Edit the domain Group Policy settings to allow yourself to view only the objects of interest.

8. You are the administrator for a small organization with four servers. You have one file server named StormSrvA that runs Windows Server 2016. You have a junior administrator who needs to do backups on this server. You need to ensure that the junior admin can use Windows Server Backup to create a complete backup of StormSrvA. What should you configure to allow the junior admin to do the backups?

   A. The local groups by using Computer Management

   B. A task by using Authorization Manager

   C. The User Rights Assignment by using the Local Group Policy Editor

   D. The Role Assignment by using Authorization Manager

9. Miguel is a junior-level system administrator, and he has basic knowledge about working with Active Directory. As his supervisor, you have asked Miguel to make several security-related changes to OUs within the company's Active Directory domain. You instruct Miguel to use the basic functionality provided in the Delegation of Control Wizard. Which of the following operations are represented as common tasks within the Delegation of Control Wizard? (Choose all that apply.)

   A. Reset passwords on user accounts.

   B. Manage Group Policy links.

   C. Modify the membership of a group.

   D. Create, delete, and manage groups.

10. You are the primary system administrator for a large Active Directory domain. Recently, you have hired another system administrator upon whom you intend to offload some of your responsibilities. This system administrator will be responsible for handling help desk calls and for basic user account management. You want to allow the new employee to have permissions to reset passwords for all users within a specific OU. However, for security reasons, it's important that the user not be able to make permissions changes for objects within other OUs in the domain. Which of the following is the best way to do this?

   A. Create a special administration account within the OU and grant it full permissions for all objects within Active Directory.

   B. Move the user's login account into the OU that the new employee is to administer.

   C. Move the user's login account to an OU that contains the OU (that is, the parent OU of the one that the new employee is to administer).

   D. Use the Delegation of Control Wizard to assign the necessary permissions on the OU that the new employee is to administer.

Chapter

20

Maintaining Active Directory

THE FOLLOWING 70-742 EXAM OBJECTIVES ARE COVERED IN THIS CHAPTER:

✓ **Maintain Active Directory**

- This objective may include but is not limited to: Back up Active Directory and SYSVOL; manage Active Directory offline; perform offline defragmentation of an Active Directory database; clean up metadata; configure Active Directory snapshots; perform object- and container-level recovery; perform Active Directory restore; configure and restore objects by using the Active Directory Recycle Bin; configure replication to Read-Only Domain Controllers (RODCs); configure Password Replication Policy (PRP) for RODC; monitor and manage replication; upgrade SYSVOL replication to Distributed File System Replication (DFSR).

✓ **Configure Active Directory in a complex enterprise environment**

- This objective may include but is not limited to: Configure a multi-domain and multi-forest Active Directory infrastructure; deploy Windows Server 2016 domain controllers within a pre-existing Active Directory environment; upgrade existing domains and forests; configure domain and forest functional levels; configure multiple user principal name (UPN) suffixes; configure external, forest, shortcut, and realm trusts; configure trust authentication; configure SID filtering; configure name suffix routing; configure sites and subnets; create and configure site links; manage site coverage; manage registration of SRV records; move domain controllers between sites; configure account policies.

Microsoft has designed Active Directory to be an enterprise-wide solution for managing network resources. In previous chapters, you saw how to create Active Directory objects based on an organization's logical design. Domain structure and organizational unit (OU) structure, for example, should be designed based primarily on an organization's business needs.

Now it's time to learn how Active Directory can map to an organization's *physical* requirements. Specifically, you must consider network connectivity between sites and the flow of information between domain controllers (DCs) under less-than-ideal conditions. These constraints determine how domain controllers can work together to ensure that the objects within Active Directory remain synchronized no matter how large and geographically dispersed the network.

Fortunately, through the use of the Active Directory Sites and Services administrative tool, you can quickly and easily create the various components of an Active Directory replication topology. Using this tool, you can create objects called *sites*, place servers in sites, and create connections between sites. Once you have configured Active Directory replication to fit your current network environment, you can sit back and allow Active Directory to make sure that information remains consistent across domain controllers.

This chapter covers the features of Active Directory, which allow system administrators to modify the behavior of replication based on their physical network design. Through the use of sites, system and network administrators will be able to leverage their network infrastructure best to support Windows Server 2016 and Active Directory.

So far, you have learned the steps necessary to install the Domain Name System (DNS) and to implement the first Active Directory domain. Although I briefly introduced multidomain Active Directory structures earlier, I focused on only a single domain and the objects within it.

Many businesses find that using a single domain provides an adequate solution to meet their business needs. By working with *trees* and *forests*, however, large organizations can use multiple domains to organize their environments better.

Overview of Network Planning

Before I discuss sites and replication, you need to understand some basic physical and network concepts.

The Three Types of Networks

When designing networks, system and network administrators use the following terms to define the types of connectivity between locations and servers:

Local Area Networks   A *local area network (LAN)* is usually characterized as a high-bandwidth network. Generally, an organization owns all of its LAN network hardware and software. Ethernet is by far the most common networking standard. Ethernet speeds are generally at least 10 Mbps and can scale to multiple gigabits per second. Currently, the standard for Ethernet is the 10 Gigabit Ethernet, which runs at 10 times the speed of Gigabit Ethernet (1 GB). Several LAN technologies, including routing and switching, are available to segment LANs and to reduce contention for network resources.

Wide Area Networks   The purpose of a *wide area network (WAN)* is similar to that of a LAN, that is, to connect network devices. Unlike LANs, however, WANs are usually leased from third-party telecommunications carriers and organizations known as *Internet service providers (ISPs)*. Although extremely high-speed WAN connections are available, they are generally costly for organizations to implement through a distributed environment. Therefore, WAN connections are characterized by lower-speed connections and, sometimes, nonpersistent connections.

The Internet   The *Internet* is a worldwide public network infrastructure based on the *Internet Protocol (IP)*. Access to the Internet is available through Internet service providers (ISPs). Because it is a public network, there is no single "owner" of the Internet. Instead, large network and telecommunications providers constantly upgrade the infrastructure of this network to meet growing demands.

Organizations use the Internet regularly to sell and market their products and services. For example, it's rare nowadays to see advertisements that don't direct you to one website or another. Through the use of technologies such as *virtual private networks (VPNs)*, organizations can use encryption and authentication technology to enable secure communications across the Internet.

Exploring Network Constraints

In an ideal situation, a high-speed network would connect all computers and networking devices. In such a situation, you would be able to ensure that any user of your network, regardless of location, would be able to access resources quickly and easily. When you are working in the real world, however, you have many other constraints to keep in mind, including network bandwidth and network cost.

Network Bandwidth

Network bandwidth generally refers to the amount of data that can pass through a specific connection in a given amount of time. For example, in a WAN situation, a T1 may have 1.544 Mbps (megabits per second), while a DSL might have a bandwidth of 56 Kbps or 57.6 Kbps (kilobits per second) or more. On the other hand, your LAN's Ethernet connection may have a bandwidth of 100 Mbps or 1000 Mbps. Different types of networks work at different speeds. Therefore, it's imperative that you always consider network bandwidth when thinking about how to deploy domain controllers in your environment.

Network Cost

Cost is perhaps the single largest factor in determining a network design. If cost were not a constraint, organizations would clearly elect to use high-bandwidth connections for all of their sites. Realistically, trade-offs in performance must be made for the sake of affordability. Some factors that can affect the cost of networking include the distance between networks and the types of technology available at locations throughout the world. In remote or less-developed locations, you may not even be able to get access through an ISP or telecom beyond a satellite connection or dial-up, and what is available can be quite costly. Network designers must keep these factors in mind, and they must often settle for less-than-ideal connectivity.

You have considered the monetary value of doing business. Now let's consider another aspect of cost. When designing and configuring networks, you can require certain devices to make data-transport decisions automatically based on an assigned network cost. These devices are commonly known as *routers*, and they use routing protocols to make routing decisions. One of the elements a router uses to configure a routing protocol is its ability to adjust the cost of a route. For example, a router may have multiple ways to connect to a remote site, and it may have multiple interfaces connected to it, each with different paths out of the network to which it is connected locally. When two or more routes are available, you can set up a routing protocol that states that the route with the lower cost is automatically used first.

Another cost is personnel. Do you have the personnel to do the job, or do you need to hire a consultant? Remember that even if you use individuals already on staff, they will be spending time on these projects. When your IT team is working on a project, this is a cost because they cannot also be working on day-to-day tasks.

All of these factors play an important role when you make your Active Directory implementation decisions.

Overview of Active Directory Replication and Sites

Now I need to address two topics that not only are covered heavily on the Microsoft exams but are two areas that all IT administrators should understand. Understanding Active Directory replication and sites can help you fine-tune a network to run at peak performance.

Replicating Active Directory

Regardless of the issues related to network design and technological constraints, network users have many different requirements and needs that must be addressed. First, network resources, such as files, printers, and shared directories, must be made available. Similarly, the resources stored within Active Directory, and its security information in particular, are required for many operations that occur within domains.

With these issues in mind, take a look at how you can configure Active Directory to reach connectivity goals using replication.

Active Directory was designed as a scalable, distributed database that contains information about an organization's network resources. In previous chapters, you saw how you can create and manage domains and how you can use domain controllers to store Active Directory databases.

Even in the simplest of network environments, you generally need more than one domain controller. The major reasons for this are *fault tolerance* (if one domain controller fails, others can still provide services as needed) and performance (the workload can be balanced between multiple domain controllers). Windows Server 2016 domain controllers have been designed to contain read-write copies as well as read-only copies of the Active Directory database. However, the domain controllers must also remain current when objects are created or modified on other domain controllers.

To keep information consistent between domain controllers, you use *Active Directory replication*. Replication is the process by which changes to the Active Directory database are transferred between domain controllers. The result is that all of the domain controllers within an Active Directory domain contain up-to-date information and achieve convergence. Keep in mind that domain controllers may be located very near to each other (for example, within the same server rack), or they may be located across the world from each other. Although the goals of replication are quite simple, the real-world constraints of network connections between servers cause many limitations that you must accommodate. If you have a domain controller on your local LAN, you may find that you have Gigabit Ethernet, which runs at 1000 Mbps between your server connections, whereas you may have a domain controller on the other side or a WAN where the network link runs at a fraction of a T1, 56 Kbps. Replication traffic must traverse each link to ensure convergence no matter what the speed or what bandwidth is available.

Throughout this chapter, you will study the technical details of Active Directory replication. You will also learn how to use the concept of sites and site links to map the logical structure of Active Directory to a physical network topology to help it work efficiently, no matter the type of link with which you are working.

Understanding Active Directory Site Concepts

One of the most important aspects of designing and implementing Active Directory is understanding how it allows you to separate the logical components of the directory service from the physical components.

The logical components—Active Directory domains, OUs, users, groups, and computers—map to the organizational and business requirements of a company.

The physical components, on the other hand, are designed based on the technical issues involved in keeping the network synchronized (that is, making sure that all parts of the network have the same up-to-date information). Active Directory uses the concept of sites to map to an organization's physical network. Stated simply, a *site* is a collection of well-connected subnets. The technical implications of sites are described later in this chapter.

It is important to understand that no specified relationship exists between Active Directory domains and Active Directory sites. An Active Directory site can contain many domains. Alternatively, a single Active Directory domain can span multiple sites. Figure 20.1 illustrates this very important characteristic of domains and sites.

FIGURE 20.1 Potential relationships between domains and sites

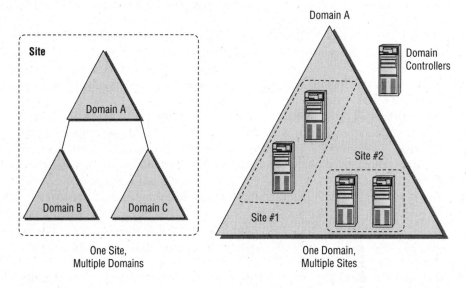

One Site,
Multiple Domains

One Domain,
Multiple Sites

There are two main reasons to use Active Directory sites: service requests and replication.

Service Requests

Clients often require the network services of a domain controller. One of the most common reasons for this is that they need the domain controller to perform network authentication. If your Active Directory network is set up with sites, clients can easily connect to the domain controller that is located closest to them. By doing this, they avoid many of the inefficiencies associated with connecting to distant domain controllers or to those that are located on the other side of a slow network connection. For example, by connecting to a local domain controller, you can avoid the problems associated with a saturated network link that might cause two domain controllers to be out of sync with each other.

Replication

As mentioned earlier, the purpose of Active Directory replication is to ensure that the information stored on all domain controllers within a domain remains synchronized. In environments with many domains and domain controllers, multiple communication paths usually connect them, which makes the synchronization process more complicated. A simple method of transferring updates and other changes to Active Directory involves all of the servers communicating directly with each other as soon as a change occurs; they can all update with the change and reach convergence again. This is not ideal, however, because it places high requirements on network bandwidth and is inefficient for many network environments that use slower and more costly WAN links, especially if all environments update at the same time. Such simultaneous updating could cause the network connection at the core of your network to become saturated and decrease the performance of the entire WAN.

Using sites, Active Directory can automatically determine the best methods for performing replication operations. Sites take into account an organization's network infrastructure, and Active Directory uses these sites to determine the most efficient method for synchronizing information between domain controllers. System administrators can make their physical network design map to Active Directory objects. Based on the creation and configuration of these objects, the Active Directory service can then manage replication traffic in an efficient way.

Whenever a change is made to the Active Directory database on a domain controller, the change is given an update sequence number. The domain controller can then propagate these changes to other domain controllers based on replication settings.

Windows Server 2016 uses a feature called *linked value replication* that is active only when the domain is in the Windows Server 2003, Windows Server 2008, Windows Server 2008 R2, Windows Server 2012, Windows Server 2012 R2, or Windows Server 2016 domain functional level. With linked value replication, only the group member is replicated. This greatly enhances replication efficiency and cuts down on network traffic utilization. Linked value replication is automatically enabled in Windows Server 2003, Windows Server 2008/2008 R2, Windows Server 2012/2012 R2, and Windows Server 2016 functional-level domains.

Planning Your Sites

Much of the challenge of designing Active Directory is related to mapping a company's business processes to the structure of a hierarchical data store. So far, you've seen many of these requirements. What about the existing network infrastructure, however? Clearly, when you plan for and design the structure of Active Directory, you must take into account your LAN and WAN characteristics. Let's see some of the ways that you can use Active Directory sites to manage replication traffic.

Synchronizing Active Directory is extremely important. To keep security permissions and objects within the directory consistent throughout the organization, you must use replication. The Active Directory data store supports *multimaster replication*; that is, data can be modified at any domain controller within the domain because replication ensures that information remains consistent throughout the organization.

Ideally, every site within an organization has reliable, high-speed connections with the other sites. A much more realistic scenario, however, is one in which bandwidth is limited and connections are sometimes either sporadically available or completely unavailable.

Using sites, network and system administrators can define which domain controllers are located on which areas of the network. These settings can be based on the bandwidth available between the areas of the network. Additionally, these administrators can define *subnets*—logically partitioned areas of the network—between areas of the network. Subnets are designed by subdividing IP addresses into usable blocks for assignment, and they are also objects found within the Sites and Services Microsoft Management Console (MMC) in the Administrative Tools folder. Windows Server 2016 Active Directory services use this information to decide how and when to replicate data between domain controllers.

Directly replicating information between all domain controllers might be a viable solution for some companies. For others, however, this might result in a lot of traffic traveling over slow or undersized network links. One way to synchronize data efficiently between sites that have slow connections is to use a *bridgehead server*. Bridgehead servers are designed to accept traffic between two remote sites and then to forward this information to the appropriate servers. Figure 20.2 provides an example of how a bridgehead server can reduce network bandwidth requirements and improve performance. Reduced network bandwidth requirements and improved performance can also be achieved by configuring replication to occur according to a predefined schedule if bandwidth usage statistics are available.

FIGURE 20.2 Using a bridgehead server

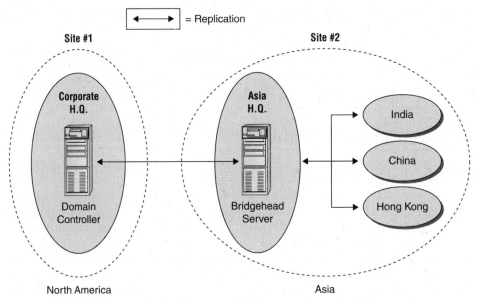

Bridgehead servers do not fit a normal hub-and-spoke WAN topology. Such a topology usually involves a core site (for example, company headquarters) with remote sites as links one off from the core. However, you can use a bridgehead server design to fit a distributed star, where you have a hub-and-spoke topology design with additional spokes coming out of the first set of spokes. Doing so would make some of your spoke sites into smaller core sites. It is at these sites that you would place your bridgehead servers. In Figure 20.2, you can see that your Asia headquarters site is also where you can connect to India, China, and Hong Kong, thus making the Asia headquarters the ideal site for the bridgehead server.

In addition to managing replication traffic, sites offer the advantage of allowing clients to access the nearest domain controller. This prevents problems with user authentication across slow network connections, and it can help find the shortest and fastest path to resources such as files and printers. Therefore, Microsoft recommends that you place at least one domain controller at each site that contains a slow link. Preferably, this domain controller also contains a copy of the global catalog so that logon attempts and resource search queries do not occur across slow links. The drawback, however, is that deploying more copies of the global catalog to servers increases replication traffic.

Through proper planning and deployment of sites, organizations can best use the capabilities of the network infrastructure while keeping Active Directory synchronized.

Understanding Distributed File System Replication

DFS Replication (DFSR) was created to replace the File Replication Service (FRS) that was introduced in the Windows 2000 Server operating systems. DFSR is a state-based, multimaster replication engine that supports replication scheduling and bandwidth throttling. DFSR has the ability to detect insertions, removals, and rearrangements of data in files. This allows DFS Replication to replicate only the changed file blocks when files are updated.

The DFS Replication component uses many different processes to keep data synchronized on multiple servers. To understand the DFSR process, it is helpful to understand some of the following concepts:

- DFSR is a multitasker replication engine, and changes that occur on one of the members are then replicated to all of the other members of the replication group.

- DFSR uses the update sequence number (USN) journal to detect changes on the volume, and then DFSR replicates the changes only after the file is closed.

- Before sending or receiving a file, DFSR uses a staging folder to stage the file.

- When a file is changed, DFSR replicates only the changed blocks and not the entire file. The RDC protocol is what helps determine the blocks that have changed in the file.

- One of the advantages of DFSR is that it is self-healing and can automatically recover from USN journal wraps, USN journal loss, or loss of the DFS Replication database.

- Windows Server 2016 DFSR includes the ability to add a failover cluster as a member of a replication group.

- Windows Server 2016 DFSR allows for read-only replicated folders on a particular member in which users cannot add or change files.

- In Windows Server 2016, it is possible to make changes to the SYSVOL folder of an RODC.

The Dfsrdiag.exe command-line tool includes three Windows Server 2016 command-line switches that provide enhanced diagnostic capabilities for DFSR:

Dfsrdiag.exe ReplState   When you use the ReplState switch, a summary of the replication status across all connections on the specified replication group member is provided. The ReplState switch takes a snapshot of the internal state of the DFSR service, and the updates that are currently being processed (downloaded or served) by the service are shown in a list.

Dfsrdiag.exe IdRecord   When replicating a file or folder, the DFSR service creates an ID record, and an administrator can use this ID record to determine whether a file has replicated properly to a specific member. The IdRecord switch returns the DFSR ID record for the file or folder that you specify by using its path or its unique identifier (UID).

Dfsrdiag.exe FileHash   The FileHash switch, when used against a particular file, will compute and display the hash value that is generated by the DFSR service. An administrator can then look at the hash values to compare two files. If the hash values for the two files are the same, then the two files are the same.

Implementing Sites and Subnets

Now that you have a good idea of the goals of replication, take a look at the following quick overview of the various Active Directory objects that are related to physical network topology.

The basic objects that are used for managing replication include the following:

Subnets   A *subnet* is a partition of a network. As I started to discuss earlier, subnets are logical IP blocks usually connected to other IP blocks through the use of routers and other network devices. All of the computers that are located on a given subnet are generally well connected with each other.

    It is extremely important to understand the concepts of TCP/IP and the routing of network information when you are designing the topology for Active Directory replication.

Sites   An Active Directory site is a logical object that can contain servers and other objects related to Active Directory replication. Specifically, a *site* is a grouping of related subnets. Sites are created to match the physical network structure of an organization. Sites are primarily used for slow WAN links. If your network is well connected (using fiber optics, Category 6 Ethernet, and so on), then sites are not needed.

Site Links   A *site link* is created to define the types of connections that are available between the components of a site. Site links can reflect a relative cost for a network connection and can also reflect the bandwidth that is available for communications.

All of these components work together to determine how information is used to replicate data between domain controllers. Figure 20.3 provides an example of the physical components of Active Directory.

FIGURE 20.3   Active Directory replication objects

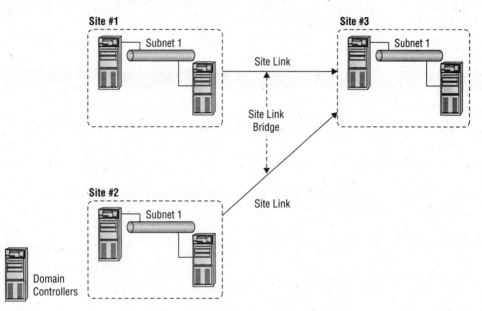

Many issues are related to configuring and managing sites, and all of them are covered in this chapter. Overall, using sites allows you to control the behavior of Active Directory replication between domain controllers. With this background and goal in mind, let's look at how you can implement sites to control Active Directory replication so that it is efficient and in sync.

If you do not have replication set up properly, after a while you will experience problems with your domain controllers. An example of a common replication problem is event log event ID 1311, which states that the Windows NT Directory Services (NTDS) Knowledge Consistency Checker (KCC) has found (and reported) a problem with Active Directory replication. This error message states that the replication configuration information in Active Directory does not accurately reflect the physical topology of the network. This error is commonly found on ailing networks that have replication problems for one reason or another.

Creating Sites

The primary method for creating and managing Active Directory replication components is to utilize the Active Directory Sites and Services tool or the MMC found within the Administrative Tools folder. Using this administrative component, you can graphically create and manage sites in much the same way that you create and manage OUs.

Exercise 20.1 walks you through the process of creating Active Directory sites. For you to complete this exercise, the local machine must be a domain controller. Also, this exercise assumes that you have not yet changed the default domain site configuration.

 Do not perform any testing on a production system or network. Make sure you test site configuration in a lab setting only.

EXERCISE 20.1

Creating Sites

1. Open the Active Directory Sites and Services tool from the Administrative Tools program group.

2. Expand the Sites folder.

3. Right-click the Default-First-Site-Name item and choose Rename. Rename the site CorporateHQ (see Figure 20.4).

FIGURE 20.4   Renaming the site to CorporateHQ

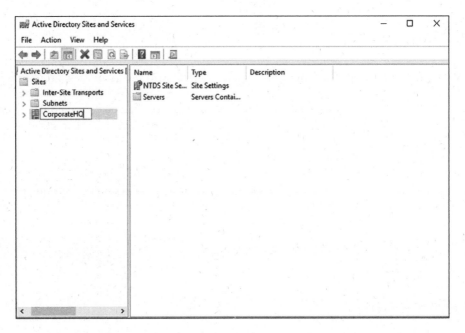

4. Create a new site by right-clicking the Sites object and selecting New Site.

5. In the New Object – Site dialog box, type **Farmington** for the site name. Click the DEFAULTIPSITELINK item, and an information screen pops up. Then click OK to create the site. Note that you cannot include spaces or other special characters in the name of a site.

6. Notice that the Farmington site is now listed under the Sites object.

7. Create another new site and name it **Portsmouth**. Again, choose the DEFAULTIPSITELINK item. Notice that the new site is listed under the Sites object.

8. When you have finished, close the Active Directory Sites and Services tool.

Creating Subnets

Once you have created the sites that map to your network topology, it's time to define the subnets that define the site boundaries.

Subnets are based on TCP/IPv4 or TCP/IPv6 address information. For example, the IPv4 address may be 10.10.0.0, and the subnet mask may be 255.255.0.0. This information specifies that all of the TCP/IP addresses that begin with the first two octets are part of the same TCP/IP subnet. All of the following TCP/IP addresses would be within this subnet:

- 10.10.1.5
- 10.10.100.17
- 10.10.110.120

The Active Directory Sites and Services tool expresses these subnets in a somewhat different notation. It uses the provided subnet address and appends a slash followed by the number of bits in the subnet mask. In the example in the previous paragraph, the subnet would be defined as 10.1.0.0/16.

Remember that sites typically represent distinct physical locations, and they almost always have their own subnets. The only way for a domain controller in one site to reach a DC in another site is to add subnet information about the remote site. Generally, information regarding the definition of subnets for a specific network environment will be available from a network designer. Exercise 20.2 walks you through the steps that you need to take to create subnets and assign subnets to sites. To complete the steps in this exercise, you must have completed Exercise 20.1.

EXERCISE 20.2

Creating Subnets

1. Open the Active Directory Sites and Services tool from the Administrative Tools program group.

2. Expand the Sites folder. Right-click the Subnets folder and select New Subnet.

3. In the New Object – Subnet dialog box, you are prompted for information about the IPv4 or IPv6 details for the new subnet. For the prefix, type **10.10.1.0/24** (you are staying with the more commonly used IPv4). This actually calculates out to 10.10.1.0 with the mask of 255.255.255.0. Click the Farmington site and then click OK to create the subnet.

4. In the Active Directory Sites and Services tool, right-click the newly created 10.10.1.0/24 subnet object and select Properties.

5. On the subnet's Properties dialog box, type **Farmington 100 MB LAN** for the description. Click OK to continue.

6. Create a new subnet using the following information:

   Address: **160.25.0.0/16**

   Site: **Portsmouth**

   Description: **Portsmouth 100Mbit LAN**

7. Finally, create another subnet using the following information:

   Address: **176.33.0.0/16**

   Site: **CorporateHQ**

   Description: **Corporate 100Mbit switched LAN**

8. When finished, close the Active Directory Sites and Services tool.

So far, you have created the basic components that govern Active Directory sites and subnets. You also linked these two components by defining which subnets belong in which sites. These two steps—creating sites and creating subnets—form the basis of mapping the physical network infrastructure of an organization to Active Directory. Now look at the various settings that you can make for sites.

Configuring Sites

Once you have created Active Directory sites and have defined which subnets they contain, it's time to make some additional configuration settings for the site structure. Specifically, you'll need to assign servers to specific sites and configure the site-licensing options. By placing servers in sites, you tell Active Directory replication services how to replicate information for various types of servers. Later in this chapter, you'll examine the details of working with replication within and between sites.

In Exercise 20.3, you will add servers to sites and configure CorpDC1 options. To complete the steps in this exercise, you must have completed Exercise 20.1 and Exercise 20.2.

EXERCISE 20.3

Configuring Sites

1. Open the Active Directory Sites and Services tool from the Administrative Tools program group.

2. Expand the Sites folder and click and expand the Farmington site.

3. Right-click the Servers container in the Farmington site and select New ≻ Server. Type **FarmingtonDC1** for the name of the server and then click OK.

4. Create a new Server object within the CorporateHQ site and name it **CorpDC1**. Note that this object also includes the name of the local domain controller.

5. Create two new Server objects within the Portsmouth site and name them **PortsmouthDC1** and **PortsmouthDC2**.

6. Right-click the CorpDC1 server object and select Properties. On the General tab of the CorpDC1 Properties box, select SMTP in the Transports Available For Inter-site Data Transfer box and click Add to make this server a preferred IP bridgehead server. Click OK to accept the settings.

7. When you have finished, close the Active Directory Sites and Services tool.

With the configuration of the basic settings for sites out of the way, it's time to focus on the real details of the site topology—creating site links and site link bridges.

Configuring Replication

Sites are generally used to define groups of computers that are located within a single geographic location. In most organizations, machines that are located in close physical proximity (for example, within a single building or branch office) are well connected. A typical example is a LAN in a branch office of a company. All of the computers may be connected using Ethernet, and routing and switching technology may be in place to reduce network congestion.

Often, however, domain controllers are located across various states, countries, and even continents. In such a situation, network connectivity is usually much slower, less reliable, and more costly than that for the equivalent LAN. Therefore, Active Directory replication must accommodate this situation accordingly. When managing replication traffic within Active Directory sites, you need to be aware of two types of synchronization:

Intrasite   *Intrasite replication* refers to the synchronization of Active Directory information between domain controllers that are located in the same site. In accordance with the concept of sites, these machines are usually well connected by a high-speed LAN.

Intersite   *Intersite replication* occurs between domain controllers in different sites. Usually, this means there is a WAN or other type of low-speed network connection between the various machines. Intersite replication is optimized for minimizing the amount of network traffic that occurs between sites.

In the following sections, you'll look at ways to configure both intrasite and intersite replication. Additionally, you'll see features of Active Directory replication architecture that you can use to accommodate the needs of almost any environment.

Intrasite Replication

Intrasite replication is generally a simple process. One domain controller contacts the others in the same site when changes to its copy of Active Directory are made. It compares the update sequence numbers in its own copy of Active Directory with those of the other domain controllers; then the most current information is chosen by the DC in question, and all domain controllers within the site use this information to make the necessary updates to their database.

Because you can assume that the domain controllers within an Active Directory site are well connected, you can pay less attention to exactly when and how replication takes place. Communications between domain controllers occur using the *Remote Procedure Call (RPC) protocol.* This protocol is optimized for transmitting and synchronizing information on fast and reliable network connections. The RPC protocol provides for fast replication at the expense of network bandwidth, which is usually readily available because most LANs today are running on Fast Ethernet (100 Mbps) at a minimum.

Intersite Replication

Intersite replication is optimized for low-bandwidth situations and network connections that have less reliability. Intersite replication offers several features that are tailored toward these types of connections. To begin with, two different protocols may be used to transfer information between sites:

RPC over IP   When connectivity is fairly reliable, IP is a good choice. IP-based communications require you to have a live connection between two or more domain controllers in different sites and let you transfer Active Directory information. RPC over IP was originally designed for slower WANs in which packet loss and corruption may often occur.

Simple Mail Transfer Protocol   *Simple Mail Transfer Protocol (SMTP)* is perhaps best known as the protocol that is used to send and receive email messages on the Internet. SMTP was designed to use a store-and-forward mechanism through which a server receives a copy of a message, records it to disk, and then attempts to forward it to another email server. If the destination server is unavailable, it holds the message and attempts to resend it at periodic intervals.

This type of communication is extremely useful for situations in which network connections are unreliable or not always available. For example, if a branch office in Peru were connected to the corporate office through a dial-up connection that is available only during certain hours, SMTP would be a good choice for communication with that branch.

SMTP is an inherently insecure network protocol. Therefore, if you would like to ensure that you transfer replication traffic securely and you use SMTP for Active Directory replication, you must take advantage of Windows Server 2016's Certificate Services functionality.

Other intersite replication characteristics are designed to address low-bandwidth situations and less-reliable network connections. These features give you a high degree of flexibility in controlling replication configuration. They include the following:

- Compression of Active Directory information. This compression is helpful because changes between domain controllers in remote sites may include a large amount of information and also because network bandwidth tends to be less available and more costly.

- Site links and site link bridges help determine intersite replication topology.

- Replication can occur based on a schedule defined by system administrators.

You can configure intersite replication by using the Active Directory Sites and Services tool. Select the name of the site for which you want to configure settings. Then right-click the NTDS Site Settings object in the right window pane and select Properties. By clicking the Change Schedule button in the NTDS Site Settings Properties dialog box, you'll be able to configure how often replication occurs between sites (see Figure 20.5).

FIGURE 20.5   Configuring intersite replication schedules

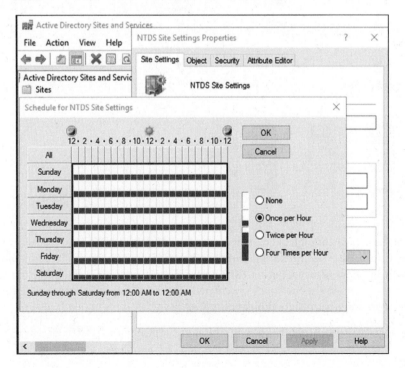

You will see how to set the replication schedule in Exercise 20.4.

In the following sections, you will see how to configure site links and site link bridges as well as how to manage connection objects and bridgehead servers.

Creating Site Links and Site Link Bridges

The overall topology of intersite replication is based on the use of site links and site link bridges. *Site links* are logical connections that define a path between two Active Directory sites. Site links can include several descriptive elements that define their network characteristics. *Site link bridges* are used to connect site links so that the relationship can be transitive. Figure 20.6 provides an example of site links and site link bridges.

FIGURE 20.6   An example of site links and site link bridges

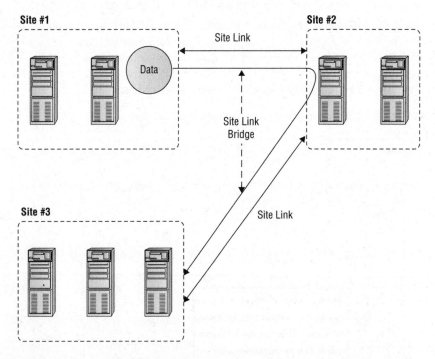

Both of these types of logical connections are used by Active Directory services to determine how information should be synchronized between domain controllers in remote sites. The Knowledge Consistency Checker (KCC) uses this information, which forms a replication topology based on the site topology created. The KCC service is responsible for determining the best way to replicate information within sites.

When creating site links for your environment, you'll need to consider the following factors:

Transporting Information   You can choose to use either RPC over IP or SMTP for transferring information over a site link. You will need to determine which is best based on your network infrastructure and the reliability of connections between sites.

Assigning a Cost Value   You can create multiple site links between sites and assign site links a cost value based on the type of connection. The system administrator determines the cost value, and the relative costs of site links are then used (by the system) to determine the optimal path for replication. The lower the cost, the more likely the link is to be used for replication.

For example, a company may primarily use a T1 link between branch offices, but it may also use a slower and circuit-switched dial-up ISDN connection for redundancy (in case the T1 fails). In this example, a system administrator may assign a cost of 25 to the T1 line and a cost of 100 to the ISDN line. This ensures that the more reliable and higher-bandwidth T1 connection is used whenever it's available but that the ISDN line is also available.

Determining a Replication Schedule   Once you've determined how and through which connections replication will take place, it's time to determine when information should be replicated. Replication requires network resources and occupies bandwidth. Therefore, you need to balance the need for consistent directory information with the need to conserve bandwidth. For example, if you determine that it's reasonable to have a lag time of six hours between when an update is made at one site and when it is replicated to all others, you might schedule replication to occur once in the morning, once during the lunch hour, and more frequently after normal work hours.

Based on these factors, you should be able to devise a strategy that allows you to configure site links.

Exercise 20.4 walks you through the process of creating site links and site link bridges. To complete the steps in this exercise, you must have completed Exercises 20.1, 20.2, and 20.3.

EXERCISE 20.4

Creating Site Links and Site Link Bridges

1. Open the Active Directory Sites and Services tool from the Administrative Tools program group.

2. Expand the Sites, Inter-site Transports, and IP objects. Right-click the DEFAULTIPSITELINK item in the right pane and select Rename. Rename the object **CorporateWAN**.

3. Right-click the CorporateWAN link and select Properties. In the General tab of the CorporateWAN Properties dialog box, type **T1 Connecting Corporate and Portsmouth Offices** for the description. Remove the Farmington site from the link by highlighting Farmington in the Sites In This Site Link box and clicking Remove. For the Cost value, type **50** and specify that replication should occur every **60** minutes. To create the site link, click OK.

4. Right-click the IP folder and select New Site Link. In the New Object – Site Link dialog box, name the link **CorporateDialup**. Add the Farmington and CorporateHQ sites to the site link and then click OK.

5. Right-click the CorporateDialup link and select Properties. In the General tab of the CorporateDialup Properties dialog box, type **ISDN Dialup between Corporate and Farmington** for the description. Set the Cost value to **100** and specify that replication should occur every **120** minutes. To specify that replication should occur only during certain times of the day, click the Change Schedule button.

6. In the Schedule For Corporate Dialup dialog box, highlight the area between 8:00 a.m. and 6:00 p.m. for the days Monday through Friday and click the Replication Not Available option. This will ensure that replication traffic is minimized during normal work hours.

7. Click OK to accept the new schedule and then click OK again to create the site link.

8. Right-click the IP object and select New Site Link Bridge. In the New Object – Site Link Bridge dialog box, name the site link bridge **CorporateBridge**. Note that the CorporateDialup and CorporateWAN site links are already added to the site link bridge. Because there must be at least two site links in each bridge, you will not be able to remove these links. Click OK to create the site link bridge.

9. When finished, close the Active Directory Sites and Services tool.

Creating Connection Objects

Generally, it is a good practice to allow Active Directory's replication mechanisms to schedule and manage replication functions automatically. In some cases, however, you may want to have additional control over replication. Perhaps you want to replicate certain changes on demand (for example, when you create new accounts). Or you may want to specify a custom schedule for certain servers.

Connection objects provide you with a way to set up these different types of replication schedules. You can create connection objects with the Active Directory Sites and Services tool by expanding a server object, right-clicking the NTDS Settings object, and selecting New Active Directory Domain Services Connection.

Within the properties of the connection object, which you can see in the right pane of the Active Directory Sites and Services tool, you can specify the type of transport to use for replication (RPC over IP or SMTP), the schedule for replication, and the domain controllers that participate in the replication. Additionally, you can right-click the connection object and select Replicate Now.

Moving Server Objects Between Sites

Using the Active Directory Sites and Services tool, you can easily move servers between sites. To do this, simply right-click the name of a domain controller and select Move. You can then select the site to which you want to move the domain controller object.

Figure 20.7 shows the Move Server dialog box. After the server is moved, all replication topology settings are updated automatically. If you want to choose custom replication settings, you'll need to create connection objects manually (as described earlier).

FIGURE 20.7   Choosing a new site for a specific server

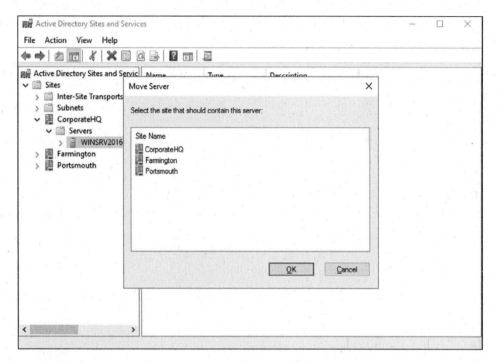

In Exercise 20.5, you move a server object between sites. To complete the steps in this exercise, you must have completed the previous exercises in this chapter.

EXERCISE 20.5

Moving Server Objects Between Sites

1. Open the Active Directory Sites and Services administrative tool.

2. Right-click the server named PortsmouthDC1 and select Move.

3. In the Move Server dialog box, select the Farmington site and then click OK. This moves this server to the Farmington site.

4. To move the server back, right-click PortsmouthDC1 (now located in the Farmington site) and then click Move. Select Portsmouth for the destination site.

5. When finished, close the Active Directory Sites and Services administrative tool.

Creating Bridgehead Servers

By default, all of the servers in one site communicate with all of the servers in another site. You can, however, further control replication between sites by using bridgehead servers. As mentioned earlier in the chapter, using bridgehead servers helps minimize replication traffic, especially in larger distributed star network topologies, and it allows you to dedicate machines that are better connected to receive replicated data. Data is replicated between sites every 180 minutes by default. Figure 20.8 provides an example of how bridgehead servers work.

FIGURE 20.8   A replication scenario using bridgehead servers

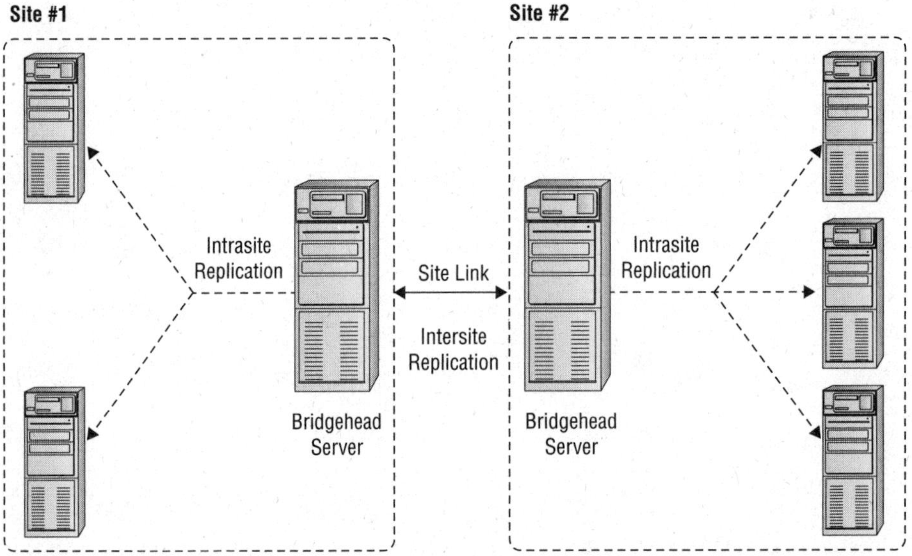

You can use a bridgehead server to specify which domain controllers are preferred for transferring replication information between sites. Different bridgehead servers can be selected for RPC over IP and SMTP replication, thus allowing you to balance the load. To create a bridgehead server for a site, simply right-click a domain controller and select Properties, which brings up the bridgehead server's Properties dialog box. To make the server a bridgehead server, just select one or both replication types (called *transports*) from the left side of the dialog box and click the Add button to add them to the right side of the dialog box.

RODCs and Replication

I have talked quite a bit about read-only domain controllers (RODCs) throughout the book. It's important that you understand that since RODCs don't actually commit changes against the Active Directory Domain Services (AD DS) database within your environment, then replication to and from your primary domain controller (PDC) and your RODCs can occur only one way. This is referred to as *unidirectional replication*. Any writable domain controller that serves as a replication partner to one of your RODCs will never pull changes from that RODC by design. This helps ensure that no malicious or corrupt changes that are made from an RODC are replicated throughout your entire forest. The RODC performs normal inbound replication for AD DS and Sysvol changes. Any other shares on an RODC that you configure to replicate using DFS Replication would still use bidirectional replication.

RODCs come with additional configuration settings like the *Password Replication Policy (PRP)*. The PRP is used to determine which user's credentials can be cached locally on a specific RODC. By default, an RODC will not cache an Active Directory user's credentials. That would defeat the purpose of an RODC. When a user wants to authenticate to an RODC, the authentication request is forwarded to a writable domain controller for authentication. If the request succeeds, it is then passed back to the RODC, and then that user will be able to log in to the domain.

Nonetheless, it is possible to allow certain user credentials to be cached on an RODC by configuring the PRP. Once a user has been added to the Allowed RODC Password Replication group, then that user's credentials will be cached, and that RODC would be able to authenticate that user locally again in the future. Because the RODC maintains only a subset of user credentials, if the RODC is compromised or stolen, only the user accounts that had been cached on the RODC must have their passwords changed. To configure an RODC PRP, open the properties of an RODC computer object in Active Directory and select the Password Replication Policy tab.

Configuring Server Topology

When you are using environments that require multiple sites, you must carefully consider where you place your servers. In doing so, you can greatly improve performance and end user experience by reducing the time they must spend performing common operations, such as authentication or searching Active Directory for resources.

There are two main issues to consider when you are designing a distributed Active Directory environment. The first is how you should place domain controllers within the network environment. The second is how to manage the use of global catalog servers. Finding the right balance between servers, server resources, and performance can be considered an art form for network and system administrators. In the following sections, you'll look at some of the important considerations that you must take into account when you design a replication server topology.

Placing Domain Controllers

Microsoft highly recommends that you have at least two domain controllers in each domain of your Active Directory environment. As mentioned earlier in this chapter, using additional domain controllers provides the following benefits:

- Increased network performance:
    - The servers can balance the burden of serving client requests.
    - Clients can connect to the server closest to them instead of performing authentication and security operations across a slow WAN link.

- Fault tolerance (In case one domain controller fails, the other still contains a valid and usable copy of the Active Directory database.)

- In Windows Server 2016, RODCs help increase security when users connect to a domain controller in an unsecured remote location.

Placing Global Catalog Servers

A *global catalog (GC)* server is a domain controller that contains a copy of all of the objects contained in the forest-wide domain controllers that compose the Active Directory database. Making a domain controller a GC server is simple, and you can change this setting quite easily. That brings us to the harder part—determining which domain controllers should also be GC servers.

Where you place domain controllers and GC servers and how many you deploy are important network planning decisions. Generally, you want to make GC servers available in every site that has a slow link. This means the most logical places to put GC servers are in every site and close to the WAN link for the best possible connectivity. However, having too many GC servers is a bad thing. The main issue is associated with replication traffic—you must keep each GC server within your environment synchronized with the other servers. In a very dynamic environment, using additional GC servers causes a considerable increase in network traffic. Therefore, you will want to find a good balance between replication burdens and GC query performance in your own large multidomain environment.

To create a GC server, simply expand the Server object in the Active Directory Sites and Services tool, right-click NTDS Settings, and select Properties to bring up the NTDS Settings Properties dialog box (see Figure 20.9). To configure a server as a GC server, simply place a check mark in the Global Catalog box.

FIGURE 20.9   Enabling the global catalog on an Active Directory domain controller

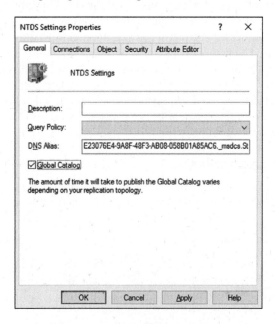

Accommodating a Changing Environment

You're a system administrator for a medium-sized business that consists of many offices located throughout the world. Some of these offices are well connected because they use high-speed, reliable links, while others are not so fortunate. Overall, things are going well until your CEO announces that the organization will be merging with another large company and that the business will be restructured. The restructuring will involve opening new offices, closing old ones, and transferring employees to different locations. Additionally, changes in the IT budget will affect the types of links that exist between offices. Your job as the system administrator is to ensure that the network environment and, specifically, Active Directory keep pace with the changes and ultimately outperform them.

An important skill for any technical professional is the ability to adapt quickly and efficiently to a changing organization. When a business grows, restructures, or forms relationships with other businesses, often many IT-related changes must also occur. You may have to create new network links, for example.

Fortunately, Active Directory was designed with these kinds of challenges in mind. For example, you can use the Active Directory Sites and Services administrative tool to reflect physical network changes in Active Directory topology. If a site that previously had 64 Kbps of bandwidth is upgraded to a T1 connection, you can change those characteristics for the site link objects. Conversely, if a site that was previously well connected is reduced to a slow, unreliable link, you can reconfigure the sites, change the site link transport mechanisms (perhaps from IP to SMTP to accommodate a nonpersistent link), and create connection objects (which would allow you to schedule replication traffic to occur during the least busy hours).

Suppose further that many of your operations move overseas to a European division. This might call for designating specific domain controllers as preferred bridgehead servers to reduce the amount of replication traffic over costly and slow overseas links.

Sweeping organizational changes inevitably require you to move servers between sites. For example, an office may close and its domain controllers may move to another region of the world. Again, you can accommodate this change by using Active Directory administrative tools. You may change your OU structure to reflect new logical and business-oriented changes, and you can move server objects between sites to reflect physical network changes.

Rarely can the job of mapping a physical infrastructure to Active Directory be "complete." In most environments, it's safe to assume that you will always need to make changes based on business needs. Overall, however, you should feel comfortable that the physical components of Active Directory are at your side to help you accommodate these changes.

Using Universal Group Membership Caching

To understand how Universal Group Membership Caching (UGMC) works, you must first understand how authentication works. When a user tries to authenticate with a domain controller, the first action that takes place is that the domain controller checks with the global catalog to see to which domain the user belongs.

If the domain controller (the one to which the user is trying to authenticate) is not a GC, then the domain controller sends a request to the GC to verify the user's domain. The GC responds with the user's information, and the domain controller authenticates the user (if the user belongs to the same domain as the domain controller).

There are two ways to speed up the authentication process. First, you can make all of the domain controller's global catalogs. But then you end up with a lot of GC replication traffic. This becomes even more of an issue if you have multiple sites. Now replication traffic can be too large for your site link connections.

Thus, if you have a slower site link connection or multiple domains, you can use Universal Group Membership Caching. If you are using UGMC, after a domain controller communicates with the global catalog, the domain controller will then cache the user's credentials for eight hours by default. Now if the user logs off the domain and then logs back into the domain, the domain controller will use the cached credentials and not ask the global catalog. The downside to using UGMC is that it is for authentication only. Global catalogs help speed up Active Directory searches, and they work with Directory Service–enabled applications (applications that have to work with Active Directory) such as Exchange and SQL.

Domain Controller Cloning

Throughout the book, I have talked about why so many organizations are switching to virtualization in their server rooms. Virtualization allows an administrator to take one physical server and turn it into multiple virtual servers by using Windows Server 2016.

In Windows Server 2016, administrators can now easily and safely create replica domain controllers by copying an existing virtual domain controller. Before Windows Server 2012, an administrator would have to deploy a server image that they prepared by using sysprep.exe. After going through the process of using sysprep.exe, the administrator would have to promote this server to a domain controller and then complete additional configuration requirements for deploying each replica domain controller.

Domain controller cloning allows an administrator to deploy rapidly a large number of domain controllers. To set up domain controller cloning, you must be a member of the Domain Admins group or have the equivalent permissions. The administrator must then run Windows PowerShell from an elevated command prompt.

Only Windows Server 2012 or Windows Server 2016 domain controllers that are hosted on a VM-compatible hypervisor can be used as a source for cloning. You should also make sure that the domain controller that you choose to clone is in a healthy state (use computer management to see the computer's state).

The following example is used to create a clone domain controller named TestClone with a static IP address of 10.0.0.5 and a subnet mask of 255.255.0.0. This command also configures the DNS Server and WINS server configurations.

```
New-ADDCCloneConfigFile -CloneComputerName "TestClone" -Static -IPv4Address
"10.0.0.5" -IPv4DNSResolver "10.0.0.1" -IPv4SubnetMask "255.255.0.0" -
PreferredWinsServer "10.0.0.1" -AlternateWinsServer "10.0.0.2"
```

 When you are ready to clone a domain controller, I recommend you visit Microsoft's TechNet site for all of the PowerShell commands needed to complete this entire process.

Configuring DNS SRV Records

When setting up Active Directory, there are a few DNS Service (SRV) records that are needed. SRV records show that a machine is running a specific service. There are a few services that are needed for the network to properly function. DNS must have service records for the domain controllers, global catalogs, PDC emulator, and the Kerberos KDC service.

The easiest way to configure the SRV records is to have these machines all be DNS clients. DNS clients will send their client information to the DNS server by default. But if the servers are not DNS clients or for some reason they do not register with DNS, you may need to manually create these SRV records. To manually create the SRV records, complete the following steps:

1. Open the DNS management tool by clicking Start ➢ Administrative Tools ➢ DNS.

2. Expand the Forward Lookup Zone and expand your zone name.

3. Right click _TCP and choose Other New Record.

4. Choose SRV record.

5. Enter the SRV record information.

Monitoring and Troubleshooting Active Directory Replication

For the most part, domain controllers handle the replication processes automatically. However, system administrators still need to monitor the performance of Active Directory replication because failed network links and incorrect configurations can sometimes prevent the synchronization of information between domain controllers.

You can monitor the behavior of Active Directory replication and troubleshoot the process if problems occur.

About System Monitor

The Windows Server 2016 System Monitor administrative tool was designed so that you can monitor many performance statistics associated with using Active Directory. Included within the various performance statistics that you can monitor are counters related to Active Directory replication.

Troubleshooting Replication

A common symptom of replication problems is that information is not updated on some or all domain controllers. For example, a system administrator creates a user account on one domain controller, but the changes are not propagated to other domain controllers. In most environments, this is a potentially serious problem because it affects network security and can prevent authorized users from accessing the resources they require.

You can take several steps to troubleshoot Active Directory replication. These steps are discussed in the following sections.

Verifying Network Connectivity

For replication to work properly in distributed environments, you must have network connectivity. Although ideally all domain controllers would be connected by high-speed LAN links, this is rarely the case for larger organizations. In the real world, dial-up connections and slow connections are common. If you have verified that your replication topology is set up properly, you should confirm that your servers are able to communicate. Problems such as a failed dial-up connection attempt can prevent important Active Directory information from being replicated.

Verifying Router and Firewall Configurations

Firewalls are used to restrict the types of traffic that can be transferred between networks. They are mainly used to increase security by preventing unauthorized users from transferring information. In some cases, company firewalls may block the types of network access that must be available for Active Directory replication to occur. For example, if a specific router or firewall prevents data from being transferred using SMTP, replication that uses this protocol will fail.

Examining the Event Logs

Whenever an error in the replication configuration occurs, the computer writes events to the Directory Service and File Replication Service event logs. By using the Event Viewer administrative tool, you can quickly and easily view the details associated with any problems in replication. For example, if one domain controller is unable to communicate with another to transfer changes, a log entry is created.

Verifying That Information Is Synchronized

It's often easy to forget to perform manual checks regarding the replication of Active Directory information. One of the reasons for this is that Active Directory domain controllers have their own read-write copies of the Active Directory database. Therefore, if connectivity does not exist, you will not encounter failures while creating new objects.

It is important to verify periodically that objects have been synchronized between domain controllers. This process might be as simple as logging on to a different domain controller and looking at the objects within a specific OU. This manual check, although it might be tedious, can prevent inconsistencies in the information stored on domain controllers, which, over time, can become an administration and security nightmare.

Verifying Authentication Scenarios

A common replication configuration issue occurs when clients are forced to authenticate across slow network connections. The primary symptom of the problem is that users complain about the amount of time it takes them to log on to Active Directory (especially during a period when there's a high volume of authentications, such as at the beginning of the workday).

Usually, you can alleviate this problem by using additional domain controllers or reconfiguring the site topology. A good way to test this is to consider the possible scenarios for the various clients that you support. Often, walking through a configuration, such as "A client in Domain1 is trying to authenticate using a domain controller in Domain2, which is located across a slow WAN connection," can be helpful in pinpointing potential problem areas.

Verifying the Replication Topology

The Active Directory Sites and Services tool allows you to verify that a replication topology is logically consistent. You can quickly and easily perform this task by right-clicking NTDS Settings within a Server object and choosing All Tasks ➤ Check Replication. If any errors are present, a dialog box alerts you to the problem.

Another way to verify replication is by using the command-line utility Repadmin. Table 20.1 shows some of the Repadmin commands.

TABLE 20.1   Repadmin commands

Command	Description
Repadmin Bridgeheads	Lists the bridgehead servers for a specified site.
Repadmin dsaguid	Returns a server name when given a GUID.
Repadmin failcache	Shows a list of failed replication events.
Repadmin istg	Returns the server name of the Inter-Site Topology Generator (ISTG) server for a specified site. The ISTG manages the inbound replication connection objects for the bridgehead servers in a site.

TABLE 20.1 Repadmin commands *(continued)*

Command	Description
Repadmin kcc	Forces the Knowledge Consistency Checker (KCC) to recalculate replication topology for a specified domain controller. The KCC modifies data in the local directory in response to system-wide changes.
Repadmin latency	Shows the amount of time between replications.
Repadmin queue	Shows tasks waiting in the replication queue.
Repadmin querysites	Uses routing information to determine the cost of a route from a specified site to another specified site or to other sites.
Repadmin replicate	Starts a replication event for the specified directory partition between domain controllers.
Repadmin replsummary	Displays the replication state and relative health of a forest.
Repadmin showrepl	Displays replication partners for each directory partition on a specified domain controller.

Reasons for Creating Multiple Domains

Before you look at the steps that you must take to create multiple domains, become familiar with the reasons an organization might want to create them.

In general, you should always try to reflect your organization's structure within a single domain. By using organizational units (OUs) and other objects, you can usually create an accurate and efficient structure within one domain. Creating and managing a single domain is usually much simpler than managing a more complex environment consisting of multiple domains.

That being said, you should familiarize yourself with some real benefits and reasons for creating multiple domains and some drawbacks of using them.

Reasons for Using Multiple Domains

You might need to implement multiple domains for several reasons. These reasons include the following considerations:

Scalability   Although Microsoft has designed Active Directory to accommodate millions of objects, this may not be practical for your current environment. Supporting thousands of users within a single domain requires more disk space, greater central processing unit (CPU) usage, and additional network burdens on your domain controllers (computers containing Active Directory security information). To determine the size of the Active Directory domain your network can support, you need to plan, design, test, and analyze within your own environment.

Reducing Replication Traffic   All of the domain controllers in a domain must keep an up-to-date copy of the entire Active Directory database. For small to medium-sized domains, this is generally not a problem. Windows Server 2016 and Active Directory manage all of the details of transferring the database behind the scenes. Other business and technical limitations might, however, affect Active Directory's ability to perform adequate replication. For example, if you have two sites that are connected by a slow network link (or a sporadic link or no link at all), replication is not practical. In this case, you would probably want to create separate domains to isolate replication traffic. Sporadic coverage across the wide area network (WAN) link would come from circuit-switching technologies such as Integrated Services Digital Network (ISDN) technologies. If you didn't have a link at all, then you would have a service provider outage or some other type of disruption. Separate domains mean separate replication traffic, but the amount of administrative overhead is increased significantly.

Because it's common to have WAN links in your business environment, you will always need to consider how your users authenticate to a domain controller (DC). DCs at a remote site are commonly used to authenticate users locally to their local area network (LAN). The most common design involves putting a DC at each remote site to keep authentication traffic from traversing the WAN. If it is the other way around, the authentication traffic may cause users problems if WAN utilization is high or if the link is broken and no other way to the central site is available. The design you are apt to see most often is one in which each server replicates its database of information to each other's server so that the network and its systems converge.

However, it's important to realize that the presence of slow WAN links alone is *not* a good reason to break an organization into multiple domains. The most common solution is to set up site links with the Sites and Services Microsoft Management Console (MMC). When you use this MMC, you can manage replication traffic and fine-tune independently of the domain architecture.

You would want to use a multidomain architecture, such as when two companies merge through an acquisition, for the following reasons:

Meeting Business Needs   Several business needs might justify the creation of multiple domains. Business needs can be broken down even further into organizational and political needs.

One of the organizational reasons for using multiple domains is to avoid potential problems associated with the Domain Administrator account. At least one user needs to have permissions at this level. If your organization is unable or unwilling to trust a single person to have this level of control over all business units, then multiple domains may be the best answer. Because each domain maintains its own security database, you can keep permissions and resources isolated. Through the use of trusts, however, you can still share resources.

A political need for separate domains might arise if you had two companies that merged with two separate but equal management staffs and two sets of officers. In such a situation, you might need to have Active Directory split into two separate databases to keep the security of the two groups separate. Some such organizations may need to keep the internal groups separate by law. A multidomain architecture provides exactly this type of pristinely separate environment.

Many Levels of Hierarchy   Larger organizations tend to have complex internal and external business structures that dictate the need for many different levels of organization. For example, two companies might merge and need to keep two sets of officers who are managed under two different logical groupings. In the, "Administer Active Directory" chapter, I showed you that you can use OUs to help group different branches of the company so that you can assign permissions, delegations, or whatever else you can think of without affecting anyone else. Managing data becomes much easier when you're using OUs, and if you design them correctly, OUs will help you control your network right from one console. You may need only one level of management—your company may be small enough to warrant the use of the default OU structure you see when Active Directory is first installed. If, however, you find that you need many levels of OUs to manage resources (or if large numbers of objects exist within each OU), it might make sense to create additional domains. Each domain would contain its own OU hierarchy and serve as the root of a new set of objects.

Decentralized Administration   Two main models of administration are commonly used: a centralized administration model and a decentralized administration model. In the centralized administration model, a single IT organization is responsible for managing all of the users, computers, and security permissions for the entire organization. In the decentralized administration model, each department or business unit might have its own IT department. In both cases, the needs of the administration model can play a significant role in whether you decide to use multiple domains.

Consider, for example, a multinational company that has a separate IT department for offices in each country. Each IT department is responsible for supporting only the users and computers within its own region. Because the administration model is largely decentralized, creating a separate domain for each of these major business units might make sense from a security and maintenance standpoint.

Multiple DNS or Domain Names   Another reason you may need to use a multidomain architecture is if you want or plan to use multiple DNS names within your organization. If you use multiple DNS names or domain names, you must create multiple Active Directory domains. Each AD domain can have only one *fully qualified domain name (FQDN)*. An FQDN is the full name of a system that consists of a local host, a second-level domain name, and a top-level domain (TLD). For example, corp.WillPanek.com is an FQDN, .com is the TLD, www is the host, and WillPanek is the second-level domain name.

Legality   One final reason you may need to use a multidomain architecture is legality within your organization. Some corporations have to follow state or federal regulations and laws. For this reason, they may need to have multiple domains.

Drawbacks of Multiple Domains

Although there are many reasons why it makes sense to have multiple domains, there are also reasons why you should not break an organizational structure into multiple domains, many of which are related to maintenance and administration. Here are some of the drawbacks to using multiple domains:

Administrative Inconsistency   One of the fundamental responsibilities of most system administrators is implementing and managing security. When you are implementing Group Policy and security settings in multiple domains, you want to be careful to ensure that the settings are consistent. In Windows Server 2016, security policies can be different between and within the same domains. If this is what the organization intended, then it is not a problem. However, if an organization wants to make the same settings apply to all users, then each domain requires a separate GPO with similar security settings.

Increased Management Challenges   Managing servers, users, and computers can become a considerable challenge when you are also managing multiple domains because many more administrative units are required. In general, you need to manage all user, group, and computer settings separately for the objects within each domain. The hierarchical structure provided by OUs, on the other hand, provides a much simpler and easier way to manage permissions.

Decreased Flexibility   Creating a domain involves the *promotion* of a DC to the new domain. Although the process is quite simple, it is much more difficult to rearrange the domain topology within an Active Directory environment than it is simply to reorganize OUs. When planning domains, you should ensure that the domain structure will not change often, if at all.

Now that you have examined the pros and cons related to creating multiple domains, it is time to see how to create trees and forests.

Creating Domain Trees and Forests

So far, this chapter has covered some important reasons for using multiple domains in a single network environment. Now it's time to look at how to create multidomain structures such as domain trees and domain forests.

Regardless of the number of domains you have in your environment, you always have a tree and a forest. This might surprise those of you who generally think of domain trees and forests as belonging only to Active Directory environments that consist of multiple domains. However, recall that when you install the first domain in an Active Directory environment, that domain automatically creates a new forest and a new tree.

In the following sections, you will learn how to plan trees and forests and how to promote domain controllers to establish a tree and forest environment.

Planning Trees and Forests

You have already seen several reasons why you might want to have multiple domains within a single company. What you haven't yet seen is how multiple domains can be related to each other and how their relationships can translate into domain forests and trees.

A fundamental commonality between the various domains that exist in trees and forests is that they all share the same Active Directory global catalog (GC). This means that if you modify the Active Directory schema, these changes must be propagated to all of the domain controllers in all of the domains. This is an important point because adding and modifying the structure of information in the GC can have widespread effects on replication and network traffic. Also, you need to ensure that any system you use in the GC role can handle it—you might need to size up the system's hardware requirements. This is especially true if there are multiple domains.

Every domain within an Active Directory configuration has its own unique name. For example, even though you might have a sales domain in two different trees, the complete names for each domain will be different (such as `sales.WillPanek1.com` and `sales.WillPanek2.com`).

In the following sections, you'll look at how you can organize multiple Active Directory domains based on business requirements.

Using a Single Tree

The concept of domain trees was created to preserve the relationship between multiple domains that share a common contiguous namespace. For example, you might have the following DNS domains (based on Internet names):

- `mycompany.com`
- `sales.mycompany.com`
- `engineering.mycompany.com`
- `europe.sales.mycompany.com`

Note that all of these domains fit within a single contiguous namespace. That is, they are all direct or indirect children of the `mycompany.com` domain. In this case, `mycompany.com` is called the *root domain*. All of the direct children (such as `sales.mycompany.com` and `engineering.mycompany.com`) are called *child domains*. Finally, *parent domains* are the domains that are directly above one domain. For example, `sales.mycompany.com` is the parent domain of `europe.sales.mycompany.com`. Figure 20.10 provides an example of a domain tree.

To establish a domain tree, you must first create the root domain for the tree. Then you can add child domains off this root. These child domains can then serve as parents for further subdomains. Each domain must have at least one domain controller, and domain controllers can participate in only one domain at a time. However, you can move a domain controller from one domain to another. To do this, you must first demote a domain controller to a member server and then promote it to a domain controller in another domain.

FIGURE 20.10   A domain tree

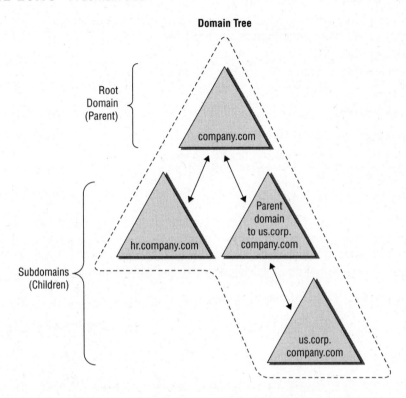

 You will learn how to demote a domain controller later in this chapter in the section "Demoting a Domain Controller."

Domains are designed to be logical boundaries. The domains within a tree are, by default, automatically bound together using a two-way transitive trust relationship, which allows resources to be shared among domains through the use of the appropriate user and group assignments. Because trust relationships are transitive, all of the domains within the tree trust each other. Note, however, that a trust by itself does not automatically grant any security permissions to users or objects between domains. Trusts are designed only to *allow* resources to be shared; you must still go through the process of sharing and managing them. Enterprise administrators must explicitly assign security settings to resources before users can access resources between domains.

Using a single tree makes sense when your organization maintains only a single contiguous namespace. Regardless of the number of domains that exist within this environment and how different their security settings are from each other, they are related by a common name. Although domain trees make sense for many organizations, in some cases the network namespace may be considerably more complicated. You'll look at how forests address these situations next.

Using a Forest

Active Directory forests are designed to accommodate multiple noncontiguous namespaces. That is, they can combine domain trees into logical units. An example might be the following tree and domain structure:

- Tree: Organization1.com
  - Sales.Organization1.com
  - Marketing.Organization1.com
  - Engineering.Organization1.com
  - NorthAmerica.Engineering.Organization1.com
- Tree: Organization2.com
  - Sales.Organization2.com
  - Engineering.Organization2.com.

Figure 20.11 provides an example of how multiple trees can fit into a single forest. Such a situation might occur in the acquisition and merger of companies or if a company is logically divided into two or more completely separate and autonomous business units.

FIGURE 20.11 A single forest consisting of multiple trees

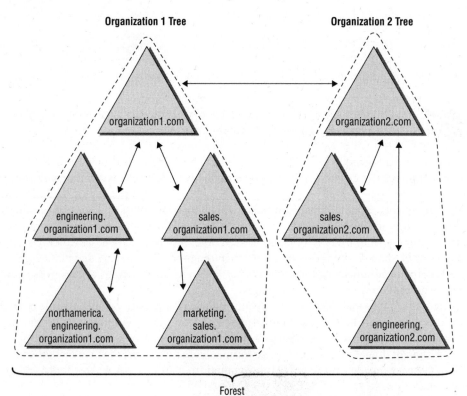

All of the trees within a forest are related through a single forest root domain. This is the first domain that was created in the Active Directory environment. The root domain in each tree creates a transitive trust with the forest root domain. The result is a configuration in which all of the trees within a domain and all of the domains within each tree trust each other. Again, as with domain trees, the presence of a trust relationship does not automatically signify that users have permissions to access resources across domains. It allows only objects and resources to be shared. Authorized network administrators must set up specific permissions.

All of the domains within a single Active Directory forest have the following features in common:

Schema   The *schema* is the Active Directory structure that defines how the information within the data store is structured. For the information stored on various domain controllers to remain compatible, all of the domain controllers within the entire Active Directory environment must share the same schema. For example, if you add a field for an employee benefit plan number, all domain controllers throughout the environment need to recognize this information before you can share information among them.

Global Catalog   One of the problems associated with working in large network environments is that sharing information across multiple domains can be costly in terms of network and server resources. Fortunately, Active Directory uses the global catalog (GC), which serves as a repository for information about a subset of all objects within *all* Active Directory domains in a forest. System administrators can determine what types of information should be added to the defaults in the GC. Generally, they decide to store commonly used information, such as a list of all of the printers, users, groups, and computers. In addition, they can configure specific domain controllers to carry a copy of the GC. Now if you have a question about where to find all of the color printers in the company, for example, all you need to do is to contact the nearest GC server.

Configuration Information   Some roles and functions must be managed for the entire forest. When you are dealing with multiple domains, this means that you must configure certain domain controllers to perform functions for the entire Active Directory environment. I will discuss some specifics of this later in this chapter.

The main purpose of allowing multiple domains to exist together is to allow them to share information and other resources. Now that you've seen the basics of domain trees and forests, take a look at how domains are actually created.

The Promotion Process

A domain tree is created when a new domain is added as the child of an existing domain. This relationship is established during the promotion of a Windows Server 2016 computer to a domain controller. Although the underlying relationships can be quite complicated in larger organizations, the Server Manager's Active Directory Installation Wizard makes it easy to create forests and trees.

Using the Active Directory Installation Wizard, you can quickly and easily create new domains by promoting a Windows Server 2016 stand-alone server or a member server to a domain controller. When you install a new domain controller, you can choose to make it part of an existing domain, or you can choose to make it the first domain controller in a new domain. In the following sections and exercises, you'll become familiar with the exact steps you need to take to create a domain tree and a domain forest when you promote a server to a domain controller.

Creating a Domain Tree

In previous chapters, you learned how to promote the first domain controller in the first domain in a forest, also known as the root. If you don't promote any other domain controllers, then that domain controller simply controls that one domain and only one tree is created. To create a new domain tree, you need to promote a Windows Server 2016 computer to a domain controller. In the Active Directory Installation Wizard, you select the option that makes this domain controller the first machine in a new domain that is a child of an existing domain. As a result, you will have a domain tree that contains two domains—a parent and a child, or two trees if you don't create a child domain.

Before you can create a new child domain, you need the following information:

- The name of the parent domain
- The name of the child domain (the one you are planning to install)
- The file system locations for the Active Directory database, logs, and shared system volume
- DNS configuration information
- The NetBIOS name for the new server
- A domain administrator username and password

Exercise 20.6 walks you through the process of creating a new child domain using Server Manager. This exercise assumes you have already created the parent domain and you are using a server in the domain that is not a domain controller.

EXERCISE 20.6

Creating a New Subdomain

1. Open Server Manager.

2. Click item 2, Add Roles And Features.

3. Make sure that the Role-Based Or Feature-Based Installation button is selected and click Next.

4. At the Select Destination screen, click Next.

5. At the Select Server Roles screen, check the Active Directory Domain Services check box. A box will appear stating that you need to install additional roles. Click the Add Features button. Then click Next.

6. At the Add Roles And Features Wizard screen, click Next.

7. At the Confirmation screen, click the Install button.

8. When the installation is complete, click the Close button.

9. Close Server Manager and restart the machine.

10. Log in and restart Server Manager.

11. In the Roles And Server Groups area, click the AD DS link.

12. In the Servers section, click the More link next to Configuration Required For Active Directory Domain Services.

13. At the All Servers Task Details screen, click the Promote This Server To A Domain Controller link.

14. At the Deployment Configuration screen, click the radio button Add A New Domain To An Existing Forest. In the Select Domain Type drop-down, chose Child Domain and then choose your parent domain. In the New Domain Name box, type in the name of your new domain. I used NewHampshire. Click the Next button.

15. At the Domain Controller Options screen, I set the following options:

    Domain Functional Level: Windows Server 2016

    Domain Name System (DNS) Server: Checked

    Global Catalog (GC): Checked

    Site Name: CorporateHQ

    Password: **P@ssw0rd**

    Click Next.

16. At the DNS screen, click Next.

17. At the Additional Options screen, accept the default NetBIOS domain name and click Next.

18. At the Paths screen, accept the default file locations and click Next.

19. At the Review Options screen, verify your settings and click Next.

20. At the Prerequisites Check screen, click the Install button (as long as there are no errors).

21. After the installation completes, the machine will automatically reboot. Log in as the administrator.

22. Close Server Manager.

Joining a New Domain Tree to a Forest

A *forest* is one or more trees that do not share a contiguous namespace. For example, you could join the `organization1.com` and `organization2.com` domains together to create a single Active Directory environment.

Any two trees can be joined together to create a forest, as long as the second tree is installed after the first and the trees have noncontiguous namespaces. (If the namespaces were contiguous, you would actually need to create a new domain for an existing tree.) The process of creating a new tree to form or add to a forest is as simple as promoting a server to a domain controller for a new domain that does *not* share a namespace with an existing Active Directory domain.

 The command-line tool adprep.exe is used to prepare a Microsoft Windows 2003, 2008, or 2008 R2 forest or a Windows 2003, 2008, or 2008 R2 domain for the installation of Windows Server 2016 domain controllers.

To add a new domain to an existing forest, you must already have at least one other domain, which is the root domain. Keep in mind that the entire forest structure is destroyed if the original root domain is ever removed entirely. Therefore, you should have at least two domain controllers in the Active Directory root domain; the second serves as a backup in case you have a problem with the first, and it can also serve as a backup solution for disaster recovery and fault tolerance purposes. Such a setup provides additional protection for the entire forest in case one of the domain controllers fails.

Adding Additional Domain Controllers

In addition to the operations you've already performed, you can use the Active Directory Installation Wizard to create additional domain controllers for any of your domains. There are two main reasons to create additional domain controllers:

Fault Tolerance and Reliability   You should always consider the theory of *disaster recovery (DR)* and have a plan, sometimes referred to as a *disaster recovery plan (DRP)*. If you're part of one of those organizations that rely upon their network directory services infrastructures, you need Active Directory to provide security and resources for all users.

For this reason, downtime and data loss are very costly. Through the use of multiple domain controllers, you can ensure that if one of the servers goes down, another one is available to perform the necessary tasks, such as user authentication and resource browsing. Additionally, data loss (perhaps from hard disk drive failure) will not result in the loss or unavailability of network security information because you can easily recover Active Directory information from the remaining, still-functional domain controller.

Performance   The burden of processing login requests and serving as a repository for security permissions and other information can be quite extensive, especially in larger businesses. By using multiple domain controllers, you can distribute this load across multiple systems. Additionally, by strategically placing domain controllers, you can greatly increase response times for common network operations, such as authentication and browsing for resources.

As a rule of thumb, you should always plan and design your infrastructure to have at least two domain controllers per domain. For many organizations, this provides a good balance between the cost of servers and the level of reliability and performance. For larger or more distributed organizations, however, additional domain controllers greatly improve performance.

Demoting a Domain Controller

In addition to being able to promote member servers to domain controllers, the Active Directory Installation Wizard can do the exact opposite, that is, demote domain controllers.

You might choose to demote a domain controller for a couple of reasons. First, if you have determined that the role of a server should change (for example, from a domain controller to a member or stand-alone server that you might make into a web server), you can easily demote it to make this happen. Another common reason to demote a domain controller is if you want to move the machine from one domain to another. You cannot do this in a single step: First you need to demote the existing domain controller to remove it from the current domain and then promote it into a new domain. The result is that the server is now a domain controller for a different domain.

To demote a domain controller, you simply access the Active Directory Installation Wizard. The wizard automatically notices that the local server is a domain controller, and it asks you to verify each step you take, as with most things you do in Windows. You are prompted to decide whether you really want to remove this machine from the current domain. Note that if the local server is a global catalog server, you will be warned that at least one copy of the GC must remain available so that you can perform logon authentication.

By default, at the end of the demotion process, the server is joined as a member server to the domain for which it was previously a domain controller. If you demote the last domain controller in the domain, the server becomes a stand-alone server.

Planning for Domain Controller Placement

You are the senior system administrator for a medium-sized Active Directory environment. Currently the environment consists of only one Active Directory domain. Your company's network is spread out over 40 different sites throughout North America. Recently, you've received complaints from users and other system administrators about the performance of Active Directory–related operations. For example, users report that it takes several minutes to log on to their machines between 9 a.m. and 10 a.m., when activity is at its highest. Simultaneously, system administrators complain that updating user information within the OUs for which they are responsible can take longer than expected.

Fortunately, Active Directory's distributed domain controller architecture allows you to optimize performance for this type of situation without making dramatic changes to your environment. You decide that the quickest and easiest solution is to deploy additional domain controllers throughout the organization. The domain controllers are generally placed within areas of the network that are connected by slow or unreliable links. For example, a small branch office in Des Moines, Iowa, receives its own domain controller. The process is quite simple: You install a new Windows Server 2016 computer and then run the Active Directory Installation Wizard in Server Manager to make the new machine a domain controller for an existing domain. Once the initial directory services data is copied to the new server, it is ready to service requests and updates of your domain information.

Note that there are potential drawbacks to this solution; for instance, you have to manage additional domain controllers and the network traffic generated from communications between the domain controllers. It's important that you monitor your network links to ensure that you've reached a good balance between replication traffic and overall Active Directory performance. In later chapters, you'll see how you can configure Active Directory sites to map Active Directory operations better to your physical network structure.

Removing a domain from your environment is not an operation that you should take lightly. Before you plan to remove a domain, make a list of all of the resources that depend on the domain and the reasons why the domain was originally created. If you are sure that your organization no longer requires the domain, then you can safely continue. If you are not sure, think again, because the process cannot be reversed and you could lose critical information!

Managing Multiple Domains

You can easily manage most of the operations that must occur *between* domains by using the Active Directory Domains and Trusts administrative tool. On the other hand, if you want to configure settings *within* a domain, you should use the Active Directory Users and Computers tool. In the following sections, you'll look at ways to perform two common domain management functions with the tools just mentioned: managing *single-master operations* and managing *trusts*. You'll also look at ways to manage UPN suffixes in order to simplify user accounts, and you'll examine GC servers in more detail.

Managing Single-Master Operations

For the most part, Active Directory functions in what is known as *multimaster* replication. That is, every domain controller within the environment contains a copy of the Active Directory database that is both readable and writable. This works well for most types of information. For example, if you want to modify the password of a user, you can easily do this on *any* of the domain controllers within a domain. The change is then automatically propagated to the other domain controllers.

However, some functions are not managed in a multimaster fashion. These operations are known as *operations masters*. You must perform single-master operations on specially designated domain controllers within the Active Directory forest. There are five main single-master functions: two that apply to an entire Active Directory forest and three that apply to each domain.

 To see what domain controllers hold which operation master roles, type `Netdom Query FSMO` at a command prompt or in a PowerShell window.

Forest Operations Masters

You use the Active Directory Domains and Trusts tool to configure forest-wide roles. The following single-master operations apply to the entire forest:

Schema Master   Earlier you learned that all of the domain controllers within a single Active Directory environment share the same schema. This ensures information consistency. However, developers and system administrators can modify the Active Directory schema by adding custom information. A trivial example might involve adding a field to employee information that specifies a user's favorite color.

When you need to make these types of changes, you must perform them on the domain controller that serves as the *Schema Master* for the environment. The Schema Master is then responsible for propagating all of the changes to all the other domain controllers within the forest.

Domain Naming Master   The purpose of the *Domain Naming Master* is to keep track of all the domains within an Active Directory forest. You access this domain controller whenever you need to add/remove new domains to a tree or forest.

Domain Operations Masters

You use the Active Directory Users and Computers snap-in to administer roles within a domain. Within each domain, at least one domain controller must fulfill each of the following roles:

Relative ID (RID) Master   Every security object within Active Directory must be assigned a unique identifier so that it is distinguishable from other objects. For example, if you have two OUs named IT that reside in different domains, you must have some way to distinguish easily between them. Furthermore, if you delete one of the IT OUs and then later re-create it, the system must be able to determine that it is not the same object as the other IT OU. The unique identifier for each object is made up of a domain identifier and a relative identifier (RID). RIDs are always unique within an Active Directory domain and are used for managing security information and authenticating users. The *RID Master* is responsible for creating these values within a domain whenever new Active Directory objects are created.

PDC Emulator Master   Within a domain, the *PDC Emulator Master* (also referred to as the PDC Emulator) is responsible for maintaining backward compatibility with Windows 95, 98, and NT clients. The PDC Emulator Master is also responsible for processing password changes between a domain user account and all of the domain controllers throughout the domain.

The PDC Emulator Master is also the default time server for all of the domain controllers in the domain. This is why it's a good practice to make sure that your PDC emulator has the proper time. It's the system that all others will rely on for time accuracy.

The PDC Emulator Master serves as the default domain controller to process authentication requests if another domain controller is unable to do so. The PDC Emulator Master also receives preferential treatment whenever domain security changes are made. PDC emulators are also the preferred point of contact for many services and applications that run on the domain.

Infrastructure Master   Whenever a user is added to or removed from a group, all of the other domain controllers should be made aware of this change. The role of the domain controller that acts as an *Infrastructure Master* is to ensure that group membership information stays synchronized within an Active Directory domain.

Unless there is only one domain controller, you should not place the Infrastructure Master on a global catalog server. If the Infrastructure Master and global catalog are on the same domain controller, the Infrastructure Master will not function.

Another service that a server can control for the network is the Windows Time service. The Windows Time service uses a suite of algorithms in the Network Time Protocol (NTP). This helps ensure that the time on all computers throughout a network is as accurate as possible. All client computers within a Windows Server 2016 domain are synchronized with the time of an authoritative computer.

Assigning Single-Master Roles

Now that you are familiar with the different types of single-master operations, take a look at Exercise 20.7. This exercise shows you how to assign these roles to servers within the Active Directory environment. In this exercise, you will assign single-master operations roles to various domain controllers within the environment. To complete the steps in this exercise, you need one Active Directory domain controller.

EXERCISE 20.7

Assigning Single-Master Operations

1. Open the Active Directory Domains and Trusts administrative tool.

2. Right-click Active Directory Domains And Trusts and choose Operations Masters.

3. In the Operations Masters dialog box, note that you can change the operations master by clicking the Change button. If you want to move this assignment to another computer, first you need to connect to that computer and then make the change. Click Close to continue without making any changes.

4. Close the Active Directory Domains and Trusts administrative tool.

5. Open the Active Directory Users and Computers administrative tool.

6. Right-click the name of a domain and select Operations Masters. This brings up the RID tab of the Operations Masters dialog box.

    Notice that you can change the computer that is assigned to the role. To change the role, first you need to connect to the appropriate domain controller. Notice that the PDC and Infrastructure roles have similar tabs. Click Close to continue without making any changes.

7. When you have finished, close the Active Directory Users and Computers tool.

Remember that you manage single-master operations with three different tools. You use the Active Directory Domains and Trusts tool to configure the Domain Name Master role, while you use the Active Directory Users and Computers snap-in to administer roles within a domain. Although this might not seem intuitive at first, it can help you remember which roles apply to domains and which apply to the whole forest. The third tool, the Schema Master role, is a bit different than these other two. To change the Schema Master role, you must install the Active Directory Schema MMS snap-in and change it there.

Seizing Roles

Changing roles from one domain controller to another is really simple. An administrator goes into Active Directory or PowerShell and changes an FSMO role from one machine to another. The problem happens when a machine with one of the roles crashes and goes down. You can't just switch the role from a machine that is not working.

So, what is an administrator to do? Well, at that point, what you need to do is seize control of the role. You do this through the use of PowerShell. Let's look at how to seize a role using PowerShell.

Normally, I would show you how to seize control of an FSMO role using an exercise, but since you probably don't have dozens of Microsoft Windows Server 2016 domain controllers just lying around, I will show you how to seize control through a step-by-step process.

To show you how to set up a step-by-step process, you first have to know what FSMO roles are assigned to what FSMO numbers. The following roles each have a corresponding number:

FSMO role	Number
PDCEmulator	0
RIDMaster	1
InfrastructureMaster	2
SchemaMaster	3
DomainNamingMaster	4

Now that you know the role and the number associated to it, you just need to know the PowerShell commands to seize control of the role. The following is an example of how to use PowerShell commands to seize control of one of the FSMO roles.

I am using the `-Identity` switch to specify the target domain controller (I am calling my target domain controller DC1) and the `-OperationMasterRole` to specify which role to transfer. I've also used the `-Force` command because my current FSMO holder is offline. I will be moving all of the roles to the target domain controller, DC1.

1. On a domain controller, log in as an administrator and start PowerShell with elevated privileges.

2. In PowerShell, type the following command:

   ```
   Move-ADDirectoryServerOperationMasterRole -Identity DC1 -OperationMasterRole
   0,1,2,3,4 -Force
   ```

3. Either type **Y** on each role move prompt or type **A** to accept all prompts.

4. After a few minutes, all of the FSMO roles should be successfully moved.

Finally, I want to show you a couple of useful PowerShell commands so that you can view which domain controller owns which FSMO role.

```
Get-ADForest DomainName | FT SchemaMaster,DomainNamingMaster
Get-ADDomain DomainName | FT PDCEmulator,RIDMaster,InfrastructureMaster
```

Managing Trusts

Trust relationships make it easier to share security information and network resources between domains. As was already mentioned, standard transitive two-way trusts are automatically created between the domains in a tree and between each of the trees in a forest. Figure 20.12 shows an example of the default trust relationships in an Active Directory forest.

FIGURE 20.12   Default trusts in an Active Directory forest

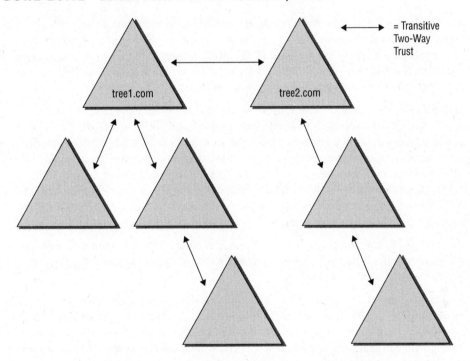

When configuring trusts, you need to consider two main characteristics:

Transitive Trusts   By default, Active Directory trusts are *transitive trusts*. The simplest way to understand transitive relationships is through this example: If Domain A trusts Domain B and Domain B trusts Domain C, then Domain A implicitly trusts Domain C. If you need to apply a tighter level of security, trusts can be configured as intransitive.

One-Way vs. Two-Way   Trusts can be configured as one-way or two-way relationships. The default operation is to create *two-way trusts* or *bidirectional trusts*. This makes it easier to manage trust relationships by reducing the trusts you must create. In some cases, however, you might decide against two-way trusts. In one-way relationships, the trusting domain allows resources to be shared with the trusted domain but not the other way around.

When domains are added together to form trees and forests, an automatic transitive two-way trust is created between them. Although the default trust relationships work well for most organizations, there are some reasons you might want to manage trusts manually:

- You may want to remove trusts between domains if you are absolutely sure you do not want resources to be shared between domains.

- Because of security concerns, you may need to keep resources isolated.

In addition to the default trust types, you can configure the following types of special trusts:

External Trusts   You use *external trusts* to provide access to resources on a Windows NT 4 domain or forest that cannot use a forest trust. Windows NT 4 domains cannot benefit from the other trust types that are used in Windows Server 2016. Thus, in some cases, external trusts could be your only option. External trusts are always nontransitive, but they can be established in a one-way or two-way configuration.

Default SID Filtering on External Trusts   When you set up an external trust, remember that it is possible for hackers to compromise a domain controller in a trusted domain. If this trust is compromised, a hacker can use the security identifier (SID) history attribute to associate SIDs with new user accounts, granting themselves unauthorized rights (this is called an *elevation-of-privileges attack*). To help prevent this type of attack, Windows Server 2016 automatically enables SID filter quarantining on all external trusts. SID filtering allows the domain controllers in the trusting domain (the domain with the resources) to remove all SID history attributes that are not members of the trusted domain.

Realm Trusts   *Realm trusts* are similar to external trusts. You use them to connect to a non-Windows domain that uses Kerberos authentication. Realm trusts can be transitive or nontransitive, one-way or two-way.

Cross-Forest Trusts   *Cross-forest trusts* are used to share resources between forests. They have been used since Windows Server 2000 domains and cannot be nontransitive, but you can establish them in a one-way or a two-way configuration. Authentication requests in either forest can reach the other forest in a two-way cross-forest trust. If you want one forest to trust another forest, you must set it (at a minimum) to at least the forest function level of Windows Server 2003.

Selective Authentication vs. Forest-Wide Authentication   Forest-wide authentication on a forest trust means that users of the trusted forest can access all of the resources of the trusting forest. Selective authentication means that users cannot authenticate to a domain controller or resource server in the trusting forest unless they are explicitly allowed to do so. Exercise 20.8 will show you the steps necessary to change forest-wide authentication to selective authentication.

Shortcut Trusts   In some cases, you may actually want to create direct trusts between two domains that implicitly trust each other. Such a trust is sometimes referred to as a *shortcut trust,* and it can improve the speed at which resources are accessed across many different domains. Let's say you have a forest, as shown in Figure 20.13.

FIGURE 20.13   Example of a forest

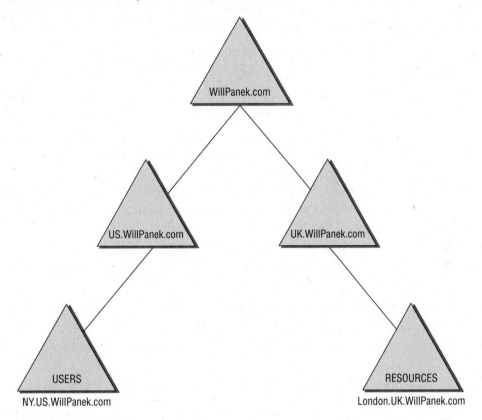

Users in the NY.us.WillPanek.com domain can access resources in the London.uk.WillPanek.com domain, but the users have to authenticate using the parent domains to gain access (NY.us.WillPanek.com to us.WillPanek.com to WillPanek.com to uk.WillPanek.com to finally reach London.uk.WillPanek.com). This process can be slow. An administrator can set up a one-way trust from London.uk.WillPanek.com (trusting domain) to NY.us.WillPanek.com (trusted domain) so that the users can access the resources directly.

> Perhaps the most important aspect to remember regarding trusts is that creating them only *allows* you to share resources between domains. The trust does not grant any permissions between domains by itself. Once a trust has been established, however, system administrators can easily assign the necessary permissions.

Exercise 20.8 walks you through the steps necessary to manage trusts. In this exercise, you will see how to assign trust relationships between domains. To complete the steps in this exercise, you must have domain administrator access permissions.

EXERCISE 20.8

Managing Trust Relationships

1. Open the Active Directory Domains and Trusts administrative tool.

2. Right-click the name of a domain and select Properties.

3. Select the Trusts tab. You will see a list of the trusts that are currently configured. To modify the trust properties for an existing trust, highlight that trust and click Properties.

4. The Properties window for the trust displays information about the trust's direction, transitivity, and type along with the names of the domains involved in the relationship. Click Cancel to exit without making any changes.

5. To create a new trust relationship, click the New Trust button on the Trusts tab. The New Trust Wizard appears. Click Next to proceed with the wizard.

6. On the Trust Name page, you are prompted for the name of the domain with which the trust should be created. Enter the name of the domain and click Next.

7. On the Trust Type page, you would normally choose the Trust With A Windows Domain option if you know that the other domain uses a Windows domain controller. Choose Realm Trust. Click Next when you have finished.

8. On the Transitivity Of Trust page, you choose whether the trust is transitive or nontransitive. Choose the Nontransitive option and click Next to continue.

9. On the Direction Of Trust page, you select the direction of the trust. If you want both domains to trust each other, you select the Two-Way option. Otherwise, you select either One-Way: Incoming or One-Way: Outgoing, depending on where the affected users are located. For the sake of this exercise, choose One-Way: Incoming and then click Next.

10. On the Trust Password page, you need to specify a password that should be used to administer the trust. Type **P@ssw0rd** and confirm it. Note that if there is an existing trust relationship between the domains, the passwords must match. Click Next to continue.

11. Now you see the Trust Selections Complete page that recaps the selections you have made. Because this is an exercise, you don't actually want to establish this trust. Click Cancel to cancel the wizard without saving the changes.

12. Exit the trust properties for the domain by clicking Cancel.

To Enable Selective Authentication

1. In the console tree, right-click the name of a domain and select Properties.

2. Select the Trusts tab. Under either Domains Trusted By This Domain (Outgoing Trusts) or Domains That Trust This Domain (Incoming Trusts), click the forest trust that you want to administer and then click Properties.

3. On the Authentication tab, click Selective Authentication and then click OK.

Managing UPN Suffixes

User principal name (UPN) suffixes are the part of a user's name that appears after the @ symbol. For example, the UPN suffix of wpanek@WillPanek.com would be WillPanek.com. By default, the UPN suffix is determined by the name of the domain in which the user is created. In this example, the user wpanek was created in the domain WillPanek.com, so the two pieces of the UPN logically fit together. However, you might find it useful to provide an alternative UPN suffix to consolidate the UPNs forest-wide.

For instance, if you manage a forest that consists of WillPanek.com and WillPanek2.com, you might want all of your users to adopt the more generally applicable WillPanek.com UPN suffix. By adding additional UPN suffixes to the forest, you can easily choose the appropriate suffix when it comes time to create new users. Exercise 20.9 shows you how to add additional suffixes to a forest.

EXERCISE 20.9

Adding a UPN Suffix

1. Open the Active Directory Domains and Trusts administrative tool.

2. Right-click Active Directory Domains And Trusts in the left side of the window and select Properties.

3. On the UPN Suffixes tab of the Active Directory Domains And Trusts Properties dialog box, enter an alternative UPN suffix in the Alternative UPN Suffixes field. Click the Add button to add the suffix to the list.

4. To remove a UPN suffix, select its name in the list and click the Remove button.

Name Suffix Routing

Name Suffix Routing is a mechanism that is used to manage how authentication requests are routed across Active Directory forests that are joined together by forest trusts. To simplify the administration of authentication requests, when you create a forest trust, all unique name suffixes are routed by default. A *unique name suffix* is a name suffix within a forest, such as a user principal name (UPN) suffix, service principal name (SPN) suffix, or Domain Name System forest, or a domain tree name that is not subordinate to any other name suffix. Name Suffix Routing is managed from the Active Directory Domains and Trusts Administrative Console.

Managing Global Catalog Servers

One of the best features of a distributed directory service like Active Directory is that you can store different pieces of information in different places within an organization. For example, a domain in Japan might store a list of users who operate within a company's

Asian operations business unit, while one in New York would contain a list of users who operate within its North American operations business unit. This architecture allows system administrators to place the most frequently accessed information on domain controllers in different domains, thereby reducing disk space requirements and replication traffic.

However, you may encounter a problem when you deal with information that is segmented into multiple domains. The issue involves querying information stored within Active Directory. For example, what would happen if a user wanted a list of all the printers available in all domains within the Active Directory forest? In this case, the search would normally require information from at least one domain controller in each of the domains within the environment. Some of these domain controllers may be located across slow WAN links or may have unreliable connections. The result would include an extremely long wait while retrieving the results of the query, that is, if any results came up without the query timing out.

Fortunately, Active Directory has a mechanism that speeds up such searches. You can configure any number of domain controllers to host a copy of the GC. The GC contains all of the schema information and a subset of the attributes for all domains within the Active Directory environment. Although a default set of information is normally included with the GC, system administrators can choose to add additional information to this data store if it is needed. To help reduce replication traffic and to keep the GC's database small, only a limited subset of each object's attributes is replicated. This is called the *partial attribute set (PAS)*. You can change the PAS by modifying the schema and marking attributes for replication to the GC.

Servers that contain a copy of the GC are known as *GC servers*. Now whenever a user executes a query that requires information from multiple domains, they need only contact the nearest GC server for this information. Similarly, when users must authenticate across domains, they do not have to wait for a response from a domain controller that may be located across the world. The result is that the overall performance of Active Directory queries improves.

Exercise 20.10 walks you through the steps that you need to take to configure a domain controller as a GC server. Generally, GC servers are useful only in environments that use multiple Active Directory domains.

EXERCISE 20.10

Managing GC Servers

1. Open the Active Directory Sites and Services administrative tool.

2. Find the name of the local domain controller within the list of objects, typically under Default First Site Name ➢ Servers, and expand this object. Right-click NTDS Settings, and select Properties.

3. In the NTDS Settings Properties dialog box, type **Primary GC Server for Domain** in the Description field. Note that there is a check box that determines whether this computer contains a copy of the global catalog. If the box is checked, then this

domain controller contains a subset of information from all other domains within the Active Directory environment. Select the Global Catalog check box and then click OK to continue.

4. When you have finished, close the Active Directory Sites and Services administrative tool.

Managing Universal Group Membership Caching

Many networks run into problems with available network bandwidth and server hardware limitations. For this reason, it may not be wise to install a GC in smaller branch offices. Windows Server 2016 can help these smaller sites by deploying domain controllers that use *Universal Group Membership Caching (UGMC)*.

Once enabled, Universal Group Membership Caching stores information locally when a user attempts to log on for the first time. With the use of a GC, the domain controller retains the universal group membership for that logged-on user.

The next time that user attempts to log on, the authenticating domain controller running Windows Server 2016 will obtain the universal group membership information from its local cache without the need to contact a GC. By default, the universal group membership information is retained on the domain controller for eight hours.

There are several advantages of using Universal Group Membership Caching:

Faster Logon Times   Because the domain controller does not need to contact a global catalog, logon authentication is faster.

Reduced Network Bandwidth   The domain controller does not have to handle object replication for all of the objects located in the forest.

Ability to Use Existing Hardware   There is no need to upgrade hardware to support a GC.

Exercise 20.11 shows you the steps necessary to configure Universal Group Membership Caching.

EXERCISE 20.11

Managing Universal Group Membership Caching

1. Open the Active Directory Sites and Services administrative tool.

2. Click Sites and then click CorporateHQ. In the right pane, right-click NTDS Settings and choose Properties.

3. In the NTDS Site Settings Properties dialog box, check the box Enable Universal Group Membership Caching and then click OK to continue.

4. When you have finished, close the Active Directory Sites and Services administrative tool.

Upgrading Existing Domains and Forests

Now that you have a new operating system to which you can upgrade, it's important that you take some time to learn about the different ways you can get your infrastructure up-to-date. There are quite a few upgrade paths to consider. Table 20.2 illustrates the most commonly used in-place upgrade paths for upgrading your domain controllers from Windows Server 2008 to Windows Server 2016. The in-place upgrades hold true only for 64-bit versions of Server 2008 to Server 2016. You cannot in-place upgrade domain controllers that run either Windows Server 2003 or a 32-bit version of Windows Server 2008. If your current environmental configurations fall outside of the possibility of an in-place upgrade, then you will need to install new domain controllers on the most up-to-date Windows Server OS and then delete the old ones.

TABLE 20.2 Supported domain controller in-place upgrade paths

If you are running these editions...	You can upgrade to these editions...
Windows Server 2008 Standard with SP2 or Windows Server 2008 Enterprise with SP2	Windows Server 2016 Standard or Windows Server 2016 Datacenter
Windows Server 2008 Datacenter with SP2	Windows Server 2016 Datacenter
Windows Web Server 2008	Windows Server 2016 Standard
Windows Server 2008 R2 Standard with SP1 or Windows Server 2008 R2 Enterprise with SP1	Windows Server 2016 Standard or Windows Server 2016 Datacenter
Windows Server 2008 R2 Datacenter with SP1	Windows Server 2016 Datacenter
Windows Web Server 2008 R2	Windows Server 2016 Standard
Windows Server 2012/2012 R2 Standard	Windows Server 2016 Standard
Windows Server 2012/2012 R2 Datacenter	Windows Server 2016 Datacenter

When preparing for your domain controller upgrade, make sure you make a full backup of your Active Directory environment prior to performing the task. If you have never actually performed a full backup and restore of your Active Directory environment, then I recommend doing so by following the instructions later in this chapter. You never know if a backup actually works until you perform the restore, and you should never make infrastructure changes without a backup of your current configuration.

Maintain Active Directory

If you have deployed Active Directory in your network environment, your users now depend on it to function properly in order to do their jobs. From network authentications to file access to print and web services, Active Directory has become a mission-critical component of your business. Therefore, the importance of backing up the Active Directory data store should be evident.

As I discussed in earlier chapters, it is important to have multiple domain controllers available to provide backup in case of a problem. The same goes for Active Directory itself—it too should be backed up by being saved. This way, if a massive disaster occurs in which you need to restore your directory services, you will have that option available to you.

Backups are just good common sense, but here are several specific reasons to back up data:

Protect Against Hardware Failures   Computer hardware devices have finite lifetimes, and all hardware eventually fails. MBTF is the average time a device will function before it actually fails. There is also a rating derived from benchmark testing of hard disk devices that tells you when you may be at risk for an unavoidable disaster. Some types of failures, such as corrupted hard disk drives, can result in significant data loss.

Protect Against Accidental Deletion or Modification of Data   Although the threat of hardware failures is very real, in most environments, mistakes in modifying or deleting data are much more common. For example, suppose a system administrator accidentally deletes all of the objects within a specific OU. Clearly, it's very important to be able to retrieve this information from a backup.

Keep Historical Information   Users and system administrators sometimes modify files and then later find out that they require access to an older version of the file. Or a file is accidentally deleted and a user does not discover that fact until much later. By keeping multiple backups over time, you can recover information from prior backups when necessary.

Protect Against Malicious Deletion or Modification of Data   Even in the most secure environments, it is conceivable that unauthorized users (or authorized ones with malicious intent!) could delete or modify information. In such cases, the loss of data might require valid backups from which to restore critical information.

Windows Server 2016 includes a Backup utility that is designed to back up operating system files and the Active Directory data store. It allows for basic backup functionality, such as scheduling backup jobs and selecting which files to back up. Figure 20.14 shows the main screen of the Windows Server 2016 Backup utility.

In the following sections, we'll look at the details of using the Windows Server 2016 Backup utility and how you can restore Active Directory when problems do occur.

FIGURE 20.14   The main screen of the Windows Server 2016 Backup utility

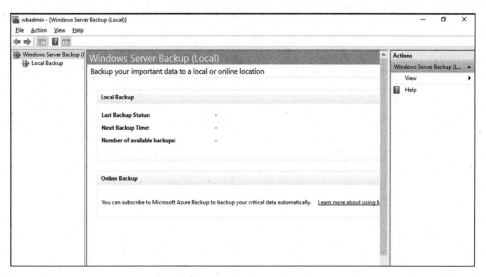

Overview of the Windows Server 2016 Backup Utility

Although the general purpose behind performing backup operations—protecting information—is straightforward, system administrators must consider many options when determining the optimal backup-and-recovery scenario for their environment. Factors include what to back up, how often to back up, and when the backups should be performed.

In the following sections, you'll see how the Windows Server 2016 Backup utility makes it easy to implement a backup plan for many network environments.

Although the Windows Server 2016 Backup utility provides the basic functionality required to back up your files, you may want to investigate third-party products that provide additional functionality. These applications can provide options for specific types of backups (such as those for Exchange Server and SQL Server) as well as disaster recovery options, networking functionality, centralized management, and support for more advanced hardware.

Backup Types

One of the most important issues you will have to deal with when you are performing backups is keeping track of which files you have backed up and which files you need to back up. Whenever a backup of a file is made, the archive bit for the file is set. You can view the attributes of system files by right-clicking them and selecting Properties. By clicking the

Advanced button in the Properties dialog box, you will access the Advanced Attributes dialog box. Here you will see the option Folder Is Ready For Archiving. Figure 20.15 shows an example of the attributes for a folder.

FIGURE 20.15   Viewing the Archive attributes for a folder

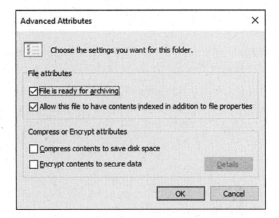

Although it is possible to back up all of the files in the file system during each backup operation, it's sometimes more convenient to back up only selected files (such as those that have changed since the last backup operation). When performing backups, you can back up to removable media (DVD) or to a network location.

It is recommended by Microsoft to do a backup to a network location. The reason for this is that if your company suffers from a disaster (fire, hurricane, and so forth), your data can all still be lost—including the backup. If you back up to a removable media source, a copy of the backup can be taken offsite. This protects against a major disaster.

 Although Windows Server 2016 does not support all of these backup types, it's very important that you understand the most common backup types. Most Administrators use third-party software for their backups. That's why it's important to know all of the different types.

Several types of backups can be performed:

Normal   Normal backups (also referred to as *system* or *full backups*) back up all of the selected files and then mark them as backed up. This option is usually used when a full system backup is made. Windows Server 2016 supports this backup.

Copy   *Copy backups* back up all of the selected files but do not mark them as backed up. This is useful when you want to make additional backups of files for moving files offsite or you want to make multiple copies of the same data for archival purposes.

Incremental   *Incremental backups* copy any selected files that are marked as ready for backup (typically because they have not been backed up or they have been changed since the last backup) and then mark the files as backed up. When the next incremental backup is run, only the files that are not marked as having been backed up are stored. Incremental backups are used in conjunction with normal (full) backups.

The most common backup process is to make a full backup and then make subsequent incremental backups. The benefit to this method is that only files that have changed since the last full or incremental backup will be stored. This can reduce backup times and disk or tape storage space requirements.

When recovering information from this type of backup method, a system administrator must first restore the full backup and then restore each of the incremental backups.

Differential   *Differential backups* are similar in purpose to incremental backups with one important exception: Differential backups copy all of the files that are marked for backup but do not mark the files as backed up. When restoring files in a situation that uses normal and differential backups, you need only restore the normal backup and the latest differential backup.

Daily   *Daily backups* back up all of the files that have changed during a single day. This operation uses the file time/date stamps to determine which files should be backed up and does not mark the files as having been backed up.

Backing Up System State Data

When you are planning to back up and restore Active Directory, be aware that the most important component is known as the *System State data*. System State data includes the components upon which the Windows Server 2016 operating system relies for normal operations. The Windows Server 2016 Backup utility offers you the ability to back up the System State data to another type of media (such as a hard disk or network share). Specifically, it will back up the following components for a Windows Server 2016 domain controller:

Active Directory   The *Active Directory data store* is at the heart of Active Directory. It contains all of the information necessary to create and manage network resources, such as users and computers. In most environments that use Active Directory, users and system administrators rely on the proper functioning of these services in order to do their jobs.

Boot Files   *Boot files* are the files required for booting the Windows Server 2016 operating system and can be used in the case of boot file corruption.

COM+ Class Registration Database   The *COM+ Class Registration database* is a listing of all of the COM+ Class registrations stored on the computer. Applications that run on a Windows Server 2016 computer might require the registration of various share code components. As part of the System State backup process, Windows Server 2016 stores all of the information related to Component Object Model+ (COM+) components so that it can be quickly and easily restored.

Registry   The Windows Server 2016 *Registry* is a central repository of information related to the operating system configuration (such as desktop and network settings), user settings, and application settings. Therefore, the Registry is absolutely vital to the proper functioning of Windows Server 2016.

Sysvol Directory   The *Sysvol directory* includes data and files that are shared between the domain controllers within an Active Directory domain. Many operating system services rely on this information in order to function properly.

Bare Metal Backups and Restores

One of the options you have in Windows Server 2016 is to do a *Bare Metal Restore (BMR)*. This is a restore of a machine after the machine has been completely wiped out and formatted. This type of restore is done usually after a catastrophic machine failure or crash.

Windows Server 2016 gives you the ability to backup all of the files needed for a Bare Metal Restore by choosing the Bare Metal Recovery checkbox (see Figure 20.16).

FIGURE 20.16   Bare Metal Recovery option

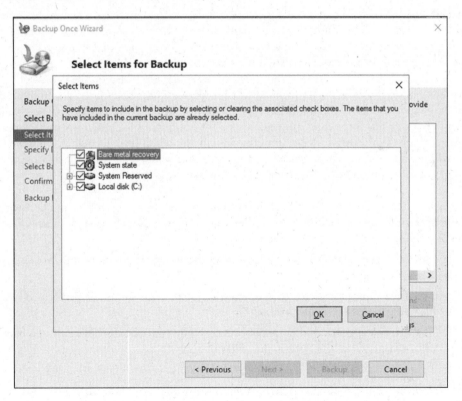

When you choose the Bare Metal Restore option in Windows Server 2016, all of the sub-options (System State, System Reserved, and Local Disk) automatically get checked.

When preparing your network for a Bare Metal Backup, you want to make sure that you have everything you need on hand to complete this type of restore. You may want to keep a copy of the server software, server drivers, and so forth on hand and ready to go, just in case you have to do a full restore.

Scheduling Backups

In addition to specifying which files to back up, you can schedule backup jobs to occur at specific times. Planning *when* to perform backups is just as important as deciding *what* to back up. Performing backup operations can reduce overall system performance; therefore, you should plan to back up information during times of minimal activity on your servers.

To add a backup operation to the schedule, you can simply click the Add button on the Specify Backup Time window.

Restoring System State Data

In some cases, the Active Directory data store or other System State data may become corrupt or unavailable. This could be due to many different reasons. A hard disk failure might, for example, result in the loss of data. Or the accidental deletion of an OU and all of its objects might require a restore operation to be performed.

The actual steps involved in restoring System State data are based on the details of what has caused the data loss and what effect this data loss has had on the system. In the best-case scenario, the System State data is corrupt or inaccurate but the operating system can still boot. If this is the case, all you must do is boot into a special *Directory Services Restore Mode (DSRM)* and then restore the System State data from a backup. This process will replace the current System State data with that from the backup. Therefore, any changes that have been made since the last backup will be completely lost and must be redone.

In a worst-case scenario, all of the information on a server has been lost or a hardware failure is preventing the machine from properly booting. If this is the case, here are several steps that you must take in order to recover System State data:

1. Fix any hardware problem that might prevent the computer from booting (for example, replace any failed hard disks).

2. Reinstall the Windows Server 2016 operating system. This should be performed like a regular installation on a new system.

3. Reinstall any device drivers that may be required by your backup device. If you backed up information to the file system, this will not apply.

4. Restore the System State data using the Windows Server 2016 Backup utility.

I'll cover the technical details of performing restores later in this section. For now, however, you should understand the importance of backing up information and, whenever possible, testing the validity of backups.

Backing Up and Restoring Group Policy Objects

Group Policy Objects (GPOs) are a major part of Active Directory. When you back up Active Directory, GPOs can also get backed up. You also have the ability to back up GPOs through the Group Policy Management Console (GPMC). This gives you the ability to back up and restore individual GPOs.

To back up all GPOs, open the GPMC and right-click the Group Policy Objects container. You will see the option Back Up All. After you choose this option, a wizard will start, asking you for the backup location. Choose a location and click Backup.

To back up an individual GPO, right-click the GPO (in the Group Policy Objects container) and choose Backup. Again, after you choose this option, a wizard will start, asking you for the backup location. Choose a location and click Backup.

To restore a GPO, it's the same process as above except, instead of choosing Backup, you will choose either Manage Backups (to restore all GPOs) or Restore (for an individual GPO).

Setting Up an Active Directory Backup

The Windows Server 2016 Backup utility makes it easy to back up the System data (including Active Directory) as part of a normal backup operation. We've already covered the ideas behind the different backup types and why and when they are used.

Exercise 20.12 walks you through the process of backing up the domain controller. In order to complete this exercise, the local machine must be a domain controller, and you must have a DVD burner or network location to back up the System State.

 The Windows Server 2016 Backup utility is not installed by default. If you have already installed the Windows Server 2016 Backup utility, skip to step 9.

EXERCISE 20.12

Backing Up Active Directory

1. To install the Windows Server 2016 Backup utility, click the Start Key ➢ Server Manager.

2. In the center console, click the link for Add Roles And Features.

3. At the Select Installation Type screen, choose role-based or feature-based installation and click Next.

4. The Select Destination Server screen appears. Choose Select A Server From The Server Pool, and choose your server under Server Pool. Click Next.

5. Click Next at the Select Server Roles screen.

6. At the Select Features screen, scroll down and check the box next to Windows Server Backup. Click Next.

EXERCISE 20.12 *(continued)*

7. At the Confirmation screen, click the checkbox to Restart the destination server auto-matically. This will bring up a dialog box. Click Yes, and then click the Install button.

8. Click the Close button when finished. Close Server Manager.

9. Open Windows Backup by clicking the Windows Key ➤ Administrative Tools ➤ Windows Server Backup.

10. On the left-hand side, click Local Backup. Then, under Actions, click Backup Once.

11. When the Backup Once Wizard appears, click Different Options and click Next.

12. At the Select Backup Configuration screen, choose Custom and click Next.

13. Click the Add Items button. Choose System State and click OK. Click Next.

14. At the Specify Destination Type, choose Remote Shared Folder. Click Next.

15. Put in the shared path you want to use and click Next.

16. At the Confirmation screen, click the Backup button.

17. Once the backup is complete, close the Windows Server Backup utility.

Restoring Active Directory

Active Directory has been designed with fault tolerance in mind. For example, it is highly recommended by Microsoft that each domain have at least two domain controllers. Each of these domain controllers contains a copy of the Active Directory data store. Should one of the domain controllers fail, the available one can take over the failed server's functionality. When the failed server is repaired, it can then be promoted to a domain controller in the existing environment. This process effectively restores the failed domain controller without incurring any downtime for end users because all of the Active Directory data is replicated to the repaired server in the next scheduled replication.

In some cases, you might need to restore Active Directory from a backup. For example, suppose a system administrator accidentally deletes several hundred users from the domain and does not realize it until the change has been propagated to all of the other domain controllers. Manually re-creating the accounts is not an option because the objects' security identifiers will be different (and all permissions must be reset). Clearly, a method for restoring from backup is the best solution. You can elect to make the Active Directory restore authoritative or nonauthoritative, as described in the following sections.

Overview of Authoritative Restore

Restoring Active Directory and other System State data is an important process should system files or the Active Directory data store become corrupt or otherwise unavailable. Fortunately, the Windows Server 2016 Backup utility allows you to restore data easily from a backup, should the need arise.

I mentioned earlier that in the case of the accidental deletion of information from Active Directory, you might need to restore the Active Directory from a recent backup. But what happens if there is more than one domain controller in the environment? Even if you did perform a restore, the information on this domain controller would be seen as outdated and it would be overwritten by the data from another domain controller. This data from the older domain controller is exactly the information you want to replace. The domain controller that was reloaded using a backup would have an older time stamp, and the other domain controllers would re-delete the information from the backup.

Fortunately, Windows Server 2016 and Active Directory allow you to perform what is called an *authoritative restore*. The authoritative restore process specifies a domain controller as having the authoritative (or master) copy of the Active Directory data store. When other domain controllers communicate with this domain controller, their information will be overwritten with Active Directory data stored on the local machine.

Now that you have an idea of how an authoritative restore is supposed to work, let's move on to looking at the details of performing the process.

Performing an Authoritative Restore

When you are restoring Active Directory information on a Windows Server 2016 domain controller, make sure that Active Directory services are not running. This is because the restore of System State data requires full access to system files and the Active Directory data store. If you attempt to restore System State data while the domain controller is active, you will see an error message.

In general, restoring data and operating system files is a straightforward process. It is important to note that restoring a System State backup will replace the existing Registry, Sysvol, and Active Directory files, so that any changes you made since the last backup will be lost.

In addition to restoring the entire Active Directory database, you can also restore only specific subtrees within Active Directory using the restoresubtree command in the ntdsutil utility. This allows you to restore specific information, and it is useful in case of accidental deletion of isolated material.

Following the authoritative restore process, Active Directory should be updated to the time of the last backup. Furthermore, all of the other domain controllers for this domain will have their Active Directory information overwritten by the results of the restore operation. The result is an Active Directory environment that has been recovered from media.

Overview of Nonauthoritative Restore

Now that you understand why you would use an authoritative restore and how it is performed, it's an easy conceptual jump to understand a *nonauthoritative restore*. Remember that by making a restore authoritative, you are simply telling other domain controllers in the domain to recognize the restored machine as the newest copy of Active Directory for replication purposes. If you only have one domain controller, the authoritative restore process becomes moot; you can simply skip the steps required to make the restore authoritative and begin using the domain controller immediately after the normal restore is complete.

If you have more than one domain controller in the domain and you need to perform a nonauthoritative restore, simply allow the domain controller to receive Active Directory database information from other domain controllers in the domain using normal replication methods.

Active Directory Recycle Bin

The Active Directory Recycle Bin is a great feature that allows an administrator to restore an Active Directory object that has been deleted.

Let's say that you have a junior administrator who has been making changes to Active Directory for hours. The junior admin then deletes an OU from Active Directory. You would then have to reload the OU from a tape backup, or even worse, you may have to reload the entire Active Directory (depending on your backup software), thus losing the hours of work the junior admin has completed.

The problem here is that when you delete a security object from Active Directory, the object's Security ID (SID) gets removed. All users' rights and permissions are associated with the users' SID number and not their account name. This is where the AD Recycle Bin can help.

The *Active Directory Recycle Bin* allows you to preserve and restore accidentally deleted Active Directory objects without the need of using a backup.

The Active Directory Recycle Bin works for both the Active Directory Domain Services (AD DS) and the Active Directory Lightweight Directory Services (AD LDS) environments.

By enabling (disabled by default) the Active Directory Recycle Bin, any deleted Active Directory objects are preserved and Active Directory objects can be restored, in their entirety, to the same condition that they were in immediately before deletion. This means that all group memberships and access rights that the object had before deletion will remain intact.

To enable the Active Directory Recycle Bin, you must do the following (you must be a member of the Schema Admins group):

- Run the adprep /forestprep command to prepare the forest on the server that holds the schema master to update the schema.

- Run the adprep /domainprep /gpprep command to prepare the domain on the server that holds the infrastructure operations master role.

- If a read-only domain controller (RODC) is present in your environment, you must also run the adprep /rodcprep command.

- Make sure that all domain controllers in your Active Directory forest are running Windows Server 2016, Windows Server 2012 / 2012 R2, or Windows Server 2008 R2.

- Make sure that the forest functional level is set to Windows Server 2016, Windows Server 2012 / 2012 R2, or Windows Server 2008 R2.

Restartable Active Directory

Administrators have the ability to stop and restart Active Directory in the Windows Server 2016 operating system without the need to reboot the entire system. Administrators can perform these actions either by using the Microsoft Management Console (MMC) snap-ins or the command line.

With *Restartable Active Directory Services*, an administrator has the ability to stop Active Directory Services so that updates and other tasks can be applied to a domain controller. One task that an administrator can perform while Active Directory is stopped is an offline defragmentation of the database.

One of the advantages of a Restartable Active Directory is that other services running on the same server do not depend on Active Directory to continue to function properly while Active Directory is stopped. An administrator has the ability to stop and restart the Active Directory Domain Services in the Local Services MMC snap-in.

Offline Maintenance

As you learned in the preceding section, there are times when you have to be offline to do maintenance. For example, you need to perform authoritative and nonauthoritative restores while the domain controller is offline. The main utility we use for offline maintenance is ntdsutil.

Ntdsutil.exe

The primary method by which system administrators can do offline maintenance is through the ntdsutil command-line tool. You can launch this tool by simply entering ntdsutil at a command prompt. For the commands to work properly, you must start the command prompt with elevated privileges. The **ntdsutil** command is both interactive and context sensitive. That is, once you launch the utility, you'll see an ntdsutil command prompt. At this prompt, you can enter various commands that set your context within the application. For example, if you enter **domain management**, you'll be able to enter domain-related commands. Several operations also require you to connect to a domain, a domain controller, or an Active Directory object before you perform a command.

Table 20.3 provides a list of some of the domain-management commands supported by the ntdsutil tool. You can access this functionality by typing the command at an elevated command prompt. Once you are in the ntdsutil prompt, you can use the question mark to see all of the commands available.

TABLE 20.3   Ntdsutil offline maintenance commands

Ntdsutil **Domain Management Command**	**Purpose**
Help or ?	Displays information about the commands that are available within the Domain Management menu of the ntdsutil utility.
Activate instance %s	Sets NTDS or a specific AD LDS instance as the active instance.

TABLE 20.3 Ntdsutil offline maintenance commands *(continued)*

Ntdsutil **Domain Management Command**	**Purpose**
Authoritative restore	Sets the domain controller for the authoritative restore of the Active Directory database.
Change service account	This allows an administrator to change the AD LDS service account to username and password. You can use a "NULL" for a blank password, and you can use * to prompt the user to enter a password.
configurable settings	Allows an administrator to manage configurable settings.
DS behavior	Allows an administrator to view and modify AD DS or AD LDS behavior.
files	This command allows an administrator to manage the AD DS or AD LDS database files.
Group Membership Evaluation	Allows an administrator to evaluate the security IDs (SIDs) in a token for a given user or group.
LDAP policies	Administrators can manage the Lightweight Directory Access Protocol (LDAP) protocol policies.
metadata cleanup	Removes metadata from decommissioned domain controllers.
security account management	This command allows an administrator to manage SIDs.
Set DSRM Password	Resets the Directory Service Restore mode administrator account password.

Active Directory Database Mounting Tool

One issue that an administrator may run into when trying to restore Active Directory is the need to restore several backups to compare the Active Directory data that each backup contains. Windows Server 2016 has a utility called the Active Directory database mounting tool (Dsamain.exe), which can resolve this issue.

The Dsamain.exe tool can help the recovery processes by giving you a way to compare data as it exists in snapshots (taken at different times) so that you have the ability to decide which Active Directory database to restore.

Creating snapshots on a regular basis will allow you to have enough data so that you can keep accurate records of how the Active Directory database changes over time. The ntdsutil utility allows you to take snapshots by using the ntdsutil snapshot operation.

 NOTE You are not required to run the ntdsutil snapshot operation to use Dsamain.exe. You have the ability to use a backup of the Active Directory database.

You must be a member of the Domain Admins group or the Enterprise Admins group to view any snapshots taken due to the fact that these snapshots contain sensitive Active Directory data.

Compact the Directory Database File (Offline Defragmentation)

One task that all of us have been doing for years is the process of defragging the operating systems that we run. We have used the defragmentation utility since Windows NT. Defragging a system helps return free space from data to the hard drive.

You can also use the defragmentation process to compact the Active Directory database while it's offline. Offline defragmentation helps return free disk space and check Active Directory database integrity.

To perform an offline defragmentation, you would use the ntdsutil command. When you perform a defragmentation of the Active Directory database, a new compacted version of the database is created. This new database file can be created on the same machine (if space permits) or on a network location. After the new file is created, copy the compacted Ntds.dit file back to the original location.

It is a good practice, if space allows, to maintain a copy of the older, original database file. You can either rename the older database file and keep it in its current location or copy the older database file to an alternate location.

Monitoring Replication

At times you may need to keep an eye on how your replication traffic is working on your domain controllers. We are going to examine the replication utility that you can use to help determine if there are problems on your domain.

Repadmin Utility

The Repadmin utility is included when you install Windows Server 2016. This command-line tool helps administrators diagnose replication problems between Windows domain controllers.

Repadmin allows administrators to view the replication topology of each domain controller as seen from the domain controller's perspective. Administrators can also use Repadmin to create the replication topology manually. By manually creating the replication topology, administrators can force replication events between domain controllers and view the replication metadata vectors.

To access the Repadmin utility, open a command prompt using an elevated privilege (Run ➤ CMD). At the command prompt, type **Repadmin.exe**, and all of the available options will appear.

Using the ADSI Editor

Another utility (explained earlier in the chapter) that allows you to manage objects and attributes in Active Directory is the Active Directory Service Interfaces Editor (ADSI Edit). Earlier we used ADSI Edit (Adsiedit.msc) to create multiple password policies to allow for fine-grained password policies. ADSI Edit allows you to view every object and attribute in an Active Directory forest.

One advantage to using the Adsiedit.msc MMC snap-in is that this tool allows you to query, view, create, and edit attributes that are not exposed through other Active Directory Microsoft Management Console (MMC) snap-ins.

ADSI Edit allows you to administer an AD LDS instance. To do this, you must first connect and bind to the instance. After you connect and bind to the instance, you can administer the containers and objects within the instance by browsing to the containers or objects and then right-clicking them. To complete this task, you must be a member of the Administrators group for the AD LDS instance.

Wbadmin Command-Line Utility

The wbadmin command allows you to back up and restore your operating system, volumes, files, folders, and applications from a command prompt.

You must be a member of the Administrators group to configure a backup schedule. You must be a member of the Backup Operators or the Administrators group (or you must have been delegated the appropriate permissions) to perform all other tasks using the wbadmin command.

To use the wbadmin command, you must run wbadmin from an elevated command prompt (to open an elevated command prompt, click Start, right-click Command Prompt, and then click Run As Administrator). Table 20.4 shows some of the wbadmin commands.

TABLE 20.4   Wbadmin commands

Command	Description
Wbadmin enable backup	Configures and enables a daily backup schedule.
Wbadmin disable backup	Disables your daily backups.

Command	Description
Wbadmin start backup	Runs a one-time backup.
Wbadmin stop job	Stops the currently running backup or recovery operation.
Wbadmin get items	Lists the items included in a specific backup.
Wbadmin start recovery	Runs a recovery of the volumes, applications, files, or folders specified.
Wbadmin get status	Shows the status of the currently running backup or recovery operation.
Wbadmin start systemstaterecovery	Runs a system state recovery.
Wbadmin start systemstatebackup	Runs a system state backup.
Wbadmin start sysrecovery	Runs a recovery of the full system state.

Summary

In this chapter, I discussed the purpose of Active Directory replication. As you have learned, replication is used to keep domain controllers synchronized, and it is important in Active Directory environments of all sizes. Replication is the process by which changes to the Active Directory database are transferred between domain controllers.

This chapter also covered the concepts of sites, site boundaries, and subnets. In addition to learning how to configure them, you learned that subnets define physical portions of your network environment and that sites are defined as collections of well-connected IP subnets. Site boundaries are defined by the subnet or subnets that you include in your site configuration.

I also covered the basics of replication and the differences between intrasite and intersite replication. Additionally, I covered the purpose and use of bridgehead servers in depth. Although replication is a behind-the-scenes type of task, the optimal configuration of sites in distributed network environments results in better use of bandwidth and faster response by network resources. For these reasons, you should be sure you thoroughly understand the concepts related to managing replication for Active Directory.

I covered the placement of domain controllers and global catalog servers in the network and how, when placed properly, they can increase the performance of Active Directory operations.

I also showed how to monitor and troubleshoot replication. The Windows Server 2016 System Monitor administrative tool was designed so that you can monitor many performance statistics associated with using Active Directory.

The chapter also covered the basics of linking multiple domains in trees and forests. You now know why you would want to plan for them and the benefits and drawbacks of using only one domain or of having a multidomain environment. For example, you might decide to have multiple domains if you have an acquisitions-and-mergers situation where you need to keep multiple administrators. In addition, by using multiple domains, organizations can retain separate security databases; however, in such cases, they are also able to share resources between domains.

You can use multiple domains to provide two major benefits for the network directory services—security and availability. These benefits are made possible through Active Directory and the administrative tools that can be used to access it.

System administrators can simplify operations while still ensuring that only authorized users have access to their data. Multiple domains can interact to form Active Directory trees and forests, and you can use the Active Directory Installation Wizard to create new Active Directory trees and forests.

Exam Essentials

Understand the reasons for using multiple domains.   There are seven primary reasons for using multiple domains: They provide additional scalability, they reduce replication traffic, they help with political and organizational issues, they provide many levels of hierarchy, they allow for decentralized administration, they preserve legality, and they allow for multiple DNS or domain names.

Understand the drawbacks of using multiple domains.   With multiple domains, maintaining administrative consistency is more difficult. The number of administrative units multiplies as well, which makes it difficult to keep track of network resources. Finally, it is much more difficult to rearrange the domain topology within an Active Directory environment than it is simply to reorganize OUs.

Know how to create a domain tree.   To create a new domain tree, you need to promote a Windows Server 2016 computer to a domain controller, select the option that makes this domain controller the first machine in a new domain, and make that domain the first domain of a new tree. The result is a new domain tree.

Know how to join a domain tree to a forest.   Creating a new tree to form or add to a forest is as simple as promoting a server to a domain controller for a new domain that does *not* share a namespace with an existing Active Directory domain. To add a domain to an existing forest, you must already have at least one other domain. This domain serves as the root domain for the entire forest.

Understand how to manage single-master operations.   Single-master operations must be performed on specially designated machines within the Active Directory forest. There are five main single-master functions: two that apply to an entire Active Directory forest

(Schema Master and Domain Naming Master) and three that apply to each domain (RID Master, PDC Emulator Master, and Infrastructure Master).

Understand how to manage trusts.   When configuring trusts, you'll need to consider two main characteristics: transitivity and direction. The simplest way to understand transitive relationships is through this example: If Domain A trusts Domain B and Domain B trusts Domain C, then Domain A implicitly trusts Domain C. Trusts can be configured as nontransitive so that this type of behavior does not occur. In one-way relationships, the trusting domain allows resources to be shared with the trusted domain. In two-way relationships, both domains trust each other equally. Special trusts include external trusts, realm trusts, cross-forest trusts, and shortcut trusts.

Understand how to manage UPN suffixes.   By default, the name of the domain in which the user is created determines the UPN suffix. By adding additional UPN suffixes to the forest, you can easily choose more manageable suffixes when it comes time to create new users.

Understand how to manage global catalog servers.   You can configure any number of domain controllers to host a copy of the global catalog (GC). The GC contains all of the schema information and a subset of the attributes for all domains within the Active Directory environment. Servers that contain a copy of the GC are known as GC servers. Whenever a user executes a query that requires information from multiple domains, they need only contact the nearest GC server for this information. Similarly, when users must authenticate across domains, they will not have to wait for a response from a domain controller that may be located across the world. The result is increased overall performance of Active Directory queries.

Understand universal group membership caching.   You can enable a domain controller as a Universal Group Membership Caching server. The Universal Group Membership Caching machine will then send a request for the logon authentication of a user to the GC server. The GC will then send the information back to the Universal Group Membership Caching server to be cached locally for eight hours (by default). The user can then authenticate without the need to contact the GC again.

Understand the purpose of Active Directory replication.   Replication is used to keep domain controllers synchronized, and it is important in Active Directory environments of all sizes. Replication is the process by which changes to the Active Directory database are transferred between domain controllers.

Understand the concept of sites, site boundaries, and subnets.   Subnets define physical portions of your network environment. Sites are defined as collections of well-connected IP subnets. Site boundaries are defined by the subnet or subnets that you include in your site configuration.

Understand the differences between intrasite and intersite replication.   Intrasite replication is designed to synchronize Active Directory information to machines that are located in the same site. Intersite replication is used to synchronize information for domain controllers that are located in different sites.

Understand the purpose of bridgehead servers.   Bridgehead servers are designed to accept traffic between two remote sites and then to forward this information to the appropriate servers. One way to efficiently synchronize data between sites that are connected with slow connections is to use a bridgehead server.

Implement site links, site link bridges, and connection objects.   You can use all three of these object types to finely control the behavior of Active Directory replication and to manage replication traffic. Site links are created to define the types of connections that are available between the components of a site. Site links can reflect a relative cost for a network connection and can reflect the bandwidth that is available for communications. You can use site link bridges to connect site links so that the relationship can be transitive. Connection objects provide you with a way to set up special types of replication schedules such as immediate replication on demand or specifying a custom schedule for certain servers.

Configure replication schedules and site link costs.   You can create multiple site links between sites, and you can assign site links a cost value based on the type of connection. The system administrator determines the cost value, and the relative costs of site links are then used to determine the optimal path for replication. The lower the cost, the more likely the link is to be used for replication. Once you've determined how and through which connections replication will take place, it's time to determine *when* information should be replicated. Replication requires network resources and occupies bandwidth. Therefore, you need to balance the need for consistent directory information with the need to conserve bandwidth.

Determine where to place domain controllers and global catalog servers based on a set of requirements.   Where you place domain controllers and global catalog servers can positively affect the performance of Active Directory operations. However, to optimize performance, you need to know the best places to put these servers in a network environment that consists of multiple sites.

Monitor and troubleshoot replication.   The Windows Server 2016 System Monitor administrative tool is designed so that you can monitor many performance statistics associated with using Active Directory. In addition to this monitoring, you should always verify basic network connectivity and router and firewall connections and also examine the event logs.

Understand the various backup types available with the Windows Server 2016 Backup utility.   The Windows Server 2016 Backup utility can perform full and incremental backup operations. Some third-party backup utilities also support differential and daily backups. You can use each of these operations as part of an efficient backup strategy.

Know how to restore Active Directory.   Restoring the Active Directory database is considerably different from other restore operations. To restore some of or the entire Active Directory database, you must first boot the machine into Directory Services Restore mode.

Understand the importance of an authoritative restore process.   You use an authoritative restore when you want to restore earlier information from an Active Directory backup and you want the older information to be propagated to other domain controllers in the environment.

Understand offline maintenance using `ntdsutil`.   The ntdsutil command-line tool is a primary method by which system administrators perform offline maintenance. Understand how to launch this tool by entering **ntdsutil** at a command prompt.

Review Questions

You can find the answers in the Appendix.

1. You need to deactivate the UGMC option on some of your domain controllers. At which level in Active Directory would you deactivate UGMC?

    A.   Server

    B.   Site

    C.   Domain

    D.   Forest

2. You work for an organization with a single domain forest. Your company has one main location and two branch locations. All locations are configured as Active Directory sites, and all sites are connected with the DEFAULTIPSITELINK object. Your connections are running slower than company policy allows. You want to decrease the replication latency between all domain controllers in the various sites. What should you do?

    A.   Decrease the replication interval for the DEFAULTIPSITELINK object.

    B.   Decrease the replication interval for the site.

    C.   Decrease the replication schedule for the site.

    D.   Decrease the replication schedule for all domain controllers.

3. You need to enable three of your domain controllers as global catalog servers. Where would you configure the domain controllers as global catalogs?

    A.   Forest, NTDS settings

    B.   Domain, NTDS settings

    C.   Site, NTDS settings

    D.   Server, NTDS settings

4. Daniel is responsible for managing Active Directory replication traffic for a medium-sized organization that has deployed a single Active Directory domain. Currently, the environment is configured with two sites and the default settings for replication. Each site consists of 15 domain controllers. Recently, network administrators have complained that Active Directory traffic is using a large amount of available network bandwidth between the two sites. Daniel has been asked to meet the following requirements:

    - Reduce the amount of network traffic between domain controllers in the two sites.

    - Minimize the amount of change to the current site topology.

    - Require no changes to the existing physical network infrastructure.

Daniel decides that it would be most efficient to configure specific domain controllers in each site that will receive the majority of replication traffic from the other site. Which of the following solutions meets the requirements?

A.   Create additional sites that are designed only for replication traffic and move the existing domain controllers to these sites.

B.   Create multiple site links between the two sites.

C.   Create a site link bridge between the two sites.

D.   Configure one server at each site to act as a preferred bridgehead server.

5.   Which of the following does not need to be created manually when you are setting up a replication scenario involving three domains and three sites?

A.   Sites

B.   Site links

C.   Connection objects

D.   Subnets

6.   Which of the following services of Active Directory is responsible for maintaining the replication topology?

A.   File Replication Service

B.   Knowledge Consistency Checker

C.   Windows Internet Name Service

D.   Domain Name System

7.   A system administrator for an Active Directory environment that consists of three sites wants to configure site links to be transitive. Which of the following Active Directory objects are responsible for representing a transitive relationship between sites?

A.   Additional sites

B.   Additional site links

C.   Bridgehead servers

D.   Site link bridges

8.   You have configured your Active Directory environment with multiple sites and have placed the appropriate resources in each of the sites. You are now trying to choose a protocol for the transfer of replication information between two sites. The connection between the two sites has the following characteristics:

▪   The link is generally unavailable during certain parts of the day because of an unreliable network provider.

▪   The replication transmission must be attempted whether the link is available or not. If the link was unavailable during a scheduled replication, the information should automatically be received after the link becomes available again.

▪   Replication traffic must be able to travel over a standard Internet connection.

Which of the following protocols meets these requirements?

A. IP

B. SMTP

C. RPC

D. DHCP

9. A system administrator suspects that there is an error in the replication configuration. How can the system administrator look for specific error messages related to replication?

A. By using the Active Directory Sites and Services administrative tool

B. By using the Computer Management tool

C. By going to Event Viewer ➤ System Log

D. By going to Event Viewer ➤ Directory Service Log

10. Christina is responsible for managing Active Directory replication traffic for a medium-sized organization. Currently, the environment is configured with a single site and the default settings for replication. The site contains more than 50 domain controllers, and the system administrators are often making changes to the Active Directory database. Recently, network administrators have complained that Active Directory traffic is consuming a large amount of network bandwidth between portions of the network that are connected by slow links. Ordinarily, the amount of replication traffic is reasonable, but recently users have complained about slow network performance during certain hours of the day.

Christina has been asked to alleviate the problem while meeting the following requirements:

- Be able to control exactly when replication occurs.

- Be able to base Active Directory replication on the physical network infrastructure.

- Perform the changes without creating or removing any domain controllers.

Which two of the following steps can Christina take to meet these requirements? (Choose two.)

A. Create and define connection objects that specify the hours during which replication will occur.

B. Create multiple site links.

C. Create a site link bridge.

D. Create new Active Directory sites that reflect the physical network topology.

E. Configure one server at each of the new sites to act as a bridgehead server.

Chapter

21

Implementing GPOs

THE FOLLOWING 70-742 EXAM OBJECTIVES ARE COVERED IN THIS CHAPTER:

✓ **Create and manage Group Policy Objects (GPOs)**

- This objective may include but is not limited to: Configure a central store; manage starter GPOs; configure GPO links; configure multiple local Group Policies; back up, import, copy, and restore GPOs; create and configure a migration table; reset default GPOs; delegate Group Policy management; detect health issues using the Group Policy Infrastructure Status dashboard

✓ **Configure Group Policy processing**

- This objective may include but is not limited to: Configure processing order and precedence; configure blocking of inheritance; configure enforced policies; configure security filtering and Windows Management Instrumentation (WMI) filtering; configure loopback processing; configure and manage slow-link processing and Group Policy caching; configure client-side extension (CSE) behavior; force a Group Policy update

✓ **Configure Group Policy settings**

- This objective may include but is not limited to: Configure software installation; configure folder redirection; configure scripts; configure administrative templates; import security templates; import a custom administrative template file; configure property filters for administrative templates

✓ **Configure Group Policy preferences**

- This objective may include but is not limited to: Configure printer preferences; define network drive mappings; configure power options; configure custom registry settings; configure Control Panel settings; configure Internet Explorer settings; configure file and folder deployment; configure shortcut deployment; configure item-level targeting

For many years, making changes to computer or user environments was a time-consuming process. If you wanted to install a service pack or a piece of software, unless you had a third-party utility, you had to use the *sneakernet* (that is, you had to walk from one computer to another with a disk containing the software).

Installing any type of software or company-wide security change was one of the biggest challenges faced by system administrators. It was difficult enough just to deploy and manage workstations throughout the environment. Combine this with the fact that users were generally able to make system configuration changes to their own machines; it quickly became a management nightmare!

For example, imagine that a user noticed that they did not have enough disk space to copy a large file. Instead of seeking assistance from the IT help desk, they may have decided to do a little cleanup on their own. Unfortunately, this cleanup operation may have resulted in deleting critical system files! Or, consider the case of users who changed system settings "just to see what they did." Relatively minor changes, such as modifying TCP/IP bindings or Desktop settings, could cause hours of support headaches. Now multiply these (or other common) problems by hundreds (or even thousands) of end users. Clearly, system administrators needed to have a secure way to limit the options available to users of client operating systems.

How do you prevent problems such as these from occurring in a Windows Server 2016 environment? Fortunately, there's a readily available solution delivered with the base operating system that's easy to implement. Two of the most important system administration features in Windows Server 2016 and Active Directory are *Group Policy* and *Security Policy*. By using *Group Policy Objects (GPOs)*, administrators can quickly and easily define restrictions on common actions and then apply them at the site, domain, or organizational unit (OU) level. In this chapter, you will see how group and security policies work, and then you will look at how to implement them within an Active Directory environment.

Introducing Group Policy

One of the strengths of Windows-based operating systems is their flexibility. End users and system administrators can configure many different options to suit the network environment and their personal tastes. However, this flexibility comes at a price—generally, end users on a network should not change many of these options. For example, TCP/IP configuration and security policies should remain consistent for all client computers. In fact, end users really don't need to be able to change these types of settings in the first place because many of them do not understand the purpose of these settings.

Windows Server 2016 *group policies* are designed to provide system administrators with the ability to customize end-user settings and to place restrictions on the types of actions that users can perform. Group policies can be easily created by system administrators and then later applied to one or more users or computers within the environment. Although they ultimately do affect Registry settings, it is much easier to configure and apply settings through the use of Group Policy than it is to make changes to the Registry manually. To make management easy, Microsoft has set up Windows Server 2008, Windows Server 2008 R2, Windows Server 2012, Windows Server 2012 R2, and Windows Server 2016 so that Group Policy settings are all managed from within the Microsoft Management Console (MMC) in the Group Policy Management Console (GPMC).

Group policies have several potential uses. I'll cover the use of group policies for software deployment, and I'll also focus on the technical background of group policies and how they apply to general configuration management.

Let's begin by looking at how group policies function.

Understanding Group Policy Settings

Group Policy settings are based on *Group Policy administrative templates*. These templates provide a list of user-friendly configuration options and specify the system settings to which they apply. For example, an option for a user or computer that reads Require A Specific Desktop Wallpaper Setting would map to a key in the Registry that maintains this value. When the option is set, the appropriate change is made in the Registry of the affected users and computers.

By default, Windows Server 2016 comes with several administrative template files that you can use to manage common settings. Additionally, system administrators and application developers can create their own administrative template files to set options for specific functionality.

Most Group Policy items have three different settings options (see Figure 21.1):

Enabled   Specifies that a setting for this GPO has been configured. Some settings require values or options to be set.

Disabled   Specifies that this option is disabled for client computers. Note that disabling an option *is* a setting. That is, it specifies that the system administrator wants to disallow certain functionality.

Not Configured   Specifies that these settings have been neither enabled nor disabled. Not Configured is the default option for most settings. It simply states that this group policy will not specify an option and that other policy settings may take precedence.

FIGURE 21.1   Group Policy configuration settings

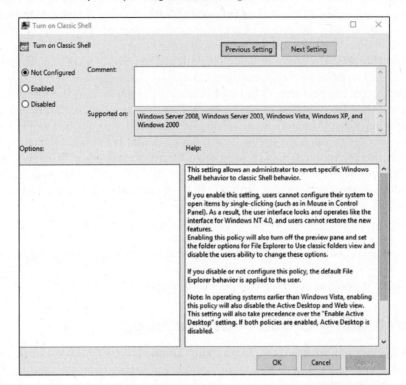

The specific options available (and their effects) will depend on the setting. Often, you will need additional information. For example, when setting the Account Lockout policy, you must specify how many bad login attempts may be made before the account is locked out. With this in mind, let's look at the types of user and computer settings that can be managed.

Group Policy settings can apply to two types of Active Directory objects: User objects and Computer objects. Because both users and computers can be placed into groups and organized within OUs, this type of configuration simplifies the management of hundreds, or even thousands, of computers.

The main options you can configure within user and computer group policies are as follows:

Software Settings   The *Software Settings* options apply to specific applications and software that might be installed on the computer. System administrators can use these settings to make new applications available to end users and to control the default configuration for these applications.

Windows Settings   The *Windows Settings* options allow system administrators to customize the behavior of the Windows operating system. The specific options that are available here are divided into two types: user and computer. User-specific settings let you configure Internet Explorer (including the default home page and other settings). Computer settings include security options, such as Account Policy and Event Log options.

Administrative Templates *Administrative templates* are used to configure user and computer settings further. In addition to the default options available, system administrators can create their own administrative templates with custom options.

Group Policy Preferences The Windows Server 2016 operating system includes *Group Policy preferences (GPPs)*, which give you more than 20 Group Policy extensions. These extensions, in turn, give you a vast range of configurable settings within a Group Policy Object. Included in the new Group Policy preference extensions are settings for folder options, mapped drives, printers, the Registry, local users and groups, scheduled tasks, services, and the Start menu.

Besides providing easier management, Group Policy preferences give an administrator the ability to deploy settings for client computers without restricting the users from changing the settings. This gives an administrator the flexibility needed to decide which settings to enforce and which not to enforce.

Figure 21.2 shows some of the options you can configure with Group Policy.

FIGURE 21.2   Group Policy options

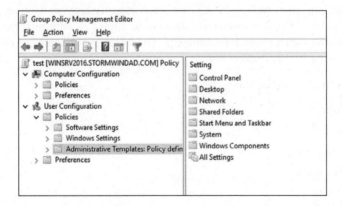

ADMX Central Store Another consideration in GPO settings is whether to set up an *ADMX Central Store*. GPO administrative template files are saved as ADMX (.admx) files and AMXL (.amxl) for the supported languages. To get the most benefit out of using administrative templates, you should create an ADMX Central Store.

You create the Central Store in the SYSVOL folder on a domain controller. The Central Store is a repository for all of your administrative templates, and the Group Policy tools check it. The Group Policy tools then use any ADMX files that they find in the Central Store. These files then replicate to all domain controllers in the domain.

If you want your clients to be able to edit domain-based GPOs by using the ADMX files that are stored in the ADMX Central Store, you must be using Windows Vista, Windows 7,

Windows 8, Windows 10, Server 2008, Server 2008 R2, Server 2012, Windows Server 2012 R2, or Server 2016.

Security Template *Security templates* are used to configure security settings through a GPO. Some of the security settings that can be configured are settings for account policies, local policies, event logs, restricted groups, system services, and the Registry.

Starter GPOs *Starter Group Policy Objects* give administrators the ability to store a collection of administrative template policy settings in a single object. Administrators then have the ability to import and export starter GPOs to distribute the GPOs easily to other environments. When a GPO is created from a starter GPO, as with any template, the new GPO receives the settings and values that were defined from the administrative template policy in the starter GPO.

Group Policy settings do not take effect immediately. You must run the gpupdate command at the command prompt or wait for the regular update cycle in order for the policy changes to take effect.

The Security Settings Section of the GPO

One of the most important sections of a GPO is the Security Settings section. The Security Settings section, under the Windows Settings section, allows an administrator to secure many aspects of the computer and user policies. The following are some of the configurable options for the Security Settings section:

Computer Section Only of the GPO

- Account Policies
- Local Policies
- Event Policies
- Restricted Groups
- System Services
- Registry
- File System
- Wired Network
- Windows Firewall with Advanced Security
- Network List Manager Policies
- Wireless Networks
- Network Access Protection
- Application Control Policies

- IP Security Policies
- Advanced Audit Policy Configuration

Computer and User Sections of the GPO

- Public Key Policies
- Software Restriction Policy

Restricted Groups

The *Restricted Groups* settings allow you to control group membership by using a GPO. The group membership I am referring to is the normal Active Directory groups (domain local, global, and universal). The settings offer two configurable properties: Members and Members Of.

The users on the Members list do not belong to the restricted group. The users on the Members Of list do belong to the restricted group. When you configure a Restricted Group policy, members of the restricted group that are not on the Members list are removed. Users who are on the Members list who are not currently a member of the restricted group are added.

Software Restriction Policy

Software restriction policies allow administrators to identify software and to control its ability to run on the user's local computer, organizational unit, domain, or site. This prevents users from installing unauthorized software. Software Restriction Policy is discussed in greater detail later in this chapter in the section "Implementing Software Deployment."

Client-Side Extensions

In Windows Server, group policies are designed using both server-side and client-side extensions (CSEs). The server-side elements include a user interface for creating each Group Policy Object (GPO). When a Windows client system logs into the Active Directory network, the client-side extensions (normally a series of DLL files) receive their GPOs and the GPOs make changes to the Windows client systems.

Within GPOs, there are computer policies that exist for each CSE. The policies normally include a maximum of three options: Allow Processing Across A Slow Network Connection, Do Not Apply During Periodic Background Processing, and Process Even If The Group Policy Objects Have Not Changed.

Group Policy Objects

So far, I have discussed what group policies are designed to do. Now it's time to drill down to determine exactly how you can set up and configure them.

To make them easier to manage, group policies may be placed in items called *Group Policy Objects (GPOs)*. GPOs act as containers for the settings made within Group Policy files, which simplifies the management of settings. For example, as a system administrator, you might have different policies for users and computers in different departments. Based on these requirements, you could create a GPO for members of the Sales department and another for members of the Engineering department. Then you could apply the GPOs to the OU for each department. Another important concept you need to understand is that Group Policy settings are hierarchical; that is, system administrators can apply Group Policy settings at four different levels. These levels determine the GPO processing priority.

Local   Every Windows operating system computer has one Group Policy Object that is stored locally. This GPO functions for both the computer and user Group Policy processing.

Sites   At the highest level, system administrators can configure GPOs to apply to entire sites within an Active Directory environment. These settings apply to all of the domains and servers that are part of a site. Group Policy settings managed at the site level may apply to more than one domain within the same forest. Therefore, they are useful when you want to make settings that apply to all of the domains within an Active Directory tree or forest.

Domains   Domains are the third level to which system administrators can assign GPOs. GPO settings placed at the domain level will apply to all of the User and Computer objects within the domain. Usually, system administrators make master settings at the domain level.

Organizational Units (OUs)   The most granular level of settings for GPOs is the OU level. By configuring Group Policy options for OUs, system administrators can take advantage of the hierarchical structure of Active Directory. If the OU structure is planned well, you will find it easy to make logical GPO assignments for various business units at the OU level.

Based on the business need and the organization of the Active Directory environment, system administrators might decide to set up Group Policy settings at any of these four levels. Because the settings are cumulative by default, a User object might receive policy settings from the site level, from the domain level, and from the OUs in which it is contained.

You can also apply Group Policy settings to the local computer (in which case Active Directory is not used at all), but this limits the manageability of the Group Policy settings.

Group Policy Inheritance

In most cases, Group Policy settings are cumulative. For example, a GPO at the domain level might specify that all users within the domain must change their password every 60 days, and a GPO at the OU level might specify the default desktop background for all users and computers within that OU. In this case, both settings apply, so users within the OU are forced to change their password every 60 days and have the default Desktop setting.

What happens if there's a conflict in the settings? For example, suppose you create a scenario where a GPO at the site level specifies that users are to use red wallpaper and another GPO at the OU level specifies that they must use green wallpaper. The users at the OU layer would have green wallpaper by default. Although hypothetical, this raises an important point about *inheritance*. By default, the settings at the most specific level (in this case, the OU that contains the User object) override those at more general levels. As a friend of mine from Microsoft always says, "Last one to apply wins."

Although the default behavior is for settings to be cumulative and inherited, system administrators can modify this behavior. They can set two main options at the various levels to which GPOs might apply.

Block Policy Inheritance   The *Block Policy Inheritance* option specifies that Group Policy settings for an object are not inherited from its parents. You might use this, for example, when a child OU requires completely different settings from a parent OU. Note, however, that you should manage blocking policy inheritance carefully because this option allows other system administrators to override the settings made at higher levels.

Force Policy Inheritance   The *Enforced option* (sometimes referred as *No Override*) can be placed on a parent object, and it ensures that all lower-level objects inherit these settings. In some cases, system administrators want to ensure that Group Policy inheritance is not blocked at other levels. For example, suppose it is corporate policy that all network accounts are locked out after five incorrect password attempts. In this case, you would not want lower-level system administrators to override the option with other settings.

System administrators generally use this option when they want to enforce a specific setting globally. For example, if a password expiration policy should apply to all users and computers within a domain, a GPO with the *Force Policy Inheritance* option enabled could be created at the domain level.

You must consider one final case: If a conflict exists between the computer and user settings, the user settings take effect. If, for instance, a system administrator applies a default desktop setting for the Computer policy and a different default desktop setting for the User policy, the one they specify in the User policy takes effect. This is because the user settings are more specific, and they allow system administrators to make changes for individual users regardless of the computer they're using.

Planning a Group Policy Strategy

Through the use of Group Policy settings, system administrators can control many different aspects of their network environment. As you'll see throughout this chapter, system administrators can use GPOs to configure user settings and computer configurations. Windows Server 2016 includes many different administrative tools for performing these tasks. However, it's important to keep in mind that, as with many aspects of using Active Directory, a successful Group Policy strategy involves planning.

Because there are thousands of possible Group Policy settings and many different ways to implement them, you should start by determining the business and technical needs of your organization. For example, you should first group your users based on their work functions. You might find, for example, that users in remote branch offices require particular network configuration options. In that case, you might implement Group Policy settings best at the site level. In another instance, you might find that certain departments have varying requirements for disk quota settings. In this case, it would probably make the most sense to apply GPOs to the appropriate department OUs within the domain.

The overall goal should be to reduce complexity (for example, by reducing the overall number of GPOs and GPO links) while still meeting the needs of your users. By taking into account the various needs of your users and the parts of your organization, you can often determine a logical and efficient method of creating and applying GPOs. Although it's rare that you'll come across a right or wrong method of implementing Group Policy settings, you will usually encounter some that are either better or worse than others.

By implementing a logical and consistent set of policies, you'll also be well prepared to troubleshoot any problems that might come up or to adapt to your organization's changing requirements. Later in this chapter, you'll learn about some specific methods for determining effective Group Policy settings before you apply them.

Implementing Group Policy

Now that I've covered the basic layout and structure of group policies and how they work, let's look at how you can implement them in an Active Directory environment. In the following sections, you'll start by creating GPOs. Then you'll apply these GPOs to specific Active Directory objects, and you'll take a look at how to use administrative templates.

Creating GPOs

In Windows Server 2000 and Windows Server 2003, you could create GPOs from many different locations. For example, you could use Active Directory Users and Computers to create GPOs on your OUs along with other GPO tools. In Windows Server 2016, things are simpler. You can create GPOs for OUs in only one location: the Group Policy Management Console (GPMC). You have your choice of three applications for setting up policies on your Windows Server 2016 computers.

Local Computer Policy Tool ·This administrative tool allows you to quickly access the Group Policy settings that are available for the local computer. These options apply to the local machine and to users who access it. You must be a member of the local Administrators group to access and make changes to these settings.

Administrators may need the ability to work on Multiple Local Group Policy Objects (MLGPOs) at the same time. To do this, you would complete the following steps. (You can't configure MLGPOs on domain controllers.)

1. Open the MMC by typing **MMC** in the Run command box.

2. Click File and then click Add/Remove Snap-in.

3. From the available snap-ins list, choose Group Policy Object Editor and click Add.

4. In the Select Group Policy Object dialog box, click the Browse button.

5. Click the Users tab in the Browse For The Group Policy Object dialog box.

6. Click the user or group for which you want to create or edit a local Group Policy and click OK.

7. Click Finish and then click OK.

8. Configure the multiple policy settings.

Group Policy Management Console   You must use the GPMC to manage Group Policy deployment. The GPMC provides a single solution for managing all Group Policy–related tasks, and it is also best suited to handle enterprise-level tasks, such as forest-related work.

The GPMC allows administrators to manage Group Policy and GPOs all from one easy-to-use console whether their enterprise solution spans multiple domains and sites within one or more forests or is local to one site. The GPMC adds flexibility, manageability, and functionality. Using this console, you can also perform other functions, such as backup and restore, importing, and copying.

Auditpol.exe   Auditpol.exe is a command-line utility that works with Windows Vista, Windows 7, Windows 8, Windows 10, Windows Server 2008, Windows Server 2008 R2, Windows Server 2012, Windows Server 2012 R2, and Windows Server 2016. An administrator has the ability to display information about policies and also to perform some functions to manipulate audit policies. Table 21.1 shows some of the switches available for auditpol.exe.

TABLE 21.1   Auditpol.exe switches

Switch	Description
/?	This is the Auditpol.exe help command.
/get	This allows you to display the current audit policy.
/set	This allows you to set a policy.
/list	This displays selectable policy elements.
/backup	This allows you to save the audit policy to a file.
/restore	This restores a policy from a previous backup.
/clear	This clears the audit policy.
/remove	This removes all per-user audit policy settings and disables all system audit policy settings.
/ResourceSACL	This configures the Global Resource SACL.

NOTE   You should be careful when making Group Policy settings because certain options might prevent the proper use of systems on your network. Always test Group Policy settings on a small group of users before you deploy them throughout your organization. You'll probably find that some settings need to be changed to be effective.

Exercise 21.1 walks you through the process of installing the Group Policy Management MMC snap-in for editing Group Policy settings and creating a GPO.

EXERCISE 21.1

Creating a Group Policy Object Using the GPMC

1. Click the Windows button and choose Administrative Tools ➢ Group Policy Management. The Group Policy Management tool opens.

2. Expand the Forest, Domains, *your domain name,* and North America containers. Right-click the Corporate OU and then choose Create A GPO In This Domain, And Link It Here.

3. When the New GPO dialog box appears, type **Warning Box** in the Name field. Click OK.

4. The New GPO will be listed on the right side of the Group Policy Management window. Right-click the GPO and choose Edit.

5. In the Group Policy Management Editor, expand the following: Computer Configuration ➢ Policies ➢ Windows Settings ➢ Security Settings ➢ Local Policies ➢ Security Options. On the right side, scroll down and double-click Interactive Logon: Message Text For Users Attempting To Log On.

6. Click the box Define This Policy Setting In The Template. In the text box, type **Unauthorized use of this machine is prohibited** and then click OK. Close the GPO and return to the GPMC main screen.

7. Under the domain name (in the GPMC), right-click Group Policy Objects and choose New.

8. When the New GPO dialog box appears, type **Unlinked Test GPO** in the Name field. Click OK.

9. On the right side, the new GPO will appear. Right-click Unlinked Test GPO and choose Edit.

10. Under the User Configuration section, click Policies ➢ Administrative Templates ➢ Desktop. On the right side, double-click Hide And Disable All Items On The Desktop and then click Enabled. Click OK and then close the GPMC.

Note that Group Policy changes may not take effect until the next user logs in (some settings may even require that the machine be rebooted). That is, users who are currently working on the system will not see the effects of the changes until they log off and log in again. GPOs are reapplied every 90 minutes with a 30-minute offset. In other words, users who are logged in will have their policies reapplied every 60 to 120 minutes. Not all settings are reapplied (for example, software settings and password policies).

Linking Existing GPOs to Active Directory

Creating a GPO is the first step in assigning group policies. The second step is to link the GPO to a specific Active Directory object. As mentioned earlier in this chapter, GPOs can be linked to sites, domains, and OUs.

Exercise 21.2 walks you through the steps that you must take to assign an existing GPO to an OU within the local domain. In this exercise, you will link the Test Domain Policy GPO to an OU. To complete the steps in this exercise, you must have completed Exercise 21.1.

EXERCISE 21.2

Linking Existing GPOs to Active Directory

1. Open the Group Policy Management Console.

2. Expand the Forest and Domain containers and right-click the Africa OU.

3. Choose Link An Existing GPO.

4. The Select GPO dialog box appears. Click Unlinked Test GPO and click OK.

5. Close the Group Policy Management Console.

Note that the GPMC tool offers a lot of flexibility in assigning GPOs. You can create new GPOs, add multiple GPOs, edit them directly, change priority settings, remove links, and delete GPOs all from within this interface. In general, creating new GPOs using the GPMC tool is the quickest and easiest way to create the settings you need.

To test the Group Policy settings, you can simply create a user account within the Africa OU that you used in Exercise 21.2. Then, using another computer that is a member of the same domain, you can log on as the newly created user.

Forcing a GPO to Update

There will be times when you need a GPO to get processed immediately. If you are testing a GPO, you will not want to wait for the GPO to process in its own time or you may not want to have to log off the domain and log back onto the domain just to get the GPO processed.

Windows Server 2016 has changed how GPOs get processed. In a Windows Server 2016 domain, when a user logs onto the domain, the latest version of the Group Policy gets downloaded from the domain controller, and it writes that policy to the local store.

If you have your GPOs set up and running in synchronous mode, then the next time the computer restarts, it will use the most recently downloaded GPO from the local store and not download the GPO from the domain. This is a new feature in Windows Server 2016, and it helps to reduce the time it takes to log onto the domain because the GPO policy doesn't need to be downloaded each time.

So, now that you understand how GPOs get processed in Windows Server 2016, let's look at a few different ways that you can force a GPO to get processed immediately.

Forcing the GPO from the Server

Windows Server 2016 has an MMC called Group Policy Management Console (GPMC), and by using this MMC, you can remotely refresh an organizational unit (OU) and force the GPO on all users and computers within that OU. The GPMC remote refresh automatically updates all settings, including security settings, which are configured in the GPO that is linked to the OU. In the OU's context menu, you can choose to refresh remotely the OU and the GPOs associated with that OU. When you remotely refresh an OU, the following steps occur:

1. Windows Server 2016 does an Active Directory query, and that query returns a list of all users and computers that belong to the OU.

2. Windows Management Instrumentation (WMI) queries all users and computers that are currently logged into the domain and creates a list that will be used.

3. Using the list that was created in step 2, a remote scheduled task is created, and a GPUpdate.exe /force is executed on all of the users and computers that are logged into the domain. The remote scheduled task is then scheduled to execute with a 10-minute random delay to help decrease the load on network traffic.

 When you are using the GPMC to force a GPO update, you do not have the ability to change the 10-minute random delay, but if you force the GPO through the use of PowerShell, you have the ability to set the delay.

Another way that you can force a GPO to update immediately is to use Windows PowerShell. By using the PowerShell command Invoke-GPUpdate cmdlet, you cannot only force the GPO but also set the parameters to be more granular.

Forcing the GPO from the Client

As an administrator, you have the ability also to force a GPO onto a client machine on which you may be working. The GPUpdate.exe command allows you to run a GPO on a client machine. The GPUpdate command will run on all Windows client machines from

Windows Vista to Windows Server 2016. Table 21.2 shows some of the GPUpdate switches you can use.

TABLE 21.2   GPUpdate.exe switches

Switch	Description
/target:{Computer | User}	Updates only the User or Computer policy settings for the computer or user specified.
/force	Forces the GPO to reapply all policy settings. By default, only policy settings that have changed are applied.
/wait: \<VALUE\>	Determines the number of seconds that the system will wait after a policy is processed before returning to the command prompt.
/logoff	The domain user account will automatically log off the computer after the Group Policy settings are updated.
/boot	The computer will automatically restart after the Group Policy settings are applied.
/sync	This switch forces the next available foreground policy application to be done synchronously. Foreground policies are applied when the computer boots up and the user logs in.
/?	Displays help at the command prompt.

Managing Group Policy

Now that you have implemented GPOs and applied them to sites, domains, and OUs within Active Directory, it's time to look at some ways to manage them. In the following sections, you'll look at how multiple GPOs can interact with one another and ways that you can provide security for GPO management. Using these features is an important part of working with Active Directory, and if you properly plan Group Policy, you can greatly reduce the time the help desk spends troubleshooting common problems.

Managing GPOs

One of the benefits of GPOs is that they're modular and can apply to many different objects and levels within Active Directory. This can also be one of the drawbacks of GPOs if they're not managed properly. A common administrative function related to using GPOs is finding all of the Active Directory links for each of these objects. You can do this when you are viewing the Linked Group Policy Objects tab of the site, domain, or OU in the GPMC (shown in Figure 21.3).

FIGURE 21.3   Viewing GPO links to an Active Directory OU

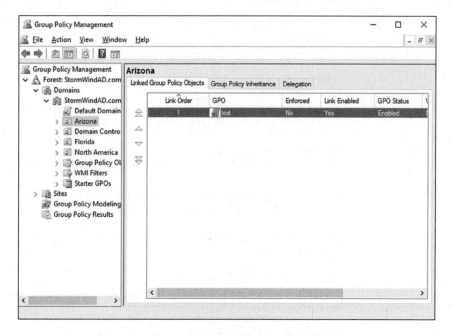

In addition to the common action of delegating permissions on OUs, you can set permissions regarding the modification of GPOs. The best way to accomplish this is to add users to the Group Policy Creator/Owners built-in security group. The members of this group are able to modify security policy.

Windows Management Instrumentation

Windows Management Instrumentation (WMI) scripts are used to gather information or to help GPOs deploy better. The best way to explain this is to give an example. Let's say you wanted to deploy Microsoft Office 2016 to everyone in the company. You would first set up a GPO to deploy the Office package (explained later in the section "Deploying Software Through a GPO").

You can then place a WMI script on the GPO stating that only computers with 10 GB of hard disk space actually deploy Office. Now if a computer has 10 GB of free space, the Office GPO would get installed. If the computer does not have the 10 GB of hard disk space, the GPO will not deploy. You can use WMI scripts to check for computer information such as MAC addresses. WMI is a powerful tool because if you know how to write scripts, the possibilities are endless. The following script is a sample of a WMI script that is checking for at least 10 GB of free space on the C: partition/volume:

```
Select * from Win32_LogicalDisk where FreeSpace > 10737418240 AND Caption = "C:"
```

Security Filtering of a Group Policy

Another method of securing access to GPOs is to set permissions on the GPOs themselves. You can do this by opening the GPMC, selecting the GPO, and clicking the Advanced button in the Delegation tab. The Unlinked Test GPO Security Settings dialog box appears (see Figure 21.4).

FIGURE 21.4   A GPO's Security Settings dialog box

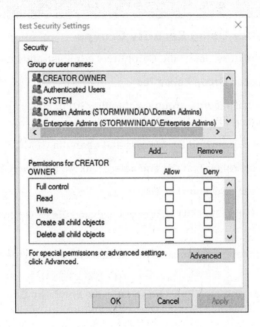

The following permissions options are available:

- Full Control
- Read
- Write
- Create All Child Objects
- Delete All Child Objects
- Apply Group Policy

You might have to scroll the Permissions window to see the Apply Group Policy item. Of these, the Apply Group Policy setting is particularly important because you use it to filter the scope of the GPO. *Filtering* is the process by which selected security groups are included or excluded from the effects of the GPOs. To specify that the settings should apply to a GPO, you should select the Allow check box for both the Apply Group Policy setting and the Read setting. These settings will be applied only if the security group is also contained within a site, domain, or OU to which the GPO is linked. To disable GPO access for a group, choose Deny for both of these settings. Finally, if you do not want to specify either Allow or Deny, leave both boxes blank. This is effectively the same as having no setting.

In Exercise 21.3, you will filter Group Policy using security groups. To complete the steps in this exercise, you must have completed Exercises 21.1 and 21.2.

EXERCISE 21.3

Filtering Group Policy Using Security Groups

1. Open the Active Directory Users and Computers administrative tool.

2. Create a new OU called **Group Policy Test**.

3. Create two new global security groups within the Group Policy Test OU and name them **PolicyEnabled** and **PolicyDisabled**.

4. Exit Active Directory Users and Computers and open the GPMC.

5. Right-click the Group Policy Test OU and select Link An Existing GPO.

6. Choose Unlinked Test GPO and click OK.

7. Expand the Group Policy Test OU so that you can see the GPO (Unlinked Test GPO) underneath the OU.

8. Click the Delegation tab and then click the Advanced button in the lower-right corner of the window.

9. Click the Add button and type **PolicyEnabled** in the Enter The Object Names To Select field. Click the Check Names button. Then click OK.

10. Add a group named **PolicyDisabled** in the same way.

11. Highlight the PolicyEnabled group and select Allow for the Read and Apply Group Policy permissions. This ensures that users in the PolicyEnabled group will be affected by this policy.

12. Highlight the PolicyDisabled group and select Deny for the Read and Apply Group Policy permissions. This ensures that users in the PolicyDisabled group will not be affected by this policy.

13. Click OK. You will see a message stating that you are choosing to use the Deny permission and that the Deny permission takes precedence over the Allow entries. Click the Yes button to continue.

14. When you have finished, close the GPMC tool.

Delegating Administrative Control of GPOs

So far, you have learned about how to use Group Policy to manage user and computer settings. What you haven't done yet is to determine who can modify GPOs. It's important to establish the appropriate security on GPOs themselves for two reasons:

- If the security settings aren't set properly, users and system administrators can easily override them. This defeats the purpose of having the GPOs in the first place.

- Having many different system administrators creating and modifying GPOs can become extremely difficult to manage. When problems arise, the hierarchical nature of GPO inheritance can make it difficult to pinpoint the problem.

Fortunately, through the use of delegation, determining security permissions for GPOs is a simple task. Exercise 21.4 walks you through the steps that you must take to grant the appropriate permissions to a user account. Specifically, the process involves delegating the ability to manage Group Policy links on an Active Directory object (such as an OU). To complete this exercise, you must have completed Exercises 21.1 and 21.2.

EXERCISE 21.4

Delegating Administrative Control of Group Policy

1. Open the Active Directory Users and Computers tool.

2. Expand the local domain and create a user named **Policy Admin** within the Group Policy Test OU.

3. Exit Active Directory Users and Computers and open the GPMC.

4. Click the Group Policy Test OU and select the Delegation tab.

5. Click the Add button. In the field Enter The Object Name To Select, type **Policy Admin** and click the Check Names button.

6. The Add Group Or User dialog box appears. In the Permissions drop-down list, make sure that the item labeled Edit Settings, Delete, Modify Security is chosen. Click OK.

7. At this point you should be looking at the Group Policy Test Delegation window. Click the Advanced button in the lower-right corner.

8. Highlight the Policy Admin account and check the Allow Full Control box. This user now has full control of these OUs and all child OUs and GPOs for these OUs. Click OK.

   If you just want to give this user individual rights, then, in the Properties window (step 8), click the Advanced button and then the Effective Permissions tab. This is where you can also choose a user and give them only the rights that you want them to have.

9. When you have finished, close the GPMC tool.

Understanding Delegation

Although I have talked about delegation throughout the book, it's important to discuss it again in the context of OUs, Group Policy, and Active Directory.

Once configured, Active Directory administrative delegation allows an administrator to delegate tasks (usually administration related) to specific user accounts or groups. What this means is that if you don't manage it all, the user accounts (or groups) you choose will be able to manage their portions of the tree.

It's important to be aware of the benefits of Active Directory Delegation (AD Delegation). *AD Delegation* will help you manage the assignment of administrative control over objects in Active Directory, such as users, groups, computers, printers, domains, and sites. AD Delegation is used to create more administrators, which essentially saves time.

For example, let's say you have a company whose IT department is small and situated in a central location. The central location connects three other smaller remote sites. These sites do not each warrant a full-time IT person, but the manager on staff (for example) at each remote site can become an administrator for their portion of the tree. If that manager administers the user accounts for the staff at the remote site, this reduces the burden on the system administrator of doing trivial administrative work, such as unlocking user accounts or changing passwords, and thus it reduces costs.

Controlling Inheritance and Filtering Group Policy

Controlling inheritance is an important function when you are managing GPOs. Earlier in this chapter, you learned that, by default, GPO settings flow from higher-level Active Directory objects to lower-level ones. For example, the effective set of Group Policy settings for a user might be based on GPOs assigned at the site level, at the domain level, and in the OU hierarchy. In general, this is probably the behavior you would want.

In some cases, however, you might want to block Group Policy inheritance. You can accomplish this easily by selecting the object to which a GPO has been linked. Right-click the object and choose Block Inheritance. By enabling this option, you are effectively specifying that this object starts with a clean slate; that is, no other Group Policy settings will apply to the contents of this Active Directory site, domain, or OU.

System administrators can also force inheritance. By setting the Enforced option, they can prevent other system administrators from making changes to default policies. You can set the Enforced option by right-clicking the GPO and choosing the Enforced item (see Figure 21.5).

FIGURE 21.5   Setting the Enforced GPO option

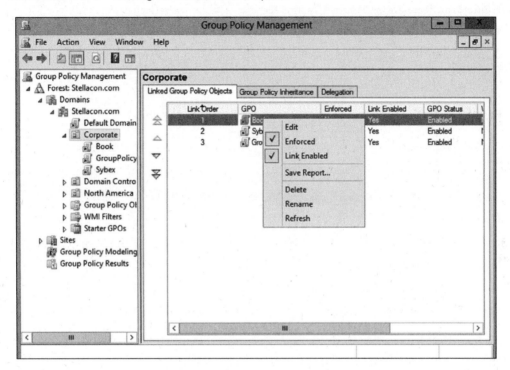

Assigning Script Policies

System administrators might want to make several changes and implement certain settings that would apply while the computer is starting up or the user is logging on. Perhaps the most common operation that logon scripts perform is mapping network drives. Although users can manually map network drives, providing this functionality within login scripts ensures that mappings stay consistent and that users only need to remember the drive letters for their resources.

Script policies are specific options that are part of Group Policy settings for users and computers. These settings direct the operating system to the specific files that should be processed during the startup/shutdown or logon/logoff processes. You can create the scripts by using the *Windows Script Host (WSH)* or with standard batch file commands. WSH allows developers and system administrators to create scripts quickly and easily using Visual Basic Scripting Edition (VBScript) or JScript (Microsoft's implementation of JavaScript). Additionally, WSH can be expanded to accommodate other common scripting languages.

To set script policy options, you simply edit the Group Policy settings. As shown in Figure 21.6, there are two main areas for setting script policy settings.

Startup/Shutdown Scripts   These settings are located within the Computer Configuration ➤ Windows Settings ➤ Scripts (Startup/Shutdown) object.

Logon/Logoff Scripts   These settings are located within the User Configuration ➤ Windows Settings ➤ Scripts (Logon/Logoff) object.

FIGURE 21.6   Viewing Startup/Shutdown script policy settings

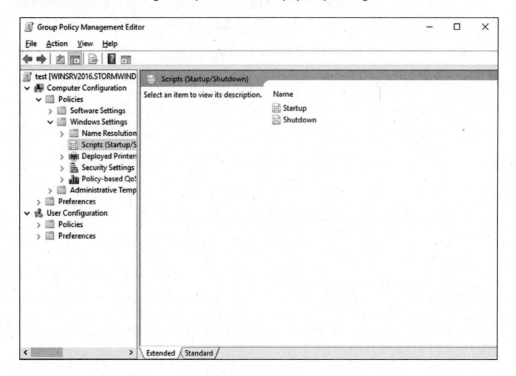

To assign scripts, simply double-click the setting and its Properties dialog box appears. For instance, if you double-click the Startup setting, the Startup Properties dialog box appears (see Figure 21.7). To add a script filename, click the Add button. When you do, you will be asked to provide the name of the script file (such as `MapNetworkDrives.vbs` or `ResetEnvironment.bat`).

Note that you can change the order in which the scripts are run by using the Up and Down buttons. The Show Files button opens the directory folder in which you should store the Logon script files. To ensure that the files are replicated to all domain controllers, you should be sure you place the files within the SYSVOL share.

FIGURE 21.7   Setting scripting options

Understanding the Loopback Policy

There may be times when the user settings of a Group Policy Object should be applied to a computer based on its location instead of the User object. Usually, the user Group Policy processing dictates that the GPOs be applied in order during computer startup based on the computers located in their organizational unit. User GPOs, on the other hand, are applied in order during logon, regardless of the computer to which they log on.

In some situations, this processing order may not be appropriate. A good example is a kiosk machine. You would not want applications that have been assigned or published to a user to be installed when the user is logged on to the kiosk machine. *Loopback Policy* allows two ways to retrieve the list of GPOs for any user when they are using a specific computer in an OU.

Merge Mode   The GPOs for the computer are added to the end of the GPOs for the user. Because of this, the computer's GPOs have higher precedence than the user's GPOs.

Replace Mode   In Replace mode, the user's GPOs are not used. Only the GPOs of the Computer object are used.

Managing Network Configuration

Group policies are also useful in network configuration. Although administrators can handle network settings at the protocol level using many different methods, such as Dynamic Host Configuration Protocol (DHCP), Group Policy allows them to set which functions and operations are available to users and computers.

Figure 21.8 shows some of the features that are available for managing Group Policy settings. The paths to these settings are as follows:

Computer Network Options   These settings are located within the Computer Configuration ➤ Administrative Templates ➤ Network ➤ Network Connections folder.

User Network Options   These settings are located within User Configuration ➤ Administrative Templates ➤ Network.

Here are some examples of the types of settings available:

- The ability to allow or disallow the modification of network settings.

  In many environments, the improper changing of network configurations and protocol settings is a common cause of help desk calls.

- The ability to allow or disallow the creation of Remote Access Service (RAS) connections.

FIGURE 21.8   Viewing Group Policy User network configuration options

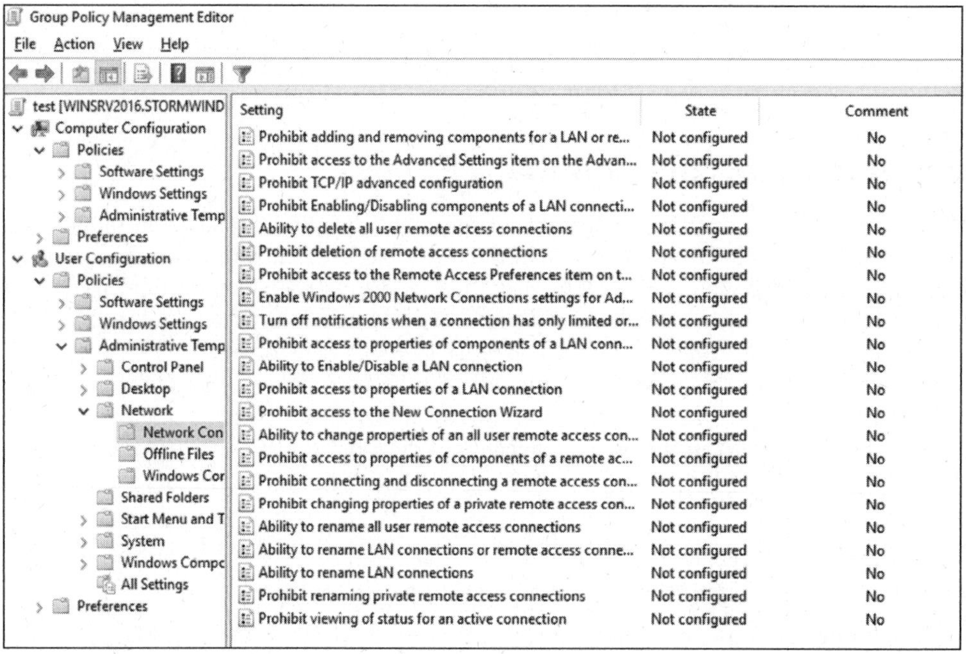

This option is useful, especially in larger networked environments, because the use of modems and other WAN devices can pose a security threat to the network.

- The ability to set offline files and folders options.

  This is especially useful for keeping files synchronized for traveling users, and it is commonly configured for laptops.

Each setting includes detailed instructions in the description area of the GPO Editor window. By using these configuration options, system administrators can maintain consistency for users and computers and avoid many of the most common troubleshooting calls.

Configuring Network Settings

In Windows Server 2016, you can set a lot of user and network settings by using GPOs. Some of the different settings that can be configured are configure printer preferences, defining network drive mappings, configuring power options, setting custom registry settings, munipulating Control Panel settings, configuring Internet Explorer settings, settings for file and folder deployment, setting up shortcut deployments and configuring item-level targeting.

To configure any of these settings, open the Group Policy Management Console and choose the GPO you want to edit. Once you start editing, you can configure any of these network settings.

Automatically Enrolling User and Computer Certificates in Group Policy

You can also use Group Policy to enroll user and computer certificates automatically, making the entire certificate process transparent to your end users. Before proceeding, you should understand what certificates are and why they are an important part of network security.

Think of a digital certificate as a carrying case for a public key. A certificate contains the public key and a set of attributes, including the key holder's name and email address. These attributes specify something about the holder: their identity, what they're allowed to do with the certificate, and so on. The attributes and the public key are bound together because the certificate is digitally signed by the entity that issued it. Anyone who wants to verify the certificate's contents can verify the issuer's signature.

Certificates are one part of what security experts call a *public-key infrastructure (PKI)*. A PKI has several different components that you can mix and match to achieve the desired results. Microsoft's PKI implementation offers the following functions:

Certificate Authorities   CAs issue certificates, revoke certificates they've issued, and publish certificates for their clients. Big CAs like Thawte and VeriSign do this for millions of users. If you want, you can also set up your own CA for each department or workgroup in your organization. Each CA is responsible for choosing which attributes it will include in a certificate and what mechanism it will use to verify those attributes before it issues the certificate.

Certificate Publishers   They make certificates publicly available, inside or outside an organization. This allows widespread availability of the critical material needed to support the entire PKI.

PKI-Savvy Applications These allow you and your users to do useful things with certificates, such as encrypt email or network connections. Ideally, the user shouldn't have to know (or even be aware of) what the application is doing—everything should work seamlessly and automatically. The best-known examples of PKI-savvy applications are web browsers such as Internet Explorer and Firefox and email applications such as Outlook.

Certificate Templates These act like rubber stamps. By specifying a particular template as the model you want to use for a newly issued certificate, you're actually telling the CA which optional attributes to add to the certificate as well as implicitly telling it how to fill some of the mandatory attributes. Templates greatly simplify the process of issuing certificates because they keep you from having to memorize the names of all of the attributes you may potentially want to put in a certificate.

Learn More About PKI

When discussing certificates, it's also important to mention PKI and its definition. The exam doesn't go deeply into PKI, but I recommend you do some extra research on your own because it is an important technology and shouldn't be overlooked. PKI is actually a simple concept with a lot of moving parts. When broken down to its bare essentials, PKI is nothing more than a server and workstations utilizing a software service to add security to your infrastructure. When you use PKI, you are adding a layer of protection. The auto-enrollment Settings policy determines whether users and/or computers are automatically enrolled for the appropriate certificates when necessary. By default, this policy is enabled if a certificate server is installed, but you can make changes to the settings, as shown in Exercise 21.5.

In Exercise 21.5, you will learn how to configure automatic certificate enrollment in Group Policy. You must have first completed the other exercises in this chapter in order to proceed with Exercise 21.5.

EXERCISE 21.5

Configuring Automatic Certificate Enrollment in Group Policy

1. Open the Group Policy Management Console tool.

2. Right-click the North America OU that you created in the previous exercises in this book.

3. Choose Create A GPO In This Domain And Link It Here and name it **Test CA**. Click OK.

4. Right-click the Test CA GPO and choose Edit.

5. Open Computer Configuration ➤ Policies ➤ Windows Settings ➤ Security Settings ➤ Public Key Policies.

6. Double-click Certificate Services Client – Auto-Enrollment in the right pane.

7. The Certificate Services Client – Auto-Enrollment Properties dialog box will appear.

8. For now, don't change anything. Just become familiar with the settings in this dialog box. Click OK to close it.

Redirecting Folders

Another set of Group Policy settings that you will learn about are the *folder redirection settings*. Group Policy provides a means for redirecting the Documents, Desktop, and Start Menu folders, as well as cached application data, to network locations. Folder redirection is particularly useful for the following reasons:

- When they are using roaming user profiles, a user's Documents folder is copied to the local machine each time they log on. This requires high bandwidth consumption and time if the Documents folder is large. If you redirect the Documents folder, it stays in the redirected location, and the user opens and saves files directly to that location.

- Documents are always available no matter where the user logs on.

- Data in the shared location can be backed up during the normal backup cycle without user intervention.

- Data can be redirected to a more robust server-side administered disk that is less prone to physical and user errors.

When you decide to redirect folders, you have two options: basic and advanced.

- Basic redirection redirects everyone's folders to the same location (but each user gets their own folder within that location).

- Advanced redirection redirects folders to different locations based on group membership. For instance, you could configure the Engineers group to redirect their folders to //Engineering1/Documents/ and the Marketing group to //Marketing1/Documents/. Again, individual users still get their own folder within the redirected location.

To configure folder redirection, follow the steps in Exercise 21.6. You must have completed the other exercises in this chapter to proceed with this exercise.

EXERCISE 21.6

Configuring Folder Redirection in Group Policy

1. Open the GPMC tool.

2. Open the North America OU and then edit the Test CA GPO.

3. Open User Configuration ➢ Policies ➢ Windows Settings ➢ Folder Redirection ➢ Documents.

4. Right-click Documents, and select Properties.

EXERCISE 21.6 *(continued)*

5. On the Target tab of the Documents Properties dialog box, choose the Basic – Redirect Everyone's Folder To The Same Location selection from the Settings drop-down list.

6. Leave the default option for the Target Folder Location drop-down list and specify a network path in the Root Path field.

7. Click the Settings tab. All of the default settings are self-explanatory and should typically be left at the default setting. Click OK when you have finished.

Folder Redirection Facts

Try not to mix up the concepts of *folder redirection* and *offline folders*, especially in a world with ever-increasing numbers of mobile users. Folder redirection and offline folders are different features.

Windows Server 2016 folder redirection works as follows: The system uses a pointer that moves the folders you want to a location you specify. Users do not see any of this—it is transparent to them. One problem with folder redirection is that it does not work for mobile users (users who will be offline and who will not have access to files they may need).

Offline folders, however, are copies of folders that were local to you. Files are now available locally to you on the system you have with you. They are also located back on the server where they are stored. The next time you log in, the folders are synchronized so that both folders contain the latest data. This is a perfect feature for mobile users, whereas folder redirection provides no benefit for the mobile user.

Managing GPOs with Windows PowerShell Group Policy Cmdlets

As stated earlier in this book, *Windows PowerShell* is a Windows command-line shell and scripting language. Windows PowerShell can also help an administrator automate many of the same tasks that you perform using the Group Policy Management Console.

Windows Server 2016 helps you perform many of the Group Policy tasks by providing more than 25 cmdlets. Each of these cmdlets is a simple, single-function command-line tool.

The Windows PowerShell Group Policy cmdlets can help you perform some of the following tasks for domain-based Group Policy Objects:

- Maintain, create, remove, back up, and import GPOs

- Create, update, and remove GPO links to Active Directory containers

- Set Active Directory OUs and domain permissions and inheritance flags
- Configure Group Policy registry settings
- Create and edit Starter GPOs

The requirement for Windows PowerShell Group Policy cmdlets is Windows Server 2016 on either a domain controller or a member server that has the GPMC installed. Windows 7, Windows 8, and Windows 10 also have the ability to use Windows PowerShell Group Policy cmdlets if they have Remote Server Administration Tools (RSAT) installed. RSAT includes the GPMC and its cmdlets. PowerShell is also a requirement.

Item-Level Targeting

Administrators have the ability to apply individual preference items only to selected users or computers using a GPO feature called item-level targeting. *Item-level targeting* allows an administrator to select specific items that the GPO will look at and then apply that GPO only to the specific users or computers. Administrators have the ability to include multiple preference items, and each item can be customized for specific users or computers to use.

The target item has a value that belongs to it, and the value can be either true or false. Administrators can get even more granular by using the operation command of AND or OR while building this GPO, and this will allow an administrator to combine the targeted items with the preceding one. Once all of the conditions are executed, if the final value is false, then the GPO is not applied. If the final value is true, the GPO is applied to the users or computers that were previously determined. Administrators have the ability to item-level target the following items:

- Battery Present Targeting
- Computer Name Targeting
- CPU Speed Targeting
- Date Match Targeting
- Disk Space Targeting
- Domain Targeting
- Environment Variable Targeting
- File Match Targeting
- IP Address Range Targeting
- Language Targeting
- LDAP Query Targeting
- MAC Address Range Targeting
- MSI Query Targeting
- Network Connection Targeting
- Operating System Targeting

- Organizational Unit Targeting
- PCMCIA Present Targeting
- Portable Computer Targeting
- Processing Mode Targeting
- RAM Targeting
- Registry Match Targeting
- Security Group Targeting
- Site Targeting
- Terminal Session Targeting
- Time Range Targeting
- User Targeting
- WMI Query Targeting

Administrators can easily set up item-level targeting by following these steps:

1. Open the Group Policy Management Console. Select the GPO that will contain the new preferences by right-clicking the GPO and then choose Edit.

2. In the console tree under Computer Configuration or User Configuration, expand the Preferences folder and then browse to the preference extension.

3. Double-click the node for the preference extension and then right-click the preference item and click Properties.

4. In the Properties dialog box, click the Common tab.

5. Select Item-Level Targeting and then click Targeting.

6. Click New Item. If you are configuring multiple targeted items, on the Item Option menu, click the logical operation (AND or OR). Then click OK when finished.

7. Click the OK button on the Properties dialog box, and you are all set.

Back Up, Restore, Import, Copy, and Migration Tables

One of the biggest advantages of using the Group Policy Management Console is that it is a one-stop shopping utility. You can do everything you need to do for GPOs in one location. The GPMC not only allows you to create and link a GPO but also lets you back up, restore, import, copy, and use migration tables.

Backing Up a GPO

Since this book is about Windows Server 2016 and everything you should do to set up the server properly, then you most likely already understand what backups can do for you.

The reason we back up data as an administrator is in the event of a crash or major error that requires us to reload data to the server. Backups should be done daily on all data that is important to your organization. Backups can be done either by using Windows Server 2016's backup utility, or you can purchase third party software/hardware to back up your data.

I am an IT Director, and data recoverability is one of the most critical items that I deal with on a daily basis. I use a third-party hardware device from a company called Unitrends. This is just one of many companies that helps protect an organization's data.

This hardware device does hourly backups for all of my servers. One of the nice features of the Unitrends box is that it backs up onto the hardware device and then sends my data up to the cloud automatically for an offsite backup. This way, if I need to recover just one piece of data, I can grab it off the hardware device. But if I have a major issue, such as a fire that destroys the entire server room, I have an offsite backup from which I can retrieve my data.

It's the same for GPOs. You need to make sure you back up your GPOs in the event of an issue that requires you to do a reload. To back up your GPOs manually, you can go into the GPMC MMC and, under Group Policy Objects, you can right click and choose Backup All or right click on the specific GPO and choose Backup.

Restoring a GPO

There may be times when you have to restore a GPO that was previously backed up. There are normally two reasons why you have to restore a GPO—you accidently deleted the GPO, or you need to restore the GPO to a previous state. (This normally happens if you make changes and it causes an issue.) Restoring a GPO is simple.

1. Open the Group Policy Management Console.

2. In the console tree, right-click Group Policy Objects and choose Manage Backups.

3. Choose the backup you want to restore and click the Restore button.

Importing or Copying GPOs

As an administrator, there may be times when you need to import or copy a GPO from one domain to another domain. Administrators do this so that the second domain has the same settings as the first domain.

An administrator can use the import or copy-to-transfer settings from one GPO to another GPO within the same domain, to a GPO in another domain in the same forest, or to a GPO in a domain in a different forest.

Importing or copying a GPO is an easy process. To do this, an administrator completes the following steps:

1. Open the Group Policy Management Console.

2. In the console tree, right-click Group Policy Objects and choose either Import Settings or Copy.

Migration Tables

One issue that we run into when copying or moving a GPO from one system to another is that when some GPOs are built, they are domain specific. This can be a problem when they are moved to a system in another domain. This is where migration tables can help you out.

Migration tables will tell you how domain specific settings should be treated when the GPO is moved from the domain in which it was created to another domain.

Migration tables are files that are used to map previous domain information (such as users and groups) to the new domain's object-specific data. Migration tables have mapping entries that map the old data to the new data.

Migration tables store their mapping data in an XML format, and the migration tables have their own extension name, `.migtable`. If you want to create your own migration table, you can use the *Migration Table Editor (MTE)*. The MTE is an easy-to-use utility for configuring or just viewing migration tables.

It does not matter if you decide to copy or import a GPO, migration tables apply to any of the settings within the GPO. However, if you copy a GPO instead of move it, you have the option of bringing the Discretionary Access Control List (DACL) option over with the copy.

If you are looking at using migration tables, there are three settings that can be used:

Do Not Use A Migration Table   If an administrator chooses this option, the GPO is copied over exactly as is. All security objects and UNC paths are copied over without any modification.

Use A Migration Table   If an administrator chooses this option, the GPO has all of the options that can be in the migration table mapped.

Use A Migration Table Exclusively   If an administrator chooses this option, all security principals and UNC path information in the GPO are chosen. If any of this information is not included in the migration table, the operation will fail.

To open the Migration Table Editor, perform the following steps:

1. Open the Group Policy Management Console.

2. In the console tree, right-click Group Policy Objects and choose Open Migration Table Editor.

Resetting the Default GPO

There may be a time when you need to reset the default GPO to its original settings. This is easy to do as long as you understand how to use the DCGPOFix command-line utility. This command-line utility is just what it spells—it fixes the domain controller's GPO. To use this command, you would use the following syntax:

```
DCGPOFix [/ignoreschema] [/target: {Domain | DC | Both}] [/?]
```

So, let's take a look at the switches in the previous command. The /ignoreschema switch ignores the current version of the Active Directory Schema. The reason you use this switch is because this command works only on the same schema version as the Windows version in which the command was shipped. By using this switch, you don't need to worry about what schema you have on the system.

The next switch is [/target: {Domain | DC | Both}]. This switch specifies the GPO you are going to restore. An administrator has the ability to restore the Default Domain Policy GPO, the Default Domain Controllers GPO, or both. The final switch, /?, displays the help for this command.

Deploying Software Through a GPO

It's difficult enough to manage applications on a stand-alone computer. It seems that the process of installing, configuring, and uninstalling applications is never finished. Add in the hassle of computer reboots and reinstalling corrupted applications, and the reduction in productivity can be substantial.

Software administrators who manage software in network environments have even more concerns.

- First, they must determine which applications specific users require.

- Then, IT departments must purchase the appropriate licenses for the software and acquire any necessary media.

- Next, the system administrators need to install the applications on users' machines. This process generally involves help desk staff visiting computers, or it requires end users to install the software themselves. Both processes entail several potential problems, including installation inconsistency and lost productivity from downtime experienced when applications were installed.

- Finally, software administrators still need to manage software updates and remove unused software.

One of the key design goals for Active Directory was to reduce some of the headaches involved in managing software and configurations in a networked environment. To that end, Windows Server 2016 offers several features that can make the task of deploying software easier and less error prone. Before you dive into the technical details, however, you need to examine the issues related to software deployment.

The Software Management Life Cycle

Although it may seem that the use of a new application requires only the installation of the necessary software, the overall process of managing applications involves many more steps. When managing software applications, there are three main phases to their life cycle, as follows:

Phase 1: Deploying Software The first step in using applications is to install them on the appropriate client computers. Generally, some applications are deployed during the initial configuration of a PC, and others are deployed when they are requested. In the latter case, this often used to mean that system administrators and help desk staffs have to visit client computers and manually walk through the installation process. With Windows Server 2016 and GPOs, the entire process can be automated.

Before You Install, Stop

It is important to understand that just because you can easily deploy software, it does not necessarily mean you have the right to do so. Before you install software on client computers, you must make sure you have the appropriate licenses for the software. Furthermore, it's important to take the time to track application installations. As many system administrators have discovered, it's much more difficult to inventory software installations after they've been performed. Another issue you may encounter is that you lack available resources (for instance, your system does not meet the minimum hardware requirements) and that you face problems such as limited hard disk space or memory that may not be able to handle the applications that you want to load and use. You may also find that your user account does not have the permission to install software. It's important to consider not only how you will install software but also whether you can.

Phase 2: Maintaining Software   Once an application is installed and in use on client computers, you need to ensure that the software is maintained. You must keep programs up-to-date by applying changes due to bug fixes, enhancements, and other types of updates. This is normally done with service packs, hot fixes, and updates. As with the initial software deployment, software maintenance can be tedious. Some programs require older versions to be uninstalled before updates are added. Others allow for automatically upgrading over existing installations. Managing and deploying software updates can consume a significant amount of the IT staff's time.

Using Windows Update

Make sure that you learn about Windows Update, a service that allows you to connect to Microsoft's website and download what your system may need to bring it up to compliance. This tool is helpful if you are running a stand-alone system, but if you want to deploy software across the enterprise, the best way to accomplish this is first to test the updates you are downloading and make sure you can use them and that they are not bug ridden. Then you can use a tool such as the Windows Server Update Service (WSUS), which was formerly called the Software Update Services (SUS).

You can check for updates at Microsoft's website (http://update.microsoft.com). Microsoft likes to ask many types of questions about WSUS on its certification exams. WSUS is described in detail in other Sybex certification books.

Phase 3: Removing Software   The end of the life cycle for many software products involves the actual removal of unused programs. Removing software is necessary when applications become outdated or when users no longer require their functionality. One of the traditional problems with uninstalling applications is that many of the installed files may not be removed. Furthermore, the removal of shared components can sometimes cause other programs to stop functioning properly. Also, users often forget to uninstall applications that they no longer need, and these programs continue to occupy disk space and consume valuable system resources.

The Microsoft Windows Installer (MSI) manages each of these three phases of the software maintenance life cycle. Now that you have an overview of the process, let's move forward to look at the steps involved in deploying software using Group Policy.

The *Microsoft Windows Installer* (sometimes referred to as Microsoft Installer or Windows Installer) is an application installation and configuration service. An instruction file (the Microsoft Installer package) contains information about what needs to be done to install a product. It's common to confuse the two.

The Windows Installer

If you've installed newer application programs (such as Microsoft Office 2016), you've probably noticed the updated setup and installation routines. Applications that comply with the updated standard use the *Windows Installer specification* and MSI software packages for deployment. Each package contains information about various setup options and the files required for installation. Although the benefits may not seem dramatic on the surface, there's a lot of new functionality under the hood.

The Windows Installer was created to solve many of the problems associated with traditional application development. It has several components, including the Installer service (which runs on Windows 2000, XP, Vista, Windows 7, Windows 8, Windows 10, Windows Server 2003, Windows Server 2008, Windows Server 2008 R2, Windows Server 2012, Windows Server 2012 R2, and Windows Server 2016 computers), the Installer program (msiexec.exe) that is responsible for executing the instructions in a *Windows Installer package*, and the specifications third-party developers use to create their own packages. Within each installation package file is a relational structure (similar to the structure of tables in databases) that records information about the programs contained within the package.

To appreciate the true value of the Windows Installer, you'll need to look at some of the problems with traditional software deployment mechanisms and then at how the Windows Installer addresses many of them.

Application Installation Issues

Before the Windows Installer, applications were installed using a setup program that managed the various operations required for a program to operate. These operations included copying files, changing registry settings, and managing any other operating system changes that might be required (such as starting or stopping services). However, this method had several problems:

- The setup process was not robust, and aborting the operation often left many unnecessary files in the file system.

- The process included uninstalling an application (this also often left many unnecessary files in the file system) and remnants in the Windows registry and operating system folders. Over time, these remnants would result in reduced overall system performance and wasted disk space.

- There was no standard method for applying upgrades to applications, and installing a new version often required users to uninstall the old application, reboot, and then install the new program.

- Conflicts between different versions of *dynamic link libraries (DLLs)*—shared program code used across different applications—could cause the installation or removal of one application to break the functionality of another.

Benefits of the Windows Installer

Because of the many problems associated with traditional software installation, Microsoft created the *Windows Installer*. This system provides for better manageability of the software installation process and allows system administrators more control over the deployment process. Specifically, the Windows Installer provides the following benefits:

Improved Software Removal   The process of removing software is an important one because remnants left behind during the uninstall process can eventually clutter up the registry and file system. During the installation process, the Windows Installer keeps track of all of the changes made by a setup package. When it comes time to remove an application, all of these changes can then be rolled back.

More Robust Installation Routines   If a typical setup program is aborted during the software installation process, the results are unpredictable. If the actual installation hasn't yet begun, then the installer generally removes any temporary files that may have been created. However, if the file copy routine starts before the system encounters an error, it is likely that the files will not be automatically removed from the operating system. In contrast, the Windows Installer allows you to roll back any changes when the application setup process is aborted.

Ability to Use Elevated Privileges   Installing applications usually requires the user to have Administrator permissions on the local computer because file system and registry changes are required. When installing software for network users, system administrators have two options. First, they can log off of the computer before installing the software and then log back on as a user who has Administrator permissions on the local computer. This method is tedious and time-consuming. The second option is to give users Administrator permissions temporarily on their own machines. This method could cause security problems and requires the attention of a system administrator.

Through the use of the Installer service, the Windows Installer is able to use temporarily elevated privileges to install applications. This allows users, regardless of their security settings, to execute the installation of authorized applications. This saves time and preserves security.

Support for Repairing Corrupted Applications   Regardless of how well a network environment is managed, critical files are sometimes lost or corrupted. Such problems can prevent applications from running properly and can cause crashes. Windows Installer packages provide you with the ability to verify the installation of an application and, if necessary, replace any missing or corrupted files. This support saves time and lessens end-user headaches associated with removing and reinstalling an entire application to replace just a few files.

Prevention of File Conflicts   Generally, different versions of the same files should be compatible with each other. In the real world, however, this isn't always the case. A classic problem in the Windows world is the case of one program replacing DLLs that are used by several other programs. Windows Installer accurately tracks which files are used by certain programs and ensures that any shared files are not improperly deleted or overwritten.

Automated Installations   A typical application setup process requires end users or system administrators to respond to several prompts. For example, a user may be able to choose the program group in which icons will be created and the file system location to which the program will be installed. Additionally, they may be required to choose which options are installed. Although this type of flexibility is useful, it can be tedious when you are rolling out multiple applications. By using features of the Windows Installer, however, users are able to specify setup options before the process begins. This allows system administrators to ensure consistency in installations, and it saves users time.

Advertising and On-Demand Installations   One of the most powerful features of the Windows Installer is its ability to perform on-demand software installations. Prior to the Windows Installer, application installation options were quite basic—either a program was installed or it was not. When setting up a computer, system administrators would be required to guess which applications the user might need and install all of them.

The Windows Installer supports a function known as advertising. *Advertising* makes applications appear to be available via the Start menu. However, the programs themselves may not actually be installed on the system. When a user attempts to access an advertised application, the Windows Installer automatically downloads the necessary files from a server and installs the program. The result is that applications are installed only when they are needed, and the process requires no intervention from the end user.

To anyone who has managed many software applications in a network environment, all of these features of the Windows Installer are likely welcome ones. They also make life easier for end users and application developers; they can focus on the "real work" that their jobs demand.

Windows Installer File Types

When performing software deployment with the Windows Installer in Windows Server 2016, you may encounter several different file types.

Microsoft Windows Installer Packages   To take full advantage of Windows Installer functionality, applications must include Microsoft Windows Installer packages. Third-party application vendors and software developers normally create these packages, and they include the information required to install and configure the application and any supporting files.

Microsoft Transformation Files   *Microsoft Transformation (MST) files* are useful when you are customizing the details of how applications are installed. When a system administrator chooses to assign or publish an application, they may want to specify additional options for the package. For example, if a system administrator wants to allow users to install only the Microsoft Word and Microsoft PowerPoint components of Office 2016, they could specify these options within a transformation file. Then, when users install the application, they will be provided only with the options related to these components.

Microsoft Patches   To maintain software, patches are often required. Patches may make Registry and/or file system changes. *Patch files (MSP)* are used for minor system changes and are subject to certain limitations. Specifically, a patch file cannot remove any installed program components and cannot delete or modify any shortcuts created by the user.

Initialization Files   To provide support for publishing non–Windows Installer applications, *initialization files* can be used. These files provide links to a standard executable file that is used to install an application. An example might be \\server1\software\program1\ setup.exe. These files can then be published and advertised, and users can access the *Add Or Remove Programs* icon to install them over the network.

Application Assignment Scripts   *Application assignment scripts (AAS)* store information regarding assigning programs and any settings that the system administrator makes. These files are created when Group Policy is used to create software package assignments for users and computers.

Each of these types of files provides functionality that allows the system administrator to customize software deployment. Windows Installer packages have special properties that you can view by right-clicking the file in File Explorer and choosing Properties (see Figure 21.9).

FIGURE 21.9   Viewing the properties of an MSI package file

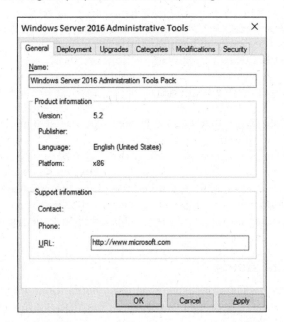

Deploying Applications

The functionality provided by Windows Installer offers many advantages to end users who install their own software. However, that is just the beginning in a networked environment. As you'll see later in this chapter, the various features of Windows Installer and compatible packages allow system administrators to determine central applications that users will be able to install.

There are two main methods of making programs available to end users using Active Directory: assigning and publishing. Both assigning and publishing applications greatly ease the process of deploying and managing applications in a network environment.

In the following sections, you'll look at how the processes of assigning and publishing applications can make life easier for IT staff and users alike. The various settings for assigned and published applications are managed through the use of GPOs.

Assigning Applications

Software applications can be assigned to users and computers. *Assigning* a software package makes the program available for automatic installation. The applications advertise their availability to the affected users or computers by placing icons within the Programs folder of the Start menu for Windows 8 (and before) and Windows Server 2012/2012 R2, and within the Apps area on Windows 10 and Windows Server 2016.

When applications are assigned to a user, programs will be advertised to the user regardless of which computer they are using. That is, icons for the advertised program will appear regardless of whether the program is installed on that computer. If the user clicks an icon for a program that has not yet been installed on the local computer, the application will automatically be accessed from a server and it will be installed.

When an application is assigned to a computer, the program is made available to any users of the computer. For example, all users who log on to a computer that has been assigned Microsoft Office 2016 will have access to the components of the application. If the user did not previously install Microsoft Office 2016, they will be prompted for any required setup information when the program first runs.

Generally, applications that are required by the vast majority of users should be assigned to computers. This reduces the amount of network bandwidth required to install applications on demand and improves the end-user experience by preventing the delay involved when installing an application the first time it is accessed. Any applications that may be used by only a few users (or those with specific job tasks) should be assigned to users.

Publishing Applications

When applications are *published*, they are advertised, but no icons are automatically created. Instead, the applications are made available for installation using the Programs and Features icon in Control Panel.

Implementing Software Deployment

So far, you have become familiar with the issues related to software deployment and management from a theoretical level. Now it's time to drill down into the actual steps required to deploy software using the features of Active Directory and the GPMC. In the following sections, you will walk through the steps required to create an application distribution share point, to publish and assign applications, to update previously installed applications, to verify the installation of applications, and to update Windows operating systems.

Preparing for Software Deployment

Before you can install applications on client computers, you must make sure that the necessary files are available to end users. In many network environments, system administrators create shares on file servers that include the installation files for many applications. Based on security permissions, either end users or system administrators can then connect to these shares from a client computer and install the needed software. The efficient organization of these shares can save the help desk from having to carry around a library of DVDs, and it allows you to install applications easily on many computers at once.

One of the problems in network environments is that users frequently install applications whether or not they really need them. They may stumble upon applications that are stored on common file servers and install them out of curiosity. These actions can often decrease productivity and may violate software licensing agreements. You can help avoid this by placing all of your application installation files in hidden shares (for example, software$).

Exercise 21.7 walks you through the process of creating a software distribution share point. In this exercise, you will prepare for software deployment by creating a directory share and placing certain types of files in this directory. To complete the steps in this exercise, you must have access to the Microsoft Office 2013 or Microsoft Office 2016 installation files (via DVD or through a network share) and have 2,000 MB of free disk space. For this exercise, I used Microsoft Office 2016.

EXERCISE 21.7

Creating a Software Deployment Share

1. Using File Explorer, create a folder called **Software** that you can use with application sharing. Be sure that the volume on which you create this folder has at least 2,000 MB of available disk space.

2. Create a folder called **Office 2016** within the Software folder.

3. Copy all of the installation files for Microsoft Office 2016 from the DVD or network share containing the files to the Office 2016 folder you created in step 2. If you prefer, you can use switches to install all of the Office 2016 installation files.

4. Right-click the Software folder (created in step 1) and select Share. In the Choose People On Your Network To Share With dialog box, type **Everyone**, and click the Add button. Next click the Share button. When you see a message that the sharing process is complete, click Done.

Software Restriction Policies

One of the biggest problems that we face as IT managers is users downloading and installing software. Many software packages don't cause any issues and are completely safe. Unfortunately, many software packages do have viruses and can cause problems. This is where software restriction policies can help. Software restriction policies help to identify software and to control its ability to run on a local computer, organizational unit, domain, or site.

Software restriction policies give administrators the ability to regulate unknown or untrusted software. Software restriction policies allow you to protect your computers from unwanted software by identifying and also specifying what software packages are allowed to be installed.

When configuring software restriction policies, an administrator is able to define a default security level of Unrestricted (software is allowed) or Disallowed (software is not allowed to run) for a GPO. Administrators can make exceptions to this default security level. They can create software restriction policy rules for specific software.

To create a software policy using the Group Policy Management Console, create a new GPO. In the GPO, expand the Windows Settings for either the user or computer configuration section, expand Security, right-click Software Restriction Policy, and choose New Software Restriction Policy. Set the policy for the level of security that you need.

Using AppLocker

AppLocker is a feature in Windows 7, Windows 8, Windows 10, Windows Server 2012/2012 R2, and Windows Server 2016. It is the replacement for software restriction policies. *AppLocker* allows you to configure a Denied list and an Accepted list for applications. Applications that are configured on the Denied list will not run on the system, whereas applications on the Accepted list will operate properly.

The new capabilities and extensions of the AppLocker feature help reduce administrative overhead and help administrators control how users can access and use files, such as EXE files, scripts, Windows Installer files (MSI and MSP files), and DLLs.

Group Policy Slow Link Detection

When setting up GPOs, most of us assume that the connection speeds between servers and clients are going to be fast. In today's world, it is unlikely to see slow connections between locations, but they are still out there. Sometimes connection speeds can cause issues with the deployment of GPOs, specifically ones that are deploying software.

A setting in the Computer and User section of the GPO called *Group Policy Slow Link Detection* defines a slow connection for the purposes of applying and updating GPOs. If the data transfer rate from the domain controller providing the GPO to the computer is slower than what you have specified in this setting, the connection is considered to be a slow connection. If a connection is considered slow, the system response will vary depending on the policy. For example, if a GPO is going to deploy software and the connection is considered slow, the software may not be installed on the client computer. If you configure this option as 0, all connections are considered fast connections.

Publishing and Assigning Applications

As mentioned earlier, system administrators can make software packages available to users by using publishing and assigning operations. Both of these operations allow system administrators to leverage the power of Active Directory and, specifically, GPOs to determine which applications are available to users. Additionally, OUs can provide the organization that can help group users based on their job functions and software requirements.

The general process involves creating a GPO that includes software deployment settings for users and computers and then linking this GPO to Active Directory objects.

Exercise 21.8 walks you through the steps required to publish and assign applications. In this exercise, you will create applications and assign them to specific Active Directory objects using GPOs. To complete the steps in this exercise, you must have completed Exercise 21.7.

EXERCISE 21.8

Publishing and Assigning Applications Using Group Policy

1. Open the Active Directory Users and Computers tool from the Administrative Tools program group (using the Windows key).

2. Expand the domain and create a new top-level OU called **Software**.

3. Within the Software OU, create a user named **Jane User** with a login name of **juser** (choose the defaults for all other options).

4. Exit Active Directory Users and Computers and open the Group Policy Management Console.

5. Right-click the Software OU and choose Create A GPO In This Domain And Link It Here.

6. For the name of the new GPO, type **Software Deployment**.

7. To edit the Software Deployment GPO, right-click it and choose Edit. Expand the Computer Configuration ➤ Policies ➤ Software Settings object.

8. Right-click the Software Installation item and select New ➤ Package.

9. Navigate to the Software share you created in Exercise 21.7.

10. Within the Software share, double-click the Office 2016 folder and select the appropriate MSI file depending on the version of Office 2016 you have. Office 2016 Professional is being used in this example, so you'll see that the OFFICEMUI.MSI file is chosen. Click Open.

11. In the Deploy Software dialog box, choose Advanced. (Note that the Published option is unavailable because applications cannot be published to computers.) Click OK to return to the Deploy Software dialog box.

12. To examine the deployment options of this package, click the Deployment tab. Accept the default settings by clicking OK.

13. Within the Group Policy Object Editor, expand the User Configuration ➤ Software Settings object.

14. Right-click the Software Installation item and select New ➢ Package.

15. Navigate to the Software share you created in Exercise 21.7.

16. Within the Software share, double-click the Office 2016 folder and select the appropriate MSI file. Click Open.

17. For the Software Deployment option, select Published in the Deploy Software dialog box and click OK.

18. Close the GPMC.

The overall process involved with deploying software using Active Directory is quite simple. However, you shouldn't let the intuitive graphical interface fool you—there's a lot of power under the hood of these software deployment features! Once you've properly assigned and published applications, it's time to see the effects of your work.

Applying Software Updates

The steps described in the previous section work only when you are installing a new application. However, software companies often release updates that you need to install on top of existing applications. These updates usually consist of bug fixes or other changes that are required to keep the software up-to-date. You can apply software updates in Active Directory by using the Upgrades tab of the software package Properties dialog box found in the Group Policy Object Editor.

In Exercise 21.9, you will apply a software update to an existing application. You should add the upgrade package to the GPO in the same way you added the original application in steps 8 through 12 of Exercise 21.8. You should also have completed Exercise 21.8 before attempting this exercise.

Applying Software Updates

1. Open the Group Policy Management Console from the Administrative Tools program group.

2. Click the Software OU, right-click the Software Deployment GPO, and choose Edit.

3. Expand the Computer Configuration ➢ Policies ➢ Software Settings ➢ Software Installation object.

4. Right-click the software package and select Properties from the context menu to bring up the Properties dialog box.

5. Select the Upgrades tab and click the Add button.

6. Click the Current Group Policy Object (GPO) radio button in the Choose A Package From section of the dialog box or click the Browse button to select the GPO to which you want to apply the upgrade. Consult your application's documentation to see whether you should choose the Uninstall The Existing Package, Then Install The Upgrade Package radio button or the Package Can Upgrade Over The Existing Package radio button.

7. Click Cancel to close the Add Upgrade Package dialog box.

8. Click Cancel and exit the GPMC.

You should understand that not all upgrades make sense in all situations. For instance, if the Panek 2015 files are incompatible with the Panek 2018 application, then your Panek 2015 users might not want you to perform the upgrade without taking additional steps to ensure that they can continue to use their files. In addition, users might have some choice about which version they use when it doesn't affect the support of the network.

Regardless of the underlying reason for allowing this flexibility, you should be aware that there are two basic types of upgrades that are available for administrators to provide to the users:

Mandatory Upgrade Forces everyone who currently has an existing version of the program to upgrade according to the GPO. Users who have never installed the program for whatever reason will be able to install only the new, upgraded version.

Nonmandatory Upgrade Allows users to choose whether they would like to upgrade. This upgrade type also allows users who do not have their application installed to choose which version they would like to use.

Verifying Software Installation

To ensure that the software installation settings you make in a GPO have taken place, you can log into the domain from a Windows 10, Windows 8, or Windows 7 computer that is within the OU to which the software settings apply. When you log in, you will notice two changes. First, the application is installed on the computer (if it was not installed already). To access the application, a user needs to click one of the icons within the Program group of the Start menu. Note also that applications are available to any of the users who log on to this machine. Second, the settings apply to any computers that are contained within the OU and to any users who log on to these computers.

If you publish an application to users, the change may not be as evident, but it is equally useful. When you log on to a Windows 7, Windows 8, or Windows 10 computer that is a member of the domain, and when you use a user account from the OU where you published the application, you will be able to install any of the published applications automatically. On a Windows 10, Windows 8, or Windows 7 computer, you can do this by accessing the Programs icon in Control Panel. By clicking Add New Programs, you access a display of the applications available for installation. By clicking the Add button in the Add New Programs section of the Programs dialog box, you will automatically begin the installation of the published application.

Configuring Automatic Updates in Group Policy

So far you've seen the advantages of deploying application software in a group policy. Group policies also provide a way to install operating system updates across the network for Windows 10, Windows 7, Windows 8, Windows Server 2008/2008 R2, Windows Server 2012/2012 R2, and Windows Server 2016 machines using Windows Update in conjunction with Windows Server Update Service (WSUS). WSUS is the newer version of SUS, and it is used on a Windows Server 2016 system to update systems. As you may remember, WSUS and SUS are patch-management tools that help you deploy updates to your systems in a controlled manner.

Windows Update is available through the Microsoft website, and it is used to provide the most current files for Windows operating systems. Examples of updates include security fixes, critical updates, updated help files, and updated drivers. You can access Windows Update by clicking the Windows Update icon in the system tray.

WSUS is used to leverage the features of Windows Update within a corporate environment by downloading Windows updates to a corporate server, which in turn provides the updates to the internal corporate clients. This allows administrators to test and have full control over what updates are deployed within the corporate environment.

Within an enterprise network that is using Active Directory, you would typically see automatic updates configured through Group Policy. Group policies are used to manage configuration and security settings via Active Directory. Group Policy is also used to specify what server a client will use for automatic updates.

If the WSUS client were part of an enterprise network that is using Active Directory, you would configure the client via a group policy.

Configuring Software Deployment Settings

In addition to the basic operations of assigning and publishing applications, you can use several other options to specify the details of how software is deployed. In the following sections, you will examine the various options that are available and their effects on the software installation process.

The Software Installation Properties Dialog Box

The most important software deployment settings are contained in the Software Installation Properties dialog box, which you can access by right-clicking the Software Installation item and selecting Properties from the context menu. The following sections describe the features contained on the various tabs of the dialog box.

Managing Package Defaults

On the Deployment tab of the Software Installation Properties dialog box, you'll be able to specify some defaults for any packages that you create within this GPO. Figure 21.10 shows the Deployment options for managing software installation settings.

FIGURE 21.10   Deployment tab of the Software Installation Properties dialog box

The following options are used for managing software installation settings:

Default Package Location   This setting specifies the default file system or network location for software installation packages. This is useful if you are already using a specific share on a file server for hosting the necessary installation files.

New Packages   These settings specify the default type of package assignment that will be used when you add a new package to either the user or computer settings. If you'll be assigning or publishing multiple packages, you may find it useful to set a default here. Selecting the Advanced option (see Figure 21.11) enables Group Policy to display the package's Properties dialog box each time a new package is added.

FIGURE 21.11   Advanced Deployment dialog box

Installation User Interface Options   When installing an application, system administrators may or may not want end users to see all of the advanced installation options. If Basic is chosen, the user will be able to configure only the minimal settings (such as the installation location). If Maximum is chosen, all of the available installation options will be displayed. The specific installation options available will depend on the package itself.

Uninstall Applications When They Fall Out Of The Scope Of Management   So far, you have seen how applications can be assigned and published to users or computers. But what happens when effective GPOs change? For example, suppose User A is currently located within the Sales OU. A GPO that assigns the Microsoft Office 2013 suite of applications is linked to the Sales OU. You decide to move User A to the Engineering OU, which has no software deployment settings. Should the application be uninstalled or should it remain?

If the Uninstall Applications When They Fall Out Of The Scope of Management option is checked, applications will be removed if they are not specifically assigned or published within GPOs. In this example, this means Office 2013 would be uninstalled for User A. If this box is left unchecked, however, the application will remain installed.

Managing File Extension Mappings

One of the potential problems associated with using many different file types is that it's difficult to keep track of which applications work with which files. For example, if you received a file with the filename extension .abc, you would have no idea which application you would need to view it.

Fortunately, through software deployment settings, system administrators can specify mappings for specific *filename extensions*. For example, you could specify that whenever users attempt to access a file with the extension .vsd, the operating system should attempt to open the file using Visio diagramming software. If Visio is not installed on the user's machine, the computer can automatically download and install it (assuming that the application has been properly advertised).

This method allows users to have applications automatically installed when they are needed. The following is an example of a sequence of events that might occur:

1. A user receives an email message that contains a PDF (.pdf) file attachment.

2. The computer realizes that the PDF file does not have the appropriate viewing application for this type of file installed. However, it also realizes that a filename extension mapping is available within the Active Directory software deployment settings.

3. The client computer automatically requests the PDF software package from the server, and it uses the Microsoft Windows Installer to install the application automatically.

4. The computer opens the attachment for the user.

Notice that all of these steps were carried out without any further interaction with the user.

You can manage filename extension mappings by right-clicking the Software Installation item, selecting Properties, and then clicking the File Extensions tab.

Creating Application Categories

In many network environments, the list of supported applications can include hundreds of items. For users who are looking for only one specific program, searching through a list of all of these programs can be difficult and time-consuming.

Fortunately, methods for categorizing the applications are available on your network. You can easily manage the application categories for users and computers by right-clicking the Software Installation item, selecting Properties, and then clicking the Categories tab.

Figure 21.12 shows you the categories tab of the Software Installation package. When creating categories, it is a good idea to use category names that are meaningful to users because it will make it easier for them to find the programs they're seeking.

FIGURE 21.12   The Categories tab of the Software Installation Properties dialog box

Once the software installation categories have been created, you can view them by clicking the Programs or Programs And Features icon in Control Panel. When you click Add New Programs, you'll see that several options appear in the Category drop-down list. Now when you select the properties for a package, you will be able to assign the application to one or more of the categories.

Removing Programs

As discussed in the beginning of the chapter, an important phase in the software management life cycle is the removal of applications. Fortunately, if you use the GPMC and the Windows Installer packages, the process is simple. To remove an application, you can right-click the package within the Group Policy settings and select All Tasks ➤ Remove. This brings up a removal text box (see Figure 21.13).

FIGURE 21.13   Removing a software package

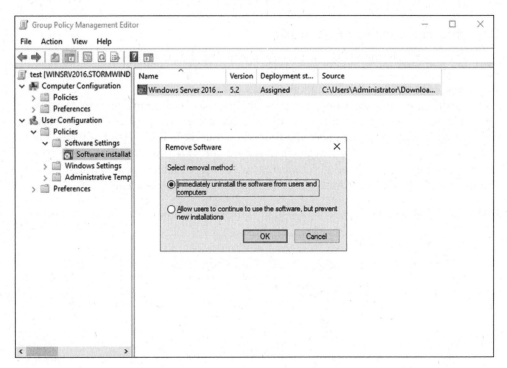

When choosing to remove a software package from a GPO, you have two options, shown here:

Immediately Uninstall The Software From Users And Computers   System administrators can choose this option to ensure that an application is no longer available to users who are affected by the GPO. When this option is selected, the program will be uninstalled automatically from users and/or computers that have the package. This option might be useful, for example, if the license for a certain application has expired or if a program is no longer on the approved applications list.

Allow Users To Continue To Use The Software, But Prevent New Installations This option prevents users from making new installations of a package, but it does not remove the software if it has already been installed for users. This is a good option if the company has run out of additional licenses for the software but the existing licenses are still valid.

If you no longer require the ability to install or repair an application, you can delete it from your software distribution share point by deleting the appropriate Windows Installer package files. This will free up additional disk space for newer applications.

Microsoft Windows Installer Settings

Several options influence the behavior of the Windows Installer; you can set them within a GPO. You can access these options by navigating to User Configuration ➤ Administrative Templates ➤ Windows Components ➤ Windows Installer.

The options are as follows:

Always Install With Elevated Privileges This policy allows users to install applications that require elevated privileges. For example, if a user does not have the permissions necessary to modify the Registry but the installation program must make Registry changes, this policy will allow the process to succeed.

Prevent Removable Media Source For Any Install This option disallows the installation of software using removable media (such as a CD-ROM or DVD-ROM). It is useful for ensuring that users install only approved applications.

Prohibit Rollback When this option is enabled, the Windows Installer does not store the system state information that is required to roll back the installation of an application. System administrators may choose this option to reduce the amount of temporary disk space required during installation and to increase the performance of the installation operation. However, the drawback is that the system cannot roll back to its original state if the installation fails and the application needs to be removed.

Specify The Order In Which Windows Installer Searches This setting specifies the order in which the Windows Installer will search for installation files. The options include *n* (for network shares), *m* (for searching removal media), and *u* (for searching the Internet for installation files).

With these options, system administrators can control how the Windows Installer operates for specific users who are affected by the GPO.

Troubleshooting Group Policies

Because of the wide variety of configurations that are possible when you are establishing GPOs, you should be aware of some common troubleshooting methods. These methods will help isolate problems in policy settings or GPO links.

One possible problem with GPO configuration is that logons and system startups may take a long time. This occurs especially in large environments when the Group Policy settings must be transmitted over the network and, in many cases, slow WAN links. In general, the number of GPOs should be limited because of the processing overhead and network requirements during logon. By default, GPOs are processed in a synchronous manner. This means that the processing of one GPO must be completed before another one is applied (as opposed to asynchronous processing, where they can all execute at the same time).

When a group policy gets processed on a Windows-based operating system, client-side extensions are the mechanisms that interpret the stored policy and then make the appropriate changes to the operating system environment. When an administrator is troubleshooting a given extension's application of policy, the administrator can view the configuration parameters for that extension in the operating system's Registry. To view the extension in the Registry, you would view the following key:

```
HKEY_LOCAL_MACHINE\Software\Microsoft\Windows \CurrentVersion\Group Policy
```

The most common issue associated with Group Policy is the unexpected setting of Group Policy options. In Windows Server 2000, administrators spent countless hours analyzing inheritance hierarchy and individual settings to determine why a particular user or computer was having policy problems. For instance, say a user named wpanek complains that the Run option is missing from his Start menu. The wpanek user account is stored in the New Hampshire OU, and you've applied group policies at the OU, domain, and site levels. To determine the source of the problem, you would have to sift through each GPO manually to find the Start menu policy as well as to figure out the applicable inheritance settings.

Windows Server 2016 has a handy feature called *Resultant Set of Policy (RSoP)* that displays the exact settings that actually apply to individual users, computers, OUs, domains, and sites after inheritance and filtering have taken effect. In the example just described, you could run RSoP on the wpanek account and view a single set of Group Policy settings that represent the settings that apply to that account. In addition, each setting's Properties dialog box displays the GPO from which the setting is derived as well as the order of priority, the filter status, and other useful information, as you will see a bit later.

RSoP actually runs in two modes:

Logging Mode   *Logging mode* displays the actual settings that apply to users and computers, as shown in the example in the preceding paragraph.

Planning Mode   *Planning mode* can be applied to users, computers, OUs, domains, and sites, and you use it before you apply any settings. As its name implies, planning mode is used to plan GPOs.

Additionally, you can run the command-line utility gpresult.exe to get a quick snapshot of the Group Policy settings that apply to a user and/or computer. Let's take a closer look at the two modes and the gpresult.exe command.

RSoP in Logging Mode

RSoP in logging mode can query policy settings only for users and computers. The easiest way to access RSoP in logging mode is through the Active Directory Users and Computers tool, although you can run it as a stand-alone MMC snap-in if you want.

To analyze the policy settings for wpanek from the earlier example, you would right-click the user icon in Active Directory Users and Computers and select All Tasks ➢ Resultant Set of Policy (Logging). The Group Policy Results Wizard appears. The wizard walks you through the steps necessary to view the RSoP for wpanek.

The Computer Selection page, shown in Figure 21.14, requires you to select a computer for which to display settings. Remember that a GPO contains both user and computer settings, so you must choose a computer to which the user is logged on in order to continue with the wizard. If the user has never logged on to a computer, then you must run RSoP in planning mode because there is no logged policy information yet for that user.

FIGURE 21.14   The Computer Selection page of the Group Policy Results Wizard

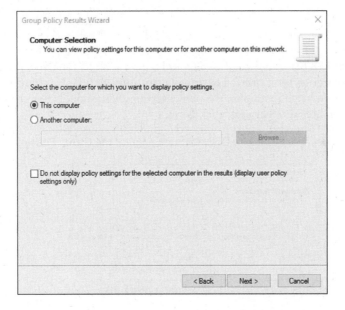

The User Selection page, shown in Figure 21.15, requires you to select a user account to analyze. Because I selected a user from the Active Directory Users and Computers tool, the username is filled in automatically. This page is most useful if you are running RSoP in MMC mode and don't have the luxury of selecting a user contextually.

FIGURE 21.15 The User Selection page of the Group Policy Results Wizard

The Summary Of Selections page, shown in Figure 21.16, summarizes your choices and provides an option for gathering extended error information. If you need to make any changes before you begin to analyze the policy settings, you should click the Back button on the Summary screen. Otherwise, click Next.

FIGURE 21.16 The Summary Of Selections page of the Group Policy Results Wizard

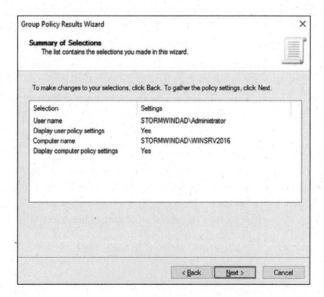

After the wizard completes, you will see the window shown in Figure 21.17. This window displays only the policy settings that apply to the user and computer that you selected in the wizard. You can see these users and computers at the topmost level of the tree.

FIGURE 21.17   The User Selection page for the administrator on computer WinSRV2016

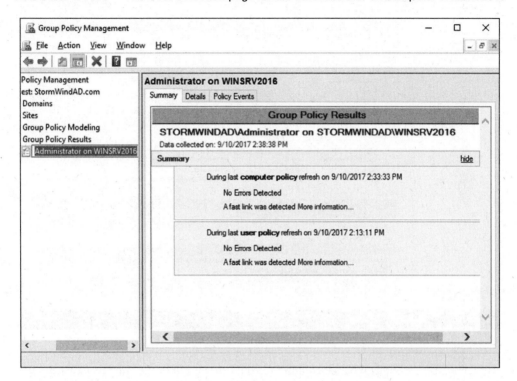

Any warnings or errors appear as a yellow triangle or red X over the applicable icon at the level where the warning or error occurred. To view more information about the warning or error, right-click the icon and select Properties.

You cannot make changes to any of the individual settings because RSoP is a diagnostic tool and not an editor, but you can get more information about settings by clicking a setting and selecting Properties from the context menu.

The Details tab of the user's Properties window, shown in Figure 21.18, displays the actual setting that applies to the user in question based on GPO inheritance.

RSoP in Planning Mode

Running RSoP in planning mode isn't much different from running RSoP in logging mode, but the RSoP Wizard asks for a bit more information than you saw earlier.

FIGURE 21.18 The Details tab of the object's Properties window

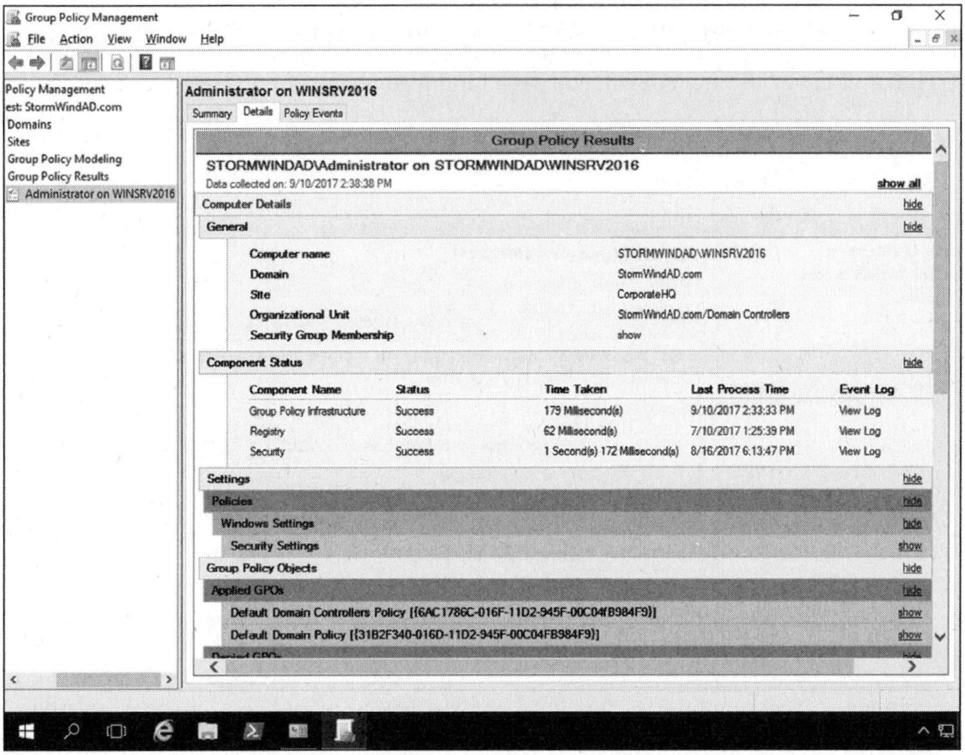

In the former example, wpanek couldn't see the Run option in the Start menu because his user account is affected by the New Hampshire GPO in the San Jose OU. As an administrator, you could plan to move his user account to the North America OU. Before doing so, you could verify his new policy settings by running RSoP in planning mode. Run the RSoP on the user wpanek under the scenario that you've already moved him from the San Jose OU to the North America OU. At this point, you haven't actually moved the user, but you can see what his settings would be if you did.

Using the *gpresult.exe* Command

The command-line utility gpresult.exe is included as part of the RSoP tool. Running the command by itself without any switches returns the following Group Policy information about the local user and computer:

- The name of the domain controller from which the local machine retrieved the policy information

- The date and time at which the policies were applied

- Which policies were applied
- Which policies were filtered out
- Group membership

You can use the switches shown in Table 21.3 to get information for remote users and computers and to enable other options.

TABLE 21.3 gpresult switches

Switch	Description
/S *systemname*	Generates RSoP information for a remote computer name.
/USER *username*	Generates RSoP information for a remote username.
/x /h filename	Generates a report in either XML (/x) or HTML (/h) format. The filename and location is specified by the *filename* parameter.
/V	Specifies verbose mode, which displays more verbose information such as user rights information.
/Z	Specifies an even greater level of verbose information.
/SCOPE MACHINE	Displays maximum information about the computer policies applied to this system.
/SCOPE USER	Displays maximum information about the user policies applied to this system.
>*textfile.txt*	Writes the output to a text file.

Table 21.3 is not a complete list. To see a complete list of the gpresult.exe command, visit Microsoft at www.microsoft.com.

For example, to obtain information about user wpanek in a system called WILLPANEK, you would use the command gpresult/S WILLPANEK/USERwpanek.

Through the use of these techniques, you should be able to track down even the most elusive Group Policy problems. Remember, however, that good troubleshooting skills do not replace planning adequately and maintaining GPO settings!

Using the Group Policy Infrastructure Status Dashboard

In Windows Server 2016, the Group Policy Management MMC also allows you to see the Active Directory Domain Services Infrastructure status. To see the Group Policy Infrastructure Status Dashboard, open the Group Policy Management Console. Click on a GPO and then click the Status Tab. You would then click the Detect Now button to see the Infrastructure Dashboard (see Figure 21.19).

FIGURE 21.19   The Infrastructure Dashboard

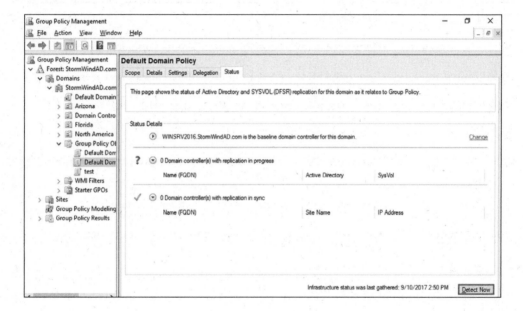

Summary

In this chapter, you examined Active Directory's solution to a common headache for many systems administrators: policy settings. Specifically, I discussed topics that covered Group Policy.

I covered the fundamentals of Group Policy including its fundamental purpose. You can use Group Policy to enforce granular permissions for users in an Active Directory environment. Group policies can restrict and modify the actions allowed for users and computers within the Active Directory environment.

Certain Group Policy settings may apply to users, computers, or both. Computer settings affect all users who access the machines to which the policy applies. User settings affect users regardless of the machines to which they log on.

You learned that you can link Group Policy Objects to Active Directory sites, domains, or OUs. This link determines to which objects the policies apply. GPO links can interact through inheritance and filtering to result in an effective set of policies.

The chapter covered inheritance and how GPOs filter down. I showed you how to use the Enforced option on a GPO issued from a parent and how to block a GPO from a child.

You can also use administrative templates to simplify the creation of GPOs. There are some basic default templates that come with Windows Server 2016.

In addition, administrators can delegate control over GPOs in order to distribute administrative responsibilities. Delegation is an important concept because it allows for distributed administration.

You can also deploy software using GPOs. This feature can save time and increase productivity throughout the entire software management life cycle by automating software installation and removal on client computers. The Windows Installer offers a more robust method for managing installation and removal, and applications that support it can take advantage of new Active Directory features. Make sure you are comfortable using the Windows Installer.

You learned about publishing applications via Active Directory and the difference between publishing and assigning applications. You can assign some applications to users and computers so that they are always available. You can also publish them to users so that the user can install them with minimal effort when required.

You also learned how to prepare for software deployment. Before your users can take advantage of automated software installation, you must set up an installation share and provide the appropriate permissions.

The final portion of the chapter covered the Resultant Set of Policy (RSoP) tool, which you can use in logging mode or planning mode to determine exactly which set of policies applies to users, computers, OUs, domains, and sites.

Exam Essentials

Understand the purpose of Group Policy.   System administrators use Group Policy to enforce granular permissions for users in an Active Directory environment.

Understand user and computer settings.   Certain Group Policy settings may apply to users, computers, or both. Computer settings affect all users that access the machines to which the policy applies. User settings affect users, regardless of which machines they log on to.

Know the interactions between Group Policy Objects and Active Directory.   GPOs can be linked to Active Directory objects. This link determines to which objects the policies apply.

Understand filtering and inheritance interactions between GPOs.   For ease of administration, GPOs can interact via inheritance and filtering. It is important to understand these interactions when you are implementing and troubleshooting Group Policy.

Know how Group Policy settings can affect script policies and network settings. You can use special sets of GPOs to manage network configuration settings.

Understand how delegation of administration can be used in an Active Directory environment. Delegation is an important concept because it allows for distributed administration.

Know how to use the Resultant Set of Policy (RSoP) tool to troubleshoot and plan Group Policy. Windows Server 2016 includes the RSoP feature, which you can run in logging mode or planning mode to determine exactly which set of policies applies to users, computers, OUs, domains, and sites.

Identify common problems with the software life cycle. IT professionals face many challenges with client applications, including development, deployment, maintenance, and troubleshooting.

Understand the benefits of the Windows Installer. Using the Windows Installer is an updated way to install applications on Windows-based machines. It offers a more robust method for making the system changes required by applications, and it allows for a cleaner uninstall. Windows Installer–based applications can also take advantage of new Active Directory features.

Understand the difference between publishing and assigning applications. Some applications can be assigned to users and computers so that they are always available. Applications can be published to users so that the user may install the application with a minimal amount of effort when it is required.

Know how to prepare for software deployment. Before your users can take advantage of automated software installation, you must set up an installation share and provide the appropriate permissions.

Know how to configure application settings using Active Directory and Group Policy. Using standard Windows Server 2016 administrative tools, you can create an application policy that meets your requirements. You can use automatic, on-demand installation of applications as well as many other features.

Create application categories to simplify the list of published applications. It's important to group applications by functionality or the users to whom they apply, especially in organizations that support a large number of programs.

Review Questions

You can find the answers in the Appendix.

1. The process of assigning permissions to set Group Policy for objects within an OU is known as _____.

    A. Promotion

    B. Inheritance

    C. Delegation

    D. Filtering

2. Which of the following statements is true regarding the actions that occur when a software package is removed from a GPO that is linked to an OU?

    A. The application will be automatically uninstalled for all users within the OU.

    B. Current application installations will be unaffected by the change.

    C. The system administrator may determine the effect.

    D. The current user may determine the effect.

3. You are the network administrator for your organization. You are working on creating a new GPO for the sales OU. You want the GPO to take effect immediately. Which command would you use?

    A. GPForce

    B. GPUpdate

    C. GPResult

    D. GPExecute

4. You are the network administrator for your organization. You are working on creating a new GPO for the Marketing OU. You want the GPO to take effect immediately, and you need to use Windows PowerShell. Which PowerShell cmdlet command would you use?

    A. Invoke-GPUpdate

    B. Invoke-GPForce

    C. Invoke-GPResult

    D. Invoke-GPExecute

5. You are the network administrator, and you have decided to set up a GPO with item-level targeting. Which of the following is *not* an option for item-level targeting?

    A. Battery Present Targeting

    B. Computer Name Targeting

    C. CPU Speed Targeting

    D. DVD Present Targeting

6. You are the network administrator for a large organization that uses Windows Server 2012 R2 domain controllers and DNS servers. All of your client machines currently have the Windows XP operating system. You want to be able to have client computers edit the domain-based GPOs by using the ADMX files that are located in the ADMX Central Store. How do you accomplish this task? (Choose all that apply.)

   A. Upgrade your clients to Windows 8.

   B. Upgrade your clients to Windows 7.

   C. Add the client machines to the ADMX edit utility.

   D. In the ADMX store, choose the box Allow All Client Privileges.

7. You work for an organization with a single Windows Server 2016 Active Directory domain. The domain has OUs for Sales, Marketing, Admin, R&D, and Finance. You need the users in the Finance OU only to get Microsoft Office 2016 installed automatically onto their computers. You create a GPO named OfficeApp. What is the next step in getting all of the Finance users Office 2016?

   A. Edit the GPO, and assign the Office application to the user's account. Link the GPO to the Finance OU.

   B. Edit the GPO, and assign the Office application to the user's account. Link the GPO to the domain.

   C. Edit the GPO, and assign the Office application to the computer account. Link the GPO to the domain.

   D. Edit the GPO, and assign the Office application to the computer account. Link the GPO to the Finance OU.

8. You are hired as a consultant to the ABC Company. The owner of the company complains that she continues to have desktop wallpaper that she did not choose. When you speak with the IT team, you find out that a former employee created 20 GPOs and they have not been able to figure out which GPO is changing the owner's desktop wallpaper. How can you resolve this issue?

   A. Run the RSoP utility against all forest computer accounts.

   B. Run the RSoP utility against the owner's computer account.

   C. Run the RSoP utility against the owner's user account.

   D. Run the RSoP utility against all domain computer accounts.

9. You are the network administrator for a large organization that has multiple sites and multiple OUs. You have a site named SalesSite that is for the sales building across the street. In the domain, there is an OU for all salespeople called Sales. You set up a GPO for the SalesSite, and you need to be sure that it applies to the Sales OU. The Sales OU GPOs cannot override the SalesSite GPO. What do you do?

   A. On the GPO, disable the Block Child Inheritance setting.

   B. On the GPO, set the Enforce setting.

   C. On the GPO, set the priorities to 1.

   D. On the Sales OU, set the Inherit Parent Policy settings.

10. You are the administrator for an organization that has multiple locations. You are running Windows Server 2012 R2, and you have only one domain with multiple OUs set up for each location. One of your locations, Boston, is connected to the main location by a 256 Kbps ISDN line. You configure a GPO to assign a sales application to all computers in the entire domain. You have to be sure that Boston users receive the GPO properly. What should you do?

   A. Disable the Slow Link Detection setting in the GPO.

   B. Link the GPO to the Boston OU.

   C. Change the properties of the GPO to publish the application to the Boston OU.

   D. Have the users in Boston run the `GPResult/force` command.

Chapter

22

Understanding Certificates

THE FOLLOWING 70-742 EXAM OBJECTIVES ARE COVERED IN THIS CHAPTER:

✓ **Install and configure AD CS**

    ▪ This objective may include but is not limited to: Install Active Directory Integrated Enterprise Certificate Authority (CA); install offline root and subordinate CAs; install standalone CAs; configure Certificate Revocation List (CRL) distribution points; install and configure Online Responder; implement administrative role separation; configure CA backup and recovery.

✓ **Manage certificates**

    ▪ This objective may include but is not limited to: Manage certificate templates; implement and manage certificate deployment, validation, and revocation; manage certificate renewal; manage certificate enrollment and renewal for computers and users using Group Policies; configure and manage key archival and recovery.

In this chapter, I will discuss certificate services and the importance of securing the corporate *public key infrastructure (PKI)* environment. The Windows 2016 PKI implementation resides in Active Directory Certificate Services (AD CS). PKI is the collection of technology, protocols, services, standards, and policies that control the issuing and management of public and private keys using digital certificates, which are the core of PKI. Encryption is used to protect data messages. While certificates provide a certain level of security, they are still vulnerable.

Features of Windows Server 2016 Certificate Services

Active Directory Certificate Services is a server role included in Windows Server 2016. AD CS allows administrators to customize, issue, and manage public key certificates. AD CS issues digital certificates for authentication, encryption and decryption, and signing.

The following are just some of the features regarding Active Directory Certificate Services (AD CS) in Windows Server 2016:

Server Core and Minimal Server Interface Support   You can install and deploy any of the six AD CS role services to any version of Windows Server 2016, including Server Core and Minimal Server Interface. The Minimal Server Interface looks and feels like a Server Core installation with most of the GUI management utilities intact. Windows Server 2016 Minimal Server Interface reduces the attack surface and lowers the footprint by removing components such as File Explorer and Internet Explorer and their supporting libraries.

Site-Aware Certificate Enrollment   Windows 8/8.1/10 and Windows Server 2016 computers default to using certificate authorities within their sites when requesting certificates. However, you must configure site information on the certificate authorities' objects within Active Directory for the site-awareness feature to be worthwhile. Once configured, computers running Windows 8/8.1/10 and Windows Server 2016 request certificates from a certificate authority running in the same site as the computer.

Automatic Certificate Renewal for Non-Domain-Joined Computers   Certificate Enrollment Web Services (CES) allows non-domain-joined computers and computers not directly connected to the corporate network to request and retrieve certificates.

AD CS in Windows Server 2016 includes the ability for these clients to renew certificates automatically for non-domain-joined computers.

Enforcement of Certificate Renewal with the Same Key   In earlier versions of Windows, clients that received certificates from templates that were configured for renewal with the same key had to renew their certificates using the same key, or renewal would fail.

With Windows 8/8.1/10 or Windows Server 2016, you can continue this behavior, or you can configure certificate templates to give higher priority to Trusted Platform Module (TPM)–based KSPs for generating keys. Moreover, using renewal with the same key, administrators can rest assured that the key remains on TPM after renewal.

This feature allows you to enforce renewal with the same key, which can reduce administrative costs (when keys are renewed automatically) and increase key security (when keys are stored using TPM-based KSPs).

Internationalized Domain Names (IDNs)   International languages often contain characters that cannot be represented using ASCII encoding, which limits the function of these languages when enrolling for a certificate. Windows Server 2016 now includes support for international domain names.

Default Security Increased on the Certificate Authority Role Service   Certificate authorities running on Windows Server 2016 include increased RPC (Remote Procedure Call) security. Increased RPC security on the CA requires that all clients must encrypt the RPC communication between themselves and the CA when requesting certificates.

Active Directory Certificate Services Roles

The Active Directory Certificate Services role provides six role services to issue and manage public key certificates in an enterprise environment. These roles are listed in Table 22.1 and described in the following sections.

TABLE 22.1   AD CS roles

Role Service	Description
Certificate Authority (CA)	The CA service includes root and subordinate CAs for issuing certificates to users, computers, and services. This role service also manages certificate validity.
Web Enrollment	This is a web-based interface to enable users to enroll, request, and retrieve certificates as well as retrieve certificate revocation lists from a CA using a web browser.
Online Responder	The Online Responder service retrieves revocation status requests for specific certificates and the status of these certificates, and it returns a signed response with the requested certificate status information.

TABLE 22.1 AD CS roles *(continued)*

Role Service	Description
Network Device Enrollment Service (NDES)	NDES enables routers and other non-domain-joined network devices to acquire certificates.
Certificate Enrollment Policy Web Server (CEP)	CEP enables users and computers to inquire about certificate enrollment policy information.
Certificate Enrollment Web Services (CES)	CES enables users and computers to enroll for certificates with the HTTPS protocol. CEP and CES can be used together to support certificate enrollment for non-domain-joined computers and computers not directly connected to the corporate network.

Planning the Certificate Authority Hierarchy

A *certification authority (CA)* is a trusted server designed to grant certificates to individuals, computers, or organizations to certify the identity and other attributes of the certificate subject.

A CA receives a certificate request, verifies the requester's identity data according to the policy of the CA, and uses its private key to apply its digital signature to the certificate. The CA issues the certificate to the subject of the certificate as a security credential within a PKI environment. A CA is also responsible for revoking certificates and publishing a *certificate revocation list (CRL)*.

A CA can be a third-party issuer, such as VeriSign, or you can create your own CA by installing Active Directory Certificate Services. Every CA also has a certificate confirming its identity, issued by another trusted CA or root CAs.

Cryptography

The Cryptography options for a certificate authority provide increased deployment flexibility to those with a more advanced understanding of cryptography. You can implement cryptographic options by using cryptographic service providers (CSPs) or key storage providers (KSPs).

CSPs are hardware and software components of Windows operating systems that provide generic cryptographic functions. CSPs can provide a variety of encryption and signature algorithms. Key storage providers can provide strong key protection on computers running Windows Server 2012/2016, Windows Server 2008/2008 R2, Windows Vista, Windows 7, Windows 8/8.1 or Windows 10. Figure 22.1 shows some of the Cryptography options in the AD CS installation.

FIGURE 22.1   Cryptography for CA screen

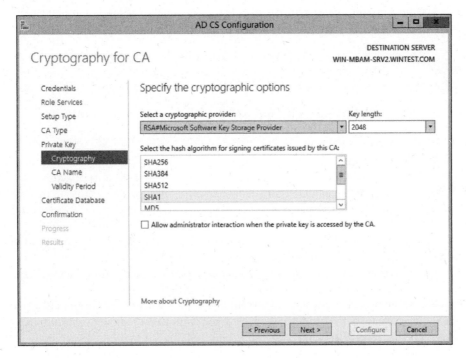

Here are the options:

Select a Cryptographic Provider   Windows Server 2016 provides many CSPs and KSPs, and you can install additional CSPs or KSPs provided by third parties. In Windows Server 2016, the algorithm name is listed in the provider list. All providers with a number sign (#) in the name are cryptography next-generation (CNG) providers. CNG providers can support multiple asymmetric algorithms. CSPs implement only a single algorithm.

Key Length   Each CSP and KSP supports different character lengths for cryptographic keys. Configuring a longer key length hardens against an attack by a hacker to decrypt the key and also degrades the performance of cryptographic operations.

Select The Hash Algorithm For Signing Certificates Used By This CA   The CA uses hash algorithms to sign CA certificates and issues certificates to ensure that an external identity has not tampered with a certificate. Each CSP can support different hash algorithms.

Make sure that your applications, your devices, and all operating systems that may request certificates from this certificate authority support the selected hash algorithm.

Allow Administrator Interaction When The Private Key Is Accessed By The CA   Use this option to help secure the CA and its private key by requiring an administrator to enter a password before every cryptographic operation.

> Exercise caution with this setting because this requires user interaction each time the certificate authority accesses the private key. A certificate authority signs each issued certificate. To sign the issued certificate, the certificate authority must access the private key.

Private Key

A certificate authority uses its assigned certificate to generate and issue certificates. The certificate used by the CA includes a public key and a private key. The private key should be available only to the owner. The public key is publicly available to other entities on the network.

For example, a user's public key can be published within a certificate in a folder so that it is accessible to other people in the organization. The sender of a message can retrieve the user's certificate from Active Directory Domain Services, obtain the public key from the certificate, and then encrypt the message by using the recipient's public key.

Data encrypted with a public key can be decrypted only with the mathematically paired private key. Certificate authorities use their private key to create a digital signature in the certificate when issuing certificates.

Enterprise Certificate Authorities

Enterprise certificate authorities (CAs) publish certificates and CRLs to Active Directory. Enterprise CAs access domain data stored in Active Directory. Enterprise CAs engage certificate templates when issuing certificates. The enterprise CA uses default configuration data in the certificate template to create a certificate with the appropriate attributes for that certificate type.

If you want to enable automatic certificate approval and automatic user certificate enrollment, use enterprise CAs to issue certificates. These features are available only when the CA infrastructure is integrated with Active Directory. Additionally, only enterprise CAs can issue certificates that enable smart card logon because this process requires the CA to map the user account in Active Directory to the smart card certificates.

A *root CA*, sometimes called a *root authority*, is the most trusted CA type in an organization's PKI. The root CA is the only CA that signs its own certificate. The physical security and the certificate issuance policy of a root CA should be tightly reinforced. If the root CA is compromised or if it issues a certificate to an unauthorized identity, any certificate-based security in your organization is compromised by the exposed private key. The best practice is to deploy a second PKI tier to issue certificates from other CAs, called *subordinate CAs* (see Figure 22.2).

FIGURE 22.2   Two-tier PKI hierarchy model

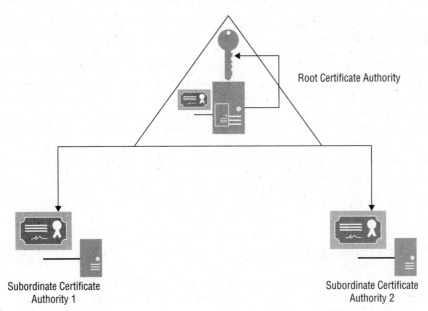

Root Certificate Authority

Subordinate Certificate
Authority 1

Subordinate Certificate
Authority 2

A *subordinate CA* is one that has received its signing certificate by a root CA, third-party CA, or stand-alone CA in your organization. Subordinate CAs normally issue certificates for specific purposes, such as secure email, SSL, Wireless 801.x security, or smart card authentication. Subordinate CAs can also issue certificates to other, more subordinate CAs. A root CA, the subordinate CAs certified by the root, and subordinate CAs certified by other subordinate CAs form a certification hierarchy.

Stand-alone certificate authorities are not integrated into Active Directory and do not support certificate templates. If you deploy stand-alone CAs, you must include all the information about the requested certificate type in the certificate request. By default, all submitted certificate requests to a stand-alone CA are placed in a pending queue, awaiting a CA administrator's approval. Stand-alone CAs can issue certificates automatically upon request, but this is not recommended because the requests are not authenticated.

Because stand-alone CAs are not Active Directory integrated, a stand-alone CA would seem like a less appropriate choice for an enterprise. However, stand-alone root CAs offer a layer of protection when a powered-down stand-alone CA is less likely to be compromised and does not have a footprint in Active Directory. More organizations are deploying *offline stand-alone root CAs* that are brought online only temporarily for re-issuing signing certificates to subordinate CAs. Some organizations permanently keep the offline stand-alone root CA disconnected from the network and distribute signing certificates only via removable media such as CDs, DVDs, or USB flash drives. Offline root CAs have the following characteristics:

- Deployed as a stand-alone root CA

- Deployed on a non-domain-joined server to avoid being offline or powered down for long periods without requiring computer password synchronizations

Real World Scenario

Protect the Offline Root CA

Best practice strongly recommends you securely store and back up the offline standalone root CA. A large Medical center implemented their offline stand-alone root CA solution by installing their root CA on a laptop. They routinely kept the laptop in the datacenter until a new administrator discovered and returned laptop to the help desk for repurposing. Needless to say, the laptop was re-imaged, and the entire PKI infrastructure was wiped out. No one was aware until the subordinate CA's certificate had expired a year later and certificates could no longer be issued. You can avoid this catastrophic scenario by securely storing and backing up the offline stand-alone CA.

Two-Tier and Three-Tier Models

It's acceptable for a single enterprise to have multiple PKIs. Multiple PKIs result in one root CA for each PKI and possibly multiple subordinate CAs that chain to their respective roots.

Organizations also may choose a third-tier CA hierarchy model, which involves adding a CA policy server. CA policy servers are designed to implement specific certificate policies that can include certificate life cycle, encryption type, key length, and some approval workflow.

Validity Period

All certificates issued by a certification authority have a validity period. The *validity period* is a time range that specifies how long PKI clients can accept the certificate as an authoritative credential based on the identity stated in the subject of the certificate. This assertion presumes the certificate is not revoked before the validity period ends and the issuing CA remains trusted. The validity period limits the time in which an issued certificate is exposed to the possibility of being compromised.

All CAs have an expiration date based on its CA certificate's validity ending period. This rule affects the CA's ability to issue certificates and not the validity period of its CA certificate. Because of this rule, organizations must plan for the renewal of every certificate issued to a CA in the certification hierarchy to ensure the existing trust chains and to extend the lifetimes of CAs.

Active Directory Certificate Services enforces a rule that a CA never issues a certificate past the expiration date of its own certificate. Because of this behavior, when a CA's certificate reaches the end of its validity period, all certificates issued by the CA will also expire. Certificates issued by the now-expired CA will not be honored as valid security credentials.

Active Directory Certificate Services allows for the maximum validity periods shown in Table 22.2, which are based on the type of certificate. You configure these validity periods using certificate templates.

TABLE 22.2 AD CS maximum validity periods

Certificate Type	Maximum Validity Period
Root certificate authority	Determined during CA deployment
Subordinate CA Internet Protocol Security Enrollment agent Domain controller	Up to five years, but never more than the root CA's or the issuing CA's validity period
All other certificates	One year, but never more than the root CA's or issuing CA's validity period

Certificate Validation

PKI trust requires a certificate to be validated for both its expiration and its overall chain of trust. When a certificate user leaves the company, you will want to make sure that no one can use that certificate for authentication and revoke the certificate. Revocation checking is one of the key components of PKI.

Certificate revocation uses certificate revocation lists. CRLs contain a list of certificates that are no longer valid, and the CRL can become large. To solve this, you can access a delta CRL that contains changes or new revocations. So when discussing CRLs, there are two main types:

Base CRLs A Base CRL is a CRL that contains all non-expired revoked certificates.

Delta CRLs A Delta CRL is a CRL that contains all non-expired certificates that have been revoked since the last base CRL was published.

CRLs are accessed through *CRL distribution points (CDPs)*, which are part of a CA role in Windows Server 2016. HTTP, FTP, LDAP, or file-based addresses may be used as URLs. Only newly issued certificates will recognize new changes in the CRL URL; old certificates will use the old URL for revocation list operations.

When setting up the CRL, you can set a time interval for how often the servers check the CRL. This is referred to as the CRL publication interval or Delta CRL publication interval. So if you want to have your certificate servers check the CRL more or less frequently, set the publication interval.

Online Responders

When a new certificate is issued, the computer queries the issuing CA to find out whether the certificate has been revoked. Traditionally, certificate revocation checking can be done by retrieving certificate revocation lists that are published in Lightweight Directory Access Protocol (LDAP) or Hypertext Transfer Protocol (HTTP) or by using a newer HTTP method named the Online Certificate Status Protocol (OCSP).

OCSP is a lightweight HTTP protocol that responds faster and more efficiently than downloading a traditional CRL. An *online responder* is a trusted server that receives and responds to individual client requests for the status of a certificate. An OCSP responder retrieves CRLs and provides digitally signed real-time certificate revocation status responses to clients based on a given certificate authority's CRL. The amount of data retrieved per request remains constant regardless of the number of revoked certificates.

Online responders process certificate status requests more efficiently than direct access to CRLs in several scenarios (http://technet.microsoft.com/en-us/library/cc725958.aspx):

- When clients have slow VPN connections or do not have the high-speed connections required to download large CRLs

- When network utilization peaks because revocation-checking activity is high, such as when large numbers of users log on or send signed email simultaneously

- When revocation data for certificates is needed from a non-Microsoft certification authority

- When revocation data is needed to verify individual certificate status requests rather than all revoked or suspended certificates

Installing AD CS

Server Manager provides a graphical user interface to install Active Directory Certificate Services on local and remote computers running Windows Server 2016. The Remote Server Administration Tools for Windows Server 2016 also includes Server Manager, which allows you to run Server Manager on a computer running Windows 8/8.1. In Exercise 22.1, you'll install an AD CS role on the local computer using Server Manager.

EXERCISE 22.1

Installing AD CS Through Server Manager

1. Start Server Manager.

2. Click Manage and click Add Roles And Features.

3. The Add Roles And Features Wizard shows the Before You Begin screen. Click Next.

4. Click Role-Based Or Feature-Based Installation on the Select Installation Type screen. Click Next.

5. Click the server on which you want to install Active Directory Certificate Services from the Server Pool list on the Select Destination Server screen. Click Next.

6. Select the Active Directory Certificate Services check box on the Select Server Roles screen.

   Server Manager prompts you to add more features associated with this role, such as management tools. Leave the default selections. Click Add Features to close the dialog. Click Next on the Select Server Roles screen.

7. Click Next on the Select Features screen.

8. Server Manager displays the Active Directory Certificate Services screen. This screen provides a simple role introduction and noteworthy information, such as that the name of the certificate authority cannot be changed. Click Next.

9. From the Select Role Services screen, select the check boxes next to the AD CS role services you want to install on the computer. Click Next.

10. Read the Confirm Installation Selections screen. This screen provides a list of roles, role services, and features that the current installation prepares on the computer. Click Install to start the installation.

Installation Using Windows PowerShell

A major benefit gained from basing Windows Server 2016's Server Manager on Windows PowerShell is consistency of installation. Server Manager relies on its Windows PowerShell foundation as the underlying engine responsible for installing any of the Active Directory Certificate Services role services. However, you cannot use Server Manager to install roles and features on a Windows Server 2016 core installation.

The Server Manager module for Windows PowerShell provides cmdlets to install, view, and remove features and roles included in Windows Server 2016. You can use these cmdlets on any installation of Windows Server 2016 because it provides Windows PowerShell in all installation types. Also, these cmdlets can install, view, and uninstall Active Directory Certificate Services role services from remote computers running Windows Server 2016.

To view the installation state of Active Directory Certificate Services using Windows PowerShell, follow these steps:

1. Open an elevated Windows PowerShell console. (On Server Core installations, type **PowerShell** in the command console.)

2. In the Windows PowerShell console, type the following command and press Enter:

```
Get-WindowsFeature *adcs-cert*
```

The Windows PowerShell cmdlet outputs three columns of information: Display Name, Name, and Install State. The Display Name column is a user-friendly name that describes the feature or service role's use. The Name column represents the name of the component. You use this name with the `Install-WindowsFeature` and `Remove-WindowsFeature` cmdlets. Use the Install State column to determine the installation state of the role or service role.

Typically, the Install State column shows one of three install states: Removed, Available, and Installed. The Removed install state designates that its associated role or feature is not included in the current installation of Windows. You cannot install the associated role or feature without the installation media or Internet connectivity to Windows Update if the feature or role is removed. The Available installation state indicates that the role or feature is staged in the current installation of Windows; however, it is currently not installed. The Installed installation state indicates that the role or feature is installed on the current installation of the computer and is ready, or it has been deployed or configured.

The Active Directory Certificate Services entry from the cmdlet's output represents the parent role. Six child role services appear underneath the parent role. A lowercase *x* appears between the opening and closing square brackets in the parent role if any of the six child role services are installed. The cmdlet also places a lowercase *x* between the opening and closing square brackets for any installed child role service. You should interpret entries without a lowercase *x* between the opening and closing square brackets as not installed. Check the install state to determine whether the role or role service is staged on your installation of Windows.

To install Active Directory Certificate Services using Windows PowerShell, follow these steps:

1. Open an elevated Windows PowerShell console.

2. Use the `Get-WindowsFeature` cmdlet to ensure that the Active Directory Certificate Services role's installation state is Available.

3. In the Windows PowerShell console, type the following command and press Enter:

   ```
   Install-WindowsFeature adcs-cert-authority -IncludeManagementTools
   ```

4. Use the `Get-WindowsFeature` cmdlet to verify the installation.

The preceding command instructs the Server Manager module of Windows PowerShell to take the staged binaries for the Certificate Authority role service and install them to the current computer.

 It's important to remember the `-IncludeManagementTools` argument when installing a feature using Windows PowerShell. The Server Manager module for Windows PowerShell does not install a feature or role management tool by default. The `Install-WindowsFeature` cmdlet does not install the role management tool without this argument. The Server Manager GUI automatically selects installing the role management tool for you, and it gives you a choice of not to install it before completing the installation.

You can install any of the other child role services using the `Install-WindowsFeature` cmdlet simply by replacing the `adcs-cert-authority` argument with the associated name of the child role service. The following example installs the Active Directory Certificate Services Web Enrollment role service:

```
Install-WindowsFeature adcs-web-enrollment -IncludeManagementTools
```

 The role and feature installation experience is consistent on Windows Server 2016 using the Server Manager module for Windows PowerShell. You can use the same syntax to install a feature or role listed using `Get-WindowsFeature`.

Configuring Active Directory Certificate Services

You begin the Active Directory Certificate Services deployment by starting the AD CS Configuration Wizard (Exercise 22.2). To start the wizard, click the Configure Active Directory Certificate Services On The Destination Server link shown in the Action Flag dialog. The wizard shows the current destination for the role deployment in the Destination Server portion of the screen.

EXERCISE 22.2

Configuring AD CS Through Server Manager

1. After the AD CS installation is successful, click the Configure Active Directory Certificate Services On The Destination Server link.

2. The Credentials screen of the AD CS Configuration Wizard displays the required credentials to perform specific AD CS role services deployment. The wizard shows your current credentials in the Credentials portion of the screen. Click Change if your current credentials do not match the credentials needed for the current role service deployment. Otherwise, continue by clicking Next.

3. Select the check boxes for the Certification Authority and Online Responder role services.

4. The Setup Type screen of the AD CS Configuration Wizard shows the two types of certificate authorities you can configure with Active Directory Certificate Services: enterprise or stand-alone. An enterprise certificate authority must run on domain-joined computers and typically remains online to issue certificates or certificate policies. Select Enterprise and click Next.

5. In the Setup Type dialog box, select Enterprise CA and click Next.

6. In the CA Type dialog box, click Root CA and click Next.

EXERCISE 22.2 *(continued)*

7. In the Private Key dialog box, verify that Create A New Private Key is selected and click Next.

8. Select the RSA# Microsoft Software Key Storage Provider.

9. Windows Server 2012 includes a number of CSPs and KSPs, and you can install additional CSPs or KSPs provided by third parties. In Windows Server 2016, the provider list includes the name of the algorithm. All providers with a number sign (#) in the name are CNG providers. CNG providers can support multiple asymmetric algorithms. CSPs implement only a single algorithm.

10. Select a key length of 2048.

11. Each CSP and KSP supports different character lengths for cryptographic keys. Configuring a longer key length can enhance security by making it more difficult for a hacker or disgruntled employee to decrypt the key, but it can also slow down the performance of cryptographic operations.

12. Select the SHA1 hash algorithm and click Next.

13. Enter a name for the root CA server and click Next.

14. In the Certificate Request dialog box, verify that Save A Certificate Request To File On The Target Machine is selected and click Next.

15. In the CA Database dialog box, verify the location for the log files in the Certificate Database Log Location box and click Next.

16. In the Confirmation dialog box, click Configure.

17. In the Results dialog box, click Close.

The CA uses hash algorithms to sign CA certificates and issues certificates to ensure that an external identity has not tampered with a certificate. Each CSP can support different hash algorithms. Make sure your applications, devices, and all operating systems that may request certificates from this certificate authority support the selected hash algorithm.

Use the Create A New Private Key option when creating or reinstalling a certificate authority.

Certificate Authority Name

Names for CAs cannot exceed 64 characters in length. You can create a name by using any Unicode character, but you might want the ANSI character set if interoperability is a concern.

In Active Directory Domain Services (AD DS), the name you specify when you configure a server as a CA (Figure 22.3) becomes the common name of the CA, and this name is reflected in every certificate the CA issues. Because of this behavior, it is important that you do not use the fully qualified domain name (FQDN) for the common name of the CA. Hackers can acquire a copy of a certificate and use the FQDN of the CA to compromise security.

FIGURE 22.3   Specifying the name of the CA

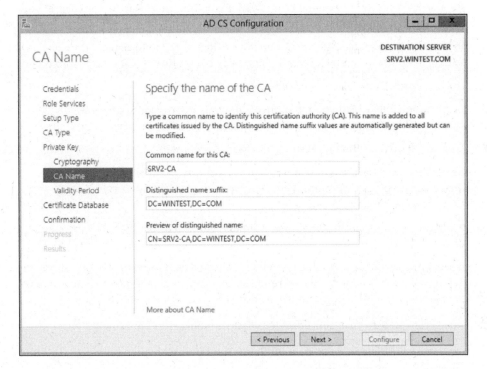

The CA name does not have to be the computer's name. Changing the name after installing Active Directory Certificate Services (AD CS) will invalidate every certificate issued by the CA.

Group Policy Certificate Auto-Enrollment

Many certificates can be distributed without the client interaction. These can include most types of certificates issued to computers and services as well as many certificates issued to users.

To enroll clients automatically for certificates in a domain environment, you must do the following:

- Configure a certificate template with auto-enroll permissions
- Configure an auto-enrollment policy for the domain

Membership in Domain Admins or Enterprise Admins, or equivalent, is the minimum required to complete this procedure. In Exercise 22.3 we are going to configure a group policy to support the auto-enrollment feature.

EXERCISE 22.3

Configure an Auto-Enrollment Group Policy for a Domain

1. On a domain controller running Windows Server 2016, click Start ≻ Administrative Tools ≻ Group Policy Management.

2. In the console tree, double-click Group Policy Objects in the forest and domain containing the Default Domain Policy Group Policy Object (GPO) that you want to edit.

3. Right-click the Default Domain Policy GPO and click Edit.

4. In the Group Policy Management Console (GPMC), go to User Configuration ≻ Windows Settings ≻ Security Settings and click Public Key Policies.

5. Double-click Certificate Services Client – Auto-Enrollment.

6. Select the Enroll Certificates Automatically check box to enable auto-enrollment. If you want to block auto-enrollment from occurring, select the Do Not Enroll Certificates Automatically check box.

7. If you are enabling certificate auto-enrollment, you can select the following check boxes:

"Renew expired certificates, update pending certificates, and remove revoked certificates enables auto-enrollment for certificate renewal, issuance of pending certificate requests, and the automatic removal of revoked certificates from a user's certificate store."

"Update certificates that use certificate templates enables auto-enrollment for issuance of certificates that supersede issued certificates."

8. Click OK to accept your changes.

Key-Based Renewal for Non-Domain-Joined Computers

Windows Server 2016 combines automatic certificate renewal with AD CS Certificate Enrollment Web Services to enable non-domain-joined computers to renew their certificates automatically before they expire like Internet-facing web servers.

Many organizations and service providers maintain servers that require SSL certificates. These servers are not typically joined to the same domain as an issuing certificate authority, and they do not have identity records or accounts in the organization's Active Directory. This means they cannot benefit from today's automatic certificate renewal, which is based on secured certificate templates in Active Directory. As a result, these organizations manage and renew SSL certificates manually, a time-intensive and error-prone process. Neglecting to renew a single SSL certificate can cause a massive and costly system outage.

Currently, Certificate Enrollment Web Services supports three types of server-side authentication modes:

- Windows integrated (Kerberos)
- Certificate-based
- Username and password

These authentication mode options, however, are not viable choices when the client is not joined to a domain and the enterprise certificate authority makes authorization decisions using templates that are based on the Active Directory group membership of the requestor.

Consider the following authentication options for automatic renewal:

Windows Integrated This authentication option is not suitable for auto renewal because the two domains to which the certificate authority and the requesting server belong do not have a trust relationship between them or the requesting server is not joined to any domain.

Certificate-Based The initially enrolled server certificate is not suitable for authentication because it contains no identity information within it that can be mapped to a directory account object.

Username And Password Usernames and passwords can be cached within the system's identity vault and used for authentication to the enrollment server. However, passwords usually have shorter lifetimes than server SSL certificates. (Both default and recommended settings for passwords are shorter than the default and recommended certificate lifetime.) Thus, by the time renewal happens, the password will likely have changed.

Anonymous This authentication option is not suitable since MS CEP and CES do not support this option, making automatic renewal impossible for these targeted server systems.

Enforcement of Certificate Renewal with Same Key

Windows 8/8.1/10 and Windows Server 2016 provide an efficient mechanism to increase the security of renewing hardware-based certificates. This is accomplished by enforcing the certificate renewal to occur for the same key. This guarantees the same assurance level for the key throughout its life cycle. Additionally, Windows Server 2016's Certificate Template Management Console supports CSP/KSP ordering that clients may choose for generating a private/public key pair. This way, you can give a higher priority to hardware-based keys (Trusted Platform Module or smart card) over software-based keys.

Cryptographic Service Provider/Key Service Provider Ordering

Another problem addressed in Windows Server 2016 is GUI support for CSP/KSP ordering. With increased interest in the deployment of Trusted Platform Module in enterprise scenarios, providing a mechanism for prioritizing TPM-based keys over other types of keys has become a "must-have" for certificate enrollment based on certificate templates. This is important from the client perspective when enrolling for a non-exportable key. You want to have assurance that the non-exportable keys are generated in the TPM and are not software based (assuming that no malware is involved and the user is not malicious).

Currently this prioritization is captured as an attribute of a certificate template object in Active Directory; however, a user interface does not exist for modifying such properties, and Microsoft does not support it. Windows Server 2016's Certificate Template Management Console fully supports CSP/KSP ordering.

Managing Certificate Authority: Certificate Templates Overview

Enterprise certificate authorities issue certificates from certificate templates, a preconfigured list of certificate settings. This allows administrators to enroll users and computers for certificates without the need to create complex certificate requests. Windows Server 2016 AD CS does include a minor user interface change and the Active Directory Certificate Services Administration module for Windows PowerShell. The new Compatibility tab in the Certificate Templates Management Console lets you identify incompatible certificate template settings between different versions of Windows-based certificate recipients and the certificate authority. The AD CS Administration module for Windows PowerShell lets you manage common AD CS management tasks using Windows PowerShell.

Certificate Template Compatibility

Multiple versions of certificate templates have been released for the family of Windows Server products. New certificate template versions include settings that control the features relevant to each new certificate authority. However, not all features are compatible with all certificate authorities and certificate requests. Therefore, it can be difficult to determine which certificate templates are compatible with different versions of certificate authorities and different Windows-based certificate requestors.

Version 2 certificate templates are customizable certificate templates that are supported with Windows Server 2008 Enterprise CAs or Windows Server 2003 Enterprise edition CAs. Version 2 certificate templates enable advanced CA features, such as key archiving and recovery and certificate auto-enrollment.

> To use version 2 templates, Active Directory must be upgraded to support Windows Server 2008 or Windows Server 2003 schema changes. Standard editions of Windows Server 2008 and Windows Server 2003 support only version 1 certificate templates, which are not customizable and do not support key archival or automatic enrollment.

Version 3 certificate templates were new to Windows Server 2008. Version 3 certificate templates function similarly to version 2 templates, and they support new Active Directory Certificate Services features available in Windows Server 2008. These features include CNG, which introduces support for Suite B cryptographic algorithms such as elliptic curve cryptography (ECC).

The Windows Server 2016 Certificate Template Management Console includes a new certificate template Compatibility tab that lets you select the Windows operating system of the certificate authority and the Windows operating system of the certificate recipient.

The Certificate Template Management Console determines incompatible settings between the selections and shows a list of template settings that the management console adds or removes from template selection.

You view the compatibility table from the Certificate Template Management Console. You can launch the Certificate Template Management Console by typing **certtmpl.msc** in the Run dialog or on the Start screen and pressing Enter.

Creating Certificate Templates

When creating a new certificate template, you copy an existing template similar to the configuration defaults needed for your particular application. It is best to review the default list of certificate templates and find the template that best matches your application's requirements.

The Request Handling tab (Figure 22.4) in the Certificate Templates Management console has the Renew With Same Key Certificate Template Configuration option. This certificate template option becomes visible in the user interface when you configure the Certification Authority and the Certificate Recipient options to Windows Server 2016 and Windows 8/8.1, Windows 10 respectively.

FIGURE 22.4   Request Handling tab of the Certificate Templates Management console

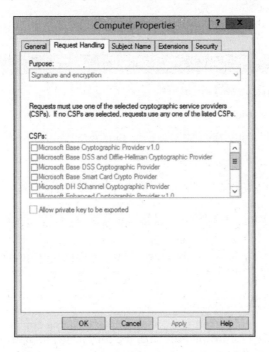

You will create an example certificate template in Exercise 22.4.

EXERCISE 22.4

Creating a Certificate Template

1. Start the Certificate Templates snap-in, read through the certificate templates titles, and choose the Computer Template.

2. In the details pane, right-click an existing certificate and click Duplicate Template.

3. Choose to duplicate the template as a Windows Server 2008–based template.

4. On the General tab, enter the template display name and the template name and click OK.

5. Define any additional attributes for the newly created certificate template.

Publishing the Certificate Template

After creating a certificate template and applying the proper security permissions, you will want to deploy the new certificate template by publishing to the Active Directory where it can be shared with other Enterprise CAs. The following exercise will take us through the steps to perform the task.

In Exercise 22.5, you will deploy a certificate template.

EXERCISE 22.5

Publishing a Certificate Template

1. In Server Manager, click Tools and then Certification Authority.

2. In the Certification Authority MMC, expand the CA Server Name.

3. Select the Certificate Templates container.

4. Right-click the Certificate Templates container and then click New Certificate Template To Issue.

5. In the Enable Certificate Templates dialog box, select the certificate template or templates that you want the CA server to issue and click OK. The newly selected certificate template or templates should appear in the details pane on the right.

 If a certificate template is not displayed in the Enable Certificate Templates dialog box, the replication of the certificate template may not have finished on all domain controllers in the forest.

Certificate Revocation

Revocation renders a certificate invalid and lists the revoked certificate in the CRL. You can revoke a certificate in the Certificate Authority snap-in with the steps shown in Exercise 22.6.

EXERCISE 22.6

Revoking a Certificate

1.   Start the Certification Authority snap-in.

2.   In the console tree, click the issuing certificate container.

3.   In the right pane, select and right-click the target certificate.

4.   Select All Tasks.

5.   Select Revoke Certificate.

6.   In the Certificate Revocation dialog box, you must select one of the following reason codes:

     Unspecified: Default reason code. This lacks information during future audits.

     Key Compromise: Select this when you think the key has been compromised.

     CA Compromise: Select this when you suspect the issuing CA of being compromised.

     Change of Affiliation: Select this when the person has exited the organization or changed roles.

     Superseded: Select this when issuing a new certificate to replace an existing certificate.

     Cease of Operation: Select this when the issuing device or server has been decommissioned.

     Certificate Hold: Select this to suspend an existing certificate temporarily.

7.   Click OK.

Display the Current Site Name for Certificate Authorities

Enter the following command to display current site names for one or more certificate authorities:

```
Certutil -ping caDnsName, [caDnsName, ...]
```

The command utilizes the DsGetSiteName API on each named certificate authority. After determining the site for all the certificate authorities, certutil.exe uses the DsQuerySitesByCost API to obtain the client's site costs for all the name certificate authorities.

CA Policy Auditing

PKI auditing logging is not enabled on the Windows 2016 CA server by default. After the auditing is enabled, all the events will be logged in the Security log.

Exercise 22.7 covers the steps that the CA administrator must complete to enable auditing.

EXERCISE 22.7

Configuring CA Policy Auditing

1. Enable Object Access/Success Auditing in the CA machine's local security policy:

   a. Start mmc.exe.

   b. Add the snap-in Group Policy Object Editor and select the Local Computer GPO.

   c. Under the path Computer Configuration\Windows Settings\ Security Settings\Local Policies\Audit Policy, enable success auditing for Object Access.

2. Enable auditing on the CA:

   a. Start the CA Management snap-in.

   b. Open the CA Properties dialog.

   c. On the Auditing tab, check the Change CA Configuration and Change CA Security Settings options.

Backing Up the Certificate Authority Server

The AD CS certificate authority deployment creates a database. The CA records certificates issued by the CA, private keys archived by the CA, revoked certificates, and all certificate requests to the database regardless of issuance status.

Configure the database location on an NTFS partition on the server's disk drives to provide the best security possible for the database file. Specify the location for the database in the Certificate Database Location box. By default, the wizard configured the database location to systemroot\system32\certlog. The name of the database file uses the CA's name, with an .edb extension.

The certificate database uses a transaction log to ensure the integrity of the database. The CA records its transactions in its configured log files. The CA then commits each transaction from the log file into the database. The CA then updates the last committed transaction in the database, and the process continues.

The CA database logs are selected when restoring the CA from a backup. If a CA is restored from a backup that is one month old, then the CA database can be updated with more recent activity recorded in the log to restore the database to its most current state.

When you back up a CA, the existing certificate database logs are truncated in size because they are no longer needed to restore the certificate database to its most current state.

The recommended method to back up a CA is to leverage the native Backup utility (included with the operating system) to back up the entire server, including the system state, which contains the CA's data. However, the Certificate Authority snap-in can be used to back up and restore the CA, but this backup method is intended only in cases where you want to migrate CA data to different server hardware. The public key and private key are backed up or restored using the PKCS #12 PFX format.

The Backup Or Restore Wizard will ask you to supply a password when backing up the public and private keys and CA certificates. This password will be needed to restore the CA.

Start the Certificate Authority snap-in for Exercise 22.8, which explains how to back up a CA.

EXERCISE 22.8

Backing Up the Certificate Authority Server

1. Start the Certification Authority MMC.

2. In the left pane, right-click the name of the server; then choose All Tasks ➢ Back Up CA.

3. When the Certification Authority Backup Wizard appears, click Next.

4. At the Items To Back Up screen, click the Private Key And CA Certificate check box. Next to the Back Up To This Location field, click the Browse button. Choose a location for your backup and click OK. Click Next.

5. At the Select A Password screen, enter and confirm a password. For this exercise, enter **P@ssw0rd**. Click Next.

Configuring and Managing Key Archive and Recovery

The key archive stores a certificate's subject name, public key, private key, and supported cryptographic algorithms in its CA database. This procedure can be performed manually or automatically, depending on the configuration. If the certificate template requires key archiving, then the process requires no manual intervention. However, key archiving can also be performed manually if the private key is exported and then sent to an administrator for import into the CA database.

There is also a Key Recovery Agent template available in the standard templates within Active Directory Certificate Services. The Key Recovery Agent template enables Domain Admins and Enterprise Admins to export private keys. Additionally, you can add other accounts and groups to have the necessary permissions (Read and Enroll) through the Security tab of the template.

The Key Recovery Agent template also needs to be enabled, as with other certificate templates, through the Certification Authority tool by selecting Certificate Template To Issue. See "Publishing a Certificate Template" earlier in this chapter for more details on enabling a certificate template on a CA.

With the Key Recovery Agent template in place, the following process must take place for key archiving and recovery:

1. Request a key recovery agent certificate using the Certificates snap-in.

2. Issue the key recovery agent certificate using the Certification Authority tool.

3. Retrieve the enrolled certificate using the Certificates snap-in.

4. Configure the CA for key archiving and recovery.

The final step, configuring the CA for key archiving and recovery, takes place in the Properties dialog box of each CA that will need to archive and recover keys. Specifically, the Recovery Agents tab configures the behavior of the CA when a request includes key archiving.

Each Key Recovery Agent certificate should be added using the Add button on the Recovery Agents tab.

PowerShell for AD CS

Table 22.3 will show you just some of the available PowerShell commands for maintaining an Active Directory Certificate Server.

TABLE 22.3 PowerShell Commands for AD CS

Command	Description
Add-CAAuthorityInformationAccess	This command allows an administrator to configure the Authority Information Access (AIA) or Online Certificate Status Protocol (OCSP) URI on a CA.
Add-CACrlDistributionPoint	Administrators can use this command to add a certificate revocation list (CRL) distribution point.
Add-CATemplate	This command allows an administrator to add a certificate template to the CA.
Backup-CARoleService	This command can be used to back up the CA database and private key information.

Command	Description
Confirm-CAEndorsementKeyInfo	Administrators can use this command to check the endorsement certificate of a TPM on the local CA.
Get-CAAuthorityInformationAccess	This command allows an admin to view the Authority Information Access (AIA) and Online Certificate Status Protocol (OCSP) URI information set.
Get-CACrlDistributionPoint	Administrators can use this command to view all the locations set for the CRL distribution point (CDP).
Get-CATemplate	This command allows an admin to view the list of templates set on the CA for issuance of certificates.
Remove-CAAuthorityInformationAccess	Administrators can use this command to remove Authority Information Access (AIA) or Online Certificate Status Protocol (OCSP) URI from the CA.
Remove-CACrlDistributionPoint	This command allows an administrator to delete the URI for the certificate revocation list (CRL) distribution point (CDP) from the CA.
Remove-CATemplate	Administrators can use this command to delete the templates from the CA.
Restore-CARoleService	This command allows an administrator to restore the CA database and private key information.

Summary

In this chapter, I discussed the certificate authority role and some of the new features in Microsoft Windows Server 2016, including additional management options, new certificate templates, and better support for globalized organizations with limited IDN support. I also covered the details of the same-key certificate renewal requirement and the effects of the new increased default security settings on the CA role service.

I also showed you just some of the PowerShell commands that you can use to configure and modify the Active Directory Certificate Server.

Exam Essentials

Understand the concepts behind certificate authority.   Certificate authority servers manage certificates. Make sure you understand why companies use certificate servers and how they work.

Understand certificate enrollment.   You need to understand the many different ways to issue certificates to users and computers. You also need to understand the differences between installing certificates using GPOs, auto-enrollment, and web enrollment.

Review Questions

You can find the answers in the Appendix.

1. You are the network administrator for a large organization. You need to add a certificate template to the Certificate Authority. What PowerShell command would you use?

    A. Get-CSTemplate

    B. Add-CSTemplate

    C. Add-CATemplate

    D. New-Template

2. Channel Fishing Company wants to configure a CA server in the DMZ to issue certificates to remote users. How would you accomplish this? (Choose all that apply.)

    A. You should consider having the Certificate Enrollment Policy Web Server role included in the solution.

    B. You should consider having the online responder included in the solution.

    C. You should consider having the Network Device Enrollment Service included in the solution.

    D. You should consider having the web service included in the solution.

    E. You should consider having the Certificate Enrollment Web Service included in the solution.

    F. You should consider having the Web Enrollment service included in the solution.

3. The certificate revocation list (CRL) polling begins to consume bandwidth. What steps should you consider to reduce network traffic?

    A. You should consider implementing the Certificate Enrollment Policy Web Server role and Certificate Enrollment Web Services role.

    B. You should consider implementing an online responder.

    C. You should consider implementing an online issuing CA and a root CA.

    D. You should consider publishing more CRLs.

4. ABC Industries wants configuration modifications of the Certification Authority role service to be logged. How would you implement this? (Choose all that apply.)

    A. You should consider enabling auditing of system events.

    B. You should consider enabling logging.

    C. You should consider enabling auditing of object access.

    D. You should consider enabling auditing of privilege use.

    E. You should consider enabling auditing of process tracking.

5. You are the network administrator for an Active Directory forest named WillPanek.com. The forest contains a single domain. The domain contains a single Windows Server 2016 server named Server1. An administrator named John Smith plans to set up Server1 as a stand-alone certification authority (CA). You need John Smith to set up Server1 as a stand-alone CA. What group does John Smith need to be part of to configure Server1 as a stand-alone CA?

   A. Administrators group on Server1

   B. Domain Admins group in WillPanek.com

   C. Cert Publishers group on Server1

   D. Key Admins group in WillPanek.com

6. You are the network administrator for WillPanek.com. You set up an enterprise certification authority (CA) named ServerCA1. You are planning to issue certificates based on the User certificate template. You need to make sure that the issued certificates are valid for two years and that they also support auto-enrollment. What should you do first?

   A. Run the certutil.exe command and specify the resubmit parameter.

   B. Duplicate the User certificate template.

   C. Add a new certificate template for CA1 to issue.

   D. Modify the Request Handling settings for the CA.

7. You have set up an enterprise root certification authority (CA) named Server1. Computers on the network have successfully enrolled and received certificates that will expire in one year. The certificates are based on a template named CA_Template1. You need to ensure that new certificates based on CA_Template1 are valid for three years. What should you do to make sure that they are valid for three years?

   A. Modify the Validity period for the certificate template.

   B. Instruct users to request certificates by running the certreq.exe command.

   C. Instruct users to request certificates by using the Certificates console.

   D. Modify the Validity period for the root CA certificate.

8. You are the network administrator for a large company. You need to make sure that certificate clients check the CRL at least every 30 minutes to see whether a certificate has been revoked or not. Which of the following should you configure to accomplish this goal?

   A. Key recovery agent

   B. CRL publication interval

   C. Delta CRL publication interval

   D. Certificate templates.

9. You are the network admin for your company. You need to see all of the location sets for the CRL distribution point (CDP). What PowerShell command would you use?

    A. View-CACrlDistributionPoint

    B. See-CACrlDistributionPoint

    C. Add-CACrlDistributionPoint

    D. Get-CACrlDistributionPoint

10. You are the network admin for your company. You need to see the list of templates set on the CA for issuance of certificates. What PowerShell command would you use?

    A. Get-CATemplate

    B. View-CATemplate

    C. Add-CATemplate

    D. New-CATemplate

Chapter

23

Configure Access and Information Protection Solutions

THE FOLLOWING 70-742 EXAM OBJECTIVES ARE COVERED IN THIS CHAPTER:

✓ **Install and configure Active Directory Federation Services (AD FS)**

- This objective may include but is not limited to: Upgrade and migrate previous AD FS workloads to Windows Server 2016; implement claims-based authentication, including Relying Party Trusts; configure authentication policies; configure multi-factor authentication; implement and configure device registration; integrate AD FS with Microsoft Passport; configure for use with Microsoft Azure and Office 365; configure AD FS to enable authentication of users stored in LDAP directories.

✓ **Implement Web Application Proxy (WAP)**

- This objective may include but is not limited to: Install and configure WAP; implement WAP in pass-through mode; implement WAP as AD FS proxy; integrate WAP with AD FS; configure AD FS requirements; publish web apps via WAP; publish Remote Desktop Gateway applications; configure HTTP to HTTPS redirects; configure internal and external Fully Qualified Domain Names (FQDNs).

✓ **Install and configure Active Directory Rights**

- This objective may include but is not limited to: Install a licensor certificate AD RMS server; manage AD RMS Service Connection Point (SCP); manage AD RMS templates; configure Exclusion Policies; back upand restore AD RMS.

In this chapter, I will discuss Active Directory Federation Services and how to set up relying party trusts with certificates. I will also discuss rights management, which Microsoft created to further protect documents, email, and web pages from unauthorized copying, printing, forwarding, editing, deleting, and so forth.

Finally, I will talk about using the Web Application Proxy and how this can be setup in conjunction with AD FS for greater control of which applications get accessed through AD FS.

Implement Active Directory Federation Services

Active Directory Federation Services (AD FS) demands a great deal of preparation and planning to ensure a successful implementation. The type of certificate authority used to sign the AD FS server's certificate must be planned. The SSL encryption level must be negotiated with the partnering organization. For instance, how much Active Directory information should be shared with the partnering organization? What should the DNS structure look like to support federation communications? You must explore all of these questions before implementing AD FS. In the followings sections, I will discuss how to deploy AD FS and the configurations used to set up a federated partnership between businesses.

What Is a Claim?

A *claim* is an identifiable element (email address, username, password, and so on) that a trusted source asserts about an identity, such as, for example, the SID of a user or computer. An identity can contain more than one claim, and any combination of those claims can be used to authorize access to resources.

Windows Server 2016 extends the authorization identity beyond using the SID for identity and enables administrators to configure authorization based on claims published in Active Directory.

Today, the claims-based identity model brings us to cloud-based authentication. One analogy to the claim-based model is the old airport check-in procedure:

1. You first check in at the ticket counter.

2. You present a suitable form of ID (driver's license, passport, credit card, and so on). After verifying that your picture ID matches your face (authentication), the

agent pulls up your flight information and verifies that you've paid for a ticket (authorization).

3. You receive a boarding pass (token). The boarding pass lets the gate agents know your name and frequent flyer number (authentication and personalization), your flight number and seating priority (authorization), and more. The boarding pass has barcode information (certificate) with a boarding serial number proving that the boarding pass was issued by the airline and not a (self-signed) forgery.

Active Directory Federation Service is Microsoft's claims-based identity solution providing browser-based clients (internal or external to your network) with transparent access to one or more protected Internet-facing applications.

When an application is hosted in a different network than the user accounts, users are occasionally prompted for secondary credentials when they attempt to access the application. These secondary credentials represent the identity of the users in the domain where the application is hosted. The web server hosting the application usually requires these credentials to make the most proper authorization decision.

AD FS makes secondary accounts and their credentials unnecessary by providing trust relationships that send a user's digital identity and access rights to trusted partners. In a federated environment, each organization continues to manage its own identities, but each organization can also securely send and accept identities from other organizations. This seamless process is referred to as *single sign-on (SSO)*.

Windows Server 2016 AD FS federation servers can extract Windows authorization claims from a user's authorization token that is created when the user authenticates to the AD FS federation server. AD FS inserts these claims into its claim pipeline for processing. You can configure Windows authorization claims to pass through the pipeline as is, or you can configure AD FS to transform Windows authorization claims into a different or well-known claim type.

Claims Provider

A *claims provider* is a federation server that processes trusted identity claims requests. A federation server processes requests to issue, manage, and validate security tokens. Security tokens consist of a collection of identity claims, such as a user's name or role or an anonymous identifier. A federation server can issue tokens in several formats. In addition, a federation server can protect the contents of security tokens in transmission with an X.509 certificate.

For example, when a Stellacon Corporation user needs access to Fabrikam's web application, the Stellacon Corporation user must request claims from the Stellacon Corporation AD FS server claims provider. The claim is transformed into an encrypted security token, which is then sent to Fabrikam's AD FS server.

Relying Party

A *relying party* is a federation server that receives security tokens from a trusted federation partner claims provider. In turn, the relying party issues new security tokens that a local relying party application consumes. In the prior example, Fabrikam is the relying party that relies on the Stellacon's claims provider to validate the user's claim. By using a relying-party federation server in conjunction with a claims provider, organizations can offer web single sign-on to users from partner organizations. In this scenario, each organization manages its own identity stores.

Endpoints

Endpoints provide access to the federation server functionality of AD FS, such as token issuance, information card issuance, and the publishing of federation metadata. Based on the type of endpoint, you can enable or disable the endpoint or control whether the endpoint is published to AD FS proxies.

Table 23.1 describes the property fields that distinguish the various built-in endpoints that AD FS exposes. The table includes the types of endpoints and their methods of client authentication. Table 23.2 describes the AD FS security modes.

TABLE 23.1   AD FS Endpoints

Name	Description
WS-Trust 1.3	An endpoint built on a standard Simple Object Access Protocol (SOAP)–based protocol for issuing security tokens.
WS-Trust 2005	An endpoint built on a prestandard, SOAP-based protocol for issuing security tokens.
WS-Federation Passive/SAML Web SSO	An endpoint published to support protocols that redirect web browser clients to issue security tokens.
Federation Metadata	A standard-formatted endpoint for exchanging metadata about a claims provider or a relying party.
SAML Artifact Resolution	An endpoint built on a subset of the Security Assertion Markup Language (SAML) version 2.0 protocol that describes how a relying party can access a token directly from a claims provider.
WS-Trust WSDL	An endpoint that publishes WS-Trust Web Services Definition Language (WSDL) containing the metadata that the federation service must be able to accept from other federation servers.
SAML Token (Asymmetric)	The client accepts a SAML token with an asymmetric key.

TABLE 23.2   AD FS Security Modes

Name	Description
Transport	The client credentials are included at the transport layer. Confidentiality is preserved at the transport layer (Secure Sockets Layer [SSL]).
Mixed	The client credentials are included in the header of a SOAP message. Confidentiality is preserved at the transport layer (SSL).
Message	The client credentials are included in the header of a SOAP message. Confidentiality is preserved by encryption inside the SOAP message.

Claim Descriptions

Claim descriptions are claim types based on an entity's or user's attribute like a user's email address, common name or UPN. AD FS publishes these claims types in the federation metadata and most common claim descriptions are pre-configured in the AD FS Management snap-in.

The claim descriptions are published to federation metadata which is stored in the AD FS configuration database. The claim descriptions include a claim type URI, name, publishing state, and description.

Claim Rules

Claim rules define how AD FS processes a claim. The most common rule is using a user's email address as a valid claim. The email address claim is validated through the partner's Active Directory email attribute for the user's account. If there is a match, the claim is accepted as valid.

Claim rules can quickly evolve into more complex rules with more attributes such as a user's employee ID or department. The key goal of claim rules is to process the claim in a manner that validates the user's claim and to assemble a user's profile information based on a sufficient number of attributes to place the user into a role or group.

The Attribute Store

Attribute stores are the repositories containing claim values. AD FS natively supports Active Directory, by default, as an attribute store. SQL Server, AD LDS, and custom attribute stores are also supported.

AD FS Role Services

The AD FS server role includes federation, proxy, and web agent services. These services enable the following:

- Web SSO
- Federated web-based resources

- Customizing the access experience
- Managing authorization to access applications

Based on your organization's requirements, you can deploy servers running any one of the following AD FS role services:

Active Directory Federation Service   Microsoft federation solution for accepting and issuing claims based token for users to experience a single sign-on to a partnered web application.

Federation Service Proxy   The Federation Service Proxy forwards user claims over the internet or DMZ using WS-Federation Passive Requestor Profile (WS-F PRP) protocols to the internal ADFS farm. Only the user credential data is forwarded to the Federation Service. All other datagram packets are dropped.

Claims-Aware Agent   The claims-aware agent resides on a web server with a claims-aware application to enable the Microsoft ASP.NET application to accept AD FS security token claims.

Windows Token-Based Agent   The Windows token-based agent resides on a web server with a Windows NT token-based application to translate an AD FS security token to an impersonation-level Windows NT token-based authentication.

What's New for AD FS in Windows Server 2016?

The Active Directory Federation Services role in Windows Server 2016 introduces the following new features:

- HTTP.SYS
- Server Manager integration
- AD FS deployment cmdlets in the AD FS module for Windows PowerShell
- Interoperability with Windows authorization claims
- Web proxy service

HTTP.SYS

Prior AD FS versions relied on IIS components for the AD FS claim functions. Microsoft has improved the overall claims handling performance and SSO customization by building the AD FS 3.0 code on top of the standard kernel mode driver—HTTP.SYS. This approach also avoids the huge security "no-no" of hosting IIS on a domain controller.

The classic netsh HTTP command can be entered to query and configure HTTP.SYS. AD FS proxy server introduces interesting deployment nuisances and "gotchas" with HTTP.SYS, which I will discuss in the "Web Proxy Service" section.

Improved Installation Experience

The installation experience for Active Directory Federation Services 3.0 was cumbersome, requiring multiple hotfixes, as well as .NET Framework 3.5, Windows PowerShell, and the

Windows Identity Foundation SDK. Windows Server 2016's AD FS role includes all of the software you need to run AD FS for an improved installation experience.

Web Proxy Service

The kernel mode (HTTP.SYS) in Windows Server 2016 includes server name indication (SNI) support configuration. I strongly recommend verifying that your current load balancer/ reverse proxy firmware supports SNI. This prerequisite is a sore spot for most AD FS 3.0 upgrade projects in the field. Therefore, it's worthwhile checking the following:

- Your preferred load balancer/device needs to support SNI.

- Clients and user agents need to support SNI and should not become locked out of authentication.

- All SSL termination endpoints vulnerable to the recent heartbleed bug (http:// heartbleed.com) need to be patched, exposing OpenSSL libraries and certificates.

AD FS Dependency Changes in Windows Server 2016

Active Directory Federation Services was built on a claim-based identity framework called *Windows Identity Foundation (WIF)*. Prior to Windows Server 2016, WIF was distributed in a software development kit and the .NET runtime. WIF is currently integrated into version 4.5 of the .NET Framework, which ships with Windows Server 2016.

Windows Identity Foundation

WIF is a set of .NET Framework classes; it is a framework for implementing claims-based identity for applications. Any web application or web service that uses .NET Framework version 4.5 or newer can run WIF.

New Claims Model and Principal Object

Claims are at the core of .NET Framework 4.5. The base claim classes (`Claim`, `ClaimsIdentity`, `ClaimsPrincipal`, `ClaimTypes`, and `ClaimValueTypes`) all live directly in `mscorlib`. Interfaces are no longer necessary to plug claims in the .NET identity system. `WindowsPrincipal`, `GenericPrincipal`, and `RolePrincipal` now inherit from `ClaimsPrincipal`, `WindowsIdentity`, and `GenericIdentity`, and `FormsIdentity` now inherit from `ClaimsIdentity`. In short, every principal class will now serve claims. The integration classes and interfaces (`WindowsClaimsIdentity`, `WindowsClaimsPrincipal`, `IClaimsPrincipal`, and `IClaimsIdentity`) have thus been removed. The `ClaimsIdentity` object model also contains various improvements, which makes it easier to query the identity's claims collection.

As you climb further up "Mount Federation," you will realize that not all vendor SAML flavors are compatible, and configuration challenges can bring even the most seasoned system integrators to their knees. SAML deserves an entire book, so to avoid this chapter reaching encyclopedia size, I will touch on just a few pointers.

AD FS negotiates SAML authentication in order of security strength from the weakest to the strongest, as shown in Table 23.3. The default mode, Kerberos, is considered the strongest method. The authentication precedence can be tuned by executing the PowerShell command Set-AD FSProperties –AuthenticationContextOrder to select an order to meet your organization's security requirements.

TABLE 23.3   SAML-supported authentication methods

Authentication Method	Authentication Context Class URI
Username/password	urn:oasis:names:tc:SAML:3.0:ac:classes:Password
Password-protected transport	urn:oasis:names:tc:SAML:3.0:ac:classes: PasswordProtectedTransport
Transport Layer Security (TLS) Client	urn:oasis:names:tc:SAML:3.0:ac:classes:TLSClient
X.509 certificate	urn:oasis:names:tc:SAML:3.0:ac:classes:X509
Integrated Windows authentication	urn:federation:authentication:windows
Kerberos	urn:oasis:names:tc:SAML:3.0:classes:Kerberos

Active Directory Federation Services Installation

I will now describe how to install and deploy Active Directory Federation Services roles on computers running Windows Server 2016 (see Exercise 23.1). You will learn about the following:

- Deploying AD FS role services using Windows PowerShell
- Supporting upgrade scenarios for AD FS

EXERCISE 23.1

Installing the AD FS Role on a Computer Using Server Manager

1.   Start Server Manager.

2.   Click Manage and click Add Roles And Features. Click Next.

3.   The Add Roles And Features Wizard shows the Before You Begin screen. Click Next.

4.   Click Role-Based Or Feature-Based Installation on the Select Installation Type screen. Click Next.

5.   Click the server on which you want to install Active Directory Federation Services from the Server Pool list on the Select Destination Server screen. Click Next.

6. Select the Active Directory Federation Services check box on the Select Server Roles screen. Server Manager will prompt you to add other features associated with this role, such as management tools. Leave the default selections. Click Add Features to close the dialog.

7. Click Next on the Select Server Roles screen.

8. Click Next on the Select Features screen.

9. Server Manager shows the Active Directory Federation Services screen. This screen displays simple role introduction and important AD FS configuration information. Click Next.

10. From the Select Server Roles screen, select the check box next to the AD FS role services to install on the computer. Click Next.

11. Server Manager prompts you to add other features associated with this role, such as management tools. Leave the default selections. Click Add Features to close the dialog.

12. Read the Confirm Installation Selections screen. This screen provides a list of roles, role services, and features that the current installation prepares on the computer. Click Install to begin the installation.

Role Installation Using Windows PowerShell

To view the installation state of AD FS using Windows PowerShell, open an elevated Windows PowerShell console, type the following command, and press Enter:

```
Get-WindowsFeature "adfs*","*fed*"
```

Upgrading to Windows AD FS 2016

Windows Server 2016's AD FS role supports upgrading version 3.0 of Active Directory Federation Services. You cannot upgrade versions of AD FS prior to version 3.0 using Windows Server 2016.

Table 23.4 represents the support upgrade matrix for the AD FS role in Windows Server 2016.

TABLE 23.4   Support upgrade matrix for the AD FS role in Windows Server 2016

AD FS and Operating System Version	Windows Server 2016 Upgrade Supported
AD FS 3.0 running on Windows Server 2008	Yes
AD FS 3.0 running on Windows Server 2008 R2	Yes

TABLE 23.4   Support upgrade matrix for the AD FS role in Windows Server 2016 *(continued)*

AD FS and Operating System Version	Windows Server 2016 Upgrade Supported
AD FS 3.0 Proxy running on Windows Server 2008	Yes
AD FS 3.0 Proxy running on Windows Server 2008 R2	Yes
AD FS 1.1 running on Windows Server 2008	No
AD FS 1.1 running on Windows Server 2008 R2	No
AD FS 1.1 Proxy running on Windows Server 2008	No
AD FS 1.1 Proxy running on Windows Server 2008 R2	No
AD FS 1.1 Web Agents on Windows Server 2008 or Windows Server 2008 R2	Yes

Configuring Active Directory Federation Services

Windows Server 2016 delineates role installation and role deployment. Role installations make staged role services and features available for deployment. Role deployment enables you to configure the role service, which enables the role service in your environment. AD FS in Windows Server 2016 uses the same deployment tools as AD FS 3.0. However, an entry point to start these tools is included in Server Manager. Server Manager indicates that one or more role services are eligible for deployment by showing an exclamation point inside a yellow triangle on the Action Flag notification. Click the action flag to show the role services you can deploy.

AD FS Graphical Deployment

The Run The AD FS Management snap-in link in Windows Server 2016 Server Manager is how you perform the initial configuration for the AD FS roles using the graphical interface. Alternatively, you can start the AD FS management console using the AD FS Management tile on the Start screen. The Start screen tile points to the Microsoft.IdentityServer.msc file located in the C:\windows\adfs folder.

To configure AD FS, select Start ➢ Run and type **FsConfigWizard.exe**; alternatively, click the FsConfigWizard.exe file located in the C:\windows\adfs folder.

Exercise 23.2 uses the AD FS Federation Server Configuration Wizard. To complete this exercise, you'll need an active SSL certificate assigned to the server and a managed service account for AD FS service.

EXERCISE 23.2

Configuring the AD FS Role on the Computer Using Server Manager

1. Select Create The First Federation Server In The Federation Server Farm.

2. Select the administrative account with permissions to configure the AD FS server and click Next.

3. Select the server certificate from the SSL certificate drop-down list.

4. Select the AD FS service name from the drop-down list.

5. Type **ADFS-Test** in the federation service's Display Name field and click Next.

6. Select Create A Database On This Server Using Windows Internal Database and click Next.

7. Click Next on the Review Options screen.

8. If the prerequisites check is successful, click Configure on the Prerequisite Check screen.

9. If the Result screen displays "This Server was successfully configured," you can click Close.

Deployment Using Windows PowerShell

Windows Server 2016 includes the Active Directory Federation Services module for Windows PowerShell when you install the AD FS role using Server Manager. The AD FS module for Windows PowerShell includes five new cmdlets to deploy the AD FS role:

- Add-AdfsProxy
- Add-AdfsFarmNode
- Export-AdfsDeploymentSQLScript
- Install-AdfsStand-alone
- Install-AdfsFarm

These AD FS cmdlets provide the same functionality as the command-line version of the AD FS Federation Server Configuration Wizard, fsconfig .exe. The AD FS role in Windows Server 2016 includes fsconfig.exe to remain compatible with previously authored deployment scripts. New deployments should take advantage of the deployment cmdlets included in the AD FS module for Windows PowerShell.

Add-AdfsProxy Configures a server as a federation server proxy.

FederationServiceName Specifies the name of the federation service for which a server proxies requests.

FederationServiceTrustCredentials Specifies the credentials of the Active Directory identity that is authorized to register new federation server proxies. By default, this is the account under which the federation service runs or an account that is a member of the Administrators group on the federation server.

ForwardProxy Specifies the DNS name and port of an HTTP proxy that this federation server proxy uses to obtain access to the federation service.

Add-AdfsFarmNode Adds this computer to an existing federation server farm.

CertificateThumbprint Specifies the value of the certificate thumbprint of the certificate that should be used in the SSL binding of the default website in IIS. This value should match the thumbprint of a valid certificate in the Local Computer certificate store.

OverwriteConfiguration Must be used to remove an existing AD FS configuration database and overwrite it with a new database.

SQLConnectionString Specifies the SQL Server database that will store the AD FS configuration settings. If not specified, AD FS uses Windows Internal Database to store configuration settings.

ServiceAccountCredential Specifies the Active Directory account under which the AD FS service runs. All nodes in the farm must have the same service account.

PrimaryComputerName Specifies the name of the primary federation server in the farm that this computer will join.

PrimaryComputerPort Specifies the value of the HTTP port that this computer uses to connect with the primary computer in order to synchronize configuration settings. Specify a value for this parameter only if the HTTP port on the primary computer is not 80.

Active Directory Federation Services Certificates

There are three types of certificates used by an AD FS implementation:

- Service communications
- Token decrypting
- Token signing

The service communications certificate is required for communication with web clients over SSL and with web application proxy services using Windows Communication Foundation (WCF) components. This certificate is specified at configuration time for AD FS.

The token decrypting certificate is required to decrypt claims and tokens received by the federation service. The public key for the decrypting certificate is usually shared with relying parties and others to encrypt the claims and tokens using the certificate.

The token signing certificate is required to sign all claims and tokens created by the server. You can have multiple token encrypting and signing certificates for an implementation, and new ones can be added within the AD FS management tool, shown in Figure 23.1.

FIGURE 23.1   Active Directory Federation Certificate Console screen

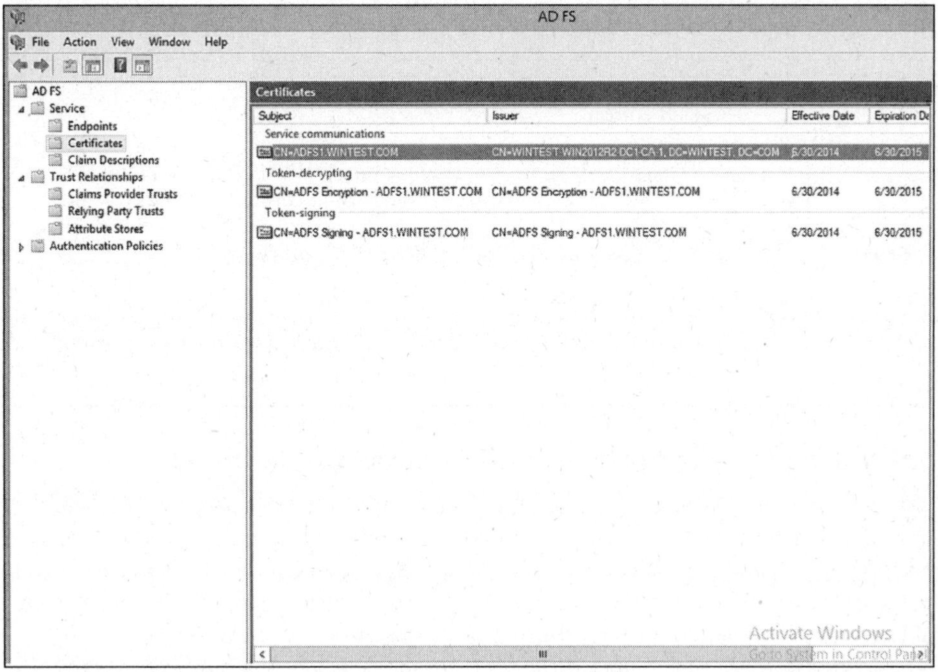

Relying-Party Trust

The federation service name originates from the SSL certificate used for AD FS. The SSL certificate can be template-based and needs to be enrolled and used by IIS.

The next step in setting up AD FS is to configure a relying-party trust. A relying-party trust can be configured with a URL acquired from the relying party. The URL contains the federation metadata used to complete the federation trust configuration. The federation metadata may also be exported to a file that can then be imported into the relying-party trust. There is also a manual option for configuring a relying-party trust.

See Table 23.5 for the Federation Metadata fields.

TABLE 23.5   Federation Metadata Fields

Field	Description
Display Name	This is the friendly display name given to this relying party trust.
Profile	Select AD FS Profile for the standard Windows Server 2012 AD FS, or select AD FS 1.0 And 1.1 Profile for AD FS configurations that need to work with older versions of AD FS.

TABLE 23.5   Federation Metadata Fields *(continued)*

Field	Description
Certificate	This is the optional certificate file from the relying party for token encryption.
URL	This is the URL for the relying party. WS-Federation Passive Protocol URL or SAML 2.0 WebSSO protocols are supported.
Identifiers	This is the unique identifier used for this trust.
Authorization Rules	Selecting this permits all users to access the relying party or denies all users access to the relying party, depending on the needs of this trust.

Configuring Claims Provider and Transform Claims Rules

Claims provider trust rules are configured within the AD FS management console and are configured on a per-trust basis. Planning claims rules involves determining what claims are needed by the relying party to complete the authentication and authorization process and which users will need access to the relying-party trust. The relying party determines what claims need to be received and trusted from the claims provider.

Trust rules start with templates as the basis for the rule. There are different types of claims templates depending on the type of rule being used. The claims rule templates for transforms are described in Table 23.6.

TABLE 23.6   Transform claims rule templates

Template	Description
Send LDAP Attributes as Claims	Attributes found in an LDAP directory (such as Active Directory) can be used as part of the claim.
Send Group Membership as Claim	The group memberships of the logged-in user are sent as part of the claim.
Transform an Incoming Claim	This is used for configuring a rule to change an incoming claim. Changes include both the type and the value of an incoming claim.
Pass Through or Filter an Incoming Claim	This performs an action such as pass-through or filter on an incoming claim based on certain criteria, as defined in the rule.
Send Claims Using a Custom Rule	This creates a rule that's not covered by a predefined template, such as an LDAP attribute generated with a custom LDAP filter.

Defining Windows Authorization Claims in AD FS

Windows Server 2016 stores information that describes Windows authorization claims in the configuration partition of Active Directory. Windows refers to this information as *claim types*; however, Active Directory Federation Services typically refers to this information as claim descriptions (see Figure 23.2). There are more than 40 new claims descriptions available in the AD FS Windows Server 2016 release.

FIGURE 23.2 AD FS claim descriptions

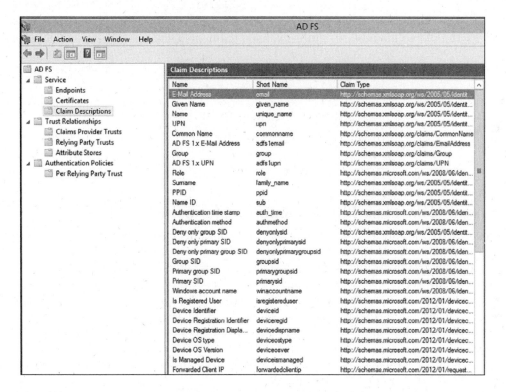

The Active Directory Federation Services role included in Windows Server 2016 lets you configure AD FS to include Windows authorization claims in the AD FS claim pipeline. To simplify this configuration, you can create *claim descriptions* in AD FS. Claim types in Windows authorization claims are analogous to claim descriptions in AD FS. The Windows authorization claim ID maps to the AD FS claim description's claim identifier (see Figure 23.3).

To simplify AD FS configuration using Windows authorization claims, create a claim description in AD FS for each Windows authorization claim you intend to deploy in AD FS.

FIGURE 23.3   Adding a claim description

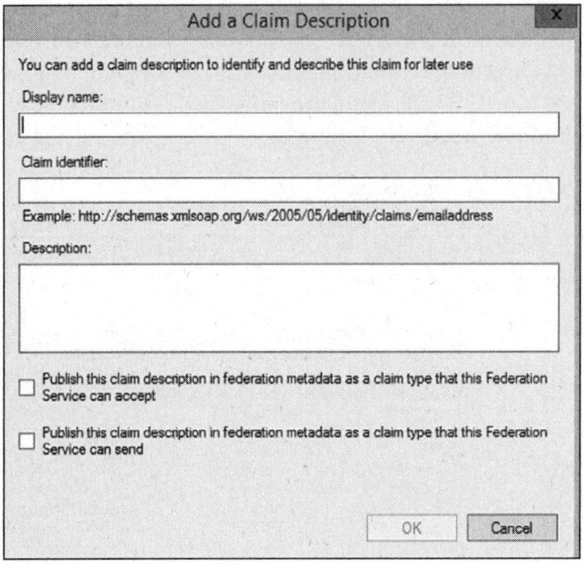

Create Claim Pass-Through and Transformation Rules

You need to configure a claim rule with the Active Directory Claims Provider Trusts Wizard to insert Windows authorization claims into the AD FS claims pipeline.

Creating a claim description makes it easier to select the incoming claim type. Alternatively, you can type the claim type ID directly in the Incoming Claim Type list. A *pass-through claim rule* enables the Windows authorization claim to enter the AD FS claim pipeline. A pass-through claim leaves the claim type ID intact. Therefore, the pass-through claim ID begins with ad://ext, whereas most claim description URIs begin with http://. In addition, you can create a claim transformation claim rule on the Active Directory Claim Provider Trust Wizard to transform a Windows authorization claim into a well-known claim description (see Figure 23.4).

Creating a claims provider trust claim rule enables the Windows authorization claim to enter the AD FS claim pipeline. However, this does not ensure that AD FS sends the Windows authorization claim. AD FS claim processing begins with the claims provider. This allows the claim to enter the pipeline. Claim processing continues for the targeted relying party—first with the issuance authorization rules and then with the issuance transform rules.

You can configure Windows authorization claims in claims rules configured on a relying party. By default, a relying party does not have any issuance transform rules. Therefore, AD FS drops all claims in the pipeline destined for a relying party when the relying party does not have any rules that pass incoming claims. Additionally, issuance authorization rules determine whether a user can receive claims for a relying party and, therefore, access the relying party.

FIGURE 23.4 Claim transformation claim rule

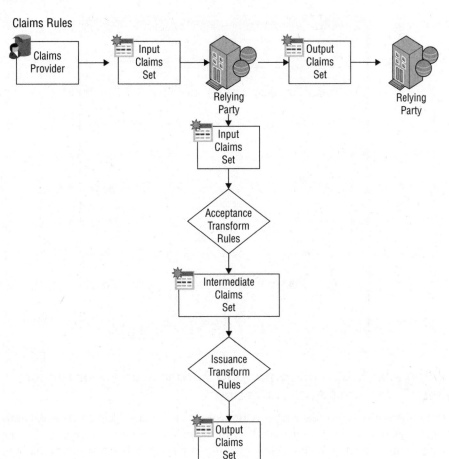

Choose the claims types from the list of inbound rules created in the Active Directory claims provider trust that you want to send to the designated relying party. Then create rules that continue to pass the selected claim types through the pipeline to the relying party. Alternatively, you can create a rule that passes all the inbound claims to the relying party (see Figure 23.5).

 The AD FS role in Windows Server 2016 cannot provide claim information when the incoming authentication is not Kerberos. Clients must authenticate to AD FS using Kerberos authentication. If Windows authorization claims are not entering the AD FS claim pipeline, then make sure the client authenticates to AD FS using Kerberos and the correct service principal name is registered on the computer/service account.

FIGURE 23.5   Editing the claims rules

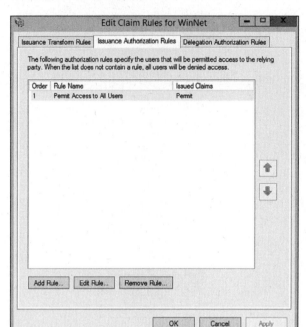

Enabling AD FS to Use Compound Authentication for Device Claims: Compound Authentication

Windows Server 2016 enhances Kerberos authentication by introducing compound authentication. Compound authentication enables a Kerberos TGS request to include two identities: the identity of the user and the identity of the user's device. Windows accomplishes compound authentication by extending Kerberos Flexible Authentication Secure Tunneling (FAST) or Kerberos armoring.

During normal Kerberos authentication, the Kerberos client requesting authentication for a service sends the ticket-granting service (TGS) a request for that service. Using Kerberos armoring, the TGS exchange is armored using the user's ticket-granting ticket (TGT). Prior to sending the ticket-granting service reply (TGS-REP) to the client, the KDC checks the 0x00020000 bit in the value of the msDS-SupportedEncryptionTypes attribute of the security principal's object running the service. An enabled bit means that the service can accept compound authentication. The KDC sends the TGS-REP, which includes the service's ability to support compound authentication.

The Kerberos client receives the ticket-granting service TGS-REP that includes compound authentication information. The Kerberos client then sends another ticket-granting service request (TGS-REQ), with the difference being that this TGS-REQ is armored with the device's TGT rather than the user. This allows the KDC to retrieve authentication information about the principal and the device.

The Active Directory Federation Services role included in Windows Server 2016 automatically enables compound authentication when creating an AD FS web farm. During the creation of the first node in the farm, the AD FS configuration wizard enables the compound authentication bit on the msDS-SupportedEncryptionTypes attribute on the account that you designate to run the AD FS service. If you change the service account, then you must manually enable compound authentication by running the Set-ADUser -compoundIdentitySupported:$true Windows PowerShell cmdlet.

In Exercise 23.3, you will learn how to configure multifactor authentication.

EXERCISE 23.3

Configuring Multifactor Authentication

1. In the AD FS Management Console, traverse to Trust Relationships And Relying Party Trusts.

2. Select the relying party trust that represents your sample application (claimapp) and then either by using the Actions pane or by right-clicking this relying party trust, select Edit Claim Rules.

3. In the Edit Claim Rules For Claimapp window, select the Issuance Authorization Rules tab and click Add Rule.

4. In the Add Issuance Authorization Claim Rule Wizard, on the Select Rule Template screen, select Permit Or Deny Users Based On An Incoming Claim Rule Template and click Next.

5. On the Configure Rule screen, complete all of the following tasks and click Finish.

    a. Enter a name for the claim rule, for example **TestRule**.

    b. Select Group SID As Incoming Claim Type.

    c. Click Browse, type in **Finance** for the name of your AD test group, and resolve it for the Incoming Claim Value field.

    d. Select the Deny Access To Users With This Incoming Claim option.

    e. In the Edit Claim Rules For Claimapp window, make sure to delete the Permit Access To All Users rule that was created by default when you created this relying party trust.

Verify Multifactor Access Control Mechanism

In this phase, you will verify the multifactor access control policy that you set up in the previous phase. You can use the following procedure to verify that a test AD user can access your sample application because the test account belongs to the Finance group. Conversely, you will use the procedure to verify that AD users who do not belong to the Finance group cannot access the sample application.

1. On your client computer, open a browser window and navigate to your sample application: `https://webserv1.contoso.com/claimapp`. This action automatically redirects the request to the federation server, and you are prompted to sign in with a username and password.

2. Type in the credentials of a test AD account to be granted access to the application.

3. Type in the credentials of another test AD account that does not belong to the Finance group.

At this point, because of the access control policy that you set up in the previous steps, an access denied message is displayed for an AD account that does not belong to the Finance group. The default message text is "You are not authorized to access this site. Click here to sign out, and sign in again or contact your administrator for permissions." However, this text is fully customizable.

Workplace Join

Today's employees are mobile and remote, working across a plethora of consumer platforms. The age of bring your own device (BYOD) is here to stay. CIOs, IT security workers, and administrators cringe at the idea of storing company data on unmanaged devices. The Workplace Join feature adds a safety measure to ensure that only registered devices have access to company data.

For Workplace Join to work, a certificate is placed on the mobile device. AD FS challenges the device as a claims-based authentication to applications or other resources without requiring administrative control of the device.

Device Registration Service

Workplace Join is supported by the Device Registration Service (DRS) included with the Active Directory Federation Services role in Windows Server 2016. When a device is set up with Workplace Join, the DRS registers a device as an object in Active Directory and sets a certificate on the consumer device that is used to represent the device identity. The DRS is meant to be both internal and external facing.

DRS requires at least one global catalog server in the forest root domain. The global catalog server is needed to run the PowerShell cmdlet `-Initialize-ADDeviceRegistration` during AD FS authentication.

Workplace Join Your Device

For Workplace Join to succeed, the client computer must trust the AD FS SSL certificate. It must also be able to access and validate revocation information for the certificate from the CRL.

In Exercise 23.4, you will configure the DRS.

> ### EXERCISE 23.4
>
> **Workplace Joining a Device**
>
> 1. Start a Windows PowerShell command window and type
>
>   **Initialize-ADDeviceRegistration.**
>
> 2. When prompted for a service account, type **contoso\fsgmsa$**.
>
> 3. On the AD FS server, in the AD FS Management console, navigate to the Authentication Policies tab. Select Edit Global Primary Authentication. Select the Enable Device Authentication check box and click OK.
>
> Finally, you will need to make sure you have the following DNS records for the DRS.
>
> | Entry | Type | Address |
> | --- | --- | --- |
> | adfs1 | A | IP address of the AD FS server |
> | enterpriseregistration | Alias (CNAME) | adfs1.contoso.com |
>
> 4. Log on to the client with your Microsoft account.
>
> 5. On the Start screen, start the Charms bar and then select the Settings charm. Select Change PC Settings.
>
> 6. On the PC Settings screen, select Network and click Workplace.
>
> 7. In the Enter Your UserID To Get Workplace Access Or Turn On Device Management box, type the user's UPN or email address—for example, **RobertM@contoso.com**—and click Join.
>
> 8. When prompted for credentials, type the user's UPN or email address—for example, **roberth@contoso.com**—and a password such as **P@ssword**. Click OK.
>
> 9. You should now see the message "This device has joined your workplace network."

Active Directory Rights Management Services

Active Directory Rights Management Services (AD RMS), included with Microsoft Windows Server 2016, helps safeguard sensitive information created and distributed using AD RMS–enabled applications such as Word, Outlook, or InfoPath, similar to Adobe Acrobat's permissions for print, save, fill-form, and copy functions. Unlike traditional file permission methods, RMS rights stay with the content and ensure exclusive access to the intended recipient.

Application developers may enable their applications to work with RMS extensions. AD RMS uses policies managed from the RMS server to provide a consistent experience for users across the enterprise.

You can enforce AD RMS usage policy templates directly to protect confidential information. You can install AD RMS easily using Server Manager, and you can administer it through the MMC snap-in. These three new administrative roles allow you to delegate AD RMS responsibilities:

- AD RMS Enterprise Administrators
- AD RMS Template Administrators
- AD RMS Auditors

AD RMS integrates with AD FS, which allows two organizations to share information without requiring AD RMS in both organizations.

Self-enrollment AD RMS server enrollment allows for the creation and signing of a server licensor certificate (SLC). This SLC enables the AD RMS server to issue certificates and licenses whenever required.

Considerations and Requirements for AD RMS

Before installing Active Directory Rights Management Services on Windows Server 2016 for the first time, you must meet several requirements:

AD RMS Server   Install the AD RMS server as a member server in the same Active Directory domain as the user accounts that will be using rights-protected content.

AD RMS Service Account   Create a domain user account that has no additional permissions that can be used as the AD RMS service account. I recommend using a group-managed service account to ensure that the account password is managed by Active Directory and that it does not require a manual password change by an administrator.

If you are registering the AD RMS service connection point during installation, the user account installing AD RMS must be a member of the AD DS Enterprise Admins group or equivalent.

Which Database AD RMS Will Store Configuration Data   Microsoft SQL Server 2008 or newer and WID are supported databases for the AD RMS configuration data. Windows Internal Database is more suitable for small and/or test environments. If you are using an external SQL database server for the AD RMS databases, the user account installing AD RMS must have the right to create new databases.

AD RMS URL   Reserve a URL for the AD RMS cluster that will be available throughout the lifetime of the AD RMS installation. Make sure the reserved URL differs from the computer name.

Cryptographic Mode   Mode 1 is composed of RSA 1024-bit keys and SHA-1 hashes. Mode 2 includes RSA 2048-bit keys and SHA-256 hashes for a more secure and recommended option.

Location for Cluster Key Storage By default, the cluster key is stored within AD RMS. You may also deploy a cryptographic service provider to store the cluster key. However, you will have to distribute the key manually when installing additional AD RMS servers.

Cluster Key Password The Cluster Key password helps to encrypt the cluster key, and it must be provided when adding AD RMS servers to the cluster. The Cluster Key password must also be provided when recovering an AD RMS cluster from backup.

Cluster Name Choose the fully qualified domain name to be hosted on the AD RMS server. An SSL certificate should be configured with the FQDN of the AD RMS server. The cluster address and port cannot be changed after AD RMS is deployed. A non-SSL address can be configured, but you will lose the AD RMS with Identity Federation functionality.

AD RMS Add-On for Internet Explorer

The Windows Rights Management Add-on (RMA) for Internet Explorer enables rights-protected content to be viewed only. Because you can only view and not alter these restricted files, this prevents sensitive documents, web-based information, and email messages from being forwarded, edited, or copied by unauthorized individuals. For you to run RMA for Internet Explorer successfully, you must first install the Windows Rights Management (RM) client. The Extensible Rights Markup Language (XrML) is the XML verbiage used by AD RMS to express usage rights for rights-protected content.

AD RMS Requirements

AD RMS requires an AD RMS–enabled client. Windows Vista, Windows 7, and Windows 8/8.1 include the AD RMS client by default. If you are not using Windows Vista, Windows 7, Windows 8/8.1/10 Windows Server 2008, Windows Server 2008 R2, Windows Server 2012/2012 R2, or Windows Server 2016, you can download the AD RMS client for previous versions of Windows from Microsoft's Download Center.

   File System: The NTFS file system is recommended.

   Messaging: Message Queuing.

   Web Services: Internet Information Services (IIS). ASP.NET must be enabled.

Active Directory Domain Services

AD RMS must be installed in an Active Directory domain in which the domain controllers are running Windows Server 2008 or above. All users and groups that use AD RMS to acquire licenses and publish content require an email address configured in Active Directory.

   Database Server: AD RMS requires a SQL database server. Microsoft SQL Server 2005 or above are all supported SQL versions.

The new AD RMS administrative roles are as follows:

AD RMS Service Group   When the AD RMS role is installed onto a server, a local AD RMS service account is created and added to the local AD RMS service group. The server uses the service account to start services at system startup and cannot be the same account used to install the service.

AD RMS Enterprise Administrators   The AD RMS policies and settings are managed by members of the local AD RMS Enterprise Administrators group. When AD RMS is installed onto the server, the user account installing the role is added to the AD RMS Enterprise Administrators group. Only administrators who manage RMS should be added to this group.

AD RMS Template Administrators   Users who belong to the local AD RMS Templates Administrators group are allowed to manage rights policy templates. AD RMS template administrators have the rights to read cluster data, list rights policy templates, create new rights policy templates, modify existing rights policy templates, and export rights policy templates.

AD RMS Auditors   The local AD RMS Auditors role allows administrators who have this right to manage logs and reports. The AD RMS Auditors role is a read-only role that is restricted to running reports available on the AD RMS cluster, reading cluster information, and reading logging settings.

Installing AD RMS

AD RMS deployment is described as a root cluster, which is not used in terms of failover or network balancing clustering. An AD RMS root cluster manages all of the AD RMS licensing and certificate provisions for the forest. There can be only one AD RMS root cluster per AD forest. After a root cluster is deployed, there is the option of installing additional licensing-only clusters, which issue licenses to clients for publishing their content.

Now that you have a basic understanding of AD RMS, let's take the next step and install it. In Exercise 23.5, you will install AD RMS using the Server Manager MMC.

EXERCISE 23.5

Installing an AD RMS Role on the Local Computer Using Server Manager

1. Start Server Manager. Click Manage and then click Add Roles And Features.

2. The Add Roles And Features Wizard shows the Before You Begin screen. Click Next.

3. Select the Active Directory Rights Management Services Role and click Next.

4. Add the required Active Directory Rights Management Services by default and click Add Features.

5. Click Next.

6. On the screen that explains ADRMS, click Next.

7. On the Select Role Services screen, by default Active Directory Rights Management Server is selected. Identity Federation Support uses AD FS federated trust between organizations to establish user identities and provide access to the RMS-protected content across the federation. Click Next.

8. Click Next on the Web Server (IIS) screen.

9. At the confirmation screen, click Install.

10. Once the installation is complete, click Close.

11. While still in Server Manager, click the AD RMS link on the left side.

12. Click the More About The AD RMS Service Account link next to Configuration Required For Active Directory Rights Management Service.

13. Under Action, click the Perform Additional Configuration link.

14. At the AD RMS introduction screen, click Next.

15. On the Create Or Join An AD RMS Cluster screen, choose Create A New AD RMS Cluster. (The other choice will not be available because you are installing the first AD RMS server and must start the cluster.) Click Next.

16. AD RMS uses a database to store configuration and policy information. At the Select Configuration Database screen, choose Use Windows Internal Database on this server. (The other option is to use a third-party database engine or MSSQL.) Click Next.

17. On the Specify Service Account screen, choose the service account that AD RMS will use. Click the Specify button and type in an administrator account and password other than the ones with which you are currently logged in. Click Next.

18. At the Cryptographic Mode screen, choose Cryptographic Mode 2 (RSA 2048-bit keys/SHA-256 hashes) and click Next.

19. At the Configure AD RMS Cluster Key Storage screen, choose Use AD RMS Centrally Managed Key Storage and click Next.

20. Next you will be asked to enter a password in the AD RMS Cluster Key Password field. The AD RMS cluster key password is used to encrypt the AD RMS cluster key that is stored in the AD RMS database. Type **P@ssw0rd**, confirm it, and click Next.

21. On the Select Website screen, click default website and click Next. AD RMS needs to be hosted in IIS. This will set up a default website for AD RMS.

22. On the Specify Cluster Address screen, choose whether to use a secure or a nonsecure website. Choose the Use An SSL-Encrypted Connection (https://) check box. In the Internal Address box, type in the server name and click the Validate button. After the address is verified, click Next.

23. The Choose A Server Authentication Certificate For SSL Encryption screen appears. If you receive a message stating the certificate for this server is already created, just click Next. If the message doesn't appear, choose one of your certificates and click Next.

24. The Name The Server Licensor Certificate screen appears. Accept the default server and click Next.

25. You have the option to register AD RMS now or later. If you register the server now, AD RMS will take effect immediately. If you register the server later, AD RMS will not work until you register. You will not register during this exercise. Choose Register Later and click Next.

26. At the Configure Identity Federation Support screen, specify the name of the web server that Identity Federation will use and click the Validate button. The Next button will become available once the server is validated. If an error appears during validation, it will not affect this exercise. Click Next.

27. At the Confirm Installation Selections screen, verify all of your settings and click Install.

28. The install progress screen appears. When the install is complete, click Close.

29. Close the Server Manager MMC.

Managing AD RMS: AD RMS Service Connection Point

The *service connection point (SCP)* is used to store the URL of the AD RMS cluster. The SCP is stored as an object in Active Directory. The SCP can be configured when AD RMS is being installed or later through the Active Directory Rights Management Services console. Only one SCP can exist in an Active Directory forest.

The AD RMS SCP can be registered automatically during AD RMS installation, or it can be registered after installation has finished. To register the SCP, you must be a member of the local AD RMS Enterprise Administrators group and the Active Directory Domain Services (AD DS) Enterprise Admins group, or you must have been given the appropriate authority.

Managing the SCP is accomplished on the SCP tab of the AD RMS cluster's Properties dialog box.

If a client computer is not located within the Active Directory forest, you must use registry keys to point the AD RMS client to the AD RMS cluster. These registry keys are created in HKEY_Local_Machine\Software\Microsoft\MSDRM\ServiceLocation. Create a key called Activation with the value of http(s)://<your_cluster>/_wmcs/certification, where <your_cluster> is the URL of the root cluster used for certification.

AD RMS Templates

As you know, a template is a mold that you can use over and over again. AD RMS templates are no different. Before you start creating AD RMS templates, you must first create a shared directory where the templates can be stored. An administrator can then create AD RMS rights policy templates on the AD RMS cluster and export those templates to the shared directory. If your users are connected to the company intranet and they are using AD RMS–enabled applications, they can access the AD RMS templates right from the shared directory as long as they have read access to the shared folder. If your users are not connected to the company intranet, just copy the template to their computers, and this will allow AD RMS–enabled applications to continue to function properly.

When publishing protected content, the author selects the rights policy template to apply from the templates that are available on the local computer. Visibility of the templates is controlled via NTFS permissions. If the user does not have NTFS read access, the respective template will not be visible in an RMS-aware application.

When a user attempts to use protected content, the RMS-enabled application obtains the latest version of the rights policy template that was used to publish the content from the configuration database. The RMS-enabled application then applies its settings to the content. When the rights policy template is modified on the RMS server, RMS updates the template accordingly, in both the configuration database and the shared folder.

If a rights policy template is deleted, it is removed from the configuration database and also from the shared folder (that is specified as the file location for storing copies of templates) location when the template is deleted.

When working with rights policy templates, perform the following tasks:

1. Create and edit rights policy templates.

2. When creating a rights policy template, define the users and rights that apply. Also define how the rights policy template is to be applied to content.

3. Edit the rights policy templates later when they need to be updated.

4. Create as many rights policy templates as are required to manage rights in the organization, but consider that some applications are limited in the number of templates that can be displayed in the application's user interface. If more than a few templates are created in a cluster, you might want to scope the different templates to different groups of users by modifying NTFS permissions.

5. When a template is no longer appropriate, archive the rights policy template and update the distribution of the rights policy templates to the clients so that users do not try to protect content with the retired template. Users attempting to use content protected with the template will still be able to do so because the archived template is still accessible to the RMS servers issuing licenses.

6. If usage of all documents protected with a template is no longer desired, you can delete the template instead of archiving it. Make sure you understand that if users try to access data that is from a deleted template, that data will not be accessible because the template is gone.

See Table 23.7 for a description of the RMS template rights.

TABLE 23.7   Description of rights in RMS templates

Right	Description
Full control	If established, this right enables a user to exercise all rights in the license, whether or not the rights are specifically established to that user.
View	If this right is established, the AD RMS client enables protected content to be decrypted. Usually, when this right is established, the RMS-aware application will allow the user to view protected content.
Edit	If this right is established, the AD RMS client enables protected content to be decrypted and re-encrypted by using the same content key. Usually, when this right is established, the RMS-aware application will allow the user to change protected content and then save it to the same file. This right is effectively identical to the Save right.
Save	If this right is established, the AD RMS client enables protected content to be decrypted and then re-encrypted by using the same content key. Usually, when this right is established, the RMS-aware application will allow the user to change protected content and then save it to the same file. This right is effectively identical to the Edit right.
Export (Save As)	If this right is established, the AD RMS client enables protected content to be decrypted and then re-encrypted by using the same content key. Usually, when this right is established, the RMS-aware application will allow the user to use the Save As feature to save protected content to a new file.
Print	Usually when this right is established, the RMS-aware application will allow the user to print protected content.
Forward	Usually when this right is established, the RMS-aware application will allow an email recipient to forward a protected message.
Reply	Usually when this right is established, the RMS-aware application will allow an email recipient to reply to a protected message and include a copy of the original message.
Reply All	Usually when this right is established, the RMS-aware application will allow an email recipient to reply to all recipients of a protected message and include a copy of the original message.
Extract	Usually when this right is established, the RMS-aware application will allow the user to copy and paste information from protected content.

Right	Description
Allow Macros	Usually when this right is established, the RMS-aware application will allow the user to run macros in the document or use an editor to modify macros in the document.
View Rights	If this right is established, the AD RMS client enables a user to view the user rights that are assigned by the license.
Edit Rights	If this right is established, the AD RMS client enables a user to edit the user rights that are assigned by the license.

Backing Up AD RMS

Follow these steps to allow you to recover from any AD rights management server failure:

1. Record your cluster key password and store it in a safe manner.
2. Export the trusted publishing domain (see Exercise 23.8).
3. Create database backups.

Record and Store Your Cluster Key Password

During installation, take note of the cluster key password and securely store it. If you inherited the AD RMS server and the cluster key password hasn't been documented, you should change it before backup. To accomplish this, start the Active Directory Rights Management Services console under ServerName ➢ Security Policies ➢ Cluster Key Password. Click Change Cluster Key Password.

Create a Backup of the AD RMS Database

AD RMS uses three databases in the database server:

Configuration Database   This is a critical component of an AD RMS installation. The database stores, shares, and retrieves all configuration data and other data that the service requires to manage account certification, licensing, and publishing services for a whole cluster.

Directory Services Database   This contains information about users, identifiers (such as email addresses), security IDs, group membership, and alternate identifiers. This information is a cache of directory services data.

Logging Database   This is all of the historical data about client activity and license acquisition. For each root or licensing-only cluster, by default AD RMS installs a logging database in the same database server instance hosting the configuration database.

In Exercise 23.6, we will perform a backup of the RMS database.

EXERCISE 23.6

Backing Up an AD RMS Database

1. Log on to the SQL server.

2. Click Start ➢ All Programs ➢ Microsoft SQL Server and select SQL Server Management Studio. The Connect To Server dialog box will appear. Verify that the server name is correct and that authentication is set for Windows Authentication.

3. Click Connect.

4. Expand the Databases node.

5. Right-click DRMS_Config_rms_domain_com_443, select Tasks, and then select Back Up.

6. Click Add in the Destination section and select the location.

7. Click OK to finish the backup.

8. Repeat these steps to back up the logging and directory services cache database.

 If you cannot restore the configuration database, you can recover your AD RMS infrastructure with the exported TPD and the cluster key password.

AD RMS Trust Policies

Trust policies are implemented to define how content licensing requests are processed throughout the enterprise, including rights-protected content from other AD RMS clusters. Trust policies are defined as follows:

Trusted User Domains   A trusted user domain (TUD) is the boundary mechanism for the AD RMS root cluster to process client licensor certificates or use licenses from users whose rights account certificates (RACs) were issued by another AD RMS root cluster. You must import the server licensor certificate of the AD RMS cluster to be trusted, to define your TUD.

Trusted Publishing Domains   A trusted publishing domain (TPD) is another boundary type for one AD RMS cluster to issue licenses against publishing licenses issued by another AD RMS cluster. You must also import the server licensor certificate and private key of the server to be trusted, to define the TPD.

Windows Live ID   Microsoft offers an online RMS service for an AD RMS user to send rights-protected content to another user with their Windows Live ID. The Windows Live ID recipient is then able to read rights-protected content from the originating AD RMS cluster registered through Microsoft's online RMS service. This extended AD RMS implantation does not allow the Windows Live ID user to create rights-protected content from the on-premise AD RMS cluster.

Federated Trust   With a federated trust established between AD forests, users from one organization can share rights-protected content with another organization without requiring AD RMS implementation on both sides of the trust.

Microsoft Federation Gateway   Microsoft also offers federated trust through the Microsoft Federation Gateway, which is essentially a trusted broker between organizations. Microsoft Federation Gateway handles all of the identity verifications with all participating Microsoft federated organizations. Microsoft federated organizations can take advantage of this gateway by filtering lists to select which domains can receive certificates or licenses from the on-premise AD RMS cluster.

Managing Trusted User Domains   Trusted user domains enable trust between domains running AD RMS, and they are often used to connect users between forests. TUD management is accomplished in the AD RMS Management console. TUD information is exported to a .bin file and then subsequently imported using the Import Trusted User Domain dialog box.

Adding a Trusted User Domain   By default, Active Directory Rights Management Services (AD RMS) will not process requests from users whose rights account certificate was issued by a different AD RMS installation. However, you can add user domains to the list of trusted user domains, which allows AD RMS to process such requests.

For each TUD, you can also add and remove specific users or groups of users. In addition, you can remove a TUD; however, you cannot remove the root cluster for this Active Directory forest from the list of TUDs. Every AD RMS server trusts the root cluster in its own forest. In Exercise 23.7 we'll add a TUD into the test domain.

EXERCISE 23.7

Adding a Trusted User Domain

Before getting started, the TUD of the AD RMS installation should already be exported and available.

1. Start the Active Directory Rights Management Services console and expand the AD RMS cluster.

2. In the console tree, expand Trust Policies and click Trusted User Domains.

3. In the Actions pane, click Import Trusted User Domain.

4. In the Trusted User Domain File dialog box, type the path to the exported server licensor certificate of the user domain to trust or click Browse to locate it.

5. In Display Name, type a name to identify this trusted user domain. If you would like to extend this trust to federated users, select Extend Trust To Federated Users Of The Imported Server.

6. Click Finish.

Exporting the Trusted User Domain

TUDs allow an AD RMS cluster to issue licenses to users whose rights account certificate was established by another server in an AD RMS cluster. Exporting a TUD's key and importing it into another AD RMS cluster allows the cluster to process requests for use licenses from users whose rights account certificates are in a different cluster.

Membership in the local AD RMS Enterprise Admins group, or equivalent, is the minimum required to complete this procedure. In Exercise 23.8, we will export the TUD and store the data in a location you provide.

EXERCISE 23.8

Exporting the Trusted User Domain

1. Start the Active Directory Rights Management Services console and expand the AD RMS cluster.

2. In the console tree, expand Trust Policies and click Trusted User Domains.

3. In the Actions pane, click Export Trusted User Domain.

4. The Save As dialog box appears. I recommend you modify the .bin filename to include the name of your server, such as ADRMS_Cluster1_LicensorCert.bin.

5. Click Save to save the file with the name and location you specified.

Exporting the Trusted Publishing Domain

Unlike a trusted user domain, a trusted publishing domain enables an AD RMS cluster to issue licenses as if it was a different AD RMS cluster. To accomplish this, both the certificate and the private key need to be imported. This is different from a TUD scenario, where only the certificate is imported.

Importing a TPD is accomplished within the AD RMS Management console using the Import Trusted Publishing Domain dialog box. Saving a copy of the trusted publishing domain can be done from within the AD RMS administration console. In Exercise 23.9, we will export the TPD.

EXERCISE 23.9

Exporting the Trusted Publishing Domain

1. Start the AD RMS administration console.

2. In the console tree view, select the Trusted Publishing Domains node.

3. In the details pane on the right, select Export Trusted Publishing Domain. The Export Trusted Publishing Domain dialog box will appear.

4. From the Export Trusted Publishing Domain dialog box, click Save As. The Export Trusted Publishing Domain File Save As dialog box will appear. On the left pane, select the folder you want to save the trusted publishing domain.

5. In File Name enter a filename; then verify the XML File (*.xml) type is selected for Save As Type.

6. Click Save. This will close the Export Trusted Publishing Domain As dialog box.

7. In the Export Trusted Publishing Domain dialog box, enter a password in the Password box.

8. Enter a password again in the Confirm Password dialog box.

9. Click Finish.

Adding a Trusted Publishing Domain

Exercise 23.10 assumes you have exported the trusted publishing domain of another AD RMS cluster (as described in the preceding section). Membership in the local AD RMS Enterprise Admins group, or equivalent, is the minimum required to complete this procedure.

EXERCISE 23.10

Adding the Trusted Publishing Domain

1. Start the Active Directory Rights Management Services console and expand the AD RMS cluster.

2. In the console tree, expand Trust Policies and click Trusted Publishing Domains.

3. In the Actions pane, click Import Trusted Publishing Domain.

4. In the Trusted Publishing Domain File dialog box, type the path to the trusted publishing domain file or click Browse to locate it. This file contains the licensor certificate, private key (if the key is stored in software), and rights policy templates. This file is encrypted.

5. In Password, type the password required to decrypt this file.

6. In Display Name, type a name to identify this trusted user domain.

7. Click Finish.

Managing Distributed and Archived Rights Policy Templates

Rights policy templates are managed in the AD RMS Management console. Planning and overviews of rights policies are available here:

http://technet.microsoft.com/en-us/library/ee221094

http://technet.microsoft.com/en-us/library/dd996658

You can designate the location for the templates as well as set whether the templates can be exported by using the properties of the Rights Policy Template tab.

Configuring a Web Application Proxy

One of the advantages of using the Remote Access role service in Windows Server 2016 is the Web Application Proxy. Normally, your users access applications on the Internet from your corporate network. The *Web Application Proxy* reverses this feature, and it allows your corporate users to access applications from any device outside the network.

Administrators can choose which applications to provide reverse proxy features, and this allows administrators the ability to give access selectively to corporate users for the desired application that you want to set up for the Web Application Proxy service.

The Web Application Proxy feature allows applications running on servers inside the corporate network to be accessed by any device outside the corporate network. The process of allowing an application to be available to users outside of the corporate network is known as *publishing*.

Web Application Proxies work differently than a normal VPN solution because when an administrator publishes applications through Web Application Proxy, end users get access only to applications that the administrator published. Administrators have the ability to deploy the Web Application Proxy alongside a VPN as part of your Remote Access deployment for your organization.

Web Application Proxy can function as an AD FS proxy, and it also preauthenticates access to web applications using Active Directory Federation Services (AD FS).

Publishing Applications

One disadvantage to corporate networks are that the machines that access the network are normally devices issued by the organization. That's where Web Application Proxy publishing can help.

Web Application Proxy allows an administrator to publish an organization's applications, thus allowing corporate end users the ability to access the applications from their own devices. This is becoming a big trend in the computer industry called *bring your own device (BYOD)*.

In today's technology world, users are buying and using many of their own devices, even for business work. Because of this, the users are comfortable with their own devices. Web Application Proxy allows an organization to set up applications and enable their corporate users to use these applications with the devices the users already own, including computers, tablets, and smartphones.

The client side is easy to use as long as the end user has a standard browser or Office client. End users can also use apps from the Microsoft Windows Store that allow the client system to connect to the Web Application Proxy.

Configuring Pass-Through Authentication

Now when setting up the Web Application Proxy (see Figure 23.6) so that your users can access applications, you must have some kind of security or everyone with a device would be able to access and use your applications.

FIGURE 23.6   Example of Web Proxy setup

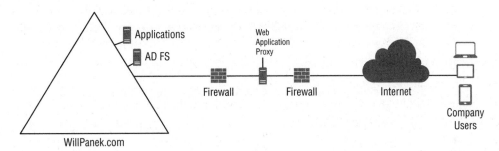

Because of this, Active Directory Federation Services (AD FS) must always be deployed with Web Application Proxy. AD FS gives you features such as single sign-on (SSO). *Single sign-on* allows you to log in one time with a set of credentials and use that set of credentials to access the applications over and over. To use a Web Application Proxy, you should set your firewall to allow for ports 443 and 49443.

When an administrator publishes an application using the Web Application Proxy, the method that users and devices use for authentication is known as preauthentication. The Web Application Proxy allows for two forms of preauthentication:

AD FS Preauthentication   AD FS preauthentication requires the user to authenticate directly with the AD FS server. After the AD FS authentication happens, the Web Application Proxy then redirects the user to the published web application. This guarantees that traffic to your published web applications is authenticated before a user can access it.

Pass-Through Preauthentication   When using Pass-through Preauthentication, a user is not required to enter credentials before they are allowed to connect to published web applications.

Pass-through authentication is truly a great benefit for your end users. Think of having a network where a user has to log in every time that user wants to access an application. The more times you make your end users log into an application, the more chances there are that the end user will encounter possible issues. Pass-through authentication works in the following way:

1. The client enters a URL address on their device, and the client system attempts to access the published web application.

2. The Web Application Proxy sends the request to the proxy server.

3. If the backend server needs the user to authenticate, the end user needs to enter their credentials only once.

4. After the server authenticates the credentials, the client has access to the published web application.

To access applications easily that are published by the Web Application Proxy and use the AD FS preauthentication, end users need to use one of the following types of clients:

▪ Any HTTP client that supports redirection (web browsers). When Web Application Proxy receives an incoming message, the Web Application Proxy redirects the user to an authentication server and then back to the original web address authenticated.

▪ Rich clients that use HTTP basic.

▪ Clients that uses MSOFBA.

▪ Clients that use the Web Authentication Broker for authentication like Windows Store apps and RESTful applications.

Authentication Capabilities

One of the great advantages of using AD FS for authentication is that your organization gets to also benefit from all of the different features that AD FS provides including:

Workplace Join This feature in AD FS allows users to join devices to the corporate network that would not normally be domain-joined. An example of this is a user's home computer. Once an administrator enables this feature, the AD FS admin will be able to configure all applications that require devices to be registered before they can gain access to published applications.

Single Sign-On The Single Sign-On (SSO) feature allows users to enter their credentials only once but then be authenticated to all supported published applications. SSO is a feature that is used heavily when connecting your corporate network to another network (like the cloud). Users sign in once but have access to both networks.

Multifactor Authentication (MFA) AD FS gives an administrator the ability to require users to authenticate with more than one authentication scheme (smart card).

Multifactor Access Control Authorization claim rules allow an administrator to control access in AD FS. Once these claim rules are implemented, they are used to issue or deny claims. This will help determine whether a user or a group of users will be allowed to access to the AD FS secured resources. Authorization rules can only be set on relying party trusts.

One thing an administrator should remember, when you decide to publish applications using the Web Application Proxy, an administrator is not required to configure any of the AD FS authentication features mentioned above.

This allows the network administrators to allow access to devices that are not able to join the workplace, or provide additional factors of authentication (kiosk machines).

All of the above features can be combined to allow for stricter security on applications or ignored for less security on applications.

PowerShell Commands

Table 23.8 shows you just some of the available PowerShell commands available for AD FS and the Web Application Proxy.

TABLE 23.8 PowerShell Commands

Command	Description
Add-AdfsAttributeStore	Administrators can use this command to add an attribute store to the Federation Service.
Add-AdfsCertificate	This command allows an administrator to add a new certificate to the AD FS server for signing, decrypting, or securing communications.
Add-AdfsClaimsProviderTrust	Administrators can use this command to add a new claims provider trust to the Federation Service.
Add-AdfsClient	This command allows an admin to register an OAuth 2.0 client with AD FS.
Add-AdfsFarmNode	Administrators can use this command to add a computer to an existing federation server farm.
Add-AdfsNativeClientApplication	This command allows an admin to add a native client application role to an application in AD FS.
Add-AdfsServerApplication	Administrators can use this command to add a server application role to an application in AD FS.
Disable-AdfsCertificateAuthority	This command allows an admin to disable a certificate authority.
Disable-AdfsLocalClaimsProviderTrust	This command allows an administrator to disable a local claims provider trust.
Disable-AdfsRelyingPartyTrust	Administrators can use this command to disable a relying party trust of the Federation Service.
Enable-AdfsApplicationGroup	This command allows an administrator to enable an application group in AD FS.

TABLE 23.8   PowerShell Commands *(continued)*

Command	Description
Enable-AdfsClaimsProviderTrust	Administrators can use this command to enable a claims provider trust in the Federation Service.
Enable-AdfsLocalClaimsProviderTrust	This command allows an administrator to enable a local claims provider trust.
Get-AdfsApplicationGroup	Administrators can use this command to view an application group.
Get-AdfsAttributeStore	This command allows an administrator to view the attribute stores of the Federation Service.
Get-AdfsAuthenticationProvider	Administrators can use this command to view a list of all authentication providers in AD FS.
Get-AdfsCertificate	This command allows an administrator to view the certificates from AD FS.
Get-AdfsCertificateAuthority	Administrators can use this command to view a certificate authority.
Get-AdfsClient	This command allows an administrator to view registration information for an OAuth 2.0 client.
Get-AdfsFarmInformation	Administrators can use this command to view AD FS behavior level and farm node information.
Initialize-ADDeviceRegistration	Admins can use this command to initialize the Device Registration Service configuration in the Active Directory forest.
New-AdfsApplicationGroup	This command creates a new application group.
New-AdfsClaimRuleSet	Administrators can use this command to create a set of claim rules.
New-AdfsOrganization	This command allows an administrator to create a new organization information object.

Command	Description
Register-AdfsAuthenticationProvider	Administrators can use this command to register an external authentication provider in AD FS.
Remove-AdfsApplicationGroup	This command allows an administrator to remove an application group.
Set-AdfsFarmInformation	This command allows an admin to remove a stale or offline farm node from the farm information table.
Set-AdfsProperties	Administrators can use this command to set the properties that control global behaviors in AD FS.
Set-AdfsServerApplication	This command allows an administrator to modify configuration settings for a server application role of an application in AD FS.
Set-AdfsWebConfig	Administrators can use this command to modify web customization configuration settings

Summary

In this chapter, I discussed the Active Directory Federation Services, which provides Internet-based clients with a secure identity access solution that works on both Windows and non-Windows operating systems.

I also talked about Active Directory Rights Management Services. I explained that AD RMS is included with Microsoft Windows Server 2016 and discussed how it allows administrators or users to determine what access to give other users in an organization.

Finally, I talked about the Web Application Proxy. The Web Application Proxy allows an administrator to publish an organization's applications, thus allowing corporate end users the ability to access the applications from their own devices.

Exam Essentials

Understand Active Directory Federation Service.   Active Directory Federation Service gives users the ability to do a single sign-on and access applications on other networks without needing a secondary password. Organizations can set up trust relationships with other trusted organizations so that a user's digital identity and access rights can be accepted without a secondary password.

Know how to install Active Directory Rights Management Services.   Active Directory Rights Management Services, included with Microsoft Windows Server 2016, allows administrators and users to determine what access (open, read, modify, and so on) they give to other users in an organization. This access can be used to secure email messages, internal websites, and documents.

Understand what Web Application Proxy.   The Web Application Proxy allows your corporate users to access applications from any device outside the network.

Review Questions

You can find the answers in the Appendix.

1. ABC Industries wants configuration modifications of the Certification Authority role service to be logged. How would you implement this? (Choose all that apply.)

   A. You should consider enabling auditing of system events.

   B. You should consider enabling logging.

   C. You should consider enabling auditing of object access.

   D. You should consider enabling auditing of privilege use.

   E. You should consider enabling auditing of process tracking.

2. Federation proxy services are installed through which of the following?

   A. Separate Active Directory Federation Proxy install download

   B. Server Manager ➤ Remote Access ➤ Web Proxy

   C. Server Manager ➤ Active Directory Federation Services ➤ Active Directory Proxy services

   D. Windows PowerShell ➤ Install-Windows-Feature Web Proxy

3. The new Workplace Join feature supports which of following? (Choose all that apply.)

   A. Federates an iPhone to the corporate intranet

   B. Allows Windows 8 clients to process claim-based trusts

   C. Allows Windows 8 clients to form claim-based trusts automatically with the home domain

   D. None of the above

4. You install and configure four Windows Server 2016 servers as an AD FS server farm. The AD FS configuration database is stored in a Microsoft SQL Server 2012 database. You need to ensure that AD FS will continue to function in the event of an AD FS server failure. You also need to ensure that all four servers in the AD FS farm will actively perform AD FS functions. What should you include in your solution?

   A. Windows Failover Clustering

   B. Windows Identity Foundation 3.5

   C. Network Load Balancing

   D. Web Proxy Server

5. Your network contains an Active Directory domain named contoso.com. You plan to deploy a Windows 2016 Active Directory Federation Services (AD FS) farm that will contain eight federation servers. You need to identify which technology or technologies must be deployed on the network before you install the federation servers. Which technology or technologies should you identify? (Choose all that apply.)

   A. Network Load Balancing

   B. Microsoft Forefront Identity Manager 2010

   C. Windows Internal Database feature

   D. Microsoft SQL Server 2016

   E. The Windows Identity Foundation 3.5 feature

6. You are the system administrator at JavaCup, which hosts a web RMS-aware application that the JavaCup forest and Boston Tea Company forest users need to access. You deploy a single AD FS server in the JavaCup forest. Which of the following is a true statement about your AD FS implementation? (Choose all that apply.)

A. You will configure a relying-party server on the JavaCup AD FS server.

B. The AD FS server in the Boston Tea Company forest functions as the claims provider.

C. The AD FS server in the Boston Tea Company forest functions as the relying-party server.

D. You will configure a claims provider trust on the JavaCup AD FS server.

7. You store AD FS servers in an OU named Federation Servers. You want to auto-enroll the certificates used for AD FS. Which certificates should you add to the GPO?

A. The CA certificate of the forest

B. The third-party (VeriSign, Entrust) CA certificate

C. The SSL certificate assigned to the AD FS servers

D. The Token Signing certificate assigned to the AD FS Servers

8. You plan to implement Active Directory Rights Management Services (AD RMS) across the enterprise. You need to plan the AD RMS cluster installations for the forest. Users in all domains will access AD RMS–protected documents. You need to minimize the number of AD RMS clusters. Which of the following will help you determine how many AD RMS root clusters you require?

A. You need at least one AD RMS root cluster for the enterprise.

B. You need at least one AD RMS root cluster per forest.

C. You need at least one AD RMS root cluster per domain.

D. You need at least one AD RMS root cluster per Active Directory site.

E. An AD RMS root cluster is not required.

9. You have a server named Server1 that runs Windows Server 2016. You need to configure Server1 as a Web Application Proxy. Which server role or role service should you install on Server1?

A. Remote Access

B. Active Directory Federation Services

C. Web Server (IIS)

D. DirectAccess and VPN (RAS)

10. Your network contains an Active Directory forest named `WillPanek.com`. The forest contains a member server on the perimeter network named Server1 that runs Windows Server 2016. The administrator installs the Active Directory Federation Services server role on Server1 along with the Web Application Proxy. Which two inbound TCP ports should you open on the firewall? Each correct answer presents part of the solution. (Choose two.)

A. 443

B. 390

C. 8443

D. 49443

Appendix

Answers to the Review Questions

Chapter 1: Installing Windows Server 2016

1. B. Windows Server 2016 Server Core is a more secure, slimmed-down version of Windows Server. Web versions of Windows Server 2016 are not available. You would use Windows Server 2016 Standard as a Web server.

2. A. The only way you can change between Server Core and the Desktop Experience is to reinstall the server. Converting from Server Core to Desktop Experience by running a PowerShell command is no longer available.

3. B. Microsoft recommends that you upgrade your Windows Server 2012 or Windows Server 2012 R2 Standard server to Windows Server 2016 Standard.

4. A. Windows Server 2012 R2 Datacenter was designed for organizations that are seeking to migrate to a highly virtualized, private cloud environment. Windows Server 2012 R2 Datacenter has full Windows Server functionality with unlimited virtual instances.

5. D. Windows Server 2016 Essentials is ideal for small businesses that have as many as 25 users and 50 devices. Windows Server 2016 Essentials has a simpler interface and preconfigured connectivity to cloud-based services but no virtualization rights.

6. C. Windows Server 2016 Essentials is ideal for small businesses that have as many as 25 users and 50 devices. It has a simple interface, preconfigured connectivity to cloud-based services, and no virtualization rights.

7. A, B, C, D. All four answers are advantages of using Windows Server 2016. Server Core is a smaller installation of Windows Server and therefore all four answers apply.

8. B. Windows Server 2016 Features On Demand allows an administrator not only to disable a role or feature but also to remove the role or feature's files completely from the hard disk.

9. D. Windows Server 2016 Nano Server uses the Current Branch for Business (CBB) servicing model. This version of servicing is a more aggressive version and it was specifically designed with the cloud in mind. As the cloud continues to quickly evolve, the CBB servicing model is meant for that lifecycle.

10. C. Windows Server 2016 has a type of domain controller called a read-only domain controller (RODC). This gives an organization the ability to install a domain controller in an area or location (onsite or offsite) where security is a concern.

Chapter 2: Installing in the Enterprise

1. D. You would use the Sysprep utility. The /generalize options prevents system-specific information from being included in the image.

2. A. The DISM utility with the /get-ImageInfo displays information about images in a WIM or VHD file..

3. A. SIM is a graphical utility that can be used to create an answer file. Answer files can be used to automate the installation routine so that no user interaction is required.

4. C. Windows System Image Manager (SIM) is used to create unattended answer files in Windows Server 2016. It uses a GUI-based interface to set up and configure the most common options that are used within an answer file.

5. A. The /unattend option can be used with the Setup.exe command to initiate an unattended installation of Windows Server 2016. You should also specify the location of the answer file to use when using the Setup.exe utility.

6. D. Once you have a reference computer installed, you can use the System Preparation Tool to prepare the computer to be used with disk imaging. Image Capture Wizard is a utility that can be used to create a disk image after it is prepared using the System Preparation Tool. The image can then be transferred to the destination computer(s).

7. C. Unique information is stripped out of the installation image when you use the System Preparation Tool to create a disk image—for example, the unique SID that is applied to every computer. Unique information is then generated when the target computer is installed.

8. B. When you configure your WDS server, the remote installation folder should not reside on the system partition.

9. C. You would configure formatting and partitioning information in the Windows PE component of the answer file. The options specified in this configuration pass will occur before the image will be copied to the local computer.

10. B. The /generalize option prevents system-specific information from being included in the image. The Sysprep.exe command can be used with a variety of options. You can see a complete list by typing **sysprep/?** at a command-line prompt.

Chapter 3: Configuring Storage and Replication

1. A. The iSCSI default port is TCP 3260. Port 3389 is used for RDP, port 1433 is used for Microsoft SQL, and port 21 is used for FTP.

2. A. The Get-ShieldedVMProvisioningStatus command allows you to view the provisioning status of a shielded virtual machine.

3. B. The Set-VMNetworkAdapter command allows an administrator to configure features of the virtual network adapter in a virtual machine or the management operating system.

4. C. This `Set-VMProcessor` command allows an administrator to configure the processors of a virtual machine. While the virtual machine is in the OFF state, run the Set-VMProcessor command on the physical Hyper-V host. This enables nested virtualization for the virtual machine.

5. C. The `Set-VMSwitch` cmdlet allows an administrator to configure a virtual switch.

6. D. The `Optimize-VHD` command allows an administrator to optimize the allocation of space in virtual hard disk files, except for fixed virtual hard disks.

7. B. The `Get-Package` command allows an administrator to view a list of all software packages that have been installed by using Package Management.

8. D. The `Get-WindowsFeature` cmdlet allows an administrator to view a list of available and installed roles and features on the local server.

9. D. The `iscsicli addisnsserver server_name` command manually registers the host server to an iSNS server. `refreshisnsserver` refreshes the list of available servers. `removeisnsserver` removes the host from the iSNS server. `listisnsservers` lists the available iSNS servers.

10. D. The `Set-VMHost` cmdlet allows an administrator to configure a Hyper-V host. These settings include network settings network adapters.

Chapter 4: Understanding Hyper-V

1. B, D. Hyper-V can be installed on the Standard or Datacenter Editions of Windows Server 2016. Itanium, x86, and Web Editions are not supported.

2. C. The external virtual network type will allow the virtual machine to communicate with the external network as it would with the Internet, so A is wrong. The internal-only network type allows communication between the virtual machines and the host machine. Because the question says that only communication between the virtual machines should be allowed, the only valid answer is private virtual machine network. The last option, public virtual machine network, does not exist in Hyper-V.

3. A. This question focuses on the fact that you cannot change the memory if the virtual machine is running, paused, or saved. The only valid answer is to shut it down and then change the memory.

4. A. The only virtual hard disk that increases in size is the dynamically expanding disk. Thus, this is the only valid answer to this question. The fixed-size disk creates a disk of the size you specify, the differencing disk is a special disk that stores only the differences between it and a parent disk, and the physical disk uses a physical drive and makes it available to the virtual machine.

5. C. Physical hard disks cannot be configured using the Virtual Hard Disk Wizard, the Edit Virtual Hard Disk Wizard, or the New Virtual Machine Wizard. You can configure and attach a physical disk only by using the virtual machine's settings.

6.   B. Hyper-V is not supported on Itanium-based systems, thus he cannot install it.

7.   A, B, C. The minimum CPU requirement for running Hyper-V is a x64-based processor (Itanium is not supported), hardware Data Execution Protection must be enabled, and hardware-assisted virtualization must be enabled. There is no minimum requirement for a dual-core processor.

8.   C. This question relates to the setup command used to install the Hyper-V server role on a Windows Server 2016 Server Core machine. It's important to remember that these commands are case sensitive, and that the correct command is `start / wocsetup Microsoft-Hyper-V`, which is option C. All of the other commands will fail to install Hyper-V on a Server Core machine.

9.   A, C, D. The Hyper-V Manager is available only for Windows Server 2012 R2/2012/2008 R2/2008, Windows 10, Windows 8, and Windows 7. There is no version available that runs on Windows Server 2003.

10. C. The virtual network type in which the machines communicate with each other and with the host machine is called internal only. In a private virtual network, the virtual machines can communicate only with each other, not with the network or the host machine. The external network type defines a network where the virtual machines can communicate with each other, with the host machine, and with an external network like the Internet.

Chapter 5: Configuring High Availability

1.   A. To create a new NLB cluster, you would use the PowerShell command `New-NlbCluster`.

2.   D. Software Load Balancing allows administrators to have multiple servers hosting the same virtual networking workload in a multitenant environment. This allows an administrator to set up high availability.

3.   A. The maximum number a single cluster can support is 32 computers.

4.   B. If an administrator decides to use the drainstop command, the cluster stops after answering all of the current NLB connections. So the current NLB connections are finished but no new connections to that node are accepted.

5.   D. If you want to stop the entire cluster from running, while in the NLB manager (type **NLBmgr** in Run command), you would right-click on the cluster, point to Control Hosts, and then choose Stop.

6.   A. The PowerShell command `Stop-VMReplication` will stop virtual machine replication from happening.

7.   D. The `Enable-VMReplication` command allows an administrator to enable virtual machine migration on a virtual machine host.

8.   B. To use unicast communication between NLB cluster nodes, each node must have a minimum of two network adapters.

9. D. Setting the cluster affinity to Single will send all traffic from a specific IP address to a single cluster node. Using this affinity will keep a client on a specific node where the client should not have to authenticate again. Setting the filtering mode to Single would remove the authentication problem but would not distribute the load to other servers unless the initial server was down.

10. C. When setting the affinity to Class C, NLB links clients with a specific member based on the Class C part of the client's IP address. This allows an administrator to set up NLB so that clients from the same Class C address range can access the same NLB member. This affinity is best for NLB clusters using the Internet.

Chapter 6: Understanding Clustering

1. D. The `Enable-VMReplication` PowerShell command allows an administrator to configure the automatic replication of a cluster.

2. A, B. The first PowerShell command, `(Get-Cluster).CrossSiteDelay`, is what is used to set the amount of time between each heartbeat sent to nodes. This value is in milliseconds (default is 1000).

   The second PowerShell command, `(Get-Cluster).CrossSiteThreshold`, is the value that you set for the number of missed heartbeats (default is 20) before the node is considered offline.

3. D. A Windows Server 2016 cluster consisting of servers running the x64 version can contain up to 64 nodes.

4. A. The `Enable-ClusterStorageSpacesDirect` command allows an administrator to enable highly available storage spaces that use directly attached storage, Storage Spaces Direct (S2D), on a cluster.

5. B. The storage tests require the clustered disk resource to be offline. If you need to run the storage tests, the Validate a Configuration Wizard will prompt you to make sure you want to take the resources offline.

6. A, C. SQL Server and Exchange Server are supported only on failover clusters. Websites and VPN services are network-based services, so they are better suited for NLB clusters.

7. A. Administrators would use the `Test-Cluster` command to complete validation tests for a cluster.

8. B. The cluster heartbeat is a signal sent between servers so that they know that the machines are up and running. Servers send heartbeats and after five nonresponsive heartbeats, the cluster would assume that the node was offline. Cross-Site Heartbeating is the same signal but with longer timeouts to allow for cluster nodes in remote locations.

9. B. Up to two votes can be lost before quorum can no longer be achieved. These votes can come from the file share witness or a cluster node.

10. B. In a three-node cluster, only one node can be offline before quorum is lost; a majority of the votes must be available to achieve quorum.

Chapter 7: Configuring Windows Containers

1. C. Administrators can set any configuration option for the daemon in a JSON format.

2. A. The docker create command gives you the ability to create a new container.

3. D. The Get-Container PowerShell command allows an administrator to view information about containers.

4. D. The docker run command executes commands in a Dockerfile. The Docker build command allows you to compile and create an image and the docker rm command allows you to delete an image.

5. A. The docker images command gives you the ability to see your images. The docker info command allows you to see how many images you have on a host but it does not give you details about the images.

6. C. The Docker build command allows you to compile and create an image. The docker run command executes commands in a Dockerfile, and the docker rm command allows you to delete an image.

7. A. The docker run command executes commands in a Dockerfile. The Docker build command allows you to compile and create an image, and the docker rm command allows you to delete an image.

8. C. The Remove-Container command gives you the ability to delete a container.

9. B. The docker pull microsoft/windowsservercore command allows you to grab an image of Windows Server Core from the Docker website.

10. C. Windows Server 2016 and Windows 10 Professional and Enterprise (Anniversary Edition) allow you to set up containers.

Chapter 8: Maintaining Windows Server

1. B, E. You can set the Registry key HKEY_LOCAL_MACHINE\Software\Policies\ Microsoft\Windows\WindowsUpdate\AU\UseWUServer to 0 to use the public Windows Update server, or you can set it to 1, which means that you will specify the server for Windows Update in the HKEY_LOCAL_MACHINE\Software\Policies\Microsoft\Windows\ WindowsUpdate key. The WSUServer key sets the Windows Update server using the server's HTTP name, such as, for example, http://intranetSUS.

2. C. Server Manager is the one place where you install all roles and features for a Windows Server 2016 system.

3. C. All options are valid steps to complete the configuration except option C because SERVERB cannot automatically draw updates from whichever sources are on SERVERA.

4. B, D, F. Option A schedules the updates to occur at a time when the computers are generally not connected to the corporate network. Options C and E require more user interaction than would be considered minimal. By setting updates to occur with no user interaction at noon, you satisfy the requirements.

5. D. You can recover system state data from a backup, which always includes the Active Directory database. In this case, Event Viewer and System Monitor wouldn't help you recover the database, but they might help you determine why the hard drive crashed in the first place.

6. C. The Update Source And Proxy Server option allows you to specify where you will be receiving your updates (from Microsoft or another WSUS server) and your proxy settings if a proxy server is needed.

7. A. Using images allows you to back up and restore your entire Windows Server 2016 machine instead of just certain parts of data.

8. C. The Backup Once link allows you to start a backup on the Windows Server 2016 system.

9. D. If you need to back up and restore your Windows Server 2016 machine, you need to use the Windows Server Backup MMC.

10. B. The primary method by which system administrators create and manage application data partitions is through the `ntdsutil` tool.

Chapter 9: Understanding Monitoring

1. D. All of the applications that are running on the Windows Server 2016 machine will show up under the Details tab. Right-click the application and end the process.

2. A. If you use MBSA from the command-line utility `mdsacli.exe`, you can specify several options. You type **mdsacli.exe/hf** (from the folder that contains `Mdsacli.exe`) and then customize the command execution with an option such as `/ixxxx.xxxx.xxxx.xxxx`, which specifies that the computer with the specified IP address should be scanned.

3. A. Performance Monitor allows you to watch the resources on your system. You can add as many objects and counters that you want to view.

4. B. `Perfmon.exe` is the command-line command to start Performance Monitor.

5. D. All of the users that are running applications on the Windows Server 2016 machine will show up under the Users tab. Right-click the user and click the Disconnect button if you need them to be disconnected.

6. B. The Resource Monitor is another utility that allows you to view the resources on your server. You can use Resource Monitor to watch the system's CPU, Memory, Disk, and Network.

7. D. Resmon.exe is the command-line command to start Resource Monitor.

8. D. By using the Microsoft Message Analyzer, you can view all of the network packets that are being sent to or from the local server. Based on this information, you can determine the source of certain types of traffic, such as pings. The other types of monitoring can provide useful information, but they do not allow you to drill down into the specific details of a network packet, and they don't allow you to filter the data that has been collected based on details about the packet.

9. A. Microsoft Baseline Security Analyzer is a free download that you can get from Microsoft's website.

10. D. All of the users that are running applications on the Windows Server 2016 machine will show up under the Users tab. Right-click the user and click the Disconnect button if you need them to be disconnected.

Chapter 10: Configuring TCP/IP

1. D. To calculate the network mask, you need to figure out which power number (2x) is greater than or equal to the number you need. Since we are looking for 1000, 210 = 1024. You then add the power (10) to the current network mask (53 + 10 = 63).

2. A. When you look at an IPv6 address, the first sections tell you the IPv6 address space prefix. Fd00:: /8 is the unique local unicast prefix, and this allows the server to communicate with all local machines within your intranet.

3. C. The unique local address can be FC00 or FD00, and it is used like the private address space of IPv4. Unique local addresses are not expected to be routable on the global Internet, but they are used for private routing within an organization.

4. A. A Class B address with a default subnet mask of 255.255.0.0 will support up to 65,534 hosts. To increase the number of networks that this network will support, you need to subnet the network by borrowing bits from the host portion of the address. The subnet mask 255.255.252.0 uses 6 bits from the host's area, and it will support 64 subnets while leaving enough bits to support 1,022 hosts per subnet. The subnet mask 255.255.248.0 uses 5 bits from the hosts and will support 32 subnetworks while leaving enough bits to support 2,046 hosts per subnet. 255.255.252.0 is the better answer because it leaves quite a bit of room for further growth in the number of networks while still leaving room for more than 1,000 hosts per subnet, which is a fairly large number of devices on one subnet. The subnet mask 255.255.254.0 uses 7 bits from the host's area and will support 126 networks, but it will leave only enough bits to support 500 hosts per subnet. The subnet mask 255.255.240.0 uses 4 bits from the hosts and will support only 16 subnetworks, even though it will leave enough bits to support more than 4,000 hosts per subnet.

5. A. The network mask applied to an address determines which portion of that address reflects the number of hosts available to that network. The balance with subnetting is always between the number of hosts and individual subnetworks that can be uniquely represented within one encompassing address. The number of hosts and networks that are made available depends on the number of bits that can be used to represent them. This scenario requires more than 35 networks and fewer than 1,000 workstations on each network. If you convert the subnet masks as described in the chapter, you will see that the mask in option A allows for 64 networks and more than 1,000 hosts. All of the other options are deficient in either the number of networks or the number of hosts that they represent.

6. A. The subnet mask 255.255.255.192 borrows 2 bits from the hosts, which allows you to build four separate networks that you can route through the Windows server. This will allow you to have 62 hosts on each segment. A mask of 255.255.255.128 would have been even better, with two subnets of 126 hosts each, but that wasn't an option and this solution gives you room for growth in the number of subnets. The subnet mask 255.255.255.224 borrows 3 bits from the hosts. This allows you to create 8 networks, which you don't need, and it leaves only enough bits for 30 hosts. The subnet mask 255.255.255.252 borrows 6 bits from the hosts. This allows you to create 64 networks, which you don't need, and it leaves only enough bits for 2 hosts. The subnet mask 255.255.255.240 borrows 4 bits from the hosts. This allows you to create 16 networks, which you don't need, and it leaves only enough bits for 14 hosts per subnet.

7. B, C, D. When you add up the locations that currently need to be given a network address, the total is 3,150, and the maximum number of hosts at any one of these locations is fewer than 1,000. The subnet masks need to support those requirements. Assuming that you choose the Class A private address space 10.0.0.0/8, the subnet masks given in options B, C, and D will provide the address space to support the outlined requirements. The subnet mask 255.255.240.0 supports 4,096 subnets and more than 4,000 hosts. The subnet mask 255.255.248.0 supports 8,192 subnets and 2,046 hosts. The subnet mask 255.255.252.0 supports more than 16,000 subnets and more than 1,000 hosts. Although each of these subnet masks will work, at the rate that this company is growing, 255.255.252.0 is probably the best mask to prepare for the future. It's unlikely that there will ever be more than 1,000 hosts on any given network. In fact, that number would probably cause performance problems on that subnet. Therefore, it's better to have more subnets available to deploy as the company grows. The subnet mask 255.255.224.0 supports 2,048 subnets— an insufficient number to cover the locations. The subnet mask 255.255.254.0 supports 32,768 subnets, but only 500 hosts per subnet, which are not enough hosts to cover all of the locations.

8. C. The CIDR /27 tells you that 27 1s are turned on in the subnet mask. Twenty-seven 1s equals 11111111.11111111.11111111.11100000. This would then equal 255.255.255.224.

The network address 192.168.11.192 with a subnet mask of 255.255.255.224 is perfect for Subnet A because it supports up to 30 hosts. The network address 192.168.11.128 with a subnet mask of 255.255.255.192 is perfect for Subnet B because it supports up to 62 hosts. The network address 192.168.11.0 with a subnet mask of 255.255.255.128 is perfect for Subnet C because it supports up to 126 hosts.

9. C. You need to configure a subnet mask that can accommodate 3,500 clients. The way to figure it out is to use the formula of 2x-2=Mask Number. So 3,500 clients means it is 212-2=4094. 4094 (power of 12) is the first Power number that is greater than 3,500. So since it is 212, that means that our subnet mask has 12 zeros. So it looks like the following; 11111111.11111111.11110000.00000000. This translates into 255.255.240.0.

10. B, D. If the first word of an IPv6 address is FE80 (actually the first 10 bits of the first word yields 1111 1110 10 or FE80:: /10), then the address is a link-local IPv6 address. If it's in EUI-64 format, then the MAC address is also available (unless it's randomly generated). The middle FF:FE is the filler and indicator of the EUI-64 space, with the MAC address being 00:03:FF:11:02:CD. Remember also the 00 of the MAC becomes 02 in the link-local IPv6 address, flipping a bit to call it local.

Chapter 11: Configuring DNS

1. B. Because of the .(root) zone, users will not be able to access the Internet. The DNS forwarding option and DNS root hints will not be configurable. If you want your users to access the Internet, you must remove the .(root) zone.

2. C. Active Directory Integrated zones store their records in Active Directory. Because this company only has one Active Directory forest, it's the same Active Directory that both DNS servers are using. This allows ServerA to see all of the records of ServerB and ServerB to see all the records of ServerA.

3. D. The Secure Only option is for DNS servers that have an Active Directory Integrated zone. When a computer tries to register with DNS dynamically, the DNS server checks Active Directory to verify that the computer has an Active Directory account. If the computer that is trying to register has an account, DNS adds the host record. If the computer trying to register does not have an account, the record gets tossed away and the database is not updated.

4. A. If you need to complete a zone transfer from Microsoft DNS to a BIND (Unix) DNS server, you need to enable BIND secondaries on the Microsoft DNS server.

5. B. Conditional forwarding allows you to send a DNS query to different DNS servers based on the request. Conditional forwarding lets a DNS server on a network forward DNS queries according to the DNS domain name in the query.

6. B. On a Windows Server 2016 DNS machine, debug logging is disabled by default. When it is enabled, you have the ability to log DNS server activity, including inbound and outbound queries, packet type, packet content, and transport protocols.

7. D. Active Directory Integrated zones give you many benefits over using primary and secondary zones, including less network traffic, secure dynamic updates, encryption, and reliability in the event of a DNS server going down. The Secure Only option is for dynamic updates to a DNS database.

8. A. Windows Server 2016 DNS supports two features called DNS Aging and DNS Scavenging. These features are used to clean up and remove stale resource records. DNS zone or DNS server aging and scavenging flags old resource records that have not been updated in a certain amount of time (determined by the scavenging interval). These stale records will be scavenged at the next cleanup interval.

9. C. The dnscmd /zoneexport command creates a file using the zone resource records. This file can then be given to the Compliance department as a copy.

10. D. Stub zones are very useful for slow WAN connections. These zones store only three types of resource records: NS records, glue host (A) records, and SOA records. These three records are used to locate authoritative DNS servers.

Chapter 12: Configuring DHCP

1. C. Out of the possible answers provided, the only DHCP configuration option that would be both fault tolerant and redundant is DHCP failover.

2. C. Admins can use the Set-DhcpServerv4Scope command to configure the settings of an existing IPv4 scope.

3. D. Microsoft recommends the 80/20 rule for redundancy of DHCP services in a network. Implementing the 80/20 rule calls for one DHCP server to make approximately 80 percent of the addresses for a given subnet available through DHCP while another server makes the remaining 20 percent of the addresses available.

4. A. DHCP can become a single point of failure within a network if there is only one DHCP server. If that server becomes unavailable, clients will not be able to obtain new leases or renew existing leases. For this reason, it is recommended that you have more than one DHCP server in the network. However, more than one DHCP server can create problems if they both are configured to use the same scope or set of addresses. Microsoft recommends the 80/20 rule for redundancy of DHCP services in a network. To do this, you run the Configure Failover Wizard.

5. B. DHCP can't be loaded onto a Nano Server. You can load DHCP on a Server Core server (Server with no GUI desktop) or a server with the GUI desktop.

6. A. 003 Router is used to provide a list of available routers or default gateways on the same subnet.

7. D. Admins can use the Set-DhcpServerv4Scope command to configure the settings of an existing IPv4 scope.

8. B. 006 DNS is used to provide a list of available DNS servers to your scope settings or to your server settings.

9. B. Reservations are set up by using the machine's network adapter's MAC address. Every network adapter has its own MAC address. So when the network card got replaced, the new MAC address needs to be put into the current reservation.

10. C. Conflict Detection Attempts specifies how many ICMP echo requests (pings) the server sends for an address it is about to offer. The default is 0. Conflict detection is a way to verify that the DHCP server is not issuing IP addresses that are already being used on the network. Since you only have one DHCP server, lower the value to zero (0).

Chapter 13: Implement IP Address Management

1. B. Administrators can use the Set-IpamBlock PowerShell command to configure an IP address block in IPAM.

2. C. Administrators can use the Add-IpamRange PowerShell command to add an IP address range to an IPAM server.

3. D. Administrators can use the Set-IpamDiscoveryDomain PowerShell command to change the IPAM discovery configuration.

4. A. Administrators can use the Get-IpamDnsZone PowerShell command to view the DNS zone information from IPAM database.

5. C. Administrators need to create and links IPAM group policies (GPOs) for provisioning. To do this, you can either manually create the GPOs or run the Invoke-IpamGpoProvisioning PowerShell command.

6. C. The IPAM ASM Administrators group is specifically designed for the delegation of IPAM Address Space Management. The IPAM Administrators group would give her domain account way too much access within the environment, and the other two possible answers would not provide her with enough permissions to perform her required responsibilities.

7. B. Out of the three real possible deployment methods—Distributed, Centralized, and Hybrid—only the Centralized deployment method allows one primary IPAM server to manage the entire enterprise. The Distributed method places an IPAM server at each site location, and the Hybrid method uses a primary server with an additional IPAM server at each site location within the enterprise.

8. A. The Set-IPAMConfiguration command is used if the GPOs are already created. If you need to create the GPOs, you use the Invoke-IpamGpoProvisioning.

9. C. After you have successfully installed and provisioned your IPAM server, the next logical step in the IPAM deployment configuration is to configure and run server discovery.

10. A. The Move-IpamDatabase command allows an admin to move an IPAM database to a SQL Server database.

Chapter 14: Configuring Network Access

1. B. Using single tenant mode allows you to deploy the RAS Gateway as an edge VPN server, an edge DirectAccess server, or both simultaneously.

2. A. The Get-BgpRouter PowerShell command allows you to see the configuration information for BGP routers.

3. B. Administrators use the Get-DAClient command to see the list of client security groups that are part of the DirectAccess deployment and the client properties.

4. D. Logman creates and manages Event Trace Session and Performance logs and allows an administrator to monitor many different applications through the use of the command line.

5. D. The higher the RADIUS priority number, the less that the RADIUS server gets used. To make sure that RADIUS ServerD is only used when ServerB and ServerC is unavailable, you would set the RADIUS priority from 1 to 10. This way it will only get used when ServerB and ServerC is having issues or is unresponsive.

6. B. SSTP is secure sockets and secure sockets uses port 443.

7. C. The Get-RemoteAccess command shows the configuration of a DirectAccess and VPN server.

8. B. The Set-DAServer command allows an administrator to set the properties specific to the DirectAccess server.

9. C. Administrators use the Set-VpnAuthType command to set the authentication type to be used for a VPN connection.

10. D. The Add-RemoteAccessRadius command allows an administrator to add a new external RADIUS server for VPN or DirectAccess connectivity.

Chapter 15: Understanding File Services

1. C. You need to publish shares in the directory before they are available to the users of the directory. If NetBIOS is still enabled on the network, the shares will be visible to the NetBIOS tools and clients, but you do not have to enable NetBIOS on shares. Although replication must occur before the shares are available in the directory, it is unlikely that the replication will not have occurred by the next day. If this is the case, then you have other problems with the directory as well.

2. A. The Sharing tab contains a check box that you can use to list the printer in Active Directory.

3. B. The Get-FsrmQuota command allows you to view the quotas on the FSRM server.

4. C. The New-FsrmFileGroup command allows an administrator to create a file group.

5. A. Administrators can use the New-FsrmQuotaTemplate command to create a new quota template on FSRM.

6. C. An administrator can use the Remove-FsrmClassificationRule command to delete the FSRM classification rule.

7. B. Offline files give you the opportunity to set up files and folders so that users can work on the data while outside the company walls. Offline files allows a user to work on files while at home without the need to be logged into the network.

8. A, B, C, D. Improved security, quotas, compression, and encryption are all advantages of using NTFS over FAT32. These features are not available in FAT32. The only security you have in FAT32 is shared folder permissions.

9. B. Disk quotas allow you to limit the amount of space on a volume or partition. You can set an umbrella quota for all users and then implement individual users' quotas to bypass the umbrella quota.

10. B. Cipher is a command-line utility that allows you to configure or change EFS files and folders.

Chapter 16: Configuring High Availability

1. A. To create a new NLB cluster, you would use the PowerShell command New-NlbCluster.

2. B, D. Answers B and D are the only versions that are real. There is no 2016 Small Business Server or Virtual Edition. The Windows Server 2016 server for virtualization is Hyper-V.

3. A. The maximum number a single cluster can support is 32 computers.

4. B. If an administrator decides to use the drainstop command, the cluster stops after answering all of the current NLB connections. So the current NLB connections are finished but no new connections to that node are accepted.

5. D. If you want to stop the entire cluster from running, while in the NLB manager (type **NLBmgr** in Run command), you would right click on the cluster, point to Control Hosts, and then choose Stop.

6. A. The PowerShell command Stop-VMReplication will stop virtual machine replication from happening.

7. B, D. Websites and Terminal Services are all designed to work with NLB clusters. Database servers like SQL Server do not work on NLB clusters.

8. B. To use unicast communication between NLB cluster nodes, each node must have a minimum of two network adapters.

9. D. Setting the cluster affinity to Single will send all traffic from a specific IP address to a single cluster node. Using this affinity will keep a client on a specific node where the client should not have to authenticate again. Setting the filtering mode to Single would remove the authentication problem but would not distribute the load to other servers unless the initial server was down.

10. C. When setting the affinity to Class C, NLB links clients with a specific member based on the Class C part of the client's IP address. This allows an administrator to setup NLB so that clients from the same Class C address range can access the same NLB member. This affinity is best for NLB clusters using the Internet.

Chapter 17: Implementing Software Defined Networking

1. D. The New-NetworkControllerNodeObject command is the PowerShell command that allows you to setup a new Network Controller.

2. B. Remote Access Server (RAS) gateways are used for bridging traffic between virtual and non-virtual networks. Organizations can use Software Load Balancing (SLB) to evenly distribute network traffic between the virtual network resources.

3. B. Network Controllers are new to Windows Server 2016. Network Controllers allow an administrator to have a centralized virtual and physical datacenter infrastructure. This allows administrators to manage, configure, and troubleshoot all of their infrastructure components from one location.

4. A. The only virtual hard disk that increases in size is the dynamically expanding disk. Thus this is the only valid answer to this question. The fixed-size disk creates a disk of the size you specify, the differencing disk is a special disk that stores only the differences between it and a parent disk, and the physical disk uses a physical drive and makes it available to the virtual machine.

5. C. Physical hard disks cannot be configured using the Virtual Hard Disk Wizard, the Edit Virtual Hard Disk Wizard, or the New Virtual Machine Wizard. You can configure and attach a physical disk only by using the virtual machine's settings.

6. B. Hyper-V is not supported on Itanium-based systems, thus he cannot install it.

7. A, B, C. The minimum CPU requirement for running Hyper-V is a x64-based processor (Itanium is not supported), hardware Data Execution Protection must be enabled, and hardware-assisted virtualization must be enabled. There is no minimum requirement for a dual-core processor.

8. C. This question relates to the setup command used to install the Hyper-V server role on a Windows Server 2016 Server Core machine. It's important to remember that these commands are case sensitive, and that the correct command is start /wocsetup Microsoft-Hyper-V, which is option C. All of the other commands will fail to install Hyper-V on a Server Core machine.

9.   B. In single tenant mode, the RAS Gateway is used as the exterior or Internet facing VPN or DirectAccess edge server.

10. C. The virtual network type in which the machines communicate with each other and with the host machine is called internal only. In a private virtual network, the virtual machines can communicate only with each other, not with the network or the host machine. The external network type defines a network where the virtual machines can communicate with each other, with the host machine, and with an external network like the Internet.

Chapter 18: Installing Active Directory

1.   A, B, C, D. The forest and function levels have to be Windows 2003 or newer to install an RODC.

2.   B. A domain controller can contain Active Directory information for only one domain. If you want to use a multidomain environment, you must use multiple domain controllers configured in either a tree or a forest setting.

3.   D. NTFS has file-level security, and it makes efficient usage of disk space. Since this machine is to be configured as a domain controller, the configuration requires at least one NTFS partition to store the Sysvol information.

4.   A, D. To convert the system partition to NTFS, you must first use the CONVERT command-line utility and then reboot the server. During the next boot, the file system will be converted.

5.   B, E. The use of LDAP and TCP/IP is required to support Active Directory. TCP/IP is the network protocol favored by Microsoft, which determined that all Active Directory communication would occur on TCP/IP. DNS is required because Active Directory is inherently dependent on the domain model. DHCP is used for automatic address assignment and is not required. Similarly, NetBEUI and IPX/SPX are not available network protocols in Windows Server 2016.

6.   A, C. The Sysvol directory must be created on an NTFS partition. If such a partition is not available, you will not be able to promote the server to a domain controller. An error in the network configuration might prevent the server from connecting to another domain controller in the environment.

7.   B, C. You need to run the Adprep command when installing your first Windows Server 2016 domain controller onto a Windows Server 2008 R2 domain. Adprep /rodcprep actually gets the network ready to install a read-only domain controller and not a GUI version.

8.   A. You'll need to use Active Directory Federation Services (AD FS) in order to implement federated identity management. Federated identity management is a standards-based and information technology process that will enable distributed identification, authentication, and authorization across organizational and platform boundaries. The AD FS solution in Windows Server 2016 helps administrators address these challenges by enabling organizations to share a user's identity information securely.

9. B. The HOSTS file is a text-file-based database of mappings between hostnames and IP addresses. It works like a file-based version of DNS. DNS resolves a hostname to an IP address.

10. A. You only need to give them rights to the WillPanek.com zone using the DNS snap-in. If they do not have any rights to the WillPanekAD.com zone, they will not be able to configure this zone in any way.

Chapter 19: Administer Active Directory

1. A. A computer account and the domain authenticate each other by using a password. The password resets every 30 days. Since the machine has not connected to the domain for 16 weeks, the computer needs to be rejoined to the domain.

2. C. Checking the box Account Never Expires will prevent this user's account from expiring again.

3. D. The dsadd command allows you to add an object (user's account) to the Active Directory database.

4. A. Distribution groups are for emails only, and distribution groups cannot be assigned rights and permissions to objects.

5. A. Inheritance is the process by which permissions placed on parent OUs affect child OUs. In this example, the permissions change for the higher-level OU (Texas) automatically caused a change in permissions for the lower-level OU (Austin).

6. B, E. Enabling the Advanced Features item in the View menu will allow Isabel to see the LostAndFound and System folders. The LostAndFound folder contains information about objects that could not be replicated among domain controllers.

7. A. Through the use of filtering, you can choose which types of objects you want to see using the Active Directory Users and Computers tool. Several of the other choices may work, but they require changes to Active Directory settings or objects.

8. A. To allow the junior admin to do backups, their account needs to be part of the Backup Operators local group. To add their account to the local group, you need to use Computer Management.

9. A, B, C, D. All of the options listed are common tasks presented in the Delegation of Control Wizard.

10. D. The Delegation of Control Wizard is designed to allow administrators to set up permissions on specific Active Directory objects.

Chapter 20: Maintaining Active Directory

1. B. The NTDS settings for the site level are where you would activate and deactivate UGMC.

2. A. By decreasing the replication interval for the DEFAULTIPSITELINK object, you will decrease the replication latency for all sites using the DEFAULTIPSITELINK.

3. D. In the Active Directory Sites and Services console, the Server NTDS settings are where you would activate and deactivate global catalogs.

4. D. Preferred bridgehead servers receive replication information for a site and transmit this information to other domain controllers within the site. By configuring one server at each site to act as a preferred bridgehead server, Daniel can ensure that all replication traffic between the two sites is routed through the bridgehead servers and that replication traffic will flow properly between the domain controllers.

5. C. By default, connection objects are automatically created by the Active Directory replication engine. You can choose to override the default behavior of Active Directory replication topology by manually creating connection objects, but this step is not required.

6. B. The Knowledge Consistency Checker (KCC) is responsible for establishing the replication topology and ensuring that all domain controllers are kept up-to-date.

7. D. Site link bridges are designed to allow site links to be transitive. That is, they allow site links to use other site links to transfer replication information between sites. By default, all site links are bridged. However, you can turn off transitivity if you want to override this behavior.

8. B. Simple Mail Transfer Protocol was designed for environments in which persistent connections may not always be available. SMTP uses the store-and-forward method to ensure that information is not lost if a connection cannot be made.

9. D. The Directory Service event log contains error messages and information related to replication. These details can be useful when you are troubleshooting replication problems.

10. A, D. By creating new sites, Christina can help define settings for Active Directory replication based on the environment's network connections. She can use connection objects to define further the details of how and when replication traffic will be transmitted between the domain controllers.

Chapter 21: Implementing GPOs

1. C. The Delegation of Control Wizard can be used to allow other system administrators permission to add GPO links.

2. C. The system administrator can specify whether the application will be uninstalled or whether future installations will be prevented.

3.   B. You would use `GPUpdate.exe /force`. The `/force` switch forces the GPO to reapply all policy settings. By default, only policy settings that have changed are applied.

4.   A. You would use the Windows PowerShell `Invoke-GPUpdate` cmdlet. This PowerShell cmdlet allows you to force the GPO to reapply the policies immediately.

5.   D. DVD Present Targeting is not one of the options that you may consider when using item-level targeting.

6.   A, B. If you want your clients to be able to edit domain-based GPOs by using the ADMX files that are stored in the ADMX Central Store, you must be using Windows 10, Windows 8, Windows 7, or Windows Server 2008/2008 R2/2012/2012 R2/2016.

7.   D. If you assign an application to a user, the application does not get automatically installed. To have an application automatically installed, you must assign the application to the computer account. Since Finance is the only OU that should receive this application, you would link the GPO to Finance only.

8.   C. The Resultant Set of Policy (RSoP) utility displays the exact settings that apply to individual users, computers, OUs, domains, and sites after inheritance and filtering have taken effect. Desktop wallpaper settings are under the User section of the GPO, so you would run the RSoP against the user account.

9.   B. The Enforced option can be placed on a parent GPO, and this option ensures that all lower-level objects inherit these settings. Using this option ensures that Group Policy inheritance is not blocked at other levels.

10.   A. If the data transfer rate from the domain controller providing the GPO to the computer is slower than what you have specified in the slow link detection setting, the connection is considered to be a slow connection, and the application will not install properly.

Chapter 22: Understanding Certificates

1.   C. The Add-CATemplate command allows an administrator to add a certificate template to the CA.

2.   A, E. Certificate Enrollment Web Services with the Certificate Enrollment Policy Web Server role is the preferred Microsoft solution for issuing certificates through the internet.

3.   B. The online responder uses a lightweight HTTP protocol that responds faster and more efficiently than downloading a traditional CRL.

4.   B, C. To enable auditing, you must check the boxes for Success Audits and Failure Audits on the Events tab of the Federation Service Properties dialog box. You must also enable Object Access Auditing in Local Policy or Group Policy.

5.   A. To configure a server as a stand-alone CA server, you need to be an administrator on that server.

6. B. Since you are planning to issue certificates based on a User certificate template, you need to first copy that template so that you can alter it to the new settings.

7. A. You change the validity period of a certificate template, an administrator needs to modify the validity period setting for the certificate template.

8. C. The reason that you check the Delta CRL is because the Delta CRL shows any changes since the last CRL update. So if you want clients to verify the CRL every 30 minutes, you would want to set the Delta CRL publication interval.

9. D. Administrators can use the `Get-CACrlDistributionPoint` command to view all the locations set for the CRL distribution point (CDP).

10. A. Administrators can use the `Get-CATemplate` command to view the list of templates set on the CA for issuance of certificates.

Chapter 23: Configure Access and Information Protection Solutions

1. B, C. To enable AD FS auditing, you must check the boxes for Success Audits and Failure Audits on the Events tab of the Federation Service Properties dialog box. You must also enable Object Access Auditing in Local Policy or Group Policy.

2. B. Federation Proxy Services are installed under Remote Access as a web application proxy server in Windows Server 2016.

3. A, B, C. By using Workplace Join, information workers can join their personal devices with their company's workplace computers to access company resources and services. When you join your personal device to your workplace, it becomes a known device and provides seamless second-factor authentication and single sign-on to workplace resources and applications.

4. C. Network Load Balancing (NLB) is the only support Microsoft solution for providing high availability across an ADFS server farm. Windows Failover Clustering does not currently support ADFS as one master server is allowed to write to the configuration database per farm.

5. D. The AD FS configuration database stores all of the configuration data. It contains information that a federation service requires to identify partners, certificates, attribute stores, claims, and so forth. You can store this configuration data in either a Microsoft SQL Server 2005 or newer database or the Windows Internal Database feature that is included with Windows Server 2008/2008 R2, Windows Server 2012/2012 R2, and Windows Server 2016. The Windows Internal Database supports only up to five federation servers in a farm.

6. A, B. The relying-party server is a member of the Active Directory forest that hosts resources that a user in the partner organization wants to access. In this case, the relying party server should be the JavaCup AD FS server. A claims provider provides users with claims. These claims are stored within digitally encrypted and signed tokens. In this case, Boston Tea Party is the claims provider.

7. A. The Forest CA certificate is the only certificate that is automatically trusted, does not require user interaction and digital signature does not change in this scenario.

8. B. Licensing Server/Cluster is the component in charge of delivering publishing and use licenses. Several clusters can be installed per forest depending on the technical needs (servers' workload and bandwidth constraints).

9. A. To use the Web Application Proxy, you must install the Remote Access role.

10. A, D. To use a Web Application Proxy and AD FS, you should set your firewall to allow for ports 443 and 49443.

Index

Comprehensive Online Learning Environment

Register to gain one year of FREE access to the online interactive learning environment and test bank to help you study for your MCSA Windows Server 2016 certification exams—included with your purchase of this book!

The online test bank includes:

- **Assessment Test** to help you focus your study to specific objectives
- **Chapter Tests** to reinforce what you've learned
- **Practice Exams** to test your knowledge of the material
- **Digital Flashcards** to reinforce your learning and provide last-minute test prep before the exam
- **Searchable Glossary** to define the key terms you'll need to know for the exam
- **Videos** created by the author to accompany many of the chapter exercises

Register and Access the Online Test Bank

To register your book and get access to the online test bank, follow these steps:

1. Go to bit.ly/SybexTest.
2. Select your book from the list.
3. Complete the required registration information including answering the security verification proving book ownership. You will be emailed a pin code.
4. Go to http://www.wiley.com/go/sybextestprep and find your book on that page and click the "Register or Login" link under your book.
5. If you already have an account at testbanks.wiley.com, login and then click the "Redeem Access Code" button to add your new book with the pin code you received. If you don't have an account already, create a new account and use the PIN code you received.

SYBEX®
A Wiley Brand